48th Power Sources Conference 2018

Denver, Colorado, USA
11-14 June 2018

ISBN: 978-1-7138-0810-7

Printed from e-media with permission by:

Curran Associates, Inc.
57 Morehouse Lane
Red Hook, NY 12571

Some format issues inherent in the e-media version may also appear in this print version.

Power Sources Conference
Palisades Convention Management
411 Lafayette Street, Suite 201
New York, NY 10003

Phone: (212) 460-8090 ext. 202
Email: mgoldfarb@pcm411.com

Additional copies of this publication are available from:

Curran Associates, Inc.
57 Morehouse Lane
Red Hook, NY 12571 USA
Phone: 845-758-0400
Fax: 845-758-2633
Email: curran@proceedings.com
Web: www.proceedings.com

TABLE OF CONTENTS

What Can We Learn from the Samsung Galaxy Note7 Battery Safety Event

Shmuel De-Leon
Shmuel De-Leon Energy, Ltd.
www.sdle.co.il
shmuel@sdle.co.il

Abstract: *Samsung Galaxy Note 7 battery safety event is the worst ever consumer electronic recall. In this paper we review step by step the crisis, the follow-up investigation results and corrective actions. The author is bringing his review of what we should learn from that safety event which can also be simply in the military battery market.*

Temperature Adjustable Thermal Management System with Thermal Runaway Protection for Li Ion Packs

Mark Hartmann
Outlast Technologies LLC
Golden, CO 80403
MHH@OUTLAST.COMM /303-381-2129

Abstract: *Lithium-ion batteries are the preferred choice in many applications due to their energy density, higher voltage, and negligible memory effects. Most commercial lithium-ion cell chemistries will start to degrade at or above 60°C and leads to rapid loss of capacity over subsequent charge/discharge cycles. Additionally, thermal runaway and propagation is a priority safety concern due to the possibility of serious fire, explosion and injury in the event the cells are physically damaged or short circuited. Thermal management of lithium-ion battery packs using latent heat systems (LHS®) systems has proven highly effective for both improved pack performance and prevention of thermal runaway or propagation. In addition to prevention of thermal runaway and improved cell life, these systems provide for more homogenous pack temperatures, electrically insulative properties and less complex BMS system requirements*

Keywords: thermal runaway; thermal propagation; Li ion; Lithium; thermal management; fast charging; discharge capacity.

Introduction

Lithium-ion (Li-Ion) batteries are nearly universally used as the rechargeable energy storage in consumer goods, ranging in applications from cell phones to children's toys. Their success over other rechargeable batteries, in nearly every consumer goods market, has led to a renewed expectation of better battery performance: faster charging, longer cell life, higher voltage and improved safety. Larger power demands and increasing cell density of lithium-ion battery packs result in high operating temperatures, especially under peak loads and because of the susceptibility of most commercial lithium-ion cell chemistries to degrade or age at or above 60°C, this leads to rapid loss of capacity and cell life over subsequent charge/discharge cycles (C/D cycles) [1].

Large packs containing multiple cells (Fig 1) have an inherent problem during use in that the center or inner cells cannot effectively dissipate their heat during C/D cycles due to surrounding cells blocking that heat dissipation, and also the surrounding cells themselves creating heat during their C/D cycles. This creates multiple problems such as hot cells and hot spots within the pack that can cause cell degradation leading to loss of cell life and cell energy capacity. The C/D capacity (i.e. Wh/kg or Ah) of a cell is also proportional to its temperature with higher temperature cells having higher capacity. Therefore, non-homogenous pack temperatures lead to uneven C/D capacity in a pack. Depending on the application, this non-homogeneity requires complex battery management systems (BMS) to measure, monitor and control the various cells and their C/D rates and capacities.

Figure 1, Large Multicell Pack

One of the most catastrophic failures of a lithium-ion battery system is a cascading thermal runaway event where failure in one individual cell causes multiple cells in a battery fail. Thermal runaway can occur due to exposure to excessive temperatures, external shorts due to faulty wiring, or internal shorts due to cell defects. Thermal runaway events, especially in large multicell packs, result in the explosive release of significant energy in the form of heat and also toxic flammable gases that can lead catastrophic and life threating failure of battery packs.

It can be shown that correctly engineered passive thermal management systems based on latent heat absorption, storage and dissipation can provide sufficient cyclable energy capacity to absorb cell heat during charge/discharge cycles to reduce peak temperatures by 10-15°C. This temperature control leads to less cell degradation, and depending on the cell and environment can lead to a >40% increase in cell life. These systems also encase each cell in the pack which provides consistent thermal absorption properties leading to homogenous cell temperatures throughout the pack.

These same systems when optimized with the incorporation of absorption/degradation mechanisms, electrically insulative properties, fire retardant properties, and latent heat absorption properties at the correct latent heat absorption temperatures - the system can withstand

and absorb sufficient explosive energy to prevent a damaged or short-circuited cell from thermally propagating to adjacent cells and starting them on fire.

Pack Temperature Control and Cell Life Improvement

In order to test the effect of thermal control on the cells and packs, 18650 cells from the same manufacturing lot were tested in air as a control and held in an LHS® thermal management matrix (Fig. 2).

Figure 2, Example of Cells and Matrix

The LHS® Matrix had a 42-45°C transition/absorption temperature with 75-80 Joules/gram of latent energy capacity. Four LGDAHB41865 1.5Ah Li-ion cells (3.7V, 6 Ah) were connect in parallel on an Arbin® BT cell testing device. Thermocouples were attached to cell surface between the cell and the LHS® Matrix carrier. The charge/discharge cycle protocol consisted of: cells rest for 1 minute before charging at 6A till voltage reaches 4.2V, then trickle charge until current drops to 0.25A. Cells rest for 30 seconds before discharging at 80A until voltage of 2.5V is achieved. The cells rest for 10 minutes before looping back to the charge cycle. This repeats for 1000 cycles. As shown in Figures 3 and 4, the thermal management effect reduces peak cell temperatures, provides even cell temperatures throughout the pack, and improves cell energy capacity, i.e. cell life by reducing degradation due to cycling thermal exposure. Figure 3 shows the temperature profile for control cell versus LHS® temperature managed cells. The control cell in air reaches peak temperatures in the range of 60-65°C, whereas all of the cells in the LHS® matrix are 10-15°C lower and peak temperatures remain in the 48-53°C range. This work also shows the ability to even out the temperature of the pack with the interior cells within 1-2°C of the exterior cells. Figure 4 shows the improvement in cell discharge capacity over cycling lifetime. By reducing cell temperature, i.e. degradation, a >40% improvement in cell life and discharge capacity can

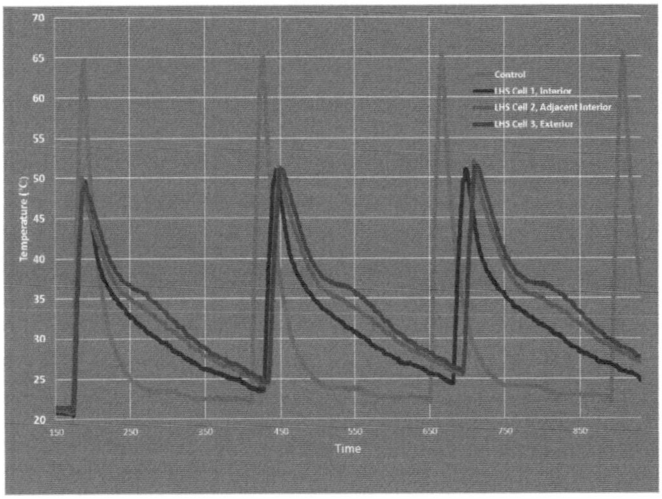

Figure 3, Charge/Discharge temp. profile and pack homogeneity

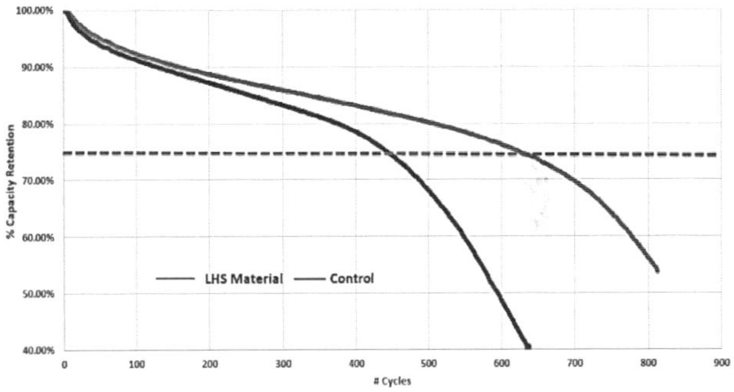

Figure 4, Cell Discharge Capacity

be realized, as measured by number of cycles above 75% capacity.

Nail Penetration and Thermal Propagation Testing for 18650 Cylindrical Cells

In order to show the ability of the material to prevent thermal runaway and propagation, nail penetration was conducted using a custom-built testing instrument.

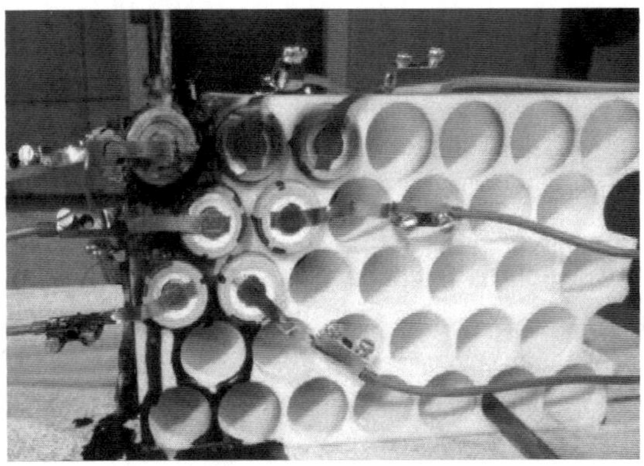

Figure 5, After Nail Penetration

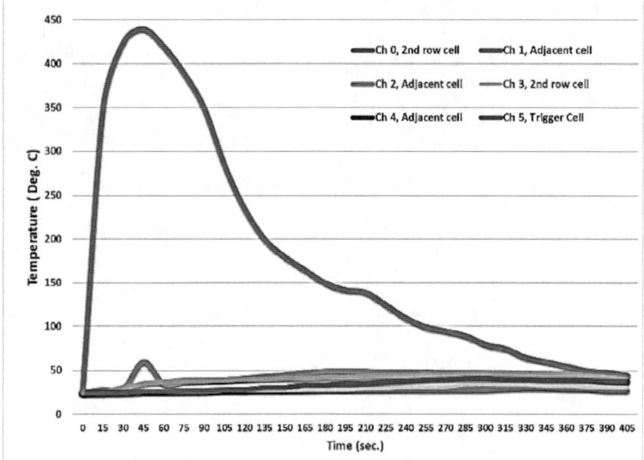

Figure 6, Nail Penetration Temp. Profile

A 5-ton hydraulic press modified with a linear actuator was used for cell penetration. The pack under test was secured and cell perpendicularly oriented to the nail. The nail was made of hardened tool steel 0.150" in diameter with a 0.025" diameter tip. The nail was penetrated at a speed of 23 inches/minute into the cell about 50% through or about the middle of the cell, at which point the nail movement was stopped. Nail penetration testing perpendicular to the cell axis will more severely short circuit the internal foils of the cell jellyroll creating a more intense and explosive thermal runaway event [2]. Cell temperatures were monitored and are shown in figure 6. As shown in figure 5 and 6, there was no adjacent cell propagation and adjacent cells did not overheat and remained below 80°C.

Thermal Management and Nail Penetration Testing for Pouch Cells

The LHS® Matrix composite material can also be formed into sheets for use with pouch cell applications. These sheets are simply placed between the pouches and can be thicknesses of 1-5 mm depending on size, cell configuration and cell energy capacity. The LHS® material has slight elastomeric properties which allow for pouch cell expansion and contraction.

Both thermal management and nail propagation testing were performed on 4 Ah Polymer Li-ion 6745135-10C pouch cells. Cells were tested with a 2.5 mm layer of LHS® material on either side of cell or between cells for nail penetration testing.

Charge/discharge cycle testing consisted of a constant current of 1.25A (~0.3C) to 4.2V then constant voltage till current drops to 200 mA. Cell rests for 1 minute then is discharged at constant current of 30A (7.5C) to 2.75 volts. Cell is let cool until below 30°C and cycles are repeated.

As can be seen in figures 7 and 8, the LHS® material consistently keeps the pouch cells cooler which leads to longer cell life. Charge/discharge peak temperatures reach 53-55 °C for the control material while the LHS® material yields 10-12 °C lower peak temperatures with readings in the 43-44 °C range.

These lower temperatures lead to less cell degradation and therefore longer cell life with approximately 35% increase in cell life as shown by increased cycle count above 75% discharge capacity retention.

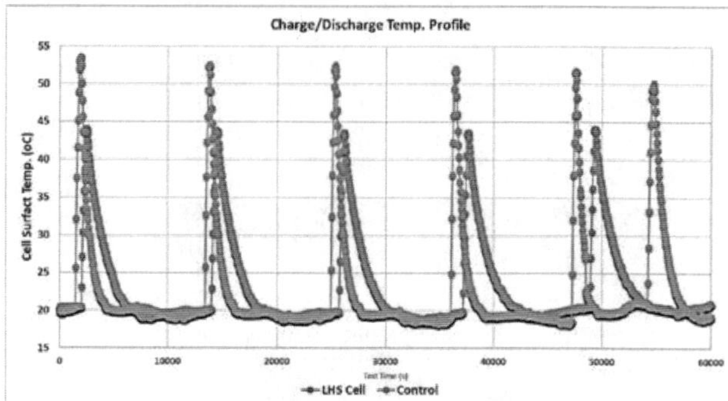

Figure 7, Pouch Cell Discharge Cycle Testing

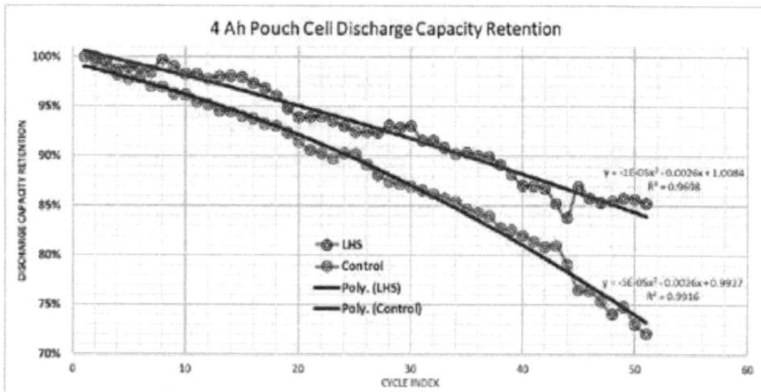

Figure 8, Cell Discharge Capacity Retention

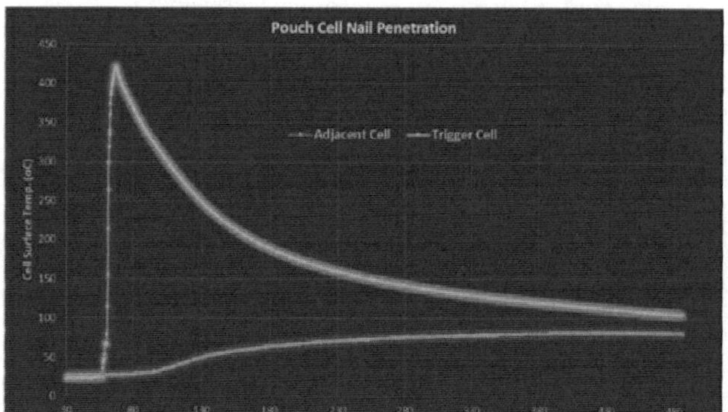

Figure 9, Pouch Cell Nail Penetration Test

Similar nail penetration was performed on the pouch cells as previously described for the cylindrical cells. Figure 9 shows the temperature profile of the top trigger cell and the adjacent pouch cell. The adjacent cell did not exceed 90°C and did not propagate, vent or go into thermal runaway.

Conclusions

Latent Heat Systems (LHS®) passive thermal management, when properly designed and engineered can provide significant benefits in pack safety and performance. Benefits of this technology include:

- Eliminates Thermal Runaway
- >40% Improved Battery Life
- Significant Reduction in Cell Thermal Degradation
- Electrically Insulative, not Conductive
- Superior Thermal Mitigation during High Charge/Discharge Cycles.
- Homogeneous Cell Temperatures Across Battery Pack
- Recyclability and Reuse of Shape Stable Matrix and Fill & Flow products.

References

1. Ling, Z., Zhang, Z., Shi, G., Fang, X., Wang, L., Gao, X., Fang, Y., Xu, T., Wang, S. & Liu, X. "Review on thermal management systems using phase change materials for electronic components, Li-ion batteries and photovoltaic modules". *Renewable and Sustainable Energy Reviews*, vol. 31, 427-438, 2014.
2. Lei, B., Zhao, W. "Experimental analysis of thermal runaway in 18650 cylindrical li-Ion cells using an accelerating rate calorimeter, *Batteries*, vol. 3, issue 2, June 2017.

Consumer Battery Fires-Failure Trends

Michael D. Eskra
Paula K. Ralston
Eskra Technical Products, Inc.
Saukville, WI 53080
mike.eskratechnical@gmail.com / 1-262-235-4068

Abstract: Batteries are everywhere in our daily lives. Most of the devices aid to make our daily lives more enjoyable. However, there are daily occurrences of batteries doing damage to structures and bodily harm to users. In most instances, the losses represented are at a low level of damage. The end users demand more and more portable power, and the battery industry has responded. Unfortunately, at the same time, the overall quality of the industry as a whole has significantly decreased. The result is that failures are becoming more catastrophic, with higher loss of property, personal injury and life. This paper will discuss the most common failure modes we have been identifying in the consumer space and how the occurrence could have been mitigated.

Keywords: Battery fires; lithium battery fires; lithium battery explosions, consumer battery fires; battery management failures; battery fire mitigation

Introduction: All batteries can cause a fire or be involved in a personal injury if misused or otherwise managed improperly. The lithium ion chemistry however has become increasingly used by commercial packagers and designers.

Lithium ion batteries have unique characteristics of operation which allow them to be used under a wide range of operational conditions. Under normal operation, most users find them to be rather ubiquitous, and embedded in their daily lives.

There are hundreds of papers devoted to safe operational conditions and battery management along with which reactions occur during overcharge and over discharge. It is unfortunate that many of the multitude of the products which are used by consumers and purchased as COTS for the US military, disregard basic safe practices for battery management. These digressions and lack of respect for the millions of dollars previously spent on research to understand the safety issues of lithium ion cost the American consumer billions of dollars annually with occasional loss of life, dismemberment, or need for reconstructive surgery.
Litigation takes various forms costing time and millions of dollars. Chinese companies continue to produce poorly designed and assembled batteries which are subsequently packaged into toys, tools and computers for children, businesses, consumers and our government. Much of the real cost is unrecoverable due to limitations of law, and other factors.

The use of these power sources as COTS further spreads the risk. Packaging of foreign cells into larger battery systems without a thorough examination significantly increases that risk.

What We Found: Failures which are plaguing the consumer marketplace can be lumped into groups. The failure modes appear to us to go through cycles. Early on failures revolved around parallel cells which were being subjected to uneven heating. This caused the PTC's of individual cells to change resulting in over discharge of one of the parallel cells. While these failures continue, they are being overshadowed by other failure modes.

Typically overcharge does not occur in battery systems until one or more cells in a series string fails through degradation, or initial lack of capacity matching. Subsequently the weakest cells get reversed. Very few consumer or commercial fires that we have seen are due to overcharging. The mechanisms and time required for an overcharge cell to burst and catch fire will usually be noticed prior to the actual initiation of the fire occurring.

Chinese cells, in particular, have a great deal of contamination. ETP has found eye lashes, copper ribbon of 100um, calcium oxides and lime have been found in many different brands of batteries examined.

Mismatched cells during initial battery pack assembly coupled with battery monitoring systems which do not limit cell overcharge and subsequent recharge is the leading failure modes of lithium batteries. ETP has investigated many first charge failures of name brand battery powered devices. The typical fire scenario will come to us as the individual purchased a new brand name tool, brought it home and plugged it in to charge. They then went to a neighbor's house or down to the dock. Fifteen minutes later their house, garage or hangar was engulfed with fire.

These types of fires can easily be contributed to infant mortality of a cell or battery. Our investigation leads us to several other possibilities. Using CT scans of the individual cells recovered from the battery pack along with other evidence. Procuring and testing of exemplars of identical products gives us insight on how the lithium ion battery business has morphed.

Foreign materials embedded into the cells and poor quality manufacturing certainly causes some fires. Mismatched cells put together into 12 to 48 volt battery packs with weak battery management strategies contribute to most of the major losses we have seen to date.

Figure 1 shows a CT scan image of a brand new RC battery. These are used in many households throughout the world. Please note that the alignment is poor.

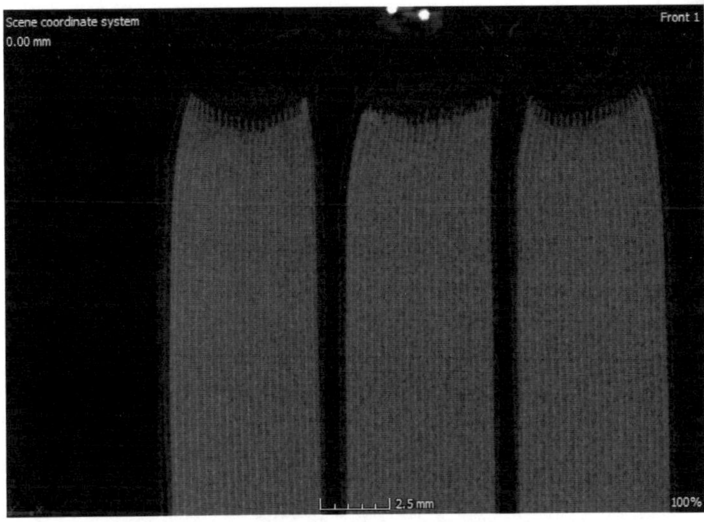

Figure 1. CT Image of a New RC Battery

Figure 2, below shows an arc area of an electrode of the battery in Figure 1, a zero cycle RC battery.

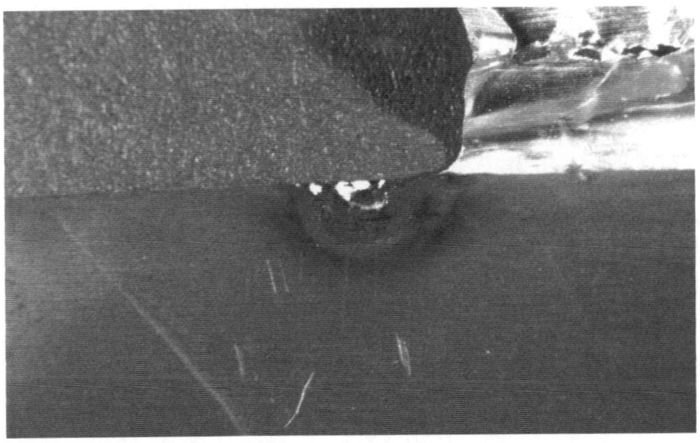

Figure 2. Figure 1 Battery Teardown

Figure 3 shows a view of a contaminant which was found in another battery. These types of contaminants can be found in nearly every battery we have torn down. These types of contaminations can easily pierce a separator, causing shorting in a cell.

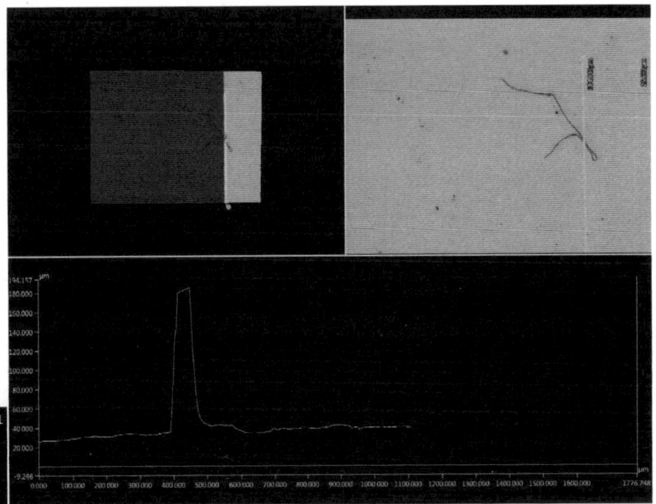

Figure 3. Keyence Images of Contaminants.

The contaminants found in cells coming from China are not restricted in size or type. Figure 4, shows a large ceramic contaminant that was found in a battery. Subsequent analysis of 10 other exemplar batteries found numerous similar or more dangerous contaminants. Interestingly, these types of contaminants can be tolerated if the battery is not fully charged or discharged and packaged in a typical three or four layer film. This battery however was packaged in the film and then subsequently wrapped in several layers of glass wrap and charged to 4.25 V and discharged to 2.5 V. This wide range of operation increases the stresses available to drive the contamination through multiple layers of separators and electrodes.

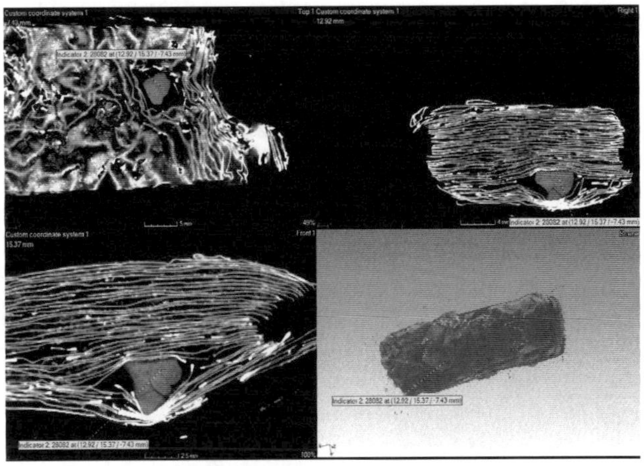

Figure 4. Pouch Cell Contamination

Larger battery modules and system do not appear to be immune to the failings of matching cells and contamination. Figure 5 shows an IR image of an operational large format battery module which clearly shows what happens when cells are not matched and are cycled.

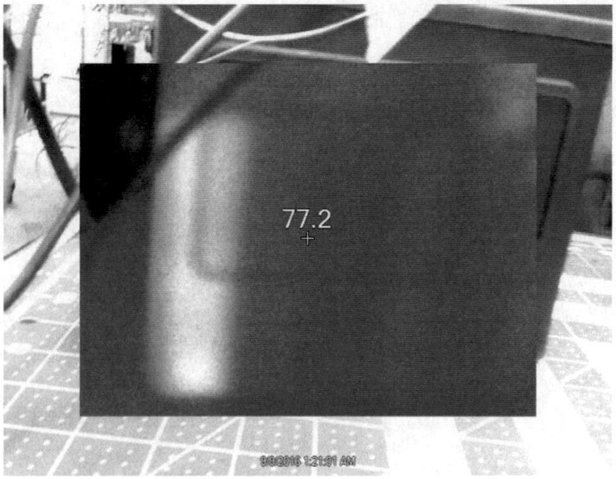

Figure 5. IR Photo Of Module

The typical failure will follow as the module is discharged, destroying the Solid Electrode Interface (SEI) and likely plating copper on the cathode. Upon recharge the SEI layer will not reform properly, causing further shorting. This battery's management system looks at every cell but does not appear to react to protect the battery from thermal runaway or other damage. If this battery was in a high voltage string it would have likely already failed.

Summary: Lithium Ion batteries can be a great technology if proper battery management and quality is adhered too. It is necessary to ensure proper cell matching and have a thorough understanding of the inherent failure modes of the technology. Unfortunately many of the battery management strategies developed for other chemistries become catastrophic failure modes with lithium ion.

The concept of using commercial off the shelf (COTS), batteries for the US military was based upon cells and batteries manufactured in Japan. Presently the majority of the batteries produced are made by the Chinese which are rapidly replicating and expanding cell and battery capability with little regard to quality and safety. The cells, batteries and products which they export vary greatly with little relevant quality control, a lack of interest on overall safety.

Acknowledgement: Eskra Technical Products, Inc. has assembled this work from some of the many hundreds of battery incidents it has investigated on behalf of its clients.

Safety of High Energy Soldier Wearable Batteries

David B. Shoemaker, Dr. Tony Thampan, Dr. Ashley Ruth
U.S. Army Communications-Electronics Research Development and Engineering Center
Power Division – Command Power and Integration

Abstract: *Safety and weight are two main concerns for the soldier when it comes to the conformal wearable battery (CWB) that they wear and use to power most of the equipment on themselves. Currently, the soldier wears the CWB in front of his/her ballistic plate. This is due to the possible case in which the battery may be shot and flame as a result. Having the battery on the outside of the ballistic plate makes it easier for the soldier to get rid of the flaming battery. However, there is a tradeoff of reducing the chance of flaming when shot. The CWB currently uses very small capacity cells, around 1.1Ah. In an effort to reduce the weight of the battery and increase energy density, larger capacity cells were used in this testing. In order to improve the ballistic protection of the CWB, during testing, the battery was placed behind the ballistic plate and a small amount of fireproof material was coated on the cells. The combination of these factors has been able to increase the energy density of the prototype CWB to approximately 156 Wh/Kg and stop flaming/smoking when the ballistic plate/battery system is shot. With the CWB now placed behind the ballistic plate, the battery no longer sees the bullet penetration, which significantly reduces the chance of flaming, but the fireproof material was added as an extra layer of protection against the backface deflection impact from the plate. Bullet penetration testing was performed on the ballistic plate and CWB system, both in front of and behind the ballistic plate to show the level of difference in battery protection. Little or no flaming/smoking was observed for the behind the plate configuration when combined with the fireproof material, but smoking or flaming was observed when the same type of CWB was placed in front of the ballistic plate. The change in the system configuration allows the battery to be more energy dense without compromising safety. This paper will be discussing the results of the bullet penetration tests, with a specific focus on how the addition of the fireproof material inside the battery can help ensure a lower failure rate.*

Keywords: conformal wearable battery, backface deflection

Introduction

The soldier burden of today is increasing with the number of devices that are to be worn. One of the main goals of CERDEC Power is to make the batteries safer and lighter for the soldier. They need to be lighter, provide more run-time, be safer, and not be a burden. One of the central batteries for the soldier is the Conformal Wearable Battery (CWB).

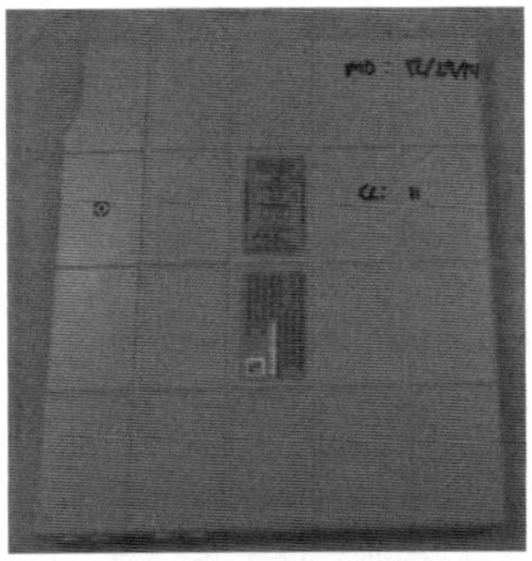

Figure 1) Current Inventus conformal wearable battery.

Currently 148Wh and 1.18Kg, the CWB has the ability to flex and conform to the shape of the human body and is coupled with a ballistic armor plate whenever worn by the soldier. The CWB has a military requirement to not flame for at least two minutes after being shot by a 7.62mm rifle round and is normally worn on the outside of the ballistic plate. In order to accomplish this, the current manufacturer of the CWB is required to use small capacity cells in conjunction with a proprietary additive that they externally apply to their cells before packaging.

The purpose of the testing performed is to try and increase the energy density of the CWB by increasing the capacity of the cells used internally, without introducing a risk to safety.

Hypothesis and Test Plan

Since the current configuration of the CWB has it directly exposed to gunfire, with the ballistic plate against the human body, CERDEC Power wanted to experiment what type of safety is added by placing the battery behind the ballistic plate in combination with larger capacity cells. Increasing the capacity of the cells is well known to introduce more of a risk of flaming when a battery is punctured or penetrated. However, if the battery never sees the full force of the bullet, then increasing the capacity of the cells should prove to be an improvement rather than a liability. Instead, the battery would only see the backside impact from where the bullet strikes the ballistic plate.

In order to test this hypothesis, proper safety countermeasures were evaluated. Commercial grade Kevlar was looked at as a potential material for the battery sleeve that would house the cells. Kevlar has the properties of being non-flammable, and also adds to some of the ballistic protection. While Kevlar will not stop a direct hit from a rifle round, the ballistic plate will absorb the brunt of the impact, while the Kevlar only has to handle the shock from the BFD. When hermetically sealed, the non-flammable property of Kevlar should be able to snuff out any sort of flame that might have been started inside of the battery if one of the cells gets crushed from the backside impact. Four different grades of Kevlar were used in testing. Grade 1 was the strongest and thickest Kevlar and Grade 4 was the thinnest and weakest Kevlar. In this testing, the Kevlar was not hermetically sealed.

Figure 2.a) Grade 1 Kevlar CWB sleeve.

Fireproof materials were also looked at as a possible way to suppress any sort of heat build-up that may occur if one or multiple cells are damaged. Both a commercial, low-cost fireproof spray and a high strength, moderate cost fireproof grease were evaluated.

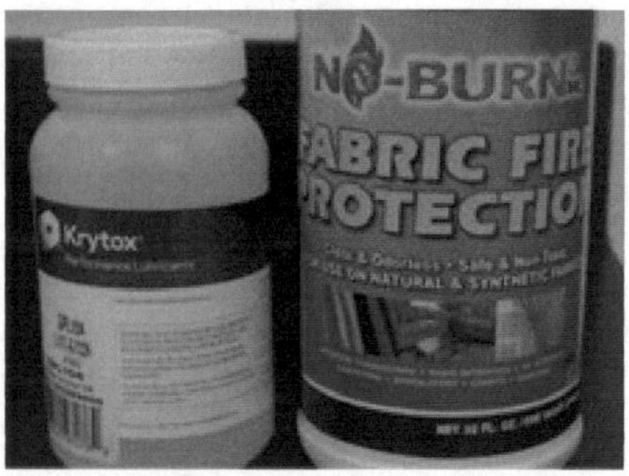

Figure 2.b) (Left) fireproof Krytox™ grease. (Right) commercial fireproof spray.

With the current capacity of cells in the CWB being around 1.1Ah, larger capacities were used for this experiment: 3.3Ah and 1.9Ah. All of the cells were standard lithium ion commercial grade. To fit into the 214mm X 193mm footprint of the CWB, 24x of the 1.9Ah cells were used, which equated to 169Wh of energy and roughly 1.18Kg. For the 3.3Ah cells, 16x were used, which equated to 195.4Wh and roughly 1.25Kg.

Figure 2.c) (Left) 3.3Ah cell. (Right) 1.9Ah cell.

Inside of the prototype CWB, a dummy circuit board that flexes was used. All of the cells inside of the battery were charged to 100% and were wired together as a normal battery pack would be, but no electronics were included. The thickness of the battery sleeve and the circuit board were representative of the actual thicknesses that are used in the official Army CWB.

Figure 2.d) Internal cells wired together.

Test Results

Once the prototype CWB's were constructed, they were taken to HP White Laboratory to be shot by professionals with the required round and velocity called out in MIL-PRF 32383/4A. The batteries were shot both behind the ballistic plate and in front of the ballistic plate. Some of the batteries that were tested had fireproof material applied to the cells, while others did not. Different grades of Kevlar were used as the sleeve material for the batteries that were tested, and some of the batteries had the 1.9Ah cells and some of them had the 3.3Ah cells.

Figure 3) Battery behind ballistic plate about to be shot for ballistic testing.

The CWB's with Kevlar Grades 1 and 2, 3.3Ah cells, behind the plate, and with the Krytox™ fireproof grease performed the best. The CWB's with Kevlar Grade 3, 1.9Ah cells, in front of the plate, and without any fireproof material performed the worst. If the CWB smoked or flamed in less than two minutes after being shot behind the plate, then the "in front of the plate" test was not performed since the battery already failed at that point.

Table 1. First Round, Shot Without Fireproof Material

Kevlar Grade and Cell Capacity	Behind Plate	In Front of Plate
Grade 1 – 1.9Ah	Fail	N/A
Grade 1 – 3.3Ah	Pass	Fail
Grade 2 – 1.9Ah	Pass	Fail
Grade 2 – 3.3Ah	Pass	Fail
Grade 3 – 1.9Ah	Fail	N/A
Grade 3 – 3.3Ah	Pass	Fail
Grade 4 – 1.9Ah	Pass	Fail
Grade 4 – 3.3Ah	Pass	Fail

Figure 4) 159Wh/Kg battery with grade 2 Kevlar sleeve shot behind the ballistic plate.

After the initial testing, in which none of the CWB's had a fireproof material applied, both the commercial fireproof spray and the Krytox™ fireproof grease were used for the following round of testing. While the commercial spray added some protection against flame, the batteries still smoked a little bit when shot behind the ballistic plate. The 3.3Ah CWB that had Krytox™ applied, performed much better both behind the ballistic plate as well as in front of the ballistic plate. Even though the 3.3Ah Krytox™ CWB smoked a little when shot in front of the CWB, it only smoked a little bit for a few seconds and no flame was ever seen. Throughout all of the testing that was performed, the 1.9Ah cells seemed to perform worse than the 3.3Ah cells.

Table 2. Second Round, Shot With Fireproof Material

Kevlar Grade, Cell Capacity, Fireproof Type	Behind Plate	In Front of Plate
Grade 2 – 1.9Ah – Comm. Spray	Fail	N/A
Grade 2 – 3.3Ah – Comm. Spray	Fail	N/A
Grade 2 – 1.9Ah – Krytox™ Grease	Fail	N/A
Grade 2 – 3.3Ah – Krytox™ Grease	Pass	Fail

After seeing the benefit that the Krytox™ fireproof grease had for the 3.3Ah cells in the second round of testing, CERDEC Power decided to use only 3.3Ah cells and only Krytox™ fireproof grease in the next round of testing. All four grades of Kevlar were tested as well, and the data shows that during the first and third round of testing, the Grade 3 Kevlar proved to not be protective enough to prevent failure.

Table 3. Third Round, Shot With Only Krytox™ Grease and Only 3.3Ah

Kevlar Grade and Cell Capacity	Behind Plate	In Front of Plate
Grade 1 – 3.3Ah	Pass	Fail
Grade 2 – 3.3Ah	Pass	Fail
Grade 3 – 3.3Ah	Fail	Fail
Grade 4 – 3.3Ah	Pass	Fail

Fourth round testing is still planned to be conducted. This testing will involve only look at using Kevlar Grades 1 and 2, since they proved to have the best success rates. Also, only 3.3Ah cells will be used and Krytox™ fireproof grease.

Backface Deflection

One of the added benefits of having the battery configured behind the ballistic plate is that it acts as a cushion against the backside impact from the plate when the bullet strikes it. Testing was performed to see what the backside deflection of multiple configurations would be.

- With the ballistic plate alone – 24mm of BFD
- With the battery in front of the ballistic plate – 24mm of BFD
- With the battery behind the ballistic plate – average was 12mm of BFD

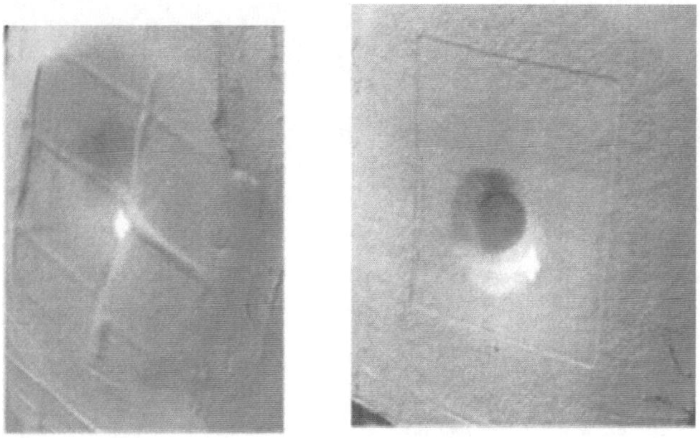

Figure 5) (Left) backface deflection with battery behind ballistic plate (12mm deep). (Right) backface deflection with battery in front of ballistic plate (24mm deep).

This is a critical benefit for any soldier that has to wear the ballistic plate/CWB system. There was a significant difference in impact to the clay mold that was used in the testing.

Conclusions

Testing is still ongoing for the evaluation of a higher energy dense fireproof CWB. Kevlar Grades 1 and 2 were found to be the most effective battery sleeve choices. Cells of capacity 3.3Ah consistently performed better than cells of capacity 1.9Ah. Cells coated with the Krytox™ fireproof grease performed better than the cells coated with the commercial fireproof spray or cells that weren't coated with a fireproof material at all. It was also clearly evident that having the ballistic plate placed in front of the battery significantly decreased the likelihood that the battery would catch on fire after bullet impact. In addition to protecting the integrity of the battery, having the ballistic plate in front significantly reduced the backface deflection normally seen by the soldier.

By using higher capacity cells, the energy density of the CWB will increase, which will make the CWB much lighter for the soldier. By placing the battery behind the ballistic plate, the CWB will be less susceptible to flaming upon impact and the soldier will be more protected from the backface deflection of the ballistic plate. CERDEC Power's goal is to make the batteries safer and lighter for the soldier.

Reference

1. MIL-PRF 32383/4A. Oct. 2015

Remaining Useful Life Prediction of Lithium-Ion Batteries Using Multiple Model Particle Filter

Chao Hu[1,2], Hui Ye[3], Gaurav Jain[3], and Craig Schmidt[3]
[1] Department of Mechanical Engineering, Iowa State University, Ames, IA 50011
[2] Department of Electrical and Computer Engineering, Iowa State University, Ames, IA 50011
[3] Medtronic Energy and Component Center, Brooklyn Center, Minnesota 55430
chaohu@iastate.edu / 1-515-294-0771

Abstract: *This paper presents a model-based method for remaining useful life (RUL) prediction of lithium-ion (Li-ion) batteries in implantable medical devices. The model-based method is developed on and evaluated against data from two sets of Li-ion prismatic cells used in implantable applications. The first set consists of eight cells whose rates of capacity fade appear to be stable and gradually decrease over a 10-year test duration; the second set comprises eight cells from Manufacturer X whose rates of capacity fade appear to show sharp increase after some period over a 1.8-year test duration. The method employs a multiple model particle filter with fixed-lag smoothing for updating multiple capacity fade models and predicting the probability distribution of RUL. It is demonstrated that the method is capable of adapting capacity fade models to changes in the rate of capacity fade over the lifetime of a single cell, as well as to variations in the trend of capacity fade across different cells from different manufacturers.*

Keywords: capacity fade, online prognostics, remaining useful life, lithium-ion battery.

Introduction

When a lithium-ion (Li-ion) battery is used as the power source in an implantable medical device, it is very important to be able to track the capacity fade of the battery and assess its remaining useful life (RUL) throughout the lifetime [2,2]. This can provide information to the patient and his/her health care provider regarding when and how a replacement of the device might be needed. The need for predictable capacity fade models and ability to predict RUL is particularly significant given long targeted lifetime of implanted devices (typically 10 years; up to 25 years in some cases) and large variation in use conditions (many cycles versus few cycles over a certain calendar time) depending on the therapy needs. Examples of implantable medical devices that may be powered by a Li-ion battery include neurological stimulators, spinal stimulators, cardiac stimulators such as pacemakers and defibrillators, and diagnostic devices such as cardiac monitors.

In this paper, a model-based method is employed for online prognostics of Li-ion batteries in implantable medical devices. A generic particle filter is adopted to implement recursive Bayesian filtering for batteries whose capacity fade behavior can be represented by a single fade model, and a multiple model particle filter (MMPF) with fixed-lag smoothing is proposed for batteries whose capacity fade behavior switches between multiple fade models. The effectiveness of the proposed method is demonstrated by leveraging daily cycling data from eight fresh cells from Medtronic, PLC (hereafter referred to as the MDT cells) as well as eight fresh/post-explant cells from Manufacturer X (hereafter referred to as the Mfg. X cells) [2]. A large difference in the capacity fade behavior is seen between the two manufacturers' data sets used in this paper and hence these data sets serve as excellent test cases for developing robust prognostic techniques applicable to wide variety of fade characteristics.

Technical Approach

Given the estimates of battery capacities at the current and previous charge/discharge cycles, the proposed method employs a recursive Bayesian filtering technique, namely particle filters, to recursively update the parameters of empirical capacity fade models and extrapolate the updated models for prediction of RUL [2]. The updating of a capacity fade model enables adapting the model to track the fade trends of individual battery cells and tailoring the predictions of RUL to the fade behavior of these individual cells.

Capacity Fade Models: This study involves the use of two empirical models, denoted as Models 1 and 2, that can be used to represent the capacity fade behavior of Li-ion battery. These two models are described as follows.

Model 1 (Exponential/linear hybrid model): Model 1 assumes capacity loss can be expressed as a hybrid of exponential and linear functions of cycle number, and takes the following form [2-4]

$$c_k = \frac{C_k}{C_0} = 1 - \alpha\left[1 - \exp(-\lambda k)\right] - \beta k \tag{1}$$

where C_k is the capacity at the kth charge/discharge cycle, C_0 is the initial capacity, α is the coefficient of the exponential component of capacity fade, λ is the exponential capacity fade rate, β is the coefficient of the linear component of capacity fade, and c_k is the normalized capacity at the kth cycle. In recursive Bayesian filtering with Model 1, we treat the parameters of the fade model, α, λ, and β, as the state variables, $\mathbf{x}$, and recursively update the posterior distribution of $\mathbf{x}$ with the capacity measurement, y.

Model 2 (Linear model): Model 2 is of a simpler form than Model 1, and assumes capacity loss has a linear relationship with the cycle number. In this model, the normalized capacity c_k of a battery cell at the cycle k is formulated as [2]

$$c_k = \gamma - \beta k \tag{2}$$

where γ and β are the intercept and negative of the slope of the linear model, respectively. This model is capable of representing that linear fade behavior, where capacity decreases linearly with cycle. In Model 2, the model parameters that need to be updated are γ and β, and these are considered as the state variables, $\mathbf{x}$.

State-State Model and Generic Particle Filter: In our task of battery prognostics, we treat the fade model parameters (i.e., α, λ and β in Model 1 or γ and β in Model 2) as the system states $\mathbf{x}$, and the normalized capacity, y, as the system measurement. A discrete state-space model that consists of system transition and measurement functions can then be written for Model 1 as [1,2]

$$\begin{aligned} \text{Transition:} \quad & \alpha_k = \alpha_{k-1} + u_{1,k}, \\ & \lambda_k = \lambda_{k-1} + u_{2,k}, \\ & \beta_k = \beta_{k-1} + u_{3,k} \\ \text{Measurement:} \quad & y_k = \underbrace{1 - \alpha_k\left[1 - \exp\left(-\lambda_k k\right)\right] - \beta_k k}_{c_k} + v_k \end{aligned} \tag{3}$$

and for Model 2 as

$$\begin{aligned} \text{Transition:} \quad & \gamma_k = \gamma_{k-1} + u_{4,k}, \ \beta_k = \beta_{k-1} + u_{5,k} \\ \text{Measurement:} \quad & y_k = \underbrace{\gamma_k - \beta_k k}_{c_k} + v_k \end{aligned} \tag{4}$$

Here, y_k is the capacity measurement (or the mean of the estimate by the sparse capacity estimator) at the kth charge/discharge cycle, and u_1, u_2, u_3, u_4, u_5 and v are the Gaussian noise variables with zero means.

The inference tasks described in Eqs. (3) and (4) are to learn on the fly the capacity fade behavior of a cell by tracking the evolution of the fade parameters (or states), $\mathbf{x}$, based on the capacity estimate (or measurement), y, from the cell. In a Bayesian framework, the posterior probability distribution functions (PDF) of the states given the past measurements, $p(\mathbf{x}_k \mid \mathbf{y}_{1:k})$, constitutes a statistical solution to this inference problem and properly captures the uncertainty of the states. Recursive Bayesian filtering enables a continuous update of the posterior PDF with new measurements. It is often difficult or even impossible to derive an analytical form of the updated posterior $p(\mathbf{x}_k \mid \mathbf{y}_{1:k})$. It is, however, easier to draw samples (or particles) from the true posterior (or a distribution proportional to the posterior) and devise an approximation to the posterior based on the particles. This is the basic idea of particle filters, which implement recursive Bayesian filtering by sequential Monte Carlo simulation [0,5]. In particle filters, the state posterior is built based on a set of particles and their associated weights, expressed as

$$p\left(\mathbf{x}_k \mid \mathbf{y}_{1:k}\right) \approx \sum_{j=1}^{N_P} w_k^j \delta\left(\mathbf{x}_k - \mathbf{x}_k^j\right) \tag{5}$$

where $\{\mathbf{x}_k^j\}_{j=1:N_P}$ and $\{w_k^j\}_{j=1:N_P}$ are respectively the particles and weights estimated at the kth measurement step, N_P is the number of particles, and δ is the Dirac delta function. The basic ideas of generic particle filter are that 1) the posterior distribution of the states $\mathbf{x}$ at any time can be approximated with a finite number (N_P) of Monte Carlo samples (or particles) and their associated weights, and 2) the chronological behavior of these particles can be modeled sequentially according to the dynamics described by the state transition equations (e.g., Eq. (3) for Model 1 and Eq. (4) for Model 2 in the task of battery prognostics).

Fixed-Lag Multiple Model Particle Filter: The multiple model particle filter (MMPF) has been proposed in several earlier studies [6,7] on nonlinear filtering with switching dynamic models. In these studies, the MMPF aimed at addressing hybrid state estimation problems where the (augmented) state vector consists of both a vector of state variables (e.g., the fade model parameters in the task of battery prognostics) and a vector of model variables (e.g., the fade model in effect). Let us define the augmented state vector as $\boldsymbol{\psi}_k = [\mathbf{x}_k^{\mathrm{T}}, m_k]^{\mathrm{T}}$, where $m_k \in \{1, 2, \ldots, S\}$ with S being the number of candidate fade models ($S = 2$ in this study). The main difference between the MMPF and the generic particle filter lies in that the former allows for the use of multiple transition/measurement models that better captures the complex dynamics of a system than the use of a single model. At each measurement step, a transition/measurement model is weighed according to how well the observations predicted by the model match the actual measurements. For example, if the fade model m_k at the kth charge/discharge cycle matches the best with the capacities measured from a battery cell, then the fade behavior of the cell is deemed to be best represented by the model m_k at cycle k.

Given the past and current measurements $\mathbf{y}_{1:k}$ at step k and D future measurements $\mathbf{y}_{k+1:k+D}$, a fixed-lag smoothing step estimates the posterior distribution of the states $p(\mathbf{x}_k \mid \mathbf{y}_{1:k+D})$ [8,9]. Here, D is a fixed time delay that is often predefined based on prior knowledge about the system dynamics. In our task of battery prognostics, the main objective of updating the parameters of a fade model is not to match the model-predicted capacity at the current cycle with the actual measurement. Rather, it is for the updated model to capture the capacity fade trend including and beyond the current cycle (i.e., the model shall match the capacity measurements at multiple cycles starting from the current cycle). To properly update and evaluate multiple fade models for battery prognostics, this study integrates the fixed-lag smoothing step with the MMPF. The basic ideas of the fixed-lag MMPF procedure are that 1) the posterior distribution of the states $\mathbf{x}$ at step k is estimated using measurements up to a future step $k + D$, and 2) a resampling step is used to reassign particles to different measurement models, allowing a better model to possess a larger number of particles.

Experimental Results

The performance of the proposed method is evaluated based on data from daily cycling of two sets of Li-ion prismatic cells in implantable applications: 1) eight fresh MDT cells whose rates of capacity fade appear to gradually decrease over a 10-year test duration; and 2) eight fresh/post-explant Mfg. X cells whose rates appear to sharply increase after some period over a 1.8-year test duration [2]. The daily cycling data used in this evaluation were gathered by the authors at MDT, and the evaluation was conducted by the author at the Iowa State University (ISU). This section reports the results of this evaluation.

Cycling Data: This study involved testing two sets of eight Li-ion cells with hermetically sealed prismatic cases: 1) eight fresh MDT cells; and 2) two fresh Mfg. X cells and six post-explant Mfg. X cells [2]. These two sets of cells were subject to full depth of charge/discharge cycling with a nominally daily discharge rate under 37 °C in the lab. This represents a high end use condition for typical implantable neurostimulator devices. The discharge capacities of a subset of these cells are plotted against the cycle number in Fig. 1. Note that, for confidentiality reasons, the discharge capacity of a cell in Fig. 1 and in the discussions thereafter is presented after being normalized by the beginning-of-life (BOL) discharge capacity of the cell. It can be seen that the two fresh Mfg. X cells (Mfg. X cells 1 and 2) exhibit a three-stage fade behavior (see Fig. 1(b)), that is, the rate of capacity fade was initially high (stage 1), but slowed down quickly after around 50 cycles (stage 2), and at around 150 cycles, started to increase and stayed constant after around 250 cycles (stage 3) [2]. This pattern contrasts with the almost continuous decrease in the rate of capacity fade (i.e., capacity fade slows down with ageing) observed from the MDT cells (see Fig. 1(a)).

RUL Prediction Results on MDT Cells: The generic particle filter was used to update the parameters of the first capacity fade model (Model 1) in Eq. (1), and the updated model was projected to a capacity threshold (i.e., 75% of the initial discharge capacity) for RUL prediction [2]. The RUL prediction at cycle 1000 is shown in Fig. 2(a), where the prediction at cycle 1000 yields an accurate prediction of life, a slightly conservative solution that includes the true end of service (EOS) cycle (i.e., 2780 cycles or approximately 8.2 years). Figure 2(b) plots the RUL predictions (means ± three standard deviations) at multiple cycles throughout the lifetime. The graph shows that the RUL prediction keeps being updated over time, and that as the battery approaches its EOS cycle, the mean prediction tends to converge to the true value.

RUL Prediction Results on Mfg. X Cells: The fixed-lag MMPF was used to update the parameters of the empirical capacity fade models (Models 1 and 2) in Eqs. (1) and (2), and the updated models were projected to a capacity threshold for RUL prediction [2]. The capacity projections based on the updated particles at cycle 200 (or at 0.8 years) and cycle 400 (or at 1.5 years) are shown as two gray curves in Fig. 3(a). The updated particles at cycle 200 yield a shorter predicted life than the true life (i.e., 420 cycles versus 519 cycles). This is mainly because the dominant fade model at cycle 200 (see Fig. 3(c)), Model 1, projects an exponential fade whose rates accelerate over cycle (see the capacity projection in Fig. 3(a)), and this projected fade over-predicts the capacity fade at the later cycles. In contrast, the dominant model at cycle 400 (see Fig. 3(c)), Model 2, better captures the linear fade at the later cycles, and the extrapolation of the model yields a predicted life much closer to the true life (i.e., 516 cycles versus 519 cycles).

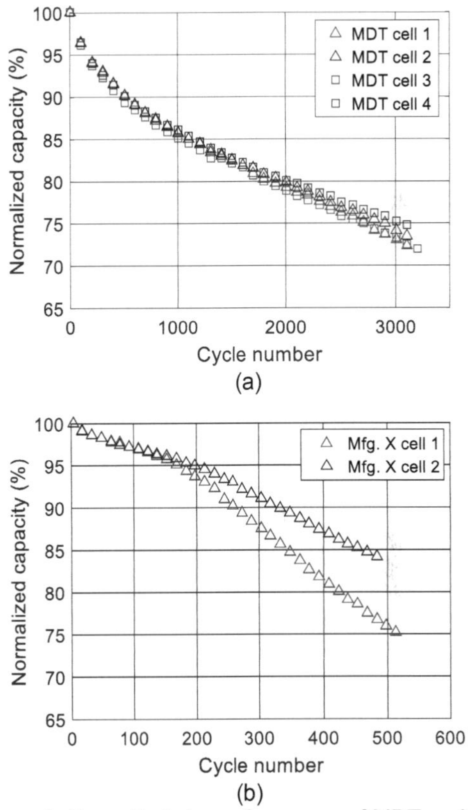

Figure 1. Capacity fade performance of MDT and Mfg. X cells cycled with a nominally daily discharge rate: (a) MDT cells 1–4 and (b) Mfg. X cells 1 and 2 (fresh cells) [2]. For the ease of visualization, capacity measurements are plotted every 100 (10) daily cycles for MDT (Mfg. X) cells.

Acknowledgements

This research was in part supported by the US National Science Foundation (NSF) Grant Nos. CNS-1566579 and ECCS-1611333. Any opinions, findings or conclusions in this paper are those of the authors and do not necessarily reflect the views of the sponsoring agency.

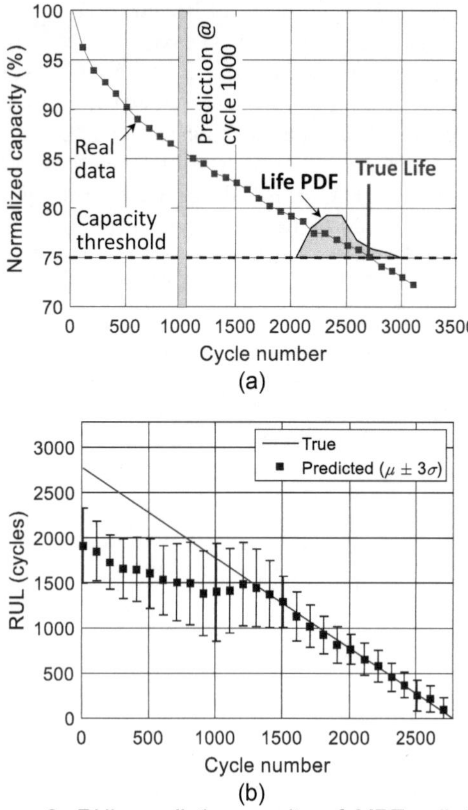

Figure 2. RUL prediction results of MDT cell 1 using generic particle filter [2]. Figure (a) plots the RUL prediction at cycle 1000 and (b) plots the RUL predictions at multiple cycles. Error bars in (b) indicate intervals of ± three standard deviations around mean RUL predictions.

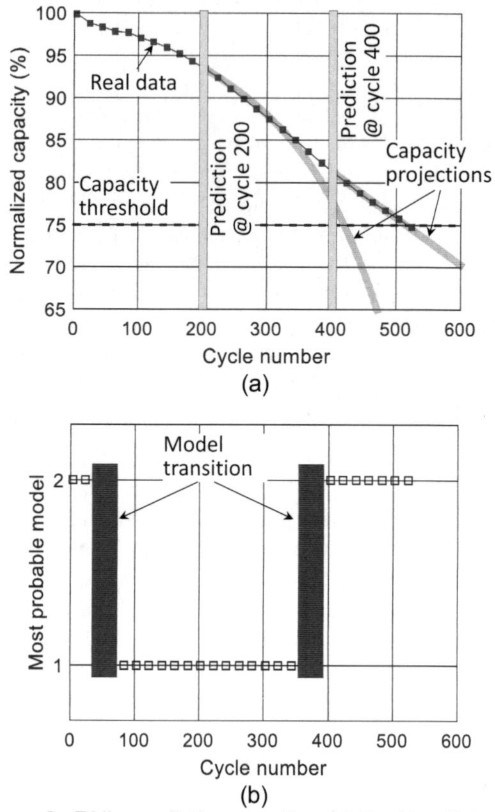

Figure 3. RUL prediction results of Mfg. X cell 1 using multiple model particle filter [2]. Figure (a) plots the mean capacity projections starting from cycles 200 and 400, respectively and (b) plots the most probable fade models at multiple cycles.

References

1. Hu, C., Jain, G., Tamirisa, P. and Gorka, T., 2014. Method for estimating capacity and predicting remaining useful life of lithium-ion battery. *Applied Energy*, *126*, pp.182-189.
2. Hu, C., Ye, H., Jain, G. and Schmidt, C., 2018. "Remaining useful life assessment of lithium-ion batteries in implantable medical devices," *Journal of Power Sources*, *375*, pp.118-130.
3. Hu C., Jain G., Schmidt C., Strief C., and Sullivan M., 2015, "Online Estimation of Lithium-Ion Battery Capacity Using Sparse Bayesian Learning," *Journal of Power Sources*, v289, p105–113.
4. Jason Brown, Erik Scott, Craig Schmidt, William Howard, 2006, "A Practical Longevity Model for Lithium-Ion Batteries: De-coupling the Time and Cycle-Dependence of Capacity Fade," 208th ECS Meeting, Abstract #239.
5. O. Cappe, S. J. Godsill, and E. Moulines, 2007, "An overview of existing methods and recent advances in sequential Monte Carlo," *IEEE Proceedings*, v95, n5, p899–924.
6. McGinnity S and Irwin G W 2000 Multiple model bootstrap filter for maneuvering target tracking IEEE Trans. Aerosp. Electron. Syst. 36 1006–12
7. Bores Y and Driessen J N 2003 Interacting multiple model particle filter IEE Proc. Radar Sonar Navig. 150 344–9.
8. Doucet, A., Gordon, N. J., & Krishnamurthy, V. (2001). Particle filters for state estimation of jump Markov linear systems. *IEEE Transactions on signal processing*, *49*(3), 613-624.
9. Doucet, A., & Johansen, A. M. (2009). A tutorial on particle filtering and smoothing: Fifteen years later. *Handbook of nonlinear filtering*, *12*(656-704).

An Analysis of Hybridization Methods and Techniques for CF_x-MnO_2 Blends

Paula C. Latorre and Terrill B. Atwater
U.S. Army Communications-Electronics Research, Development, and Engineering Center
Power Division – Command, Power, and Integration Directorate

Abstract: *Batteries are typically the limiting factor in the performance of most commercial and military portable electronic equipment. This is a result of the restrictions on the size, weight, and configuration placed on the power source by the equipment. Because of its high energy density, lithium carbon fluoride (CF_x, $0.6 < x < 1.3$) is one of the most promising non-rechargeable electrochemical systems to meet growing portable energy needs. Blending the CF_x chemistry with manganese dioxide (MnO_2) has become a very popular technique used to mitigate some undesirable properties of CF_x, such as poor performance at low temperature. The purpose of this paper is to analyze varying hybridization methods of CF_x-MnO_2. Coin cells were fabricated using three different hybridization methods: homogeneous blended cathode, heterogeneous blended cathode, and separate cells. Ratios of CF_x-MnO_2 were also varied to evaluate their electrochemical properties. Cells were discharged from 0.5-4.0 mA/cm2 under both constant current and pulsed loads. The pulse capability of these experimental cells reveals the thermodynamic and kinetic properties of the system. Optimal CF_x blends should therefore have an operating discharge potential between 2.0-2.5 V (i.e., similar thermodynamics and kinetics) in order to have a uniform integrated hybrid chemistry. Results show similar performance among each Li/CF_x-MnO_2 fabrication method.*

Keywords: Li/CF_x; Li/CF_x-MnO_2; cathode blend; hybrid battery; lithium batteries

Introduction

Advances in the capabilities of portable electronic systems continue to increase those systems' power and energy requirements. The military continues to need reliable, safe, and efficient power sources with high energy densities, high power, and low weight that will enable the Warfighter to complete his or her mission. Additionally, the power source must also be able to operate over an extremely wide temperature range, from -30 to 55°C. These requirements drastically limit the available battery technologies that can be utilized by the military. The U.S. Army is currently relying on Li/SO_2 and Li/MnO_2 for non-rechargeable batteries to power portable electronic systems. These chemistries have relatively limited energy densities, and with increasing technology-driven requirements, the need for a higher energy power source has become more prevalent.

Li/CF_x systems are known to have a high theoretical specific capacity (864 mAh/g) when compared to other primary chemistries [1]. This chemistry has been demonstrated to have double to triple the capacity and energy of Li/SO_2 systems; however, it has limited operability at low temperatures and it requires a high level of heat mitigation. Additionally, resources are scare due to high manufacturing costs. Hybridization of this chemistry focuses on providing a cost effective solution by retaining the chemistry's high performance characteristics while removing or mitigating its weaknesses. This paper investigates the various fabrication and hybridization methods of the Li/CFx-MnO2 blended battery to determine optimal performance.

Background

Carbon fluorides have some very desirable properties, including high energy density and operation under a wide temperature range. Some disadvantages of pure Li/CF_x batteries include their low-medium discharge rates, initial voltage delays at low temperatures, and high cost. Some methods to improve the electrochemical performance of CF_x include carbothermal treatment [2, 3], enhanced surface treatment [4], and the replacement of graphite to carbon nanostructures, which improves rate capability [5].

Another common practice to increase the electrochemical performance of CF_x is mixing the cathode with another active cathode material such as MnO_2 [6], $Ag_2V_4O_{11}$ (SVO) [7-10], or MoO_3 [11]. This effort uses a variety of fabrication methods to hybridize CF_x with MnO_2. The hybridization of CF_x-MnO_2 has been a common practice in industry in the attempt to produce safe and reliable, high-capacity primary lithium batteries with a wide temperature range. A hybrid takes advantage of the beneficial characteristics of both cathode materials. Inherently, the hybrid will have advantages over single component cathode systems and will mitigate limitations of these systems. The same phenomena applies in rechargeable systems. H. Y. Trans investigated the blended cathode system of $LiMn_2O_4$ and $LiNi_{0.8}Co_{0.15}Al_{0.05}O_2$, where the two materials were selected in order to compensate for the negative characteristics of the other [12]. A hybrid CF_x-MnO_2 system will therefore have greater cathode efficiency, higher initial voltage, lower material costs, and greater pulse and rate capabilities.

This effort continues the evaluation of the hybridization of CF_x due to its high energy characteristics. This office has been investigating hybrids and hybridization techniques for many years [13-15]. Generally, a hybrid cathode is fabricated by mixing or blending active components together to form a uniform homogeneous mixture. In a blended cathode system, the lithium extraction in one parent cathode material may impact the other. Additionally, lithium diffusion may also impact the discharge profile of the blended cathode system, specifically with respect to its cell voltage in comparison to its parent cathode components. Because of the complex nature of blended cathode systems, it is an active research area for both primary and rechargeable systems [16]. Additionally, many studies are also using mathematical modeling to characterize the interaction of parent cathodes to optimize the blended hybrid system [17].

However, there are limited reports of the electrochemical effects on the hybrid system created by varying the cathode arrangement, with the exception of Li and Feng [17], who investigated various heterogeneous arrangements of CF_x-MnO_2 and their respective effects on electrochemical performance. The results indicated that a mixed parallel arrangement provides the best rate performance.

Another hybrid battery system that industry has commonly utilized is the combination of a battery and a supercapacitor, known as a hybrid energy storage system (HESS). Similarly to blended hybrid cathode systems, HESS components also complement each other and bring out advantageous electrical properties [19]. To our knowledge, this hybridization method has not been utilized solely with batteries, specifically in regards to CF_x and MnO_2 battery systems. This work focuses on three different hybridization techniques in order to understand and analyze their electrochemical effects.

Experimental

This effort focuses on the fabrication of three varying assembly techniques for the development of a blend or hybrid CF_x-MnO_2 battery system. Active materials of both MnO_2 and CF_x, where $1.05 < x < 1.2$, were received from multiple sources and integrated into conventional 2025 coin cells with a surface area of 2.0 cm^2. Coin cells were fabricated using three different hybridization methods and will be referred to as homogeneous blend, heterogeneous blend (internal hybrid), or external hybrid (separate cells).

The first hybridization method consists of a homogeneous mixture of active cathode material. Various cathode samples were synthesized in multiple ratios of CF_x to MnO_2. The blended cathode was then incorporated into experimental coin cells. The second method consists of a heterogeneous blend of active materials as shown in Figure 1. Separate cathodes of CF_x and MnO_2 were fabricated and then assembled in concentric rings. The ratio of CF_x to MnO_2 was varied by changing the diameter of each ring or circle. The subsequent heterogeneous cathodes were then incorporated into experimental coin cells. The final hybridization method consists of separate CF_x and MnO_2 cathodes incorporated into coin cells and welded in parallel to form a hybrid battery system.

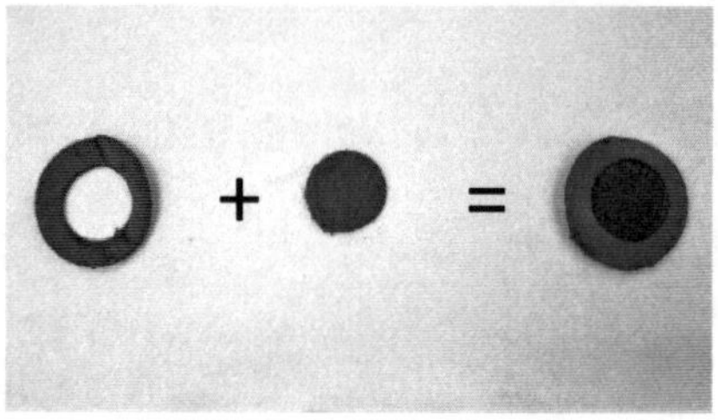

Figure 1. Hybridization method 2, showing a CF_x ring (left) paired with an MnO_2 disc (middle) to form a heterogeneous cathode mixture (right).

All experimental cells were composed of a pure lithium anode separated from the cathode by a nonwoven glass separator. The cathode was fabricated using a solid state process. The active material, carbon (pure black), and polytetrafluoroethylene (PTFE) were mixed together in an 85:10:5 weight ratio, respectively. The cathode mixture was rolled to approximately 0.04 cm and dried in a vacuum oven for a minimum of four hours. A 0.075 cm thick lithium foil was cut using a 16 mm diameter hole punch. The cathode was cut into 2.0 cm^2 discs, resulting in a 0.09-0.13 g cathode for the coin cells. A 0.01 cm nonwoven glass separator served both as the separator and as a wick for the electrolyte. The electrolyte used was 1 molar $LiPF_6$ in proportional mixtures of dimethyl carbonate and ethylene carbonate.

Before testing, cell impedance and OCV were measured for each cell using a Solartron Model 1260 Impedance Analyzer. Cells were discharged with an ARBIN MSTAT4 battery cycler system controlled by MITS Pro software. All tests were performed at room temperature. The cells were discharged to either 1.0 V or 0 V. Cells were discharged based on observed loads in actual operating environments. Batteries used in communication electronic equipment will more commonly experience a varying current or pulse load. Typically, batteries are not hybridized and thrive in continuous load applications; however, with the advancement in technology and the push for a common power architecture and power management, varying loads are becoming more prevalent. During a continuous discharge, a hybrid battery would be underutilized; however, a hybridized battery can more efficiently distribute a pulse or sporadic load. Therefore, discharge rates were determined by scaling down the cell loading experienced in a battery pack. The discharge rates consisted of a pulse or constant current draw between 0.4 and 3.0 mA/cm^2. A minimum of three cells were used for each test condition.

Results

Li/CF_x-MnO_2 coin cells were fabricated using a homogeneous blended cathode containing 60%, 50%, and 30% CF_x. These cells were then discharged at ambient temperature at a continuous current of 2 mA and 8 mA until a 1 V cutoff. Additionally, some cells were discharged under a pulse load of 8 mA for 1 min, followed by a 1 mA load for 7 min until a cutoff of 1 V was reached. Voltage and load distributions were determined based on the scale-down from cell loading in a typical Li/CF_x pack.

Figure 2 shows the electrochemical characterization of the Li/CF_x-MnO_2 cells containing a homogeneous blended cathode with varying concentrations of CF_x. In both figures, the discharge profiles demonstrate two voltage plateaus; the first occurs with the activation of MnO_2 and the second with the activation of CF_x.

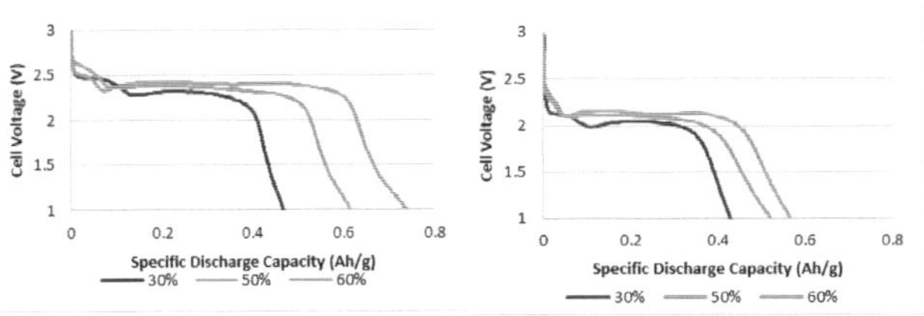

Figure 2. The discharge profiles of homogeneous cathode blends of Li/CF_x-MnO_2 coin cells tested at 2 mA (1mA/cm^2) (left) and 8 mA (4mA/cm^2) (right) continuously. Curves represent varying weight ratios of CF_x in the sample.

The left image in Figure 2 shows that the specific discharge capacities of the cells at a 2 mA continuous load are between 0.46 and 0.74 mAh/g. Each representative cell contained varying ratios of CF_x in the cathode blend: 60%, 50%, and 30%, by weight. As expected, the specific capacities increase with increasing CF_x concentration in the cell. Similarly, the nominal operating voltage also increases slightly with CF_x concentration. The right image in Figure 2 shows that the specific discharge capacities of the cells at an 8 mA continuous load are between 0.43 and 0.57 mAh/g.

Li/CF_x cells were also discharged in a pulse profile to determine the system's thermodynamics and kinetics. The pulse discharge consisted of an 8 mA high discharge for 1 min followed by a 1 mA "rest" for 7 min. The average current distribution across the cell was 1.87 mA. During a duty cycle, the kinetics of the cell are attributed to the high discharge rate, whereas under no current or low discharge rates, the cell recovery is attributed to thermodynamics.

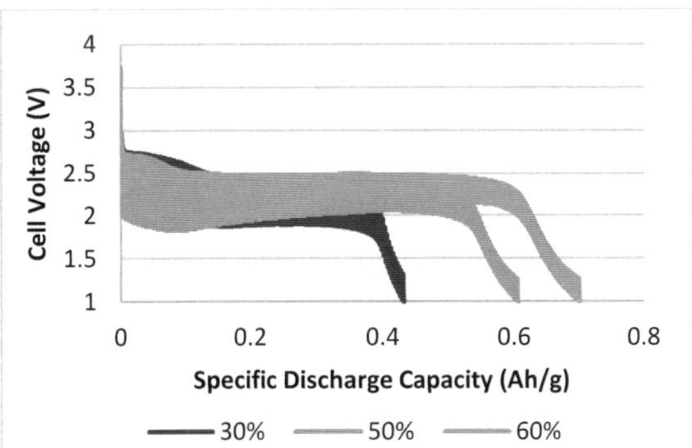

Figure 4. The discharge profiles of homogeneous cathode blends of Li/CF_x-MnO_2 in coin cells discharged at 8 mA for 1 min followed by 1 mA for 7 min. Curves represent varying ratios of CF_x in sample.

Figure 4 shows the pulse discharge profile of Li/CF_x-MnO_2 cells containing a homogeneous blended cathode with varying concentrations of CF_x to a 1 V cutoff, with the observed specific capacity being similar to that of the 2 mA test. The differential potential between high and low discharge was approximately 0.5 V, with higher differential voltages seen during early discharge. Therefore, the thermodynamics and kinetics of Li/CF_x were more balanced and consistent once the differential potential stabilized. This occurred once the cell discharged approximately 20% of its available capacity.

Li/CF_x-MnO_2 cathodes were fabricated using the heterogeneous blended method of hybridization. Figure 5 shows representative x-ray images of the cathode in CT slices. This method was used to aid in the visualization of the cathode morphology. The right image shows the CF_x outer ring surrounded by the highly dense MnO_2 center. The thickness of the cathode slightly varied and some sporadic particles of MnO_2 can be seen.

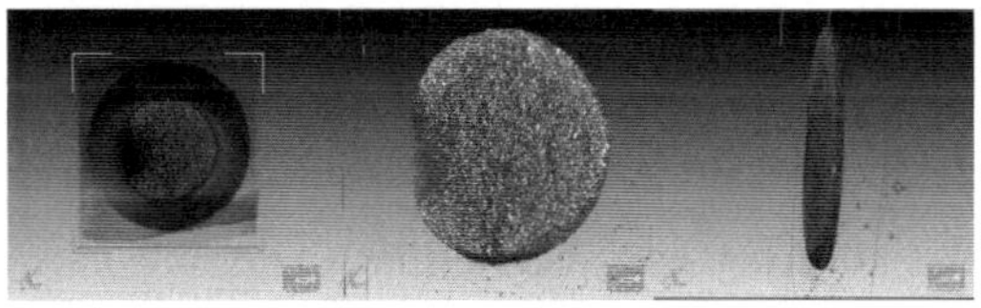

Figure 5. The CT images of the heterogeneous cathode mixture (left), zoomed in on centralized MnO_2 and side profile of MnO_2.

Li/CF_x-MnO_2 electrochemical coin cells were then made using the heterogeneous blended cathodes. Figure 6 shows the pulse discharge profile of Li/CF_x-MnO_2 cells containing a homogeneous blended cathode to a 1 V cutoff. Each representative cell contained varying ratios of CF_x in the cathode blend: 80%, 50%, and 27% by weight with a specific capacity of 0.43-0.79 Ah/g. The observed cell performance is similar to the performance of homogeneously blended Li/CF_x-MnO_2 cells.

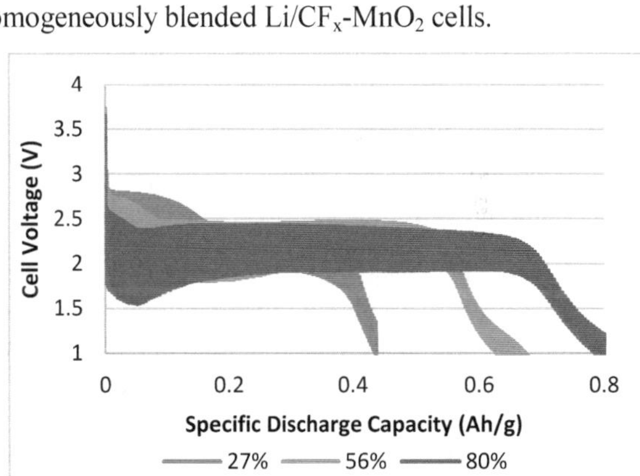

Figure 6. The discharge profiles of homogeneous cathode blends of Li/CF_x-MnO_2 coin cells discharged at 8 mA for 1 min followed by 1 mA for 7 min. Curves represent varying ratios of CF_x in sample.

Figure 7 shows the discharge profile of two representative external hybrid cell packs discharged under a pulse profile (16 mA for 1 min followed by 2 mA for 7 min) down to 1 V. These cell packs contained a $LiCF_x$ cell in parallel with an MnO_2 cell with 40% CF_x active material. Cells delivered approximately 0.51 Ah/g.

Figure 8 shows the discharge profile of four MnO_2 coin cells in parallel with five CF_x coin cells to demonstrate an optimized cell pack with respect to OCV.

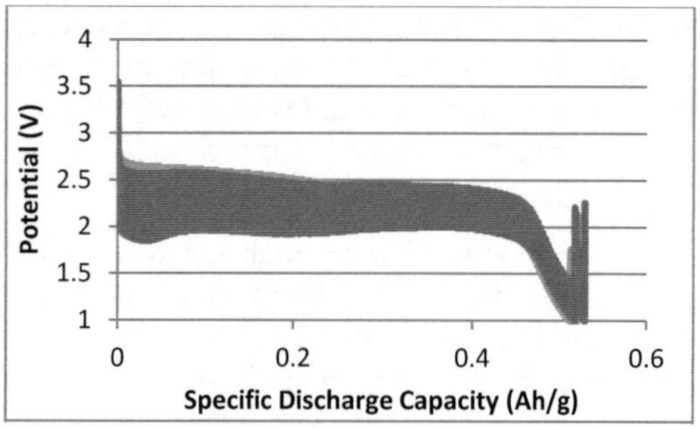

Figure 7. The discharge profiles of hybrid cell packs of Li/CF_x and MnO_2 coin cells discharged at 16 mA for 1 min followed by 2 mA for 7 min.

The external hybrid cell packs were discharged under a pulse profile (16 mA for 1 min followed by 2 mA for 7 min) down to 5 V (1-1.25V across each cell). These cell packs contained approximately 50% CF_x active material and lasted approximately 19.3 hours (1Wh/g) to a cutoff of 5 V. The differential potential was approximately 1.4 V consistently. Therefore, the thermodynamics and kinetics of the cell pack were very well balanced and constant throughout discharge.

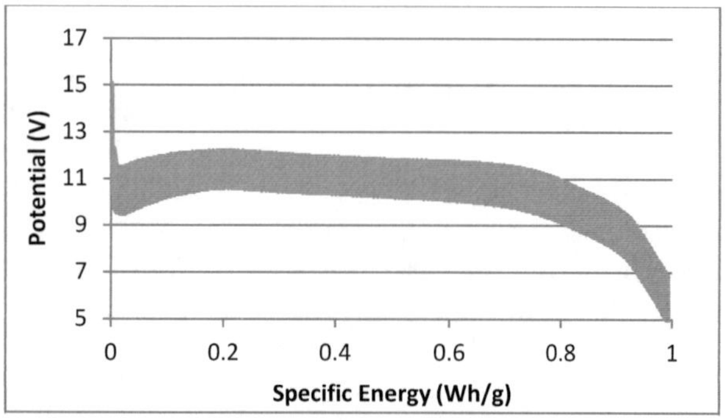

Figure 8. The discharge profile of hybrid cell packs of Li/CF_x and MnO_2 coin cells discharged at 16 mA for 1 min followed by 2 mA for 7 min.

Figure 9 shows a comparison of the specific capacity of all cells tested under a pulse profile in this effort. The graph shows a similar linear correlation for cells fabricated using the homogeneous and heterogeneous blended cathodes.

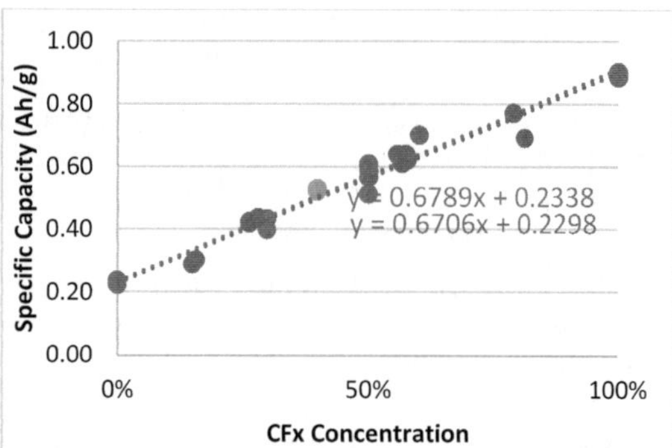

Figure 9. Specific capacity plotted as a function of CF_x present in hybrid cell systems: homogeneous blend cells (blue), heterogeneous blend cells (red), and external hybrid cells (green).

Conclusion

An ideal candidate for cathode hybridization should have a discharge profile within the thermodynamic and kinetic profile of the primary material. The resultant hybrid would have equal or narrower differential discharge potentials, demonstrating similar thermodynamics and kinetics. All hybrid fabrication methods demonstrated similar performances given the same CF_x concentration, with most of the variation occurring in the first 20% of discharge.

References:

1. P. Lam, and R. Yazami. *J. Power Sources* 153.2 (2006): 354-359.
2. Sheng S. Zhang et al. *J. Power Sources* 188 (2009): 601-605.
3. Sheng S. Zhang et al. *J. Power Sources* 191 (2009): 648-652.
4. Q. Zhang et al *J. Power Sources* 195 (2010): 2914-2917.
5. Y. Li et al. *J. Power Sources* 196 (2011): 2246-2250.
6. A. Kozawa, *J. Electrochemical Society*. 134 (1987) 780.
7. H. Gan, R.S. Rubino, E.S. Takeuchi, *J. Power Sources* 146 (2005) 101.
8. K. Chen, D.R. Merritt, W.G. Howard, C.L. Schmidt, P.M. Skarstad, *J. Power Sources* 162 (2006) 837-840.
9. P.M. Gomadam, D.R. Merritt, E.R. Scott, C.L. Schmidt, P.M. Skarstad, J.W. Weidner, *J. Power Sources* 174 (2007) 872.
10. P. Meduri, et al. *Electrochemistry Communications* 13.12 (2011): 1344-1348.
11. S.J. Ebel, S.A. Smesko, E.S. Takeuchi, 1997 (U. S. Patent 5,667,916).
12. H.Y. Tran et al., *J. Electrochemical Society* 158 (2011) A556–A561.
13. T. B. Atwater, P. J. Cygan, and F. C. Leung, *J. Power Sources* 91.1 (2000): 27-36.
14. L. P. Jarvis, T. B. Atwater, and P. J. Cygan, *J. Power Sources* 79.1 (1999): 60-63.
15. L. P. Jarvis, T. B. Atwater, and P. J. Cygan, *Aerospace and Electronic Systems Magazine, IEEE* 15.9 (2000): 37-41.
16. S. B. Chikkannanavar et al., *J. Power Sources* 248 (2014) 91-100.
17. P. M. Gomadom et al., *J. Power Sources* 174 (2007) 872-876.
18. Yu Li and Wei Feng., *J. Power Sources* 274 (2015) 1292-1299.
19. L. Kouchachvili, W. Yaici, E. Entchev., *J. Power Sources* 374 (2018)

Li / CF_x Cells for Extreme Low Temperature and High Power Applications

Ryo Tamaki, Hiroshi Nakahara, Som Mohanty
EnerSys
12744 San Fernando Rd, Sylmar, California, USA, 91342
ryo.tamaki@enersys.com / 1-818-833-2028

Abstract: *EnerSys developed Li / CF_x cells capable of high power an d low temperature discharge that still retain advantage of high energy utilizing two different approaches, one with a novel electrode architecture in combination with a new active material and a new electrolyte, another with a novel hybrid electrode design with lithium vanadium oxide (LVO). The new Li / CF_x cells perform well at extreme low temperatures, even at -70°C, a property not know in conventional Li / CF_x cells.*

Keywords: lithium CFx cells, high power, low temperature, lithium vanadium oxide, hybrid electrode

Introduction

CF_x is attractive as a choice of the Li-ion cathode material because of its high theoretical specific capacity, 865mAh/g, and low self-discharge rate during storage and wide temperature range capability. However, CF_x has poor high rate capability and low temperature performance. CF_x is an insulating material which has high electrical resistivity and low ionic conductivity. Therefore in the beginning of discharge, before conductive amorphous carbon formation, the initial voltage drop is usually observed. Conductive amorphous carbon forms during discharge as shown below [1].

$$CF_x + x\mathrm{Li}^+ + xe^- \rightarrow XC + x\mathrm{LiF}$$

Conventional Li / CF_x cells are comprised of CF_x material that are either pressed into thick pellets or wound pressed electrodes with non-woven separator into a cylindrical shape. These cells perform well for long term discharge but cannot perform very well under high power discharge nor at low temperatures because of the dense and thick electrode structures.

Comparatively there are also Li / MnO_2 cells. These cells are able to deliver high power, but do not have as much capacity as CF_x cells especially after storage at higher temperatures.

EnerSys developed new Li / CF_x cells capable of high power and low temperature discharge that still retain its advantage of high energy, a property not found in conventional Li / CF_x cells.

Two different approaches were utilized to achieve the desired performances.

1) An unique electrode fabrication approach:

In order to develop a Li / CF_x cell that is capable of high power and discharge at low temperatures, a unique method of electrode fabrication was used. Instead of pressing pellets for electrodes, the CF_x material was coated on aluminum substrate to prepare an electrode with a thin layer of CF_x (**Figure 1**). The thin layer electrode enables it to handle a much higher current load than a conventional pelletized electrode. The improvement in the high current capability is clearly observed in AC impedance measurement at 1k*Hz*. The impedance/area of the coated electrode is much lower than that of the pelletized electrode with values of 0.2mΩ/mm^2 for the coated electrode and 500 mΩ/mm^2 for the pelletized electrode.

Figure 1. The top figure shows the flexibility of this thin film coated electrode. This characteristic allows the electrode to be wound into a jellyroll and fitted inside a D-cell can as shown in the bottom figure.

In addition to the unique electrode processing methods, a higher surface area CF_x material was also utilized (**Figure 2**). The precursor carbon was carefully chosen to provide desired properties such as crystallinity, particle size / surface area, in addition to a careful control the fluorination degree.

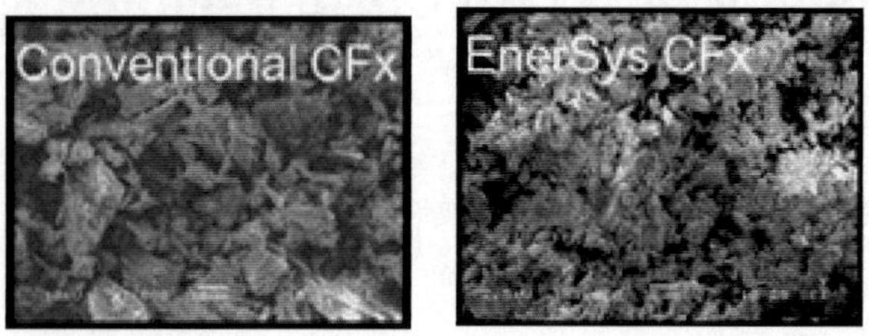

Figure 2. A unique high surface area CFx powder, comparison with conventional CFx powder.

EnerSys's Li / CF_x cells also contain specialized low viscosity electrolyte and a microporous separator film. These are key elements to the cell's high power and low temperature capabilities (**Figure 3**).

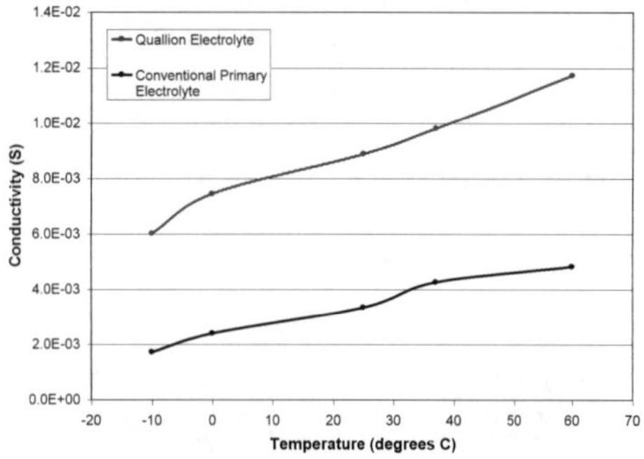

Figure 3. A comparison of EnerSys low temperature electrolyte with a conventional electrolyte conductivities.

AA cell was prepared with the new designs with capacity of 2.5Ah, achieving volumetric energy density of 966 Wh/L and the specific energy density of 385 Wh/kg, numbers equivalent or exceeding conventional CFx cells.

Most importantly, the cell achieved a wide range of temperature discharge capability, ranging from -70°C up to 60°C (**Figure 4**). Especially, the low temperature performance is unprecedented, 89% of the capacity at -40°C and 38% retention at -70°C (Table 1).

Table 1. Capacities of AA cell prepared with the new design at various temperatures

Temperature	Capacity (Ah)	Capacity (% of 2.5Ah)
60 °C	2.58	103
25 °C	2.64	105
-40 °C	2.22	89
-70 °C	0.92	38

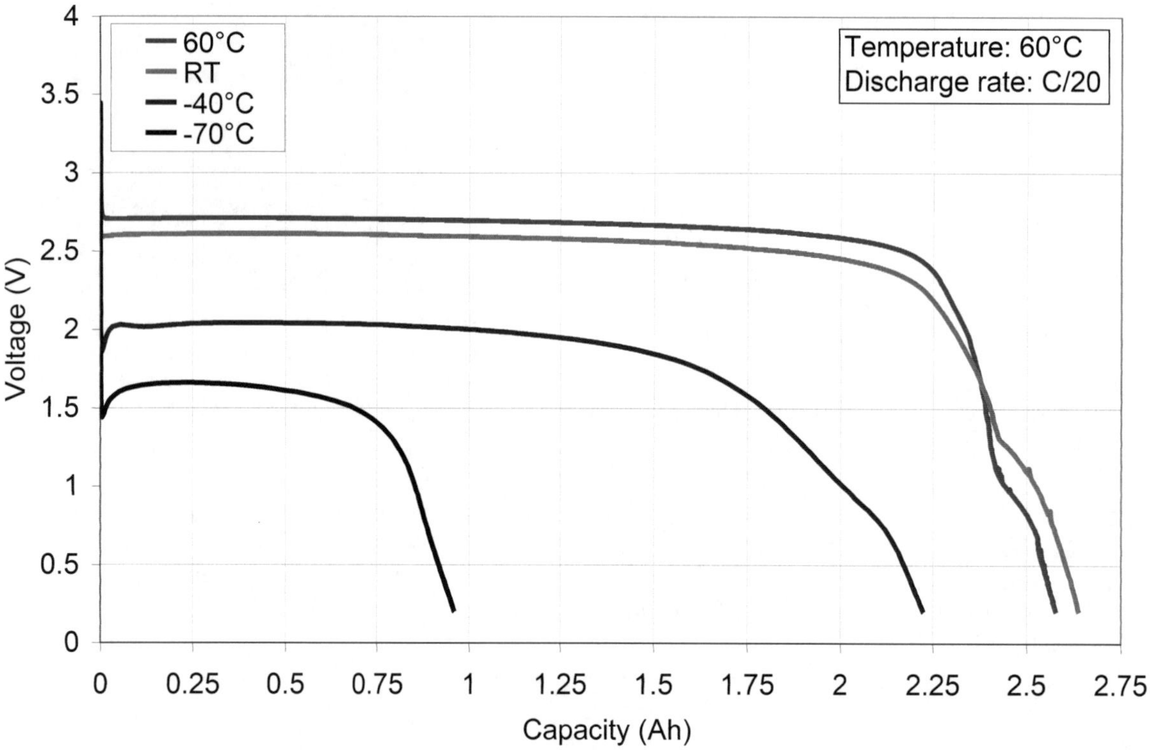

Figure 4. Wide range temperature performance of AA cell prepared with the new designs.

2) A hybrid electrode approach:

In order to mitigate the initial voltage drop and to improve the high rate capability, CF_x was mixed with lithium vanadate. Among several potential cathode materials, vanadium oxides are promising positive materials because of their high capacity, high power capabilities, good cycle life, facile preparation and stability in air [2-5]. LVO has a monoclinic crystal structure of P21/m and the crystal unit of $V_3O_8^-$ in b-c planes stacked in the direction of axis to form the layer structure [6, 7]. $V_3O_8^-$ is linked by Li^+ at the octahedral site. Excess lithium corresponding to 0.2 moles of Li occupies the tetrahedral sites between layers. In highly crystalline LVO, preexisting lithium does not hinder lithium insertion during the discharge process and acts as a pillar to stabilize the host structure during the lithium insertion and extraction process, promoting good cycle life [8]. In addition to improve the high rate capability and to mitigate the initial voltage drop of CF_x through the addition of lithium vanadate, the discharge capability at low temperature is also improved by the addition of lithium vanadate and low temperature electrolyte.

$Li_{1+x}V_3O_8$ has a theoretical capacity of 360mAh/g that corresponds to the following reaction:

$$Li_{1+x}V_3O_8 + 3Li+ + 3e^- \leftrightarrow Li_4V_3O_8$$

When CF_x and LVO are mixed in a single electrode, LVO responds to a high power load with it's high rate capability, then LVO is charged by CF_x as LVO voltage drops below thta of CF_x at lower SOC (**Figure 5**) through the following reaction.

$$Li_{1+y}V_3O_8 + (CF)_x \rightarrow Li_{1+y-x}V_3O_8 + xC + xLiF$$

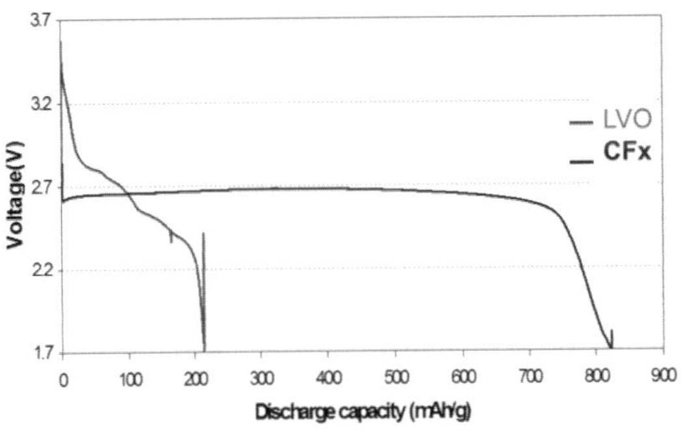

Figure 5. Voltage profiles of LVO and CF_x

When subjected to C/3 continuous discharge at room temperature, LVO / CF_x hybrid electrode was able to demonstrate more than 700mAh/g capacity while pure CF_x electrode failed to show any discharge capacity.

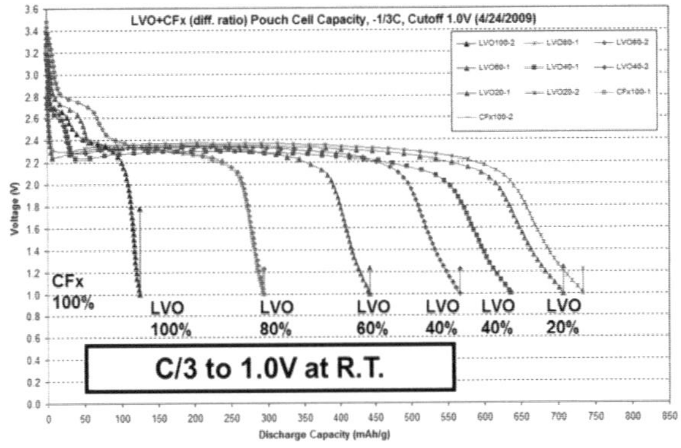

Figure 6. Discharge curves of the hybrid cell with different LVO/CF_x ratios

The hybrid electrode also demonstrated much higher pulse capability. For example, during four 1.5C pulse discharge test, the hybrid electrode cell performed well without significant voltage delay. The addition of LVO did not have an adverse effect on the storage capability, showing the capacity retention more than a year without any capacity fade. The cell with the hybrid electrode demonstrated remarkable low temperature performance, even at an extremely severe condition of -29°C, not observed in conventional Li/CF_x cells.

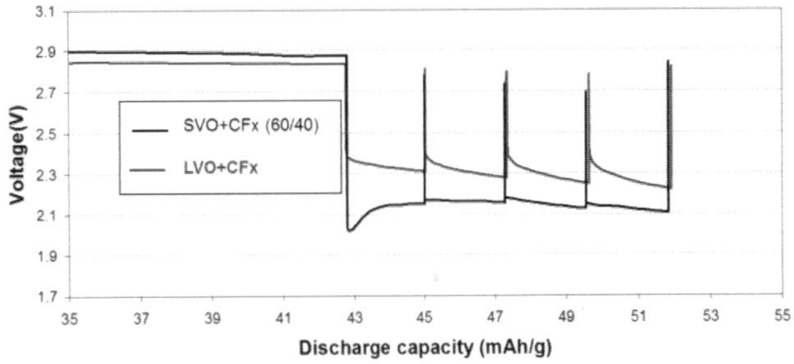

Figure 7. Response of LVO/CF_x hybrid cell to 1.5C rate pulse

References

1. N. Tsuyoshi, N. Watanabe, "*Graphite Fluorides and Carbon -Fluorine Compounds*", CNC Press, Florida, 1991..
2. G. Pistoia, M. Pasquali, G. Wang, L. Li, *Journal of The Electrochemical Society*, 137 (1990) 2365-2370.
3. G. Pistoia, M. Pasquali, M. Tocci, R.V. Moshtev, V. Maner, *Journal of The Electrochemical Society*, 132 (1985) 281-284.
4. S. Panero, M. Pasquali, G. Pistoia, *Journal of The Electrochemical Society*, 130 (1983) 1225-1227.
5. G. Pistoia, S. Panero, M. Tocci, R.V. Moshtev, V. Manev, *Solid State Ionics*, 13 (1984) 311-318.
6. L.A. de Picciotto, K.T. Adendorff, D.C. Liles, M.M. Thackeray, *Solid State Ionics*, 62 (1993) 297-307.
7. A. Wadsley, *Acta Crystallographica*, 10 (1957) 261-267.
8. J. Kawakita, T. Miura, T. Kishi, *Journal of Power Sources*, 83 (1999) 79-83.

Effects of Low Temperature Discharge on Performance of Lithium Oxyhalide Primary Cells

Arden P. Johnson and Yufei Wang
Electrochem Solutions, Inc.
670 Paramount Drive, Raynham, MA 02767
ajohnson@electrochemsolutions.com / 1-781-830-5830

Abstract: *Lithium oxyhalide primary batteries can function at temperatures well below 0°C, though with reduced running voltage and rate capability. In this talk we show discharge results comparing the capabilities of the different oxyhalide chemistries in the temperature range from 0°C down to -40°C, with a focus on identifying detrimental effects of low temperature discharge. We include results from mixed temperature testing in which the cells are first discharged at very low temperature and then at a higher temperature; the results help establish whether starting the battery discharge in cold conditions will harm the subsequent performance of the batteries.*

Keywords: lithium primary battery; thionyl chloride; sulfuryl chloride; low temperature.

Introduction

General effects of temperature on cell discharge: Chemical reaction rates decrease at low temperatures, and both the oxidation-reduction reactions and charge transfer processes that occur during battery discharge occur more slowly. As a consequence, the closed-circuit voltages when a load is applied are lower, and this in turn results in lower capacity being obtained to a given cut-off voltage. All batteries show diminished performance under low temperature conditions. Indeed, many familiar battery chemistries cannot operate at all below about 0°C. Only a few battery types can deliver usable performance in the cold environments that can occur, for example, in the winter, at high altitudes, or in the Arctic.

Lithium oxyhalide primary cells: In lithium oxyhalide primary batteries, the anode is lithium metal, while the active cathode material is an oxidizing liquid that also serves as the electrolyte.[1,2,3] During discharge, the liquid cathode undergoes reduction at the surface of a porous carbon structure, and solid reduction products are deposited on the surface of the carbon. The electrolytes, thionyl chloride and sulfuryl chloride, remain liquid to very low temperatures (sulfuryl chloride freezes at -54°C, while thionyl chloride freezes at -105°C), and in principle the cells can operate down to those low temperatures. However, because of the limited chemical kinetics under those conditions, the solid discharge products can end up poorly distributed in the carbon, with solids that deposit on the outer surface of the carbon blocking access to pores that are deeper in the carbon structure. As a result, the discharge efficiency can end up much lower than it would be at higher temperatures. This phenomenon is referred to as "cathode freeze-over." It is irreversible, so excessive blockage that occurs at low temperature will continue to limit the cell performance even if the operating temperature is later increased. The possible harmful effects of low temperature discharge can be a particular concern in situations where cells have been stored in a cold environment and have then been placed into use while they are still cold.

The present work compares the capabilities of three lithium oxyhalide systems: thionyl chloride ("QTC"); "BCX," a thionyl chloride-based system with a bromine-chlorine additive; and sulfuryl chloride ("CSC"). Cells containing these electrolytes were discharged at various temperatures from room temperature (RT, 23°C) down to -40°C, under both constant current and constant power loads, and also under a pulsed discharge condition. Because the voltage profile of the three electrolyte types is different, the capacity that is obtained can vary considerably, because it depends strongly on the voltage cut-off. We also include results for tests in which the discharge was started at -40°C, but the temperature was then increased after several hours. These results provide a basis for assessing what effect the initial low temperature discharge had on subsequent performance.

Experimental

All of the discharge results described here were obtained using DD-sized (33.5 mm diameter, 111.5 mm length) cells from standard Electrochem production lots. The low temperature tests were conducted in Tenney environmental chambers, with temperatures controlled within ±0.5°C. The room temperature tests were carried out in a room that is maintained at 23±2°C. Cells in the low temperature tests were allowed to stand at the test temperature for at least four hours before any discharge load was applied. The discharge control and data-collection were conducted using battery testing equipment from Maccor.

Five cells of each of the three cell types were tested under each test condition. In the graphs shown here, only one discharge curve for each cell type is shown. In every case the curve that was closest to the average of the five cells tested is shown.

Low Temperature Discharge

Constant Current Discharge: Constant current is the discharge condition most typically shown on manufacturers' datasheets. The lithium oxyhalide chemistries generally give a very flat voltage profile under constant current discharge. In the case of BCX, the bromine-chlorine additive gives a higher voltage plateau at the beginning of the discharge, followed by a lower voltage plateau that continues through the remainder of the discharge.

Figures 1-4 show discharge at 500 mA for each cell type at RT, 0°C, -20°C, and -40°C. Although the relative performance of the three cell types is different at the different temperatures, BCX clearly gives the best performance at -40°C. Note that in the case of constant current discharge, the run-time is directly proportional to the capacity that is delivered.

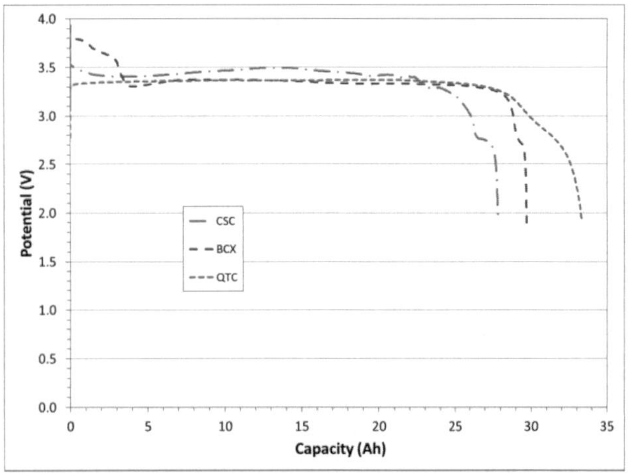

Figure 1. DD cells, 500 mA, 23°C.

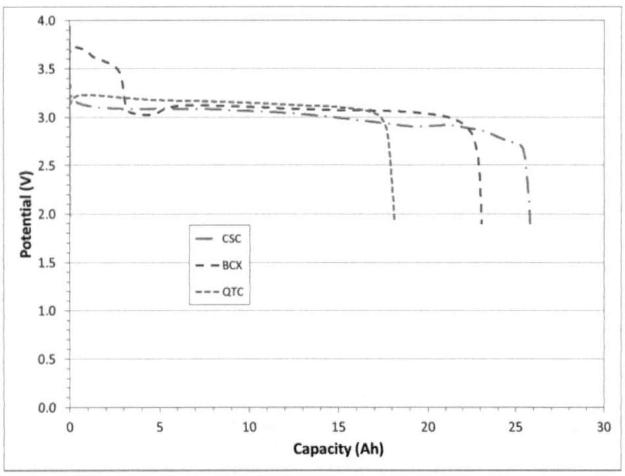

Figure 2. DD cells, 500 mA, 0°C.

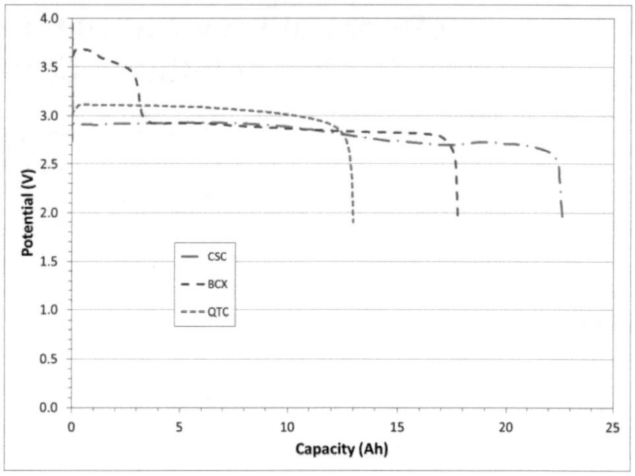

Figure 3. DD cells, 500 mA, -20°C.

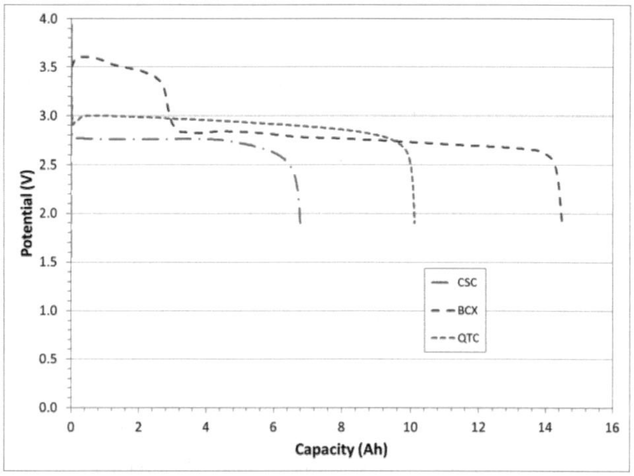

Figure 4. DD cells, 500 mA, -40°C.

Constant Power Discharge: Discharge under a constant power load is different from constant current discharge in that the amount of current drawn from the cell changes as the voltage changes. Because the voltage profile of the oxyhalide cells is flat, however, the two types of discharge condition generally give very similar behavior. In the case of BCX, the initial high voltage plateau in discharge curve provides an advantage to that chemistry because less current is required to maintain the constant power, and a cell with the same capacity can thus deliver a longer run-time.

Figures 5-8 show discharge for the three cell types under a constant power load of 3.6 W. This corresponds to a current level of slightly more than 1 A that increases as the discharge proceeds.

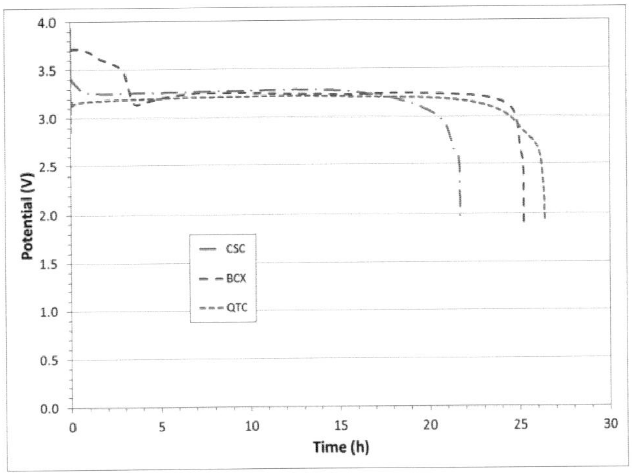

Figure 5. DD cells, 3.6 W, 23°C.

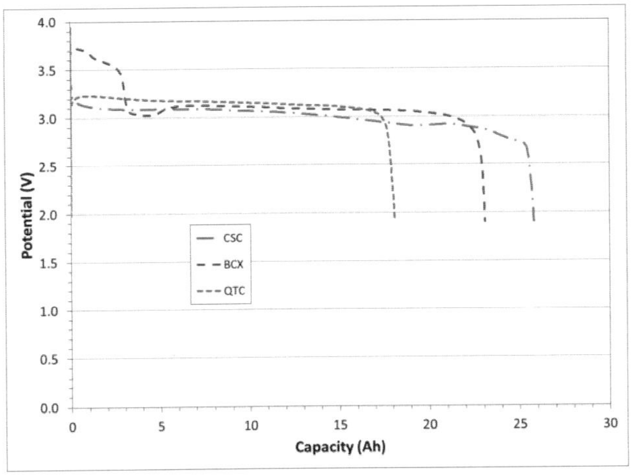

Figure 6. DD cells, 3.6 W, 0°C.

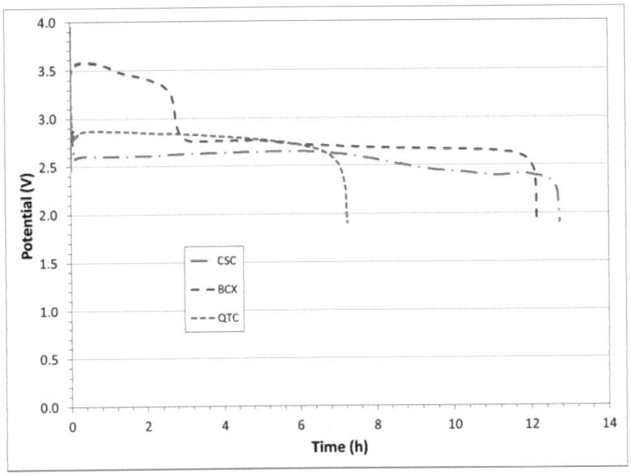

Figure 7. DD cells, 3.6 W, -20°C.

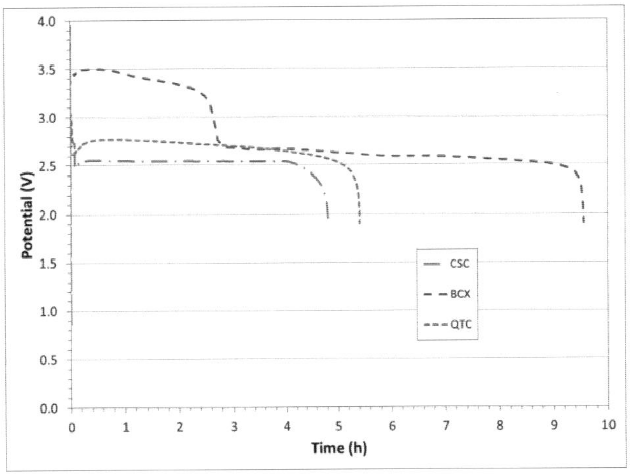

Figure 8. DD cells, 3.6 W, -40°C.

Figure 9 shows discharge of BCX cells at 0°C under a constant power load of 3.6 W and a constant current load of 1.25 A. The voltage profiles and the run-times obtained under these two conditions were nearly identical.

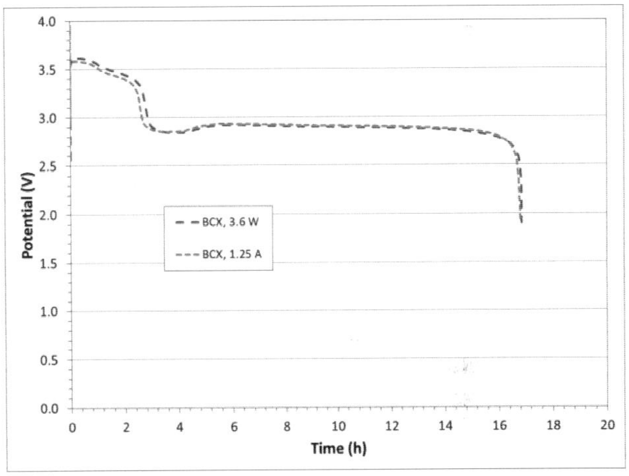

Figure 9. BCX DD cells, 3.6 W vs. 1.25 A at 0°C.

Pulsed Discharge: Under pulsed discharge conditions, the amount of capacity that can be obtained from the cell is determined by when the voltage drops below the voltage cut-off of the device during the heaviest pulse. Because the voltages are lower overall at cold temperatures, modest differences in the voltage drop that occurs during the pulsing can lead to dramatic differences in when the device cut-off is reached.

Figure 10 shows an example of pulsed discharge at 0°C. If the voltage cut-off is taken as 2.0 V, the CSC cell gives the longest run-time, but in the case of a 2.5 V cut-off it is the BCX cell that give the best performance.

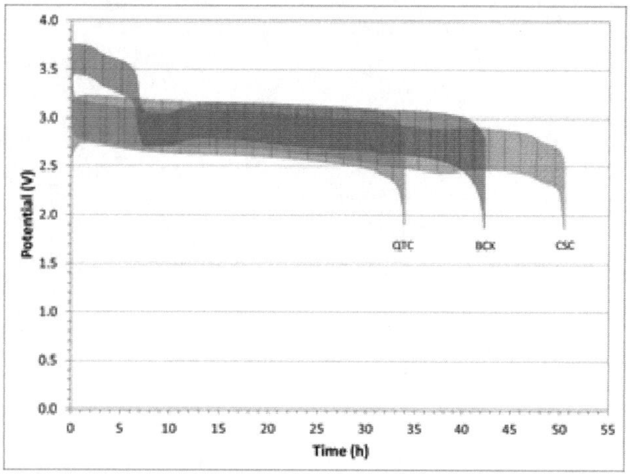

Figure 10. DD cells, pulsed discharge, 0°C.

Mixed Temperature Discharge

Figures 11 and 12 show discharge results for tests in which the cell was discharged under a 3.6 W load for several hours at -40°C, and the temperature was then ramped up to 0°C or RT over the course of two hours, after which the discharge was allowed to proceed until the cells dropped below a final cut-off of 2.0 V. These conditions are intended to simulate a scenario in which cells that have been stored in a cold environment are installed in a tool and the tool is powered up so that its operation can be assessed before the tool is deployed into a warmer environment. Such scenarios are common, for example, in the case of pipeline inspection in northern regions.

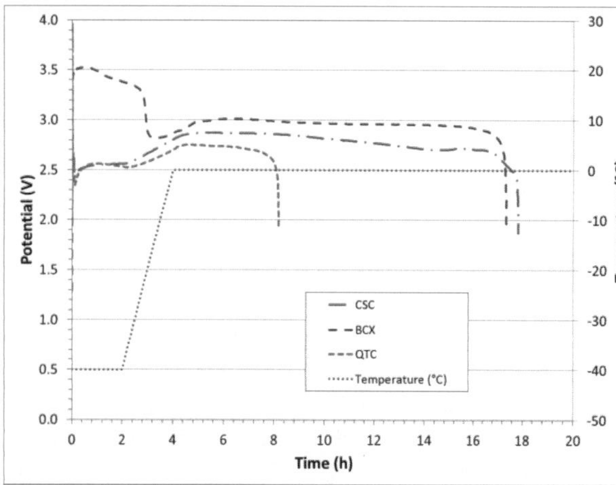

Figure 11. DD cells, 3.6 W: 2 h at -40°C, 2 h ramp to 0°C, discharge to end-of-life at 0°C.

In the first test, the cells were run at -40°C for two hours before the temperature was increased. The voltages of the cells increased with the temperature, and the final capacities obtained were close to 100% of the expected higher temperature capacity.

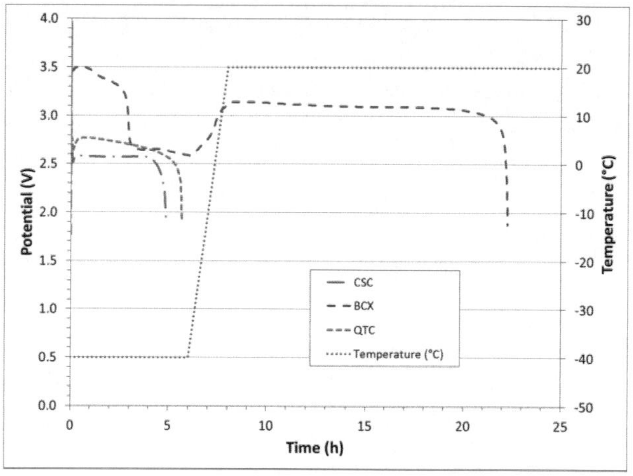

Figure 12. DD cells, 3.6 W: 6 h at -40°C, 2 h ramp to 23°C, discharge to end-of-life at 23°C.

In the second test, the cells were allowed to run for six hours at -40°C before the temperature was increased. During that six hours, the QTC and CSC cells dropped below 2.0 V, and did not restart. The BCX cells, however, remained at usable voltages throughout, and delivered their full higher temperature capacity with no apparent harm from the low temperature discharge.

Conclusions

Both the running voltage and the capacity will decrease when a battery is run at low temperatures. Lithium oxyhalide cells can operate at extremely low temperatures, but the performance available from the cell is very sensitive to the cut-off voltage of the device. Excessive discharge at very low temperature can lead in some cases to reduced capacity due to cathode freeze-over.

Acknowledgements

The authors wish to thank Jim Stawitzky for tabulating information from customers about typical cell usage under low temperature field conditions.

References

1. T. B. Reddy, "Lithium/Thionyl Chloride (Li/$SOCl_2$) Batteries", in D. Linden, T. B. Reddy, *Linden's Handbook of Batteries*, 4th Ed., McGraw-Hill, New York, pp.14.26-14.42, 2011.
2. T. B. Reddy, "Lithium/Oxychloride Batteries", in D. Linden, T. B. Reddy, *Linden's Handbook of Batteries*, 4th Ed., McGraw-Hill, New York, pp.14.42-14.47, 2011.
3. A. P. Johnson, "Lithium-Sulfur/Chlorine", in J. Garche, P. Moseley, Z. Ogumi, D. Rand, B. Scrosati, Eds., *Encyclopedia of Electrochemical Power Sources*, Vol. 4, Elsevier, Amsterdam, pp. 111-119, 2009.

Novel Hybrid Cathode Incorporating Carbon Monofluoride and Phthalocyanine for Primary Lithium Batteries

Joseph Fellner
Air Force Research Laboratory
2130 8th Street
Wright-Patterson AFB, OH 45433-7103
joseph.fellner@us.af.mil

Max Tsao
University of Dayton Research Institute
300 College Park
Dayton, OH 45469-0101

Abstract: *A novel hybrid cathode for primary lithium batteries has been developed through the incorporation of both carbon monofluoride (CF_x) and copper phthalocyanine (CuPc) with some discharge capacities in excess of 3000 mAh/g. This hybrid cathode utilizes nascent carbon produced during discharge of CF_x to enhance the electronic conductivity and performance of the lower voltage CuPc. The synergistic behavior between the two cathode materials is believed to be the primary contributor to the observed high discharge capacity. Experiments are in progress to further elucidate and understand this mechanism.*

Keywords: carbon monofluoride; graphene; synergistic; primary; phthalocyanine; lithium; battery

Introduction

Yamaki and Yamaji were the first to report that a series of phthalocyanines (Pc) could function as high capacity primary battery cathodes in non-aqueous electrolytes with capacities ranging from 450 to 1710 mAh/g [1]. They also showed that these cathodes could function reversibly, but at a much lower capacity and limited cycle life. Recent efforts have shown the effect of conductive carbon on the capacity of iron phthalocyanine (FePc) primary batteries with discharge capacity of up to 2000 mAh/g observed using nanographene platelets [2]. The effort in this paper sought to further enhance the rate and capacity of primary batteries by the use of carbon monofluoride (CF_x) and copper phthalocyanine (CuPc) in a hybrid battery configuration in which a non-provisional patent application was recently submitted [3].

Experimental

Testing was performed with CR2032 coin cells which enabled quick assembly for characterization and failure analysis. The CR2032 coin cells contained two 500 μm thick stainless steel spacers, a wave spring, and an O-ring for sealing. A Hohsen crimper was used to crimp and seal the cells. The cathodes for the coin cells consisted of active material, carbon additive, and binder. Cathodes were produced by solution casting using a doctor blade to spread the mixture to the appropriate thickness. After casting, the cathodes were dried overnight in a vacuum oven. The anodes were lithium metal punched out to the appropriate size from a bulk lithium foil roll. Celgard 2300 was used as the separator. 1 M lithium bis(fluorosulfonylimide) in 1,2-dimethoxyethane (1M LiFSI/DME) was used as the electrolyte.

Electrochemical studies were accomplished using a Maccor 2300 Battery Test System, Gamry Reference 6000, or Landt Instruments CT2001A Battery Testing System. Powder XRD analysis was performed using a Bruker D8 Discover and SEM images were obtained using a JEOL JSM-606.

Results and Discussion

Baseline discharge curves of both CuPc and CF_x are shown below in Figures 1 and 2, respectively.

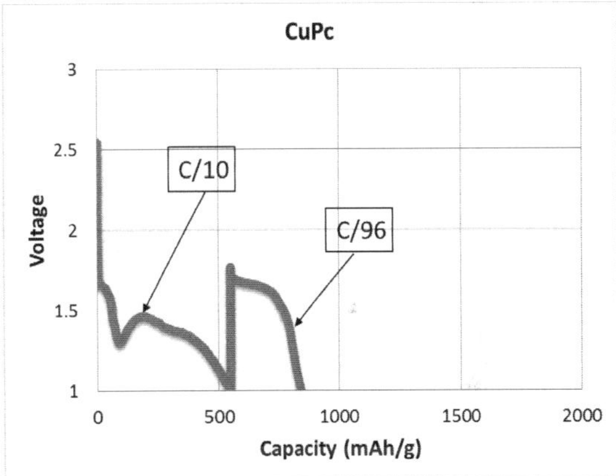

Figure 1. Baseline coin cell discharge curve of 60 wt% CuPc with 30 wt% carbon black and 10 wt% PVDF.

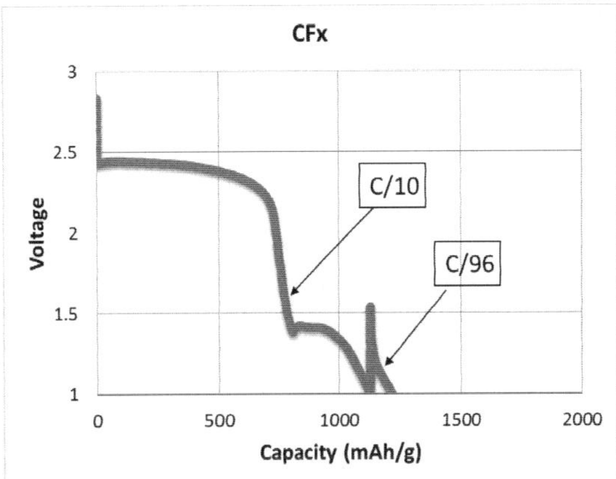

Figure 2. Baseline coin cell discharge curve of 60 wt% CF_x with 30 wt % carbon black and 10 wt % PVDF.

The CuPc has an operating voltage of around 1.65 V that continuously slopes downward at the C/10 discharge rate, whereas a slightly higher operating voltage and flatter curve is observed at the C/96 rate. For CF_x, there is a very flat plateau near 2.4 V, followed by a shorter plateau near 1.4 V. Little capacity for the CF_x cell remains at the C/96 rate, indicating the cell has mostly expended its energy at the C/10 rate.

With the expectation that performance would be improved, hybrid cathode cells were then produced for comparison with the baseline cells. Cathode mixtures contained active material ratios of 7:3 wt% and 1:1 wt% of CF_x to CuPc, and the cells were discharged under the same previously described conditions. The results are shown below in Figure 3.

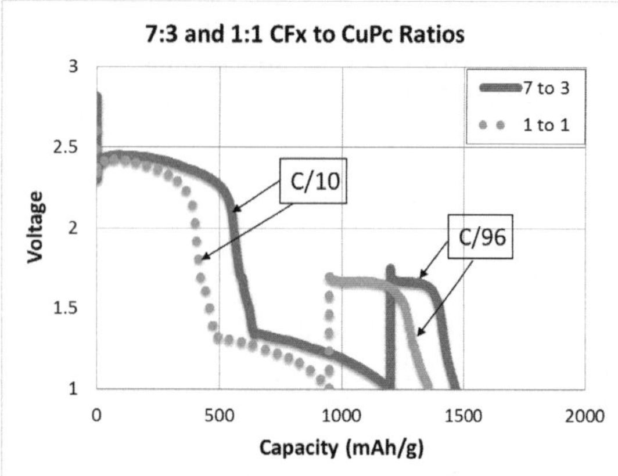

Figure 3. Comparison of coin cell discharge curves of 7:3 to 1:1 wt % ratio CF_x to high purity CuPc; 60 wt% total active material, 30 wt% carbon black, and 10 wt % PVDF.

In the case of no interaction between the two cathode materials, the observed discharge capacity would have been expected to follow the rule of mixtures, resulting in approximately 1103 and 1028 mAh/g of cathode material for the 7:3 wt% and 1:1 wt% ratios of CF_x and CuPc, respectively. Instead, an increase of at least 30% occurred in the capacity of the hybrid cathode cells. This behavior is believed to be the result of a synergistic effect between the nascent carbon formed during discharge and the CuPc molecules. The 7:3 ratio cell had longer plateaus at both 2.4 V and 1.3 V, and outperformed the 1:1 ratio in both rate and total capacity, so the 7:3 ratio was used for future experiments.

To further explore this effect, varying forms of CF_x were examined for their potential to interact with the copper phthalocyanine. These forms are synthesized through the incorporation of different carbon sources during the formation reaction with fluorine. The CF_x explored for this study was from produced from either petroleum coke (Carbofluor 1000 from ARC Chemicals), carbon fibre (Carbofluor 4000 from ARC Chemicals), or graphite. A comparison of the discharge results from the various forms of CF_x compared to graphite is shown below in Figure 4.

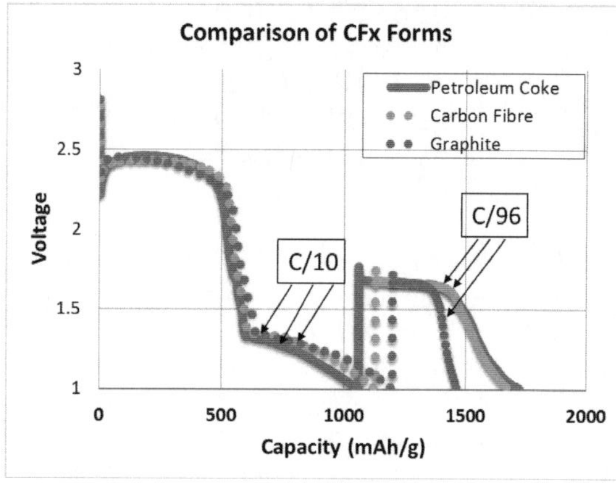

Figure 4. Comparison of coin cell discharge curves of various forms of CF_x with 7:3 wt% ratio CF_x to high purity CuPc; 60 wt% total active material, 30 wt% carbon black, and 10 wt% PVDF.

Both the petroleum coke and carbon fibre forms of CF_x appear to outperform the graphite CF_x in terms of total capacity, although the graphite form has the highest C/10 capacity. The graphite version may therefore enhance the rate capability of the hybrid cell in a greater fashion than it does the capacity. Although previous studies have shown similar performance among the various CF_x powders by themselves [4], disparate morphologies between them may influence interactions with the phthalocyanine molecules. Properties such as degree of fluorination, which affects the amount of fluorine available to participate in the redox reaction, and electrical conductivity are both potentially factors as well.

Mass produced commercially available phthalocyanines were purchased for comparison to the extremely high purity phthalocyanines typically used in the experiments. Heliogen Blue K 7090 from BASF is a copper phthalocyanine pigment used primarily in the dye industry, and its performance compared to high purity CuPc is shown below in Figure 5.

The Heliogen Blue K 7090 appeared to slightly outperform the high purity copper phthalocyanine in total capacity, although it had worse C/10 rate performance. In our previous experiments, nano-sized CuPc crystals were shown to be important in improving rate and capacity performance. As such, the high purity CuPc had been mechanically ground into a fine powder using a SPEX SamplePrep 8000M Mixer/Mill high intensity ball miller as it initially consisted primarily of multiple micron-sized crystals. In contrast, it was not deemed necessary to ground the BASF Heliogen Blue K 7090, as it already consisted of some nano-sized crystals in its as received form. This may help explain the disparity in rate performance.

An explanation for the increased capacity performance of the Heliogen version may involve several factors. It is known from Yamaki et. al that the β polymorph of CuPc slightly outperforms the α polymorph [1]. However, mechanical grinding or ball milling can convert the stable β phase into a metastable α phase [5]. Although both the Heliogen and high purity CuPc were received in the β phase, the high intensity milling of the high purity CuPc resulted in some conversion to the α phase, which was confirmed through powder XRD analysis. By maintaining the β phase of the Heliogen sample, this perhaps contributed to the increased capacity. It is also possible that impurities not disclosed in the Heliogen pigment may have influenced performance.

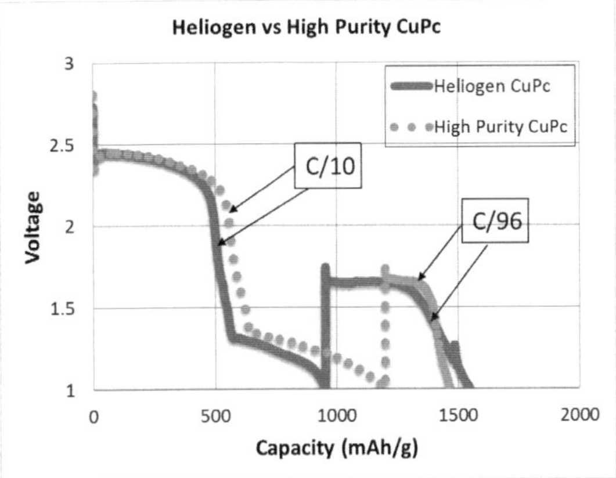

Figure 5. Comparison of coin cell discharge curves of Heliogen and high purity CuPc with 7:3 wt% ratio graphite CF_x to CuPc; 60 wt% total active material, 30 wt% carbon black, and 10 wt% PVDF.

Examination of different binders was also performed to determine their effect on cell performance. PVDF is the most commonly used binder for battery cathodes, and is well known for its temperature and chemical stability [6]. Its performance was compared to 2 million M_w polyethylene oxide (PEO), which is a binder that sees some usage in battery applications but significantly falls short of PVDF as it does not possess the same favorable characteristics. The high purity CuPc and graphite CF_x combination was used for this test, with the results shown below in Figure 6.

Total capacity of cells using PEO as a binder outperformed PVDF by a significant margin. The capacity increase may be explained by the behavior of the PVDF in the 1,2-dimethoxyethane, in which there is no significant swelling of the binder [6]. This characteristic results in blocked pores in the cathode that can no longer be filled with electrolyte. Thus, degradation of cell performance may have arisen by cutting off access to certain parts of the cathode. In contrast, the PEO has increased swellability, allowing electrolyte to fill portions of the pores occupied by binder, thereby improving cathode performance.

Graphene has exhibited unique properties that make it attractive as a candidate in a variety of applications. Hence, experiments were undertaken that focused on the usage of graphene as a conductive additive to improve the conductivity of the cathode and thereby increase performance. For these cells, nano graphene platelets (N002-PDR) from Angstron Materials were substituted in place of the standard carbon black. The cell discharge results are shown below in Figure 7.

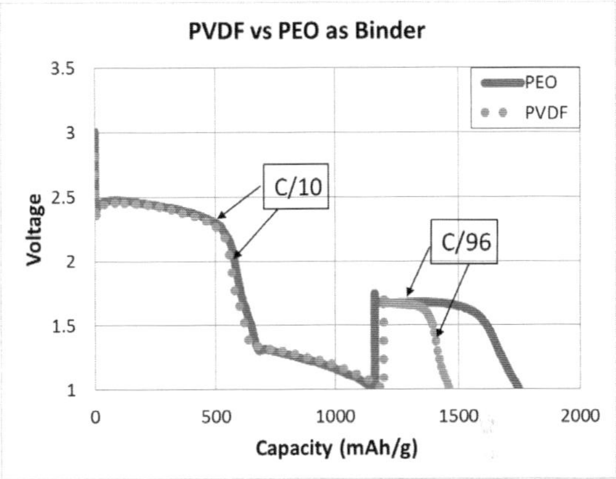

Figure 6. Comparison of coin cell discharge curves using PVDF and PEO as binders with 7:3 wt% ratio CF_x to CuPc; 60 wt% total active material, 30 wt% carbon black, and 10 wt% binder.

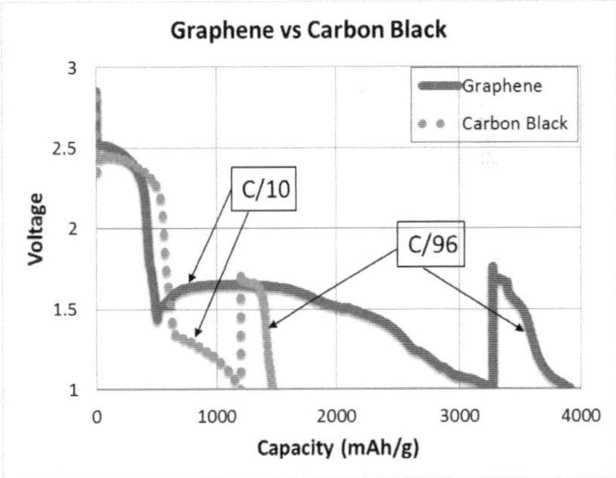

Figure 7. Comparison of coin cell discharge curves of graphene and carbon black as conductive additives, with 7:3 wt% ratio graphite CF_x to high purity CuPc; 60 wt% total active material, 30 wt% conductive material, and 10 wt% PVDF.

The cell containing graphene showed a tremendous amount of improvement in the capacity, in particular within the operating voltage window for CuPc. In contrast, the CF_x portion of the discharge experienced a slightly lowered capacity, which indicates that the beneficial influence of the graphene was an interaction with the CuPc. Jomphoak performed DFT calculations in agreement with this observation, in which the CuPc would adsorb onto a sheet of graphene [7]. This adsorption resulted in a lowering of the HOMO and LUMO gap, leading to greater electrical conductivity. Another factor that may have contributed to the results seen in this study is the thickness of the cathode used for the test. The exceptionally low density of the nano graphene platelets resulted in cathodes that were thinner than those used for previous tests. Difficulties had arisen in the preparation of thicker cathodes, including poor adhesion and severe cracking of the film during drying. Fabrication methods are still being refined to combat these issues to allow for a more direct comparison between cathodes of the same thickness.

Summary and Conclusions

A synergistic enhancement of capacity has been demonstrated in the discharge performance of a lithium primary battery by use of a hybrid cathode consisting of an active material mixture of CF_x and CuPc. A modest 30-75% synergistic increase in capacity of the hybrid cathode is demonstrated when using 30 wt% carbon black as the conductive additive. An unexplained synergistic capacity increase of greater than 250% for the hybrid cathode is observed when using 30 wt% graphene as the conductive additive. Not presented in this paper due to space limitations is the result of greater than 100% synergistic capacity increase for the hybrid cathode when using 30 wt% carbon nanotubes as the conductive additive. Computational modeling and additional experiments are underway to help explain this phenomenon.

Acknowledgements

The authors would like to thank AFOSR program officer Dr. Kenneth Caster for support through UDRI's contract FA8650-12-C-2612.

References

1. Yamaki, J. I. and Yamaji, A., "Phthalocyanine cathode materials for secondary lithium cells," *Journal of the Electrochemical Society,* vol. 129, no. 1, pp. 5-9, 1982.
2. Crowther, O., Du, L. S., Moureau, D. M. , Bicaku, I., Salomon, M., Lawson, J. W. Lucente, L. R., Mock, K., Fellner, J. P., and Scanlon, L. G., "Effect of conductive carbon on capacity of iron phthalocyanine cathodes in primary lithium batteries," *Journal of Power Sources,* vol. 217, pp. 92-97, 2012.
3. Fellner, J. P. and Tsao, M., "Hybrid primary lithium battery". United States of America Patent Application 15/903539, 23 February 2018.
4. Read, J., Marx, M., Wolfenstine, J., Zhang, S. and Foster, D., "Performance evaluation of commercial CF_x materials in lithium batteries," Army Research Laboratory Technical Report ARL-TR-5001, 2009.
5. Blackburn, J., Irvine, A., Sutcliffe, M. and McLaren, G., "Process of producing a phthalocyanine pigment". United States of America Patent 4,158,572, 19 June 1979.
6. Lacey, M., Jeschull, F., Edström, K. and Brandell, D., "Porosity blocking in highly porous carbon black by PVdF binder and its implications for the Li-S system," *The Journal of Physical Chemistry C,* vol. 118, pp. 25890-25898, 2014.
7. Jomphoak, A., Maezono, R. and Onjun, T., "Density functional theory of graphene/Cu phthalocyanine composite material," *Surface & Coatings Technology,* vol. 306, pp. 236-239, 2016.

Dry Electrode Coating Technology

Hieu Duong, Joon Shin & Yudi Yudi
Maxwell Technologies, Inc.
3888 Call Fortunada, San Diego, CA 92123
hduong@maxwell.com / 1-858-503-3296

Abstract: *In this paper we report a truly solventless dry battery electrode (DBE) coating technology developed by Maxwell Technologies that can be scalable for classical and advanced battery chemistry. Unlike conventional slurry cast wet coated electrode, Maxwell's DBE offers significantly high loading and produces a thick electrode that allows for high energy density cells without compromising physical properties and electrochemical performance. Maxwell's DBE exhibits better discharge rate capability than those of wet coated electrode. Maxwell has demonstrated scalability by producing robust self-supporting dry coated electrode film in roll form with excellent long-term electrochemical cycle performance, and established large pouch cell prototypes in greater than 10Ah format.*

Keywords: Dry battery electrode; dry coated electrode; wet coated electrode; lithium ion battery

Introduction

Within this decade, there has been immense effort focused on reducing the cost of energy storage devices. The goal towards energy independence through electrification of automobiles for widespread adoption has greatly incentivized this endeavor. Strategies ranging from novel materials investigation to advanced cell manufacturing development span the cost reduction effort. Maxwell Technologies is actively engaged in this global cost reduction effort through its development and refinement of its proprietary dry electrode fabrication technology.

Classical slurry wet coating technology has drawbacks such as solvent toxicity, reactivity between electrode material and solvent and unwanted changes of physicochemical properties of coated electrodes. Maxwell's proprietary solvent-free coating technology resolves such issues [1-3]. Maxwell dry coating technology offers manufacturing cost and performance differentiation as well as novel battery chemistry enablement [4]. This paper provides the initial foundation and validation for the application of dry coated electrode technology in lithium-ion batteries.

Maxwell Technologies is a San Diego-based ultracapacitor manufacturer that uses a proprietary solvent-free electrode production process. Advanced process development without the need for solvents has enabled Maxwell's dry coating electrode production lines to operate at high throughput using a minimal manufacturing footprint. This unique electrode manufacturing process does not introduce any volatile waste products into the atmosphere or require complex manufacturing plant arrangements. It begins with dry raw materials and maintains its liquid-free state throughout the subsequent processing steps to ultimately produce a robust high-performance ultracapacitor electrode.

For the past several years, Maxwell has been engaged in research and development efforts to expand the application space of its dry coating electrode process technology to apply to battery electrode manufacturing processes. Cell performance using prototype dry coated lithium-ion battery electrodes has been demonstrated. Dry coated electrode configuration with various architectures using a wide range of materials can be produced at thicknesses ranging from about 50 microns to about 1 millimeter. In addition to manufacturing flexibility, the cohesion and adhesion properties of electrodes derived from the dry coating process are superior in the presence of electrolyte at high temperatures compared with those produced using the wet coating technology.

This unique electrode process technology offers significant saving in manufacturing cost and helps curb CO_2 pollution in the battery electrode manufacturing process. By eliminating the use of any solvents, and the associated coating and drying complexity inherent in wet coating technology, the dry coating electrode process is environmentally friendly, and can be readily installed and commissioned with a much lower start-up capital investment. Thus, dry coating electrode manufacturing is economically attractive and socially responsible.

This paper provides recent progress in high energy dry coating electrode technology and its capacity for the enablement of advanced battery chemistries as evidenced by cell performance results witnessed from dry coated lithium-ion battery electrodes.

Experimental

Maxwell's proprietary dry coating electrode technology is comprised of three steps: (i) dry powder mixing, (ii) powder to film formation and (iii) film to current collector lamination; all executed in a solventless fashion. Maxwell's dry coating electrode process is scalable, and can accommodate current lithium ion battery chemistry and advanced battery electrode materials. In this report, the robustness of the dry coating electrode process is demonstrated using a host of commercially available anode materials such as silicon based materials and lithium titanate (LTO), as well as cathode materials such as layered $Li(Ni_xMn_yCo_z)O_2$ (NMC), $LiNi_{0.8}Co_{0.15}Al_{0.05}O_2$ (NCA),

LiFePO$_4$ (LFP) and sulfur. All dry powder materials were mixed using Maxwell's proprietary dry coating process to yield a final powder mixture consisting of active material, binder and conductive additive as shown in Fig. 1 (top). This powder mixture was calendered to form a continuous self-supporting dry coated electrode film that is wound in roll form (Fig. 1, bottom). A wide range of dry coated electrode configurations can be produced by the adjustment of film processing conditions to control material loading weights and active layer thickness.

Figure 1. Dry powder mixture comprised of active materials, conductive carbon and polymer binder (top) and a roll of free-standing dry coated electrode film fabricated from a pilot scale roll-to-roll equipment (bottom).

Figure 2. Dry battery electrode NMC roll (left) and graphite roll (right) double sided laminated onto current collector which is ready for cell assembly.

Once a film with target specification is achieved, it is laminated onto a current collector to yield an electrode, Fig. 2, that is ready for cell production.

All laminated dry coated electrodes were dried under vacuum at 120°C overnight to remove any ambient moisture before being assembled into pouch cell in an Ar-filled glove box for the small cell format or in dry-room conditions for the large cell format.

Electrochemical testing for rate capability and cycle life was carried out using an Arbin system at room temperature.

Results and discussion

Various dry coated battery electrodes were fabricated, including NMC811, NCA, LFP, LTO, sulfur/carbon and silicon composite, using Maxwell's dry coating electrode technology. Maxwell's dry coating electrode technology can be used to produce advanced high capacity NMC811 cathode and silicon-graphite composite anode that can deliver designed discharge capacity. Fig. 3 highlights discharge voltage profile for two advanced high capacity materials. The NMC811 dry coated electrode exhibited typical discharge profile with stable voltage plateau at the end of the discharge process. The Si/Graphite composite dry coated electrode produced electrochemical characteristic of Li delithiation of silicon at around 0.5V that significantly enhances energy density. Evaluations of cycling performance of high capacity NMC811 and Si/Graphite composite dry coated electrode are underway.

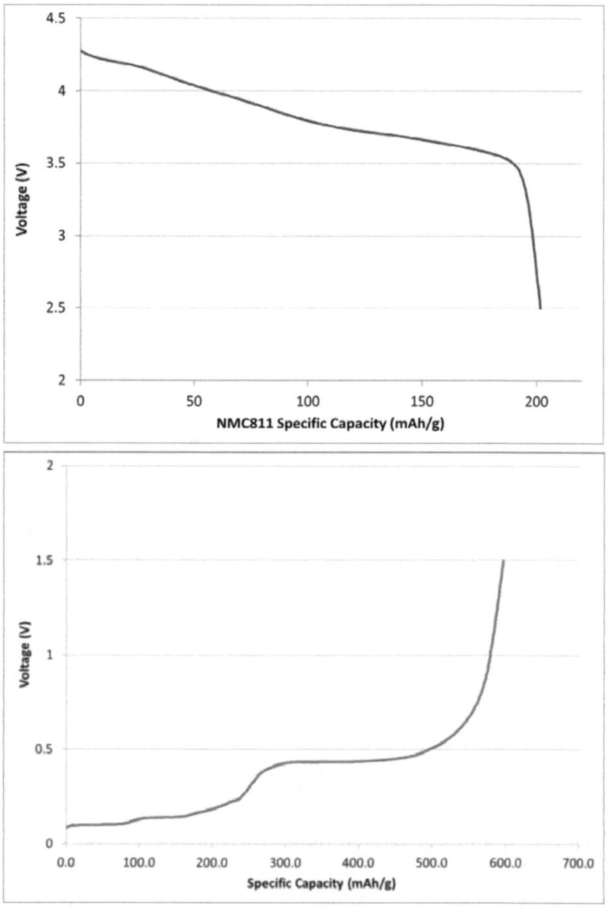

Figure 3. Discharge voltage profile of dry coated NMC811 cathode (top) and dry coated silicon-graphite composite anode (bottom) half-cell.

Maxwell's dry coating electrode technology renders a unique electrode micro-structure in which the polymer binder network allows for high ionic conductivity and intimate electronic contact between active materials and the conductive carbon network. As a solvent-free process, the polymer binder is not dissolved; as a result, the binding mechanism is an inter-connecting network comprised of point-contacts with the active material particle surface. This dry binding structure is less obtrusive and, consequently, enables lithium ions better access to the active material particles. This feature is especially advantageous for high rate performance in high energy density electrodes. A comparative example between a dry coated versus wet coated electrode is captured in Fig. 4. Both types of electrode were prepared using NMC111 for the cathode and graphite for the anode at equaled concentration with different binder materials. A constant current at 0.1C was applied to charge the cell to 100% SOC prior to discharge at each C-rate. Under low constant current discharge, both coated electrode types yielded cell discharge capacity of 105 mAh, used to normalize as 100% capacity retention at 0.1C. This discharge rate test results indicate that the dry coated electrodes delivered higher power than wet coated electrodes in a high energy density electrode configuration.

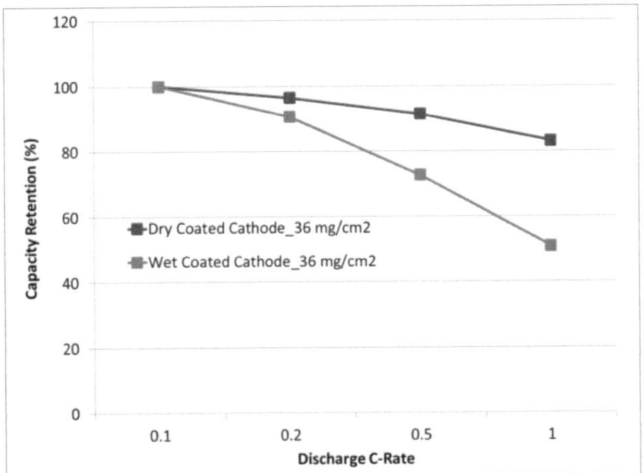

Figure 4. Discharge rate performance of dry coated NMC111/graphite full-cell in comparison to wet coated NMC111/graphite full-cell. Electrode loading is 5mAh/cm^2. Cut-off voltage was 4.2V and 2.8V for charge and discharge, respectively.

Additionally, a higher rate capability has been demonstrated by dry coated electrode with areal capacity of 4 mAh/cm^2, as shown in Fig. 5. Capacity retention for a set of five cells incorporating dry coated electrodes at 2C discharge is above 90%. The lower charge transfer and contact resistance in the dry coated electrode offer higher energy density cell designs with improved power capability.

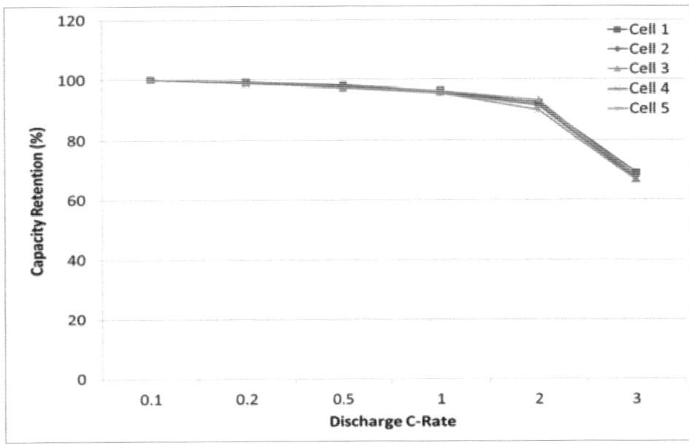

Figure 5. Rate performance of dry coated NMC111 (94 wt.% loading)/graphite (96 wt.% loading) electrode in prototype pouch cell: NMC111 electrode loading is 27 mg/cm^2 (4mAh/cm^2). The cell was charged to 4.2V at constant current followed by constant voltage at 4.2V and discharged to 2.8V.

In addition to higher power performance demonstrated in high energy density cells using dry coating, electrodes derived from a solvent-free process can also be robustly cycled at 100% DOD using a charge/discharge rate of 0.5C/1C, respectively. It can be observed in Fig. 6 that a full-cell with a specific capacity of 4 mAh/cm^2 can deliver nearly 90% of its original capacity after 2000 cycles.

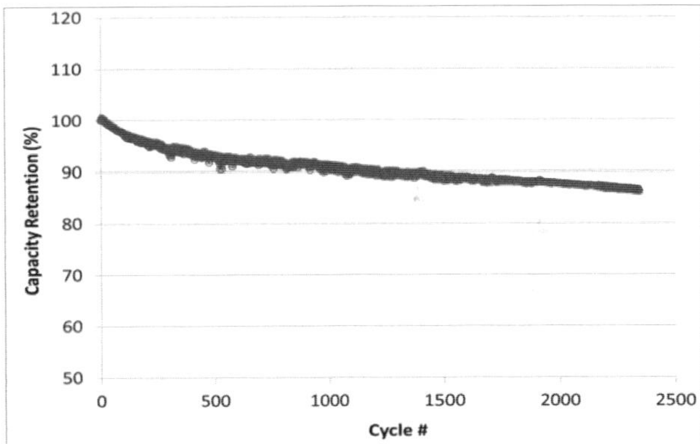

Figure 6. Cycle performance of dry coated NMC/graphite electrode in a prototype pouch cell at constant current 0.5C charge/1C discharge: Electrode loading- 4mAh/cm^2. Cut-off voltage was 4.2V and 2.7V for charge and discharge, respectively.

Discussion

Maxwell Technologies has successfully expanded its proprietary dry electrode process used to productize ultracapacitors to include lithium based battery electrode production. It has been demonstrated that this unique dry electrode process can be applied to both classical and advanced battery materials, and is scalable to roll-to-roll production. Maxwell's dry coated battery electrode offers extraordinary benefits, including manufacturing cost reduction, elimination of solvent toxicity, enabling the application of liquid sensitive battery chemistries and enhancing cell performance, particularly at high loading weights when compared to conventional wet coated electrode in discharge rate studies. These results suggest that dry coated electrodes exhibit lower particle-to-particle contact resistance and charge transfer impedance, likely due to a uniform network of interconnects between binder and active material particles. Additionally, prolonged cycle life performance of dry coated electrodes in small prototype pouch cells and large format pouch cells, ≥10Ah, is under evaluation.

References

1. Park, D., Canas N.A., Wagner N., Friedrich K.A.,"Novel Solvent-free Direct Coating Process for Battery Electrodes and Their Electrochemical Performance," J. Power Sources, vol. 306, pp. 758-763, 2016.
2. Al-Shroofy M., Zhang Q., Xu J., Chen T., Kaur A.P., Cheng Y., "Solvent-free Dry Powder Coating Process for Low-cost Manufacturing of $LiNi_{1/3}Mn_{1/3}Co1/3O_2$ Cathodes in Lithium-ion Batteries," J. Power Sources, vol. 352, pp. 187-193, 2017.
3. Ludwig B., Zheng Z., Shou W., Wang Y., Pan H., "Solvent-Free Manufacturing of Electrodes for Lithium-ion Batteries," Nature, Scientific Reports 6, no. 23150, pp 1-10
4. Duong H., Suszko A., Feigenbaum H., "Dry Electrode Process Technology," 229th ECS meeting, vol. A05, P-475, May 2016.

The Effect of Grain Size on the Electrochemical and Mechanical Properties of Cubic $Li_7La_3Zr_2O_{12}$

Jeff Wolfenstine and Jan L. Allen

Army Research Laboratory
2800 Powder Mill Road
Adelphi, MD 20783

Abstract: The effect of grain size on the ionic conductivity, critical current and fracture toughness of high relative density (>97%) cubic $Li_7La_3Zr_2O_{12}$ was determined at room temperature. It was observed that for grain sizes less than about 150 μm that both the ionic conductivity and critical current increased with increasing grain size. Above 150 μm they were independent of grain size. A reverse trend was observed for fracture toughness but, at a lower grain size (40 μm). The smaller grain size samples exhibited the highest fracture toughness values. At larger grain sizes fracture toughness was independent of grain size.

Keywords: fracture; conductivity; grain boundary

Introduction

$Li_7La_3Zr_2O_{12}$ (LLZO) is receiving considerable attention as a solid-state Li-ion conducting electrolyte because of its high ionic conductivity and adequate mechanical properties. It is possible that the electrical and mechanical properties may vary with LLZO grain size. It is the purpose of this paper to examine the effect of LLZO grain size on ionic conductivity, fracture toughness and critical current (current at which lithium dendrites/filaments form on charging).

Experimental

Cubic Al-doped LLZO with nominal composition of $Li_{6.25}Al_{0.25}La_3Zr_2O_{12}$ was prepared using a solid-state synthetic technique [1]. This composition was chosen due to its high ionic conductivity and stability against metallic Li. The calcined powders were hot-pressed at temperatures between 1100-1300°C under a uniaxial pressure of 62 MPa for 1 h. In addition, one of the pellets was heated at 1350°C for 50 h under LLZO powders to further increase the grain size. The pellets were polished through 0.5 μm diamond prior to electrical and mechanical testing.

The grain size of the LLZO specimens was characterized using electron backscatter diffraction (EBSD). The impedance spectra of the different grain size samples at room temperature was characterized in the frequency range of 1Hz to 7 MHz using a 100 mV AC amplitude. From this information and the sample dimensions the total conductivity was determined. The fracture toughness as a function of grain size was determined using the indentation technique with a Vickers indenter. The applied load was 0.196 N, chosen to produce measurable crack lengths with a crack radius about 2–3 times larger than the half diagonal for all the measurements. The critical current was determined as function of grain size using Li/LLZO/Li cells. The DC current was increased until a drop in voltage resulted. The current at which the drop in voltage occurred was defined as the critical current.

Results and Discussion

After hot-pressing the resulting LLZO pellets were single phase with relative densities between 96-99% and grain sizes in the range between 5 to 80 μm. The heat-treated LLZO sample had a grain size of about 600 μm. Figure 1 is a plot of total conductivity of LLZO as a function of grain size.

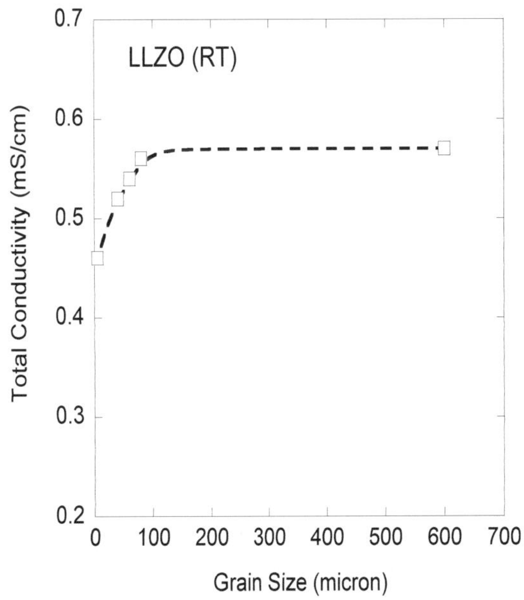

Fig.1. LLZO total conductivity versus grain size.

From Figure 1 it is observed that the total conductivity increases with grain size up to about 150 μm after which it is independent of grain size. Attempts to separate the total conductivity into lattice and grain boundary resistance components were not successful. However, it is highly likely in a first approximation that the lattice resistance is constant for all grain sizes and thus, the increase in total conductivity is associated with a decrease in the grain boundary resistance as the grain size increases. Above 150 μm the LLZO grain boundary resistance is negligible and hence, LLZO behaves like a single crystal where lattice resistance controls conductivity. Such behavior is in good agreement with previous work on another solid-state Li-ion conductor $Li_{0.33}La_{0.57}TiO_3$ [2].

Figure 2 is plot of fracture toughness for LLZO as a function of grain size.

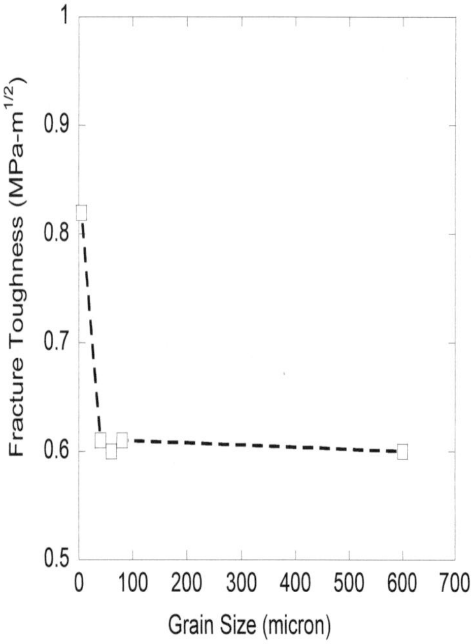

Fig. 2. Fracture toughness of LLZO as a function of grain size.

From Figure 2 it is observed that fracture toughness decreases with grain size up to about 40 μm, after which it is independent of grain size. Examination of fracture surfaces of LLZO samples with grain sizes of 40 μm and greater revealed 100% transgranular fracture mode. Examination of the fracture surface of the 5 μm sample revealed that the majority of the fracture mode was transgranular however, some evidence of intergranular fracture was observed. Hence, it is highly likely that the higher fracture toughness of the 5 μm grain size sample compared to the larger grain sizes is associated with the intergranular fracture component. It is general accepted that the presence of weak grain boundaries (e.g., those which exhibit intergranular fracture) will deflect cracks leading to increased fracture toughness values compared to the case where the fracture mode is transgranular [3]. This is most likely what is happening in our case. At grain sizes above 40 μm the fracture toughness (≈0.60 MPa-$m^{1/2}$) should correspond to the value for a LLZO single crystal. Single crystal values for ceramics range from, 0.5 to 2.5 MPa-$m^{1/2}$ [3]. Thus, the fracture toughness for LLZO at large grain sizes is at the low end of typical values for ceramic single crystals. This is likely a result of the covalent bonding in LLZO.

Before testing for the critical current as a function of the grain size the LLZO pellets were heated in a glove box at 400°C for 3 h. This step helps to reduce the interfacial impedance between Li/LLZO by removing a surface layer of Li_2CO_3 which can form if LLZO is exposed to ambient atmosphere. After this heat-treatment Li is pressed onto LLZO and heated under a small stress at 175°C for 12 h before testing. This step helps increase the contact area between Li and LLZO. After this two-step process the area specific resistance of Li/LLZO is less than 5 ohm/cm^2, whereas without this treatment it can be range from hundreds to thousands of ohm/cm^2 [1]. Figure 3 is a plot of LLZO critical current as a function of grain size.

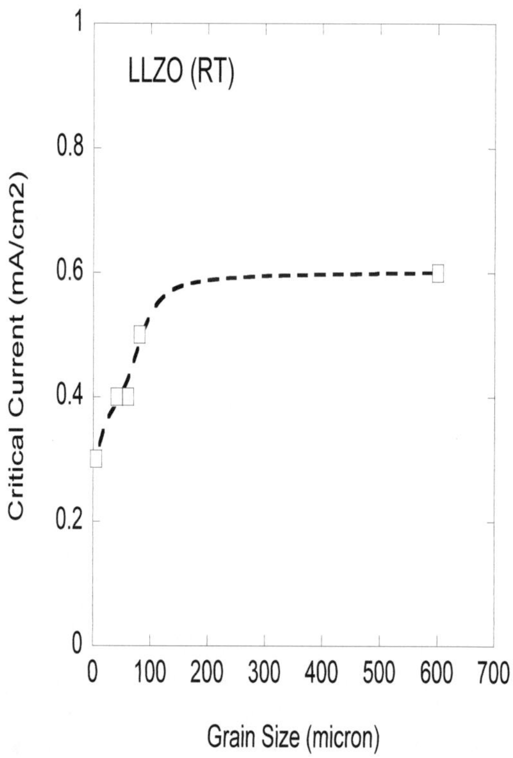

Fig. 3. Critical current of LLZO as function of grain size.

The onset of a critical current was confirmed not only by the decrease in voltage but also by a change in the shape of the AC impedance curve. Below the critical current the impedance spectra showed normal behavior, with distinct semi-circles whereas when the critical current was reached the impedance spectra changed to more like that of a resistor (e.g., single point). In addition, below the critical current the LLZO sample faces in contact with Li were white, above the critical current black spots appeared on the LLZO sample faces in contact with Li. From Figure 3 several important points are noted. Firstly, as the grain size increases from 5 to about 150 μm the critical current increases. Secondly, above 150 μm the critical current becomes independent of grain size behaving like a single crystal. This observations suggests that elimination of grain boundaries is key to achieving high current densities. A comparison of Figures 1 and 3 reveals a similar trend in that both show that as grain size increases critical current and conductivity increase. This suggest that both critical current and conductivity are influenced by the same phenomena. It was suggested earlier that the increase in conductivity with grain size shown in Figure 1 is associated with a reduction in the number of high resistance grain boundaries. Thus, it appears that the reduction in the number of high resistance grain boundaries also causes the critical current to increase with grain size. At large grain sizes the effect of grain boundaries is negligible and hence, the critical current reaches single crystal values.

Summary

The effect of grain size on the ionic conductivity, critical current and fracture toughness current of high relative density (>97%) cubic $Li_7La_3Zr_2O_{12}$ was determined at room temperature. It was observed that for grain sizes less than about 150 μm that both the ionic conductivity and critical current increased with increasing grain size. Above 150 μm they were independent of grain size. It is suggest that the increase in both critical current and conductivity with increasing grain size is associated with a reduction in the number of high resistance grain boundaries. It is observed that fracture toughness decreases with grain size up to about 40 μm, after which it is independent of grain size. It is suggested that the increase in fracture toughness with decreasing grain size is associated with increasing the number of weak grain boundaries.

Acknowledgements

JW and JLA would like to acknowledge support of the U. S. Army Research Laboratory.

References

1. A. Sharafi, C. G. Haslam, R. D. Kearns, J. Wolfenstine, J. Sakamoto (2017) J. Mater. Chem. A 5:21491.

2. A. C. Sutorik, M. D. Green, C. Cooper, J. Wolfenstine, G. Gilde (2012) 47:6992.

3. Y. Kim, H. Jo, J. L. Allen, H. Choe, J. Wolfenstine, J. Sakamoto (2016) J. Am. Ceram. Soc. 99:1367.

Low Cost, High Speed, Agile Automated Laser Electrode Cutter

Stephen Cordova, Steven C. Arzberger and Weibing Xing
stephenc@adatech.com, stevena@adatech.com, weibingx@adatech.com
ADA Technologies, Inc.
11149 Bradford Road,
Littleton, CO 80127
Phone: (303) 792-5615
Fax: (303) 792-5633

Abstract:

ADA Technologies, Inc. (ADA) designed, developed and fabricated a prototype, agile Automated Laser Electrode Cutter (ALEC) as a precursor to commercial unit sales. The ALEC is a critical first unit of a series of custom and enabling Industrial Automation Equipment (IAE) offerings, designed to modernize Lithium-Ion (Li-ion) battery fabrication. It replaces "lifetime buy" systems (e.g., matched die sets) and thus, minimizes up-front and tooling cost and expedites product development timelines; this yields rapid, agile, flexible, cost-effective and high quality Li-ion battery manufacture. The ADA Agile Manufacturing Environment enables the rapid fabrication of disparate electrochemical systems with automated systems to achieve low-cost, high quality products serving customer needs such as low volume (initial) production and part obsolescence challenges.

Keywords: laser; electrode cutter; automated; high speed; manufacturing; additive manufacturing; thin film; laser welding; laser processing, industrial automation equipment

Introduction

ADA Technologies, Inc. (ADA) designed, developed and fabricated a prototype ALEC to demonstrate low-cost, automated, high-speed and -throughput electrode processing capable of producing high quality electrodes in an additive manufacturing environment. Our design uses the latest in laser technology and scanhead systems coupled to innovative designs for automation, to realize a system with unparalleled performance in a compact and cost-effective (1/10th the cost of current laser cutter systems) format. The system will yield high quality cuts with excellent tolerances, reliability and repeatability, with minimum maintenance. The elimination of sharp edges, burrs and debris will ensure safe operation, minimizing the chances of cell failure and thermal runaway. The system is designed autonomous, delivering electrodes for planar and cylindrical cells of virtually any size and shape. It is compact (bench top size), durable and robust. This enables facile integration into battery assembly/manufacturing lines. A low cost, high speed (4-5 m/s cutting, 10's of electrodes/min.), high precision, flexible (easily variable cutting speeds/geometry), durable electrode cutter with unsurpassed cutting quality has been demonstrated.

Identification & Significance of the Problem or Opportunity

Increased Li-Ion Battery Prevalence: The US military goal to "establish a long-term, viable, world-class, domestic manufacturer of high energy density Li-ion batteries that is responsive to customer requirements with respect to performance, reliability, quality, delivery and price"[1] strongly indicates the Department of Defense (DoD) is increasingly becoming dependent on Li-ion batteries. Applications range from small, Class I unmanned air vehicle (UAV) platforms to reconnaissance satellites, fighter aircraft platforms (JSF), next-generation hybrid and electric drive (HEV) ground vehicles, and power sources for dismounted soldiers – to name a few (**Figure 1**).

Figure 1. Various Li-ion applications.

The Increasing Focus on Li-ion Battery Electrode Cutting Technologies: Compromising manufacturing technologies are often the reason for Li-ion battery failures. One of the biggest hindrances at present lies in the technology of electrode cutting. While traditional mechanical die-cutting technologies provide adequate quality and consistency in lower-energy battery systems, this manufacturing technology represents one of the main impediments toward realizing the full potential of Li-ion chemistries. An enabling electrode cutting technique is essential to achieve

[1] Defense Production Act Title III: "Lithium Ion Battery Production for Military Applications" Project Solicitation Number: BAA-11-17-PKM, posted on July 11, 2001 and retrieved from: https://www.fbo.gov/index?s=opportunity&mode=form&id=da412ded9d7cb11819b2060fab691771&tab=core&_cview=1

exceptional tolerances with minimal edge debris and shards for minimizing catastrophic cell failure (hard short) or possible prolonged self-discharge (soft short). It is also important to replace "lifetime buy" systems such as dies to enable rapid, agile, flexible, cost-effective and high quality Li-ion battery manufacturing for the rapidly evolving needs of the US military. Hence, it is imperative to develop next-generation, cost-effective, flexible electrode cutting technologies, to enable a rapidly, advancing US military through rapid innovation in Li-ion battery design, while enhancing quality and tolerances.

Laser Cutting of Electrodes

Laser cutting is the cutting technology of choice in many industries where speed and precision are emphasized. The technology is proven as a highly efficient and reliable manufacturing method that can potentially contribute to significant cost savings and quality improvements. This is because it requires no consumables (*i.e.*, dies that wear out) and permits greater manufacturing flexibility; for example, computer "CAD style" software can generate special part designs and permit rapid development via iteration, with no new tooling costs. Recent advances in commercial lasers and power sources permit the technology to be applied to Li-ion battery electrode cutting.

Fundamentals of Laser-Assisted Cutting: High quality laser ablation cutting is dependent on many factors, including: laser power, wavelength and type; beam quality, optics and power delivery method; and expulsion of melt, and material to be processed, *etc*. For Li-ion battery electrode cutting, the unit must provide sufficient intensity for electrode ablation, without excessive intensity as this may damage the product from excess heat. Intensity (laser power per unit area) can be expressed as:

$$\text{Intensity} = \frac{\textbf{\textit{Laser Power (W)}}}{\textbf{\textit{Irradiated Area (cm}}^2\textbf{\textit{)}}}$$

Hence, for effective electrode laser cutting, it is imperative to minimize the irradiated area by decreasing the spot size and providing a nominal amount of power for ablation; this serves to maximize cut speed, reduce cost and minimize the heat affected zone (HAZ).

Conventional Laser Cutting (Gantry-Driven Lasers): With gantry-driven lasers (*e.g.*, **Figure 2**), the cut head includes fixed beam delivery optics and a cut, gas delivery system that ejects the melt from the kerf. The cut head is typically mounted on a robot or the vertical axis of a Computer Numeric Control (CNC) machine tool system, which uses moving linear axes. This system has the advantage of an on-axis optical system with a very small spot size. The spot size can be moved over very large fields since the beam is always orthogonal to the work piece. Optics focus the collimated laser beam on the work piece to achieve a small spot size.[5] Many difficulties arise with gantry-driven lasers, including achieving high speeds, precision and accuracy due to the movement of large masses over the cutting field, and cost. The moving linear axes are expensive and generate a large HAZ due to the relatively slow speeds. These systems are massive and bulky, requiring more workspace. Their accuracy is low and deteriorates with increasing unit size. Dynamics of the system constrain the maximum possible speed and acceleration. The programming of the cut-path also requires special attention, as the cutting path geometry becomes complex due to the momentum generated from the relatively large mass. Besides common process parameters such as laser power, speed and spot size, *etc*., for conventional and remote laser cutting process, there are a number of other critical factors that affect the cut quality. For example, factors include nozzle size, distance of nozzle tip to the top of material surface, cutting gas type, gas pressure, and flow rate, *etc*. Compared to remote cutting, the achievable cutting speed is significantly less due to limitations in the available power and maximum repetition rate.[6] Gantry-driven lasers are large, expensive and most deleteriously suffer from slow scan speeds that are not amenable to high speed Li-ion electrode cutting.

Remote Laser Cutting: Remote cutting technology is a relatively new laser cutting process that replaces the gantry for laser light positioning and focuses the laser beam with quick moving mirrors. Remote laser cutting systems are capable of achieving spot speeds as fast as several meters/second. Due to low interaction time between the laser beam and component, the material is partially evaporated and desorbed, which leads to cleaner cuts and less edge burr effects than traditional gantry-driven laser cutting systems. The essential components that have led to the success of remote cutting technology, include advancements in: (1) optical beam scanning systems and (2) high brightness lasers that provide highly efficient beam delivery.[7]

Figure 2. Typical gantry-driven laser.

Remote cutting uses well-established galvanometer scanner technology comprised of high-performance rotary motors that produce high dynamic beam deflection. The low mass and inertia of these systems enable high speeds (up to 15 m/s) and acceleration (up to 10 g). The material is cut by a combination of very high energy densities in a very small laser spot and very high speed beam movement; it does not require any cutting gas as the melt in the cut kerf is partially vaporized and ejected by very high vapor pressure under extreme conditions of temperature and melt pool dynamics. The image field size and working distance are directly proportional to the F-Theta focusing lens focal length, and are not adjustable. A larger field size requires a longer focal length, which requires better beam quality to generate small spot sizes. With the availability of high power and brightness lasers, such as fiber and disk lasers with excellent beam quality, it is possible to achieve very small spot sizes < 20 μm with high power intensities (>10^8 W/cm^2).[7]

The downside of current remote laser cutting systems is that they use F-Theta lenses that can't adjust or achieve a large image field size to spot size ratio. A higher power continuous wave laser is also necessary, which substantially raises the cost of remote laser systems in comparison to gantry-driven laser systems. Further, these units are large, often requiring water-cooling systems that fill a large room. Finally, the increased power and larger spot size promote a much larger HAZ. This diminishes precision, accuracy and potentially compromises safety, once the electrodes are used in a Li-ion cell. *Hence, it is desirable to use advancements in laser cutting technologies that can address the current limitations and deliver high-quality, low-cost Li-ion battery electrode manufacture.*

ADA Automated Laser Electrode Cutter (ALEC)

Approach: In contrast to the abovementioned laser cutting techniques, a 3-axis scanhead coupled to a relatively low power pulsed laser offers tremendous advantages. The ADA ALEC design significantly increases the image field size to spot ratio, which leads to desirable increases in cut quality and customization and flexibility. It is compact in size and significantly less expensive than existing systems. Because it is specifically tailored for electrode cutting for Li-ion batteries, the ALEC rapidly processes high quality electrodes for planar prismatic and cylindrical cells. We designed the ALEC to serve as a standalone unit (*i.e.*, R&D processing unit) or as an integrated production Li-ion electrode fabrication unit (**Figure 3**).

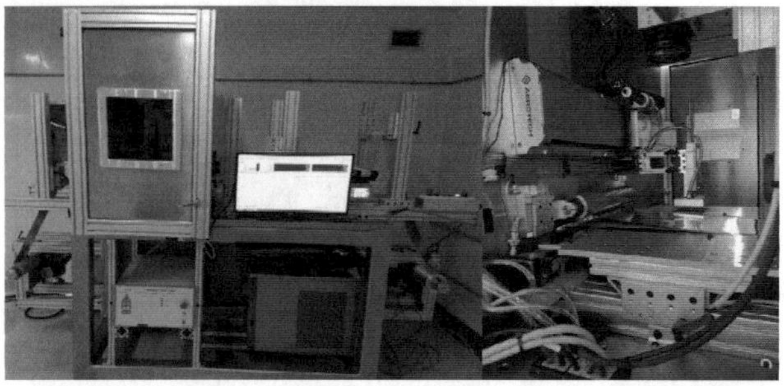

Figure 3. ADA's Automated Laser Electrode Cutter.

ADA ALEC Performance Parameters: The ADA ALEC offers very high cutting speeds (up to 5 m/s) for Li-ion electrodes, while maintaining a very high cut quality (**Table 1**). We optimized cut speeds to ~ 2 m/s to process cathode and anode based electrodes. We further demonstrated planar electrode fabrication (**Figure 4**) at a rate of 13 electrodes per minute (including pick-and-place) and slit electrodes (**Figure 5**) at a rate of ~ 50, 18650 electrodes per minute.

Table 1. ALEC electrode cut speeds.

Electrode Type	*Max Cut Speed (m/s)*	*Optimized Cut Speed (m/s)*	*Electrodes per Minute*	*Notes*
Planar	5	2	13	~ 140 cm^2 Electrode Area
Slit	5	2.5	~ 50	18650 Electrode Processed

*Optimized cut speed determined by electrode cut completion; no perforations, scalloped edges or "hanging shards".

Figure 4. Still screenshot of ALEC, planar Li-ion electrodes (right) and cutting (left) .

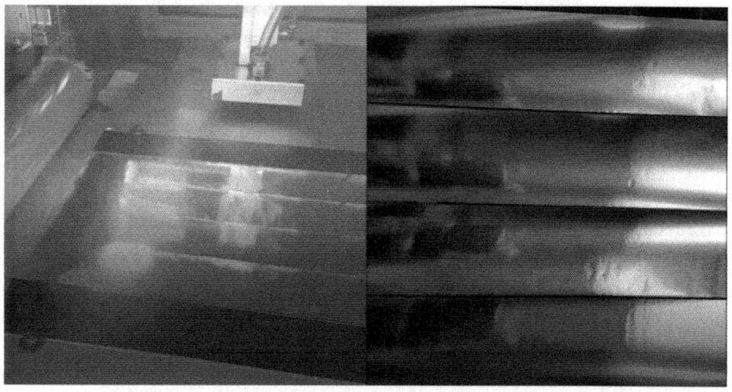

Figure 5. Still screenshot of ALEC, slit Li-ion electrodes.

The ADA ALEC is equipped with state-of-the-art (SOTA) components that afford an ability to process high-energy (thick electrodes) and -power (thin coatings) at production volumes (**Table 1**), and maintains high-cut quality and rapid transference between disparate formats/footprints. **Figure 6** compares the electrode cut quality and other attributes prepared from stamping and laser cutting. Laser cut electrodes offer exceptional tolerance and precision, while stamped electrodes show a comparatively large deviation along a linear cut with the potential for shards or incomplete cuts. The cut quality varies with die use, progressively worsening with time. The ADA ALEC offers superior reliability with little to no required maintenance, whereas dies require substantial maintenance due to pronounced wear. The laser cutter processes virtually any size electrode via rapid and simple software manipulation. Stamped electrodes, on the other hand, require a pair of dies for each cell footprint; this severely limits cell design flexibility. Finally, laser cut electrodes posses substantially better cut-quality, a fact that is most prominently observed on thin power electrodes, without the formation of shards, burrs or furled edges; this essentially eliminates safety concerns and leads to higher performance products.

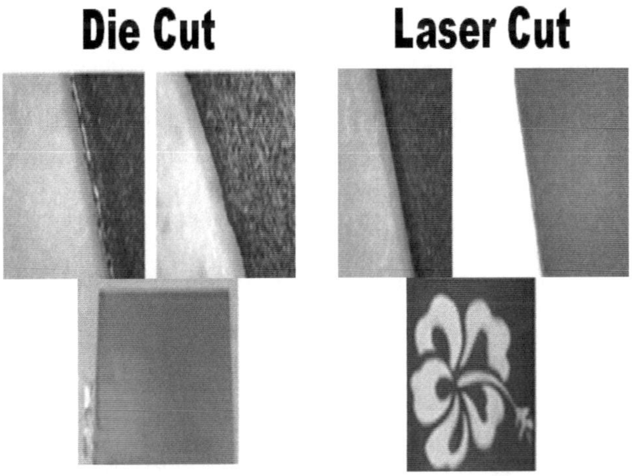

Figure 6. Comparison of die cut (left) and laser cut electrodes with the ADA ALEC (right).

The ADA ALEC provides unprecedented flexibility due to the wide range of scanhead software capabilities. Using the simple and efficient CAD style software and laser output (laser power, scan speed and waveform), a user can rapidly machine electrodes/substrates in a variegated manner. This represents a demonstration of some of the expansive capability of this machine. These advanced capabilities have the potential to open new areas of research in energy storage, among others.

As an example of our engineering design efforts, we incorporate a position based output (PSO), rather than time-based, for the pulsed laser to precisely cut electrodes and minimize the HAZ on linear and radii components (**Figure 7**). We further position electrical components away from the thermally-sensitive scanhead to prevent drift (**Figure 8**).

We processed the upper limit of SOTA manufactured Li-ion electrode thicknesses, including anodes prepared from loading ~ 20 mg/cm^2 and cathodes of ~ 30 mg/cm^2 at rates as high as 3 m/s. Due to the extreme cutting speeds, we optimized mechanical electrode processing, via pick-and-place and web handling, while minimizing cost.

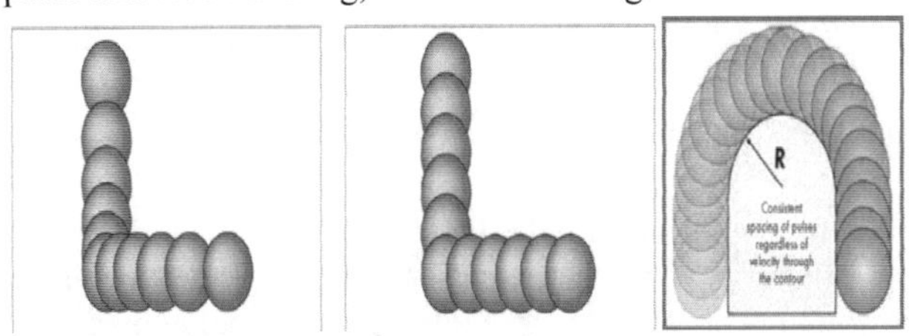

Figure 7. Examples of time-based (left) and position based (center) laser firing, and specific example of PSO around a radius (right).

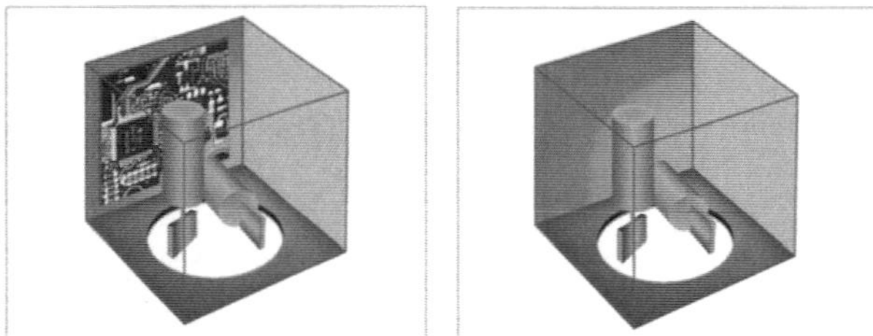

Figure 8. Scanhead examples depicting scanhead electronics (left) and exterior (right).

Acknowledgements

The authors wish to thank Mather "Matt" Hutchens and Traci Myers of the Defense Logistics Agency (DLA) for their continued support and funding (contract SP4701-16-C-0084) in the development of the ADA ALEC.

References

1. "Possible Solutions for the Battery Problem on the Boeing 787," © 2013 Isidor Buchmann
2. *Lithium-Ion Batteries Hazard and Use Assessment* by Celina Mikolajczak, et al. (Springer, 2012)
3. Vesely, B., "Fault Tree Analysis (FTA): Concepts and Applications," Presentation to NASA by Underwriters Laboratory. Web: 30 May 2013. http://www.hq.nasa.gov/office/codeq/risk/docs/ftacourse.pdf
4. http://www.ntsb.gov/investigations/fulltext/hzb0501.htm
5. Rahul Patwa1, Hans Herfurth1, Henrikki Pantsar1, (2012). High Speed Laser Cutting of Electrodes for Advanced Batteries, Fraunhofer Center for Laser Technology, University of Michigan, College of Engineering, Ann Arbor, MI
6. Herfurth H.J., Patwa R., Pantsar H. (2010), Laser cutting of electrodes for advanced batteries, in Proceedings of the LPM, Germany
7. Rahul Patwa1, Hans Herfurth1, Henrikki Pantsar1, (2012). High Speed Laser Cutting of Electrodes for Advanced Batteries, Fraunhofer Center for Laser Technology, University of Michigan, College of Engineering, Ann Arbor, MI.

Safety Enhanced, Block Copolymer Derived Nanoporous Battery Separators

Weibing Xing, Stephen Cordova, and Steve C. Arzberger
weibingx@adatech.com, stevea@adatech.com, stephenc@adatech.com
ADA Technologies, Inc.
11149 Bradford Road, Littleton, CO 80127
Phone: (303) 792-5615 / Fax: (303) 792-5633

Abstract: *To meet US military and consumer needs for high performance and safe lithium (Li) or lithium-ion (Li-ion) batteries, ADA Technologies, Inc. (ADA) is working to develop a family of block copolymer-derived, nanoporous separators. The molecular level controlled material synthesis and processing allow high tunability in separator's physical properties rendering desirable performance and safety characteristics including uniform and narrow pore size distribution, high electrolyte wettability, and highly tunable thermal shutdown temperatures. The use of low cost precursors allows economical scale-up. The block copolymer derived nanoporous separator represents a promising technology that affords high energy density, high rate capability, long cycle life and unprecedented safety characteristics for the next generation Li-ion batteries.*

Keywords: lithium battery; lithium ion battery; block copolymer derived separator; nanoporous separator; rapid thermal shutdown; tunable thermal shutdown temperature

Introduction

A battery separator physically and electronically separates the anode and cathode but permits lithium ion (Li^+) transport between them. Battery separators play a critical role in battery safety by providing, *e.g.*, thermal shutdown functionality in abusive events or, by preventing lithium metal dendrites or other defects in the cell from penetrating the membrane; such can cause internal short circuit leading to uncontrolled thermal runaway, as in the case of Boeing 787 Dreamliner [1] or Samsung Galaxy Note 7 [2] battery fire incidents (**Figure 1**).

Figure 1. Boeing 787 Dreamliner (left) and Samsung Galaxy Note 7 (right) battery fire incidents.

One of the challenges with designing safe battery separators is a trade-off between mechanical robustness and porosity/transport properties. For example, high separator tortuosity is good for dendrite resistance but can lead to higher separator resistance [2]. Separator design is further complicated by additional constraints including tolerance to abuse conditions, stable at high voltages (*e.g.*, > 4V), chemically inert to other cell materials, and low cost to meet the performance and cost targets. There is a need to tailor design battery separators that enable high energy and power with engineered functionality for safety, without adversely affecting cost.

Separator Sample Preparation

There are a number of different types of state-of-the-art (SOA) Li-ion battery separators, such as, microporous, non-woven, ion exchange, polymer, *etc.* [3]. SOA Li-ion battery separators are typically produced via dry processes involving extruding, annealing and stretching steps, or wet process consisting of mixing, heating, extruding and additive removal steps.

We investigated a new approach to prepare Li-ion battery separators based on block polymer synthesis routes [4, 5, 6]. As illustrated in **Figure 2**, there are a number of advantages of block polymer derived nanoporous separators including (i) Selectively remove sacrificial block copolymers (*e.g.*, polylactic acid, PLA) to realize a nanoporous membrane/separator (*e.g.*, polyethylene, PE), which allows precisely controlled separator porosity by controlling the sacrificial copolymer fraction. (ii) The ability to attach functional polymer branches to the backbone to fine tune separator properties (*e.g.*, thermal shutdown temperature). (iii) Use multiple blocks, and/or control polymer crystallinity to enhance mechanical properties.

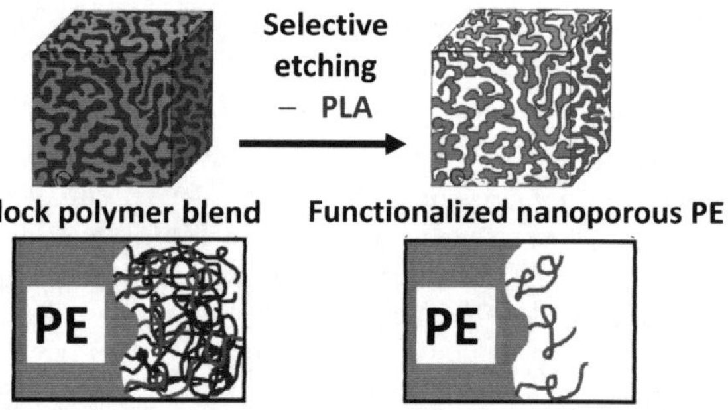

Figure 2. Schematic of block copolymer derived separator fabrication processes.

Our first generation (Gen1) triblock copolymer derived separator was synthesized according to the synthesis procedure in Ref. 4. A poly(lactide)-b-polyethylene-b-poly(lactide), or PLA-PE-PLA (LEL), triblock copolymer was first synthesized as a precursor via a Ru-catalyzed ring opening metathesis polymerization (ROMP). The PLA sacrificial block was then selectively removed which resulted in a linear PE based, nanoporous polyethylene (NPE) separator.

In our safety enhanced, second generation (Gen2) copolymer derived separator preparation, a branched block polymer was introduced into the block copolymer chain to fine tune the separator' melting point [7], which led to desired thermal shutdown safety characteristics of the resultant NPE separator.

Scanning Electron Microscopy (SEM)

Figure 3 shows SEM images of a Gen1 NPE separator (A, B) and a commercial PP/PE/PP trilayer separator (C, D). The NPE separator was in the range of 20 – 30 μm thick. The commercial trilayer separator was 25 μm thick. The NPE separator adopted a disordered bicontinuous morphology, with a percolating pore structure derived ultimately from the thermodynamic incompatibility and resulting microphase separation of polylactide and polyethylene. The NPE separator exhibited a narrower pore size distribution and higher void fraction, as expected based on a high weight fraction of polylactide in the block polymer precursor, compared with the commercial separator which exhibited a broad pore size distribution and relatively low void fraction, consistent with the mechanism of pore formation being voiding during cold drawing.

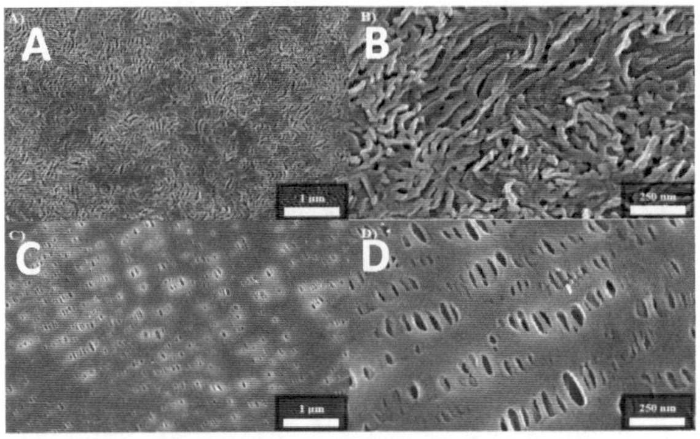

Figure 3. SEM of a Gen 1 NPE separator (A, B) and a commercial trilayer separator (C, D).

Separator Electrolyte Wettability Evaluation

Figure 4 shows electrolyte wicking observation (left, top views) and contact angle observation (right, horizontal views) of a Gen1 NPE (A, B) and a commercial trilayer (C, D) separator. The electrolyte is a conventional Li-ion battery electrolyte. The top views (left) clearly show much better electrolyte wicking (absorbing) of the NPE separator, compared with the commercial counterpart. The horizontal views (right) are intended to provide estimate of contact angle measurement. The contact angles were estimated to be 31° for the NPE separator and 69° for the commercial separator. A smaller contact angle is desirable since it corresponds to a larger differential pressure that drives deeper penetration of the electrolyte into the cylindrical capillary pores of the separator. Therefore, a smaller contact angle corresponds to a higher electrolyte wettability.

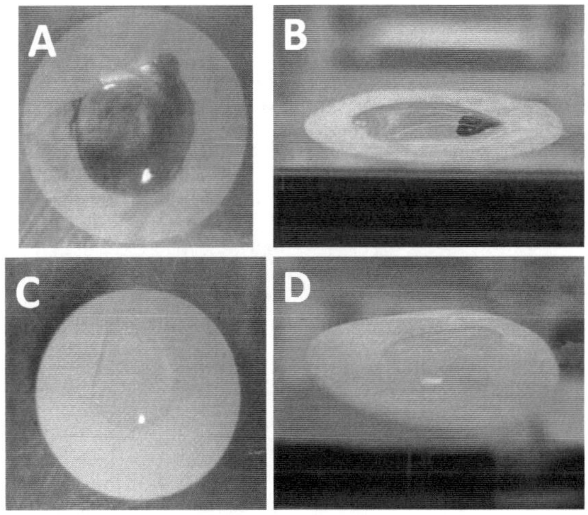

Figure 4. Electrolyte wicking observation of an NPE (A, B) and a commercial trilayer (C, D) separator.

Separator Thermal Shutdown Evaluation

We used an electrochemical impedance technique to measure the separator impedance as a function of separator shutdown temperature on Gen1 and Gen2 NPE separators and a commercial PP/PE/PP trilayer separator. To ensure the high temperature tolerance (up to 150°C), we used high temperature enduring wires and connectors (alligator clips). An environmental (EV) chamber (Espec model BTZ-133) was used to control the temperature of the separator cells. To ensure the proper separator thermal shutdown characterization, we used a specially formulated electrolyte for high temperature endurance (no deterioration at the temperature of evaluation) while providing high ionic conductivity (to ensure good signal to noise ratio to capture the thermal shutdown event of the separator). A supporting separator with higher melting point than the sample separator was used in the separator cells to maintain dimensional stability. We defined the separator thermal shutdown temperature, T_{sd}, as the onset temperature of the impedance rise.

Shutdown Temperature Measurement Results

Figure 5 shows separator cell impedance as a function of temperature for NPE separators and a commercial PP/PE/PP trilayer separator. To ensure the accurate measurement of separator thermal shutdown temperature, the temperature of the EV chamber was programmed to increase at a rate of 0.5°C/min. The onset of the impedance rise occurred at 80°C for Gen2, 115°C for Gen1, and 130°C for the trilayer separator samples, respectively. The increase of the separator impedance is due to separator thermal shutdown, *i.e.*, micropore closing due to the melting/shrinking of the separator, which impedes the ionic motion. As a result, the separator cell impedance increases as the temperature approached the thermal shutdown onset. It is interesting to note that the separator impedance increased by one to two orders of magnitude at the peak of the thermal shutdown, compared with the initial impedance value. The drastic separator impedance increase as a result of separator thermal shutdown is responsible for providing the safety feature to the otherwise normal operation of Li and/or Li-ion batteries. The enhanced thermal shutdown features seen in the NPE separators render earlier, much more rapid thermal shutdown at abusive events (*e.g.*, short circuit, overcharge), which leads to much improved safety characteristics for Li and/or Li-ion batteries.

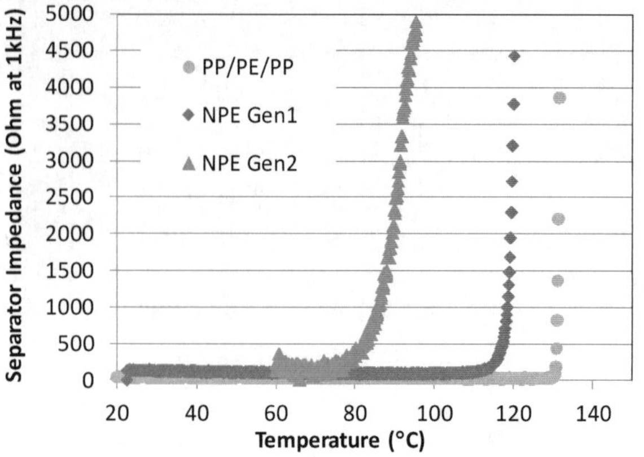

Figure 5. Impedance *vs.* temperature for NPE and commercial trilayer separators.

The 130°C T_{sd} of the PP/PE/PP trilayer is assigned to the melting point of the PE layer. It can therefore be concluded that the molecularly engineered NPE separators (both Gen1 and Gen2) derived from block copolymer architecture successfully modified the PE melting temperature.

Since NPE Gen1 separator was synthesized via the removal of a sacrificial polymer block in the LEL triblock copolymer, this result suggests that, by controlling L-to-E ratios, the resultant NPE separator thermal shutdown temperature (melting point), along with other physical properties such as porosity, tensile strength, *etc.*, can be fine-tuned at the molecular level. In general, the melting point of a polymer is dependent on molecular weight, crystal size (or crystallinity), and stiffness. Physical characterizations of the Gen1 separator suggest that values of these physical parameters were reduced, which resulted in the lowered T_{sd}. The lower T_{sd} of Gen1 NPE separator is qualitatively agreeable with a differential scanning calorimetry (DSC) measurement. For Gen2 NPE, the branched polymer unit effectively disrupted the crystallinity of the otherwise linear polyethylene backbone, which contributes, at least partially, to the further lowering of the thermal shutdown temperature. This study clearly demonstrates the powerfulness of the molecular/nano scale material engineering that can be utilized to fine tune thermal shutdown temperature of the NPE separators.

Hybrid Separator Architectures

ADA employed a hybrid approach to address the multifaceted requirements for a high performance and safe battery separator. We combined the rapid thermal shutdown NPE separator with a supporting separator that is highly porous, mechanically and thermally robust. In specific, the supporting separator was selected so that it possessed a much higher thermal shutdown temperature than NPE. This was done so that, in a battery abusive event, the resultant hybrid separator would have a rapid thermal shutdown afforded by the NPE separator while maintaining the mechanical integrity without dimensional change afforded by the supporting separator.

Figure 6 shows impedance *vs.* temperature of a commercial, PE based, inorganic (silica) filler modified supporting separator. The 144°C T_{sd} of the supporting separator is 64°C, 29°C and 14°C higher than the Gen2 NPE, Gen1 NPE and a typical PE separator, respectively. The increased T_{sd} of the supporting separator is due to the incorporation of the inorganic fillers. Due to its high T_{sd}, the supporting separator is ideally suited for the hybridization architecture. In a thermal abuse event, the NPE separator will provide battery rapid thermal shutdown while the support separator maintains mechanical integrity, due to its much higher T_{sd}; this physically separates the anode and the cathode to prevent possible battery internal short due to otherwise thermal shrinkage of the polymer separator.

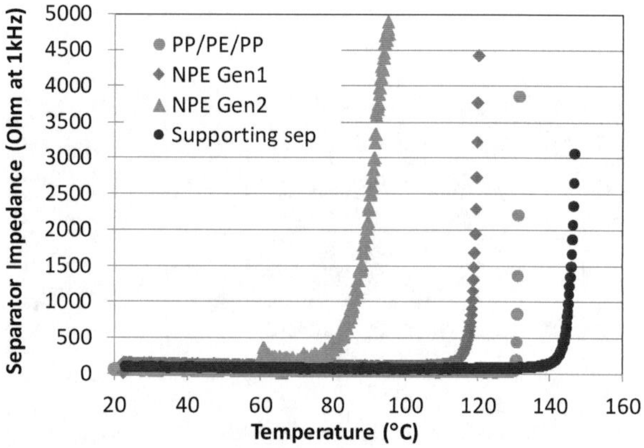

Figure 6. Impedance *vs.* temperature for NPE and supporting separators.

Electrochemical Evaluation of NPE Separators

Figure 7 shows charge/discharge voltages *vs.* specific capacity during formation for Gen1 NPE and a commercial trilayer separator in Li/$LiCoO_2$ (LCO) half cells at room temperature (RT).

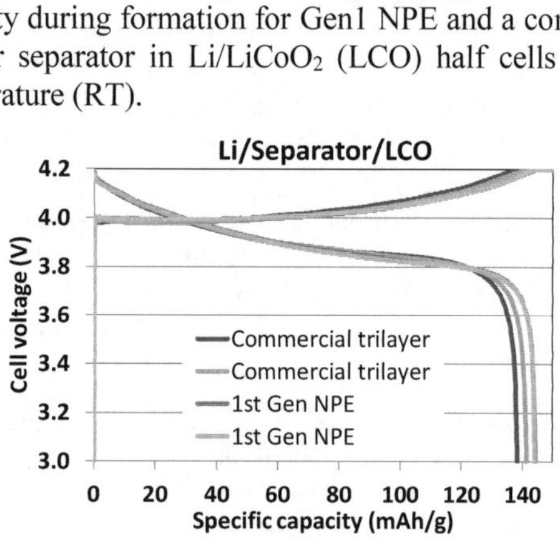

Figure 7. Voltage profiles for Li/LCO half cells.

The NPE-based cells displayed characteristic LCO voltage profiles *vs.* Li and a slightly higher specific capacity (123.2 mAh/g, based on LCO active weight) than the trilayer separator cells. This result is very encouraging since it is the first demonstration of the NEP separator in a Li cell.

Electrochemical Evaluation of Hybrid Separators

Figure 8 shows charge/discharge voltages *vs.* specific capacity during formation for a graphite/LCO full cell using a NPE-based hybrid separator. The hybrid separator based Li-ion full cell showed a characteristic graphite/LCO voltage profiles and a good discharge specific capacity of ~ 120 mAh/g (based on LCO active mass). This represents the first successful demonstration of this class of hybrid separator in a real Li-ion full cell.

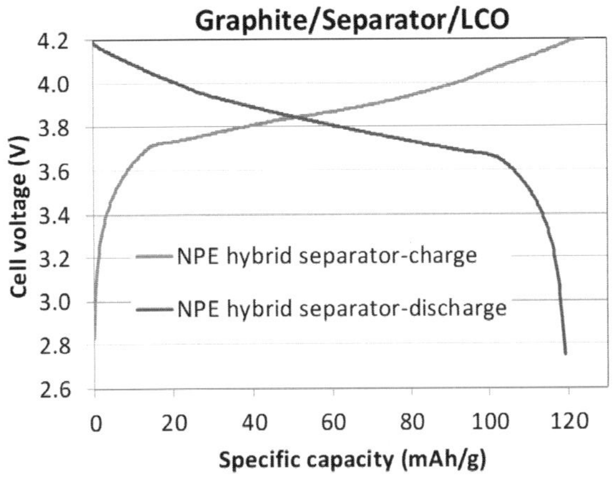

Figure 8. Charge/discharge voltages *vs.* specific capacity during formation of a graphite/LCO full cell.

Figure 9 shows discharge capacity retention (% *vs.* C/4 rate) as a function of C rate for NPE-based hybrid and a trilayer separator in graphite/LCO full cells. The NPE-based hybrid separator demonstrated superior rate capability than the commercial trilayer separator at C rates ≥ 5C. At 20C rate, the NPE hybrid separator based Li-ion cells demonstrated an impressive rate capability of > 73% capacity retention, 2.5x that of the trilayer. The excellent rate performance of the NPE-based hybrid separator highlights the great potential of the ADA separator technology.

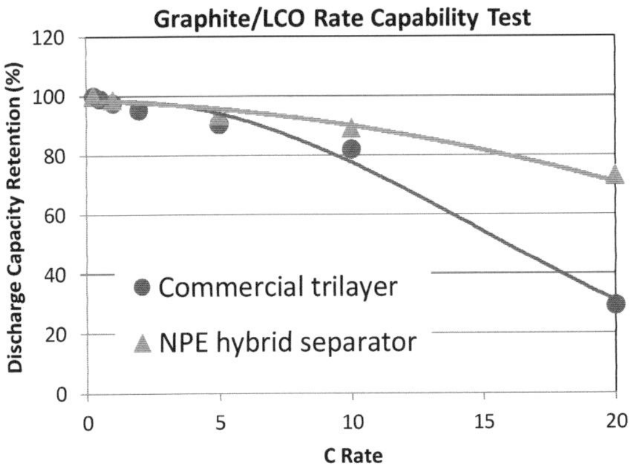

Figure 9. Rate capacity test for graphite/LCO full cells.

Figure 10 shows discharge capacity retention (% *vs.* the initial capacity) *vs.* cycle number of the Li-ion full cells using NPE-based hybrid separator and a trilayer separator (as control). The cells were cycled at 0.5C charge/1C discharge at RT. The NPE hybrid separator based Li-ion full cells showed excellent cycle life performance with 88% capacity retention after 300 cycles, which is comparable to the commercial trilayer. This result illustrates an excellent chemical compatibility (*e.g.*, electrolyte) and electrochemical compatibility (*e.g.*, cycle voltage range) of the NPE-based hybrid separator to Li-ion batteries.

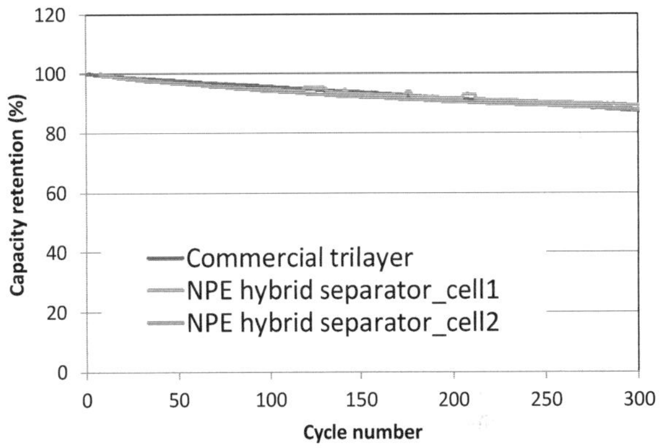

Figure 10. Cycle life of graphite/LCO full cells.

Conclusions

The strategy of preparing block copolymer derived nanoporous separators provides a very promising and powerful tool to allow exquisite tuning of performance and safety features (*e.g.*, thermal shutdown temperature) of the nanostructured separator. The NPE-based hybrid separator architecture will afford an unprecedented performance and safety characteristics for the next generation Li-ion batteries.

Acknowledgements

The authors would like to acknowledge Dr. Mike Larsen and Dr. Marc Hillmyer of the University of Minnesota for NPE separator sample preparation and physical characterizations.

References

1. "FAA Grounds Boeing 787 Dreamliner for Battery Problems", Aviation International News, January 2013
2. https://www.scribd.com/document/368235555/Case-Study-Samsung-Galaxy-Note-7-Exploding-Batteries-PR-Response
3. Pankaj Arora and Zhengming (John) Zhang, Chem. Rev. 104, 4419 (2004).
4. Louis M. Pitet, Mark A. Amendt, and Marc A. Hillmyer, J. AM. CHEM. SOC. 132, 8230 (2010).
5. Bielawski, C. W.; Grubbs, R. H. Prog. Polym. Sci. 32, 1–29 (2007).
6. Pitet, L. M.; Hillmyer, M. A. Macromolecules, 42, 3674–3680 (2009).
7. Wang, Y.; Hillmyer, M. A. ACS Macro Lett. 2017, 6, 613

Advanced Lithium Ion Manufacturing Processes for High Performing Batteries

Pu Zhang, Robert Sosik, Chris Silkowski, Hong Wang, Felix Nunez, and Michael Wixom

Navitas Systems
4880 Venture Drive, Ann Arbor, MI, 48108
pzhang@navitassys.com

Abstract: *The commercial success of lithium ion batteries hinges on significant improvements in both cost and energy density. The electrode coating operation presents the highest leverage opportunity to address both challenges. Navitas ASG has recently demonstrated and scaled up two advanced electrode fabrication processes. One process uses microwave drying to efficiently transfer drying energy into the electrode bulk. The advantages of this approach include 200-500% increase in drying throughput, plus the ability to extend electrode thickness by at least 50% beyond the limits of conventional slot die coating. Data will be presented comparing microwave-dried electrodes to commercial state of the art electrodes for electrode loading ranging from 3 to 8 mAh/cm2. The second process is a dry electrode fabrication process in which active materials, conductive additives, and binder are dry-mixed and roll-milled to form a continuous sheet of free standing electrode material. In addition to eliminating the need to dry and recover NMP, this process enables the fabrication of electrodes with limited stability to solvents or ambient air.*

Guidelines for Safe, High Performing Li-ion Battery Designs for Manned Vehicles

Jacob J. Darst[1], James C. Thomas[1], Donal P. Finegan[2], and Eric C. Darcy[1]

1. NASA Johnson Space Center, 2101 E NASA Pkwy, Houston, TX 77058, USA
2. National Renewable Energy Laboratory, 15013 Denver W Parkway, Golden, CO 80401, USA

Corresponding author email: eric.c.darcy@nasa.gov

Abstract: *New design features and test methods are in development at NASA to take advantage of the newest high power and energy dense commercial Li-ion cell designs and to achieve passively thermal runaway (TR) propagation resistant (PPR) designs for manned missions requiring high power/voltage. The goal is to minimize the parasitic mass and volume of the battery components; thus reaching a balance between high battery specific power (W/kg) and energy (Wh/kg) as well as power (W/L) and energy density (Wh/L). Current 18650 cell designs achieve > 275 Wh/kg, > 725 Wh/L, but present high risks of side wall breaching during TR which can defeat many other safety features resulting in nearly immediate TR propagation. This work seeks to better understand the phenomena of cell side wall breaches and to determine the effectiveness of promising battery design features for achieving safe, high performing battery designs for high voltage/power applications.*

Keywords: Li-ion; thermal runaway propagation; side wall breaches; interstitial heat sinks, battery design guidelines.

Introduction

NASA was successful in establishing guidelines that designers can readily follow for achieving batteries that are passively thermal runaway (TR) propagation resistant (PPR) and prevent flames and sparks from exiting the battery enclosure for low power/voltage applications with low mass/volume penalties.[1]

However, many of NASA's higher power and more energy demanding applications (e.g., Robonaut, RoboSimian, Valkyrie, Mars Chariot Rover and Resource Prospector, and especially NASA electrified aircraft flight projects such as X-57 Electric Airplane) are significantly mass/volume constrained and require more effective thermal management features for both performance and safety. In addition, due to their high voltage, have electrocution and corona discharge hazards. The initial battery designs for Robonaut, Robosimian, and X-57 have been demonstrated (either by intentional test or by catastrophic failure) to not achieve PPR status against a single cell TR event.[2,3]

Why aren't the guidelines and experience from the previous work sufficient?

a) The phenomena and factors driving the propensity of 18650 cell side wall breaches are not well-understood and uncertainty exists about which cell design features mitigate them.[4]
b) Recent calorimetric experiments indicate that introducing a bottom vent feature on 18650 cells reduces total heat output.[5]
c) Risk of side wall breaches with 0.5mm spacing between very high energy-density 18650 cell designs (>700 Wh/L) with an interstitial metallic heat sink was shown to not propagate, albeit with low safety margins for protecting adjacent cells.[6]
d) The solution of adding a snug fitting full length steel sleeve on each cell as structural support has been successfully vetted and adopted for the Orion Command Module battery but comes at significant mass and volume penalties that are too severe for these new applications.[6]
e) Fusible links integrated into the nickel (Ni) bussing sufficiently protects parallel cells in medium and low power applications, but may generate too much heat for high power applications due to their high resistance.[7]
f) The high temperature materials utilized for the cell TR ejecta vectoring protects adjacent cells in the previous assessment, but also presents insufficient safety margins for achieving 0.5mm cell spacing.[6]
g) The current guidelines do not address electrocution and corona discharge hazards.

Prototype Battery Brick Design

The most recently tested heat sink system is depicted in Figure 1. System components include the metallic interstitial bore casing, (50) 18650 lithium-ion cells with mica strips, (25) ceramic bushings, (2) fiberglass capture plates, and (6) nickel bus plates with fusible links in the negative cell weld terminal. Aluminum 6061T6 alloy with an anodized coating as the interstitial heat sink has enabled assemblies achieving > 190 Wh/kg. Substituting to a beryllium-aluminum alloy, with higher conductivity, melting point, and strength and lower density can enable > 200 Wh/kg.[1] The unique geometry of the 50-cell brick shown in Figure 1 allows all cells to have a minimum neighbor limit of three and can also be tessellated in multi-brick systems to yield overall rectangular geometries. Cell-to-cell spacing in the system has been iteratively reduced to the current value of 0.37 mm.

Traditional designs include a mica sleeve around the cells to electrically insulate them from the interstitial material, but thermal analysis suggests the presence of an air gap protects adjacent cells while swelling of the trigger cell and its ejected contents promote heat dissipation to the heat sink.[3] Accordingly, to replace fully circumferential mica sleeves, thin mica strips are wound around cells in a spiral pattern and glued to their surface (Figure 5).

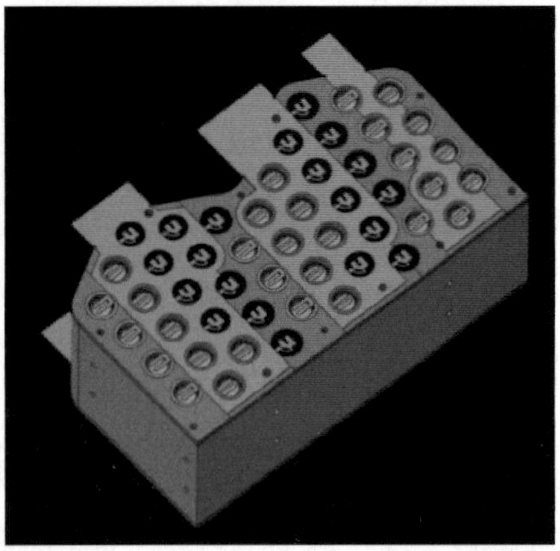

Figure 1. Battery Brick Assembly. CAD model depicting the interstitial bore casing, cells, ceramic bushings, capture plates, and nickel bussing plates in a 5s10p configuration.

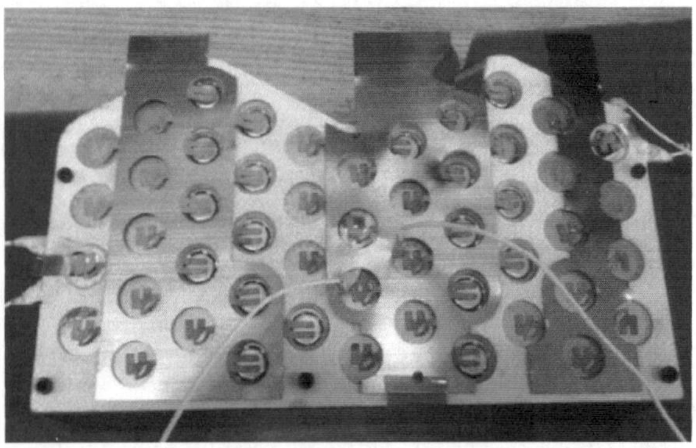

Figure 2. Photo of battery brick as prepared for testing.

Prototype Battery Brick Verification

The battery brick assembly shown in Figures 1 and 2 contained three 'trigger' cells implanted with internal short circuit devices[4] for initiating thermal runaway. The key component of the device is a wax disc inside which melts when heated > 57 °C, inducing a hard internal short between anode active material and cathode current collector, which initiates thermal runaway. Previous tests have shown that heating normal cells into thermal runaway while inside interstitial aluminum heat sink is extremely difficult due to its very facile heat dissipation.[3] The locations of the trigger cells included a corner cell, side cell, and middle cell, which can be seen in Figure 2 where heater wires stem from the system. Three separate experiments were conducted by charging the battery to 100% state-of-charge and initiating a thermal runaway event in each trigger cell with a small custom bottom heater. The temperature of the cells neighboring the trigger cells and the temperature of the test article at key locations was measured with K-type thermocouples, and the voltage of each trigger cell bank was recorded during each experiment. A snapshot of the third test (corner trigger cell) during the thermal runaway event is depicted in Figure 3.

Thermal runaway propagation from cell to cell was not observed in any of the three single cell trigger events conducted. Instantaneous temperatures as high as 450 and 750 °C were recorded at the terminals of neighboring cells during thermal runaway events initiated by the edge and middle trigger cells, respectively. These high temperatures stemmed from direct contact of thermocouple junctions with combusting ejecta, or with flames, or due to diagnostic cables exposed to the ejecta. Nevertheless, the temperature readings quickly decreased due to rapid heat dissipation throughout the system. The open-cell voltage (OCV) of each bank dipped and immediately recovered which indicates effective electrical isolation of the trigger cell by the cell fusible link designed into the negative cell termination connection of each nickel bus plate. The lack of thermal runaway propagation and open circuit voltage bounce-back serve as verification of the current metallic interstitial system and its corresponding design parameters. However, post-test examination capacity cycling of the adjacent cells indicated a few of the 12 total cells would not accept a charge suggesting low margins against propagation. These cells were located next to the side and corner trigger cells.

Figure 3. Video snapshot of the battery brick assembly during the single cell thermal runaway event.

Latest Design Methods

Numerous cell and pack level features are being developed and incorporated in new batteries for improved TR performance and greater energy density.

Previous generations of high performance battery packs were built using highly insulating interstitial materials that limited energy transfer to adjacent cells; newer development designs tend to favor a highly conductive and diffusive pack featuring a solid metal conductive heat sink as an intercell interstitial material.

The goal in using these conductive heat sinks is to allow heat (from either TR or nominal cycling) to be dissipated away quickly from the target cell and distributed evenly across the other healthy cells in the pack, while simultaneously removing this energy from the pack itself via thermal links to the case and vehicle structure itself. The solid metal heatsink also serves to prevent expansion of the cells and contain side-breach events during TR.

The latest of these designs featuring aluminum interstitial material couples this with a hexagonal packing arrangement (Figure 4).

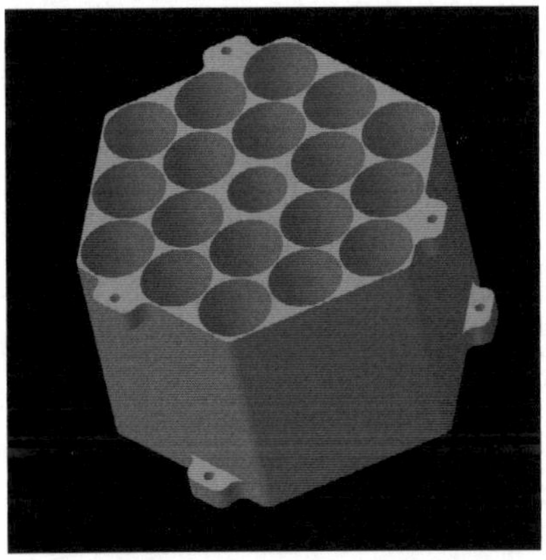

Figure 4. Hexagonal aluminum interstitial heat sink.

The hexagonal packing offers the tightest possible arrangement of cylinders in a plane, while also being able to be tessellated infinitely to allow larger batteries to be constructed from these smaller interlocking modular banks. The design also allows for stacking of modules in "decks", giving even more options for use.

In an 18650 cell, the entire cell can is polarized negative, which creates a short risk to chassis when cells are embedded in these conductive heat sinks. To prevent this electrical shorting, the surface is hard-anodized, and several additional processes are performed on the cells themselves.

The cells are coated with a thin paraxylene layer approximately 1 thousandth of an inch thick via chemical vapor deposition. This coating is abrasion resistant, inert, and electrically isolating, and is too thin to impact normal vent and burst operation of the cell.

In addition to the paraxylene, the cells are wrapped with a helical strip of mica paper. The mica is both electrically and thermally isolating, and retains its mechanical strength up to 900°C. The helical wrap serves a double function: it lightens the pack by using less material than a full sleeve, and serves to create a critical dead air gap in between the cells and the heat sink. As shown in Figure 5 the cell mica paper wrapping that ensures the air gap and is less likely to be damaged when inserting the cell assembly in the snug fitting bores of the heat sink.

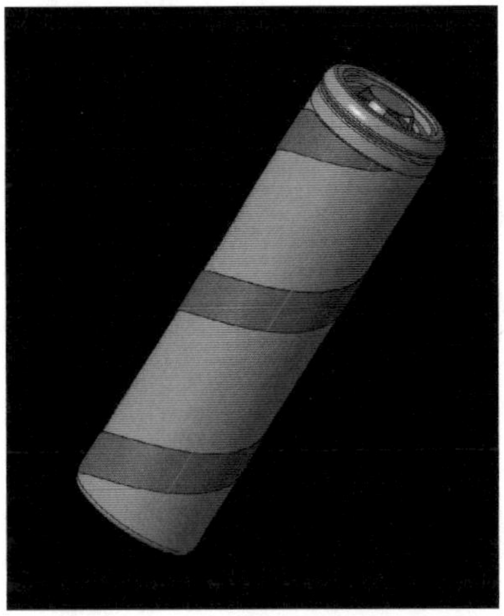

Figure 5. Spiraling mica paper wrapped around an 18650 cell.

These features combine to make the heat sink effective at wicking away heat during nominal operations as well as TR, but insulating enough to prevent damage to adjacent cells during a single-cell TR event. In addition to nominal TR protection, the design must be prepared against abnormal venting and failure.

In certain high energy cells, can breaching is occasionally observed in the spin groove below the positive terminal of the cell. This failure results in hot ejected material being sprayed diagonally in an uncontrolled manner and impinging upon neighboring cells. To mitigate the consequence of this failure, a number of features are being developed.

Offsetting the positive end of the 18650 cells from the negative end of adjacent cells helps protect the neighboring cells from being exposed to direct contact with ejected material from the failed cells. It is worth noting that this is only effective in modules in which cells are oriented with their positives faced both up and down in banks; if positives faced the same direction, the lower cell would always be able to impinge on the higher cell.

As seen in Figure 6, the spin groove is raised far away from adjacent negative ends, preventing direct impingement. This is sufficient if cells are packed in a checkerboard pattern with adjacent positive terminals spaced far away from each other, but the increased safety comes at a cost of space efficiency and interstitial mass.

In a hexagonal packed structure, it is inevitable there will be adjacent positive cell headers, making additional controls necessary (see Figure 7.) To address this concern, short and thin stainless steel tubes are placed over the spin groove, acting as a blast shield for ejecta, redirecting it upwards in a safe direction (Figure 8.)

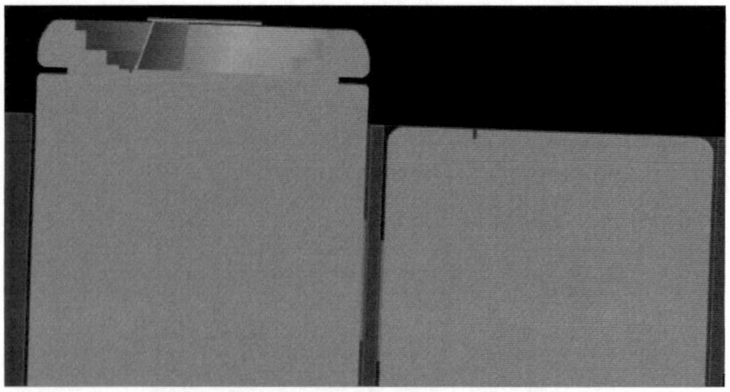

Figure 6. Offset alignment of adjacent cells as protection against spin groove breaches during TR.

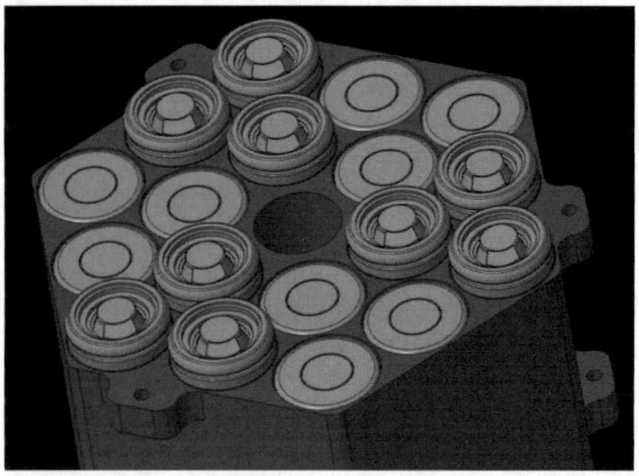

Figure 7. Battery packaging showing groups of cells with the vulnerable spin grooves in very close proximity.

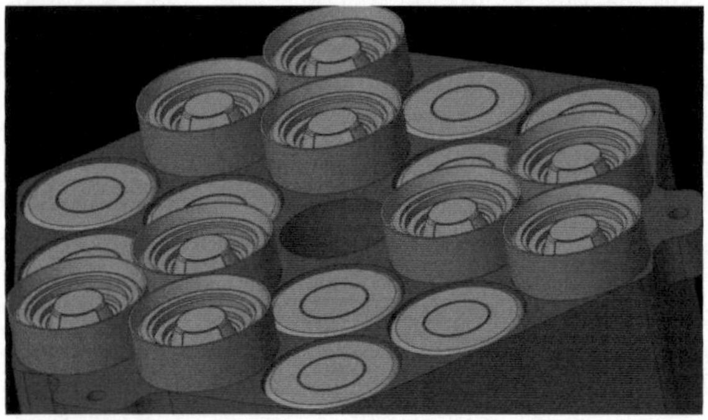

Figure 8. Short steel tubes protecting the spin groove area of a TR cell from impinging on adjacent cells.

There is concern that when axial compression of the cells leading up to and during TR events is sufficient to prevent the free expansion of the header crimp, the resultant higher burst pressures create greater energy release and consequently a more violent TR than nominal conditions. To fasten cells in place securely while minimizing the amount of header compression, a frangible tab has been built into the capture plates for the modules, covering the positive button of the cell. A plastic washer is sandwiched between the top of the cell and the capture plate; this applies uniform pressure to the tabs during TR by providing a buffer between the cell buttons and the tabs themselves. During TR the header attempts to swell and lengthen, causing the washer to shear off the tabs, giving the header the room it needs to expand (see Figure 9).

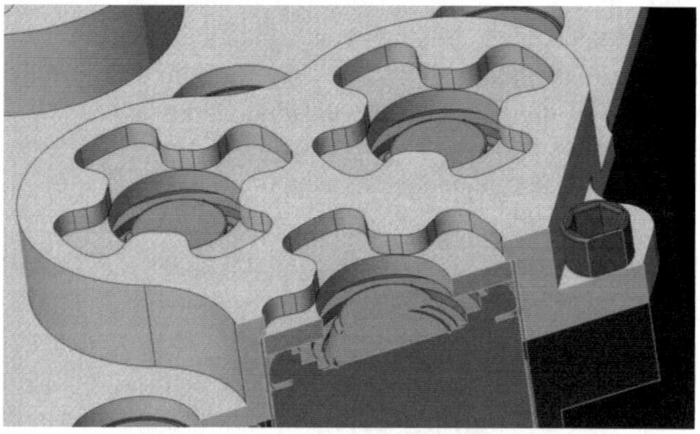

Figure 9. Plastic washer and frangible tabs in capture plate.

Conclusions

Safe, high performing (>160 Wh/kg) battery designs are possible with metal interstitial heat sinks.

Acknowledgements

This effort is funded by NASA Engineering Safety Center.

References

1. Darcy, E., and Scharf, S. "Safe, High Performing Li-Ion Battery Designs: Summary of 2015 Findings," *2015 NASA Aerospace Battery Workshop*, Huntsville, AL, Nov 2015.
2. http://www.dailymail.co.uk/sciencetech/article-3883158/Nasa-reveals-shocking-video-secretive-military-RoboSimian-EXPLODING-batteries-catch-fire.html
3. Darcy, E., "Safe Battery Design Guidelines for Achieving Passive TR Propagation Resistance," *2nd International Battery Safety Workshop, Albuquerque*, NM, May, 2017.
4. Finegan, E., et.al., "Characterising TR within Li-ion cells by inducing and monitoring internal short circuits." *Energy Environ. Sci.*, **10**, 1377, 2017.
5. Walker, W., et.al., "Statistical Characterization of 18650-Format Li-ion Cell TR Energy Distributions," *NASA Aerospace Battery Workshop*, Nov 2017.
6. Darcy, E., "*Insights from Safety Tests with an On-demand Internal Short Circuit Device in 18650 Cells.*" International Battery Seminar, Fort Lauderdale, FL, 2017.
7. Darcy, E., and Keyser, M., "*Driving Factors for Achieving Safe, High Performing Li-ion Battery Designs*," More Electric Aircraft USA, Seattle, WA, Aug, 2016.

Copper Dissolution Investigations in Large-Format Lithium-ion Cells

Christopher E. Hendricks[a,b], Azzam N. Mansour[a], Daphne A. Fuentevilla[a], Jonathan K. Ko[a], and Gordon H. Waller[a]
a – Naval Surface Warfare Center, Carderock Division
9500 MacArthur Blvd, West Bethesda, MD 20817
b – Center for Advanced Life Cycle Engineering
University of Maryland, College Park, MD 20742
christopher.hendricks@navy.mil / 1-301-227-3985

Abstract: Lithium-ion batteries are seeing increased use in military applications, but safety concerns are a huge impediment for their widespread adoption, especially in the U.S. Navy and U.S. Marine Corps. Although lithium-ion technologies offer undeniable improvements in energy density and lifetime, the effect of unintended battery abuse on host platforms needs to be assessed and quantified. Overdischarge is well known as one of several possible failure mechanisms [1]. However, it is less well studied than failure mechanisms, such as overcharge and thermal abuse, which consistently elicit worst-case-scenario responses. As a result, it is still unclear how the battery's performance and safety is impacted by storage at low voltages. Because overdischarge can occur naturally through self-discharge of the batteries, it is a much more likely failure mechanism than overcharge, which is heavily regulated by the battery's charging software and hardware. With batteries potentially stored for months or years at a time in an inactive state, it is critical to understand the effects of overdischarge on the battery's performance and safety. In this paper, we examine individual cells that have been overdischarged and held at different voltage levels (0.25 V and 0 V) for over six months, and study the chemical state of the dissolved copper through X-ray absorption fine structure (XAFS) spectroscopy of the anodes. In most cases, copper was found in a non-conductive species, with copper hydroxide $Cu(OH)_2$ as the dominant species. The presence of these species on electrode surfaces suggests both a performance and safety hazard is present even before voltage reversal, due to the potential for inhibited lithium intercalation and the creation of potential nucleation sites for lithium dendrite growth. The threshold for whether recharge is advisable depends on the anode to cathode balance ratio and the chemistry of the particular cell design

Keywords: Lithium-ion batteries; copper dissolution; overdischarge; X-ray absorption fine structure

Introduction

Overdischarge, unlike conventional lithium-ion abuses such as overcharge, high temperature, or short circuit, does not immediately result in a dramatic thermal runaway event that leads to fire and gas generation. Instead, the effects from overdischarge become apparent only on subsequent recharge, if there are any noticeable effects at all. Overdischarge does not immediately result in thermal runaway; however, it is one of the more likely failure mechanisms to occur and its effects on battery performance and safety have not been fully characterized.

Overdischarge of lithium-ion batteries can be separated into two different categories. The first overdischarge situation occurs when the battery's voltage falls below the battery's low voltage cutoff (approximately 2.5 Volts for most lithium-ion chemistries), but remains above 0 Volts (V). This scenario can occur due to parasitic loads or simply long-term storage. The second is overdischarge into voltage reversal, or forced overdischarge, where the cell voltage drops below 0 V. In this situation, a power supply of some type is needed to force the battery's voltage to a negative value.

Reports of overdischarge into reversal clearly show the dissolution of copper and formation of internal short circuits. In [2], cells were discharged at a constant current to as much as -100% state-of-charge (SOC), and later recharged to estimate the resistance of copper short circuits. Cells overdischarged to less than -12% SOC exhibited short circuits with resistances on the order of a few ohms, whereas the cells overdischarged beyond -15% SOC could not be fully recovered. The presence of copper on both the anode and cathode was confirmed by SEM as well as XRD. The authors note that the SOC% is very much dependent on the ratio of anode to cathode active material, as the copper dissolution threshold is related to the voltage of the anode vs. Li/Li^+.

Studies of cells overdischarged without going into voltage reversal have also reported the dissolution of copper from the anode's copper current collector; however, the formation of short circuits is not well documented. In [3], failure of overdischarged cells was attributed to copper dissolution and plating, which led to gas generation due to electrolyte decomposition. The gas generation and electrolyte decomposition were documented; the copper dissolution and plating was hypothesized. Researchers in [4] demonstrated dissolution of copper in small lithium-ion cells and confirmed its presence through EDX measurements of disassembled cells. Studies of both bare copper [5,6] and graphite-coated copper [7, 8] were performed to identify copper dissolution rates and initiation voltages. The presence of graphite inhibits copper dissolution to some extent and shifts the copper oxidation by 50 mV to approximately 3.65 V vs. Li/Li^+.

In this paper, we describe X-ray absorption fine structure (XAFS) measurements on overdischarged electrodes to identify the chemical state of dissolved copper in the electrodes. Previous work on the same large-format, lithium-ion cell has shown that copper dissolution occurs at voltages below 0.5 V for a cathode-rich NCA cell [10]. The presence of copper on both the anode and cathode of overdischarged cells was confirmed via X-ray photoelectron spectroscopy (XPS).

Experimental

Large-format (>30 Ampere-hour) lithium-ion cells were overdischarged to 0.25 V or 0 V for a time period of at least 6 months. The cells were then either disassembled immediately following storage or were charged and discharged prior to disassembly. Disassembly was carried out in an argon-filled glovebox with oxygen levels less than 1 ppm. Cells were disassembled at 0% SOC or lower and a Dremel tool with a non-conducting cutting disk was used to remove the top and bottom of the cell and score along the length of the casing. The cell casing was pried open using non-conductive tools, and the jelly roll was unwound to gather samples. Samples were removed from near the exterior (closest to outer case), middle, and interior (closest to mandrel) of the jelly roll.

XAFS Sample Preparation – Reference powders were obtained for a number of copper compounds including $Cu(OH)_2$, Cu_2O, CuO, and CuF_2. The powders were manually ground with a mortar and pestle and sifted to particle sizes less than 20 μm in diameter using an ultrasonic sifter. Each compound was mixed with boron nitride and pressed into a 5 mm x 12 mm free-standing pellet using a force of 1.5 metric tons. The pellet was mounted in between two pieces of Scotch-brand tape to avoid contamination.

Graphitic electrode sample preparation – Samples from the graphitic electrode were collected by peeling off one side of the electrode from the current collector using Scotch-brand tape. The XAFS samples then consisted of a layer of Scotch-tape and an electrode that is approximately 90 μm thick mounted onto a sample holder.

Copper measurement – X-ray absorption fine structure (XAFS) measurements were performed under general user proposal # 48045 at the 5-BM-D beamline at Argonne National Laboratory's Advanced Photon Source. Copper was measured in fluorescence mode using a Cambera passivated implanted planar silicon (PIPS) detector to measure the intensity of the fluorescence photons from the sample. Ion chamber detectors were used to measure the intensity of the incident X-rays, the transmitted X-rays through the sample, and the transmitted X-rays through a copper reference foil (for calibration purposes). The X-ray cross section was approximately 1mm x 7mm, and the center of the samples was located by scanning the sample for the point of maximum fluorescence. Scans were performed between 8.779 keV and 10.079 keV with 5 eV steps in the pre-edge region, 0.5 eV steps in the XANES region, and 0.05 $Å^{-1}$ in the EXAFS region.

Results and Discussion

Copper dissolution in the electrodes was measured in fluorescence mode on three different samples from each cell. For most samples, the spectra were nearly identical for different regions within the cell. However, the cells that were recharged from an overdischarged state showed some differences. In all cases, the three spectra are averaged together for the plots in this section.

The cells overdischarged to 0 or 0.25 V are normalized and their X-ray Absorption Near Edge Structure (XANES) is plotted in Figure 1. All of the samples have the same overall spectra; however, the pre-edge shoulder at 8982 eV was more pronounced for some of the samples. Figure 2 shows one of the 0 V cells plotted against reference compounds. The left plot shows the normalized absorption in the XANES region and the right plot shows the 1st derivative. It is evident that the pre-edge shoulder is associated with Cu_2O (labeled A in the plot), indicating that some portion of the copper in the electrode can be attributed to this species. Cu_2O does not explain the full spectra, which suggests that another species is present. Figure 2 also includes the spectra for $Cu(OH)_2$, and the small shoulder before the Cu K-edge (labeled B in the plot) and the electrode's behavior above the Cu K-edge (labeled C in the plot) provides evidence for the presence of $Cu(OH)_2$ in addition to Cu_2O.

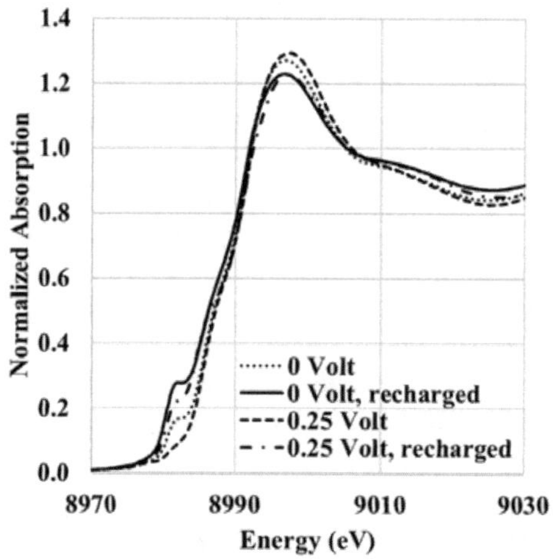

Figure 1: Cu K-edge XANES data of overdischarged large-format, lithium-ion, NCA cells

The Fourier transform of the k^3-weighted $\chi(k)$ of the Cu K-edge EXAFS region in the left plot of Figure 3 shows a large peak between 1 and 2 Å with smaller peaks between 2

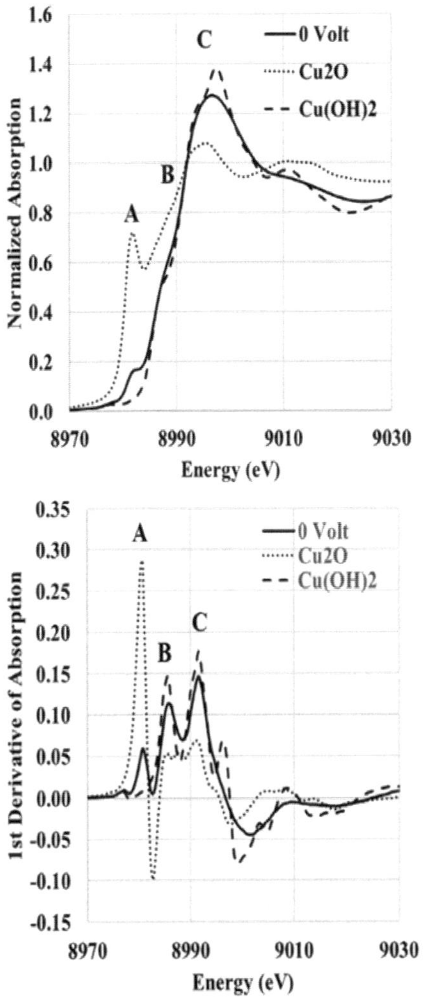

Figure 2: Cu K-edge XANES (top) and derivative of XANES (bottom) comparison of 0 V overdischarged lithium-ion cell with reference materials.

and 4 Å. By plotting the reference materials in the top plot in Figure 3 along with a representative 0 V and 0.25 V cell sample, it is possible to more clearly see the presence of $Cu(OH)_2$ in the extended region of the spectra. Furthermore, the peak is much more pronounced in the 0.25 V cell compared to the 0 V cell, indicating that the 0 V cells contain less $Cu(OH)_2$ than the 0.25 V cells. The lack of significant contribution above 2 Å is indicative of the highly disordered or amorphous nature of the $Cu(OH)_2$ species. Table 1 gives the parameters obtained when fitting the model to the experimental data.

When fitting the model, data was used from all samples with a fixed many bodied amplitude reduction factor (S_0^2) and the fractions of Cu in $Cu(OH)_2$ and Cu_2O were allowed to vary and were later converted to mole fractions of $Cu(OH)_2$ and Cu_2O as seen in Table 2. All samples shared common values for coordination distance (R), mean squared relative displacement or disorder (σ^2), and inner

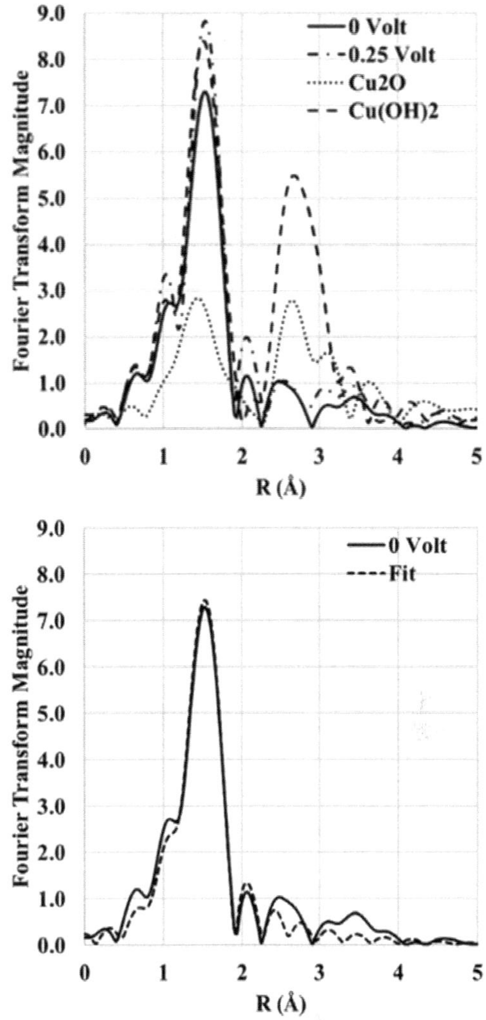

Figure 3: Fourier transform of k^3-weighted Cu K-Edge EXAFS spectra comparison with reference samples of Cu_2O and $Cu(OH)_2$ (top) and simulated Fourier transform.

potential correction (E_0). This allowed us to fit a common model that assumed all samples contained the same compounds (Cu_2O and $Cu(OH)_2$) in varying concentrations. The goodness of fit is reported as an R-factor which is defined as the sum of squares residual between measured and modeled data normalized by the magnitude of the measured data. A low R-factor confirms that our simplifying assumptions are reasonable. The most amount of $Cu(OH)_2$ was seen in the 0.25 V cell that was not recharged. The least amount of $Cu(OH)_2$ was present in the 0 V sample that was recharged. The act of recharging a cell following overdischarge appears to result in an increase in Cu_2O in the anodes; however, further investigations are required to determine the mechanism responsible for this result. Additionally, discharging to 0 V appears to generate more Cu_2O than comparable 0.25 V cells.

Table 1: Local structure parameters calculated from simulated Fourier transforms of EXAFS spectra for 0 V, 0 V recharged, 0.25 V, and 0.25 V recharged cells (uncertainties reported in parentheses). Mole fraction and R-factor from the 0.25 V cell. Other parameters are shared for all cells.

	S_0^2	Mole Fraction	N	R (Å)[a]	σ^2 (Å^2)	E_0 (eV)	R-Factor
$Cu(OH)_2$	0.86	0.829(0.13)	4	1.939 (0.004)	0.0031(0.0010)	0.5(0.4)	0.014
			1	2.335 (0.004)	0.036(0.0182)		
Cu_2O		0.171(0.13)	2	1.805 (0.004)	0.0028(0.0014)		

[a] R for reference spectra are 1.960, 2.356, and 1.826

Table 2: Mole fractions for different overdischarge conditions

Storage Condition	Mole Fraction ($Cu(OH)_2$)	Mole Fraction (Cu_2O)	R-Factor
0 V	0.709(0.08)	0.291(0.08)	0.0018
0.25 V	0.829(0.13)	0.171(0.13)	0.014
0 V, recharged	0.563(0.06)	0.437(0.06)	0.0020
0.25 V, recharged	0.664(0.09)	0.336(0.09)	0.032

Conclusions

The dissolution of copper was confirmed by XAFS analysis of overdischarged lithium-ion cell anodes. Cupric oxide (Cu_2O) and copper hydroxide ($Cu(OH)_2$) were detected in all samples; however, the concentration of the species varied depending on the cell voltage and whether the cell was recharged after an overdischarge event. In most cases $Cu(OH)_2$ was the dominant species in the anodes. Due to the non-conductive nature of these compounds, it is not evident that a hard internal short circuit is the primary failure mechanism of cells overdischarged between 0.5 V and 0 V. The presence of these species on electrode surfaces; however, does present a performance and safety risk due to inhibited lithium intercalation and the creation of potential nucleation sites for lithium dendrite growth. Due to the uncertainty in these types of failures, recharging an overdischarged cell is not advised. The exact threshold for whether recharge is advisable depends on the anode to cathode balance ratio and the chemistry of the cell. As a result, the voltage at which a battery can be recharged and used must be determined on a case-by-case basis, specific to the cell design and manufacturer.

Acknowledgements

The authors acknowledge support under the Naval Innovative Science and Engineering (NISE) program, managed by the NSWC Carderock Division Director of Research, Jack Price. The XAS experiments were performed at the DuPont-Northwestern-Dow Collaborative Access Team (DND-CAT) located at Sector 5 of the Advanced Photon Source (APS). DND-CAT is supported by Northwestern University, E.I. DuPont de Nemours & Col, and the Dow Chemical Company. This research used resources of the Advanced Photon Source, a U.S. Department of Energy (DOE) Office of Science User Facility operated for the DOE Office of Science by Argonne National Laboratory under Contract No. DE-AC02-06CH11357.

References

1. C. Mikolajczak, M. Kahn, K. White, R. Long, "Lithium-Ion Batteries Hazard and Use Assessment," Springer, New York (2011).
2. R. Guo, L. Lu, M. Ouyang, and X. Feng, Mechanism of the entire overdischarge process and overdischarge-induced internal short circuit in lithium-ion batteries, Sci. Rep. 6 (30248) (2016) pp. 1-9
3. K. Kumai, H. Miyashiro, Y. Kobayashi, K. Takei, and R. Ishikawa, "Gas generation mechanism due to electrolyte decomposition in commercial lithium-ion cell," J. Power Sources 81-82 (1999) pp. 715-719.
4. H. Maleki and J. N. Howard, Effects of overdischarge on performance and thermal stability of a Li-ion cell, J. Power Sources 160 (2006) pp. 1395-1402.
5. M. Zhao et al., Electrochemical stability of copper in lithium-ion battery electrolytes, J. Electrochem. Soc., Vol. 147 (8) (2000) pp. 2874-2879.
6. M. Zhao et al., Quantitation of the dissolution of battery-grade copper foils in lithium-ion battery electrolytes by flame atomic absorption spectroscopy, Electrochimica Acta, Vol. 49 (2004) pp. 683-689.
7. M. Zhao et al., Electrochemical stability of graphite-coated copper in lithium-ion battery electrolytes, J. Electrochem. Soc., Vol. 147 (11) (2000) pp. 3983-3988.
8. M. Zhao et al., Quantitation of the dissolution of the graphite-coated copper foil in lithium-ion battery electrolytes by flame absorption spectroscopy, Electrochimica Acta, Vol. 49 (2004) pp. 677-681.
9. K. R. Crompton, and B. J. Landi, Opportunities for near zero volt storage of lithium ion batteries, Energy and Environ. Sci. 7 (2016) pp. 2219-2239
10. D. Fuentevilla, C. Hendricks, A. Mansour, Quantifying the impact of overdischarge on large format lithium-ion cells, ECS Transactions 69 (20) (2015) pp. 1-4.
11. B. Ravel and M. Newville, ATENA, ARTEMIS, HEPHAESTUS: data analysis for X-ray absorption spectroscopy using IFEFFIT, J. of Sync. Rad. 12 (2005), pp. 537-541.

Safer by Design: Limited Thermal Event Propagation in NMC Pouch-Based Batteries

Jon Diller
Spear Power Systems LLC
4020 E 138th Street, Grandview, Missouri, USA 64030
jdiller@spearps.com / 1-913-636-9574

Abstract: *Lithium ion cells are an enabling technology, but their safety must be managed. Techniques for controlling the propagation of a thermal event from cell to cell are well known as applied to cylindrical cells. Pouch cells offer several advantages, but the prevention of event cascade is less widely understood. This paper describes the need for and a methodology for achieving the control of thermal event propagation with pouch cells.*

Keywords: lithium; battery; pouch; cell; cells; thermal event; cascade; NMC; propagation

Introduction

The lithium ion battery (LIB) is an enabling technology at the heart of both the information age and the green revolution. Without this remarkable energy storage medium our phones would still be the size of briefcases, and we would be years from practical vehicles that can run purely on clean, renewable energy. Further, the defense of our nation relies on advanced technologies like unmanned vehicles and directed energy weapons which would be difficult to realize without the unique combination of energy and power density available from an LIB.

Safety: Like the more familiar energy storage medium gasoline, LIBs are potentially volatile when abused, so their safety must be carefully managed. Large batteries, such as those used for vehicles, consist of an arrangement of many cells. If one of those cells experiences a thermal event following severe abuse, neighboring cells may also be affected, and a massive fire can propagate through the entire battery pack.

LIB safety is primarily a function of the collection of electronics and software known as the battery management system (BMS); this is both preventative, as the advanced BMS manages the charge and discharge of the battery via interactive communications with the power source/supply, and limiting, since the BMS monitors both the voltage and temperature of each cell or parallel cell group and switches the battery off prior to truly unsafe conditions being met.

The product of a thermal event in a single cell can be managed. Temperatures can be reduced, flame suppressed, and hazardous gasses can be vented to a safer location. However, similar measures robust enough to contain a full-battery fire would increase the weight and size of a LIB such that its advantages over other storage technologies would be largely offset.

To be truly effective, then, the safety mechanism of an LIB must be three layered: a BMS which is robust and redundant, to minimize the chance of a thermal event and terminate function early in an event's evolution; a mechanical design which incorporates features to mitigate and control the products of a single-cell thermal event; and a proven mechanism for prevention of the propagation of a thermal event to neighboring cells.

Cell formats: Such propagation control is well known in application to LIBs which use cylindrical cells. These cells, which take the form of small tubes or cans and which are of limited energy storage capacity, can be housed in a block of material which moves heat away rapidly from a burning cell and prevents propagation to neighboring cells not in parallel. This is established in multiple embodiments and the subject of various patents[1].

However, cylindrical cells have certain limitations in comparison to pouch cells – flat battery cells that are for example used in cell phones. A pouch cell, which is available in larger capacities than its cylindrical counterpart, can deliver much more energy than a cylindrical cell during a thermal event. Battery packs using pouch cells are often designed to be highly space- and weight-efficient. Retaining that advantage while preventing propagation of a thermal event is a challenge which has not been extensively addressed by the industry.

This paper explores a proven means of limiting propagation between pouch cells, and as such enables its reader to understand that the advantages of pouch cells can be combined with even greater safety than cylindrical cells offer, if the battery pack maker is sufficiently adept.

Cell Formats

Cylindrical cells are quite familiar to laypersons. They consist of two electrodes, or current collectors, which take the form of long strips of foil. These electrodes are coated with materials which allow them to store and discharge energy. The coated electrodes are rolled up, flooded with electrolytes which carry the charge from one electrode to the other, and sealed in a metal can. This format is used with alkaline primary cells – the familiar 'coppertops' nobody has enough of on Christmas morning – and is also the technology at the heart of Tesla's innovative automobiles.

Pouch cells might be a bit harder for the average person to recognize – but are probably closer to him or her physically, as they are the energy storage that makes flat, capable cellular phones possible. These cells contain the same electrodes as cylindrical cells, but they are stacked flat and placed in a plastic pouch, which is flooded with the same electrolytes and sealed.

Pouch cells have several advantages over cylindrical cells. Since their electrodes are stacked flat, rather than wound upon itself, it is much more available to thermal movement. The entire surface may be cooled, whereas in a cylindrical cell the terminals of the electrode are the dominant thermal path. This surface area advantage permits more efficient and rapid cooling.

This also means that the heat is more evenly distributed across the cell, and the collection of heat in isolated areas can be avoided. This extends the life of the cell (chemistry for chemistry, pouch cells typically have from twice to an order of magnitude more cycles available to the user) and probably has influence on the safety of the cell [cf. Lian et al[2], wherein it is established that aging reduces the temperature at which cylindrical cells can encounter a thermal event].

Furthermore, the path for heat generated by the electrochemical action of the cell is much shorter in a pouch cell than a wound cylindrical format. Figure 1 illustrates the very direct path heat, as facilitated by the thermal spreader, may take to the external thermal mass, in contrast to the arduous path followed by heat through a spiral-wound electrode to the positive and negative terminals of a cylindrical cell.

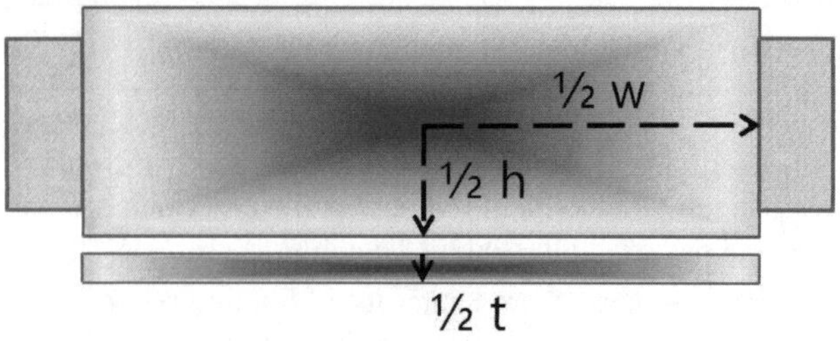

Figure 1: Thermal Path through Pouch Cell

The second key advantage of pouch cells is that they are available in much larger formats, and hence greater capacity, than cylindrical cells. As mentioned, a 5 Amp-hour (Ah) cylindrical cell may be considered very capacious; 200 Ah pouch cells are readily available. The principal benefit conferred by this difference is that fewer pouch cells need to be placed in parallel to achieve a given capacity.

Since cylindrical cells have limited capacity, large numbers of cells are often bussed in parallel to meet the current requirements of a given application. Since as mentioned the primary thermal path of a cylindrical cell exits at its terminal, and since busing must be highly electrically conductive to carry large currents, there is a substantial thermal path from cell to cell within a parallel group of cylindrical cells. As a result, it is usually only possible to limit a thermal event to a given parallel cell group[3]; and if the group has many participants, the thermal event may be large enough to propagate to the entire pack. Limiting the number of cells in parallel while accomplishing the task of the energy storage system, as is possible with large capacity pouch cells, is a path to making thermal event propagation easier to control, thus making the battery safer.

Technique

In larger battery packs, pouch cells are generally arranged in modules. These modules consist of a stack of cells, which are bused together and enclosed in a container. The module has two essential functions related to safety: maintaining the temperature of the cell and managing the potential byproducts of a thermal event.

Thermal Management: Pouch cells exist in two primary variants: those with their connection features, or tabs, on one side of the pouch, and those with tabs on opposing sides. The tabs are significant to the thermal behavior of the cell because they tend to be the point at which heat generated by the movement of current is concentrated. In order to produce the most consistent aging of the electrodes in the cell, and to permit the thermal management of the cell, a thermal spreader is placed against each face of the cell.

The thermal spreader, a thin sheet of thermally conductive material, extends beyond the cell stack. The portion of the spreader that so extends contacts a separate thermal mass, such as a cooling plate. This permits removal of the heat generated by the cell.

In addition to the thermal spreader, a thermal barrier is interspersed between the cell and spreader layers. This inhibits movement of thermal energy in the direction of neighboring cells, so that heat is directed to the external thermal mass.

The essence of propagation limitation between cells in a pack is to remove heat so quickly and efficiently that neighboring cells do not reach the temperature threshold at which they in turn would enter thermal runaway. Design elements that have been shown by experimentation to be most influential to the success of this approach include the selection of highly conductive thermal spreader material and an external thermal mass which is effective without adding excessive weight to the system.

Test Methodology

One of the most developed and deployed methods for propagation testing has been defined by the Norwegian Maritime Authority in its circular RSV 12-2016[5]. This standard is used to validate large battery packs used in passenger vessels and workboats throughout Norway, a country which has been on the leading edge of maritime electrification.

The NMA circular demands that the battery pack be tested with live modules abutting the unit under test representing the installed configuration in a ship. Provisions are allowed by the circular for the manufacturer to represent additional modules with thermal masses. In the example of Spear's "Trident" system below three modules are stacked vertically, and a thermal mass is placed on either side to simulate other modules in the system.

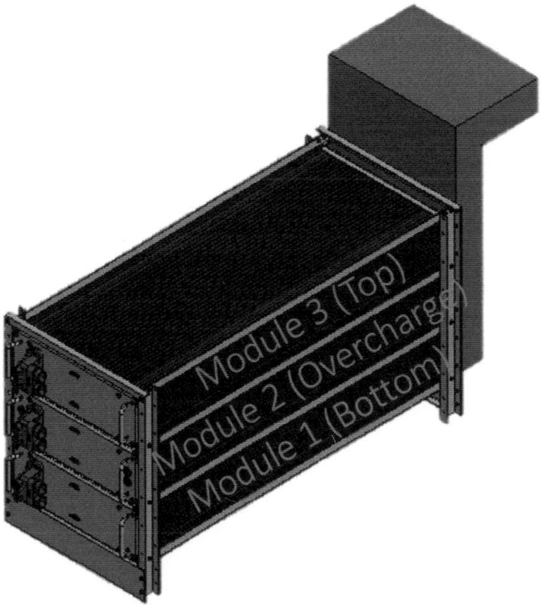

Figure 2: NMA Test Module Arrangement

All modules are tested at full charge, and the test is performed at the maximum temperature specified for operation by the battery manufacturer. The BMS must be disabled. In order to demonstrate the worst-case scenario, including the loss of auxiliary system power, the active cooling systems are disabled for the test; this is not a requirement of the circular but may be pursued by battery system manufacturers who want to ensure the credibility of the test.

The center cell (or parallel cell group) in the center module is intentionally abused by overcharging. The maximum charge current specified by the manufacturer is applied at 150% of the specified maximum voltage until a thermal event occurs.

This technique is preferred to initiation by penetration of a conductive element (often referred to as nail penetration tests). Nail penetration tests are highly variable depending on their methodology and the nature of the cell, and in the opinion of some authorities "are easily gamed[6]." Overcharge is considered a worst-case methodology of initiating a thermal event, since the cell's stored energy can reach twice the nominal 'fully charged' level before the event occurs.

The standard of the circular is that a fire initiated in this fashion should not propagate to adjacent modules; the NMA does not yet demand limitation of propagation to a single parallel cell group. However, using the technique described above, it has been possible to repeatedly empirically demonstrate a strict propagation limitation which surpasses the NMA standard.

Test Results

Spear's "Trident" marine battery system was tested for propagation in the course of its certification for marine safety. The test was performed as prescribed by the NMA circular according to their "Propagation Test 1" standards, with the additional restriction of the disabling of the modules' active cooling features. Only the passive interaction of the thermal spreader with the stagnant ambient air was present.

In repeated testing witnessed by representatives of the maritime certifying authority DNV-GL, thermal events were initiated that took the form of full thermal runaway – the venting of combustible gasses and their ignition. In one of three tests, the cell core of one of the cells in a parallel group of two ejected, demonstrating the module's ability to contain and control the molten ejecta.

At the conclusion of each test the module was disassembled to the cell level. Figure 3 shows the condition of the cells after one of the tests. As shown, the center pair experienced the thermal event, and the four pairs to the top and bottom in the figure were progressively adjacent.

Figure 3: Cells after NMA Test

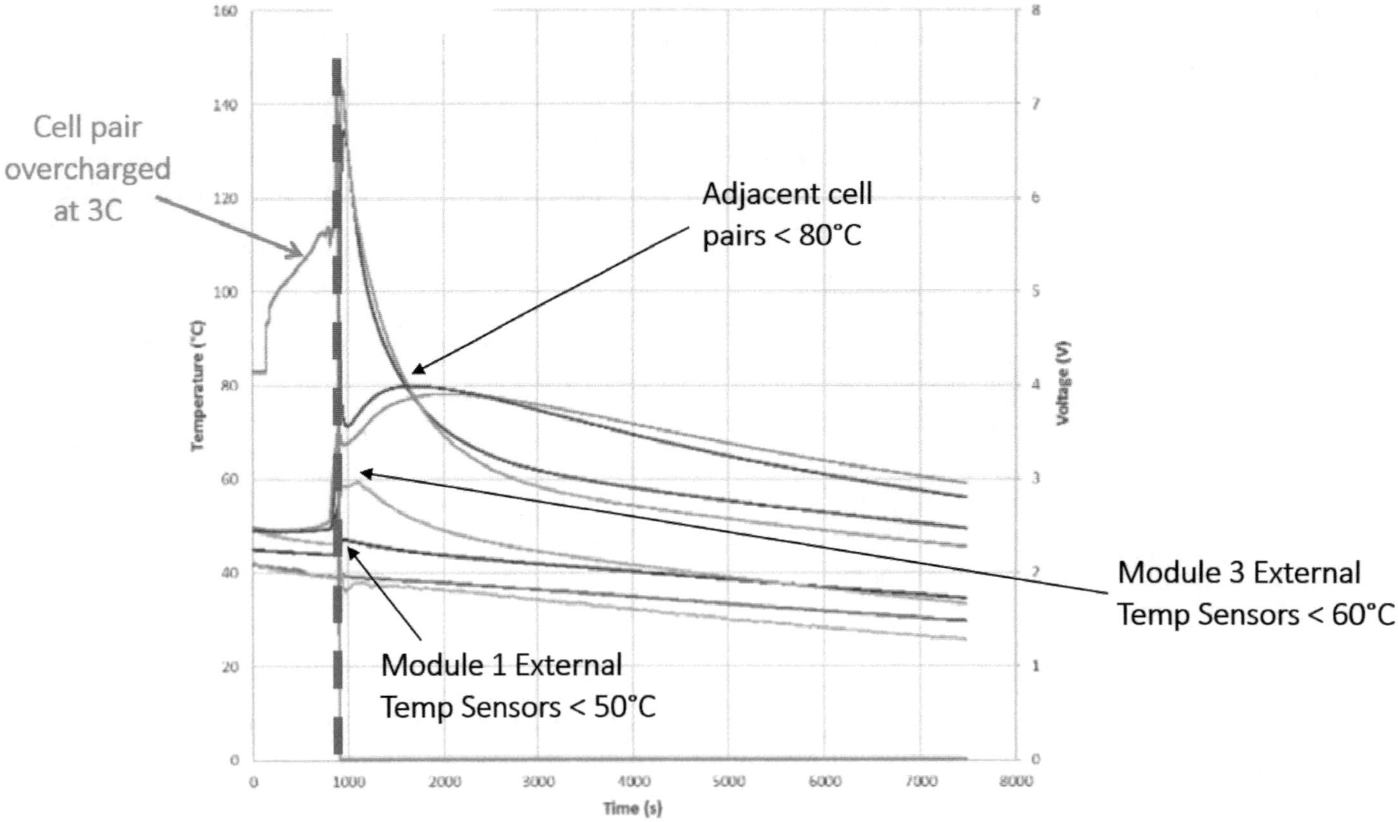

Figure 4: Typical Data from NMA Test

As illustrated in Figure 4, the temperature of the cells immediately adjacent to the fire did not rise above 80°C. The module above the fire remained below 60° C, and the module below remained below 50° C, very close to ambient temperatures.

Conclusions

Using techniques well established by an advanced subset of battery suppliers, the propagation of a thermal event in a battery pack based on pouch cells can be demonstrated with high confidence. While the significant energetic content of pouch cells makes safety a primary concern in their use, proven approaches exist to provide the degree of safety demanded by military and transportation contexts, while retaining the advantages pouch cells confer to certain applications.

References

1. Al Hallaj, S. et al.: Thermal modeling and design considerations of lithium-ion batteries, Journal of Power Sources, 83 (1999) pp. 1-8
2. Lian, T., J. Gakkestad, and S. Forseth, "Safety Aspects of New and Cyclic Aged 18650 Lithium-Ion Cells," presentation at 2nd Oil & Gas, Marine, Subsea, and Aquaculture Battery Conference, Oslo, Aug. 24, 2017
3. Lamb, J., C. Orendorff, L. A. Steele, and S. Spangler, "Failure Propagation in Multi Cell Lithium Ion Batteries," *Journal of Power Sources,* vol. 283, no. C, 2014
4. Finegan, D.P., et al "Identifying the Cause of Rupture of Li-ion Batteries During Thermal Runaway," *Advanced Science*, published online Oct 27, 2017, onlinelibrary.wiley.com/doi/full/10.1002/advs.201700369
5. Norwegian Maritime Authority Circular RSV 12-2016, retrieved online from www.sdir.no/en/shipping/legislation/directives/guidelines-for-chemical-energy-storage---maritime-battery-systems/ Mar. 10, 2018
6. Rona, M., Y. E. Hyung, and B. Barnett, "the Relationship of Nail Penetration Tests to the Safety of Li-Ion Cells." *Proceedings of the 2013 DOE Annual Merit Review Meeting,* Lexington, MA, May 2012, retrieved online from www.energy.gov/sites/prod/files/2014/03/f13/es142_sriramulu_2013_p.pdf, Mar. 9, 2018.

Safety Aspects of Cyclic Aged Commercial Lithium-ion Cells

Torleif Lian[1], Preben J. S. Vie[2], Martin Gilljam[1], Sissel Forseth[1]

[1]Norwegian Defence Research Establishment (FFI)
P.O.Box 25, N-2027 Kjeller, Norway

[2]Institute for Energy Technology
P.O.Box 40, N-2027 Kjeller, Norway

Contact Author E-mail: torleif.lian@ffi.no

Abstract: *The fact that aging of lithium-ion cells leads to a reduced capacity and cell life, is extensively covered in the literature by several research groups, e.g. Vetter [1]. The safety effects of ageing are far less studied, with only a handful of empirical studies published, e.g. [2-4].*

In this paper we describe a test methodology to evaluate the effects of cyclic aging on safety properties of lithium-ion cells. We also describe a systematic approach to study how different temperatures are affecting the safety aspect during cyclic aging of a cylindrical lithium-ion power cell.

Our work has revealed new and potentially dangerous safety aspects in cyclic aged lithium-ion batteries. A decrease of thermal stability was found in one test series where cells were cycled with high current at a low temperature (5 °C), although within the limits of the cell manufacturer's data sheet. The thermal stability decrease was rather large and potentially dangerous. As a result, one of the cells experienced severe disintegration of the cell cylinder can during the test.

The decrease in thermal stability could be dangerous and should be an end of life criteria. An uncycled cell in a battery module may withstand the heat from a neighboring thermal runaway cell, while a cycled cell may be driven into thermal runaway. A cycled cell could also have a higher risk of evolving a dangerous internal short-circuit, as less heat is needed to send the cell into thermal runaway. It is of vital importance to develop new diagnostic tools capable of detecting and possibly avoiding a dangerous drop in thermal stability in cyclic aged lithium-ion cells.

Keywords: Safety aspects; accelerated rate calorimetry; cyclic ageing.

Introduction

It is a well-known fact that lithium-ion cells/batteries could have safety issues. Several battery fire incidents have been reported [5][6]. There are many factors that could make a lithium-ion cell unstable and eventually start a fire. These are factors like; overcharge, overload, heat exposure, external shorts, overdischarge (followed by a charge) and internal shorts. If the cell/battery system is not able to handle the heat generation caused by these factors, this could evolve into decomposition of the cell material, physical reactions like ventilation, gassing, fire and in rare cases even explosions. Figure 1 shows different factors which could make a lithium-ion cell unstable (yellow and blue circles) and the potential physical consequences (red figures).

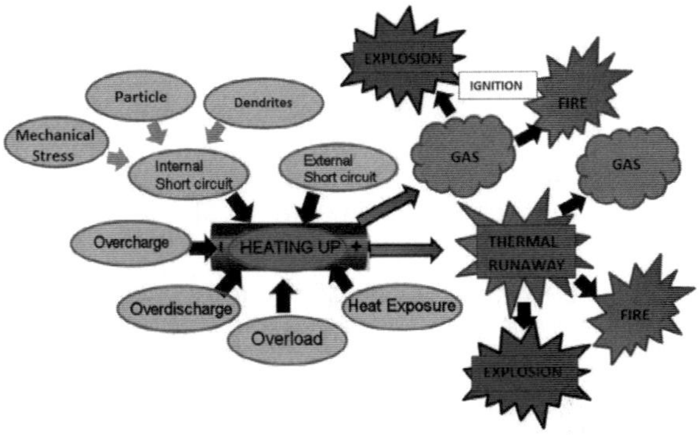

Figure 1. Overview of different factors that could affect the stability of a lithium-ion cell (yellow and blue circles) and the reaction pattern leading to different physical reactions (red figures).

Most of these factors could be controlled by battery management system (BMS). Therefore, the likelihood of a fire in a lithium-ion cell is very low. But an internal short under development cannot be detected by the BMS or any other commercially available systems today [7]. The internal short could be caused by defects from production (*e.g.* particles) or as a result of cyclic degradation (mechanical stress or lithium dendrites) of the cell (blue circles shown in Figure 1). The probability of a safety issue (fires and explosions) is one in 1 million to one in 10 million [8], but should not be ignored especially when the battery is used in sensitive platforms or in considerable sizes.

In Norway there are economic incentives for changing from fossil fuel to electrical power in maritime platforms. These maritime platforms are very sensitive to fire, and the Norwegian Maritime Authorities (NMA) requires that a battery powered propulsion system should be as safe as a conventional propulsion line. Since the development of an internal short in a lithium-ion battery cannot be detected, the physical reaction from a lithium-ion battery has to be managed by robust battery design. The battery design needs to be approved in a propagation tests as verification of the design [9]. During a propagation test one or several lithium-ion cells are forced into fire either by heating or overcharge. The acceptance criterion is; no spread of fire between modules (propagation). Additionally, NMA requires an explosion analysis to determine the amount and composition of the gases released in the battery space in the case of a non-propagating battery fire.

The degradation effects of cyclic ageing of lithium-ion cells are complicated and not fully understood [10, 11]. If the thermal stability or physical response of the cell changes, it could change the ability to pass a propagation test. The thermal stability for uncycled cell materials and cells is well documented [2, 12-15], but the effect of cyclic ageing on thermal stability is far less studied [2, 16-18].

The cyclic ageing reported in the literature was performed on small cylindrical 18650 cells. Literature on cyclic ageing of larger format lithium-ion cells has not been found. The 18650 cell is normally not used in larger energy storage systems for the maritime industry due to increased complexity and cost. There is a strong need to understand the safety aspects of cyclic aged large format power capable lithium-ion cells in the field of maritime applications.

This paper describes a test methodology to evaluate the effects of cyclic aging on lithium-ion cell's safety properties. It also describes a systematic approach to study how different temperatures are affecting the safety properties during cyclic aging of a 30 Ah cylindrical power lithium-ion power cell.

Experimental

Development of a methodology to evaluate the effects of cyclic aging on lithium-ions cell's safety properties: A test series with five different lithium-ion cells with same form factor (18650), different cathode chemistries and electrical energy content were evaluated with respect to thermal stability and physical response. All cells were tested at a 100% SoC. The energy densities and the cathode chemistries for the cells are given in Table 1.

Table 1. Cathode chemistry, anode chemistry, number of tested cells and energy density for the five lithium-ion 18650 cells in the test series.

Cathode material	Anode material	Energy density [Wh/Kg]	Number of tested cells
$LiFePO_4$ (LFP)	Graphite	93	5
$LiNi_{0.8}Co_{0.15}Al_{0.05}O_2$ (NCA)	Graphite	254	6
$LiMn_{0.33}Ni_{0.33}Co_{0.33}O_2$ (NMC)	Graphite	162	6
$LiCoO_2$ (LCO)	Graphite	193	4
$LiMn_{0.33}Ni_{0.33}Co_{0.33}O_2$ (NMC) $LiMn_2O_4$ (LMO)(1:1)	Graphite	119	3

The thermal stability of the cells were determined using an accelerating rate calorimeter (ARC). The ARC measures the thermal response as a result of controlled heating (heat, seek and wait procedure). Heating is conducted in 5 °C steps, in each step the instrument waits for 60 minutes before entering a seek mode looking for exothermic reactions. When the cell starts to self-heat (0.02 °C/min), the temperature of the ARC follows the temperature of the cell, *i.e.* adiabatic conditions. If the exothermic reaction inside the cell halts, the controlled heating phase starts over. This continues either to the occurrence of the next exothermic response, or to the maximum achievable temperature of the ARC (250 °C).

EUCAR hazard level was used to rate the physical response of the lithium-ion cell. See Table 2 for a simplified definition of these hazard levels. For this test only hazard levels four to six were used.

Table 2. Description of EUCAR hazard levels used to measure the physical response from lithium-ion cells in this test [19].

Hazard level	Description	Classification Criteria & Effect
4	Venting	No fire or flame, no rupture, no explosion. Weight loss ≥ 50 % of electrolyte weight
5	Fire or flame	No rupture, no explosion (*i.e.*, no flying parts).
6	Rupture	No explosion, but flying parts of the active mass
7	Explosion	Explosion (*i.e.* disintegration of the cell)

Evaluation of the effect of cyclic aging under different temperatures for a 30 Ah power lithium-ion cell: The cells were cycled at 5 and 45 °C at 1C charge (CC-CV) and 1C discharge rates. Every 100-300 cycles all cells were characterized at 25 °C measuring remaining capacity at 1C and C/10 discharge rates.

Results and discussion

Development of a methodology to evaluate the effects of cyclic aging on lithium-ions cell's safety properties: Figure 2 shows the heat rate as a function of temperature for five different 18650 lithium-ion cells. Included in the Figure is also the EUCAR hazard level. From Figure 2 it can be concluded that safety considerations based only on heat rates from cells with different cathode chemistries could give an insufficient basis for rating a cell's safety properties. The cell with the highest energy density (NCA cell) had the highest EUCAR hazard level but a lower heat rate than the LCO cell (green line in Figure 2). Lithium iron phosphate (LFP) cell with the lower electrical energy density had the lowest hazard level and heat rate, indicating that the electrical energy content in the cell could affect the safety properties of lithium-ion cells. The tested cells in this test series were of the same form factor and size. But different form factors, internal structure and cell sizes could affect the mechanical stress inside the lithium-ion cell.

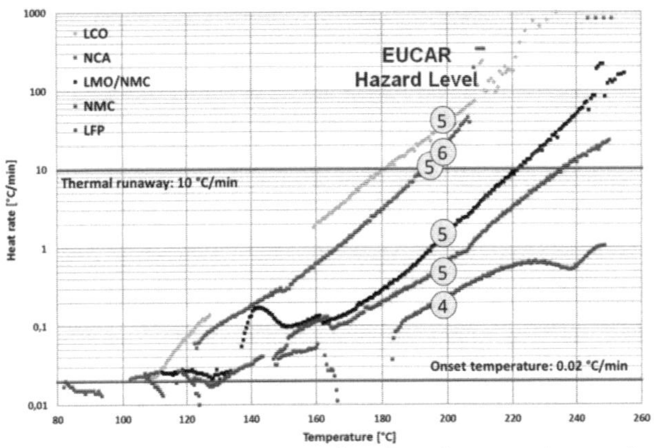

Figure 2. The heat rate as a function of temperature and physical result as defined by EUCAR hazard levels for five different lithium-ion 18650 cells.

Based on ARC results from the five different lithium-ion cells with equal form factor (18650) and the possibility of increased mechanical stress inside a cell (due to SEI increase), the following factors were used for the evaluation of internal shorts on the safety properties of a 30 Ah cylindrical cyclic aged lithium-ion cell:

- Change of thermal stability of the cell
- Reduced electrical energy content in the cell
- Increased mechanical stress inside the cell

Evaluation of the effect of cyclic aging under different temperatures for one 30 Ah circular power lithium-ion cell: One cell from the different cyclic aging series was evaluated with respect to; change of electrical energy content in the cell, change in thermal stability of the cell and change in mechanical stress inside the cell. The results are described in the following sections. The following sections compare the safety properties of these cells as new and cyclic aged.

The electrical energy losses in the cyclic aged 30 Ah cells are presented in Table 3.

Table 3: Energy loss (SoH) as a function of cyclic ageing conditions for the 30 Ah cell at 1C charge and discharge cycling.

Cyclic conditions: Temperature	**5 °C**	**45 °C**
Energy after cycling: SoH	71.8 %	77.1 %
Number of cycles	3000	2900

ARC tests were conducted on two cells from the cyclic aged test series and compared with the results from new cells. Figure 3 presents the results from the ARC test of new and cyclic aged 30Ah cells. The cyclic aged cell at 45 °C show similar heat rates between 140 to 167 °C and a decrease in heat rates in the temperature region between 167 – 250 °C compared to uncycled cells. The decrease in heat rates could be explained as a result of cathode material /electrolyte loss during cyclic ageing [20].

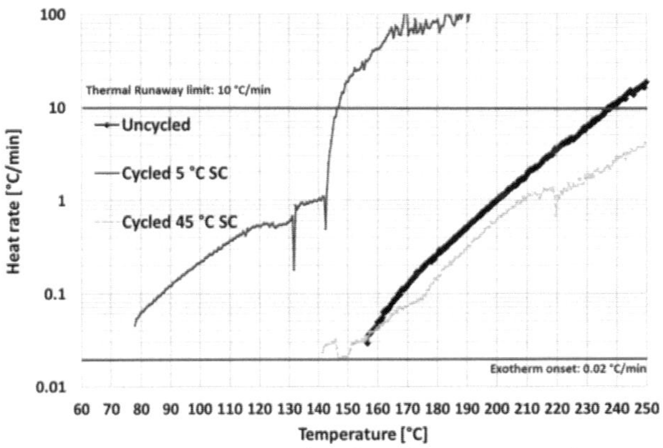

Figure 3. Heat rates as a function of temperature for new and cyclic aged 30 Ah cells (cycled 5 and 45 °C).

The cyclic aged cell at 5 °C shows higher heat rates at all temperatures compared to uncycled cells. The onset temperature is reduced from 155 to 77 °C and the thermal runaway temperature drops from 238 to 147 °C. The acceleration response of the heat rates between 142 – 150 °C could be due to a short circuit inside the cell. The cell tested at 5 °C experienced severe disintegration at the end of the ARC test. Figure 5 shows a picture of the cyclic aged cell at 5 °C condition after the ARC test.

Figure 5. ARC tested 30 Ah cyclic aged cell at 5 °C cycling condition with severe disintegration.

The cyclic 5 °C condition aged cell's response to controlled heating corresponds to EUCAR hazard level 7. However, an evaluation of physical reactions demands at least three parallel tests and the results from this test doesn't fulfill this requirement. The combination of these findings could point towards a new potentially dangerous response of cyclic aged lithium-ion cells.

The cell was too big for the X-ray topography machine. Consequently, none of the cells were examined and evaluated with respect to mechanical stress.

Conclusion

This paper describes a test methodology to evaluate the effects of cyclic aging on lithium-ion cell's safety properties. It also describes a systematic approach to study how different temperatures are affecting the safety properties during cyclic aging of 30 Ah cylindrical lithium-ion power cells.

New potentially dangerously safety aspects have been found in cyclic aged lithium-ion batteries. Decrease in thermal stability was found at low temperature cycling even if the cells were tested within the limits of the data sheet. The decrease in thermal stability was rather large and potentially dangerous for the cell tested at 5 °C. As a result, one of the cells with decreased thermal stability experienced severe disintegration of the cell can cylinder during the test.

The decrease in thermal stability could be dangerous and should be an end of life criteria. An uncycled cell in a battery module may withstand the heat from a neighboring thermal runaway cell, while a cycled cell may be driven into thermal runaway. It is of vital importance to develop new diagnostic tools capable of detecting and possibly avoiding a dangerous drop in thermal stability in cyclic aged lithium-ion cells.

Acknowledgements

The authors want to acknowledge the funding received for the SafeLiLife project (project no. 228739) from the Research Council of Norway. We also want to acknowledge MoZEES, a Norwegian Centre for Environment-friendly Energy Research, co-sponsored by the Research Council of Norway (project number 257653) and 40 partners from research, industry and public sector.

References

1. Vetter, J., et al., *Ageing mechanisms in lithium-ion batteries.* Journal of Power Sources, 2005. **147**(1-2): p. 269-281.
2. Fleischhammer, M., et al., *Interaction of cyclic ageing at high-rate and low temperatures and safety in lithium-ion batteries.* Journal of Power Sources, 2015. **274**: p. 432-439.
3. Friesen, A., et al., *Influence of temperature on the aging behavior of 18650-type lithium ion cells: A comprehensive approach combining electrochemical characterization and post-mortem analysis.* Journal of Power Sources, 2017. **342**: p. 88-97.
4. Gilljam, M., et al., *7E. Effect of electrical energy and aging on cell safety*, in *Safety of Lithium Batteries*, J. Garche and K. Brandt, Editors. 2017, Elsevier.
5. *Auxiliary Power Unit Battery Fire, Japan Airlines Boeing 787-8, JA829J, Boston, Massachusetts, January 7, 2013.* . 2014, National Transportation Safety Board.
6. Smith, B., *Chevrolet Volt Battery Incident Overview Report.* 2012, NHTSA.
7. Ansean, D., et al., *Operando lithium plating quantification and early detection of a commercial LiFePO4 cell cycled under dynamic driving schedule.* Journal of Power Sources, 2017. **356**: p. 36-46.
8. Wang, Q., et al., *Thermal runaway caused fire and explosion of lithium ion battery.* Journal of Power Sources, 2012. **208**: p. 210-224.
9. NorwegianMaritimeAuthority, *Guidelines for chemical energy storage - maritime battery systems.* 2016, Circular-Series V, 2016/8065, RSV 12-2016.
10. Peled, E. and S. Menkin, *Review-SEI: Past, Present and Future.* Journal of the Electrochemical Society, 2017. **164**(7): p. A1703-A1719.
11. Gilbert, J.A., I.A. Shkrob, and D.P. Abraham, *Transition Metal Dissolution, Ion Migration, Electrocatalytic Reduction and Capacity Loss in Lithium-Ion Full Cells.* Journal of the Electrochemical Society, 2017. **164**(2): p. A389-A399.
12. Roeder, P., et al., *Impact of delithiated Li0FePO4 on the decomposition of LiPF6-based electrolyte studied by accelerating rate calorimetry.* Journal of Power Sources, 2013. **236**: p. 151-157.
13. Roth, E.P. and D.H. Doughty, *Thermal abuse performance of high-power 18650 Li-ion cells.* Journal of Power Sources, 2004. **128**(2): p. 308-318.
14. Mendoza-Hernandez, O.S., et al., *Cathode material comparison of thermal runaway behavior of Li-ion cells at different state of charges including over charge.* Journal of Power Sources, 2015. **280**(0): p. 499-504.
15. Zaghib, K., et al., *Enhanced thermal safety and high power performance of carbon-coated LiFePO4 olivine cathode for Li-ion batteries.* Journal of Power Sources, 2012. **219**: p. 36-44.
16. Börner, M., et al., *Correlation of aging and thermal stability of commercial 18650-type lithium ion batteries.* Journal of Power Sources, 2017. **342**: p. 382-392.
17. Friesen, A., et al., *Impact of cycling at low temperatures on the safety behavior of 18650-type lithium ion cells: Combined study of mechanical and thermal abuse testing accompanied by post-mortem analysis.* Journal of Power Sources, 2016. **334**: p. 1-11.
18. Friesen, A., et al., *Al2O3 coating on anode surface in lithium ion batteries: Impact on low temperature cycling and safety behavior.* Journal of Power Sources, 2017. **363**: p. 70-77.
19. Doughty, D.H. and C.C. Crafts, *SANDIA REPORT SAND2005-3123 Unlimited Release Printed August 2006 FreedomCAR Electrical Energy Storage System Abuse Test Manual for Electric and Hybrid Electric Vehicle Applications.* 2006.
20. MacNeil, D.D. and J.R. Dahn, *The reaction of charged cathodes with nonaqueous solvents and electrolytes - I. Li0.5CoO2.* Journal of the Electrochemical Society, 2001. **148**(11): p. A1205-A1210.

Rechargeable, Aqueous Zinc–Ion Batteries with Pulse-Power Capability Enabled by Nanostructured Manganese Oxides and Mixed-Salt Electrolytes

Jeffrey W. Long,[1] Jesse S. Ko,[2] Megan B. Sassin,[1] Joseph F. Parker,[1] and Debra R. Rolison[1]

[1]Surface Chemistry Branch – Code 6170
[2]NRL-NRC Postdoctoral Associate
U.S. Naval Research Laboratory
Washington, DC 20375, USA
Contact Author Email: jeffrey.long@nrl.navy.mil

Abstract: *Zinc-ion cells comprising mild Zn^{2+}-containing aqueous electrolytes and nanostructured manganese oxides (MnOx) as the active cathode material offer a compelling energy-storage solution with the advantages of low cost, low toxicity components, and extended rechargeability. Here, we describe the performance of zinc-ion cells based on advanced MnOx@carbon three-dimensional electrode architectures that impart supercapacitor-like function when used with Zn^{2+}-based electrolytes that also contain alkali metal salts (e.g., Na_2SO_4). Prior half-cell and full-cell characterization demonstrated the promise of such cathodes, but some long-term capacity fade was noted with extended electrochemical cycling and ascribed to slow dissolution of MnOx over multiple discharge excursions. To mitigate such effects, we explored the additions of $MnSO_4$ to an established electrolyte mixture of $ZnSO_4$ and Na_2SO_4, as tested in two-terminal Swagelok cells. We show that capacity fade is lessened with the new three-component electrolyte mixture, while the power capabilities of the MnOx@carbon electrode architectures are also preserved.*

Keywords: zinc–ion battery; hybrid electrochemical energy storage; manganese oxides; pulse-power capability

Introduction

The alkaline Zn/MnO_2 battery remains a ubiquitous energy-storage solution for civilian and military applications, yet lacks the extended rechargeability and high-power capability demanded by many emerging technologies. The inherent cost and safety advantages of zinc and manganese oxide (MnO*x*) electrodes can be translated to next-generation rechargeable "zinc-ion batteries" by replacing the traditional alkaline electrolyte with mild aqueous electrolytes containing simple Zn^{2+} salts (*e.g.*, $ZnSO_4$). By pairing such electrolytes with particular forms of MnO*x* that facilitate reversible charge-storage reactions involving Zn^{2+} ions, the rechargeability of Zn/MnO*x* systems can be extended to hundreds or thousands of cycles.[1,2]

One limitation of Zn-ion cells reported to date is the sluggish nature of the Zn^{2+}-based redox reactions at MnO*x*, which restricts pulse power and increases charge–discharge voltage hysteresis (thereby reducing energy efficiency). We address these shortcomings by adopting electrode designs comprising nanoscale birnessite–type MnO*x*, coating the surfaces of an ultraporous carbon nanofoam (here designated as "MnO*x*@CNF").[3,4] When such electrodes are cycled in aqueous 1 M $ZnSO_4$, they exhibit characteristic electrochemical signatures for Zn^{2+}-based redox, with MnO*x*-normalized capacity approaching theoretical (308 mAh g^{-1}) for a one-electron $Mn^{3+/4+}$ reaction.[5]

While MnO*x*@CNF electrodes can operate at higher rates than typical powder-composite MnO*x* electrodes, capacity still falls as current demand is increased beyond a 1*C* rate (308 mAg^{-1}). We find that addition of Na_2SO_4 to the $ZnSO_4$-based electrolyte boosts high-rate performance, as mediated by pseudocapacitance reactions at the MnO*x*.[5] Thus, at low rates, Zn^{2+}-based redox provides high capacity while at demanding current density, pseudocapacitance dominates charge delivery and supports pulse-power requirements.

Herein, we report how the addition of a third salt, $MnSO_4$, to the $Na_2SO_4/ZnSO_4$ electrolyte mixture improves the cycling stability of MnO*x*@CNF electrode, which otherwise undergoes slow capacity fade due to reductive dissolution of the MnO*x* with extensive cycling. Two-terminal cells comprising zinc foil anode, MnO*x*@carbon cathode, and the three-component electrolyte mixture noted above are subjected to galvanostatic charge–discharge cycling over a range of *C*-rates and up to 100 total cycles. The presence of Mn^{2+} in the electrolyte suppresses MnO*x* dissolution, resulting in stable cycling, while the Na^+ component of the aqueous electrolyte supports pseudocapacitance reactions that can be tapped at increasing charge–discharge rates.

Experimental

MnOx@CNF Electrode Preparation: Birnessite-type manganese oxide–coated carbon nanofoam (MnO*x*@CNF) electrodes were prepared as previously described.[3–6] Briefly, fiber-paper-supported carbon nanofoams of the one-ply "40/500" type,[7] which express a hierarchical distribution of pore sizes (10–80 nm) and high specific surface area (262 m^2 g^{-1}), were first infiltrated with aqueous 0.1 M Na_2SO_4 for 8 h under vacuum. The 0.1 M Na_2SO_4 solution was then replaced with 0.1 M $NaMnO_4 \cdot H_2O$ + 0.1 M Na_2SO_4 and soaked under ambient temperature and pressure conditions for 20 h before being thoroughly washed with de-ionized water. After multiple rinse cycles, the MnO*x*@CNF electrodes were dried overnight under flowing N_2.

Zinc-Ion Cell Evaluation: A two-terminal cell configuration was prepared using a PFA Swagelok® assembly with titanium rods serving as the current collectors. The as-prepared MnO*x*@CNF papers were used as the positive terminal by punching out a 0.5 cm × 0.5 cm piece and adhering it onto a ⅜" diameter titanium foil using carbon epoxy (DAG EB-020A). A ½" diameter zinc foil was used directly as the negative terminal. A glass-fiber separator (Whatman) was soaked in a mixed supporting electrolyte of 0.75 M Na_2SO_4, 0.20 M $ZnSO_4$, and 0.05 M $MnSO_4$. The prototype zinc-ion cells (Schematic 1) were cycled using an Arbin BT2000 battery cycler within cut-off voltages between 0.9 and 1.9 V. All C-rates are normalized to the one-electron theoretical capacity of MnO*x* (308 mAh g^{-1}).

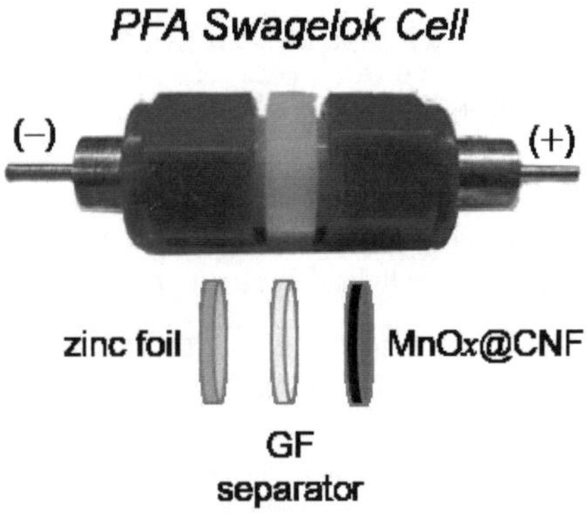

Schematic 1. Illustration of a prototype zinc-ion rechargeable cell comprising a zinc foil anode, glass-fiber separator, and a MnO*x*@CNF electrode.

Results and Discussion

Manganese oxide-coated carbon nanofoam electrodes, expressed as a mesoporous, 3D interconnected network of conductive carbon and charge-storing oxide (Figure 1) facilitates key attributes of charge-storage such as high conductivity and improved electrolyte accessibility throughout the electrode volume. The MnO*x* coating in the MnO*x*@CNF electrode serves as a versatile charge-storing material that sustains both Na^+-supported pseudocapacitance and Zn^{2+}-based battery-like mechanisms. The combination of Na^+ and Zn^{2+} salts enables high specific capacity at slow rates, while moderate capacity is retained at higher rates, as supported by fast pseudocapacitive charge-storage processes.[5]

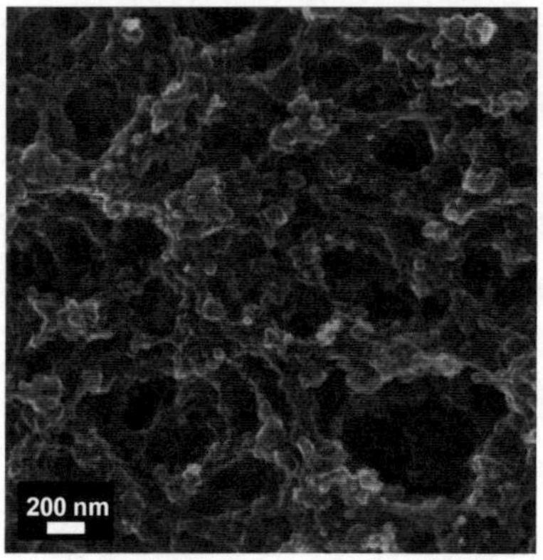

Figure 1. Scanning electron micrograph of the MnO*x*@CNF electrode.

The electrolyte plays a critical role in facilitating these multiple and rate-distinct charge–storage mechanisms. We find that incorporating $MnSO_4$ at low concentration further mitigates capacity loss upon continuous charge–discharge cycles. To explore this hypothesis, we evaluated two-terminal Zn-ion cells that incorporate 0.75 M Na_2SO_4 + 0.20 M $ZnSO_4$ + 0.05 M $MnSO_4$ as the electrolyte. We first subjected these cells to a series of galvanostatic charge–discharge profiles with increasing *C*-rates from 1C to 20C, as shown in Figure 2. At the lowest rate (1C), this prototype cell delivers theoretical capacity for MnO*x* when normalized to the mass of the oxide (~40% of the mass of the positive electrode). At more challenging *C*-rates, specific capacity decreases, but ~100 mAh g^{-1} is still available at 20C, similar to analogous tests with 0.75 M Na_2SO_4 + 0.25 M $ZnSO_4$ (absent $MnSO_4$).[5]

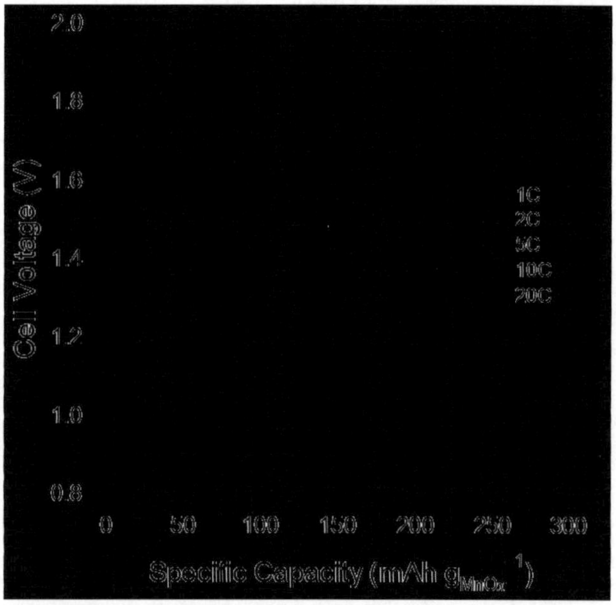

Figure 2. Corresponding charge–discharge profiles of Zn/MnO*x* prototype cell at imposed *C*-rates from 1C–20C.

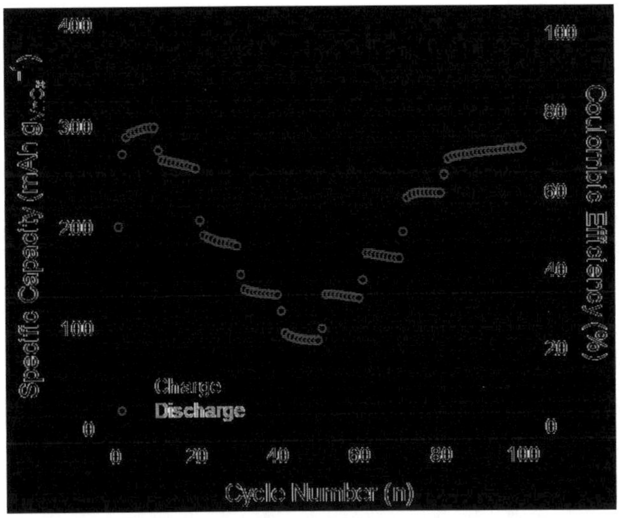

Figure 3. Specific capacity (and coulombic efficiency) *vs.* *C*-rate trends for Zn/MnO*x* prototype cells from 1C to 20C. Note that the few stray coulombic efficiency data points arise at the first cycle of each transition between

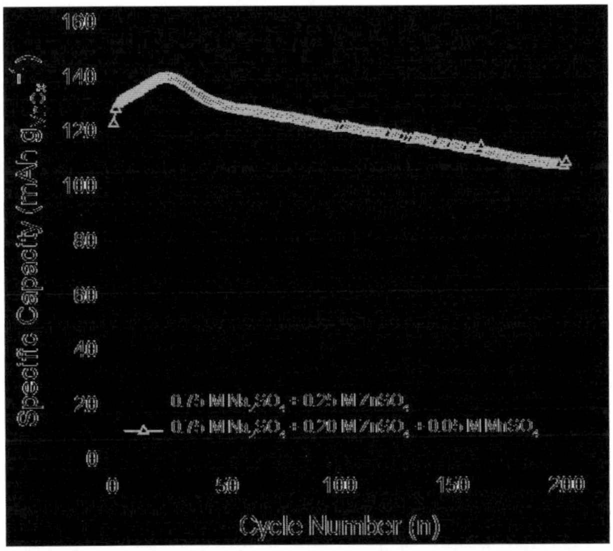

Figure 4. 200 cycles at 10C for Zn||MnO*x*@CNF with 0.75 M Na_2SO_4 + 0.20 M $ZnSO_4$ + 0.05 M $MnSO_4$ or 0.75 M Na_2SO_4 + 0.20 M $ZnSO_4$ supporting electrolyte.

The Zn/MnO*x* cells were also subjected to a series of increasing *C*-rates (10 cycles at each rate) followed by reversing the sequence back towards low *C*-rates; the MnO*x*-normalized capacity values for this series are summarized in Figure 3. Adding $MnSO_4$ to the mixed Na^+/Zn^{2+} electrolyte noticeably enhances cyclability even within the first 10 cycles at 1C, compared to our earlier study without added $MnSO_4$.[5]

In subsequent segments of charge–discharge at increasing *C*-rates, specific capacity holds steady through the 10-cycle step with minimal loss. When the *C*-rate sequence is reversed back to 1C, we observe a return to a specific capacity of ~280 mAh g^{-1}, near theoretical value, after 100 total cycles at varying rate. Without $MnSO_4$, capacity only recovers to ~240 mAh g^{-1} after a similar charge–discharge sequence.[5] Note that coulombic efficiency is maintained near 100% throughout this charge–discharge cycling test.

In separate experiments, MnO*x*@CNF electrodes were cycled continuously at a 10C rate for 200 cycles in either 0.75 M Na_2SO_4 + 0.20 M $ZnSO_4$ + 0.05 M $MnSO_4$ or 0.75 M Na_2SO_4 + 0.25 M $ZnSO_4$ supporting electrolyte (Figure 4). Without added $MnSO_4$ in the electrolyte, initial capacity is slightly higher at ~150 mAh g^{-1} and steadily declines to ~110 mAh g^{-1} at the end of the sequence. When the MnO*x*@CNF electrode is cycled in-cell in the presence of added $MnSO_4$, the initial capacity rises from ~125 to 140 mAh g^{-1} over the first few dozen cycles, then exhibits a more shallow decay of capacity with subsequent charge–discharge cycles. These results are consistent with the earlier report of Pan *et al.*, who first demonstrated that the addition of Mn^{2+} helps to suppress MnO*x* dissolution/degradation in $ZnSO_4$-based aqueous electrolytes.[2]

In conclusion, we demonstrate that an optimized supporting electrolyte of $Na_2SO_4/ZnSO_4$ with the addition of $MnSO_4$ extends cycle life for two-terminal zinc-ion prototype cells that incorporate a zinc foil anode and an advanced MnO*x*@CNF cathode. The electrochemical performance of these prototype cells offer desirable attributes for next-generation hybrid electrochemical energy–storage devices capable of delivering both high specific capacity and high-rate capability.

Acknowledgements

The information, data, and work presented herein were funded by the U.S. Office of Naval Research.

References

1. Xu, C., Li, B., Du, H., and Kang, F., "Energetic Zinc Ion Chemistry: The Rechargeable Zinc Ion Battery." *Angewandte Chemie, International Edition,* vol. 41, pp. 933–935, 2012.
2. Pan, H., Shao, Y., Yan, P., Cheng, Y., Han, K.S., Nie, Z., Wang, C., Yang, J., Li, X., Bhattacharya, P., Mueller, K.T., and Liu, J., "Reversible Aqueous Zinc/Manganese Oxide Energy Storage from Conversion Reactions." *Nature Energy*, vol. 1, article no. 16039, 2016.
3. Fischer, A.E., Pettigrew, K.A., Rolison, D.R., Stroud, R.M., and Long, J.W., "Incorporation of Homogeneous, Nanoscale MnO_2 within Ultraporous Carbon Structures *via* Self-Limiting Electroless Deposition: Implications for Electrochemical Capacitors." *Nano Letters*, vol. 7, pp. 281–286, 2007.
4. Fischer, A.E., Saunders, M.P., Pettigrew, K.A., Rolison, D.R., and Long, J.W., "Electroless Deposition of Nanoscale MnO_2 on Ultraporous Carbon

Nanoarchitectures: Correlation of Evolving Pore–Solid Structure and Electrochemical Performance." *Journal of the Electrochemical Society*, vol. 155, pp. A246–A252, 2008.

5. Ko, J.S., Sassin, M.B., Parker, J.F., Rolison, D.R., and Long, J.W., "Combining Battery-Like and Pseudocapacitive Charge Storage in 3D MnO*x*@Carbon Electrode Architectures for Zinc-Ion Cells." *Sustainable Energy & Fuels*, vol. 2, pp. 626–636, 2018.
6. Sassin, M.B., Hoag, C.P., Willis, B.T., Kucko, N.W., Rolison, D.R., and Long, J.W., "Designing High-Performance Electrochemical Energy-Storage Nanoarchitectures to Balance Rate and Capacity." *Nanoscale*, vol. 5, pp. 1649–1657, 2013.
7. Lytle, J.C., Wallace, J.M., Sassin, M.B., Barrow, A.J., Long, J.W., Dysart, J.L., Renninger, C.H., Saunders, M.P., Brandell, N.L., and Rolison, D.R., "The Right Kind of Interior for Multifunctional Electrode Architectures: Carbon Nanofoam Papers with Aperiodic Submicrometre Pore Networks Interconnected in 3D." *Energy & Environmental Science*, vol. 4, pp. 1913–1925, 2011.

Optimizing Coulombic Efficiency of All-Iron Redox-Flow Cell

Buddhinie S. Jayathilake[a], Billal Zayat[a], Edward. J. Plichta[b], Mary A. Hendrickson[b] and S. R. Narayanan[a]

[a]Loker Hydrocarbon Research Institute, Department of Chemistry, University of Southern California, Los Angeles, California 90089, USA

[b]RDECOM CERDEC CP&I, Aberdeen Proving Ground, Maryland 21005, USA

srnaraya@usc.edu / 1- 213-740-5965

Abstract: *The all-iron redox flow battery is an attractive, eco-friendly and inexpensive solution for large-scale energy storage because of the favorable earth abundance of iron-based materials. A major technical challenge for the deployment for a continuously operable battery is the parasitic evolution of hydrogen at the iron electrode during battery charging. During repeated cycling, the hydrogen evolution reaction not only lowers the coulombic efficiency, but also causes the capacity to fade due to changes in electrolyte composition. We have found that the increase of charging current density has a significant beneficial impact on the coulombic efficiency. We attribute this increase in efficiency to the increase of surface pH that shifts the equilibrium potential for iron deposition favorably to more negative values. We demonstrated that by regulating the flow rate of the electrolyte, the surface pH can be controlled and the coulombic efficiency values can be optimized. We present here understanding of the observed trends and differences in coulombic efficiency.*

Keywords: All-iron redox flow battery, aqueous redox flow battery, energy storage, large-scale energy storage

Introduction

Redox flow batteries based on metal ions and organic redox molecules using both aqueous and non-aqueous electrolytes are being studied widely for grid-scale energy storage applications.[1-6] Iron-based redox flow batteries are particularly attractive because iron is inexpensive and abundantly available. An aqueous iron-chloride redox flow rechargeable battery based on the Fe(III)/Fe(II) redox couple at the positive electrode and the Fe(II)/Fe(0) redox couple at the negative electrode (Eqs. 1 and 2) with a nominal cell voltage of 1.21 V is a promising low-cost, durable and eco-friendly energy storage system for large-scale applications.

Positive Electrode:

$$Fe^{3+} + e^{-} \leftrightarrows Fe^{2+} \qquad E^0 = 0.77\ V \qquad (1)$$

Negative Electrode:

$$Fe^{2+} + 2e^{-} \leftrightarrows Fe^{0} \qquad E^0 = -0.44\ V \qquad (2)$$

The specific energy of a 3 M solution of iron (II) chloride is 257 Wh/kg. At a bulk price of iron (II) chloride of $ 3/kg, the material cost of the iron chloride is estimated to be $10/kWh. If an efficient cell that can operate at high current density can be designed, a system cost of $100/kWh is potentially reachable with the all-iron redox flow battery.

The all-iron flow battery system was introduced by Savinell and Hrushka in 1981.[7] During the charging of this battery, iron is electrodeposited from solutions of iron (II) chloride at the negative electrode while iron (II) chloride is converted to iron (III) chloride at the positive electrode. During discharge, elemental iron at the negative electrode is returned to the solution as iron (II) chloride, while iron (III) chloride is reduced to iron (II) chloride at the positive electrode. The earliest experiments on the all iron flow battery system deployed iron chloride solutions and a porous separator between the two electrodes.[7, 8] However, as we described in our previous publication, an iron-chloride flow cell, assembled with an anion exchange membrane (Figure 1) prevents crossover of iron species and avoids capacity losses due to self-discharge.[9]

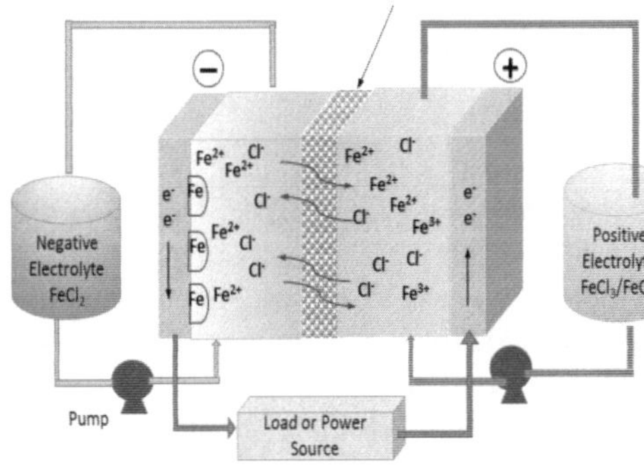

Figure 1. Scheme of all iron redox flow cell

The main obstacle for commercial deployment of the all-iron flow battery is the competitive hydrogen evolution reaction (HER) at the negative electrode that occurs during the charging process. HER lowers the round-trip coulombic efficiency and generates hydroxide ions in the negative electrolyte. Precipitation of iron hydroxides occurs with the increase of the pH. Since the charge lost to hydrogen gas produced is not easily recoverable during discharge, accumulation of iron (III) occurs in the positive electrolyte chamber, progressively resulting in capacity imbalance during prolonged cycling Therefore, during long-term operation, HER causes the pH to increase, results in capacity fade due to changes in electrolyte composition, and also leads to capacity imbalance between the positive and negative electrodes. Thus, for the continuous operation of this battery for thousands of cycles without onerous capacity re-balancing schemes and re-adjustment of pH, we must suppress hydrogen evolution completely at the negative electrode.

HER can be suppressed during iron deposition by the prevention of hydrogen adsorption on to the electrode surface. Effects of electrolyte composition, temperature and current density on coulombic efficiency were reported in our previous studies.[9] With increasing the bulk pH of the electrolyte, we have found that the coulombic efficiency of the iron-plating electrode can be increased. Because, upon increasing the pH value, the equilibrium potential for the hydrogen evolution reaction (as given by the Nernst Equation) shifts by 59 mV per pH unit and HER could be minimized. However, the benefit of increasing charging current density on the surface pH was not recognized. With the understanding gained from experimental and simulated data of the near surface pH, we present here the dependence of coulombic efficiency on the activity of iron (II) and diffusion layer thicknesses at the negative electrode. Further, we show that the iron (II) hydrolysis influences the charge transfer process during iron deposition. The activity and diffusion coefficient of iron (II) varies with the concentration of iron (II), along with electrolyte density, viscosity, conductivity and electrolyte pH. Understanding the observed differences in coulombic efficiency was used to model the performance of the iron redox flow battery to identify the optimum operating point.

Experimental Methods

To study the coulombic efficiency of iron deposition and dissolution we used a three-electrode arrangement. The working electrodes was made of impervious graphite (Graphitestore, GT001672) to mimic an electrode substrate with high hydrogen overpotential. We used a mild- steel mesh as the counter electrode and a silver/silver chloride reference electrode. The use of a mild-steel counter electrode ensured that the composition of the solution and the pH stayed relatively constant because mild steel underwent dissolution to iron (II) under anodic conditions, and supported the electrodeposition of iron during cathodic polarization. The electrolyte solution consisted of iron (II) chloride (0.6-3.0 M) and ammonium chloride (2 M).

The coulombic efficiency of electro-deposition of iron on a graphite-working electrode was determined over the range of 10-50 mA/ cm^2. Iron was electrodeposited by passing a fixed amount of charge of 60 Coulombs and this was followed by anodic dissolution at 20 mA/ cm^2. The coulombic efficiency was calculated, from the ratio of the charge delivered during the anodic stripping step, $Q_{stripping}$, to the charge uptake during electrodeposition of iron, $Q_{deposition}$, as per Eq. 3.

$$\%\ \text{Coulombic efficiency} = (Q_{stripping}/\ Q_{deposition}) * 100 \qquad (3)$$

The experiments with the three-electrode cell were performed using a potentiostat (VMC-4, Ametek). During preparation and testing, the electrolyte was de-aerated using argon gas to prevent the air oxidation of Fe (II). The electrolyte was stirred using a magnetic stirrer bar to avoid being limited by mass transport of iron (II). The pH near the cathode surface and in the bulk electrolyte during charging, discharging and potentiodynamic polarization studies was measured using two pH-sensing glass electrodes (Thermo Scientific Orion-ROSS Ultra pH/ATC Triode). Electrochemical impedance under potentiostatic conditions was measured over the frequency range of 100 kHz to 0.1 mHz using an iron-plated graphite rod working electrode at -0.9 V vs the silver/silver chloride electrode at different concentrations of iron(II) chloride in the range of 0.6 to 3.0 M in 2 M ammonium chloride solution.

Results and Discussion

Figure 2 shows the increase of coulombic efficiency with increasing current density. However, the observed electrode potentials for charging is more negative at higher current densities.

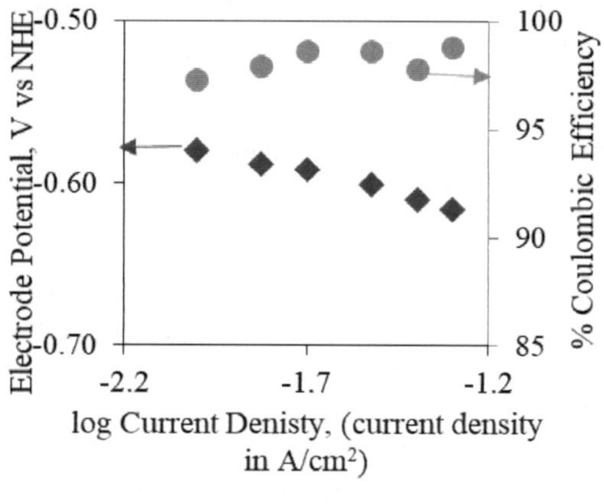

Figure 2. Coulombic efficiency and electrode potential of iron deposition and dissolution using 3 M $FeCl_2$ and 2 M NH_4Cl

Concentration of iron (II) at the electrode surface (C^s_{Fe}) under steady-state conditions can be calculated using the Nernst diffusion layer model (Eq. 4). With increasing the charging rate, concentration of iron (II) near the electrode surface decreases and this will result in lowering of the proton concentration by reduced hydrolysis. Thus, the near surface pH is a function of the activity of iron(II) near the electrode surface and depends on the current density (I), the hydrolysis constant (K_h) for iron (II), the diffusion layer thickness (δ) and the diffusion coefficient of iron (II) (D). Therefore, at a given electrolyte composition, higher charging rates can result an enhancement of the near surface pH as per Eq. 5 due to decrease of the iron (II) concentration.

$$C^{s}_{Fe} = C^{*}_{Fe(II)} - (I \gamma_{eff} \delta / n F D)) \quad (4)$$

Near-surface pH =

$$- (1/2) \log[(C^{*}_{Fe(II)} - (I \gamma \delta / n F D)) K_h'] \quad (5)$$

$$K_h' = K_h * \gamma \quad (6)$$

Where $C^{*}_{Fe(II)}$ is the bulk iron(II) concentration, γ_{eff} is the coulombic efficiency, K_h' is the conditional hydrolysis constant and γ is the activity coefficient of iron(II).

The predicted equilibrium potentials of iron deposition and HER at different activities of iron (II) chloride based on the Nernst equation are listed in Table 1. The results in Figure 3 show that the actual overpotential for iron deposition reaction increased slowly with increasing the current density. In contrast, there is a decrease of the actual overpotential applied to the HER at the electrode surface because of the increase of the near electrode surface pH.

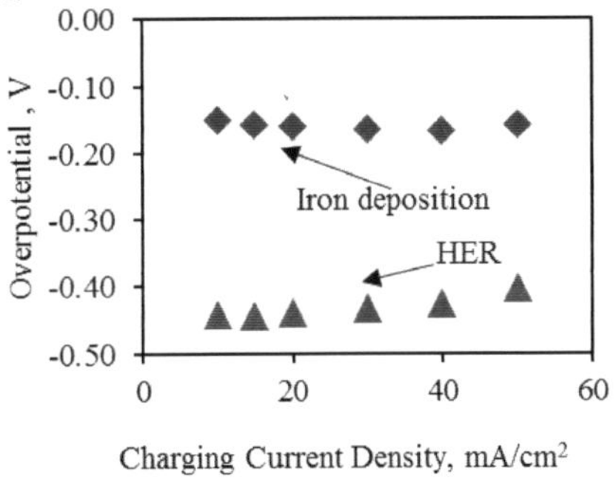

Figure 3. Over potential of iron deposition HER on iron using 3 M $FeCl_2$ and 2 M NH_4Cl

Table 1. Predicted equilibrium potentials of iron deposition and hydrogen evolution on iron

Activity of iron (II)	Electrolyte pH	Predicted equilibrium potential of iron deposition, V vs NHE	Predicted equilibrium Potential of HER, V vs NHE
0.60	*3.21*	*-0.447*	*-0.189*
1.00	*2.9*	*-0.440*	*-0.171*
2.00	*2.6*	*-0.431*	*-0.153*
2.50	*2.21*	*-0.449*	*-0.130*
2.99	*2.00*	*-0.426*	*-0.118*

The Butler-Volmer equation can be modified based on the steady-state mass transport conditions using the limiting current density ($I_{lim,}$) and exchange current density (I_o) to obtain Tafel equation for HER and iron deposition (Eq.7 & 8).

$$\eta = -[RT/ (\alpha nF) \ln(I_o)] - [RT/ (\alpha n F) \ln(I/ (C^s/C^*))] \quad (7)$$

$$\eta = -[RT/(\alpha nF) \ln(I_o)] - [RT/(\alpha nF) \ln(I/(1- I/I_{lim,c}))] \quad (8)$$

Where C^s is the surface concentration, α is the transfer coefficient, η: overpotential, R is the gas constant and T is the absolute temperature. The effect of mass transport limitation on the current can be corrected to yield a current-potential curve that is just associated with charge transfer, η vs ln (I/ (C^s/C^*), and this Tafel plot can be used to estimate the exchange current density.

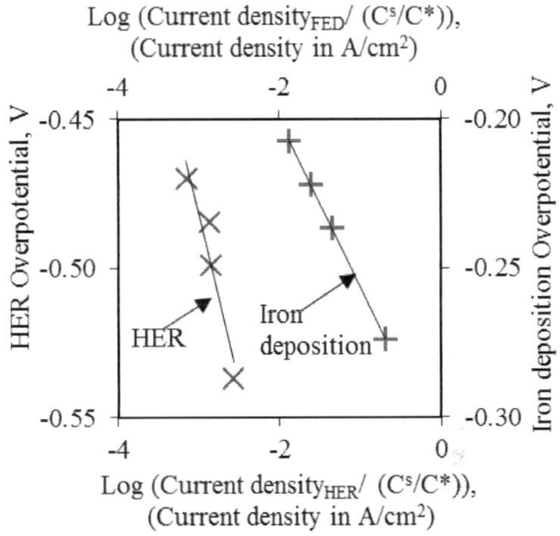

Figure 4. Tafel lines of iron deposition (FED) and HER on iron in 1 M $FeCl_2$ and 2 M NH_4Cl

Since the total cathodic current during charging is divided between iron deposition and hydrogen evolution, the partial current densities for the foregoing processes can be extracted from the total current using the coulombic efficiency values. The logarithm of these partial current density values vs. overpotential may then be plotted separately. The current density values can be corrected for mass transport limitations to obtain the kinetic current, $I/(1-I/I_{lim})$, as in Eq. 8 to generate the Tafel lines for both these competitive reactions (Figure 4). From these Tafel plots, the exchange current densities for HER ($i_{0\ HER}$) and iron deposition ($i_{0\ FED}$) in 1 M $FeCl_2$ were determined to be 8.9×10^{-8} and 2.8×10^{-6} A/cm^2, respectively.

However, due to the decrease of the bulk concentration of iron (II) during charging, the exchange current densities of iron deposition and HER can vary. We found that when iron (II) concentration is changed from 3 M (pH=2) to 1 M (pH=2.9), $i_{0\ FED}$ decreased by 4 fold. Further, the $i_{0\ HER}$ on iron in 3 M $FeCl_2$ is 50 times lower compared to that of the reported value in 0.01 N HCl.[10] Even though, the electrolyte pH is similar (pH=2) in both these electrolytes, the decrease of HER can be due to the presence of iron (II) in the electrolyte. By EIS analysis (Table 2) of iron deposition at different states of charge we found the charge-transfer resistance (R_{ct}) decreased with increasing concentration of iron (II) chloride. Consequently, the overpotential for iron deposition would be lower for any given current density and hence also a higher coulombic efficiency of iron deposition.

Table 2. EIS data of iron deposition

$FeCl_2$ concentration, M	*R_{ct}, Ω cm^2*
0.6	*12.1*
1.0	*12.0*
2.0	*4.9*
3.0	*4.7*

Decreased diffusion layer thickness resulting from increased stirring rates resulted in lowering of coulombic efficiency (Figure 5). Demonstration of the effect of stirring rate on surface pH proves that by regulating the flow rates of the electrolytes in the all iron redox flow cell, the coulombic efficiency at a given current density can be controlled.

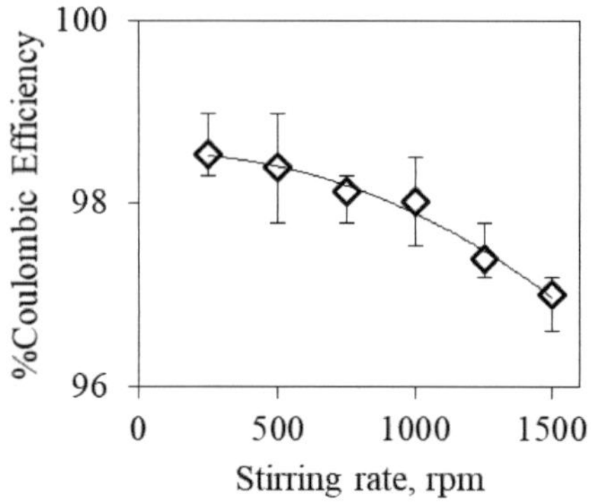

Figure 5. Coulombic efficiency of iron deposition and dissolution at different stirring rates in 3 M $FeCl_2$ and 2 M NH_4Cl

With the conversion of iron (II) chloride to metallic iron the electrode potential for iron deposition shifts to more negative values at all the current densities (Figure 6). The observation of a more negative potential at higher states of charge suggests that a higher value of current for hydrogen evolution will be sustained at higher values of SOC. The decrease of the coulombic efficiency at 20 mA/cm^2 with increasing SOC is consistent with this negative shift of the electrode potential. However, as mentioned here earlier, the equiilibrium potential for iron deposition and HER are a function of the activity of Fe(II) (Eq.4) and the degree of hydrolyis. Table 1 shows that with increasing the % SOC the iron deposition and HER equilibrium potentials shift to values that are more negative. Even though, a higher electrode potential was required for charging at a low iron (II) concentration, we can expect that the coulombic efficiency to be stable because the surface pH increased with state-of-charge due to decreased hydrolysis. In fact, we observe a coulombic efficiency of 98 +/-1% from 0 to 80% SOC at 30 and 40 mA/cm^2 (Figure 6).

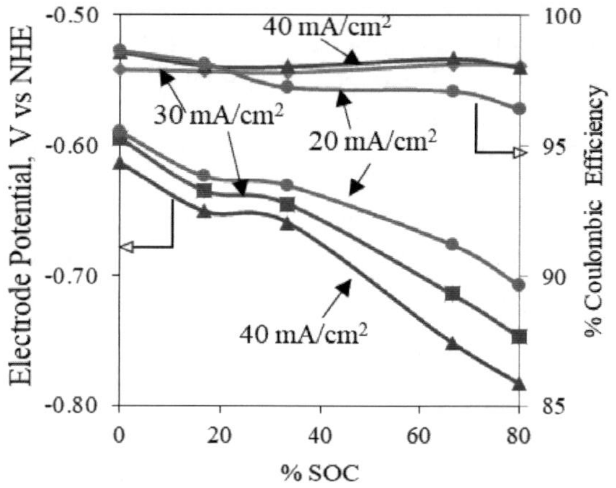

Figure 6. Coulombic efficiency and electrode potential of iron deposition and dissolution in 3-0.6 M $FeCl_2$ and 2 M NH_4Cl

Conclusions

Our study provides understanding on the effect of electrolyte composition and pH changes near the electrode surface on the coulombic efficiency of the iron electrode of an all-iron flow battery. We could verify that improved kinetics of iron deposition lowers the HER at the beginning of the charging process. Further, with increasing the SOC, the increase in pH results in increased coulombic efficiency at the higher charging current densities. We also confirmed that surface pH is a key factor affecting coulombic efficiency. We also show that from 0 to 80% state-of-charge and charging at 30 and 40 mA/cm^2, a steady coulombic efficiency of 98+/-1% could be observed.

Acknowledgements

The authors acknowledge the financial support for this study from the U.S. Army RDECOM CERDEC CP&I and the Loker Hydrocarbon Research Institute, University of Southern California. We also thank Donald Wiggins and Michael Cowan of the USC Dornsife Machine shop for support with the fabrication of the electrodes.

References

1. P. K. Leung, M. R. Mohamed, A. A. Shah, Q. Xu, and M. B. Conde-Duran, *J. Power Sources*, **274** 651-658 (2015).
2. H. S. Lim, A. M. Lackner, and R. C. Knechtli, *J. Electrochem. Soc.*, **124** (8), 1154-1157 (1977).
3. B. Yang, L. Hoober-Burkhardt, S. Krishnamoorthy, A. Murali, G. K. S. Prakash, and S. R. Narayanan, *J. Electrochem. Soc.*, **163** (7), A1442-A1449 (2016).
4. G. P. Rajarathnam, M. E. Easton, M. Schneider, A. F. Masters, T. Maschmeyer, and A. M. Vassallo, *RSC Advances*, **6** (33), 27788-27797 (2016).
5. S. Selverston, R. Savinell, and J. Wainright, *J. Power Sources*, **324** 674-678 (2016).
6. P. Leung, A. A. Shah, L. Sanz, C. Flox, J. R. Morante, Q. Xu, M. R. Mohamed, C. Ponce de León, and F. C. Walsh, *J. Power Sources*, **360** 243-283 (2017).
7. L. Hruska and R. Savinell, *J. Electrochem. Soc.*, **128** (1), 18-25 (1981).
8. K. L. Hawthorne, T. J. Petek, M. A. Miller, J. S. Wainright, and R. F. Savinell, *J. Electrochem. Soc.*, **162** (1), A108-A113 (2015).
9. A. K. Manohar, K. M. Kim, E. Plichta, M. Hendrickson, S. Rawlings, and S. R. Narayanan, *J. Electrochem. Soc.*, **163** (1), A5118-A5125 (2016).
10. N. Pentland, J. M. Bockris, and E. Sheldon, *Journal of The Electrochemical Society*, **104** (3), 182-194 (1957).

Design and Performance of Large Format Nickel-Zinc Batteries

Eivind Listerud and Adam Weisenstein
ZAF Energy Systems
8125 E 26th Street, Joplin, MO 64804
Contact Author e-mail: eivind.listerud@zafsys.com

Abstract

Nickel-Zinc batteries possess good characteristics in terms of energy density, cost and safety, but has typically suffered from poor cyclability, mainly due to the instability of the Zinc anode. ZAF Energy Systems has recently developed large format prismatic cells with capacities of 147Ah and 165Ah, respectively, that have energy densities between 70 Wh/kg to 90 Wh/kg. These cells have good cycle capability and recent testing also shows the versatility of the Nickel-Zinc system in terms of high rate discharges over a wide temperature range.

Keywords: Nickel-Zinc; batteries; rechargeable; large format.

Introduction

The energy and power density of the Nickel-Zinc (Ni-Zn) battery is very attractive to users looking for an alternative to Lead-Acid batteries. Its safety and relatively lower cost have also drawn the attention of those looking for an alternative to Lithium-Ion. Until recently, poor cycle life has limited the adaptation of Ni-Zn. The cycling issues have their roots in zinc migration and dendritic growth, causing cell shorting and loss in capacity. In addition, there has also been a tendency to have the cells dry out due to electrode gassing. In recent years there have been developments in the Ni-Zn community that have resolved these issues and shown that the cycle performance can match and even exceed those of Lead-Acid batteries[1,2,3]. The use of additives has been instrumental in this effort. Additives have been used both in the Zinc anode and the electrolyte and they have helped in stabilizing the zincate ions and reducing the migration of zinc. The additives also help to reduce hydrogen gassing, thus avoiding dry out conditions. This improvement in the electrolyte, combined with the use of a recombination coil, that recombines oxygen and hydrogen to form water and rehydrate the cell, allows for a sealed and maintenance free design with extensive cycle life. This paper will discuss some of these recent developments and show performance characteristics and cycle data collected as part of these efforts.

Historical Limitation and Mitigation Strategy

The main failure mode in Ni-Zn batteries is typically an accelerated capacity fade during long term cycling. This is usually related to the zinc in the negative electrode. Zinc is unstable in a potassium hydroxide solution and becomes a soluble ion that tends to migrate to the positive electrode on discharge and plate back on the negative electrode on charge. It typically does so unevenly, creating so-called shape change in the electrode structure, leading to uneven current density and even isolated regions of zinc that causes an unrecoverable capacity loss. In addition, the zinc solubility process tends to drive dendritic growth that will create shorts and, subsequently, capacity loss during cycling. ZAF Energy Systems utilizes several mitigation strategies to contain the zinc to the negative electrode. One is the use of additives in the anode that works to control the distribution of the nucleation sites and distribute the zinc evenly, thus limiting the potential growth sites for dendrites. Other additives are included in the electrolyte and works to stabilize the zinc, lowering the propensity of the zinc to migrate away from the anode. These additives also lower the molarity of the electrolyte. Lower molarity is better in terms of stability; however, this must be balanced with other performance requirements.

The separator design is also critical in inhibiting the migration of zinc and the dendritic growth. The tortuosity and the pore size of the separator are key factors in the design tradeoff between performance and zinc containment. Typically, there is a multicomponent separator system that works both as a zinc barrier and an electrolyte reservoir.

Another typical failure mode often seen in Ni-Zn cells is cell dry-out due to electrode gassing. During overcharge and severe over-discharge, the electrolyte will gas on the electrodes. Repeated occurrences will dehydrate the cell, increase impedance, and cause loss of performance. ZAF has approached this issue with additives to the anode material, minimizing the gassing, as well as the use of a recombination coil, which recombines the oxygen and hydrogen to form water that goes back into the electrolyte. This allows for a sealed and maintenance free design.

Large Format Cells

In recent years ZAF Energy System has taken these developments from the small lab scale cell level and incorporated these improvements into large G31 format cells and batteries. A single G31 cell is 4.6 cm thick, with a height of 23.7 cm and a width of 17.1 cm. The cell can be seen in Figure 1. It has a nominal voltage of 1.7V and seven cells are connected in series to make up a 12V G31 battery. ZAF is currently building and testing two different Generation 1 versions in this geometric format. One is a 147Ah hybrid power cell, targeted mainly for the heavy truck market, with a design that balances both power and energy. With a weight of 3.42 kg per cell, it has a nominal energy density of about 73 Wh/kg at a C/3-rate. The other is a 165Ah energy cell, targeted mainly for deep cycle applications, with an energy density of 81 Wh/kg at a C/3-rate.

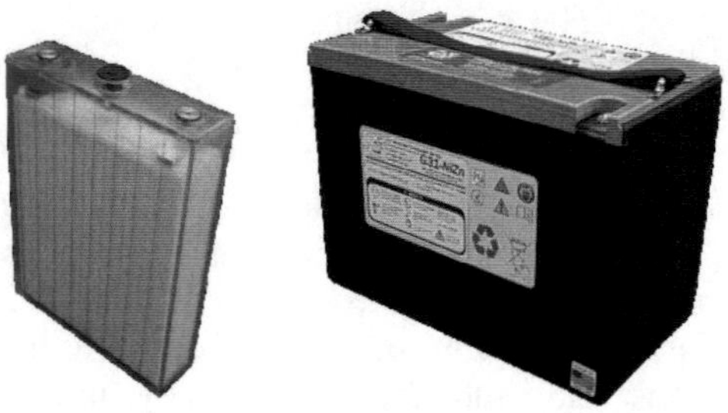

Figure 1: G31 format cell and battery. Each battery contains 7 cells.

Results and Discussion

ZAF has been able to scale the performance and the characteristics seen in small R&D pouch cells up to large format prismatic cells with capacities greater than 150Ah. These cells are now manufactured in a production environment and are undergoing extensive testing that shows the characteristics of what current Ni-Zn technology can do in a practical cell. Following is a brief overview of some of the key performance features of these Ni-Zn cells.

General Rate Characterization: A 147Ah hybrid power cell was discharged at various C-rates while at room temperature. The nominal rate for this cell is C/3, or 49A, with a nominal voltage of 1.7V. Typical cut-off voltage is about 1.25V, but when discharged at rates above 3C, the cut-off is typically lowered to 1.0V. Discharging below 1.0V is not recommended, mainly to optimize cycle life. However, there is generally no safety risk in doing so, although at very low voltages there is a chance for gassing. The various voltage curves can be seen in Figure 2. While this cell is not optimized for truly high rates, it still delivers about 90% of nameplate capacity at a 6C rate (882A). In a constant power mode, this cell can deliver 1200W for more than 5 minutes down to 1.0V.

Cycle Life: Cycle life has long been the Achilles heel of the Ni-Zn battery. Rooted in the developments in the early 2000s to stabilize the zinc in the electrolyte and thereby reducing its solubility[3], ZAF's recent R&D effort and technology transfer to a large format practical cell have demonstrated the cycle potential of the Ni-Zn system. Ongoing cycle testing shows cycle life performance that makes Ni-Zn viable for many applications in terms of life cycle cost.

Figure 3 shows the 10% depth-of-discharge (DOD) cycle performance data of a 100Ah prototype cell. It was first discharged to a 50% state-of-charge (SOC), then discharged 10 Ah and charged 10Ah at a 1C-rate repeatedly, only allowed to top charge after every 1000th cycle. No overcharge was allowed during the 10% charge segments. After about 8000 cycles a significant degradation in performance can be seen. After 8500 cycles the reduction in mass was measured to be only 1.07%, indicating insignificant loss of electrolyte during cycling and the ability of the cell design to control gassing and prevent dry out.

Figure 4 shows the cycle life performance of a 165Ah energy cell after about 100 cycles. This test is ongoing at a C/3 charge and discharge rate with a 100% DOD while at room temperature. The discharge capacity, shown in blue, indicate only a slight degradation of 2-3 Ah at this point and the discharge efficiency (Ah out/Ah in) has been above 0.98. This data underscores the ability of the Ni-Zn cell to handle deep cycles well, something that makes it a viable option in numerous Lead-Acid applications.

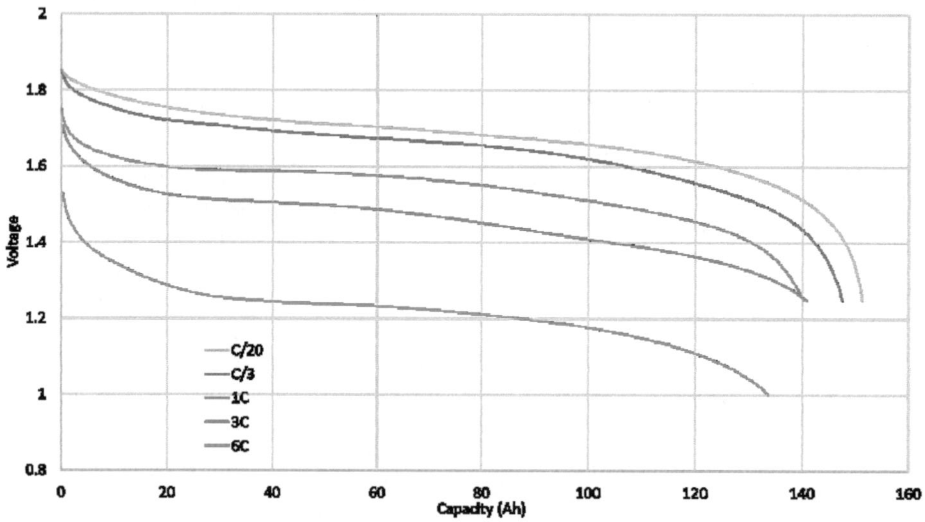

Figure 2: Voltage versus capacity at various discharge rates while at room temperature.

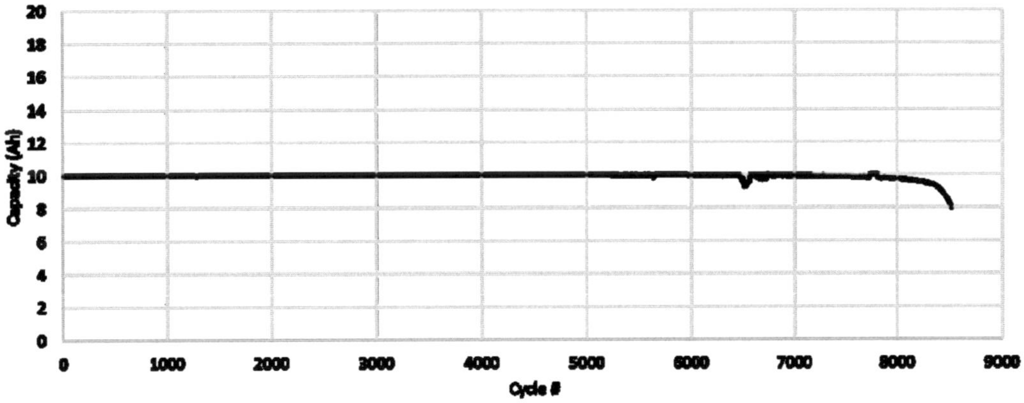

Figure 3:10% DOD cycle test performance at 1C charge and discharge rate.

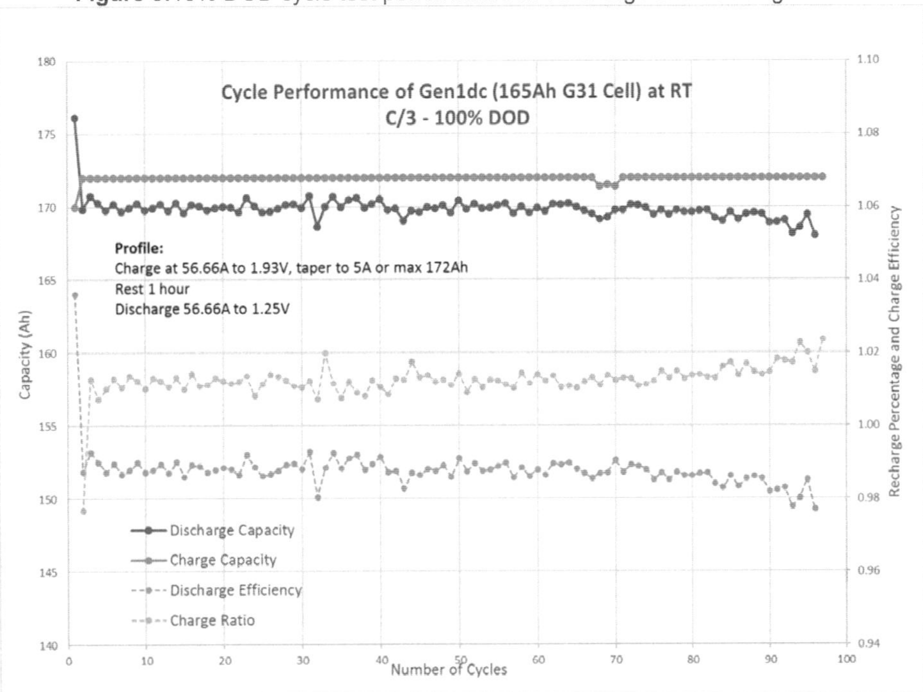

Figure 4: 100% DOD cycle test performance at C/3 charge and discharge rate.

Temperature Effect: The Ni-Zn cell has a wide operating temperature range from -30°C to 75°C. General characteristics at a nominal C/3 rate is shown in Figure 5. At -30°C the cell will deliver about 60% of nameplate capacity. At higher rates, like those considered in cold crank applications (CCA), the Ni-Zn system can deliver useful power for significant time. Figure 6 shows CCA data at -18°C, where it can deliver 900A for about 50 seconds. At -30°C, the cell can deliver 700A for more than 30 seconds, as seen in Figure 7. This is a very attractive capability in a cell package that nominally exceeds 70 Wh/kg. The cold soak was for 24 hours and no heaters or warm-up current were allowed before the 700A load was applied. The same cell can also operate at 75°C. Cells are currently undergoing the SAE J2801 cycle test, performed continuously at 75°C. This test is intended to test batteries to some of the harshest conditions under the hood of a car. After 12 weeks of cycling there is still not any significant degradation in the voltage profiles. It is noteworthy that the cell design being cycled at 75°C, is the same cell design that performed the CCA results in Figures 6 and 7. There has been no modifications to the electrolyte or other cell components, underscoring the versatility and the wide operating environment of this design. ZAF believes that similar CCA results can be achieved at -40°C with its forthcoming Generation 2 technology.

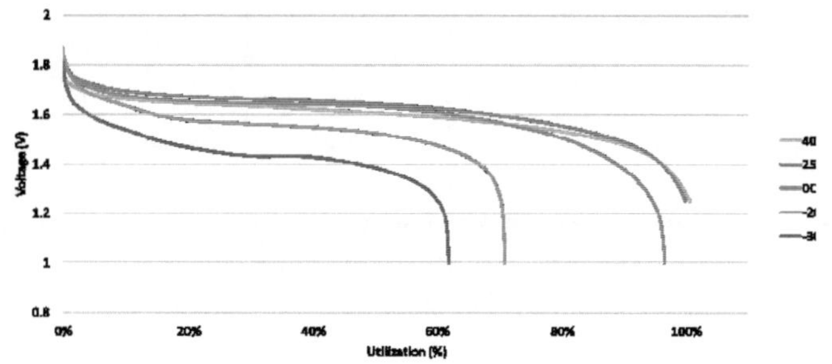

Figure 5: Capacity utilization as a function of temperature.

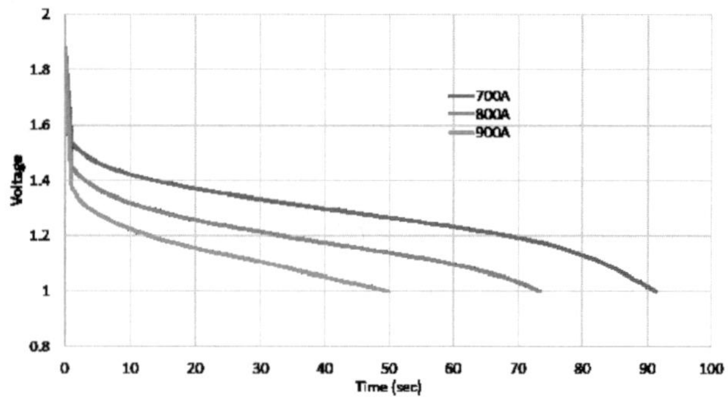

Figure 6: CCA data at -18°C

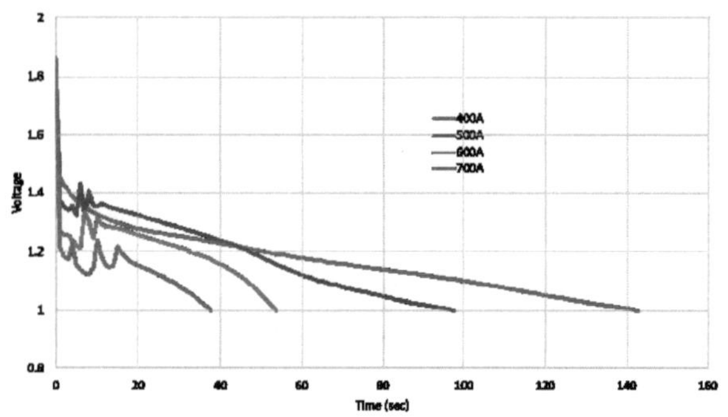

Figure 7: CCA data at -30°C

Charge acceptance: The constant current, constant voltage (CCCV) schedule is commonly used when charging nickel-zinc cells.. Figure 8 shows the charge profile at various C-rates for a G31 cell. If the current is 1C or less, the voltage is held at about 1.93V or lower. At higher charge rates, the voltage is allowed to increase during the constant current phase. During 2C and 3C charge the voltage is allowed to go to 2V. During the constant voltage portion the voltage is held at 1.93V or lower. While nominal charge rate for this specific cell design is C/3, the data shows that 80% SOC can be attained in less than 1.5 hours by charging at a 1C-or 2C-rate. The subsequent discharges give 100% of rated capacity at a C/3 rate. This charge acceptance rate separates Ni-Zn from typical Lead-Acid batteries and becomes very useful in industrial equipment applications, where it allows for faster turnaround time of equipment and maximized operating hours when using multiple shifts.

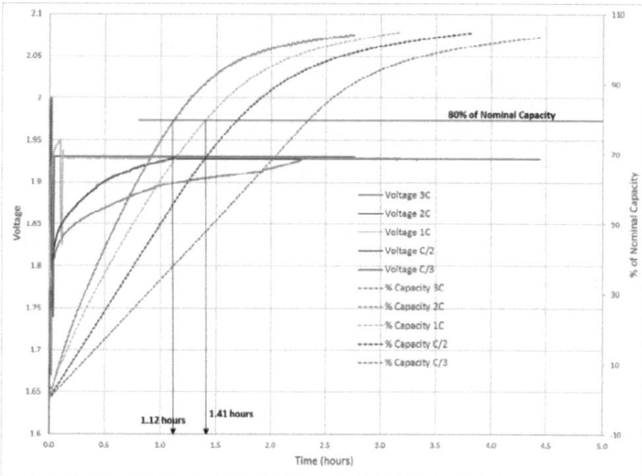

Figure 8: Charge profiles of a 147Ah G31 Ni-Zn cell at various C-rates.

Conclusion

Large format Ni-Zn cells have been built and tested, showing good cycle capability at 100% DOD and an operational temperature range from -30°C to 75°C. Particularly the CCA capability at -30°C indicates a versatile design, given a nominal density above 70Wh/kg. The ability to charge to 80% of nameplate capacity in less than 1.5 hours is also particularly attractive when turnaround time is critical. ZAF is currently in the process of building and testing their Generation 2 technology in the same cell format. Preliminary results show that 195Ah can be delivered at a nominal rate of C/3 in a G31 format cell. It is anticipated that these cells will have improved energy density, as well as better cycle life and rate capability.

References

1. J. Phillips and S. Mohanta, *Nickel-Zinc Batteries*, Linden's Handbook of Batteries, 4th Ed., Thomas B. Reddy, Ed., McGraw Hill, 2011, New York.
2. D. Coates and A. Charkey, *Nickel-Zinc Batteries*, Linden's Handbook of Batteries, 3rd Ed., David Linden and Thomas B. Reddy, Eds., McGraw Hill, 2001, New York.
3. D. Coates and A. Charkey, "Nickel-Zinc Batteries for Commercial Applications," Intersociety Energy Conversion Engineering Conference (IECEC), Vancouver, BC, Canada, August 1999.

Green Seal® Technology: Revolutionizing Battery Design

Maria Penafrancia Roma, Julius Regalado and Edward Shaffer II
Advanced Battery Concepts LLC
8 Consumers Energy Parkway, Clare, MI, 48617
mroma@advancedbatteryconcepts.com / 1-989-424-6645

Abstract: *A new battery design geared towards large-format energy applications has increased the performance of lead batteries and transformed the way they are made. The bipolar battery design termed "GreenSeal®" has allowed it to break the specific energy density bar of 50 Wh/kg, lower the weight by 35%, reduce the lead content by 46% and increase the cycle life by 300%. Material substitutions and cell design modifications reduce the amount of lead used but still deliver equivalent capacity. GreenSeal® technology facilitates high voltage battery designs up to 96V and a wide-range of large format battery types. This patented cell assembly process allows for a completely sealed, leak-free absorbed glass mat (AGM) battery design that can withstand severe impact conditions and high-vibration applications making it safer for abusive usages and harsh environments. The construction of bipolar electrodes uses common materials used in the lead battery industry with a more precise, cleaner process compared to traditional lead grid production. Integration with an existing battery production facility is not capital intensive and 100% of the materials are recyclable. Construction of a 1.5kWh bipolar battery for golf cart (GC) applications using GreenSeal® technology and processes resulted a in specific energy density of 55 Wh/kg and a cycle life predicted to be greater than premium products commercially available on the market.*

Keywords: bipolar lead battery; GreenSeal®; golf cart battery; lead acid battery; VRLA; AGM

Introduction

Power and energy dominate the resource demand pyramid today and will continue to do so over the next 10 years and beyond. Powered by the growth of portable consumer products, progress in electric vehicle (EV) development, as well as the expansion of energy storage systems (ESS), worldwide rechargeable battery demand is predicted to reach up to 775 GWh by 2025 [1]. Although the greatest growth is anticipated to be from lithium ion batteries (LIB), lead acid batteries (LAB) will still retain a majority share of 600GWh, or approximately 75% of the projected demand. For the lead battery industry, this means an $85B market ripe for the taking. The outlook may seem optimistic and encouraging but there are serious challenges that the industry must urgently resolve. Low product performance, strict environmental regulations, and poor profitability are among the major issues that make new and emerging battery chemistries very attractive alternative energy sources [2]. A bipolar battery design increases performance by increasing material utilization and energy density due to the uniform current flow across the electrode. GreenSeal® Technology utilizes these advantages to address LAB challenges through product and process designs based on sound engineering and scientific principles. The key advantage over other bipolar technologies under development is the ability of GreenSeal® technology to use existing raw materials and innovative production processes that easily scale up cell design prototypes to multi-cell large format products [3]. The objectives are to meet higher performance requirements not only of existing applications but also of emerging high growth markets at commercial levels while managing environmentally friendly operations. In this study, 1.5kWh GreenSeal® bipolar batteries are designed, assembled, and tested. Results are compared with commercially available products.

Materials and Methods

A traditional GC battery configuration is termed prismatic and flooded when there is free electrolyte present. On the other hand, within a prismatic AGM configuration there is no free moving electrolyte as it is adsorbed/absorbed within the separator and electrodes, (fill level < 100% of saturation volume). Table 1 shows a range of claimed and computed technical data for available GC batteries on the market.

Table 1. Claimed product performance of commercially available GC batteries

Battery Type	Prismatic Flooded	Prismatic AGM VRLA
Voltage, V	6	6
C/20 Capacity, Ah	225-242	190-225
C/20 Energy, Wh	1350-1452	1140-1350
Reserve Capacity, min	447-562	380-500
Weight, kg	28-32	30-33
Specific energy, Wh/kg	43-48	36-45

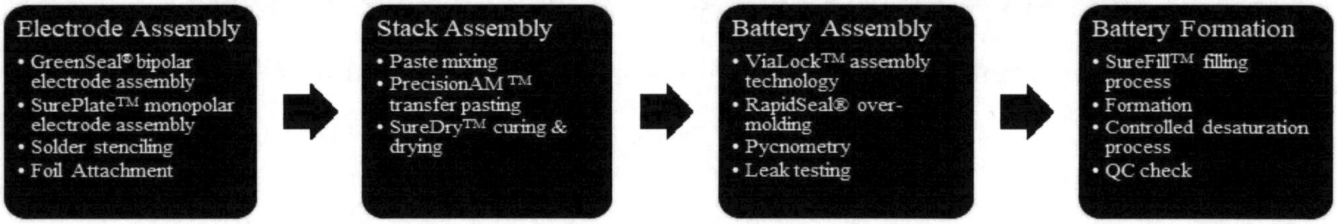

Figure 1. GreenSeal® Technology Process Flow

Materials: One of the most popular batteries on the market was used as a benchmark product. Using GreenSeal® Technology, a bipolar battery was designed to an equivalent C/20 Rate of 1350 Wh (6v-225Ah vs. 48V-28.1Ah).

Method: GreenSeal® has a total suite of technology that is used to assemble and produce a bipolar lead acid battery [4]. It starts with a design to determine the bipolar plate and battery configuration using models developed to compute power, energy as a function of size, discharge rate, and temperature. The model uses a modified Peukert equation to provide discharge data, energy density, cold cranking ampere (CCA) capacity, and reserve capacity in minutes (RCM) at 25A discharge. The next step is to assemble the actual batteries for testing: electrode assembly, stack assembly, battery assembly, and battery formation, which can all be further broken down into sub-processes as shown in Figure 1.

Electrode Assembly: Unlike prismatic batteries, GreenSeal® bipolar batteries do not need cast or expanded lead grids but instead use injection molded polymer substrates with Pb foils on both sides as electrodes. One side is designated as the positive electrode and the other as the negative electrode. Electrical connections between the two sides are achieved by stenciling a quaternary Pb-based solder into the substrate, which is then reflowed under heat and pressure after Pb foil attachment. This alone reduces the amount of lead used by about 7 kg or 88 %. Moreover, no casting, grid punching, or grid expanding machines are needed to make bipolar electrodes.

Stack Assembly: Pasting of the active material is accomplished through another unique process, PrecisionAM™ Pasting (patent pending). In this process, active material paste is transferred directly onto the bipolar electrode assembly. This process does not utilize belt pasters and does not generate waste slurries. Paste thickness is controlled by a constant depth in the machine and less than 2% variation in the paste weight has been measured. Active material adhesion is best achieved by stacking the electrodes under pressure while undergoing the curing and drying process. Unlike traditional processes, lead plates are not manually handled or exposed to the environment after pasting. Lead dust generated after curing due to stacking at the enveloping and cast-on-strap (COS) lines is eliminated.

Battery Assembly: After curing and drying, the stacked bipolar electrodes are encased with the same polymer material as the electrode in the RapidSeal® process (patent pending), where cells are isolated ionically from each other. Previously developed bipolar batteries failed due to edge seal rupture, which allowed not only electrolyte to cross into cells but also oxygen ingress. With GreenSeal® technology, this issue is resolved.

Battery Formation: The final process involves the transformation of cured and dried paste into active material through the input of electric energy. Sulfuric acid is introduced into the battery by the SureFill™ [5] process, which saturates the AGM separator and the paste material with electrolyte. To achieve the designed battery performance, an optimized formation schedule is implemented, battery temperature is strictly regulated, and a desaturation process is strictly controlled.

Figure 2. A GreenSeal® GC2 48V 1350 Wh Module

Battery Testing: A series of short-term and long-term tests are scheduled to characterize the performance of the battery's capacity, durability, and reliability.

Table 2. Schedule of short-term and long-term testing

Short Term	Long Term
Capacity Workup Test	Cycle Life
Energy Capacity-Peukert Sweep	Vibration Life
Tafel testing	Stand Life
Power Testing (IEC 61056)	Float Life

Results

Capacity tests show higher power and energy performances of the GreenSeal® GC2-48V with 31.8Ah at the C20 rate, yielding an energy value of 1526Wh. This exceeds the design capacity of 1350Wh, translating into a specific energy density of 55 Wh/kg, which is 30% better than the highest rated commercial AGM battery. A comparison of the Peukert power curves in Figure 3 shows that GreenSeal® can deliver 38% more energy than commercial batteries on the 2-hour rate. Moreover, computations of the power index ($V^2/4R$) show that GreenSeal® is about 300% higher than the highest rated AGM battery. The GreenSeal® GC2 curve is predicted from actual Peukert sweep while other AGM and flooded (FLD) batteries are based on published discharge data.

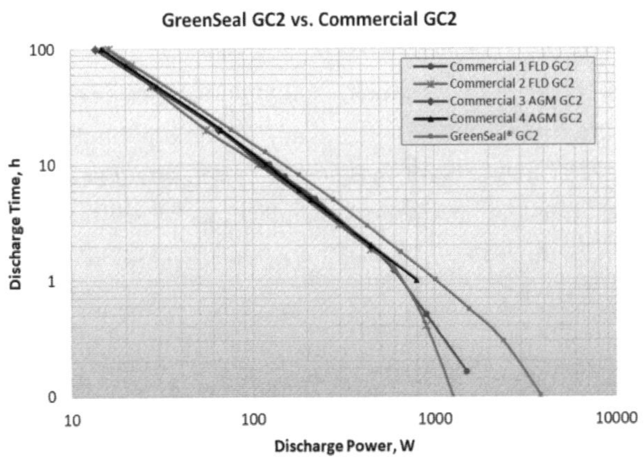

Figure 3. Peukert Power Curves

The increase in specific energy density in the GreenSeal® battery is due to the 46% decrease in lead content in this design. This is a result of the elimination of top lead or cast-on-strap (COS) configurations to connect cells in series, in addition to the elimination of lead based grids serving as electrodes. This change in the cell interconnection design results in an almost 10kg lead reduction per battery. This is made possible by multiple solder joint connections across the surface of the plate which allow a more uniform electron flow across the electrode in contrast to the traditional pathway from the grids to the lugs.

Life Cycle Testing: Cycle life performance using the BCIS-06 Cycle Life [6] tests show that the GreenSeal® GC2-48V has 2.3x more life than the leading AGM battery as shown in Figure 4.

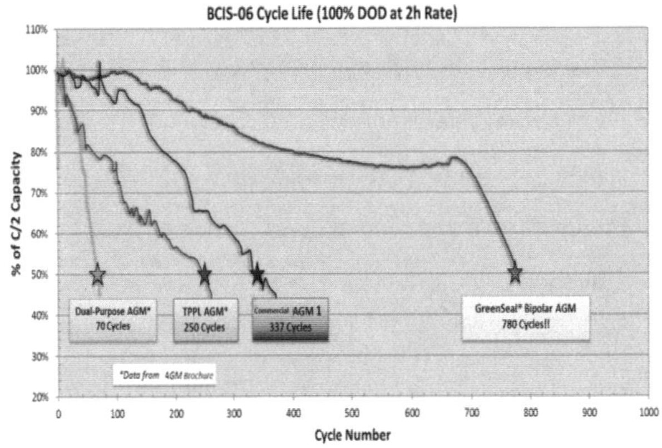

Figure 4. BCIS-06 Cycle Test Results

Vibration Testing: Another measure of durability is the vibration resistance to extreme stress conditions. Results of the SAE J930 Test (Vibration Life for Storage Batteries for Off Road Self Propelled Work Machines) [7] show that GreenSeal® GC2-48V batteries exceeded commercial GC2 batteries by 20x (Table 3). This test is an 18-hour test at a 5.0 peak G-force on the vertical axis at 30-36 Hz.

Previous long-term test data on developmental prototypes have shown that batteries designed and assembled with the GreenSeal® Technology perform on par with or better than the leading AGM brands. One example is the stand life data, which has shown values exceeding other battery chemistries.

Table 3. Summary of Results of Battery Tests

Product Name	Prismatic AGM VRLA	GreenSeal ® 48V GC
Battery Type	Prismatic AGM VRLA	Bipolar AGM VRLA
Specific energy, Wh/kg	36-45	55
Cycle Life, 100% DOD C2 to 50% capacity	75-250	780
Vibration Life SAE J930 Level 2	10-30 h	620h
Stand Life Test -% Loss , dV/mo,25°C	1-3%	0.50 % (> 2 yrs)

Stand Life Testing: This test measures the self-discharge rate of the battery in an open circuit. There are several test standards available but in this experiment, open circuit voltage (OCV) monitoring at 25°C in air shows less than a 0.5% change in OCV in over 2 years, a value which is almost 6x lower than other AGM batteries. This behavior is a function of the GreenSeal® battery design and configuration and can still be improved with stricter controls on the levels of impurities in the raw materials.

Summary

Undeniably, there are clear advantages of this design over existing products made from established production processes, even at research and prototype stages:

- Higher energy density – 30% better
- Longer Cycle Life – 300% increase
- Better vibration resistance – 20x more resistance
- Extended Stand Life – 6x longer
- Reduced Lead Usage – 46% less

As the technology matures and transitions into the manufacturing phase, the opportunity for the first movers to exceed the incumbent legacy technology benchmarks for performance and reduced manufacturing cost is considerable. GreenSeal® solves the century-old puzzle that the original bipolar battery patent holder, P. Kapitsa [8] and his successors were never able to unravel. Moreover, this technology utilizes a majority of the raw materials of existing LAB manufacturing operations and thus uses the same environmental infrastructure presently in place. In fact, it also provides a relief from stricter regulatory controls by reducing lead usage, using cleaner operations, and minimizing hazardous waste handling.

Future Actions

While waiting for the results of ongoing long-term validation tests, existing data have shown that there are additional opportunities to improve battery energy and power densities. After considering the data gathered from process and product validation runs, design recalculations have shown that a 70Wh/kg energy density can be achieved. This is possible with the following improvements: use of lower density substrate materials, higher purity raw materials, and energy- or power-enhancing paste additives. There are also opportunities to optimize electrode configuration, active material utilization, and formation processes. In the future, there are several prospects for expansion to other applications. While the bipolar battery design with GreenSeal® technology is projected to serve emerging markets like grid storage and electric mobile transports, existing military applications can also greatly benefit from the new lead battery design.

Acknowledgement

The authors would like to acknowledge Advanced Battery Concepts, LLC for allowing the publication of design and validation results for this report.

References

1. Pillot, C., "The Rechargeable Battery Market and Main Trends 2015-2025", 18th International Meeting on Lithium Batteries, Chicago, IL, June 20, 2016.
2. Shaffer, E., "Approaches to Improving Lead Battery Performance", The Battery Show, North America 2017, Novi, MI, September 11, 2017.
3. Shaffer, E., "Advanced Battery Concepts, LLC and GreenSeal® Battery Technology", 2018 NAATBatt International Annual Meeting & Conference, San Antonio, TX, March 21, 2017.
4. Shaffer, E., Brecht, W., "Bipolar Battery Assembly", US Patent No. 8357469, January 22, 2013.
5. Shaffer, E., Hobday, D., "Bipolar Battery Assembly", US Patent No. 9553329, January 24, 2017.
6. BCIS-06 , "Cycle Life Testing of Electric Vehicle & Cycling Batteries, rev. May 10, 2010
7. SAE J930, "Storage Batteries for Off-Road Self-Propelled Work Machines", 2016 Ed. May 1, 2016.
8. Kapitsa, P. L., Proceedings of the Royal Society A, 105, 691, 1924.

Nanoscale Material Design of Zinc Anodes for High-energy Rechargeable Aqueous Batteries

Nian Liu
Georgia Institute of Technology
nian.liu@chbe.gatech.edu

Abstract: *Zn-based batteries are a safe alternative to Li-ion due to compatibility with aqueous electrolyte. Also, theoretical volumetric energy density of Zn-based batteries (e.g. Zn-air) is more than twice the one of conventional Li-ion batteries and is ~85% of Li-sulfur batteries. However, the rechargeability of Zn anode is limited by passivation and dissolution. In this presentation, we will show a series of our recent efforts on improving the rechargeability of aqueous Zn anodes via nanoscale materials design and synthesis. The first example is our ZnO@TiN core/shell nanorod anode. The small diameter (<500 nm) of ZnO prevents passivation and allows full utilization of active materials, while the thin and conformal titanium nitride (TiN) coating mitigates Zn dissolution in alkaline electrolyte, mechanically maintains the nanostructure, and delivers electron to nanorods. As a result, the ZnO@TiN core/shell nanorod anode achieves superior battery performance compared with bulk Zn foil or uncoated ZnO nanorod anode. It delivers excellent long-term electrochemical performance (more than 7,500 cycles) as cycled under start-stop conditions. The second example is an ion-sieving carbon nanoshell coated ZnO nanoparticle anode, synthesized in a scalable way. The small size of ZnO prevents passivation, while microporous carbon shell slows down Zn species dissolution. This new Zn anode outperforms bare ZnO nanoparticles and Zn foil (with 1.6 times and 6 times longer cycle life, respectively) in a coin cell configuration with limited electrolyte. The third example is a lasagna-like ZnO-graphene oxide composite anode, where ZnO was confined in the graphene oxide framework. This lasagna-Zn anode achieves a high volumetric capacity of 890 Ah/L and capacity retention of 88% after 150 cycles. The remarkable performance achieved in coin-type cells with limited electrolyte is attributed to the mitigation of ZnO dissolution by graphene oxide confinement. The nanostructure designs shown in this presentation are expected to inspire the design of other electrodes for post-Li-ion batteries.*

Solvent-free and Non-sintered All Solid State Battery

Pu Zhang, Robert Sosik, Felix Nunez and Michael Wixom

Navitas Systems
4880 Venture Drive, Ann Arbor, MI, 48108
pzhang@navitassys.com

Abstract: *All-solid Li batteries are produced using solvent-free (dry) process without sintering or vapor phase processing to form solid state electrolyte. The solid-state electrolyte (SSE) material is a doped sulfide with high Li ion conductivity and chemical stability. A cathode-separator bilayer is fabricated, followed by a single-step lamination to a protected lithium metal anode. This innovative approach circumvents the mechanical limitations of handling a free-standing SSE, the processing limitations of vapor deposition, and the thermal expansion incompatibilities associated with sintering. Initial lab prototype full cells have been produced with multi-cm electrode footprint. Performance and cycle life data will be presented.*

Voltage Tunable Inductors for MHz Adaptive Power Systems

Neville Sun[1,*], Yuan (Daniel) Gao[2,*], Alexei Matyushov[1], Xiaoling (Amy) Shi[2], Nian Sun[1], Mohan Sanghadasa[3]

[1] ECE Department, Northeastern University, Boston, MA 02115
[2] Winchester Technologies LLC, Winchester, MA 01890
[3] AMRDEC, U.S. Army RDECOM, Redstone Arsenal, AL 35898
dan@winchestertech.org / 1-781-862-5971
* Neville Sun and Yuan (Daniel) Gao contributed equally to this work.

Abstract: *This work presents a class of voltage tunable magnetoelectric inductors with textured multiferroic composites cores consisting of Metglas/piezoelectric laminate/Metglas. These inductors demonstrate excellent performance with a wide operation frequency range of DC->10MHz. A large inductance tunable range $\Delta L/L_{min}$ of up to 290% was achieved in a Metglas/PMN-PT/Metglas inductor under 600 V, while a thinner PMN-PT layered structure exhibits an inductance tunability of 50% with a low voltage of 60 V. An extremely low DC resistance of 38 mΩ has also been demonstrated. These multiferroic tunable power inductors with low driving voltage will allow for the next generation compact and lightweight power systems for electronic warfare and communication systems.*

Keywords: textured composites; magnetoelectric inductor; tunability; piezoelectric; low voltage.

Introduction

Passive inductors with large tunability are desired to provide adaptability for different circuit conditions. They will add a major leap in size optimization, controllability, and circuit design strategies [1]. In particular, tunable inductors are imperative in adaptive inductive power supply systems [2, 3]. The resonant frequency of the tank circuit, the inverter frequency, the inverter duty cycle, or the rail voltage of the DC power source can be adapted to varied loads that are added or removed from the system, and hence, increase the current slew rate and reduce the number of components significantly.

It has been demonstrated that by using a textured magnetization for the core of the inductor [1, 3-8], an optimal profile of inductance versus load current can be achieved, which minimizes system loss resulting in less weight imposed by heat sinks and batteries. Profiles of inductance versus input voltage or switching frequency can also be synthesized to maximize the efficiency. Liu *et al.* [6] have demonstrated an electrically tunable ME inductor comprising of a ring-type PZT/MnZn-ferrite/PZT laminate composite, showing a tunability of 56% through interface-strain coupling. Lou *et al.* [7] have reported a compact and power-efficient solenoid-type ME inductor based on a Metglas/PZT/Metglas multiferroic composite, which exhibited giant tunability up to 450% as well as an improved quality factor. Due to big eddy current loss, its operating frequency range was limited to 100~200 kHz. Later, Lin *et al.* [3] reported a method to extend operating frequency up to 10 MHz with the same inductor structure by reducing the thickness of Metglas ribbons. Most recently, Yan *et al.* [1] have demonstrated a ring-type ME inductor using a Metglas/PMN-PT composite, achieving extremely large inductance tunability of up to 1150% under moderate voltage. However, these tunable ME inductors have drawbacks such as: (1) requiring abnormally high applied voltage; (2) low frequency (<MHz); and (3) high DC resistance that severely limits power efficiency.

In this work, electrostatically tunable solenoid ME inductors with textured multiferroic composite core consisting of two layers of amorphous Metglas ribbons and one thin PMN-PT slab have been demonstrated to have large tunable inductance range of 50% with a very low voltage of 60 V. Along with a significantly improved operating frequency of up to 10 MHz and a very low DC resistance of 38 mΩ have also been observed.

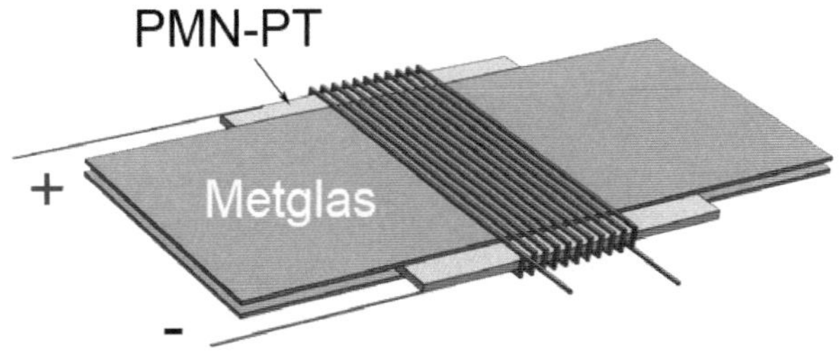

Figure 1. Schematic of ME tunable inductor based on a Metglas/(011)PMN-PT/Metglas multiferroic composite structure with the coil wrapped around the center

Experiment

Two variations of d_{31} Mode (TE Transverse Extension) (011)-cut PMN-PT single crystal slabs are used as the piezoelectric layer. Both slabs had a length and width of 10 mm, but with different thicknesses of 0.5 mm and 0.05 mm. The double sided polish and gold coated PMN-PT is poled along the thickness direction by the manufacturer. The iron-based amorphous alloy magnetic core is composed of a 23 μm thick commercially available Metglas 2605SA1 ribbon that is magnetically annealed along the length direction. One layer of Metglas (8 mm x 20 mm) is bonded to both sides of the PMN-PT with a 1:6 ratio of West System's 206 Slow Hardener and 105 Epoxy Resin. A 26 AWG copper wire is wrapped around the ME composite 10 times with a calculated DC resistance of 38 mΩ. A

Stanford Research Systems high voltage power supply (Model PS310) is used to apply a DC voltage ranging from -600 to 600 V across the thickness direction of the PMN-PT slab. The inductance and quality factor are measured by a HP4194A impedance/gain-phase analyzer.

Results and Discussion

Figure 1 illustrates the Metglas/PMN-PT/Metglas ME composite structure with a solenoid copper coil wrapped around the center of the magnetic core. The PMN-PT has been poled along the thickness direction and can have compressive stress along the in-plane direction. The magnetic flux direction is parallel to the [100] in-plane direction of the PMN-PT. The inductance tunability is defined as $(L-L_{min})/L_{min}$.

Figures 2(a) and (c) show the change in inductance of the 500 μm and 50 μm thick (011) PMN-PT, respectively, at different applied electric fields between 10 kHz to 10 MHz. Figures 2(b) and (d) show the corresponding quality factor of the 500 μm and 50 μm thick (011) PMN-PT, respectively. At 10 kHz, the inductance for the 500 μm thick PMN-PT is 3.6 μH at 0 kV/cm to 0.93 μH at 12 kV/cm demonstrating a tunability of 290% with an applied voltage of 600 V. The inductance for the 50 μm thick PMN-PT is 2.9 μH at 0 kV/cm to 2.04 μH at 12 kV/cm demonstrating a tunability of 46% with an applied voltage of 60 V.

The decay in inductance starts around 50 kHz at lower electric fields while the working frequency is much wider at higher electric fields. The decline in inductance at high frequencies is attributed to the large eddy current screening effect, which lowers the effective permeability [3]. The critical frequency limit is also dependent on the effective permeability when the magnetic layer thickness is larger than its skin depth due to the strong magnetic loss from the eddy current at high frequencies [7]. Due to the nature of the skin depth given by $\delta \propto \sqrt{1/\mu_r}$, a lower permeability ($\mu_r$) increases the skin depth resulting in an improved quality factor.

A unique trait of the ME composite for PMN-PT is demonstrated when a negative electric field is applied on a positively poled ME tunable inductor, as shown in figure 2(c). There is a large increase in inductance from 0 kV/cm to 2 kV/cm as opposed to the typical decrease. The inductance then returns to its zero electric field value from 2 kV/cm to 4 kV/cm. This effect is achieved when a negative electric field is applied from 0 kV/cm to -2 kV/cm and back to 0 kV/cm so that a remnant low-inductance state is attained. Applying a positive electric field near the coercive field, which is 2 kV/cm for PMN-PT, generates a new remnant high-inductance state with an increased inductance value. The enhanced inductance can be maintained through this technique while the change in quality factor remains linear.

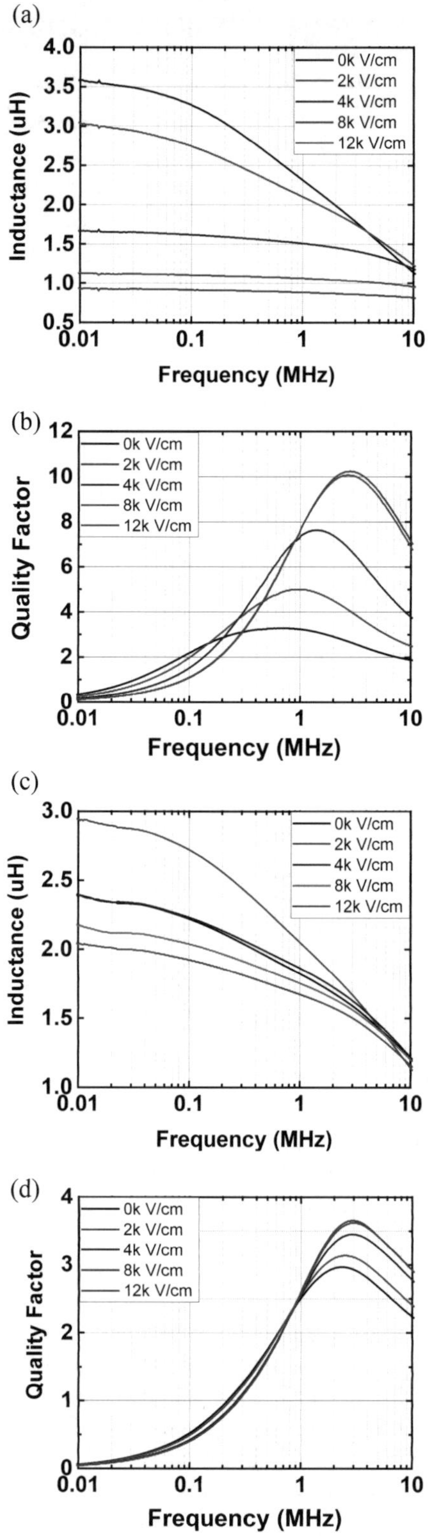

Figure 2. (a) Inductance vs. frequency and (b) quality factor under different electric fields (0, 2, 4, 8, and 12 kV/cm) for 10 windings of a 500 μm thick (011) PMN-PT core; (c) Inductance vs. frequency and (d) quality factor under different electric fields (0, 2, 4, 8, and 12 kV/cm) for 10 windings of a 50 μm thick (011) PMN-PT core

The origin of electrostatic tunability of multiferroic composite devices stems from the theory of magneto-electric (ME) coupling. Several correlations to explain the tunability of inductance in magnetostrictive/piezoelectric composites comes from the stress coupling of the permeability in the magnetic phase according to the magnetic anisotropy, strain coupling between the piezoelectric and magnetic phase, and the piezoelectric strain coefficient of the piezoelectric phase. Dominant factors for producing a shift in inductance are mostly attributed to material composition, for example, (1) shape anisotropy k_d, (2) magnetocrystalline anisotropy k_u caused by the demagnetization effect, and (3) stress induced anisotropy K_σ. It is important to note that the physical dimensions of the ME composites is negligible compared to the change in permeability of the material.

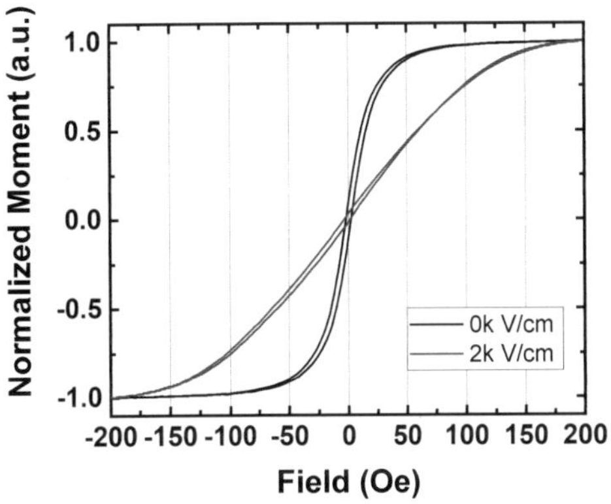

Figure 3. Magnetic hysteresis loops measured at different electric fields along the in-plane direction of the (011) PMN-PT

Figure 3 shows a magnetic hysteresis loop change measured by a vibrating-sample magnetometer (VSM) of the Metglas/PMN-PT composite where different electric field applied to the thickness direction can alter the in-plane magnetocrystalline anisotropy. The change in anisotropy of the core couples to the change in Metglas permeability, which is the root of the frequency dependent inductance transition. On a more fundamental level, the electric field induces a strain in the PMN-PT core due to either the piezoelectric effect or ferroelectric domain switching [9]. An interfacial strain coupling between the PMN-PT and Metglas alters the ME anisotropy of the Metglas. The ME change can be equated to an effective magnetic field (H_{ME}) [10]

$$H_{ME} = \frac{3\lambda_s(\sigma_{100} - \sigma_{011})}{M_S}$$

where λ_s is the magnetostriction, σ_{100} and σ_{011} are the in-plane stress directions, and M_s is the saturation magnetization. Applying an electric field to the (011) PMN-PT will create either a positive or negative H_{ME} due to the compressive strain/stress along the in-plane direction [11]. The compressive strain/stress is more effective along the magnetically annealed easy axis due to the positive magnetostriction λ_s. The Metglas has its own intrinsic anisotropy field H_a that contributes to the total effective magnetic field H_{eff}.

$$H_{eff} = H_{ME} + H_a$$

The effective permeability of the ME composite is inversely proportional to H_{eff}, therefore, the inductance will increase linearly with the change in μ_{eff} [7, 12].

$$\mu_{eff} = \frac{4\pi M_S}{H_{eff}} + 1$$

The final inductance value can be estimated with the following equation [7]

$$L = \mu_0 \frac{N^2 A\left(2\mu_{eff} t + (d - 2t)\right)}{dl}$$

where μ_0 is the permeability of vacuum, N is the number of coil turns, A is the cross-sectional area of the coil, t is the total thickness of the Metglas, d is the core thickness, and l is the length of the coil. Based on these equations, using a material with the lowest magnetocrystalline anisotropy will produce the highest tunability because it will have high initial permeability, but with a low cut-off frequency. Metglas has demonstrated very large tunability due to its high permeability but cannot be effectively used at high frequencies.

The tunability of the inductance is highly dependent on the ME coupling strength where the control of electric polarization is directly influenced by the elastic coupling at the interface between the piezoelectric phase and the magnetic phase. A disparity between the estimated change in inductance comes from the difference in mechanical properties that affect the transfer efficiency [13]. While other papers used ethyl cyanoacrylate glue during the bonding process, the benefit of using epoxy resin is the ability to create a thinner and stronger bonding interface between the Metglas and PMN-PT. More importantly, it is a nonvolatile solvent that does not shrink after curing, which reduces the strain mismatch at the interface caused by thermal expansion, atomic inter-diffusion, and the chemical reactions between the layers. However, there is still a substantial improvement if a piezoelectric single crystal interface is used instead of an epoxy resin bond because its soft nature dampens the generated strain resulting in lower efficiency.

In the real world, tuning inductors using voltages up to 600 V is not ideal. Table 1 compares the required voltage needed for the largest tunability percentage and the tunability at a more acceptable voltage requirement of 30 V. The main issue for thicker cores is that the tunability is extremely low, typically less than 6%, when using a voltage of around 30 V. Due to the contribution of magnetoelastic stress induced anisotropy, the thinner 50 μm PMN-PT slab has a different total anisotropy of the material. Essentially, the reduced thickness scales the tunability range to lower applied voltages while maintaining similar applied electric field values.

Table 1. Comparison of specifications of different ME inductor structures and their ability to tune at low voltages

Core Material	Core thickness (μm)	DC Resistance	Inductance (μH)	Voltage for Largest Tunability	Low Voltage Tunability	Reference
PZT Slab	500	13.3 Ω	30 - 200	450 % at 1 kHz (600 V)	1.7% (30 V)	[7]
PZT Slab	250	1.3 Ω	1.8 - 6	370 % at 10 kHz (400 V)	5% (30 V)	[3]
PMNPT slab	500	1 Ω	8.8 - 28.1	250 % at 1 kHz (600 V)	2.4% (30 V)	[8]
PMNPT slab	500	38 mΩ	0.93 - 3.6	290 % at 10 kHz (600 V)	5.61% (30 V)	This Work
PMNPT slab	50	38 mΩ	2.04 - 2.9	46 % at 10 kHz (60 V)	36.1% (30 V)	This Work

Conclusion

Low voltage ME tunable inductors composed of Metglas/(011) PMN-PT/Metglas has been investigated in this paper. The tunable inductance of the ME composites is attributed to the in-plane lattice-strain change and the stress coupling of the permeability in the magnetic phase in the bonded structure. While the 500 μm PMN-PT has exhibited a tunability of 290% at 600 V, their tunability at a more acceptable applied voltage of 30 V for conventional power electronics is well below 6%. Using a 50 μm thick PMN-PT core allows for a tunable inductance greater than 36% with a smaller applied voltage of only 30 V. This new technique opens up a pathway to achieve a low voltage tunable inductor for real world power-efficient adaptive power electronics and multiband RF communication systems.

Acknowledgements

This work was supported by the Army SBIR program under Award #W31P4Q-18-C-0012.

References

1. Yan, Y., LD. Geng, L. Zhang, X. Gao, S. Gollapudi, H. Song, S. Dong, M. Sanghadasa, K. Ngo, Y. U. Wang, and S. Priya, "Correlation between Tunability and Anisotropy in Magnetoelectric Voltage Tunable Inductor (VTI)," *Scientific Reports*, 7: 16008, pp. 1-10, 2017.
2. Baarman, D. W., "Methods of Administering Dalbavancin for Treatment of Skin and Soft Tissue Infections," *U.S. Patent*, 0130914, Sep. 2004.
3. Lin, H., J. Lou, Y. Gao, R. Hasegawa, M. Liu, B. Howe, J. Jones, G. Brown, and N. Sun, "Voltage Tunable Magnetoelectric Inductors with Improved Operational Frequency and Quality Factor for Power Electronics," *IEEE Trans. Magnetics*, Vol. 51, No. 1, pp. 1-5, 2015.
4. Saito, Y., H. Takao, T. Tani, T. Nonoyama, K. Takatori, T. Homma, T. Nagaya, and M. Nakamura, "Lead-free piezoceramics," *Nature*, vol. 432, pp. 84-87, Nov. 2004.
5. Ma, J., J. Hu, Z. Li, and C. W. Nan, "Recent progress in multiferroic magnetoelectric composites: from bulk to thin films," *Adv. Mater.*, vol. 23, pp. 1062-1087, 2011.
6. Liu, G. X., X. X. Cui, and S. X. Dong, "A Tunable Ring-type Magnetoelectric Inductor," *J. Appl. Phys.* 108, 094106, 2010.
7. Lou, J., D. Reed, M. Liu, and N. Sun, "Electrostatically Tunable Magnetoelectric Inductors with Large Inductance Tunability," *Appl. Phys. Lett.* 94, 112508, 2009.
8. Peng, B., C. Zhang, Y. Yan, and M. Liu, "Voltage-Impulse-Induced Nonvolatile Control of Inductance in Tunable Magnetoelectric Inductors," *Phys. Rev. Appl.* 7, 044015, pp. 1-7, 2017.
9. Hu, J. M., L. Q. Chen, and C. W. Nan, "Multiferroic Heterostructures Integrating Ferroelectric and Magnetic Materials," *Adv. Mater.* 28, 15, 2016.
10. Liu, M., O. Obi, Z. H. Cai, J. Lou, G. M. Yang, K. S. Ziemer, and N. Sun, "Electrical Tuning of Magnetism in Fe_3O_4/PZN-PT Multiferroic Heterostructures Derived by Reactive Magnetron Sputtering," *J. Appl. Phys.* 107, 073916, 2010.
11. Wu. T., A. Bur, P. Zhao, K. P. Mohanchandra, K. Wong, K. L. Wang, C. S. Lynch, and G. P. Carman, "Giant Electric-field-induced Reversible and Permanent Magnetization Reorientation on Magnetoelectric Ni/(011)$[Pb(Mg_{1/3}Nb_{2/3})O_3]_{(1-x)}$-$[PbTiO_3]_x$ Heterostructure," *Appl. Phys. Lett.* 98, 012504, 2011.
12. Vroubel M., Y. Zhuang, B. Rejaei, and J. N. Burghartz, "Integrated tunable magnetic RF inductor," *IEEE Electron Device Lett.* 25, 787, 2004.
13. Shirahata Y., R. Shiina, D. L. Gonzalez, K. J. A. Franke, E. Wada, M. Itoh, N. A. Pertsev, S. van Dijken, and T. Taniyama, "Electric-field switching of perpendicularly magnetized multilayers," *NPG Asia Mater.* 7, e198, 2015.

Soteria Architecture Cell Materials

Carl C. Hu
Soteria Battery Innovation Group, Inc.
Greenville, SC 29615
carl.hu@soteriabig.com / 1-864-609-4809

Abstract: *Lithium ion batteries have utilized a layered construction with metal foil current collectors and poly separators for quite some time. In the presence of any defect which causes a short between the layers large currents will be delivered to the defect from the cell and any external cells in parallel via the solid metal conductors. The heat generated causes the separator to shrink and enlarge the short while the current collectors continue to be good conductors in the presence of the generated heat. This can lead to thermal runaway with temperatures rapidly rising until the flammability point of various cell materials is exceeded. Substantial safety and performance benefits can be achieved by using separators that do not shrink under high temperatures, and current collectors that break their conductivity under these conditions.*

Keywords: Current Conductor; Fuse; Safety; Light Weight; Energy Density.

Introduction

Traditional Lithium-ion cells use solid metal foils for current collectors and plastic separators as components of the basic cell sandwich structure. The metals are excellent at delivering current and are typically made of aluminum on the cathode side and copper on the anode side. Both metals have high melting temperatures with aluminum around 660 degrees C and copper close to 1085 degrees C. Current 1st generation separators exhibit significant shrinkage around 130 degrees C and 2nd generation (ceramic coated) separators add about 45 degrees C to this, maintaining their dimensions until around 175 degrees C.

The combination of the materials in a cell lead to a positive feedback loop under certain failure conditions. When an interlayer short develops, the solid metal conductors deliver higher than normal cell operational currents to the location of the short causing rapid heating of the immediate area around the defect. The quick rise in temperature causes significant shrinkage of the separator whose effect is to bring more of the positive and negative parts of cell into contact. This temperature rise is not sufficient to degrade the solid metal conductors, so they continue to efficiently delivery whatever current is available into the defect area. This forms a rapid positive feedback system that can see temperatures quickly rise past separator shutdown regions to the ignition point of the materials the cell is composed of and a thermal runaway is initiated. The elements are shown in the following diagram:

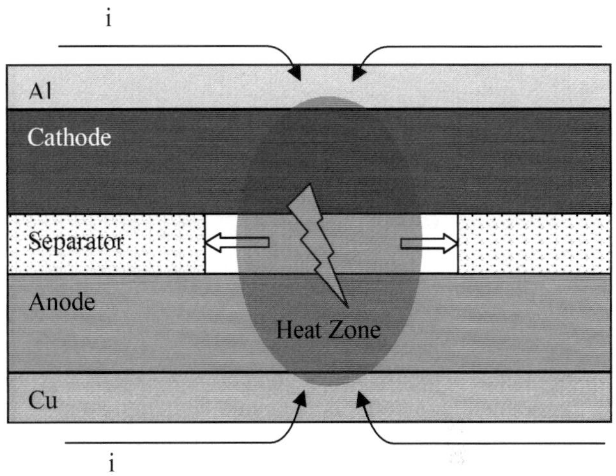

Figure 1. Defect in traditional cell architecture leading to thermal runaway

Note that i, the current delivered into the defect, can include not just the capacity of the cell but also any cells that are in parallel to the failing cell unless isolation is employed between parallel cells at the pack level. The short or defect (represented by the lightning bolt in the figure) can be any low impedance path through the separator between any of the materials of the cell but is most troublesome when conduction is made to one of the metal current collectors.

Possible latent defects include metal debris in the active materials and burrs in the foils that pass the hi pot test at manufacturing time but become active later. Damage to the cell in the form of a cell penetration by a conductive element, such as the well know nail penetration test also cause a similar positive feedback loop.

The Soteria Architecture

Soteria architecture cells are cells made with 3rd generation non-woven separators and metallized film current collectors. The combination of the two result in a cell architecture that breaks the positive feedback loop associated with thermal runaways. Each element contributes to the safety while also providing benefits to the energy density of the cell as the materials weigh less than those they replace. Safety is improved to the point where cell operation after catastrophic shorting is possible and demonstrated.

3rd Generation Separators

3rd generation separators exhibit much lower shrinkage to much higher temperatures than 1st and 2nd generation separators, as seen in figure 2.

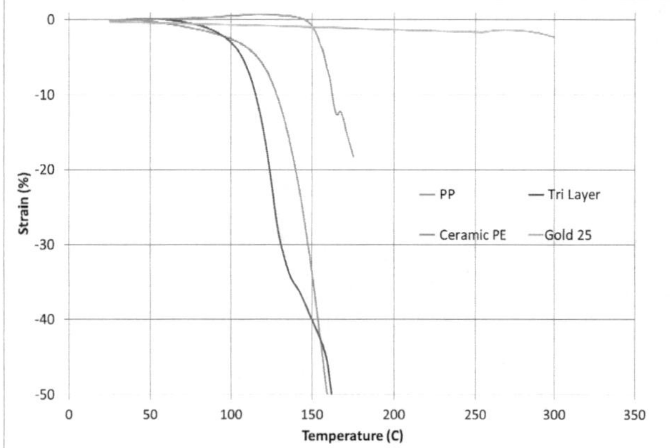

Figure 2. Shrinkage vs. Temperature in 1st, 2nd, and 3rd Generation Separators

Of note is that the ceramic coated separator extends the performance of plastic separators 45 degrees C or so, but when they reach a critical temperature, their strain slope is similar to the non-coated plastic. The non-woven 3rd generation separators exhibit very little shrinkage up to 300 degrees C and beyond and provide a much larger temperature margin to a shorted cell. Figure 3 shows post nail penetration separator differences between a Gen3 and Gen 2 separator.

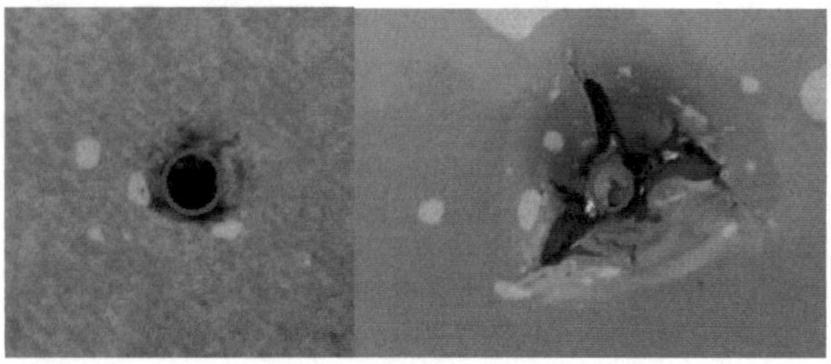

Figure 3. Post Nail Penetration Gen 3 (left) Gen 2 (right) Separators

The red circles designate the approximate size of the nail. Note the Gen2 separator has pulled away from the mechanical puncture area and also split as a result of the heating introduced into the short area no doubt enhanced by the extra area of the exposed electrodes.

The temperature stability of 3rd generation separators prevents one component of the thermal runaway positive feedback cycle, the enlarging of the shorted area due to heating. This is one pillar of the safety realized with Soteria architecture cells.

Metallized Film Current Collectors

The other pillar responsible for the safety is the use of metallized film current collectors. These are replacements for the copper and aluminum foils currently used. The metallized film consists of a substrate, like polyester, that is coated with a thin metal on both sides. This provides a electrical conductor capable of carrying the normal operating currents of the cell without any heating. However, when the current density is exceeded due to a shorting defect, the conductor disintegrates and breaks the conduction path from the rest of the cell.

Figure 4. Scanninng Electron Microscope Photo of Metallized Film conductor

Both the thickness of the metal coating and the thickness and composition of the substrate are engineered quantities to adopt to the applications requirements. For our first cell builds, we have chosen 10um thick polyester substrate coated with 500nm of aluminum on each side for the cathode current collector and 700nm of copper on the same substrate for the anode. The thickness of metal on both sides is on the order of 1/10 the metal used in equivalent solid foil current collectors.

The effect of the thin metal coupled with the polyester substrate is to become a fuse when current density exceeds designed limits. There are two methods that act in concert to achieve this. First, when the temperature rise due to the increased current density reaches around 100 degrees C, the polyester begins to shrink. Next, as the heating continues, the metal coating exceeds its ability to carry current and disintegrates. The effect is that the conductor breaks where current density exceeds set levels. Increasing the metal thickness will move the current density limit up while decreasing the thickness will reduce the limit.

In Figure 5, a test strip that is 4 squares long is subject to steady state current with temperature and failure point monitored. A 10um film with 0.5um aluminum on both sides is compared to an equivalent 17um aluminum foil

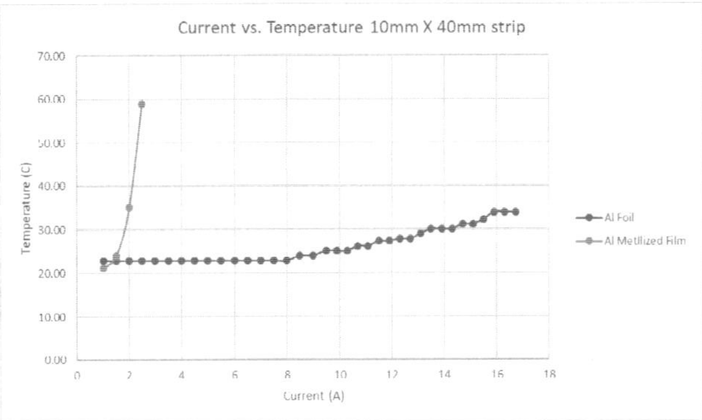

Figure 5. Metaillized Aluminum Film (.5um/10um/.5um vs. Foil (17um) Current Characteristics

Note that the film quickly heats and fails around the 2A point, while the foil exhibits minor heating and no failure up to 17A where the test was discontinued. This is steady state performance. Transient response is even better. In a test simulating a short forming in an active cell, the energy pulse necessary to blow the conductor is on the order of 4uJ for a sharpened point short on aluminum film and 40uj on copper film.

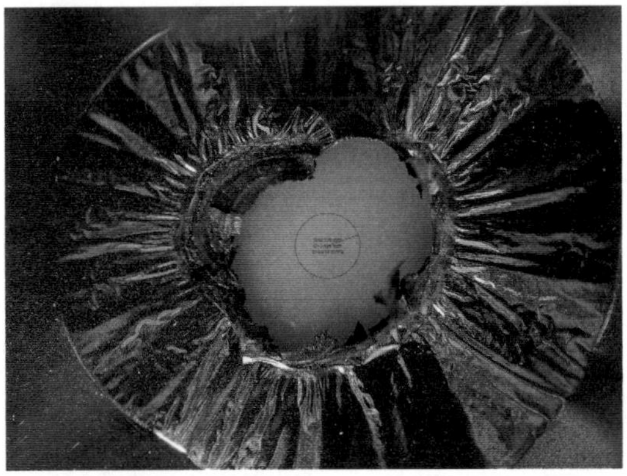

Figure 6. Metaillized Aluminum Film Point Short Area

Cell Testing

Cells using combinations of Soteria metallized current collectors in all combinations were built and tested. The cells were hand coated NMC pouch cells of ~500mah capacity with low rate (C/5) electrodes. Control cells using conventional foils for current collectors were built in the same batch to serve as a comparison. Cells all performed similarly in electrical testing with a few exceptions.

The DC impedance of the Soteria cells was a surprise given that the metallized foil conductors exhibit roughly 25 times the impedance of the solid foils. In Figure 7, we see the average DC impedance of each of the cell combinations with the control cells (both conductors solid foil) being the highest.

In figure 8, we see the 48 hour self discharge curves of all the cell build combinations, with the control cells being the most discharged at the end of the test period.

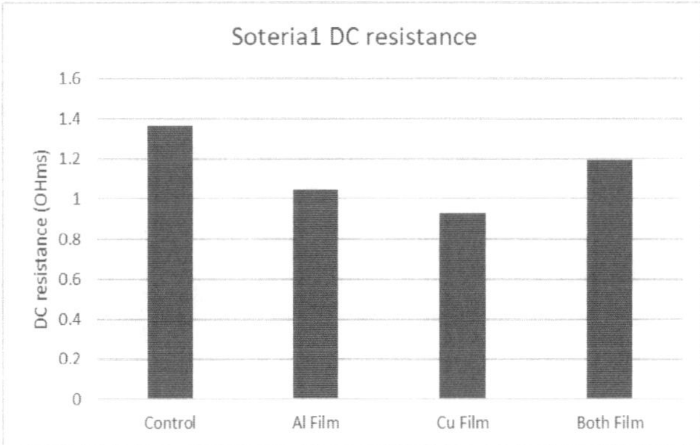

Figure 7. 48 hour Self Discharge Curves

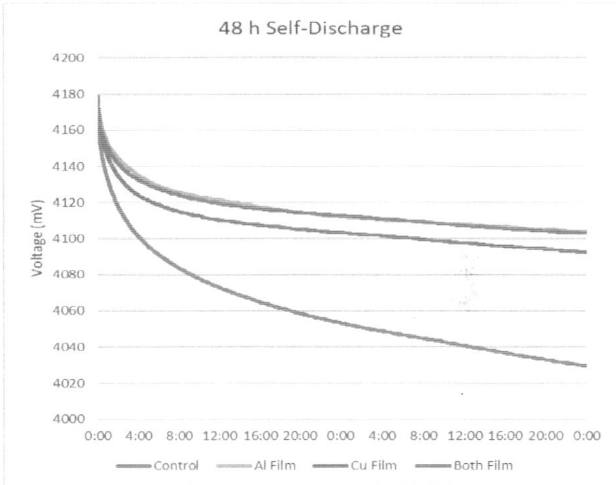

Figure 8 . 48 hour Self Discharge Curves

Cell Abuse Testing

Cells were subjected to nail penetration testing in the fully charged state. Recall that the subject cells are capable of C/5 rates due to their hand coated manufacturing. In figure 9, we see the voltage at the terminals of a control cell and a Soteria cell in response to a 3mm nail being driven completely through the cells.

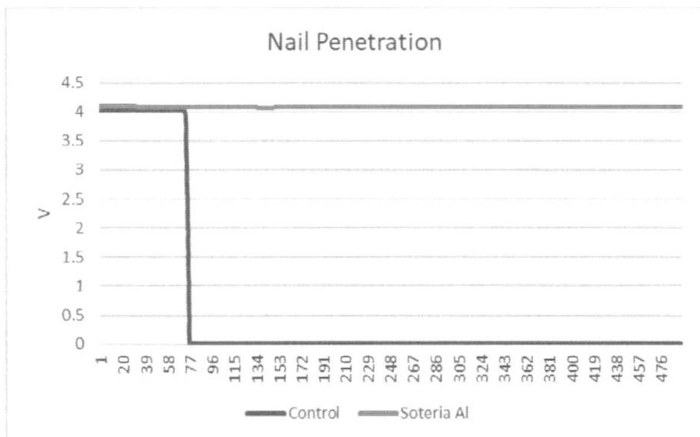

Figure 9. Nail Penetration Test voltages

The control cell immediately goes to 0 volts and begins heating, as shown in Figure 10, left. The Soteria cell exhibits no detectable change in its terminal voltage, and remained at room temperature throughout the duration of the test as seen in Figure 10, right below.

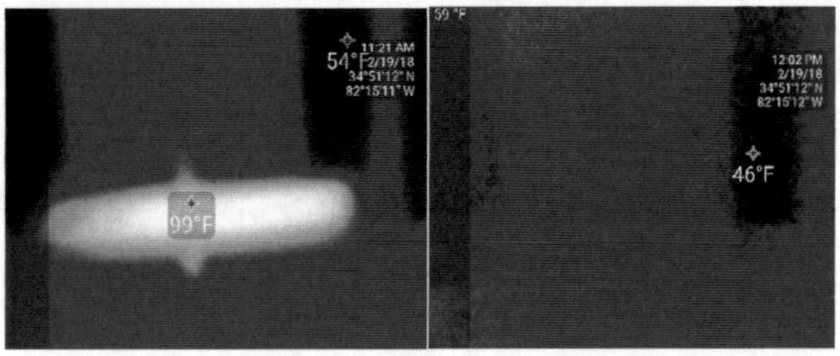

Figure 10. Control Cell (left) and Soteria (right) Thermal Image of Nail Penetration Test

The Soteria cell functioned as a cell during and after the nail penetration test. The cell, with the nail still embedded, was still functional and delivering power, of course at a reduced level, and eventually, due to electrolyte loss stopped functioning.

Material Data

Soteria cell materials are production friendly on current roll to roll cell manufacturing equipment. Dreamweaver Gold separator has been used in production environments successfully. Both copper and aluminum coated films have been built into cells and will be used in a series of cell builds that progressively prove out more elements of the production process.

Film Property	10 um Soteria Aluminum	10 um Soteria Copper
Thickness (um)	10	11
Metal Coating Thickness(nm)	500	700
Weight (g/m^2)	16	29
Tensile strength (N/mm^2)	160	>150
Elongation (%)	>50	>50
Resistance, double sided (mΩ/□)	26	11

Figure 11. Soteria Metallized Foil Material Data

Note that the 10um Soteria aluminum film has very similar tensile strength to 15um thick aluminum foil, typically quoted at 150N/mm^2. This similarity in strength with better elasticity yields similar coating and handling properties on roll to roll coating equipment.

Basic Membrane Property	Unit of Measure	USABC Requirements	Dreamweaver Gold™ 20
Thickness (12.6 psi)	µm	<25	22
Thickness (25 psi)	µm	<25	21
Gurley (JIS)	seconds		300
Porosity	%		37%
Pore Size	µm	<1.0	0.4
TD Shrinkage @ 280 C/1 Hour	%		1
MD Shrinkage @ 280 C/1 Hour	%		2
TD Strength	Kgf/cm^2		500
MD Strength	Kgf/cm^2	>70	800
Young's Modulus	Kgf/cm^2	>5,000	15,000
Melt Integrity	C	>200	500
Puncture Strength	gf	>300	
Moisture Content	%	<0.0005	6%

Figure 12. Dreamweaver Gold 20 Material Data

Both materials are lighter than the materials they replace while being dimensionally similar which results in an energy density increase at the cell level. Depending on the characteristics of the cell, energy densities can increase 10-20%.

Summary

Soteria architecture cells are built with existing manufacturing infrastructure friendly materials that replace currently used separators and foils. The result is a safer, lighter cell. Current cells that adopt the architecture can expect increased energy density due to lighter weight and a new level of safety that extends to the possibility of operation after damage.

Bio-Silica from Cultured Diatoms for Energy Storage - Flexible Electrodes and Supercapacitors

Emine Karaman[1], Zhiqian Wang[1], Giuseppe L. Di Benedetto[2], James L. Zunino, III[2], Xianyang Meng[1] and Somenath Mitra[1]*

[1] Department of Chemistry and Environmental Science
New Jersey Institute of Technology, Newark, NJ 07102.
[2] Advanced Materials Technology Branch
U.S. Army Armament Research, Development and Engineering Center, Picatinny Arsenal, NJ 07806
somenath.mitra@njit.edu / 1-973-596-5611

Abstract: *U.S. Army weapons systems require new, enhanced capabilities in order to combat current and future threats. With these new, enhanced capabilities, complex electronics packages are introduced that, in turn, require unique power sources. These power sources need to not only perform to meet mission requirements, but also be low-cost and reliable. U.S. Army ARDEC and New Jersey Institute of Technology are jointly investigating the research and development of low-cost advanced materials to enable flexible electrochemical supercapacitors. Silica from cultured diatom (CD), which possesses porous structure as well as high surface area were used as supercapacitor development. Iron oxide was loaded onto cultured diatom (CD-FeO_x) through precipitation reaction between $FeCl_3$ and NaOH and heating, forming uniform metal oxide layer that contributed significantly to supercapcitor performance through pseudocapacitance. The large surface area of CD also provide double-layer capacitance. CD-FeO_x containing 49% CD showed a specific capacitance more than 400% higher than pure CD. Supercapacitors were tested for more than 1000 cycles and 90% of the original performance was retained. Flexible supercapacitor electrodes were also made using this CD-FeO_x composite.*

Keywords: supercapacitor; diatom; algae; iron oxides; flexible; three-dimensional structures

Introduction

Supercapacitors, based on double-layer and pseudocapacitance, have been part of high-performance energy storage device advancement. Research has shown that electroactive materials and appropriate substrates both play critical roles in designing high-performance supercapacitors [1, 2] by providing short ion-electron pathway and high surface area [3, 4]. Hence smaller and porous electrode structures are desired.

Metal oxides of high specific capacitance including Mn, Ru, and Fe are promising supercapacitor electrode materials [5, 6]. Among them, iron oxides (FeO_x) are attractive electrode candidates for supercapacitor applications because of their variable valence, low cost, eco-friendly attributes and abundance in nature. Therefore, the development of FeO_x-based electroactive nanomaterials with porous three-dimensional structures has the potential to improve supercapacitor performance. Metal oxides can be loaded on various substrates such as carbon nanotube [7], graphene oxide [8], and silica [9]. Among them, silica has advantages like simple treatment methods, abundance in nature, as well as less expensive processes. Hence, silica materials, especially nano-grade and mesoporous particles, are attractive substrates for metal compounds [10, 11].

Though silica can be synthesized via chemical methods [10, 12], the processes could be expensive, toxic and complicated. Sustainable natural silica sources, such as biosilica from diatomaceous earth (DE) and biosilica from cultured diatom (CD) cells, are much preferred. DE diatom silica frustules persist after the decay of the organic matter and is geochemically incorporated into rocks [13]. Furthermore, DE has well-organized condensed silica structure with impurities which can be removed by chemical processes. In contrast, CD frustules are not condensed and contain free silanol groups, which provide a viable source of nano grade silica for surface modifications [14]. Because Diatom Phaeodactylum tricornutum is cultured in seawater environment, the reaction between NaOH and $FeCl_3$ in original culture media only leaves NaCl, a major component of seawater, in the aqueous phase. Hence, this in-situ synthesis method brings minimum toxicity and pollution.

The objective of this research was to develop cultured diatom loaded with FeO_x (CD-FeO_x) for supercapacitor development.

Experimental

Diatom Phaeodactylum tricornutum strain and culturing

Diatom Phaeodactylum tricornutum was obtained from the Carolina Biological Center, NC, U.S.A. Aquil, artificial seawater media was prepared based on trace metal physiology following the previous report method [15].

Synthesis of CD and CD-FeOx composite

Diatom Phaeodactylum tricornutum was cultured and maintained in Aquil until it reaches peak growth value. Then, diatom culture was flocculated with one molar NaOH and the culture was separated by gravitational settling. The resulting slurry was treated with concentrated H_2SO_4 and heated for 2 h at 200 °C, filtered, washed with Milli-Q water to neutral and dried under vacuum. The acid treatment allowed all the organic matter to decompose and the silica to functionalize.

For CD-FeO_x composite, diatom Phaeodactylum tricornutum was flocculated with $FeCl_3$ and then NaOH was added until the pH reached 9. The culture was shaken overnight continuously. The resulting diatom-FeO_x mixture was separated and washed with Milli-Q water. The slurry was thermally treated at 70 °C in an oven for 6 hr, dried 12 h in a speedvac (Savant AS160) under vacuum. It was further treated with 30% H_2O_2, washed until a neutral pH and then dried at 70 °C for 2 h. To take advantage of the biosilica structure in their natural environment, $FeCl_3$ interacted with live cultured diatom cells directly. Iron oxide precipitated on the diatom surface at alkaline pH and the composite was formed by heating, which was followed by H_2O_2 treatment.

Characterization

The CD, DE and CD-FeO_x were characterized using a scanning electron microscope (SEM, LEO 1530 VP, Carl Zeiss SMT Inc., Peabody, MA). The Brunauer, Emmett and Teller (BET) specific surface area of the samples were measured using Quantachrome NOVA 3000 series (Model N32-11) High-Speed Gas Sorption Analyzer (Boynton Beach, FL). MTI Battery Analyzer (Richmond, CA) was used for Galvano static charge-discharge measurements. Quantitative determination of iron element in composites was carried on Atomic absorption (AA) spectrometer (Perkin Elmer Analyst 400). Cyclic voltammetry (CV) was tested on a Homiangz 320C electrochemical analyzer versus Ag-AgCl reference electrode in 2 M Na_2SO_4 electrolyte.

Electrode preparation and cell fabrication

The electrode paste was prepared by mixing 82% silica material, 10% carbon black, and 8% polyethylene oxide (PEO) in poly(3,4-ethylenedioxythiophene)-poly(styrenesulfonate) solution (PEDOT: PSS). The typical dry electrode was 10 mg. Stainless steel cylinders were used as current collectors together with glass microfiber filters separators, and 1 M Na_2SO_4 as the electrolyte. Cyclic CV electrodes contained 73% diatom composites, 15% polyvinylidene fluoride (PVDF) binder and 12% carbon black. The total weight of each CV electrode was 3 mg. Flexible electrodes were prepared by casting the electrode slurry onto the stainless steel 316 current collectors, which was stuck to the adhesive side of polyethylene terephthalate (PET) film coated with ethylene vinyl acetate copolymer (EVA) resin. The typical electrode area was 16 mm × 16 mm and the weight of each electrode after drying was 7.7 mg. After applying the slurry onto the current collector, the electrodes were allowed to dry at room temperature for 12 h and then processed under vacuum (9.893 kPa) condition for the last 5 min. The components were thermally sealed, with glass microfiber separator between electrodes, to make a complete supercapacitor.

Results and Discussion

Material Characterization

Living Phaeodactylum tricornutum diatom was cultured in the laboratory-simulated seawater environment as shown in Fig. 1a. Then $FeCl_3$ and NaOH was added, filtered, washed and heated to synthesize iron oxides. After the loading of FeO_x, the resulted CD-FeO_x showed a color similar to Fe_2O_3.

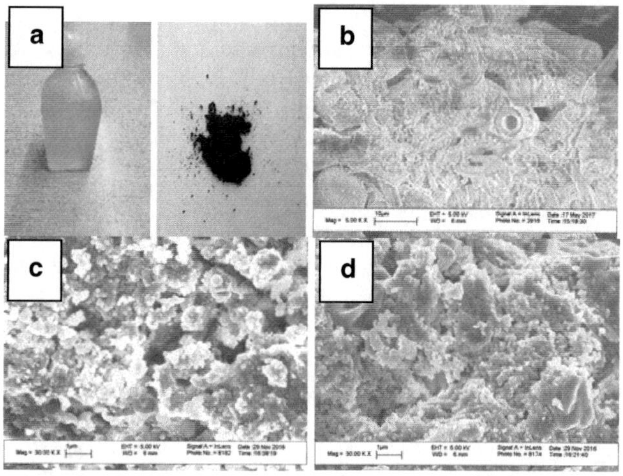

Figure 1. a) Living Phaeodactylum tricornutum diatom culture and synthesized CD-FeO_x; SEM images of b) DE; c) CD; d) CD-FeO_x.

DE has semi-cylindrical structures with a large void volume (Fig. 1b) and particles are in micron grade. Fig. 1c and Fig. 1d represent SEM images of CD and CD-FeO_x composite, respectively. CD, with smaller particles than DE, formed porous structures which were attributed to the numerous skeletal pores as well as the formation of the interparticle pores during agglomeration. This structure was beneficial for the synthesis of the 3D nanocomposite for capacitor applications such as the loading of FeO_x proposed here by providing larger surface area. Fig. 1d indicates that the FeO_x precipitated on the CD surface after acid and heat treatment. The surface is also well porous, which is desired for supercapacitor electrodes.

The BET analysis was conducted to determine the specific surface area, and DFT method was applied to calculate pore volume of samples. CD had relatively larger surface area compared with DE and the CD-FeO_x had the largest surface area of 186.62 $m^2\ g^{-1}$, followed by that of CD (20.86 $m^2\ g^{-1)}$. The DE frustules, tend to be more heterogeneous and have a wide range of properties because of their geological history, and in this case showed a lower surface area of only 0.71 $m^2\ g^{-1}$ than CD. Hence, the CD composite with both large surface area and the unique porous structure was selected as substrate for iron oxides. Besides larger specific surface area, the porous nanostructured materials were expected to provide short diffusion paths for electrons and ion transport leading to fast redox reactions and charge/discharge rates that would provide high specific capacitance. The surface area and pore volume of CD increased significantly after the loading of FeO_x, which would further enhance electrode properties.

Electrochemical properties of CD, DE, and CD-FeO$_x$

CV response of CD and DE are presented in Fig. 2a. The CD electrodes exhibited larger current density than those made of DE. The smaller pore volume of DE sample might have hindered effective transport of the electrolytes. Fig. 2b shows the influence of FeO_x layer on performance at the scan rate of 50 mV s^{-1}. As expected, the electrode containing FeO_x exhibited an approximately rectangular shape and substantially larger current as determined by the enclosed area than two other samples indicating that the FeO_x enhanced the charge-discharge process. A bulge at -0.4 V also demonstrated the existence of pseudocapacitance from FeO_x.

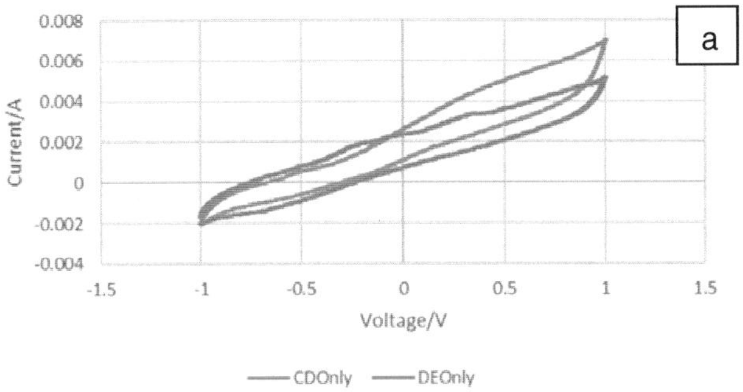

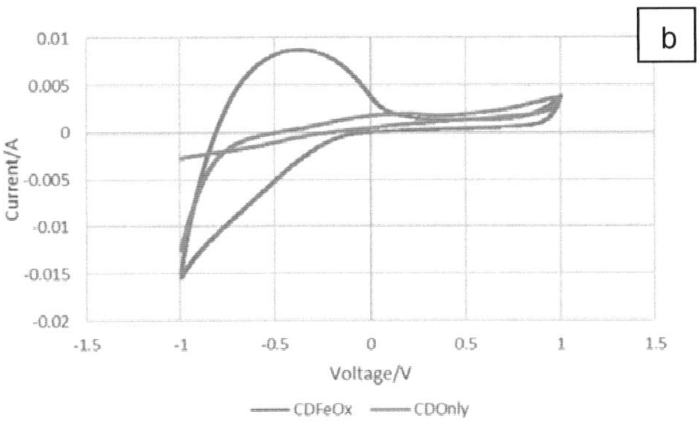

Figure 2. CV at 50 mV s^{-1} scan rate: a) CD and DE; b) CD-FeO_x composite and CD Only.

In another test, the specific capacitance C_s (F g^{-1}) of CD, DE and CD-FeO_x were calculated based on equation (1) [16] and the integration of the CV curves in three electrode configurations at the scan rate of 100 mV s^{-1}.

$$Cs = \frac{1}{mv(Vf - Vi0)} \int_{Vi0}^{Vf} I(V)dV \quad (1)$$

where m (g) is the mass of the electroactive materials in the electrodes, V_{i0} (V) is the initial and V_f (V) is the final cutoff voltages in cyclic voltammetry, I (A) is the instantaneous current, and v (V s^{-1}) is the scan rate. It was found that the specific capacitance of CD was much higher than DE composite electrode. CD-FeO_x composite electrode showed maximum specific capacitance of 70.2 F g^{-1} at the scan rate 100 mV s^{-1}.

After Atomic Absorption analysis (AA) and calculations, it was found that CD-FeO_x in the composite contained 51% iron oxides, and the rest CD. The specific capacitance of CD-FeO_x was 70.2 F g^{-1}, implying that the loaded FeO_x on CD had a specific capacitance of 124.4 F g^{-1} itself. The metal oxide contributed much to the total performance.

Fig. 3 shows cycling characteristics of supercapacitors in which electrodes CD and CD-FeO_x. The CD-FeO_x supercapacitors showed better supercapacitive behavior compared to CD only due to both pseudocapacitance and double-layer capacitance.

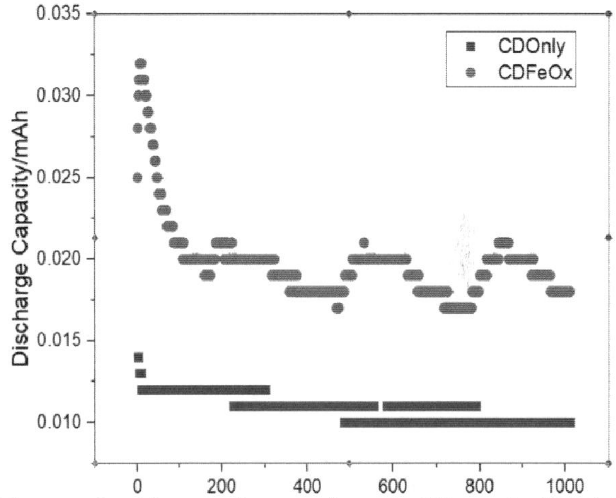

Figure 3. Measured capacity of CD and CD-FeO_x composite under 0.1 A g^{-1}.

Flexible Supercapacitor Development

Diatom material has the potential to be implemented in various configurations and structures. The flexible electrode fabricated from CD-FeO_x is shown in Fig. 4. The assembled capacitor in Fig. 4 showed similar performance to the rigid capacitor. The cell remained functional under bending conditions. The system also showed good stability as well as flexibility with CD-FeO_x materials, which provides pathways for electrolyte mobility. Further improvement can be made by improving packaging.

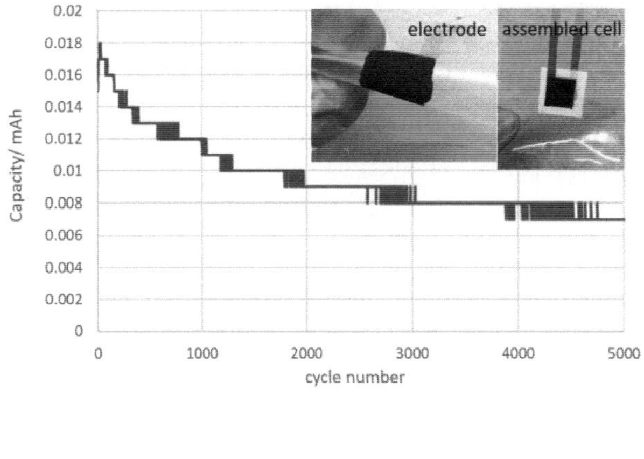

DISTRIBUTION A. Approved for public release: distribution unlimited.
UNCLASSIFIED

Figure 4. Cycling data of flexible CD-FeO_x capacitor under current density of 0.1 A g^{-1}

Conclusions

Biosilica was studied as a potential substrate material for metal oxide loading, which could be used for supercapacitor electrodes. The FeO_x-CD composite containing 49% silica showed improved capacitor performance by 400% compared with supercapacitor made from CD only. The resulted material was also used to fabricate flexible, thin-film supercapacitors successfully. It is concluded that this simple, scalable and low-cost synthetic approach can be readily applied to other metal-oxides and insoluble salts increase electrochemical properties of the biosilica.

References

1. Wang, H.; Xu, Z.; Yi, H.; Wei, H.; Guo, Z.; Wang, X., One-step preparation of single-crystalline Fe_2O_3 particles/graphene composite hydrogels as high performance anode materials for supercapacitors. *Nano Energy* **2014,** *7* (Supplement C), 86-96.
2. Padwal, P. M.; Kadam, S. L.; Mane, S. M.; Kulkarni, S. B., Enhanced specific capacitance and supercapacitive properties of polyaniline–iron oxide (PANI–Fe_2O_3) composite electrode material. *Journal of Materials Science* **2016,** *51* (23), 10499-10505.
3. Wu, Z.; Wang, Z.; Yu, F.; Thakkar, M.; Mitra, S., Variation in chemical, colloidal and electrochemical properties of carbon nanotubes with the degree of carboxylation. *Journal of Nanoparticle Research* **2017,** *19* (1).
4. Frackowiak, E.; Béguin, F., Carbon materials for the electrochemical storage of energy in capacitors. *Carbon* **2001,** *39* (6), 937-950.
5. Simon, P.; Gogotsi, Y., Materials for electrochemical capacitors. *Nat Mater* **2008,** *7* (11), 845-854.
6. Evanko, B.; Yoo, S. J.; Chun, S.-E.; Wang, X.; Ji, X.; Boettcher, S. W.; Stucky, G. D., Efficient Charge Storage in Dual-Redox Electrochemical Capacitors through Reversible Counterion-Induced Solid Complexation. *Journal of the American Chemical Society* **2016,** *138* (30), 9373-9376.
7. Fan, Y.; Su, F.; Li, K.; Ke, C.; Yan, Y., Carbon nanotube filled with magnetic iron oxide and modified with polyamidoamine dendrimers for immobilizing lipase toward application in biodiesel production. **2017,** *7*, 45643.
8. Vélez, G. Y.; Encinas, A.; Quintana, M., Immobilization of Metal and Metal Oxide Nanoparticles on Graphene. In *Functionalization of Graphene*, Wiley-VCH Verlag GmbH & Co. KGaA: 2014; pp 219-254.
9. Li, F.; Xing, Y.; Huang, M.; Li, K. L.; Yu, T. T.; Zhang, Y. X.; Losic, D., MnO_2 nanostructures with three-dimensional (3D) morphology replicated from diatoms for high-performance supercapacitors. *J. Mater. Chem. A* **2015,** *3* (15), 7855-7861.
10. Zhi, J.; Deng, S.; Wang, Y.; Hu, A., Highly Ordered Metal Oxide Nanorods inside Mesoporous Silica Supported Carbon Nanomembranes: High Performance Electrode Materials for Symmetrical Supercapacitor Devices. *The Journal of Physical Chemistry C* **2015,** *119* (16), 8530-8536.
11. Zhao, J.; Zhang, Y.; Wang, T.; Li, P.; Wei, C.; Pang, H., Reed Leaves as a Sustainable Silica Source for 3D Mesoporous Nickel (Cobalt) Silicate Architectures Assembled into Ultrathin Nanoflakes for High-Performance Supercapacitors. *Advanced Materials Interfaces* **2015,** *2* (2), 1400377-n/a.
12. Zhao, D.; Feng, J.; Huo, Q.; Melosh, N.; Fredrickson, G. H.; Chmelka, B. F.; Stucky, G. D., Triblock Copolymer Syntheses of Mesoporous Silica with Periodic 50 to 300 Angstrom Pores. *Science* **1998,** *279* (5350), 548-552.
13. Wang, Y.; Cai, J.; Jiang, Y.; Jiang, X.; Zhang, D., Preparation of biosilica structures from frustules of diatoms and their applications: current state and perspectives. *Applied Microbiology and Biotechnology* **2013,** *97* (2), 453-460.
14. Losic, D.; Yu, Y.; Aw, M. S.; Simovic, S.; Thierry, B.; Addai-Mensah, J., Surface functionalisation of diatoms with dopamine modified iron-oxide nanoparticles: toward magnetically guided drug microcarriers with biologically derived morphologies. *Chemical Communications* **2010,** *46* (34), 6323-6325.
15. Price, N. M.; Harrison, G. I.; Hering, J. G.; Hudson, R. J.; Nirel, P. M. V.; Palenik, B.; Morel, F. M. M., Preparation and Chemistry of the Artificial Algal Culture Medium Aquil. *Biological Oceanography* **1989,** *6* (5-6), 443-461.
16. Chen, W.; Fan, Z.; Gu, L.; Bao, X.; Wang, C., Enhanced capacitance of manganese oxide via confinement inside carbon nanotubes. *Chemical Communications* **2010,** *46* (22), 3905-3907.

Li-ion battery failure: Linking external risks to internal events

Donal Finegan[1], Will Walker[2], Jacob Darst[2], Rhodri Jervis[3], Thomas M.M. Heenan[3], Jennifer Hack[3], Alexander Rack[4], Paul R. Shearing[3], Matthew Keyser[1], Eric Darcy[2]

1. National Renewable Energy Laboratory, 15013 Denver W Parkway, Golden, CO 80401, USA
2. NASA Johnson Space Center, 2101 E NASA Pkwy, Houston, TX 77058, USA
3. Electrochemical Innovation Laboratory, Department of Chemical Engineering, University College London, London, WC1E 7JE, UK
4. The European Synchrotron (ESRF), 71 Avenue des Martyrs, 38000 Grenoble, France

Corresponding author email: donal.finegan@nrel.gov

Abstract

In this work, we use a novel single-cell calorimeter to decouple the heat output from 18650 cell casings and their ejected material. The results from this heat distribution calorimeter (HDC) reveal the relationship between the quantity of material ejected and total heat output, as well as the fraction of the total heat that is ejected. 18650 cells were examined. When used in combination with an internal short circuiting (ISC) device, results clarify risks associated with thermal runaway of 18650 cells when thermal runaway is initiated at different locations.

The HDC was designed to operate in-situ for simultaneous high-speed synchrotron X-ray imaging experiments at The European Synchrotron (ESRF), where we conducted extensive testing involving calorimetric measurements in concert with radiographic visualizations. This set of experiments allowed patterns in heat and mass distribution to be linked with internal structural dynamics during thermal runaway, providing insight into the mechanisms that lead to ejection and the rate of propagation of thermal runaway within cells. This is the first time that internal structural dynamics are used to describe external risks relating to heat generation and material ejection. The results from this work deepen our understanding of battery failure and on how potential hazards associated with thermal runaway can be mitigated.

Keywords: Li-ion battery, thermal runaway, X-ray imaging, calorimetry

Introduction

Now, more than ever, there is a need for high energy density Li-ion cells to operate safely and reliably under a range of demanding conditions. Their ubiquity in a wide range of applications, spanning from portable electronics to defense and aerospace, means that catastrophic failure can have severe consequences and shake user confidence. Recent high profile events such as the grounding of the Boeing Dreamliner fleet[1] and the recall of Samsung smartphones[2] following battery failures demonstrate the high risks and costs. Consequently, a thorough understanding of the failure mechanisms of Li-ion batteries is needed to progress towards safer and more reliable Li-ion cells and modules.

Current abuse testing methods include thermal, mechanical and electrical, all of which are stimulated by external conditions and exhibit a high degree of variability in the magnitude of failure. To attain more control of the failure mechanisms, improve consistency, and to more accurately replicate in-field failure scenarios, an internal short circuiting (ISC) device was developed at NREL and the NASA Johnson Space Center[3]. This ISC device is selectively positioned within 18650 test cells to determine the influence of the location of failure initiation on the risk of certain unfavorable failure mechanisms, such as bursting and local side-wall breaches, that are difficult to reliable induce using conventional abuse testing methods. High-speed synchrotron X-ray imaging is used to capture the internal structural dynamics, allowing, for the first time, internal events to be linked to external risks.

Experimental

Preparation of cells

An ISC device was integrated into 3.35 Ah 18650 test-cells that achieve >265 Wh kg^{-1} and >700 Wh L^{-1}. To determine the location where initiation of thermal runaway poses the greatest external risk, the ISC device was positioned in 4 different locations within the cell; 6 layers and 3 layers radially in from the casing at the middle, and 6 layers radially in from the casing at the top and bottom of the electrode assembly (Figure 1). The ISC device used here creates a short circuit between the positive current collector and the graphite active material on the negative electrode, which is deemed the most likely type of short for initiation of thermal runaway[4]. The internal short occurs when the ISC device reaches 57 ˚C and a wax interface between the positive and negative sides melts and exposes a conducting path[3].

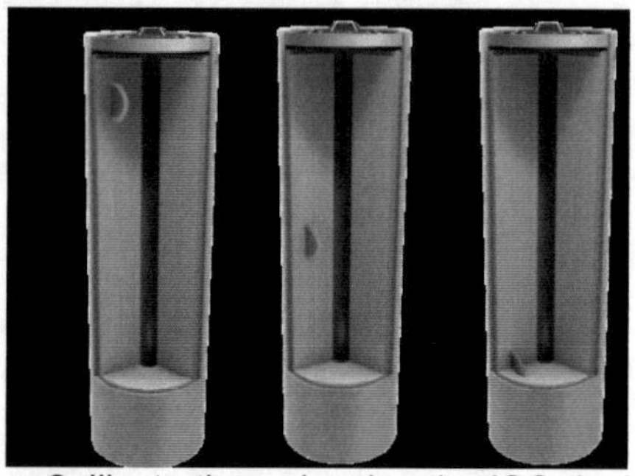

Figure 2. Illustrations showing the ISC device at the top, middle and bottom of 18650 cells.

Calorimetry and thermal abuse

To determine the risks associated with overall heat generation and the distribution of heat generated from ejected and non-ejected materials, calorimetry was carried out in a single-cell calorimeter that can decouple the heat output from the casing of cells and their ejected contents (Figure 2). This calorimeter was designed to capture the heat from contents ejected from the top and bottom of 18650 cells. The cells were placed inside an aluminum cell chamber which was thermally isolated from the sections that capture ejected contents allowing distinct heat measurements using a ceramic bushing. The cell chamber was heated using four heating cartridges, to which 1 kW of power was supplied continuously (at 250 V and 4 A) until the cell underwent thermal runaway. Upon thermal runaway, the power supply was immediately turned off and the subsequent heat from the cell and its ejected content was measured.

The heat from each component of the calorimeter was measured, allowing quantification of the total heat output, as well as the fractions of heat that arose from the cell, contents ejected from the top of the cell, and contents ejected from the bottom of the cell. As the calorimeter is contructed of aluminum, which weakly attenuates high energy X-rays, simultaneous high-speed X-ray imaging could be carried out, allowing heat generation and temperatures to be characterized with respect to internal phenomena.

X-ray imaging

High-speed X-ray imaging was carried out at beamline ID19 at The European Synchrotron (ESRF). The cells were imaged under a polychromatic beam with a pixel size of 11.35 μm and a frame rate of 2000 fps with a FOV of 1822 × 1140 pixels (horizontal×vertical). A PCO.Dimax (PCO AG, Germany) detector and scintillator were used for high-speed imaging experiments. Radiographs were flat-field corrected and enhanced using MATLAB's adaptive histogram equalization (adapthisteq) function.

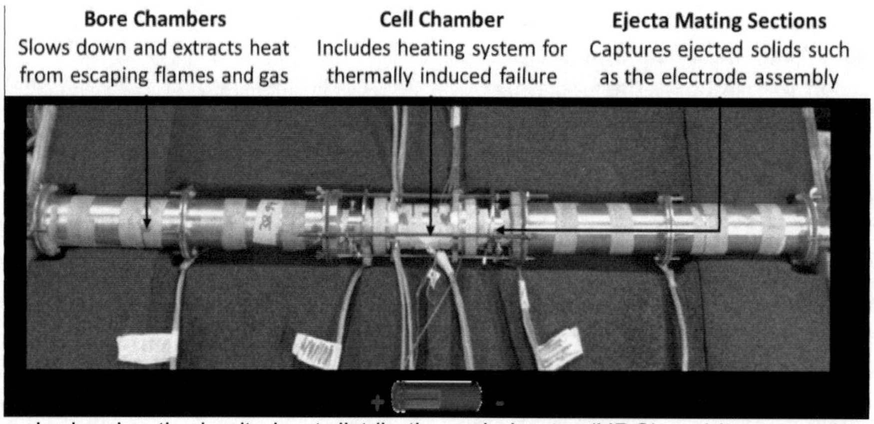

Figure 1. Photograph showing the in-situ heat distribution calorimeter (HDC) and its respective components. The illustration of an 18650 cell shows the cells orientation within the device.

Results and Discussion

Cells with the ISC device placed near the top were found to be most susceptible to breaches occurring on the spin-groove and the top button. Using high-speed radiography at 2000 fps, the internal structural dynamics that lead to side-wall and spin-groove breaches were captured. For example, in Figure 3a an 18650 cell with a breach through its spin-groove and top button is shown. In the following time-stamped radiographs in Figure 3b-f the stages leading to the breach are captured. The yellow streamlines in Figure 3 illustrate the flow of materials that is more clearly observed in the live high-speed videos. Initially, the fluidized reacting material flows from the bulk electrode assembly towards the vent, deflecting off the spin-groove fold (Figure 3c). At the point of deflection, the metal spin-groove melts and the flow of material begins to escape through the side of the cell (Figure 3d). This flow continues to deflect until a full breach penetrates through the top button of the cell (Figure 3e-f).

Similarly, when the ISC device is placed near the base of the cell (Figure 1c), the risk of the 18650 cell undergoing a breach on the base plate increases. High-speed radiography during the formation of a base-plate breach also confirms that the equivalent point of deflection (where fluidized reacting material flows from the electrode assembly towards the base, deflecting off the base plate, and thereafter flowing up through the assembly core towards the vent) is the most susceptible region for breach formation. This is due to the enhanced conductive heat transfer that arises upon renewed contact of hot reacting material with the steel casing of the cell.

Positioning of the ISC device influences where initiation occurs, and hence the location from which the fluidized reaction zone evolves. This in turn, determines the flow dynamics inside the cell during thermal runaway, affecting the risk of side-wall breaches occurring at different locations around the surface of the cell casing.

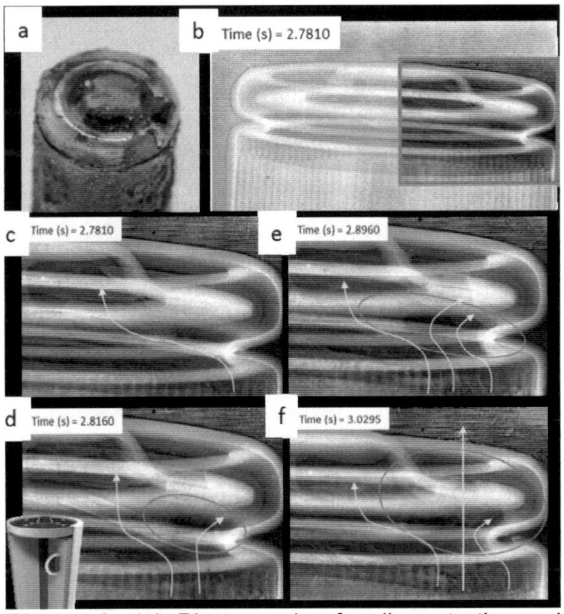

Figure 3. (a) Photograph of cell post- thermal runaway. (b-f) Time-stamped radiographs showing the top of a cell (ISC device located 6 layers in at top), where the region highlighted by the red circle shows a hole forming on the spin-groove, through which ejecting material flows, as highlighted by the yellow streamlines.

The location of the ISC device also influences the distribution of heat generated during thermal runaway between the positive end, cell chamber, and negative end of the calorimeter (Figure 4a). For example, in Figure 4b the total heat output from cells with the ISC device placed 3 layers and 6 layers radially in and mid-way along the length of the cell, is shown. And Figure 4c, the heat output from the cells where the ISC device is placed 6 layers radially in from the casing and near the top, middle and bottom along the length of the cell is shown. The average total heat output from data in Figure 4 are presented in Table 1, along with the distribution of heat output between the cell casing, and material ejected into the positive and negative ends of the calorimeter. The results clearly show that the percentage of heat ejected via the positive or negative end of the cell is influenced by the position of the ISC device in the cell. For example, the heat ejected via the negative end is much higher when the ISC device is placed near the bottom, and lowest when the ISC device is placed near the top.

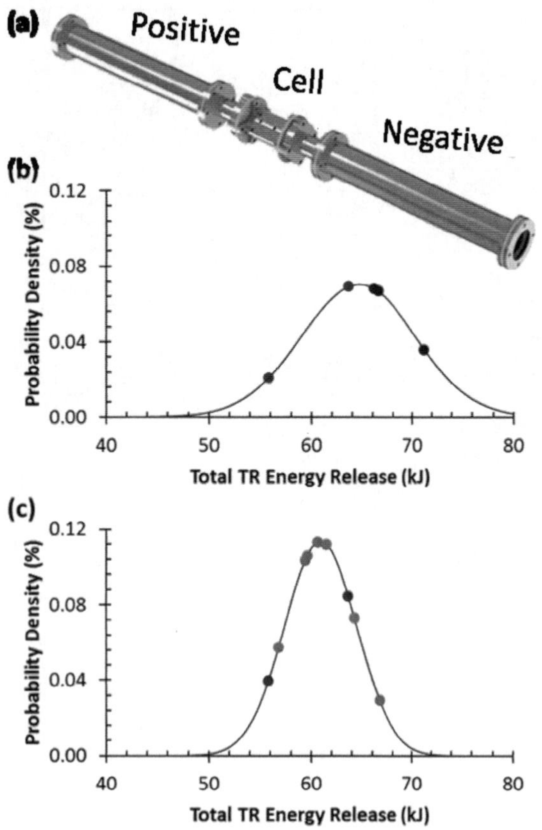

Figure 4. (a) Illustration showing the components of the calorimeter. (b) Statistical plot showing the heat output and distribution of heat output for 18650 cells with the ISC device placed 3 layers in and 6 layers in at the middle, and (c) 6 layers in at the top, middle and bottom.

	3 layers	6 layers		
	Middle	Middle	Top	Bottom
Cells tested	3.0	4.0	2.0	3.0
Total (kJ)	67.9	59.7	62.1	61.4
Std. Dev. (kJ)	5.5	5.5	2.1	1.0
Cell casing avg. (%)	26.3	22.9	37.2	36.2
Std. Dev. (%)	6.5	6.5	8.3	1.7
Pos. ejecta avg. (%)	72.5	75.1	51.0	32.5
Std. Dev. (%)	5.6	5.6	22.0	4.3
Neg. ejecta avg. (%)	1.2	2.1	11.7	31.4
Std. Dev. (%)	1.0	1.0	13.7	3.2

Table 1. Table showing the distribution of heat captured in each section of the calorimeter for cells with the ISC device placed 3 layers and 6 layers in, as well as 6 layers in at top, and bottom of the cell. The number of cells tested along with the standard deviation of each averaging measurement is shown.

Conclusions

Regions within 18650 cells that deflect the flow of hot ejecting material such the spin-groove and the base-plate, incur an increased risk of side-wall breaches. The location of thermal runaway initiation has a significant influence on the risk of breaching at certain locations as well as the distribution of heat between ejected and non-ejected material. The ISC devices provide excellent control of when and where thermal runaway will initiate, and can be used to test module vulnerabilities against, for example, top or bottom breaches. The combined approach of using ISC-induced thermal runaway, high-speed radiography, and single-cell calorimetry can provide a comprehensive description of battery failure and associated risks.

Acknowledgements

These experiments were performed on the ID19 beamline at the ESRF, Grenoble, France. We are grateful to Alexander Rack for help using this beam-line. The authors would like to give acknowledgement to the NASA Engineering and Safety Center (NESC) who sponsored and lead the technical assessment.

References

[1] NTSB, in: M. Boston (Ed.), Office of Aviation Safety, 2013.
[2] J. Chamary, in, Forbes, Why are Samsung's Galaxy Note 7 Phones Exploding?, 2016.
[3] D.P. Finegan, et al., Energy & Environmental Science, 10 (2017) 1377-1388.
[4] S. Santhanagopalan, P. Ramadass, J. Zhang, Journal of Power Sources, 194 (2009) 550-557.

Implementation of Internal Short Circuit Detection for Enhanced Safety in DOD Batteries

Christopher H. McCoy[1], Thomas Kotwal[2], Suresh Sriramulu[1], and Brian Barnett[1]
[1]CAMX Power LLC
[2]TIAX LLC
35 Hartwell Avenue, Lexington MA 02421
mccoy.chris@camxpower.com

Abstract: *We present test results for implementations of two distinct technologies for sensitive detection of incipient internal short circuits in high cell count 18650 cell-based batteries of interest to the U. S. Navy. Results demonstrating high-sensitivity detection performance are reported, including detection in actively cycling batteries and batteries with 100-cell parallel connectivity.*

Keywords: lithium-ion; internal short circuit; battery safety; early detection.

Introduction

The superior energy and power on both a weight and volume basis of lithium-ion (Li-ion) battery technology has made this chemistry the clear choice for a number of DoD applications. However, utilization of this high-performance battery chemistry has been limited by safety concerns. Under certain triggers/abuses, Li-ion cells can experience thermal runaway, i.e., a rapid increase in cell temperature accompanied by venting, vent-with-flame, ejection of cell parts, fire and explosion. Internal short circuits (most typically attributable to metal contaminants in the cell) are the most commonly identified mechanism by which such events (i.e., safety failures) occur in the field. Internal short circuits causing failures in the field typically develop after some period of normal cell operation and occur in cells that passed all manufacturing safety and quality control screening. No adequate safety test to screen for future internal short development has been available, in part because these conditions develop slowly in the field and are not detectable at the point of manufacture.

Challenges of detection of internal shorts: Certain hurdles must be overcome for an internal short to be detected with sufficient sensitivity that early warning of a fault condition can be delivered. When a short first appears, is small in magnitude, high in resistance and drawing little current, its electrical signature is heavily masked by higher currents associated with normal cell operation, which are typically many orders of magnitude higher. Further, a minor short (e.g., 1000 ohms) has essentially negligible impact on cell impedance characteristics (e.g., 1ppm at 1kHz on a cell with 1 mΩ internal resistance) unless impedance data are acquired at very low frequencies with accompanying lengthy acquisition times (e.g., hours or longer depending on cell characteristics). The default approach for detection of internal shorts is to monitor cell voltage over a sufficiently long period of time that voltage loss due to the internal short can be identified and sufficiently quantified (requiring, of course, that the cell is at rest and fully equilibrated). This engineering perspective, coupled with actual laboratory trials, led us to look for other means to achieve the sensitivity and rapidity of detection viewed as necessary for in-pack safety monitoring. In doing so, we identified reliable electrical signals that are obtained only when internal shorts are present in a cell. This knowledge has been utilized in the development of two distinct, non-invasive and chemistry-agnostic technologies for sensitive early detection of internal shorts in Li-ion batteries before the shorts pose a thermal runaway threat. We have advanced these technologies to the point that they are ready for implementation in battery systems. These technologies are based on extensive research into the underlying electrochemistry governing internal shorts, and on experience gained through safety audits of failures of Li-ion batteries in the field. They comprise hardware and software developed to acquire and interpret the specific electrical markers we have identified that indicate that internal shorts exist in a cell and deliver warning signals proportional to short severity. These technologies can be integrated with standard battery management electronics employed in Li-ion battery packs and provide early warning of incipient internal shorts that may lead to unsafe conditions.

Characteristics of internal shorts: We have been studying the nature and underlying electrochemistry of particle-induced internal shorts in lithium-ion cells for a number of years. Figure 1 depicts, in a generic manner, evolution of a fault that progresses to cell failure - thermal runaway, often accompanied by release of significant heat, sparks, flame, particulate matter, toxic and hot flammable gases, stage 3 in Figure 1. This heat release can drive neighboring cells to failure (stage 4) and, in the worst case, can progress to a large-scale fire or equipment damage in a process known as *cascading* or *propagation*, presenting catastrophic hazards to surrounding assets and to personnel. The evolution of a fault progressing to cell failure, as depicted in Figure 1, can be viewed in terms of four stages. First, the fault initiates. This fault could be the very first point of formation of, for example, an internal short resulting from Foreign Object Debris (FOD). In stage 1 the fault grows in severity until reaching stage 2 where the fault has become "critical" in that it is severe enough to trigger a thermal runaway. In stage 3, the cell exhibits thermal runaway, which may then result in cascading/propagation of the failure to adjacent cells (stage 4) and, potentially, the rest of the battery in a worst-case incident. The greatest opportunity to manage a fault in a cell, and avoid a catastrophic failure of even one cell, is obtained when the fault is detected at or near the point of initiation, where the fault is still small and harmless. Later detection (i.e., the longer one waits), increases risks. For example, waiting until a first cell actually fails at stage 3 (smoke, flame, etc.,), may not allow sufficient opportunity for productive intervention to avoid widespread violent failure.

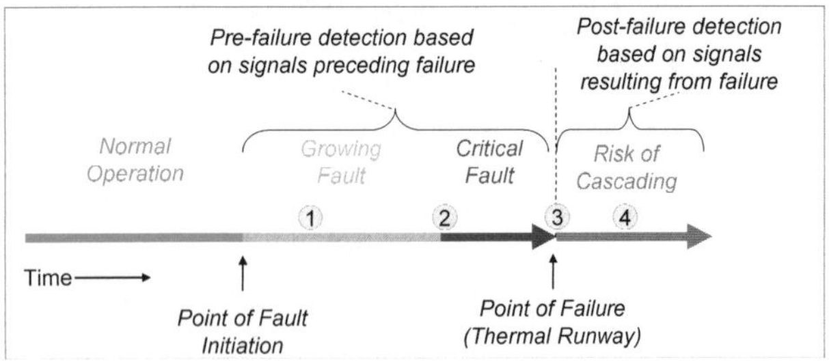

Figure 1. Representation of the timeline of a single-cell failure (thermal runaway) with subsequent risk of cascading of failure to other cells. CAMX Power technologies support pre-failure detection of faults in cells, i.e., stage 1, identifying a fault well before any cell gets "close" to thermal runaway, providing more time to implement preventive actions to suppress cascading of thermal runaway.

We have developed methodologies to reproduce particle-induced internal short-based cell failures in our laboratories, for commercial cells as well as our own 18650s. Using these methodologies, we have created well over 1000 particle-induced shorts in our laboratories under a variety of conditions. From this body of work, we have found that internal shorts typically progress through several phases, initiating as very minor cell faults of high resistance (thousands of ohms or more), growing slowly for a period of time, followed by a period of more rapid growth, sometimes abruptly, to higher severity (or runaway). Aspects of this pattern of short development are seen in the data shown in Figure 2. Internal short detection of utility to deliver enhanced safety profiles for in-pack monitoring applications requires sufficient sensitivity to identify shorts *before* they grow large enough to present an imminent threat of runaway and while productive intervention to avoid catastrophic cell failure is still possible.

We have developed two distinct technologies for in-pack monitoring of lithium-ion batteries for the presence of internal short circuits. The technologies are referred to as the Universal Detection Technology (UDT), so-named because of its applicability to batteries of any cell configuration, and the Real-time Detection Technology (RDT), which provides real-time monitoring for internal shorts whether the battery is at rest, being charged, or delivering power. Both technologies are chemistry agnostic (and demonstrated for a wide range of lithium-ion chemistry variants), functional over a wide range of temperature (demonstrated from -30°C to +55 °C to-date), and sensitive enough to detect internal shorts three orders of magnitude weaker in severity than the levels needed to trigger a thermal runaway.

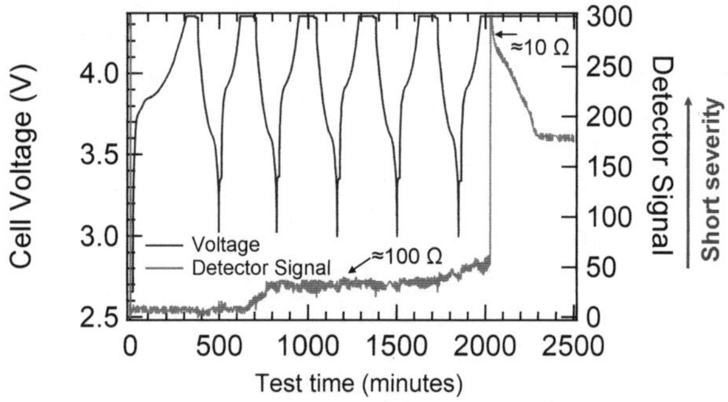

Figure 2. Cell voltage and output from our detection technologies monitoring a short created in a Li-ion cell by implantation of a metal particle. The detection signal (lower trace) shows the short initiate in the second cycle, grow to a moderate level (~ 100 Ω) for several cycles, and then abruptly spike to more dangerous levels (~ 10 Ω) in the sixth cycle

RDT offers real-time monitoring for the presence of internal short circuits and can operate continuously whether the battery is at rest, being charged, or delivering power, and successfully detects internal shorts even under demanding, complex and rapidly changing charge/discharge profiles. Implementation of RDT involves placement of a small number of sensors in the battery. UDT was developed in response to tight cost constraints encountered in discussions with major automotive manufacturers considering implementing internal short circuit detection in plug-in hybrid electric and other battery electric vehicle platforms. UDT offers the lowest cost and ease of implementation and can be integrated with existing battery management electronics designs, utilizing monitoring connections typically already in place in the form of cell/block voltage measurement connections. We now report UDT and RDT implementations for high cell count 18650 cell-based battery systems representative of lithium-ion power sources used in autonomous underwater vehicle applications.

UDT and RDT Implementations for a 100P Block-Based AUV Battery System

Figure 3 shows a sub-scale battery representative of a UAV battery based on blocks of 100 parallel 18650 cells. This 100-cell module was equipped with our present-generation standard UDT implementation. Internal short detection trials were conducted to demonstrate the functionality and efficacy of the UDT safety monitoring system. These trials included quantifying sensitivity of detection response as a function of short resistance as well as checking for cell position dependence of detection response. The latter test can be important because some battery designs create differing electrical environments at different positions within the cell array. In Figure 4, test data are shown for the response to internal shorts ranging from 50 to 500Ω in resistance. For reference, prior work in our laboratories (including experimentally validated finite element analysis modeling) has shown that the threshold for thermal runaway in an 18650 cell (in free air) is an internal short of about 4Ω. Thus, a short detected at the 500Ω level is over two orders of magnitude weaker than that required to trigger a thermal runaway. Data in Figure 5 show testing at each of the three potentially electrically distinct groups of cell locations. For this battery, no positional dependence was observed, and detection response was uniform across the battery.

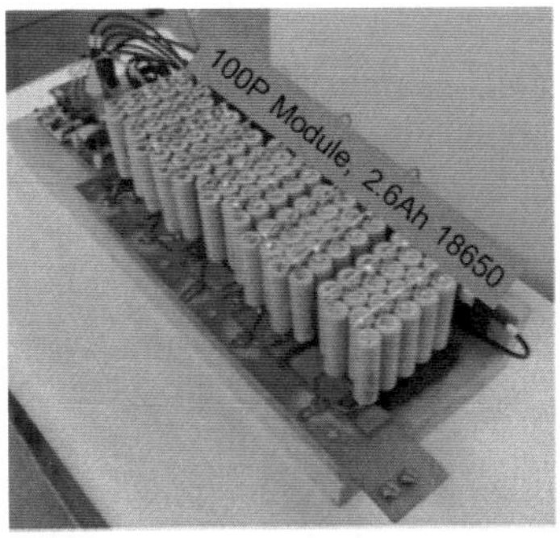

Figure 3. 100P battery based on 2.6Ah 18650 cells.

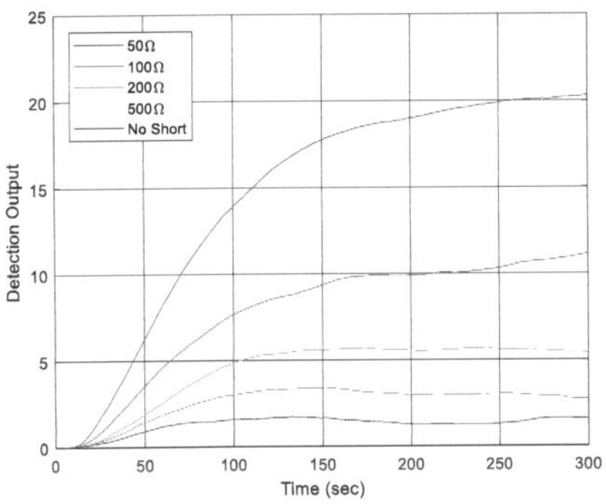

Figure 4. Test data (battery in Fig. 3) showing successful detection of internal shorts (simulated via electronic surrogates) for resistances ranging from 50 to 500Ω.

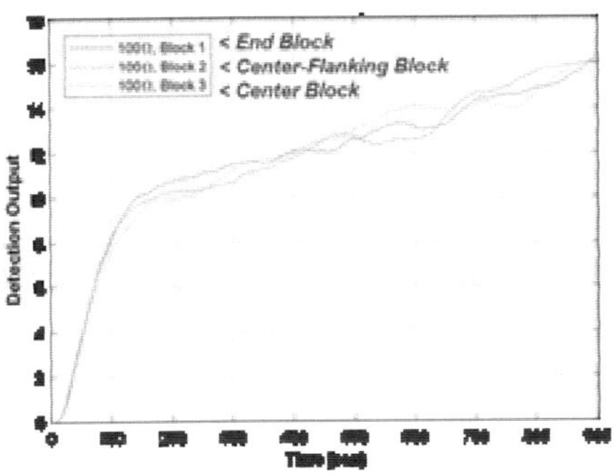

Figure 5. Test data (battery fig. 3) showing uniformity of response to a 100 ohm simulated short.

In a separate set of detection trials, the 100P battery was equipped with an RDT system. Detection trials were conducted in all battery states – rest, charge, and discharge. Figure 6 shows real-time response of the RDT system to 100Ω shorts applied to each of the five blocks of the 100P battery. The applied short is immediately detected with essentially uniform response at each position. Figure 7 shows real-time detection, with response scaling with short magnitude of three *simultaneously applied* shorts.

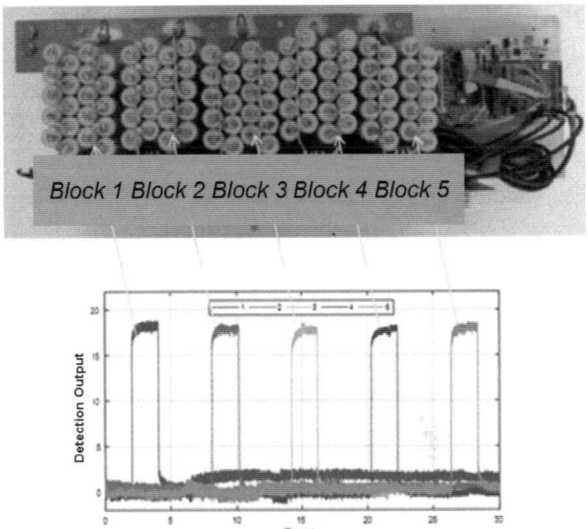

Figure 6. Test data for a 100P module equipped with our RDT system showing successful detection of 100Ω simulated shorts with testing at each block of cells.

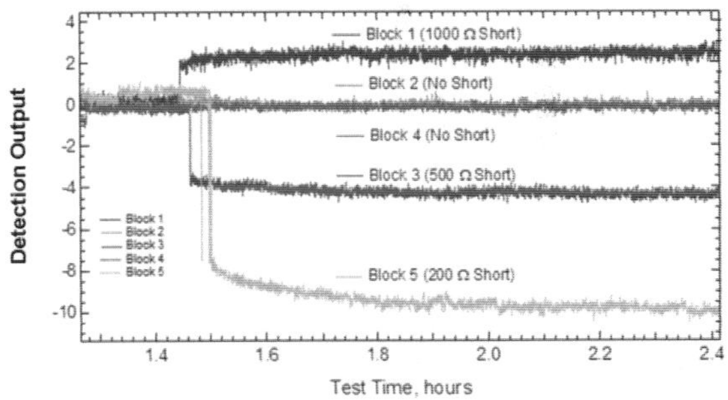

Figure 7. Test data for a 100P module equipped with our RDT system showing successful detection and independent quantification in real time of three simultaneously applied shorts.

The sensitivity and rapidity of detection illustrated by the data in Figures 6-8, including detection while the battery is actively cycling, are a function of the intrinsic capabilities of our RDT system enhanced by designing the specific implementation of the 100P battery with safety monitoring in mind. We have developed a set of general design principles to optimize sensitivity of our RDT safety monitoring system that, as we validated in testing of the battery under field-use charge-discharge protocols, are also entirely aligned with maximizing charge acceptance and power delivery of the battery, and with minimization of internal losses in the cell array.

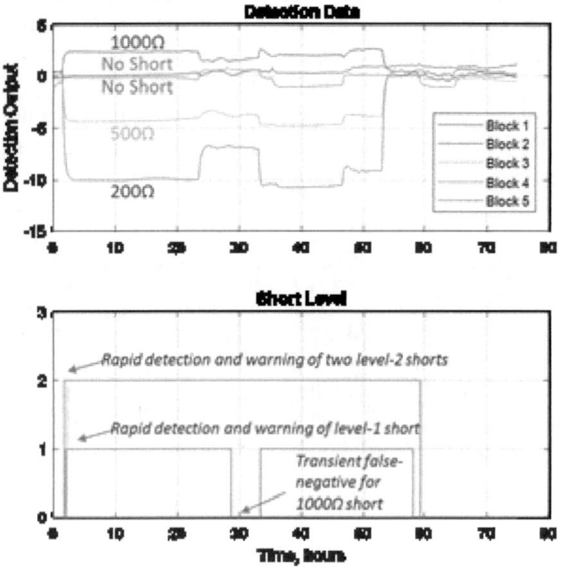

Figure 8. Test data for 100P RDT-equipped module showing successful real-time detection while the pack is actively cycling of three simultaneously applied shorts (200, 500, and 1000Ω). Cycling protocol (from ≈ hour 1 to 55): 13A (C/20) discharge with 100A, 1 minute pulses every 6 hours; 52A (C/5) charge. (top) Detection algorithm data. (bottom) Warning level output. Note that even with the battery actively cycling, only at the 1000Ω level is detection response to the short beginning to become intermittent.

Another example of UDT safety monitoring implemented in an AUV Battery System

Figure 9 shows test data demonstrating high-sensitivity detection of internal shorts as weak as 3000Ω in a AUV battery module of approximately 30 cells with mixed series-parallel connectivity. The design of this battery system differed significantly from our prior 100P example. Incorporation of additional electronics and the manner in which the cells were grouped in series-parallel connectivity created differences in electrical environment as a function of position within the cell array and circuitry. Recognizing this electrical variation, we tested detection sensitivity at each of the six electrically distinct environments within the battery. Not surprisingly, the differences in cell electrical environments affected detection response to some degree, as is evident in the data in Figure 9. However, in all cases, a simulated internal short of 3000Ω was definitively detected (i.e., gave rise to a detection response unambiguously distinct from the no-short condition) at all positions in the battery. The success of our UDT implementations in two markedly different battery systems illustrates the broad applicability of this technology.

Summary

The work we have described led to important advancements in our detection technologies including: (1) Successful extension of both internal short circuit detection technologies to high cell-count battery systems via development of the necessary technical understanding, performance models, and experimentally validated implementation guidelines; (2) Development of high-sensitivity implementations of internal short circuit detection technology expandable to battery systems of arbitrary size and cell count relevant to AUVs and many other applications; and (3) Design and implementation of a next-generation UDT and RDT hardware systems.

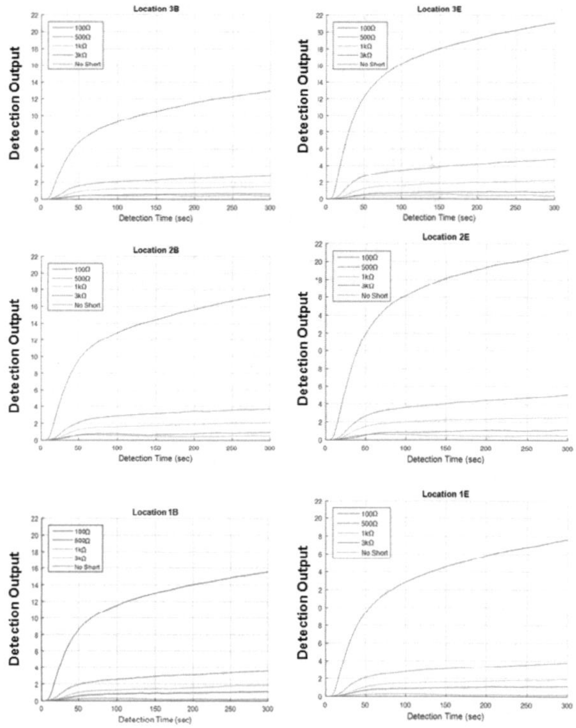

Figure 9. Test data for a UDT-equipped 18650 cell-based battery module showing successful detection of shorts as weak as 3,000Ω. The battery design inherently resulted in differences in local electrical environments as a function of cell position, resulting in some variation in detection response, as expected.

In conclusion, we have demonstrated that high cell count battery systems including those with highly parallel designs can be equipped with safety monitoring that delivers rapid, sensitive detection of internal short circuits well before such shorts reach levels posing imminent risk to the safety of a battery. We have demonstrated detection of shorts as weak as 3000Ω, and have demonstrated rapid, real-time detection of shorts to 1000Ω in an actively cycling 100-parallel cell battery.

Acknowledgements

The authors gratefully acknowledge support of the United States Navy (contracts N00024-16-C-4039 and N00024-16-P-4512) to develop adaptations of our detection technologies for Navy energy storage systems.

State-of-Health for Battery Strings with Rapid Multispectral Impedance Measurements

Jon P. Christophersen[1], Sergiy V. Sazhin[2], Chinh D. Ho[2], Christopher E. Hendricks[3]

[1]Dynexus Technology
Boulder CO 80503, USA

[2]Idaho National Laboratory
Idaho Falls, ID 83415

[3]University of Maryland
College Park, MD 20742, USA

Contact Author Email: jon.christophersen@dynexustech.com

Abstract: *Inline Rapid Impedance Spectroscopy (iRIS^{TM}) is a sensor that enables multispectral impedance measurements for onboard diagnostic applications. The purpose of this study was to assess the iRIS^{TM} tool as a noninvasive method for determining string health within a battery module. Three groups of single lithium-ion cells were subjected to accelerating aging protocols at different temperatures using both calendar- and cycle-life profiles. Aging was periodically stopped for performance assessments at the reference temperature. This included iRIS^{TM} measurements on each cell and various cell string configurations. The strings included series-connected "healthy" cells and a mixture of "healthy" and "faulty" cells, where faulty cells were aged at higher acceleration rates compared to the healthy ones. The results clearly demonstrated that strings with faulty cells show an increased impedance compared to healthy strings as a function of aging.*

Keywords: rapid; multispectral; impedance; cell stings; battery; state-of-health.

Introduction

The use of energy storage devices relies on accurate sensor technology to assess its performance, reliability, and remaining capability or life. Electrochemical impedance spectroscopy (EIS) is a well-established method to assess battery health. It usually consists of a sinusoidal excitation signal that covers a broad range of discrete frequencies and measures the battery response. A full spectral sweep can range from minutes to hours depending on system settings. The results from impedance measurements yield valuable information about the battery's characteristics and degradation as a function of time and use [1-2]. Due to the measurement duration, onboard applications of EIS have usually relied on either single frequency measurements or a small subset of targeted frequencies. These data can be used for internal core temperature estimation [3-4], safety and stability [5-6], or state of charge (SOC) and state of health (SOH) estimation [2, 7-9].

Inline Rapid Impedance Spectroscopy (iRIS^{TM}) techniques have recently been developed for near real-time monitoring and control [10-11]. It is based on a small, portable hardware platform that injects an excitation signal consisting of a sum of sinusoids at targeted frequencies and measures the system's response. The prototype iRIS^{TM} current excitation signal generally consists of harmonic sinusoids. Although previous studies used an octave harmonic separation [10-11], this study uses a "high-definition" excitation signal that includes non-octave harmonics. To ensure each frequency of interest has sufficient energy in the overall excitation signal, the number harmonics was limited to 28 discrete frequencies between 0.1 and 1638.4 Hz. The measurement duration is only one period of the lowest frequency (i.e., 10 seconds in this case). The voltage response of the battery is captured to determine the impedance as a function of frequency based on synchronous detection. With harmonic separation, each frequency of interest in the response can be treated independently with no crosstalk error [10-11]. Impedance spectra from iRIS^{TM} have been shown to match with conventional EIS instruments [10].

The iRIS^{TM} prototype sensor has been successfully validated on single cells and shows promise as an onboard diagnostic and prognostic tool. To meet onboard requirements, 50-V hardware platforms were developed for module-level applications. The goal of this work is to assess the capability of the prototype iRIS^{TM} 50-V platform to track aging on cell string architectures under different aging scenarios.

Experimental

Testing was performed with commercially available Sanyo 18650 high-power lithium-ion cells. They are rated at 1.25 Ah with a voltage range 2.5 to 4.2 V. A total of 10 cells were subjected to life aging at the specified conditions identified in Table 1. Six "A cells" were aged at a reference temperature of 30°C. Two "B cells" and two "C cells" were aged at elevated temperatures of 40 and 50°C, respectively. The cells were allowed to equilibrate at the designated temperature for at least 4 hours prior to testing.

Table 1. Cell test groups for aging

Group	# of Cells	Temperature
A	6	30°C
B	2	40°C
C	2	50°C

Aging was primarily based on the Plug-In Hybrid Electric Vehicle (PHEV) Manual developed for the U.S. Advanced Battery Consortium [12]. Accelerated life testing initially consisted of calendar aging at 60% state-of-charge (SOC) and the designated test temperature (Table 1). The cells rested at open-circuit conditions with a pulse per day to observe changes in the discharge and recharge resistances and to reset at 60% SOC [12]. After approximately six months of aging, the calendar-life test was switched to cycle-life using the same designated test temperatures to help accelerate some of the aging mechanisms. Rather than using the PHEV profile, the cells were subjected to 100% charge/discharge cycles with a 2C discharge rate. The cells were charged using the manufacturer's recommendation.

Immediately prior to the start of calendar-life aging, and approximately once a month during aging (i.e., every 32 days during calendar life, or after 300 full charge/discharge cycles), reference performance tests (RPTs) were conducted at 30°C to gauge degradation rates. As part of the RPT, iRIS™ measurements were conducted at 60% SOC on each cell and various string configurations based on a combination of cells from different aging groups. Table 2 shows the different string configurations of up to four cells. Reference conditions consist of healthy cell strings (i.e., only Group A cells during calendar aging). Faulty conditions consist of a combination of healthy cells and one cell that was subjected to harsher aging conditions. Note that parallel cell configurations were also considered, but the resolution of the existing iRIS™ prototype was not able to observe changes at the lower impedance. New, high-resolution system designs are being developed to address this issue in future studies.

Table 2. Various cell configurations for rapid impedance measurements

Measurement Type	Single or Series-Connected Cells
Single-cell measurement	A1, A2, A3, A4, A5, A6, B1, B2, C1, C2
2 Cell Series (same group conditions)	A5-A6; B1-B2; C1-C2
2 Cell Series (different group conditions)	A6-B1; A6-C1
3 Cell Series (same group conditions)	A4-A5-A6
3 Cell Series (different group conditions)	A4-A5-B2; A4-A5-C2
4 Cell Series (same group conditions)	A1-A2-A3-A4
4 Cell Series (different group conditions)	A1-A2-A3-B2; A1-A2-A3-C2

Results

Rapid impedance spectra at the beginning of aging (RPT1) and at the end of aging (RPT12) for a representative cell from Group A are shown in Figure 1. For analytical purposes, several metrics are considered, including ohmic resistance (R_{Ω}), charge transfer resistance (R_{CH_TR}) and total resistance (R_{TOTAL}) which is a sum of R_{Ω} and R_{CH_TR}. These metrics are identified in Figure 1 for the RPT12 spectrum. The values for all impedance metrics increase with cell age under both calendar- and cycle-life protocols. R_{CH_TR} increases more than R_{Ω}, which is consistent with previously reported results [4].

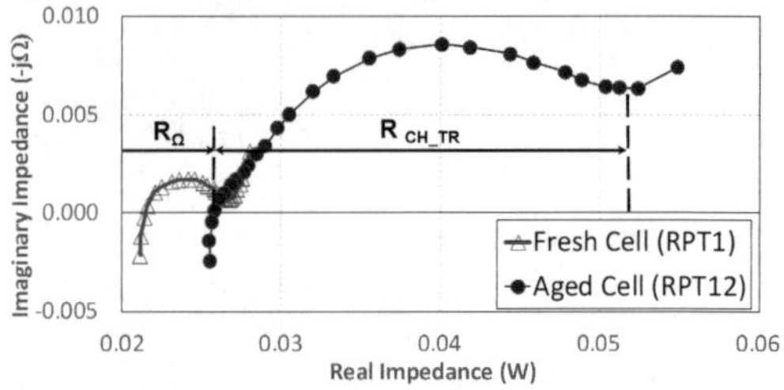

Figure 1. Impedance spectra for cell A6 (fresh and aged)

Figure 2 shows the total resistance (R_{TOTAL}) as a function of both calendar- and cycle-life aging for a representative cell from each temperature group in Table 1. Calendar aging yielded linear degradation rates with an obviously higher rate at 50°C. These trends are consistent with Belt et. al. who reported increased degradation rates for elevated temperatures using a similar cell chemistry based on standard PHEV metrics (i.e., capacity fade and pulse resistance) [13]. When the cells were switched to cycling at RPT7, the degradation rate remained relatively linear, but the 50°C rate slowed down and the 30°C rate increased significantly. Belt also noted increased degradation rates at 30°C and slower resistance growth at elevated temperatures during charge depletion cycling [13].

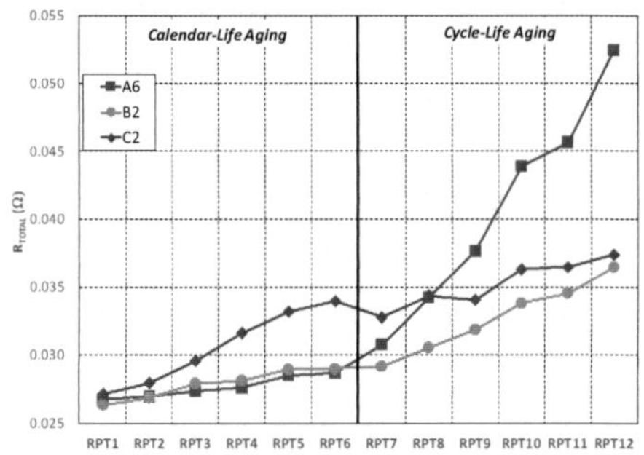

Figure 2. Rapid total impedance at 60% SOC for cells in different age groups.

Table 3 summarizes the percent-change in impedance rise for calendar- and cycle-life aging, respectively. Calendar-life is based on impedance growth from RPT1 to RPT6; cycle-life is the impedance growth between RPT7 and RPT12. The R_{CH_TR} constituent shows a higher percent-growth than R_{Ω} at each condition regardless of temperature or aging condition. Under calendar-life conditions, all three impedance types (R_{TOTAL}, R_{Ω}, and R_{CH_TR}) increase with increasing temperature. However, when the cells were switched to cycle-life aging after RPT6, the reverse effect is observed and the impedance growth reduces with increasing temperature. Hence, transitioning from calendar-life to cycle-life at RPT6 for these cells fundamentally changes the mechanism of aging [13].

Table 3. Rate of impedance increase under aging

Type	Calendar-LifeAging (%)			Cycle-Life Aging (%)		
	A	B	C	A	B	C
R_{TOT}	6.5	12.3	24.9	73.7	25.5	16.4
R_{Ω}	1.9	8.9	21.0	17.0	13.3	12.0
R_{CH_TR}	25.7	27.0	40.8	234.1	72.9	36.2

Nevertheless, the purpose of this study is to evaluate the capability of the iRIS™ sensor to detect a faulty cell within a string. A cell is considered faulty if it has a higher impedance. This approach simulates a scenario where some cells in a pack undergo accelerated degradation compared to neighboring cells (e.g., due to thermal imbalance or an internal soft short). Figure 3(a) depicts results for 2-, 3- and 4-cell serial connections of A and C cells during calendar-life aging. From Figure 2, the C cell impedance is higher than the A cells under calendar life conditions. Thus, low-impedance (i.e., healthy) strings would only consist of A cells, whereas faulty strings would include one or more C cells. As shown in Figure 3(a), the strings with faulty cells show higher overall impedance compared to the corresponding healthy strings in all cases.

The C cells showed significantly slower degradation rates compared to the A cells once the aging protocol was switched to cycling. Figure 3(b) shows the same string connections during cycling. As expected, the C cells now show lower impedances. When A cells are included in the string, the overall impedance increases in all cases.

The impedance of the A cells is also significantly higher than the B cells during cycling (Figure 2), especially at the end of aging (RPT12). Figure 4 shows string comparisons between the A and B cells during cycle-life aging. In this case, the B cells are healthy and the A cells are faulty. As with Figure 3, the strings with faulty cells can be easily detected. They have a higher rapid impedance measurement response compared to the strings with healthy cells or at least one healthy cell among the faulty cells.

Results in Figures 3 and 4 demonstrate that strings with a cell(s) having advanced degradation can be readily identified from the R_{TOTAL} measurement. The constituents of R_{TOTAL} (i.e., R_{Ω}, and R_{CH_TR}) could also be used as detection metrics and, in some cases (depending on chemistry, etc.), may provide better results.

Discussion

Results from this study demonstrate that a rapid multispectral impedance measurement may be an effective and noninvasive method to quickly identify strings within a module that have faulty cells. Note, however, that this approach requires isolating strings within the module architecture (e.g., [14]). The approach would also greatly benefit from higher resolution, especially for parallel-connected cell configurations. Conceptual designs for a high-resolution iRIS™ have been developed to enable higher sensitivity and better detection of cell imbalance and/or faulty cells in future studies. This upgrade should enable accurate impedance measurements for parallel configurations that are less than a milliohm. It also includes new analysis programs that enable non-harmonic excitation signals to provide more detail within frequency regions of interest.

For this study, the same equipment was used to evaluate cell configurations with voltages ranging from approximately 4V (single cell) to 16V (4-cell string). Thus, the same system can be used to identify an anomalous operation at the module level, and, with appropriate wiring, identify key faulty cells within the module. This identification coupled with intelligent battery management systems would allow safe and hassle-free operation of battery architectures.

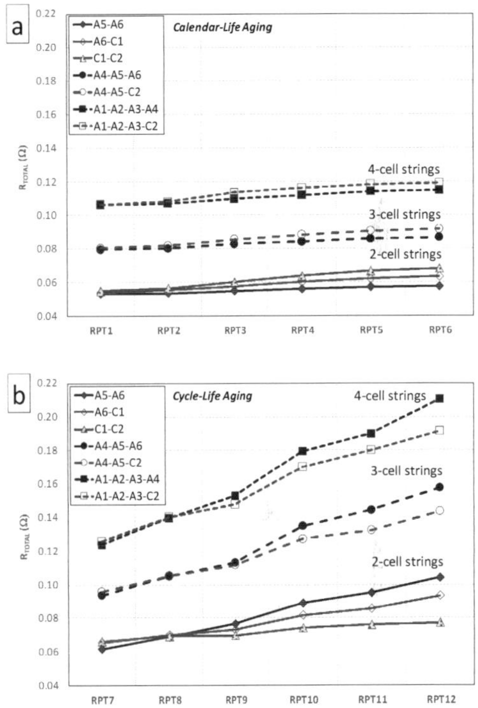

Figure 3. Rapid total impedance for 2-, 3- and 4-cell series connections for (a) calendar- and (b) cycle-life conditions.

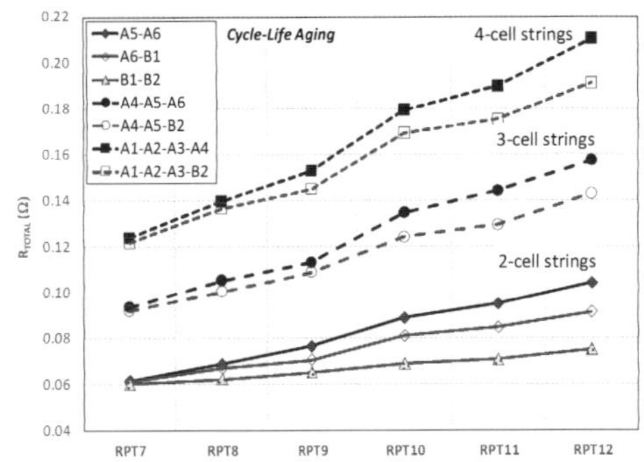

Figure 4. Rapid total impedance for 2-, 3- and 4-cell series connections cycle-life conditions.

Conclusion

Inline Rapid Impedance Spectroscopy (iRIS™) is a non-invasive method that could be helpful in determining aging or state-of-health of single cells and cell strings. Rapid impedance measurements can be performed in several seconds rather than in minutes or hours for conventional impedance measurements. The prototype 50-V iRIS™ platform was applied to strings where at least one cell was aged at a different rate. The results clearly indicated an increased impedance when faulty cells were included.

The iRIS™ sensor is useful for studying aging mechanisms under different operating conditions. It is generally applicable to any battery chemistry and design, though the required measurement frequencies may need adjusting. The method and associated hardware could be used as an onboard application for electric drive vehicles, stationary energy storage, military and aeronautic purposes, maritime applications, and portable electronic devices. Another promising application of this method may be as a diagnostic tool for the first responders on electric drive vehicles accidents or for grid storage and other battery-related accidents.

Acknowledgements

Funding was provided from Vehicle Technologies Office of the Energy Efficiency and Renewable Energy Office of the U.S. Department of Energy. This manuscript has been authored by Battelle Energy Alliance, LLC under Contract No. DE-AC07-05ID14517 with the U.S. Department of Energy. The United States Government retains and the publisher, by accepting the article for publication, acknowledges that the United States Government retains a nonexclusive, paid-up, irrevocable, world-wide license to publish or reproduce the published form of this manuscript, or allow others to do so, for United States Government purposes. The authors wish to thank Dr. Eric Dufek (INL) and Dr. John Morrison (Montana Tech) for constructive comments toward the preparation of this paper.

References

1. Christophersen, J. P., et. al., "Electrochemical impedance spectroscopy testing on the Advanced Technology Development Program lithium-ion cells," *Proceedings of the IEEE Vehicular Technology Conference*, Vancouver, Canada, Sept. 24-28, 2002, pp. 1851-1851.
2. Huang, W., and J. A. Abu Qahouq, "An Online Battery Impedance Measurement Method Using DC–DC Power Converter Control," *IEEE Transactions on Industrial Electronics*, vol. 61, no. 11, pp. 5987-5995, 2014.
3. Beelen, H.P.G.J., et. al., "A comparison and accuracy analysis of impedance-based temperature estimation methods for Li-ion batteries," *Applied Energy*, vol. 175, pp. 128-140, 2016.
4. Zhu, J. G., et. al., "A new lithium-ion battery internal temperature on-line estimate method based on electrochemical impedance spectroscopy measurement," *J. Power Sources*, vol. 274, pp. 990-1004, 2015.
5. Lamb, J., et. al., "Determination of battery stability with advanced diagnostics," SAND2017-6959, July 2017.
6. Love, C. T., and K. Swider-Lyons, "Battery Health Monitoring System and Method," US 9,465,077 B2, October 2016.
7. Singh, P., C. Fennie Jr., and D. E. Reisner, "Method and System for Determining State-of-Health of a Nickel-Metal Hydride Battery using an Intelligent System," US 7,051,008 B2, May 2006.
8. Tachibana, K., and K. Matsuki, "Development of in situ a.c. impedance measurement system under constant-current conditions and its application to galvanostatic discharge of electrolytic manganese dioxide in alkaline solution," *J. Power Sources*, vol. 74, no. 1, pp. 29-33, 1998.
9. Burkum, M. E., and C. M. Gabriel, "Apparatus and Method for Measuring Battery Condition," US 4,697,134, Sept. 1987.
10. Christophersen, J. et. al., "Rapid Impedance Spectrum Measurements for State-of-Health Assessment of Energy Storage Devices," *SAE Int. J. Passeng. Cars - Electron. Electr. Syst.*, vol. 5, no. 1, pp. 246-256, 2012.
11. Christophersen, J. et. al., "Long-Term Validation of Rapid Impedance Spectrum Measurements as a Battery State-of-Health Assessment Technique,," *SAE Int. J. Alt. Power*, vol. 2, no. 1, pp. 146-155, 2013.
12. "Battery Test Manual for Plug-In Hybrid Electric Vehicles", Revision 1, INL-EXT -07-12536, 2010.
13. Belt, J., V. Utgikar, and I. Bloom, "Calendar and PHEV cycle life aging of high-energy, lithium-ion cells containing blended spinel and layered-oxide cathodes," *J. Power Sources*, vol. 196, no. 23, pp. 10213-10221, 2011.
14. Christophersen, J. P., et. al., "Apparatuses and Methods for Testing Electrochemical Cells by Measuring Frequency Response," US 2014/0358462 A1, December 2014.

Development of a Nonflammable Electrolyte for Li-Ion Batteries

Christopher M. Lang, Peter D. Moran, Jake T. Herb
Physical Sciences Inc.
20 New England Business Center
Andover, MA USA 01810-1077
lang@psicorp.com / 1-978-738-8125

Abstract: *Safe, high performance lithium ion batteries are required to power next generation technologies. However, increasing a battery's energy density tightens the required build tolerances and utilization of flammable electrolytes increases the potential for catastrophic system failure. This presentation will discuss Physical Sciences Inc.'s efforts to develop an electrolyte that increases battery safety. PSI will show that the electrolyte developed is non-flammable as a liquid, aerosol, and on ejection from a cell following formation and cycling. Electrochemical test data will highlight that efficient cycling performance can be achieved. Finally, the impact of the PSI electrolyte on cell safety under abuse conditions will be discussed.*

Keywords: Lithium ion; non-flammable electrolyte; safety; abuse tolerance.

Introduction

Rechargeable lithium ion batteries are the preferred option to meet the energy and power density requirements of current and next generation electric vehicles. However, these batteries typically utilize flammable electrolytes that can ignite and initiate violent battery failure under abuse conditions. Non-flammable electrolytes are required to prevent catastrophic failure.

PSI has developed a non-flammable electrolyte that enables efficient cycling performance and does not ignite as a liquid, aerosol, or on ejection from a cell (see Figure 1). The subsequent section briefly outlines the tests carried out to date by PSI to demonstrate this technology. The conference talk will provide more detail on the tests performed and the results achieved.

Overview of Presentation

In order for an electrolyte to be used in a lithium ion battery it must support stable SEI formation and efficient reversible lithium ion insertion and removal from the anode and cathode. PSI has identified a quick screening method to determine the feasibility of using various ionic liquids (ILs) together with conventional electrolytes in lithium ion cells to form a non-flammable electrolyte. Testing demonstrated the need for additives and a modified formation technique to enable stable cycling and the successful use of ILs. Using these developed techniques PSI has demonstrated equivalent performance of conventional and IL based electrolytes as shown in Figure 2. PSI has also demonstrated extended stable cycling performance as shown in Figure 3 and enhanced power at room temperatures.

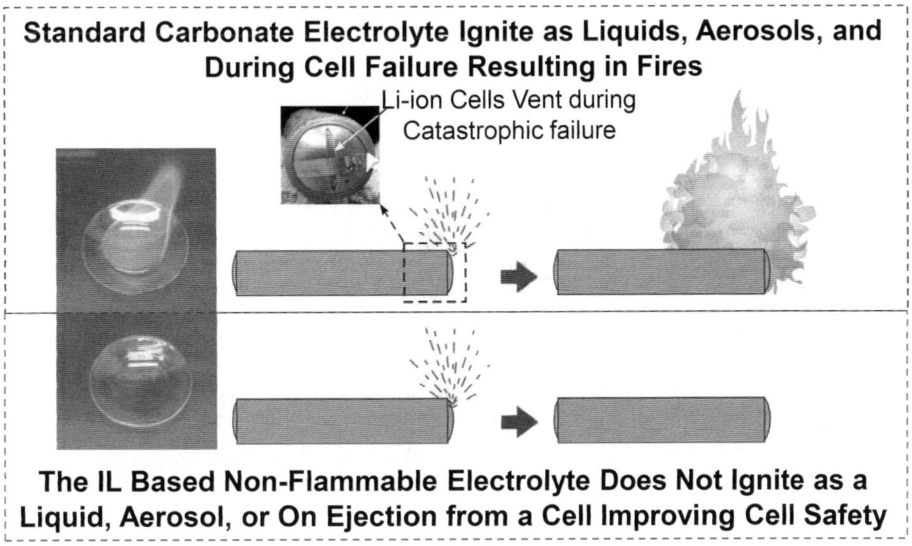

Figure 1. PSI's non-flammable electrolyte increases cell safety.

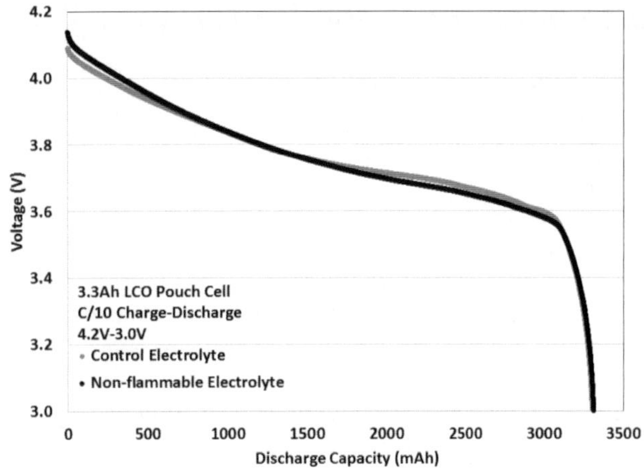

Figure 2. PSI non-flammable electrolyte (Black) delivers equivalent performance to control carbonate electrolyte (Blue) during C/10 cycling.

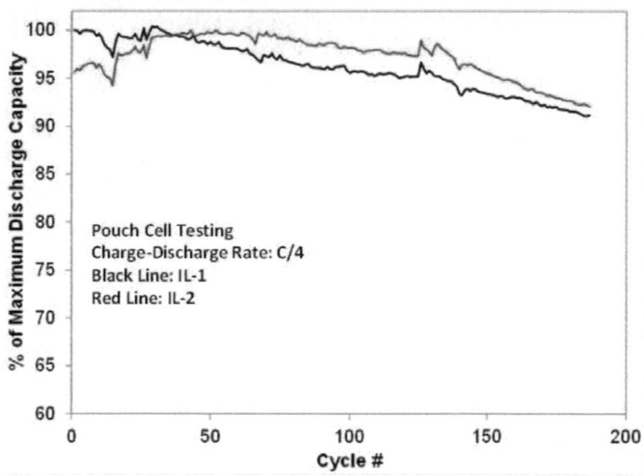

Figure 3. Stable performance on extended cycling using the non-flammable electrolyte.

In addition to a review of the electrochemical testing, PSI will present the results of safety abuse testing. Testing demonstrated that the PSI is non-flammable as a liquid, aerosol, and on ejection from a cycled cell (see Figure 4). The conference talk will provide additional information on these tests and other tests carried out to demonstrate the abuse tolerance and electrochemical performance of the PSI electrolyte.

Acknowledgments

This material is based upon work supported by the United States Air Force under Contract Numbers FA8650-15-C-2553 and FA8650-14-M-2489. Any opinions, findings and conclusions or recommendations expressed in this material are those of the author(s) and do not necessarily reflect the views of the United States Air Force.

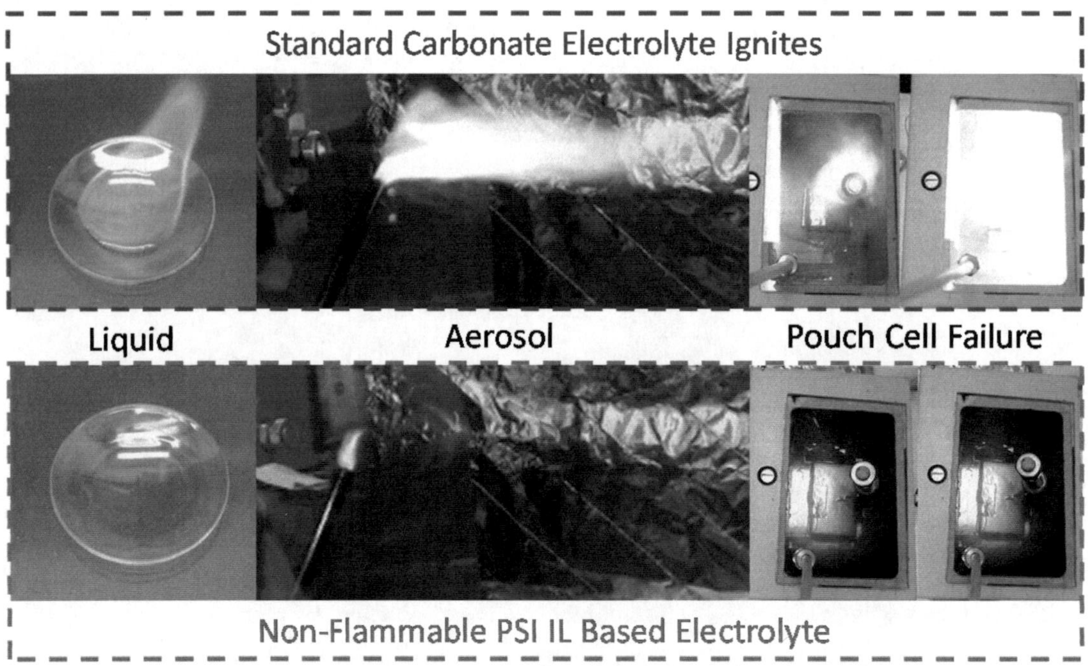

Figure 4. The PSI non-flammable electrolyte does not ignite as a liquid, aerosol, or on ejection from a cell, improving cell safety.

Failure Analysis During Mechanical Abuse of Lithium Ion Batteries

Jane Rempel[a], Richard Stringfellow[b], Sam Hui[b], Jacky Lau[b], Suresh Sriramulu[a] and Brian Barnett[a]
[a]CAMX Power, 35 Hartwell Avenue, Lexington, MA 02421; [b]TIAX LLC, 35 Hartwell Avenue, Lexington, MA 02421
e-mail: rempel.jane@camxpower.com, phone: (781)879-1238

Abstract: *Understanding Li-ion cell response to mechanical abuse scenarios is critical to understanding cell safety. In this paper we discuss the time scale for internal short circuit formation under different abuse scenarios and the resulting thermal response of the cell. We discuss response to mechanical abuse of 18650 and 26650 cells with different cathode chemistries. We present FEA modeling results that combine a dynamic stress/displacement model with an electrical/thermal model to better understand cell response to mechanical abuse.*

Keywords: Li-ion, lithium ion, 18650; abuse testing;

Introduction

High specific and volumetric energy and power density of lithium-ion batteries has made them the technology of choice for a number of DoD applications. However, this high energy content also leads to safety concerns regarding Li-ion battery use. Indeed, such safety concerns are limiting the widespread use of Li-ion batteries in many DoD applications. Under certain triggers and electrical or mechanical abuse scenarios, Li-ion cells can undergo thermal runaway, i.e., a rapid increase in cell temperature accompanied by venting, vent-with-flame, ejection of cell parts, fire and explosion. Formation of internal short circuits, either spontaneously in the field from metal contaminants or during abuse (e.g. nail penetration, mechanical crush or impact), results in heat dissipation via IR heating both at the location of the short and throughout the cell. Based on our previous FEA modeling of internal shorts, if the power dissipation in the short is sufficient to raise the local temperature of the cell above the decomposition temperature of the components (anode, cathode, and electrolyte), exothermic reactions are initiated and, in the worse cases, can lead to a thermal runaway event.

An improved understanding of the processes underlying initiation of thermal runaway from mechanical abuse (such as penetration, impact, crush, etc.) is needed to make significant improvements in Li-ion battery safety. We have previously carried out detailed work employing a combination of well-controlled testing, high-speed photography, and FEA modeling to understand the progression to thermal runaway following nail penetration.[i] Here, we describe more recent work related to mechanical abuse of Li-ion cells.

CAMX Power, in collaboration with its affiliated company TIAX, has designed, fabricated, and installed two specially designed test stations for mechanical crush and impact. These test stations incorporate instrumentation that allows us to obtain an improved understanding of the electrical and thermal response of Li-ion cells to mechanical deformation. The custom-made impact test station includes temperature, voltage, and acceleration monitoring along with high-speed video capture (Figure 1). The test station is designed such that the size, weight, shape, and drop height of the impactor can be adjusted. Similarly, the custom-made battery crush test station includes temperature, voltage, displacement and force monitoring along with high-speed video capture (Figure 2). The crush test station can be set up to carry out both traditional UL-based flat plate crush as well as a slow crush with a round bar. The ability to capture high speed video and acquire detailed information on cell voltage allows us to accurately determine the time scale for electrical shorting and resulting thermal response.

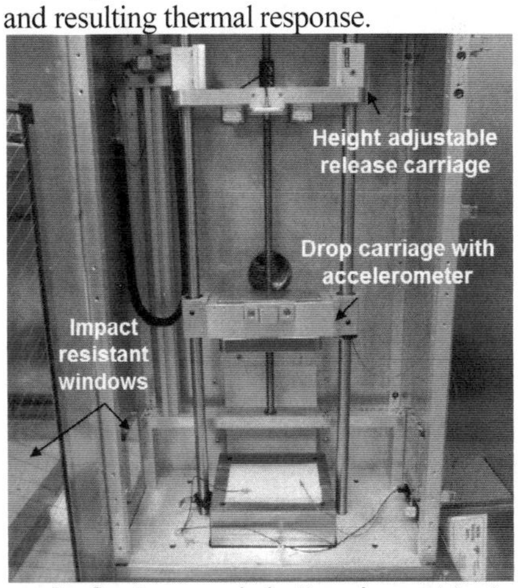

Figure 1. Custom-made battery impact tester that includes temperature, voltage, and acceleration monitoring along with high speed video capture.

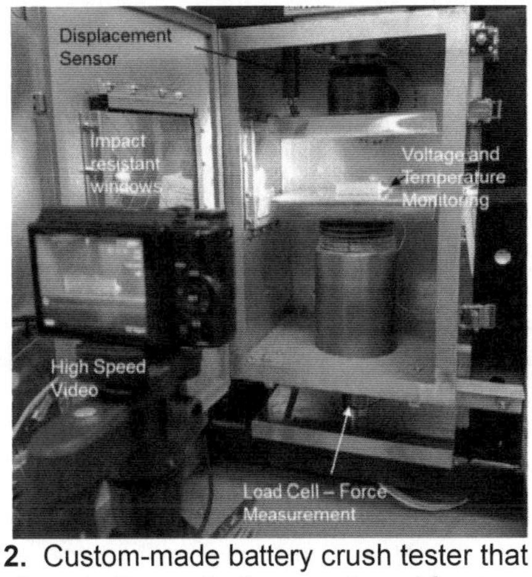

Figure 2. Custom-made battery crush tester that includes temperature, voltage, displacement, and force monitoring along with high speed video capture.

Table 1. Summary of observations for mechanical abuse testing of commercial 2.6Ah 18650 cells. Slow crush with a round bar results in a more violent thermal event than other mechanical abuse tests like flat plate crush and impact.

2.6Ah Commercial 18650 Cells	Shorting Time Scale	Event
Crush test (flat plate, ~25kN)	None	- No voltage drop or temperature rise
Round bar crush (5/8" diameter, <13kN)	100ms	- Localized heating at the short leading to thermal runaway - Sparks and fire; rupture of the cell casing
Impact test (20lb, 2ft, 5/8" diameter)	5ms	- Cell temperature began to increase in ~1s - Cell heating to ~120°C over ~35s (uniform resistive heating) - Followed by separator shutdown and voltage recovery

Comparison of Mechanical Abuse Scenarios

Comparisons of the electrical and thermal response of commercial 2.6Ah 18650 cells to different mechanical abuse scenarios are shown in Table 1. For example, commercial cells easily pass the UL specified flat plate crush and impact tests, with no voltage drop or temperature rise during flat plate crush test. We observed slow cell heating but no violent thermal event during impact testing. On the other hand, slow crush with a round bar results in a violent thermal runaway. We are exploring the relationship of such results to features of 18650 cells by fabricating custom-designed 18650 cells on our cell prototyping line.

Flat Plate Crush

Crushing a fully charged 2.6Ah 18650 cell under 13kN UL target force results in ~20% deformation but does not lead to any cell shorting or cell heating. Increasing the force further to >20kN (greater than maximum measurable by the load cell in our crush tester), led to net deformation by ~25% with no shorting or temperature rise. Measured displacement (i.e. cell deformation) as a function of applied force and the cell's voltage and thermal response are shown in Figure 3.

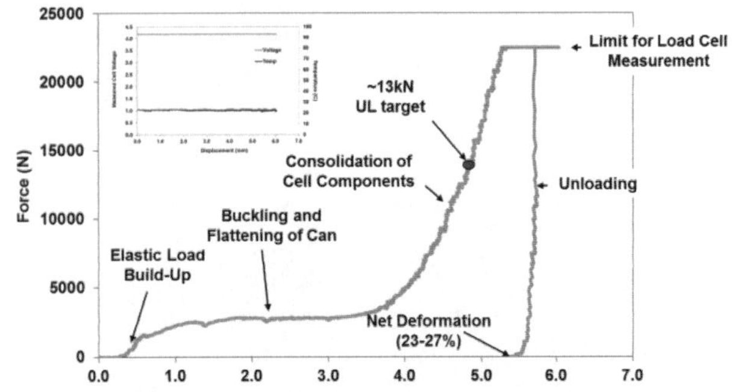

Figure 3. Flat plate crush of a 2.6Ah commercial 18650 cell charged to 4.2V. Measured cell deformation as a function of applied force. Inset shows voltage and temperature profiles as a function of displacement.

Round Bar Crush

We also carried out slow crush experiments using a round bar positioned across an 18650 cell. Unlike uniform flat plate crush, localized slow deformation of a 2.6Ah commercial 18650 leads to cell shorting and a violent thermal runaway event with fire and rupture of the 18650 can (Figure 4). Data acquired during a round bar crush experiment show that cell shorting proceeds over approximately 100ms (Figure 5), followed by cell heating (detected 1s after initial voltage drop) and eventually thermal runaway that results in cell rupture. Note that we observe similar time scale for shorting in nail penetration tests that can result in thermal runaway events.

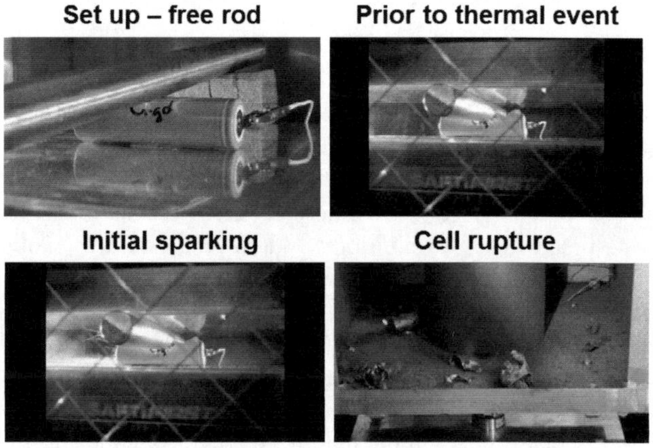

Figure 4. Round bar crush of a fully charged 2.6Ah commercial 18650 cell that results in violent thermal runaway with fire and rupture of the cell casing.

Impact Test

We also carried out impact testing following the UL specification wherein a 20lb weight is dropped onto the cell from a height of 2ft, with a 5/8" diameter round bar positioned over the 18650 cell, with its axis perpendicular to that of the cell. Unlike the UL test, we also instrumented the drop weight with an accelerometer that allows us to determine the precise time of impact and the dynamic force-displacement response of the cell. Note that results of the UL test can depend on the positioning of the round bar and the 18650 cell. To minimize the interaction between the drop mass and the 5/8" bar, we replaced the bar with a mounted impactor having the same diameter (Figure 6). Note that the mounted impactor did not change the voltage or thermal response observed during testing. In all cases, during an impact test of a fully charged 2.6Ah 18650 cell we observed formation of a hard short within 5ms of impact, followed by slow uniform cell heating to ~120°C followed by separator shutdown, slow cool down and voltage recovery (Figure 6).

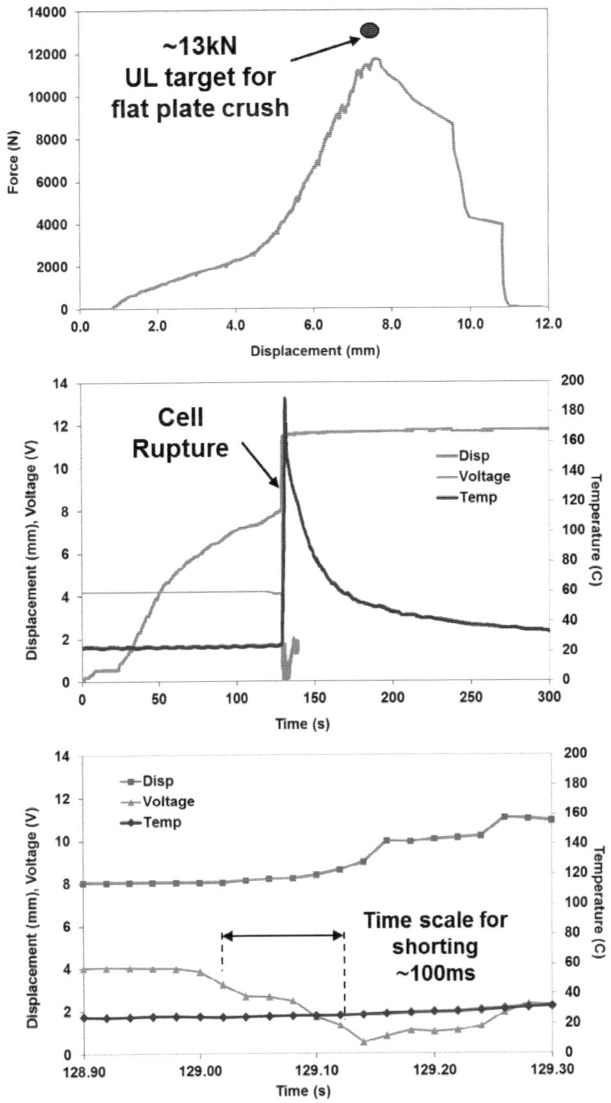

Figure 5. Round bar crush of a fully charged 2.6Ah commercial 18650 cell results in cell shorting during approximately 100ms followed by thermal runaway. Note that temperature rise is only observed ~1s after initial voltage drop. Top: cell displacement as a function of applied force. Middle/Bottom: displacement, voltage, and surface temperature as a function of time.

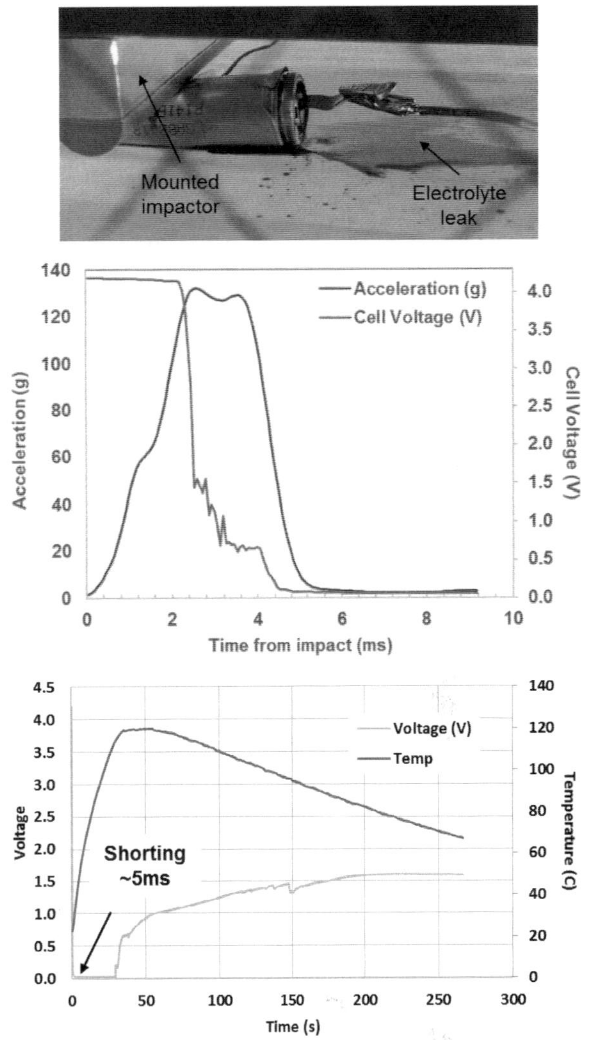

Figure 6. Time scale analysis of cell shorting during an impact test (20lb weight, 2ft height, 5/8" diameter impactor). Cell shorts in <5ms followed by delayed onset of temperature rise (detected after 1s following impact) with slow cell heating to ~120°C followed by separator shutdown and voltage recovery. Typical maximum displacement of ~25% with only one cell experiencing electrolyte leaking (40% displacement).

Table 2. Summary of observations for mechanical abuse testing of different commercial 26650 cells.

26650 Cell Type	**Crush test (flat plate, ~13kN)**	**Round bar crush (5/8" diameter, <13kN)**	**Impact test (20lb, 2ft, 5/8" diameter)**
2.5Ah Commercial LFP 26650	No voltage drop or temperature rise. (12% displacement)	Cell venting with sparks and smoke.	Slow voltage drop over ~10min accompanied by uniform slow cell heating to ~5°C above ambient. (18% displacement)
4Ah Commercial NCM-111* 26650	Cell shorting, slow temperature rise of ~30°C above ambient in ~7 minutes. (12% displacement)	Voltage drop but no temperature rise.	No voltage drop or temperature rise. (21% displacement)
5Ah Commercial NCM-622* 26650	Cell shorting, temperature rise of ~30°C above ambient in ~1 minute. (13% displacement)	No voltage drop or temperature rise.	No voltage drop or temperature rise. (22% deformation)

Mechanical Abuse Testing 26650 vs. 18650 Cell Size

We tested several different cathode materials (including NCA, NCM) in 18650 cells produced in CAMX Power cell prototyping facility. In all cases, we observed the most violent thermal runaway behavior with a slow round bar crush. Impact testing resulted in benign failure that produced hard shorting with slow cell heating to ~120°C. We also evaluated different commercial 26650 cells under a variety of mechanical abuse scenarios. A summary of the results is shown in Table 2. During impact and round bar crush abuse scenarios, deformation of the 26650 cells resulted in significantly less severe thermal response than the 18650 cells across the various cathode chemistries.

Modeling Thermal Response to Mechanical Abuse

To get a better understanding of the cell response during mechanical abuse, we developed a mechanical FEA model and coupled it with our previously developed electrical/thermal cell model. The model simulates 18650 cell response during impact, allowing us to identify regions of the cell where internal shorts are likely to form. The distribution of maximum principal strain following impact is shown in Figure 7. Areas of highest strain are most likely to experience electrode tearing that can lead to shorting. Cell geometry based on the mechanical simulation of impact test was used as an input to our electrical/thermal model that includes uniform IR heating in the cell bulk, localized IR heating in the short volume, and thermal decomposition reactions with electrolyte for the anode and cathode electrodes. Comparison of the thermal FEA model predictions to the measured temperature rise in the commercial 2.6Ah 18650 cell is shown in Figure 8. Modeled temperature at the cell edge (where the thermocouple is usually positioned during testing) is in close agreement with the experiments.

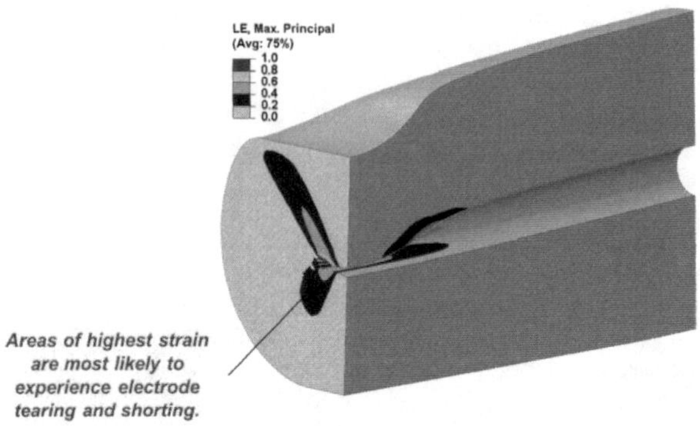

Figure 7. FEA model of mechanical deformation during round bar impact of the 18650 cell. Strain analysis shown.

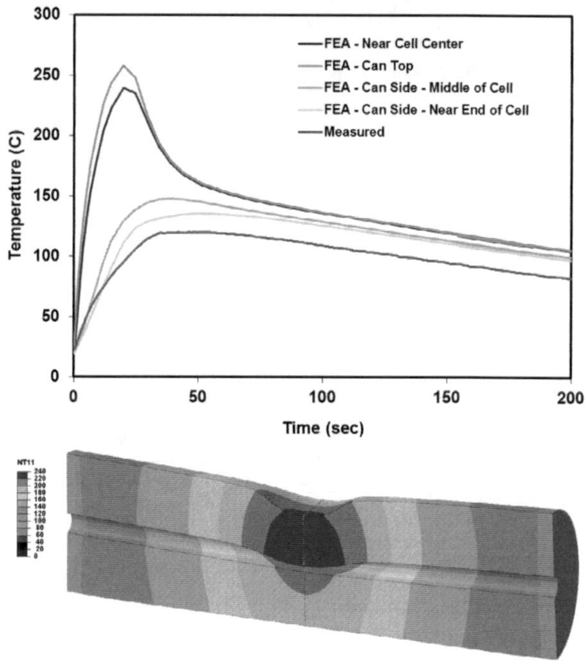

Figure 8. Top: comparison of the FEA model predictions of the cell temperature vs. measured values. Bottom: temperature profile when temperature reaches maximum.

Summary

A combination of custom-built highly instrumented test equipment, FEA modeling, and our ability to fabricate Li-ion cells (18650 and pouch designs) is leading to an improved understanding of thermal runaway of Li-ion cells following mechanical abuse. Our work to date indicates that the thermal response of a cell to mechanical abuse strongly depends on the nature of the internal short circuits that form within the cell on impact. Low resistance hard shorts that form during high velocity impact result in mostly uniform heat dissipation and benign cell failure. However, slow localized crushing leads to short formation that can result in primarily localized cell heating at the site of the short that can allow for enough local heat dissipation to set off the exothermic thermal decomposition reactions of cell components leading to thermal runaway.

Acknowledgements

We gratefully acknowledge financial support for some of the work presented in this document from the U.S. Army under Contract No. W911QX-15-C-0020.

---

[i] B. Barnett, S. Sriramulu, R. Stringfellow, C. McCoy, and D. Ofer, "Mechanisms of Safety, Predictions of Impending Thermal Runaway and Integrity of Safety Testing," 16th International Meeting on Lithium Batteries (IMLB-16), Jeju Island, Korea, June 2012.

IPOWER: Dismounted Soldier Energy Analysis and Mission Planning Tools

Richard O. Stroman[1], Christopher Buesser[4], Eric Leadbetter[2], Daniel Milliken[5] and José Collazo[3]

[1]Chemistry Div. and [2]Information Technology Div., U.S. Naval Research Laboratory, Washington DC, 20375

[3]Communications-Electronics Research, Development, and Engineering Center, Aberdeen Proving Gnd. MD 21005

[4]Excet Inc., 6225 Brandon Ave Ste 360, Springfield, VA 22150 [5]GTS LLC, Wall Township NJ 07727

Abstract: *The U.S. Naval Research Laboratory began working with the US Army Research Development and Engineering Command, Communications-Electronics Research, Development and Engineering Center in 2014 to simulate how Soldiers use energy. Several tools have resulted from this collaboration and the most recent is IPOWER: Intelligent Power Optimization with Environmental Reactivity. IPOWER combines earlier efforts (step-wise state integration, nonlinear component models, and climate data) with optimization algorithms, portability to mobile devices, and a simple user interface. The resulting tools enable Soldiers and decision makers to plan energy-aware missions in the field, analyze prospective Soldier power systems and components, or quantitatively explore energy-related "what if" scenarios. Features include algorithms that optimize the minimum-weight equipment for an anticipated mission and a climate database that enables effective use of energy harvesters and batteries by predicting the energy they will likely provide.*

Keywords: energy; power; soldier; model; simulation; mission; optimize.

Introduction

Advances in electronics and communications technology have resulted in high power demands, thus increasing the types and weight of batteries carried by the Soldier. The routes to reducing weight are clear: greater energy storage, more efficient loads, adjustable duty cycles, centralized power sources, and/or more intelligent energy management. Many research programs have focused on energy storage and efficiency; the U.S. Naval Research Laboratory has been working since 2014 to develop tools that help Soldiers, engineers, materiel developers, requirements developers, and logisticians make intelligent energy management decisions. These tools have relied on various incarnations of the NRL Soldier Power Simulation (SPS), a time-domain simulation of a dismounted Soldier power system. [1, 2]

The most recent tool is IPOWER (Intelligent Power Optimization with Environmental Reactivity). IPOWER combines SPS with an intuitive graphical user interface, a verified database of equipment and environmental data, and optimization algorithms. Equipment in the database includes loads (e.g. a PRC-154 radio), harvesters (e.g. solar panel) and batteries (e.g. BB-2525 or BB-2590). On a desktop computer, IPOWER enables users to create a mission scenario, simulate it, and quantify the energy consumed and harvested by the simulated soldier as a function of time throughout the mission. The "mission optimizer" an efficient algorithm to search the soldier equipment space and identify the minimum weight combination of energy sources (batteries and harvesters) that will satisfy the power required by the simulated mission.

The core simulation and database management are a portable C++ object module that can be compiled to run on a variety of platforms. A REST HTTP API supports local or remote interaction through a custom user interface. IPOWER most often runs on a computer for acquisitions or logistics analyses, but it can also run on a mobile device such as a smartphone or tablet. On mobile devices the user interface presents fewer options to configure the same underlying simulation optimization features. The mobile version supports mission planning, resourcing decisions, and situational awareness. For example, optimization results can guide the selection of equipment for the mission, or the "power plan" or "sustainment curve" predicted by IPOWER can be referenced during the mission to understand whether the soldier has an energy surplus or deficit and react accordingly

Desktop Workflow

The simulation process follows three steps: (1) Mission Definition, (2) Equipment Selection, and (3) Analysis & Results. The mission and equipment together form the mission scenario.

Mission Definition: The mission dictates where the soldier is, when they are there, and what they do there. The simplest mission is a start time and an end time in the same location, but the mission can be defined as a series of waypoints where each has a different arrival time, departure time, and location. Simulations with the desktop version of IPOWER usually assume a single location; the waypoint functionality was added primarily to support integration with other mission planning applications.

Another element of the mission is the soldier timeline. IPOWER assumes the Soldier might engage in a finite number of standard activities during a mission. Users assemble a schedule of soldier activities by assigning these pre-defined "mission blocks" to portions of the mission timeline. Fig 1 (top) shows the screen where the activity timeline is assembled.

Equipment Selection: Equipment falls into three categories: loads, energy harvesters, and batteries. Users are presented with a menu from which they can select equipment in the database. Loads are selected first because their inclusion is

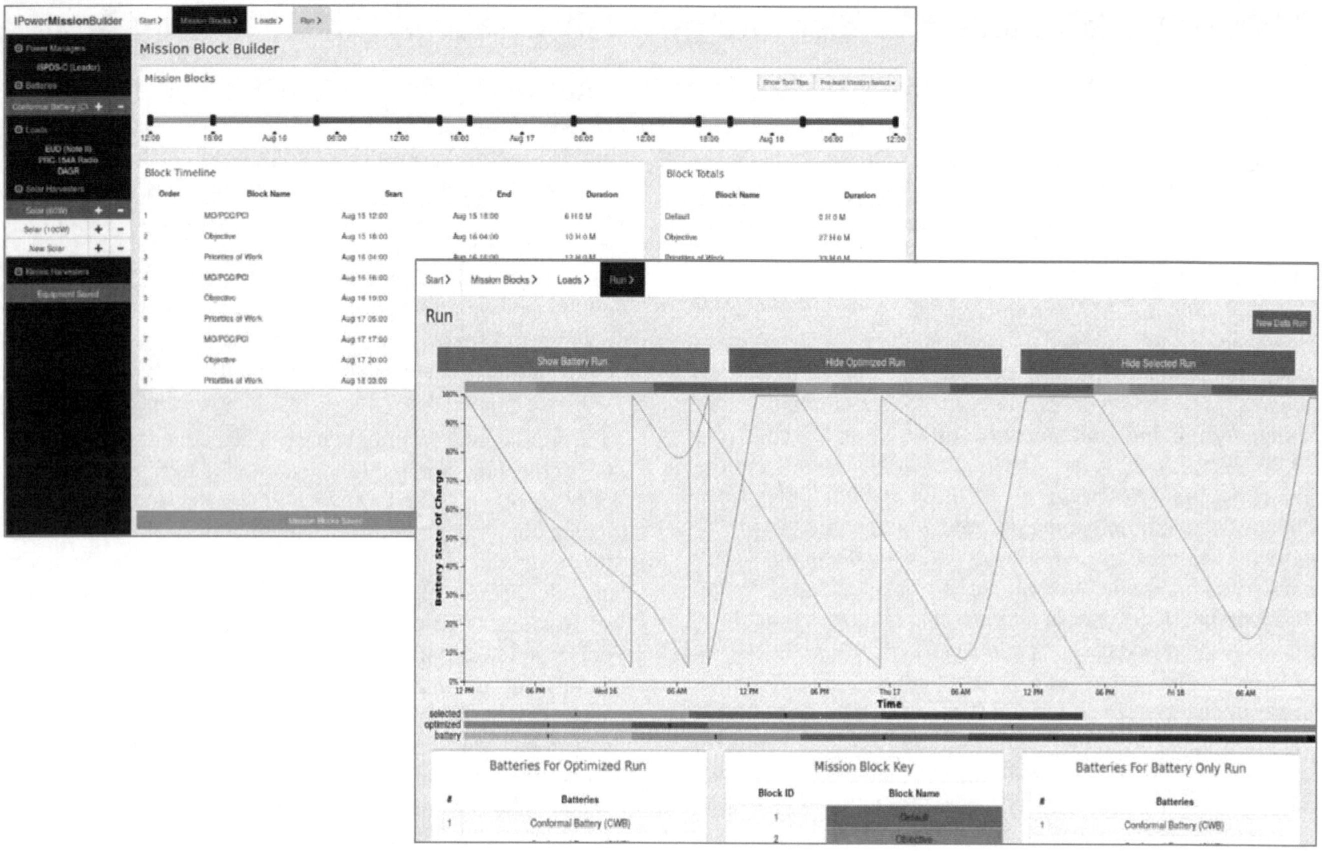

Figure 1. Mission definition screen where users assemble the mission timeline for the desktop version of IPOWER (top) and output screen where results are displayed for the desktop version of IPOWER (bottom).

driven *a priori* by the mission objectives. Next, energy harvesters (if any) are selected. Finally, the user may choose one or more batteries for the simulation, or rely on IPOWER to select the least weight combination that completes the mission. Batteries are always assumed to be fully charged at the start of the mission, but partially charged batteries could easily be added as a new feature.

Each piece of equipment has a schedule of "active times" when it will be used during the mission. Users define the active times for equipment on a timeline in much the same way they define soldier activities. The soldier activity timeline is displayed alongside the equipment activity timelines so users can align equipment activity with soldier activities during the mission.

Analysis & Results: Once the mission scenario is complete, users press the "New Data Run" button to run the simulation and optimization functions. Results are displayed in an output window as shown in Fig. 1 (bottom). The simulation produces three sets of results that make different assumptions about the way the soldier satisfies his or her energy needs.

- Selected run assumes the batteries originally selected by the user for this mission scenario are carried.
- Battery run identifies the minimum number of batteries the soldier must carry to complete the mission, and assumes that number is carried.
- Optimized run identifies the minimum weight combination of energy sources (batteries and energy harvesters) that will satisfy the mission energy required, given all the equipment in the database, and assumes that equipment is carried.

The main result is a plot of battery state of charge (SoC) throughout the mission. One SoC curve is generated for each set of results. Discontinuities in the SoC curves are due to disconnecting one battery from the power manager and connecting another battery (swaps). The color bar displayed across the top of the SoC plot shows the soldier activity timeline so users can understand how changes in battery SoC correlate to soldier activity. The color bars at the bottom of the SoC plots show which batteries are used during each portion of the mission. For example, the green bar shows when the three batteries selected by the user are connected to the power manager. The blue line shows when the optimized batteries are connected, and comparing the green and blue bars shows that the optimized result uses one fewer battery because it uses a solar panel to harvest energy (rising SoC) when the sun rises at about 06:00. Below the SoC plot are tables listing the energy sources for each result, and the weight of each energy source load-out.

Mobile Device Workflow

The IPOWER workflow on mobile devices differs to accommodate the smaller screen. For example, users do not define a mission timeline of activities; instead, average power is assumed for each load during its active times.

Mission Definition: The configure mission screens shown in Fig. 2 present users with a map of the mission region. Users can select locations to create waypoints, and then define an arrival and a departure time for each waypoint. The mission location and timeline are derived from the waypoints.

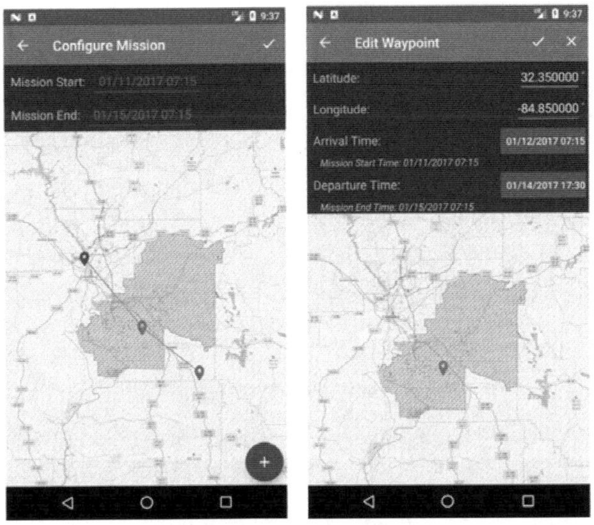

Figure 2. Configure mission screens where mission waypoints (and the mission start/end points) are defined.

Equipment Selection: Fig. 3 shows the main and equipment selection screens in the IPOWER smartphone app. The main screen shows the present estimated mission endurance as a percentage of the mission duration specified by the user, and the weight of all selected equipment. Users can tap the green circle marked with "+" to open the equipment selection screen where all of the equipment in the database is displayed. The IPOWER simulation and optimization functions run every time a change is made to the mission, and equipment in the optimal minimum weight load-out is placed at the top of the list and marked by a star to guide the user's equipment selection. Users are not forced to choose the minimum weight equipment set, but keeping them informed enables them to better understand their options.

The IPOWER smartphone app has an active times selection feature (shown in Fig. 4) for solar energy harvesters. When users add a solar panel to the equipment set, the anticipated power production by the solar panel is plotted as function of time for the mission, based on solar irradiance data in the environmental database. Users select the active times for the solar panel by adding blue dots to the power curve and moving them. This approach enables the user to understand how the utility of the solar panel varies during the mission, so they can plan the mission to take maximum advantage of the solar panel (to the extent the mission objectives allow).

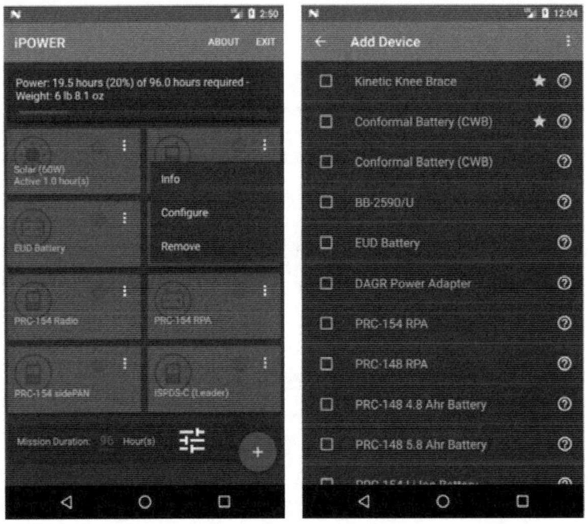

Figure 3. Main screen (left) and mission configuration screen (right) for the mobile version of IPOWER.

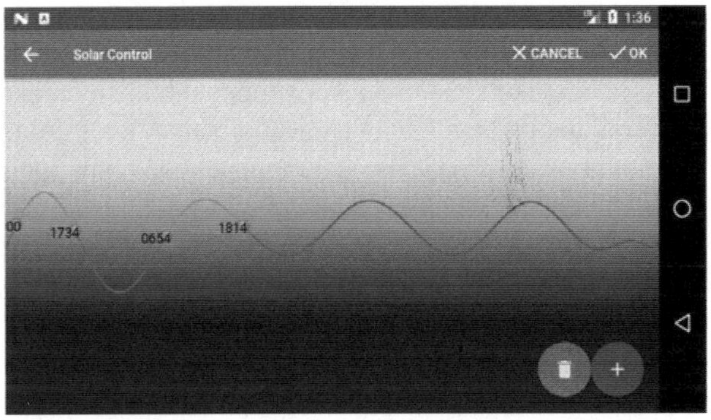

Figure 4. Active time selection feature for solar panels. Blue dots indicate start/end of active periods with time overlaid (i.e. activity on day two from 0654 to 1814).

Databases and Administration Tool

IPOWER is supported by a device database and an environmental database. The device database contains power consumption measurements for various loads under conditions that approximate Soldier activities. The environmental database contains temperature and solar irradiance data from the National Weather Service and National Renewable Energy Laboratory, respectively. The environmental data is indexed to position (latitude and longitude) and time (hourly intervals) and was averaged over 15 years to generate a "model year" dataset. IPOWER interpolates in the model year dataset to estimate the temperature and solar flux at each time step and location in the mission.

Equipment Models

The parameters that dictate power consumption and production vary from one equipment class to another, but soldier activity and active state are common among all of them. Soldier activity can, for example, dictate different power flows when the soldier is "moving to contact" or engaged in "priorities of work." SPS uses the soldier activity timeline determine the activity at each time step and then parameterize the equipment models at that time step. Similarly, "active state" dictates whether equipment is active or inactive during a soldier activity.

Loads: Each loads draws power at a rate dictated by a load model parameterized by soldier activity. Sophisticated load models that can resolve complex power consumption curves (such as differences between a radio transmitting and receiving) have been developed, but have not yet been implemented because most loads are fairly consistent. Loads with inconsistent power consumption tend to correlate well with soldier activity and are therefore captured by the present approach.

Some load power variation is presently out of scope and therefore not captured by the SPS. For example, the PRC-154 radio power consumption changes with network topology or topographical interference. In such cases a nominal power value is used.

Energy Harvesters: Harvesters are separated into two classes: solar harvesters and kinetic harvesters. Solar harvesters are photovoltaic solar panels, whereas kinetic harvesters include knee-brace, rucksack, and other energy harvesters that convert soldier motion into electrical power.

Solar panel power production is estimated at each time step via Eq. 1, where I_{ga} is the global horizontal irradiance, A_{panel} is the solar panel area, and $\eta_{panel}(T)$ is the panel efficiency as a function of temperature.

$$P_{solar} = I_{ga} A_{panel} \eta_{panel}(T) \quad (1)$$

This assumes solar panels are deployed horizontally (i.e., on flat ground) but could include an incidence angle. The conventional method in Eq. 2 estimates the panel efficiency, where $\eta_{@\,25°C}$ is the efficiency at 25°C and C_T is the temperature coefficient expressed as a percentage.

$$\eta_{solar}(T) = \eta_{@\,25°C} + 100C_T(T - 25) \quad (2)$$

The kinetic energy harvester models are similar to the load models in that they only depend on soldier activity. The average rate of power generation for each kinetic harvester, for each soldier activity, is defined in the database and retrieved during execution. This model could be expanded to more accurately capture performance - for example, using terrain to include the influence of ascent/descent rate.

Battery Model: The battery has the most detailed model to capture real world performance as accurately as possible. SOC is tracked by integrating the flow of charge into/out of the battery and comparing to the total charge capacity of the battery. Charge capacity varies with ambient temperature and SOC according to an empirical model created through battery measurements in an environmental chamber. Batteries are considered discharged when SOC reaches an adjustable lower bound *or* terminal voltage reaches the minimum. They are charged until they reach 100% SOC or the terminal voltage reaches the maximum.

While some averaging is implicit in the load and energy harvester models, battery measurements are used directly in an empirical model to characterize the expected terminal voltage. Prior to running the SPS, battery capacity, open circuit voltage (OCV), and equivalent series resistance (ESR) interpolants are constructed from battery measurements stored in SPSDB. The ALGLIB library is used for interpolation. Interpolants are used with the battery SOC and ambient temperature to estimate OCV and ESR at each time step. OCV and ESR are then used to calculate battery terminal voltage from battery power via Eq. 3.

$$V_{bat}(t) = \frac{1}{2}\left(V_{ocv}(t) + \sqrt{V_{ocv}(t)^2 - 4P_{batt}(t)R_{esr}(t)}\right) \quad (3)$$

Battery terminal voltage limits charge and discharge, but it is also used to calculate battery current via Eq. 4

$$I_{bat}(t) = P_{batt}(t)/V_{batt}(t) \quad (4)$$

The battery current is then used to estimate the total charge removed from (or added to) the battery via Eq. 5.

$$Q_{bat}(t) = Q_{batt}(0) + \int_0^t I_{bat}(t)dt \quad (5)$$

Finally, the battery state of charge is calculated via Eq. 6.

$$SOC(t, T) = Q_{batt}(t)/Q_{batt,total}(T) \quad (6)$$

The only battery with a full fidelity model in the present IPOWER library is the Conformal Wearable Battery (CWB). This could be expanded to include other common batteries through the same measurement process.

Looking Forward

Work on IPOWER is continuing in 2018 with the inclusion of discrete devices with their native batteries, an expansion to simulate a platoon, and incorporation into a service architecture to support applications in the TAK (Tactical Assault Kit) environment.

Acknowledgements

The authors thank the Department of Defense Operational Energy Capabilities Investment Fund, Soldier and Small Unit Operational Energy Program for funding this work in FY17. The authors also thank Program Executive Office Soldier, Project Manager Soldier Warrior for funding continued work in FY18.

References

1. R. O. Stroman, E. Leadbetter, and C. Buesser, *IPOWER: Energy Analysis and Mission Planning Tools for Dismounted Soldiers*, NRL Memorandum Report NRL/MR/6110--18-9781 (2018).

2. R. O. Stroman, D. J. Milliken, E. Leadbetter, K. Swider-Lyons, J. Novoa, *Energy-Informed Soldier Mission Planning Through Simulation*, Proc. of 47th Power Sources Conference, Orlando FL (2016).

3. R. O. Stroman and K. Swider-Lyons, *Soldier Power Simulation Program*, NRL Memorandum Report NRL/MR/6113--16-9688 (2016).

Performance Enhancement of Impulse Loaded Energy Harvesters through Time Varying Impedance

Dr. Nathan Sharpes
Communications-Electronics Research, Development, and Engineering Center (CERDEC)
US Army RDECOM
Aberdeen Proving Ground, Maryland 21005, USA

Abstract: *A mechanical linkage is modified, to incorporate a novel strategy to achieve a variable effective impedance of a biomechanical impulse loaded (heel-strike) shoe-mounted energy harvester. The theorized design is numerically modeled over a range of pinion gear geometries and gear train ratios. It is found that a range of pinion geometries produce similar results, though there remains a trade-off between pinion geometry, gear train ratio, performance, and subjective feel of the device.*

Keywords: Energy Harvesting; Dismounted Soldier; Soldier Power; Soldier Lethality; Wearable; Biomechanics; Human-Powered.

Introduction

Energy harvesting, or deriving energy (typically in an electrical form) from the ambient environment, has found application in scenarios where energy demands occur in remote settings. These situations arise when it is not feasible to run a power line, deliver fuel, or otherwise resupply a location in a desirable time frame. For example, off-grid camps may make use of wind or solar power to fulfil their energy requirements, or an autonomous sensor may supply its own energy by harnessing ambient temperature gradients or vibrations. Mobile environments are also an excellent candidate for energy harvesting, in circumstances where it is not feasible to carry sufficient energy for a given timeframe. The dismounted Soldier on a multi-day mission is an example of such circumstances, whereby it is not always feasible, from a pack weight standpoint, to carry a portable generator and fuel, or several sets of spare batteries. As wind and solar power often require stationary positions, thus hindering mobility, it is an attractive option to produce energy while the Soldier is in motion, preeminently by harvesting energy from the Soldier's motion (gait) itself. Such energy harvesters, though, must be carefully designed to work with the body so as to not cause additional burden on the Soldier, causing them to work harder (i.e. increase metabolic rate) to produce this electrical power, negating its usefulness.

A popular method of energy harvesting from human motion is to utilize the heel-strike– the beginning of the gait cycle where the heel contacts the ground after the swing phase. During this time, relatively high forces are generated for a short period. This impulse load has been harvested previously by piezoelectric, electromagnetic, and fluidic devices.[1] Though, the mechanical impedance of such designs, and their interaction with the body, have been largely ignored; resulting in either rigid devices, yielding the feeling of walking barefoot on concrete, or devices too compliant, yielding the feeling of walking barefoot on sand. The former yields joint and soft tissue discomfort, while the latter increases fatigue. It is therefore proposed that an equilibrium exists, whereby the energy harvester impedance to mechanical motion would mimic the feel of the shoe without the energy harvester (i.e. cushioning yet supportive).

A mechanical linkage [2] is modified, to incorporate a novel strategy to achieve a variable effective impedance (i.e. effective gear ratio) between force input (heel-strike) and the electromagnetic generator (source of mechanical impedance). It is hypothesized that optimal performance can be achieved with an initially high gear ratio, which overcomes the inertia of the generator, progressing to a lower ratio before the end of the heel-strike, maximizing the speed of the generator. This approach maximizes generated electrical power while varying impedance to enhance comfort. The proposed device is intended to integrate into either the combat boot insoles and/or midsole, as illustrated in Figure 1 below, along with labeled components.

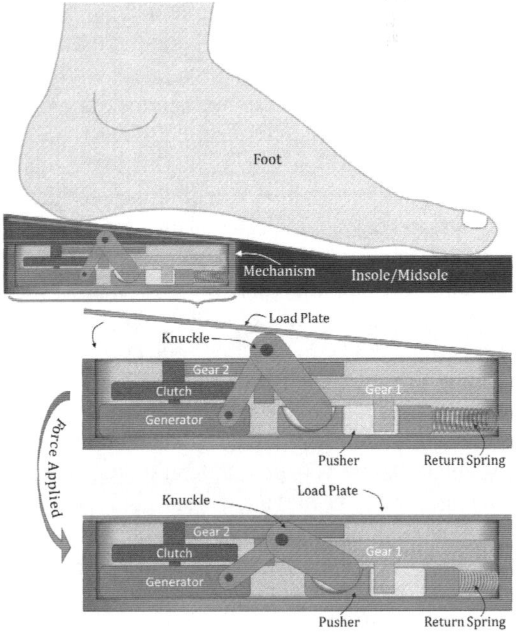

Figure 1. Illustration of system described herein.

Description of Mechanism Function

The primary purpose of the mechanism illustrated in Figure 1 is to convert the vertical compressive force of the heel-strike to rotary motion to spin the generator. To this end, in response to force from the foot, the load plate depresses, elongating the knuckle and moving the pusher forward. This movement converts the vertical linear force of the heel-strike to a horizontal linear force. The pusher has an integrated toothed rack, which interfaces with the pinion of gear 1. The horizontal translation of the pusher, thus, causes gear 1 to rotate. This motion converts the horizontal linear force, to rotational torque. With these two steps, the desired conversion of vertical linear force to rotary motion is achieved. The subsequent interaction between gear 1 and gear 2, and gear 2 and the pinion of the clutch, allows for the application of a set gear ratio. This ratio is adjusted during design and modeling, though is not time varying, but constant during mechanism operation. The clutch transfers torque when spun in one direction, and freewheels (transfers no torque) when spun in the other direction. This function allows the generator to continue to rotate under its own inertia for a period of time after the heel-strike is over, and also allows the pusher/knuckle to be reset by the return spring without engaging the generator, which may still be spinning. Without the clutch, the generator would be abruptly stopped when load plate was fully depressed and spun in opposite direction when the mechanism is reset, requiring a larger return spring, a parasitic loss to the system in terms biomechanical force input to electrical conversion. The mechanism is returned to its initial state when the heel is lifted off the ground as the foot pushes-off and swings forward for the next step.

Design Improvement Strategy

A constant gear ratio is not a desirable trait for an impulse loading system, such as this one, whereby no steady-state-like behavior is ever reached. This system is considered an impulse loading system because heel-strikes deliver a pulse of force to the system, followed a period of inactivity before the next successive heel-strike occurs. Due to the relatively long period of inactivity between heel-strikes, the generator comes to a stop between each step. Thus, the inertia of the generator and gear-train must be overcome during each heel-strike. A high gear ratio is optimal for overcoming generator inertia and maximize comfort, while a low gear ratio is optimal to maximize generator rotation speed and subsequently power output. It can therefore be concluded that a constant gear ratio is inherently a compromise between two opposing requirements (i.e. comfort and power output). The concept is qualitatively depicted in Figure 2. It is shown how a high gear ratio reaches a low maximum speed quickly and how a low gear ratio has the potential for high maximum speed if under steady state conditions, however under impulse conditions slowly only reaches a lower speed. There is naturally, then, an optimum, in terms of generator speed and subsequently power output, between the two extremes of gear ratio.

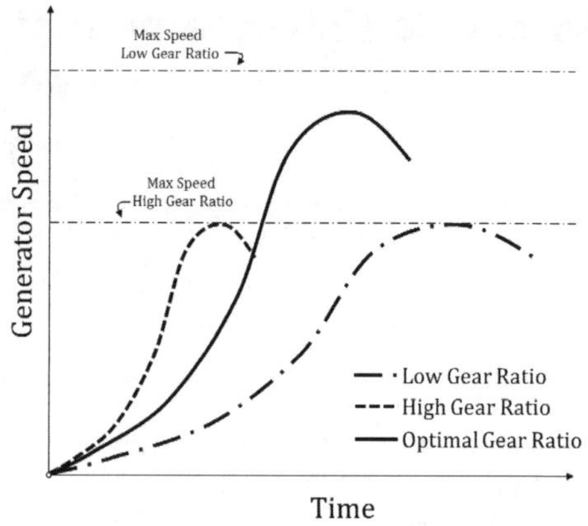

Figure 2. Qualitative plot of possible and achievable generator speeds for Low, High, and Optimal gear ratios.

To address the drawbacks of a constant gear ratio, it was sought to find a way to obtain a variable gear ratio, such that a high ratio would be available initially, then transferring to a lower gear ratio at the completion of the heel-strike. To realize such performance, a geometrically varying gear geometry is needed. The concept generated was a non-circular pinon on gear 1, paired with an accordingly-shaped pusher rack. While there are many geometries which would allow this strategy to vary the gear ratio, and indeed one could find an optimized geometry for a given impulse [3], in this work, a spiral of linearly varying radius is explored. Figure 3 illustrates the proposed design using a spiral pinion gear, compared to a circular one, and the resulting effective gear ratio as a function of the input displacement.

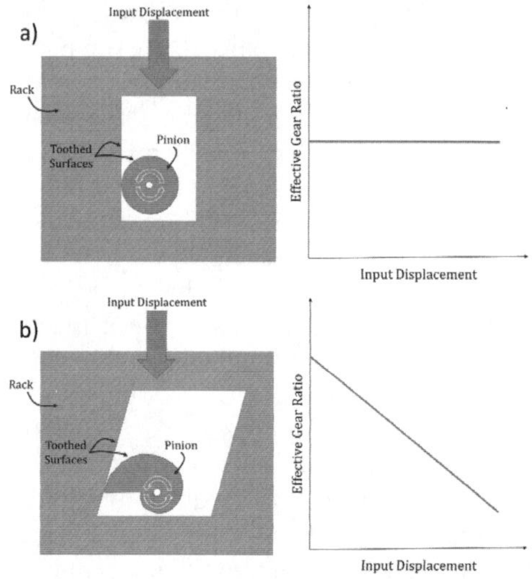

Figure 3. Illustration of a) traditional rack with circular pinion, b) non-circular pinion with accommodating rack, and resulting effective gear ratios.

Model Setup

As most mechanical systems, this system is modeled as a spring-mass-damper system, though in two rotary frames of reference, because of the gear ratios. Summing the moments about the generator axis and accounting for the gear ratio, GR, the equations below are derived.

$$J\ddot{\theta} + c\dot{\theta} = \frac{f(t)r(t)}{GR} \quad (1)$$

$$\theta = \gamma \cdot GR \quad (2)$$

$$x = \theta \cdot r(t) \quad (3)$$

Here, J, is the moment of inertia of the generator, c, the damping of the generator, $f(t)$, the time varying input force, $r(t)$, the time varying pinion radius, γ, the rotation angle of the pinion, θ, the rotation angle of the generator, and, x, the horizontal translation of the pusher.

There is no energy storage term in the model, as there are no springs in the gear train. This leads to the assumption that the gears, shafts, and connections between are rigid. An additional assumption is that the inertia of the generator is much greater than the gear train, leading to the assumption of negligible inertia of the gear train. A final assumption is that the damping of the generator is much greater than friction damping in the system, leading to the assumption that the generator is the only source of damping.

The force applied to the heel during a walking gait of self-selected speed is shown below in Figure 4. This curve is an average for 13 Soldiers wearing a commonly worn combat boot, without any pack weight. This data was measured and analyzed by the author and will be published in greater detail in an upcoming journal article.

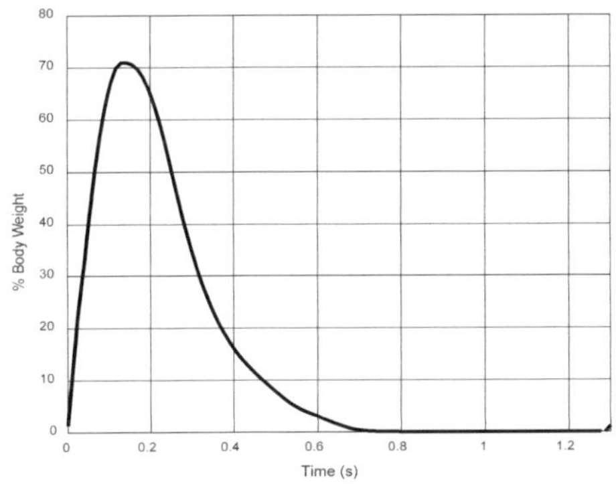

Figure 4. Typical force applied to heel during a neutral walking gait in combat boots (experimentally measured).

The curve above is taken to be $f(t)$ when multiplied by a body weight. For the purpose of this study, an average Soldier body weight of 160 pounds was used.[4] The radius of the pinion gear, $r(t)$, is varied between an initial radius of r1 and an ending radius r2. Values are varied between 5-30 mm, or the smallest practical radius possible and the largest radius able to feasibly integrate into the insole/boot.

Strictly speaking, an impulse is characterized by a force magnitude acting over a period of time, typically followed by some period of zero force (like is shown in Figure 4). In reality, there is often a limiting displacement associated with a given impulse. For example, a piston has a fixed stroke length, a lever has a finite amount of travel, and indeed even the human body can only exert forces over the length of a limb. For the case of the mechanism in Figure 1, a certain combination of load plate deflection, knuckle, and pusher geometry, yields a certain amount of pusher travel.

It can then be said that the range of pusher travel is a limiting factor of the system. In fact, there are three limiting factors of the system:

1) Range - The available travel of the pusher rack, denoted as x_{max}
2) Angle - Since the pinion gear is a spiral, it can only rotate approximately 270° (3π/2 radians) before it interferes with the rack, denoted as θ_{max}
3) Force - The force impulse returns to zero before either range or angle maximums are reached

Range is a limiting factor if the arc length of the pinion is longer than the rack's travel. If the opposite is true, the pinion will reach its full allowable rotation before full travel is achieved. It can also be the case the gear ratio is such that generator damping limits how fast the load plate can depress, thus the heel-strike would be over before the mechanism is fully actuated.

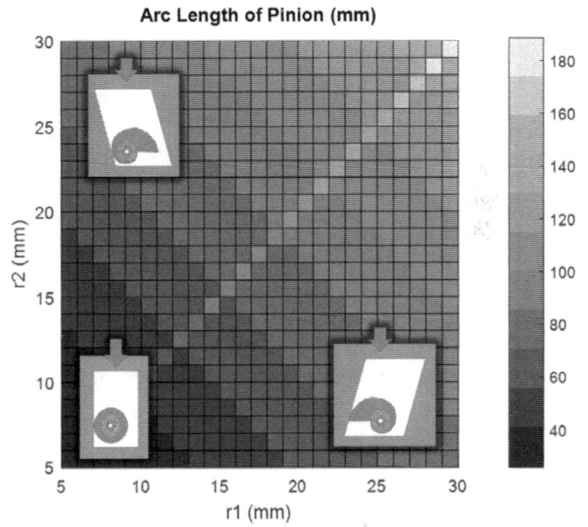

Figure 5. Arc length of considered pinion geometries.

In Figure 5 above, the arc length of the consider pinion geometries is given. Above the diagonal are geometries which go from small to large radius, while below the diagonal are geometries which go from large to small radius. Along the diagonal, the beginning and ending radii are the same, resulting in a standard circular pinion. Note that for such cases, the arc length is significantly larger. This is because there is so angle limiting factor for circular gears. Thus the arc length is calculated over 360° rather than 270°.

Model Results and Discussion

The 625 pinion gear geometry combinations are simulated across time for gear train ratios of 1-30 (note: $GR = 30$ is a 1:30 gear ratio, i.e. 1 revolution of the input yields 30 revolutions of the output), using the model parameters given in Table 1, below, and forcing function of Figure 4.

Table 1. Model parameters

J $(N \cdot m \cdot s^2)$	c $(N \cdot m \cdot s)$	x_{max} (mm)	θ_{max} (rad)	
			$r1 \neq r2$	$r1 = r2$
5×10^{-4}	5×10^{-3}	30	$3\pi/2$	∞

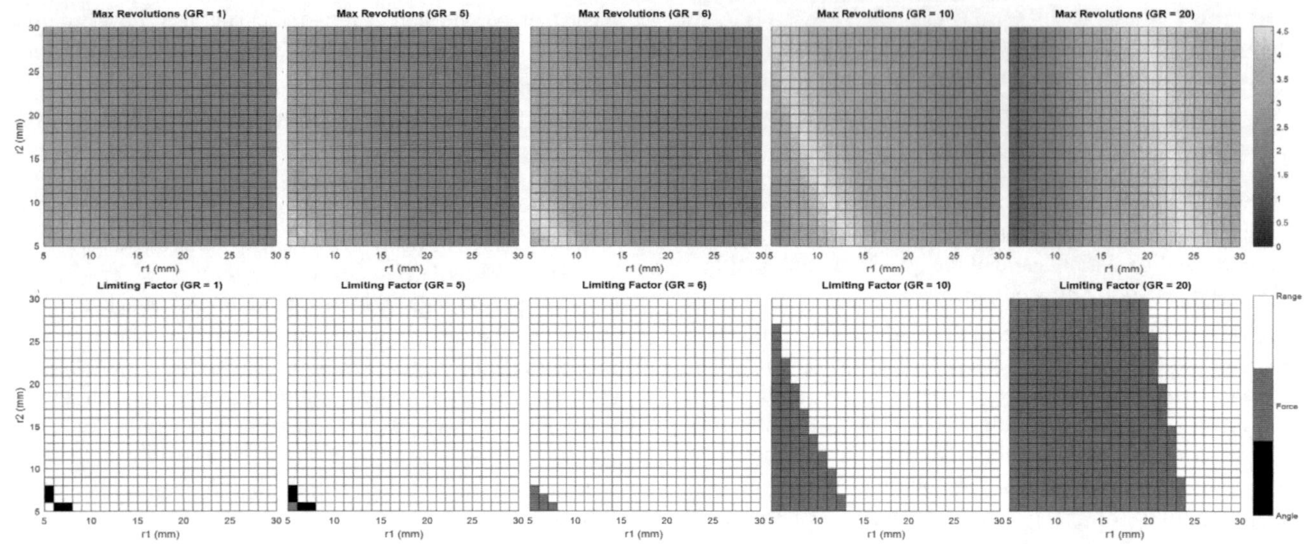

Figure 6. Maximum revolutions of generator and limiting factor for select gear train ratios.

The key measure of performance is the number of times the generator rotates for the given impulse, which can be thought of as analogous to energy converted. A summary of selected results are shown above in Figure 6. Here, the best results, in terms of most generator revolutions, are found to occur at either the smallest pinion gear possible, or at the boundary between force and range limits. This is an intuitive result, as one can imagine how, to convert the most energy, it is best to use the entire impulse and displacement available.

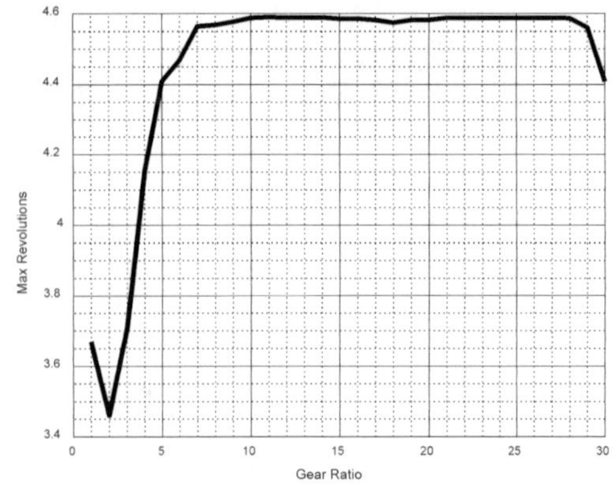

Figure 7. Maximum performance for each gear train ratio.

A plot of the maximum performance for each gear ratio is shown, above, in Figure 7. Here, it is found that, compared no gear train ratio (i.e. a gear ratio of one), an approximately 20% improvement can be had by employing a gear train ratio across all considered pinion geometries.

Though, as was discussed in the introduction, power output is not the only parameter which should be considered, but also the impedance or feel of the system. Since the forcing function is prescribed, one must look to the system acceleration to gauge what kind of reactionary forces would act on the Soldier. High accelerations indicate that the system has low impedance, and therefore a smaller effect on, and would be less noticeable by, the Soldier. Figure 8, shows the acceleration of the generator at the instance after heel-strike begins and is given as a function of gear train ratio and initial pinion radius.

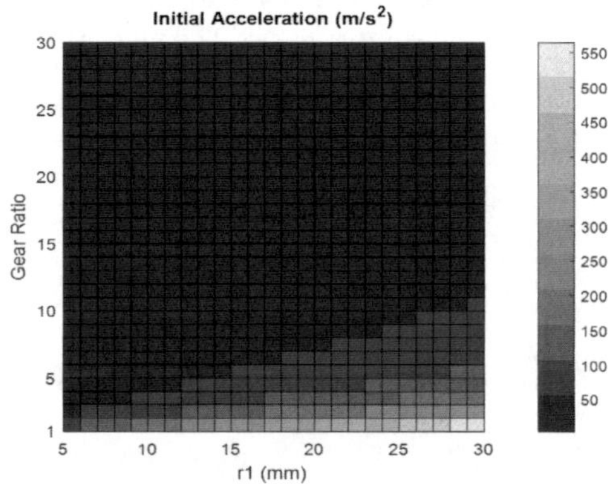

Figure 8. Initial acceleration of the generator at beginning of heel-strike, as a function of $\boldsymbol{r1}$ and $\boldsymbol{GR}$.

Here, it is evident that a system which GR closer to one, and a large $r1$ would presumably have the best feel, though, such a system would have poor performance (see Figure 6). Further analysis is required to find the optimal trade-off between pinion geometry, gear train ratio, performance, and subjective feel of the device.

References

1. Paradiso, J. A., & Starner, T. "Energy scavenging for mobile and wireless electronics", *IEEE Pervasive computing*, *4*(1), 18-27. (2005).
2. Stanton, M. J., Alexander, H., Williams, S., Stroup, S., & Golden, A. "Foot-powered energy generator", *U.S. Patent No. 9,190,886*. (2015).
3. Handžić, I., & Reed, K. B. "Kinetic shapes: analysis, verification, and applications", *Journal of Mechanical Design*, *136*(6), 061005. (2014).
4. White, R.M. and E. Churchill, "The body size of soldiers: US army anthropometry-1966", *DTIC Document*, (1971).

Experimental Verification of the Magnetic Field of an Electromagnetic Alternator

Christopher Mullen
Communications-Electronics Research, Development and Engineering Center
U.S. Army RDECOM

Abstract:
Generating electrical power for Soldier-wearable or man-portable devices often requires customized electromagnetic generators to integrate into confined spaces, and it is beneficial to have finite element modeling resources available to verify possible interference between the generator and other electronic equipment. The purpose of this research is to validate multi-physics software simulation using experimental data. The ability to model and simulate magnetic fields enables integration of energy harvesting devices on the Soldier without fear of magnetic deviation before a prototype is produced. In this study, an electromagnetic alternator is modeled in SolidWorks 3D CAD Software and imported into the ANSYS Maxwell 3D design space. Using Maxwell's equations, a finite element analysis determines the simulated magnetic field. The magnets are 3/8-inch^3 neodymium cube magnets. The experiment uses a 3D printed rotor and stator, for the magnets and coil of wire to be attached, and a Gauss meter is used to measure the magnetic field of the alternator assembly. The results of both the simulation and the experiment are presented; there was good agreement found between the FEA model and experimental results.

Keywords: Simulation; electromagnetism; experimental verification; permanent magnets; alternator; generator; Finite Element Analysis; FEA; FEM

I. Introduction & Theory

Electromagnetic alternators and electric motors are commonly found in vehicles, UXVs, and generators. Soldiers depend on them to be successful in their missions. The use of permanent magnets (PMs) has become widespread in alternator design and is the most common ferromagnetic material used for its superior performance [1].

Finite Element Analysis (FEA) has been a useful tool for modeling and simulation since the 1960's. As computers have become more powerful, simulation has become more commonplace. The benefit of simulation includes the optimization of a part or system before prototyping, potentially saving hours of work and material costs [2]. For military applications, building more than a single prototype can be cost-prohibitive, so utilizing simulation to avoid design problems can be helpful during the development phase.

This paper is organized in the following manner. In Section II, the design method is discussed which outlines the geometry and material properties of the magnet. In Section III the results of the simulation are discussed, followed by the results of the experiment in Section IV. Section V is the discussion and conclusion of the results.

In this research, ANSYS Maxwell 3D multi-physics software is used to create a simulation of a magnetostatic system. Four magnets, installed at 90 degrees from each other, in a rotor made from 3D printed ABS plastic are designed in the software, and the results are obtained. Electromagnetic problems solve Maxwell's equations, starting with the basic field equations [3]:

$$\nabla \times \boldsymbol{E} = -\frac{\partial \boldsymbol{B}}{\partial t} \tag{1}$$

$$\nabla \cdot \boldsymbol{B} = 0 \tag{2}$$

$$\nabla \times \boldsymbol{H} = \boldsymbol{J} \tag{3}$$

where **E** represents electric field strength, **B** is the magnetic flux density, **H** is the magnetic field strength, and **J** is the electric current density. These equations consider the constitutive relations:

$$\boldsymbol{B} = \mu \boldsymbol{H} \tag{4}$$

$$\boldsymbol{J} = \sigma \boldsymbol{E} \tag{5}$$

For static applications, as in this paper, the change in magnetic flux density with respect to time is zero. Using these relationships, the following FEA equation is built

$$KA = f \tag{6}$$

where K respresents the element stiffness matrix, A represents the magnetic vector potential, and f is the force vector [4]. Equation 6 is calculated at each node in the design space to solve for the magnetic vector potential.

II. Design Method

Four neodymium magnets are installed in a 3D printed ABS plastic rotor, as seen in Figure 1. The outer diameter of the rotor is 3.75 in, and the dimensions of each Neodymium cube magnet is 3/8 in^3. There is a slight difference between simulation and experimental geometries due to a thin Nickel (Ni-Cu-Ni) coating that covers the magnets, which is not considered in the simulation.

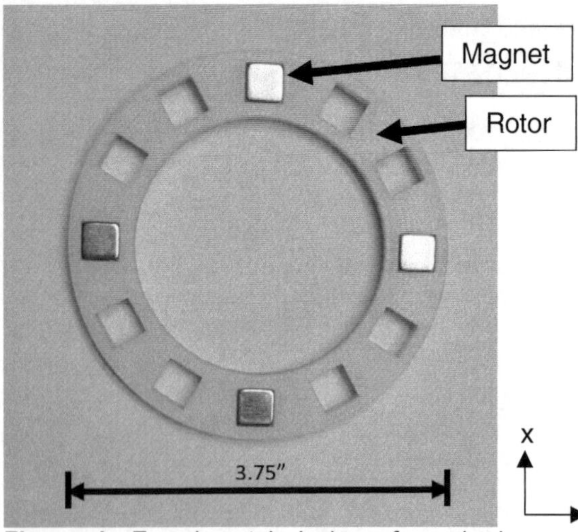

Figure 1: Experimental design of neodymium magnets installed in a rotor made of 3D printed ABS plastic.

The magnetization direction of the experimental design is on the z-axis, with the north pole of the magnet coming out of the paper. Table 1 lists material properties.

Table 1: Material Properties of magnet and rotor

	Description	Units
Magnet Material	NdFeB	
Grade	N42	
Brmax*	13,200	Gauss
BHmax*	42	MGOe
Rotor Material	ABS Plastic	
*** from K&J Magnetics**		

A F.W. Bell 5170 Gauss/Tesla Meter was used to measure the magnetic flux of one of the magnets, where each number (1 through 9) in Figure 2 denote the location of where data was taken. After each set of nine data points was collected, the distance from the magnet would increase by a 0.1 inch interval and the nine points would be taken from the new distance. A General No. 147 Digital Caliper was used to measure the distance from the magnet while taking measurements with the Gauss Meter. This process was repeated until the magnetic flux was negligible, which was determined to be 0.4 inches.

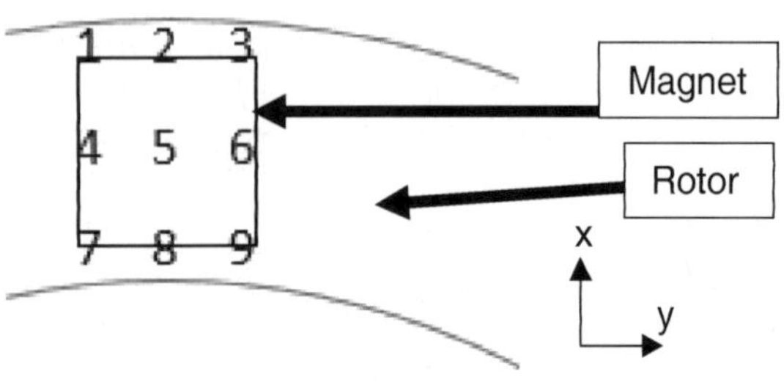

Figure 2: Location of data extraction during experimental collection as well as in the simulation.

Regarding the simulation, both two and three-dimensional analyses were conducted. The domain of each simulation is large enough to reduce artificial flux confinement error. The units of each simulation are in inches. The alignment of the magnetic poles between the 2D and 3D models differs in that the magnets in the 2D model is designed for a radial coil winding while the 3D model is designed for an axial coil winding. In the 2D model, each magnet has their south pole facing the rotor's center. The magnetization direction in the 3D model is oriented on the z-axis in the same way as the experimental setup.

III. Finite Element Analysis Results

The results of the 2D simulation is shown in Figure 3. The simulation generated 800 total elements, 17 on average per magnet, 196 for the rotor, and the remaining 536 on the surrounding region. In addition to showing the magnetic flux density (in teslas), the figure also shows the flux lines (in Wb/m). The flux density is strongest at the surface of the rotor with a value of 0.257 T. The flux decays exponentially as distance from the magnet surface increases.

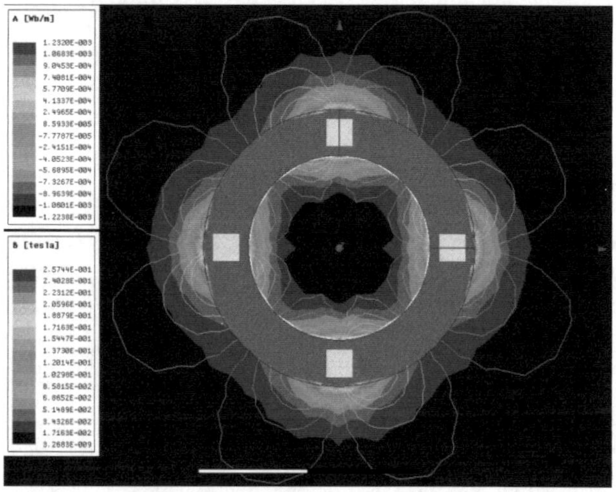

Figure 3: ANSYS Maxwell 2D results of magnets and rotor.

The results of the 3D simulation are shown in Figure 4. There were 32,618 elements generated, with an average of 305 elements per magnet, 2,803 elements for the rotor, and the remaining 28,595 elements belong to the rest of the domain.

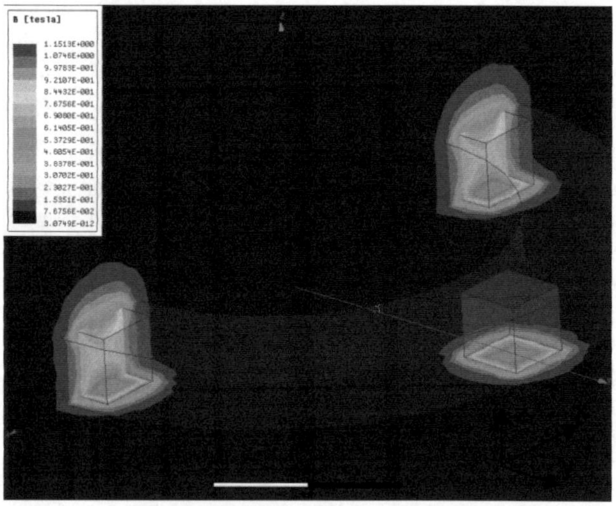

Figure 4: ANSYS Maxwell 3D results of magnets and rotor.

Figure 4 shows a cross-section of two of the magnets so that magnetic flux in the positive z-direction is revealed in addition to the magnetic flux on the x and y-axes. The maximum magnetic flux density is 1.15 T, located at the surface of the magnet.

The simulation allows magnetic flux density information to be captured at specific locations. Simulation data is pulled from the same nine locations as the experimental collection points. The simulation data is listed in Table 2.

Table 2. Simulation data of magnetic flux from one magnet (T)

Location	$4x10^{-4}$ inch	0.1 inch	0.2 inch	0.3 inch	0.4 inch
1	0.3487	0.1584	0.0849	0.054	0.033
2	0.5587	0.2145	0.1047	0.066	0.038
3	0.3635	0.1537	0.0876	0.052	0.033
4	0.5040	0.2241	0.1164	0.062	0.040
5	0.5064	0.2713	0.1414	0.081	0.048
6	0.6072	0.2071	0.1063	0.064	0.038
7	0.3546	0.1536	0.0918	0.048	0.035
8	0.5598	0.2171	0.1108	0.062	0.038
9	0.3648	0.1603	0.0845	0.050	0.035

IV. Experimental Results

The results of the experiment are listed in Table 3. The magnetic flux density data is obtained at each of the nine locations shown in Figure 2.

Table 3. Experimental data of magnetic flux from one magnet (T)

Location	Magnet Surface	0.1 inch	0.2 inch	0.3 inch	0.4 inch
1	0.380	0.125	0.066	0.046	0.029
2	0.370	0.166	0.097	0.052	0.036
3	0.310	0.104	0.056	0.038	0.027
4	0.479	0.133	0.076	0.042	0.027
5	0.494	0.255	0.134	0.064	0.034
6	0.250	0.108	0.092	0.047	0.028
7	0.455	0.121	0.048	0.031	0.023
8	0.237	0.144	0.073	0.038	0.023
9	0.228	0.079	0.042	0.027	0.019

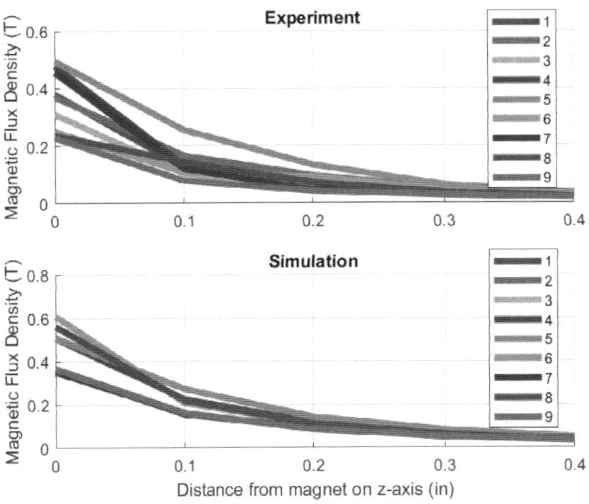

Figure 5: Comparison of Experimental and Simulation magnetic flux data.

Figure 5 shows a subplot comparison of the magnetic flux density between the experimental and simulation results. The results show the relationship between magnetic flux and distance from the magnet in the z-direction. Numbers in the legend correspond to the nine locations in Figure 2.

In Figure 6, the resulting line plots are a subtraction of experimental minus simulation results for each of the nine locations. The figure illustrates the difference between experimental and simulation results.

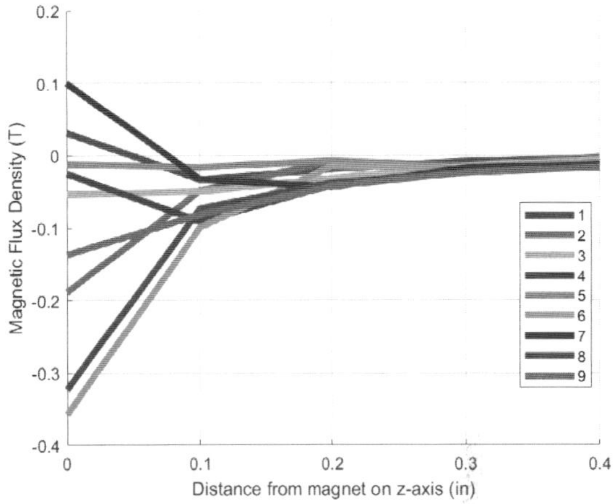

Figure 6: Experimental values minus Simulation values.

V. Discussion and Conclusion

The flux lines and magnetic field in Figure 3 are theoretically accurate, as the flux moves from North to South, avoiding similar adjacent poles. As complexity of the model increases, it will be more efficient to use symmetry to decrease calculation times. The maximum magnetic flux value in the 2D model is quite low, but this result is due to the distance between the rotor surface and the magnet.

Figure 4 shows a 3D simulation with a maximum magnetic flux of 1.15 T. This is more than double any experimental and simulation value listed in Tables 2 and 3. The reason for the discrepancy is that the simulation data on the magnet surface in Table 2 was taken at 4.0×10^{-4} inches (10 μm) away from the surface. In that distance, the magnetic flux density decreases by more than half.

The simulation and experimental data are within the same order of magnitude and have similar trends for each of the nine data points. In Figure 5, both sets of data show an exponential decay in the magnetic flux as distance from the magnet on the z-axis increases. However, Figure 6 sheds light on where most of the discrepancy comes from, and that is at the surface of the magnet. As measurements are taken farther away from the surface, agreement between simulation and experiment increases.

Possible sources of error include not taking into consideration the coating on the magnet nor the plastic coating on the Gauss meter. Even a slight difference in where the experimental data is taken can produce vastly different values given how quickly the magnetic flux decreases with greater distance. Experimental data was taken by hand, holding a sensor mounted on a wand, which introduces human error. Mounting the Gauss meter wand on a robotic arm to take steady measurements would most likely increase accuracy.

Lastly, the exact point where a measurement is taken experimentally is not as exact as in the simulation. In the simulation, it is possible to obtain flux information at a single point in space. The Gauss Meter is unable to be as precise, and the exact spot that data is being collected from cannot be determined for smaller magnets like the ones used in this study. The FEA simulation has shown to be a good tool and will be useful for future models.

References

1. Bastos, J. P., "Electromagnetic Modeling by Finite Element Methods," *CRC press*, 2003
2. Cook, R., Malkus, D, Plesha, M., Witt, R, "Concepts and applications of finite element analysis," 4th ed., *John Wiley & Sons, Inc*, 2002
3. ANSYS Application Brief, "ANSYS Maxwell Magnetic Field Formulation," *http://www.ansys.com/-/media/Ansys/corporate/resourcelibrary/techbrief/tb-ansys-maxwell-magneticfield-formulation.pdf*, 2013
4. Lee, J., Dede, E.M., Nomura, T., "Simultaneous Design Optimization of Permanent Magnet, Coils, and Ferromagnetic Material in Actuators," *Transactions on Magnetics,* Vol. 47, pp 4712-4716.

Characterization of Energy Harvesting Ruck Sack

Alexis Moy, Julianne Douglas, Nathan Sharpes, Christopher Mullen

CERDEC CP&I Power

Abstract: *The technology of today's Soldier is increasingly advanced and capable, continually increasing their power demand. The increase in demand subsequently increases the number of batteries that the Soldier carries. The current solution is to simply carry more batteries, resulting in an excess of battery weight and volume carried by the Soldier. In the field, on a Soldier's mission, they must decide between carrying new technology and packing mission essentials such as food, water and ammo. One of the promising advances in power and energy options is energy harvesting. Previous ruck sack integrated power options utilize a suspended pack mass (suspended by springs and rails), rack and pinion based energy harvester, that would stores energy based on the movement of the Soldier's body relative to the ruck sack, to charge these new technologies carried by the Soldier. As harvesting technology continues to advance, a Soldier can generate more energy based on the same movement by employing a linear magnet and coin configuration (linear alternator), rather than a rack and pinion, to capture and store energy to charge the Soldier's systems.*

Based on data that was taken in this study of a linear alternator based energy harvesting ruck (EHR) sack, there are several interesting discoveries stemming from the information analyzed. It is shown that the relative velocity between the Soldier and suspended ruck sack, with different stroke and frequency inputs, had different power outputs. Shown in the graphs presented, there is a maximum power output around a velocity (walking speed) of 3.75 in/s at each of the different weights presented, all at a torso angle of 5 degrees. Any velocity higher than 3.75 in/s showed a drop in power output. It is also seen that frequency change has a greater impact on power output than stroke. In this paper, the results will show the coupling of the EHR with the magnetic coils as well as the maximum power than can be generated during ideal conditions in the field. US Army CERDEC intends to further develop this technology with ergonomic and technologic upgrades before it is put into the Soldiers hands.

Formation of Joint Munitions Power Sources Integrated Product Team

Anthony Pergolizzi
U.S. Army Armament Research, Development and Engineering Center
Army Fuze Management Office
Picatinny Arsenal, NJ 07806
Anthony.J.Pergolizzi.civ@mail.mil / 973-724-2361

Abstract: The US Department of Defense (DoD) has recently formed an integrated product team (IPT) to address a need for better military battery solutions. Munitions batteries have seen little technological advances in an era of great technical growth. These designs and chemistries were developed decades ago and often do not meet the requirements of modern munitions. The increased power demands, enhanced capabilities, extended shelf life and environmental ruggedness of modern weapons represents a unique challenge to the current battery industrial base. Bullets and projectiles with smart capabilities are becoming smaller while requiring more power in a shorter timeframe.

To meet shelf life requirements, munitions batteries are often designed as reserve cells which activate when the munition is fired. These reserve cells remain in an inactive state until power is required. Once activated, they need to provide power in a short amount of time and provide this power to the munition throughout its mission. The reserve nature of munitions batteries and the unique environments they are required to survive represents significant design challenge. This is often in direct contrast with commercial primary and secondary battery solutions which are designed to keep costs as low as possible.

The challenge for the Joint Munitions Power IPT is to develop better munitions batteries at an affordable cost. This team seeks to engage more traditional battery manufacturers and academia to help solve this problem. Our goal is to leverage manufacturing lessons learned and commercial battery expertise to build better and more cost effective munitions batteries.

Keywords: military; munitions; power source; batteries; joint service, integrated product team

Space-based Energy Storage Technology Development at the U.S. Air Force Research lab

Jessica L. Buckner, David M. Wilt, Jacqueline H. Cromer, Kyle H. Montgomery
Air Force Research Laboratory
Space Vehicles Directorate
3550 Aberdeen Ave SE, Kirtland AFB, NM 87117
Email: AFRL.VSSVOrgMailbox@us.af.mil

Abstract: *The mass of a spacecraft power system is one of the largest contributing components to the overall spacecraft mass. The increasing need for power and emphasis on reduction of size and mass of power system components necessitates development of advanced energy storage systems capable of achieving higher specific energy. Combinations of advanced materials, cell designs, and new chemistries are needed to accomplish this goal. To meet present and future space power requirements, improvements to Li-ion, hybrid technologies, and next generation chemistries that drive specific energy density to and above 400 Wh/kg while maintaining cycle life and safety requirements are being pursued. Aspects of battery technology of interest to space applications, associated challenges, and opportunities are discussed, with attention given to progress and initiatives at the Air Force Research Lab, Space Vehicles Directorate.*

Keywords: space batteries; Li-ion; next generation chemistries; space power systems

Introduction

Batteries used in space applications have unique performance requirements, including extended cycle life, long storage times, radiation tolerance, high reliability, and demonstrated safety [1, 2]. A variety of battery chemistries have been used for space applications, to include nickel-cadmium (Ni-Cd), nickel-hydrogen (Ni-H_2), and lithium ion (Li-ion). The Air Force (AF) has used Ni-H_2 batteries since the mid-1980s for heritage spacecraft. Ni-H_2 batteries are secondary batteries stored in pressurized vessels with a specific energy of 55-60 Wh/kg, over-charge and over-discharge abuse tolerance, long life, and extensive flight heritage [3]. Environmental concerns with Ni-H_2 electrodes in conjunction with the higher performance that Li-ion batteries offer prompted the examination of Li-ion cells for AF space vehicles [4-6].

Li-ion offers higher specific energy (>150 Wh/kg), lower self-discharge, and mass savings over Ni-H_2, but is sensitive to over-charge and over-discharge, requires sophisticated battery management systems to manage safety concerns, and lacks flight heritage on AF space vehicles. National and international government agencies, such as NASA and the European Space Agency (ESA), as well as commercial companies, have been using Li-ion since the early 2000s. The AF has yet to launch a heritage space vehicle with Li-ion batteries on board, but an upcoming flight will begin to supplement ground testing data and gain Li-ion much needed flight heritage on AF space vehicles.

A key contrast to batteries used for AF space vehicles versus terrestrial applications is the cycle life requirements. Low earth orbit (LEO) missions average 6000 cycles per year, at 30-40% depth of discharge (DOD), for a nominal 10 year mission life [7]. Geosynchronous earth orbit (GEO) satellites expect roughly 2700 charge and discharge cycles per mission, at 60% depth of discharge, for a nominal 15 year mission life. All AF missions require a 20% reserve capacity requirement. Rigorous on-ground qualification and life cycle testing up to 70% mission life is required before launch. In addition, if any component of the battery is altered (electrodes, separator, electrolyte, etc.), the battery must be re-qualified and life cycle tested. These requirements often lead to technology obsolescence and transition challenges for new Li-ion technologies.

Batteries for energy storage are essential to a successful mission, powering the spacecraft in eclipse, and storing energy generated by the solar panels when in sunlight. The power system accounts for about one-third of the dry mass of a space vehicle, meaning improvements to specific energy can greatly reduce mass and cost of launch. Several 200-300 Wh/kg battery technologies exist, but few can achieve the cycle life necessary for AF space vehicles. Furthermore, performance increases in Li-ion chemistries have become incremental in recent years, prompting exploration beyond Li-ion. This paper focuses on the energy storage development efforts within the Space Vehicles Directorate of the Air Force Research Laboratory (AFRL), specifically focusing on improvements to Li-ion, hybrid, and next generation technologies. AFRL continues to team with companies like Quallion, Yardney, Lynntech Inc., ADA Technologies, and Solid Power as well as a variety of universities for technology development. AFRL has interest and efforts in energy generation and power management technologies, however this paper will focus on the energy storage component of the power system.

Advanced Li-ion

AFRL is exploring a variety of Li-ion technologies that can improve specific energy while providing cycling stability compatible with LEO and GEO missions, including efforts to create electrodes that are less affected by solid electrolyte interphase (SEI) formation, oxidation, and other detrimental side reactions. AFRL is working with Lynntech Inc. to create a high energy density lithium manganese rich, nickel manganese cobalt oxide (LMR-NMC) cathode, and optimize it to improve the structural instability and low contact area associated with inefficient material utilization and capacity fade with cycling (Fig. 1). Several methods have been explored to achieve this, including templating techniques for high surface area mesoporous structures LMR-NMC and anode structures. Paired with a silicon or graphite anode, the LMR-NMC cathode has demonstrated a specific energy >300 Wh/kg. Other solutions to capacity fade that are also of interest to AFRL include electrode pre-treatments and surface coatings, pre-lithiation, and sacrificial materials.

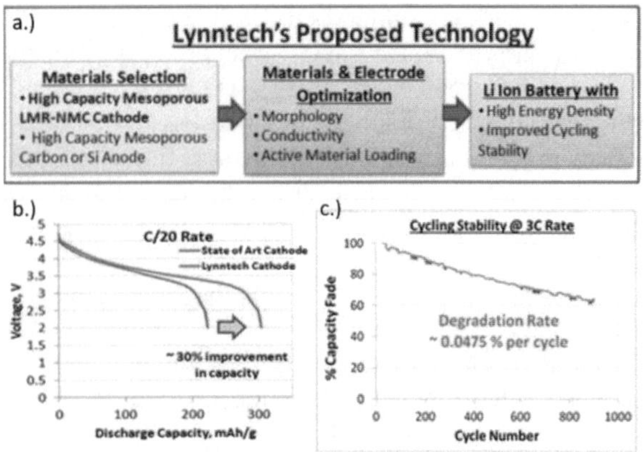

Figure 1. (a) Lynntech's proposed technology, (b) Discharge capacity of conventional vs Lynntech cathode, and (c) Capacity fade as a function of cycle number at 3C rate.

AFRL is working with Rochester Institute of Technology (RIT) to develop Li-ion cells with improvements to the cathode, anode, and current collector that can operate at 400 Wh/kg [8]. For the cathode, a variety of methods to synthesize $AlPO_4$ coated $LiCoO_2$ (LCO) were explored, increasing the capacity of the LCO cathode from 150 mAh/g to ~225 mAh/g, increasing the charge voltage from 3.6 to 3.9 V, and demonstrating significantly better cycling stability compared to the untreated LCO. A replacement for the copper foil of the anode was also investigated. Multiwall carbon nanotube (MWCNT) papers have several advantages over copper current collectors, presenting an order of magnitude lower areal density, stability at high potential, and low mass. In a dual phased approach to improve energy density of the anode, plasma enhanced chemical vapor deposition (PECVD) was used to deposit high capacity silicon on the MWCNT paper current collector, yielding an active mass loading up to 76% and an extraction capacity of 1673 mAh/g. Areal capacity was limited to 3.1 mAh/cm^2 due to internal stresses at the deposited layer. Surface modification of the MWCNT sheet for improved silicon adhesion and added coating steps prior to PECVD for deeper silicon penetration into the MWCNT sheet will be employed in the future.

Near Zero Volt Storage for Li-ion Cells

Development efforts with RIT also focused on near zero volt Li-ion storage [8-10]. In a discharged, near zero volt state, safety risks associated with Li-ion batteries decrease significantly and can enable easier transport and launch of Li-ion batteries. RIT's approach involves management of the amount of reversible lithium excess (RLE) in a cell to prevent the anode potential exceeding the potential at which dissolution of standard copper current collectors occurs at room temperature (3.1 V vs Li/Li$^+$). Other zero-volt technologies are available, but these often involve material substitutions, reduced performance, or cell re-design. Cathodes composed of LCO, nickel cobalt aluminum oxide (NCA), and HE5050, a high energy density lithium rich cathode, paired with a mesocarbon microbead (MCMB) anode all demonstrated 0-1% capacity loss upon multiple 3-day and 7-day zero volt storage periods, with strong recharge performance at a C/10 charge rate and variable discharge rates (C/10, C/2, 1C and 5C). RLE and conventional LCO/MCMB cells were subjected to 500 LEO cycles at 30% DOD (Fig. 2). Results indicate that the near zero volt storage period has no effect on cycling stability versus the conventional cell. Small satellite flight opportunities are being explored to study the trade between cycle life and zero volt storage time and gain the technology flight heritage.

Figure 2. (a) Cycle schedule flow chart, (b) Discharge

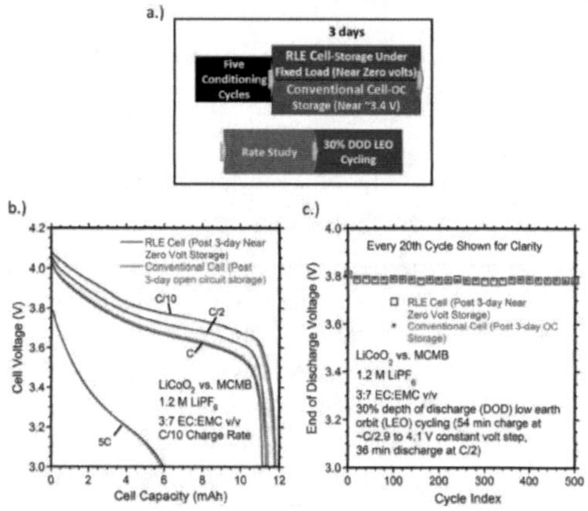

profiles of RLE and conventional cell after 3-day near zero volt storage for RLE and open circuit storage for conventional cell, and (c) End of discharge voltage for 30% DOD LEO cycling of RLE and conventional cell. Figure reproduced from [9].

Beyond the approaches to Li-ion outlined above, AFRL has interest in advanced electrode structures and modification, including templated and core shell structures, surface modification, and additives. Silicon, germanium, carbon based and other anodes with high specific capacity and energy are also of interest. First principles, chemistry specific models that can predict the performance of new Li-ion chemistries based on operating conditions (cycling protocol, temperature, etc.) are of interest. Data from the simulations can improve confidence in emerging chemistries and supplement on-ground cycling data.

Solid State Batteries

Solid state batteries can provide improved safety, higher voltage, and longer cycle life, but suffer from poor transport and require higher temperatures to operate. AFRL is working with University of Colorado-Boulder to develop an all solid state battery [11], with much of the effort focused on evaluating and increasing the specific and areal capacity of metallic silicon and tin additives anodes. While silicon is attractive for its low operating potential, abundance, and high theoretical specific capacity (3579 mAh/g for $Li_{15}Si_4$), tin has outstanding electrical conductivity and Li-ion diffusivity with relatively large theoretical specific capacity (991 mAh/g for $Li_{4.4}Sn$) [12, 13]; yet, both silicon and tin experience large volumetric expansion upon lithiation, which is problematic for cycling stability. UC Boulder combined silicon and tin nanopowders to create an anode of silicon within a tin matrix. Because Sn lithiates at higher voltages than silicon, the pressure derived from the expansion of tin upon lithiation creates an in situ pressure on the silicon to enable greater reversibility. A solid state cell employing a $77.5Li2S$-$22.5P_2S_5$ glassy solid state electrolyte and InLi counter electrode was cycled at 60ºC, realizing an active material first cycle specific capacity of over 1000 mAh/g, compared to 800 mAh/g previously achieved for pure tin, and excellent reversibility (Fig. 3). Addition of silicon lowered the anode voltage from 0.79 V vs. Li to 0.53 V vs. Li, improving applicability for high energy applications. Future work will include optimization of silicon-tin anodes with various encapsulation and synthesis techniques for improved reversibility.

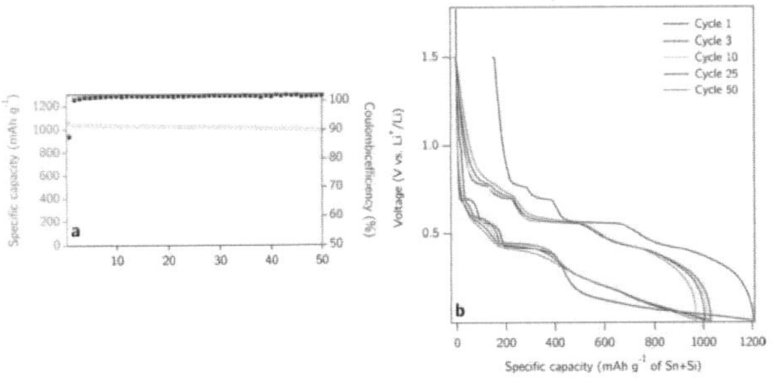

Figure 3. (a) Cycle performance and coulombic efficiency of Sn:Si:SSE [7(3:1):3] anode in all solid state Li-ion battery at 60C with C/20 rate, and (b) Corresponding voltage profiles of the Sn:Si:SSE anode. Figure reproduced from [11].

Pseudocapacitors

In addition to battery technologies, AFRL is developing capacitor technologies of benefit to pulse power and energy buffer applications. Ultracapacitor technologies have several advantages over traditional batteries, including cycle life >500,000, high power density, and minimal degradation with cycling. Pseudocapacitors fill the gap between batteries and ultracapacitors, storing more charge than ultracapacitors, but charging and discharging more quickly than a battery. AFRL is working with ADA Technologies to advance a hybrid pseudocapacitor technology with goals of >50 Wh/kg specific energy, specific power >10 kW/kg, and cycle life >500,000. Atomic layer deposition (ALD) was used to coat transition metal oxides on activated carbon cathodes; this coating enables electrochemical energy storage via Faradaic redox reactions involving electron charge transfer versus physical charge storage at the electric double layer in ultracapacitors, increasing device specific capacity and energy. The solid electrolyte and anode will also be optimized for the ALD coated cathode. Thus far, an energy density of 57 Wh/kg, 4.5 kW/kg specific power, and 30,000 charge and discharge cycles have been demonstrated at the cell level (Fig. 4). Future work will focus on fabrication and electrochemical characterization of a prototype cell in the BB-2590 form factor, commonly used in military applications, and a technology demonstration on an upcoming small satellite flight.

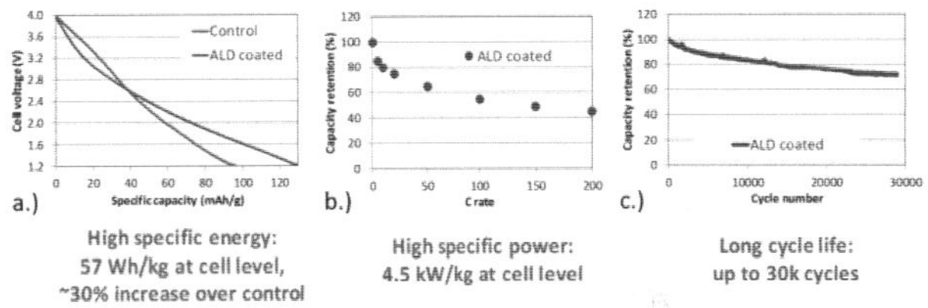

Figure 4. (a) Specific energy of ALD coated cathode vs. control cathode, (b) Capacity retention vs. C-rate for ALD coated cathode, and (c) Capacity retention vs. cycle number for ALD coated cathode.

Nanocapacitors

Advanced, next generation energy storage technologies with the potential to achieve record power and energy density are pursued by AFRL. Nanocapacitors developed with the University of Illinois Urbana-Champaign (UIUC) possess high power density similar to a capacitor, with charge and discharge times reliant on the speed of electron movement, and a theoretical energy density in the tens of thousands of Wh/kg, equivalent to the energy density of a material's covalent bonds [14]. The theoretical energy density, reliability, and cycle efficiency of nanocapacitors offer a promising alternative to Li-ion batteries, though research and development to understand the fundamental mechanisms of device operation, including quantum charge effects, must be explored.

Experimental and theoretical studies of the charge transfer mechanisms are underway. Si-SiO_2-Si, Al-Al_2O_3-Al, and Al-Al_2O_3-Graphene (plate-dielectric-plate) nanocapacitors have been fabricated and characterized to understand leakage current, dielectric strength, and self-repair. One interesting property of the nanocapacitors is charge storage in the dielectric, evidenced by hysteresis of current-voltage curves and time dependent (I~1/t) discharge of the dielectric (Fig. 3) [15]. Two models representing separate charge storage and transfer phenomena have been developed; one model represents charge trapping in the dielectric as a function of thickness, and the other explores charge transfer by cold field emission. AFRL is working to mature the latter model to compare to experimental data obtained from UIUC. Future work will expand on graphene as a plate material, lowering the leakage current, measuring the dielectric breakdown voltage, understanding the mechanism of self repair and recovery after failure, additional charge storage in the dielectric, and model development and validation from UIUC and AFRL.

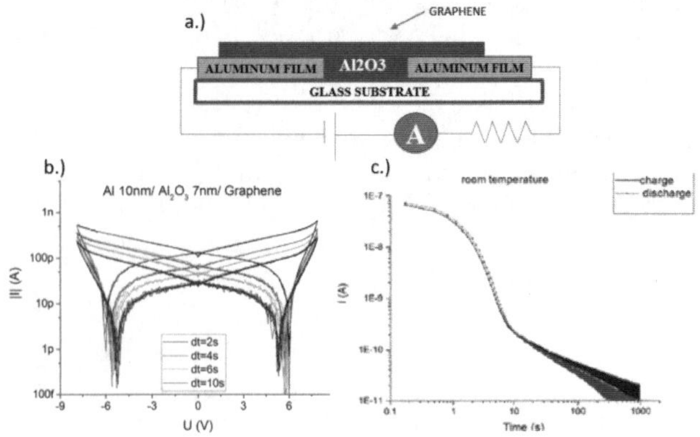

Figure 5. (a) Schematic of Al-Al_2O_3-Graphene nanocapacitor, (b) Current-voltage curve with hysteresis, demonstrating charge storage in the dielectric, and (c) Discharge behavior of capacitor, with exponential discharge at first and power law (I~1/t) discharge at t~10 sec. Figure reproduced from [15].

Outlook

The Air Force is pursuing a development path in support of the Space Warfighting Construct (SWC), where space capabilities and services will be available from a variety of satellite types, including traditional AF vehicles (GPS, AEHF, etc.) as well as smaller spacecraft in a variety of orbits. As the Air Force shifts towards proliferation of smaller assets, novel spacecraft power technologies that can provide enhanced capabilities on small scales are required, allowing for rapid technology demonstrations to provide validation and flight heritage to new battery technologies.

Implementation of the SWC will require changes to the conventional spacecraft development process. While 10-15 year missions have been successful for heritage AF space vehicles, the significant cost and schedule overheads are not compatible with the SWC. Small satellite lifetimes do not typically exceed 5 years, and extensive and costly qualification measures for heritage satellites are likely not necessary. AFRL is working with internal and industry partners to evaluate emerging battery technologies and assess flight opportunities as they relate to the SWC.

Conclusion

AFRL continues to invest in new technologies that push towards higher energy and power density to enable enhanced capabilities for AF space vehicles. The number of technologies and cell designs that have potential for specific energy >400 Wh/kg continue to grow, but few offer the cycle stability necessary for LEO and GEO missions. The SWC provides expanding opportunities for advanced energy storage system technology demonstrations and transition into AF space vehicles. AFRL, Space Vehicles Directorate continues to evaluate and develop new and advanced energy storage technologies for use on traditional and small AF space vehicles.

References

[1] R. Bugga, M. Smart, J. Whitacre, and W. West, "Lithium Ion Batteries for Space Applications," in *2007 IEEE Aerospace Conference*, 2007, pp. 1-7.

[2] Air Force Space Command, "Lithium-ion Battery for Spacecraft Application," Space and Missile Systems Center, 2008.

[3] A. H. Zimmerman, *Nickel-Hydrogen Batteries: Principles and Practice*: AIAA, 2009.

[4] A. Manthiram, "An Outlook on Lithium Ion Battery Technology," *ACS Central Science,* vol. 3, pp. 1063-1069, 2017.

[5] R. Wenige, Schilbach, M., Weidner, P.F., "Power Storage for Small Satellites: Comparison of NiH2 and Li-ion Batteries," presented at the 5th International Symposium of the International Academy of Astronautics, Berlin, 2005.

[6] M. Wasz, "Coping with T30 Obsolescence in 2013," in *NASA Aerospace Battery Workshop*, Huntsville, AL, 2010.

[7] Y. Borthomieu, "14 - Satellite Lithium-Ion Batteries A2 - Pistoia, Gianfranco," in *Lithium-Ion Batteries*, ed Amsterdam: Elsevier, 2014, pp. 311-344.

[8] B. J. Landi, Ganter, M., Schauerman, C., Crompton, K., Leggiero, A., Staub, J., "High Capacity Cathode and Carbon Nanotube-Supported Anode for Enhanced Energy Density Batteries," Defense Technical Information Center, 2017.

[9] K. R. Crompton, Landi, B.J., "Opportunities for near zero volt storage of lithium ion batteries," *Ener. Envir. Sci.,* vol. 9, 2016.

[10] K. R. Crompton, J. W. Staub, M. P. Hladky, and B. J. Landi, "Lithium rich cathode/graphite anode combination for lithium ion cells with high tolerance to near zero volt storage," *Jour. Power Sources,* vol. 343, pp. 109-118, 2017.

[11] J. Whiteley, J. Woo Kim, D. Molina Piper, and S.-H. Lee, "High-Capacity and Highly Reversible Silicon-Tin Hybrid Anode for Solid-State Lithium-Ion Batteries," *Jour. Electrochem. Soc.,* vol. 163, pp. A251-A254, 2016.

[12] M. N. Obrovac, Christensen, L., "Structural Changes in Silicon Anodes during Lithium Insertion/Extraction," *Electrochem. Solid State Lett.,* vol. 7, pp. A93-A96, 2004.

[13] A. Kamali and D. J. Fray, "Tin-based materials as advanced anode materials for lithium ion batteries: A review," *Rev. Adv. Matl. Sci.,* vol. 27, 2011.

[14] A. Hubler, "Synthetic atoms: Large energy density and a record power density," *Complexity,* vol. 18, pp. 12-14, 2013.

[15] A. Hubler, "Arrays of Synthetic Atoms: Nanocapacitor batteries with Large Energy Density and Small Leak Currents," Defense Technical Information Center, 2017.

Overview of Power in Fuze and Munitions Applications

Bradley Armstrong
Army Fuze Management Office
Armaments Research Development & Engineering Center (ARDEC)
Picatinny Arsenal, NJ 07806
bradley.a.armstrong.civ@mail.mil / 973-724-2174

Abstract: This paper presents an overview of power source capability needs for U.S. ARDEC munitions. It addresses the stringent requirements for gun launched and hand-emplaced munitions, capability gaps, and organizational structure in place to promote advancement of munitions power sources.

Keywords: fuze; fuzing; munitions; power; battery; reserve battery; gun launched;

Introduction

The U.S Army Armament Research, Development and Engineering Center (ARDEC) is an internationally acknowledged hub for the advancement of armament technologies and engineering innovation. ARDEC's portfolio includes such items as hand-emplaced munitions, small to medium cal munitions, mortars and artillery all of which utilize a fuze. As fuzing has become more advanced coupled with munitions integrating advanced sensing and guidance technologies, the demand for power sources has and will continue to increase. As a result, the ARDEC Fuze Division has been given the mission for developing power sources for these advanced munition systems.

ARDEC has therefore invested in a variety of power source technologies which range from energy harvesting devices, reserve power sources and, in some applications, primary active batteries. Balancing system level needs and requirements is of utmost importance to properly identify which type of power source is appropriate for the application. This is the primary reason ARDEC openly investigates all types of technologies to ensure the best solution is selected.

ARDEC utilizes the Army Research Lab to provide additional support for reserve batteries to supplement development and production efforts. To ensure staying at the forefront of technology, ARDEC is actively involved with a variety of organizations and working groups.

Within the Government, ARDEC is an active member of the Technology Coordinating Group V with the Department of Energy; active participant in supporting the formation of a tri-service Munitions Power Sources IPT; and active in supporting Joint Fuze Technology Program efforts and proposals.

Industry plays a critical role in shaping and realizing power solutions that meet the needs of the munitions supported by ARDEC. To engage industry ARDEC is heavily dependent on executing Small Business Innovative Research efforts, ManTech efforts, Foreign Comparative Test programs and utilizing the DOTC, which enables opportunities to solicit a variety of technology solutions from the entire National Armaments Consortium (NAC).

Due to the unique set of requirements of the Army's gun launched munitions, active batteries typically are not used due to degradation during storage or poor performance over temperature. As a result, reserve batteries are generally the only viable option to meet the Army's needs. The presentation discusses this unique set of requirements and highlights associated challenges.

ARDEC is planning S&T objectives and capability needs across the family of power sources for short-term (<5 yrs), mid-term (5-10 yrs), and long-term (10+ yrs) to ensure that power sources, which are a critical enabling technology for advanced munitions, are available to support future program needs.

Acknowledgements

Author Bradley Armstrong acknowledges Mr. Craig Doremus and the ARDEC Fuze Division for contributions to the presentation and paper.

Power Quality in a Tactical Application: What is PQ? Why is it Important?

Walter Magill, Louie Leitao
NOVA Power Solutions, Inc.
23020 Eaglewood Ct, Suite 100, Sterling, VA 20166
Walt.magill@novapower.com

Abstract: It is generally accepted that power quality is critical to the reliability and efficiency of operational warfighting capability. However, relatively little is understood about the relationship and interaction of modern combat capability and the electrical systems they are dependent on. The failure of power and systems engineering to understand this relationship has resulted in increased cost and decreased capability throughout the US Department of Defense.

In recent years there has been significant R&D investments made in advanced battery chemistries, technologies and renewable energy sources for the warfighter. With the anticipation these new technologies bring, the concern for clean, conditioned power, or "Power Quality", must remain as part of the discussion.

This article will discuss the most common power anomalies, or Power Quality issues experienced by field deployed DoD installations, and the catastrophic results these anomalies can cause with mission critical systems when they are not addressed. Potential solutions will also be discussed. Achieving consistent power quality across the electrical system is critical to reducing the cost of operations and maximizing capability.

What is Power Quality? Power Quality can be described as the amount of distortion in voltage, current or frequency from a power source. The power source can be an electrical utility grid, generator or any other energy generating source.

The power provided to mission critical systems should be consistently maintained as a clean, conditioned, regulated signal, or sine wave regardless of the state of the power source. The power signal should maintain a constant voltage and frequency with no distortion of the waveform and no interruption of power to the mission critical system (during blackout/brownout). Common power anomalies can include, harmonic distortion, switching transients, line noise, frequency variations, power surges, power sags, high voltage spikes, brownouts and power failures (blackouts).

Benefits of improved power quality include greatly reduced, or eliminated unplanned down time, increased life cycle/Mean Time Between Failure (MTBF) of mission critical systems and cost savings through reduced energy usage and cooling requirements.

Many Commercial Off the Shelf (COTS) power conditioners, or Uninterruptible Power Supplies (UPS) will convert the output signal from a sinewave to a stepped AC wave when operating on battery power as shown in **Figure 1**. Many times, this output transition will create a switching transient shown in **Figure 2**. When this transient is supplied to the input of the mission critical system, it will cause damage to the internal components. As this event happens multiple times, it will cause catastrophic equipment failure in the mission critical system, which in turn, will cause unplanned down time for the mission, and at worst case, loss of life for the warfighter. Many of these COTS systems are currently deployed in DoD applications, because the initial cost is very inexpensive.

Only after there is a catastrophic system failure are these systems replaced with ruggedized power conditioners.

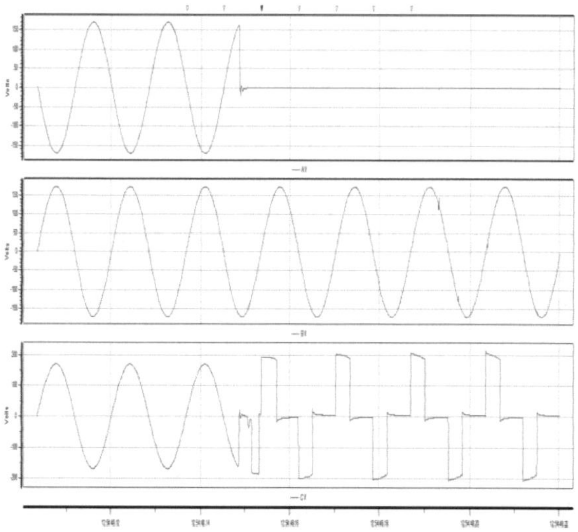

Figure 1: Stepped AC sinewave output of COTS UPS when operating on battery, shown in lower waveform.

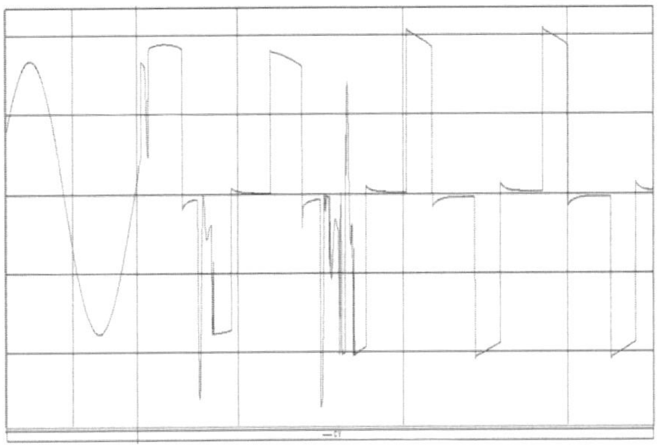

Figure 2: Switching transient on COTS UPS system output caused by transfer to battery power.

Many DoD applications use a generator as a power source. It is common that power produced from a generator will have fluctuating frequency and voltage output as seen in **Figure 3**. Any mission critical system must have a power conditioning element installed between the generator and the mission critical system (load) to correct or regulate any fluctuation or deviation in the power. Many COTS UPS systems have a passive filtering circuit that provides very limited conditioning, and only under certain conditions. To properly correct these voltage and frequency fluctuations, and to protect the mission critical system a power conditioner, or UPS with an active filtering circuit must be utilized.

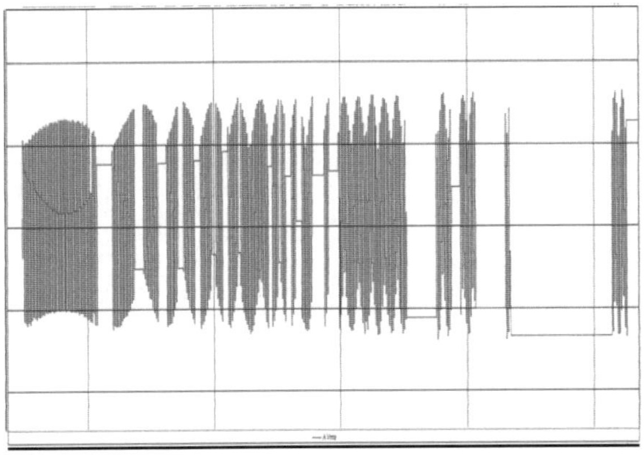

Figure 3: Generator output with frequency deviation and voltage fluctuation.

Many times, a utility power grid will produce line noise, or "dirty power" due to any number of circumstances. Line noise is characterized by "notching" in the waveform when measured with an oscilloscope as shown in **Figure 4**. This condition is very common in foreign utility grids, because of poor equipment condition, overloading or poor connections, to name a few. Line noise can be especially detrimental to sensitive mission critical systems if not corrected. As described in the previous paragraph, a power conditioner with active filtering is necessary to correct this condition.

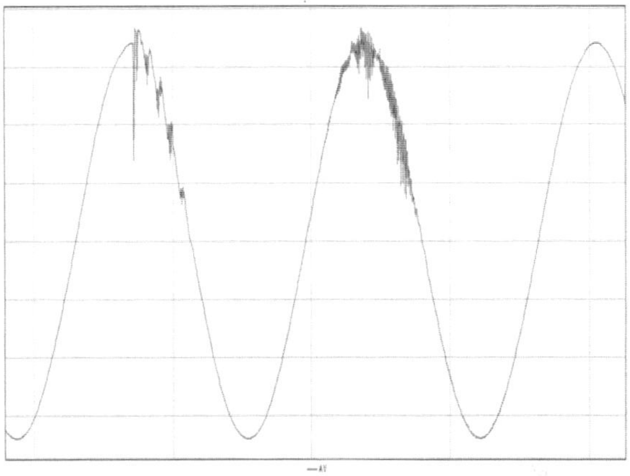

Figure 4: Line noise shown with notching of the waveform.

Another common power anomaly is harmonics. Harmonics are characterized by a distortion in the voltage, current or frequency waveform as shown in **Figure 5**. Harmonics are caused by non-linear loads such as switch mode power supplies, variable frequency drives or variable speed drives. These systems can be connected on the system load, or they can be "reflected" from other areas within the electrical distribution network. Active filtering within a power conditioner is required to correct any harmonic distortion.

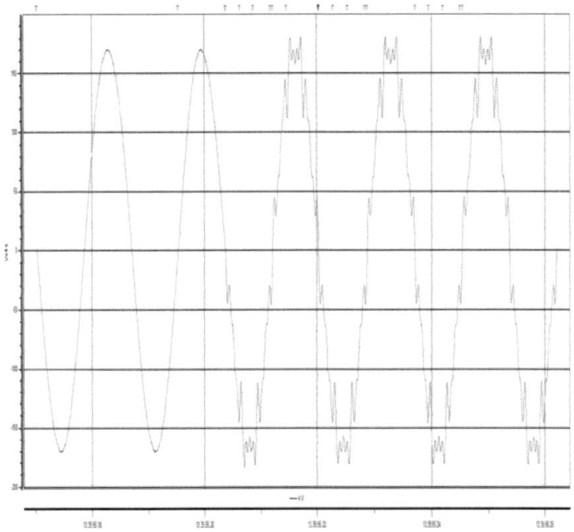

Figure 5: Common harmonic distortion caused by connected equipment in electrical distribution system.

Why is Power Quality Important? Clean power quality will ensure that the mission critical system will operate efficiently and will protect the integrity of your data. The net effect of improved power quality is a reduction of maintenance costs and conversely, an increased life cycle of the mission critical systems.

Results of poor power quality are well documented. If the power supply in a mission critical system, for example, is repeatedly exposed to varying degrees of poor power quality, including line noise, transients or harmonic distortion, sensitive components such as transistors and IC chips on circuit boards and power supplies will suffer damage as shown in **Figure 6** and **Figure 7**.

Figure 6: Blown transistor caused by generator frequency deviation.

Figure 7: 70% of electronic equipment failures are attributed to power quality issues.

What can be Done to Improve Power Quality? There are many steps that can be taken to improve power quality, chief among them is to install a power conditioner that can isolate, correct and/or mitigate any power quality issues from affecting the mission critical system. Not all power conditioners are created equal. Many times, system engineers may believe all that is required to meet the specifications for an application is a system that can provide battery backup during a loss of input power (UPS). Most COTS UPS systems, however do not have the active filtering, conditioning and isolation characteristics that are required to meet rugged military standards.

Nova Power Solutions provides true power quality as part of our equipment capability solution, which provides power conditioning 100% of the time. All Nova Power systems are designed with double conversion technology which isolates the load from harmful input harmonics and frequency distortion. Isolation transformers can also be integrated, which will isolate the distribution system from faults and harmonic effects of the load. When input power falls out of tolerance, and the power conditioner/UPS transfers to battery power, Nova Power systems do not create a switching transient on the output from the battery transfer. This will help to increase life cycle of the mission critical systems. Because Nova Power systems have a more tolerant rectifier input circuit, they will not transfer to battery power during minor input events, or fluctuations. This will increase the life cycle of the batteries within the system.

Nova Power Solutions offers power condition, conversion, backup and distribution systems. All Nova Power systems are ruggedized and tested to meet various military standards. Nova Power provides custom, scalable solutions to fit a wide range of applications. They are particularly suited for shipboard, tactical military and similar rugged environments. Nova Power has been providing systems for military and heavy industrial applications for over 30 years. With this experience we have a deep understanding of logistics and supply chain management and support the product through its entire life cycle.

Investigation of Energy Conversion Characteristics of Reversible Energy Storage System Comprised of Electrolysis, Hydrogen Storage Alloy, and Fuel Cell

***Sungbaek Cho*[1], *Gwangwoo Han*[2], *Joongmyeon Bae*[2,*]**

[1] Convergence Technology Collaboration Center, Institute of Defense Advanced Technology Research, Agency for Defence Development, Daejeon 34186, Republic of Korea

[2] Department of Mechanical Engineering, KAIST, Daejeon 34141, Republic of Korea

Contact author e-mail: jmbae@kaist.ac.kr

Abstract: *Hydrogen is a very promising source of energy owing to its high energy density, environmental friendliness and renewable nature. However, the storage and transport of hydrogen is the most critical issue to be resolved in the realization of the hydrogen energy network because conventional gas cylinders for storage and transportation have low hydrogen densities and are difficult to handle. Hydrogen is a key performance-limiting factor of a fuel cell that generates electricity through the electrochemical reactions of hydrogen and oxygen gases. In this study, a reversible energy storage system with high energy density was fabricated and evaluated. The purpose of an evaluation is to assess the energy charge and discharge characteristics and feasibility of the system. The system is composed of water electrolyzer, hydrogen storage alloys, and the fuel cell. The hydrogen is formed from water and stored in the hydrogen storage alloys. In order for the fuel cell to work, the hydrogen reacts with the oxygen to form both water and heat while creating electricity. As a result, we can make the reversible energy storage system to combine the electrolyzer and the fuel cell into one device using only water as a fuel.*

Keywords: energy storage system; high energy density; electrolyzer; hydrogen storage alloy; fuel cell

Introduction

Hydrogen is attracting great attention as a next-generation energy source because it can be stored at a high energy storage density and there are various application including fuel for power generation and transportation. In particular, fuel cells using hydrogen as a fuel are highly efficient, quiet and eco-friendly, and are used in a variety of fields including automobiles, auxiliary power sources, and submarines. However, there is a disadvantage in that the charging hydrogen is restricted due to the lack of infrastructure. Therefore, in this study, we proposed a new concept of reversible energy storage system which can charge and discharge energy through water without the need of hydrogen supply. In the charging process, water is converted into hydrogen through electrochemical reaction and stored in the hydrogen storage alloy. During the discharge process, the stored hydrogen is converted into electric energy and water. In this study, experimental studies on energy charge and discharge characteristics using water electrolysis, hydrogen storage alloy and fuel cell were carried out and the feasibility of this reversible energy storage system was examined.

System process layout

The core components of this system are water electrolysis, hydrogen storage alloy, and fuel cell. The charging part is comprised of a pressurized-type water electrolyzer and BOPs (balance of plant) including a water booster pump and the dryer module as shown in Fig. 1. The discharging part consists of an AB_5 type hydrogen storage alloy based hydrogen storage cylinder, PEMFC (polymer electrolyte membrane fuel cell) stack which can be operated without humidifying device, and a PCS (power conditioning system). In the charging process, water is converted into hydrogen through electrochemical reaction in the electrolyzer of the charging unit and hydrogen is stored in the hydrogen storage alloy of the discharging unit. During the discharge process, the stored hydrogen is converted into electricity and water through electrochemical reaction in the PEMFC stack of the discharging unit. During the entire process, hydrogen was used as an intermediate medium.

In order to design a reversible energy storage system capable of charging energy with high volumetric energy density while being easy to charge and discharge, the characteristics of the hydrogen storage alloy are the most important. In particular, the hydrogen storage density of the hydrogen storage alloy should be high at room temperature and relatively low pressure. In case of AB_5 type hydrogen storage alloy, it has a plateau pressure of 30 bar or less at near ambient temperature conditions [1]. To charge hydrogen to the AB_5 type hydrogen storage alloy via water electrolyzer without hydrogen compressor, pressurized-type electrolyzer system can be applied. By eliminating hydrogen compressor, system efficiency and noise emission problem could be significantly enhanced [2]. For the discharging part, PEMFC stack has the advantage of being able to convert hydrogen to electric power under ambient temperature and pressure conditions. In addition, it can also be used for small scale mobile applications with fast startup times. To sum up, the integration of electrolyzer system, hydrogen storage alloy, and PEMFC could be an effective combination for implementing a high energy density reversible energy storage system.

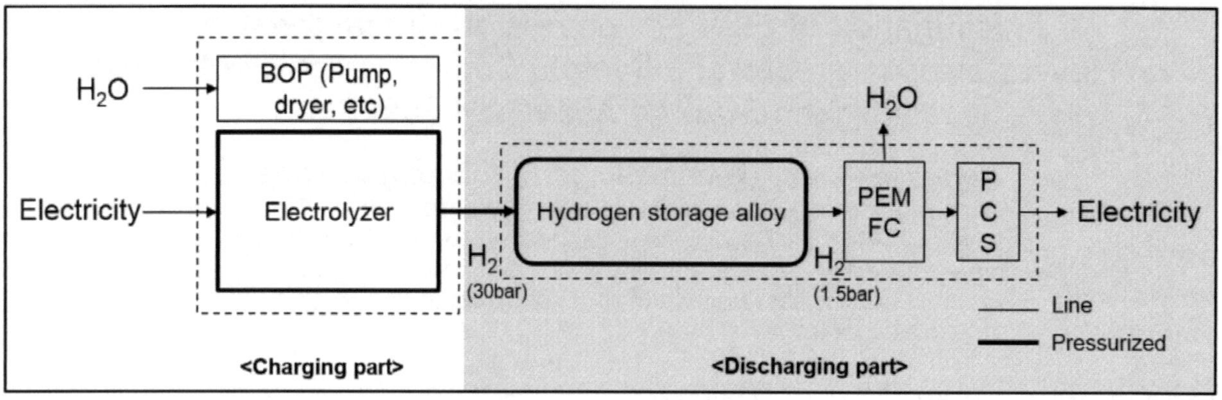

Figure 1. System process flow diagram

In this study, experimental studies were carried out to confirm energy charging and discharging characteristics when core components were integrated. Form the experimental results, effective design direction for enhancing energy conversion characteristics of this system were proposed.

Experimental set-up

1) Charging experiments

In order to study the hydrogen charging characteristics when electrolyzer and hydrogen storage alloy were integrated, experimental set-up was prepared as shown in Fig. 2. The electrolyzer system consists of an electrolysis stack module, a dryer module for producing high purity hydrogen, and a control module. It can produce 250 NL/hour of hydrogen and consumes 1.3 kW of power. 1kg of AB_5 type hydrogen storage alloy was loaded on autoclave and operating conditions were 30 bar and ambient temperature environments. In the hydrogen charging experiments, the longitudinal and radial temperature gradients of the autoclave were measured. Moreover, the hydrogen charging rate and hydrogen charged amount were checked by measuring the hydrogen flow rate of the and the weight change of the autoclave.

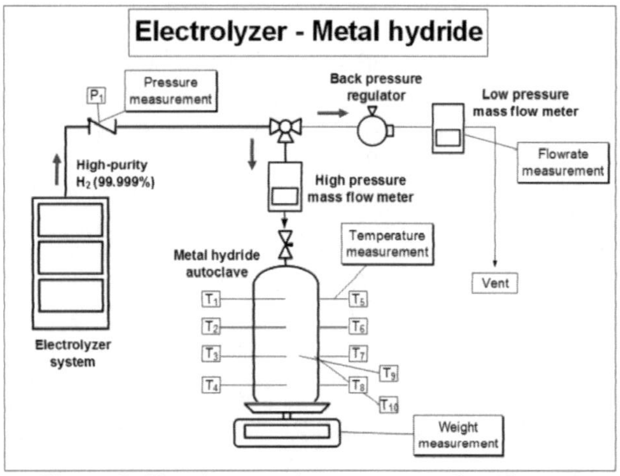

Figure 2. Charging experiments process flow diagram

2) Discharging experiments

The discharging experimental setup was prepared as shown in Fig. 3 to study the energy conversion characteristics when hydrogen storage alloy and PEMFC were integrated. During the hydrogen discharging process, the pressure from the autoclave was reduced to 1.5 barA using a micro regulator, and the flow rate was controlled through the MFC (mass flow controller). The temperature change, mass change, and flow rate of the autoclave were measured during discharging process to understand the discharge characteristic. In addition, the amount of electric energy converted from the chemical energy of the hydrogen through the fuel cell was also measured.

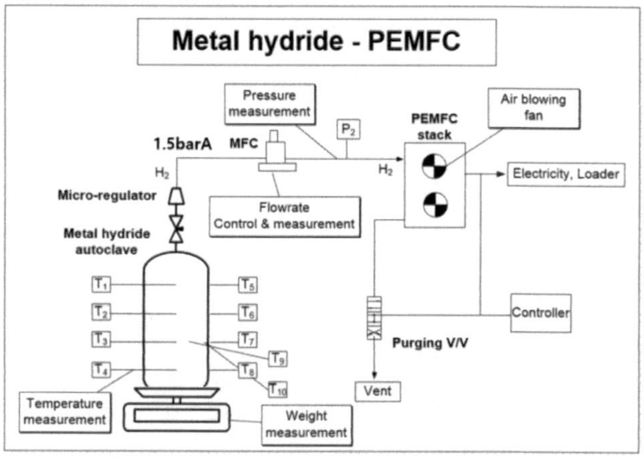

Figure 3. Discharging experiments process flow diagram

Conclusion

The present work proposed an effective concept for developing high volumetric energy density energy storage system, which is composed of electrolysis, hydrogen storage alloy, and fuel cell. In addition, energy charging and discharging characteristics were experimentally studied. During the experiments, about 1.4 wt.% of hydrogen storage density was confirmed, which can ensure energy storage density of approximately 1.5 kWh/L based on the hydrogen storage system volume. However, there was an initial rapid temperature rise up to 65°C and it took more than three hours to fully charge. This is because when the temperature rises, the amount of hydrogen that can be stored under a pressure of 30 bar is limited due to the PCT (pressure-concentration-temperature) characteristic of the hydrogen storage alloy. During the hydrogen discharge, the temperature of the hydrogen alloy decreased to minus 1°C at a fixed flow rate, and the flow rate was lower than the set value. Therefore, it was concluded that the thermal management of the hydrogen storage system is required for effective heat dissipation/heat absorption in order to secure fast hydrogen charging time and long operating time.

Acknowledgements

This work was supported by the Agency for Defense Development (ADD) in South Korea.

References

1. Guillaume, D., Claude, E., Christophe, P., Serguey, G., Pierre, M, "Hydrogen-based PEM auxiliary power unit," International Journal of Hydrogen Energy, vol. 34, pp.4983-4989, 2009
2. Marcelo, C., David, L. F., Jurgen, M., Detlef, S., "A comprehensive review on PEM water electrolysis" International Journal of Hydrogen Energy, vol. 38, pp.4901-4932, 2013

Thermal Management of Hydrogen Storage System Based on Metal Hydride

Heesook Roh[1], Seongbaek Cho[1], Joong Bae Kim[2], Mingeon Kim[2] and Bong Jae Lee[2*]

[1]Convergence Technology Collaboration Center,
Institute of Defense Advanced Technology Research,
Agency for Defense Development
Daejeon 34186, Republic of Korea

[2]Department of Mechanical Engineering,
Korea Advanced Institute of Science and Technology,
Daejeon 34141, Republic of Korea

Contact Author Email : bongjae.lee@kaist.ac.kr
Contact Author phone number : +82-42-350-3239

Abstract: *Hydrogen energy is a promising energy source for the next-generation weapon system of less noise and high energy density. In the area of the hydrogen energy, the hydrogen storage technique is the most important part of the practical applications. The previous techniques of the hydrogen storage, for example, liquid hydrogen tank, gaseous hydrogen tank and cryoadsorption have several disadvantages such as low energy density and the high cost for the installation. On the other hands, Metal hydrides facilitate to make the high energy density hydrogen storage through the simple system. In addition, the metal hydrides have long cycle life and they have superior stability from the unexpected external impact. Therefore, the metal hydrides are suitable for the power source of the next-generation military weapon system. The metal hydrides accompany the exothermic (or endothermic) reaction during the absorption (or desorption) process. Considering the fact that the thermal conductivity of the metal hydrides for the hydrogen storage system is usually less than 1 W/m·K, an appropriate thermal management is necessary to the hydrogen storage system of metal hydrides. In this research, we propose to enhance the effective thermal conductivity of the metal hydride for the thermal management of hydrogen storage system. The effect of the thermal management is verified through the transient simulation results with the enhanced effective thermal conductivity of the metal hydride.*

Keywords: metal hydride; thermal management; effective thermal conductivity

Introduction

Hydrogen energy has been in the limelight for a major power source of the next-generation weapon system with less noise and high energy density. The hydrogen storage system is the most important part of utilizing the hydrogen energy. High-pressure compression, liquefaction, chemical hydride, metal hydride are general methods of hydrogen storage technology. Comparing to the hydrogen tank of liquid hydrogen, the metal hydride has advantages such as the safety, high energy density, and thus, the hydrogen storage in the metal hydrides can be a potential solution for the energy source of future weapon systems.

The hydrogen storage system based on metal hydride accompanies the exothermic and endothermic processes in charging and discharging operations. In addition, the maximum pressure of the hydrogen charging and the stable flow rate in discharge mode are sensitive to the temperature of the metal hydride. Furthermore, the metal hydride changes its form from bulk solid to powder after several cycles of charging/discharging processes. Due to the extremely low thermal conductivity of the metal hydrides [1,2], the heat generated from the metal hydride cannot be easily transferred to the exterior, and the high temperature region in the storage system inevitably occurs. Therefore, the hydrogen storage system based on metal hydride should be equipped with the thermal management for the efficient operation.

There are several studies to propose the thermal management designs such as the internal heat path, exterior fin structure and external forced convection with a fan. Raju et al. suggested that the metal hydride storage with spiral shape of the internal heat exchanger [3]. Keshari et al. also proposed the internal heat exchanger consisting of pin fin tube in the storage [4]. However, the previous studies have a critical limitation that they designed the excessive thermal management for the hydrogen storage based on the metal hydride. Due to the excessive thermal management such as the heat exchanger, it is inevitable to loss the volume for the metal hydride and decrease the energy density.

The present work aims to propose the thermal management of hydrogen storage based on the metal hydride for efficient operation. For the thermal management of the hydrogen storage, we suggest to enhance the thermal conductivity of the metal hydride. In order to verify the effect of the enhanced thermal conductivity of the metal hydride, the thermal analysis with the commercial simulation tool (ANSYS) was conducted. The effective thermal conductivity of the metal hydride was assumed 5 and 10 times larger than the metal hydride. In addition, the quantified heat generation and absorption rates which were obtained from the hydrogen charge and discharge experiments and fitting process, were used in the simulation. Finally, the effect of the thermal management is be found as the decreases of the maximum temperature in the charge process according to the increases of the effective thermal conductivity in the simulation result. Even in the discharge process, the effect of the thermal management is verified as the increases in the minimum temperature according to the increases of the effective thermal conductivity.

Experiments

The metal hydride container was manufactured with the stainless steel (SUS316) and the shape of the container is cylindrical. The total height of the container is 170 mm, and its diameter and wall thickness are 60.5 mm and 5 mm, respectively. The metal hydride used in this work is AB_5 type and the thermal conductivity of the metal hydride in packed condition was measured by the laser flash method. The thermal conductivity of the packed metal hydride is 0.15 W/m·K. The charge and discharge processes were performed at a constant hydrogen inlet pressure of 30 bar and a constant mass flow rate condition. The thermocouple (K type) is positioned at the center of the container, and temperature of the metal hydride had been measured while the charge and discharge processes. The mass flow rate in the charge process was also precisely measured by the mass flow meter. Lastly, the heat generation and absorption rates were estimated from the measured mass flow rates and theoretical reaction heat of formation.

Results and Discussion

In the thermal management of the hydrogen storage based on the metal hydride, both of the internal and external heat transfer issues exist. The present work focus on the internal thermal management of the hydrogen storage based on the metal hydride with the assumption of free convection at the external surface. In order to propose the efficient thermal management of the hydrogen storage, we determined the enhanced thermal conductivity of the metal hydride as 5 and 10 times larger than the before. It is easy to obtain those values of the effective thermal conductivity by adding little amount of the high-thermal-conductivity materials, such as carbon nanotubes, copper, and graphite to the metal hydride powdwer.

To validate the effect of the thermal management, the simulations were performed using the simulation tool (ANSYS) using the estimated heat generation and absorption rates. However, the calculated temperature of the metal hydride from the simulation is slightly different with the experimental results. Therefore, we performed the fitting procedure of the heat generation and absorption rates in order to make the similar trends of temperature curves in the experimental results. The maximum temperature of the simulation results using the fitted conditions are shown in Fig. 1.

Finally, the effect of the thermal management is verified in the same transient simulation model with the different effective thermal conductivity ($\boldsymbol{k_{eff}/k = 5}$ **or 10**) of the metal hydride. When the hydrogen is charging to the metal hydride container, the maximum temperature of the metal hydride decreases by almost 20°C with the increase of the

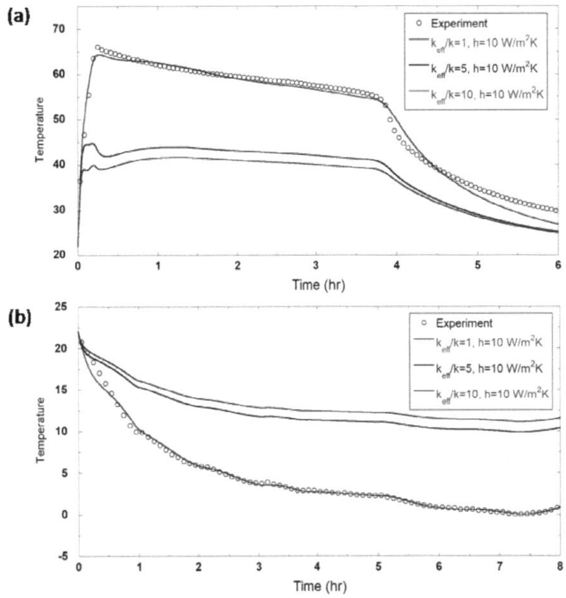

Figure 1. Center temperature variation according to thermal management: (a) charge process, (b) discharge process.

effective thermal conductivity by factor of 5. On the other hands, the minimum temperature of the metal hydride increases in the desorption process in the same condition as shown in Fig. 1. Therefore, we can conclude that the thermal management makes the hydrogen storage system to operate in the appropriate temperature range for the metal hydride.

Conclusion

The present work demonstrated effects of the effective thermal conductivity of metal hydrides by analyzing the maximum temperature in the hydrogen storage tank during the charging process. It was shown that by increasing the effective conductivity by factor of 5, the maximum temperature in the tank can be decreases by almost 20°C as compared to the case with intrinsic metal hydride.

Acknowledgements

This work was supported by the Agency for Defense Development (ADD) in South Korea.

References

1. Jinsong Zhang, Timothy S. Fisher, P. Veeraraghavan, Jay P. Gore and Issam Mudawar, 2005, "A Review of Heat Transfer Issues in Hydrogen Storage Technologies," *Journal of Heat Transfer*, Vol. 127, No. 12, pp. 1391~1399.
2. E. Hahne and J. Kallweit, 1998, "Thermal conductivity of metal hydride materials for storage of hydrogen: Experimental investigation," *International Journal of Hydrogen Energy*, Vol. 23, No. 2, pp. 107~114.

3. Mandhapati Raju and Sudarshan Kumar, 2012. "Optimization of heat exchanger designs in metal hydride based hydrogen storage systems," *International Journal of Hydrogen Energy*, Vol. 37, No. 3, pp. 2767~2778.

4. Vikas Keshari and M. P. Maiya, 2017, "Numerical Simulation of Metal Hydride Hydrogen Storage Device with Pin Fin Tube Heat Exchanger," *3rd World Congress on Mechanical, Chemical, and Material Engineering (MCM'17)*, Rome, Italy pp. 126-1~9.

$LiNi_{0.33}Mn_{0.33}Co_{0.33}O_2$ (NMC) Submicronic Particles Synthesis and Implementation of the Li-ion Battery Electrode by Using Printing Process

David Peralta, Jean-François Colin, Frédéric Fabre, Benjamin Amestoy and Jérémie Salomon
CEA Tech Liten, 17 rue des Martyrs, 3800 Grenoble, France
jeremie.salomon@cea.fr

Abstract: *In order to promote the screen printing process for flexible Li-ion battery development and on the other hand to improve the electrochemical behavior of the positive electrode, submicronic particles of* $LiNi_{1/3}Mn_{1/3}Co_{1/3}O_2$ *(NMC) were synthesized by using an easy and scalable coprecipitation synthesis protocol. Disaggregated particles of 200 nm were obtained and were characterized. The disaggregate morphology of this material makes easier the accessibility of the lithium insertion planes, and consequently, the high Crate behavior is clearly improved, compared to commercialized materials. In addition, an environmentally-friendly water-based NMC formulation was developed and the positive electrode was implemented by screen printing. The electrochemical behavior of this electrode was assessed both in half-cell and in Li-ion system configurations, leading to promising results: good Crate behavior and very stable capacity until 200 cycles at C/5 and 1D are observed in Li-ion pouch-cell configuration with a positive active material loading of 19 mg/cm². Thus, the use of submicronic NMC can be envisaged for energy battery while maintaining the power behavior induced by the particles size.*

Keywords: coprecipitation, submicronic particles, water-based formulation, screen printing, thin and flexible Li-ion battery.

Introduction

The growth of the flexible and wearable electronic market particularly in the field of creative industries (automotive, art, fashion, luxury, sports…) leads to the development of advanced power sources with various form factors and aesthetic diversity which can be easily accommodated and integrated to the electronic devices [1,2]. Today, particular attention is taken on the development of thin and flexible battery such as solid state battery (SSB) and thin film battery (TFB). SSB is a safety power source containing a solid electrolyte based on a crystalline polymer, glassy polymer or a ceramic [3,4]. Major bottlenecks remain as the lower ionic conductivity of the solid electrolyte than liquid electrolyte at ambient temperature, the lack of flexibility and the SSB production scale up is today not viable. In contrast, TFB is developed with the aim at providing a flexible or bendable battery technology with similar electrochemical performances as conventional Li-ion battery [5,6]. In order to overcome the safety issue linked to the use of a liquid electrolyte, the strategy adopted was to develop battery structure based on a polymer gel electrolyte [7,8]. Compared to a conventional Li-ion battery which is produced by coating the electrode slurries onto their proper current collectors and winding or stacking the electrodes with the separator to form a battery cell which usually has a form factor limited to cylindrical or prismatic shapes, TFB technology has a great potential to be produced at low cost from functional inks at using high throughput processes such as wet printing technologies [9-11], with the aim at proposing various form factors.

In this study, submicronic NMC particles were synthesized in order to develop a specific ink compatible with high throughput processes, containing smaller size particle aggregations than conventional ink based on micro-sized active materials. In addition, the literature reports the morphology effect of NMC materials on their electrochemical performances, from the nano-sized particles [12,13] to large, more or less dense agglomerates [14,15]. The use of cathode material nanoparticles can enhance the electrochemical performances of the battery. Thus, submicronic active materials could bring up a technological breakthrough in high energy, lithium rechargeable printed batteries for flexible components.

Also this study relates the development of an aqueous based ink formulation in order to reduce the cost production of the NMC electrode and for environmental aspects linked to the use of N-methyl-2-pyrrolidone (NMP), solvent very toxic and difficult to remove, in conventional battery production. Screen printed electrodes were implemented from optimized submicronic NMC aqueous based ink.

Experimental

In this study, submicronic $LiNi_{1/3}Mn_{1/3}Co_{1/3}O_2$ particles were produced by a very simple and scalable coprecipitation synthesis which is shared into two steps: the synthesis of a $Ni_{1/3}Mn_{1/3}Co_{1/3}(OH)_2$ in a stirring tank reactor and the calcination of this metal mix hydroxide with LiOH in order to produce the expected NMC oxide. Disaggregated particles with submicronic sizes are obtained by accurately controlling the synthesis parameters of these two steps. SEM picture of Figure 1.a reveals that well monodispersed flake-shaped particles are successfully synthesized. PSD measurement shows that the particles size is lower than 200 nm (Figure 1.b). X-ray powder diffraction analysis reveals that the material crystallizes in the well-known R-3m space group without any crystalline impurity phase detected (Figure 2).

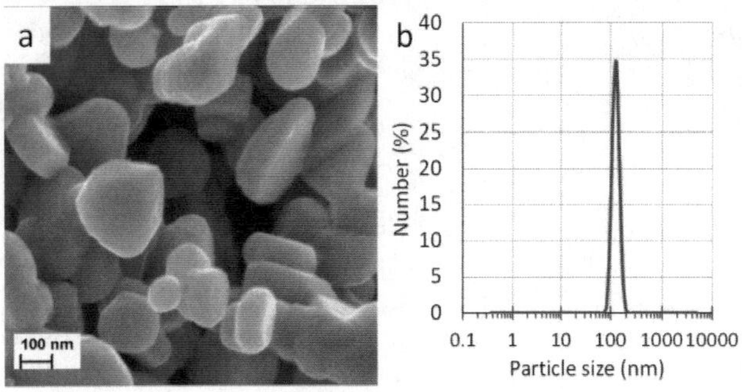

Figure 1. SEM picture (a) and PSD diagram (b) of the submicronic NMC material.

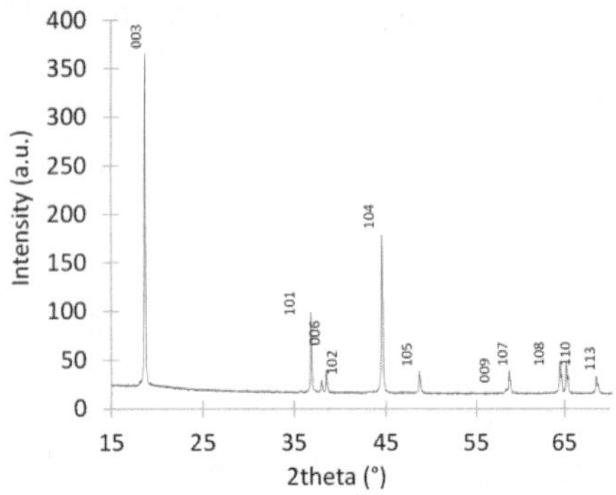

Figure 2. XRD diffractogram of the submicronic NMC material.

The electrochemical behavior of the submicronic NMC material was assessed in half-cell configuration between 4.3 and 3V vs Li/Li^+ from standard electrode based on polyvinylidene fluoride (PVdF) and NMP formulation. The electrode was prepared by coating the PVdF-NMP based ink onto standard aluminium foil with using Doctor-Blade coater. Compared to commercial reference composed of dense and spherical micro-sized particles, submicronic NMC exhibits higher capacity retention with a better Crate behavior at high discharge current (Figure 3.a). Both the electrodes were prepared in the same conditions and present the same loading (5 mg/cm²). The Crate behavior of the submicronic NMC is probably induced by the lithium mobility in the material: a higher content of lithium is removed and reinserted in the submicronic material and this difference is emphasized when the imposed current increases. The submicronic NMC exhibits analog cycle life behavior as the commercial reference at the discharge rate of 1D with charge at C/5 (Figure 3.b). This result shows that the amount of side reactions did not increase during the cycling, as it could be expected with high specific surface materials due to the higher interactions of the particles with the electrolyte.

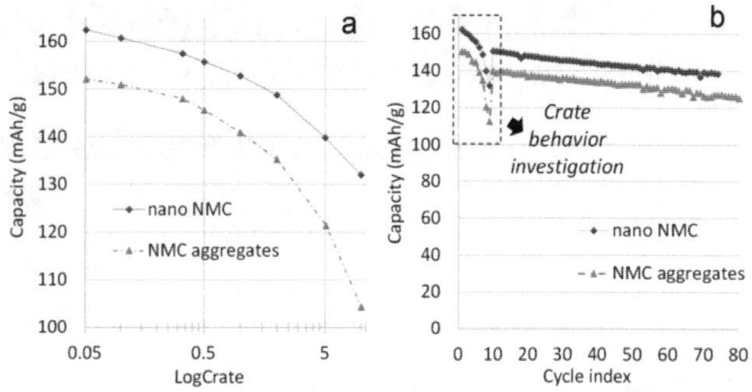

Figure 3. Half-cell characterization of submicronic NMC between 4.3 and 3V vs Li/Li^+ compared to commercial reference: Crate capability (a) and cycle life at C/5 and 1D (b).

In this work, aqueous based formulation was developed in order to reduce the manufacturing cost of the battery as well as for environmental issues linked to the use of NMP (highly toxic, difficult to extract and to recycle…). However, Li-containing materials are very sensitive to water, leading to strongly alkaline slurries during the electrode formulation step [16]. Electrode manufacturing process has to be adjusted consequently to avoid aluminium current collector corrosion. One solution to overcome the corrosion issue consists in monitoring the pH of the aqueous ink before the electrode processing [17]. The aqueous based formulation is composed of 92 wt% of submicronic NMC, 4 wt% of electronic conductors (among VGCF from Showa Denko and C65 from Timcal) and 4 wt% of binder (mixture of CMC and TRD202A latex supplied by JSR). The ink solid content was increased from typically 46 to 50 wt% in order to get the most adapted viscosity and rheology to the screen printing process. The pH is regulated by adding phosphoric acid to lower below 10. The ink is immediately screen printed to avoid the pH recovery. The viscosity and rheological behaviors of the submicronic NMC based aqueous ink were characterized. A shear thinning behavior is observed when the shear rate increases and viscosity of 3.5 Pa.s is measured at 100 s^{-1} (Figure 4.a). This indicates that the ink, highly viscous at the rest, can flow under the shear effect to pass through the screen and to be easily transferred on the aluminum foil. The rheological behavior assessed by oscillatory shear measurement at frequency sweep (Figure 4.b) exhibits a viscoelastic character. The loss modulus G" dominates over the storage modulus G'. This behavior is typical for fluid type systems which do not reveal a yield point. Theoretically, particles sedimentation can occur but no rheological changes were observed in one week of rest.

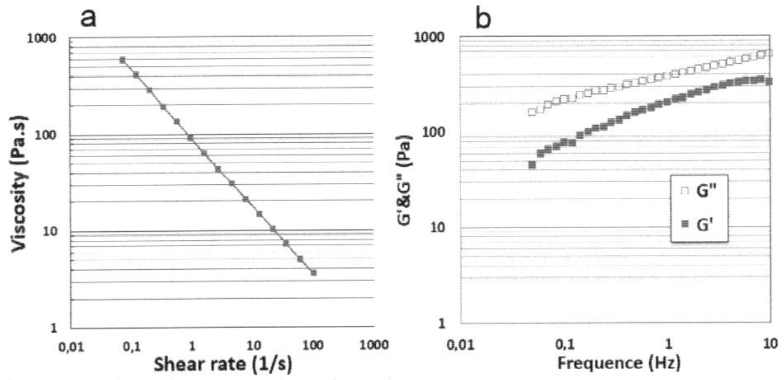

Figure 4. Flow measurement (a) and oscillatory shear experiment at frequency sweep (b) of the submicronic NMC based aqueous ink.

Screen printed electrodes were realized by using a DEK 248 semi-auto screen printer. Stencil screens with square patterns (3.5 x 3.5 cm²) and different thicknesses were used in function of the desired active material loading. For instance, a 200 µm-thick stencil screen leads to printed electrode with active material loading of 16.9 mg/cm². Picture of submicronic NMC printed electrodes is shown in Figure 5.a. One can note that the patterns are homogeneous and very well defined. Characterization of the pattern by optical microscopy allows to confirm the good resolution of the edges (Figure 5.b). The electrode profile, thickness, roughness and surface homogeneity were characterized by stylus profilometry (Figure 6).

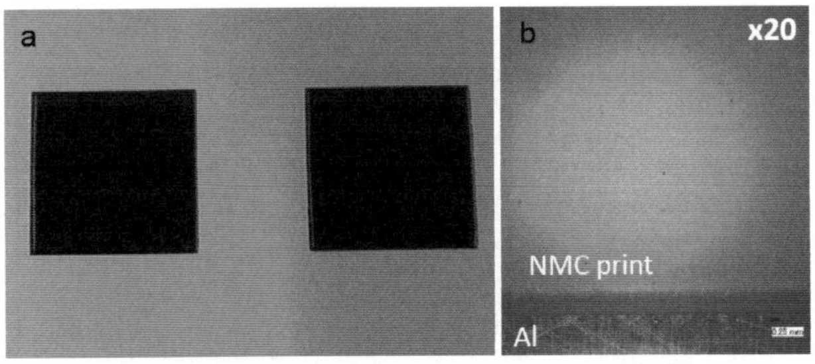

Figure 5. Picture (a) and optical microscopy characterization (b) of the submicronic NMC printed electrode.

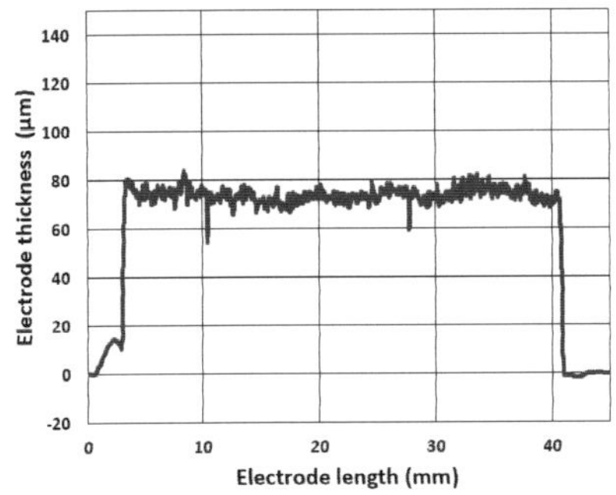

Figure 6. Stylus profile of the submicronic NMC printed electrode with active material loading of 16.9 mg/cm².

Firstly, the electrochemical behavior of the submicronic NMC printed electrode was investigated in lithium metal coin cell configuration between 4.3 and 3V. Specific capacities of 166 mAh/g with irreversible capacity of 8% were measured at C/20 and D/20 (Figure 7.a). The aqueous formulation provides equivalent Crate behavior as the PVdF-based formulation (Figure 7.b), which is a remarkable result considering the sensitivity of the Li-containing material toward water and the aluminum corrosion risk. A higher capacity retention of the aqueous formulation measured at high Crate (10D) can be highlighted. Figures 7.c and 7.d show the effect of the active material loading on the electrochemical performances. It was observed in Figure 7.c that the higher the loading, the lower is the capacity retention at high Crate. This is easily explained by mass transport limitations of lithium ion in the electrolyte phase as well as the impedance for electrons in the solid phase of thick electrodes [18]. One can note that the capacity retention at 2D of the submicronic NMC with an active material loading of 16.9 mg/cm² (corresponding to a surface capacity of 2.8 mAh/cm²) remains attractive because 66% of the initial capacity is restituted. Cycle life test performed at C/5 and 1D (100% DOD) shows very good cycling behavior until active material loading of 16.9 mg/cm² (Figure 7.d). The overall results indicate that the submicronic NMC can be envisaged for energy battery, 16.9 mg/cm² is considered as a high active material loading, while maintaining the power behavior induced by the size of the particles. On the other hand, aqueous formulation as well as the screen printing process did not mitigate the electrochemical performances.

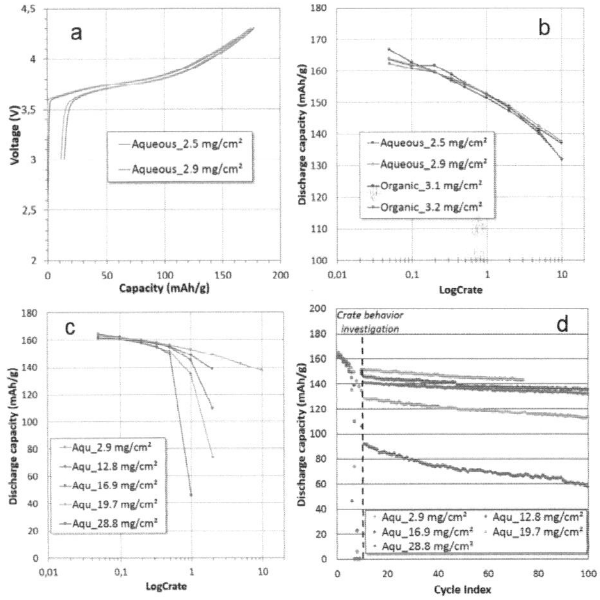

Figure 7. Half-cell characterization of the printed NMC electrode between 4.3 and 3V vs Li/Li^+: charge and discharge curves at C/20 (a), Crate behavior of aqueous and PVdF-based formulations (b), Crate behavior (c) and cycle life at C/5 and 1D (d) in function of the active material loading.

To complete the investigation, the electrochemical performances of the submicronic NMC electrode, formulated in aqueous media and produced by screen printing, were assessed in Li-ion system in pouch-cell configuration. The active material loading of the positive electrode is 18.8 mg/cm² (3.1 mAh/cm²) for a total surface of 12.25 cm². A standard graphite electrode with the adequate loading was placed in opposite of the positive electrode. Graphite electrode is also produced by screen printing from an aqueous based ink. A standard separator supplied by Celgard® and a standard electrolyte composed of 1 mol/L of $LiPF_6$ in EC/PC/DMC with a volume ratio of 1/1/3 with 2 wt% of VC were used. The electrochemical behavior of the Li-ion pouch cell was assessed between 4.2 and 3V vs Li/Li^+. Total capacity of 29 mAh was measured at low discharge rate (D/20). Crate behavior of the prototype is relatively correct considering the high active material loading of the positive electrode: 87% of the initial capacity was restituted at a discharge rate of 1D (Figure 8.a). Cycle life test performed at C/5 and 1D (100% DOD) is very promising because very stable capacity is observed until 200 cycles (Figure 8.b).

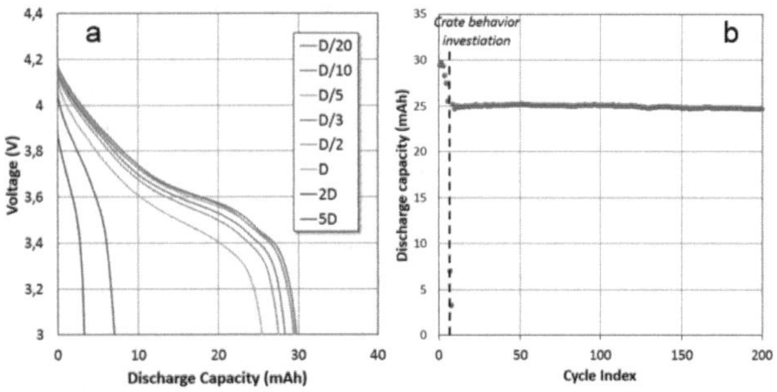

Figure 8. Half-cell characterization of submicronic NMC between 4.2 and 3V (graphite anode): Crate capability in pouch cell configuration (a) and cycle life in pouch cell configuration at C/5 and 1D (b).

Conclusion

Submicronic NMC particles were synthesized and the electrochemical behavior of the material was compared to commercial micro-sized NMC. Aqueous based formulation was specifically developed for this submicronic material leading to very promising performances in half-cell and Li-ion configuration. The electrodes were realized by screen printing with the aims at promoting the use of high throughput process in order to produce printed batteries for flexible components.

Acknowledgements

The study has been performed within the BASMATI project. This project has received funding from the European Union's Horizon 2020 research and innovation programme under grant agreement No 646159.

References

1. Jeong G., Kim Y.-U., Kim H., Kim Y.-J., and Sohn H.-J., *Energy Environ. Sci.*, Vol. 4, pp. 1986-2002, 2011.
2. Wang Y., Liu B., Li Q., Cartmell S., Ferrara S., Deng Z. D., and Xiao J., *J. Power Sources*, Vol. 286, pp. 330-345, 2015.
3. Kamaya N., Homma K., Yamakawa Y. Hirayama M. Kanno R., Yonemura M., Kamiyama T., Kato Y., Hama S., Kawamoto K., and Mitsui A., *Nature Materials*, Vol. 10, pp. 682-686, 2011.
4. Xie H., Yang C., Fu K., Yao Y., Jiang F., Hitz E., Liu B., Wang S., and Hu L., *Adv. Energy Mater.*, 1703474, 2018.
5. Koo M., Park K., Lee S. H., Suh M., Jeon D. Y., Choi J. W., Kang K., and Lee K. J., *Nano Letters*, Vol. 12, pp. 4810-4816, 2012.
6. Hu L., Wu H., La Mantia F., Yang Y., and Cui Y., *ACS Nano*, Vol. 10, pp. 5843-5848, 2010.
7. Kim H.-S., Periasamy P., and Moon S.-I., *J. Power Sources*, Vol. 141, pp. 293-297, 2005.
8. Long L., Wang S., Xiao M., and Meng Y., *J. Mater. Chem. A*, Vol. 4, pp. 10038-10069, 2016.
9. Huang J., Yang J., Li W., Cai W., and Jiang Z., *Thin Solid Films*, Vol. 516, pp. 3314-3319, 2008.
10. Park M.-S., Hyun S.-H., and Nam S.-C., *Electrochimica Acta*, Vol. 52, pp. 7895-7902, 2007.
11. Kang K.-Y., Lee Y.-G., Shin D. O., Kim J.-C., and Kim K. M., *Electrochimica Acta*, Vol. 138, pp. 294-301, 2014.
12. Wei G.-Z., Lu X., Ke F.-S., Huang L., Li J.-T., Wang Z.-X., Zhou Z.-Y., and Sun S.-G., *Adv. Mater.*, Vol. 22, pp. 4364-4367, 2010.
13. Yang Z., Lu J., Bian D., Zhang W., Yang X., Xia J., Chen G., Gu H., and Ma G., *J. Power Sources*, Vol. 272, pp. 144- 151 , 2014.
14. Cho T. H., Park S. M., Yoshio M., Hirai T., and Hideshima Y., *J. Power Sources*, Vol. 142, pp. 306-312, 2005.
15. Hou P., Wang X., Song D., Shi X., Zhang L., Guo J., and Zhang J., *J. Power Sources*, Vol. 265, pp. 174-181, 2014.
16. Loeffler N., Von Zamory J., Laszczynski N., Doberdo I., Kim G.-T., Passerini S., *J. Power Sources.*, Vol. 248, pp. 915–922, 2014.
17. Loeffler N., Kim G.-T., Mueller F., Diemant T., Kim J.-K., Behm R.J., et al., *ChemSusChem.*, Vol. 9, pp. 1112–1117, 2016.
18. Singh M., Kaiser J., and Hahn H., *J. Electrochemical Soc.*, Vol. 162(7), pp. A1196-A1201, 2015.

Carbon Free Silica Supported Pt Bifunctional Electrocatalyst for Unitized Regenerative Fuel Cells

Sung-Hee Roh[1] and Ho-Young Jung[2]
[1]College of General Education, Chosun University,
309 Pilmoon-daero, Dong-gu, Gwangju, 61452, Republic of Korea
[2]Department of Environment & Energy Engineering, Chonnam National University,
77 Yongbong-ro, Buk-gu, Gwangju, 61186, Republic of Korea
jungho@jnu.ac.kr / 82-62-530-5968

Abstract: *A novel catalyst based on platinum bearing sulfonated SiO_2 as supporter is investigated for the aim of stabilizing and improving unitized regenerative fuel cell (URFC) round-trip efficiency. The major strategy is to apply a proton conducting site onto Pt catalyst structure, thereby a facile transport for proton can be carried out into electrode for oxygen reduction or out of electrode for oxygen evolution reaction. Moreover, the use of SiO_2 is aimed to overcome corrosion issue of carbon supporter. As a result, catalyzing performance is enhanced in oxygen reduction and oxygen evolution reactions. Additionally, cell resistance is reduced compared to non-sulfonated supporter which is attributed to the proton conductive -SO_3H group. Interestingly, our catalyst possesses measured electrochemical active surface (EAS) area of 22.96 m^2 g^{-1} which is pretty close to that of commercial Pt black measured to be 23.02 m^2 g^{-1}. Therefore, our catalyst is expected to further improve operating performance of the commercial URFC.*

Keywords: sulfonated silica; platinum; electrocatalyst; unitized regenerative fuel cell;

Introduction

The reduction of carbon dioxide emission turns out to be the ultimate mission at present, hence the use of non-carbon energy source is conceptually applied to guarantee carbon-free emission for hydrogen fuel cell. Since the whole process from hydrogen production to final application (fuel cell) is borne with complexity, the URFC has therefore developed to combine hydrogen fuel production using water electrolysis and electricity generation from its fuel to compete with rechargeable batteries [1]. Nonetheless, the practical application of URFC still need to surpass the current stumbling-block that is consented to be stability, corrosion, and degradation issues in membrane electrode assembly (MEA), especially from the conventional Pt catalyst supported by carbon which is firstly perspective for high surface area, thermal and mechanical stability, and electrical conductivity, yet then corrosion during high operational voltage is observed for this catalyst material.

Addressing above drawbacks of URFC, our group attempted to rectify by proposing a robust and efficient electrocatalyst material. We remain Pt because it is a well-performed catalyst and continued to be explored at present [2]. In fact, the major problem originates from carbon supporter, hence the present study merely devises the use of alternative supporter of SiO_2-SO_3H to utilize stability of silica. Although SiO_2 possesses inferior electrical conductivity to carbon material, it is feasible to preserve the "high ionic conductivity" concept for sulfonated silica by applying proton sources due to incorporating sulfonic acid functional group [3].

Experimental

Triblock copolymer Pluronic® P123 (poly(ethylene oxide)-poly(propylene oxide)-poly(ethylene oxide)) ($EO_{20}PO_{70}EO_{20}$, molecular mass = 5800 g/mol, Aldrich), tetraethyl orthosilicate (TEOS) ($Si(OC_2H_5)_4$, 98%, Aldrich), hydrochloric acid (HCl), (3-mercaptopropyl)trimethoxysilane (MPTMS) ($C_6H_{16}O_3SSi$, 95%, Aldrich), concentrated sulfuric acid (H_2SO_4), ethanol (CH_3CH_2OH), hydrogen peroxide (H_2O_2, 30%), isopropyl alcohol (C_3H_8O, 99.5%), platinum chloride (H_2PtCl_6, 99.99%, SigmaeAldrich), Nafion™ ionomer (5 wt% Nafion™ dispersion, DuPont Co., Ltd.), and de-ionized (DI) water were used as received.

The chemical routes for preparation of supporter and electrocatalyst are illustrated in Figure 1 [4]. The same procedure is applied for non-sulfonated silica supported Pt catalyst as in Figure 1b.

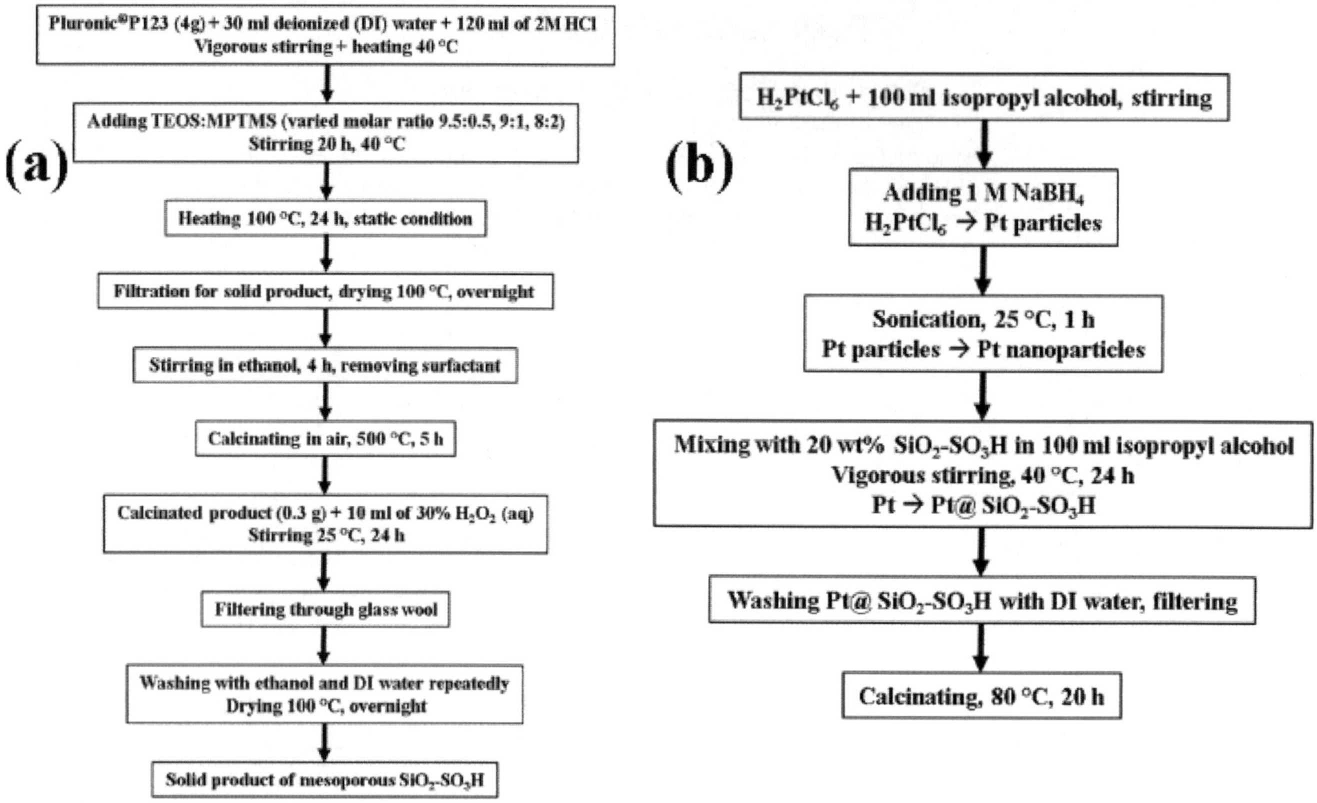

Figure 1. Synthetic procedure of (a) sulfonated silica and (b) electrocatalyst of Pt/SiO_2-SO_3H.

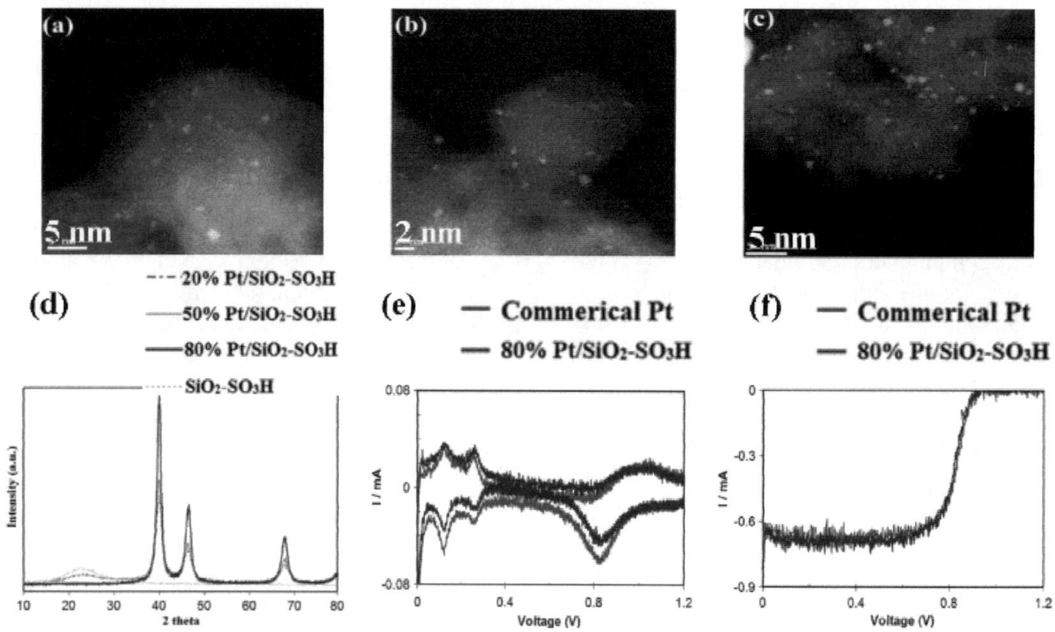

Figure 2. HAADF-STEM of (a) 20, (b) 50, and (c) 80 wt% Pt nanoparticles; (d) XRD of various Pt concentrations on SiO_2-SO_3H; (e) CV and (f) LSV of Pt black and 80 wt% Pt/SiO_2-SO_3H catalyst.

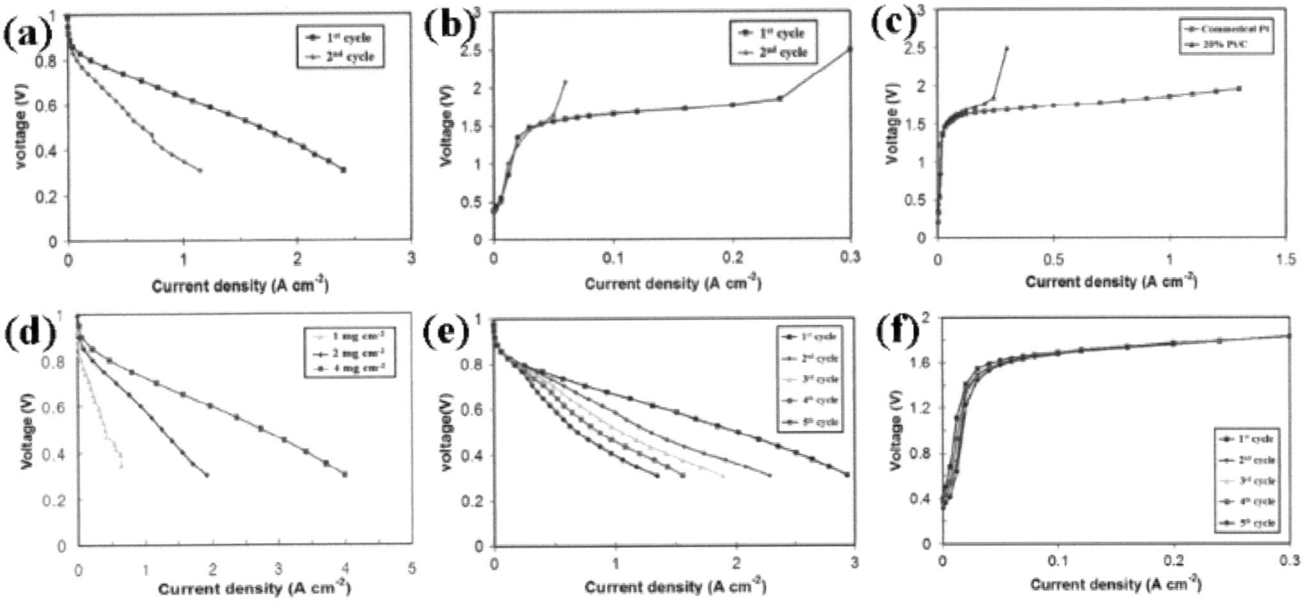

Figure 3. Polarization curves for (a) FC mode and (b) WE mode using 20 wt% Pt/C catalyst; (c) WE mode of Pt/C and commercial Pt catalyst; (d) FC mode with different loadings of commercial Pt catalyst (1, 2, and 4 mg cm^{-2}); the cyclic stability of the unit cell performance test of the Pt/SiO_2-SO_3H (e) fuel cell mode and (f) water electrolyzer mode.

Results and discussion

The formation of as-mentioned synthetic sulfonated electrocatalyst material is confirmed by X-ray diffraction (XRD) (Rigaku X-ray diffractometer employing CuKα radiation) and transmission electron microscopy (TEM) (JOEL-2100F microscope), and electrochemical properties are also examined using cyclic voltammetry (CV) and linear sweep voltammetry (LSV) in 0.5 M H_2SO_4 at a scan rate of 5 mV s^{-1} (Pine Potentiostat-Model AFCBP1) as shown in figure 2. From TEM (Figure 2a, b, c), we can conclude nano-sized Pt evenly distributed on surface of the silica. In XRD patterns (Figure 2d), peaks of Pt are detected at 39.52°, 46.12°, and 67.51° in 2theta. Also, the Si signal presents at the same 2theta as Pt in 20wt% Pt on supporter. However, this overlay is not observed in higher Pt contents. The EAS areas are calculated based on charge area Q (μC cm^{-2}), ratio of electron amount (210 μC cm^{-2}), and Pt loading L (mg cm^{-2}) in the electrode according to relation of EAS = Q/(210×L) from CV as shown in Figure 2e. The catalyst 80 wt% Pt/SiO_2-SO_3H gives 22.96 m^2 g^{-1} pretty close to 23.02 m^2 g^{-1} for Pt black. The LSV shows analogy in curves of commercial Pt and 80 wt% Pt/SiO_2-SO_3H as shown in Figure 2f. The LSV analogy reveals that catalyst synthesized in this work possessing comparable ORR performance to the commercial Pt product.

Gas diffusion layers (GDLs) are coated with various catalyst amount. Then Nafion 112 membrane is attached to coated GDL by hot-pressing at 140 °C, 800 psi for 3 min. The humidified H_2 and O_2 are drawn with 150 ml min^{-1} in flow rate into 5-cm^2 unit cell and water flow is 60 ml min^{-1}. Conventional 20 wt% Pt/C catalyst performance is significantly decreased after just one cycle for fuel cell (FC) mode in URFC as in **Figure 3a**. In polarization curve, the current density at 0.7 V drops from 650 to 250 mA cm^{-2}. The severer performance degradation is observed for Pt/C catalyst in WE mode as in **Figure 3b** after two-time cycling. In addition, the 20 wt% Pt/C catalyst exhibit inferior performance compared to commercial Pt black in water electrolyzer (WE) mode as shown in **Figure 3c**. According to this result, the corrosion issue of carbon supported can be visible, i.e. the upper limit voltage is reached within just a small current density. Additionally, the optimum loading of commercial Pt catalyst is confirmed in **Figure 3d**. The catalyst content of 4 mg cm^{-2} manifests the best performance in polarization curve, specifically 1200 mA cm^{-2} at 0.7 V. Meanwhile, catalyst loadings of 1 mg cm^{-2} and 2 mg cm^{-2} show lower current densities 175 mA cm^{-2} and 570 mA cm^{-2} at 0.7 V.

Notably, the developed catalyst shows stable performance in cycling. In FC mode, the smaller current density is obtained at a certain voltage as number of cycle increases as in Figure 3e. In other words, the slope of polarization curve is increased resulting in the raise in resistance. The causes for this issue can be accounted for interfacial delamination between membrane and electrode, cracking of Nafion binder, corrosion of bipolar plate, gas diffusion packing or hot water and humidified gas [5]. Specifically, the current densities drop from 800 to 350 mA cm^{-2} after five cycles. More greatly, the performance of URFC using our catalyst is remarkably stable after five-time cycling as in figure 3f. The stability obtained in WE mode can be contributed by the SiO_2 supporter which is resistant to corrosion. According to all cycling data, the round-trip efficiency is calculated based on ratio of FC voltage to WE voltage in percentage. The results are tabulated in table and indicate that Pt/SiO_2-SO_3H exhibits the highest efficiency due to corrosion-resistant and proton conductivity.

Table 1. URFC voltage and round-trip energy conversion efficiencies for different catalyst at 0.2 mA cm^{-2}.

Electrocatalyst	VFC (V)	VWE (V)	Efficiency (%)
Pt/C	0.800	1.765	45.32
Pt/SiO_2-SO_3H	0.818	1.773	46.13

Conclusion The major drawback of conventional URFC catalyst has been addressed and we therefore propose an improvement by synthesis of a novel and stable catalyst Pt/SiO_2-SO_3H yet still maintaining "high conductivity" aspect of carbon supporter. The electrocatalyst formation and microstructre have been confirmed using XRD and TEM. Additionally, the electrochemical properties of the synthetic catalyst have been observed to be comparable to commercial Pt black catalyst, specifically the EAS area of our catalyst of 22.96 m^2 g^{-1} is approximate to 23.02 m^2 g^{-1} of conventional Pt black catalyst. As a result, Pt/SiO_2-SO_3H has performed better than conventional Pt/C catalyst, specifically greater round-trip efficiency. Furthermore, sulfonated electrocatalyst shows stable performance during five cycles in URFC operation. Therefore, currently synthetic Pt/SiO_2-SO_3H catalyst can be recommended to be promising solution for solving degradation and low activity issues in conventional URFC.

Acknowledgements
This research was supported by Basic Science Research Program through the National Research Foundation of Korea (NRF) funded by the Ministry of Education (2015061146). Additionally, this work was supported by the New & Renewable Energy Core Technology Program of the Korea Institute of Energy Technology Evaluation and Planning (KETEP), granted financial resource from the Ministry of Trade, Industry & Energy, Republic of Korea. (No. 20153030031670 & No. 20172420108550).

References
1. Burke K.A., "Unitized Regenerative Fuel Cell System Gas Storage / Radiator Development", Sae Tech Pap Ser 2004.
2. Liu J, Jiao M, Lu L, Barkholtz HM, Li Y, Jiang L, et al, "High performance platinum single atom electrocatalyst for oxygen reduction reaction" Nat Commun 2017;8:1–9.
3. Marschall R, Rathouský J, Wark M, "Ordered Functionalized Silica Materials with High Proton Conductivity", Chem Mater 2007;19:6401–7.
4. Oh YK, Hong LY, Asthana Y, Kim DP, "Synthesis of super-hydrophilic mesoporous silica via a sulfonation route", J Ind Eng Chem 2006;12:911–7.
5. Jung HY, Kim JY, Park JK, "Effect of Nafion dispersion solvent on the interfacial properties between the membrane and the electrode of a polymer electrolyte membrane-based fuel cell" Solid State Ionics 2011;196:73–8.

Low Permeable Composite Membrane with Sulfonated Poly(phenylene oxide) (sPPO) and Sulfonated Silica for the Operation of Redox Flow Battery

***Sung-Hee Roh*[1], *Ho-Young Jung*[2]**
[1]College of General Education, Chosun University
309 Pilmoon-daero, Dong-gu, Gwangju, Republic of Korea, 61452
[2]Department of Environment & Energy Engineering, Chonnam National University
77 Yongbong-ro, Buk-gu, Gwangju, Republic of Korea, 61186
jungho@jnu.ac.kr / 82-62-530-1865

Abstract: *The present work focus on improving performance of sulfonated poly(phenylene oxide) (sPPO) electrolyte membrane in terms of proton conductivity and vanadium permeability by applying sulfonated silica (sSiO2) into sPPO to form an inorganic-organic composite membrane. The membrane properties are enhanced through increases in water uptake (WU), ion-exchange capacity (IEC), ion conductivity (IC). Greater number of sulfonic acid functional group from sSiO2 helps to increased hydrophilicity of sPPO membrane, therefore, resulting high ion conductivity can be obtained. Moreover, potential is confirmed by the transport of electron and ion through the operation of vanadium redox flow battery (VRFB). It shows that the vanadium permeability of composite membrane is significantly improved compared to Nafion 212 membrane. According to acquired experimental results, the study demonstrates a potential candidate for low cost membrane in VRFB application.*

Keywords: sulfonated silica; poly(phenylene oxide); ion conductivity; vanadium permeability;

Introduction

Among the various types of energy storage systems, vanadium redox flow battery (VRFB) has been regarded as a promising system due to its operational safety, flexible construction and easy maintenance [1]. In VRFB, the active materials (AMs) are dissolved in electrolyte solutions and circulated through cell separated by an insulating polymer electrolyte membrane.

Owing to mobile condition of AMs and different redox species in both sides, their diffusion must be controlled to avoid unexpected transport caused by concentration and electric potential gradients through polymer electrolyte membrane. This crossing transport makes redox reaction to occur without releasing electron to external circuit, thus leading to decaying cell capacity. Furthermore, reaction kinetic must remain rapid to efficiently utilize energy from VRFB. Therefore, the proton conduction is required to keep pace with energy transfer to external load. To sum up the two critical issues, low electrolyte crossover and high IC are of importance and in duty of polymer electrolyte membrane (PEM).

Hitherto, Nafion membrane has been regared as unique commercial candidate in VRFB market [2]. In operation, it shows excellent IC, yet Nafion dissatisfies expectation in vanadium permeability and price [2]. Accordingly, an alternative PEM should be suggested to replace Nafion and overcome current drawbacks.

The focus now is shifted to hydrocarbon PEM due to lower permeability and fluorine free structure for being eco-friendly [3]. Among hydrocarbon PEM, PPO possesses low cost and good mechanical strength. Moreover, incorporating PPO with sulfonic acid functional groups grants the polymer ability to conduct ion [4].

Currently, the concept of compositing polymer with supporting component is an upgrading version of hydrocarbon PEM [2]. Silica has been reported as helpful additive to suppress the permeability of polymer electrolyte membrane in the operation of VRFB, yet IC was recorded in a decreased value [5]. For this issue, our work has been solved by sulfonating silica so that IC can be improved. In this research, we further enhance sPPO membrane in IC and vanadium permeability for the sake of actualizing this low cost membrane application in VRFB through facile compositing process with $sSiO_2$.

Experimental

Materials: Poly(phenylene oxide) (PPO, Hanil, Korea), chloroform (CH_3Cl, 99%, Sigma Aldrich, USA), chlorosulfonic acid (CSA) (HSO_3Cl, 98%, Kanto Chemical, Japan), sodium hydroxide (NaOH, 98%, Daejung, Korea), silicon oxide (SiO_2, >99.9%, Ditto technology), ethanol (C_2H_5OH, 94%, OCI company, Korea), sulfuric acid (H_2SO_4, 95%, Duksan, Korea), N,N-dimethyl acetamide (DMAc) ($CH_3CON(CH_3)_2$, 99.5%, Daejung, Korea), hydrogen peroxide (H_2O_2, 30%, Daejung, Korea), vanadyl sulfate ($VOSO_4$, 98%, NeWell, Korea) and magnesium sulfate ($MgSO_4$, 99%, Duksan, Korea) were used as received.

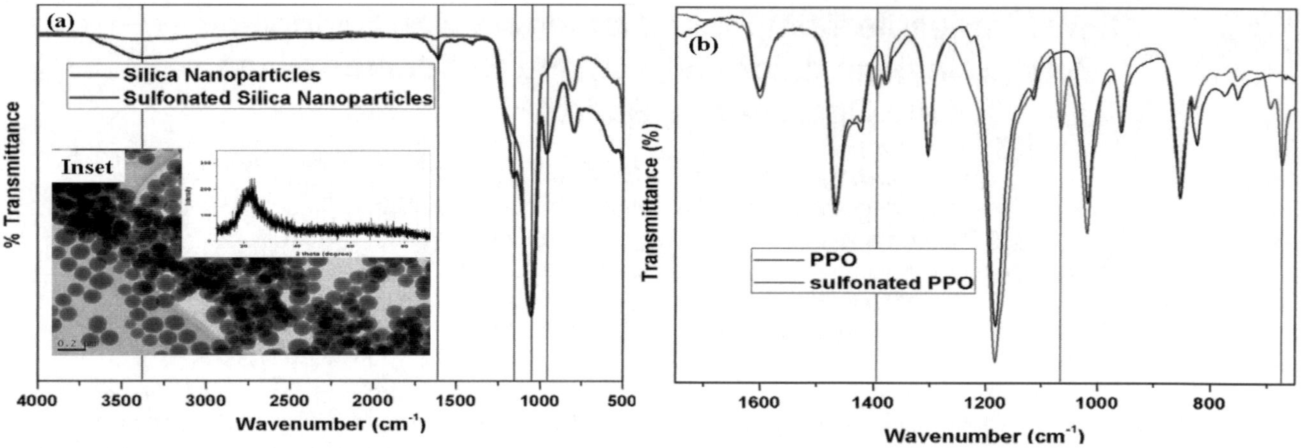

Figure 1. FT-IR of (a) SiO_2 and $sSiO_2$; (b) PPO and sPPO; the inset is TEM and XRD pattern of SiO_2

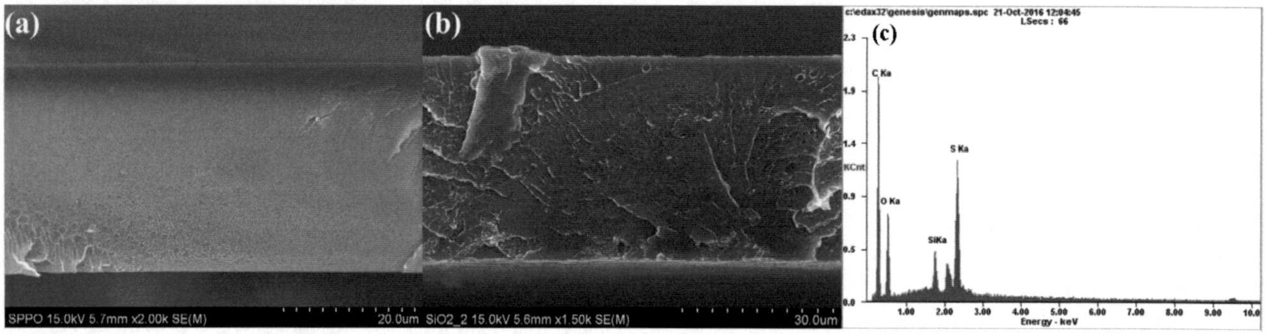

Figure 2. Cross-sectional SEM image of (a) sPPO; (b) sPPO-$sSiO_2$ membranes and (c) EDX of sPPO-$sSiO_2$ membrane

Preparation of sPPO and $sSiO_2$: The PPO was sulfonated with CSA in chloroform. sPPO precipitated in chloroform and was washed with DI water then dried at 80 °C for 24 h. The dried product was then treated in 1 M NaOH for 24 h. Afterwards, treated sPPO was washed with DI water and dried at 50 °C for 12 h. Nano-particle SiO_2 was sulfonated with process: annealing at 550 °C to eliminate impurities, treating with ethanol, sonicating in methanol with 0.5 M H_2SO_4 solution for 1 h, vaporizing to obtain nano-sized $sSiO_2$. Finally, the composite membrane was obtained by blending sonicated nano $sSiO_2$ particle in DMAc with sPPO/DMAc solution to form casting solution followed by drying thin layer of casting solution on glass plate in oven at 110 °C for 24 h. The obtained film in oven was pre-treated with H_2O_2, and protonated with H_2SO_4.

Vanadium permeability test: Fully-hydrated membranes (5 x 4 cm^2) were placed in VRFB unit cell circulated by 1.5 M $VOSO_4$ and 1.5 M $MgSO_4$ solution (both salts in 3.0 M H_2SO_4) through opposite sides. The crossover of V^{4+} through membrane was recorded by increase of V^{4+} concentration in $MgSO_4$ tank. Concentration of vanadium ion in enrichment tank was measured to determine vanadium permeability.

Results and discussion

Structural and microstructural analyses

In Fourier-transform infrared (FT-IR) spectroscopy, additional peaks at 961, 1000 – 1300, 1169 cm^{-1} are attributed to stretching vibration of -SO_3H, Si-O-Si, Si-O-SO_3H, respectively. This information can confirm sulfonation of SiO_2 as shown in **Figure 1a**. Additionally, the broad peak at 3380 cm^{-1} can reveal presence of sulfonic group in $sSiO_2$. Size of SiO_2 particles is observed through transmission electron microscope (TEM) at even size and of 100 nm in diameter. The identification of $sSiO_2$ material is confirmed in X-ray diffraction (XRD) pattern at 22.4° in 2theta as shown in inset of **Figure 1a**. In the same manner for sPPO, additional peaks at 674, 1065, 1175 cm^{-1} are attributed to stretching vibration of C-S, -SO_3H asymmetry, -SO_3H overlapped in the aromatic ether band, respectively. This information can confirm the formation of sPPO as shown in **Figure 1b.**

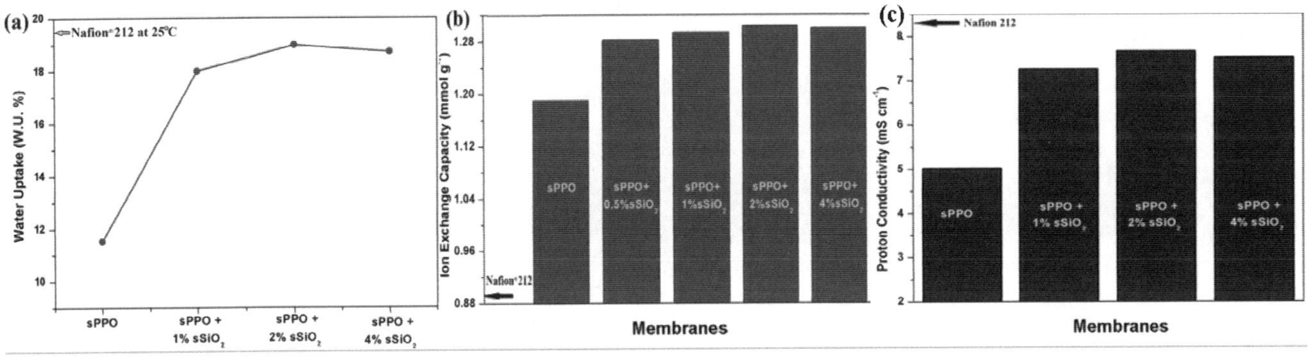

Figure 3. (a) WU; (b) IEC; (c) IC of sPPO and varied ratio of $sSiO_2$-sPPO membranes

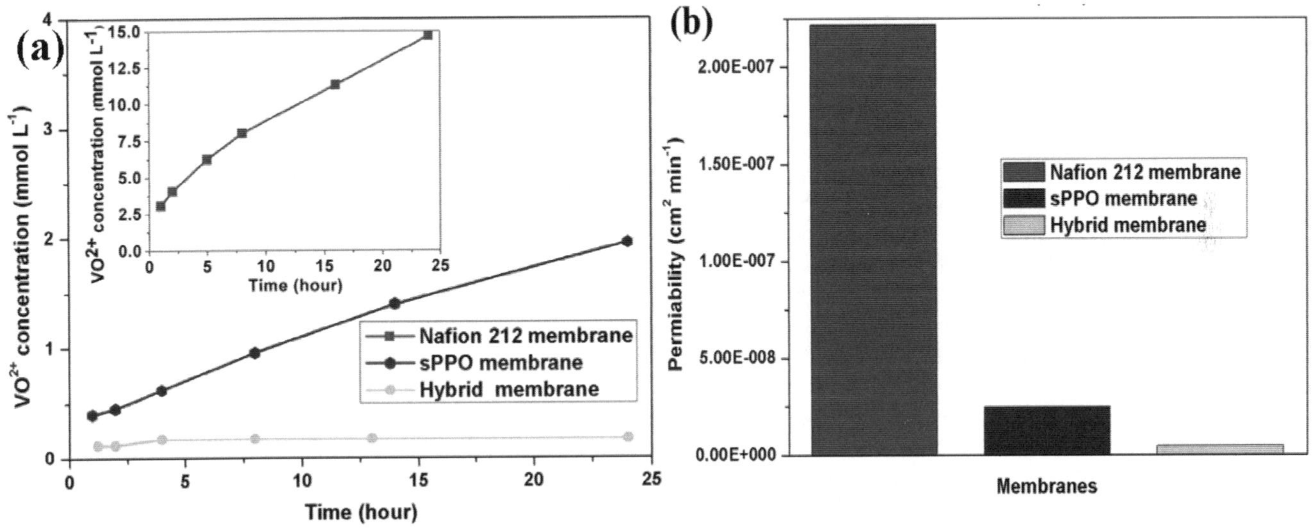

Figure 4. (a) VO^{2+} crossover of membranes through time; (b) permeability of membranes

Scanning electron microscope (SEM) apparently shows distinction between smooth cross-sectional image of sPPO membrane and rugged morphology due to silica particle incorporation of sPPO-$sSiO_2$ membrane as shown in **Figure 2a and b**. Furthermore, elemental composition (EDX) proves the existence of $sSiO_2$ in sPPO membrane through observation of Si and S elements as shown in **Figure 2c**.

Physicochemical properties of membranes

When being introduced $sSiO_2$ as hydrophilic additive, composite $sSiO_2$-sPPO membrane manifests an increased electrostatic interaction, especially with water as can be seen an augment in WU measurement in **Figure 3a.** However, only a slight divergence is observed among sPPO embedded $sSiO_2$ membranes due to small different amounts of inorganic material applied. Notably, the WU gets declined as $sSiO_2$ content reaching 4 wt%. In high loading, hydrogen bond is favored to form upon large network of OH dipole moment belonging to sulfonic groups of sPPO and $sSiO_2$. Thus, a number of hydrophilic functional groups are deactivated and water interaction accordingly goes downward. In alignment with WU, IEC of sPPO membrane is accorded increment due to incorporation with $sSiO_2$. The 4 wt% loading is again observed off the peak from 2 wt% $sSiO_2$ due to same reason as the case of WU, i.e. hydrogen bonding as shown in **Figure 3b**. Similar to WU and IEC, IC measurement shows the same pattern seen by remarkable leap from pure sPPO membrane to sPPO - 1wt% $sSiO_2$, followed by inappreciable increment to 2 wt% $sSiO_2$, then the incremental trend turns reversed for the 4 wt% loading of inorganic additive as shown in **Figure 3c**. Indeed, these properties rely on hydrophilicity of sulfonic group. The greater amount of hydrophilic group provides more ion-exchanging sites so that ability to exchange and conduct ion is improved. Notwithstanding, ion conduction is also related to tortuosity which takes effect when proton pathway gets stuck due to many silica particles as in 4 wt%

$sSiO_2$. Therefore, hydrogen bonding deactivating availability of ion-exchanging site and increasing tortuosity are accounted for drop of IC for sPPO - 4 wt% $sSiO_2$ membrane.

Vanadium permeability

The applicability of composite membrane to VRFB is proved via lower vanadium crossover as well as vanadium permeability (4.76 x 10^{-9} cm^2/min) compared to pure sPPO (2.50 x 10^{-8} cm^2/min) and Nafion 212 (2.22 x 10^{-7} cm^2/min) membranes as shown in **Figure 4**. This beneficial effect of sPPO-$sSiO_2$ membrane is attributed to ion-blocking due to silica nano-particles. In essence, the desired features from tiny dimension and hydrophilicity render nano $sSiO_2$ particles easily evenly distribute and well interact with hydrophilic polymer. The pores in sPPO membrane is thus largely filled with hydrophilic silica. Therefore, more vanadium ion is blocked to transfer through sPPO-$sSiO_2$ membrane.

Conclusion

In this work, $sSiO_2$ and sPPO were successfully synthesized from their non-sulfonated states, i.e. SiO_2 and PPO, respectively. The formation of nano-sized $sSiO_2$ particles was confirmed by characteristic peak in XRD, small size measured in TEM and additional peaks in FT-IR. The acquisition of sPPO was verified through fingerprint wavenumber of sulfonic group in IR spectrum. SEM image and EDX analyses proved the preparation of composite membrane containing silica inorganic additive. As expected, electrostatic interaction with water and ion-exchanging ability of sPPO embedded $sSiO_2$ have increased due to hydrophilicity of additional sulfonic group from sulfonated silica and have been proved by WU and IEC measurement. Inherited from enhanced WU and IEC, IC was apparently improved by incorporating $sSiO_2$. Importantly, vanadium crossover experiment has revealed feasible application of our composite membrane to VRFB because permeability was observed to be reduced by employing sPPO-$sSiO_2$ membrane. The reduction in vanadium permeability for composite membrane is due to ion-blocking effect of nano silica particle and have confirmed better performance than Nafion and pure sPPO membrane. In conclusion, we have applied sulfonated silica particle to low-cost hydrocarbon polymer to achieve the improved physicochemical properties and vanadium permeability so as to propose a promising alternative for commercial VRFB application.

Acknowledgements

This work was supported by KEPRI (Korea Electric Power Research Institute) granted financial resource from KEPCO(Korea Electric Power Corporation), Republic of Korea (No. R16EA06). The Energy Efficiency & Resources Core Technology Program of the Korea Institute of Energy Technology Evaluation and Planning (KETEP) granted financial resource from the Ministry of Trade, Industry & Energy, Republic of Korea (No. 20152010103210 & No. 20172420108550).

References

1. Alotto, P., Guarnieri, M., Moro, F., "Redox flow batteries for the storage of renewable energy: A review", *Renew Sustain Energy Rev* 29, pp. 325–335, 2014.
2. Prifti, H., Parasuraman, A., Winardi, S., Lim, T.M., Skyllas-Kazacos, M., "Membranes for redox flow battery applications", *Membranes* 2, pp. 275–306, 2012.
3. Cunha, Á., Martins, J., Rodrigues, N., Brito, F.P., "Vanadium redox flow batteries: a technology review", *Int J Energy Res* 39, pp.889–918, 2014
4. Yang, S., Gong, C., Guan, R., Zou, H., "Sulfonated poly(phenylene oxide) membranes as promising materials for new proton exchange membranes", *Polym Adv Technol* 17, pp. 360–365, 2006
5. Teng, X., Dai, J., Bi, F., Jiang, X., Song, Y., Yin, G., "Ultra-thin polytetrafluoroethene/Nafion/silica membranes prepared with nano SiO_2 and its comparison with sol–gel derived one for vanadium redox flow battery", *Solid State Ionics* 280, pp. 30–36, 2015.

Ballistic Testing of Pressurized Hydrogen Storage Cylinders

Benjamin Paczkowski
Fuel Cell Technologies, Ground Vehicle Power and Mobility
US Army Tank Automotive Research, Development and Engineering Center
Warren, Michigan, USA, 48397
benjamin.v.paczkowski.civ@mail.mil / 1-586-282-1695[1]

Disclaimer: Reference herein to any specific commercial company, product, process, or service by trade name, trademark, manufacturer, or otherwise, does not necessarily constitute or imply its endorsement, recommendation, or favoring by the United States Government or the Department of the Army (DoA). The opinions of the authors expressed herein do not necessarily state or reflect those of the United States Government or the DoA, and shall not be used for advertising or product endorsement purposes.

Abstract: *Hydrogen fuel cells have potential as future power sources for military vehicles and power generation systems. Hydrogen storage as a compressed gas presents several safety concerns in military applications. In order to optimize future design and integration work, these risks need to be investigated and understood. This work investigates the behavior of a pressurized hydrogen storage cylinder when penetrated by a ballistic threat, perhaps the greatest safety concern in a military application.*

Keywords: fuel cells; fuel processing and storage; hydrogen storage; hydrogen safety; ballistic test

Introduction

The United States Army Tank Automotive Research, Development and Engineering Center (TARDEC) has been investigating hydrogen fuel cells for primary and auxiliary power sources in ground vehicles. Specifically, polymer electrolyte membrane (PEM) fuel cells have been under study, as they operate cooler, quieter and more efficiently than gasoline or diesel burning engines. PEM fuel cells require ultra-high purity (99.999% or greater) hydrogen in order to operate, as any impurities can damage the catalyst inside. In order to supply this hydrogen to the fuel cell, hydrogen is stored on the vehicle in storage cylinders and compressed to either 5,000 pounds per square inch (psi) or 10,000 psi depending on the application. This high pressure method of storing hydrogen is a safety issue that warrants thorough testing.

Currently there are two tank designs (types) used for storing hydrogen, depending on the pressure. Cylinders that store hydrogen at 5,000 psi are typically Type III tanks, while those that store it at 10,000 psi are Type IV. Type III tanks are composed of an aluminum liner wrapped with carbon fiber and resin; Type IV tanks contain a composite liner also wrapped in carbon fiber and resin. The cylinders tested demonstrate pressurized storage and can be used to answer several frequently asked questions regarding the safety of pressurized hydrogen storage.

As part of the manufacturing and certification process, cylinder builders are required to subject the storage tanks to several abusive tests but some possible military applications can be more abusive than the tests required for certification. Several investigations have been conducted to investigate the safety of hydrogen cylinders for commercial and civilian use [1-4], yet none have investigated cylinders pressurized with hydrogen exposed to incendiary rounds or rocket propelled grenades. In order to test the safety of hydrogen storage cylinders in a military application, several different types and makes of cylinder were subjected to live fire testing. The purpose of this testing was to discover any safety issues that result from a tank being punctured by several types of ballistic rounds and a rocket propelled grenade (RPG) while pressurized with hydrogen gas.

Test Conditions

In order to perform testing in a safe and controlled manner, a surface danger zone (SDZ) of 100 yards was established to prevent any possible injury [5]. Only remotely controlled equipment (cameras) were permitted inside the SDZ while the range was hot. To capture data, a high speed camera and several real time cameras were placed in doghouses around the range, focused on the cylinder and impact zone. A thermal camera was placed downrange in order to monitor possible thermal events, such as a flame due to hydrogen's nature to burn in the ultraviolet spectrum causing difficult visualization in daylight [6].

During ballistic testing, the launcher was placed just outside the SDZ, allowing the launcher to be reloaded in case of a miss or unconfirmed hit on the pressurized cylinder. Some of the cylinders had electronic pressure release devices that could not be opened on the test site. As such, the range was only declared safe after penetration and venting of the cylinder's contents was confirmed via video review. A static RPG was used to simulate an RPG strike directly on a cylinder. The RPG was placed within a few inches of the cylinder, armed, and then remotely detonated. Table 1 presents the type of cylinder, pressure, and round fired for each test.

Table 1: Initial cylinder and test conditions

Manufacturer	Type	Pressure (psig)	Round Type
Quantum	IV	0 (empty)	7.62 M80 Ball
Worthington	III	3,500	7.62 AP
Quantum	IV	3,200	7.62 API
Luxfur	IV	3,100	7.62 AP
Worthington	III	3,200	7.62 AP
Quantum	IV	3,000	RPG

Results

After several practice shots to sight in the launcher, an empty Quantum tank was used as a control for the test. Two (2) 7.62 ball rounds and one 7.62 armor piercing (AP) round were fired at the cylinder in order to determine if the round could penetrate a tank. The results of these shots were inconclusive. The rounds all clearly struck the cylinder, yet an entry was not clear. Several attempts to probe the entry holes could not determine if the round had completely penetrated the wall of the cylinder. It was thought that the composite liner inside the cylinder had swollen around the entry hole, prohibiting a probe to go through the wall. Though penetration was unable to be determined, the test was continued as several cylinders were equipped with electronic pressure releases that could not be safely depressurized in the field. 7.62 AP rounds were chosen as the default round to increase the probability of penetration. After the test concluded, the control cylinder was cut open to determine if the rounds had penetrated since the entry holes could not be probed in the field. Upon opening the cylinder, a single round was found inside, the armor piercing round. The entry hole had not swollen, the carbon fiber wrapping of the tank layered back on top of itself making it difficult to probe through. The inside of the cylinder was inspected and no other entry holes were found where the two other rounds had hit the outside of the cylinder. The liner did become slightly delaminated from the wrapping due to the impact even though the cylinder was not pressurized.

Figure 1: Control cylinder after three initial test shots. The arrows indicate where the rounds hit the cylinder.

The first test with a pressurized cylinder involved a Type III tank that was penetrated with the AP round. The tank began to vent instantly and the round visibly bounced around inside the cylinder, ricocheting off of the aluminum liner leaving marks on the outer composite wrap where it dented the liner. The round did not exit the cylinder. The liner remained intact except for a few broken fibers at the entry hole. There was no fire observable or detected. The temperature of tank changed drastically as the gas escaped from the entry hole, as was expected. The tank took approximately 5 minutes to vent its contents to the atmosphere.

The second test of a pressurized cylinder was a Type IV tank penetrated by an armor piercing incendiary (API) round. The

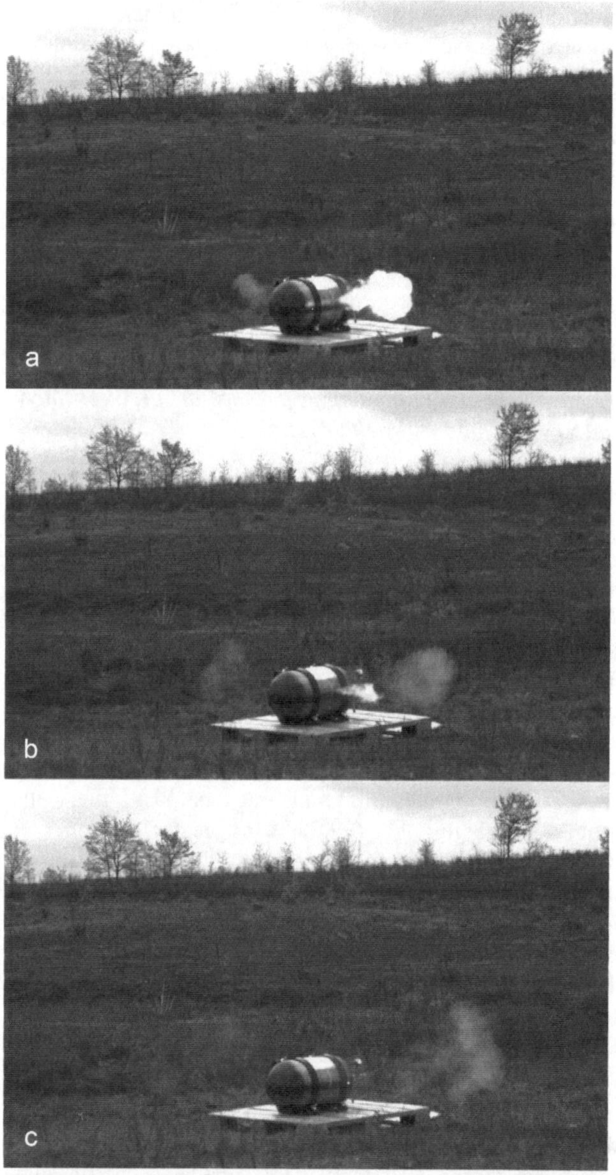

Figure 2: 7.62 API test after impact: (a) the initial flame jet after penetration along with visible exit plume, (b) flame jet sustained briefly while particulates burn off and transitions to a near-invisible hydrogen flame, (c) small flame from a residual particle passing through the near-invisible hydrogen flame.

round penetrated both walls of the cylinder, clearly entering and exiting. The entry hole immediately began to vent, the venting hydrogen mixed with the air, and the incendiary nature of the round ignited the escaping gas mixture. The gas venting from the exit hole did not ignite. The flame was visible after it ignited due to the particulates in the air around the penetration and then quickly became invisible after the particulates burned off. The sustained flame was detectible on the thermal camera and as some residual carbon fiber exited the tank, as seen in Figure 2c. The escaping gas continued to burn for 20 minutes after the initial penetration until all of the hydrogen had been consumed. The flame jet never grew larger than shown in Figure 2b, shrinking gradually as the hydrogen concentration decreased.

The third cylinder tested was also a Type IV tank from a different manufacturer. A 7.62 AP round was fired at it and it penetrated both walls of the cylinder, clearly entering and exiting. The round first penetrated the steel mounting strap used to hold the cylinder to the pallet before passing through the cylinder wall and through the other side. The exit hole had several strands of frayed carbon fiber wrapping surrounding it, along with bubbles trapped in the surface resin layer due to the venting hydrogen. The tank vented completely in about 5 minutes with no indication of ignition.

The final cylinder tested with a 7.62 AP round was a Type III tank from the same manufacturer as the first test. The tank was penetrated through one of the straps holding it to the pallet and out through the opposing wall. The tank vented completely in about 5 minutes without any ignition of the hydrogen.

The static RPG was fired at a Type IV cylinder. The RPG detonation caused a large jet of liquid metal to be shot through the cylinder. This jet can be seen in Figure 3a. After the RPG was fired, a large cloud of debris and flame enveloped the test site. After the debris began to clear, the burning hydrogen could be observed. A tail of flame was observed coming from the exit hole formed by the RPG. After the hydrogen had completely evacuated the cylinder,

Figure 3: RPG impact: (a) the initial detonation of the RPG with initial jet, (b) flame tail sustained briefly after RPG penetration.

Figure 4: Cylinder before and after RPG test: (a) cylinder before test, (b) cylinder with entry hole from RPG, (c) exit hole from RPG.

which took around one minute, the cylinder was observed to be intact. Figure 4 shows large entrance and exit holes and a strip of the outer layer of carbon fiber wrap on the top side of the cylinder was missing in between the holes. The cylinder did not rupture or burst in a destructive manner, even with the close proximity of the explosive.

Conclusions

In the ballistic live fire test, hydrogen storage tanks pressurized with hydrogen were exposed to three common types of 7.62 rounds, M80 ball, armor piercing, and armor piercing incendiary. It was found that M80 ball rounds may not penetrate Type IV tanks. Only the armor piercing round penetrated the cylinder. When penetrated by AP rounds, the cylinder will vent quickly without producing a flame. The cylinder will not catastrophically fail when pierced by a round, retaining its structural integrity and venting its contents safely. A recommended best practice for future fuel cell vehicle design is to add a vertical vent path around the hydrogen storage cylinders to the roof of the vehicle in order to allow hydrogen to escape quickly in the event of a hit, reducing the chance for hydrogen to accumulate to flammable and explosive concentrations in air [7].

Perhaps the largest threat to hydrogen storage cylinders are armor piercing incendiary rounds. When penetrated with an API round, the gas escaping from the entrance hole could possibly ignite and burn for 20 to 30 minutes. Due to hydrogen's nature to burn in the ultraviolet, a flame is invisible to the naked eye in daylight and faint in dark conditions making it difficult to identify. A thermal or ultraviolet camera is required to determine if there is a flame present. In order to reduce the chance of a complete vehicle fire, it is recommended to surround the cylinders in nonflammable material and a vertical vent, as mentioned previously. While this is a dangerous case, the buoyant nature of hydrogen causes it to travel away from the cylinder and upwards when penetrated [7]. This behavior reduces the risk of a total vehicle fire when compared to liquid fuels, which can pool below the vehicle, spread to other extremely flammable components (such as tires), and result in the entire vehicle becoming engulfed in flames [8]. Hydrogen flames radiate little heat, reducing the chance that nearby material will be ignited by the flame unless in extremely close proximity.

When struck by a rocket propelled grenade, a Type IV hydrogen storage cylinder will be penetrated through both walls and vent quickly with a short burn off period. The tank will not catastrophically burst and produce limited shrapnel, mostly carbon fiber and resin strands with relatively little mass and no sharp edges. Limited resources and uncertain availability of range personnel only allowed for one shot with an RPG to take place. Without a control to compare against, any claims of increased or decreased impact due to the presence of hydrogen is subjective at best. With that in mind, engineers familiar with RPG testing claimed that the impact of the RPG on the hydrogen cylinder was close to that of an impact with an inert target, signifying that hydrogen may not contribute significantly to the explosive force of the impact. Further testing is required to validate this claim.

Understanding the risks involved with hydrogen storage will allow for systems to be intelligently designed, mitigating most risks. While hydrogen presents several concerning properties, the risks associated with storing it are not entirely dissimilar to liquid fuels that are currently used. Storing the hydrogen at pressure will not cause any more significant safety issues than liquid fuel in the event of a ballistic penetration or explosion due to the inherently safe design of the storage systems.

Acknowledgements

The author would like to acknowledge Kevin Centeck, Steve Caito, Dan Maslach, and Mark Radiwan for their assistance in arranging and performing the testing.

References

1. Weyandt, N., "Compressed Hydrogen Cylinder Research and Testing in Accordance with FMVSS 304," DOT Report Number DOT HS 811 150; 2009.
2. Odegard, B. C. and G. J. Thomas, "Testing of High Pressure Hydrogen Composite Tanks," *Proceedings of the 2001 DOE Hydrogen Program Review;* 2001.
3. Zalosh R. and N. Weyandt, "Hydrogen Fuel Tank Fire Exposure Burst Test," SAE Paper Number 2005-01-1886; 2005.
4. Zalosh R., "Blast Waves and Fireballs Generated by Hydrogen Tank Rupture during Fire Exposure," *Proceedings of the 5th international seminar on fire and explosion hazards*, Edinburgh, UK, 23-27 April 2007; 2007.
5. Dadashzadeh, M., S. Kashkarov, D. Makarov, and V. Molkov, "Risk Assessment Methodology for Onboard Hydrogen Storage," *International Journal of Hydrogen Energy,* Vol. 43, pp. 6462-6475, 2018.
6. Schefer, R. W., W. D. Kulatilaka, B. D. Patterson, and T. B. Settersten, "Visible Emission of Hydrogen Flame," *Combustion and Flame,* Vol. 156, pp. 1234-1241, 2009.
7. Swain, M. R., J. Shriber, and M. N. Swain, "Comparison of Hydrogen, Natural Gas, Liquified Petroleum Gas, and Gasoline Leakage in a Residential Garage," *Energy & Fuels,* Vol. 12, pp. 83-89, 1998.
8. Suzuki, J., Y. Tamura, S. Watanabe, M. Takabayashi, and K. Sato, "Fire Safety Evaluation of a Vehicle Equipped with Hydrogen Fuel Cylinders: Comparison with Gasoline and CNG Vehicles," SAE Paper Number 2006-01-0129, 2006.

Standalone, Light-weight, Compact Power Generators

Anthony Anderson, Subir Roychoudhury, Christian Junaedi, Saurabh A. Vilekar, Tim LaBreche, Dave Spence, Rich Mastanduno and Matt Steinbroner

Precision Combustion, Inc.
410 Sackett Point Rd., North Haven, CT 06473
aanderson@precision-combustion.com

Abstract: *Precision Combustion, Inc. (PCI) is developing two platforms for compact power generators. In the first platform, we are utilizing reliable, lightweight and low-cost, commercial off-the-shelf (COTS) 4-stroke engines with modified fueling system that enables operation on JP-8/DF-2. This is made possible by PCI's novel and patented octane-matching approach. 0.5 and 1 kW prototypes have been matured. Capability for tethering 3 generators and obtaining up to 3 kW has been demonstrated. Custom power electronics enable simultaneous DC and AC outputs. MIL-SPEC environmental and power quality testing has been successfully completed. 1000-hour durability testing has indicated no abnormal wear and tear or impact on normally expected life. Maintenance intervals were between 100 – 150 hours with no irregular buildup of fuel or metals in the oil. The approach also avoids wet stacking. TEC-D (Technical Demonstration) testing at Fort Devens has also been completed without any technical issues identified during testing with various appliances.*

In a second platform, PCI is developing fuel cell based power generation systems. In this approach, practical fuels including distillate fuels such as military jet fuels (consisting of up to 3000 ppm$_w$ sulfur), diesels or kerosene are reformed into fuel cell quality reformate sans sulfur. The enabling component is our patented fuel processor design with proprietary sulfur tolerant catalyst and high capacity sulfur filter in a process intensified packaging. Current efforts are ongoing for integration and thermal management optimization along with controls and power conditioning. PCI's development for fuel cell based power generators has focused on stationary and portable power application, as well as Auxiliary Power Units (APU), ranging from 1 kW to 10 kW battery hybridized systems. Light-weight, low parasitic balance of plant components are being implemented to develop robust and practical systems. This poster will discuss operational details for both power generation platforms with system performance metrics, including volumetric and gravimetric power density and durability.

Keywords: Reforming, Fuel Processing, Power Generator, JP-8, Diesel, SOFC, Fuel Cell, APU, Generator, Portable, Power, Packable, PPG, STEP, Catalytic.

Introduction

Building upon catalytic reaction technology and fuel reformers developed by PCI (based upon PCI's patented Microlith® technology trademarked by PCI) [1], the company is developing and advancing two families of light-weight, compact power generation platforms. The first platform is based upon modified COTS gasoline generators which are catalytically enabled to be fueled with JP fuels. The second platform is a JP fuel reformer/solid oxide fuel cell power generator. Both platforms utilize the unique features of Microlith substrate technology to provide unique compact and lightweight systems

Microlith Substrate Technology

The Microlith substrate consists of a series of ultra-short-channel-length, catalytically coated metal meshes with very small channel diameters. The mesh-like substrates provide very high heat and mass transfer coefficients, low thermal mass, and extremely high rate of reactions. The use of this kind of reactor where the reacting stream is passed through the catalyst at extremely high space velocity is generically termed short contact time (SCT) approach. The ultra-short-channel-length Microlith substrate minimizes boundary layer buildup and results in remarkably high heat and mass transfer coefficients compared to other substrates (e.g., monoliths, foams, pellets). In many catalytic reactors, enhanced heat transfer properties are necessary to eliminate local hot spots and temperature excursions in the catalyst surface, and to prevent catalyst deactivation due to sintering. The Microlith substrate also provides about three times higher geometric surface area over conventional monolith reactors with equivalent volume and open frontal area. Additionally, PCI's proprietary catalyst coatings, with high surface area washcoats, allow for very low catalyst usage with rigorously demonstrated long-term mechanical, thermal, and performance durability.

The heat and mass transfer coefficients depend on the boundary layer thickness. For a conventional long channel honeycomb monolith, a fully developed boundary layer is present over a considerable length of the catalytic surface, limiting the rate of reactant transport from bulk to the active sites. This is avoided when short-channel-length catalytic screens are used. Computational Fluid Dynamics (CFD) analysis shows the difference in boundary layer formation between a monolith and Microlith screens. The resulting high heat and mass transfers on the Microlith reactor will allow for very small reactor sizes.

The use of catalyst substrates with high heat and mass transfer rates, high surface area, and low pressure drop has a significant impact on reactor performance and size. The effectiveness of the Microlith technology and long-term durability of PCI's proprietary catalyst coatings have been systematically demonstrated in different applications. These include exhaust aftertreatment [2], trace contaminant control system [3,4], catalytic combustion [5], partial oxidation of methane [6,7], liquid fuel reforming [8], CO preferential oxidation, and water gas shift reactors [9].

Catalyst coating and durability on the Microlith substrate: While state-of-the-art, high dispersion mixed oxide catalyst formulations have shown promise for catalytic applications, they are not intrinsically as active as platinum group metal (PGM)-based formulations. Although non-precious metal formulations are far less expensive, they are more susceptible to activity loss, and since they do not have the high intrinsic activity. Reformer performance and coating durability after exposure to vibration loads and multiple thermal cycles is crucial to permit high mission capability with long maintenance intervals. To date, the durability of the Microlith substrate and catalyst coating has been systematically demonstrated.

Military Power Generation

Currently, there is a power gap in the Army's generator set inventory. The U.S. Army does not have a diesel engine driven 1 kW generator set. The smallest power sources that are available are Government furnished batteries and fuel cells (25 to 300W). Currently fielded fuel cells do not operate on JP-8 or Diesel and would require the Soldier to obtain either Methanol or Propane fuel canisters to operate the fuel cells. At the upper end of the power gap are the smallest diesel generators available to the U.S. Army; the 2kW Military Tactical Generator (MTG) (NSN 6115-01435-1578) weighing 140 – 152 pounds (with 4 hours of fuel) and the 3kW MEP-831A TQG weighing 270 pounds (dry, no battery). Operation of these generators at low output can lead to accelerated maintenance and downtime due to wet stacking, a well-known failure mechanism with diesel engines operated continuously at part load.

Solution 1: Adapting spark ignited (SI) Internal Combustion (IC) engines to operate on heavy fuels such as JP-8 and DF-2 can result in lightweight, man-portable power generators. Compression ignition engines are too heavy due to the higher pressure combustion chamber. But SI engines require high octane fuels such as gasoline to avoid knocking and pre-ignition. Distillate fuels such as JP-8 have a low octane number, making them inherently unsuitable for spark ignition. Other companies and research groups have attempted to solve this problem through JP-8 vaporization, EGR, combustion chamber modification, high pressure fuel injection and other complex methods. In contrast, a different approach has been used by PCI. PCI's add-on solution is non-specific to the engine, generator, or manufacturer and can be applied to any of these regardless of displacement or rated output. Multiple engines (350 Watts, 450 Watts, 1 and 2 kW variants) have been modified to operate on JP-8. Durability over 1000+ hours with numerous start-stops has been demonstrated. Control integration has been implemented. Power output quality has been verified. Transition (turndown) from max to zero in ~1 second has been demonstrated.

The technology is scalable, generator agnostic and non-invasive (i.e. does not require combustion chamber modifications). It is a technology platform which will permit migration to applications including for UAV's, UGVs, wearable power, and towable generators.

Solution 2: A well-integrated fuel reformer/solid oxide fuel cell solution to optimize the attributes of the technologies at the system level providing compact size and lightweight package via robust thermal integration. 1, 2 and 10 kW variants are under development.

Conclusions

Operation of COTS generators and engines enables low cost and reliable commercial technology to deliver logistics fueled power solutions at power levels unmet by existing JP-8 fueled generators. Spark Ignited IC engines operating efficiently on JP-8 and other logistics and distillate fuels is a key outcome of this effort and demonstrates the viability of developing small, portable and efficient power generators operating on logistic fuels. PCI is also developing fuel cell based power generation systems for stationary and portable power application, as well as Auxiliary Power Units (APU).

Acknowledgement

We acknowledge the support of the DoD (TARDEC, CERDEC, SPAWAR and US TRANSCOM). Any opinions, findings, and conclusions or recommendations expressed in this paper are those of the authors and do not necessarily reflect the views of the DoD.

References

1. Microlith Catalytic Reaction System, Patent # 5,051,241. Sept. 24, 1991.
2. S. Roychoudhury, J. Bianchi, G. Muench, and W.C. Pfefferle, SAE, 971023 (1997).
3. R. Carter, J. Bianchi, W.C. Pfefferle, S. Roychoudhury, and J.L. Perry, SAE, 972432 (1997).
4. J.L. Perry, R.N. Carter, and S. Roychoudhury, SAE, 1999-01-2112 (1999).
5. G. Kraemer, W.C. Pfefferle, et al., Proc. Int. Joint Power Generation Conf., ASME (1997).
6. M. Lyubovsky, H. Karim, S. Roychoudhury, et al., Catal. Today, 83, 183 (2003).
7. M. Lyubovsky, S. Roychoudhury, and R. LaPierre, Catal Lett., 99, 113 (2005).
8. S. Roychoudhury, M.J. Castaldi, M. Lyubovsky, et al., J. Power Sources, 152, 75 (2005).
9. M. Castaldi, R. LaPierre, M. Lyubovsky, S. Roychoudhury, Catal. Today, 99, 339 (2005).

Capillary Pressure Versus Saturation Characterization of Molten-Salt Power Source Separator Materials

Alexander Headley, Martin Nemer, Christine Roberts, Ryan Solich
Sandia National Laboratories
Albuquerque, NM, USA, 87122
aheadle@sandia.gov / 1-505-844-5066

Abstract: *The Thermally Activated Battery Simulator (TABS) was developed to aid in battery design by modeling the thermal, mechanical, and electrochemical response of proposed batteries. While the model has been very successful, there is an ongoing effort to continue to improve its accuracy. One area of concern is the modeling of electrolyte flow between the separator and electrodes after battery activation, which may be influenced by capillary forces within the grain structure of the anode, cathode, and separator materials. However, to date, no relevant data for the capillary pressure of the battery materials has been available. This study focuses characterizing the saturation versus capillary pressure of the separator in conditions relevant to thermal battery operation. The porous plate test method, traditionally a soil characterization technique, was used with a wetting surrogate fluid to test relevant battery operation conditions at room temperature. Two potential separator materials were tested while varying the initial saturation level and confining stress. The data from these experiments provide previously unavailable parameter estimations. A companion talk discussing a full suite of soil-science techniques applied to separator physics will also be given.*

Keywords: thermal battery; separator; capillary pressure; saturation

Introduction

A thermal or molten salt battery separator is traditionally composed of electrolyte salt, often LiCl/KCl, that is solid at room temperature and magnesium oxide (MgO), an inert binder material. When the battery is activated, the electrolyte salt melts and flows to the anode and cathode, creating an ionically conductive path for charge transfer. Upon melting, the separator also compacts. Pores present in the separator initially collapse and the MgO condenses into a stress-supporting network. This process, which is summarized in [1] and [2], has a significant effect on the electrochemical performance of the battery.

The electrochemical impedance across an active battery cell is determined by the extent of the separator compression and the electrolyte saturation in each of the layers (anode, separator, and cathode). Electrolyte flows until the fluid pressure equalizes among the electrodes. As such, the relationship between fluid pressure and electrolyte saturation in a separator needs to be known to properly model electrochemical transport. Furthermore, studies have shown that the amount of electrolyte affects the separator compaction during activation, so the separator thickness in an active battery depends on the amount of fluid it contains initially [2].

Because the capillary pressure, P_c, of fluid that fills a circular pore is inversely related to the radius of curvature, R, and directly related to its surface tension, γ, ($P_c = 2\gamma/R$), the pressure required to drive a wetting fluid from a small pore is larger than for a large pore. Therefore, the pressure-saturation relationship for a material is a function of the binder microstructure as well as its packing density. Here, pressure-saturation data are measured for two different MgO samples that are packed to a range of densities to understand the effects of these factors on separator performance.

Methods

Two separate MgO materials with different microstructures were chosen for this study. These microstructures were imaged using scanning electron microscopy (Zeiss Gemini field emission SEM) (Figure 1). MgO A has a small, disc-like primary particle shape. These particles aggregate into loose, round structures about 1 μm in diameter. MgO B has a larger, flake-like character. Flakes join together at angles in the packed material. These two MgO microstructures are expected to have different pore size distributions at a given density due to differences in the packing efficiency of the structured particle aggregates.

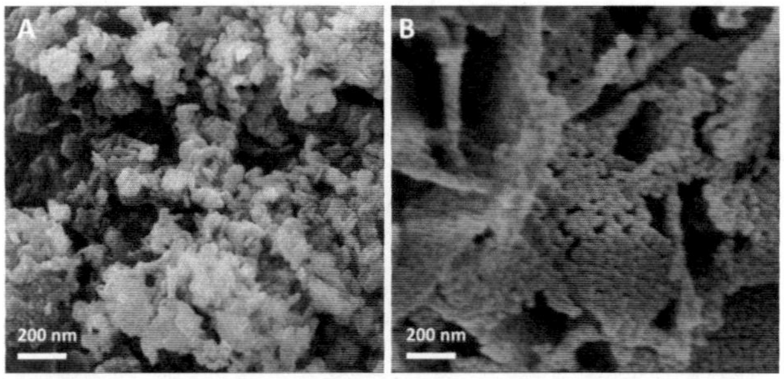

Figure 1. SEM images of MgO-A (left) and MgO-B (right) microstructures.

Eutectic electrolyte salt is difficult to use in pressure-saturation experiments due to its high melting temperature (352 °C) and corrosive nature. However, it is known that the salt thoroughly wets the MgO [4]. A surrogate fluid, 5 cSt polydimethyl siloxane (PDMS) was used as it also thoroughly wets the MgO. With knowledge of the surface tension and contact angle of both fluids, the pressure-saturation behavior measured using PDMS can be correlated to that of the electrolyte salt using the Leverett equation [3].

With this in mind, a test was developed to determine the pressure-saturation behavior of the MgO materials with respect to the initial PDMS to MgO ratio and initial axial stress. The porous plate method, a common soil science measurement technique for the determination of capillary pressure in granular materials, was used for this study. With this method, samples are placed in capillary contact with a saturated, fine grain porous plate with a high air intrusion pressure inside a sealed pressure vessel. During the course of the test, various air pressures are applied in the head space of the vessel, pushing fluid from the sample and out of the system through the porous plate. The pressure is maintained until the fluid level in the sample reaches equilibrium, at which point either the sample weight or volume of displaced fluid can be measured to determine the saturation of the sample. This process is repeated at increasing pressures to characterize the pressure-saturation curve for the sample.

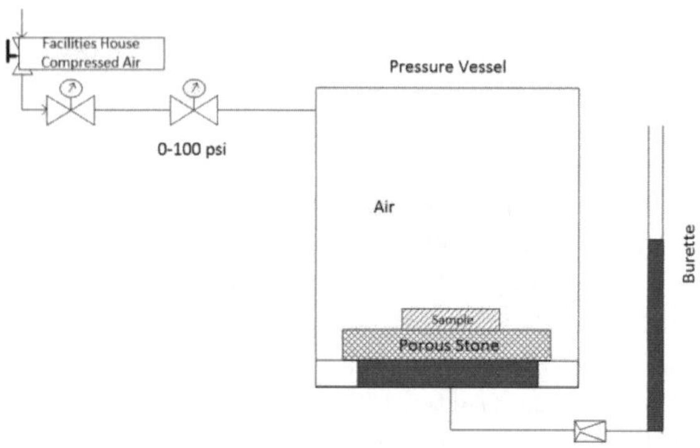

Figure 2. Schematic of a porous-plate apparatus for determining capillary pressure

A Soilmoisture Equipment Corp. (Santa Barbara, CA) pressure vessel and porous plate, as shown in Figure 2, was used for these tests. A 12" diameter, 15 bar ceramic porous plate with a sealed diaphragm underneath for fluid collection was used. This allowed twelve, 2" diameter samples to be tested simultaneously. The 15 bar rating of the stone corresponds to the minimum air intrusion pressure of the plate when saturated with water. However, as PDMS has a lower surface tension than water, this configuration allows for measurements up to approximately 375 kPa (3.75 bar) before air is pushed through the plate, ending the test. This is sufficient to cover the pressure range of interest as separators operate at high saturation levels.

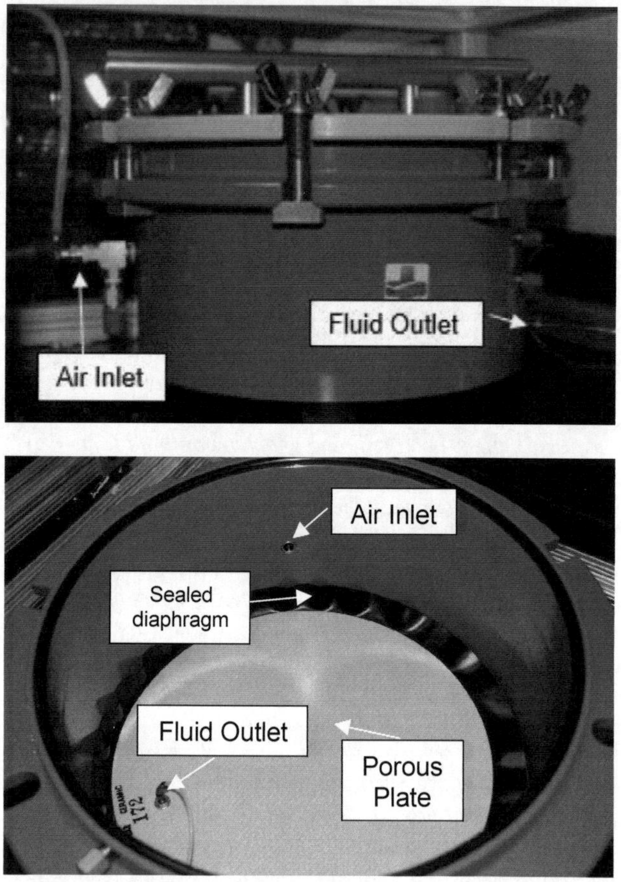

Figure 3. Soilmoisture capillary pressure test vessel outside view (top) and inside view (bottom)

For these tests, samples were mixed in initial ratios of PDMS to MgO of 2:1 or 1.5:1 by mass. Care was taken to thoroughly mix the samples such that no dry pockets of MgO remained. The mixture was loaded in to retaining rings with a fine mesh nylon filter clamped to the bottom of the ring to allow PDMS flow while limiting MgO mobility. After filling the retaining ring with the PDMS/MgO mixture, the ring was placed in a Humboldt 2" fixed-ring consolidation cell and packed to with axial loads of either 8, 14, or 28 psi with a load frame. These loads cover a range of pressures relevant to the activated thermal batteries of interest. The load was held until no there was no significant change in the height of the actuator for a minimum of 5 minutes.

After packing, the samples were submerged in PDMS in a vacuum desiccator and a vacuum was applied for 24-48 hours to displace all the air in the materials with the test fluid. This ensured that all the samples began the test fully saturated. An 80/20 mix of diatomaceous earth and kaolin clay saturated with PDMS was used as a contact agent between the samples and porous plate to give good capillary connectivity. Each air pressure was held for a minimum of 276 hours to allow the saturation level to reach equilibrium. After this time, any excess earth/clay was removed and the samples were weighed to track the loss of PDMS as a function of air pressure.

Results

The results of the measurements are shown in Figure 4. The saturations reported below are calculated as:

$$\%Sat = \frac{V_{PDMS}}{V_{pore}} = \frac{V_{PDMS}}{V_{Tot} - V_{MgO}} \quad (1)$$

Note that the sample volume was measured after the samples were tested at air pressures of 160kPa. It is possible that the sample volumes decreased from the initial value during testing.

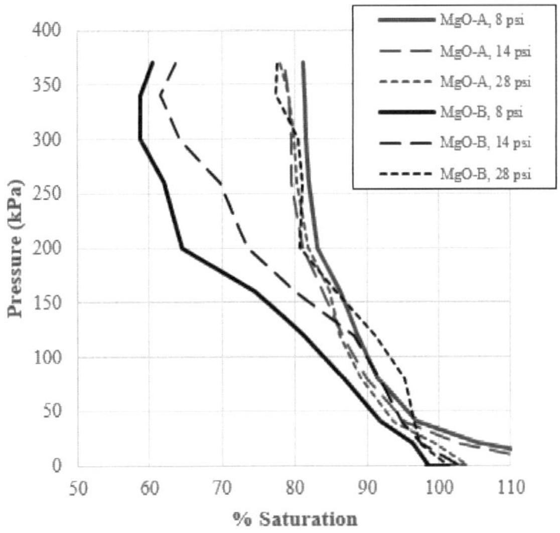

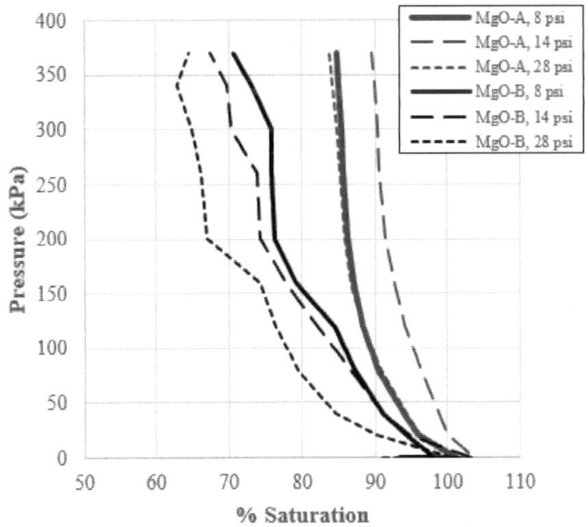

Figure 4. Measured pressure-saturation curve of PDMS fluid in MgO samples of varying initial compaction pressure. The initial ratio of fluid to MgO was 1.5:1 by mass (top) and 2:1 by mass (bottom)

In general, it can be seen that MgO-A retained more PDMS during the course of the test than MgO-B. This is in line with what would be expected from SEM imaging of the two materials. As MgO-B has larger spaces between features than MgO-A on average, the capillary pressure in the pores spaces is expected to be lower, meaning that fluid can be displaced more readily.

The effect of the initial PDMS-MgO ratio and axial loading during sample preparation is not as clear. The trend in sample porosity with consolidation pressure changes depending on the initial PDMS-MgO ratio, as highlighted in Figure 5.

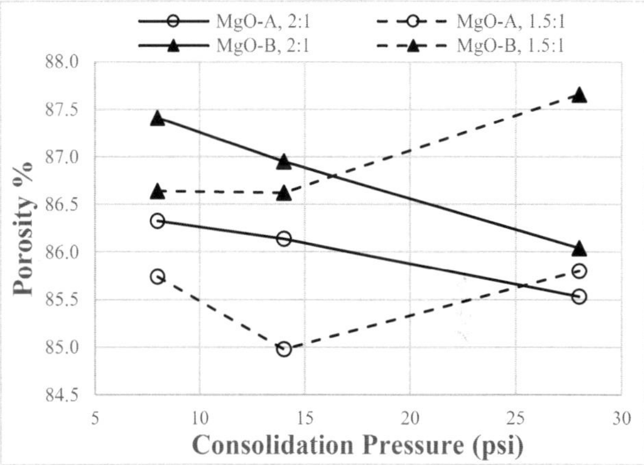

Figure 5. Sample porosity versus consolidation pressure with different MgOs and PDMS-MgO ratios

With a PDMS-MgO ratio of 2:1, the material porosity, defined here as:

$$\%Porosity = \frac{\left(V_{Tot} - V_{MgO}\right)}{V_{Tot}} \quad (2)$$

decreases as the consolidation pressure increases, suggesting that the material packs more tightly as the consolidation pressure increases. It can also be seen that MgO-B is consistently more porous than MgO-A, which is in line with the results shown in Figure 4. However, with the 1.5:1 ratio, the porosity increased as the consolidation pressure increased from 14 to 28psi. This could be due to differences in consolidation of the sample during testing caused by differences in the initial packed material structure.

With the 1.5:1 PDMS-MgO samples, little to no PDMS was pushed out of the samples during the initial axial loading step, suggesting that the mixture was not fully saturated. However, after saturation in the desiccator, air pockets in the material would be replaced with PDMS, perhaps allowing for more mobility of the MgO matrix after saturation than before. This will be explored and monitored further in future testing.

Regardless, there is a clear trend in both MgOs with regards to material porosity versus the minimum saturation level that was reached, as shown in Figure 6.

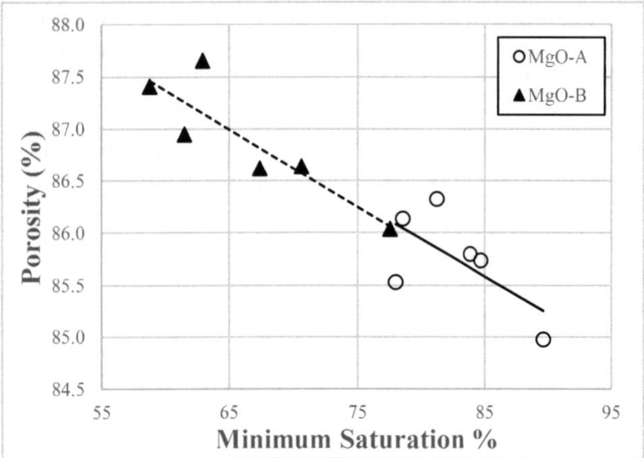

Figure 6. Sample porosity versus minimum saturation level with different MgOs

For both materials and PDMS-MgO ratios tested, as the porosity decreased, the minimum saturation level increased. This suggests that if the final packed porosity can be estimated, the pressure-saturation curve can likely be predicted with reasonable certainty as well. However, more research will be necessary to understand packing processes for these materials.

Conclusions and Future Work

Pressure-saturation measurements were performed for two different MgO materials to support separator modeling efforts for TABS. For these tests, a surrogate fluid, PDMS, replaced the electrolyte in the system such that the porous-plate method could be used. The PDMS-MgO ratio and axial consolidation pressure was also varied during sample preparation for these tests. In general, MgO-A, which is comprised of small, round structures, retained more PDMS than MgO-B, which is characterized by larger flakes of material.

It is clear that packing efficiency also plays a role in the shape of the capillary-pressure curve, but more work is needed in this area.

Future work will include further investigation of the effect of various parameters on material packing. Also, additional MgOs will be tested to better understand the effect of the basic MgO structure on fluid retention. Cathode materials will be tested in a similar fashion as well. We also intend to take X-Ray CT scans of samples to better understand the effect of saturation and axial loading on the structure of the packed material. Ultimately, this information will be used to improve electrolyte flow and mechanical modeling in TABS.

Acknowledgements

Sandia National Laboratories is a multimission laboratory managed and operated by National Technology and Engineering Solutions of Sandia LLC, a wholly owned subsidiary of Honeywell International Inc. for the U.S. Department of Energy's National Nuclear Security Administration under contract DE-NA0003525.

References

1. Roberts, C. C., et al. "Experimental Characterization of Mechanical Deformation and Fluid Transport Within Thermal Battery Constituents", SAND report SAND2017-8209, 2017.
2. Nemer, B., et al. Soil-Science (Mechanical/Capillary Pressure/Electrical) testing methods applied to Molten-Salt Power-Source Separator Materials. Proceedings of the 48th Power Sources Conference, 2018.
3. M. C. Leverett, "Capillary Behavior in Porous Solids", Trans of AIME, v 142, issue 1, 1941.
4. Chae, et. al, "Thermal batteries with ceramic felt separators – Part 1: Wetting, loading behavior and chemical stability, Ceramics International, 43 (2017). pp 4015-4022.

Manufacturing Low-Cost Nano-Coatings for High Performance Battery Materials

Meghan N. Herbert-Walters, James E. Trevey, Barbara K. Hughes

Forge Nano
Louisville, CO 80033
Email:mherbertwalters@forgenano.com

Abstract: *Lithium ion batteries used today fall short of reaching the performance requirements necessary to fully enable electric vehicles to match their combustion engine counterparts. As a result, scientific and engineering advancements must be made to enable battery technologies to meet high-energy density and longevity goals while maintaining affordability and safety. Improvements to raw materials manufacturing via precise, conformal coatings presents as an affordable means to address these issues. Forge Nano's ALD technology is a sequential chemical surface modification process that allows sub-nanometer thickness coatings to be tuned for optimal battery performance ALD-enabled electrode materials allow for higher voltage operation through surface stabilization and retardation of materials dissolution. Increased surface stability also reduces the occurrence of poisonous side reactions preventing capacity losses over multiple cycles as compared to their non-coated counterparts. In addition to improved cycling capabilities, ALD-stabilized materials also improve battery safety by preventing thermal runaway caused by high-temperature electrolyte interactions. Finally, from a manufacturing standpoint, ALD coatings have the additional potential for lowering costs through the reduction in solvent usage during battery processing, as some ALD-enabled materials benefit from reduced viscosity with coating level. In summary, the performance achievable using ALD coatings on cathode and anode particles are far superior to any alternate coating or surface modification process due to the uniformity, scalability, precision and cost.*

Lithium Ion Battery Off-Gas Monitoring for Battery Health and Safety

Scott L. Swartz, Stephen R. Cummings, Nicholas B. Frank, and William J. Dawson
Nexceris, LLC
404 Enterprise Drive
Lewis Center, OH, 43035
(614) 842-6606 (phone)
(614) 842-6607 (fax)
s.cummings@nexceris.com

Abstract: *Availability of robust and reliable gas detection for battery health monitoring is essential to the safe implementation and use of rechargeable batteries in military and commercial applications. Lithium ion batteries go through several stages leading up to the evolution of smoke and flames observed during thermal runaway, including a detectable level off-gas for the compromised cell. Leveraging its patented ceramic gas sensor technology platform, Nexceris has developed a monitoring system aimed at safety monitoring of lithium ion battery systems. Further, the off-gas monitor enables detection of electrolyte leaks from battery cells with sufficient early warning to prevent thermal runaway. A number of products have been developed to integrate this technology into energy storage systems.*

Keywords: Lithium ion; battery; off-gas; thermal runaway; monitor; rechargeable batteries; battery failure; electrical abuse; mechanical abuse; thermal abuse.

Introduction

At a high level, lithium-ion batteries failures occur in four distinct stages: battery abuse, off-gas generation, smoke generation, and fire generation (see Figure 1). Any lithium-ion battery failure is initiated by an abuse factor. There are three distinct types of abuse, including electrical, thermal, or mechanical abuse. Electrical abuse occurs when batteries are operated outside of their electrical specifications. This can include overvoltage, under voltage, or drawing too much current from the battery. Thermal abuse occurs when li-ion batteries are operated outside of their specified temperature window. Mechanical abuse is simply when a battery has been externally damaged, including crush or puncture. A very definitive signature of battery abuse is a significant drop in battery voltage, which usually indicates the beginning of a lithium-ion battery failure.

After a battery has been abused, off-gas generation occurs. In certain scenarios, such as crush or puncture of the cell, off-gas generation occurs immediately after abuse. However, in most other cases, there is a finite amount of time, usually hours or days, between initiating abuse and off-gas generation. Once abuse has occurred there is usually an increase in temperature, whether it be from ambient conditions or localized hot spots, which results when battery electrolyte solvents (DEC, EC, EMC, etc.) begin to breakdown and evaporate. With the generation of these vapors, internal cell pressure begins to increase. These vapors, or off-gas compounds, will be released externally from the cell through different mechanisms depending on the cell form factor. Hard cased cells, such as cylindrical or prismatic cells, are designed with vents to release these off-gas compounds. Soft cased cells, such as pouch cells, release off-gas compounds when the cell begins to swell and releases pressure through the weak seal points near the electrode tabs. This initial release of off-gas to the surrounding environment causes a large heat release from the battery and creates a flammable atmosphere around the batteries, further worsening the failure scenario.

The next stage of a battery failure is when the cell truly begins to experience catastrophic failure. Between off-gas generation and smoke generation, there is again a finite amount of time, usually several minutes. When smoke generation begins, the cell failure is fully developed and the cathode and anode are usually interfacing, whether it be because of dendrite formation (caused through electrical abuse), separator melting (caused through thermal abuse), or by other means. When the electrodes are touching a large amount of energy release and fire generation is imminent.

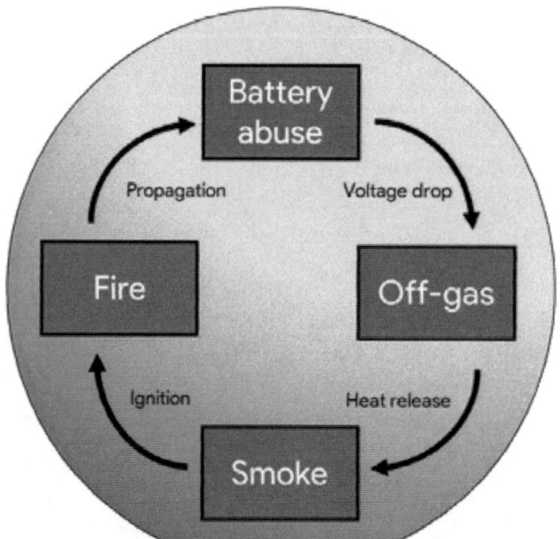

Figure 1. Stages of a battery failure.

The final stage of a battery failure is fire generation. Smoke generation and fire generation, stage three and four of a failure, are sometimes simultaneous. However, in the majority of failures observed, there is a small window of time that differentiates these stages, usually seconds. When fire generation has occurred, battery failure propagation becomes much more likely, where surrounding cells can be initiated into failure through thermal abuse resulting from the fire that the original cell generates.

Technology Overview

The starting point for this development effort was Nexceris' commercial hydrogen sensor, which was originally designed for hydrogen safety applications at concentrations approaching the lower flammability limit of hydrogen in air (which currently is sold into lead battery installations). This commercial platform was used, and modified sensor formulations were evaluated to enable detection of flammable gases emitted from lithium ion battery electrolytes, such as diethyl carbonate and dimethyl carbonate. Nexceris has assessed off-gassing characteristics over a range of operational and abuse conditions, including over-temperature, over-charging, and slow leak/pinhole tests in both pouch and cylindrical cells. Based on this sensor data collected under these conditions an advanced algorithm was developed to distinguish environmental anomalies from potential catastrophic events.

The approach was demonstrated to provide an indicator of impending catastrophic failure in time for mitigations and well in advance of conventional battery failure detection approaches. An example of this capability is shown below in Figure 2, in which a battery cell was monitored for off-gas using Nexceris' monitor while it was heated to failure at a constant rate. A change in heating rate of the battery cell temperature was observed just after 36 minutes when the cell began to self-heat (i.e., onset of thermal runaway). The monitor detected off-gas from the cell 4.5 minutes prior to the onset of thermal runaway. The stages of cell failure observed in the data in Figure 1 have proven to be repeatable. The observation that cell off-gassing is a repeatable precursor to thermal runaway has also been recognized by subject matter experts within the energy storage industry.[1] Nexceris has conducted more than fifty battery failure tests and confirmed this observation. Data from these experiments are summarized in the box and whisker plots in Figure 3. Monitoring abused cells for off-gas provides early warning prior to thermal runaway for both high and low states of charge (SOC). Median early warning for both 30% and 100% SOC are greater than five minutes which provides sufficient time for initiating mitigating actions.

Off-gas Monitor vs Smoke Detection: Off-gas monitoring within a lithium ion energy storage system provides a unique diagnostic signal which is not directly measured by the battery managements system or traditional monitoring systems utilizing smoke detection. Monitoring for cell off-gassing is a direct physical measurement of the onset of cell failure by monitoring for the initial stage in the battery failure stages described in Figure 1. If a cell continues to progress into thermal runaway, then that cell will eventually produce smoke which could be detected by a smoke detector. However, off-gas monitoring provides a unique diagnostic signal which precedes signaling from a smoke detector as show in Figure 3. Off-gas monitoring detects off-gas prior to thermal runaway, whereas, smoke detectors provide no early warning of cell failure.

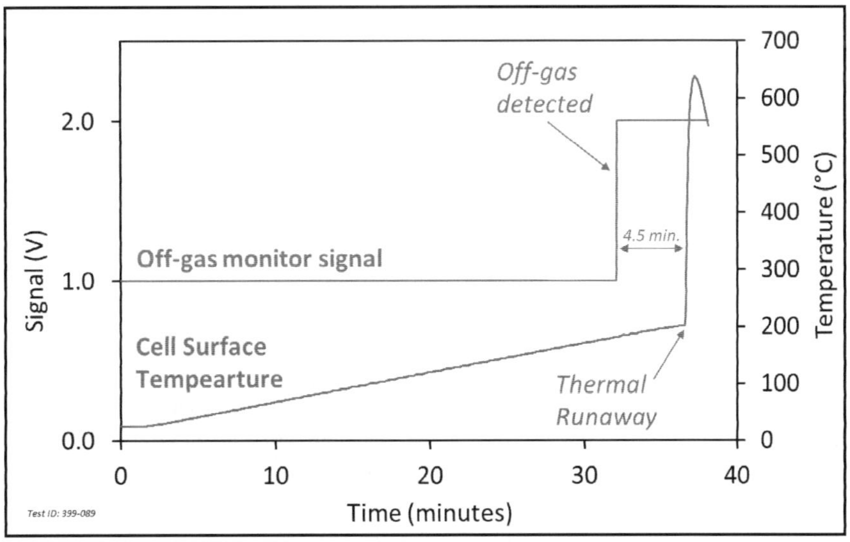

Figure 2. Results of lithium ion battery thermal runaway testing. Nexceris off-gas monitor provided 4.5 minutes of early warning prior to failure.

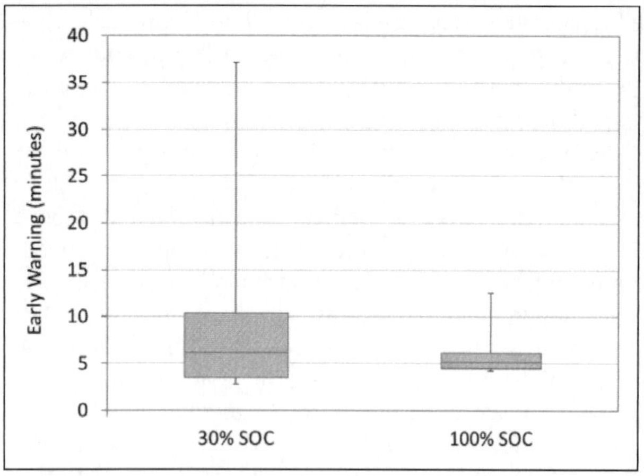

Figure 3. Early warning before thermal runaway provided by Nexceris' Li-ion Tamer off-gas monitoring system.

Stop Thermal Runaway Before It Ever Gets Started: The value of off-gas monitoring in lithium ion battery systems is that it gives warning of a cell fault ahead of thermal runaway which provides time to mitigate impending thermal runaway. Data had demonstrated that the signal provided by Nexceris' is early enough in the stages of a cell failure that thermal runaway can be prevented if the off-gas signal is used to initiate mitigating actions. This is demonstrated in the test data show in Figure 5. The cell and abuse condition for this test were identical to the test shown in Figure 2. However, during the test shown in Figure 5, the cell abuse was mitigated by removing the heat source from the cell upon detection of off-gas from Nexceris' Li-ion Tamer® off-gas monitor. This action was sufficient to prevent the cell from entering thermal runaway. The ability to prevent thermal runaway when action at the time of off-gas detection has been repeatedly demonstrated for both thermal and electrical abuse of cylindrical and pouch cell formats. The demonstration of this capability makes off-gas monitoring ideal for providing enhanced safety to lithium ion battery systems. Integrating a battery fault monitor into a lithium ion battery system provides an extra layer of defense between the battery management system and fire suppression initiated at thermal runaway when smoke detectors alarm and can prevent the fire suppression system from having to be discharged.

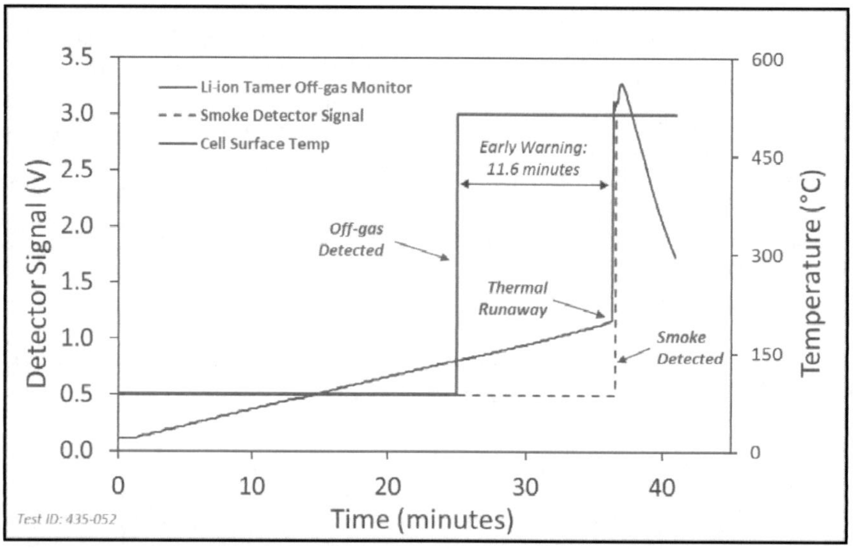

Figure 4. Early warning provided by off-gas monitoring vs smoke detection.

System Integration

Nexceris recently launched a line of off-gas monitoring products, trade-marked Li-ion Tamer®, to increase safety of lithium ion battery systems. The products are designed for integration into both battery rack systems and individual battery modules. As discussed above, utilizing the off-gas signal to isolate the cell from charge and load can prevent a cell from going into thermal runaway. Therefore, the recommended action is to use the signals from the monitoring system to actuate the contactors to isolate the battery from charge and load. A high level schematic layout of the monitoring system arrangement for battery racks is show below in Figure 6. The monitoring system consists of two off-gas monitors per rack with a centralized controller. The controller provides an output unique to each rack which enables isolation of individual racks in the event that off-gas is detected.

Li-ion Tamer® off-gas monitors are being integrated into energy storage systems to increase functional safety and defend against catastrophic failures. The system provides early warning of cell failure and has been demonstrated to stop thermal runaway before it ever gets started.

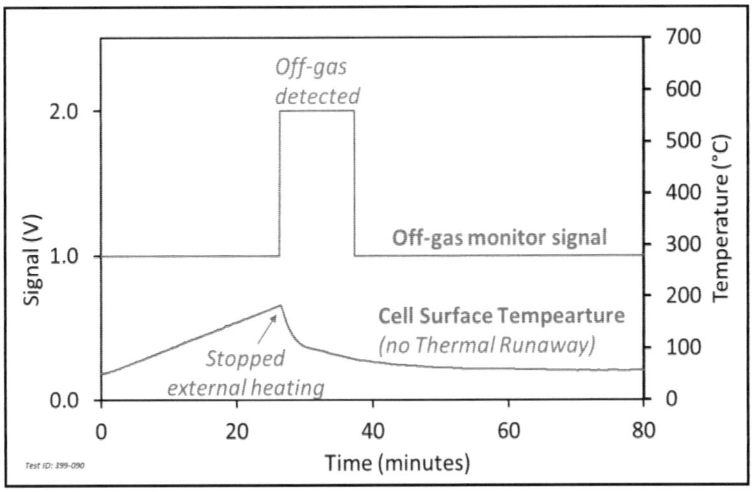

Figure 5. Preventing thermal runaway using Nexceris' Li-ion Tamer off-gas monitoring.

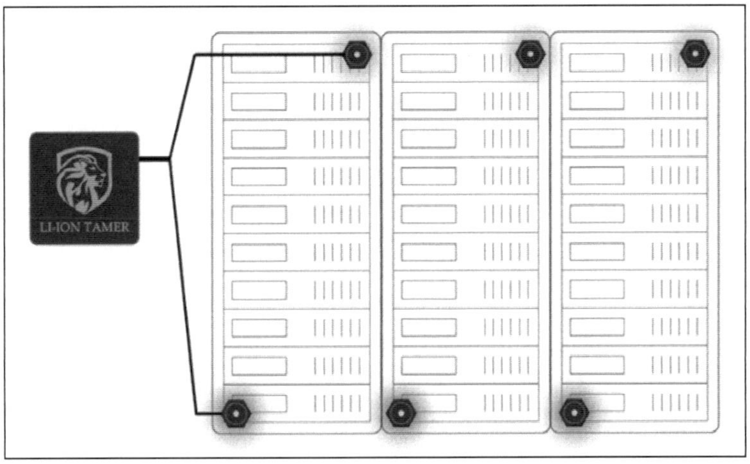

Figure 6. Li-ion Tamer rack monitoring system configuration.

Acknowledgements

Financial support for this work was provided under U.S. Department of Energy (DOE Contract No. DE-AR0000276) and by the U.S. Navy (NAVSEA Contract Numbers N65538-10-C-0035, N00024-15-C-4002, and N00024-17-C-4012).

References

1. M. Hill, Davion & Agarwal, Arun & Gully, Benjamin. (2015). A Review of Engineering and Safety Considerations for Hybrid-Power (Lithium-Ion) Systems in Offshore Applications. Oil and Gas Facilities. 4. 068-077. 10.2118/174091-PA

The "Green Latrine": Deployable Latrine with Off-Grid Photovoltaic/Thermal Energy

Michael Tomac[1*], Shannon Morse[1], David Dixon[1], Mike Farrington[2,3], Raymond Petty[2,3], Joel Bogaert[2,3], Braden Baumgardner[2,3], Reza Salavani[3]
[1]South Dakota School of Mines and Technology, 501 E St Joseph St, Rapid City, SD 57701,
[2]Universal Technology Corporation, 1270 N. Fairfield Road, Dayton, OH 45432
[3]Air Force Civil Engineer Center (AFCEC/CXAE), Tyndall AFB, FL
Presenting Author* Michael.tomac@mines.sdsmt.edu, Phone: 1-701-955-4407

Abstract: *The US Air Force has a goal of reducing field consumption of fossils fuels to improve energy efficiency and operational resiliency. One cost-effective solution is to provide field assets that can operate independent of the power grid by harnessing renewable energy. This paper details the design, construction, and assessment of a proof of concept deployable latrine powered exclusively with Photovoltaic/Thermal (PVT) energy technology that allows operation completely "off-grid". PVT arrays are traditionally used for parallel production of solar electrical power and water heating in residential recreational pools. The attachment of a heat exchanger to the back of a traditional PV panel allows for cooling of the panels, resulting in higher electrical output while simultaneously heating the water.*

A standard military portable (containerized) latrine unit was retrofitted with PVT hybrid panels that generate hot water and electricity. Potable water is the only required input. The installed electrical production capacity totaled 2.475 kW with an associated battery bank (44 kWh). The PVT added 6.0 kW of additional potential thermal energy depending upon variation in the panel flow rates and PVT configuration.

The capabilities, operating characteristics, and overall power gain of the configuration was examined during studies at Tyndall Air Force Base, Florida, and results will be presented. The system's performance is examined under varying operating scenarios to assess electrical and thermal performance. Overall energy efficiency was determined in respect to electrical capacity, electrical storage, and operating utility.

Keywords: Photovoltaic/Thermal Hybrid System; Stand-Alone System; Depth of Discharge; Sensible Heat of Water; Energy Analysis; Battery Storage; Military Energy Fuel Savings.

Introduction: In 2008, the Air Force spent $9 billion to fuel aircraft, ground vehicles, and provide utility services to installations with $1 billion of that contributing to facilities. In response to rising energy costs and energy security considerations, the Air Force is making substantial efforts in integrating energy considerations within military operations [1]. The energy-efficient "Green" Latrine was constructed to provide a deployable stand-alone latrine capable of generating its needed electricity while simultaneously producing shower-temperature water. Photovoltaic (PV) and PVT panels were selected to fit the roof space of the latrine so that sufficient energy can be generated to power the entire system. However, solar panels can only produce power when sunlight is available. In order to store the extra energy generated during the daylight, a battery system was installed. The goal of the battery bank is to store enough energy that the latrine can be self-sustained (ideally for two to three days). Thorough testing of the solar heating capability of this unit is aimed to demonstrate the enhanced solar energy capturing capability of adding a PVT hybrid system, in addition to traditional PT.

Theory: The energy storage capacity, Q, of a water storage unit at uniform temperature operating over a finite temperature difference, ΔT, is given by Equation 1[2].

$$Q = \dot{m} C_p \Delta T \qquad (1)$$

The variable $\dot{m}$ is the mass flow rate of water in the tank with units of kgs^{-1} and C_p being the heat capacity of water in units of $Jkg^{-1}K^{-1}$. Equation 2 can be used to determine the total efficiency of a PVT panel, η_{PVT}, where P is the electrical energy output of the panel, A_{PVT} is the panel surface area, and G is solar radiation.

$$\eta_E = \frac{P}{A_{PVT}\,G} \qquad \eta_{th} = \frac{Q}{A_{PVT}\,G} \qquad \eta_{PVT} = \frac{P+Q}{A_{PVT}\,G} \qquad (2)$$

The voltage differences can be used to compare the thermal-electric degradation characteristics of the Sunmodule PV panel. Equation 4 shows that there should be a decrease of 0.31% in voltage for each °C temperature increase [3].

$$TCV_{OC} = -\frac{0.31}{°C} \qquad (3)$$

Construction: The Green Latrine system was retrofitted from a standard 20-ftx8-ftx8-ft shipping container which was modified with electrical components, a plumbing system, battery storage system, and solar panels attached to the roof. The system design is illustrated in Figure 1.

Distribution A: Approved for public release; Distribution unlimited. AFCEC-201816, 17 April 2018

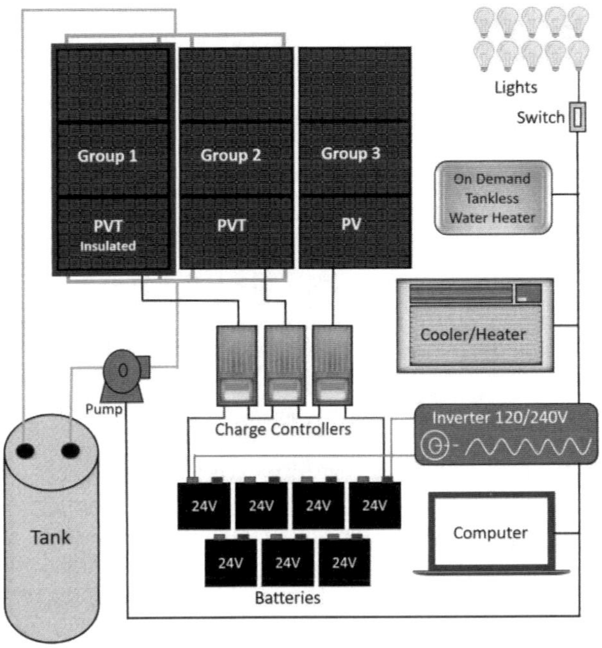

Figure 1. Flow Diagram of the Green Latrine.

Standard Sunmodule solar panels and CoolPV® PVT panels were mounted to the roof of the container structure. CoolPV® Panels are Sunmodule panels with a solar absorber attached to the backside. The power requirements of the system were compared to the rating of the CoolPV® panels to help approximate the number of panels needed for the system. At 275W nameplate and a five hours of peak power production, the power output of nine panels was 12.38 kWh which is more than the power requirement needed. Nine panels were chosen because they would easily fit on the roof of the structure.

These panels were divided into 3 groups each containing a string of three panels. The first group of panels had CoolPV® panels that were insulated with neoprene mats. The second group was un-insulated CoolPV®, and the third group contained standard solar panels without thermal absorbers. All groups were electrically separated in order to compare the benefits or deficits of each variation of solar panels based on their heating performance. Specifically, direct comparisons between PV and PVT modules can be made from experimental data along with an evaluation on the effect of insulation attached to the back of PVT modules from thermal effects of cooling and heating of the thermal absorber.

Two water heating systems were installed. The first system comprised of an on-demand tankless Stiebel Eltron mini 2.5-1, 2.4kW water heater, which was placed between the sink and storage tank. The second system design consists of six CoolPV® panels and a 20-gallon storage tank.

To determine the size of the circulating pump needed, the configuration of the fluid distribution system was estimated and compared to the head pressure of pumps available. The total pressure head, without the well pressure, was calculated to be 12.9 ft. As a result, an Astro 2 250CI 1/6 horsepower, 0.98 amp 3-speed adjustable pump was chosen. The 120 V power supplied to the circulation pump was switched by a mechanical relay in the Opto22 data acquisition system. The pump was programmed to turn on when the temperature of one of the PVT panels was a specified amount greater than the temperature of the water in the tank, thus allowing it to heat up.

The battery bank was made of 14 Apex 260 amph 12V batteries capable of storing 43.68 kWh of electrical energy. The DC power from each PV array was connected to its own Xanthax XW-MPPT60-150 maximum power point tracking (MPPT) charge controller. This monitors the system performance and provides system protection by preventing the batteries from over discharge. The charge controllers tie into the battery bank at an AIMS 6000-watt pure sine wave 120/240V split phase inverter. The system was wired to produce two separate 120 V outputs totaling 25 amps each. They were then fed into a split system of component breakers, where transducers were used to measure power. Water is often an ideal medium in which to store usable heat in stand-alone PVT systems because it can be used during the day. A summation of the load component of each element in the system was used to determine the size of the electrical system which can be seen in Table 1.

Table 1: Summation of power requirements.

Component	Quantity	Energy (kWh)
Light Bulbs	10	1.26
Pump	1	0.71
A/C Cooling	1	2.2
OPTO 22	1	0.05
Water Heater	1	2.4
TOTAL		6.62

Opto22 is a data acquisition control system that was used to acquire data while supplying 24VDC power to the electrical transducers and 5VDC to the board and associated modules. The modules included a OMR6-C mechanical relay, 2 AITM-8 thermocouple modules, and an AIMA-32 card for reading -20- to +20-mA signals. The relay was used to control the pump while the thermocouples recorded data on the temperatures of the panels and fluid outlined in the diagram below. The AIMA card was used to record outputs from the transducers and environmental data from a weather station. This data included wind speed, direction, solar irradiance, ambient temperature, relative humidity, and barometric pressure. Figure 2 is a visual representation of system layout featuring the solar panels at a 7° incline and the major components within the system design.

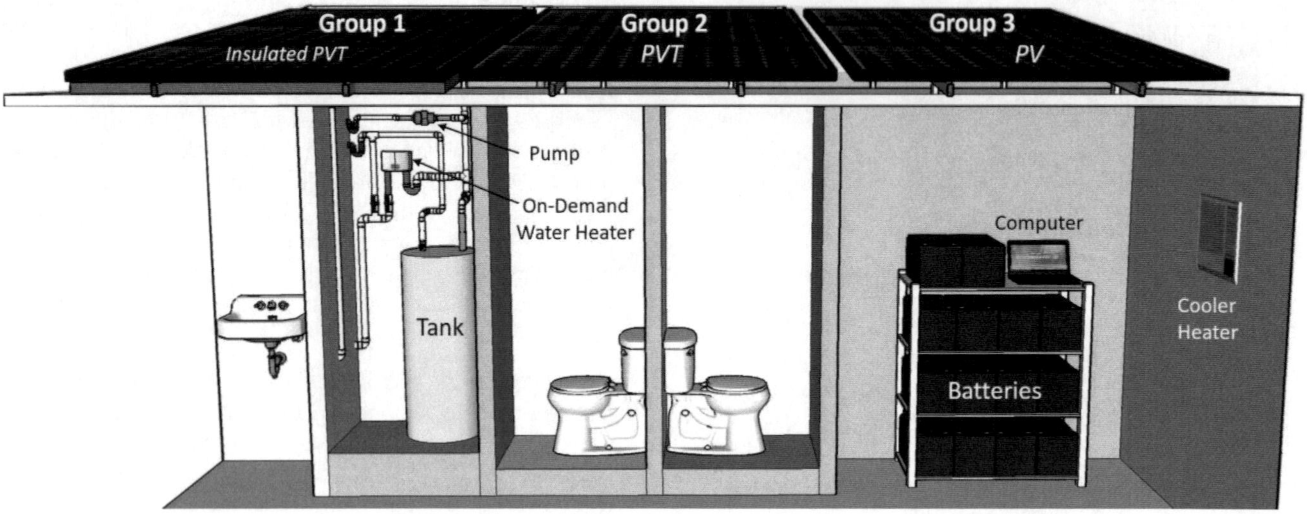

Figure 2. 3-D model of the Green Latrine Layout.

Results: The characterization of the Green Latrine system includes experiments focused on a direct comparison in power production between each group of solar panels, thermal effects, and performance of battery discharge and recharge. Thermal collector modules contain hundreds of small-diameter tubes for water to flow and collect thermal energy absorbed by the panels. The water, once having exited the panels, flows into a plumbing system that stores and provides hot water for the sink. The PVT panels cool down at night and the water in the tank should retain the heat gained from heating during the day. For this reason, a control algorithm was built to shut off the tank when the tank reached within one degree of the Group 2 surface thermocouple temperature. Table 2 shows the amount of power generated from the electrical and thermal components with 5 h of peak power production.

Table 2: Energy Production in 2017

Date	Group 1 [kWh]	Group 2 [kWh]	Group 3 [kWh]	Tank [kWh]	C*
15 Oct	2.10	1.97	1.97	4.3	C, VF
19 Oct	2.64	2.57	2.55	4.99	S, F
21 Oct	2.24	2.16	2.16	3.54	PC, VF
22 Oct	1.82	1.71	1.73	2.84	R, F
25 Oct	2.88	2.80	2.81	3.00	S, F
30 Nov	2.35	2.22	2.22	2.88	S, F
16 Dec	2.29	2.19	2.26	3.03	S, F

*C represents the Conditions: S=Sunny, C=Cloudy, R=Rain, PC=Partly Cloudy, F=Water Flow (3.6-4.2 gpm), VF=Varying Flow

In Table 2, the tank column represents the amount of energy being added to the tank just from the increase in temperature. The Group 1, Group 2, and Group 3 columns show the electrical energy generated. It is important to note that the temperature difference experienced by the tank throughout the day consistently contributes more to the total energy production than the individual electrical PV systems. This goes to show that there is indeed a benefit for using a PVT system to heat water.

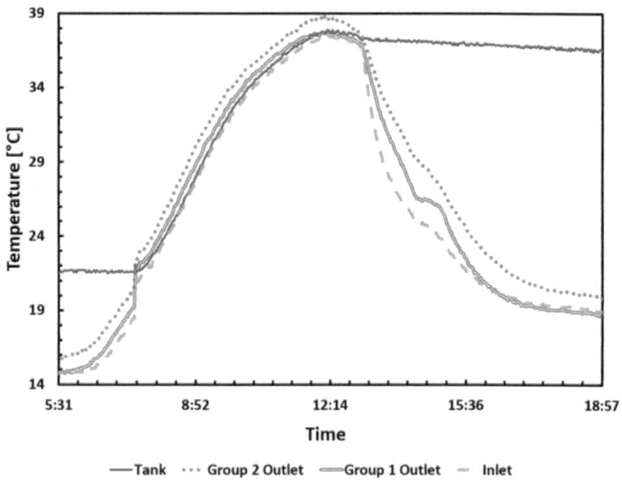

Figure 3: Temperature Profile of Water in the Latrine System on November 30, 2017.

In Figure 3, the temperature in the tank started at 21.5 °C. Once the surface temperature of the second panel in Group 2 was within 1°C of the tank temperature, the pump started and maintained an average flow rate of 4 gpm. The pump shut off when the desired shower temperature was reached in the tank. The tank was able to maintain the shower-temperature water (100°F, 39°C) into the night. The amount of energy contribution from heating the water in the tank was 2.88 kWh.

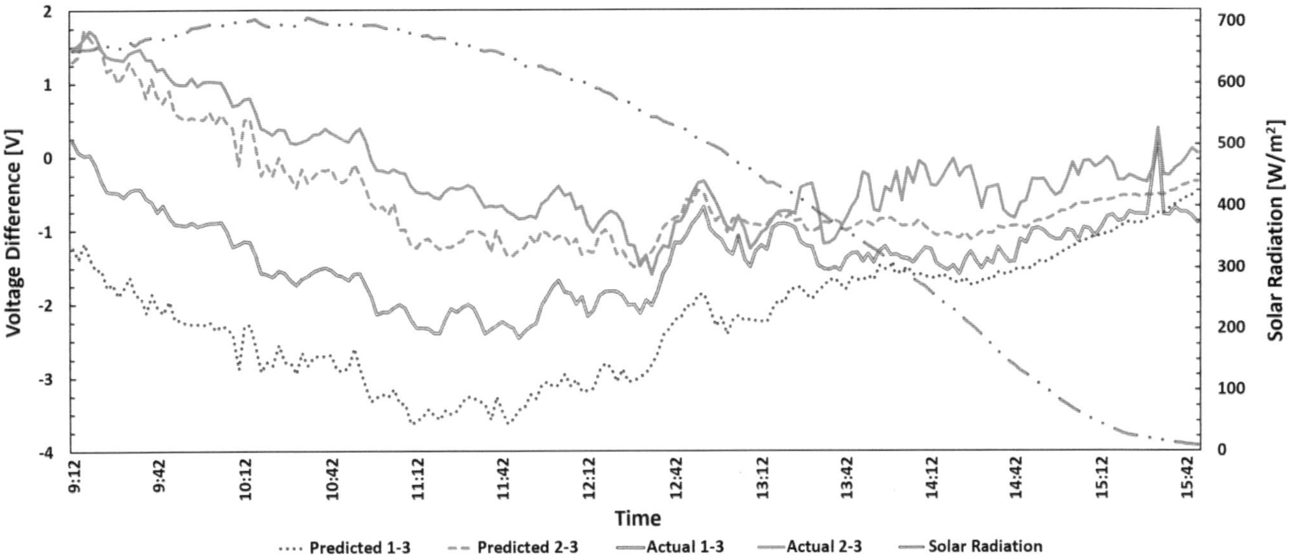

Figure 4: Voltage difference comparison between Group 1/Group 3 and Group 2/Group 3 on November 28, 2017.

A battery drain test was performed in November with a water flow rate of 3.7 gpm and a drain rate of 1.64 kW. A total of 28.85 kWh was used to keep the system running for 17 hours and 36 minutes. PV cells decrease in performance with increasing temperature. Figure 4 shows a comparison of the predicted thermal effects on the open circuit voltage by utilizing Equation 3 with the experimental results. It can be seen that the voltage difference between Group 2 and Group 3 were closely approximated. However, when using the same equation to predict the voltage difference between Group 1 and 3, a larger error can be seen during the heat of the day. One explanation for this deviation could be due to the Group 1 panels having insulation on the back to prevent heat loss during the day, therefore confirming that hotter temperatures result in lower voltages.

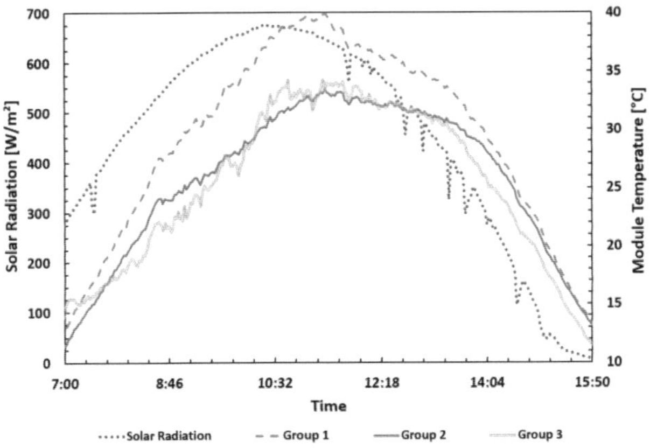

Figure 5: Module temperature comparison between Group 1, Group 2, and Group 3 on December 16, 2017.

Figure 5 shows a comparison of module temperature of the three different groups of solar panels. It can be seen that the insulated group of panels held in the most heat whereas the non-insulated PVT and PV panels have similar module temperatures. Table 3 summarizes a direct comparison of Group 1, Group 2, and Group 3 efficiencies using Equation 2.

Table 3: Module Efficiency Summary

Type	Group 1	Group 2	Group 3
Electrical	14.5$^{\psi}$, 15.6†	14.3$^{\psi}$, 15.1†	14.3$^{\psi}$, 14.8†
Thermal	39.1$^{\psi}$, 33.8†	82.6$^{\psi}$, 58.9†	-
PVT	53.6$^{\psi}$, 49.4†	96.9$^{\psi}$, 74.0†	-

$^{\psi}$ Results from November 30, 2017

† Results from December 16, 2017

Conclusion: The United States Air Force is striving to lessen their dependence on fossil fuels by decreasing fuel consumption within the military. Research has been performed on a stand-alone solar-powered latrine to determine the benefits of PVT compared to PV systems. The results of the experiments show that an addition of a thermal absorber to a PV module can increase the energy collected by the module up to 80 percent whereas PV alone has roughly 14.5 percent efficiency. However, it is not recommended to use insulation due to efficiency decrease with raising temperatures.

References

1. Donley, M.B., *Air Force Energy Plan.* Air Force Energy Plan, 2010: p. 1-38.
2. Jones, A.D., *A Thermal Model for Photovoltaic Systems.* Solar Energy, 2001. **70**(4): p. 349-359.
3. SolarWorld, *Sunmodule Protect SW 275-280 Mono Black.*

Operational Safety Analysis of Laser Power Beaming

Eric Conrad, Will Rowley, Tony Thampan

CERDEC Command, Power and Integration Directorate (CP&ID)
Aberdeen Proving Ground, MD
eric.a.conrad2.civ@mail.mil

Abstract: *In support of Chief of Staff of the Army (CSA) Science and Technology (S&T) priority areas and based on TRADOC's S&T guidance to develop new capabilities in Soldier Lethality with novel technologies such as Unmanned Systems (US) and Wireless Sensor Networks (WSN), CERDEC's Power Division is developing far field wireless energy transmission solutions via Laser Power Beaming (LPB). Far field wireless energy transmission offers the opportunity to increase the autonomy of US and WSN systems, enabling additional capability to an expeditionary maneuver force. In addition to size, weight, power and cost challenges, safety is a significant concern in developing LPB systems. This presentation contains a safety analysis of LPB along with recommendations to mitigate hazards to an acceptable risk level. It includes effects of different wavelengths, irradiance levels, reflections, hazard distances and hardware reliability. A quantitative model is also presented to evaluate the consequence of eye exposure to the "eye-safe" wavelength of 1550nm. The thermal response of the human eye to this source of radiation is used with the cumulative equivalent minutes at 43°C (CEM_{43}) metric to quantify thermal thresholds for tissue damage to the cornea and skin. Applications that bring high value to the Army in Manned Unmanned Teaming (MUM-T) operations are described and analyzed with a preliminary quantitative risk assessment.*

Experimental Particle-In-Cell Simulation of Positive Ion Influence on Vacuum Diode

Will Rowley, Eric Conrad, Tony Thampan

CERDEC Command, Power and Integration Directorate (CP&ID)
Aberdeen Proving Ground, MD
William.A.Rowley8.civ@mail.mil

Abstract: *In support of Chief of Staff of the Army (CSA) Science and Technology (S&T) priority areas [1] and based on TRADOC's S&T guidance [2] to develop new capabilities in Soldier Lethality with novel technologies such as Unmanned Systems (UMS) and Wireless Sensor Networks (WSN) [3-5], CERDEC's Power Division is developing far field wireless energy transmission solutions via Laser Power Beaming (LPB) and RF. Far field wireless energy transmission offers the opportunity to increase the autonomy of US and WSN systems, enabling additional capability to an expeditionary maneuver force.*

This presentation identifies potential LPB applications that bring increased capability to the Army. Included in the analysis is a description of system capabilities, size, weight, and power (SWaP) to determine overall feasibility and tradeoffs. Using data available from commercially available systems and current laser and photovoltaic research, power requirements of each system and accompanying loads are used to determine necessary optical power transmission as well as the total input power and cooling requirements. Furthermore these results are used to identify research gaps to be exploited for more effective LPB systems and as a guide for future prototyping and development of Army LPB systems. Additionally the presentation will also describe upcoming CERDEC/Partner demonstrations of LPB technology.

Fuel Cell Powered Small Unmanned Aerial System (*s*UAS) Lessons Learned and the Road Ahead

Deryn Chu and Rongzhong Jiang
U. S. Army Research Laboratory,
2800 Powder Mill Rd., Adelphi, MD 20783-1107
Deryn.d.chu.civ@mail.mil

Summary:
Small unmanned aerial systems (*s*UASs) have great potential for many different applications (1-3). The *s*UASs are light-weight, man-portable, and capable of carrying payloads. *s*UASs can be broadly classified by their performance characteristics such as size, weight, speed, and endurance. Currently, small UASs are powered by lithium-ion or lithium polymer batteries; however, flight endurance is limited and requires frequent battery replacement. Frequent battery replacement is due to low capacity and energy density (less than 200Wh/Kg). Numerous research and development efforts have focused on alternative power sources. These alternative power sources technologies include such as solar cells and hydrogen based polymer electrolyte membrane fuel cells. Power and energy systems for *s*UASs will be discussed and presented at the conference.

Key Words: Fuel Cells, Unmanned Aerials System

Small unmanned aerial systems (sUASs) have been used for military applications and have additional potential for commercial applications. These systems provide valuable intelligence, surveillance, reconnaissance and target acquisition (ISRTA) capabilities for infantry units at the battalion, company, and platoon levels. The small UASs need for a long range and extended endurance is important for practical applications. However, Li-ion batteries provide less than 2hrs of flight endurance for a Puma UAS platform. This restricts the endurance, range, and nature of the missions which may be performed by the UAS. Therefore, it is critical to develop and implement alternative power and energy systems for small UASs. Alternative power and energy systems used to power sUASs that have been reported in literature. These included combinations such as batteries with advanced high-efficiency solar cells, a small engine, and high power/energy density fuel cell systems. sUASs have strict specific power and energy requirements. Batteries can have a wide range of specific powers, but have limited specific energy. Fuel cells have the promise to achieve both the specific power and the specific energy requirements. Over the last decade, numerous efforts have been put forth to integrate fuel cell power systems into UASs. Defense Advanced Research Projects Agency (DARPA) and Army Research Laboratory (ARL) have jointly studied and developed fuel cells powered UASs since 2009. During this period, we considered all of the current UAS systems (Fig. 1). Based on our extensive research, we concluded the size, weight, payload, and typical flight characteristics of the Stalker UAS made it an ideal candidate to a first adopter of a fuel cell power system. There is a long list of factors that lead to this conclusion; however, two of the most critical considerations were flight altitude and noise. Altitude is an important consideration because fuel cells use oxygen from the air as an oxidant. As an UAS's altitude increases, oxygen levels in the air decrease. The lower oxygen levels can starve the fuel cell of the oxygen it needs and result in a concurrent decrease in fuel cell performance (power and efficiency). For example, the Scan Eagle typically flies above 16,000 feet (4876 meters) and the Shadow typically flies at altitudes in the 4,000 to 8,000 feet range. The Scan Eagle and Shadow UAS platforms use internal combustion engines (ICEs), which require the higher elevations to avoid detection because they make noise. Detectable noise is not desirable for small UASs operating at lower altitudes because it can compromise operational security. On the other hand, small platforms including Wasp and Raven become size (volume) limited making fuel cell power impractical at this time.

High performance fuel cell systems are a logical candidate for small UAS power systems. A fuel cell is an electrochemical device that converts chemical energy of a fuel and oxidant (O_2 from air) into electricity, water, and heat. The cell directly extracts electrons from the fuel through an electrochemical oxidation reaction at anode, and an electrochemical oxygen reduction at cathode; producing electrical power during the process. Hence the energy is directly stored in the fuel and the basic power production process involves no moving parts. This raises the expectations of a silent and vibration free operation.

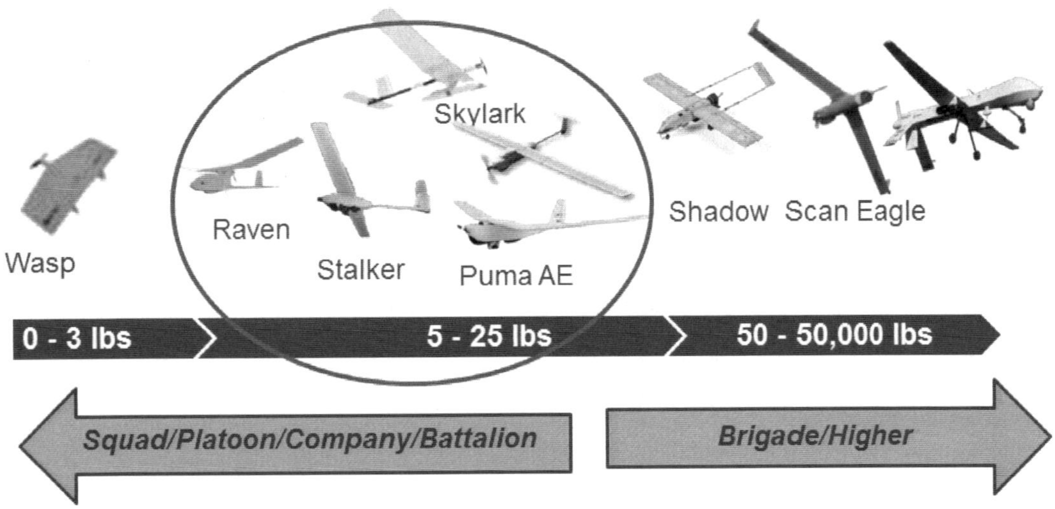

Figure 1. Different Unmanned Aerial Systems.

Considerable attention has also been paid to the type of fuel cell that would be best suited for small UAS applications. There are several types of fuel cells under development. Each type of fuel cell has its own advantages and disadvantages for potential applications. A few of the most promising types include (1) alkaline, (2) molten carbonate, (3) phosphoric acid, (4) polymer electrolyte membrane (PEM), and (5) solid oxide fuel cell (SOFC). PEMFC and SOFC are among the most mature fuel cell technologies which could be suitable for small UAS applications. PEMFCs typically require an extra high purity hydrogen (99.99%). Hydrogen itself has the highest gravimetric energy density based on a mass, however, it has the lowest volumetric energy density based on a volume. This means, such systems are either too large for small UAS or require heavy high pressures storage tanks. The transport and storage of hydrogen is extremely difficult for military missions. In this regard, SOFCs have significant advantage over PEMFCs. SOFCs have much greater fuel flexibility. This allows SOFC to operate on any combustible high energy dense fuel such as propane.

While able to use a higher energy density fuel, the SOFC has several technical impediments that needed to be resolved prior to application in UAS. The impediments include (1) development of a stack design that can tolerant thermal cycling, (2) increased stack durability and reliability such that it can survive the acceleration forces during UAS talk-off and landing (anticipate land force example: 100G 30ms impact), and (3) increased current collector and fuel cell stack tolerance of vibration and shock such that the fuel cell stack can meet the cycle lifetime while maintaining the minimum output power. All of the impediments have been addressed and resolved under the DARPA and ARL's joint program.

Present versions of the 245W fuel cell system powered Stalker small UAS have requested to participate many military exercises and theaters applications. The 245W SOFC system have already been demonstrated in Stalker sUAS platforms and have shown a remarked improvement in endurance (4x increase in flight endurance relative to Li-polymer battery for small UAS). Currently, we plan to develop and demonstrate a high power (350 W) with high efficiency and variable fuel consumption SOFC system for current and future unmanned aerial systems. The new 350W SOFC system can significantly increase specific power relative to the present 245W propane fueled SOFC system (135W/kg vs 94W/kg). An increase in system power to 350W (up from 245W) and power density to 135 W/kg mean the upgraded SOFC power source can provide new capabilities for small UAS applications. These upgrades will be incorporated in the same physical power system package (i.e., size and weight) that is used on the existing Stalker UASs.

To demonstrate and apply the new technology capabilities, the 350W fuel cell stack technology will be incorporated into a 350W portable power system. This power system will be tested/evaluated and subsequently be integrated into Stalker UAS platforms. The new high power and high efficient 350W SOFC to power Stalker UAS plan to field evaluation and demonstration in 2019. In addition, the new 350W SOFC system will also benefit other Army portable power and energy applications. The Army has long term research and development goals and programs for improving fuel cell systems for alternate power and energy. For example, the Army has a need for a soldier-carried, back-pack sized 350 watt power system with improved reliability, performance, and fuel efficiency. For soldier-carried power systems, SOFC systems can increase overall operational energy efficiency. Development a high power and high efficient SOFC system for Army applications is our ultimate goal.

Acknowledgements: The fuel cell powered small UAS system program funded by the DARPA, ARL and OSD Rapid Reaction Technology Office. SOFC system developed by the UltraElectronics AMI and integrated into the Stalker unmanned aerial system by Lockheed Martin, Inc.

References:

(1) http://www.youtube.com/watch?v=98Blu9dpwHU

(2) http://www.youtube.com/watch?v=98Blu9dpwHU&feature=player_detailpage

(3) https://www.youtube.com/watch?v=-CYT4PFV_Hs

Air Independent Power for Underwater Applications

Jonathan Reeh, Jady Stevens, John Zbranek, Brian Hennings*
Lynntech, Inc.
2501 Earl Rudder Fwy S, College Station, TX, USA, 77845, www.lynntech.com
*Corresponding Author: Email: Brian.Hennings@Lynntech.com

Abstract: *Unmanned underwater vehicles (UUV) are seeing an increased role within the Navy for many missions. The Navy is actively pursuing the development of several UUV classes that range in outer diameter from 4.785 inches up to the XLUUV. For air-independent power, these UUVs are currently battery powered and have limited mission endurance and capability due to limited energy density. Enabling enhanced missions with a better energy system will greatly increase the flexibility and utility of the UUV platform regardless of size. The additional energy can be used to extend mission duration or to employ new or additional payloads.*

A case study of a hybrid energy system that is flexible, modular, and consists of a low temperature PEM fuel cell, a battery, and advanced power management system architecture is presented. The development team has demonstrated that the system meets or exceeds the power profile for the specific Navy mission and offers more total stored energy and mission flexibility than the current batteries while increasing safety of the system. The system is scalable and the form factor can be adapted to be applicable to most UUV sizes.

Keywords: Hybrid Energy System; Fuel Cell; Chemical Hydride; Hydrogen Peroxide; UUV Energy System; Air-independent Energy System.

Introduction

Unmanned underwater vehicles (UUV) are seeing an increased role within the Navy for high-priority missions such as fleet protection, inspection/identification, oceanography, communication and navigation, payload delivery, information operations and time critical strike operations. The Navy is actively pursuing the development of four UUV classes that range in size from 9" to 48" (outer diameter). These UUVs are currently battery powered and have limited energy density, which limits mission endurance and capability.

Aside from military applications, several civilian uses exist for small autonomous, long endurance UUVs. Past uses include searching for wreckage and sunken debris, gas/oil pipeline inspection, aqueduct tunnel inspection, general marine research (shark tracking), and seafloor topographical mapping (bathymetry) [1].

For each application endurance is usually a limiting factor with current durations limited to <24 hours depending on UUV size and operational conditions. These durations are defined by current battery energy density and specific energy limitations. Another critical mission limitation is the recharging time. The size and compactness of the batteries require a recharging time of ~8 hours. Lynntech is currently developing emerging technologies which addresses the shortfalls of the current energy systems.

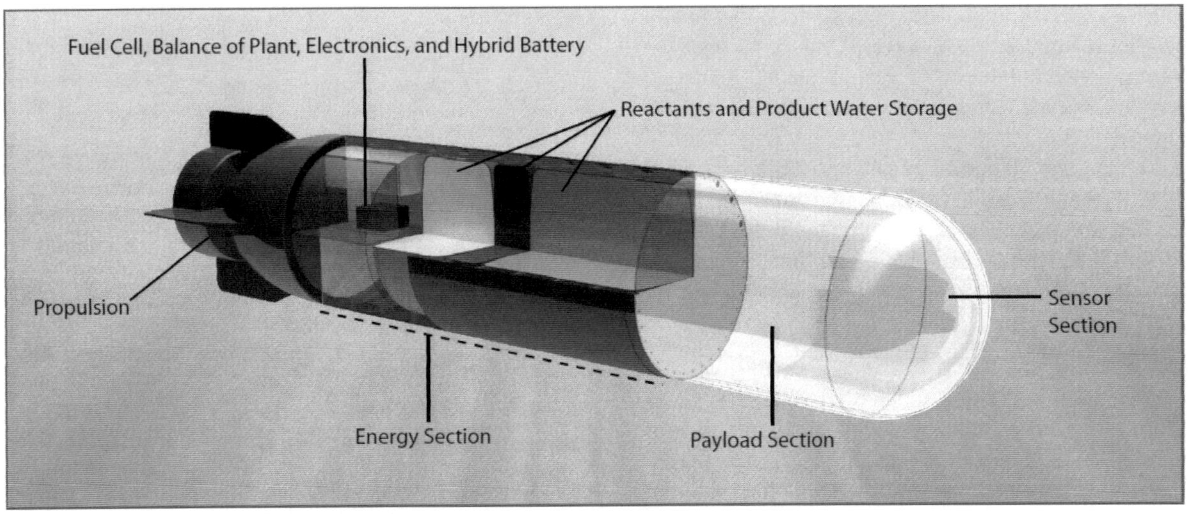

Figure 1. CAD rendering of envisioned hybrid energy system integrated into a generic UUV.

Lynntech's Hybrid Energy System Architecture

Lynntech is developing innovative hybrid energy systems that are flexible, modular, and can meet the varied power requirements as dictated by the mission while significantly increasing duration and reducing the re-deployment time (Figure 1).

One challenge in the development of a fuel cell based UUV energy system are the large transient loads. The fuel cell is not well suited to deal with these rapid, high amplitude power demands. Therefore Lynntech has developed a hybrid power system architecture which incorporates a secondary battery. The high power density battery handles the short term high power requirements of the load profile, while the high energy density fuel cell provides power at a stable rate for the base load and recharges the small battery during low power intervals.

Another challenge associated with any high energy density PEM Fuel Cell system is the safe, compact and lightweight storage of the hydrogen fuel required. To address this Lynntech has investigated several chemical hydride based fuels. By focusing on liquid based fuels, Lynntech avoids the complex and problematic processing of solids. These liquid fuels are safe to store, have high energy densities, high specific energies and can be effectively pumped into and out of the energy system for quick refueling.

When hydrogen is needed, the liquid fuel is pumped into specially designed reactors to produce high purity, pressurized hydrogen gas on demand. These reactors have been specifically designed to meet the transient loads of the UUV and can ramp from idle to full scale hydrogen production in seconds.

Since UUVs are submerged during operation, an air-independent energy system is required. Therefore, the oxidant required must also be stored onboard the UUV. Lynntech has internally developed the use of liquid peroxides to produce high purity oxygen on demand for the fuel cell. The Navy has been using peroxides as a propellant for over 50 years. However, Lynntech pumps the high gravimetric/volumetric oxygen content peroxide solution into a special reactor where the peroxide produces pure oxygen. Similar to the fuel reactor discussed previously, the peroxide reactor is capable of producing full oxygen flow within seconds to meet the transient loads. Both the fuel and peroxide are stored onboard the UUV in specially designed bladders with multiple redundant barriers and safeties to prevent mixing.

Many systems aboard the UUV produce waste heat during operation including the electronics, fuel cell, and fuel and oxidant generation systems. Lynntech removes this waste heat effectively with an integrated coolant loop and heat exchanger. Heat is actively rejected to the sea water to maintain safe temperatures for all of the internal components.

Buoyancy control is critical to any under-sea vehicle, reducing power demand and increasing stability and control. The vehicle remains neutrally buoyant throughout the mission due to a closed system design wherein all waste is retained on board. Reactant storage is designed to maintain CG of the energy section within fractions of an inch for the mission duration for predictable vehicle control.

Quick, safe refueling of the system is accomplished in ~2 hours or less with an automated refueling station that handles all reactants, waste, and purge gases. The refueling station also performs automated leak checking of the energy system as well as the hull seals.

This approach has been demonstrated to produce the desired power that follows the load profile at various power levels while significantly increasing the endurance and reducing the re-deployment time.

Performance Advantage over Current Batteries

Multiple advantages are realized over rechargeable batteries by Lynntech's hybrid energy system. Primarily the energy system scales up favorably over batteries. Since batteries have a fixed energy density and specific energy, they scale linearly in mass and volume to additional energy needs. However, after the fuel cell and BOP components are accounted for, only additional fuel and oxidant are needed to increase the energy of Lynntech's hybrid system. Figure 2 illustrates the scaling advantages of Lynntech's hybrid energy system. Assuming a UUV outer diameter of 12.75", the energy section length is increased to offer additional mission duration and energy storage. When compared to secondary batteries, Lynntech's system is projected to significantly increase the energy storage after a hull length of 30". The increased effective energy density and specific energy are also shown as a function of hull length. These projections are based on UUV energy sections with neutral buoyancy for an equivalent comparison.

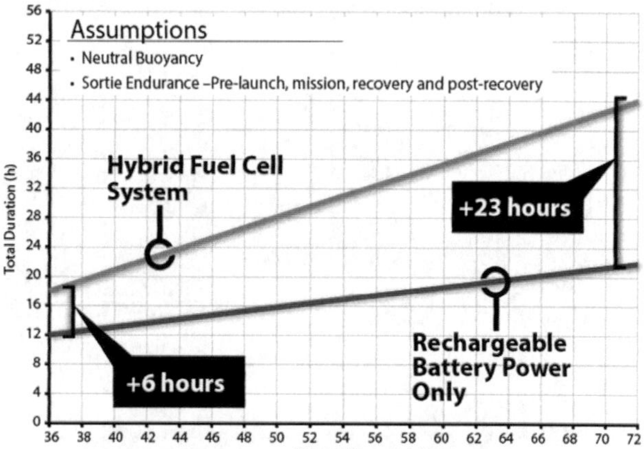

Figure 2. Lynntech's Hybrid Energy System outpaces battery-only power sources for supporting extended missions and high energy demand payloads.

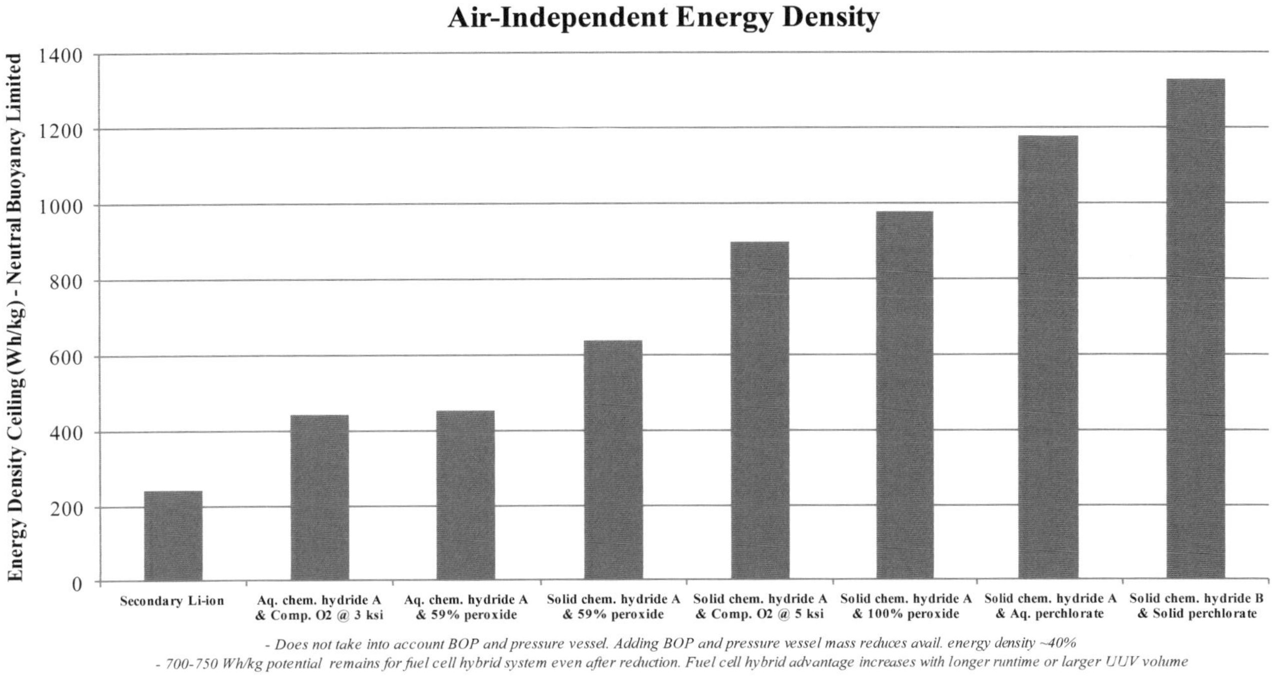

Figure 3. Lynntech's hybrid energy system can utilize a variety of high energy density reactant sources for maximum mission performance when properly matched to the vehicle and application.

Safety Advantage over Current Batteries

In Li-ion batteries, reactants are separated by very thin membranes. Overcharging can cause lithium metal to plate out at the anode and oxygen to form at the cathode, putting highly reducing and oxidizing agents in dangerously close proximity. Leakage across this membrane is a single-point failure mode that can lead to catastrophic effects.

In a hybrid fuel cell system, only very small quantities of reactants are in close proximity within the fuel cell itself. The bulk of the high energy density reactants are stored separately and protected from mixing through multiple preventative measures. Safety measures include redundant containment of each reactant as well as detection of liquid and gas leaks. This reactant storage approach not only provides much superior reactant separation, it also identifies failures before they present a significant hazard to the system or nearby personnel.

Experimental Results

Lynntech has demonstrated in the lab that the previously discussed UUV hybrid energy breadboard system meets or exceeds the power profile ranging up to ~1 kW average and has packaged the system within a 12.75" diameter hull.

The developed system is highly scalable and the form factor can be adapted to be applicable to most UUV sizes. Current efforts are focused on completing testing of the packaged prototype system in preparation for field testing. Enabling these enhanced missions will greatly increase the flexibility and utility of the UUV platform. The additional energy can be used to extend mission duration or to employ new or additional payloads.

Future Work

Future work includes transitioning from laboratory benchtop testing of the packaged hybrid energy system to integration and testing with the target vehicle system. Integrated testing will be first performed in a controlled aquatic environment. Subsequent developmental testing followed by operational testing will be performed in the open ocean to verify mission performance.

The air-independent hybrid energy system is not limited to the current 12.75" diameter vehicle application, nor is it limited to the current chemical hydride and peroxide reactant solutions. Compressed gas, chemical hydrides, and various perchlorates are all viable sources of reactant gases for the fuel cell. These reactant sources have high energy density (Wh/kg), which is needed to meet the neutral buoyancy requirement of UUVs without sacrificing power or mission duration.

Adapting the hybrid energy system for future UUV applications may include switching to an alternative reactant source. As Figure 3 illustrates, alternate reactants can further increase the ceiling of energy density for air-independent energy systems. Even taking into account the mass and volume of the fuel cell and balance-of-plant, hybrid energy systems can hold a significant energy density advantage over Li-ion battery systems. This advantage is further increased when, as in Figure 2, energy storage (runtime) is increased while keeping the same power levels.

Conclusions

Lynntech's air-independent, hybrid energy system offers distinct advantages over batteries in subsea environments.

Advantages include increased energy density/specific energy, better scaling characteristics, safer energy storage and faster turnaround time (refueling).

Other potential applications of Lynntech's hybrid energy system include stationery underwater power sources for sensor networks and UUV recharging, man portable power supplies for primary power and battery charging, as well as powering other unmanned vehicles such as Unmanned Ground Vehicles (UGVs), Unmanned Aerial Vehicles (UAVs), and Unmanned Surface Vehicles (USVs).

Acknowledgements

The authors would like to especially acknowledge the support of this work from Navy Funding (Contract N00024-14-C-4083. Miscellaneous NASA and DOD (Army, Navy, Air Force, Marines) entities are also acknowledged for previous funding of founding technologies used herein.

References

1. Woods Hole Oceanographic Systems Laboratory website. www.whoi.edu/osl/remus-auv

Lightweight System Design and Demonstration of a High Reliability, Air Independent, PEMFC Power System for an Untethered Subsea Power Node

Robert C. Utz, Robert K. Wynne, Michael C. Miller, Robert K. Sievers, & Thomas I. Valdez

Teledyne Energy Systems
Hunt Valley, MD, USA 21031
Rob.Utz@teledyne.com / 410-891-2398

Abstract: *Demand has increased in recent years for unmanned underwater vehicles (UUVs), subsea equipment, and sensors to perform activities below the surface of the ocean for defense, oil & gas, and security applications. The power required to perform tasks below the surface must be supplied by a long cable connected to either a surface ship, platform, or land-based station. Batteries can be stored on-board the vehicle to provide power but must be frequently brought to the surface to recharge due to the limited energy density of the system. Vehicle and equipment operators desire a continuous, persistent underwater presence that is either too expensive to support by ship or unachievable through batteries alone. Teledyne Energy Systems, Inc. (TESI) has developed an Untethered Subsea Power Node concept to provide a source of energy for underwater recharging of UUVs. The concept is based on the TESI ejector driven reactant (EDR) fuel cell system using passive circulation, integrated balance of plant, product water separation, and reactant humidification hybridized with a nickel-metal hydride battery.*

This paper reviews the development of the subsea power node concept and explains novel system features necessary for operating a fuel cell system in an underwater environment. Status of the building and testing of the concept prototype will be discussed. Future work will include completion of prototype testing, initial submerged operation, and a demonstration in shallow ocean water (7 m) in August 2018.

Keywords: PEM fuel cells; subsea; untethered; hydrogen; energy density; hybrid power system; lithium-free; unmanned underwater vehicles

Introduction

Demand has increased in recent years for underwater vehicles, equipment, and sensors to support a wide range of activities. The Unites States Navy is quickly accelerating acquisition of unmanned undersea vehicles (UUVs) from 7 m to 50 m in length in an effort to assemble a family of vehicles covering many defense capabilities[1]. Deployment of subsea vehicle fleets or arrays of sensors for monitoring and inspection is critical for maintaining port security[2]. The exploration and maintenance of deep water subsea oil fields requires a network of vehicles and equipment for long-term environmental monitoring and pipeline and equipment inspections[3].

All of the applications listed above require a reliable source of power to perform the desired activities. Power is delivered to equipment at subsea oil fields and remotely operated vehicles (ROVs) through long power cables connected to oil platforms, ships, or land-based stations. Tethering subsea equipment can limit the possible areas of operation to locations near existing platforms or within close proximity to land. Tethering equipment to a ship can enable access to more areas but with significantly higher operational costs.

Battery-powered subsea equipment can be used to eliminate the need to deliver power through a cable, enabling access to more subsea locations. Battery systems, in both primary and secondary form, are limited in energy density, especially when energy system neutral buoyancy is required to maintain stable vehicle buoyancy. Using battery-powered equipment keeps operational times low, typically less than 10 hours, before the vehicle needs to resurface for recharging. Battery-powered equipment must be regularly monitored by a surface ship and resurfaced for maintenance to maintain long-term operation in off-shore, deep water locations.

Centralized underwater hubs have been proposed to service underwater vehicles and sensors in the applications listed above so that ship or land based support is no longer required. The Navy is developing the Forward-Deployed Energy & Communications Outpost (FDECO) where UUVs can come to dock, recharge, and transmit and receive data[4]. The FDECO stations can be stationed across operating areas of interest, allowing UUVs to maintain a persistent presence that would not otherwise be possible due to power limitations. The Space and Naval Warfare Systems Command (SPAWAR) is also developing underwater wireless charging technologies to facilitate recharging of UUVs in an underwater environment like FDECO[5]. These proposed concepts will require an energy storage and power delivery solution that is energy dense, reliable in the challenging subsea environment, and highly efficient.

Significant interest exists for an untethered subsea power node for powering equipment at subsea oil fields and recharging fleets of underwater vehicles. Teledyne Energy Systems, Inc. (TESI) has designed and developed a hybrid power system using high performance PEM fuel cell technology hybridized with a nickel-metal hydride (NiMH) battery. Meeting the demand for untethered subsea power requires addressing system design challenges that are unique to the subsea environment in fuel cell/battery hybrid systems. This paper will outline the system design approach to satisfy this need, the plan to demonstrate system capabilities, and discuss future actions to enable operation in underwater applications of several thousand meters in depth.

System Concept

The Subsea Power Node concept is shown in Figure 1. This initial prototype concept delivers 100 kWh of energy at 3 kW. The subsea power node measures 5 foot by 4 foot by 4 foot volume and weighs approximately 800 kg in air. The untethered subsea power node incorporates the Ejector Driven Reactant (EDR) PEM fuel cell system designed and developed by TESI over the last several years. Reactants for the fuel cell are stored as gasses in 10,000 psi pressure vessels at the rear of the node. The fuel cell is combined with a series of NiMH battery packs in a hybridized solution that provides immediate power on demand while avoiding the safety issues associated with lithium-ion technology. The power can be converted to a voltage (24 to 600VDC) specified for the application through power management electronics within the battery chamber.

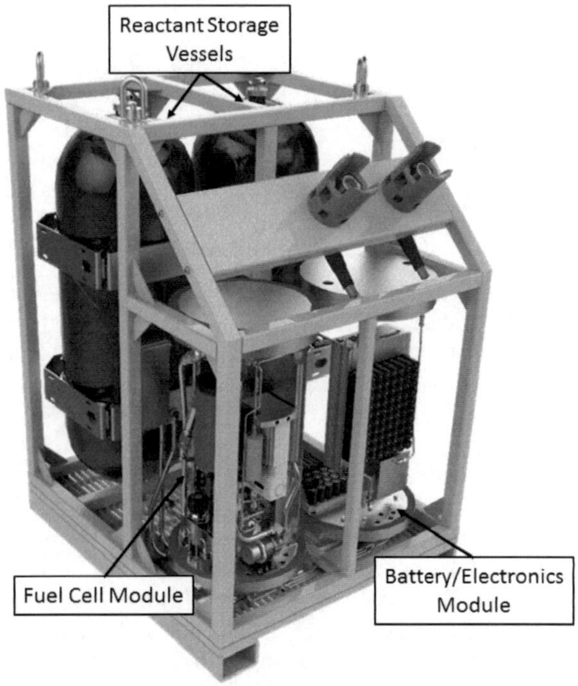

Figure 1: Untethered Subsea Power Node Concept

The TESI EDR fuel cell system can provide highly efficient and reliable power in challenging environments[6]. The system incorporates a passive integrated balance of plant design that increases system reliability and reduces parasitic power losses encouraged the pursuit of a passive balance of plant design. An advanced regulator/ejector system developed jointly with NASA Johnson Space Center provides a passive means of recirculating the reactants at high stoichiometric flow rates to maximize performance without excessive parasitic losses and lower reliability from moving parts in pumps. The water management assembly removes product water and provides humidification to incoming gases in an electrically isolated but physically connected section of the fuel cell stack. The TESI EDR fuel cell system combines the reactant circulation and water removal subsystems into a single unit integrated within the stack assembly to provide a compact system that minimizes the overall volume while increasing reliability. A conceptual model of the TESI EDR fuel cell system is shown in Figure 2. An image of the actual system during prototype testing is shown in Figure 3.

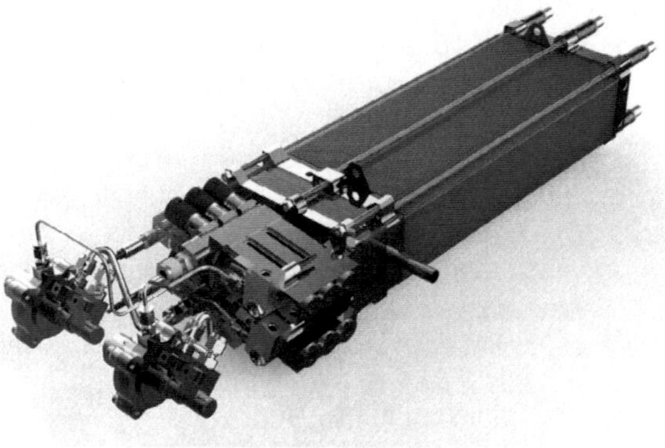

Figure 2: Conceptual model of the TESI EDR fuel cell system

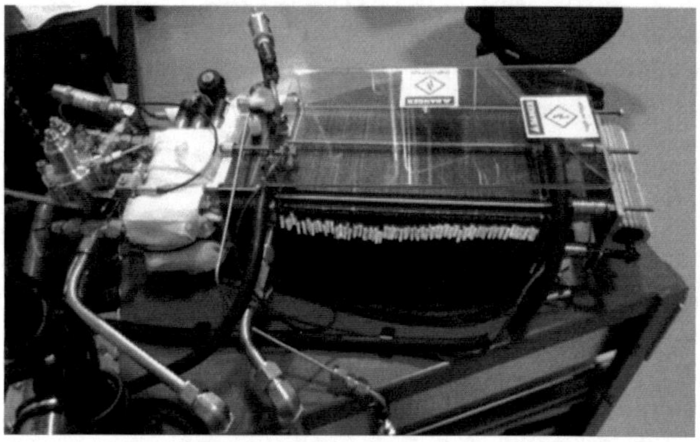

Figure 3: TESI EDR fuel cell system in prototype testing

Successfully incorporating a fuel cell system in an underwater power application requires addressing unique environmental challenges. Operation in deep ocean environments requires both structural and system configuration changes to compensate for the extreme external pressures. The high pressure hydrogen and oxygen gas pressure vessels are capable of handling external pressure at full ocean depth. The fuel cell system and supporting equipment, NiMH battery packs, and control and power electronics are contained within their own pressure vessels designed to withstand the external pressure. The transfer of power and reactants between the vessels is handled through depth-rated Teledyne ODI wet mate connectors.

The water produced by the hydrogen and oxygen in the fuel cell reaction cannot be stored inside the fuel cell housing due to volume limitations when paired with any reactant storage subsystem containing over tens of kWh. Water produced by the fuel cell with any significant quantity of reactant storage must be expelled out of the fuel cell vessel at ocean depth pressure. The reactants circulating in the fuel cell system must also be periodically exhausted outside the vessel to clear inert gas buildup and maintain high performance operation. The subsea power node expels product water and purged gasses using an in-house developed product expulsion system. This technique enables exhausting at 10,000 psi with very little power, differentiating this system from other fuel cell system manufacturers. The ability to expel water and inert gas is critical to the successful operation of the system, getting rid of the need to store unneeded mass within the subsea power node volume and minimizing overall system weight and volume.

Battery-based power systems require large increases in mass and volume to provide higher energy content. Increasing the energy content of the fuel cell based subsea power node involves simply increasing the size of the reactant storage vessels or adding more vessels. Decoupling the fuel cell system pressure vessel from the reactant storage vessels enables achievement of high energy densities without any increase in fuel cell system mass. This means that the marginal increase in volume and cost with respect to energy is relatively minor, unlocking access to MWh of energy from a single deployment on the seafloor. Figure 4 shows concepts for energy storage pods delivering 2 to 20 MWh of energy in a single package.

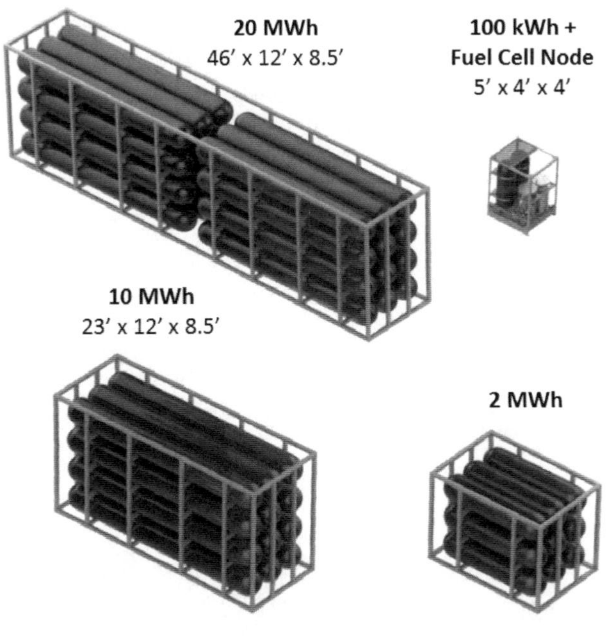

Figure 4: Subsea Power Node, Energy Storage Scalability, 2 to 20 MWh

Using pressurized hydrogen and oxygen gas provides multiple operational advantages over alternative energy storage media for both fuel cells and batteries. Measuring the reactant pressure at any time gives the system the ability to monitor the remaining energy much like a fuel gauge on a vehicle. Pressurized gas allows for refueling an energy storage pod within minutes versus several hours of recharging for a battery-based power system. This will minimize turnaround time during already infrequent maintenance periods with respect to battery-based systems. The positive buoyancy of the gas pressure vessels allows for neutrally buoyant system design when combined with the fuel cell vessel, battery packs, and supporting equipment. This increases the mobility of the unit, simplifying delivery and retrieval.

Qualification & Demonstration Testing

Proving the capabilities of this design requires a full demonstration of the TESI EDR fuel cell system with reactant storage vessels, battery packs, and supporting equipment while submerged in an underwater environment. Testing is in progress for the fuel cell system to confirm expected performance of each segment of the design individually prior to full integration. Subsea power node system components, such as the equipment vessels, reactant storage vessels, battery packs, and power management electronics are on order or are in fabrication. Once manufactured and assembled, the fully integrated system will be tested on land to confirm stable and successful power delivery through expected demand profiles. The system will be submerged in shallow water at a depth of 7 m to demonstrate power generation and delivery in an underwater environment.

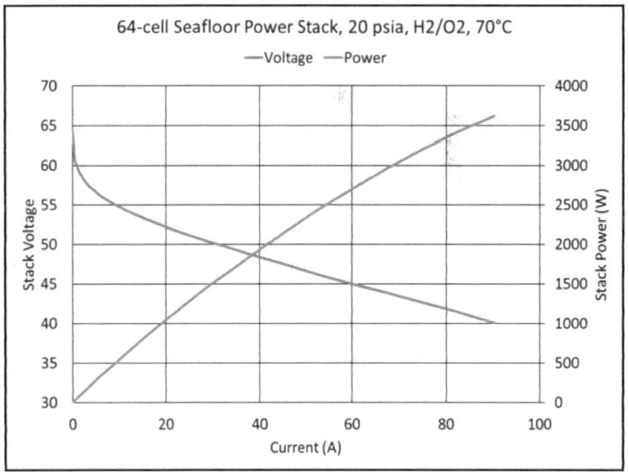

Figure 5: Fuel Cell Stack Testing - 64 cells, 20 psia, H2/O2, 70°C

Fuel Cell Stack: A stack consisting of 64 cells was built with the MEA and bipolar plate designs developed for the TESI EDR fuel cell system. The stack was tested independently of the integrated balance of plant and water management sections using actively controlled humidification, gas flow rate, and water separation. The test was done to verify MEA performance and efficiency prior to assembling the fully integrated system. A stack polarization curve is shown in Figure 5. The stack demonstrated the ability to produce 500

W of power at lower current densities favorable for minimizing long term degradation and over 3 kW of stable, continuous power to satisfy higher power demand. The stack will be paired with previously proven ejector and water management subsections to complete the TESI EDR fuel cell system in preparation for integration into the subsea power node.

Upcoming Work: Fabrication and testing of the system will continue, with a demonstration in shallow water scheduled for August 2018 at the Advanced Naval Technology Exercise (ANTX) in Newport, RI. Successful completion of the demonstration will be followed by upgrading the system design to accommodate deep water environments exceeding 2000 m. A deep-water untethered subsea power node is scheduled to be ready for ocean trials in mid-2019.

Conclusion

An untethered subsea power node concept has been developed by Teledyne Energy Systems to provide a reliable, unattended power source for subsea oil fields and underwater vehicle fleets. The subsea power provides operational advantages in the form of extended runtime for vehicles and equipment without being restricted to platform, coastal, or ship-based support. The subsea power node uses the TESI EDR fuel cell system running on high pressure hydrogen and oxygen gas storage and hybridized with a NiMH battery. The prototype design has been completed and is currently being manufactured for testing. Testing at the subsystem level is currently in progress with integrated system testing to follow. The fully integrated system will be assembled and subjected to testing in both above water and underwater environments. Future work will include upgrading the system design to withstand deeper ocean environments.

Acknowledgements

This project has been supported by Teledyne internal research and development funding.

References

1. Harper, J. "Navy Officials Speed Up Acquisition of Unmanned Maritime Systems," *National Defense Magazine*. Jan. 11 2018. http://www.nationaldefensemagazine.org/articles/2018/1/11/navy-officials-under-pressure-to-speed-up-acquisition-of-unmanned-maritime-systems
2. Whittenton, N., Granger, R., Walker, C., "Waterborne Surveillance for Enhanced Harbor Security," *Sea Technology Magazine*. 2013. https://www.sea-technology.com/features/2013/1113/3.php
3. Granger, R., Neal, N., Pomerleau R., Harald, G. "Resident AUV system with subsea dock in development," *Offshore Magazine,* Apr. 4 2014, https://www.offshore-mag.com/articles/print/volume-74/issue-4/subsea/resident-auv-system-with-subsea-dock-in-development-p1.html
4. Freedburg, S.J., "The 7-11 For Robot Subs: Underwater Plug And Stay Hubs" *Breaking Defense,* May 21 2015, https://breakingdefense.com/2015/05/the-7-11-for-robot-subs-underwater-plug-and-stay-hubs/
5. Snyder, A., "Powering Through: Navy Scientists Develop Underwater Wireless Charger", *Armed With Science*, Aug 28, 2017, http://science.dodlive.mil/2017/08/28/powering-through-navy-scientists-develop-underwater-wireless-charger/
6. Utz, R., Wynne, R., Ferguson, S., Miller, M., Sievers, R., Song, Y., "Lightweight System Design and Demonstration of a High Reliability, Air Independent, PEMFC Power System for Aerial and Space Applications" *47th Power Sources Conference*, Jun. 14 2016

Alternative Energy: Powering Army Modernization

Julianne Douglas, Dr. Nathan Sharpes, Alexis Moy, Christopher Mullen, & Christopher Hurley
Communications-Electronics Research, Development and Engineering Center
US Army Research, Development and Engineering Command
Aberdeen Proving Ground, MD, USA, 21005

Abstract: *In October 2017, the US Army began implementing pilot Cross-Functional Teams (CFTs) to modernize its materiel development strategy and rapidly transition necessary capabilities to the Warfighter* [1]. *The CERDEC Power Division is currently focused on three of the eight CFTs with definite power needs: Next Generation Combat Vehicle (NGCV), Future Vertical Lift, and Soldier Lethality* [2].

In recent years, CERDEC energy harvesting efforts have focused primarily on wearable kinetic technologies such as boot insole mechanisms and rucksack suspension tuning optimization. In addition, CERDEC has spearheaded the development, maturation, and evaluation of several photovoltaic chemistries including gallium arsenide and amorphous silicon.

As the Army implements its modernization strategy, CERDEC Power Division is preparing to support rapidly evolving Warfighter needs in a holistic manner. This paper will discuss CERDEC's recent alternative energy efforts and potential paths forward leveraging that experience to address opportunities for alternative energy within the CFTs, focusing on Soldier Lethality and the remaining CFTs to a lesser extent.

Keywords: Warfighter; CFT; Modernization; Alternative Energy; Energy Harvesting; Solar; Kinetic

Introduction

In late 2017, the US Army announced its new acquisition modernization strategy and intent to create eight Cross-Functional Teams (CFTs) as its driving force [1]. The US Army CERDEC Power Division is currently working to support at least three of those CFTs directly. They are: Next Generation Combat Vehicle (NGCV), Future Vertical Lift, and Soldier Lethality [2]. All of these CFTs have already identified significant power and energy needs or gaps. However, the primary focus of this paper will be on the Soldier Lethality (SL) CFT.

The SL CFT encompasses task force architecture, modeling and simulation, tactical (meaning Soldier and squad/small unit) power and energy, target acquisition/fire control, and considerably more, but these are the top four priorities identified at the SL CFT Workshop held on 6-8 March 2018 in Ft. Belvoir, VA, which was attended by stakeholders in government and industry. The stakeholders included representatives from the CFT leadership, user and requirements communities, as well as representatives from both the equipment capability and energy community in the science and technology, acquisition program management, and industry realms. The three main systems that the SL CFT is targeting are Next Generation Squad Weapon (NGSW), Enhanced Night Vision Goggles – Binoculars (ENVG-B), and Adaptive Soldier Architecture (ASA).

Closing the power and energy gap is a high priority issue for Soldier Lethality. Capabilities and their respective power needs are increasing rapidly following Moore's law, while S&T improvements for power generation and sources increase at far slower (more linear) rates. One of the activities that occurred during the power breakout session of the SL CFT Workshop was an estimation of the number of L91s a soldier would have to carry to power the second or third generations of NGSW and ENVG-B only over a 72-hr mission. Based on our assumptions, the energy could be approximately 400 W-hrs. That's 88.89 L91s at 15 g each (300 W-hrs/kg specific energy), totaling 1.275 kg or 2.81 lbs. of non-rechargeable L91s carried per Soldier on a three day mission. The power and energy community indicated that we can make it lighter and higher capacity (closer to 400 W-hrs/kg). Just changing to a military standard chemistry (i.e. Li/CFx at 400 W-hrs/kg) and adapting it to other form factor solutions (i.e. AA or 2/3 A) can increase the capacity and runtime by 20-30 percent without increasing weight. Alternatively, this type of solution could help unburden the Soldier if a cap is placed on the equipment power draw.

The other major outcomes for the power and energy breakout session of the SL CFT Workshop in March were as follows. Collective planning/roadmapping is needed to ensure we don't miss any opportunities due to program alignment or missing S&T insertion points for power and energy solutions into relevant capabilities. Implementation of incentivized/enforceable energy efficiency requirements language into new procurement actions. Long term, the need to replace the existing AA technology with other lightweight, high-performance power sources and investigate alternative sources and methods of supplying or recharging Soldier-carried equipment is clearly apparent.

The bottom line is: we need to close the energy gap, fast.

Alternative Energy

Alternative energy in the form of solar photovoltaics, fuel cells, biofuels, wearable kinetic energy harvesters, wind turbines, and more have been investigated and developed in CERDEC and across the DOD in the last decade and beyond. These sources may provide direct power to or recharging of tactical and logistical equipment in theater. Recharging radio and sensor batteries during operations can reduce the logistics burden/dependence on energy resupply as well as provide critical mission extending capabilities in limited resupply situations.

Basing

In theater, generator sets, vehicle alternators, and large quantities of batteries are typically used to power operations. The generator sets and vehicle alternators convert liquid fuels (typically JP-8 or similar) into the electric power needed to conduct most military operations. Typical usage implementation is one-to-one. That means one power generator or power source to power one piece of equipment or a few through a power distribution hub. A macro-scale (power for basing operations) example of modernization improvements to this paradigm is illustrated in the operational vignette below, where an intelligent microgrids is implemented (i.e. many-to-many instead of one-to-one). The CERDEC Energy Informed Operations (EIO) effort (see below) attempts to shift the paradigm on generator usage in theater by implementing standards for smart microgrids that automate energy efficiency and simultaneously track and communicate usage, priorities, refueling/resupply needs, and maintenance.

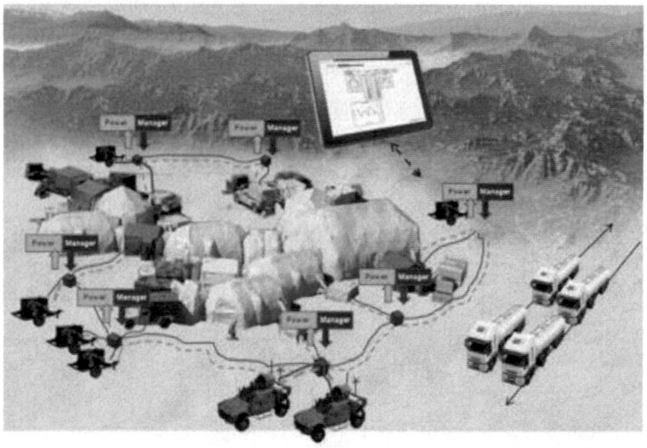

Figure 1: Energy Informed Operations (EIO) Microgrid [3]

Intelligent microgrids become very important when implementing hybrid (energy storage) and renewable energy systems, especially when combining with traditional fuel-based generation. It is fundamentally important that smart power distribution systems implement algorithms to optimize energy efficiency, not just instantaneously but also predictively, to maximize "grid" performance and health as well as maximize return on investment.

Tactical Power (Soldier and Small Unit)

On the smaller-scale side of the power spectrum (i.e. Warfighter and small unit) alternative energy technologies such as solar, fuel cells, and harvesting can be critical to satisfying the increased energy demand at the tactical edge. Figure 2 illustrates forward solar recharging of peripheral batteries during a rest period as one possible concept of operation for solar alternative energy. Typically, the bigger the solar panel, the more you can recharge. This one could be used to recharge a phone, sensors, IR, torch, or other next generation Soldier Lethality technology.

Figure 2: Example solar recharging CONOP in theater [4]

Previous and on-going technology development efforts at CERDEC relevant to the Soldier Lethality CFT include energy storage (batteries and capacitors), kinetic energy harvesters (backpacks, boots, and insoles), solar PV (c-Si, a-Si, CIGS, GaAs, perovskite, DSSC), wind, and intelligent power management (hardware and software). The graphic below illustrates some of these innovations.

Figure 3: CERDEC Power and Energy on the Battlefield

Fielded technologies that are available today include primary batteries (BA 5590, AA, and AAA), rechargeable batteries (BB-2590 and 150 W-hr Conformal Wearable Battery (CWB)), squad power generation (100-120 W Solar PV blankets), Universal Battery Chargers and Soldier Power Management and distribution systems. Another example is the 120 W solar blanket which can be used to recharge a BB-2590 in roughly 2 hours.

Some technologies that have been recently transitioned to PM SWAR for the dismounted platoon and below include: 1 kW Multi-fuel generator, 20 W Wearable Hybrid Fuel Cell, 150 and 50 Whrs versions of the rechargeable Conformal Wearable Battery (CWB), 250 Whrs non-rechargeable CWB, High capacity BA-5790, Distributed Power Manager, Universal Battery Charger.

Some rough estimates on future target metrics for power sources are as follows. Primary batteries with upwards of 600-800 Whrs/kg could sustain the power demands of future dismounted combat operations on a single battery or at dramatically reduced (less than half) the weight burden for a 72 hr mission. Rechargeable batteries of 300-500 Whrs/kg would double to triple today's capabilities. This would enable the present dismounted Soldier's load to decrease by roughly 2-6 lbs. Progress in rechargeable batteries that can face the military operational environment, especially cold weather conditions, is difficult since we do not drive the market, but extremely essential for the same reasons. The battery market is driven by the commercial and private sectors. Demand is high and growing for commercial Li-ion rechargeable batteries, while supply for commercial and military battery materials alike is not. This could lead to future scarcity or market instability. This is in addition to the fact that it far more expensive (in terms of weight and volume) to ship batteries than fuel.

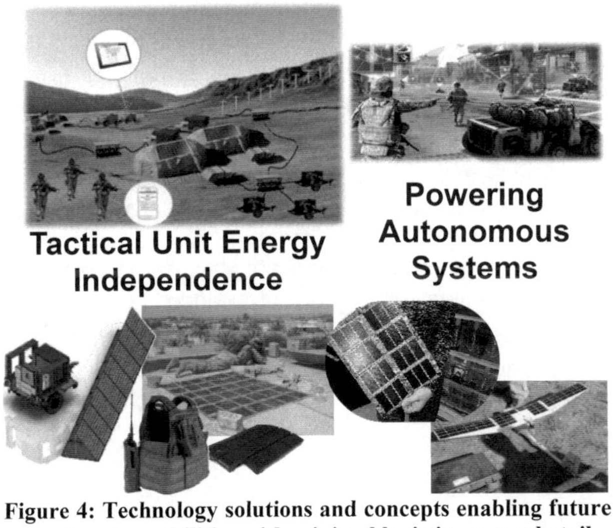

Figure 4: Technology solutions and concepts enabling future operational capabilities with minimal logistics resupply tail

Future alternative energy technologies that would be successful or worthwhile in the mid- to far-term Soldier Lethality CFT would be solar or other energy harvesting solutions enabling 2-8W at less than 0.5-1 lbs. in combination with smart power management and distribution solutions. Examples include kinetic recoil harvesting from NGSW firing rounds or acoustic or thermal harvesting from the same. An alternative high TRL, lightweight solution could also be to employ an array of high efficiency solar PV cells such as GaAs or silicon on top of the all the new NGSW technology that may be packaged in the new, larger weapon scope. The main issue with carrying solar on the Soldier or weapon is that it gets hot and produces an IR signature detectable by unfriendly forces.

Partnering agencies to CERDEC such as ARL, NSRDEC, PM SWAR, ONR, NRL, NSWC, and more have contributed to the technology developments in the power and energy area. Figure 5 depicts one of ARL's unified battlefield energy and information concepts.

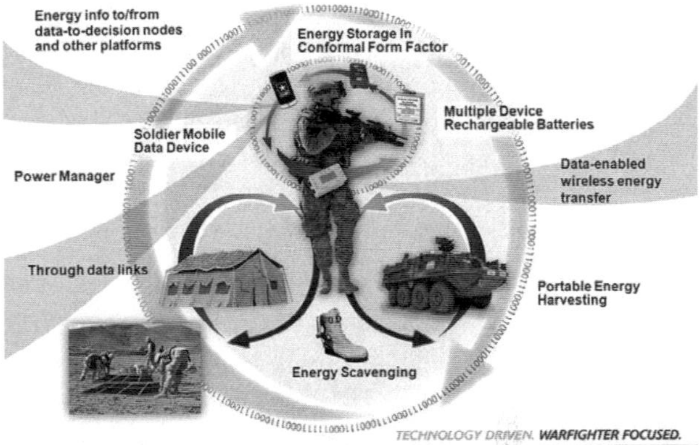

Figure 5: ARL's 2013 Smart Battlefield Energy on Demand concept [5]

There are benefits, drawbacks, and ideal usage scenarios (or concepts of operation) to any technology and power sources are no exception. Batteries are the most commonly used power source for wearable or carried electronic devices in the world. However, the majority of the world doesn't have same weight, energy density, and resupply concerns as the dismounted Warfighter. State of the art military battery chemistries are usually too expensive or niche to sell on the commercial market. Alternative energy solutions such as solar, fuel cell, and energy harvesting technologies are typically used as mission extending capabilities or in situations with limited resupply availability. They typically require hybridization with rechargeable batteries and a smart power management and distribution system.

Combining multiple power sources and/or energy consuming electronics together is always a good time to implement (or at least consider) a smart power management and distribution architecture such as ASA for Soldier Lethality CFT. The Adaptive Soldier Architecture is crucial to the CFT as it will not only provide the trade space for additional capabilities versus Soldier performance enhancement or degradation, but also—hopefully—a way to centralize and manage power and energy. In addition, it is important to be able to prioritize and gracefully provide capability degradation in low energy situations so that your primary warfighting functions are the last to be affected by power loss.

Capabilities

In addition to the expertise in the CERDEC Power Division, the facilities are well equipped to perform any power and energy investigations required to assess an application with its intended power source or generation capabilities. We preform unbiased and objective analysis of electrochemical materials and chemistries, power sources and alternative energy systems. Use these evaluations to inform the PM and user communities with new capabilities and empower the army modernization priorities.

We have the prototyping ability to do quick turnaround of systems using circuit board and 3D printing machines to get user feedback before we do large design scale ups. For example, one success story involved following up on Soldier feedback during a lab tour, we designed and prototyped an inverter with an AC outlet to securely plug into and fit on top of a BB-2590. The design was proven out, vetted by the user, and then scaled up for production.

Figure 6: Selected Power Division Capabilities

A wide variety of environmental testing is conducted in our diverse size range of environmental chambers to observe how technologies perform under various operational type conditions. Chambers with operating temperatures ranging from -50°C to +150°C gives us the capability to run desert cycle as well as extreme hot and cold weather cycling on power systems from the size of a coin to a vehicle.

The solar emulator provides the ability to repeatably test at one sun, which is equivalent to the solar radiation at noon on the equator, without regard to weather or time of year. We use it to perform apples to apples comparisons of various solar chemistries and technology implementations. We then can easily calculate equivalent average output anytime and anywhere in the world using lookup tables. This information can be used to help inform mission planning actions such as whether to pack a solar blanket or fuel for a generator set for an extended duration mission where you may have limited resupply.

The Warrior Torso Test Stand (WATTS) emulates vertical center of mass torso motion of a human tiptoeing, walking, and running including forward trunk lean angle for short and long term programmable missions. WATTS is not a replacement for human subject testing, but rather an enabler to prolonged, uncomfortable, and early prototype level testing.

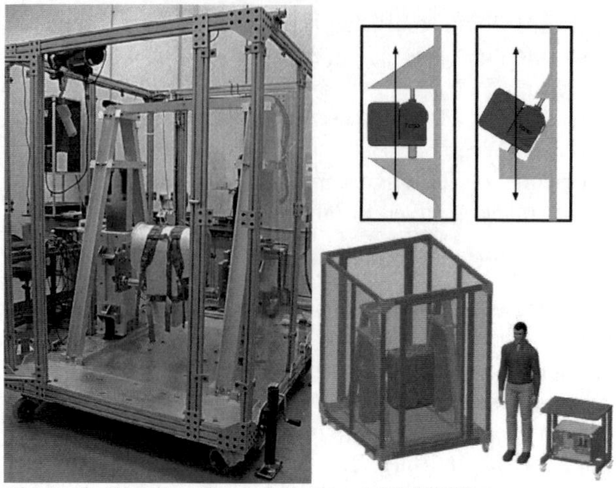

Figure 7: Warrior Torso Test Stand (WATTS)

References

[1] D. Vergun, "Cross-functional teams to spearhead modernization, says McCarthy," 13 OCT 2017. [Online]. Available: https://www.army.mil/article/195247/cross_functional_teams_to_spearhead_modernization_says_mccarthy.

[2] C. McBride, "Leaders Tapped for Eight Cross-Functional Team Pilots," 30 OCT 2017. [Online]. Available: https://www.pmpnt.army.mil/leaders-tapped-for-eight-cross-functional-team-pilots/.

[3] US Army CERDEC, [Online]. Available: https://www.cerdec.army.mil/news_and_media/Energy_Informed_Operations_Microgrid/.

[4] army-technology.com, "Wearable Solar Cells for Soldiers: Running of of Energy?," [Online]. Available: https://www.army-technology.com/features/feature-wearable-solar-cells-soldiers-running-out-of-energy/.

[5] www.arl.army.mil, "Power Up!," 23 April 2013. [Online]. Available: https://www.arl.army.mil/www/default.cfm?article=1919.

High-Performance Body Armor-Integrated, Multi-functional Batteries for Dismounted Soldier

Brian Henslee and Jacob Monat

CRG, Inc.
Miamisburg, OH, USA

Abstract: *CRG is developing a high performance, fail-safe, multifunctional, conformal battery with integrated ballistic capability that can be worn with small arms protective insert (SAPI) hard body armor plates for improved weight reduction on the dismounted soldier.*
A significant number of military assets, including multiple types of soldier-worn systems, rely heavily on power provided by rechargeable batteries. As the capabilities of these systems increase, there is an ever-increasing need for batteries with more electrical energy. Along with the increasing need for additional batteries to support these growing energy demands comes added weight, mounting space limitations, and restricted body movement for the dismounted soldier. Soldiers can carry in excess of 30 lbs. of batteries, such as the BB-2590 and Conformal Wearable Battery (CWB), to support a single mission in addition to the SAPI hard body armor weight. To further enhance the safety and protection of the warfighter, while seeking to provide further advancements in weight and space reduction without sacrificing energy storage, a more closely coupled body armor and energy storage solution is needed.

CRG's approach to meet this need is a conformal battery design which can be installed with SAPI hard body armor in existing plate carrier vests without modification. CRG's battery pack design is a thin, conformal package with ballistic capability built into a lightweight battery case. Safety is of utmost concern as this is a body-worn device, so the battery pack includes temperature monitoring and fail-safe capabilities should a ballistics event occur.

The system-level specific energy objective is to exceed 150-200 Wh/kg including the battery cells, control electronics, structural ballistic case, and connector. CRG is currently optimizing the design for weight, volume, ballistic protection, and ruggedization to support operations in a wide range of environmental conditions. Successful demonstration will show a significant weight and space reduction on the soldier compared to current soldier-worn battery solutions.

Lightweight 0.4 – 3 kW Soldier-Portable JP-8/DF-2 Generators

Timothy LaBreche, Dave Spence, Rich Mastanduno, Subir Roychoudhury

Precision Combustion, Inc.,
410 Sackett Point Rd., North Haven, CT 06473
tlabreche@precision-combustion.com

Abstract:

Precision Combustion, Inc. (PCI) has developed a line of battery-hybridized generators by utilizing reliable, lightweight and low-cost, commercial, off-the-shelf (COTS) 4-stroke engines. The fueling system is modified to operate on JP-8/DF-2 via PCI's novel and patented octane-matching approach. 0.5 and 1 kW prototypes have been matured. Capability for tethering 3 generators and obtaining up to 3 kW has been demonstrated. Custom power electronics enable simultaneous DC and AC outputs. MIL-SPEC environmental and power quality testing has been successfully completed. 1000-hour durability testing has indicated no abnormal wear and tear or impact on normally expected life. Maintenance intervals were between 100 – 150 hours with no irregular buildup of fuel or metals in the oil. The approach also avoids wet stacking. TEC-D (Technical Demonstration) testing at Fort Devens has also been completed without any technical issues identified during testing with various appliances.

The 400 W generator has a dry-weight of less than 18 pounds and is ruck-packable. It includes electric start and consumes less than 0.07 gallons of JP8 per hour. The 1 kW version weighs 30 pounds and in addition to AC, it has full range DC output as an option. Stable operation with other liquid and gaseous fuels has also been demonstrated for multi-fuel capability. Any COTS engine can be suitably adapted. The particular engines used were chosen for reliability, low noise and availability.

PCI has also developed tethering technology that leverages our power electronics to create a load-sensitive network of 1kW generators. The modular approach permits load matching so that only the generators needed are operating. This increases efficiency, reduces maintenance, and eliminates wet stacking compared to the TQG or MTG at part load. This enables multiple single soldier portable generators to be daisy-chained for producing up to 3 kW (compared to the much heavier and larger 2 kW MTG (MEP-531A; 123.5 lbs) or the 3kW TQG (MEP-831A; 304 lbs).

PCI's proven octane-matching approach is inherently superior to other "fogging" approaches for enabling spark ignited (SI) engine operation on JP-8. SI engines require octane numbers of >80 for stable operation and avoiding knock, yet JP-8 has an octane number of only ~20. PCI uses its in-situ and on-demand JP-8 upgrading reactor (the size of a D-cell battery) and an advanced direct fuel injection approach to upgrade the octane and thereby reliably operate SI engines on JP-8 or other liquid and gaseous fuels. No carburetor, special start fluids or starting procedures are required. This also allows attitude independence during operation. The JP-8 upgrading reactor is tolerant to 3000 ppm sulfur (JP-8 spec) and its performance has been proven over 1000's of hours of testing. Test data will be shared during the presentation.

Keywords: Portable, Packable, PPG, Reforming, Fuel Processing, Power Generator, JP-8, Diesel, APU

Introduction

Commercial off-the-shelf gasoline engines are inexpensive and meet the weight, size, and power output requirements for the deployed soldier. These engines however run on gasoline, a high octane fuel (octane number 85-100). As a result, these engines cannot operate with JP-8 heavy fuel, whose octane number is in the range of 15-25. Multiple alternative means developed to allow operation on JP-8 are inherently flawed due to their reliance upon approaches that do not actually overcome the core octane number problem.

PCI's approach

The octane number of JP-8 fed to the engine was directly increased to the 80+ range, suitable for operation of SI engines via "Octane Matching". The JP-8 is instantaneously (order of milliseconds) converted to high octane fuel, immediately prior to injection into the combustion chamber via an extremely compact (C-cell battery size), octane-boosting reactor. PCI's underlying CPOX reactor breakthrough has been advanced in collaboration with automotive and DoD support. 0.3 – 1 kW versions of the generator have been matured for meeting field battery charging needs with JP-8.

PCI's Fuel conditioning Module (FCM) for the Soldier Power Genset (SPG) series of generators is based on the concept of converting any spark ignited commercial off the shelf (COTS) gasoline generator to run on low octane, heavy distillate fuels such as JP8 or diesel. Over the course of the program, a kit was developed that is adaptable to run a wide range of engine makes, models and power ratings by changing a small number of components and control variables. This makes the technology relatively engine agnostic over a wide range of power levels.

In order to operate the balance of plant components during startup of the FCM a system battery was required. The battery needed to be robust enough to handle operation of these components, while also being lightweight and power dense. Once the system was operating, the control and power electronics were capable of recharging the battery. Several potential options were studied prior to the selection of a battery capable of producing the required power while still being small enough and light enough to be integrated into the generator system.

The primary requirements with respect to control and power electronics were to provide high fidelity fuel conditioner operation and reliable integration with the engine to properly meter fuel at steady state and transient conditions. The power electronics were implemented to provide reliable AC and DC power as well as providing power management between the balance of plant components and the rechargeable onboard battery. A logical stepwise progression of both hardware and software was employed over the course of the program to allow for requirements to be identified and improvements to be made through several iterations. The hardware was matured in stages and software was continuously modified and improved for maximum benefit to the genset system.

Transient response testing consisted of multiple loading cycles performed at each power level tested during durability evaluations. The transient response testing was then repeated after the testing was complete for both AC and DC power outputs. The results of this testing can be seen in Figures 1 and 2. Engine oil temperatures are also shown. Note the stable AC and DC outputs during transition.

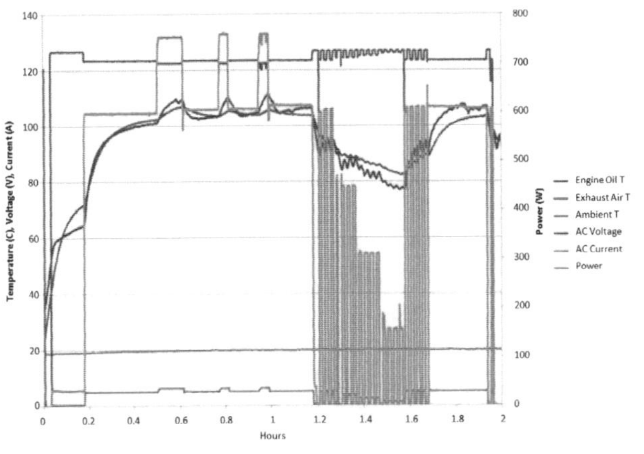

Figure 1: Max power and transient testing performed prior to the endurance test.

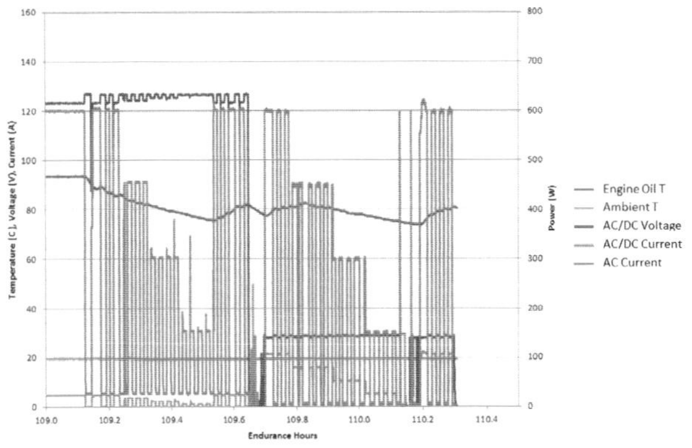

Figure 2: Transient testing performed on both AC and DC loads after the endurance testing. No change in performance was observed before and after the 100-hour test.

Engine Oil Analysis

PCI measured oil compositions on several development test engines and compared results to unused engine oil. The figures below summarize oil composition analysis measurements made on 3 different engines with run times of 94 to 335 hours. No meaningful change in oil properties were observed after operation with JP-8 (i.e. no JP-8 dilution of crankcase oil) (Figure 3). Note: Manufacturer recommended oil change interval is 100 hours. Contamination of the oil by fuel leaking past the piston rings has been a concern noted with other JP-8 conversion technologies. The oil analysis from the engines fitted with PCI's FCM showed < 1 percent fuel in the engine oil, demonstrating a key benefit to PCI fuel conditioning approach and further confirming the 100 hour oil change interval recommendation. Figure 3 shows the results of the analysis.

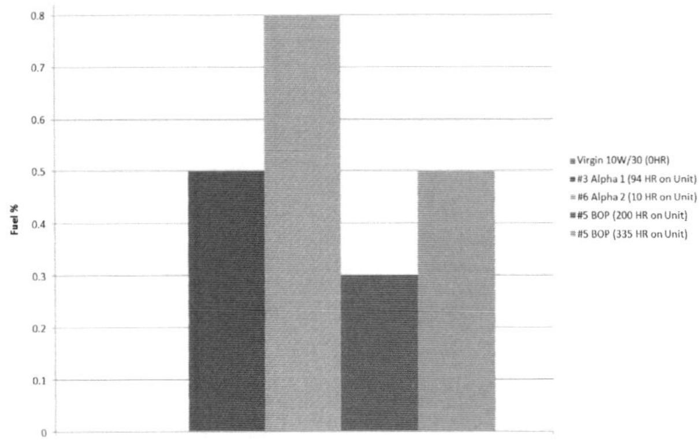

Figure 3: Results of oil analysis examining fuel percentage in engine oil over several hundred hours **showed no JP-8 dilution in crankcase oil**.

Conclusions

The feasibility of converting a lightweight gasoline engine without any internal engine modification, and operating on distillate fuels (i.e. diesel and JP-8), in addition to gasoline was clearly illustrated. Four units at TRL of 7 were developed. The generators were capable of starting and operating in varied weather and temperatures, maintaining speed and voltage during load transitions and operating safely for long periods. PCI's fuel conditioner module has also shown to be applicable to a wide range of makes, models and power outputs of gasoline generators that are readily available today.

Acknowledgements

We acknowledge the support of the DoD (CERDEC, Picatinny Arsenal, and WPAFB). Any opinions, findings, and conclusions or recommendations expressed in this paper are those of the authors and do not necessarily reflect the views of the DoD and DOE.

Advances in Betavoltaics, a Radioisotope Power Source for Long-Life and High Energy Density Applications

Tom Adams[1], Shripad Revankar[2], Darrell Cheu[2], Peter Cabauy[3] and Bret Elkind[3]

[1] Power and Energy Division
Naval Surface Warfare Center, Crane Division
Crane, IN, USA, 47522

[2] School of Nuclear Engineering
Purdue University
West Lafayette, IN, USA, 47907

[3] City Labs, Inc.
Homestead, FL, USA, 33030

Contact Author Email: thomas.e.adams@navy.mil

Abstract: *Unlike electrochemical batteries, betavoltaics and other types of radioisotope power sources can meet the demands in applications requiring long operating lifetimes and operation in extreme temperatures. State-of the-art betavoltaics are being developed with power densities of 0.1 mW/cm³ and with further refinement, 1 mW/cm³ is promising. Though the power density is much lower than lithium primary batteries, the amount of energy delivered after 10 years is at least 5000 times more than lithium batteries. A promising fit in DoD exists in smart tags and unattended ground/maritime sensors (field & forget) to significantly extend current mission lives and situational awareness resulting in huge savings while mitigating risk to Warfighters. Center for Strategic and Budgetary Assessments estimated the cost per troop in Afghanistan for 2015 is $2M. Experimental results and evaluation data will be presented and discussed, with a direction of where this technology may be utilized.*

Keywords: Betavoltaic; radioisotope power source; energy harvesting; hybrid battery; solid-state battery; beta emitter; p-n junction; latent power; low power; modelling.

Introduction

Radiation interaction with materials can have beneficial uses, such as in betavoltaic cells, a type of radioisotope power source where the kinetic energy associated with beta (*β*-) decay is converted into electricity. Novel and compelling need-based applications are emerging in the military, intelligence, commercial, and medical markets that can utilize the diminutive energy produced from such cells. Present-day sensors, medical implants and electronic devices make betavoltaics an attractive alternative to electrochemical batteries enabling applications to perform for much longer periods in extreme temperatures. Unlike conventional electrochemical batteries, commercially available betavoltaics can operate in excess of 10 years over temperatures ranging from -55°C to 150°C [1]. Because the technology is far from mature, many challenges and issues remain to increase energy density, reduce cost, and make them easier to use.

Background

The first betavoltaic battery was developed in 1953 at RCA by Rappaport. The device yielded an efficiency of only 0.2% and degraded rapidly due to radiation damage from the beta source, strontium-90 [3]. Several others continued research using ^{147}Pm but were only able to achieve <1% efficiency [4, 5]. The most promising effort in the early history of betavoltaic developments occurred ca. 1974 through research led by Olsen at the Donald W. Douglas Laboratories [6, 7]. Olsen's Betacel battery exhibited a 4% efficiency using ^{147}Pm and silicon p-n junctions. Over 285 patients received pacemakers powered by the Betacel batteries, 60 patients inside the United States. German and U.S. medical institutions were seriously considering the Betacel for wider use. The United States Atomic Energy Commission (USAEC) had authorized the licensing in the United States of a Clinical Investigation Program that allowed the implantation of 50 Betacel pacemakers per month [8]. However, strides in lithium battery development entered onto the scene and were subsequently selected for pacemakers instead [9].

Most research and development in the last 10 years has concentrated on designs using tritium; since the radiation damage is low and thus easily shielded, and available. City Labs successfully produced tritium betavoltaic prototypes in 2008 (Figure 1), that are still operating. The NanoTritium™ betavoltaic was granted a NRC General License which is approved for manufacture and sales within the United States.

Figure 1. City Labs' NanoTritium™ betavoltaics.

Theory of Operation

A direct conversion betavoltaic is comprised of two components, the p-n junction and the beta source. Electricity is produced similar to a photovoltaic using the kinetic energy of the beta particles. The basic concept of operation is shown in Figure 2. Beta particles enter the p-n junction and collide with atoms creating electron-hole pairs (EHPs) as they slow down. A 5 keV particle creates over 1000 EHPs, and deposits some energy into the lattice. In the depletion region, holes are accelerated to the p-side collector and the electrons are accelerated to the n-side collector. With a load connected, the electrons travel from the n-side, through the load and back to the p-side. The voltage developed in a betavoltaic is directly related to the quality of the semiconductor and its band-gap energy.

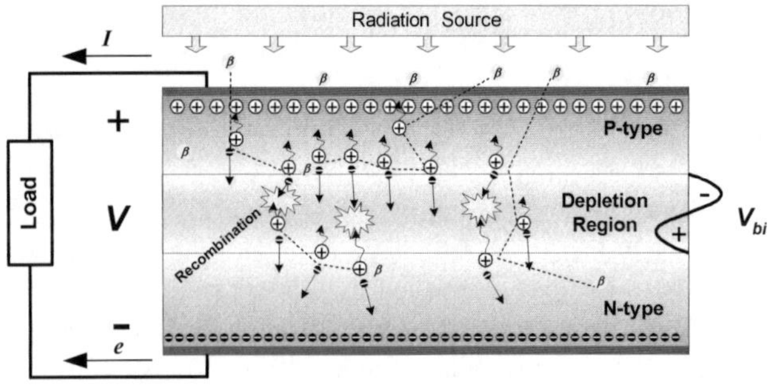

Figure 2. Overview of a betavoltaic cell.

Combining the betavoltaic in parallel with a solid-state lithium rechargeable (secondary) battery can provide latent and burst power for many applications. In a design using a Cymbet 50 µAh lithium solid-state rechargeable battery, the operating temperature is limited to 85°C, the maximum operating temperature of the battery.

Beta emitting source

When selecting a beta emitting isotope, the maximum beta energy and decay half-life are the most important criteria. The beta energy from ^{90}Sr and ^{85}Kr exceeds the minimum dislocation energy of 300 keV which results in semiconductor damage and bremsstrahlung [10] The 25-day half-life of phosphorus-33 is too short for a long operating life. Therefore, of the three potential isotopes in Table 1, tritium is the most attractive. Tritium is readily available from Ontario Power in Canada and is least expensive at $3.50/Curie (Ci). Russia is the only provider of ^{147}Pm and ^{63}Ni, which are costly at >$1000/Ci and $4000/Ci [11], respectively. Reprocessing in the U.S. would alleviate these obstacles making them attractive again for radioisotope power.

Table 1. Potential radioisotopes.

Isotope	$T_{1/2}$ (yr.)	E_{AVG} (keV)	E_{max} (keV)	Ci/g	W/g	Cost/Ci
Tritium	12.33	5.7	18.5	9,664	0.33	$3.5
Ni-63	100.1	17.1	67	59	0.006	$4,000
Pm-147	2.6	65	220	600	0.22	$1,000

In tritium based designs, the substrate material that serves as the sync or storage medium for the tritium has become a significant challenge. Tritium can be efficiently stored as a solid in metal rather than as a compressed gas. Scandium (Sc) and titanium (Ti) can store larger amounts of hydrogen by forming hydrides, ScH_2 and TiH_2. Recent designs invoking tritium stored as tritides demonstrated many practical difficulties with loading techniques and substrate damage. Air and moisture contaminate the surface which increases the activation energy necessary for diffusion. Substrates around 500 nm thick are necessary to efficiently fuel betavoltaics due to shielding from the metallic substrate. Models using MC-SET (Monte Carlo Simulation of Electron Trajectories in solids) [2] were developed to predict surface beta flux for storage materials and reported in Ph.D. dissertation.

Temperature Performance Results

Betavoltaics were evaluated under temperature from -30°C to 70°C by applying a voltage and sinking the current using a Keithley 2602B source measurement unit. For individual cells, Current-voltage (I-V) curves were acquired by stepping the voltage from 1.00 V to -0.10 V in steps of 1 mV and measuring the current. Figure 3 shows I-V curves measured on Sample BV07. From cold to hot, the open-circuit voltage, V_{oc}, decreased from 0.95V to 0.65V while the short-circuit current (I_{sc}) increased from 82 to 86 nA.

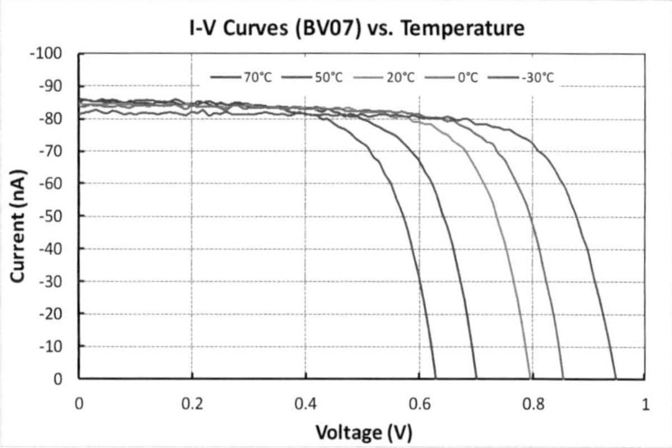

Figure 3. I-V curves of BV07 at -30°C to 70°C

Because of the strong temperature dependence on voltage, the maximum power increases with decreasing temperature. To charge a lithium solid-state rechargeable battery, six betavoltaic cells were connected in series and

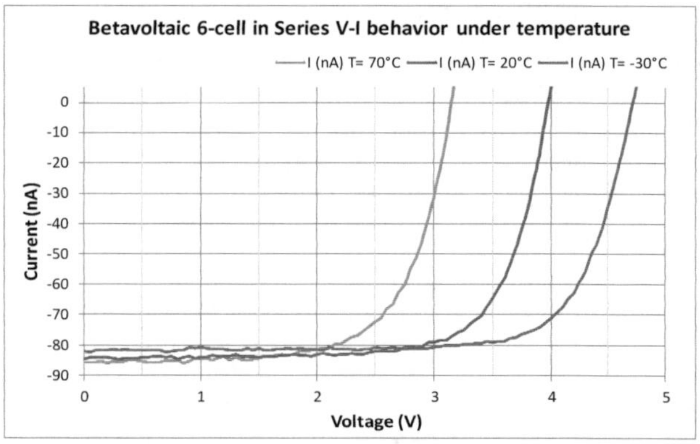

Figure 4. I-V curves of six samples (BV07-BV11) connected in series at temperatures from -30°C to 70°C

evaluated from -30°C to 70°C where they behave similar to individual cells (Figure 4). The six-cell arrangement works for temperature below room temperature but for higher temperatures, another cell is needed to boost the voltage.

The 6-cell betavoltaic was connected to a Li-SS battery in parallel to create a hybrid design. The test was done at 20°C and Li-SS battery was 90 percent charged to determine if full charge can be achieved. The result is shown in Figure 5 where the voltage increased quickly then slowed as the current decreased. The battery approached full charge to 4.0V, but fell short at the current diminished to zero. Adding another cell will provide full charge but will continue to overcharge and cause cell damage. Either voltage on betavoltaic needs to be increased or a clamping circuit needs to be developed.

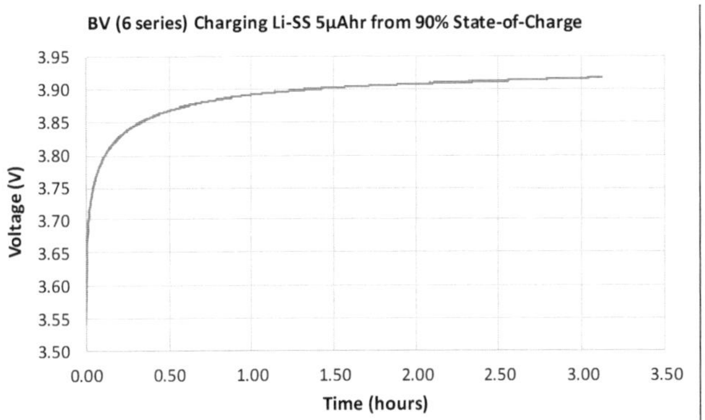

Figure 5. I-V curves of six betavoltaics connected in series at temperatures from -30°C to 70°C.

In another experiment, the internal resistance that affects the voltage was explored using a technique that maintains constant voltage over a temperature of -10°C to 50°C. A shunt resistor was placed in parallel with the betavoltaic to clamp the voltage below open-circuit voltage and cycled over the temperature range. Six betavoltaics were connected in parallel to reduce the value of the shunt resistor to what was available. The voltage followed a single cell but the current was much higher indicating that combining in parallel does not affect performance or integrity.

At 30°C, a potentiometer (outside of temperature chamber) was placed across the betavoltaic parallel stack and adjusted to obtain a voltage of 0.3 V_{oc}. Without changing the potentiometer, the open-circuit voltage was measured at -10°C and 50°C. The test was repeated with the potentiometer adjusted to provide 0.5 V_{oc}. The results in Figure 6 indicate the voltage is stable; it increases benignly as temperature increases, which is due to increasing current. The shunt resistance needed to maintain the open-circuit voltage is shown in Table 2. Higher clamped voltages vary more over temperature as the knee of the I-V curve is approached.

Using the same setup, a test was done to evaluate effects of load current on voltage stability over temperature. This time, the open-circuit voltage was set to 0.2 ,0.3, 0.4, and 0.5 V. At temperatures from -10°C and 50°C, load current was increased to 50 nA in steps of 5 nA. Results for tests at 30°C are shown in Figure 7. The voltages under 50 nA remained within 5% of open-circuit voltage.

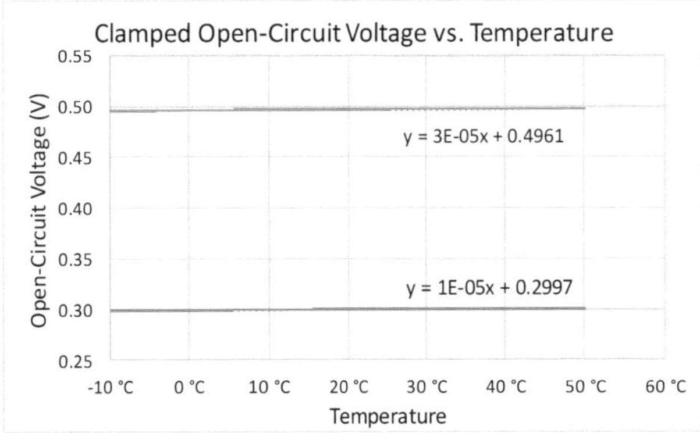

Figure 6. Clamped open-circuit voltage for 6-cell Betavoltaic over a temperature of -10°C to 50°C.

Table 2. Shunt Resistance for V_{OC} Clamping over Temperature

Voc	R_{L-10C} (MΩ)	R_{L30C} (MΩ)	R_{L50C} (MΩ)
0.2	0.506	0.506	0.506
0.3	0.774	0.767	0.768
0.4	1.041	1.042	1.057
0.5	1.322	1.369	1.466

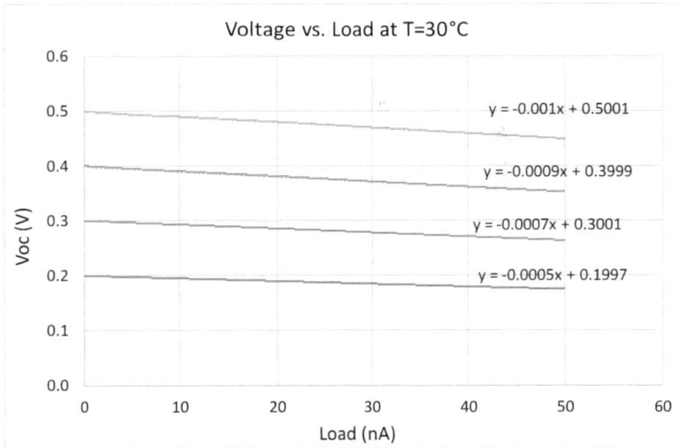

Figure 7. Sensitivity of clamped voltage for 6-cell Betavoltaic under load to 50 nA at 30°C.

Next Generation Betavoltaic

Recent advances at City Labs incorporate tritium metal hydride beta flux density and a reduction of the betavoltaic semiconductor substrate thickness from 625 microns in the P100a units (Figure 1) to 170 microns in the new 100μW betavoltaic unit (Figure 8) allowing for an increased power density level through stacking of betavoltaic semiconductors. Recent advances in tritium scandium metal hydride deposition techniques are projected to raise the current density to 100 nA/cm^2. The projected open circuit voltage for the P200 units are 0.8V,

1.6V, or 2.4V with short circuit current at inception of 156 μA, 78 μA, or 52 μA respectively. The power decay of the 100μW betavoltaic will follow the natural decay of tritium with a half-life of 12.3 years as shown in Figure 9. On-going developments are being done to reduce the semiconductor substrate down to 10 μm that will enable milliwatt power levels within the same package.

Figure 8. Render of City Labs next generation 100μW P200 betavoltaic (99mm x 45mm x 8mm, 20.1g)

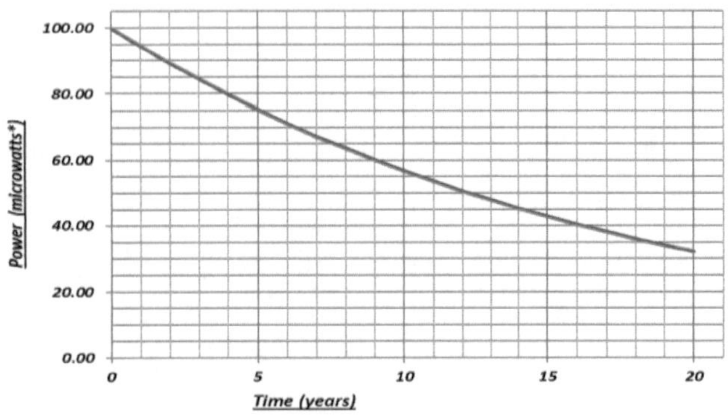

Figure 9. Projected power for Model P200 betavoltaic

Conclusion

Betavoltaics are a safe enabling technology for military and commercial applications, but the technology is far from maturity with much room for improvement. Direct replacement of batteries with betavoltaics is not straight forward and will likely require a hybrid design consisting of a betavoltaic stack and storage device (battery or capacitor) that must be able to operate in the extreme temperatures as betavoltaics. Betavoltaics have an advantage where they can operate in a constant current range with little changes in voltage. Betavoltaics can be placed in parallel and series with one another without adverse effects in performance. Paralleling multiple betavoltaics together reduces the effect of temperature on voltage which is critical in many sensor applications. The technology is developing with higher power devices and general licensed devices for less restrictive uses. Consortiums are being developed by Niowave, Inc., betavoltaic manufacturers, private industry, Department of Energy, Department of Defense, and Academia to address present challenges and advance the technology into military, commercial and medical applications.

Acknowledgements

Author Thomas Adams would like to thank Naval Surface Warfare Center, Crane Division (Crane, IN) for support and Purdue University in this research. This work was done at Purdue University (West Lafayette, IN) with Shripad Revankar, Darrell Cheu, and colleagues from City Labs, Inc. (Homestead, FL). Special appreciation goes to the Radiological and Environmental Management (REM) and PUR-1 laboratory personnel at Purdue for providing facilities and radiological guidance. Finally, author would like to thank Eli Napchan for his support in beta sources.

References

1. Olsen, L.C., P. Cabauy, and B.J. Elkind, *Betavoltaic power sources.* Physics Today, 2012. **65**(12): p. 35-38.
2. Napchan, E., *MC-SET - Monte Carlo Simulation of Electron Trajectories*, 2008, [Computer Software].
3. Rappaport, P., *The electron-voltaic effect in pn junctions induced by beta-particle bombardment.* Physical Review, 1954. **93**(1): p. 246.
4. Flicker, H., J.J. Loferski, and T.S. Elleman, *Construction of a promethium-147 atomic battery.* IEEE Transactions on Electron Devices, 1964. **11**(1): p. 2-8.
5. Manasse, F.K., J.J. Pinajian, and A.N. Tse, *Schottky barrier betavoltaic battery.* IEEE Trans. Nucl. Sci, 1976. **23**(1).
6. Olsen, L., *Betavoltaic energy conversion.* Energy Convers., v. 13, no. 4, pp. 117-127, 1973. **13**(4).
7. Olsen, L. *Advanced betavoltaic power sources.* 1974.
8. R. Franco, M.L.S. *Benefits and Risks of Promethium Battery-Powered Pacemakers.* in *Advances in Pacemaker Technology.* 1974. Erlagen Springer-Verlag.
9. Olsen, L.C. *Review of betavoltaic energy conversion.* 1993.
10. Santos, I., Marques, L. A., Pelaz, L., and Lopez, P., "Molecular dynamics study of damage generation mechanisms in silicon at the low energy regime,"pp. 37-40.
11. Bower, Kenneth E, Barbanel, Yuri A., Shreter, Yuri G., and Bohnert, George W., *Polymers, Phosphors, and Voltaics for Radioisotope Microbatteries*, CRC Press, Boca Rotan (2002).

USB 3.1 Capabilities and Considerations for the Dismounted Soldier

Dan Milliken[1] and José Collazo[2]
[1]GTS LLC, Wall Township, NJ 07727
[2]Communications-Electronics Research, Development, and Engineering Center, Aberdeen Proving Gnd. MD 21005

Abstract: *In 2017, US Army Program Executive Office (PEO), Soldier, funded a study to establish the applicability of USB 3.1 standards to the dismounted Soldier equipment set. These standards included USB 3.1 SuperSpeed data, USB Type C, and USB Power Delivery. Special focus was given to the capabilities provided by USB 3.1 data rates, and the features provided by USB Power Delivery. It was established that adoption of the new USB standards would come at a significant cost in ruggedizing the hardware, cables, and connectors to meet military standards, and that the current USB 2.0 + Power system meets the near term needs of the dismounted Soldier.*

Keywords: USB; Type-C; Data; Power Delivery; SuperSpeed; power; Soldier

Introduction

The Nett Warrior (NW) is an integrated dismounted situational awareness (SA) and mission command (MC) system for use during combat operations. Designed as a tool for leaders, NW provides unparalleled SA and MC capabilities to the dismounted leader, permitting faster and more accurate decisions during the tactical fight. With advanced navigation and information sharing capabilities, leaders are able to avoid fratricide and are more effective and more lethal in the execution of their combat missions.

The NW program delivers a SA and MC system, which has the ability to graphically display the location of an individual leader's location on a digital geo-referenced map image. Additional Soldiers, platforms, and unit locations are also displayed on the digital user interface. NW is connected through a radio that will send and receive information from one NW to another, thus connecting the dismounted leader to the network. These radios will also connect the equipped leader to higher echelon data and information products to assist in decision making and situational understanding. Soldier position location information will be added to the network via interoperability with the Army's Rifleman Radio capability. These capabilities will allow the leader to easily see, understand, and respond in the method that best suits the user and the particular mission. NW will employ a system-of-systems approach, optimizing and integrating capabilities while reducing the Soldier's combat load and logistical footprint [1].

The NW program represents an effort to adopt commercial technologies and adapt them for military use, taking advantage of the rapid innovation pace of commercial development, while providing the dismounted Soldier a rugged and reliable equipment set that can survive his or her mission.

Dismounted Soldier Baseline

The central point of the NW system (Figure 1) is the power and data manager, a USB 2.0 data hub combined with a power distribution bus. The End User Device (EUD) is the commercial smartphone that acts as the USB host on the Upstream Facing Port (UFP) of that hub. Power is provided by a Conformal Wearable Battery (CWB) and distributed to all the Downstream Facing Ports (DFPs) as well as the UFP. The CWB provides 14.8V nominal at 5A max, or 75W of power. The main power consumer of the system is the radio or radios. Power and data are distributed through shielded cables with a 6-pin ruggedized, keyed, push-pull, circular connector.

USB Implementers Forum (USB-IF)

The USB-IF is a not-for-profit organization to promote and support the Universal Serial Bus. Its main activities are the promotion and marketing of USB, Wireless USB, USB On-The-Go, and the maintenance of the specifications, as well as a compliance program.

USB-IF was formed in 1995 by the group of companies that developed USB. Notable members include Hewlett-Packard, NEC, Microsoft, Apple Inc., Intel, and Agere Systems.

Membership in the USB-IF is open to industry and academia for an annual fee. Member benefits include the issuance of a Vendor ID (VID) and ability to participate in compliance workshops. The goal of the USB-IF and the logo and compliance program is to facilitate interoperability of devices in the commercial market.

USB 3.1 Standards

The USB 3.1 Standard, introduced in November 2008, and updated in July 2013 to include USB 3.1 Generation II, defines a SuperSpeed data rates of 5 Gbit/s and SuperSpeed+ rates of 10 Gbit/s [2]. These data rates are provided by employing two additional transmit and receive differential pairs on the connector beyond the traditional USB 2.0 differential data signaling pair.

The new USB standards also sought to address a deficiency in the way USB 2.0 devices used the Vbus power line. In USB 2.0 and the USB Battery Charging (BC) Specification, Vbus provides 5V from a host to a downstream device. Vbus current is limited to 500 mA for downstream data ports, but can be up to 1500 mA for dedicated charging ports. The new standards define USB Power Delivery (PD), with the capability to negotiate Vbus up to 20 V at 5 A, as well as the ability for a device to provide power to a host.

Lastly, the USB 3.1 standard allows for alternate modes, which permit the USB data pairs to be reconfigured for other protocols including DisplayPort and Thunderbolt.

Along with the USB 3.1 data standard, a new physical interconnect was defined called USB Type-C (Figure 2). This 24-pin reversible connector would provide all the functions of USB 3.1 including SuperSpeed data, alternate mode, and PD.

Several features of the new standards necessitate the use of a newly defined Electronically Marked Cable Assemble (EMCA), or eMarker. This is an integrated circuit (IC) embedded at one or both ends of the Type-C cable, and is required whenever:

- *VBUS current of more than 3A is required*
- *USB 3.1 Gen. 2 or 10 GHz USB, is required*
- *Alternate modes are required*

The DC Electrical Requirements in the USB 3.1 specification are outlined in accordance with the Electronic Industries Alliance (EIA) standard 364. The EIA develops standards to ensure electronic equipment from different manufactures is compatible and interchangeable. As it applies to USB, these standards govern parameters like contact resistance (EIA 364-23B), insulation resistance (EIA 364-21), contact current rating (EIA 364-70), insertion and extraction forces, insertion/extraction cycles, cable flexing (EIA 364-41), among others.

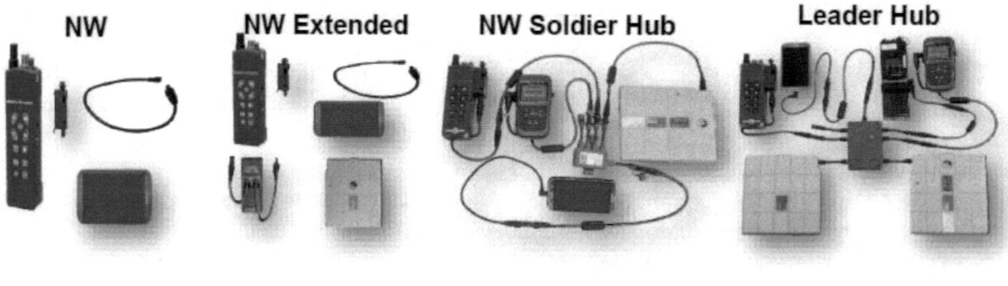

Figure 1 - Soldier baseline equipment configurations.

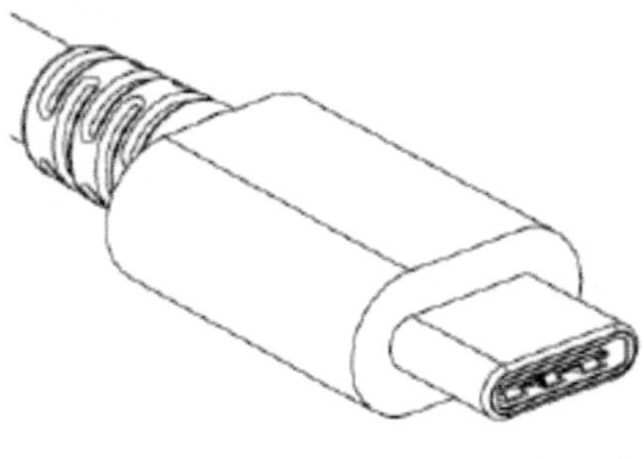

Figure 2 - USB Type C connector (USB-IF)

Analysis & Results: The Dismounted Soldier Baseline capability set was evaluated against the 480 Mbit/s bandwidth provided by the USB 2.0 data bus, as well as the 75W total power provision.

Devices, cables, and connectors for the Soldier Baseline have been specifically selected in order to meet strict military requirements including MIL-STD-810G governing environmental requirements. Some of these tests include temperature range up to 120 degrees Fahrenheit, as well as operation during subjection to rain, humidity, sand and blown dust, vibration, crash shock, and immersion. The connectors are chosen to create a watertight seal during operation. In addition, the components are subject to MIL-STD-461G tests for operation in electromagnetic fields, and radiated emissions. These test conditions represent operating modes beyond the capability of the commercial cables and connectors defined in the USB specifications. Departure from the use of the cables and connectors specified in the USB standard also creates a need for the Army to perform its own electrical compliance testing program.

In order for the Army to adopt the USB 3.1 and associated standards, the 24 pin reversible type C connector (Figure 3) would have to be scaled to a lower pin count, ruggedized, keyed connector.

A1	A2	A3	A4	A5	A6	A7	A8	A9	A10	A11	A12
GND	TX1+	TX1−	VBUS	CC1	D+	D−	SBU1	VBUS	RX2−	RX2+	GND
GND	RX1+	RX1−	VBUS	SBU2	D−	D+	CC2	VBUS	TX2−	TX2+	GND
B12	B11	B10	B9	B8	B7	B6	B5	B4	B3	B2	B1

Figure 3 - USB Type-C receptacle (front view) (USB-IF)

Pin count for the connector could be reduced as appropriate by sacrificing some of the functionality as follows:

- Type C Connector – USB 3.1 + PD - 24 Pins
- USB 3.1 Type C functional, non-reversible – 18 Pins
- USB 3.1 + PD with single GND + Vbus – 12 Pins
- USB 3.1 + PD w/o SBU – 10 Pins
- USB 2.0 + PD – 6 Pins

In order to gauge the necessity of USB 3.1 data speeds, one of the use cases considered was the need to transfer full motion video between devices. For this the required bandwidth is given by

$$H_{resolution} \times V_{resolution} \times Color\ bits \times \frac{frames}{s} = \frac{bits}{s}$$

For a 1280x720 pixel video at 24 bits of color and 30 frames per second (FPS), the required bandwidth is 663 Mbit/s. This bandwidth exceeding the 480 Mbit/s provided by USB 2.0 provides compelling reason to move toward USB 3.1.

In practice, however, video is encoded and transmitted in compressed form. h.264 MPEG encoding is considered to be widely used and representative of the state of the art of video compression. The bandwidth of an H.264 encoded video stream is approximated by

$$H_{resolution} \times V_{resolution} \times \frac{frames}{s} \times Motion\ Rank \times 0.07 = \frac{bits}{s}$$

The h.264 bandwidth estimate [3] is determined by several factors, including a "motion rank" of 1-low, 2-medium and 4-high. An example of low motion rank would be an interview with a subject talking on screen, while an example of high motion rank would be an action movie trailer or sports clip. When employing h.264 compression, the bandwidth required is 7.75 Mbit/s for the same video stream at the highest motion rank. Therefore, the USB 2.0 data bus has the capacity to handle up to 62 compressed video streams. With that in mind it was determined that the current system has enough overhead to meet today's data bandwidth needs with room to grow.

It should be noted that these calculations represent a "best case" analysis. In practice, there will be bandwidth overhead for signaling, error checking and correction (ECC), transport and session management.

Finally, USB Power Delivery provision of 100 W bi-directional power presents a unique capability but comes at a cost of cable embedded chips which increase cable cost decrease durability, and don't provide a significant capability beyond the 75W power bus in the custom architecture to justify the added investment.

Looking Forward

The US Army will continue to monitor the state of the commercial market concerning maturity of USB 3.1 devices, as well as the power and data needs of the warfighter, and adopt USB 3.1 features at appropriate technology insertion points.

Acknowledgements

The studies that provided the research for this paper were funded by US Army PEO Soldier. US Army CERDEC, The MITRE Corporation, and Protonex provided contributing research for this paper.

References

1. PEO Soldier, "Nett Warrior," [Online]. Available: http://www.peosoldier.army.mil/docs/pmswar/Nett-Warrior-Poster-061512.pdf [Accessed April 23, 2018].
2. USB-IF, "USB-IF Documents," [Online]. Available: http://www.usb.org/developers/docs/. [Accessed June 2017].
3. Adobe Systems, "h.264 Compression Primer," [Online]. Available: http://www.adobe.com/content/dam/Adobe/en/devnet/video/articles/h264_primer/h264_primer.pdf

Lithium Rechargeable Pouch Flexible Batteries

Shmuel De-Leon

Shmuel De-Leon Energy, Ltd.
www.sdle.co.il
shmuel@sdle.co.il

Abstract: *New lithium ion pouch cells in the market offer mechanical flexibility. That flexibility is require by military and consumer wearable applications. That paper review the current developments in the flexible battery filed.*

High Energy Density and Specific Energy Silicon Anode-Based Batteries

Constantin Ionel Stefan
Amprius, Inc.
225 Humboldt Ct.
Sunnyvale, CA 95136
ionel@amprius.com / 1-510-512-5484

Abstract: *Amprius' unique, patent-protected, silicon nanowire technology addresses swelling by enabling anodes to expand and contract internally, in a very robust mechanical structure. As a result, Amprius has achieved 1000 Wh/L and 400Wh/kg levels of energy density and specific energy, respectively, in lithium-ion cells with a cycle life in the hundreds of cycles. Manufacturing capacity and products are currently available for mission critical applications in aerospace and military.*

Keywords: silicon anode; lithium-ion; batteries; energy density; specific energy; power; aerospace; wearable batteries; drones.

Introduction

Current state-of-the-art lithium-ion cells with graphite anodes have specific energies of up to 250 Wh/kg. There is very limited room for improvement because the active materials are utilized at capacities close to their theoretical limits and the packaging has been substantially optimized. Hence, new materials are required to increase performance.

There is an abundance of research on active materials that can increase either the capacity (mAh/g) or the voltage (V vs. Li/Li+) of the cathode side of the cell, but these increases are rather small, around 10-20% at the component level, and about 5% at the cell level. On the anode side, there are active materials such as Si, Ge, Sn, Al and combinations of these that can offer capacities up to an order of magnitude larger than carbon. Silicon offers the most significant increase. But, despite many years of research, none of these materials, in any structure or composition, has been developed to meet the requirements of a commercial product. The key metric in the search for better materials is not only the specific energy capability, but also the cycle life and rate capability of the active material. Amprius is the first to report a stable anode made of 100% pure silicon that can cycle in a full cell for hundreds of cycles and retain more than 80% of initial capacity, at a rate and capacity loading compatible with commercial application requirements. Amprius' technology thus provides a significant step forward in lithium-ion battery development. The anode-based performance improvement is independent of the cathode material. Any increase in cathode capacity will be enhanced in a silicon battery due to the higher percentage of cathode in the cell.

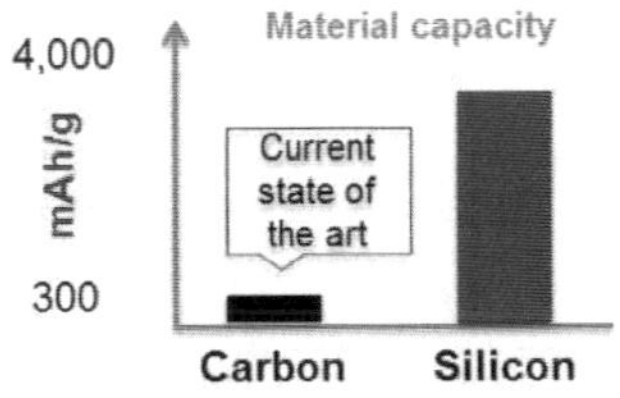

Figure 1. Silicon materials have a theoretical capacity ten times higher than that of graphite anodes

For example, when paired with commercially available cathodes (e.g., LCO and NCM type materials with a cycling capacity of 150-200mAh/g), Amprius' silicon nanowire anode-based cells have demonstrated 300-400Wh/kg - an increase of 30-50% in specific energy over state-of-the-art lithium-ion cells. Amprius' volumetric energy improvements are similarly impressive compared to carbon cells because the anode is the most voluminous component of the cell. See Figure 2. Amprius' anode takes up less space and weighs less than state-of-the-art anodes, giving the cell higher energy for a lower volume/mass (or, allowing for more run time with the same volume/mass). Amprius' silicon anode cells currently reach over 1000 Wh/L and can potentially achieve over 1200 Wh/L, depending on cell design, capacity and other cell components.

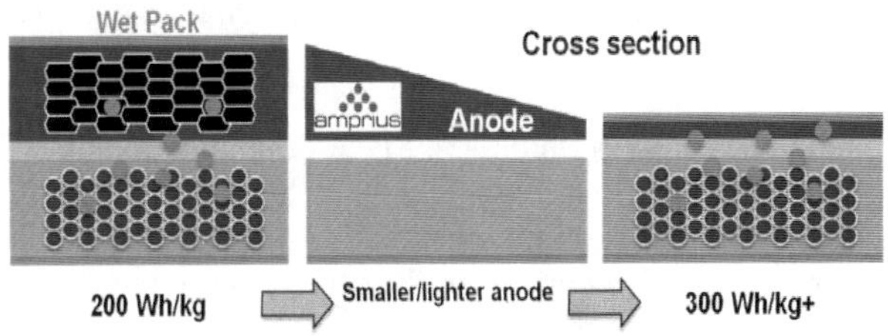

Figure 2. Amprius' silicon anode greatly decreases the size and weight of the cell, increasing energy density and specific energy.

Technical Description

Structure and Properties: The silicon nanowire structure, shown in Figure 3, includes a metallically conductive nanowire core, metallurgically connected to the current collector. This robust connection is essential in creating and maintaining a stable electrical connection and mechanical structure at the electrode level. Each silicon wire is directly connected and does not need to rely on particle-to-particle contacts for conductivity. Since this connection is very robust compared to connections between particles created by electrode calendaring and binders, the silicon material remains in electrical contact, i.e. electrochemically active, over the entire cycle life of the cell. The fast loss of electrical connectivity and changes in mechanical structure that plague the majority of other silicon technologies are virtually non-existent in the rooted silicon nanowire anodes. Moreover, this significant stability is achieved in a structure that is virtually 100% silicon, without any binder or conductive additive to dilute its active material content.

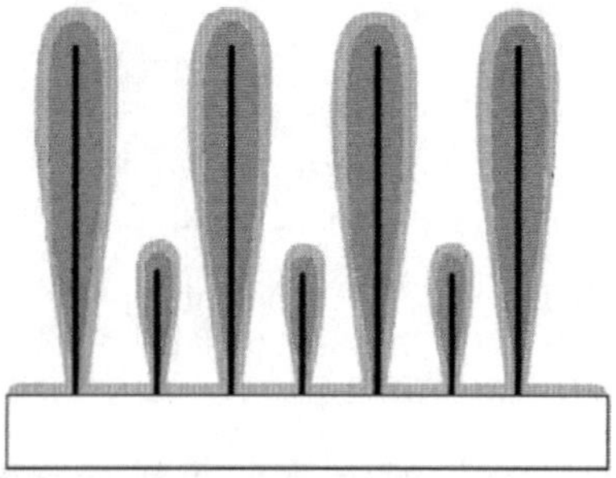

Figure 3. Amprius' growth rooted silicon nanowire structure

The silicon nanowire has a tapered shape, with a much lower thickness toward the root, where it connects to the current collector. This shape is essential in reducing the mechanical stress at the interface during lithiation/ delithiation cycles. When silicon films or particles are coated on foils as thin as those used currently in lithium ion cells, e.g. 6-12 μm in thickness, upon lithiation the foils are stretched and that leads to wrinkles, ripples and foil ripping. In the case of silicon nanowire electrodes, the minimum contact surface between the root of the silicon wire and foil eliminates mechanical stress in the foil during cell cycling.

A second feature of Amprius' silicon nanowire material is its nanostructure. The internal porosity and amorphous structure accommodate and dissipate some of the mechanical stress induced in the material during lithiation/delithiation processes. Since these processes start from the silicon/electrolyte interface, they occur mostly radially, and the stress and material swell are of the same geometry. The silicon nanowire structure can accommodate a large amount of lithium without significant radial swell. Even at full lithiation, the axial swell, which is responsible for the cell swelling, is less than 30%.

The nanowire material structure also enables a relatively high 94% first coulombic efficiency in half cells and 90% coulombic efficiency in full cells with LCO cathode. These values are competitive with graphite materials and reduce or eliminate the need for prelithiation steps that compensate for the first cycle loss in the cell fabrication. A typical first cycle at a 0.05C rate of a silicon nanowire electrode is shown in Figure 4.

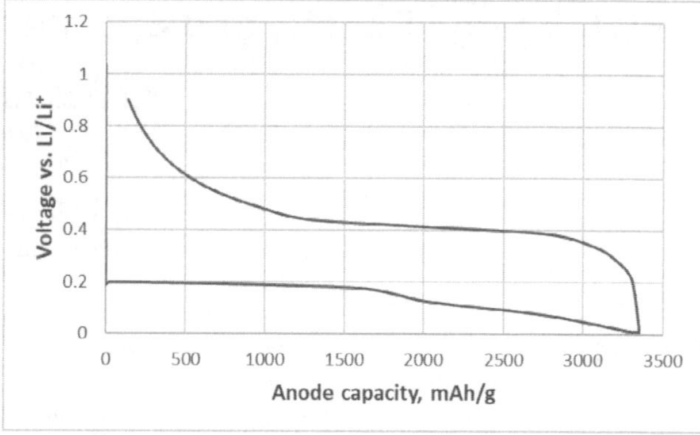

Figure 4. Silicon nanowire voltage profile in half cell, lithiated to 10mV vs. Li/Li+ electrode and delithiated to 0.9V at a 0.05C rate

Energy Density and Specific Energy: The main advantage of using silicon materials in lithium ion cells reaches the highest level with silicon nanowire technology. Since silicon is the material with the highest capacity for lithium storage, a 100% silicon anode would bring the most performance advantage to lithium ion cells. The reduction in anode thickness frees more space in the cells for the rest of the cell components, including the other active material, the cathode. As a result, cell energy can be increased in the same cell volume, or the size of the cell can be reduced while keeping the energy at the same level. Both options are a result of a significant increase in energy density. The reduction in anode volume of 2-2.5 times compared to graphite results in an increase in energy density of 30-60%, depending on the cathode material and type, loading and other cell component specifications. The cell specific energy increases as well but by a slightly smaller percentage (see Figure 5).

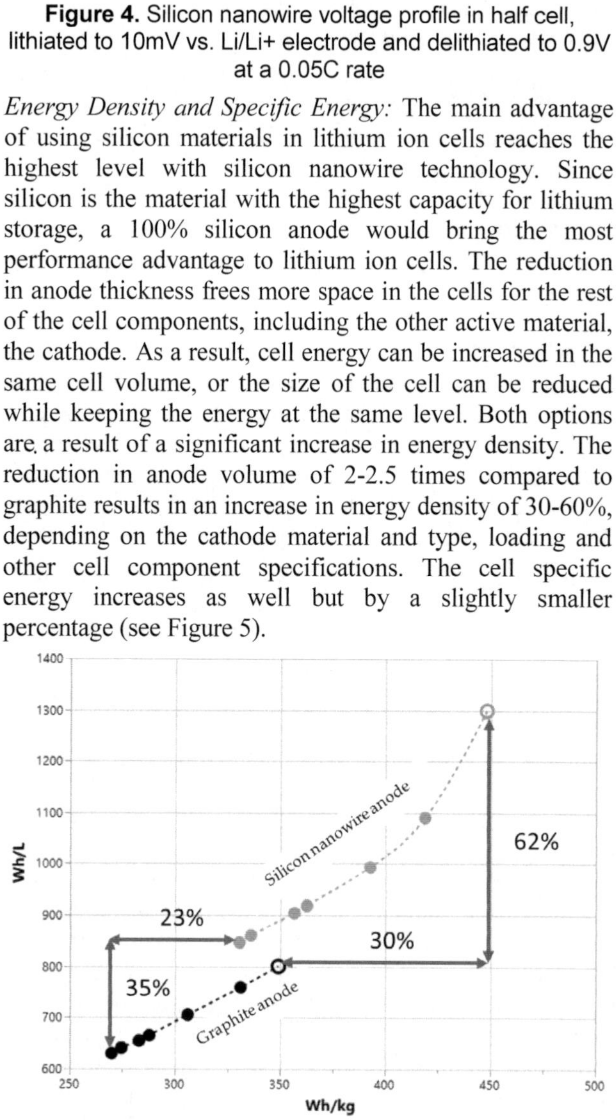

Figure 5. With the same cathode and separator components, the silicon nanowire anode technology significantly increases energy density and specific energy (solid circles are demonstrated products)

Cycle Life: The silicon nanowire anodes can cycle for hundreds of cycles in full cells due to limited swell at the material and cell level, and stable material and electrode structure. The stability of the material and partial utilization of the theoretical capacity of silicon also limit lithium consumption for SEI repair and, thus, extend the cycle life to numbers approaching those of graphite cells. In cells with LCO cathode, the cycle life depends on the cathode loading and charging voltage, which are adjusted based on the target energy density and specific energy. Moreover, the rate of lithium consumption and SEI growth are strongly affected by the cycling rate. The increase in volume and lithium consumption can be mitigated by improved electrolyte formulations. However, during anode delithiation (cell discharge), higher discharge rates lead to increased tensile stress in the outer regions of the silicon material and eventual crack formation at the surface. Crack formation is more damaging to cycle life because it increases significantly the surface area of the silicon, which leads to accelerated lithium loss and impedance increase. The nanowire structure with a porosity gradient in its structure reduces these effects, but the SEI growth is still faster than on graphite materials. Figure 6 presents cycle life curves for cells with capacities of 2.6-3.1Ah in the same form factor as a function of their energy density. The increased energy density was achieved in this case by changing the cathode loading and maximum operating voltage.

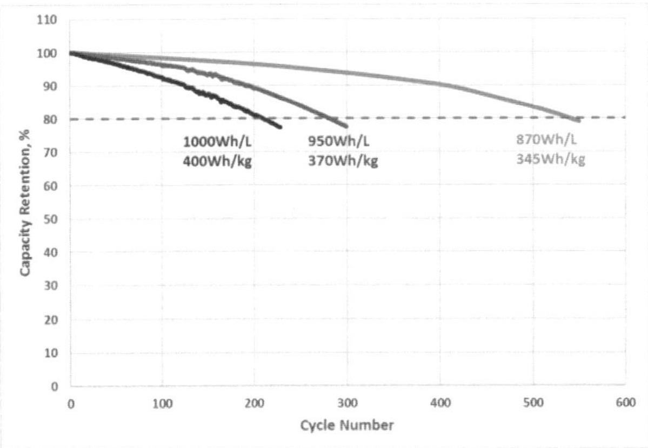

Figure 6. The cycle life of Si/LCO cells ranges from 200 to 500 cycles, and depends on cathode loading and maximum cell voltage

Rate and Power: The nanowire structure has higher surface area than typical lithium ion material structures in graphite electrodes. This advantage can be exploited in silicon nanowire cells by matching the nanowire anodes with a cathode designed for a target rate capability. For example, in cells designed mostly for high energy applications (smartphones, tablets, day-night cycling etc.), the acceptable continuous discharge rate is limited to 1C rate (see Figure 7A). However, in cells designed for power and high rate continuous discharge (drones, power tools), the continuous discharge rate can be as high as 10C (see Figure 7B). In this case, the cathode loading is lower, and the energy density and specific energy are lower than those of an energy cell.

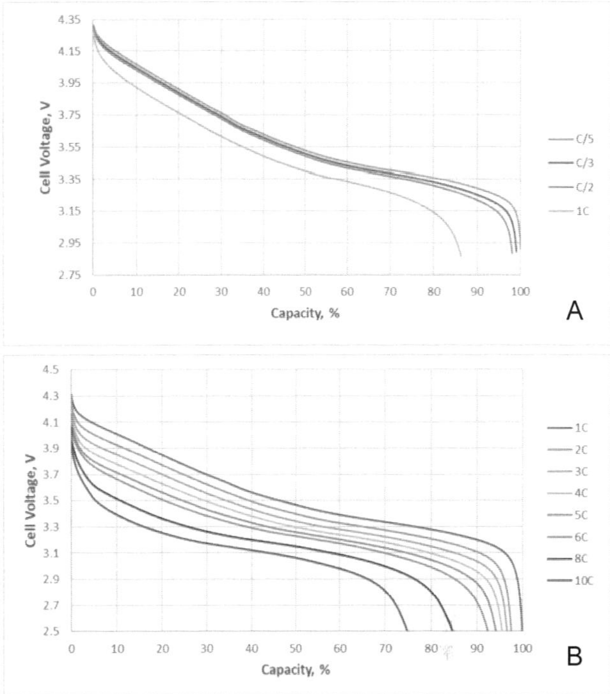

Figure 7. A – Discharge curves at different rates after charging at C/5 rate for a high energy density cell; B-Discharge curves at different rates after charging at 1C rate for a high-power density cell

The high energy density and specific energy performance of the silicon nanowire cells, coupled with its superior power performance, result in a relatively flat and wide range Ragone plot, as shown in Figure 8. This property is very appealing to a wide range of applications in aerospace and telecommunications, which can take advantage of high specific energy and energy density cells while still requiring high power for limited amount of time. The power/energy ratio is controlled by the cathode specifications because the cathode is the limiting rate component.

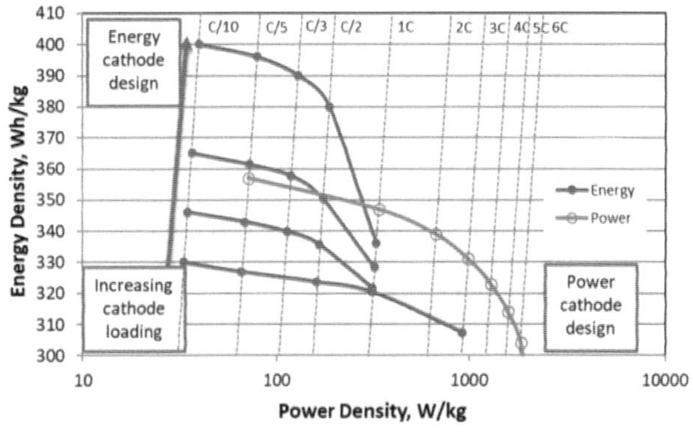

Figure 8. Energy vs. Power density curves (Ragone plot) of Si/LCO cells are controlled mostly by cathode structure, which is the limiting rate component.

Safety: Silicon nanowire cells developed in the last few years were successfully tested in multiple abuse and safety evaluation conditions, including electrical, mechanical and thermal factors. For example, 2.2Ah pouch cells with silicon nanowire anode and LCO cathode were certified to pass the tests required for air cargo shipping, according to UN 38.3 specifications. These tests include Altitude Simulation (low pressure test), Thermal Shock Test (-40°C to 72°C), Vibration, Mechanical Shock and External Short Circuit, done sequentially on the same cells, as well as Crush and Forced Discharge tests, done separately. The same type of cells also passed the suite of tests included in the UL 1642 specification. Separately, silicon nanowire cells passed other abuse and safety test, including nail penetration and overcharge to by 150% charge capacity. These results suggest that there is little argument to support the assumption that silicon materials are inherently less safe than graphite anodes.

Products: Amprius has already developed and demonstrated the performance of its patented silicon nanowire anode structure in prototype cells of different form factors, with cathodes that include LCO, NCM and NCA materials, and with capacities up to 45 Ah. Amprius has also begun commercializing its cells for high-end and mission critical applications. Some of the form factors developed are shown in Figure 9.

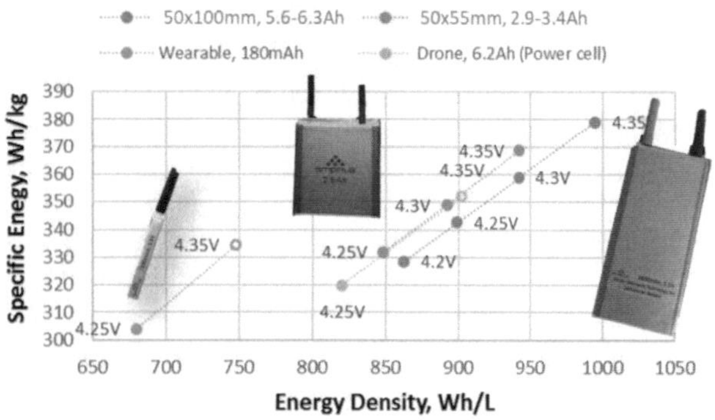

Figure 9. Silicon nanowire anodes have been assembled in cells spaning a wide range of capacities and applications. Their capacity is variable and can be controlled by voltage, without other changes to cell components.

In an Army (NSRDEC) conformal battery project, Amprius developed a 2.2 Ah cell. Amprius' cell exceeded the project's energy goal (301 Wh/kg) by 8%. Independent, third party testing houses (UL) tested and validated Amprius' cell (in the form factor developed for the project) for both performance and safety (UL 1642 and other tests, including nail penetration). Amprius' cell received the UN 38.3 certification for air transportation. The cell was designed for a 150 Wh CWB that reduced the weight of the Army's current battery pack by 40%.

Amprius developed a 5.8Ah cell under a contract with NASA Glenn Research Center, which verified that the performance (specific energy and cycle life) of Amprius' cells exceeded the project's targets; Amprius achieved >340Wh/kg and more than 200 cycles at both at 0°C and 30°C.

With USABC (Ford, GM, Fiat Chrysler and DOE) support, Amprius developed a 45 Ah cell in a standard form factor for electric vehicle applications. Cells with NCM cathodes achieved 340Wh/kg and were tested by Idaho National Laboratory and Sandia National Laboratory for performance and safety. Amprius' smaller Silicon-NCM cells passed over 500 cycles of driving cycle stress tests.

Commercial entities from the aerospace industry tested Amprius cells designed for very high specific energies (>350 Wh/kg). Amprius' cells achieved 400 Wh/kg in a 3.8Ah cell form factor and are currently powering advanced aircraft.

Summary and Conclusions

Silicon is recognized as one of the most promising materials for next generation lithium-ion battery anode to replace the conventional carbon-based anode due to its high theoretical capacity, similar discharge potential and reliable operation safety. However, in most silicon material structures and compositions, the critical drawback of huge volume expansion upon lithiation causes series of adverse consequences, leading to very poor cyclic stability.

The rooted silicon nanowire structure developed by Amprius has largely mitigated the drawbacks that afflict other silicon materials and has led to the development of lithium-ion pouch cells with energy and power performance significantly above those of commercial state of the art graphite anode cells, in most cases by 30-50% improvement. Moreover, the cycle life of these cells is closing in on graphite cell performance, already meeting the requirements of a variety of markets. Some of the silicon nanowire cell products have been already qualified for applications, including safety and abuse tolerance validation. In general, the development of first silicon nanowire products has shown that the safety and abuse tolerance of silicon nanowire cells can be as good or better than that of similar graphite cells. It is expected that, in parallel with an increase in manufacturing capability and capacity, the application scope of silicon nanowire cells will expand from premium and mission critical markets to consumer and commercial application in the next few years.

Acknowledgements

Amprius wishes to acknowledge the funding received from US Army (Contract No. W911QY-12-C-0118), NASA (Contract No. NNC16CA10C), USABC (Project No. DE-EE0006250) and DOE (Award No. DE-EE0005474).

Potassium and Cobalt-Doped Lithium Manganese Spinel Cells for Use in Rechargeable Battery Applications

Yakira J. Howarth and Terrill B. Atwater
U.S. Army Communications-Electronics Research, Development, and Engineering Center
Power Division – Command, Power, and Integration

Abstract: *Lithium manganese oxide doped with potassium and cobalt forms a promising cathode material for lithium-ion cells used in high-rate and pulse applications. The two dopants work to enhance the robustness of the spinel matrix thereby maintaining the electrochemistry's reversibility throughout abusive cycling conditions. Synthesized with the stoichiometric formula $Li_xK_yMn_{2-z}Co_zO_4$ where with x=1, y=0.1, and z=0.1-0.2, and tested in a cell against metallic lithium, the doped spinel material proves to be effective at allowing for the cell overcharge necessary to sink pulses of power from energy harvesting devices. This paper will present high-rate discharge, pulse and constant current cycling, and deep discharge test data from tests performed to gather baseline cell performance data as well as simulate the power demands of high-power and pulse technologies. It will additionally be shown that through unregulated constant voltage charging tests Li // $Li_xK_yMn_{2-z}Co_zO_4$ cells were able to successfully maintain reversibility and exhibit great potential for maximizing energy recovery in rechargeable battery applications.*

Keywords
Lithium-ion batteries; $LiK_xMn_2O_4$; Energy harvesting; Rechargeable batteries; Rechargeable lithium cells

Introduction
New and expanding Army capabilities continuously drive the need for higher-energy, higher-power, and longer-lasting power sources. The movement towards directed energy (DE) and electronic warfare (EW) technologies requires higher-rate and more robust electrochemistries to meet the demand of rapid-fire and pulse applications[1-4]. Though traditional lithium-ion batteries can often meet these energy needs, quick and sporadic discharging causes degradation of the cells, thereby limiting their effectiveness and lifespan[3-5]. In order to overcome this obstacle, a reinforced lithium-ion cathode material is being investigated to maintain its reversibility and stability when used in these abusive cycling conditions.

When doped with potassium and cobalt, lithium manganese spinel ($Li_xMn_2O_4$) cathodes are able to overcome many of the cycle-life obstacles of commercial spinel cells by preventing matrix degradation. Capacity fading in $Li_xMn_2O_4$ cells occurs due to the mechanical strain placed on the skeletal structure during the insertion and extraction of lithium upon charge and discharge, respectively[3,4,6-8]. The potassium and cobalt dopants work to both stabilize the spinel matrix as well as improve its overall rate capability for use in high-power and pulse applications.

This paper will investigate the robustness of potassium and cobalt-doped lithium manganese spinel cells when cycled in abusive conditions. $Li_xK_yMn_{2-z}Co_zO_4$ was tested against metallic lithium using active material with concentrations x=1, y=0.1, and z=0.1, z=0.14, and z=0.2 produced through a two-step synthesis method. Tests included high-rate discharge, pulse cycling, deep discharging, prolonged cycling, and unregulated constant voltage charging.

Background
Lithium manganese spinel ($Li_xMn_2O_4$) is an attractive cathode material for rechargeable lithium ion cells due to their low cost, high energy density, and environmental-friendliness[1,5,9]. The spinel structure provides a lattice for lithium intercalation where lithium is removed on charge and inserted on discharge according to the following reversible reaction

$$LiMn_2O_4 \leftrightharpoons Li_xMn_2O_4 + (1-x)Li^+ + (1-x)e^-$$

However, repeatedly inserting and extracting lithium cations to and from the spinel structure can result in irreversible lattice damage that limits a battery's cyclability and lifespan by means of "capacity fading."[3-6]

In order to prevent the degradation of the spinel matrix and cathodic capacity fading, doping the $Li_xMn_2O_4$ material was investigated as a means of stabilizing the lattice and prolonging the cells' lifespan. As part of the testing procedure, the unregulated constant voltage cycling revealed exciting results about the spinel electrochemistry's capabilities. Not only didn't the cell degrade after these abusive tests, but it was actually revived to an improved state of performance. This could lead to new conclusions about using the doped $Li_xMn_2O_4$ material in rechargeable battery applications.

Experimental

$Li_xK_yMn_{2-z}Co_zO_4$ was prepared using a two-step synthesis method where a manganese mixed metal oxide compound is first produced through a hydrothermal process and subsequently reacted with LiOH and KOH in a solid state reaction to form the final product. The cathode electrodes were then fabricated using the active $Li_xK_yMn_{2-z}Co_zO_4$ material combined with carbon black and PTFE, and formed into button cells versus metallic lithium anodes. The concentrations of lithium and potassium were chosen to be x=1 and y=0.1 based on previous research, and concentrations of z=0.1, z=0.14, and z=0.2 were used to analyze the effects of varied cobalt concentrations.

The $MnCoO_x$ mixed metal oxide precursor material was synthesized by adding ammonium hydroxide to a manganese acetate and cobalt acetate mixture dissolved in water. It was then dry mixed in a Random Orbit Mixer Mill with the appropriate concentrations of LiOH and KOH and heated at 800°C for 72 hours and 30°C for 48 hours to facilitate the chemical reaction yielding $Li_xK_yMn_{2-z}Co_zO_4$. To form the cathodes, this active ingredient was combined with carbon black, PTFE, and isopropanol using a mortar and pestle, calendared, and punched into 1.25 cm discs. This yielded 0.1 g cathodes which were pressed into coin cells welded with aluminum mesh and tested against metallic lithium pressed into nickel mesh. Three nonwoven glass separators were used between the electrodes and wicked with the electrolyte of 1 molar $LiPF_6$ in diethyl, dimethyl, and ethylene carbonates.

An ARBIN MSTAT4 Battery Cyclersystem was used for the tests. All cells were initially cycled at 2 mA between 3.5 V and 4.5 V in order to establish a baseline performance. This test was then run at different intervals throughout the cells' abusive testing in order to compare performance to the cells' baseline. The first 8 tests performed consisted of 10 charge and discharge cycles at 2 mA with a lower cutoff at 3.5 V and an upper cutoff at either 4.5, 5, or 5.25 V. Test 9 was a deep discharge test which alternated 10 cycles of discharging down to 3.5 V and 2.25 V. Tests 10-16 were unregulated constant voltage tests with a baseline test run in the middle, and tests 17-23 pulse charged and discharged the cells at constant voltage for 30 seconds, 1 minute, or 45 seconds, with a baseline test performed after each run. In total, cells were cycled 190 times and maintained their stability and functionality throughout all simulated battery conditions.

Results and Discussion

$LiK_{0.1}Mn_{2-z}Co_zO_4$ with cobalt concentrations of z=0.1, z=0.14, and z=0.2 were all cycled at 2 mA between 4.5 and 3.5 V in order to establish the cells' baseline performance before any abusive testing. The initial 10 charge and discharge cycles for a cell from the z=0.14 batch can be seen below in its differential capacity curves in Figure 1 along with an exemplary galvanostatic charge and discharge curve in Figure 2. The specific differential capacity chart plots the cell's capacity increase and decrease as a function of potential, here illustrating the reproducible thermodynamics throughout all 10 charge and discharge cycles.

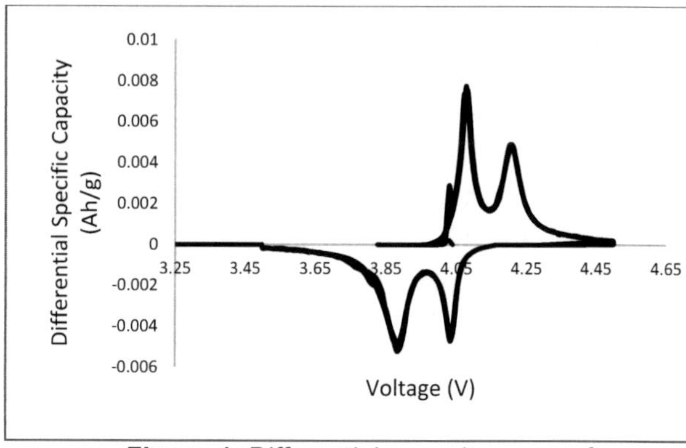

Figure 1: Differential capacity curve of Li \\ $LiK_{0.1}Mn_{1.86}Co_{0.14}O_4$ initial baseline cycling

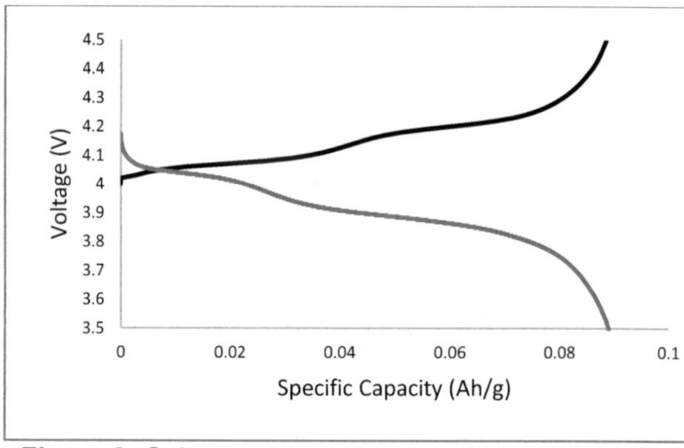

Figure 2: Galvanostatic charge and discharge curves of Li \\ $LiK_{0.1}Mn_{1.86}Co_{0.14}O_4$ initial baseline cycling

After 80 cycles of being discharged to 3.5 V, Li \\ $LiK_{0.1}Mn_{1.86}Co_{0.14}O_4$ cells were discharged down to 2.25 V to test their deep discharge ability. The cells were subsequently charged and discharged again between 4.5 and 3.5 V to demonstrate that there were no negative effects on the spinel material as a result of the deep discharge. Figure 3 shows the differential capacity curves of 10 cycles alternating between discharging down to 2.25 V and 3.5 V, and Figure 4 shows a single deep discharge down to 2.25 V followed by a normal discharge down to 3.5 V to illustrate the lack of negative effects on the cell.

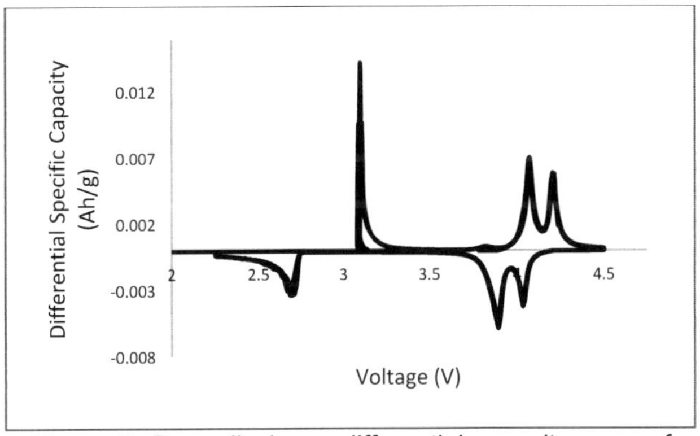

Figure 3: Deep discharge differential capacity curve of Li \\ $LiK_{0.1}Mn_{1.86}Co_{0.14}O_4$ down to 2.25 V

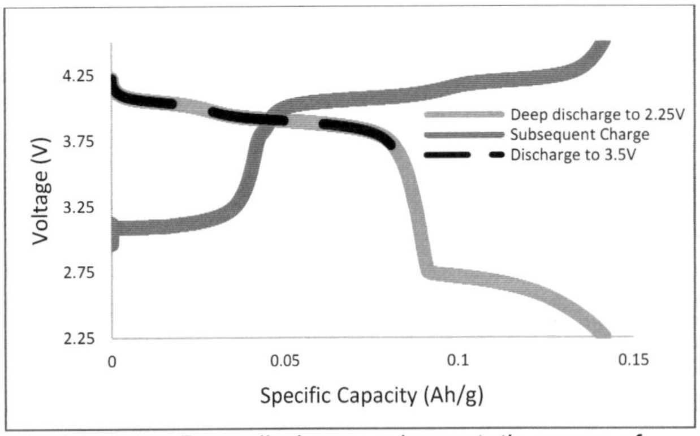

Figure 4: Deep discharge galvanostatic curves of Li \\ $LiK_{0.1}Mn_{1.86}Co_{0.14}O_4$

A series of tests were then performed holding the Li \\ $LiK_{0.1}Mn_{1.86}Co_{0.14}O_4$ cells at a constant voltage for varying lengths of time in order to demonstrate the cells' ability to function after unregulated constant voltage charging and discharging. These tests were performed after 90 cycles of 2 mA charge and discharge tests to varying voltage cutoffs. Cells were first held for 30 minutes at 4.5 V, rested for 30 minutes, held at 3.5 V for 30 minutes, and then rested for 30 minutes. This test was repeated a second time, followed by a test with a 120 minute hold at 4.5 V and 3.5 V with an hour rest after each voltage. A fourth test was performed holding the cells at 4.75 and 3.5 V for 60 minutes with 60 minute rests after each voltage. Figure 5 below shows the initial cycling differential specific capacity curves of the Li \\ $LiK_{0.1}Mn_{1.86}Co_{0.14}O_4$ cells, Figure 6 shows the cells at 70 cycles before the four voltage clamp tests, and Figure 7 shows the 12 cells after the tests. It can be seen from the initial cycling data to the data after 70 cycles that the performance began to vary between the 12 cells. After the four constant voltage tests, not only did the cells recover to their initial state, they even improved. The exact overlapping of the differential capacity curves for all 12 cells show that the thermodynamics and kinetic end-state are equivalent. These results indicate that a stable end-state exists for the spinel chemistry that a constant voltage test could initiate in order to revive and rematch separate cells that have deviated from each other.

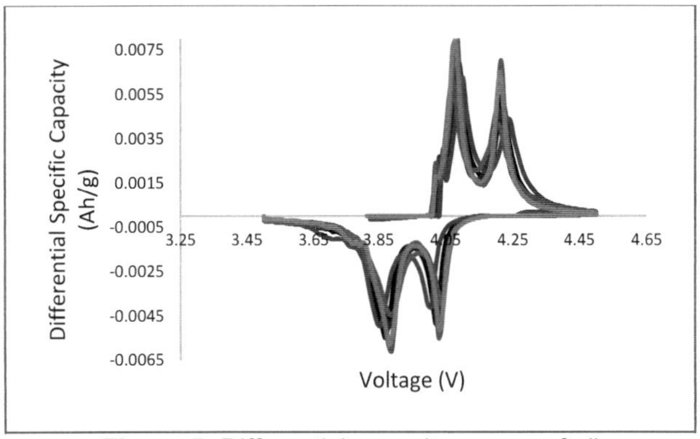

Figure 5: Differential capacity curves of all Li \\ $LiK_{0.1}Mn_{1.86}Co_{0.14}O_4$ cells' initial baseline cycling

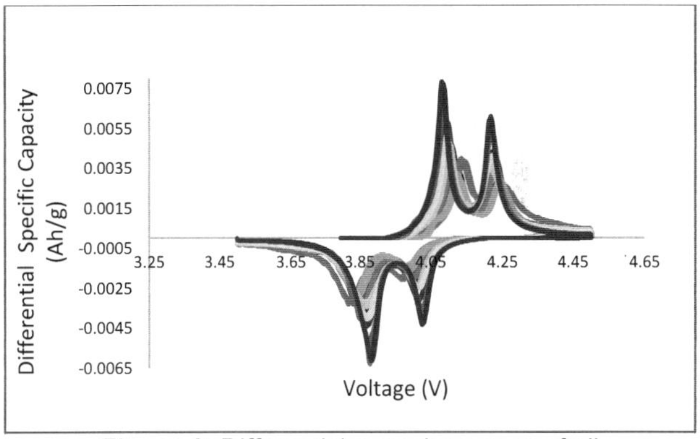

Figure 6: Differential capacity curves of all Li \\ $LiK_{0.1}Mn_{1.86}Co_{0.14}O_4$ cells after 70 cycles

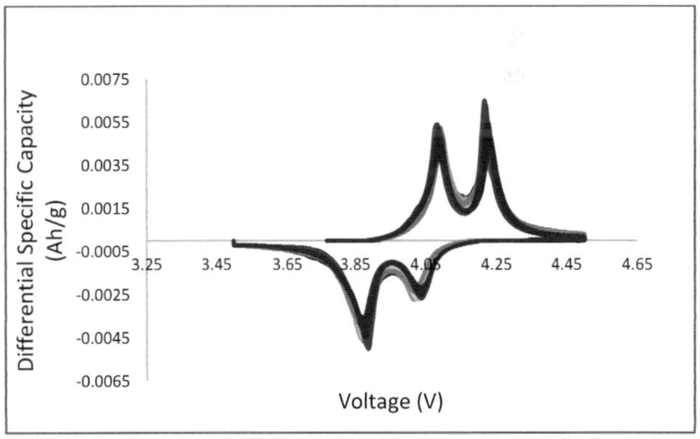

Figure 7: Differential capacity curves of all Li \\ $LiK_{0.1}Mn_{1.86}Co_{0.14}O_4$ cells after 4 unregulated constant voltage tests

Following the unregulated constant voltage tests, all cells were then subjected to abusive pulse charge and discharge cycling with varied pulse times. Figure 8 below shows an exemplary pulse test where cells were both pulse charged and pulse discharged for 1 minute pulses between 4.5 and 3.5 V. This test was following 150 cycles already performed which included all baseline cycling, unregulated voltage cycling, and pulse cycling tests. Figure 9 shows a 2 mA baseline test performed following 170 cycles and demonstrates the robustness of the cell chemisty throughout the simulated pulse applications. Though the cells lost capacity over the 170 cycles, the overlapping differential capacity curves show that the thermodynamics and kinetics of the spinel material were maintained.

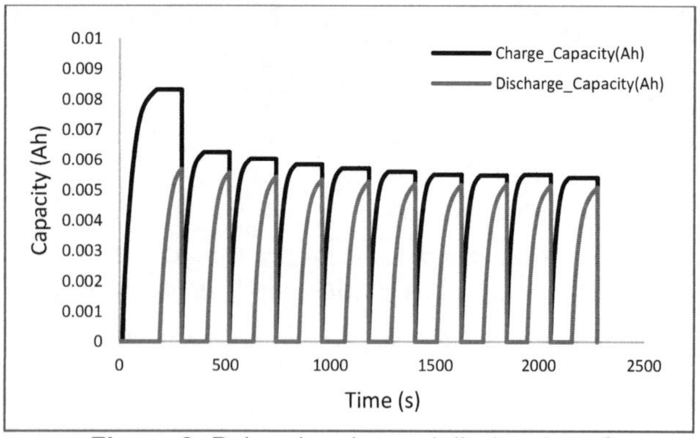

Figure 8: Pulse charging and discharging of Li \\ $LiK_{0.1}Mn_{1.86}Co_{0.14}O_4$ cell

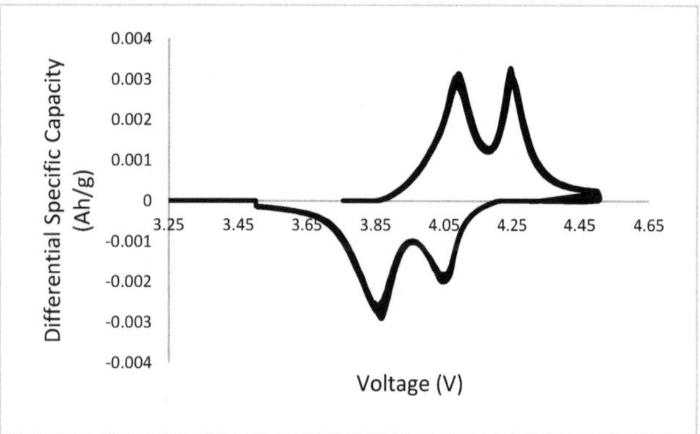

Figure 9: Baseline test differential capacity curves of all Li \\ $LiK_{0.1}Mn1.86Co_{0.14}O_4$ cells after 170 abusive cycles

Conclusion

Lithium manganese spinel doped with potassium and cobalt was synthesized and tested versus metallic lithium in order to evaluate its strengths in rechargeable battery applications. The robustness of the material was demonstrated through prolonged cycling, deep discharge, pulse charge and discharge, and unregulated constant voltage tests. Stable thermodynamics and kinetics were observed throughout abusive high-rate and pulse simulations, indicating the material's promise for use in such demanding technologies. Furthermore, not only were the cells able to operate under the unregulated constant voltage tests, but showed their ability to recover and even exceed their initial performance capabilities by reaching a stable and matching end-state. These results could have exciting implications for using the doped spinel electrochemistry in rechargeable battery applications that need exact cell matching for optimal performance. Future research into the mechanisms behind this revived thermodynamic and kinetic stability of the $Li_xK_yMn_{2-z}Co_zO_4$ material will be necessary to best optimize the performance and usage of these cells.

References

1. Atwater TB and AJ Salkind, "Advanced Manganese Oxide Material for Rechargeable Lithium Cells," *Journal of Power Sources*, vol. 162, no. 2, pp. 773-779, 2006.
2. Ohzuku T and RJ Brodd, "An Overview of Positive-Electrode Materials for Advanced Lithium-Ion Batteries," *Journal of Power Sources*, vol. 174, no. 2, pp. 449-456, 2007.
3. Fergus JW, "Recent Developments in Cathode Materials for Lithium Ion Batteries," *Journal of Power Sources*, vol. 195, pp. 939-954, 2010.
4. Dou S, "Review and Prospects of Mn-Based Spinel Compounds as Cathode Materials for Lithium-Ion Batteries," *Ionics*, vol. 21, no. 11, pp. 3001-3030, 2015.
5. Fey GTK, Lu CZ and TP Kumar, "Preparation and Electrochemical Properties of High-Voltage Cathode Materials, $LiM_yNi_{0.5-y}Mn_{1.5}O_4$ (Me=Fe, Cu, Al, Mg; *y*=0.0-0.4)," *Journal of Power Sources*, vol. 115, pp. 332-345, 2003.
6. Li X and Y Xu, "Spinel $LiMn_2O_4$ Active Material with High Capacity Retention," *Applied Surface Science*, vol. 253, pp. 8592-8596, 2007.
7. Wolska E, Tova M, Andrzejewski B, Nowicki W, Darul J, Piszora P and M Knapp, "Structural and Magnetic Properties of the Iron Substituted Lithium-Manganese Spinel Oxides," *Solid State Sciences*, vol. 8, pp. 31-36, 2006.
8. Thackeray MM, "Structural Considerations of Layered and Spinel Lithiated Oxides for Lithium Ion Batteries," *Journal of The Electrochemistry Society*, vol. 142, no. 8, pp. 2558-2563, 1995.
9. Bang HJ, Donepudi VS and J Prakash, "Preparation and Characterization of Partially Substituted $LiM_yMn_{2-y}O_4$ (M=Ni, Co, Fe) Spinel Cathodes for Li-ion Batteries," *Electrochimica Acta*, vol. 48, pp. 443-451, 2002.

Ultra-Thin, Flexible Solid-State Battery with Integrated Solar Energy Harvesting

Brian Berland[1], Calvin Sprangers[1], Alvin Compaan[2], Victor Plotnikov[2], David Carey[3], John Olenick[3], and Kathy Olenick[3]

1-ITN Energy Systems, Inc., 8130 Shaffer Parkway, Littleton, CO, USA 80127
2- Lucintech, Inc., 1510 North Westwood Avenue, Toledo, OH, USA 43606
3- ENrG, Inc, 175 Rano St., Suite 101, Buffalo, NY, USA 14207
bberland@itnes.com / 1-303-285-5107

Abstract: *With funding from the FlexTech Alliance, ITN Energy Systems and ENrG Inc. have demonstrated promising new thin, solid-state lithium rechargeable batteries (SSLB) capable of providing the high power and energy required for many flexible electronics, wireless devices/sensors, wearables, medical devices, unmanned vehicles, portable power, etc. Combining ITN's SSLB with ENrG's ultra-thin flexible ceramic solves the capacity and packaging issues that have thus far limited the thin film battery technology to niche applications. With a capacity up to 100 mAh in a thickness less than 250 microns, including hermetic packaging, the new SSLB enables energy density greater than 1,000 Wh/l while maintaining the benefits of enhanced safety and durability provided by the all solid state chemistry. Results are also presented for a new Flexible Integrated Power Pack (FIPP) that adds in-field solar recharging by combing the SSLB with Lucintech's high efficiency CdTe solar cells.*

Keywords: Solid-State Battery; Ultra-Thin Battery; High Efficiency CdTe Solar Cell; Solar Energy Harvesting; Thin, Flexible Power Source; Flexible Electronic Power

Introduction

While Li-ion batteries have changed the world we live in, the industry as a whole struggles to meet market demands for ultra-thin batteries required for the next generation of flexible electronics, medical devices, wearables, and wireless devices in support of the Internet of Things. While all device manufacturers want more power, current batteries simply have no way to achieve the desired power, particularly for applications demanding total packaged thickness less than 500 microns. Within a defined volume, the problem is one of space allocation to include: (1) the battery (power/energy), (2) hermetic, protective packaging, and (3) terminals/connections of the battery to the device.

Figure 1 shows the heart of the challenge, ***typical lithium ion packaging materials alone are ~200 microns thick. With a large customer base desiring batteries with a total packaged thickness of 100-250 microns, current battery packaging solutions use the entire thickness allotment leaving literally no room for the active battery materials.*** The emphasis traditionally has been on battery material improvements over novel packaging.

Li-Ion Battery Encapsulation Materials
(Pouch Cell Packaging)

Layers from Outside to Inside 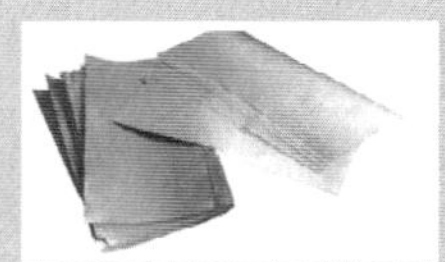	Polyamide Adhesive Aluminum Foil Adhesive Polypropylene
Thickness	**111 µm (Each Side!)**

Packaging thickness alone ~ 220 µm

Li-Ion Batteries Use Packaging that Limits Their Attainable Energy Density in a Thin, Flexible Package

Figure 1. Encapsulation materials ultimately limit the battery's total packaged thickness.[1] Much thinner batteries with higher energy density are desired for a number of markets including medical devices, wearables, flexible electronics, unmanned vehicles, portable power, etc.

The advantage of solid state batteries, and thin film solid state batteries in particular, is that there are no liquids to contain. Therefore, the substrate itself can be an integral part of the packaging without adding significant volume. As a result, thin film solid state batteries can achieve substantially higher energy density. Further, without the traditional packaging, solid state batteries can maintain the same energy density even as the total packaged thickness decreases to less than 500 microns.

Ultra-Thin Solid State Battery

In a project sponsored by the FlexTech Alliance, ITN and ENrG demonstrated the feasibility of high energy density solid state lithium batteries (SSLB) on ultra-thin, flexible yttria-stabilized zirconia substrates (YSZ). Taking advantage of the impervious nature of the YSZ, SSLB batteries are produced by vertically cells on YSZ with an sealing adhesive between layers to help protect the battery materials from moisture and oxygen. Figure 2 shows that, without the need for additional packaging, the resultant SSLB battery can be less than 100 µm total packaged thickness. To enhance the overall energy density, over 80% of the YSZ area is coated with active battery materials to achieve SSLB with a range of capacity from less than 1 mAh to greater than 1,000 mAh.

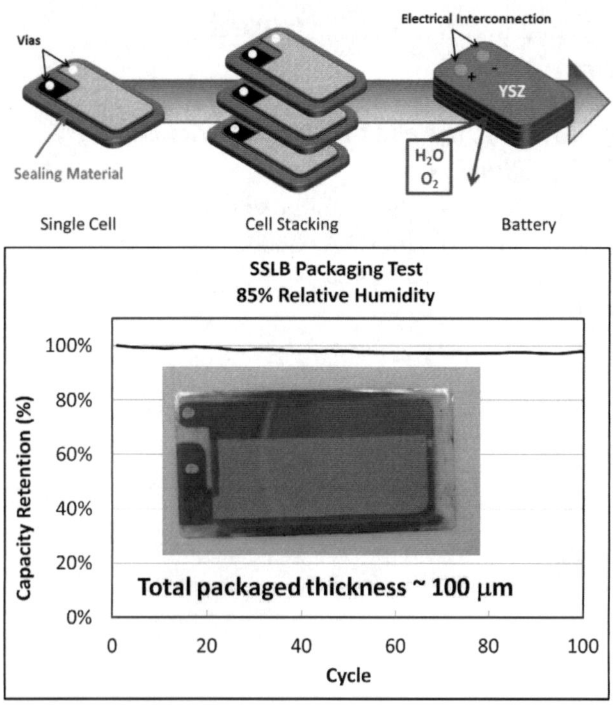

Figure 2. SSLB packaging employs YSZ as both the substrate and hermetic packaging with edge sealing adhesives between layers (top). SSLB with thickness <100 μm shows stable cycling in high humidity.

Figure 2 also shows SSLB employing this packaging scheme are able to cycle in high humidity with only minimal capacity fade. Similarly, SSLB initially powering devices in ambient have been stored, also in ambient conditions, without substantial loss of capacity for greater than eight months. Based on these tests, as well as measured water vapor transport measurements for the packaging materials and accelerated high temperature and high humidity tests, the SSLB packaging is projected to have over five year shelf life with less than one percent capacity loss.

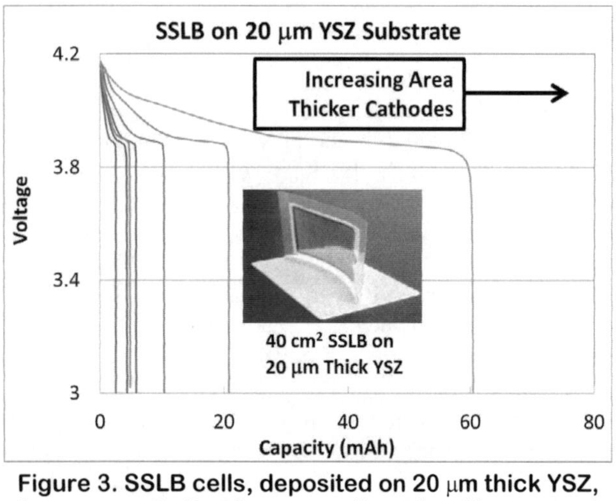

Figure 3. SSLB cells, deposited on 20 μm thick YSZ, have capacity that increases linearly with area and cathode thickness; inset is a large area SSLB.

In addition to the novel packaging, ITN and ENrG have recently deposited SSLB on YSZ substrates with a thickness of 20 microns. In some cases, the SSLB thickness is almost as thick as the substrate, leading to very high energy density. Further, the SSLB can be deposited over a range of areas and cathode thickness, all using the same materials and processes. SSLB capacity scales linearly with area and cathode thickness. Figure 3 shows SSLB cells provide very attractive single cell capacities from 1-60 mAh for cells that vary in area from 5 cm^2 to 100 cm^2.

Further, Figure 4 shows the SSLB capacity is preserved as the layers are stacked. In this case, two roughly 4 mAh cells are connected in parallel to achieve a battery with 8 mAh capacity (C/4 means the battery is discharged over 4 hours). Similar results have been achieved with up to 7 SSLB cells and with individual cell capacities up to 50 mAh. The resultant SSLB battery capacities range from 1 to 340 mAh. Consequently, a scalable range of SSLB can be provided unique to each customer's needs while maintaining standard materials and processes. Only the geometry, i.e. cell area, number of cells, etc., need modification to achieve the custom SSLB designs tailored to each application end use requirements.

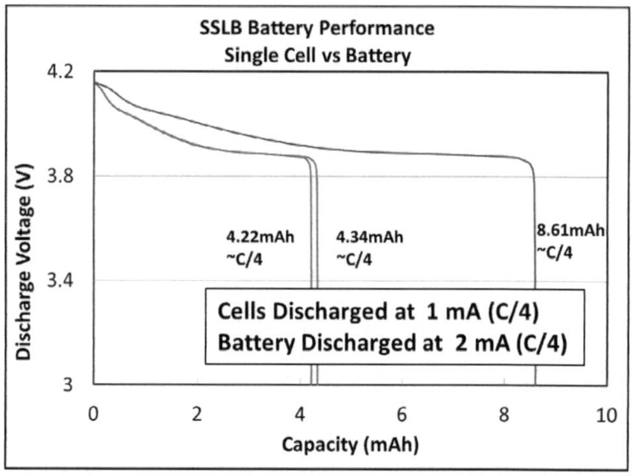

Figure 4. SSLB battery capacity scales with the number of cells in the stack.

Given the heightened concerns with lithium batteries, most recently highlighted by the Samsung Galaxy fires, we confirmed the SSLB's solid state nature is safe and avoids fires. Up to 20 mAh SSLB have passed critical safety tests such as UL1642 short circuit and crush tests with only modest heating (45°C) and no fires.

Another key advantage of the SSLB is its ability to support high power pulsing. Figure 5 shows SSLB can support prolonged high current pulses while maintaining a battery voltage greater than 3.5 V that is required for many commercial electronics. With rates as high as 10C at the beginning of life and averaging ~6C over the entire discharge range, the SSLB easily powers a range of devices from wireless sensors with RF telemetry[2] to flexible displays and smart watches.

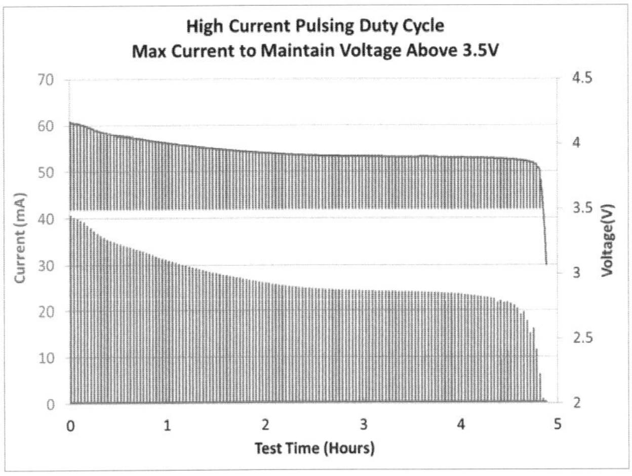

Figure 5. The low SSLB internal resistance supports repeated high current pulses over the entire discharge; in this case 40 mA pulses (10C) at the beginning of life and ~25 mA on average (6C).

Specific to the needs of the defense community, ITN and ENrG worked with the FlexTech Alliance to evaluate the potential benefits of the ultra-thin SSLB technology for powering flexible electronics. As a test case, we identified a flexible electronic print device (FEP) that requires sustained high current pulsing over long durations. Figure 6 shows the SSLB performance relative to a baseline commercial-off-the-shelf (COTS) lithium battery.

A 20 mAh SSLB was able to power the FEP for almost twice as long as was achieved with a COTS battery that also has more than eight times larger volume. Further, a range of SSLB was able to power the FEP for durations that vary linearly with the battery size. Thus, this particular customer now has new options to operate the FEP with a dramatically smaller battery, for significantly longer times in a similar footprint, or some combination of both. Similar benefits are expected for a range of defense and commercial applications.

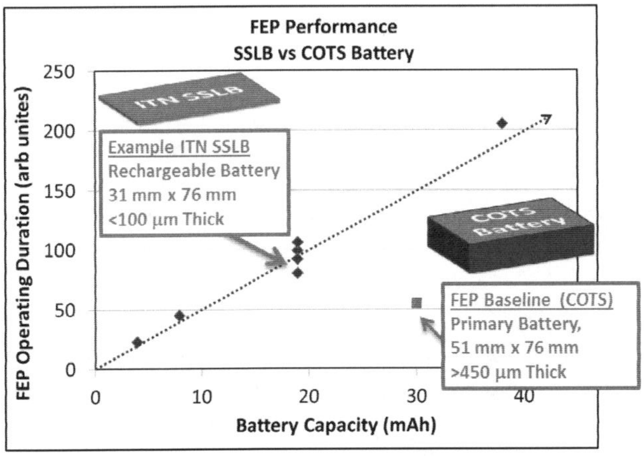

Figure 6. SSLB achieved over twice the duration with less than one-fourth the size of baseline batteries in powering a flexible electronic device test case chosen in concert with the FlexTech Alliance.

Other promising features of the new SSLB technology are:

- Rapid Charging, i.e. Charging to 75% of full capacity in ~20 minutes,
- Micro-SSLB cells with area as small as 1 mm^2 with Photolithographic Patterning, and
- Flexible power sources; SSLB with Bend Radius as small as 10 mm have been demonstrated

Ultra-Thin Solid State Battery with Integrated Solar Energy Harvesting

Recently, the SSLB has been combined with Lucintech's high efficiency CdTe solar cells to provide in-field recharging. The new product, called a Flexible Integrated Power Pack (FIPP), integrates the SSLB and CdTe PV in a single, vertically integrated package. CdTe PV was chosen not only for its high efficiency, but also due to its ability to be fabricated in a "superstrate configuration" where the thin film solar cell is deposited on the bottom side of the YSZ sheet. This enables the CdTe to share packaging with the SSLB to maximize the amount of energy generation and storage in a very thin package. Namely, the SSLB essentially serves as the backsheet for PV encapsulation eliminating the need for additional sealing adhesive and YSZ layers.

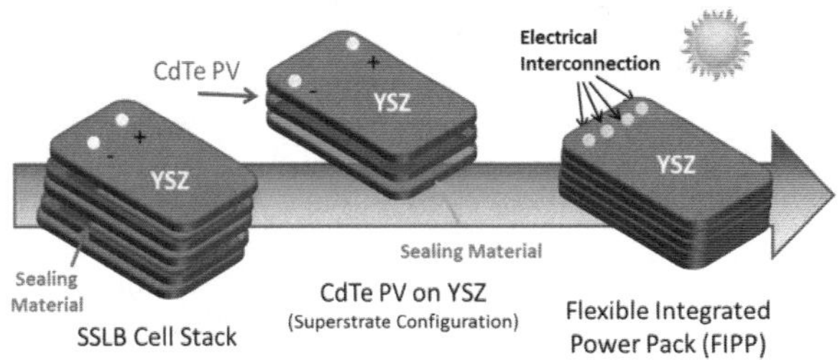

Figure 7. Flexible Integrated Power Pack (FIPP) combining the SSLB and high efficiency CdTe PV in a single vertically integrated package.

In a new project sponsored by the FlexTech Alliance, the CdTe has successfully been deposited on ultra-thin YSZ substrates (20 μm thick). Figure 7 shows that efficiencies approaching 7% at full sun (AM1.5) have been achieved with CdTe mini-modules that are 25 mm x 76 mm. These dimensions match those of a 20 mAh SSLB that is two layers thick. As the materials and process are further optimized, we expect to reach efficiencies of 10-15% by the third quarter of 2018. Similar to the SSLB, over 80% of the YSZ substrate is covered with active PV materials.

Another benefit of the thin film CdTe PV is the cells are monolithically integrated from cells into modules using a laser scribing and ink fill process. The number of cells in a mini-module can then be optimized to match the control circuitry requirements that route the PV to charge the battery as well as maintain the SSLB in desired voltage range. Using this approach, module voltages from 1-20V are possible within the package size shown in Figure 8.

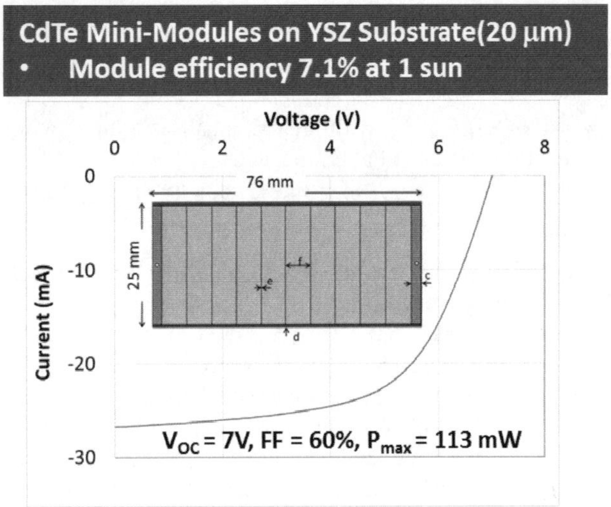

Figure 8. CdTe mini-modules on YSZ achieved ~7% efficiency. Based on recent small cells with 11% efficiency, module efficiencies approaching 20% should be possible with further optimization.

Based on a modest 14% CdTe efficiency, an ultra-thin FIPP, 31 mm x 76 mm x 250 µm, will produce ~250 mW and charge a 60 mAh battery in one hour. Figure 9 shows a control circuit that supports the critical FIPP functions:

- Solar charging of the SSLB
- Maintaining the SSLB in the desired voltage range
- Powering a Load with Either the PV or SSLB

All of this is done with a minimal number of microelectronic circuit elements vertically integrated into the FIPP or integrated with the main system electronics.

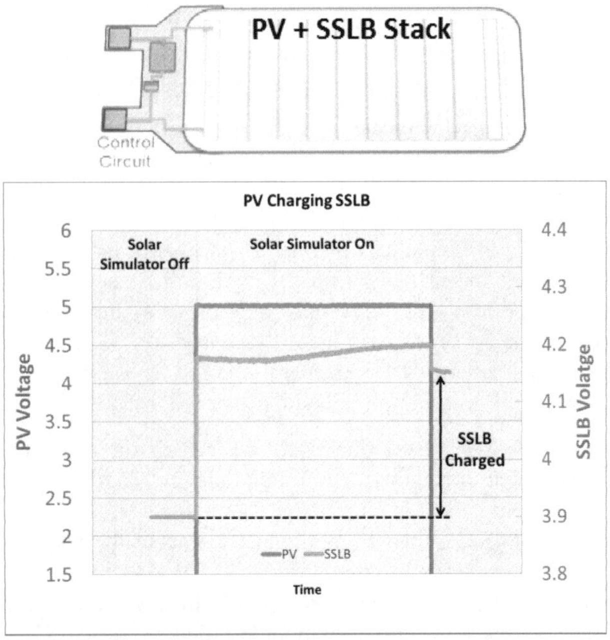

Figure 9. FIPP schematic with integrated control circuit (top); Breadboard configuration demonstration of FIPP functionality (bottom).

Summary

Promising new SSLB and FIPP products have been fabricated on ultra-thin YSZ substrates. By eliminating the need for extraneous packaging to protect these devices from water and oxygen, extraordinary energy densities have been achieved. Current SSLB products are achieving up to 600 Wh/l. Recent demonstrations of SSLB on YSZ as thin as 12 µm, in conjunction with other modest materials and process improvements, support a roadmap to SSLB energy density of greater than 1,000 Wh/l and greater than 200 Wh/kg.

Even more remarkably, the vertical integration of the CdTe PV and SSLB on YSZ substrates enables energy density >400 Wh/l, including the energy harvesting materials thickness. This is higher than many state of the art thin batteries alone. Table 1 shows some important properties for both the SSLB and SSLB + PV products.

Table 1. Example properties for a SSLB and SSLP+PV Device on Ultra-Thin YSZ. Both achieve very high energy density.

	SSLB	SSLB + PV
Substrate Area	31 mm x 76 mm	31 mm x 76 mm
Packaged Thickness	<250 µm	
Capacity/Power	SSLB Capacity: Up to 60 mAh	PV Power: Up to 215 mW
Charge Time	~1 hour	
Energy Density		
Today	600 Wh/l	>400 Wh/l
Roadmap	>1,000 Wh/l	(Includes PV)

Acknowledgements

The authors gratefully acknowledge support for this work funded in part by the FlexTech Alliance under Grants from the Air Force Research Lab and Army Research Lab:

- ARL TIA W911NF-10-3-0001
- AFRL CA FA8650-15-2-5401

In addition, we would like to thank Dr. Melissa Grupen-Shemansky for her guidance in the project including helpful input on the needs and shortcomings of current thin, flexible power sources for the flexible hybrid electronics industry.

References

1 Example of typical Li-Ion Packaging Materials, see http://www.mtixtl.com/AluminumLaminatedFilmforPolymerBatteryCase100mmWx210mmL50pcs.aspx

2 See for example, Phase II SBIR Final Report "Multifunctional Fibers for Energy Storage in Advanced EVA systems," NASA contract number NNJ07JA13C.

A New Design Approach to Li-Ion Cells for LEO Applications

Chengsong Ma[1*], Yannick Borthomieu[2]

1. Saft SDD, 107 Beaver Ct, Cockeysville, MD 21030, USA
2. Saft SDD, Rue Georges Leclanche BP1039, 86060 Poitiers Cedex 9, France
*Email: Chengsong.ma@saftbatteries.com / 1-410 568 6487

Abstract: *Saft has started to investigate a new Li-Ion cell chemistry, Lithium Titanate (LTO) for space. The new space chemistry has excellent cold temperature chargeability, and therefore the complex thermal management for a space battery can be reduced. Prove of concept LTO cells were built in 2017 and have started LEO testing up to 80% DOD discharge with different C rates. This higher percentage DOD enables Saft's LTO cells to achieve 92Wh/Kg usable energy, which is superior to existing 18650 cells for LEO applications. The early stage LEO cycling shows good capacity retention.*

Keywords: Low earth orbit; LEO; Lithium Titanate; LTO; space; Li ion batteries; high DOD; high rate discharge; thermal management.

Introduction

A graphite anode is typically used in Space Li-Ion cells, graphite anode provides energy and cycle life for batteries used at Geosynchronous orbit (GEO) and some Low earth orbit (LEO) applications. But solid electrolyte interface (SEI) formation and Li intercalation potential of graphite is only 0.15V away from the Li potential limit its use for high rate charge and discharge which is required for some LEO applications. Graphite is prone to Li plating and causes safety concerns for the cells. Li plating on the anode consumes active Li (capacity loss) and increases the internal resistance. A state-of-the-art LEO 18650 Li-Ion cell with graphite chemistry compensates for this by only using 20% depth of discharge (DOD) in order to maintain a good LEO life of 50000-70000 cycles and the usable energy is around 50Wh/kg to 75Wh/Kg at the cell level.

Lithium Titanate (LTO) has s spinal structure and it can be fast charged and discharged at high rate. This type of charge and discharge property brings more interest than a regular Li ion cell with graphite in high rate applications. Figure 1 shows the charge potential of both LTO and graphite vs Li potential. When it is at fully charge stage, graphite is very close to Li plating potential while LTO is 1.5V above. LTO does not form Lithium dendrite like graphite does. LTO does not have the type of SEI layer graphite does. LTO is safe and has excellent low temperature discharge characteristics and still maintains 80% of its capacity even at -30oC. LTO is a zero strain material when it fully charged only 0.2% volume change while graphite has 10-15% volume change at charge stage. The volume change of graphite during cycle caused SEI to crack and enable electrolyte decomposition. It caused long-term degradation in batteries with graphite anode. The zero strain property provides LTO exceptionally long cycle life than graphite.

Batteries with graphite anode use Cu foil as current collector due to Cu's stability at Li potential when graphite is fully charged. However, when a cell voltage drop to 0V anode potential will arrive above 3V vs Li and Cu will be oxidized at this potential and dissolve into electrolyte. Therefore it is not possible to store a battery with graphite anode at 0V of cell voltage.

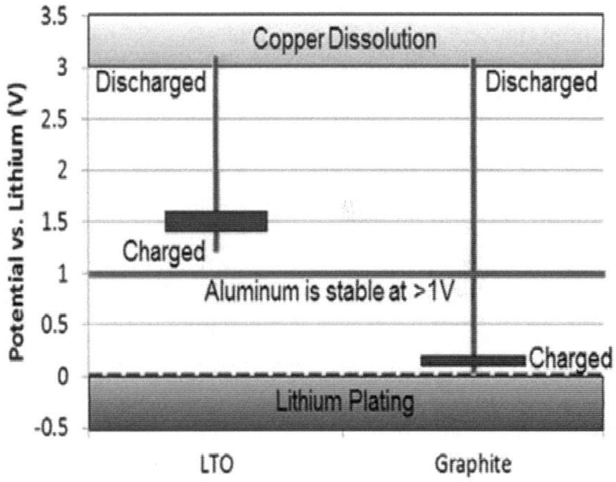

Figure 1 Voltage of LTO and graphite vs. Lithium potential

Satellite batteries are always stored on ground and on launch pad for long time. Batteries storage at very low state of charge (SOC) or even at 0V is very beneficial to human handing and space vehicle safety.

Saft has started to investigate Lithium Titanate (LTO) for space application. Since LTO is 1.5V separated from Li plating. An aluminum current collector is used for LTO anodes and makes zero voltage (0V) storage feasible (see Figure 2).

Figure 2 Saft prototype LTO cell with 0V storage capability

LTO is not sensitive to Li plating and can be used for high current pulse cycles as some special LEO applications. LTO has excellent power capability and long mission life which suit perfectly for long LEO cycles. LTO as space chemistry has excellent cold temperature chargeability and therefore the complex thermal management for a space battery can be reduced or eliminated. LTO cells can be used for radar/agile LEO satellites with short time for recharge. Space cells with graphite anode are maintained at a 20°C ambient temperature. The thermal management to maintain at 20°C is costly. At higher or lower temperatures the cells don't perform well. LTO cell has good performance in a wide temperature window which would reduce thermal management cost. Low (or no) sensitivity to rate and depth of discharge will enable LTO based space cells to discharge down to very high DOD.

The drawback of LTO chemistry is the cell voltage of 2.2V vs. 3.6V of graphite cell so more LTO cells needed for same voltage battery system. (See Figure 3)

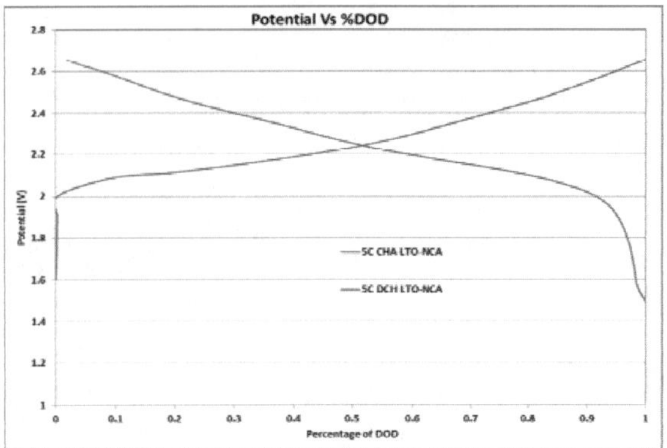

Figure 3 Voltage profile of LTO/NCA cell

Saft started working on the LTO cell development for the Navy in 2012, where our prototype cells demonstrated 80,000 cycles life at 15C pulse discharge rate with a very minor temperature rise. After 80,000 cycles our prototype cells still maintained more than 80% of original capacity as shown in Figure 4.

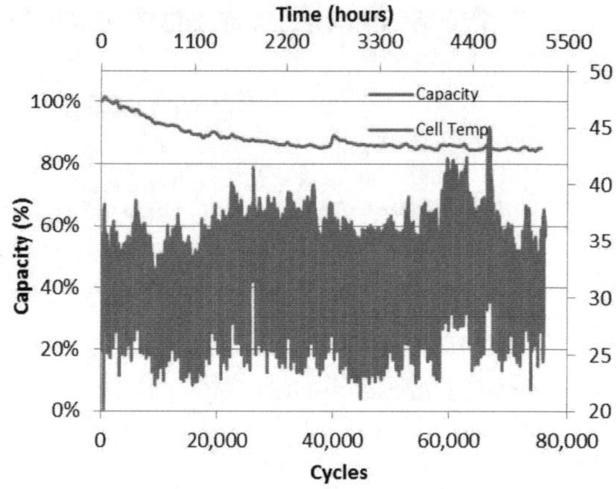

Figure 4 15C pulse cycle test of LTO cell

Prove of concept LTO cells were built in 2017 and have started LEO testing up to 80% DOD discharge with different C rates. This higher percentage DOD enables Saft's LTO cells to achieve 92Wh/Kg usable energy, which is superior to existing 18650 cells for LEO applications. The early stage LEO cycling shows good capacity retention.

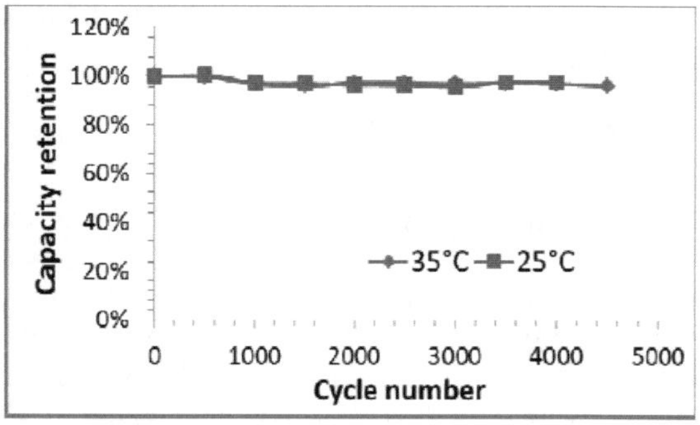

Figure 5a Saft prototype cell design-1, 0.85C charge and 1.2C discharge

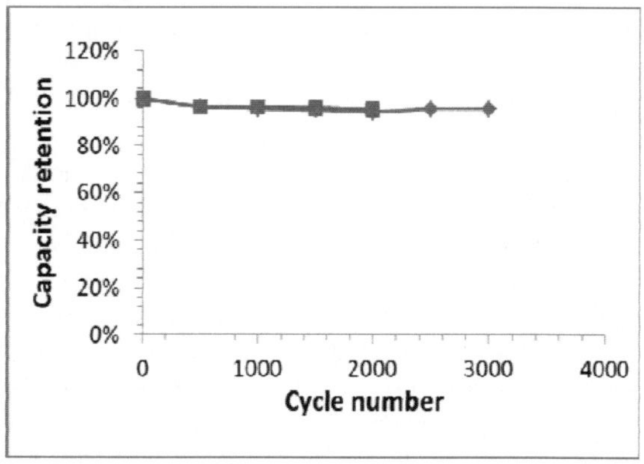

Figure 5b Saft prototype cell design-2, 0.85C charge and 1.2C discharge

Figure 5 a and b are the LEO test results of two different Saft proof of concept cells. Two different cell designs both have very good capacity retention at both 25oC and 35oC.

Table 1 Self-discharge of prototype LTO space cells

Cell number	50% SOC self-discharge (mV)
2	0.15
3	0.17
4	0.15
5	0.15
6	0.15
10	0.13
11	0.13
12	0.15
13	0.13
14	0.15
Average	0.146

The prototype LTO space cells had very low self-discharge when stored at 50% SOC as shown in Table 1.

Saft has expanded the test on LTO prototype cells to very cold and high temperature environments to check whether LTO cells survive after thermal management system removed. Figure 6 is 100% DOD cycle test at -20°C. These LTO cells maintained very good cycle life at such cold environment. There is no capacity fading after 350 cycles and cell impedance did not change.

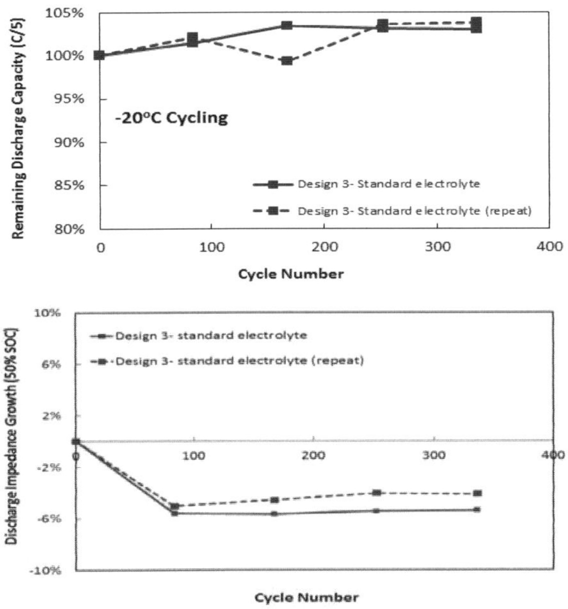

Figure 6 -20°C cycle, C/2 charge and discharge, no rest, 100% DOD

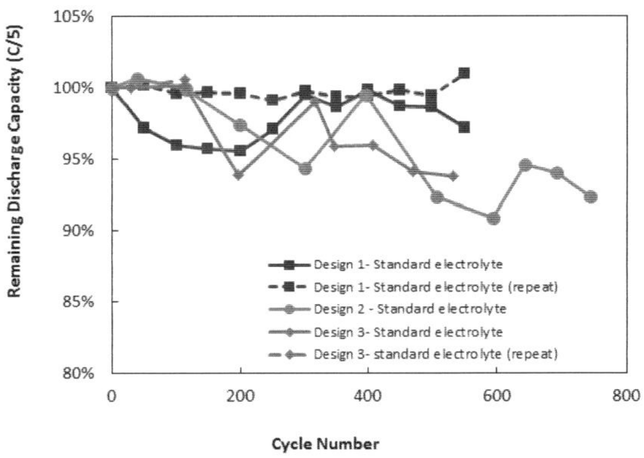

Figure 7 55°C cycle, C/2 charge and discharge no taper, 100% DOD

Figure 7 showed the cycle performance of several different designed LTO cells at 100% DOD and 55°C. Except design-1 cell most of the LTO cells showed slightly high capacity fading. It is well known that LTO can react with residual moisture in electrolyte to generate gas. LTO also can react with some of electrolyte solvents to generate gas at elevated temperature. The calculated gas generation rate in these particular cells is 0.013μmol/Ahr. Byproducts from these reactions can create a thin film on LTO particles. At high potential, electrolyte can oxidize on positive electrode, forming a film on cathode particles; oxidized species can transport to negative electrode, react with LTO and generate gas. It is very important to dry LTO electrode properly to remove residual moisture. Electrolyte salt plays an important role in suppressing gas generation rate. Saft is investigating different electrolyte salts to reduce gas generation at higher temperature.

Summary

Saft is developing a LTO based space cell with 0V storage capability. This LTO cell can be used for special high current discharge LEO applications. The temperature insensitive property of LTO will reduce the complex battery thermal management and reduce cost and weight of a space battery. A patent was filed for this application (#WO2017103641)

Acknowledgements

Authors would like to thank some early work supported from ONR. The space cell design and testing was funded under Saft incubator funding and a space customer.

Operando Spectroscopy of the Electrochemical Oxidation of Carbon Monoxide over Ni-YSZ Anode-Supported Solid Oxide Fuel Cells: A Study of Simulated Syngas Mixtures

William A. Maza[1], Daniel A. Steinhurst[2], Stanislav D. Tsoi[3], Jeffrey C. Owrutsky[3]

[1] National Research Council
Postdoctoral Fellow
U.S. Naval Research Laboratory
Washington, DC, USA

[2] Nova Research, Inc.
Alexandria, VA, USA

[3] Chemistry Division
U.S. Naval Research Laboratory
Washington, DC, USA

jeff.owrutsky@nrl.navy.mil

Abstract: *Solid oxide fuel cells (SOFCs) are attractive devices for power generation because they can operate under a variety of fuel feedstocks. Syngas (CO + H_2), as a fuel, is of particular interest as it is a major by-product of hydrocarbon logistics fuel steam reforming. However, the mechanism of electrochemical oxidation of CO in SOFCs is still not well understood. Herein,* ***operando*** *methods provide Fourier transform infrared emission spectra of the SOFC headspace together with thermal imaging data of the Ni-YSZ anode surface to probe reactions occurring in commercial anode-supported SOFCs operating on simulated syngas mixtures at 800 °C. These methods are combined with simultaneously collected electrochemical data to provide a comprehensive picture of processes occurring during fuel oxidation. Fourier transform infrared emission spectra show an increase in CO_2 and a decrease in CO with increasing cell polarization. There is less of an increase in CO_2 when CO is used as a fuel without H_2 suggesting a contribution to CO_2 production from syngas by the water-gas shift reaction as a result of H_2O formation upon polarization. Thermal imaging of the anode surface shows a small amount of surface heating ($\Delta T \sim 1$ °C) when using CO as a fuel in the absence of H_2 which is consistent with the exothermic partial oxidation of CO to CO_2. There is less of a temperature change at the anode surface with H_2 in the fuel. The results are discussed within the framework of current models of CO activation and oxidation at Ni-YSZ surfaces.*

Keywords: solid oxide fuel cell; SOFC; syngas; operando spectroscopy; infrared emission spectroscopy; thermal imaging.

Introduction

The catalyst mediated process of steam reforming of hydrocarbon feedstocks produces synthesis gas (syngas) whose composition is rich in carbon monoxide and hydrogen according to the generic scheme below [1].

$$C_nH_m + nH_2O \leftrightarrow nCO + \left(\frac{n+m}{2}\right)H_2$$

It has been shown that, in addition to H_2, CO can also serve as a fuel to operate a solid oxide fuel cell (SOFC) to generate chemically derived electrical power output [2]. Recent modelling of electrochemical data, however, suggests that the primary current generating process at low biases (relative to the open circuit potential, OCV) is H-spillover resulting from H_2 adsorption and dissociation at Ni-sites generating H_2O at the triple phase boundary (TPB) – where the Ni-anode, yttrium stabilized zirconia (YSZ) electrolyte, and gas phase reactants are all in contact [3]. Alternatively, at higher biases O-spillover – from O^{2-} ion diffusion from the YSZ bulk to vacancy sites at the YSZ surface to generate H_2O and CO_2 from Ni-adsorbed H and CO – is the major contributor to the overall SOFC current and power output.

Spectroscopic methods capable of directly observing the consumption of reactants and formation of chemical and electrochemical products under operational conditions are difficult due to the high temperatures required for SOFC operation. Both Raman and IR vibrational spectroscopic techniques have been developed in conjunction with near-infrared thermal imaging that can probe the chemical and thermal progress of high temperature catalytic and electrochemical reactions in real time [4-7]. Recently, *operando* high temperature Raman spectroscopy was used to monitor carbon deposition over a commercial Ni-YSZ anode cermet under simulated syngas mixtures of CO/H_2 at OCV and under galvanostatic polarization [8]. At OCV, coking was observed as evidenced by the presence of vibrational bands associated with ordered graphite in the presence of 14% CO and 14% H_2 at 675 °C. The intensities of these vibrational features were found to depend strongly on the applied bias suggesting a dependence on the electrochemical oxidation of CO to CO_2 or efficient oxidation of anode surface-bound carbon at higher current densities. The data presented here augment and expand on the previously reported *operando* Raman results by using *operando* Fourier transform infrared emission spectroscopy (FTIRES) and near-infrared thermal imaging (TI) to monitor the anode under OCV and galvanostatic polarizations operating under simulated syngas mixtures.

Experimental

Membrane electrode assemblies (MEAs, 25mm dia.) were acquired from FCM (fuelcellmaterials.com) and were comprised of a 400μm-thick NiO-YSZ anode electrode support, a 3μm-thick YSZ electrolyte layer, a 3μm-thick gadolinium-doped ceria (GDC) barrier layer, and a 12.5mm dia., 12μm-thick lanthanum strontium cobaltite (LSC) cathode electrode. Gold leads (99.9%, Sigma-Aldrich) and current collectors comprised of 100 mesh Au (anode, 99.99%, Fisher Scientific) and Pt (cathode, 99.9%, Sigma-Aldrich) were coupled to the anode and cathode surfaces using Au and Pt inks (Heraeus Electronics), respectively. The electrochemical cell assembly (comprising the MEAs, alumina supports, and fuel tubes), as well as the duplex TI/FTIRES instrumentation and geometry have been described in detail elsewhere [9-11]. The assembly was then heated to 800°C overnight at a rate of 1°C/min.

Galvanostatic polarization, linear sweep voltammetry (LSV), and electrochemical impedance spectroscopy (EIS) experiments were carried out with a Gamry Reference 3000 Potentiostat/Galvanostat/ZRA using a two-electrode arrangement. The partial pressures of the gases used in this study were regulated using mass flow controllers (Brooks SLA5850 and Celerity FC-260V). Gases used were of ultra-high purity quality. The fractional composition of H_2, CO, and/or CO_2 within the total headspace was varied from 0 to 40% (Ar as balance) while maintaining a total flow rate of 250sccm. On the cathode side, the gas composition was maintained constant throughout all of the experiments performed and consisted of 20% O_2 and 80% Ar with a total flow rate of 100sccm.

Results and Discussion

Linear sweep voltammetry and the power spectrum of a SOFC running under a syngas composition of 20% CO and 20% H_2 ($syngas_{1to1}$) resulted in performance parameters similar to those for a 40% H_2 fuel composition (Figure 1). Specifically, a $syngas_{1to1}$ fuel mixture produced an OCV of -1.11V, short circuit current (I_{max}) of 469mA, and a maximum power output (P_{max}) of 126mW. For comparison, under 40% H_2 the cell performed at an OCV of -1.12V, an I_{max} of 470mA, and P_{max} of 128mW. The similarity in cell performance between H_2 and $syngas_{1to1}$ has been previously reported by Weber, *et al.* [12]. A noticeable reduction in cell performance, however, was observed under 20% CO (no H_2) where the OCV is -1.08V, the I_{max} was found to be 420mA, and a resulting P_{max} of 112mW.

Electrochemical impedance spectra collected under $syngas_{1to1}$, 40% H_2, and 20% CO were fit to a circuit model consisting of an initial inductive element to treat the high frequency behavior observed, a resistive element (related to oxide migration through the YSZ electrolyte, R_{bulk}), and grouped RC elements designated as the polarization resistance (R_{pol}) which has contributions from resistances due to fuel activation, redox reactions at the TPB, and mass transport at the electrodes (see inset of Figure 2). The fits indicate similar R_{bulk} values under both $syngas_{1to1}$ and 40% H_2 (2.04Ω and 2.06Ω, respectively) whereas under 20% CO there is an increase in the R_{bulk} to 2.11Ω (Figure 2). In contrast, the R_{pol} increases from 0.79Ω to 0.91Ω between 40% H_2 and $syngas_{1to1}$. Under 20% CO, R_{pol} increases to a much larger resistance, 1.36Ω.

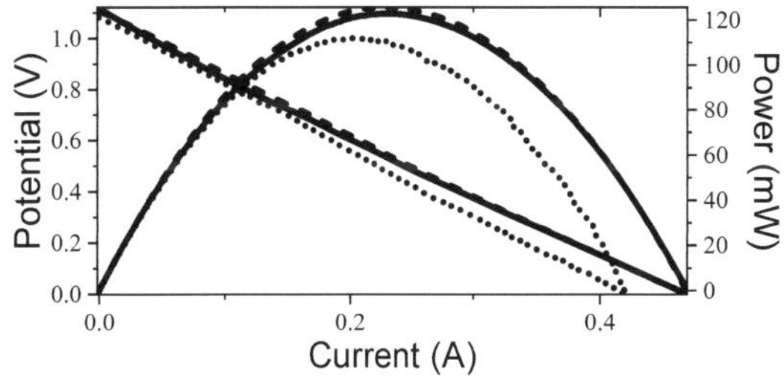

Figure 1. Linear sweep voltammetry scans of a SOFC under 40% H_2 (solid line), $syngas_{1to1}$ (dashed line), and 20% CO (dotted line) fuel conditions at 800°C.

The performance of the cell depended on the relative ratio of CO to H_2 in the syngas mixtures. At high relative CO concentrations (20% CO + 4% H_2, $syngas_{5to1}$), the I_{max} decreased to 440mA which is consistent with the reduced current observed when using CO as fuel in the absence of H_2 and is also consistent with observations made by Weber, *et al.* [12]. Interestingly, the I_{max} and the P_{max} display a maxima under $syngas_{1to1}$ (Figure 3). Both the R_{bulk} and R_{pol} were found to display minima under a $syngas_{2to1}$ mixture (20% CO + 10% H_2, Figure 3 inset).

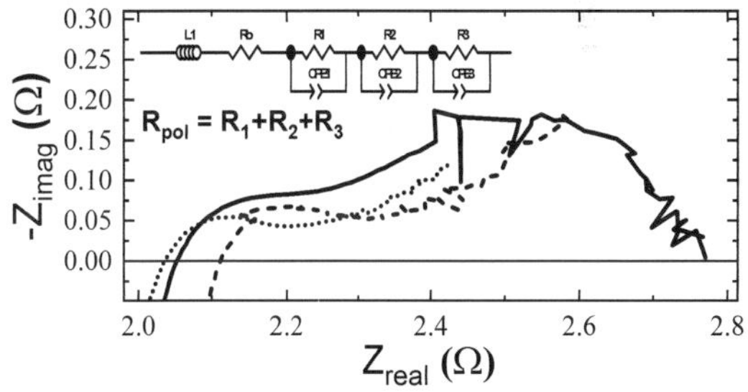

Figure 2. Nyquist plots of the EIS data obtained for a SOFC operating under 40% H_2 (solid line), $syngas_{1to1}$ (dotted line), and 20% CO (dashed line) fuels at 800°C. Inset shows the circuit model used to fit the EIS data to obtain R_{bulk} and R_{pol} parameters.

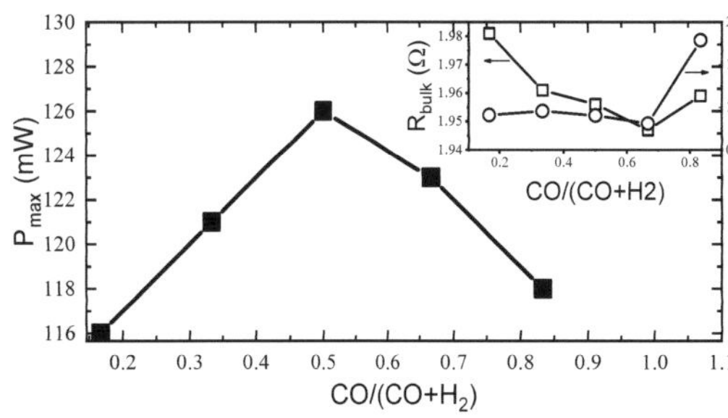

Figure 3. Maximum SOFC power output with varying CO/H_2 syngas fuel gas mixtures at 800°C. (Inset) Cell bulk (open squares) and polarization (open circles) resistances for various relative amounts of CO in CO/H_2 gas mixtures at 800°C. The partial pressures of CO and H_2 at a given CO/H_2 mixture were used to calculate the $CO/(CO+H_2)$ ratios

Near-infrared TI of the Ni-YSZ anode surface upon galvanostatic polarization displayed exothermic heating in the region of the anode adjacent to the current collector under both simulated syngas and CO alone. Differential thermal images are shown in Figure 4. Relative to open circuit conditions, there was a clear difference in the magnitude of the heating between the two fuel conditions shown at the biases probed; generally, more heating was observed in the absence rather than in the presence of H_2. In addition, the heating observed at the current collector was found to have a positive dependence on polarization. In other words, increased heating was observed with increasing polarization in both syngas fuels and CO alone, although the magnitude of the change differed between the two fuel conditions.

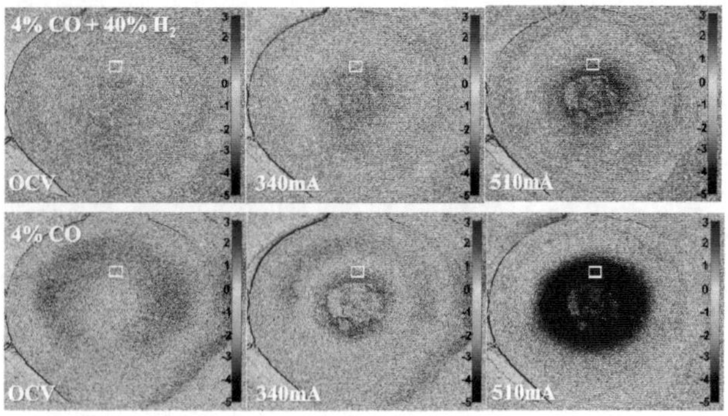

Figure 4. Near infrared thermal images of SOFC Ni-YSZ anode surface at OCV (left), 340mA (middle), and 510mA (right) galvanostatic polarization under 4% CO in the absence (bottom) and presence (top) of 40% H_2. The white box indicates the region of interest (ROI) on the anode surface from which thermal data in Figure 6 was taken. The color scale on the right represents the differential temperature relative to dry H_2 reducing conditions.

FTIRES indicated an increase in the amount of CO_2 (monitored at 2292 cm^{-1}) present upon polarization under both syngas and CO. The FTIRES difference spectra shown in Figure 5, obtained by subtracting the spectra under polarization from the spectra at OCV, also indicated an increase in the amount of water present when operating under syngas, and a noticeable decrease in the amount of CO (monitored at 2094 cm^{-1}) present where CO was used as a fuel.

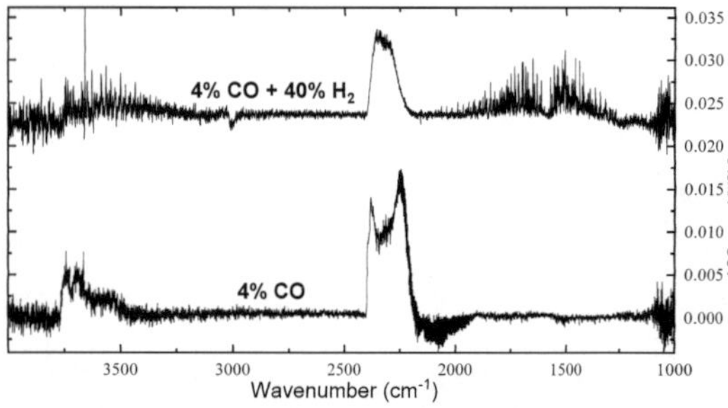

Figure 5. FTIRES difference spectra of a SOFC running under 4% CO in the presence (top) and absence (bottom) of 40% H_2 at 800°C under galvanostatic bias of 340mA.

It is known that the concentrations of both CO_2 and H_2O can vary by either electrochemical oxidation of CO and H_2, respectively, at the TPB or by shifts in the water-gas shift reaction equilibria [3, 13, 14]. Chronopotentiometric experiments were therefore carried out at varying CO/H_2 mixtures while monitoring the TI and FTIRES. This was done in an attempt to determine the origin of the change in CO_2 and H_2O signals under syngas and identify the dominant mechanism of oxidation and fuel consumption under the conditions applied. In general, higher polarizations resulted in larger changes in the H_2O content (monitored at 1507 cm^{-1}) relative to OCV at all syngas mixtures (Figure 6). The amount of H_2O formed was linearly proportional to the H_2 content of the syngas regardless of the degree of cell bias which was not that surprising.

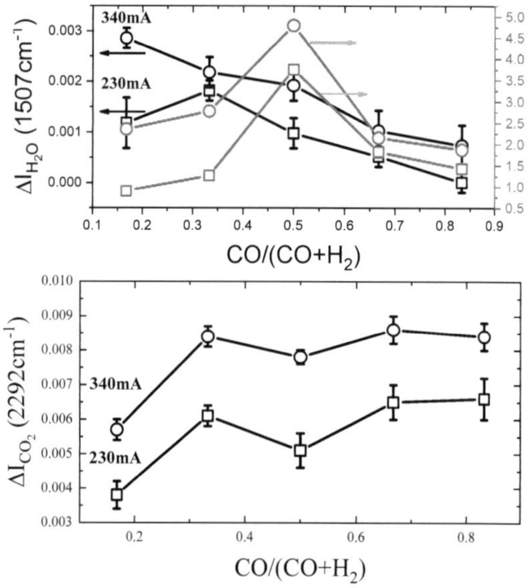

Figure 6. (Top panel) Differential H_2O content (black lines) and anode surface temperature change at the current collector (grey lines) as a function of relative CO concentration at constant current bias of 340mA (open circles) and 230mA (open squares). (Bottom panel) Differential CO_2 content at constant current bias of 340mA (open circles) and 230mA (open squares) as a function of relative CO concentration.

Interestingly, the temperature changes observed at the current collector at both high and low polarizations were largest under $syngas_{1to1}$ conditions (CO relative ratio ~0.5). This agrees with the electrochemical results shown in Figure 2 where power outputs were also maximal at a relative CO ratio of 0.5. The exothermic temperature changes over all polarizations and at all syngas mixtures (shown in Figure 4) is not surprising. It is consistent with electrochemical oxidation of CO which increases the temperature at the current collector and exothermic temperature changes from the presence of H_2 upon applying bias, has been demonstrated previously. [4]. The observed temperature increases are attributed to electrochemical oxidation of CO and H_2. What is noteworthy is 1) the peak performance and surface temperature change associated with $syngas_{1to1}$ over both CO- and H_2-rich fuels and that, in general, 2) at lower polarizations CO rich mixtures result in higher temperature changes relative to H_2-rich mixtures whereas 3) at higher polarizations the opposite is observed.

The trends in CO_2 production as a function of both the degree of cell bias and H_2 present in the syngas are also shown in Figure 6. The amount of CO_2 produced was dependent on both the amount of bias applied to the cell and the concentration of CO relative to H_2 in the syngas mixture. An asymptotic limit to the amount of CO_2 formed upon polarization was apparent when the CO accounted for approximately 30% of the total fuel present in the syngas mixture at which point, the change in CO_2 upon applying modest ($1/2*I_{max}$) and large ($3/4*I_{max}$) bias remained constant within experimental error.

In summary, there is more CO_2 and H_2O content observed at high current loads (relative to low current load) in H_2-rich syngas mixtures. In CO rich syngas mixtures, increased CO_2 content is accompanied by increased H_2O content only at high current loads; the H_2O content in H_2 deficient fuel approaches zero at lower bias. Increased current load results in increased temperature changes at the anode surface regardless of the relative CO and H_2 fuel content and reach a maximum when the relative partial pressures of CO and H_2 are equal. Similar temperature increases are observed when using both H_2 and CO alone as fuels and are related to fuel oxidation processes.

Acknowledgements

This work was supported by the Office of Naval Research (N0001418WX00063). W.A.M. would like to thank the National Research Council, U.S. Naval Research Laboratory Postdoctoral Fellowship Program for their support.

References

1. Ciferno, J.P., J.J. Marano, "Benchmarking Biomass Gasification Technologies for Fuels, Chemicals and Hydrogen Production," US Department of Energy, National Energy Technology Laboratory, 2002, https://www.netl.doe.gov/File%20Library/research/coal/energy%20systems/gasification/BMassGasFinal.pdf.
2. Jiang, Y., A.V. Virkar, "Fuel Composition and Diluent Effect on Gas Transport and Performance of Anode-Supported SOFCs," *Journal of the Electrochemical Society*, vol. 150, no. 7, pp. A942-A951, 2003.
3. Ong, K., J. Hanna, A.F. Ghoniem, "Investigation of a Combined Hydrogen and Oxygen Spillover Mechanism for Syngas Electro-Oxidation on Ni/YSZ," *Journal of the Electrochemical Society*, vol. 164, no. 2, pp. F32-F45, 2017.
4. Pomfret, M.B., J.C. Owrutsky, R.A. Walker, "In Situ Optical Studies of Solid-Oxide Fuel Cells," *Annual Review of Analytical Chemistry, Vol 3*, vol. 3, pp. 151-174, 2010.
5. Pomfret, M.B., D.A. Steinhurst, D.A. Kidwell, J.C. Owrutsky, "Thermal Imaging of Solid Oxide Fuel Cell Anode Processes," *Journal of Power Sources*, vol. 195, no. 1, pp. 257-262, 2010.
6. Pomfret, M.B., R.A. Walker, J.C. Owrutsky, "High-Temperature Chemistry in Solid Oxide Fuel Cells: In Situ Optical Studies," *Journal of Physical Chemistry Letters*, vol. 3, no. 20, pp. 3053-3064, 2012.
7. Pomfret, M.B., D.A. Steinhurst, J.C. Owrutsky, "Identification of a Methane Oxidation Intermediate on Solid Oxide Fuel Cell Anode Surfaces with Fourier Transform Infrared Emission," *Journal of Physical Chemistry Letters*, vol. 4, no. 8, pp. 1310-1314, 2013.
8. McIntyre, M.D., J.D. Kirtley, D.M. Halat, K.W. Reeping, R.A. Walker, "In Situ Spectroscopic Studies of Carbon Formation in SOFCs Operating with Syn-Gas," *Solid Oxide Fuel Cells 13 (SOFC-XIII)*, vol. 57, no. 1, pp. 1267-1275, 2013.
9. Kirtley, J.D., D.A. Steinhurst, J.C. Owrutsky, M.B. Pomfret, R.A. Walker, "In Situ Optical Studies of Methane and Simulated Biogas Oxidation on High Temperature Solid Oxide Fuel Cell Anodes," *Physical Chemistry Chemical Physics*, vol. 16, no. 1, pp. 227-236, 2014.
10. Kirtley, J.D., M.B. Pomfret, D.A. Steinhurst, J.C. Owrutsky, R.A. Walker, "Toward a Working Mechanism of Fuel Oxidation in SOFCs: In Situ Optical Studies of Simulated Biogas and Methane," *Journal of Physical Chemistry C*, vol. 119, no. 23, pp. 12781-12791, 2015.
11. Kirtley, J.D., S.N. Qadri, D.A. Steinhurst, J.C. Owrutsky, "In Situ, Simultaneous Thermal Imaging and Infrared Molecular Emission Studies of Solid Oxide Fuel Cell Electrodes," *Journal of Power Sources*, vol. 336, pp. 54-62, 2016.
12. Weber, A., B. Sauer, A.C. Muller, D. Herbstritt, E. Ivers-Tiffee, "Oxidation of H_2, CO and Methane in SOFCs with Ni/YSZ-Cermet Anodes," *Solid State Ionics*, vol. 152, pp. 543-550, 2002.
13. Suwanwarangkul, R., E. Croiset, E. Entchev, S. Charojrochkul, M.D. Pritzker, M.W. Fowler, P.L. Douglas, S. Chewathanakup, H. Mahaudom, "Experimental and Modeling Study of Solid Oxide Fuel Cell Operating with Syngas Fuel," *Journal of Power Sources*, vol. 161, no. 1, pp. 308-322, 2006.
14. Ye, X.F., S.R. Wang, J. Zhou, F.R. Zeng, H.W. Nie, T.L. Wen, "Assessment of the Performance of Ni-Yttria-Stabilized Zirconia Anodes in Anode-Supported Solid Oxide Fuel Cells Operating on H_2-CO Syngas Fuels," *Journal of Power Sources*, vol. 195, no. 21, pp. 7264-7267, 2010.

Recent Achievements with Alane (Aluminum Hydride, AlH_3) and Fuel Cell Power Systems

Daniel Braithwaite[1], Courtney A. Helland[1], Terry G. DuBois[2], Tony M. Thampan[2], Christian R. Schumacher[3]

[1]Ardica Technologies
San Francisco, CA
USA 94107
www.ardica.com

[2]CERDEC/CP&I/Power Division
Aberdeen Proving Ground, MD
USA 21005

[3]Naval Undersea Warfare Center
Newport, RI
USA 02841

Contact Author Email: daniel@ardica.com / 1-415-358-1924

Abstract: *Fuel cells have many advantages compared to conventional power sources including high efficiency and solid-state operation. Until now, a key shortcoming of fuel cell technology has been the fuel itself, as conventional methods for storing hydrogen were unsafe or impractical for portable use. This paper discusses a lightweight, energy-dense, non-toxic, recyclable, stable, and easy to transport solution for hydrogen storage. It is a material known as Alane that exists as powder and, when heated to the proper temperature, controllably releases hydrogen gas. Alane has near ideal attributes in terms of reactivity, stability, and safety - making it an excellent choice for several applications in need of a portable hydrogen supply. However, it has historically been difficult to produce efficiently. Through partnerships with leading industry experts in the government and private sector, Ardica Technologies has advanced the state of the art of Alane production. Ardica has developed a small-scale process which has been proven to yield high quality Alane that meets or exceeds the characteristics of the generally accepted gold standard reference material.*

Keywords: Alane; hydride; hydrogen; fuel cell; power system; solid-state; energy density; portable generator

Introduction

Fuel cell technology has the potential to provide an unmatched capability for supplying portable power and energy over incumbent solutions such as batteries and internal combustion engines. Fuel cells are silent and solid state, like batteries, yet can run continuously and nearly indefinitely off a chemical fuel, like internal combustion engines do. However, until now, a key limitation of fuel cell technology was the fuel itself. Traditional methods for storing hydrogen are heavy, bulky, and often dangerous due to the high pressures involved. Alane, or Aluminum Hydride (AlH_3), offers an alternative solution for storing hydrogen and is widely recognized as one of the world's most promising energy compounds [1].

Alane is a stable, non-toxic, lightweight powder that can be stored for decades at ambient temperature with no appreciable loss of hydrogen. The mechanism for releasing hydrogen from Alane is a simple, single-step decomposition reaction that easily starts, stops, and proceeds to nearly 100% completion [2]. When Alane is paired with a fuel cell to produce power, the only by-products are a minute amount of water vapor and pure aluminum powder, making it an exceptionally environmentally friendly choice. Alane-based power systems are also almost totally silent.

Without the need for heavy storage tanks, Alane allows for truly superior energy density of fuel cell power systems. The chart in Figure 1 shows a comparison of conventional hydrogen storage options versus Alane.

	Industrial Compressed Gas	Composite Tank Compressed Gas	Metal Hydride	Alane
Weight	136 lb	33 lb	43 lb	15 lb
Volume	50 L	37 L	19L	6 L
Pressure	2400 psi	4351 psi	1450 psi	0 psi
Wt % H2	1.1%	4.5%	3.4%	9.8%
Total H2	670 g	670 g	670 g	670 g
Notes	Heavy, Pressurized, Bulky, Flammable	Highest Pressure, Flammable	Small but Heavy for its size	No Pressure, Lightweight, Compact, Safe

Figure 1: Conventional hydrogen storage methods vs Alane storage. Alane safely stores hydrogen chemically bound to aluminum powder at a fraction of the weight and volume of other solutions. By storing hydrogen as a solid, Alane avoids the inherent danger of high pressure gas storage.

Alane Powered Systems

The ability to store a significant quantity of hydrogen at ambient pressure and release it in a controlled fashion lends itself to many applications. Since 2008, Ardica has worked with Army CERDEC to develop Alane powered fuel cell systems, the most notable being a soldier wearable power system known as the Ardica Wearable Power System (WPS). The WPS is a lightweight power generator that produces 20 watts of continuous electricity at 12 – 16.8V

DC. It has a flat, flexible form factor which allows the WPS to be worn either against a SAPI armor plate in the soldier's vest or elsewhere on their body. For a mission time of 72 hours at 20 W, the WPS has an energy density of 463 Wh/kg and 528 Wh/L, which is a 55% savings compared to standard batteries [3]. The WPS is a hybrid system which contains an internal battery to allow for instant power on and continuous power even when changing the fuel cartridges (i.e. "hot swap" capability). In addition, the solid-state nature of the fuel cell enables near silent operation in a wide range of environmental conditions.

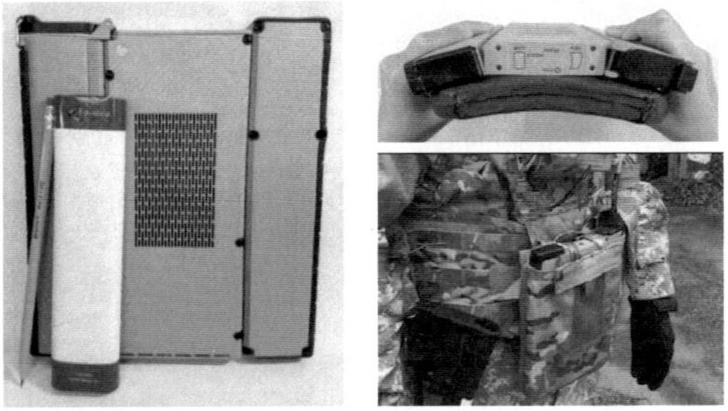

Figure 2: Ardica Wearable Power System (WPS). A 20-watt, solider wearable, portable power generator.

Alongside individual soldier wearable power systems, the Army has also shown interest in higher power generators [4] [5]. These systems would serve as portable battery chargers for groups of soldiers, from the squad level up to platoon level, for example. In Spring 2017, Ardica modeled two potential systems for meeting this Army need, a 1000-watt generator (AFC-1000) and a 500-watt generator (AFC-500). The AFC-1000 system weighs 14.3 lb and has a system volume of 732 cubic inches. The smaller AFC-500 system is slightly more than half the weight and volume of the AFC-1000 system, however two of them are still well below the incumbent solution which weighs over 30 pounds. In addition, the AFC-500s represent a more modular solution that is easier for an individual to carry. Figure 3 shows mock-up systems of both the AFC-500 and AFC-1000 compared to a generator comparable in size and weight to the current Army 1000-watt generators.

Figure 3: 500-watt AFC-500 and 1000-watt AFC-1000 compared to a typical off-the-shelf 1000-watt generator that is comparable to state-of-the-art Army generators.

In June 2017, Ardica began work with Army TARDEC on an Alane based fuel cell system for an all-terrain transport vehicle (FCATT). This vehicle will make use of a 15-kW fuel cell to give it a range of 100 to 300 miles. A traditional compressed hydrogen storage tank to carry the fuel would be too large and remote filling stations pose a challenge. An Alane solution would offer the required hydrogen without these drawbacks.

There has recently also been huge growth in unmanned aerial vehicles (UAVs). Smaller UAVs are typically powered by batteries, most often lithium-ion batteries. These solutions have short runtimes, which limit their usefulness. Larger UAVs are sometimes powered by diesel or gasoline engines, which have an acoustic and thermal signature in addition to producing carbon emissions and other pollution. Using Alane to supply hydrogen to a fuel cell in a UAV would allow for significantly higher energy storage, and thus extended runtime for the same weight. When compared to a typical lithium ion battery, a 375% increase in runtime could be achieved by switching to an Alane powered system of equivalent weight, while still maintaining the advantages of electric propulsion including low noise, low temperature, and only water vapor as an emission. In addition, simple cartridge swaps enable fast refueling, resulting in more uptime and increased productivity. Spent cartridges can be safely and easily stored until they are recycled.

Unmanned underwater vehicles (UUVs) provide another opportunity for enhanced performance with an Alane powered solution. Ardica has worked since 2015 with the Naval Undersea Warfare Center (NUWC) on concepts for Alane powered Navy systems. The Remus 600, shown in Figure 4, was identified as a platform with which to explore the performance metrics of an Alane powered fuel cell-based power system. The Remus 600 is a 12.75" diameter UUV which requires 250 watts of power. An Alane based system would provide a 1.8-2.4x improvement in runtime over the current design, which is an increase of 44 to 60 hours [6].

Figure 4: An Alane powered Remus 600 UUV would have approximately twice the runtime as the current technology

Alane Production

While Alane offers obvious tremendous performance benefits over other hydrogen storage solutions, its biggest shortcoming is that it is not readily available and has only been made by a handful of groups in the past. The Former Soviet Union (FSU), Dow Chemical, and the Office of

Naval Research (ONR) with a contractor have all made Alane before, but the fuel they produced was generally too expensive for commercial applications.

The traditional method to make Alane utilizes costly feedstocks and very dilute solutions in ether and toluene solvents. This drives up the cost in terms of safety, labor, and materials. This method is generally referred to as the "Dow Process" due to their pioneering work in this field during the 1960's [7].

Over the past several years, Ardica has partnered with SRI International and Savannah River National Lab (SRNL) to leapfrog the Dow Process to reduce costs, increase batch sizes, and improve the safety of the manufacturing steps. The result is a small-scale process which advances the state of the art in terms of production and has been proven to yield high quality Alane [8].

In general, Alane produced by the Former Soviet Union (FSU) is considered the "gold standard" to which all newly generated Alane material is compared. Ardica has conducted analytical tests for safety, performance, and thermal stability on both Ardica Alane and FSU Alane to compare and benchmark our progress. We ran several characterization tests including:

- X-Ray Diffraction (XRD)
- Thermogravimetric Analysis (TGA) / Differential Scanning Calorimetry (DSC)
- Thermal desorption-gas chromatography mass spectrometry (TD GC-MS)
- Modified bureau-of-mines (MBOM) impact
- Alleghany Ballistic Laboratory (ABL) friction
- ABL electrostatic discharge (ESD)
- Thermal stability

In third party testing, Ardica Alane compared favorably with FSU Alane in terms of performance and safety, and in certain cases, described below, exceeded the stability of the FSU Alane. The Threshold Initiation Level (TIL) approach was utilized for the impact, friction, and ESD sensitivity tests because it provides a simple and direct comparison of materials for easy ranking. In general, the TIL characterizes the minimum amount of energy required to react a sample.

XRD testing was conducted at an independent 3rd party lab, Balazs Nanoanalysis (Balazs), Fremont, CA. Three samples were tested, one of FSU Alane and two of Ardica Alane. The Ardica samples demonstrated greater than 98% content alpha Alane, which is slightly better than the FSU Alane baseline.

Balazs also conducted the TGA/DSC testing. The TGA test was conducted in a nitrogen atmosphere at a ramp of 10 °C per minute. The Ardica samples were comparable to the FSU Alane sample as both demonstrated less than 0.5% weight loss by 120 °C and between 9% and 10.5% weight loss by 210 °C.

With respect to the DSC, in contrast to the FSU result, the Ardica Alane showed two closely spaced endothermic peaks, which is characteristic of the bimodal distribution in particle size that Ardica has informally observed during production runs. This is a minor distinction and has not presented any challenges with downstream use of the material. The DSC for both the FSU and the Ardica samples was mildly endothermic as expected.

The TD GC-MS organic outgassing testing was also conducted by Balazs. Three samples were tested, one of FSU Alane and two of Ardica Alane. A sum of the organic contaminants in parts per million by weight (ppmw) was used as the critical assessment criteria. Both samples of the Ardica Alane were found to have lower total organic ppmw than the FSU baseline as shown in Table 1.

Table 1: Total Organic Outgassing measured in parts per million by weight. Both Ardica Alane samples show less total contaminants than the FSU baseline sample.

Component	**FSU**	**Ardica1**	**Ardica2**	**Units**
Low boilers C7 - C10	110.5	77.7	87.2	ppmw
Medium boilers >C10 – C20	10	16.5	31.6	ppmw
High boilers >C20	0.1	0.2	0.4	ppmw
Sum >- C7	**120.6**	**94.4**	**119.2**	**ppmw**

An MBOM impact test was conducted at an independent 3rd party lab, Safety Management Services (SMS), West Jordan, UT. Both the FSU baseline and the Ardica Alane samples did not react even at the highest setting of the MBOM impact machine. This leads us to conclude that the samples' behavior is equivalent, to the best of our measurement capabilities, and that they are both relatively insensitive to impact.

ABL friction testing was also conducted by SMS. The TIL for the Ardica Alane sample was tested to be over 30% higher than the TIL for the FSU baseline (as shown in Table 1), indicating that the Ardica material is less sensitive to friction than the FSU Alane.

Table 2: ABL friction test results. The Ardica Alane exhibited less sensitivity to friction than the FSU sample.

Material	**TIL**
FSU sample	56 lbf at 4 ft/s
Ardica sample	75 lbf at 4 ft/s

SMS also conducted ABL ESD testing. ESD testing is used to determine the response of an energetic material when subjected to various levels of electrostatic discharge energy. The TIL for both the FSU baseline and the Ardica Alane sample were relatively low, indicating that they are both ESD sensitive materials. In contrast to the FSU sample, the TIL for the Ardica Alane sample was below the machine's detection limit, so we have not yet been able to quantify its sensitivity. Through prior work, however,

Ardica has found that ESD sensitivity can be modified and improved through doping with a low weight fraction of conductive materials to meet requirements.

The most notable finding for users interested in Alane's shelf-life is the thermal stability test. For this test, a sample of known mass is placed into a sealed glass vessel. The vessel is then evacuated to a vacuum level less than 1 torr. The temperature of the vessel and sample is then regulated, measured, and maintained based on the test protocol. The pressure inside the vessel is continuously recorded to monitor the reaction of the sample over time. An independent 3rd party lab, Safety Management Services (SMS), West Jordan, UT, tested one sample of Ardica Alane and one sample of FSU Alane at temperatures ranging from 80 °C to 140 °C. At each temperature, the Ardica material was found to be more thermally stable than the FSU baseline. In fact, at 80 °C, the test results indicate that the Ardica material exhibits over two times the onset time to reaction compared to the FSU baseline.

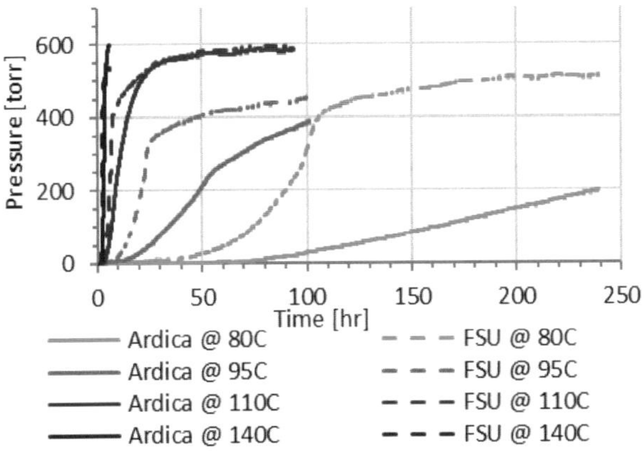

Figure 5: Thermal stability test results. The FSU Alane reacts faster than the Ardica Alane, indicating that the Ardica material is more thermally stable.

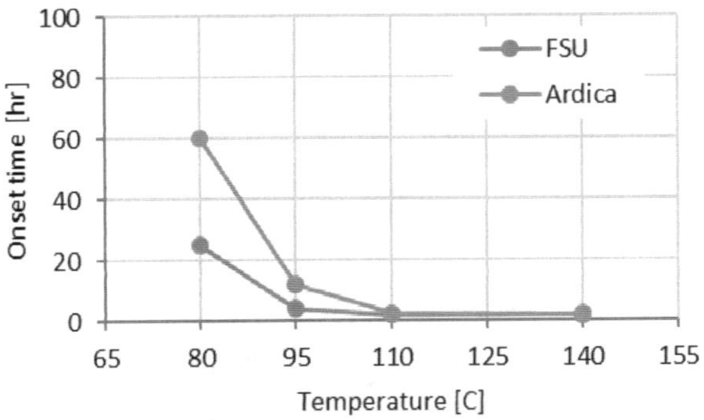

Figure 6: The onset time to reaction is extrapolated from the chart above and plotted here for reference. The onset time to reaction is longer for the Ardica Alane sample than for the FSU Alane sample, providing exceptionally superior stability at more moderate temperatures.

For longer time scales, Alane has been found to be stable for decades at room temperature. Ardica has been in possession of FSU Alane that is over 15 years old, which has generally been stored at ambient temperature. This Alane currently has a hydrogen content in the 9.5-10% range and is regularly used safely in Ardica fuel cartridges. Enough time has not yet passed to have an equivalent measurement for the freshly produced Ardica Alane, but the testing to date leads us to expect a similar result.

Acknowledgements

The authors would like to acknowledge and thank the US Army's Communication-Electronics Research, Development & Engineering Center (CERDEC) Command Power & Integration (CP&I), Power Division, PEO Soldier, Project Manager Soldier Warrior (PM-SWAR) Soldier Systems & Integration, Tank and Automotive Research, Development & Engineering Center (TARDEC), the US Navy's Naval Underwater Warfare Center (NUWC) Newport Division, the Department of Energy (DoE) Hydrogen and Fuel Cells Program and Savannah River National Laboratory (SRNL) for their early vision and ongoing support to bring this technology forward and provide new and cutting edge capabilities to the DoD and civilian marketplace.

References

1. Department of Energy, "Materials-Based Hydrogen Storage." https://energy.gov/eere/fuelcells/materials-based-hydrogen-storage. [Accessed: 24-Jan-2017].
2. J. Graetz, "New approaches to hydrogen storage," *Chem. Soc. Rev.*, vol. 38, no. 1, pp. 73–82, 2009.
3. "Army Expeditionary Warrior Experiment 2016, Wearable Power System Technology Assessment, Battle Lab Report #346", U.S. Army Maneuver Center of Excellence, February 16, 2016.
4. Huggins, James L. Jr., "Capability Development Document for Small Unit Power (SUP) Increment: 1", U.S. Army Maneuver Center of Excellence, Operational Energy Branch, Soldiers Division, June 25, 2013
5. Thompson, K., "Requirements Clarification for KPP 3 in Small Unit Power CDD", Memorandum for Program Manager PEO CS&CSS, February 8, 2017
6. Joseph Teprovich et al., "Investigation of Solid State Hydrides for Autonomous Fuel Cell Vehicles," presented at the 2017 Annual Merit Review Proceedings - Hydrogen Program, Washington DC, June 8, 2017
7. Frank M. Brower, "Preparation and Properties of Aluminum Hydride." The Dow Chemical Company, June 30, 1975
8. Ragaiy Zidan, "Formation and Regeneration of Alane," presented at the 2017 Annual Merit Review Proceedings - Hydrogen Program, Washington DC, June 8, 2017.

Standalone, Light-weight Diesel/Jet-fueled Fuel Cell Generators

Subir Roychoudhury, Christian Junaedi, Saurabh A. Vilekar, Tim LaBreche and Richard Mastanduno

Precision Combustion, Inc.
410 Sackett Point Rd., North Haven, CT 06473
sroychoudhury@precision-combustion.com

Abstract: *Precision Combustion, Inc. (PCI) is developing complete fuel cell generators with high capacity sulfur filters to enable JP-8/DF-2 use. Over the years, PCI has made significant advances in the area of fuel processing to enable use of practical fuels including distillate fuels such as military jet fuels (consisting of up to 3000 ppm$_w$ sulfur), diesels or kerosene, as well as renewable fuels such as bio-diesels. Light-weight, low parasitic balance of plant components are being implemented to develop robust and practical systems. Coupling our high power density fuel processors with suitable solid oxide fuel cells is a critical aspect for successful system development. Currently, integration and thermal management optimization is ongoing via development of reliable components and strategies that enable transients and steady state operation via suitable thermal integration for maximizing system efficiency. Meeting long-term durability, startup and cyclic requirements are key considerations. PCI has developed water recovery subsystems and robust control schemes to enable water-neutral system operation and to maximize system efficiency with state of the art fuel cells. PCI's development has focused on stationary power, lightweight generator application, and Auxiliary Power Unit (APU), ranging from 1 kW to 10 kW battery hybridized systems.*

Keywords: Reforming, Fuel Processing, Power Generator, JP-8, Diesel, SOFC, Fuel Cell, APU.

Introduction

Challenges affecting widespread deployment of fuel cell power generators include stack and reformer durability, water recovery, reliable balance of plant (pumps, blowers, heat exchangers, etc.), start/stop cycling capability, low cost, low weight, and minimizing system parasitics. Over the years, PCI has made significant advances in the area of fuel processing to enable use of practical fuels including distillate fuels such as military jet fuels (consisting of up to 3000 ppm$_w$ sulfur), diesels or kerosene, as well as renewable fuels such as bio-diesels. This is achieved by utilizing our proprietary catalyst coatings combined with unique, process-intensified and patented fuel processor designs that allow reformation of these fuels with minimal water needs (for water neutrality) while minimizing higher hydrocarbon content in the reformate to an acceptable level (depending on the fuel cell type). Sulfur cleanup is achieved to <<1 ppm$_v$ in the reformate stream in a practical and compact package. Light-weight, low parasitic balance of plant (BOP) components are being implemented to develop robust and practical systems. PCI has developed water recovery subsystems and robust control schemes to enable water-neutral system operation and to maximize system efficiency with state of the art fuel cells. Currently, integration and thermal management optimization is ongoing via development of reliable components and strategies that enable transients (e.g. startup, shutdown, load changes) and steady state operation via suitable thermal integration for maximizing system efficiency. PCI's development has focused on stationary power, lightweight generator application, and Auxiliary Power Unit (APU), ranging from 1 kW to 10 kW battery hybridized systems. In this paper, development of key components of the fuel cell generator is discussed along with test data from system operation with reforming of JP-8 containing up to 3000 ppm$_w$ sulfur, without any upstream sulfur cleanup, in an extremely compact and lightweight package.

System Components for a Complete Fuel Cell Generator

PCI's unique design enables Fuel Cell power generation with tactical fuels and diesels, integrating recent advances for development of reliable, water-neutral Fuel Cell generator. A solid model of the packaged design envisioned for the SOFC-based 1 kWe JP-8/JP-5/DF2 fueled generator is shown in Figure 1.

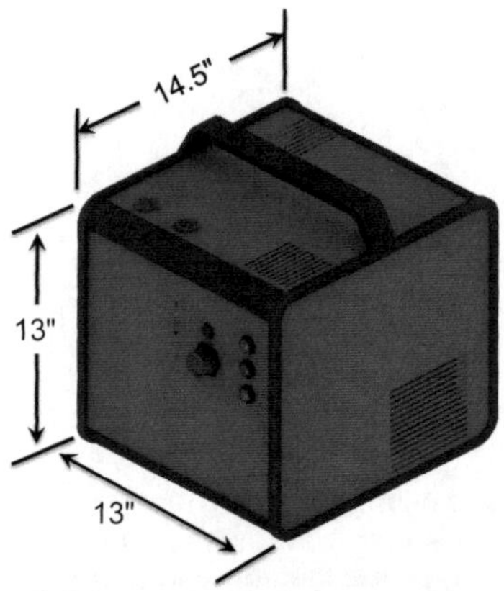

Figure 1. Solid model of fully-packaged 1 kW$_e$ Fuel Processor + SOFC + BOP integrated system. Projected dimensions and dry weight are 13"x13"x14.5" and ≤35 lbs.

The system package includes the thermally-integrated fuel reformer/processor, sulfur trap, SOFC stack, fuel and water pumps, reformer and cathode air blowers, fuel and water tanks, sensors, heat exchangers, burner, water recovery system, controls, power conditioning board, battery, and electronics.

A core innovation is PCI's Microlith® catalyst technology for coating nano-powder catalysts and sorbents on unique Microlith short contact time, high surface area substrates, enabling a number of advantages, notably, ultra-compact size, rapid transient response, high selectivity and efficiency, and robust operation including with sulfur-containing fuels. This permits a unique combination of sulfur cleanup and reforming of JP-8 with effective heat and flow balance. The catalysts have been demonstrated to be sulfur-tolerant (up to 3000 ppm_w) with stable surface area under operating temperatures for 1000's of hours. The catalyst and reactor technology in combination with "process intensification" of steam generation, sulfur cleanup, atomization and mixing, permits extremely compact system footprint. For example, a 1 kWe reformer, sulfur cleanup, fuel tank, controls, pumps, blowers, BOP components etc. has been packaged and delivered to CERDEC (Figure 2).

Figure 2. PCI's fully-packaged 1 kWe JP-8/JP-5/DF2 Fuel Reformer System for SOFC power generator. The fuel processor includes fuel tank, water tank, sulfur trap, BOP, control electronics, sensors for stand-alone operation.

For this reformer system, no upstream desulfurization was needed and it produced SOFC-quality reformate. The volume and weight of the 1 kWe fuel reformer component was 1.5 liter and 2.9 kg. It included the reforming catalyst, housing, steam generator, heat exchanger, fuel/air/steam injector, mixer, and sulfur trap. It is important to note that many of the housing components were not yet optimized for weight, and further light-weighting can be done. Durability testing, including steady state and multiple start/stop cycles, was performed on the Fuel Reformer System with JP-8 fuels for a total of 1500 hours to monitor and validate the long-term performance, BOP components and sulfur trap. Figure 3 shows the results from testing the reformer with JP-8 consisting of 400 ppm_w up to 3000 ppm_w sulfur for 210 hours. Stable product composition was observed throughout the testing, without detectable carbon formation or reformer performance degradation. Sulfur mass balance identified that almost all fuel-bound sulfur was converted to readily-removable gaseous H_2S and trace COS. The sulfur in form of H_2S was captured in a downstream, high capacity sorbent. These results demonstrate a very simple reforming system, avoiding any upstream liquid fuel desulfurization.

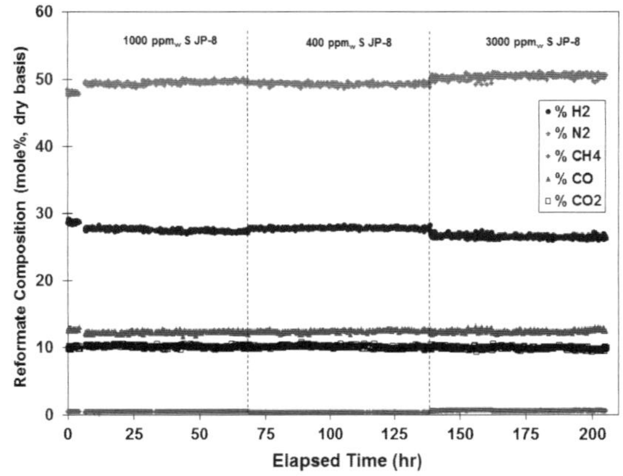

Figure 3. Stable reformate composition (mole %, dry basis) was observed during the 210-hour durability testing of the reformer with JP-8 containing 400/1000/3000 ppm_w sulfur.

Other key system components include the burner, heat exchangers and control and power electronics. PCI's dual fuel burner (Figure 4) is capable of operation with liquid fuels (diesel/JP-5/JP-8) and SOFC anode exhaust recycle (H_2, CO, CO_2, N_2, H_2O). This eliminates the need for a second burner. It is lightweight (<1 kg), capable of 10:1 turndown and is integrated with heat exchangers for both startup and steady state operation. It has a fast response time and can readily adjust to SOFC stack requirements.

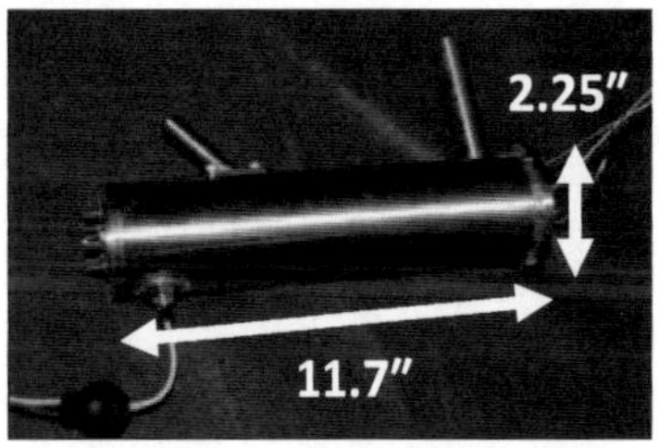

Figure 4. PCI's dual fuel burner.

Finally, feasibility of water neutrality through water recovery from anode tail gas from SOFC stacks has been demonstrated at PCI. PCI's modeling study of the integrated reformer + SOFC system indicates that 60-70% of water recovery should be sufficient to provide the required amount of water for PCI's reformer operation. System integration for flow and thermal balance of fuel processor, burner, heat exchangers, BOP, controls and power conditioning with SOFC stack are currently ongoing.

Conclusions

PCI is developing complete fuel cell generators with high capacity sulfur filters to enable JP-8/DF-2 use. Our approach enables a simple SOFC integration scheme with efficient thermal and flow balancing and water-neutral operation. Current efforts are focused on integration and thermal management optimization via development of reliable components and strategies that enable transients and steady state operation via suitable thermal integration for maximizing system efficiency.

Acknowledgement

We acknowledge the support of the DoD (ONR, TARDEC, ARL, CERDEC, NAVAIR, and WPAFB). Any opinions, findings, and conclusions or recommendations expressed in this paper are those of the authors and do not necessarily reflect the views of the DoD.

Morphology and Chemical Structure of Modified Nitrogen-Doped Graphene for Highly Active Oxygen Reduction Reactions

Harsimranjit Singh, Shiqiang Zhuang, Bharath Babu Nunna, Eon Soo Lee*

Department of Mechanical and Industrial Engineering
New Jersey Institute of Technology
Newark, NJ 07102, USA
eonsoo.lee@njit.edu / 1-973-596-3318

Abstract: *Platinum Group Metal (PGM)-based electrocatalysts have been known to exhibit exceptional catalytic performance. However, the cost of these PGM catalysts outweighs its benefits. More than three decades of catalytic research were focused on eliminating platinum altogether but was challenging because of the limited number of Non-PGM catalysts. A suitable catalyst is desired to have high chemical stability, long-term operational stability, low cost, high electrochemical performance and stability in a wide range of environmental conditions (temperature, humidity etc). Recently, it has been shown that nitrogen-doped graphene catalysts manifest remarkable oxygen reduction reaction (ORR) catalytic activity. Here, we report an inexpensive graphene- based electrocatalyst with high electrochemical performance and high durability. The N-G/MOF electrocatalyst is synthesized from graphene oxide and melamine as precursors and modified with metal-organic framework (MOF) in a high energy wet ball milling method. SEM, TEM, BET, and XPS methods are used to characterize the catalyst for physical, chemical and electrochemical properties. The electrochemical performance (current density) of N-G/MOF is better than the 10% Pt/C.*

Keywords: Cathode catalyst; Oxygen Reduction Reaction; Nitrogen-doped Graphene; Metal-Organic Framework; Ball milling; Fuel cells; Energy storage systems

Introduction

Platinum Group Metal (PGM) electrocatalysts are currently the most prominent in the cathodic Oxygen Reduction Reaction (ORR) of energy systems such as fuel cells. However, due to their excessive cost, limited reserves and sluggish reaction kinetics it is imperative to replace these catalysts with inexpensive non-PGM catalysts of similar electrochemical performance. To eliminate Pt-based catalysts, the Non-PGM catalyst should have (i) Volumetric activity larger than 1/10 that of Pt/C, (ii) Specific Surface Area larger than $200m^2/g$, (iii) High Stability in the operating conditions. Researchers have devoted several decades to synthesize a cost-effective, high performance and stable cathode catalyst. Nitrogen-doped Graphene (N-G) is one of the most aspiring metal free electrocatalysts. The active sites of N-G are nitrogen functional groups: pyridinic-N, graphitic-N, pyridinic N-O, and pyrrolic-N (N-H) [1].

N-G exhibits remarkable ORR catalytic activity and it can be further improved by enhancing the mass transport properties. This improvement can be achieved by increasing the accessibility of the active sites for the ORR. This accessibility of the ORR relevant species like H^+, O_2, e^- can be improved by increasing the specific surface area (SSA) and the porosity of the support material [2]. The approach is using a microporous metal-organic framework (MOF) such as, ZIF-8, which is a composite material consisting metal ions coordinated with rigid organic molecules to form one-dimensional, two-dimensional or three-dimensional structures [3]. Besides SSA, another big advantage of using MOF as an additive is its high chemical, and thermal stability. The resultant catalyst N-G/MOF has high performance, enhanced mass transport properties, high chemical and thermal stability.

In general, catalysts are synthesized by conventional methods like Chemical Vapor Deposition (CVD), thermal treatment and plasma treatment. In most these methods the activation energy of synthesis reaction is derived from heat energy. Various complications such as caking issue, overheating and safety are associated with these methods. Therefore, a mechano-chemical approach called ball milling is used in this research to synthesize N-G. Specifically, Nanoscale High Energy Wet (NHEW) ball milling method is implemented in which the activation energy is obtained from collisions of the grinding balls and the precursors. The parameters that control the reaction mechanism are the grinding speed and grinding time.

Experimental method

This research includes (i) the detailed method for the facile synthesis of N-G and N-G/MOF using a mechano-chemical approach (ii) the morphological study of the synthesized catalysts (N-G and N-G/MOF) through various characterization techniques such as SEM, TEM, Zetasizer, and BET. The study of the morphology of the catalyst will aid in understanding the surface structure and reaction mechanism between N-G and ZIF-8. Besides physical characterization, the elemental composition and the influence of ZIF-8 on the chemical binding of N-G is investigated through XPS technique.

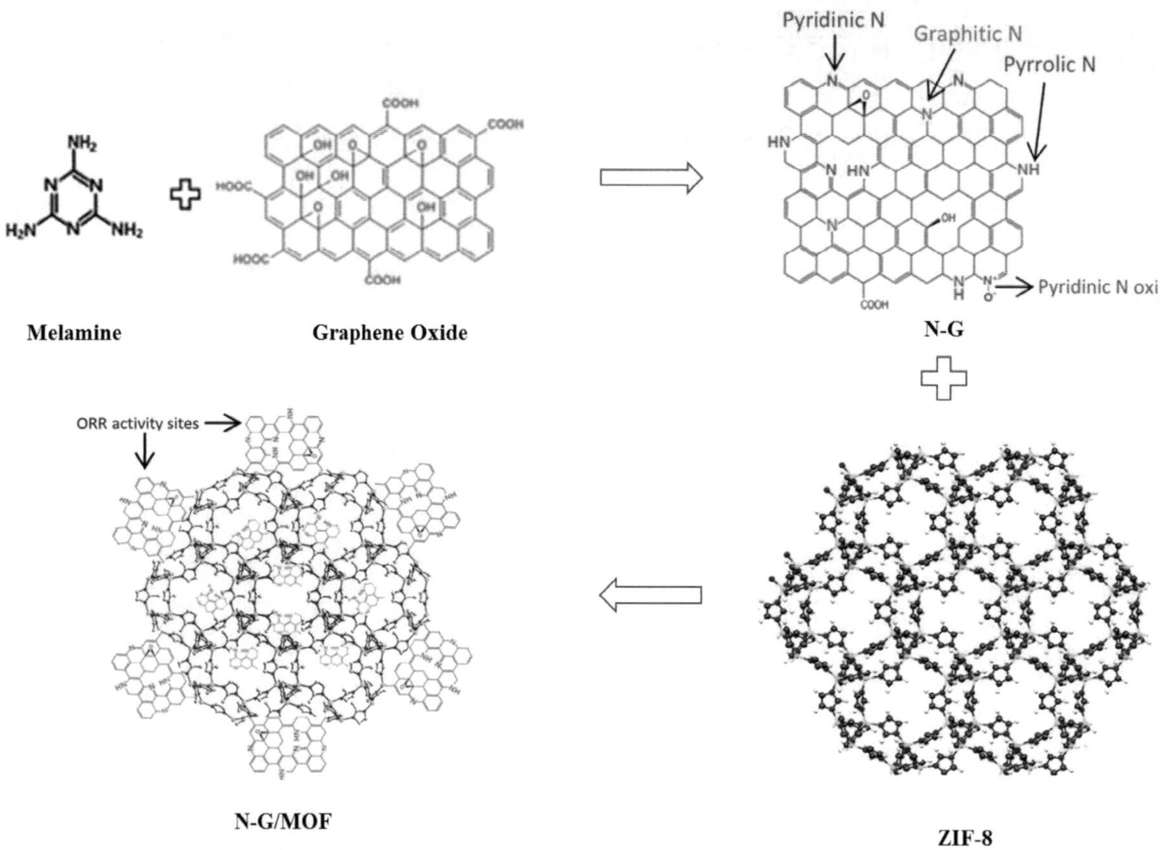

Figure 1. Schematic of synthesis of N-G and N-G/MOF by NHEW ball milling method [5]

Synthesis: N-G and N-G/MOF are synthesized through a mechano-chemical approach (Fig. 1). Unlike most of the non-PGM catalysts where graphite is used as a support material, we have used Graphene Oxide (GO) for an uninhibited doping of nitrogen. The precursors GO and Melamine (nitrogen source) are ground in a stainless-steel jar containing Zirconia balls (grinding medium) in a planetary ball milling machine. The grinding environment of the reaction is wet (deionized water), to minimize the container contamination and avoid unnecessary large aggregates of GO. Our previous research has shown that the grinding time and speed for the optimal electrochemical performance of N-G is 16 hours and 500 RPM respectively [4]. There has been a significant improvement in the volumetric catalytic activity (about $1/10^{th}$ of Pt/C) of the non-PGM electrocatalysts in the past decade. This improvement is sufficient for the practical applications of the PEM fuel cell. But it leads to thicker layers of catalyst, in which the mass transport of the oxygen becomes the performance controlling property of the catalyst. Therefore, in this research these properties are enhanced using extremely porous ZIF-8 as support for N-G. The precursors N-G and ZIF-8 are ground for 16 hours at 350 RPM for synthesizing N-G/MOF and acquiring the best electrochemical performance [5].

Results and Discussion

Particle Size characterization: The morphology of the catalysts is studied through Scanning Electron Microscope (SEM) and Transmission Electron Microscope (TEM) techniques. Fig. 2 illustrates the SEM and TEM images of the catalysts. Fig. 2(a,b) shows the surface structure of N-G catalyst. Along with creating more defects in the GO for nitrogen doping, the NHEW ball milling cleavage the graphene sheets and results in the lower surface area of the catalyst. Fig. 2(c,d) indicates the crystalline rhombic dodecahedral morphology of Zeolitic imidazolate framework-8. The resultant N-G/MOF exhibits both N-G (amorphous) and MOF (crystalline) structures (Fig. 2(e,f)). N-G/MOF structure show larger porosity than N-G with better electrochemical performance. The particle size of the electrocatalysts is analyzed through Zetasizer Nano ZS. The particle size varies on varying the grinding conditions. The average particle size of the N-G catalyst is 495.2 nm whereas the particle size of N-G/MOF is 955 nm. This increase is due to the addition of ZIF-8 particles (3090 nm). During the ball milling process, the ZIF-8 particles size changes rapidly during the initial amorphization followed by fewer changes when fully amorphized.

BET Surface area: The effect of NHEW ball milling on the surface area, pore size and pore volume of N-G catalyst is studied through the Brunauer–Emmett–Teller (BET) Autosorb instrument (Quantachrome) with N2 as an adsorbate. As shown in the table (1), the BET surface area of the GO is 347.23 m^2/g but after the synthesis of N-G, the BET surface area is reduced to 77.81 m^2/g. This reduction can be attributed to the fact that after the ball milling process (16 hours, 500RPM), the long graphene sheets are cleaved. Evidently, for practical applications the specific

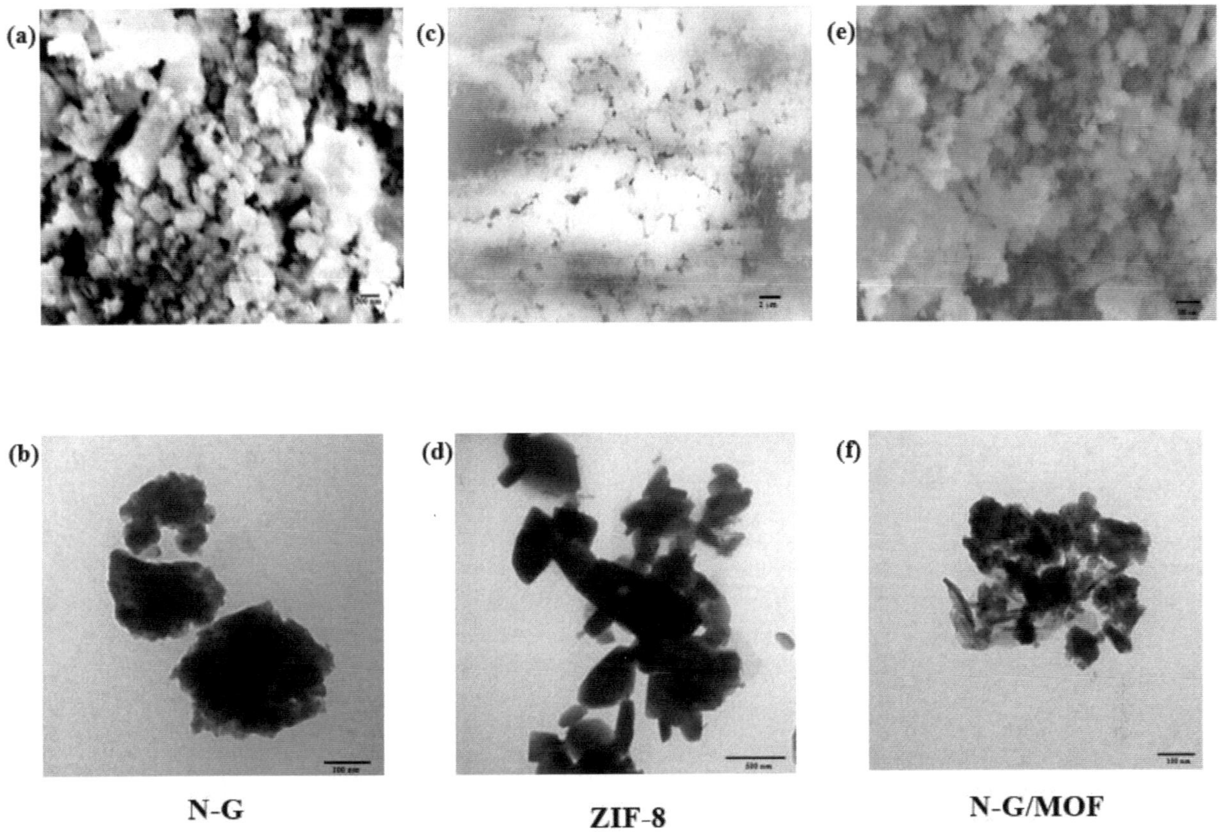

Figure 2. SEM and TEM Images of (a,b) N-G,(c,d) ZIF-8, and (e,f) N-G/MOF

surface area of the ORR electrocatalyst should be greater than 200 m^2/g [6]. Therefore, it is crucial to increase the BET surface area of N-G catalyst for enhanced ionic and electronic conductivity during ORR. This improvement is achieved by successfully incorporating ZIF-8 as a support for N-G using NHEW ball milling techniques. While evaluating the BET surface area of flexible MOF's like ZIF-8 (1775.4 m^2/g), it is very important to mention the pressure range $0.005 < P/Po < 0.02$ of the measurement. The BET surface area of the resultant N-G/MOF is 1039.79 m^2/g. It is believed that this reduction is because of NHEW ball milling the morphology of the catalyst is changed from crystalline to amorphous, which results in the loss of free volume of the porous ZIF-8 structure and, due to the dispersion of N-G particles over the ZIF-8 particles blocks the access to the internal microporous structure. However, the N-G/MOF catalyst has a significantly larger surface area for the practical applications.

XPS Characterization: Using X-ray photoelectron spectroscopy technique we can analyze the binding energies which contain the information of elemental composition and the nature of chemical bindings. Fig. 3(a) shows the N1s spectra of N-G and N-G/MOF catalyst. The active sites of the catalyst and their respective binding energies are pyridinic-N (398.4eV), graphitic-N (401eV), pyridinic N-O (402-404eV), and pyrrolic-N-H (400eV). The electrochemical performance of the N-G catalysts is determined by these active sites.

Table 1. Physical Characterizations of the precursors and catalysts

	Graphene Oxide	N-G	MOF	N-G/MOF
BET Surface Area (m^2/g)	347.23	77.81	1775.4	1039.79
Pore Volume (cc/g)	0.4	0.08	0.62	0.42
Avg. Pore Size (nm)	2.76	1.4	1.1	1.08

Fig. 3(b) indicates a new binding in the N-G/MOF chemical structure. During the synthesis process of N-G/MOF, the ZIF-8 heteroatom containing C-N-Zn is decomposed and influences the nitrogen spectra. This indicates that along with physical structure change there is also chemical structure change during the ball milling process. The new chemical bindings have different ratios of nitrogen functional groups. The electrochemical performance of the N-G/MOF is better than N-G catalyst. This adds to the ambiguity of the activity of the nitrogen

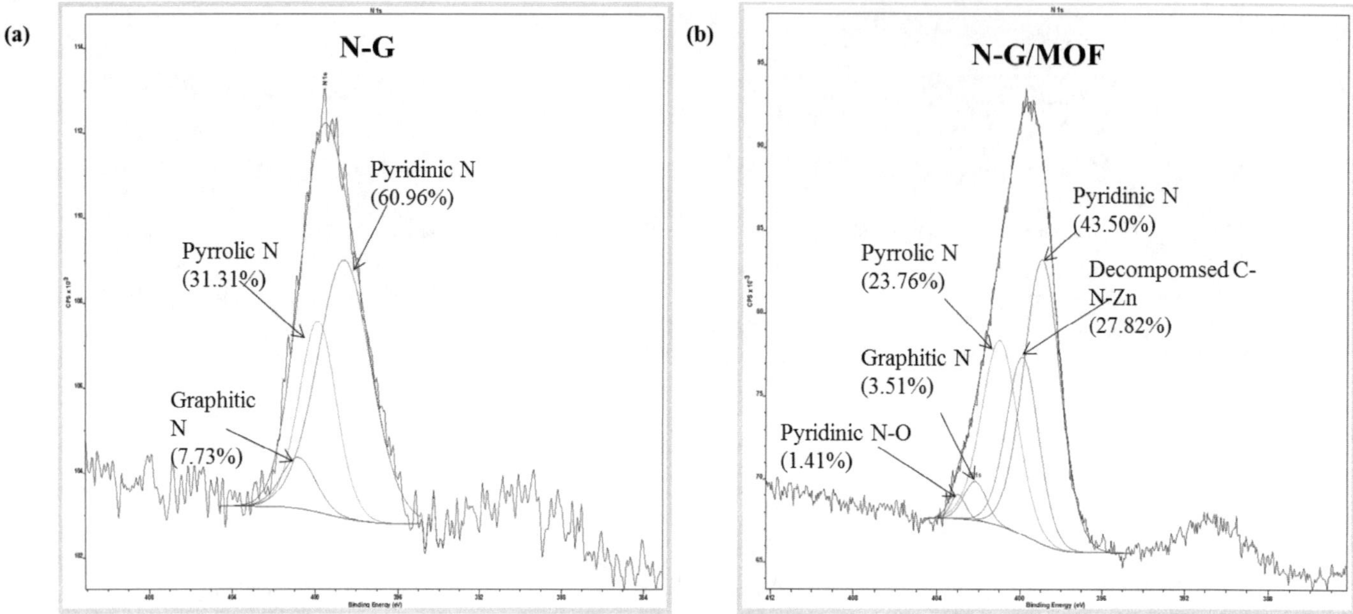

Figure 3. XPS- Nitrogen spectra of (a) N-G, (b) N-G/MOF

functional groups but it is clear that the activity of the N-G/MOF is controlled by the ratio of these functional groups.

The electrochemical performance of the N-G/MOF catalyst is comparable to the 10% Pt/C, where the current density of N-G/MOF is 5.02 mA/cm^2 and that of Pt/C is 4.3 mA/cm^2 [5].

Conclusion:

From this research we can conclude that (i) Both the physical and chemical structure of the N-G/MOF catalyst controls the electrochemical performance;(i) large BET surface area of N-G/MOF enhances the availability of the active sites to the ORR relevant species (ii) Different chemical bindings and ratios of the active sites have different electrochemical performance. The addition of metal-organic Framework in the nitrogen-doped graphene catalyst is an effective method to control the physical and chemical properties. In whole, we conclude that N-G/MOF is a promising catalyst and have the potential to replace the PGM catalysts.

Acknowledgement:

The authors acknowledge the research support from the Materials Characterization Laboratory at Otto H. York center (NJIT), Advanced Energy Systems and Microdevices Laboratory (NJIT). This research is carried out in part at the Center for Functional Materials, Brookhaven National Laboratory, which is supported by the US Department of Energy, Office of Basic Energy Sciences, under Contract No. DE-SC0012704. We would also like to thank the administrative support from the department of Mechanical and Industrial Engineering at NJIT.

References:

1. Wang H, Maiyalagan T, Wang X. Review on recent progress in nitrogen-doped graphene: synthesis, characterization, and its potential applications, 10.1021/cs200652. ACS Catalysis 2012; 2:781–794.
2. H.-W. Liang, W. Wei, Z.-S. Wu, X. Feng, and K. Müllen: Mesoporous metal–nitrogen-doped carbon electrocatalysts for highly efficient oxygen reduction reaction. J. Am. Chem. Soc. 135, 16002 (2013).
3. S.R. Batten, N.R. Champness, X.-M. Chen, J. Garcia-Martinez, S. Kitagawa, L. Öhrström, M. O'Keeffe, M. Paik Suh, and J. Reedijk: Terminology of metal–organic frameworks and coordination polymers (IUPAC Recommendations 2013). Pure Appl. Chem. 85, 1715 (2013).
4. S. Zhuang, E.S. Lee, L. Lei, B.B. Nunna, L. Kuang, and W. Zhang: Synthesis of nitrogen-doped graphene catalyst by high-energy wet ball milling for electrochemical systems. Int. J. Energy Res. 40, 2136 (2016).
5. S Zhuang, E.S. Lee, and B.B Nunna: Metal organic framework-modified nitrogen-doped graphene oxygen reduction reaction catalyst synthesized by nanoscale high-energy wet ball-milling structural and electrochemical characterization. MRS Communications, 2017.
6. P.K. Shen, C.-Y. Wang, S.P. Jiang, X. Sun and J. Zhang, Electrochemical energy: advanced materials and technologies, CRC Press, 2016.

Sates of Water in Thermally Annealed Recast Nafion® Films and Impact on Fuel Cell Performance

Xiaoming Ren, Eric Gobrogge and Frederick Beyer
US Army Research Laboratory
SEDD-C, 2800 Powder Mill Road
Adelphi, Maryland 20783, USA
contactauthors-xiaoming.ren.civ@mail.mil / 1-301-394-0379

Abstract: *The states of water in recast H^+-Nafion® ionomer films thermally annealed at temperatures up to 120°C were determined using attenuated total internal reflection FTIR (ATR-FTIR) spectroscopy. This study revealed that the Nafion films annealed at temperatures above the glass transition temperature form a more robust polymer matrix, which exerts restriction on the size of the water clusters in the ionic aggregates in the polymer films. Such morphological changes under annealing treatment were further supported by the small-angle X-ray scattering (SAXS) experiments. The impact of the annealing treatment on the recast Nafion in the fuel cell electrodes on the hydrogen/air fuel cell performance is also presented.*

Keywords: Water hydrogen bonding; Polymer morphology, SAXS, ATR-FTIR spectroscopy; Nafion, Recast ionomer; Annealing treatment; Fuel Cells.

Introduction

Perfluorosulfonic acid (PFSA) polymer electrolyte materials such as Nafion® are key components for many important electrochemical devices, such as fuel cells, electrolyzers, flow batteries, etc. (1; 2) Recast films from the ionomer solution are used in the catalyst layer to establish a three-dimensional reaction zone for enhanced catalyst utilization (3-5). The excellent transport and mechanical properties demonstrated by the PFSA polymer electrolytes are attributed to the unique phenomenon of nanoscale phase separation into the hydrophobic and hydrophilic domains upon water uptake. The hydrophobic domains are comprised of entangled and bundled poly-tetrafluoroethylene (PTFE) polymer backbone chains, which form a robust polymer framework responsible for maintaining the excellent mechanical properties of the polymer materials. While the hydrophilic domains consisting of the sulfonic acid aggregates (at the termini of the polymer side chains) and water clusters are responsible for retaining the good transport properties for protons, water, reactants and products.(6-9) Upon water uptake, a balance is maintained between the expanding force of the osmotic pressure (from solvating the sulfonic acid groups) and the restricting force of the elastic pressure (from the deformed polymer framework), resulting with the polymer morphology evolves considerably to accommodate the amount of water absorbed.

Understanding the states of water and the interaction between the water and the perfluorosulfonic acid aggregates in the polymer is essential for the development and applications of the polymer electrolyte materials. In this study, we utilized attenuated total internal reflection Fourier Transform infrared (ATR FT-IR) spectroscopy to identify and quantify the states of water in recast Nafion® films thermally annealed. Using the spectra obtained from bulk water and known concentrations of triflic acid solutions as standards, the states and distribution of water in the recast Nafion® films were quantitatively determined with Principle Component Analysis (PCA) and Multivariant Curve Resolution (MCR) methods. Additionally, small-angle X-ray scattering (SAXS) experiments were performed to verify the film morphology indicated by the ATR-FTIR experiments. H_2/air fuel cell tests were carried out to examine the impacts of the ionomer thermal annealing treatment on the H_2/air fuel cell performance stability. The results obtained in this study provide useful insights on the important roles played by water in polymer electrolyte materials.

Experimental

FTIR-ATR Measurements: All FTIR-ATR spectra were collected using a Nicolet 6700 FT-IR (Thermo Scientific) spectrometer equipped with an ATR accessory unit (specAC) with a diamond crystal reflection element at 45° incident beam angle. More than 128 scans were accumulated with a DLaTGS detector in the 4000-700 cm^{-1} range at 2 cm^{-1} resolution for each spectrum. Nafion® recast films (estimated to be at 5.0 μm) on the diamond crystal were formed by slowly evaporating the solvent from the ionomer solution (Aldrich) at room temperature. Thermal annealing of the films was carried out in an oven at a temperature ranging from 80°C to 120°C for 1.5 hs. Water uptake ((wet film mass-dry film mass)/dry film mass) by the recast film was gravimetrically determined by weighing the film deposited on a sapphire wafer. The final dry film mass was obtained after drying the film at 120°C under vacuum (0.015 torr) for 24 hs and weighed immediately in a dry room with a dew point of -89°C.

Principle Component Analysis and Multivariate Curve Resolution: Principle Component Analysis (PCA) was used to determine the minimum number of components required in a linear combination to explain the sample data variation, and a Multivariate Curve Resolution (MCR) method using alternating lease squares curve fitting was used to extract the pure component spectra and their intensities from the sample data, according to the following bilinear model:

$$D(n\ m) = C(n\ s) * ST(s\ m) + E_{rror}(n\ m) \qquad [1]$$

Where D(n m) is the sample datum matrix composed of n sample spectra at m wavenumbers, C(n s) is the intensity matrix of the s components in n samples, ST(s m) is the transposed spectrum matrix of the s principle components at m wavenumbers, and E_{rror}(n m) is the error matrix containing the difference between the sample and predicted model spectra. Data analyses were performed using an open source Matlab program (10).

Small-Angle X-Ray Scattering Experiments: Small-angle X-ray scattering (SAXS) data were collected using a Rigaku S-MAXS 3000 instrument, which uses a Rigaku MicroMax-007HF rotating Cu anode source and a Confocal Max-Flux double-focusing optic to produce photons having a wavelength, λ, of 1.542 Å. Data were collected using a Rigaku 200 mm diameter multiwire area detector at camera lengths of 1.5 m and 0.5 m. Two-dimensional data were azimuthally averaged into one-dimensional intensity (I) as a function of momentum transfer vector magnitude, q, of 0.007 $Å^{-1}$ to 0.5 $Å^{-1}$, where $q = 4\pi\sin(\theta)/\lambda$ and 2θ is the scattering angle. The scattering data were fit assuming scattering from two distinct sets of features originating from the polymer backbone PTFE crystallites and ionic aggregates. A hard sphere structure factor was used to account for interparticle scattering, both for PTFE crystallites and ionic aggregates.

Fuel Cell Preparation and Tests: Fuel cell tests were conducted at the single cell level with 5 cm^2 active electrode area using a fuel cell hardware and test station from Fuel Cell Technology Inc. (Albuquerque, New Mexico, USA). The Pt catalyzed carbon cloth gas diffusion electrode (GDE) (Fuel Cell Store, College Station, Texas, USA, 0.5 mg Pt /cm^2 using 60 wt.% Pt on carbon support as the catalyst) was spray-coated with the Nafion ionomer solution to reach a loading of 0.33 mg Nafion/cm^2, and then thermally annealed in a nitrogen atmosphere at a temperature up to 120°C for 1.5 hrs. Two identically annealed GDEs sandwiching a DuPont Nafion PFSA NR-212 membrane (1100 g/mol in equivalent weight, 50.8 um in thickness) were finally steam-pressed together at 80°C to form the MEA.

The fuel cell tests were conducted at 80°C with a hydrogen feed (80°C humidified, 150 sccm, 0 psig) at the cell anode and an air feed (80°C humidified, 250 sccm, 0 psig) at the cell cathode. Fuel cell stability tests were conducted by holding the cell at a constant cell voltage of 0.65 V.

Results and discussions

In accordance with reports in literature (11; 12), we found that 99.98% variations in the spectra of bulk water ranging from 0.3°C to 90°C can be accounted for by just two principle water components, which are labeled in this study as a high level hydrogen-bonded water (HLHW) clusters, and a low level hydrogen-bonded water (LLHW) clusters.

In an electrolyte solution, in addition to the water in the HLHW and LLHW states, some water molecules form hydration shell waters (HSW) surrounding the ionic species. In this study, we examined trifluoromethanesulfuric acid (triflic acid) solutions ranging from neat acid to a much diluted concentration. Some representative spectra are shown in Fig. 1. The states of water and the sulfonate acid groups are quantified by examining the evolution of the FT-IR absorption spectra as the water content is increased. At λ (defined as the mole ratio of $H_2O/-SO_3^-$) = 1, the sulfonic acid groups ($-SO_3H$) are completely converted to sulfonates ($-SO_3^-$) and hydroniums (H_3O^+) as evidenced by the disappearance of the S-OH stretching bands at 960 cm^{-1} and 1400 cm^{-1}, and the appearance of a $-SO_3^-$ stretching band at 1034 cm^{-1} (Fig. 1, comparing neat triflic acid to 45 m solution). At this low water content, the strong interaction between the H_3O^+ and $-SO_3^-$ induces ion-pair formation which weakens the O-H bond as reflected by the red shift of water O-H stretch to a frequency around 2800 cm^{-1}. At λ = 2, HSW starts to form around the ions, as evidenced by the appearance of the broad O-H stretching band at 3450 cm^{-1}. At λ > 2, the δ(H-O-H) (bending mode) band at 1630 cm^{-1} for hydrogen bonded water appears, and the O-H stretching region can be described by a linear combination of the pure spectra for the three states of water: HSW, LLHW, and HLHW.

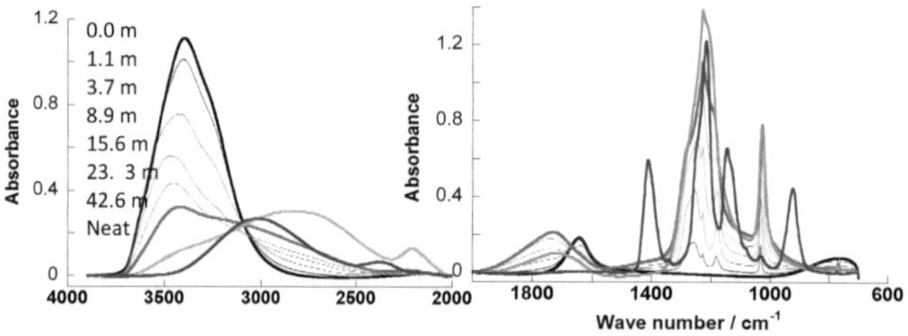

Figure 1. FT-IR absorption spectra of triflic acid and aqueous solutions collected at 22°C. The concentrations are denoted in the order of decreasing intensity for the peak around 3400 cm^{-1}.

FT-IR spectra of water OH stretch for the annealed recast Nafion® films in contact with liquid water, water vapor at 96% R.H. and dry argon are shown in Fig. 2. The water O-H stretching FT-IR spectra of the triflic acid solutions matches well with those of the recast H+-Nafion® films at similar water contents, indicating that the effects on the water O-H stretching vibrations by the polymer chains and trifluoromethyl group are not significantly different in these two electrolytes.

For the thermally annealed films, the amount of water in films in contact with water vapor at 96% R.H. decreases slightly with an increase in annealing treatment temperature. In comparison, when the films are exposed to liquid water, the water content decreases substantially with an increase in annealing treatment temperature (Figs. 2).

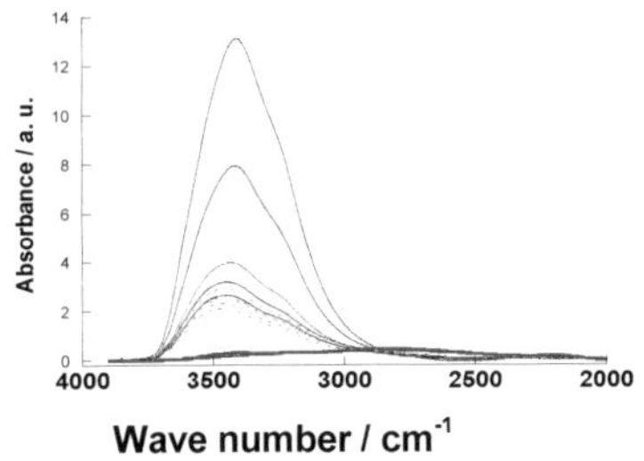

Figure 2. Water O-H bond stretching ATR FT-IR spectra of the recast H^+-Nafion® films in contact with liquid water (solid lines, blue), water vapor at 96% R.H. (dashed lines, green) and dry argon (dotted lines, red) after thermal annealing treatments at 22, 80,100, 110 and 120°C. The peak heights decrease as the treatment temperature increases.

The states of water in the recast Nafion® films were determined using the PCA-MCR method using those in the bulk water and triflic acid solutions as standards. Fig. 3 shows the distribution of water in the films in the HLHW, LLHW and HSW states as a function of the annealing treatment temperature. When exposed to liquid water, the fraction of water in HLHW state is 41% for a Nafion® film without thermal annealing treatment. As the annealing treatment temperature is increased to above 110°C, this value decreases to near zero. When exposed to water vapor at 96% R.H., water in the LLHW state decrease slightly with the increase in the annealing treatment temperature, while the waters in the HLHW remain at zero for all annealing temperatures. For all the cases, the water in the HSW state remains nearly constant in the range of $\lambda = 5\text{-}6$. With an increase in the annealing treatment temperature, not only is there less water in the films in contact with liquid water, but the bulk-like water also has a lower degree of hydrogen bonded water networks (as evaluated by the decreased ratio of $\lambda_{HLHW}/\ \lambda_{LLHW}$). At annealing temperatures above the glass transition temperature, the PTFE backbone polymer chains possess enough kinetic energy to arrange themselves and bundle together to form PTFE crystallites thereby minimizing their total surface energy. Since the water in the HLHW state only exists when the water cluster structures are sufficiently large in size to establish a high level of two- and four-hydrogen bonded water networks, our findings suggest that the thermal annealing treatment at a temperature above the glass transition temperature decreases the expandable space available. The fused joints of the PTFE polymer chains prevent the admission of enough water molecules to establish HLHW water clusters.

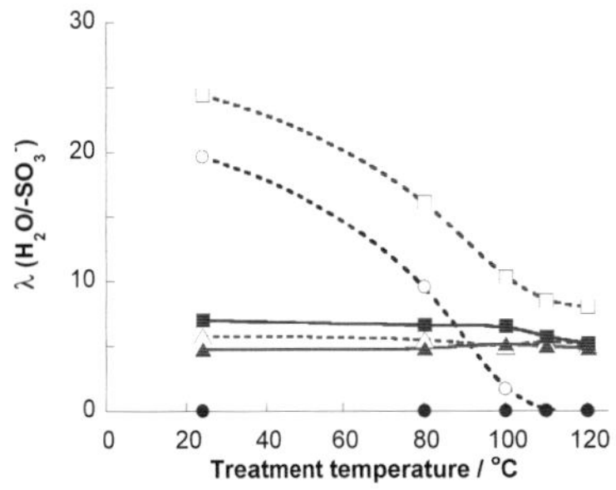

Figure 3. Number of water per sulfonic site in the HLHW (circles), LLHW (squares), and HSW (triangles) states in H^+-Nafion® recast films in contact with water vapor at 96% R.H. (solid lines with filled symbols), and with liquid water (dashed line with open symbols) at room temperature as a function of thermal annealing treatment temperature.

The impact of annealing treatment temperature on the morphology of recast Nafion films was further studied using small-angle X-ray scattering (SAXS). The azimuthally averaged data are shown in Fig. 4. Increasing the annealing temperature results in two changes to film morphology. First, the polymer matrix peak, which is due to interdomain scattering from the PTFE crystallites and is centered around $q \approx 0.06$ Å^{-1}, becomes significantly better defined and increases in intensity. Model fits to this peak indicate that the mean size of the PTFE crystallites increases with annealing temperature, while the variation in crystallite size (for 100°C and above) stays relatively steady. This demonstrates that at temperatures above 100°C, the PTFE backbone polymer chains reorganize and align with each other to form a structure with an increased PTFE crystallinity.

The second change in morphology is related to the ionic cluster peak ($q \approx 0.18$ - 0.23 Å^{-1}), which arises from scattering by clusters of the charged sulfonate groups. Annealing the films causes the ionic cluster peak to shift to higher q, indicating a decrease in the separation between the ionic aggregates. Thus from both SAXS and ATR-FTIR experiments, it can be concluded that a Nafion film treated at a higher annealing temperature forms a more robust polymer framework surrounding the ionic aggregates of decreased sizes.

The stability test of a H_2/air fuel cell prepared with non-thermally annealed recast Nafion in the catalyst layers was carried out at 80°C at a constant cell voltage of 0.65 V (Fig. 7). The VI curves taken during the stability tests are shown in Fig. 8. The cell performance loss during the stability test is clearly correlated to the decrease in the limiting current of the oxygen transport. The high levels of water uptake and dissolution rate of the non-annealed Nafion could directly contribute to the cathode flooding. The leaching of Nafion from the cathode catalyst layer assisted by the outward flow of water generated from the fuel cell reaction can cause the PTFE treated microporous layer on the cathode backing layer to lose its initial hydrophobicity.

This results in the pores being gradually filled with liquid water, which blocks the fast oxygen diffusion in the gas phase to the catalyst layer. Thus, the thermal annealing treatment of the catalyst layers is a necessary step in fabricating the fuel cell MEAs in order to stabilize the recast Nafion.

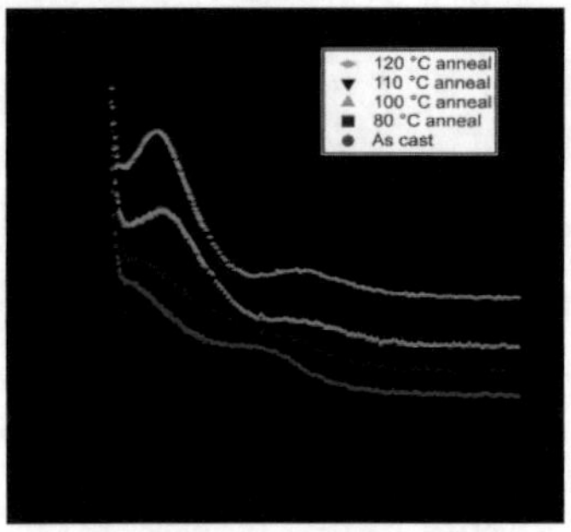

Figure 4. SAXS data collected from recast Nafion films after annealing at different temperatures. The classical Nafion scattering features, a matrix peak and an ionomer peak, are observed for samples annealed at 100°C and above. Data are shifted vertically for clarity.

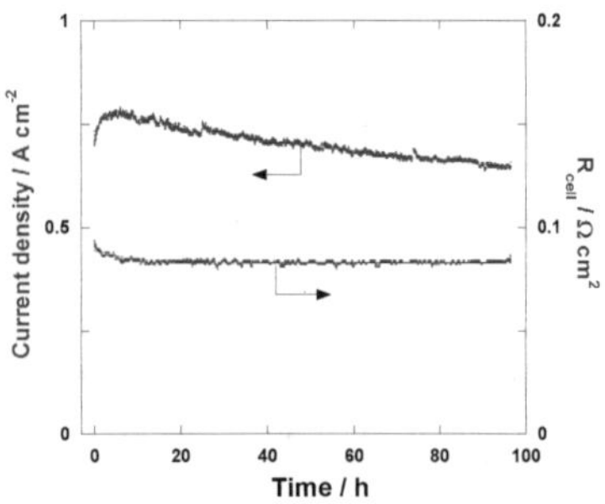

Figure 5. Cell current and area resistance measured during the stability test of a H2/air fuel cell at 80°C at a constant cell voltage held at 0.65 V. The fuel cell was prepared with the catalyst layers containing non-thermally annealed recast Nafion.

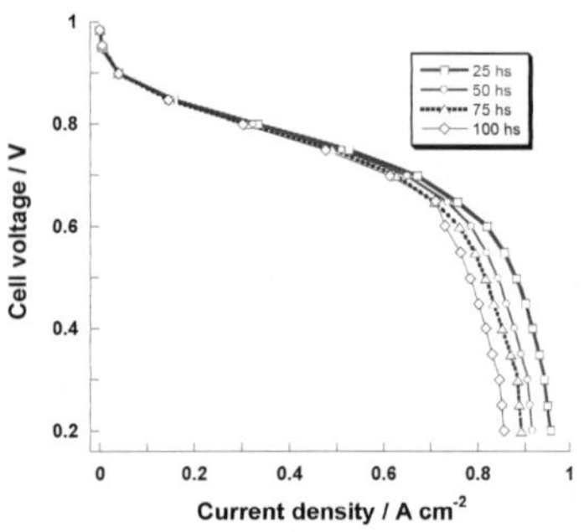

Figure 6. VI curves recorded during the course of fuel cell stability test shown in Fig. 5

Conclusions

This work demonstrated that one can use water O-H vibrational spectrum to identify and quantify the states of water in polymer electrolyte materials. The recast Nafion® films maintain a nearly constant amount of water in the HSW state at around λ = 5-6 under all the conditions examined in this study. Additional absorption of water in the Nafion® films is achieved by increasing the amount of water in the LLHW and HLHW states, both representing the bulk-like water.

Nafion films without a thermal annealing treatment have high water content in both LLHW and HLHW states when in contact with liquid water. Fuel cell stability tests on a cell prepared with the catalyst layers containing non-thermally annealed recast Nafion exhibit performance loss due to cathode flooding. The high levels of water uptake and dissolution rate of the non-annealed Nafion films could directly contribute to the cathode flooding.

Acknowledgments

The authors gratefully acknowledge the support of this work by U.S. Army Research Laboratory. The authors would also like to acknowledge the support and discussions with Dr. Cynthia Lundgren of the U.S. Army Research Laboratory, and with Dr. Jeff Owrutsky of U.S. Naval Research Laboratory.

References

1. S. Banerjee, and D. E. Curtin, *J. Fluorine Chem.*, **125**, 1211 (2004).
2. C. HeitnerWirguin, *J. Membr. Sci.*, **120**, 1 (1996).
3. X. Jian, D. L. Wood, K. L. More, P. Atanassov, and R. L. Borup, *J. Electrochem. Soc.*, **152**, A1011 (2005).
4. D. Lee, and S. Hwang, *Int. J. Hydrogen Energy*, **33**, 2790 (2008).
5. S. C. Thomas, X. Ren, and S. Gottesfeld, *J. Electrochem. Soc.*, **146**, 4354 (1999).
6. T. Okada, G. Xie, O. Gorseth, S. Kjelstrup, N. Nakamura, and T. Arimura, *Electrochim. Acta*, **43**, 3741 (1998).
7. A. Z. Weber, and J. Newman, *J. Electrochem. Soc.*, **150**, A1008 (2003).
8. X. Ren, T. D. Myles, K. N. Grew, and W. K. S. Chiu, *J. Electrochem. Soc.*, **162**, F1221 (2015).
9. G. S. Hwang, D. Y. Parkinson, A. Kusoglu, A. A. MacDowell, and A. Z. Weber, *Acs Macro Letters*, **2**, 288 (2013).
10. J. Jaumot, R. Gargallo, A. de Juan, and R. Tauler, *Chemom. Intell. Lab. Syst.*, **76**, 101 (2005).
11. Y. Marechal, *J. Mol. Struct.*, **1004**, 146 (2011).
12. W. C. McCabe, Subraman.S, and H. F. Fisher, *J. Phys. Chem.*, **74**, 4360 (1970).

Hydrogen Fuels from Solar Energy and Water: Using Inexpensive 2D Transition Metal Nitrides

Abdoulaye Djire, Hanyu Zhang, Jun Liu, Elisa Miller, and Nathan Neale*

National Renewable Energy Laboratory
Department of Chemistry and Nanoscience

Abstract: *United States is the largest user of energy in the world (more than 50% of total consumption), and any change in global energy use would require a change in U.S. production and consumption of energy. Renewable energy research is of utmost importance for developing a long-term, sustainable energy economy. Solar and wind power have shown technological and economic feasibility, as well as generation potential of relevant scale, to supply the growing global energy demand. Hydrogen as a chemical energy carrier is essential for energy storage, ammonia production, and as transportation fuel. This research aims to provide a clean, cost-effective, and locally produced solar fuel by using electroactive, two-dimensional (2D) layered transition metal nitrides (MXenes) photoelectrodes. Theoretical reports have shown that these materials, although inherently metallic, can become semiconductors via surface functionalization, and can be used as photoelectrodes for solar fuel production. Results highlighted in this presentation revealed the physical and photoelectrochemical properties of Ti4N3Tx and Ti2NTx nitrides with surface functional groups (Tx = O, OH, F). The materials showed excellent photoelectrochemical properties (i.e. solar-to-hydrogen efficiency) and good stability in aqueous media.*

Ti4N3Tx and Ti2NTx nitrides were synthesized via molten salt fluoride treatment of their corresponding Ti4AlN3 and Ti2AlN precursors. The phase purity, crystal structure, and removal of Al from the precursors were confirmed by X-ray diffraction and X-ray photoelectron analyses. Scanning electron microscopy and high-resolution transmission electron microscopy were used to access the morphologies of the layers (multilayers and single layers). Various electrochemical characterization techniques including linear sweep voltammetry, cyclic voltammetry and electrochemical impedance spectroscopy were used to evaluate the electrochemical properties of the synthesized materials.

Self-contained Energy Harvesting Sensor System

Alexa Aguilar, Tyler Larson, Andrew Davies, and Herbert L. Hess
Department of Electrical and Computer Engineering
University of Idaho
Moscow, Idaho 83844-1023
hhess@uidaho.edu / 1-208-885-4341

Abstract: *Harvesting energy from typical wireless router electromagnetic radiation. Energy that is normally considered can be exploited by capturing unused RF energy and converting it back into usable electricity. The design investigated several antenna configurations, settling on a half-wave dipole array. The resulting voltage is filtered and rectified for capacitive storage. The output of the combined network is then used for low-power applications, such as a microcontroller and sensor system. Receiving antenna concepts and naturally occurring waveguide geometries were investigated through simulations in ANSYS HFSS. A receiving antenna equivalent circuit was developed and verified in LTSPICE and then integrated with the rectifier and impedance matching model. A prototype of the receiving and conversion circuit was implemented in hardware, and a DC output of 176mV was observed on storage capacitors.*

Keywords: energy harvesting, sensor power, WiFi energy.

Introduction

Wireless communication and information exchange has become an integral part of the twenty-first century. These systems are designed for effective communication at appropriate speeds. Though they were not designed for transmission of energy, they do radiate continually at specified frequencies and known signal strengths in many buildings, populated areas, and even a few rather remote places. Receiving efficiencies for these systems, however, are quite low, and much of the transmitted power is lost during data exchanges. Knowing this, these losses can be exploited by harvesting the unused RF energy and converting it back into usable electricity.

The objective of this work is to build a proof of concept device that captures some portion of the electromagnetic energy radiated by a typical wireless network, stores it temporarily, and then uses it for a low power electronic circuit application. A sequence of functions or tasks provides an organized means to accomplish this objective as illustrated in Figure 1. The energy harvesting device has three separate subsystems:

- an antenna subsystem consisting of an optimized trace, a bandpass filter, and an impedance matching network,
- electronic energy conversion circuitry which is an isolated bridge rectifier with filtering, and
- a load such as a sensor or the unit's controller.

An antenna system captures the radiated energy in sufficient quantity to be useful for a desired application. This energy passes through a trace designed to match impedance and to minimize transmission energy losses. A bandpass filter provides single-frequency sinusoidal signal for the rectifier. The rectifier converts the energy to a direct current appropriate for energy storage and for powering an electronic load at point of use. Through both computational models (simulation) and hardware prototypes, a design was developed for capturing ambient RF energy, specifically Wi-Fi, and for filtering and rectifying that energy into a usable form of a DC voltage. Applications may then use the energy to perform desired electronic tasks. The amount of energy captured and processed is quite small, but there are tasks, such as certain sensors and data gathering functions, that perform well on the amounts and patterns of energy available with such an energy harvesting system. Therefore, the result of this work is a self-contained device that harvests energy from typical radiated wireless network signals, processes that energy to a desired form and location, and then uses that energy for a sensor and data gathering load.

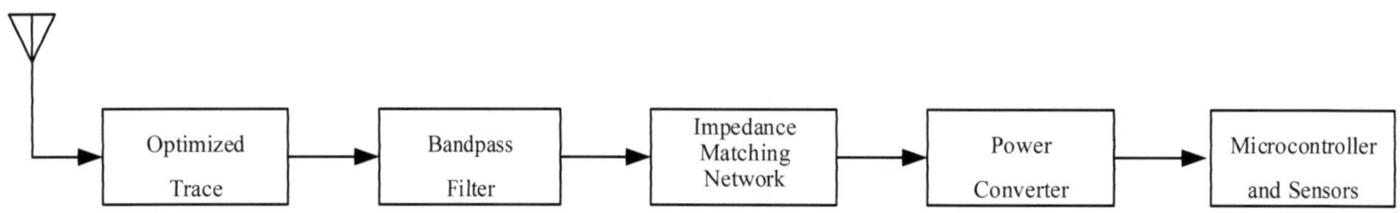

Figure 1. Energy Harvesting System Concept.

Antenna Subsystem Design

In this section, an antenna subsystem is developed, a subsystem to capture enough energy for the purpose at hand, including losses in energy conversion and transmission to point of application. Wireless routers radiate signals in a 2.4 GHz band throughout many office buildings, homes, and other places. Governments strictly regulate frequency and signal strength of these router signals as part of their spectrum management responsibilities. Likewise, manufacturers design wireless receivers for expected frequency and signal strength. Information technology specialists maintain that wireless signal strength at desired levels within many urban office buildings. Routers for home use have similar performance. This gives a predictable environment for harvesting that radiated energy.

Several possibilities were considered for the antenna subsystem, but a half-wave dipole array and a Planar Inverted F Antenna (PIFA) produces the best combination of the amount of energy captured, the radiation pattern, and simplicity. The antenna must be designed to capture the most available energy while still maintaining a manageable size, form factor, and complexity. Both dipole antennas and planar inverted-F antennas (PIFA) prove to be the best to do this at the energy levels that were considered. Dipole antennas have simplicity, but PIFA antennas match many wireless router antennas, an appropriate condition to minimize energy lost in transmission. ANSYS HFSS simulations using standard antenna models show radiation patterns for the receiver in Figure 2.[1] Using design toolboxes in MATLAB, the design of the receiver antenna was optimized for a known signal strength characteristic of wireless routers for commercial buildings. An optimized two-dipole array captures nearly an order of magnitude more energy than a single optimized dipole. The array itself is two dipole antennas configured in physical parallel with each other. Each antenna is 7.5cm in length and 6.2cm apart. The maximum power at 2.412GHz is 4.68mW. The PIFA antenna gives similar performance for a similar size.[2]

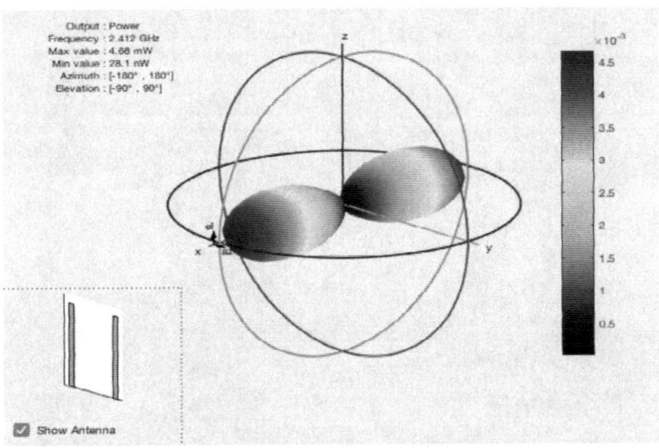

Figure 2. Two Dipole Antenna Radiation Pattern

Data of WiFi signal strength within the laboratory building is readily available from the university's Information Technology Services. For experiments, a Software Defined Radio (SDR) provide the ability to generate a known signal and then calculate its strength at the receiving antenna in the laboratory, all with a single testing device. The result of the design and testing phase of the project was the selection of a two dipole array. It provides the best tradeoff between energy captured, cost, size, and simplicity.

A microstrip trace is designed to transmit energy on the circuit board with minimal losses. It provides an appropriate impedance match to the cable capacitance of 101pF/m and inductance of 253nH/m.[2] Its S-parameters as a function of frequency are shown in Figure 3.

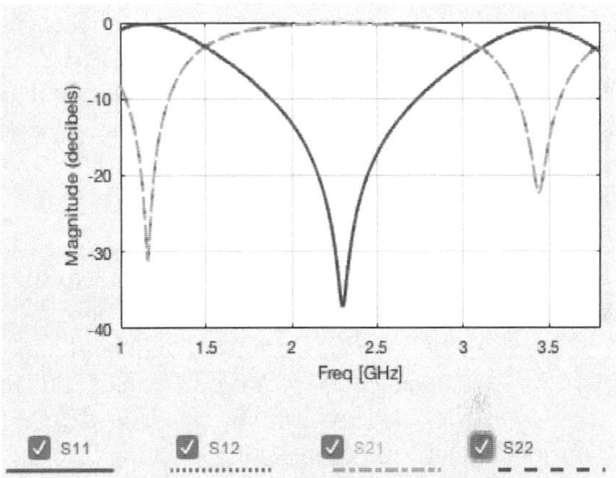

Figure 3. S Parameters of Two-Dipole Array

A third order bandpass filter provided impedance matching and eliminated possible destructive interference, providing a clean signal to the electronic energy conversion section. The design is shown in Figure 4.[1] It has a center frequency of 2.4GHz with a pass band of 0.4GHz. It provides a single frequency sinusoidal waveform to the power conversion section of the energy harvesting system.

Figure 4. Bandpass Filter.

Energy Conversion Subsystem

Though a clean signal that preserves most of the captured energy is delivered to the rectifier, this energy must be processed efficiently. A switching power converter is the obvious choice. Its switching behavior minimizes energy losses. Its flexibility provides operation at a wide range of frequencies. Its output can be readily sent to a low pass filter to gain a direct current that can charge capacitive energy storage. On the other hand, rectifying a 2.4GHz signal presents two great challenges: high frequency operation and low voltage signal strength.

The frequency provides the greatest challenge to the rectifier design. Few power electronic switching devices operate at all at 2.4GHz. Those that may operate there are not necessarily efficient. As such, either a CMOS transistor-based active rectifier or a Schottky-diode based rectifier becomes attractive. CMOS circuits abound in that frequency range; Wireless routers have CMOS chips. Schottky diodes have wide bandwidths and a very low forward voltage drop.

Signal amplitude is quite small, providing a challenge to rectifier switching device selection. Again, active CMOS rectifiers and Schottky diode rectifiers are most attractive. On larger rectifiers, a CMOS active rectifier is generally superior, but at low signal amplitude, Schottky diodes have a slight advantage to meet low forward voltage specifications here.

The rectified voltage is substantially less than any target applications may require. Therefore, a low power, low input voltage DC/DC converter follows the Schottky diode rectifier. This converter, an Analog Devices LTC3105, amplifies signals as low as 200mV, boosting them to a 3.3Volt level that is compatible with a range of applications. The LTC3105 was originally created to serve photovoltaic energy conversion and thermoelectric generation, technologies that occasionally have similar problems with voltage levels. It has a maximum power point tracker to optimize power output for very small input voltages.[3] An LT SPICE schematic model of the power conversion circuit is shown in Figure 5 and results are shown in Figure 6.[2]

Sensor Application and Experimental Results

The target application is a remote sensor system that wakes up from time to time to take a reading or send a transmission of data. The amount of energy captured is quite small. However, when integrated over a long time, sufficient energy can be accumulated to operate many low power sensors. Both the Schottky diode half bridge rectifier and the LTC3105 chip operate in a boost mode. As such, they use the series inductance of the system to force energy to accumulate on capacitors for storage. This accumulation provides enough energy to power sensor and data communication electronics designed for intermittent operation. The final design has 3 temperature sensors that send a reading to a microcontroller for processing and long term nonvolatile storage. The system reaps its own energy for sensing, energy conversion, and signal processing. It is to a degree self-contained.

Experimental is shown in Figure 7 and experimental results are shown in Figure 8. The rectifier placed a consistent 2.35Volts and 2.15Volts on capacitors C1 and C6, respectively, diagrammed in Figure 5. The system accumulated enough energy over a nine-hour period to raise an output voltage of 176 mV, just slightly short of the 200mV necessary to operate the DC/DC converter. (The LTC3105 DC/DC converter was tested and verified separately.) [3]

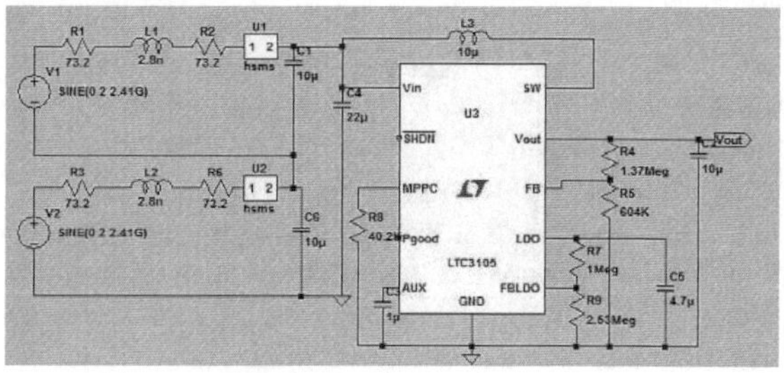

Figure 5. LT SPICE Schematic of Power Converter Subsystem.

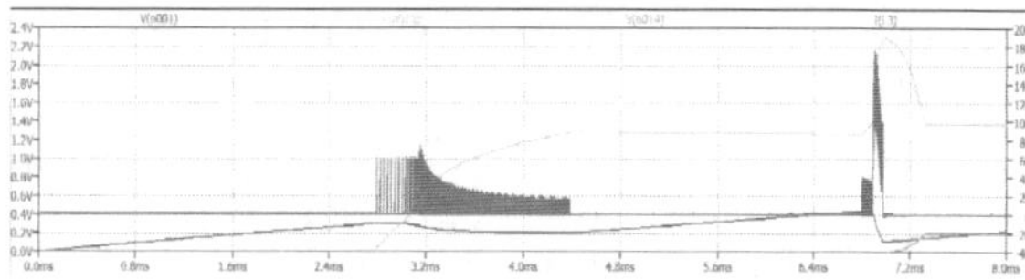

Figure 6. Simulation Results for Power Converter Subsystem

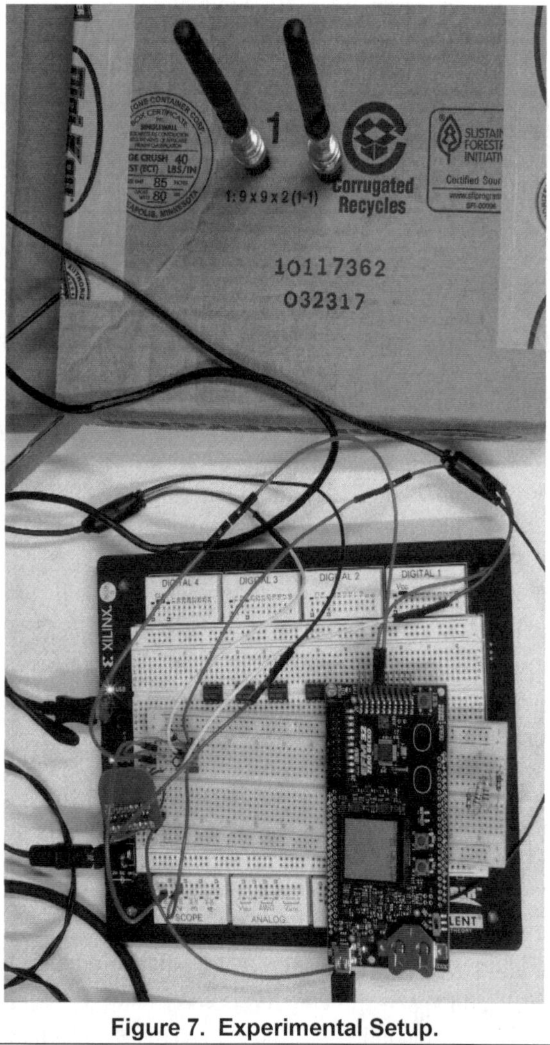

Figure 7. Experimental Setup.

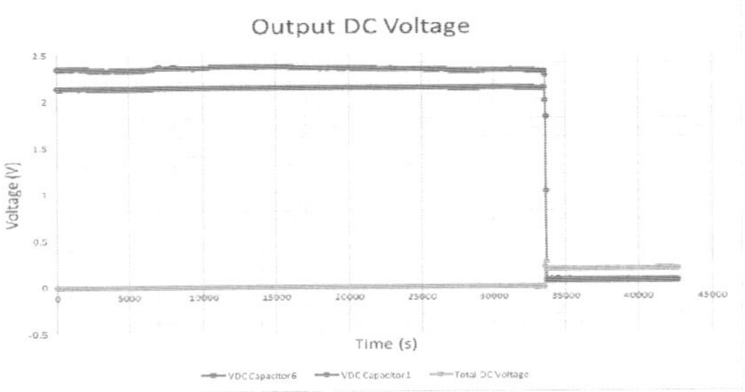

Figure 8. Experimental Results: Output Voltages

Conclusions

An energy harvesting system has been shown in this paper. It reaps energy from a typical wireless router system common to many commercial buildings and residential installations. It captures energy through three subsystems: an antenna array with microstrip transmission and a bandpass filter for signal integrity. For an antenna subsystem, it has a two-dipole array, chosen from ANSYS HFSS simulations for its energy capture, cost, size, and simplicity. A microstrip transmission line provides efficient energy transmission from the antenna and a bandpass filter yields a single frequency for rectification. Energy then feeds into a rectifier that uses a boost mode to convert the 2.4GHz signal into direct current and employing system inductance, forces that energy onto storage capacitors. A DC/DC converter with MTTP control provides amplification to levels appropriate to run a sensor system that wakes up from time to time to make readings or communicate data. The system was tested and found to provide an output voltage of 176mV in nine hours, just short of what is necessary to operate the sensor system.

References

1. Aguilar, A., T. Larsen, A. Davies, and H. Hess, "Freely Reaped Electromagnetic Energy," Proceedings of the Fourteenth International Planetary Probe Workshop, The Hague, Netherlands, June 2017.

2. Aguilar, A., T. Larsen, A. Davies, and H. Hess, "Freely Reaped Electromagnetic Energy," http://mindworks.shoutwiki.com/wiki/Freely_Reaped_Electromagnetic_Energy_(FREE)_2016-2017, Accessed 22 April 2018.

3. Analog Devices, "LTC3105 data sheet," http://www.analog.com/media/en/technical-documentation/data-sheets/3105fb.pdf, Accessed 22 April 2018.

Acknowledgements

This research was funded by the University of Idaho Faculty of Excellence in Electric Power Endowment and by alumni and faculty donations to the University of Idaho Department of Electrical Engineering. The following students performed the work on this project: Alexa Aguilar, Tyler Larsen, and Andrew Davies.

Integrated Energy Solutions for Cold Weather Operations from Soldier to Deployed Camps

Ed Andrukaitis
Defence Research and Development Canada, Department of National Defence
101 Colonel By Drive, Ottawa, Ontario, CANADA, K1A 0K2
ed.andrukaitis@forces.gc.ca

Abstract: *The Canadian Armed Forces rely on fossil fuels, such as kerosene, to meet shelter heating, lighting and cooking requirements for tactical camps in the High Arctic. Typically, these needs are met using open flame technologies inside the tent, which increases carbon monoxide / carbon dioxide levels and the risk of fire. Ninety five percent of the fuel consumed in an Arctic shelter is used to heat it. Baseline energy usage was measured for the current Army shelter system and alternative commercial shelters. Also, alternative energy systems will be evaluated to demonstrate a strategy or solution to reduce energy consumption. Results conclude that shelter design improvements can not only reduce fuel consumption significantly, but also address the military requirement of reducing the burden for deployed soldiers in austere environments, such as the High Arctic.*

Keywords: Cold weather operation; shelter heating; alternative energy systems; arctic shelter; energy audit.

Introduction

Militaries often work under very adverse conditions and different operational scenarios. The energy required to sustain such operations can be variable. This is especially true for areas in which the Canadian Armed Forces (CAF) needs to operate, such as austere environments like Canada's High Arctic. Currently, sustainment of tactical missions in the High Arctic relies on in-shelter open-flame burning of fossil fuels, such as kerosene, to provide shelter space heating and white gas (naphtha) to provide lighting and cooking fuel. The issues with this approach is that it increases the fire hazard risk and potential elevated levels of dangerous gases to CAF personnel. Also the release of GHGs in a pristine environment is counter to the new Department of National Defence (DND) Policy 'The Defence Energy and Environment Strategy' [1]. A goal for DND is to reduce the carbon footprint and reduce the burning of fossil fuels as much as possible to meet or exceed the federal targets for GHG emissions.

To identify and demonstrate suitable replacement (energy efficient, safe and reliable) solutions in cold climates, Defence Research and Development Canada (DRDC) is leading an energy survey under the Joint Arctic Experiment (JAE) project. A Canadian Government partnership involving Department of National Defence (DND), Defence Research and Development Canada (DRDC) and Natural Resources Canada (NRCan) was established under JAE. Technology insertion is being explored as well through the North American Technology and Industrial Base Organization (NATIBO) with the U.S. Army Communications-Electronics Research, Development and Engineering Center (CERDEC). NATIBO is chartered to promote a cost effective, healthy technology and industrial base that is responsive to the national and economic security needs of the United States and Canada.

Whether conducting search and rescue operations, asserting Canadian sovereignty, or during training activities, better energy efficiency systems are but one of the factors that can impact the ability of CAF members to achieve success in the North. The first steps this year were to conduct an energy and environmental audit of the tactical deployed camp during the Joint Arctic Experiment to gain an understanding of baseline energy requirements. As well, a comparative energy study between typical and energy efficient shelter systems was conducted during JAE to then perform a simulation-based analysis on possible shelter efficiency improvements, both to minimize cold exposure and reduce shelter fuel demands. Continuing into the second year of the project, alternative power systems are being evaluated for shelter lighting and cooking, such as high capacity batteries and direct methanol fuel cells. The results from this year will be discussed, along with how industry can contribute to future demonstrations.

In general, for large operational camp installations in ambient temperature ranges, the fossil fuel is used to generate electrical power for a multitude of camp functions (shelters, command post, kitchen, ablutions, etc) [2]. The last comprehensive study of camp power in cold weather environments was conducted in 2012 [3] where about 80% of the fuel is used to generate electrical power.

However, operating in the High Arctic is very different where diesel is burned directly in heaters for shelters and troop movements are conducted on snowmobiles. Thus, it is critical to limit burden on a squad operating in this austere environment. This study will monitor and record the fuel and energy consumption of shelter systems for consideration in an Arctic environment for the first time, thus providing a baseline for comparison in future studies and optimization for JAE 2019.

CAF Joint Arctic Experiment (JAE) 2018 Results

Energy Audit Analysis

The study focused this year on the smaller sleeping shelter systems likely to be deployed in High Arctic regions typically on the scale of a squad (up to 10 persons). For this size of operation, mobility via snowmobiles and reduced burden (packing weight) is essential. Thus, shelter and energy systems to provide heat, light and cooking (hot water) add significantly to this burden. As part of the experiment for JAE 2018 just completed in March, shelter systems were setup which included a typical military shelter (Bell tent design) used over 50 years by the CAF for high Arctic deployments and two commercial shelters (as shown in Figure 1). The farthest shelter (PH) in the background of the figure also comes with an insulated floor.

Figure 1: JAE18 Energy experiment showing a typical military shelter in the foreground and two common commercial shelters in background.

The commercial shelter in the middle (AO) of Figure 1, has a double walled system with an inner insulation layer and small vestibules (46 square feet each) at the entrances that help to reduce heat loss. Commercial diesel heaters (rated 30,000 BTU) were used in the commercial tents. The military tent was configured in standard issued items, with a Coleman Dual Fuel 2-Burner (rated 17,000 BTU) used for heating/lighting, a Yukon Stove (27,000 BTU) and kerosene lantern for lighting.

All the shelters were metered with sensors at various heights and locations to enable recording of temperature, as well the level of CO, CO_2 and humidity. The temperature at the Cambridge Bay location in March 2018 for the experiments ranged from about -20 to -40°C with a few days having a wind chill recorded at about -50°C. Temperatures were measured at various locations in all the shelters from ground level to the ceiling and in various locations around the perimeter and in the center of the shelters. Overall the commercial tents had a more even distribution of heat and both maintained a comfortable temperature, averaging about 15°C. The military shelter would never achieve this overall average temperature level and had a very large temperature striation that could range from below 0°C in locations at the floor level to 55°C at the very top. Furthermore, the overall consumption of fuel, as shown in Table 1, was much lower in both of the commercial shelters compared to the military tent.

Table 1. Approximate size, weight and fuel consumption for three shelter systems studied at JAE18.

Shelter	Area (sq ft)	Pack Weight (lbs)	Inside Temp range	Fuel Used (L/day)
Military-Bell tent	200	90	5-15	36*
AO-insulated	304+92+	180	15	22
PH-rigid/floor	144	600	15	14.4

+ Includes two vestibules on either end of shelter

** Two types of fuel used - naphtha and diesel (about 40:60 ratio)*

Alternative energy systems

Current operations in the High Arctic do not use electrical power for heating, lighting or cooking. As an estimated 95% of the fuel consumed in an Arctic shelter is used for heat, it is very efficient and easy to operate heaters to burn the fuel directly in an open flame in very cold environments. That being said, this requires dedicated personnel to maintain, monitor these heating systems due to risk of fire and production of CO_2 and CO in the combustion process. Thus, there is a human factors driver to try and remove open flames in shelter systems going forward and some alternative solutions were assessed during JAE18. As part of the ongoing benefit analysis a small tactical diesel generator rated at about 2KW was used in the commercial shelters to demonstrate LED lighting to replace kerosene lanterns and flameless cooking/heating methods, such as an induction stove electrically powered to replace kerosene burners (Figure 2).

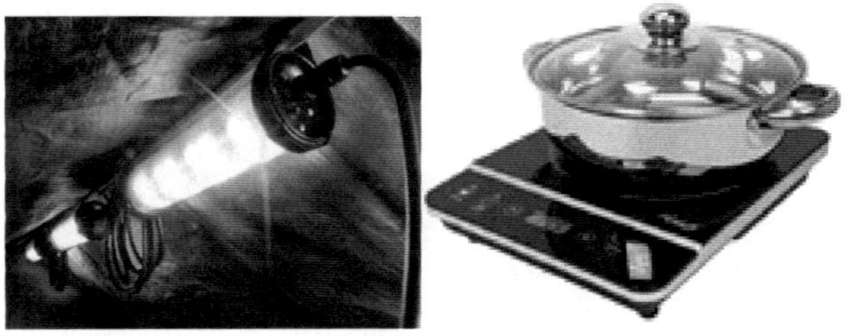

Figure 2A: Typical LED Lights, **B:** Induction Stove

It also powered required measurement equipment (data takers, 3 CO-CO_2 monitors, computer, battery charging etc.). It was difficult to quantify the lighting/cooking usage at this time and the system and electrical requirement will be optimized for JAE19 when soldiers will be using the shelter systems as well. Preliminary results show that if the generator is operated in economy mode fuel consumption was a maximum of about 7L/day to provide most of the electrical needs in a modern shelter design.

Also, energy storage in the form of newer lower operating temperature lithium batteries and very high capacity lithium batteries were examined as part of the electrical system. To demonstrate energy storage for cold weather operations, a 1.8 kWh BB-2590/U Based Portable Power System was evaluated. It uses six MOTS (military-off-the-shelf) BB 2590/U lithium rechargeable batteries commonly used in military communication equipment rated to operate down to -30° C and weighing about 18Kg (about 50% of the weight of the system is batteries). For example, this would provide about 30 hours of LED lighting in the commercial shelter or power/backup any other future electrical power needs. In the past, electrical power in High Arctic tactical operations was not required. However, with new capability (equipment) that needs significant electrical power, depending on operational needs, electric power generation systems may need to be deployed in the future.

One important reason for the slow implementation for High Arctic operations is the weight and performance/durability constraints of electrical generation/storage technologies. For example, lithium batteries designed for the commercial market have no or little capacity below -20° C. Recently with the advancement of ultra-high capacity lithium cells low temperature capacity performance has been improved to operate effectively down to -30° C as shown in Figure 3.

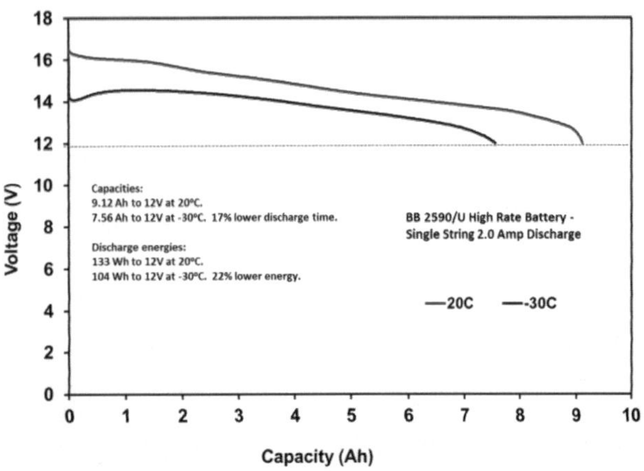

Figure 3: Typical discharge curves at 2.0 Amps for BB 2590/U high rate battery string.

The battery will only loose about 20% of its rated capacity at -30° C compared to ambient temperature. This is a large improvement in low temperature performance for lithium-ion rechargeable batteries, making them more competitive with primary (disposable) batteries in this lower temperature range.

Discussion

The first steps this year were to conduct an energy and environmental audit of the tactical deployed camp during the Joint Arctic Experiment to gain an understanding of baseline energy requirements. As well, a comparative energy study between typical and energy efficient shelter systems was conducted at JAE18 this year. Results show that significant energy (fossil fuel) consumption savings of 60 to 70% can be achieved by using modern commercial shelter designs. This can be improved even more as the heaters were perhaps somewhat oversized and a lower BTU rated heater could be used in future experiments depending on the desired comfort level. The average of 15° C reached in the commercial tents was a target that the standard military tent could not achieve in its current design/heating system layout.

But is that enough justification to make a shelter change on its own? What also needs to be taken into consideration is the packing weight/volume of the systems that are being carried by the soldier in this type of operation. The space and fact that everything needs to be carried by individuals severely restricts technology options and the fact that operations can range from 24 hours to a week or longer gives a wide window of supplies and equipment that will be transported. With this view in mind the packing weight of the shelter and its heating system need to be considered as well. Thus, when examining Table 1 and looking more at overall packing weight that includes the shelter, heating system and fuel for a 72 hour duration as an example, the weight savings of commercial systems to sustain a sleeping shelter is negligible in the one case for the double walled shelter systems and the rigidly constructed shelter system with the insulated floor is twice the overall weight. With this in mind the military Bell tent has fared well over 50+ years because of its lightweight durable design, easy setup and teardown under adverse conditions. Also from the table it is important to note the floor area of each shelter system. It can be argued that the military Bell tent is in the optimum range to accommodate a squad (up to 10 persons) comfortably in a harsh climate, who also carry with them sleeping/cold weather gear to sustain themselves in that climate. This would be conclusion if only looking at the packing weight of the shelter and heating system on its own. Also, current commercial shelters may be either too small or too large to match the weight/packing requirements for these smaller teams on deployment.

As can be seen in Figure 4, with the initial analysis of fuel consumption, there is a point over the one day operational period where fuel consumption is included in total weight. For a 24 hour mission or less, the lighter weight tent (Bell tent) has modest benefit. This is related more to setup and teardown etc. than to operational tempo and tasks. However, anything longer than 72 hours about 2/3 of the overall weight of the military tent is the fuel required for heating and for one week of operation it is over 80%.

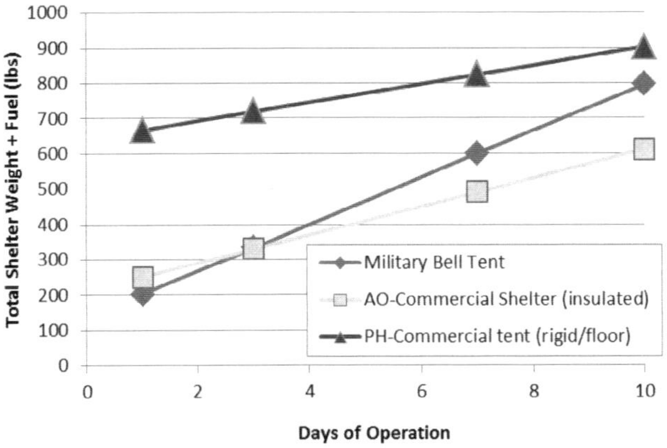

Figure 4: Comparison of total shelter system weight when fuel is included over number of operational days.

Thus, a significant amount of weight that is being carried for longer duration missions is essentially all fuel. However, the insulated shelter (AO) with a larger volume and vestibules is about the same total weight around 48hrs and already half of the total weight of the military tent system is fuel. For one week, the overall weight of fuel is 77% of the total weight of the military Bell tent system. Given the desire to reduce fossil fuel consumption as part of the Defence Energy and Environment Strategy to reduce the carbon footprint, an improvement in shelter design can yield significant energy savings, but also address the military logistics of reducing the overall packing weight of the shelter system.

Some consideration was given to other alternatives such as renewable energy (solar, wind) and thermal energy storage but were ruled out this year because the Technology Readiness Level (TRL) for tactical camps is lower than required for demonstration in the High Arctic environment with rapid assembly/tear down requirements [4]. They will be analyzed for next year's demonstration if industrial solutions are available.

Summary

To summarize, the first step this year was to conduct an energy and environmental audit of the tactical deployed camp during the Joint Arctic Experiment (JAE18) to gain an understanding of baseline energy requirements. As well, a comparative energy study between typical and energy efficient shelter systems was conducted and will continue over the next year to perform a simulation-based analysis on possible shelter efficiency improvements to minimize cold exposure and further reduce shelter fuel demands. Continuing into the second year of the project, alternative power systems are being evaluated for shelter lighting and cooking such as high capacity batteries, fuel cells and other energy conversion technologies.

There is an opportunity over the experiment to allow technology solutions from industry to contribute to future demonstrations. Future plans for JAE19 will include further shelter system measurements over an extended period of four to six weeks. The traditional military Bell tent will be modified to include better insulation and optimized heating system with reduced exposure to combustion products and open flame. There will be an opportunity for technology demonstration in the areas of thermoelectrics, micro diesel generation, PV etc.

Preliminary results conclude that shelter design improvements can not only reduce fuel consumption significantly, but also address the military requirement of reducing the burden for deployed soldiers in austere conditions such as the High Arctic. Reducing the weight burden of the shelter system, will allow the inclusion of other required capabilities for operations in the North. It will also inform the CAF on future decisions related to a range of priority areas such as equipment, training and more. The data collected over the JAE project will be vital to improving the conditions for CAF personnel and success of operations in austere environments such as Canada's High Arctic.

Acknowledgements

The author wishes to thank Natural Resources Canada (CANMet Energy) for their assistance and enormous contribution to a successful JAE18 experiment. Also, the cooperation and assistance of the CAF personnel during the Op NUNALIVUT 2018 exercise was greatly appreciated.

References

1. The Defence Energy and Environment Strategy, https://www.canada.ca/content/dam/dnd-mdn/documents/reports/2017/20171004-dees-en.pdf
2. NATO Report AC/340-N(2015)0190, Smart Energy Team (SENT) Comprehensive Report On Nations' Need for Energy in Military Activities, Focusing on a Comparison of the Effectiveness of National Approaches to Reduce Energy Consumption, 6 May 2015, 71 pages.
3. Suzanne Cassolato, Martin Kegel, Chad Abbey, Yves Brissette, Demonstration of Energy Reduction Technologies for Deployed Camps, CANMetENERGY, Varennes Research Centre, Dec 2013. 2013-178 (RP-FIN) 170-DRDC, 144 pages.
4. E. Andrukaitis, Ian Hill, Suzanne Cassolato, Mark Douglas, Evaluation of suitability/performance of deployed camp power and energy from commercial/industrial solutions-Spiral 1, DRDC-RDDC-2016-R159, August 2016

Electrochemical Evaluation of Atomizer Effect on E-Cigarette Safety

David B. Shoemaker, Yuk Chan
U.S. Army Communications-Electronics Research Development and Engineering Center
Power Division – Command Power and Integration

Abstract: *Due to a recent increase in electronic cigarette (e-cigarette) related accidents that have caused many injuries to soldiers and sailors, CERDEC Power began investigating one of the root causes of the e-cigarette failures, the atomizer. Safety tests were performed on the atomizer component of the e-cigarette to evaluate the effect that resistance has on the temperature of the system. Using atomizers of 0.8 Ohms, 1.0 Ohms, 1.5 Ohms, and 1.8 Ohms, charge tests were performed at constant voltage of 4.2V, and the atomizer was cycled 4,000 times to see if we could induce thermal runaway of the system. The results showed that the higher resistance atomizers had the least amount of failures and the lowest resulting temperatures. Nine of the fifteen atomizers of 0.8 Ohms failed, eight of the fifteen atomizers of 1.0 Ohms failed, one of the fifteen atomizers of 1.5 Ohms failed, and zero of the fifteen atomizers of 1.8 Ohms failed.*

Keywords: atomizer, e-liquid

Introduction

Many people these days have turned to e-cigarettes, or the process known as vaping, as a way to get their daily dose of nicotine. Since there aren't the carcinogens, tar, or tobacco that are present in regular cigarettes, users tend to see vaping as a healthier alternative. However, since e-cigarettes are fairly new and no federal regulations have been passed as of yet, there are many safety issues that exist within the devices due to improper user maintenance, improper batteries used, or lack of necessary electronics to regulate charging of the battery.

The e-cigarette devices have several components that must be replaced regularly, such as the battery, the atomizer, and the e-liquid. A failure to do so could result in unfavorable consequences.

Anatomy of the E-Cigarette

There is a variety of e-cigarettes that are available to consumers, but all of them have the same three necessary components. Every e-cigarette contains an atomizer, a compartment to store the e-liquid, and a battery.

The atomizer is a key component that houses the resistor coil that is responsible for elevating the temperature of the e-cigarette and vaporizing the e-liquid. The atomizer also contains the wick that absorbs the e-liquid, nicotine, and flavoring additives. Atomizers come in a range of resistances (e.g. 1.0 Ohm, 1.5 Ohm, 1.8 Ohm, etc.) and this is part of what determines the current, which in turn determines the temperature of the e-liquid.
The e-liquid storage compartment is where the vegetable glycerin, propylene glycol, nicotine, and flavor additives are added, and is located directly adjacent to the atomizer to allow for maximum heat transference.

Depending on the type of e-cigarette used, the type of battery may vary. Some e-cigarettes may have electronics built directly into the device to control charging and voltage cutoffs for the battery, and some e-cigarettes rely on the battery to have the electronics inside. Some e-cigarettes have a way to regulate what voltage or power you are using to vape, and some of the cheaper versions have a set voltage input. The voltage or power level used directly affects the life of the atomizer, as higher voltages or powers will produce higher temperatures and produce more carbon on the resistor coil's surface faster.

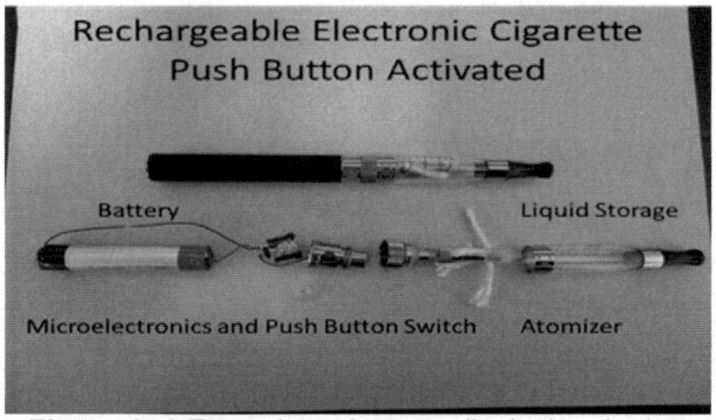

Figure 1.a) Example e-cigarette displaying the battery, storage compartment for the e-liquid, and the atomizer.

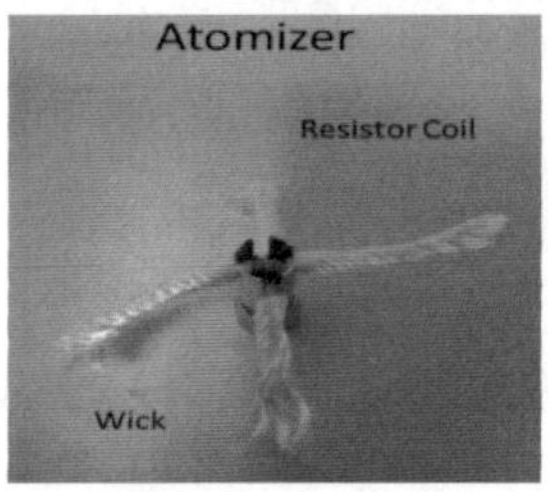

Figure 1.c) The inside of the atomizer, exposing the resistor coil and wick.

Hypothesis and Test Plan

Consumers who use their e-cigarette with the same atomizer for a duration of time will notice a build-up of carbon on the resistor coil inside. Users that vape at high voltages or high powers will build up the soot on the atomizer faster. Since carbon is an excellent electrical conductor, it will significantly reduce the resistance of the atomizer, which can often times lead to a shorting of the e-cigarette battery, and may eventually lead to thermal runaway. In order to see if this indeed would occur, CERDEC Power decided to perform simulated charge tests on the atomizer, since we believe that the degradation of the atomizer's integrity may be one of the major contributors to the battery failing in the e-cigarette.

CERDEC Power performed constant voltage testing first. The atomizer was placed in a testing simulator and charged at 4.2V for 10 seconds, and then placed on rest for 10 seconds. This process was repeated 4,000 times to simulate a person that would vape for 10 seconds at a time and rest for 10 seconds at a time. Each test lasted for 22.2 hours and the current was capped at 14A for safety reasons. A thermocouple was placed on the mouth piece to monitor touch temperature.

Atomizers of resistance 0.8 Ohm, 1.0 Ohm, 1.5 Ohm, and 1.8 Ohm were tested using an e-liquid mixture of propylene glycol and vegetable glycerin. Sixty atomizers total were tested.

- 15x 0.8 Ohm Resistors
- 15x 1.0 Ohm Resistors
- 15x 1.5 Ohm Resistors
- 15x 1.8 Ohm Resistors

Both the voltage and resistance are fixed in this portion of the experiment, and both contribute to the power of the system. Since the temperature of the e-cigarette is directly dependent on the power that the battery is delivering, and $P = V^2/R$, we know that as resistance increases, the power will decrease, which will decrease the temperature of the e-cigarette, which in turns decreases the likelihood that the atomizer will fail during the 4,000 cycles. And this is exactly what we saw during our testing

Hypothesis and Test Plan

The spikes in the graphs represent where the resistance dropped to near zero and the current spiked as a result, but was limited to 14 Amps. This is indicative of a failure. The goal of this testing is to find the optimal power or voltage level for e-cigarettes to ensure zero failures.

The most failures were seen while testing the 0.8 Ohm atomizers: 9 out of 15. The temperature of the mouthpiece was around 180°C for all of the samples.

$$P = \frac{(4.2V)^2}{0.8\Omega} = 22.05\ W$$

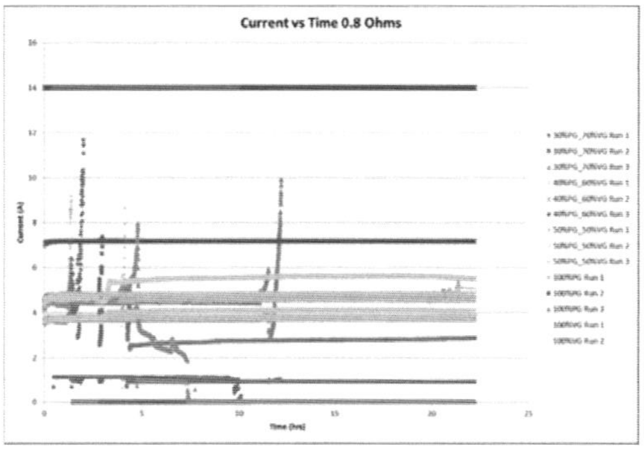

Figure 2.a) The Current vs. Time data for the 0.8 Ohm atomizers during constant voltage testing.

There were also a considerable amount of failures for the 1.0 Ohm atomizers: 8 out of 15. The temperature of the mouthpiece was around 170°C for all of the samples.

$$P = \frac{(4.2V)^2}{1.0\Omega} = 17.64\ W$$

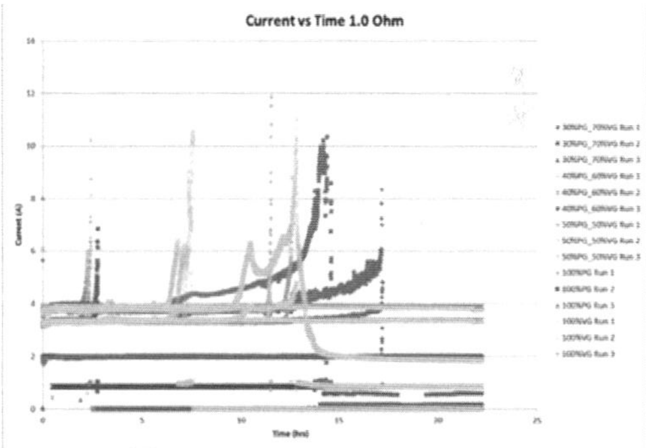

Figure 2.b) The Current vs. Time data for the 1.0 Ohm atomizers during constant voltage testing.

Increasing the resistance to 1.5 Ohm significantly decreased the number of failures: 1 out of 15. The temperature of the mouthpiece was around 110°C for all of the samples.

$$P = \frac{(4.2V)^2}{1.5\Omega} = 11.76\ W$$

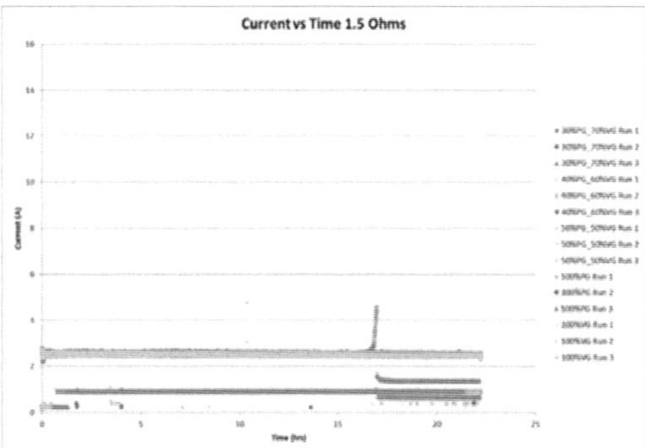

Figure 2.c) The Current vs. Time data for the 1.5 Ohm atomizers during constant voltage testing.

Increasing the resistance to 1.8 Ohm resulted in no failures: 0 out of 15. The temperature of the mouthpiece was around 60°C for all of the samples.

$$P = \frac{(4.2V)^2}{1.8\Omega} = 9.8\,W$$

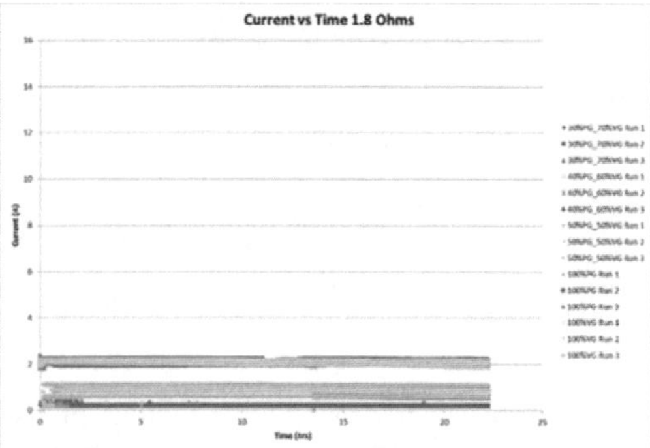

Figure 2.d) The Current vs. Time data for the 1.8 Ohm atomizers during constant voltage testing.

The higher the resistance of the atomizer, the lower the power draw, which in turn resulted in lower temperatures for the e-cigarette during charge, which is why we saw less failures

Constant Power Testing

Many of the e-cigarettes that are available on the market have a power variable setting that allows the user to select a fixed wattage at which they would vape. This allows for safer smoking conditions, since it wouldn't matter what resistance atomizer the user has, the power remains constant. If the person uses a lower resistance atomizer, then the device will automatically reduce the voltage, allowing it to keep the same wattage.

For the constant power testing, CERDEC Power chose to begin testing at a setting of 15W, and incrementally decrease the wattage by 1W until we saw a consistent sign of no failures. Iterations of at least 15 tests would be made before we had any sort of confidence in that the non-failures were consistent. If a failure happened before the 15 tests were completed, we would move on to the next lower power level to test.

Since the power was fixed, it did not matter which resistance atomizer was used, but the plan was to test resistances of 0.8 Ohm, 1.0 Ohm, 1.2 Ohm, 1.5 Ohm, and 1.8 Ohm. Following the pattern of the constant voltage test, we charged the atomizer at each power level for 10 seconds, and then rested for 10 seconds. However, we only performed 1,800 cycles during this phase of testing. If a human vapes 60 times a day, then 1,800 is representative of a month's worth of using their e-cigarette without changing out their atomizer.

Three atomizers were tested at 15W before a failure was seen. Since we are looking for 0% failures, we moved on to 14W. At 14W, four atomizers were tested before failure. At 13W, three atomizers were tested before failure. At 12W, two atomizers were tested before failure. At 11W, twelve atomizers were tested before failure.

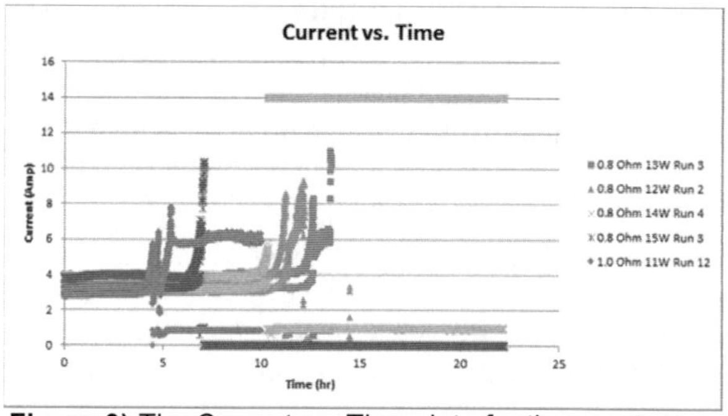

Figure 3) The Current vs. Time data for the constant power testing performed at 15W, 14W, 13W, 12W, and 11W.

During the constant voltage testing, consistent success for the 15 iterations was not seen until reaching a power level of approximately 10W, so it was not completely surprising to see some failure in power levels above 10W during the constant power testing.

A total of 46 atomizers of varying resistances were tested at the 10W power level as shown by the graphs below. There was one anomaly during the 1.8 Ohm 10W test, where there was a power miscommunication between the atomizer and the power simulation machine, which caused the current level to spike immediately. This was no counted as a failure from the power level used, but rather a machine error.

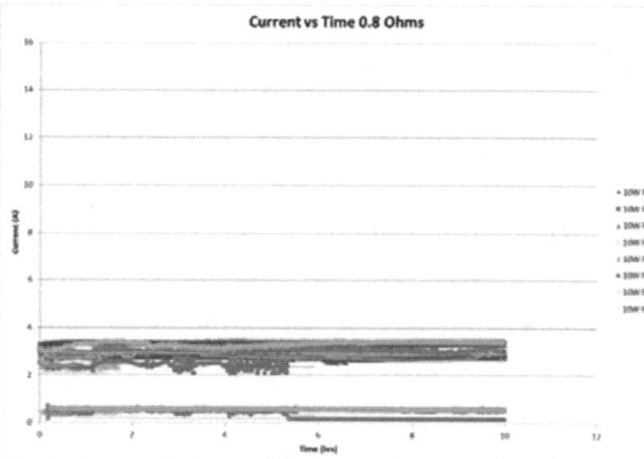

Figure 4.a) The Current vs. Time data for the 0.8 Ohm atomizers during 10W constant power testing.

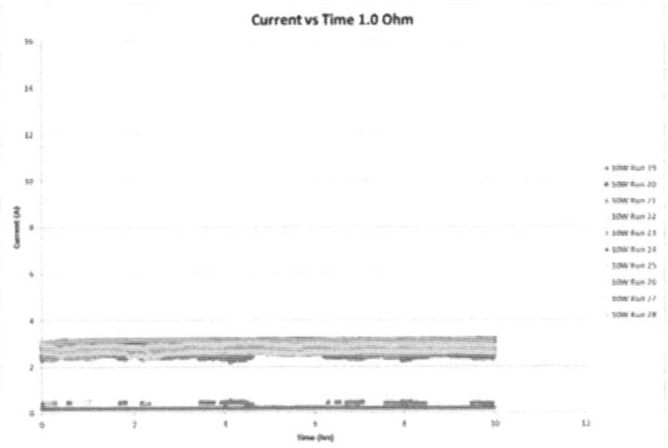

Figure 4.b) The Current vs. Time data for the 1.0 Ohm atomizers during 10W constant power testing.

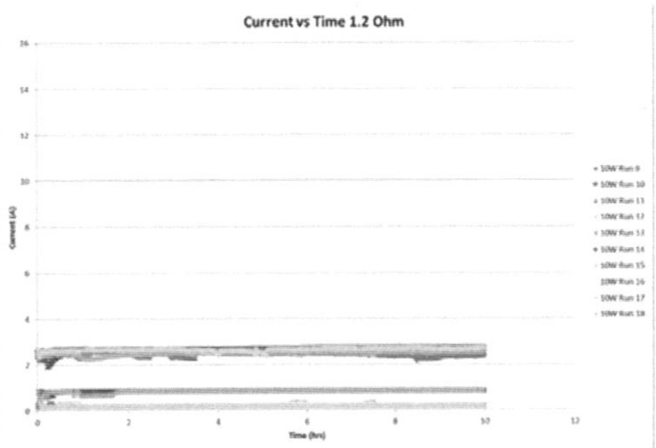

Figure 4.c) The Current vs. Time data for the 1.2 Ohm atomizers during 10W constant power testing.

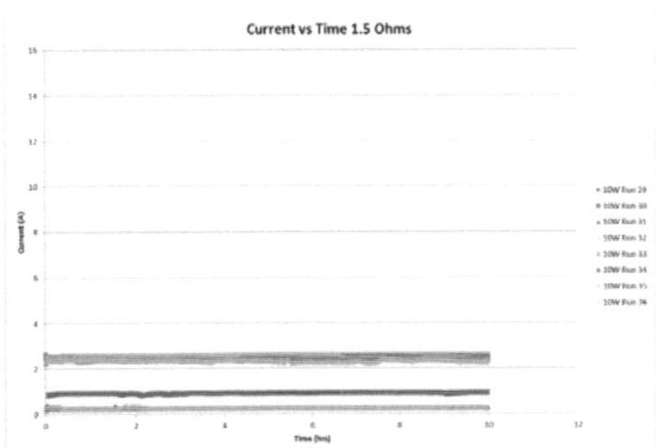

Figure 4.d) The Current vs. Time data for the 1.5 Ohm atomizers during 10W constant power testing.

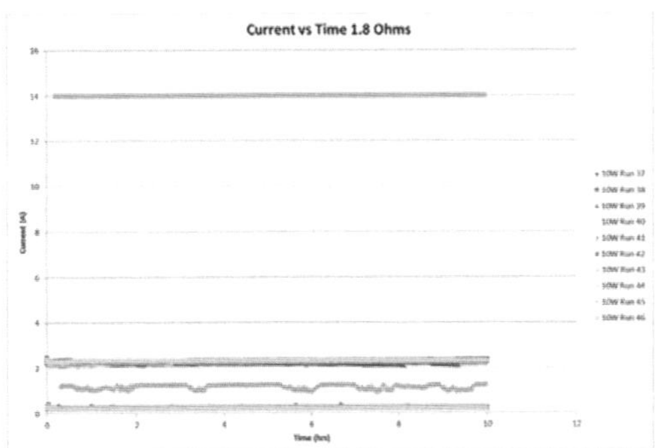

Figure 4.e) The Current vs. Time data for the 1.8 Ohm atomizers during 10W constant power testing.

Conclusions

SEM images were taken after all of the testing was performed to identify the material that was built-up on the resistor coil inside of the atomizer. CERDEC Power took the pictures using resistor coils from an atomizer that failed, an atomizer that was used but passed, and an unused atomizer.

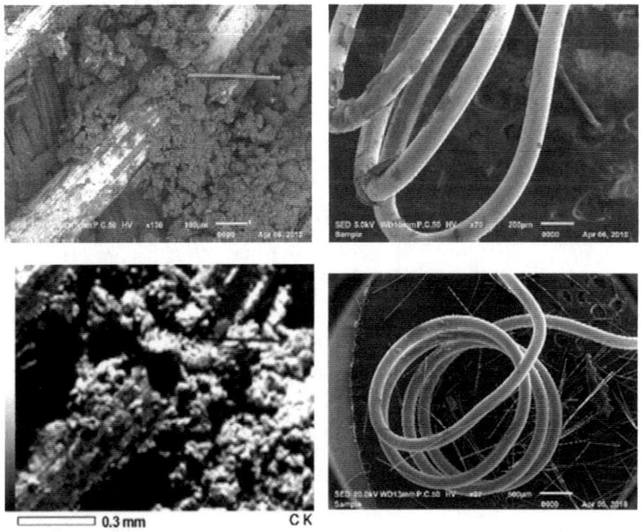

Figure 5) (Top Left) shows the large amount of Carbon build-up on an atomizer that was tested but failed. (Bottom Left) the yellow represents the Carbon that was on the surface of the atomizer that failed. (Top Right) shows the small amount of Carbon build-up on an atomizer that was tested but passed. (Bottom Right) represents an unused atomizer that has no Carbon.

More SEM imaging will be produced in the future, however, the presence of Carbon was very abundant on the surface of the atomizer that failed. Not so much on the atomizer that passed, there were trace amounts though. There was no carbon build-up on the atomizer that was unused.

After the testing of the atomizers was analyzed and evaluated, recommendations were sent to the ARMY safety office including:

- Soldiers charging with a variable voltage e-cigarette should use an atomizer of no less than 1.8 Ohms.
- Soldiers charging with a variable wattage e-cigarette should not exceed 10W.
- Soldiers should replace the atomizer in their e-cigarette monthly.

Additional testing will be performed by CERDEC Power on different e-cigarette batteries involving overcharge and overdischarge tests to evaluate the safest batteries that are available to the soldier.

Atomic Layer Deposition: A Scalable Process for Enabling the Next Generation of High Performance Materials

Barbara K. Hughes, Meghan N. Herbert-Walters, James Trevey

Forge Nano (*formerly PneumatiCoat Technologies*)

Abstract: *Atomic Layer Deposition (ALD) is a platform technology that has been widely demonstrated throughout the literature to impart significant processing and performance gains in all areas of advanced materials. Historically it has been too expensive to consider as a realistic process for commercial adoption, but Forge Nano has patented, constructed, and demonstrated the highest throughput ALD capability in the world, unlocking new potential for lower cost integration of ALD into products. In this seminar, Forge Nano will discuss ALD as a means of controlling surface phenomena and its application in energy storage. Forge Nano will discuss ALD methodologies and best-suited applications to clarify the most appropriate steps towards the industrialization of an ALD-enabled energy storage future. While there are many metrics with which to evaluate the adoption of ALD-enabled materials, all can be distilled down to three main areas: performance, safety, and cost. Forge Nano will address these areas within energy storage, focusing on Li-ion battery technology, to illustrate why ALD is a critical tool for anyone attempting to maintain an edge in a competitive market. A breaking point in ALD manufacturing has been reached, and with a never-ending outlook for technological advancement the opportunity for adoption will never be as good as it is today.*

Performance Studies of Fe-rich and Cu-rich $Cu_xFe_{1-x}F_2$ Conversion Cathode Materials

Jonathan K. Ko, Daphne A. Fuentevilla, and Azzam N. Mansour

NSWC Carderock, West Bethesda, Maryland 20817, USA

Abstract: *Lithium metal/metal fluoride batteries are potentially more energy dense compared to traditional lithium intercalation batteries; the redox chemistry in conversion materials involves multi electron transfer processes per transition metal atom (e.g., Cu^{2+} to Cu^0, Fe^{2+}/Fe^{3+} to Fe^0) while intercalation of traditional electrodes involves a single electron transfer per transition metal atom. CuF_2 is of interest as an active cathode material due to its high theoretical potential of 3.55 V [1] [2] [3]. Along with its theoretical specific capacity of 528mAh/g, CuF_2 provides a high theoretical energy density of 1874 Wh/kg. However, due to Cu dissolution, CuF_2 is not fully reversible and has poor cycle life [2]. On the other hand, FeF_2 has good cycleability but suffers from large hysteresis due to different reaction pathways during charge and discharge [4]. By substituting Cu into the Fe lattice, $Cu_xFe_{1-x}F_2$, a ternary metal fluoride, shows promise overcoming the issues with CuF_2 and FeF_2. Upon charge of $Cu_xFe_{1-x}F_2$ electrodes, initial reconversion of Fe to Fe^{2+} and Fe^{3+} is followed by reconversion of some of the Cu to Cu^{2+} while the remaining Cu provides conductive pathways during the charge process [5]. Studies have been performed on the $Cu_{0.5}Fe_{0.5}F_2$ which showed improvement over the binary CuF_2 and FeF_2. The Cu-substituted material showed low hysteresis (<150mV) which allows higher cycling efficiency [5]. In this work, we present further electrochemical testing on $Cu_{0.5}Fe_{0.5}F_2$ as well as investigations of Fe and Cu rich $Cu_xFe_{1-x}F_2$. The ternary metal fluorides are manufactured by mixing FeF_2 and CuF_2 in a high-energy ball mill until a solid solution is formed. The structure and phase purity of the materials are characterized by XRD while XPS is used to evaluate the chemistry of the solid electrolyte interfaces.*

High Voltage Double Doped Lithium Spinel Cathodes, $Li_xMn_{1.9}Co_{0.04}Fe_{0.06}O_4Cl_d$, Synthesized via Citric Acid Method

Matthew A. Limpert* and Terrill B Atwater

U.S. Army Communications Electronics Research Development and Engineering Center, Command Power and Integration, Power Division

Abstract: *Lithium spinel cathodes ($LiMn_2O_4$) are one of the studied cathode materials to replace layered mixed metal oxides ($LiMO_2$, M=Ni, Mn, or Co) as a more energy dense and environmentally friendly cathode. Doping with chlorine on the oxygen site stabilizes the structure during deep discharge (2V to 5V). Chlorine doping creates disorder on the transition metal sites enabling structural stability when saturated with lithium and places a more electronegative species in chlorine on an oxygen site, allowing larger lattice parameters and increased lithium diffusion. Doping with cobalt, nickel, and iron increases the capacity and structural stability. Using a modified citric acid sol gel method, we have synthesized double metal doped chlorinated spinel to increase both capacity and energy while maintaining structural stability from 2.5 volts to over 5 volts. The energy density of the cathode was found to be 600 Wh/kg with a capacity of 180 mAh/g on deep discharge. The differential capacity curve presents plateaus at 5V, 4V and 3V indicating that lithium is inserting into both octahedral and tetrahedral sites. The elevated charging plateau is higher than reported in literature with the minimal amounts of cobalt and iron dopants due to citric acid method. Through x-ray diffraction, scanning electron microscope, x-ray fluorescence, and electrochemical cycling, we have produced $LiMn_{1.9}Co_{0.04}Fe_{0.06}O_{4-d}Cl_d$ and revealed that it is possible to cycle with structural stability from 2.5V to over 5 Volts and possible to have over 224 cycles with 80% capacity with minimal additional dopants if a stable electrolyte can be utilized.*

Keywords: Li-Ion Battery; Lithium manganese oxide spinel; spinel cathode; iron-doping; cobalt-doping; secondary lithium battery

CONFERENCE TOPIC: Secondary Lithium Batteries; Lithium Ion Batteries

Introduction

The US Army has a need to increase life cycle, energy density, and temperature performance in soldier portable batteries. The current performance standard for the conformal wearable battery, MIL-PRF 32383/4, requires 148 Wh in a 2.6 lbs package but to increase the energy, new electrochemical materials are necessary in order to beat the standard. Standard lithium ion cathode materials use $LiNi_{0.33}Mn_{0.33}Co_{0.33}O_2$ for consumer electronics or $LiNi_{0.8}Co_{0.15}Al_{0.05}O_2$ for higher power applications such as electric vehicles. The Army increasingly requires both high capacity and high current rates as well as a wider temperature range (-20°C to 55°C) than commercial materials. Newer cathode materials will necessitate a different structure than the layered $LiMO_2$ (M=Co, Mn, Al, Ni, etc) structure that has dominated commercial industry since Panasonic introduced Li-Ion technology in 1991 with $LiCoO_2$ (LCO). Spinel materials with the format LiM_2O_4 (M=Mn, Co, Ni, Al, Fe, etc.) offer the ability to tune properties for high rates and increased energy density.

Lithium spinel, $LiMn_2O_4$ (LMO), follows an AB_2O_4 structure and offers a low cost, environmentally friendly alternative to LCO due to manganese abundance while relieving environmental concerns of using cobalt. The spinel structure consists of lithium at the 8a tetrahedral sites, manganese at the 16d octahedral sites, and oxygen surrounding the manganese[1]. A fraction of lithium can switch during cycling with manganese and dope at the octahedral site with manganese doping the tetrahedral site which can increase capacity[2]. There are many factors that contribute to electrochemical performance of the spinel: doping and the ordering of cations[3,4], oxygen vacancies[5], and surface morphology[6] to name a few. Nickel (Ni) or cobalt (Co) is commonly doped on the manganese (Mn) site to increase operational voltage (5V to 3V) and enhance rate capabilities with a specific energy of 610 Wh kg^{-1} [7,8]. The higher voltage occurs from the difference in binding energy between the energies of the top valence band such as in Ni^{2+} and Mn^{3+}[9]. Doping with Ni or Co increases disorder on the cation sites by allowing Mn^{3+} and Mn^{2+} to exist within the structure, which reduces capacity fade from lattice deformities from high rates, increases the temperature range, and widens the voltage windows[5,7]. The structural impacts of the disorder are difficult to detect in XRD but can be seen in electrochemical cycling. The disordered B-sites allows the structure to maintain integrity with lithium insertion and desertion while increasing electrical conductivity, which improves capacity retention, cycle life, and current rate capability. Iron doping has been a transition metal that was not considered for spinel material due to multiple oxidation states allowing atomic movement from different lattice sites. However, when appropriately placed it delivers rates of 10C with 100 mAh g^{-1} making it an attractive dopant[10]. Designing spinels with dopants and disorder on the B site can stabilize the structure during deep cycling, allow high cycling rates, and enable long cycle life.

The electrochemical and structural impacts of anion vacancies controls both oxygen loss and the process in which the oxygen vacancies are created[11]. There are two oxygen vacancies reported in nickel doped spinels: one bonded to Ni and two bonded to Mn, with the other one bonded to three Mn ions depending on state of lithiation[12,13]. Anion doping is an alternative to creating oxygen vacancies in spinels. It increases structural stability at higher voltages and temperatures[14]. There have been multiple contradictory reports on the roles and effects of anion doping on the performance of the spinel structure but chlorine (Cl) doping has been investigated and shows better charge retention, increased operational temperature stability, and increased voltage range[15]. This is crucial to improving capacity and energy density for future requirements.

Spinel cathodes offer a high voltage, environmentally friendly materials, and long cycle life as a replacement for commercially used layered transition metal oxide cathode. However it requires dopants such as Co, Fe, and Cl to improve its electrochemical performance to fit the future Army requirements of wide temperature range, long cycle life, high current, and large energy density.

Experimental

Developing a high voltage cathode requires dopants to tune the high rate and high voltage capabilities. Inserting low amounts of iron and cobalt as "B site" dopants with chlorine doping the oxygen site can significantly increase charge rates, cycle life, and usable capacity. Sol gel methods have been developed to decrease particle size and increase surface area but yield rates are low due to the ignition of the precursors[16,17]. Establishing a modified Pechini method that limits ignition and maintains the desired structure with cobalt, chlorine, and iron dopants to obtain the desired electrochemical properties and a high surface area high will be key.

Stoichiometric amounts of lithium nitrate, manganese nitrate, lithium chloride as 10% excess lithium, cobalt nitrate, and iron nitrate were mixed in methanol for $LiMn_{1.9}Co_{0.04}Fe_{0.06}O_{4-d}Cl_d$. The mixture was vigorously stirred, then citric acid was added in a 1:1 mol ratio with metal ions during mixing. Finally, ethylene glycol was added in a 70:1 mL of ethylene glycol to mol of metal ions before being mixed and simultaneously heated to evaporate the water and gel the liquid, completing trans esterification. The mixture was then heated to the auto ignition temperature of 300°C to ash and breakdown the powder. The remaining powder was then ground and calcined at 650°C for 10 hours with a heating/cooling rate of 10°C/min to limit chlorine loss before the formation temperature.

Samples were characterized using x-ray diffraction (XRD) to identify potential secondary phases and confirm the spinel structure. Rietveld refinement will be performed to calculate the lattice parameter of the samples. X-ray florescence (XRF) was performed to quantify the chlorine content in the sample. Scanning electron microscope (SEM) images were taken of the powder to characterize the microstructure surface of the material. Electron dispersive spectroscopy (EDS) was performed to quantify the elemental distribution in the powder.

The powders were mixed with conductive carbon and Teflon in a ratio of 80:15:5 before being placed as the cathode in a CR2032 electrochemical cell. Lithium hexafluorophosphate was the electrolyte in a glass separator and lithium metal used as the anode. EIS was performed on all made cells. Then the cells will be cycled at 1 Amp, between 5.25 Volts and 3 Volts until 60% original capacity. Cells were also be cycled between 4.5V and 2.5 V to test the structural integrity of the sample under a wide voltage range and then between 5.25V and 2.5V to test under the widest possible range.

Results

The XRD displayed in Figure 1 shows the material made via the citric acid method with the stoichiometry of $Li_xMn_{1.9}Fe_{.06}Co_{.04}O_{4-b}Cl_b$ including the XRD pattern from the International Center for Diffraction Data for $LiMn_2O_4$ spinel. Through Rietveld Refinement, the lattice parameter was calculated to be 8.182Å while $LiMn_2O_4$ spinel made using the same method was calculated to be 8.184Å. The made powder has a smaller lattice but that is a consequence of the chlorine addition and the addition of the low amounts of dopants. XRF confirmed the stoichiometry of the transition metals and the presence of chlorine in the sample. The SEM images within Figure 1 exhibit a submicron sized powder which is expected from the Pechini method. This will increase the rate capability of the material by having large surface areas for lithium reaction and diffusion, which is important for future DOD applications. EDS data shows chlorine and manganese evenly dispersed throughout the powder. Indicating that chlorine has entered the spinel structure and is not a surface coating. Iron and cobalt were not detected because of their low concentrations.

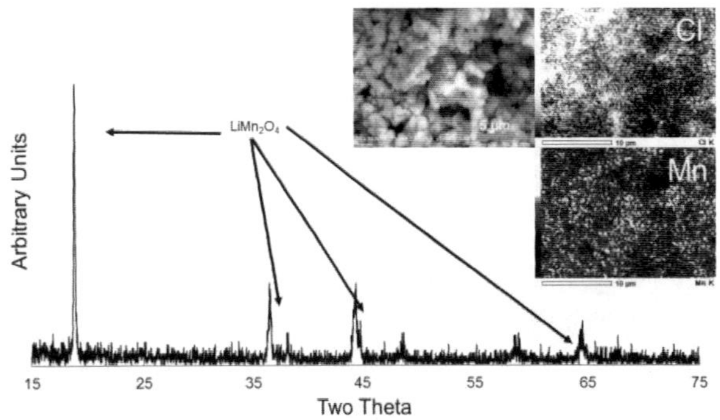

Figure 1: XRD of $Li_xMn_{1.9}Fe_{0.06}Co_{0.04}O_{4-b}Cl_b$ and enclosed SEM images of the fabricated powders

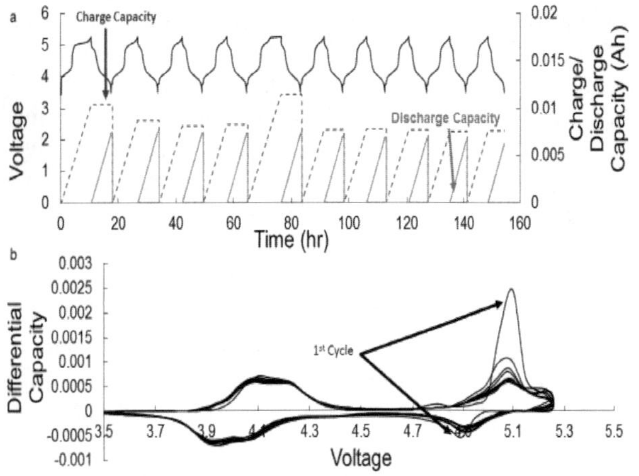

Figure 2: First 10 Charge/Discharge Cycles and the Corresponding Differential Capacity Plot

The initial ten charge/discharge cycles at 1 Amp and the differential capacity data are displayed in Figure 2 which indicate capacities of 120 mAhr/g on discharge. The energy density was found to be 425 Wh/kg when cycling to 3.5V. However, there was a large overcharge on the first cycle, demonstrating electrolyte breakdown. This increases resistance in the cell which limits rate performance and cycle life. The following cycles in the differential capacity plot show no loss in structural stability following the increased charge voltage i.e. the curves do not change shape or change magnitudes. This portends well to cycling at high voltages but will eventually cause premature failure in the cell from the increased resistances without a suitable electrolyte. The high energy when cycling at high voltage is important for the next cathode materials for the Army. This will help to decrease weight by increasing energy via the higher voltage without increasing cathode weight.

The cycling data shows the cells are capable of cycling between 5.25V and 3.5 V with two plateau regions displayed in the differential capacity plot. The four volt plateaus indicate lithium insertion into the tetrahedral 8a site at 3.95V, the next plateau is lithium inserting into the neighboring 16c tetrahedral site[18] which are both associated with the Mn^{3+}-Mn^{4+} redox couple. While the upper 5V plateau is asscociated with Co^{3+}-Co^{4+} redox couple[19]. Since the cell was made with liquid electrolyte, there is an overcharge on the first cycle above 4.75V which is electrolyte gelling and is expected since electrolytes begin to decompose at voltages above 4.5-4.75V. Electrolytes that are stable above 5V are critical to improving the actual usable capacity of high voltage doped spinels. Without the high voltage region, 20-40% of the energy is not accessible. That limits the usability of the material but can achieve over 400 Wh/kg.

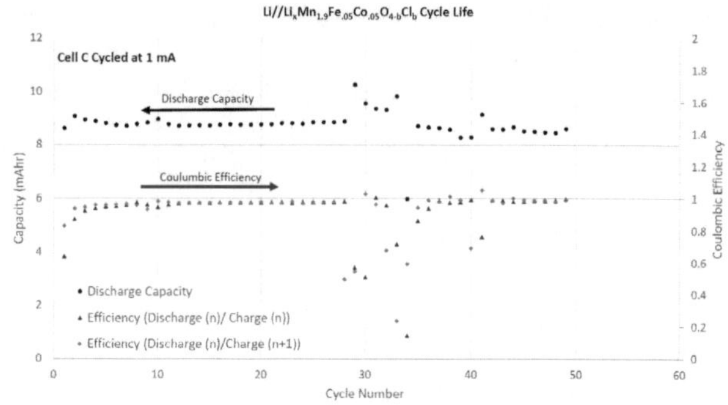

Figure 3: Capacity and Columbic Efficiency vs Cycle Count at 1 C Cycling from 5.25V to 3.5V

The capacities become unstable after the first 30 cycles as displayed in Figure 3. This is due to impedance in the cells which is seen in the differential capacity plots that demonstrate shifting peaks to the left on discharge and right on charge rather than decreasing peak sizes. That indicates an increase in resistance within the cell that is attributed to electrolyte decomposition from high voltages. The unstable capacities do not indicate structural failure in the cells but rather, instability of the electrolyte at the high voltage.

Cycling to 2.5V inserts lithium into octahedral sites which creates instability in the lattice structure. This increases the capacity by 50% by inserting 1.5 lithium per unitof cathode. Non conductive species tend to form without the dopants at those levels. In Figure 4, a cell was cycled between 4.5V and 2.5 V to test the structurale stablality at those voltages. The cell was stable and outside of the forming cycle peak at 3.8V, the thermodynamics of the cell did not change before or after the 2.5V. The cell is missing 30% of its capacity by not cycling to 5.25V

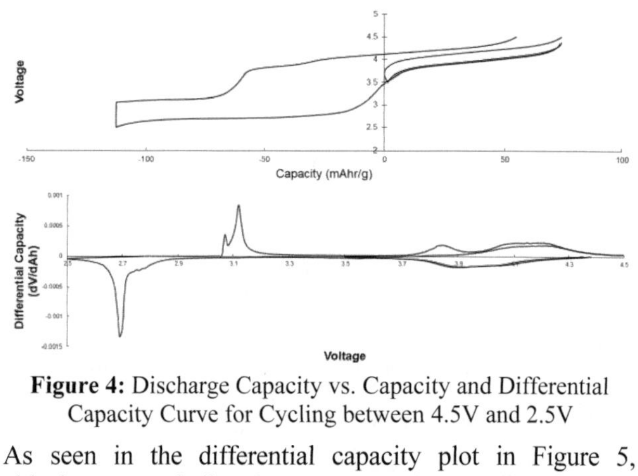

Figure 4: Discharge Capacity vs. Capacity and Differential Capacity Curve for Cycling between 4.5V and 2.5V

As seen in the differential capacity plot in Figure 5, chlorine can stabalize the structure when cycling between 5.25V to 2.5V and increase the energy to above 600 Wh/kg. This is critical to fully realizing the potential of the triple doped spinel.

The cells that were cycled between 5.25V and 2.5V achieved 180 mAhr per gram but sufferenced from the same increasing internal resistance as the cells in Figure 4. There was a passivation layer from high voltage cycling that was broken by cycle 18. The condition was exacerbated due to the wide voltage range. However, the differential capacity points to electrolyte problems again because the resistance within the cells increases and causes the unstable capacity. In order to fully realize the potential for this material, new electrolytes that are stable within this wide voltage range need to be created.

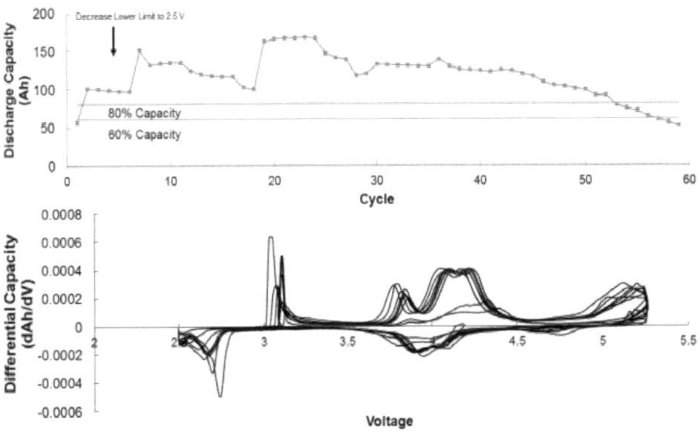

Figure 5: Discharge Capacity vs. Cycle Life and Differential Capacity Curve for Cycling between 5.25V and 2.5V

To confirm the structural stability, one cycle was performed to 2.5V and then a normal cycle to 3.5V. It was seen that this did not increase structural loss in the samples but there was the same internal resistance increases. There needs to be more studies performed on long term stability of discharging to 2.5V. However, the results indicate that the batteries can perform to 2.5 for select cycles.

Conclusions

The military has a need for high energy density materials with higher current capabilities. One material examined was a low doped lithium spinel that increased the charge to above 4.5 V and achieved 120 mAhr/g when discharged to 3.5V and 180 mAhr/g when discharged to 2.5V. However, the electrolyte decomposition limited the experiments that could be accomplished and limited cycle life experiments. In order to fully evaluate the cathode, new stable electrolytes need to be formulated.

References

1. Kelly, C.o., et al. *Thirteenth Annual Battery Conference on Applications and Advances. Proceedings of the Conference*, doi:10.1109/bcaa.1998.653890.
2. Cras, F Le, et al. *Solid State Ionics*, vol. 106, no. 1-2, Jan. 1998, pp. 1–10., doi:10.1016/s0167-2738(97)00490-6.
3. Shin, Youngjoon, and A. Manthiram. *Chemistry of Materials*, vol. 15, no. 15, 2003, pp. 2954–2961., doi:10.1021/cm0341787.
4. Oh, Si Hyoung, et al. *Journal of Alloys and Compounds*, vol. 452, no. 2, 2008, pp. 389–396., doi:10.1016/j.jallcom.2006.10.153.
5. Song, Jie, et al. *Chemistry of Materials*, vol. 24, no. 15, 2012, pp. 3101–3109., doi:10.1021/cm301825h.
6. Kunduraci, M., and G.g. Amatucci. Electrochimica Acta, vol. 53, no. 12, 2008, pp. 4193–4199., doi:10.1016/j.electacta.2007.12.057.
7. Wan, Lina, et al. *RSC Advances*, vol. 5, no. 33, 2015, pp. 25988–25997., doi:10.1039/c5ra03602j.
8. Liu, D., et al. *RSC Adv.*, vol. 4, no. 1, 2014, pp. 154–167., doi:10.1039/c3ra45706k.
9. Y. Gao, K. Myrtle, M. Zhang, J.N. Reimers, J.R. Dahn, Phys. Rev. B, 54 (1996), p. 16670
10. Liu, Jun, and Arumugam Manthiram. *The Journal of Physical Chemistry C*, vol. 113, no. 33, 2009, pp. 15073–15079., doi:10.1021/jp904276t
11. Strobel, P., et al. *Journal of Solid State Chemistry*, vol. 135, no. 1, 1998, pp. 132–139., doi:10.1006/jssc.1997.7611.
12. Wang, Zhiguo, et al. *ChemElectroChem*, vol. 2, no. 8, 2015, pp. 1182–1186., doi:10.1002/celc.201500059.
13. Wang, Zhiguo, et al. *ChemElectroChem*, vol. 2, no. 8, 2015, pp. 1182–1186., doi:10.1002/celc.201500059.
14. Hagh, Nader M., and Glenn G. Amatucci. *Journal of Power Sources*, vol. 256, 2014, pp. 457–469., doi:10.1016/j.jpowsour.2013.12.135.
15. Kong, Fantai, et al. *Chemistry of Materials*, vol. 28, no. 19, 2016, pp. 6942–6952., doi:10.1021/acs.chemmater.6b02627.
16. Hernã¡n, L. *Solid State Ionics*, vol. 118, no. 3-4, Feb. 1999, pp. 179–185., doi:10.1016/s0167-2738(98)00449-4.
17. Michalska, M., et al. *Journal of Alloys and Compounds*, vol. 632, 2015, pp. 256–262., doi:10.1016/j.jallcom.2014.12.266.
18. Bai, Ying, et al. *Transactions of Nonferrous Metals Society of China*, vol. 16, no. 2, 2006, pp. 402–408., doi:10.1016/s1003-6326(06)60069-1.
19. Aitchison, Phillip, et al. *Journal of Materials Chemistry*, vol. 9, no. 12, 1999, pp. 3125–3130., doi:10.1039/a905784f.

Electrochemical Performance of $Li_xMn_{2-y}Fe_yO_{4-z}S_z$ Cathode Material with Constant Voltage Application

Ashley L. Ruth, Paula C. Latorre, Alexandra M. Karalekas, and Terrill B. Atwater
U.S. Army Communications-Electronics Research, Development, and Engineering Center
Power Division – Command, Power, and Integration

Abstract: *Lithium manganese oxide spinel offers a three-dimensional network of lithium pathways within the structure, making it an attractive material for the positive electrode of a lithium battery. However, this material suffers from limited cyclability as a result of structural decomposition through extended cycling. Transition metal B-site doping of the AB_2O_4 spinel is a common approach for stabilizing the structure. This doping reduces the energy barriers for removing lithium from the octahedral sites and prevents the formation of manganese ions (Mn^{3+}) via the Jahn-Teller effect. This work utilizes iron (Fe) doping at the B-site while also incorporating sulfur (S) at the O-site to form more polarized metal-S bonds in order to assist with liquid-to-solid transfer of lithium ions (Li^+). These electrochemical cells are capable of achieving similar discharge capacity after a traditional 1.0 mA/cm² charge at cycle 11 when compared to the discharge at cycle 451 following an unregulated "bus bar" charge reaching 13.6 mA/cm² at its peak. This demonstrates the capability of the material to achieve high reaction rates, resulting in an improved state-of-charge capability at faster times. This performance allows for access to energy at extended cycling and across potential regimes.*

Keywords: lithium-ion battery, lithium manganese oxide spinel, spinel cathode, sulfur doping, iron doping, secondary lithium battery

Introduction

Lithium manganese oxide spinels have been utilized in cathode materials for lithium-ion batteries because of their access to high voltages, material affordability, and low toxicity while achieving comparable capacity when compared to similar lithium-ion battery chemistries [1-3]. Unfortunately, the structure suffers from capacity fading as a result of crystal degradation, either through the Jahn-Teller distortion, alternative phase formation via non-stoichiometry, or loss of crystallinity [4-6]. In an effort to combat these concerns, cycle life improvements have been achieved through stabilization of the spinel structure via transition metal doping at the B-site of the AB_2O_4 lattice [7-15]. Iron, the transition metal, is an attractive dopant because of its low toxicity and particularly because of its affordability and availability. Iron also has a high voltage redox couple of Fe^{3+} and Fe^{4+} at ~ 5.1 V, allowing for high voltage applications beyond that of the traditional spinel at 4.1 V [16-19]. Taniguchi and Bakenov demonstrate an increased capacity retention of $LiMn_{2-x}Fe_xO_4$ versus the undoped $LiMn_2O_4$ spinel over 100 cycles [20]. While B-site doping has improved cyclability, adding anion dopants could enhance cycle life and rate capability in $Li_xMn_{2-y}Fe_yO_4$ (LMFO). Our group, as well as other researchers, have added chlorine and fluorine anion dopants and demonstrated performance enhancements [9, 13-14, 21-24]. Our previous work has concluded that chlorine addition assists with the charge transfer of the lithium in and out of the lattice, and we have speculated this attribute may be influenced by a partial ionic and covalent bonding nature at the chlorine site [25]. While oxygen may be able to take advantage of p-orbitals for providing covalency, the addition of sulfur instead will provide access to d-orbitals. This can potentially enhance the covalent nature of the bond and possibly strengthen the crystal such that manganese dissolution is further prevented and can enhance cycle life. Jiang et al. demonstrates that the Mn 2p XPS spectra shift toward higher bonding energies with the addition of sulfur at the O-site of the $LiMn_2O_4$ spinel using a plasma-based synthesis, supporting the supposition that the crystal is strengthened [26]. Additionally, cyclic voltammetry data demonstrates a faster electrode reaction with the addition of S to the base spinel, $LiMn_2O_4$ [26]. Molenda et al. supports the stabilization of the base spinel structure with the substitution of sulfur for oxygen through a decrease in octahedral symmetry [27]. With the addition of a B-site dopant, Park et al. shows the synergistic effect of cation and anion site doping on the stabilization of the octahedral sites [28].

This work intends to study the addition of a sulfur anion dopant to the $Li_xMn_{2-y}Fe_yO_4$ material and its impact on cyclability and resilience to high current rates. Our method employs *in-situ* B-site doping and anion doping to synthesize the $Li_xMn_{2-y}Fe_yO_4S_z$ material.

Experimental

Iron- and sulfur-doped lithium manganese oxide spinel (LMFOS) was synthesized using a wet chemical glycine nitrate ignition synthesis. Stoichiometric amounts of $Li(NO_3)$ and $Mn(NO_3)_2{\cdot}4H_2O$ (Alfa Aesar) with $FeSO_4{\cdot}7H_2O$ and/or $Fe(NO_3)_3$ were mixed to incorporate both the iron and sulfur content, then dissolved in DI H_2O. NH_2CH_2COOH (glycine, Alfa Aesar) was dissolved into the aqueous solution as a chelating agent in a 1:1

metal ion-to-glycine ratio. The solution was heated to 80 °C until the water fully evaporated and a gel was formed. The gel was heated further to 250 °C, at which point auto-ignition occurred and a black ash was formed. The ash was collected, ground in a mortar and pestle, and fired at 600 °C for two hours to achieve the desired phase.

Phase purity was determined using x-ray diffraction (XRD, Bruker D8 Advance, Cu-kα). Sulfur content was determined from x-ray fluorescence spectroscopy (XRF, Bruker S2 Ranger) after firing for phase formation. Experimental button cells were assembled using a lithium anode separated from the cathode by a 0.01 cm nonwoven glass separator. $Li_xMn_{2-y}Fe_yO_{4-z}S_z$ cathode was fabricated by mixing together the active material, carbon, and PTFE in an 85:10:5 by weight ratio, respectively. The cathode mixture was rolled to 0.04 cm and dried in a vacuum oven. A 0.075 cm thick lithium foil was cut using a 12.7 mm hole punch. The cathode was cut into 2.0 cm^2 discs of approximately 0.13 g. The electrolyte used was 1 molar $LiPF_6$ in a 1:1:1 mixture of diethyl carbonate, dimethyl carbonate, and ethylene carbonate.

Cells were cycled with an ARBIN MSTAT4 battery cycler system controlled by MITS Pro software. The cells were charged and discharged from 4.5 V to 3.5 V or 4.5 V to 2.25 V. The charge/discharge rates were maintained at 0.5 mA/cm^2 or 1.0 mA/cm^2. A rest period of 15 minutes between charge and discharge cycles was used to allow for cells to achieve equilibrium on all experiments.

Results and Discussion

X-ray diffraction (XRD) was performed on the $Li_xMn_{2-y}Fe_yO_{4-z}S_z$ cathode material after calcination in order to confirm phase purity. Figure 1 shows the resultant diffraction spectrum as compared with the JCPDS file for $LiMn_2O_4$ spinel (PDF 01-070-3120). While a slight shift is expected due to the dopant straining of the lattice, no additional peaks are detected within the resolution of XRD, indicating relative phase purity with no secondary phases that may not participate electrochemically.

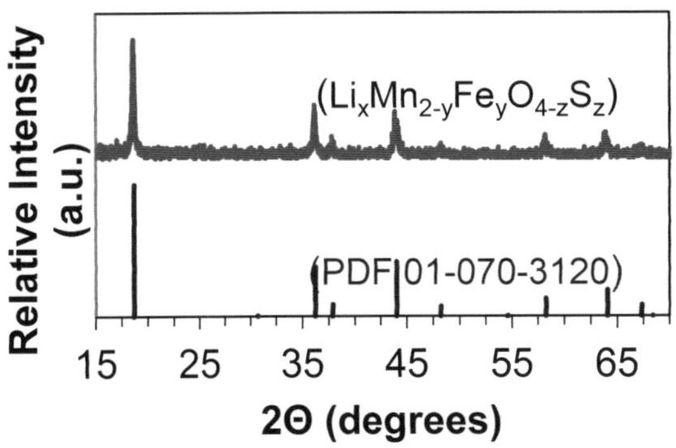

Figure 1. X-ray diffraction results for $Li_xMn_{2-y}Fe_yO_{4-z}S_z$ cathode material as compared with JCPDS file (PDF 01-070-3120) for $LiMn_2O_4$ spinel.

The energetic nature of the ignition synthesis method could have resulted in loss of the sulfur dopant. The $Li_xMn_{2-y}Fe_yO_{4-z}S_z$ cathode material was observed using XRF to confirm the maintenance of sulfur and determine its concentration after the calcination to the correct phase is complete. Figure 2 shows the elemental components of the calcined material. Si, P, and a proportional amount of S are expected background resulting from the polymer sample holder. The Pd peaks are the signature of the Pd x-ray source. As expected, there is very high (off the chart) intensity for the Mn and Fe peaks. Due to overlap of the Mn and Fe, the Fe is confirmed by the Kb1 emission at 7.06 keV. Most importantly, the S peak is enhanced beyond the background signature of the sample holder only, showing the presence of sulfur in the $Li_xMn_{2-y}Fe_yO_{4-z}S_z$ material after calcination. The values for y and z were calculated for the samples in this work to vary from $0.114 < y < 0.196$ and $0.017 < z < 0.032$. The sulfur from the sample holder is accounted for from a sulfur-to-manganese ratio respect using a similar material without sulfur doping (Figure 2B).

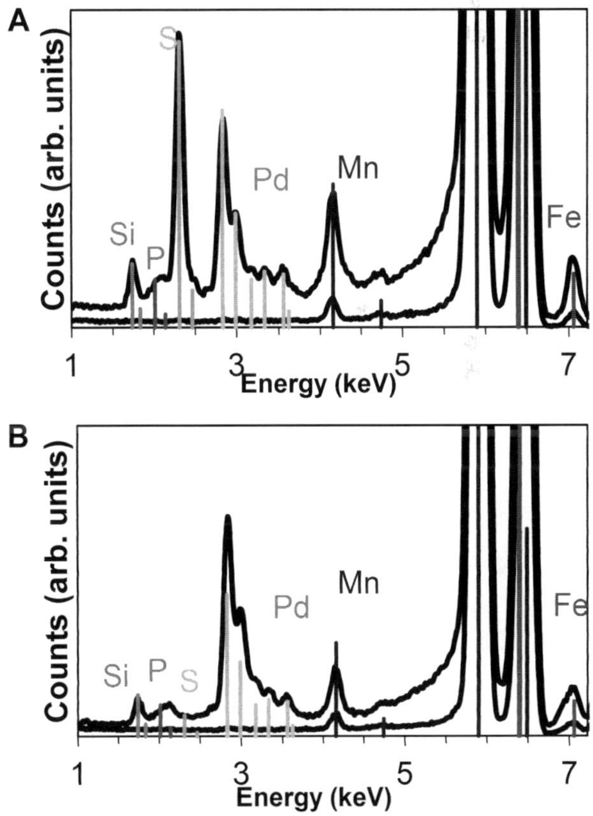

Figure 2a. X-ray fluorescence results for the $Li_xMn_{2-y}Fe_yO_{4-z}S_z$ cathode material. **Figure 2b.** X-ray fluorescence results for $Mn_{2-y-z}Fe_yNi_zO_3$ cathode precursor material for sulfur background determination.

Electrochemical measurements were performed on the $Li_xMn_{2-y}Fe_yO_{4-z}S_z$ cathode material opposite a Li metal anode and results are shown in Figures 3-5. For the highest sulfur doping level, where $z = 0.032$, cells were discharged to 2.25 V on cycles 11-20 after a traditional charge and discharge regime for 10 cycles from 4.5 V to 3.5 V at 1.0 mA/cm^2. Cycle 11 is shown in Figure 3 as the initial cycle to the lower voltage. After cycling again for 430 cycles from 4.5 V to 3.5 V, the cells were returned to deep discharge at cycles 451-460. Cycle 451 is also shown in Figure 3 as a comparison. However, for cycles 451 – 460 the cells were charged with an unregulated constant voltage charge. The current profiles for the constant voltage "bus bar" charge to 4.5 V before and after the 2.25 V discharge are shown in Figure 4. Figure 3 shows that, after advanced cycling and high rate charging, the cells demonstrate discharge profiles that are nearly identical and achieve the same capacity. This suggests that the cathode chemistry is quite robust. Figure 4 shows that the material is very capable of charging under constant voltage conditions across one voltage regime but does falter when performing the unregulated constant voltage charge across two electrochemical regimes at the higher current (22 mA versus 13.6 mA), as indicated by the undulating current. One possible explanation for the shorting behavior is that the separator used for these cells is not commercial grade and therefore not as effective at preventing dendritic shorts.

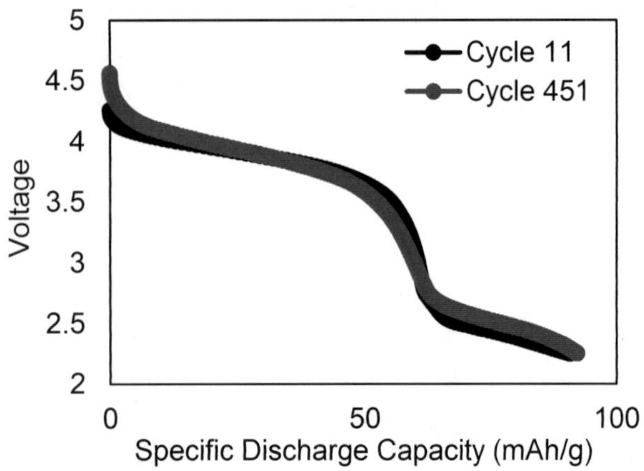

Figure 3: Discharge curves of $Li//Li_xMn_{1.804}Fe_{0.196}O_{3.968}S_{0.032}$ cell following traditional constant current charging (1.0 mA/cm^2) at cycle 11, and the 451st cycle of the same cell following a constant voltage charge with a peak in current at 13.6 mA/cm^2.

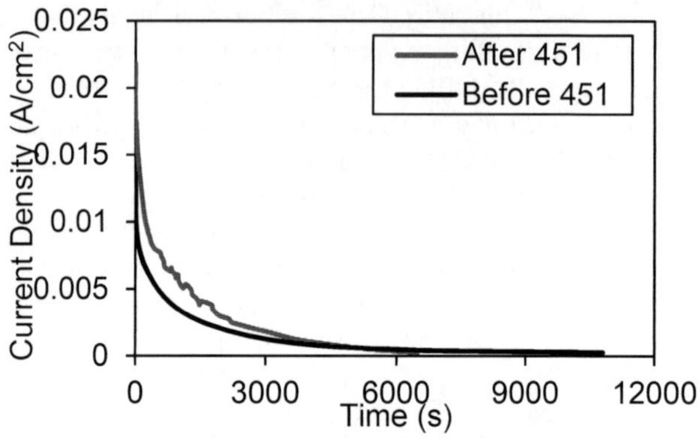

Figure 4: Current versus time for a $Li//Li_xMn_{1.804}Fe_{0.196}O_{3.968}S_{0.032}$ cell showing the 3.5 to 4.5 V constant voltage charge before cycle 451 and the 2.25 V to 4.5 V constant voltage charge after cycle 451.

Figure 5 shows the discharge capacities for 3.5 V to 4.5 V cycling at 1 mA/cm^2 for a $Li//Li_xMn_{1.886}Fe_{0.114}O_{3.983}S_{0.017}$ cell at lower doping levels of iron and sulfur. From cycles 11 to 30, the even-numbered cycles were discharged to 2.25 V (not shown to maintain resolution of the degradation on y-axis). It is evident that this lower voltage discharge did have a detrimental impact on the crystal, as there were permanent impacts on the capacity, as compared with the higher iron- and sulfur-doped material shown in Figure 3 with equally as many discharges to 2.25 V and significantly more cycles. However, when maintained at the 3.5 to 4.5 V regime from 31 through 350 cycles, the discharge capacity remains stable.

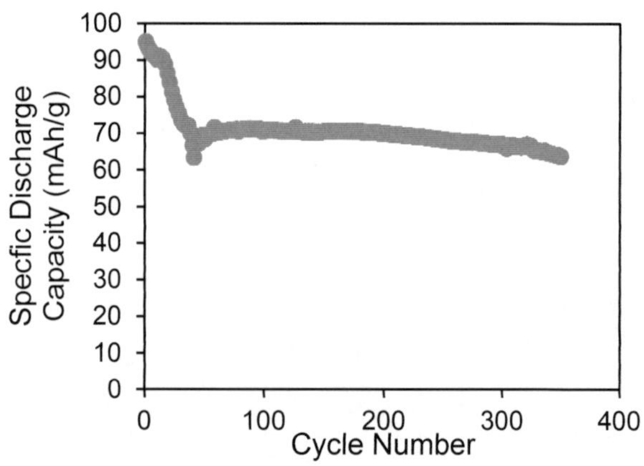

Figure 5: Discharge capacity for a $Li//Li_xMn_{1.886}Fe_{0.114}O_{3.983}S_{0.017}$ cell.

Conclusions

This work studied the impact of adding a sulfur anion dopant to the $Li_xMn_{2-y}Fe_yO_4$ material. The main goal of this effort was improved cyclability and resilience to high current rates as compared to $LiMn_2O_4$. Synthesis of the $Li_xMn_{2-y}Fe_yO_4$ material used a wet chemical glycine nitrate ignition synthesis method. This synthesis method reduces post-formulation processing and provides a homogeneous distribution of all dopants within the material.

Materials and experiments were designed to advance the theory that strengthening the $LiMn_2O_4$ crystal, such that manganese dissolution is prevented or reduced, can enhance cycle life. Oxygen can only take advantage of p-orbitals for providing covalency. This limits oxygen to a tetrahedral bond configuration. The addition of sulfur to replace oxygen provide access to d-orbitals which can potentially enhance the covalent nature of the bond, thus adding rigidity. It is through the sp^3d^2 hybrid bonds available to sulfur that the required rigidity to maintain cyclability and resilience to high current rates is established.

Testing this $Li_xMn_{2-y}Fe_yO_{4-z}S_z$ cathode material in an electrochemical cell opposite a lithium metal anode resulted in excellent capacity retention at extended cycling with constant voltage charging resulting in the mitigation of high current. Future work would include incorporating a more robust separator, as well as a high voltage electrolyte that will not degrade at advanced cycling at high voltages. Should an adequate electrolyte be used in addition to a separator that can prevent dendritic shorting across the electrodes, this $Li_xMn_{2-y}Fe_yO_{4-z}S_z$ cathode may be able to achieve a more superior rate capability in a constant voltage charging mode. More research is needed for selecting the appropriate doping levels of iron and sulfur, as it is evident that the stability of the material does depend upon the dopant concentrations.

References

[1] B. Ebin, S. Gürmen, C. Arslan, G. Lindbergh, Electrochimica Acta, 76 (2012) 368-374.

[2] H. Xia, Y.S. Meng, M.O. Lai, L. Lu, Journal of The Electrochemical Society, 157 (2010) A348-A354.

[3] D. Liu, W. Zhu, J. Trottier, C. Gagnon, F. Barray, A. Guerfi, A. Mauger, H. Groult, C.M. Julien, J.B. Goodenough, K. Zaghib, RSC Advances, 4 (2014) 154-167.

[4] H. Xia, Z. Luo, J. Xie, Progress in Natural Science: Materials International, 22 (2012) 572-584.

[5] H. Huang, C.A. Vincent, P.G. Bruce, Journal of The Electrochemical Society, 146 (1999) 3649-3654.

[6] Y. Xia, M. Yoshio, Journal of The Electrochemical Society, 143 (1996) 825-833.

[7] N.M. Hagh, G.G. Amatucci, Journal of Power Sources, 256 (2014) 457-469.

[8] S. Jayapal, R. Mariappan, S. Sundar, S. Piraman, Journal of Electroanalytical Chemistry, 720 (2014) 58-63.

[9] X. He, J. Li, Y. Cai, Y. Wang, J. Ying, C. Jiang, C. Wan, Journal of Power Sources, 150 (2005) 216-222.

[10] J. Morales, L. Sánchez, J. Tirado, Journal of Solid State Electrochemistry, 2 (1998) 420-426.

[11] J. Amarilla, J. Martin de Vidales, R. Rojas, Solid State Ionics, 127 (2000) 73-81.

[12] H.J. Bang, V. Donepudi, J. Prakash, Electrochimica Acta, 48 (2002) 443-451.

[13] G. Amatucci, A. Du Pasquier, A. Blyr, T. Zheng, J.-M. Tarascon, Electrochimica Acta, 45 (1999) 255-271.

[14] G. Amatucci, N. Pereira, T. Zheng, I. Plitz, J. Tarascon, Journal of Power Sources, 81 (1999) 39-43.

[15] C. Wu, F. Wu, L. Chen, X. Huang, Solid State Ionics, 152 (2002) 335-339.

[16] A. Eftekhari, Journal of Power Sources, 124 (2003) 182-190.

[17] M. Pico, I. Álvarez-Serrano, M. López, M. Veiga, Dalton Transactions, 43 (2014) 14787-14797.

[18] H. Kawai, M. Nagata, M. Tabuchi, H. Tukamoto, A.R. West, Chemistry of materials, 10 (1998) 3266-3268.

[19] L. Herna, J. Morales, L. Sanchez, E. Rodriguez Castello, and M.A.G. Arandab, *Journal of Materials Chemistry*, 12 (2002) 734–741.

[20] I. Taniguchi, Z. Bakenov, Powder technology, 159 (2005) 55-62.

[21] T. Atwater, P. Tavares, SAE International Journal of Materials and Manufacturing, 6 (2013) 85-89.

[22] T.B. Atwater, P.C. Tavares, in, US Patent 8,900,756, 2014.

[23] J. Son, H. Kim, Journal of Power Sources, 147 (2005) 220-226.

[24] W.-R. Liu, S.-H. Wu, H.-S. Sheu, Journal of Power Sources, 146 (2005) 232-236.

[25] A.L. Ruth, P.C. Latorre, E.D. Wachsman, T.B. Atwater, Electrochemical Society Transactions, 80 (2017), 305-316.

[26] Q. Jiang, D. Liu, H. Zhang, S. Wang. Journal of Physical Chemistry C. 119 (2015), 28776–28782.

[27] M. Molenda, R. Dziembaj, E. Podstawka, W. Łasocha, L.M. Proniewicz. Journal of Physics and Chemistry of Solids. 67 (2006) 1347–1350.

[28] S.H. Park, K.S. Park, S.S. Moon, Y.K. Sun, K.S. Nahm. Journal of Power Sources. 92 (2001) 244-249.

Safe Lithium-ion Battery Development

Umamaheswari Janakiraman, Logan Wittmaier, Mario Destephen and James Bond
Research & Development
EaglePicher Technologies
P.O. Box 47, Joplin, MO 64801-0047
mario.destephen@eaglepicher.com / 1-417-623-8000

Abstract: *The Lithium-ion battery and its safety is taken more into consideration in recent years, as it has been widely used in many different applications including consumer portable electronics. Thermal runaway of Lithium-ion batteries results from a series of chemical reactions of the internal components under abusive conditions. The heat generated from these reactions causes an increase in battery temperature along with the release of flammable gases, thereby creating a fire. EaglePicher Technologies continues to develop reduced flammability (RF) electrolytes to improve the safety of Lithium-ion batteries for Military, Navy, and Aircraft applications. The RF electrolyte, along with the improvements in cell chemistry and design, are critical components for enhancing the safety of the battery. EPT has demonstrated the safety of the advanced Lithium-ion battery by means of thermal characterization and by subjecting the battery to several abuse tests, such as external short, over charge, and heat to vent tests.*

Keywords: Lithium-ion battery; battery safety; overcharge; overheating.

Introduction

The Lithium-ion battery is a very promising energy storage medium with uses from portable electronics to passenger vehicles, including aircraft. It is getting more and more attention due to the worldwide energy shortage, as the availability of non-renewable energy sources is declining [1]. However, these batteries have not been widely deployed commercially in passenger vehicles primarily due to safety concerns [2-4]. The fire and explosion of a Lithium-ion battery is related to the flammability of the electrolyte, the rate of charge and/or discharge, and the engineering of the battery pack [6]. It can rupture, ignite, or explode when exposed to high temperatures or by short-circuiting the battery or cell. The adjacent cells may also then heat up and fail in some cases, causing the entire battery to ignite or rupture [7]. Many researchers have conducted experiments to find the exact cause of thermal runaway and the means to prevent it [8]. Thermal runaway occurs when an exothermic reaction goes out of control. Thermal runaway of a Lithium-ion battery results from a series of exothermic chemical reactions of the internal components under abusive conditions [9]. The heat generated from these reactions causes an increase in battery temperature, which increases the reaction rate further, causing a rapid temperature rise along with the release of flammable gases, thereby creating a fire or explosion [10, 11]. Lithium-ion battery safety can be improved in two ways: inherent safety methods and safety devices. Inherent safety is related to the safety of the battery's internal materials, interfaces, and overall cell design. Suppressing the decomposition of battery internal materials and interfaces is a basic way to improve the inherent safety of the battery. To improve the safety of battery cathode materials, they can be coated with a ceramic coating to minimize any side reactions with electrolyte and to improve the structural stability [12-15]. In addition to that, many researchers are working on synthesizing new cathode materials. Ways of improving anode material safety have also been studied. As anode SEI layer decomposition initiates a series of exothermic chemical reactions, many ways have been identified to modify the anode surface to improve the SEI layer stability. This includes physical coatings, such as metal oxides, and chemical coatings from electrolytes containing novel solvents and additives [16, 17]. These additives can be divided into the following categories [18]: (1) SEI formation improvers, (2) cathode protection agents, (3) $LiPF_6$ salt stabilizers, (4) safety protection agents, (5) Li deposition improvers, and (6) other agents such as solvation enhancers, aluminum corrosion inhibitors, and wetting agents.

EaglePicher has developed a Reduced Flammability (RF) electrolyte including additives and solvents from the above classes. Moreover, EaglePicher has developed a line of Lithium-ion batteries to serve both military and aerospace applications with various formats and cell electrochemistries. Through these efforts, a layered safety methodology has evolved to collectively reduce the probability of a catastrophic cell failure and the collateral damage that could possibly result. EaglePicher is presently working to augment this 'overlapping' design approach to better enable an oxide chemical cell formulation that notably improves the overall safety with a more 'energy dense' battery implementation.

Experimental

EaglePicher reduced flammability electrolyte (RF electrolyte) was formulated with a mixture of appropriate additives in carbonate solvents [19]. $LiNi_xCo_yMn_zO_2$ (NCM) cathodes, $LiNi_{0.8}Co_{0.15}Al_{0.05}O_2$ (NCA) cathodes, and graphite anodes were prepared using standard industrial processes by mixing the active material with carbon, poly(vinylidene fluoride) (PVDF), and N-methyl-2-pyrrolidinone (NMP). The resulting slurry was then coated on the current collector. Thermal properties of the different electrolyte formulations were studied using Differential Scanning Calorimetry (DSC). Flammability of the RF electrolyte and baseline electrolyte was tested using an open cup flash point test. Pouch cells and 18650 cells were constructed to do the discharge and safety tests.

Results

EaglePicher Reduced Flammability electrolyte (RF) has been evaluated by electrochemical and thermal characterization methods as is and in conjunction with anode materials. The baseline electrolyte is a typical Lithium-ion baseline electrolyte (BL) without additives. The electrochemical stability of RF electrolyte has been compared against the baseline electrolyte by a cyclic voltammetry experiment. The electrolytes were subjected to a voltage scan between 5V and 0.01V at a 1mV/s scan rate using Li/Li^+ as a reference electrode. As can be seen in Figure 1, the RF electrolyte showed better voltage stability than the BL electrolyte in the cell operational voltage window (4.3 and 2 V).

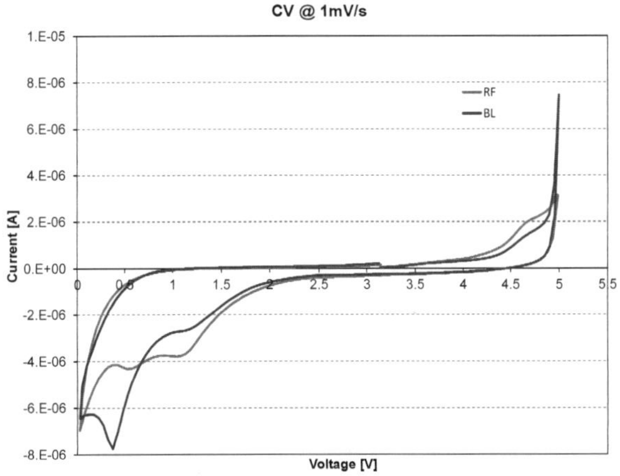

Figure 1. Cyclic voltammogram of RF and BL electrolytes @ 1mV/s.

DSC evaluation of RF and BL electrolytes was conducted in a Nitrogen atmosphere at a 20 K/min heating rate. The RF electrolyte exothermic decomposition reaction was shifted to a higher temperature and the heat output was lower than the BL electrolyte, as shown in Figure 2. This demonstrates that the thermal decomposition of the RF electrolyte is less energetic and therefore it is safer than the baseline (BL) electrolyte.

In order to understand the anode SEI layer stability, DSC evaluations were conducted on cycled anode half-cells containing a graphite anode and Lithium made with the BL and RF electrolytes. In order to evaluate the anode SEI layer thermal stability, the anode half cells were cycled at a C/10 rate for 3 cycles and stopped at the fully lithiated state of the graphite anode. As can be seen in Figure 3, the DSC of the lithiated anode showed lower heat generation for the sequence of SEI layer decomposition reactions in the presence of RF electrolyte than with the BL electrolyte.

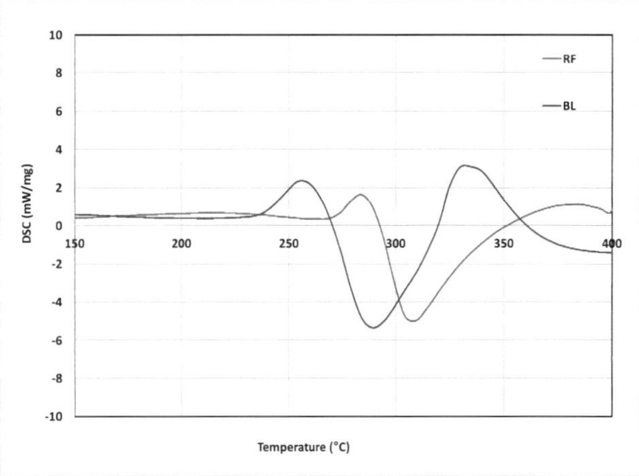

Figure 2. DSC of RF vs BL electrolyte.

As the SEI decomposition reaction initiates a chain reaction leading to thermal runaway, the observed higher anode SEI layer stability with RF electrolyte is an important factor to improve battery safety.

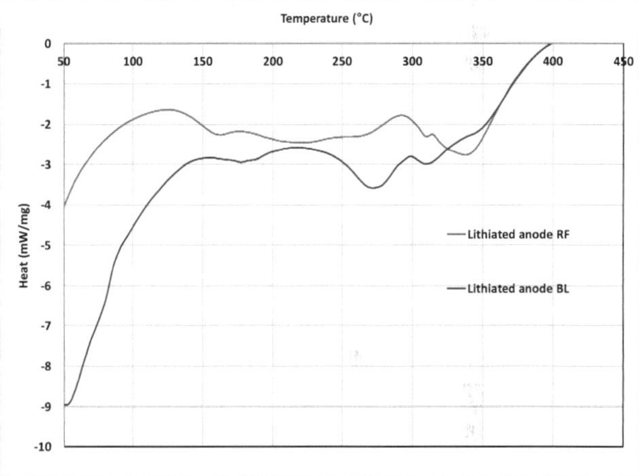

Figure 3. DSC of lithiated graphite anode with RF and BL electrolytes.

Open cup flammability tests were also performed, in which the Self Extinguishing Time (SET) of the electrolyte was measured upon igniting with a torch. The BL electrolyte caught on fire instantaneously in the presence of a flame and burned for 30s, whereas the RF electrolyte never caught on fire. This demonstrates the flame retardant capability of the RF electrolyte.

Following the characterization of electrochemical and thermal stability of RF electrolyte, the RF and BL were incorporated in NCA/graphite pouch cells and NCM/graphite cylindrical cells to evaluate their effect on the discharge capacity. The cells were tested at different rates at room temperature (RT), to evaluate the rate capability in the presence of RF and BL electrolytes. The pouch cells were tested up to a 4C rate. The RF electrolyte cells showed good capacity at all rates as shown in Figure

4. This demonstrates that EPT RF electrolyte didn't compromise the cell rate capability. The RF electrolyte cell performance is comparable to the BL electrolyte cells, in the investigated testing conditions.

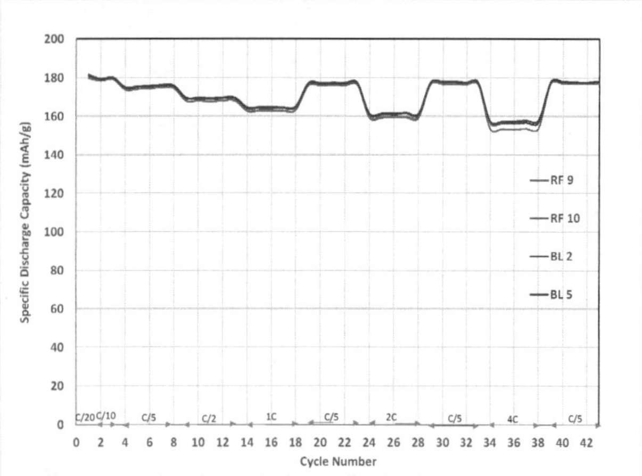

Figure 4. Specific Capacity of NCA/graphite pouch cells made with RF and BL electrolytes.

Furthermore, the pouch cells were also tested at cold and hot temperatures at different rates to evaluate the effect of RF electrolyte on temperature capability. They also showed good performance characteristics at low and high temperatures when tested at a 1C rate. Figure 5 shows the plot of average cell capacity of RF and BL cells at different temperatures. RF electrolyte is made with a combination of additives to improve safety and reduce flammability. These components have a slightly higher viscosity and density than those of the conventional Lithium-ion electrolyte. The observed good rate capability with RF electrolyte at temperatures from -20°C to 50°C demonstrates the effectiveness of the optimized EPT RF electrolyte formulation in achieving good capacity at higher rates and at colder temperatures.

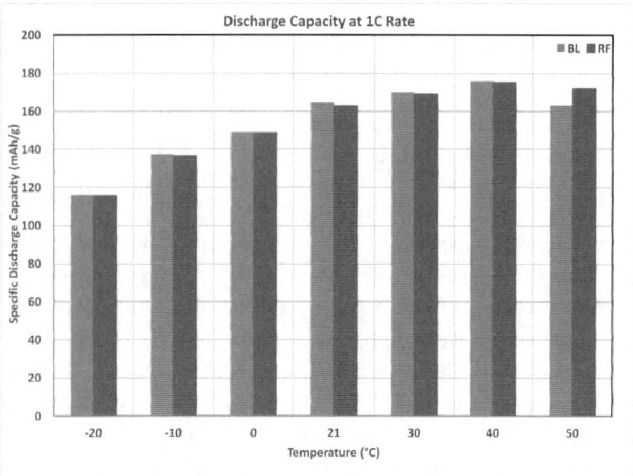

Figure 5. Specific Capacity of NCA/graphite pouch cells made with BL and RF, discharged at a 1C rate from -20°C to 50°C.

In addition to a good capacity (relative to the BL) at -20°C at a 1C rate, the RF electrolyte cells showed a higher discharge capacity at 50°C when compared to the BL cells. As in the case of the NCA pouch cells, NCM/graphite 18650 cells also showed a good capacity in the presence of RF electrolyte, when tested up to a 1C rate (Figure 6).

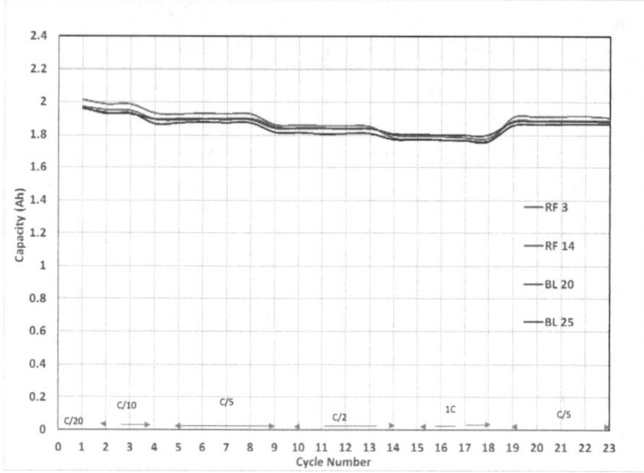

Figure 6. Capacity of NCM/graphite 18650 cells made with RF and BL electrolytes.

Following the electrical performance evaluation, the fully charged pouch cells and cylindrical cells were subjected to a series of safety tests, such as external short at 55°C, overcharge at 55°C, and overheating tests, in the presence of a spark emitter. The RF electrolyte cells passed in all of the above tests. The overheating test is the most rigorous test and it is performed as follows: cells were heated at a rate of 5–10°C/min until the cell voltage dropped. Both cells vented in the test, expelling electrolyte (see Figure 7). However, the maximum temperature was higher for the cells with the BL electrolyte (>300°C) than for the cells with the RF electrolyte.

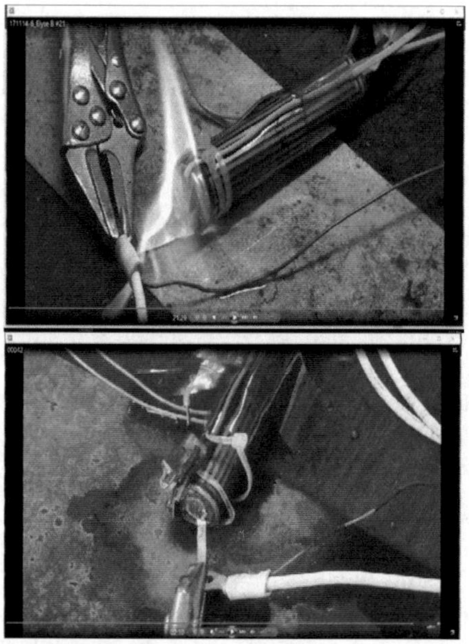

Figure 7. End of the overheating test of NCM 18650 with BL electrolyte (top) and RF electrolyte (bottom).

The RF electrolyte did not catch fire, whereas the baseline electrolyte burned completely. This proves the advantage of using the RF electrolyte in reducing the cell temperature, as shown in Figure 8, and in stopping the fire from propagating due to the reduced flammability of the leaked electrolyte.

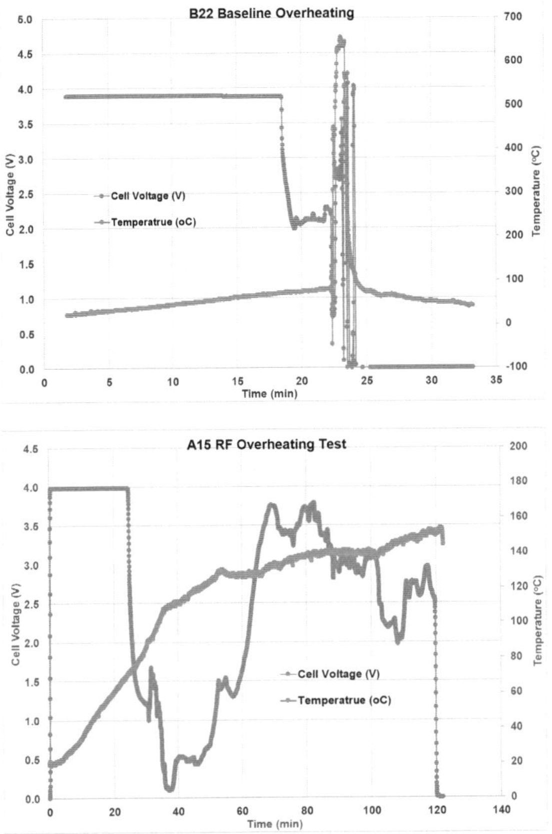

Figure 8. Overheating test of NCM 18650 cells made with BL (top) and RF (bottom) electrolytes in the presence of a spark emitter.

Summary and Outlook

EaglePicher Technologies has developed a Reduced Flammability (RF) electrolyte for Lithium-ion batteries. The RF electrolyte was tested against the BL electrolyte in NCA/graphite pouch cells and NCM/graphite 18650 cells. The RF electrolyte cells showed good rate capability, wide temperature discharge capability, and a superior high temperature performance compared to the BL cells. The RF and BL cells were tested for their response to abuse tests, such as overcharge, overheating, and external short tests. The RF electrolyte cells passed all the abuse tests without the electrolyte catching on fire while the BL electrolyte burned completely. Specifically, the overheating test of NCM 18650 cells shows the advantage of the RF electrolyte over the BL electrolyte in improving safety. The 18650 cells made with RF electrolyte lead to a lower cell temperature and a higher safety compared to the BL cell.

Acknowledgements

This work was supported in part by FAA (DTFACT-16-C-00043). The authors would like thank Mike Walz at FAA for the support.

References

1. J.Y. Lee, D. Deng, M.G. Kim, J. Cho, Energy Environ. Sci. 2 (2009) 818–837.
2. T.M. Bandhauer, S. Garimella, T.F. Fuller, J. Electrochem. Soc. 158 (2011) R1–R25.
3. J.B. Goodenough, Y. Kim, Chem. Mater. 22 (2010) 587–603.
4. J.M. Tarascon, M. Armand, Nature 414 (2001) 359–367.
5. Science Daily, American Chemical Society, 2007, http://www.sciencedaily.com/releases/2007/2012/071217110106.htm
6. P.G. Balakrishnan, R. Ramesh, T.P. Kumar, J. Power Sources 155 (2006) 401–414.
7. S.Y. Chen, Z.X. Wang, H.L. Zhao, L.Q. Chen, Prog. Chem. 21 (2009) 629–636.
8. F. Torabi, V. Esfahanian, J. Electrochem. Soc. 158 (2011) A850–A858.
9. Q. Wang, P. Ping, X. Zhaoa, G. Chub, J. Suna, Chunhua Chen., J. Power Sources 208 (2012) 210–224.
10. R.M. Spotnitz, J. Weaver, G. Yeduvaka, D.H. Doughty, E.P. Roth, J. Power Sources 163 (2007) 1080–1086.
11. B.K. Mandal, A.K. Padhi, Z. Shi, S. Chakraborty, R. Filler, J. Power Sources 161 (2006) 1341–1345.
12. C. Li, H.P. Zhang, L.J. Fu, H. Liu, Y.P. Wu, E. Ram, R. Holze, H.Q. Wu, Electrochim. Acta 51 (2006) 3872–3883.
13. Z.X. Yang, W.S. Yang, D.G. Evans, G. Li, Y.Y. Zhao, Electrochem. Commun. 10 (2008) 1136–1139.
14. W. Hong, M.C. Chen, Electrochem. Solid State 9 (2006) A82–A85.
15. J. Cho, Y.W. Kim, B. Kim, J.G. Lee, B. Park, Angew. Chem. Int. Ed. 42 (2003) 1618–1621.
16. H.J. Kweon, J. Park, J. Seo, G. Kim, B. Jung, H.S. Lim, J. Power Sources 126 (2004) 156–162.
17. J. Cho, T.J. Kim, J. Kim, M. Noh, B. Park, J. Electrochem. Soc. 151 (2004) A1899–A1904.
18. S.S. Zhang, J. Power Sources 162 (2006) 1379–1394.
19. R. Thillaiyan et al, US patent publication no. 20160336615 (pending).

Li-ion Capacitor/Li-ion Battery Hybrid Energy Storage Cell

Jim P. Zheng[(a)*], Annadanesh Shellikeri[(a)], Mark Hagen[(a)], Jin Yan[(b)], Ben Cao[(b)], Richard Jow[(c)], and Jeffrey Read[(c)]

[(a)]Department of Electrical and Computer Engineering, Florida A&M University and Florida State University, Tallahassee, FL 32310, USA; [(b)]General Capacitor LLC, Tallahassee, FL 32304, USA; and [(c)]U.S. Army Research Laboratory, Adelphi, MD 20783-1197, USA
[*]Tel: (850) 410-6464, Fax: (850) 410-6479, Email: zheng@eng.fsu.edu

Abstract: As a new generation of supercapacitor, the Li-ion capacitor (LIC) is an advanced energy storage device which consists of an electric double-layer capacitor (EDLC) cathode and a pre-lithiated anode [1,2], between which the ions shuttle during charge and discharge processes. Because of using pre-lithiated and low surface anode materials, the LIC can be charged to a maximum voltage as high as 4.0 V, which is much higher than of EDLCs and comparable to Li-ion batteries (LIBs); therefore, it allows the LIC and LIB to be assembled in one package as a LIB/LIC hybrid energy storage cell.

Keywords: Hybrid energy storage, Li-ion battery, Li-ion capacitor, high energy, long cycle life.

Introduction

Lithium (Li)-ion battery (LIB) and electric double-layer capacitor (EDLC) are the two widely used electrochemical energy storage devices. A typical LIB is made with Li intercalated anode and Li metal oxide cathode (hence the redox process or faradaic mechanism of energy storage), while the EDLC is made with a high surface area activated carbon (AC) for both anode and cathode (hence the reliance on double layer capacitance or non-faradaic form of energy storage). As a consequence of their different energy storage mechanisms, they both are distinct in their energy and power performances. LIB has a high specific energy of 100-250 $Wh \cdot kg^{-1}$; however, it has a low specific power of < 0.5 $kW \cdot kg^{-1}$ and a poor cycle life of < 5,000 cycles. EDLC has a high specific power of 10 $kW \cdot kg^{-1}$ and a long cycle life over 100,000 cycles; however, it has a much lower specific energy of < 6 $Wh \cdot kg^{-1}$ [1-4].

Moreover, energy storage devices, which can combine the advantages of LIBs and EDLCs in a single form, are highly desirable. As a new generation of supercapacitor, the Li-ion capacitor (LIC) is an advanced energy storage device which consists of an EDLC cathode and a prelithiated anode [5-6], between which the ions shuttle during charge and discharge processes. Because of using prelithiated and low surface anode materials, the LIC can be charged to a maximum voltage as high as 4.0 V, which is much higher than that of EDLCs and comparable to LIBs.

Results and Discussion

We have demonstrated a new hybrid energy storage device that combines the advantages of both the LIB and the LIC [7], thereby avoiding their inherent defects, while bridging the gap between the high energy densities offered by batteries and the high power densities seen in EDLCs. The fundamental difference between this hybrid LIC energy storage source and the LIC is that the hybrid LIC technology integrates two separate energy storage devices into one by synergistically combining battery and capacitor materials together to form a composite cathode. As seen from the potential profile of the hybrid cathode in Fig. 1, the non-faradaic capacitor material is initially charged electrostatically till the electrode potential reaches the redox reaction potential of the faradaic battery material, when the battery material is charged while maintaining a constant battery redox reaction potential. Once fully charged, the capacitor material is charged again till a limiting potential is reached for the capacitor material. Moreover, the composite cathode combines the double layer capacitance, which is surface limited, with the materials that store charge through redox reactions, which are limited by the charge transfer kinetics and diffusional processes, but are not limited to the material surface and hence, the bulk can be accessed, resulting in greater charge storage. This internal hybrid LIC device does not require any electric circuits for charge balancing and control when compared with the conventional external hybrid energy storage source. The energy density and power density of the hybrid cell can be designed to meet the requirements by a reasonable distribution of the ratio between LIB and LIC electrode materials in the internal hybrid LIC. For example, in a LIB/LIC internal hybrid cell in our recent work, made with a 20 wt.% $LiFePO_4$ (LFP) and 80 wt.% AC mixed cathode and a pre-lithiated hard carbon anode, showed the best rate performance and the specific energy increased by 40% compared with conventional LIC [8]. The LFP is a high specific capacity and high potential battery material, while the AC is a highly conductive and porous material which provides better power capability and adsorption of electrolyte, apart from contributing towards surface charge storage.

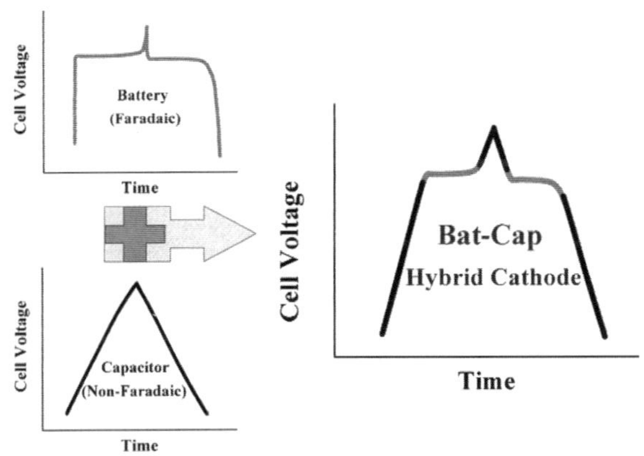

Figure 1. An illustration of a hybrid composite cathode potential profile, combining faradaic and non-faradaic types of charge storage.

Commercial active materials were used for the negative and positive electrode preparation. The composite cathode (abbreviated as LFP20 electrodes) was prepared with 20% LFP and 80% AC using a dry method of electrode fabrication. A free-standing film was first prepared by mixing 18.8 wt.% LFP (MTI Corporation), 75.2 wt.% Activated Carbon (YP-50F, Kurruray), and 6 wt.% Polytetrafluoroethylene (PTFE, DuPont™) binder. LFP nanoparticles were received from manufacturer pre-coated with a thin layer of carbon and were used as received. The carbon coating is known to have a beneficial effect on capacity [9] and rate performance [10]. This mixture was blended together until homogenous mixture was obtained. The carbon mixture was then pressed and calendared to the desired thickness at 100 °C forming the free-standing film. This film is then laminated at 200 °C to an etched aluminum current collector that has an 8-10 μm conductive coating to achieve better contact and conductivity between the current collector and the active material layer. The active material thickness achieved for the designed capacity was ~106 μm with a tap density of 0.83 $g{\cdot}cm^{-3}$.

The anode electrode consisted of hard carbon (HC) as the active material. The electrodes sheets (active material thickness ~90 μm, tap density of 0.93 $g{\cdot}cm^{-3}$) were supplied by General Capacitor LLC., Tallahassee, FL, and were used without any further processing after punching out the electrodes of desired sizes from the supplied sheets.

The electrodes were then punched from the electrode sheets to the desired dimensions (4.9 cm × 4.9 cm (active area) for anodes and 4.8 cm × 4.8 cm for cathodes, then vacuum dried at 120 °C overnight and transferred to dry room environment before final cell assembly there as shown in Fig. 2(a) and (b). For anode (Fig. 2(a)), Li metal strips (45 μm) were used as the source of Li-ion for pre-doping process. Based on the rated specific capacity of the hard carbon electrode, the weight of the Li strips to be loaded was estimated to be 7~8 wt% of the hard carbon electrode active material weight, which were pressed on to the anode surface.

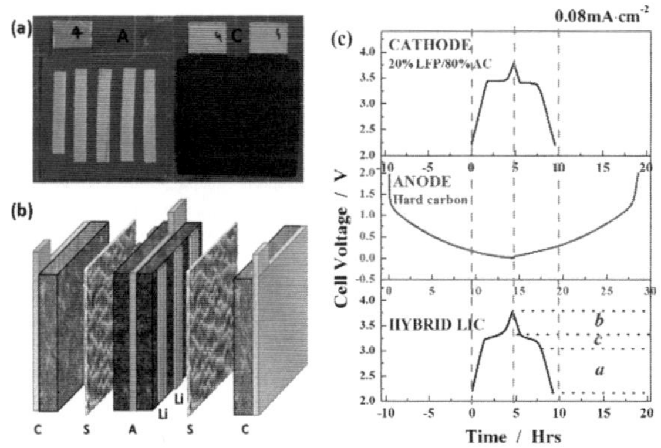

Figure 2. Cell design and assembly (a) Double sided hard carbon anode (A) loaded with Li metal strips and two single-sided LFP20 cathode (C) electrodes, (b) Assembled Cell configuration – C: LFP20 Cathode, S: Separator, A: Hard carbon Anode, Li: Li metal strips loading, and (c) Electrode capacity design and internal hybrid LIC Cell.

Fig. 2(c) illustrates the capacity matching between the LFP20 cathode and HC anode. As seen in this figure, for a fixed rate of 0.08 $mAcm^{-2}$, the hard carbon electrode is able to discharge for a time that is approximately three times that of LFP20 cathode.

Fig. 3(a) shows the rate performance recorded for the LFP20/HC full cell during the galvanostatic charge/discharge tests performed at various discharge rates ranging from 0.1C to 53C. It can clearly be inferred, that the capacity contribution by capacitor material (AC) was less sensitive than battery material when the discharge rate increased from 0.1C to 53C. A cell capacity retention of 89% was observed when the C-rate increased from 0.1C to 1.9C. The retention decreased to 75%, 66% and 52% when the C-rate increased to 9C, 20C and 53C, respectively. The lowering of the discharge curve plateau with an increase in C-rate is due to a combination of internal resistances (ohmic, charge transfer, SEI interface, diffusion) of the cell which induce IR polarization and overpotentials from both HC anode and LFP/AC cathode. For example, at much higher rates (e.g. 53C), the Li-ion solid state diffusion into the bulk of the LFP particles is a major limitation, resulting into insufficient charging/discharging during the faradaic processes, which causes a noticeable rate induced reversible capacity decay.

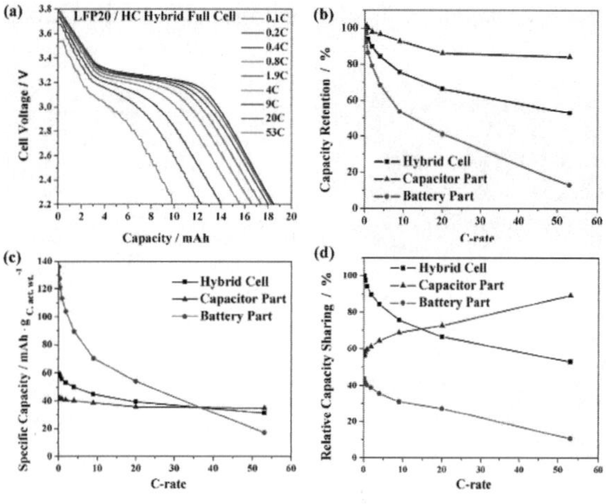

Figure 3 (a) Discharge profiles for a hybrid cell (20 wt.% LFP and 80 wt.% AC) at different charge/discharge rates from 0.1C to 53C, (b) Capacity retention, (c) Specific capacities, and (d) Relative capacity Sharing. Note: The cell, capacitor and battery parts specific capacities were calculated using LFP20, AC and LFP (including carbon coating) active material weights in cathode electrode, respectively.

From our previous study of LIC, it was known that activated carbon can be cycled over >300,000 cycles without significantly capacity decay. To study the LFP decay rate in the composite cathode and to understand the effect of C-rates on the long-term cycle life on the LFP20 composite electrode, the two LFP20/HC internal hybrid LIC full cells were assembled and cycled at two different rates, one at a low rate of 2.7 C and the other at a high rate of 43C. The discharge capacities recorded during the continuous galvanostatic charge-discharge cycling in the voltage range of 2.2-3.8 V at the two different C-rates of 2.7C (6000 cycles) and 43C (70,000 cycles) are shown in Fig. 3(a), along with their respective cycle efficiencies.

As seen in Fig. 4(a), similar to our earlier observation, the capacity of the cell cycled at a low rate of 2.7 C decays faster than that cycled at high rate of 43C, the capacity retention of the 43C rate cycled hybrid LIC being as high as 84% after 70,000 cycles (91 % after 20,000 cycles) and that being 87% for the 2.7C rate cycled cell after 6,000 cycles. Also, the coulombic efficiency of both the cells float around 100% all along during the respective cycling. In order to eliminate the effect of rate induced decay, we recorded the true capacities retained by the hybrid cells by intercepting/stopping the cycle tests after a fixed number of cycles were completed (e.g. cycle 1, 100, 500, 1,000, etc.) and performing galvanostatic charge-discharge cycling in the voltage range of 2.2-3.8 V at a slow rate of 0.2C. Once the true capacities were recorded, the long-term cycling tests were resumed. The results are presented in Fig. 4.

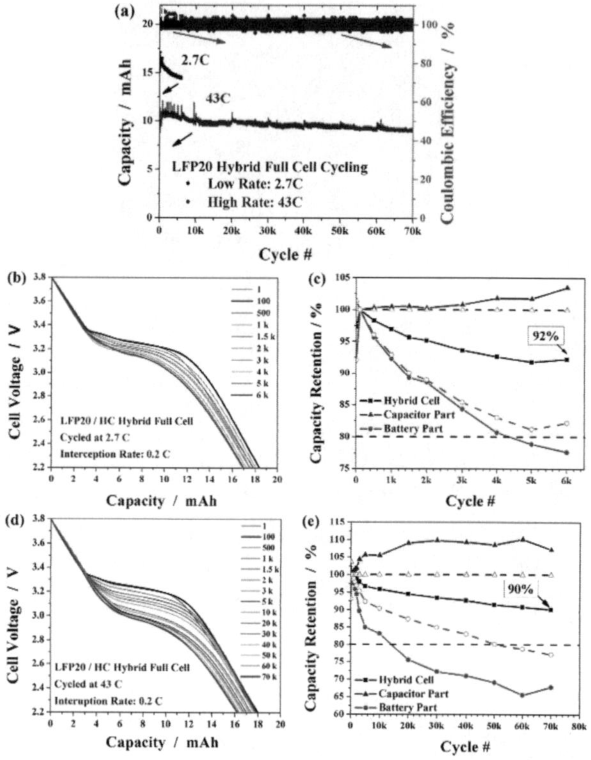

Figure 4. Hybrid LIC cycling and capacity sharing: (a) Full Cell discharge capacity and efficiency at high (43C) and low (2.7C) galvanostatic charge-discharge cycle rates, (b) Discharge voltage profiles for the 2.7C-rate cycled cell at an interception rate of 0.2C, (c) Capacity Retention for the 2.7C-rate cycled cell, and capacity sharing between the battery and capacitor material, (d) Discharge voltage profiles for the 43 C-rate cycled cell at an interception rate of 0.2C, (e) Capacity Retention for the 43C-rate cycled cell, and capacity sharing between the battery and capacitor materials. Note: The dotted lines indicate the capacitor and battery materials capacity retention rates, assuming that the capacitor material (AC) didn't undergo any capacity decay.

Conclusion

LFP20%/AC 80% composite cathode electrode was manufactured using a dry method, delivering an enhanced specific capacity of 65 $mAh \cdot g^{-1}$. An internal hybrid LIC Cell, with a 3:1 anode (HC) to the composite cathode capacity ratio design was assembled and analyzed for low and high rate performance. The pre-lithiation strategy was employed using Li-metal strips as the source of Li to compensate for the initial capacity loss. The large anode capacity and pre-lithiation design strategies enable the anode to operate in a narrow potential window to avoid Li-plating in the hybrid full cell configuration. The hybrid LIC cells showed a cell capacity retention of 94% over 1000 cycles at a low rate of 1 C, while at a high rate of 60C, it exhibited an impressive capacity retention of 92% over 100,000 cycles.

Acknowledgements
This work is supported by US Army Research Laboratory under contract No. W911NF-15-2-0103 and Office of Naval Research under contract No. N00014-17-1-2650.

References
1. G. Gourdin, P.H. Smith, T. Jiang, T.N. Tran, D. Qu, J. Electroanalytical Chemistry, 2013, **688**, p. 103.
2. Fuji heavy Industry Patent: N. Ando, S. Taguchi, Y. Hato, Organic electrolyte capacitor, EP1400996A1 (2002).
3. Y. Sun, H.-W. Lee, Z. W. Seh, N. Liu, J. Sun, Y. Li and Y. Cui, Nat. Energy, 2016, **1**, 15008.
4. V. Khomenko, E. Raymundo-Piñero, F. Béguin,J. Power Sources, 2008, **177**, 643 – 651.
5. W.J. Cao and J.P. Zheng, J P. Journal of Power Sources, 2012, **213**: 180-185.
6. H. Sun, X. M. He, J. G. Ren, J. J. Li, C. Y. Jiang, C. R. Wan, Electrochim. Acta 2007, **52**, 4312–4316.
7. J.S. Zheng, L. Zhang, A. Shellikeri, W. Cao, Q. Wu, & J.P. Zheng, Scientific Reports, 2017, **7**, 41910.
8. A. Shellikeri, J. S. Zheng, S. Yturriaga, W. Cao, J. P. Zheng., Long Cycle Life $LiFePO_4$ /AC Hybrid Cathodes for Lithium Ion Capacitors. 231st ECS Meeting, New Orleans, LA (2017).
9. H. Huang, S-C. Yin, L. F. Nazar, Approaching Theoretical Capacity of LiFePO4 at Room Temperature at High Rates. Electrochem. Solid-State Lett., 2001, **4**, A170.
10. W. J. Zhang, Comparison of the Rate Capacities of LiFePO4 Cathode Materials. *J. Electrochem. Soc.*, 2010, **157**, A1040–A1046.

High Capacity, High Power, Lithium-Ion Supercapacitor/Battery Hybrids Using Layered Hybrid Electrode for Military Applications

Denguo Wu and Jiang Fan

American Lithium Energy Corporation (ALE)
2261 Rutherford Road, Carlsbad, CA 92008
jfan@americanlithiumenergy.com

Abstract: *The performance of a lithium-ion battery and supercapacitor hybrid using a layered structural electrode was studied as a potentially strong candidate for high power military applications according to military specifications such as MIL-PRF-32143 (AT). A lithium ion battery/supercapacitor hybrid cell with 2Ah capacity (4500 F) at 20A has been designed and developed. Various kinds of hybrid designs were tested together with different electrolytes. The hybrid cell has achieved the specific energy and specific power targets: >50 Wh/kg at 10C or 20A and 3000 W/kg for more than 10 seconds. The hybrid cell lost very little capacity after over 35000 cycles of 60A charging for 30 seconds, and 60A discharging for 30 seconds between 3.8V to 2.2 V. The hybrid cell still kept about 70% of its capacity after about 35000 cycle of 10C (or 20A) continuous charging and 10C (20A) continuous dischargine between 3.8V to 2.2V. It appears highly likely that the cell cycle life with 60A charging/60A discharging for 30 seconds will achieve the target 100000 cycles. The cell abuse tolerance will be discussed.*

Keywords: High Energy; High Power; Polymer Li-Ion Cell; Li-ion Supercapacitors

Introduction

There is a strong growing need for improved power sources for military applications such as energy weapons, vertical lift aircraft and the mciro-grid. A high power battery could meet the discharge power needs, while its charging rate is limited. The supercapacitor is good in both charge and discharge power, but its energy density is too low to meet the power density needs in the highly constrained space. Therefore, there is a strong interest in combining the battery together with the supercapacitor so that the combined power source will have both high power and energy densities. In fact, many kinds of approaches have been attempted over the past several years [2]. For instance, the battery and a supercapacitor are combined t to have the required power and energy density for the target application, but this approach requires a complicated electronic controlling system, which adds not only the cost but also weight. Another approach is that the supercapacitor electrode materials were directly mixed with the battery electrode materials to form a supercapacitor/battery hybrid electrode for use in a supercapacitor/battery hybrid. The disadvantage for this kind of approaches is that it is difficult to optimize the performance of the battery and supercapacitor separately because the supercapacitor and battery electrodes are mixed together, which make this approach less attractive. ALE took a different approach in a way that both the supercapacitor electrode and battery electrode can be optimized independently, forming a solid base to take a full advantage of both supercapacitor and battery. Following are the details.

Results and Discussion

Capacity and impedance of hybrid cells with different designs:

Table 1 lists the cell capacities at the discharge currents 2A and 50A, and impedance at 1 kHz for the cells made with different hybrid electrodes. Several observations can be made: 1) the power of the hybrid cell is good when the supercapacitor electrode layer is on the top of the battery positive electrode (see HR7); 2) The power of the hybrid cell is poor when the supercapacitor electrode layer is on the top of the negative electrode (HR4); the power of the hybrid is relatively good when the battery negative electrode is on the top of supercapacitor electrode layer (HR5); and 3) the correlation between the cell impedance at 1 kHz is weak (see HR3, HR6 and HR4). The discharge capacity at 50A for HR4 is much lower than that obtained from HR3 and HR6 even the cell impedance at 1 kHz for HR 4 is much smaller than these obtained with HR3 and HR 6 cells.

Table 1 Cell information, capacity and impedance at 1 kHz

Cell ID	Supercapacitor/ Battery ratio	Imp. (mΩ)	Cap. (Ah) at 2A	Cap. (Ah) at 50A
HR1	Low	2.58	2.992	2.694
HR3	High; battery (+) layer is on the top of the capacitor layer	8.87	2.58	1.68
HR6	High; battery (+) layer is on the top of the super capacitor;	10.2	2.97	1.902
HR7	High; capacitor layer is on the top of the battery (+) layer;	3.2	2.92	2.528
HR5	Low; battery (-) electrode is on the top of super capacitor oxide layer	4.4	2.35	1.847
HR4	Low; super capacitor oxide layer on the top of the (-) battery electrode	4.7	2.45	0.402

Cell Discharge Voltage Profiles at Room Temperature:

Figure 1 presents the cell discharge voltage profiles at different currents 2A, 5A, 10A, 30A and 50A. The cell from HR1 can also be discharged at 100A for 10 seconds, which corresponds to 3000 W/kg (not shown because of the limited space).

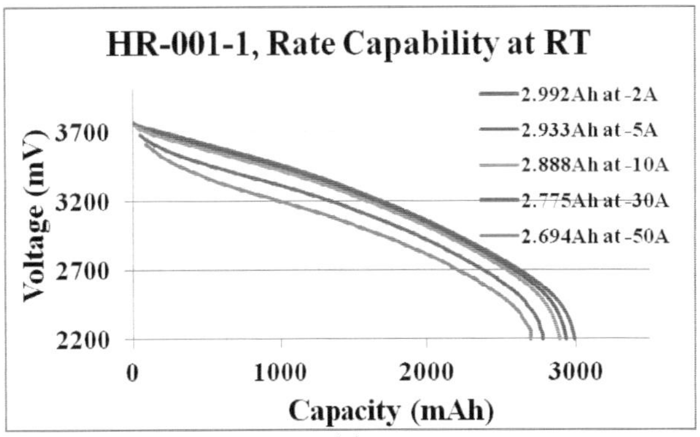

(a)

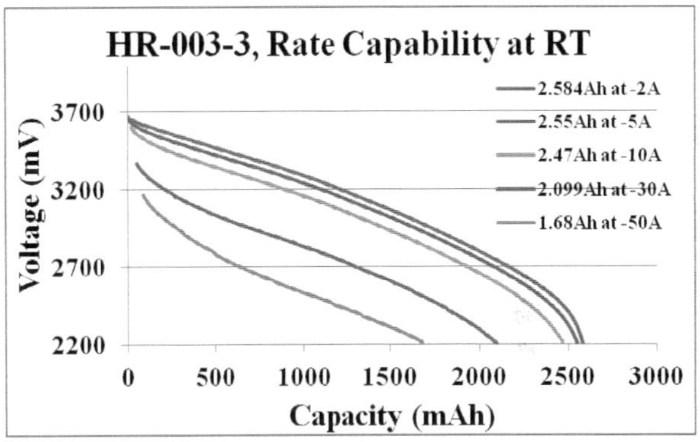

(b)

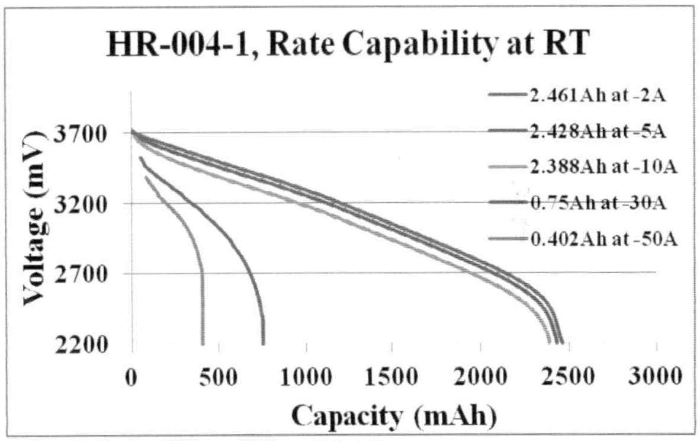

(c)

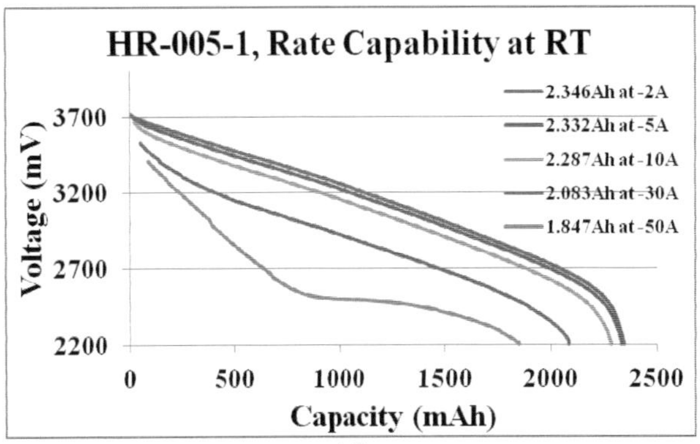

(d)

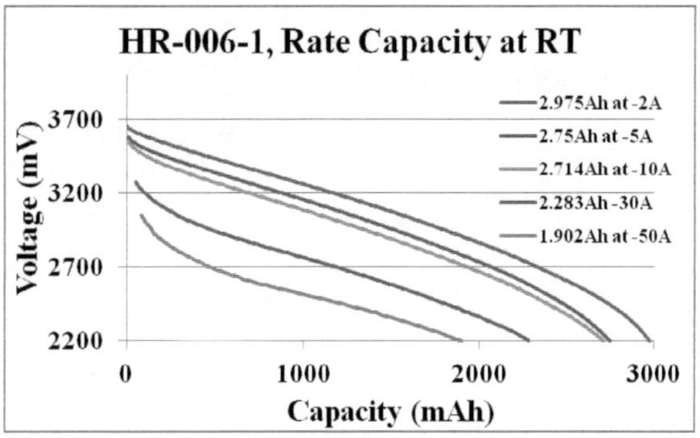

(e)

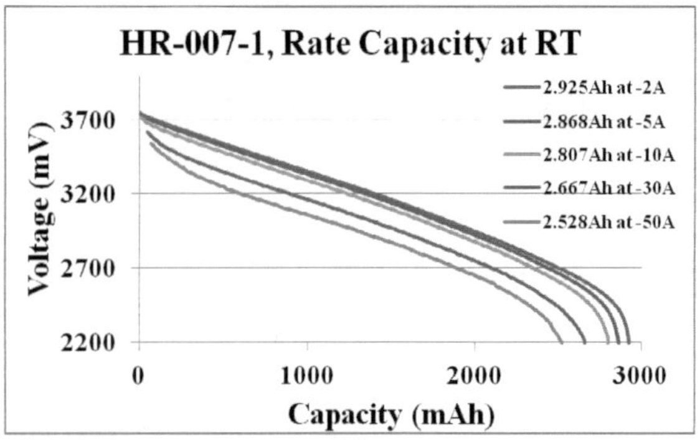

(f)

Figure 1a to f: Cell discharge voltage profiles at the different discharge currents 2, 5, 10, 30 and 50A and at room temperature.

Cell Cycle Life:

Figure 2a shows a) the hybrid cell capacity vs. the cycle number during 60A charging/60A discharging for 30 seconds at room temperature. The cell lost very little capacity after over 35000 cycles. The cell lost about 30% after over 35000 cycles during 20A charging and 20A discharging cycling. The cycle life could be improved further,

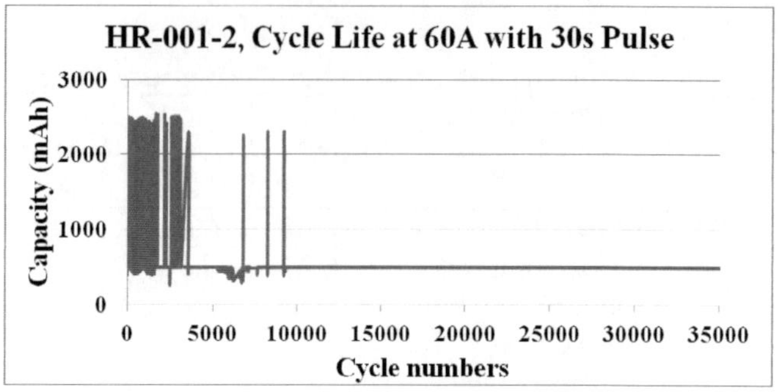

a)

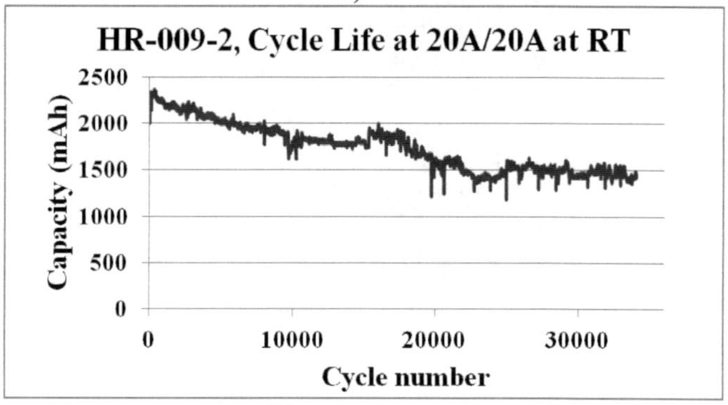

b)

Figure 2a to 2b: the cell capacity vs the cell cycle number for a) 60A charging for 30 second and 60A discharging for 30 second and at room temperature; b) 20A charging to 3.8V and 20A discharge to 2.2V.

Cell Safety

The cell abuse tolerance was also studied and will be reported during the meeting.

Conclusions

The performance of a lithium-ion battery and supercapacitor hybrid using a layered structural electrode was studied as a potentially strong candidate for high power military applications according to military specifications such as MIL-PRF-32143 (AT). The lithium ion battery/supercapacitor hybrid cell with 2Ah capacity (4500 F) at 20A has been designed and developed. Various kinds of hybrid designs were tested together with different electrolytes. The hybrid cell has achieved the specific energy and specific power targets: >50 Wh/kg at 10C or 20A and 3000 W/kg for more than 10 seconds. The hybrid cell lost very little capacity after over 35000 cycles of 60A charging for 30 seconds, and 60A discharging for 30 seconds between 3.8V to 2.2 V. The hybrid cell still kept about 70% of its capacity after about 35000 cycle of 10C (or 20A) continuous charging and 10C (20A) continuous discharging cycle between 3.8V to 2.2V. It is highly likely that the cell cycle life with 60A charging/60A discharging for 30 seconds will achieve the target 100000 cycles. The cell abuse tolerance will be discussed.

Reference

[1] MIL-PRF-32383-4

[2] Wenhua Zuo, Ruizhi Li, Cheng Zhou, Yuanyuan Li, Jianlong Xia and Jinping Liu, "Battery-Supercapacitor Hybrid Devices: Recent Progress and Future Prospects" in Adv. Sci., 2017, 4, 1600539

Acknowledagement

Authors will like to thank US Army, CERDEC, Aberdeen, MD 21005 for their partial financial support for the work per the contract GTS-S-16-11

The Effects of Potassium Ferrocyanide/Potassium Ferricyanide and their Derivatives on the Performance of Solid-State Supercapacitor

Xiangyang Zhou, Xiaoyao Qiao, Chen Zhang, and Yuchen Wang
Department of Mechanical and Aerospace Engineering, University of Miami
1251 Memorial Drive, Coral Gables, Florida, USA, FL33124
xzhou@miami.edu / 1-305-284-3287
Azzam N. Mansour, Gordon H. Waller, and Curtis A. Martin
NSWCCD, 9500 MacArthur Boulevard, West Bethesda, Maryland, USA MD20817
azzam.mansour@navy.mil / 301-227-4451

Abstract: *In previous studies, we have demonstrated that the addition of metal cyanide mediators or redox species into polymer electrolytes can effectively increase the specific energy and power of a mediator containing supercapacitor relative to a supercapacitor without a mediator. The benefits of combining mediators into the composite electrode, which contains carbon powder and polymer electrolyte, are the introduction of pseudo-capacitance, promotion of ionic and electronic conductivities, and serving as additional ion sources for electric double layer capacitance. In order to further enhance the performance of the mediator supercapacitor and to elucidate the charge/discharge mechanisms, a systematic study was conducted. In this report, we will present the research progress in three aspects: 1) synthesis of mediators in the form of* $KMFe(CN)_6$ *(M=transition metal); 2) structural characterization of the synthesized compounds using X-ray Photoelectron Spectroscopy (XPS) and X-ray diffraction (XRD); 3) experimental validation of time dependent charge and discharge process. The full cell measurements revealed that the specific energy of supercapacitors with mediators where M is Mn, Fe, Co, increased by more than 40% relative to that of supercapacitors containing* $K_3Fe(CN)_6/K_4Fe(CN)_6$.

Keywords: supercapacitor; potassium ferrocyanide, potassium ferricyanide; mediator; solid-state; XPS; XRD.

Introduction

A mediator is a redox material that undergoes fast and reversible reactions. Examples of mediator pairs are NaI/I_2, $K_4Fe(CN)_6/K_3Fe(CN)_6$. Our research group proposed a new concept of mediator supercapacitor (SC), which is composed of large amount of activated carbon and small amount of mediator [1,2]. This type of SC can be considered as an EDLC combined with a pseudocapacitor, or a hybrid SC. The Faradaic reactions can increase the capacitance of the electrodes, replenish the number of free ions in the electrolyte, and minimize reduction of ionic conductivity during the charge/discharge processes.

In previous work by Zhou's group, a couple of mediators/redox species were reported to be effective in enhancing the performance of supercapacitors. The function of mediators, including increasing capacitance of supercapacitor and promoting the ionic conductivity of the electrolyte, have been observed and analyzed.

As a mediator, Prussian blue derivatives or analogues (PBAs) have fast reversible redox kinetics and high specific capacitance. However, compared to other redox mediators, PBAs have unique advantages in practical applications:

1. PBAs are insoluble in most solvents. For other redox mediators, such as $K_3Fe(CN)_6/K_4Fe(CN)_6$ and NaI/I_2, which are soluble in an aqueous electrolyte, an expensive selective membrane must be employed to prevent the mediator-crossover issue for non- solid-state SC.

2. PBAs containing multi-valent transition metals, such as $K_2MnFe(CN)_6$, could further improve the capacitance of $K_3Fe(CN)_6$ and $K_4Fe(CN)_6$, because Mn can have oxidation states of 2+, 3+, and 4+ under normal potential range.

3. For EDLCs and pseudocapacitors, the ions are consumed to form the EDL or complete redox reactions. However, PBAs can provide extra ions to the electrolyte to maintain the concentration, as shown in the following redox reaction:

$$K_2Mn^{2+}Fe^{2+}(CN)_6 \rightarrow Mn^{3+}Fe^{3+}(CN)_6 + 2e^- + 2K^+$$

The objectives of the present research work are as follows.

1. Develop reliable and repeatable chemical synthesis procedure to produce series of transition metal based PBAs.

2. Characterize the synthesized PBAs using XPS and XRD to verify the structures and compositions of the PBAs.

3. Fabricate mediator supercapacitors using the PBAs to evaluate the performance of the mediator supercapacitors as a function of mediators.

4. Study the effect of the mediators as ion providers during charge/discharge.

Experimental Approach

Sample Preparation: The $K_4Fe(CN)_6$ and $K_3Fe(CN)_6$ mediators were obtained from Sigma-Aldrich. An attempt was made to prepare a number of $K_3Fe(CN)_6$ and $K_4Fe(CN)_6$ analogues using the following procedures:

(1) Dissolve 0.01 mole of transition metal (Mn^{2+}, Co^{2+}, Ni^{2+}, Cu^{2+}, Zn^{2+}) nitrate in 100 mL of deionized water with magnetic stirring at room temperature to get Solution 1.

(2) Dissolve 0.01 mole $K_3Fe(CN)_6$ or $K_4Fe(CN)_6$ in 100 mL of deionized water with magnetic stirring at room temperature to get Solution 2.

(3) Add these two solutions dropwise into 100 mL of deionized water with magnetic stirring at room temperature. Precipitate forms immediately but stirring continues for another 2 hours.

(4) The precipitate is centrifuged at 6500 rpm, washed with deionized water for three times, and dried in nitrogen-filled glovebox at 50°C for 1 day.

(5) The raw product is grounded by hands with a mortar and pestle and kept in a nitrogen-filled glovebox.

The general chemical reactions are shown as follow:

$$K_3Fe(CN)_6 + M(NO_3)_2 \rightarrow KMFe(CN)_6 + 2KNO_3$$

$$K_4Fe(CN)_6 + M(NO_3)_2 \rightarrow K_2MFe(CN)_6 + 2KNO_3$$

$$K_4Fe(CN)_6 + Fe(NO_3)_3 \rightarrow KFeFe(CN)_6 + 3KNO_3$$

XPS and XRD Measurements: XPS spectra were collected using Physical Electronics VersaProbe II Scanning XPS Microprobe using monochromatic Al Kα (1486 eV) X-ray source with a focused beam size of 200 microns rastered over and area of 1000 x 200 microns. The structure and phase purity of mediators were investigated by powder X-ray diffraction using the Bruker D8 Advance Diffractometer with Cu K_α X-rays (λ = 1.5404 Å).

Supercapacitor Fabrication: The electrodes were prepared using the following steps: 1) adding 0.05 g polyvinylidene fluoride (PVDF) into 3 mL N-methyl-2-pyrrolidone solvent (NMP) and stirring at 80°C until PVDF is totally dissolved (this process may take 3 hours), 2) adding 0.1 g of mediator, 0.9 g of activated carbon (AC), and 0.05 g of conductive carbon to the previous solution and stirring for 2 hours to form consistent slurry, 3) coating the composite slurry onto a 50 cm^2 carbon paper with a drawdown tool, and 4) The coated electrode is then dried in a glovebox at 80°C for 24 hours. The same procedure was used to prepare an electrode without mediators and used as a reference for comparison purposes. Two aluminum foils were used as current collectors, a PVDF with 1 M of tetraethylammonium tetrafluoroborate based polymer electrolyte membrane similar to those described in Refs. 1 and 2 were used as the separator. The SC cell was assembled in a glove box with nitrogen using a vacuum sealing machine. The specific energy was evaluated by normalizing the measured data with the total mass of the electrode including active carbon, conductive graphite, PVDF binder, and mediator. The cyclic voltammetry and galvanostatic charge/discharge (GCD) testing was conducted using Gamry model 3000 electrochemical measurement system.

Results

XPS: Based on XPS composition results (Table 1), the surface region consists mostly of C and N in accord with the stoichiometry of the cyanide group. Considering the semi-quantitative nature of XPS composition analysis, the potassium concentrations of 11.0 and 11.4 for $K_2MnFe(CN)_6$ and $K_2CoFe(CN)_6$, respectively, are in general agreement with its nominal value of 12.5. However, the potassium concentrations of 6.3 and 5.5 for $K_2CuFe(CN)_6$ and $K_2ZnFe(CN)_6$ are well below nominal value indicating that these two mediators will not form pure phases with the indicated nominal stoichiometry using the synthesis procedure described here.

Table 1. Summary of XPS composition of various mediators.

Sample	C	N	O	K	Fe	M %
$K_4Fe(CN)_6$	40.7	22.8	9.8	22.5	4.2	N/A
$K_3Fe(CN)_6$	43.8	26.5	6.6	18.5	4.7	N/A
$K_2MnFe(CN)_6$	39.0	30.7	5.9	11.0	5.8	7.6
$K_2CoFe(CN)_6$	39.1	31.7	4.1	11.4	5.5[a]	8.3[b]
$K_2CuFe(CN)_6$	43.3	33.4	5.6	6.3	6.10	5.3
$K_2ZnFe(CN)_6$	44.2	29.7	6.4	5.5	4.88	9.4
$KMnFe(CN)_6$	44.0	29.4	7.9	5.6	5.2	8.0
$KFeFe(CN)_6$	46.1	27.2	13.3	0.5	12.9	N/A
$KCoFe(CN)_6$	42.3	34.2	6.3	0.6	4.9[a]	11.7[b]
$KCuFe(CN)_6$	46.8	31.2	9.0	0.4	6.1	6.5
$KZnFe(CN)_6$	51.7	28.5	7.0	0.4	4.0	8.4

[a] The Fe $2p_{3/2}$ concentration is distorted due to interference with the Co Auger lines. [b] The Co $2p_{3/2}$ concentration is distorted due to interference with the Fe Auger line.

The potassium concentration of 5.6 is roughly close to the nominal value of 6.7 for $KMFe(CN)_6$ where M is Mn but is reduced significantly below 1 when M is Fe, Co, Cu, or Zn. Hence, the samples with potassium concentrations below 1 do not support the formation of significant quantities of $KMFe(CN)_6$. The concentrations of Fe are in qualitative agreement with nominal value for all mediators. The Mn, Cu and Zn concentrations are somewhat close to the nominal value. Note that the Fe concentration for $KFeFe(CN)_6$ is close to the nominal value of 13.3. To be noted, oxygen was found to be present in all mediators with concentrations in the range of 4.2-8.6 % except in the case of $KFeFe(CN)_6$ where the concentration is highest at 13 %. The presence of oxygen was also confirmed on the basis of XRD indicating that oxygen was not only present as surface contaminant but also in the bulk of the sample most likely in the form of adsorbed and structurally bonded water. Based on XPS results, it is more appropriate to describe the stoichiometry of the mediators as $K_xM_yFe(CN)_6{\bullet}zH_2O$ where x, y, and z depend on the transition metal component as proposed previously [3]. For simplicity, hereafter, we refer to the mediators with the desired stoichiometry throughout the paper.

Quantitative deconvolution of the Fe $2p_{3/2}$ spectra **(Figure 1)** revealed they consist of either one component or two components corresponding to Fe with oxidation state of 2+

or a mixture of 2+ and 3+, respectively. The component with biding energy near 708.8 eV is assigned to the presence of Fe^{2+} and is present in all mediators [4]. The second component with binding energy near 711 eV is assigned to $Fe^{3+}$and is present in $KMFe(CN)_6$ (M: Fe, Cu and Zn). The Mn $2p_{3/2}$ region (Figure 2) was deconvoluted into three components with binding energies near 641.7, 643.4, and 646.4 eV. The first two components correspond to the presence of Mn species with oxidation states of 2+ and 3+/4+ [5], respectively. The third component corresponds to a shake-up structure. The chemistry of Mn appears to be similar in both $KMnFe(CN)_6$ and $K_2MnFe(CN)_6$ with the majority of Mn (~75%) present in the 2+ oxidation state.

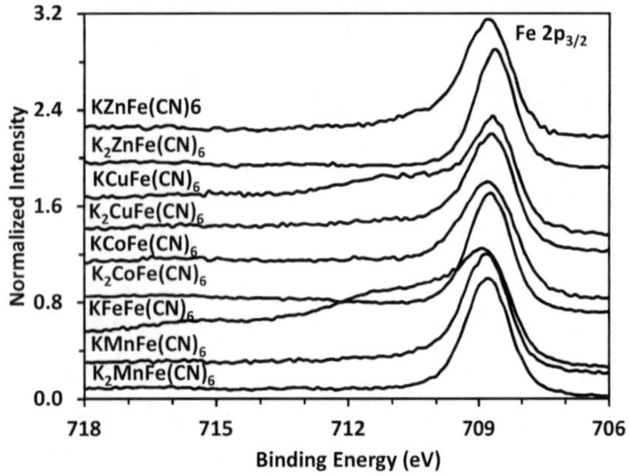

Figure 1. Fe $2p_{3/2}$ XPS region of mediators with different transition metals.

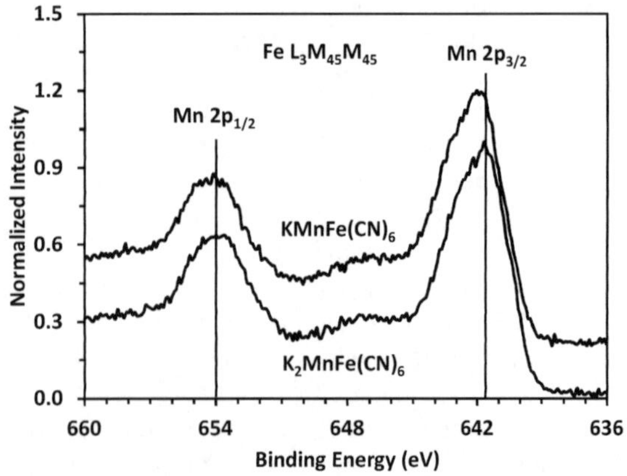

Figure 2. Mn 2p XPS region of $K_2MnFe(CN)_6$ and $KMnFe(CN)_6$ mediators.

XRD: The XRD data for the $K_2MFe(CN)_6$ (M: Mn, Co, Cu) (Figure 3), are closely related to the orthorhombic lattice assigned to $K_2MFe(CN)_6{\bullet}2H_2O$, cubic lattice assigned to $K_2CoFe(CN)_6$ and $K_2CuFe(CN)_6$. In the case of Zn mediator (Figure 3), the XRD data are closely related to the rhombohedral lattice assigned to $KZn_{1.5}Fe(CN)_6$-xH_2O (x = 2.5 and/or 4.5) [6].

XRD data for $KMFe(CN)_6$ (Figure 4) can be tentatively assigned to $Mn_{1.5}Fe(CN)_6{\bullet}2H_2O$ & $KMn(CN)_6$, $KCoFe(CN)_6{\bullet}0.5H_2O$ & $Co_{1.5}Fe(CN)_6{\bullet}6H_2O$ and $KCuFe(CN)_6{\bullet}7H_2O$ & $Cu_{1.5}Fe(CN)_6{\bullet}5H2O$, and $Zn_{1.5}Fe(CN)_6{\bullet}4.7H_2O$ & $ZnFe(CN)_5(NO)$. Some of the XRD assigned phases are consistent with the higher concentration of the metal component (Mn, Co, Cu, Zn) relative to that of Fe as shown in Table 1. To be noted, the XRD pattern of $KFeFe(CN)_6$ is similar to those of $K_2MFe(CN)_6$ (M: Mn, Co, or Cu) in Figure 3 despite that the potassium concentration based on XPS is well below the value based on nominal stoichiometry. Again, it is appropriate to describe the stoichiometry of the mediators as $K_xM_yFe(CN)_6{\bullet}zH_2O$ in agreement with XPS results

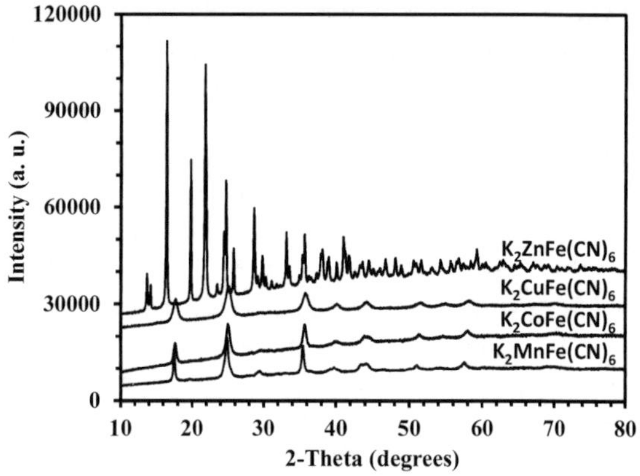

Figure 3. XRD pattern of $K_2MFe(CN)_6$ (M: Mn, Co, Cu, Zn) Mediators.

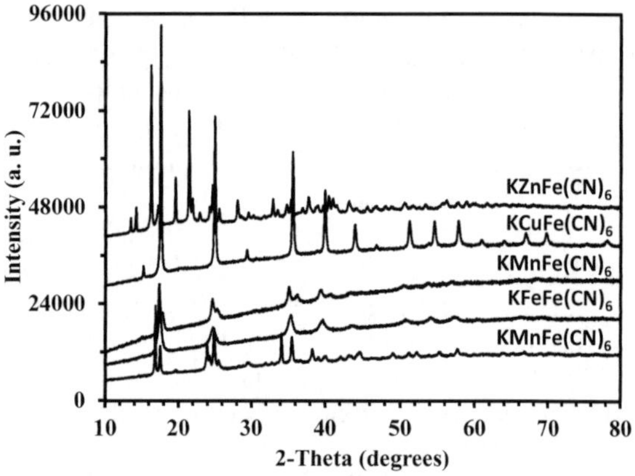

Figure 4. XRD patterns of $KMFe(CN)_6$ (M: Mn, Fe, Co, Cu, Zn) mediators.

The cyclic voltammetry curves of the SCs were generated using a Gamry electrochemical testing system at a scan rate of 10 mV s^{-1}. Clearly the specific currents for the mediator SCs (Figure 5) are much greater than that of the active carbon based SC. Small humps appearing at about 1.6 V and 1.3 V are indicative of redox reactions. GCD curves (Figure 6) clearly indicate that the specific capacitance and energy for the PB mediator SC are much greater than those of the reference SC. The specific energy values at the 0.5 A/g rate are tabulated in Table 2. The maximum value was achieved with the Mn mediator SC. It was anticipated that redox reactions for Mn can lead to multiple valence changes, such as from 2+ to 3+ and 4+.

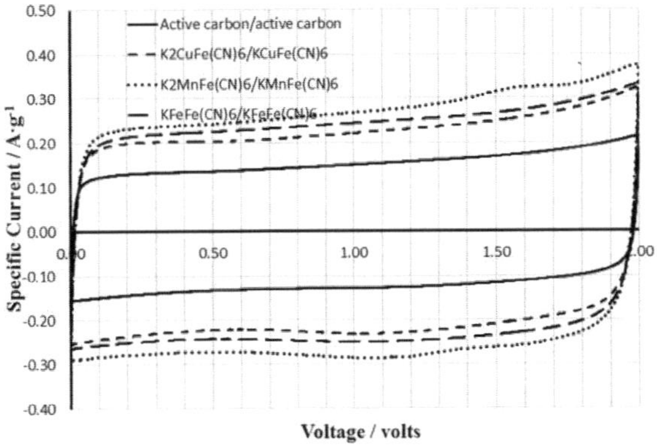

Figure 5. Cyclic voltammetry of activated carbon based SC and mediator containing SCs as indicated in the legend.

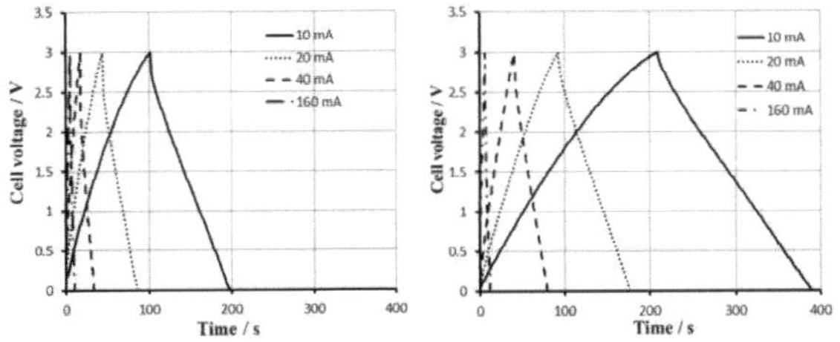

Figure 6. Galvanostatic charge/discharge of activated carbon (left) SC and $KFeFe(CN)_6$ mediator SC (right). The curves from right to left: 10, 20, 40, 80, and 160 mA.

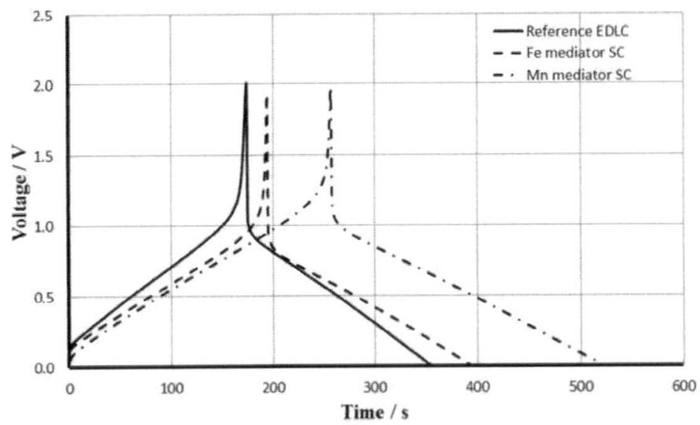

Figure 7. GCD results of three SCs with 0.1 M electrolyte concentration at charge/discharge current of 0.089A g^{-1}.

In order to evaluate the effect of ion release from mediators, GCD curves were evaluated in an electrolyte with low concentrations of ions. One set of results are shown in Figure 7. It is clear that at a low concentration of 0.1 M of tetraethylammonium tetrafluoroborate and total amount of electrolyte of 0.1 mL, the Mn mediator SC achieves the maximum specific capacitance and energy. The specific capacity of the $KFeFe(CN)_6$ mediator SC is similar to that of the activated carbon based SC. The explanation is that the $KFeFe(CN)_6$ mediators contain only 0.5 atomic % of K^+ whereas $K_2MnFe(CN)_6$ contains 11.0 atomic % of K^+. During the charging cycle, the oxidation of the mediators at the positive electrodes releases potassium ions. These released ions compensate loss of ions in the electrolyte due to formation of electrical double layers. This deficiency of ions is clearly shown by the transition from linear dependence of the cell voltage on time to exponential dependence.

Table 2. Specific energy values for mediator and activated carbon based SCs.

SC	Specific Energy $Wh{\cdot}kg^{-1}$	Anode mediator	Cathode mediator
Reference	16	Activated carbon	Active carbon
Ferrocyanide	30	$K_4Fe(CN)_6$	$K_3Fe(CN)_6$
Mn Mediator	44	$K_2MnFe(CN)_6$	$KMnFe(CN)_6$
Fe Mediator	42	$KFeFe(CN)_6$	$KFeFe(CN)_6$
Co Mediator	39	$K_2CoFe(CN)_6$	$KCoFe(CN)_6$
Cu Mediator	31	$K_2CuFe(CN)_6$	$KCuFe(CN)_6$
Zn Mediator	23	$K_2ZnFe(CN)_6$	$KZnFe(CN)_6$

Conclusions

1. Transition metal based Prussian Blue analogues were synthesized. The PB analogues were characterized using XPS and XRD to acquire the elemental compositions, oxidation states and structural information. The stoichiometry of the synthesized material has the genral formula $K_xM_yFe(CN)_6{\bullet}zH_2O$.

2. Supercapacitors were fabricated uisng the mediators. The specific capacitance and energy of the Mn and PB mediator SC is much greater than that of the active carbon based SC and greater than the $K_3Fe(CN)_6/K_4Fe(CN)_6$ mediator SC.

3. Ion release from the mediators into the electrolyte mitigates loss of ions in the electrolyte during the charging cycle.

Reference

1. Y. Yin, J. Zhou, A.N. Mansour, and X. Zhou, "Effect of NaI/I2 mediators on properties of PEO/LiAlO 2 based all-solid-state supercapacitors," J. Power Sources. Vol. 196 , pp. 5997–6002, 2011.
2. A.N. Mansour, J. Zhou, and X. Zhou, "X-ray absorption spectroscopic study of sodium iodide and iodine mediators in a solid-state supercapacitor," J. Power Sources. Vol. 245, pp. 270–276, 2014.
3. S. J. Gerber and E. Erasmus, Electronic Effects of Metal Hexacyanoferrates: An XPS and FTIR study, Mater. Chem., Vol. 203, pp. 73-81, 2018.
4. Y. Zhang, Y. Wen, Y. Liu, D. Li, J. Li, "Functionalization of single-walled carbon nanotubes with Prussian blue," Electrochem. Commun., Vol. 6, pp. 1180-1184, 2004.
5. W.-J. Li, S. L. Chou, J.-Z.Wang, J.-L.Wang, Q.-F. Gu, H.-K. Liu, S.-X. Dou, "Multifunctional conducing polymercoated $Na_{1+x}MnFe(CN)_6$ cathode forsodium-ion batteries withsuperiorperformance via a facileandone-stepchemistryapproach," Nano Energy, Vol. 13, pp. 200-207, 2015.
6. E. Garnier, P. Gravereau, A. Hardy, "Zeolitic iron cyanides: the structure of $Na_2Zn_3[Fe(CN)_6]_2.xH_2O$," Acta Crystallogr. Sect. B. Vol. 38, pp. 1401-1405, 1982.

Electrochemical Performance of Lithium-ion Capacitors Evaluated under High Stress Conditions for Fast Charge Devices

Jonathan Boltersdorf, [1] ***Samuel A. Delp,*** [1,2] ***Jin Yan,*** [3,4] ***Ben Cao,*** [3]
Jim P. Zheng, [4] ***T. Richard Jow,*** [1] ***and Jeffrey A. Read*** [1]
[1] United States Army Research Laboratory, RDRL-SED-C, Adelphi, MD 20783-1138, USA
[2] General Technical Services, Adelphi, MD 20783-1197, USA
[3] General Capacitor LLC & INTL, INC. Tallahassee, FL 32304, USA
[4] Department of Electrical and Computer Engineering, Florida A&M University-Florida State University, Tallahassee, FL 32310-6046, USA
jonathan.a.boltersdorf.civ@mail.mil / 301-394-0049

Abstract: *Lithium-ion capacitors (LICs) were investigated for high power, moderate energy density applications for fast-charge operation in extreme environments with prolonged cycle-life performance. The LICs were assembled as three-layered pouch cells in an asymmetric configuration employing Faradaic pre-lithiated hard carbon anodes and non-Faradaic ion adsorption-desorption activated carbon cathodes. The capacity retention was measured under high stress conditions, while the design factor explored was electrolyte formulation using a set of carbonates and electrolyte additives, with a focus on their stability. The rate performance was measured after the initial LIC cell formation at varied discharge rates to understand the relationship between the electrolyte formulation, the additive content, and the rate capability. The vinylene carbonate (VC) and tris (trimethylsilyl) phosphate (TMSP) additives were found to be essential to the improved electrochemical performance of the LIC cells under all testing conditions.*

Keywords: Lithium-ion capacitors; Pre-lithiation; Hybrid Capacitor; Additives; Activated Carbon; tris (trimethylsilyl) phosphate

Introduction

The lithium-ion capacitor (LIC) is hybrid battery-capacitor that has been proposed as a suitable alternative high-power power source technology with low self-discharge. [1,2] The conventional electrochemical double-layer capacitor (EDLC), also known as a supercapacitor, is composed of high surface area activated carbon (AC) electrodes that store energy in the double-layer formed at the interface of the porous AC electrodes and the electrolyte. The EDLC provides high power density and superior cycle performance using cost-effective and environmentally friendly electrode materials. However, the energy density is relatively low (~0.5 to 15 Wh/kg) compared to that of lithium-ion batteries (~100-265 Wh/kg), which limits its usage in large scale energy devices. [1-6] In contrast, the lithium-ion battery (LIB) is an electrochemical energy storage device that is formed using Li-intercalation materials as the positive electrode (e.g., $LiMn_2O_4$, $LiFePO_4$, etc.), carbonaceous materials as the negative electrode (e.g., graphite, hard carbon, etc.), and a Li-based organic electrolyte. [7-9] The LIB displays relatively high energy density and high working voltage, and a low self-discharge in comparison to EDLC devices, but limited power density and cycle life. [7,10–11] The supercapacitor electrodes of EDLCs undergo ion adsorption/desorption during the charge-discharge process, while Li-ion intercalation/de-intercalation occurs within the bulk of the electrodes in LIBs. [1-6]

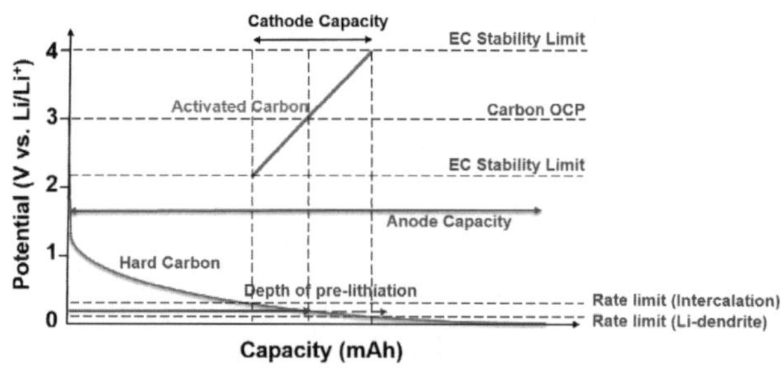

Figure 1. Schematic of LIC electrode capacity design and limits as a function of cell charge potential vs. Li/Li^+.

The LIC can accommodate both the non-faradaic (i.e., ion adsorption/desorption) and the faradaic (i.e., Li-ion insertion/extraction) processes of EDLCs and LIBs at the same time, respectively. [1,2] The advantages of the hybrid LIC device includes higher power density and longer cycle life than a LIB and higher energy density than an EDLC, as well as a higher output voltage and a wide range of operational temperatures, from -30 °C to 70 °C. [5] Factors that affect the LIC performance are the pre-lithiation process of the negative battery electrode, the carbonaceous active electrode materials, safe operational limits of the electrolyte, and the configuration of the electrodes for hybrid cell design. Pre-lithiation of the negative battery electrode (e.g., hard carbon) for LICs is required and improves the working voltage, energy density, and cycling stability. The pre-lithiated battery electrodes exhibit better retention of the irreversible capacity and lower electrode resistance. [2] Additionally, hard carbon (HC) anodes as the battery electrode exhibit high capacity, do not undergo intercalation-induced exfoliation, and have higher rate capabilities compared to graphite. [1-6] Figure 1 shows a schematic of the LIC electrode capacity design and limits as a function of cell charge potential vs. Li/Li^+ for the configuration used in this study.

The Army requires that power sources operate within extreme environments over long mission periods, be light weight/energy dense, and provide rapid charge capability to minimize the burden on the Soldier and meet specific high power density requirements. The objective of this investigation into LICs for Army applications is to optimize power density and high temperature lifetime through consistent cell design, electrolyte and additive development, and rigorous performance testing.

Experimental

The non-aqueous electrolytes were prepared using ethylene carbonate (EC), fluoroethylene carbonate (FEC), ethyl methyl carbonate (EMC), and dimethyl carbonate (DMC) as the solvents, as well as $LiPF_6$ as the salt. The electrolyte formulations utilized in this study were 1.2 M $LiPF_6$ solution in a 3EC:7EMC (3:7 wt%) mixture, 1 M $LiPF_6$ solution in FEC:4DMC (1:4 wt%) mixture, and 1 M $LiPF_6$ solutions in a EC:DMC (1:1 wt%). Additionally, vinylene carbonate (VC) and tris(trimethylsilyl) phosphate (TMSP) were added in 1 wt% to the electrolytes as the surface-electrolyte interphase (SEI) forming additives. The LIC cells were assembled with one HC double-sided negative electrode (anode) and two single-sided AC positive electrodes (cathodes) divided by sheets of microporous membrane separator, as shown in Figure 2. The AC cathodes with the composition 92:8 AC to polytetrafluoroethylene (PTFE) binder were coated on aluminum (Al) foil substrate with an area capacitance of 0.6 F/cm^2. The HC anode with a composition of 96:4 HC to carboxymethyl cellulose (CMC) binder was coated on copper foil substrates with a nickel current collector tab covered in Li-metal foil strips for pre-lithiation of the HC. Pre-lithiation of the HC anode is achieved by short-circuiting the Li-metal and the HC during the formation process, in which the Li-ions are spontaneously inserted into the HC owing to the potential difference between the Li-metal and the HC anode. The pre-lithiation step is essential to compensate for the initial loss of cyclable Li and to improve the working potential of the cell.

All of the pouch cells in this study underwent a standard formation process after electrolyte impregnation, and the final formed cells were degassed and vacuum sealed for testing using a Maccor Series 4000 tester. The rate performance of the LIC cell was measured after the formation procedure by charging the cells from 2.2 V to 3.8 V at a 1C rate (1 h) and discharging at increasing rates (1 h to 6 min) followed by the 1C rate. Critical performance tests on the cells were performed to measure the cycle life and capacity at room temperature (25 °C), high temperature (65 °C), and increasing charge potential (3.8 to 4.4 V) conditions. The float-cycle test procedures were conducted on cells by holding the cells at the charge potential (float) and periodically cycling (2.2-3.8 V) at a 10C rate to monitor the change in capacity over time.

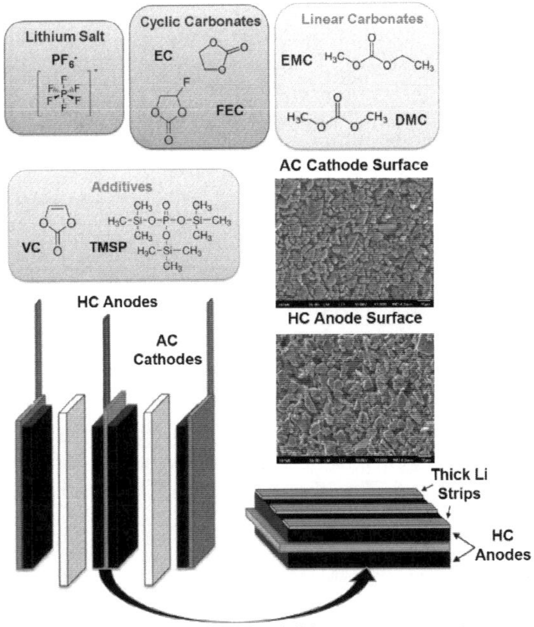

Figure 2. Electrolyte and additive components used in testing 3-layer LIC cells shown in schematic with lithium-metal strips used for lithiation of the hard carbon anode and SEM images of the electrode surfaces (scale bar = 10 μm).

Results and Discussion

The LIC cells and electrolytes were evaluated for their rate capability and stability, with the LICs discharged from 1C up to 10C, as shown in Figures 3. The FEC-based electrolyte exhibited a constant and rapid decrease in the capacity as well as an unstable coulombic efficiency at all discharge rates. Therefore, the FEC-based electrolytes were found to not be suitable electrolytes for use in the LIC cells configured in this study. In contrast, the coulombic efficiencies were >99.97% at a 10C discharge rate for all EC-based electrolytes. The capacities for the LIC cells formed with the EC:DMC electrolyte were consistently the highest for all discharge rates from 1C to 10C as compared to the cells containing the 3EC:7EMC electrolyte. The addition of the VC and TMSP additives increased the capacity of the cells in comparison to both the 3EC:7EMC and EC:DMC electrolytes at higher rates. Overall, the electrolytes with a TMSP additive displayed the highest capacity and coulombic efficiency >99.99% at a 10C discharge rate, followed by the electrolytes with the VC additive. The capacities for the electrolytes containing both the VC and the TMSP additives showed an improvement over the 3EC:7EMC and the EC:DMC base electrolytes at a 10C discharge rate. However, the mixture of the VC and TMSP additives in the electrolytes exhibited lower capacity and inconsistent/unstable coulombic efficiencies in comparison to the electrolytes with either the VC or TMSP additive alone.

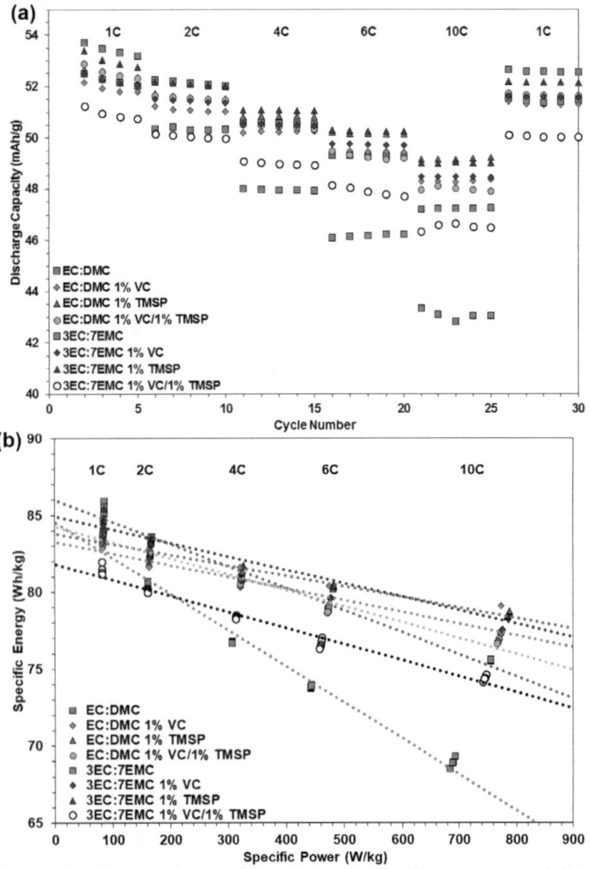

Figure 3. Comparison of the (a) rate performance and (b) specific energy/power density of the three-layer LIC cells at discharge rates ranging from 1C to 10C using EC:DMC and 3EC:7EMC base electrolytes with VC and TMSP additives.

In Figure 3b, the Ragone chart is used for comparison of the energy and power performance of the EC:DMC and 3EC:7EMC based electrolytes with the VC and TMSP additives. The charts are plotted with the specific energy and specific power obtained from the rate performance tests of the three-layer LIC cells at discharge rates ranging from 1C to 10C. Ragone charts are used to describe how much energy is available and how fast that energy can be delivered (power) per unit mass for the three-layer LIC energy storage devices. There is a linear relationship between the specific energy and specific power as a function of discharge rate, as indicated by the dotted linear trend lines fitted to the multiple data points for each electrolyte taken for the 1C to 10C discharge rates on the Ragone chart. These trend lines may aid in predicting the specific energy and power of LICs operated at a given C-rate. As observed in Figure 3a, the TMSP additive shows the best improvement in the base electrolytes.

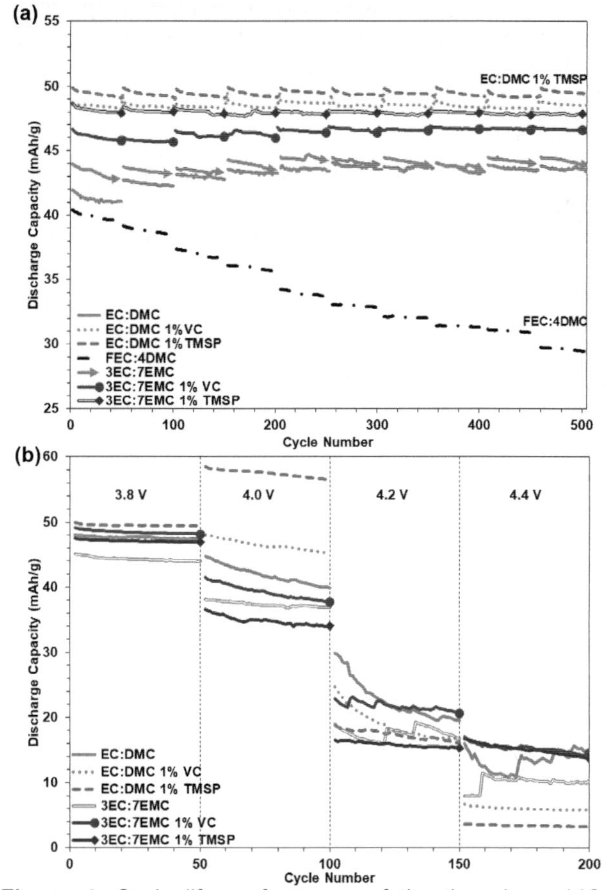

Figure 4. Cycle life performance of the three-layer LIC cells at room temperature shown by (a) alternating float-cycle at 3.8 V and (b) alternating float-cycle at increasing charge voltages at a 10C charge/discharge rate using various electrolytes with additives.

The LIC cells were tested for their cycle-life performance at 25 °C for various electrolytes and additives, as shown in Figure 4a. The cells were held at the charge potential of 3.8 V for prolonged periods of time (120 h) and periodically cycled (2.2-3.8 V) at a 10C charge/discharge rate for 50 cycles. Reproducible and stable higher rate performance is desired for faster charge/discharge of devices in high-demand field conditions. The inclusion of VC and TMSP additives in the EC:DMC and 3EC:7EMC electrolytes resulted in an increase in the specific capacity, energy, and power, as well as a more consistent and stable cycling efficiency on average (~99.992%). The LIC cells tested with the EC:DMC + TMSP electrolyte exhibited the best results compared to all other electrolyte formulations, with an average specific discharge capacity of 49.4 mAh/g, specific energy of 79.1 Wh/kg, and a specific power of 790.9 W/kg with ~99.995% coulombic efficiency after 1200 hours at 3.8 V and 500 cycles. The FEC:4DMC electrolyte is also shown for comparison. The FEC-based electrolyte was highly unstable, experienced capacity fade over time, and showed significant gas production that filled the entire pouch cell. By comparison, there was significantly less gas formation for the EC:DMC and 3EC:7EMC electrolytes and no gas formation with the addition of the VC and/or TMSP additives.

The electrochemical stability window for the LIC cells was tested at increasing charge potentials, as shown in Figure 4b. At 4.0 V, the EC:DMC electrolyte with VC (~46-48 mAh/g) and TMSP (~56-58 mAh/g) additives showed high capacity retention and increased specific energy/power compared to EC:DMC without additives (~40-45 mAh/g). All other electrolytes at 4.0 V experienced capacity loss and retained ~83-99% of the specific energy/power. The additives were not as effective in preventing the decline in cell performance and oxidation of the electrolytes at potentials above 4.0 V. Electrolyte decomposition resulted in gaseous byproducts filling the pouch cells with increasing potential until cell failure at >4.4 V.

Finally, the LIC cells have shown long cycle life (1200+ hours) in the float at 65 °C and cycle at 25 °C test procedure for fast charge/discharge (6 min), as shown in Figure 5. Gradual capacity fade was observed for all electrolytes after prolonged high temperature float at 3.8 V. Electrolytes containing DMC had better capacity retention and were more stable than those containing EMC. Therefore, the 3EC:7EMC based electrolytes were found to not be suitable electrolytes for LICs at high temperatures. Addition of both the VC and TMSP additives moderately improved the cell performance and reduced gassing of the 3EC:7EMC electrolyte. The VC and TMSP additives improved the EC:DMC electrolyte stability, reduced the capacity fade at high temperatures, and reduced the amount of gassing as a result of the surface protecting SEI formed by these additives. The EC:DMC electrolyte with a TMSP additive exhibited the best performance stability at high temperatures, retaining 70.5% of the initial performance after floating at 3.8 V for ~1200 h at 65 °C, and was found to be a promising candidate for future LIC studies.

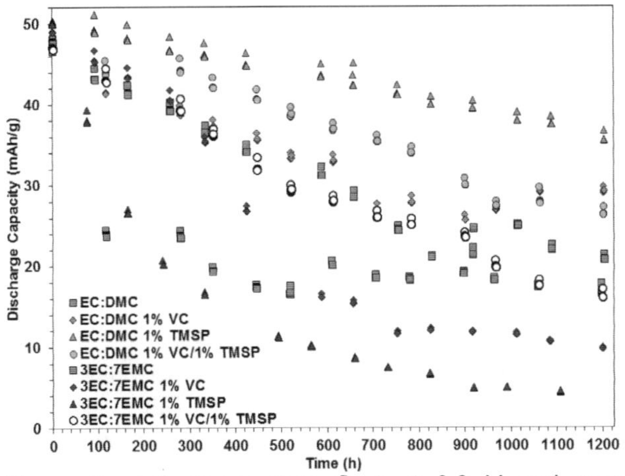

Figure 5. High temperature float at 3.8 V and room temperature cycling of the three-layer LIC cells at a 10C charge/discharge rate using various electrolytes and additives comparing the capacity retention.

Acknowledgements

Dr. Boltersdorf acknowledges support from the U.S. Army Research Laboratory postdoctoral program administered through Oak Ridge Associated Universities (***W911NF-16-2-0059***). Dr. Delp is a General Technical Services (GTS) employee working as a contractor for ARL at Adelphi, MD.

References

1. A. Byeon, M. Boota, M. Beidaghi, K. V. Aken, J.W. Lee, Y. Gogotsi, "Effect of hydrogenation on performance of TiO_2(B) nanowire for lithium ion capacitors", *Electrochem. Comm.* 60 (2015) 199–203.
2. A. Brandt, A. Balducci, U. Rodehorst, S. Menne, M. Winter, A. Bhaskar, "Investigations about the Use and the Degradation Mechanism of $LiNi_{0.5}Mn_{1.5}O_4$ in a High Power LIC", *J. Electrochem. Soc.* 161 (2014)
3. Z. Shi, J. Zhang, J. Wang, J. Shi, C. Wang, Effect of the capacity design of activated carbon cathode on the electrochemical performance of lithium-ion capacitors, *Electrochem. Acta.* 153 (2015) 476–483.
4. P.H. Smith, T.N. Tran, T.L. Jiang, J. Chung, "Lithium-ion capacitors: Electrochemical performance and thermal behavior", *J. Power Sources.* 243 (2013) 982–992.
5. Y. Firouz, N. Omar, J.M. Timmermans, P. Van den Bossche, J. Van Mierlo, "Lithium-ion capacitor - Characterization and development of new electrical model", *Energy.* 83 (2015) 597–613.
6. J. Zhang, X. Liu, J. Wang, J. Shi, Z. Shi, "Different types of pre-lithiated hard carbon as negative electrode material for lithium-ion capacitors", *Electrochem. Acta.* 187 (2016) 134–142.
7. D. Aurbach, "Review of selected electrode-solution interactions which determine the performance of Li and Li ion batteries", *J. Power Sources.* 89 (2000) 206–218.
8. J. Cabana, L. Monconduit, D. Larcher, M.R. Palacín, "Beyond intercalation-based Li-ion batteries: The state of the art and challenges of electrode materials reacting through conversion reactions", *Adv. Mater.* 22 (2010) 170–192.
9. B.L. Ellis, K.T. Lee, L.F. Nazar, "Positive electrode materials for Li-Ion and Li-batteries", *Chem. Mater.* 22 (2010) 691–714.
10. J. Jiang, Y. Li, J. Liu, X. Huang, C. Yuan, X.W. Lou, "Recent advances in metal oxide-based electrode architecture design for electrochemical energy storage", *Adv. Mater.* 24 (2012) 5166–5180.
11. B. Scrosati, J. Hassoun, Y.-K. Sun, "Lithium-ion batteries. A look into the future", *Energy Environ. Sci.* 4 (2011) 3287–3295.

Nanostructured Carbide Materials Enable High Performance Pseudocapacitors in Mg^{2+} Ion Electrolytes

Xining Zang[1], Liwei Lin[1], Mohan Sanghadasa[2]

[1]Mechanical Engineering, University of California Berkeley, CA, 94704, USA

[2]AMRDEC, U.S. Army RDECOM, Redstone Arsenal, AL 35898, USA

Contact email: xining.zang.sjtu@gmail.com ; lwlin@berkeley.edu

Abstract: *Nanostructured materials, including nano-oxides, nanostructured metal particles and etc, bring new structures and new physics. Among them, transition metal carbides (TMC) with many fascinating electronic and electrochemical properties are essential for investigation in nanoscale. Herein, we demonstrate a versatile self-assembly method to synthesize ultrathin nanoscale TMC. Such synthesized two dimensional (2D)-like Mo_2C and W_2C provide high specific capacitance in Mg^{2+} electrolyte (magnesium acetate), resulting in up to 100F/g capacitance by scan rate of 1mV/s which also illustrate the strongest intercalation with 2D-like Mo_2C. Meanwhile, such carbide-Mg^{2+} electrolyte system could achieve a high working voltage range up to 2.4V due to low hydrolysis potential in magnesium-based neutral electrolyte and stability of neutral electrolyte, resulting in a significant energy density of 20Wh/kg.*

Keywords: nanostructured materials; transition metal carbides; electrochemical energy storage; supercapacitors; magnesium ion electrolyte.

Introduction

Metal carbides from group 4, 5 and 6 transition metals are often described as the interstitial compounds, which are refractory with metallic properties[1]. It is well known that some of these metal carbides have attractive energy-related properties[2], including catalytic activity[3], storage capability[4], stability and resistance to poisoning[5, 6], while nanostructures with high surface area are desirable for various efficient clean energy applications or example, transition metal carbides (such as Mo_2C and WC) are among the family of highly-effective energy storage materials. Nanostructured molybdenum carbide and tungsten, with lower dimensions (0D/1D/2D), large surface area, hierarchical porosity and a higher ratio of active sites are desired for efficient catalyst[7, 8]. However, current manufacturing processes of these metal carbide materials, are tedious and complex[9]. In 2015, H. Wu et al demonstrated a metal-organic frameworks-assisted strategy for the synthesis of nanostructured transition metal carbides, called porous MoC_x with octahedral sub-micrometer-sized particles, by confined carburization in the MOF[9]. However, that process is very complex, requiring a high temperature (at 800°C) and removal of Cu nanoparticles by the Fe^{3+} etching process. In 2016, Q. Gong described the fabrication of W_2C nanoparticles for electrocatalytic and photoelectrochemical hydrogen evolution processes[10]. However, the selective synthesis of ultra-small and phase-pure W_2C particles require the template of multi-walled CNTs at 900°C and 320 Pa with low yields.

Meanwhile, recently, 2D transition metal carbides (MXenes), has been synthesized and demonstrated as a new class of material to provide high specific capacity. The fabrication process of MXenes, including temperatures as high as 1600°C to a MAX phase powder followed by an HF etching[11]. In general, the family of transition metal carbide materials is much larger than the MAX phase family, as many carbides with different stoichiometry cannot be derived from MAX phase. The existing of MAX phase depends highly on the kinetic stability, as well as the competing stability of other phases[12]. For example, Mo_3C_2 is one of many Molybdenum carbide phases but there is no reported or known Mo_3AC_2 phase. Meanwhile, although Tungsten carbide is very hard and stiff as widely applied for the protection of machine tools, there is no report on tungsten based MAX[13]. Other methods to make two-dimensional transition metal carbides include chemical vapor on Cu buffered Mo foil which sacrifice the extreme low yield for slow kinetics 2D structure formation[14, 15]. These robust activities seeking a path to employ "nanostructured" transition metal carbide materials towards clean energy applications indicate that advanced manufacturing for the synthesis of porous and 2D-like metal carbides are key emerging technologies for possible various energy applications.

Here in this paper, we present a self-assembly assist large scale manufacturing process to fabricate different kinds of 2D transition metal carbide, shown in **Figure 1**. Polymer with various peptide combination is employed as assembly template. Amino acid functional groups coordinate with transition metal ions. After annealing at relative low temperature, ultrathin carbides are produced.

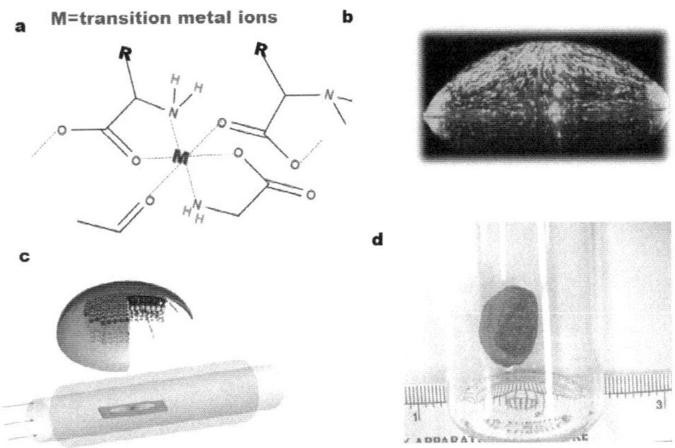

Figure 1. Schematic of the nanostructured TMC synthesis process. **(a)** Rich amino acid group coordinate with transition metal ions. Ions assemble laterally in the gelatin mediated hydrogel. **(b)** Convection in the droplet of Mo-gelatin solution. **(c)** Carbonization process is performed at a relatively low temperature of 600 °C. **(d)** 100μl Mo-gel precursor is exploded to center meter cubic after annealing at 600 °C.

Results and Discussion

Using Mo^{5+} as an example, molybdenum ion dissolved in gelatin (60%) media is calcinated at 600 °C. As shown in **Figure 2a**, large-scale (>20μm in lateral size) ultrathin (~10nm in thickness) Mo_2C is produced. If mixed with Polyvinylpyrrolidone (PVP) and Polyethylene glycol (PEO), molybdenum ions cannot be effectively convert to uniform, large area sheets (**Figure 2b-c**). Carbonized Mo-PVP hydrogel shows Mo_2C character in XRD, while the structure is much thicker and bulkier. Mo-PEO after carbonization shows chunky structure, without any crystalline phase. We also notice in **Figure 1d**, that the volume of Mo-gel expands greatly from 100μl to ~1 cm^3 after calcinated at 600 °C, resulting highly porous sponge like structure with ultrathin walls. Such process could be explained with the high surface tension which is like the pore generation in soapy water with surfactant. The few atom layer thickness at the liquid-air interface also helped the structured assembly of ultrathin carbide sheets. Besides Mo_2C, W_2C and Co_3C can be produced in the similar process, showing both large scale ultrathin nanostructure.

As synthesized nanostructured carbide materials are grinded and mixed with 1wt% percentage of polyacrylonitrile (PAN) dissolved in N-Methyl-2-pyrrolidone (NMP) as binder to make electrodes. 1mg of carbide-PAN is deposited onto carbon paper with a surface area of 1cm^2, which is dried in oven overnight. Such strips of electrodes are tested in a three-electrode system, using Ag/AgCl as reference electrodes and Pt film as contour electrode. **Figure 3a-c** show the electrochemical performance of Mo_2C with a loading of 1mg/cm^2 in different electrolytes. Surprisingly, the Mo_2C electrode shows the highest specific capacitance in magnesium acetate which is up to 118F/g at scan rate of 1mV/s. Capacitance of Mo_2C in other electrolyte of monovalent cations including H^+, Li^+ and Na^+ are similar (**Figure 3a**).The serious decay of capacitance with scan rate indicate a strong diffusive behavior of Mg^{2+}, which is analysis in **Figure 3b** and **Table 1**.

The capacitive and diffusive behaviors of the system can be analyzed following the equation[16]:

$$i(v) = k_1 v + k_2 v^{1/2} \quad (1)$$

in which k_1 and k_2 are the capacitive and diffusion constant and the integration is plot in **Figure 3b** following:

$$Q = Q^* + \alpha v^{-1/2} \quad (2)$$

The large $k_2/(k_1+k_2)$ ratio implies a capacitance mechanism dominated by diffusion.

Results in **Table 1** indicate a strong intercalation of Mg^{2+} with the carbide electrodes made of Mo_2C. $k_2/(K_1+k_2)$ is nearly 100% Li^+ shows stronger intercalation with Mo_2C, resulting higher capacitance than H^+ and Na^+. Besides the strong intercalation induced high capacity, $Mg(CH_3COO)_2$ induce the largest electrochemical window comparing to the other monovalent cation electrolytes. With up to 2.4V working voltage window, the energy density of Mo_2C-Mg is ~20Wh/kg.

Figure 2. Morphology of calcination product achieved from different hydrogel media with Mo^{5+} ions. **(a)** SEM image of ultrathin Mo_2C carbonized from Mo-gelatin gel. **(b)** SEM image of thick layer of Mo_2C carbonized from Mo-PVP gel. **(c)** SEM image of bulky amorphous Mo_2C-Carbon carbonized from Mo-PEO gel.

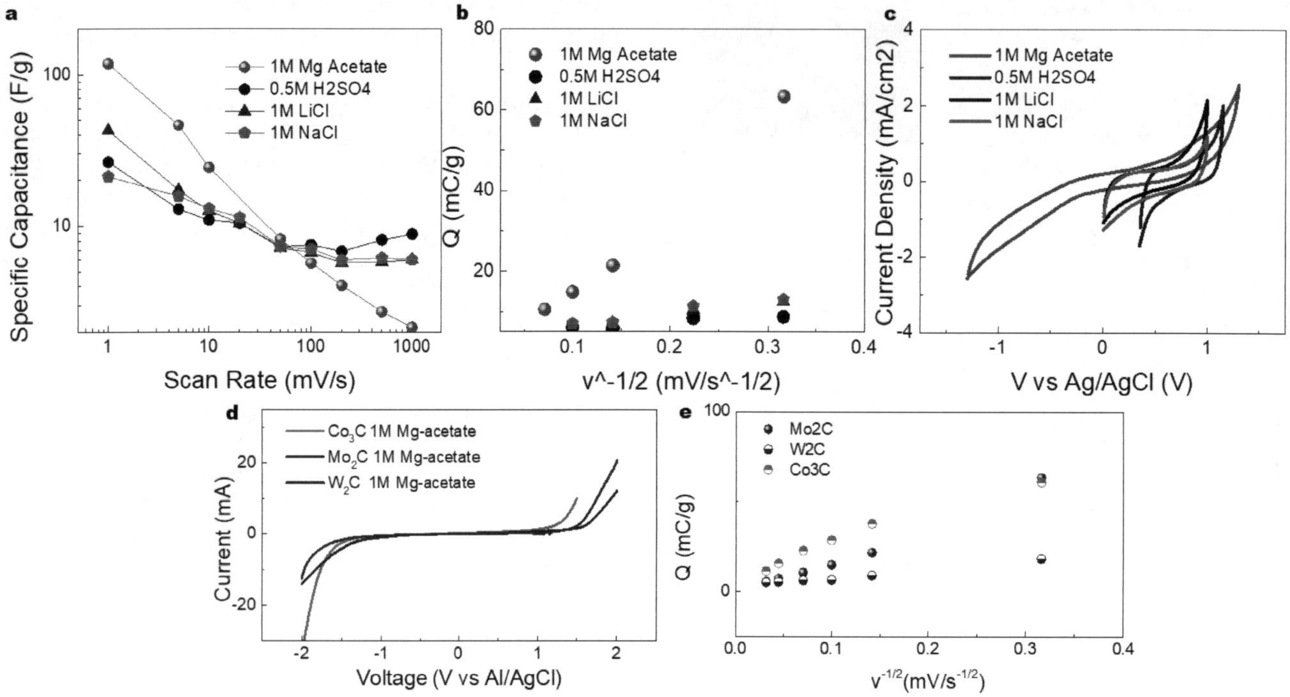

Figure 3. Electrochemical performances of nanostructured carbide in different electrolyte **(a)** Specific of Mo_2C electrode change with scan rate in different electrolyte. **(b)** Capacity of Mo_2C change with the reverse of square root of scan rate ($v^{-1/2}$) in different electrolyte. **(c)** Cyclic voltammetry (CV) curve of Mo_2C electrode in different electrolyte at a scan rate of 10mV/s. **(d)** Linear sweep voltammetry of different carbides in 1M magnesium acetate. **(e)** Capacity of different carbides change with the reverse of square root of scan rate ($v^{-1/2}$) in magnesium acetate.

Table 1. Capacitance of nanostructured molybdenum carbide in different electrolyte with 1M of cation.

Materials	Specific capacitance (F/g) scan rate 1mV/s	K_1 (capacitive)	K_2 (diffusive)
1M $Mg(CH_3COO)_2$	118.4	0.5	145.7
0.5M H_2SO_4	26.6	4.6	13.2
1M LiCl	42.78	3.3	30.9
1M NaCl	21.3	4.5	26.2

W_2C and Co_3C also shows high capacitance, high conductivity and high over 2V working range in magnesium acetate electrolyte, as shown in **Figure 4-6** and **Table 2**. Cobalt carbide shows better capacity at higher discharge rate, while down to 1mV/s Mo_2C shows slightly better capacitance. Co_3C shows extremely low series resistance (~5ohm) in $Mg(CH_3COO)_2$, while Mo_2C show ~17ohm and W_2C shows much higher series resistance in Mg^{2+} electrolyte. All three kinds of carbide show >90% diffusive capacitance in $Mg(CH_3COO)_2$, indicating strong intercalation with Mg^{2+}.

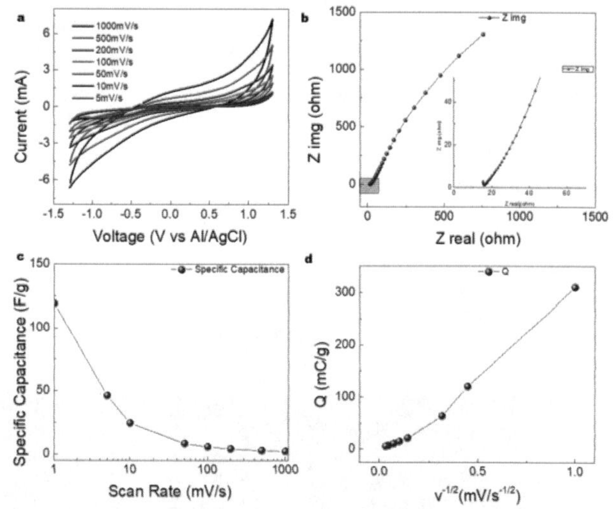

Figure 4. Electrochemical performances of nanostructured Mo_2C in 1M magnesium acetate. **(a)** Cyclic voltammetry (CV) curve of Mo_2C electrode tested at different scan rates from 5mV/s to 1000mV/s. **(b)** EIS spectrum of Nyquist plot showing impedance of the electrode. **(c)** Capacitance vs scan rate. **(d)** Capacity vs square root of scan rate reverse.

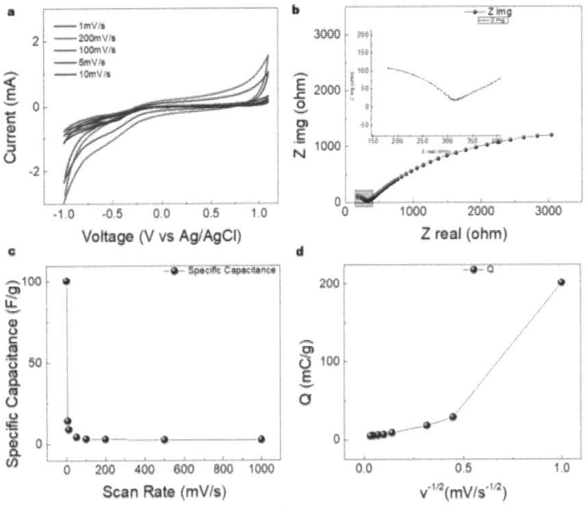

Figure 5. Electrochemical performances of nanostructured W_2C in Mg Acetate. **(a)** CV curve of W_2C electrode tested from 1mV/s to 200mV/s. **(b)** EIS spectrum of Nyquist plot of impedance. **(c)** Capacitance vs scan rate. **(d)** Capacity vs square root of scan rate reverse.

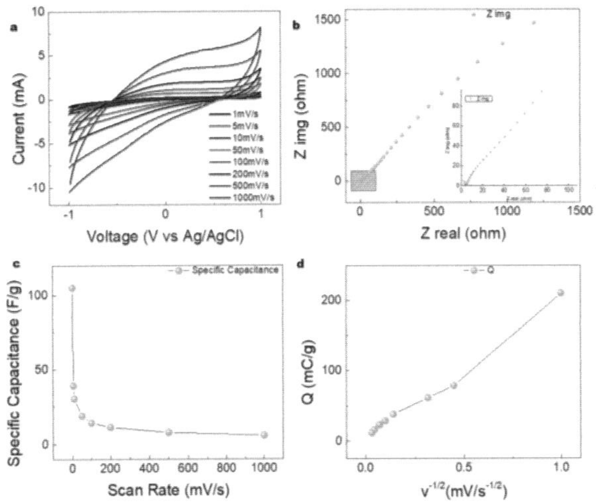

Figure 6. Electrochemical performances of nanostructured Co_3C in Mg Acetate. **(a)** CV curve of Co_3C electrode tested from 1mV/s to 1000mV/s. **(b)** EIS spectrum of Nyquist plot. **(c)** Capacitance vs scan rate. **(d)** Capacity vs square root of scan rate reverse.

Table 2. Capacitance of different nanostructured carbide in 1M Magnesium *acetate* electrolyte

Materials	Voltage window (V)	Capacitance (F/g)	$K_{2\%}$ (diffusive)
Mo_2C	2.4	118	99.6
W_2C	2.6	100	90.5
Co_3C	2.5	105	98.2

Conclusion

In this paper, we introduced a method to construct nanostructured ultrathin transition metal carbides. As synthesized nanostructured carbides show high conductivity and high capacitance in different electrolytes including 0.5M H_2SO_4, 1M LiCl, 1M NaCl, and 1M $Mg(CH_3COO)_2$. Surprisingly the nanostructured carbides show strong intercalation with Mg^{2+}, which could be promising for the design and construction of magnesium battery.

References

1. S. T. Oyama, in *The chemistry of transition metal carbides and nitrides*, Springer, 1996, 1.
2. B. Anasori, et al., 2D metal carbides and nitrides (MXenes) for energy storage, *Nat Rev Mater,* **2017**, *2*.
3. D. V. Esposito, et al., A New Class of Electrocatalysts for Hydrogen Production from Water Electrolysis: Metal Monolayers Supported on Low-Cost Transition Metal Carbides, *Journal of the American Chemical Society,* **2012**, *134*, 3025.
4. J. Halim, et al., Synthesis and Characterization of 2D Molybdenum Carbide (MXene), *Advanced Functional Materials,* **2016**, *26*, 3118.
5. F. X. Ma, et al., Hierarchical beta-Mo2C Nanotubes Organized by Ultrathin Nanosheets as a Highly Efficient Electrocatalyst for Hydrogen Production, *Angew Chem Int Edit,* **2015**, *54*, 15395.
6. C. Wan, et al., Multiple Phases of Molybdenum Carbide as Electrocatalysts for the Hydrogen Evolution Reaction, *Angew Chem Int Edit,* **2014**, *53*, 6407.
7. H. B. Zhang, et al., Active Sites Implanted Carbon Cages in Core Shell Architecture: Highly Active and Durable Electrocatalyst for Hydrogen Evolution Reaction, *Acs Nano,* **2016**, *10*, 684.
8. X. X. Zou, Y. Zhang, Noble metal-free hydrogen evolution catalysts for water splitting, *Chemical Society Reviews,* **2015**, *44*, 5148.
9. H. B. Wu, et al., Porous molybdenum carbide nano-octahedrons synthesized via confined carburization in metal-organic frameworks for efficient hydrogen production, *Nat Commun,* **2015**, *6*.
10. Q. F. Gong, et al., Ultrasmall and phase-pure W2C nanoparticles for efficient electrocatalytic and photoelectrochemical hydrogen evolution, *Nat Commun,* **2016**, *7*.
11. M. R. Lukatskaya, et al., Cation Intercalation and High Volumetric Capacitance of Two-Dimensional Titanium Carbide, *Science,* **2013**, *341*, 1502.
12. Z. M. Sun, Progress in research and development on MAX phases: a family of layered ternary compounds, *Int Mater Rev,* **2011**, *56*, 143.
13. P. Eklund, et al., The Mn+1AXn phases: Materials science and thin-film processing, *Thin Solid Films,* **2010**, *518*, 1851.
14. C. Xu, et al., Large-area high-quality 2D ultrathin Mo2C superconducting crystals, *Nat Mater,* **2015**, *14*, 1135.
15. Y. Gogotsi, Chemical vapour deposition: Transition metal carbides go 2D, *Nat Mater,* **2015**, *14*, 1079.
16. G. A. Muller, et al., High Performance Pseudocapacitor Based on 2D Layered Metal Chalcogenide Nanocrystals, *Nano Letters,* **2015**, *15*, 1911.

Sulfur-Carbon Composites and Solid State Electrolytes in Lithium Sulfur Batteries

Frank Zalar[1], Priyanka Bhattacharya[2], Jitendra Kumar[2], and Brian Henslee[1]

[1]Cornerstone Research Group, Miamisburg, OH, USA

[2]University of Dayton, Dayton, OH, USA

Abstract: *Advanced lithium battery chemistries beyond lithium-ion have demonstrated high energy density (>300 Wh/kg) but need further work to improve and demonstrate cycle life, shelf life, rate capability, and safety matching or exceeding that of lithium-ion batteries. A lithium sulfur battery can theoretically reach energy densities of 2600 Wh/kg and has high potential to meet energy density needs for portable power including electric vehicles. Nevertheless, the Li-S system has not yet been implemented because of multiple obstacles: poor electrical conductivity of elemental sulfur, lack of a system that reduces the capacity robbing polysulfide shuttle (PS) effect, a suitable electrolyte that can suppress dendrite formation, and thicker cathode layers necessary to realize the energy density of a lithium sulfur couple.*

Past research to improve sulfur cathode conductivity and eliminate the PS effect has included infusing sulfur within electrically conductive carbon micro- and nano-scale particles. This approach addresses both the PS shuttle and sulfur's poor electrical conductivity; however it presents a barrier for lithium ions, which slows reaction, reduces power, and limits cathode thickness. Effective sulfur encapsulation requires both electronic and ionic conduction to build thicker cathode structures that retain battery power, capacity, and cycle life.

Typically liquid electrolytes facilitate high sulfur loadings and cathode capacity in a lithium sulfur battery however they also encourage the polysulfide shuttle through the porous polymer separator and don't prevent dendrites. Excessive amounts of liquid electrolyte also reduce the practical energy density of a lithium sulfur cell. Solid-state electrolytes and additives have the potential to play at least three significant roles in a lithium sulfur battery: (1) provide a barrier to stop PS shuttle effect, (2) prevent lithium dendrite formation, and (3) reduction of liquid electrolyte.

This presentation will discuss the development of a lithium sulfur battery based on combining a solid state electrolyte, entrapped sulfur cathode, and a lithium metal anode necessary to meet needs for high energy density, rechargeable energy storage. New processing methods that improve performance of sulfur carbon composites for cathodes will be discussed. The feasibility of low cost practical carbon materials for sulfur carbon composite cathodes will also be discussed in relation to the new processing methods. Methods and results of using solid state electrolytes in lithium sulfur cell design will also be discussed related to their impact on liquid electrolyte reduction and cathode capacity. Finally optimization targets for a metallic lithium anode, solid electrolyte, and sulfur cathode materials will be discussed in relation to goals for cell specific energy.

Advanced Lithium Sulfur Technologies for High Rates and Long Life

Pu Zhang, Michael Wixom, Hong Wang, Felix Nunez

Navitas Systems
4880 Venture Drive, Ann Arbor, MI 48108
pzhang@navitassys.com

Abstract: Low Cost, High Energy Dense lithium, and Safe batteries are the ultimate battery solutions for many military applications. Lithium Sulfur (Li-S) has been an attractive solution due to all the mentioned qualities, with a theoretical energy density of 2600 Wh/kg and capacity of over 1600 mAh/g it is very desirable for such applications as vehicle starting, Silent Watch, portable communications power units, Unmanned Systems, and other battlefield applications. Low cost and high energy Li-S material has been in development by Navitas with significant improvements made to date. Navitas has developed Cathode and Separator technologies and processing methods that are showing superior performance over existing materials for Li-S applications. Navitas is currently working on the development and scaling this technology to production levels and all the electrodes are prepared using Navitas processes and are currently built in pilot scale with plans for scaling to production levels numbers. Navitas is working on improving the cycle life to Lithium Ion levels, which has been demonstrated in laboratory cells. This technology will be applied in portable power systems, such as the Conformal Wearable Batteries (CWB) and will provide energy density to support UAV applications.

Energy Density Limitation of Lithium-Sulfur Battery

Jim P. Zheng[(a)*], Chao Shen[(a)], Jianxin Xie[(b)], Mei Zhang[(b)], Petru Andrei[(a)], Mary A. Hendrickson[(c)], and Edward J. Plichta[(c)]

[(a)]Department of Electrical and Computer Engineering and [(b)]Department of Industrial and Manufacturing Engineering, Florida A&M University and Florida State University, Tallahassee, FL 32310, USA; [(c)]Army Power Division, Aberdeen Proving Ground, MD 21005, USA

[*]Tel: (850) 410-6464, Fax: (850) 410-6479, Email: zheng@eng.fsu.edu

Abstract: *Li-S batteries with a theoretical specific capacity of 1,672 mAh g^{-1}, are among the most promising candidates for the next generation rechargeable batteries due to their high energy density, low raw material cost and environmental friendlines. Despite this great potential, the complicated electrochemical process introduces many challenges for Li-S batteries, including low conductivity of both elemental sulfur and end discharge product Li_2S, large volume expansion of 80% upon discharge, and unfavorable redox shuttle effect due to soluble nature of intermediate LiPS.*

Keywords: Li-S battery, energy density, lithium polysulfide, solubility

Introduction

The electrolyte plays a crucial role in the electrochemical performance of Li-S batteries. Sufficient ionic conductivity, high chemical and electrochemical stability, low volatility and toxicity are required for Li-S batteries electrolytes [1]. High LiPS solubility is also generally favored since dissolved LiPS has easy access to carbon support, resulting in better utilization of active materials and faster reaction kinetics. In fact, the most widely used ether based electrolytes for Li-S cells are polar-aprotic solvents which yield high solubility for LiPS molecules. However, the soluble LiPS can also cause a severe redox shuttle effect and therefore an effective passivation layer must be present on Li anode. Currently, $LiNO_3$ is the most common electrolyte additive to help passivate Li anode surface [2].

Despite recent improvement in rechargeable Li-S batteries, to the operation of Li-S batteries under lean electrolyte conditions remains a grand challenge because the practical energy density of Li-S batteries strongly depends on the electrolyte/sulfur ratio (E/S expressed in mL g^{-1}). In the literatures, high E/S ratios are commonly used and the large excess of the electrolyte dominates in cell weight. However, in practical applications, relatively low E/S ratio must be achieved in order to increase the energy density of these batteries [3-5]. Unfortunately, E/S ratio sets an upper bound on LiPS dissolution, and the solubility of LiPS species reported in the widely used 1,2-dimethoxyethane (DME): 1,3-dioxolane (DOL) binary electrolyte ([S]=~ 6 M) [6] corresponds to an E/S ratio of 5.2 mL g^{-1}. Therefore, in order to enable full dissolution of LiPS, a minimum E/S ratio of 5.2 mL g^{-1} is required. As a result, under low E/S conditions the low LiPS solubility causes severe performance degradation and electrolyte consumption from side reactions may even result in cell dry-out and failure [7]. On the anode side, solid electrolyte interface (SEI) formed under high LiPS concentration conditions was found out to lead to gradual etching of Li metal [8]. Thus, achieving reversible electrochemistry under low E/S conditions is necessary for commercializing sulfur battery chemistries and increasing the LiPS solubility would be of great significance for a lean electrolyte operation.

Experimental

In this work, a freestanding, three-dimensional macroporous multi-walled carbon nanotube (MWCNT) foam was used as carbon host for synthesizing three types of cathodes, which were then tested under designed scenarios to demonstrate the effects of LiPS solubility on cell capacity. The combined results underlined importance of LiPS solubility on fully exploiting high capacity of Li-S cells. Finally, the specific energy of an ideal Li-S cell was reevaluated taking into account of LiPS solubility limit.

Three types of cathodes, i.e., carbon-only cathodes (denoted as C-only cathodes), sulfur cathodes with solid state LiPS loading (denoted as C/LiPS cathodes), and sulfur cathodes with sulfur loading (denoted as C/S cathodes), were employed in test. The selected LiPS species Li_2S_8 were prepared by mixing stoichiometric amounts of sulfur powder (Sigma-Aldrich) and Li_2S powder in DME solution. The precursor solution was heated at 45 °C and stirred vigorously for 48 hours to produce the dissolved solution. In an argon-filled glovebox, C/LiPS cathodes were obtained by soaking CNT foams in LiPS solution with controlled concentration for a controlled time period and finally dried overnight to evaporate solvent. The #1, #2 and #3 C/LiPS cathodes have LiPS loading of ~4 mg, 2 mg and 1 mg, respectively.

C/S cathodes were made by infiltrating sulfur into CNT foams via the melting diffusion method. Sulfur powder was placed onto punched CNT foam electrode surface and heated at 158 °C on a hot plate until designed sulfur loading was met. The electrode was rotated regularly during sulfur infiltration. The #1, #2 and #3 C/S cathodes have sulfur loading of ~4 mg, 2 mg and 1 mg, respectively.

The regular electrolyte used was composed of 1 M bis(trifluoromethane)sulfonimide Li salt (LiTFSI) and 0.1 M $LiNO_3$ in DME: DOL (1:1 v:v). The high Li salt electrolyte was composed of 5 M LiTFSI in DME: DOL (1:1 v:v). The Li_2S_8 catholyte was prepared in the described method above except that the blank electrolyte used was 0.5 M LiTFSI and 0.1 M $LiNO_3$ in DME: DOL (1:1 v:v). The as-prepared cathode was assembled with a glass fiber separator (0.26 mm) and a Li foil anode (0.25 mm) subsequently into a CR2032-type coin cell. 60 μL of desired electrolyte was used in all cells. The assembled Li-S cells were discharged in galvanostatic mode under current density of 0.4 mA cm^{-2}. The linear sweep voltammetry (LSV) measurement was conducted by Gamry Instruments-Reference 3000 at a scan rate of 0.1 mV s^{-1}.

To synthesize CNT foams, PMMA microspheres were used as a template and PAN as a precursor to create cross-links among CNTs. SEM images in Fig.1 illustrate morphology of CNT foam at different magnifications. As seen in Fig.1, the cellular microstructure of CNT foams consisted of major spherical void, which were closely packed and interconnected with each other through junctions of MWCNT walls.

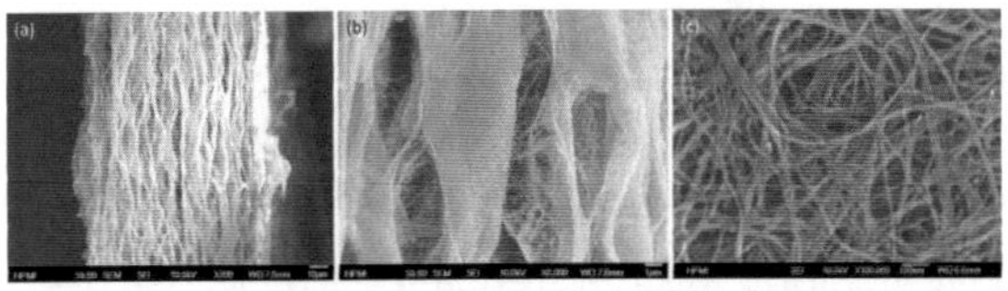

Fig. 1. SEM images of CNT foams at different magnifications.

Results and Discussion

Fig.2 plots the discharge profiles and LSV curves of Li-S cells with regular electrolyte. Both discharge profiles clearly presents two discharge plateaus, which correspond to the two cathodic peaks in their LSV curves. The specific capacity of the cell with C/S cathode was larger than that with C/LiPS cathode, the difference being due to the different starting points of reduction reaction.

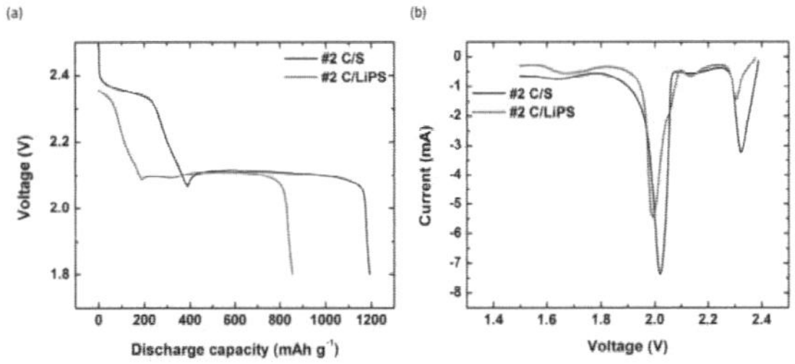

Fig. 2. (a) Voltage profiles of Li-S cells with regular electrolyte; (b) LSV curves of Li-S cells with regular electrolyte

When regular electrolyte is used, it becomes difficult to observe the over-saturation condition since either electrolyte amount is often in excess in cell assembly, or the reactions become too sluggish to fully utilize active material under low E/S conditions. One approach to create over-saturation condition is to decrease LiPS solubility in electrolyte deliberately by modifying electrolyte components. It was reported that when a high Li salt electrolyte was used, the solubility of LiPS would be reduced significantly due to common ion effect [9]. As a result, LiPS species would become mostly insoluble in electrolyte and the electrochemical reactions of Li ion intercalation would occur in solid phase. Fig. 3 (a) shows the cell performances with electrolyte containing 5 M LiTFSI. The voltage profiles still exhibit a two-stage shape, but discharge voltages shift to lower average values compared to those with regular electrolyte, which was also consistently observed by other groups in similar conditions [9,10]. The much reduced peak current intensity in Fig. 3 (b) suggests that the reaction rate was lower in high Li salt electrolyte compared to that in regular electrolyte.

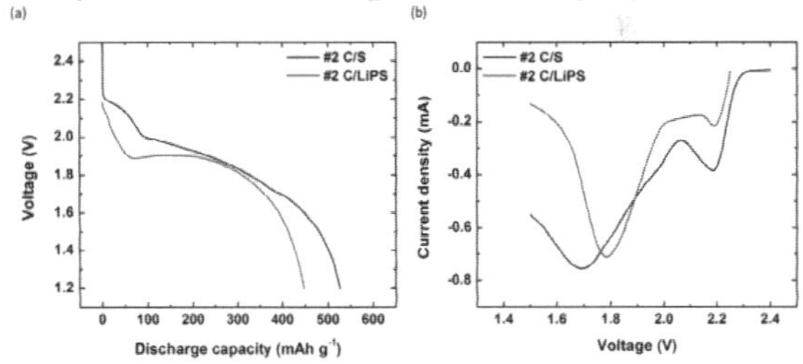

Fig. 3. (a) Voltage profiles of Li-S cells with high Li salt electrolyte; (b) LSV curves of Li-S cells with high Li salt electrolyte

In order to create an over-saturation condition with access to both liquid phase and solid phase reaction pathway needs to be created in the electrolyte. This can be realized by using a combination of a high concentration LiPS catholyte and a sulfur-containing cathode. Another set of tests was then conducted using C/S cathodes coupled with high concentration LiPS catholyte ([S] = 5 M). The extremely high concentrations of LiPS and co-salts make the solution almost saturated, thus prohibiting further dissolution of LiPS and enforcing the appearance of LiPS insoluble pathway. As seen in Fig. 5 (a), the upper plateau capacities in voltage profiles show a monotonous increasing trend with increasing cathode sulfur loading. The upper plateau can be further divided into two parts as seen in the lower-left inset. First, the solid lines in the relatively flat region at the beginning of discharge are attributed to the reduction of sulfur to Li_2S_8. It is found that the increased capacities are due to this region and the higher cathode sulfur loadings yield to larger capacity with a relatively constant sulfur conversion rate of ~ 50%. Second, the dashed oblique lines are associated with the conversion from high-order LiPS to low-order LiPS. One could see that the slopes and associated capacities remain almost unchanged in this region. The above results imply that reduction of sulfur to Li_2S_8 is not inhibited by the high concentration of Li_2S_8 catholyte. However, the generated Li_2S_8 does not further convert to low-order LiPS, indicating the full utilization of active material is prohibited owing to LiPS solubility limit. One can also observe that the overall capacities of cell with C/S cathodes decreased compared to that with a carbon-only cathode, which results from the decrease of lower plateau capacity.

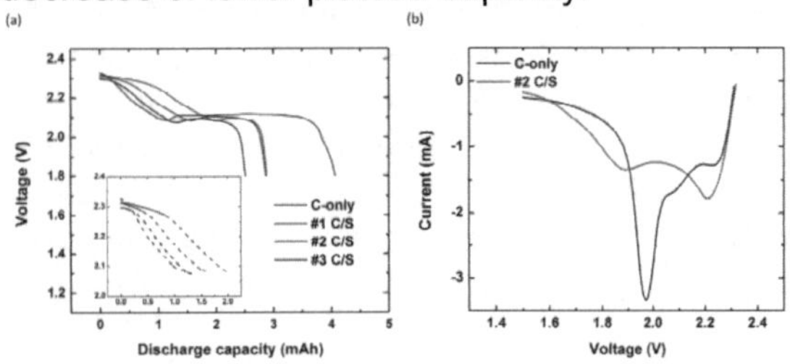

Fig. 5. (a) Voltage profiles of Li-S cells with C/S cathodes and Li_2S_8 catholyte ([S]=5 M); (b) LSV curves of Li-S cells with C/S cathodes and Li_2S_8 catholyte ([S]=5 M)

C/LiPS cathodes were later tested using Li_2S_8 catholyte with different concentrations ([S]=1 M and [S]=5 M). This scenario provides better way of understanding the discharge process since all cell capacities originate from reduction of an identical LiPS species. Fig. 6 presents the discharge profiles of Li-S cell with medium and high concentration LiPS catholyte ([S] =1 M). When catholyte concentration is [S]= 1M, the upper plateau capacity shows a monotonous increasing trend with increasing cathode LiPS loading, indicating the participation of extra LiPS from cathode.

It is because the dissolved LiPS in electrolyte was well below saturation level and therefore solid LiPS in cathode would still dissolve first and undergo the liquid phase reaction. Consequently, cathode with higher LiPS loading would deliver higher upper plateau as well as lower plateau capacity. However, the increase of the capacity of the upper plateau was not observed when a higher concentration catholyte was used. The overall capacities especially the upper plateau capacities remained almost unchanged regardless of cathode LiPS loading when catholyte concentration was increased to [S]=5 M. The distinct behaviors under different LiPS concentrations clearly demonstrate the effects of LiPS solubility on LiPS dissolution.

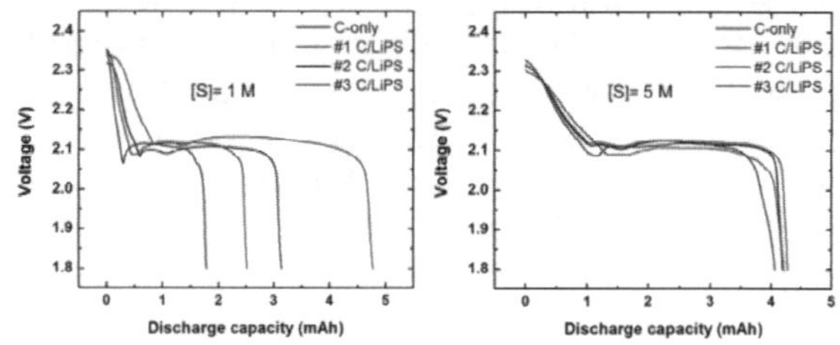

Fig. 6. Voltage profiles of Li-S cells with C/LiPS cathodes and Li_2S_8 catholyte ([S]=1 M and[S]=5 M)

When LiPS is generated as a result of sulfur reduction, the battery is unlikely to deliver its entire theoretical capacity. The LiPS must be readily reduced electrochemically, otherwise it eventually becomes “dead” sulfur source. The combined results above suggest that the LiPS-soluble reaction pathway dominates in the Li-S cell with a liquid electrolyte environment. When the LiPS solubility limit is reached, although sulfur can be reduced to solid state LiPS, the subsequent reduction reactions can occur exclusively in liquid phase and the maximum number of LiPS species available for reaction is restricted by LiPS solubility, which becomes an intrinsic limitation for Li-S cell capacity.

With above findings the theoretical energy density of Li-S cells needs to be reevaluated under low E/S conditions. Fig. 7 presents a series of specific energy calculation of an ideal Li-S cell. Here only the weight of active electrode material, i.e., sulfur and Li, as well as electrolyte weight is included in calculation.

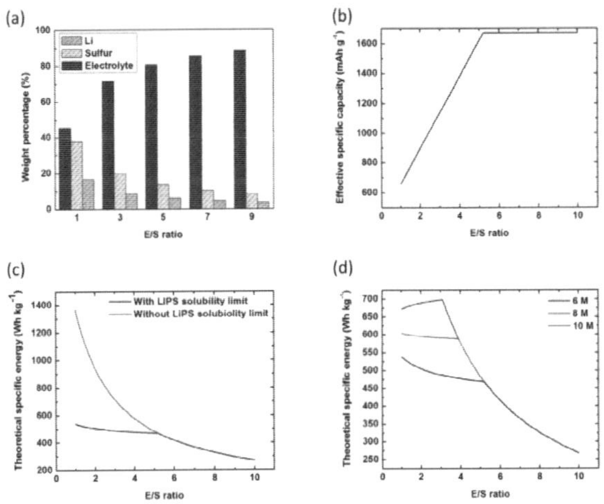

Fig. 7. Specific energy calculation of an ideal Li-S cell. (a) Weight percentage of cell components in an ideal Li-S cell under different E/S ratios. (b) Effective specific capacity of an ideal Li-S cell under different E/S ratios. (c) Specific energy of an ideal Li-S cell under different E/S ratios. (d) Specific energy of an ideal Li-S cell with different LiPS solubility.

Conclusion

The theoretical energy density of Li-S batteries strongly depends on the E/S ratio of the cell. When the minimal E/S ratio is determined by LiPS solubility in the current organic electrolyte, the theoretical energy density of Li-S batteries will become less attractive. Here some designed scenarios were evaluated for the effect of LiPS solubility on cell capacity. It revealed that the when LiPS solubility is reached, although sulfur can be reduced to solid state LiPS, it will not further contribute to cell capacity. Since lowering E/S ratio is essential to boost the energy density of Li-S batteries and LiPS solubility will be an intrinsic limit under low E/S condition, the importance of LiPS solubility cannot be overlooked. There is a pressing need for research on electrolyte and electrode chemistry to improve the reaction kinetics under LiPS-saturated or LiPS-insoluble condition.

Acknowledgments

This work was supported by US Army Power Division under contract No. GTS-S-15-014 and by the National Science Foundation under Grant No. 1609860.

References

[1]. S. Zhang, K. Ueno, K. Dokko, M. Watanabe, Adv. Energy Mater. 5 (2015) 1–28. doi:10.1002/aenm.201500117.

[2]. W. Li, H. Yao, K. Yan, G. Zheng, Z. Liang, Y.-M. Chiang, et al., Nat. Commun. 6 (2015) 7436. doi:10.1038/ncomms8436.

[3]. M. Hagen, P. Fanz, J. Tübke, J. Power Sources. 264 (2014) 30–34. doi:10.1016/j.jpowsour.2014.04.018.

[4]. B.D. McCloskey, J. Phys. Chem. Lett. 6 (2015) 4581–4588. doi:10.1021/acs.jpclett.5b01814.

[5]. D. Eroglu, K.R. Zavadil, K.G. Gallagher, J. Electrochem. Soc. 162 (2015) 982–990. doi:10.1149/2.0611506jes.

[6]. J.W. Dibden, J.W. Smith, N. Zhou, N. Garcia-Araez, J.R. Owen, Chem. Commun. 52 (2016) 12885–12888. doi:10.1039/C6CC05881G.

[7]. J. Brückner, S. Thieme, H.T. Grossmann, S. Dörfler, H. Althues, S. Kaskel, J. Power Sources. 268 (2014) 82–87. doi:10.1016/j.jpowsour.2014.05.143 Short communication.

[8]. C. Yan, X.B. Cheng, C.Z. Zhao, J.Q. Huang, S.T. Yang, Q. Zhang, J. Power Sources. 327 (2016) 212–220. doi:10.1016/j.jpowsour.2016.07.056.

[9]. E.S. Shin, K. Kim, S.H. Oh, W. Il Cho, Chem. Commun. (Camb). 49 (2013) 2004–6. doi:10.1039/c2cc36986a.

High Charge and Discharge Power Li-ion Prismatic Cells

Frank J. Puglia, Svetlana Trebukhova, Dr. Boris Ravdel, Stuart Santee, Christine Cook

EaglePicher Technologies-Yardney Technology Center
2000 South County Trail
East Greenwich RI
Phone: (401) 471-6580
Fax: (401) 471-6599

Contact Author: Frank Puglia
Email: frank.puglia@eaglepicher.com

Abstract: *More Electric Aircraft (MEA) and Directed Energy Weapons (DEW) are rapidly growing fields. Each of these needs performance that is well outside of the boundaries of commercial, Li-ion performance and even batteries for typical military applications. MEA and DEW are developing fields with highly proprietary usage profiles. To date, these applications fall into two categories. In the first category, the discharge rates are in the 20C to 50C range. These applications are often well serviced by the semi-commercial cells already being produced for specialty applications such as race cars. EaglePicher has a product line dedicated to MEA and DEW using these cells. For the highest power or high duty cycle applications, prismatic cells are preferred for both electrochemical performance and thermal management. This paper discusses the state of the art performance of EaglePicher's custom, prismatic Li-ion cells. These cells are capable of charge rates in excess of 20C and pulse discharge rates in excess of 400C. These power levels put the specific discharge power in line with the best capacitor technologies. All performance data presented is generic and not related to any specific mission or program.*

Keywords: Directed Energy, More Electric Aircraft, Power, Prismatic, Thermal, Specific Power

Introduction

The demand for high power Li-ion cells is rapidly increasing. This demand, well beyond the demand of typical consumer applications, is driven by the new requirements of Directed Energy Weapons (DEW) and More Electric Aircraft (MEA). There is also an increase in demand from commercial and military aircraft looking to reduce the cost per flight hour.

The power and temperature requirements for the MEA, DEW and traditional aircraft applications are so varied that there is no possibility of a universal solution. Aircraft applications that allow heating and have modest power requirements, typically less than a 30C peak discharge rate, are very well serviced by commercial (COTS) cells. A good example of this is the various Iron Phosphate (LFP) 26650 cells. EaglePicher's LithiumStart division provides cost effective solutions for MEA, DEW and many other applications using screened COTS cells.

The most extreme applications are often best serviced through the use of custom prismatic cells. The combination of extremely high power chemistry, novel low temperature electrolyte, thin cell design, and an efficient module heating and/or cooling system, creates a system with tremendous capability. Power levels exceeding 30kW/kg have been demonstrated. Recharge rates exceeding 30C have been shown and result in a duty cycle of nearly 50% for DEW applications. Even with this power capability, there are some applications in which a battery-capacitor hybrid system is the ideal solution. EaglePicher's Yardney Technology Center has hybrid programs underway with the AirForce (HESM), Northrop Grumman, PCKA and ElectroStandards Laboratories.

The work on prismatic cells presented herein follows the work started under a NAVAIR-Pax River SBIR for high temperature range, safe Li-ion batteries for military aircraft. Those results were published in the Power Sources paper Thermally Stable High Energy Lithium-Ion Batteries for Naval Aviation Applications. In that paper, and others, we showed how cells with a high surface area to volume ratio (i.e. thin) could dramatically change the response of a cell to a failure initiation event.

Directed Energy

There is no clearly defined requirement for a Directed Energy (DE) power supply. Some applications require very long duration power draw, often exceeding two minutes and with well controlled temperatures. The two minutes of "magazine depth" translates into just a 30C discharge rate. Some applications have total durations of less than one second, translating to a 3600C discharge rate. These applications are often best serviced with capacitors. However, Li-ion can now surpass many capacitors in specific discharge power. The majority of applications are based on discharges of 3 to 30 seconds and that balance of energy and power is ideal for Li-ion. The critical sizing factor for these applications is the number of discharges before a recharge is needed. A twenty pulse discharge magazine depth of 5 second loads is comparable in many ways to a single 36C discharge. This level of performance is easily met by many COTS cells and all of the high power prismatic cells. The original high rate chemistry, using a 2.7V cutoff, delivered comparable capacity at either continuous or pulse discharge through the 100C discharge rate. Above 100C, the capacity available was highly dependent on if the discharge was pulsed or continuous rate. Figure 1 shows the percentage of low rate capacity retained at various rates. Over 60% of the C/5 capacity is delivered at 100C but only 15% of the capacity was delivered at 167C. Figure 2 shows the performance when the discharge load is pulsed. A rest time of ten seconds was sufficient to bring the capacity of the five second pulse from 15% to 50% of the original capacity. All testing was performed at 30°C.

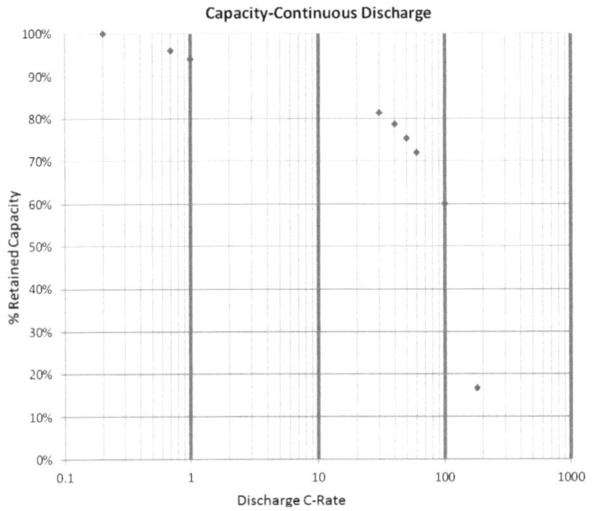

Figure 1. Original High Power Chemistry Retained Capacity as a Function of Continuous Discharge Rate (C)

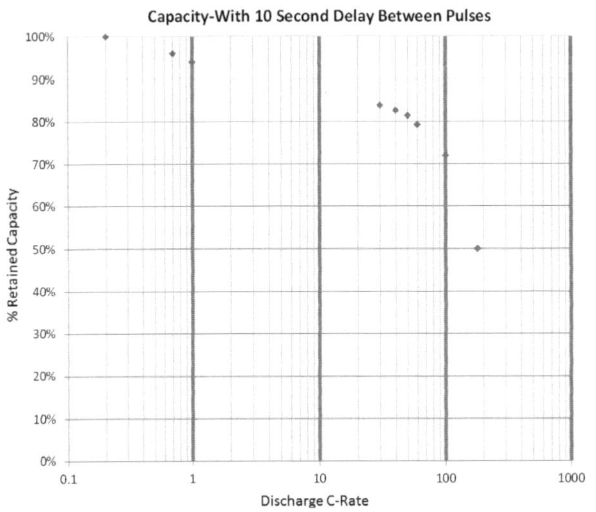

Figure 2. Original High Power Chemistry Retained Capacity as a Function of Pulsed Discharge Rate (C)

Improvements have been implemented since the original chemistry was delivered to several DEW applications. Figure 3 shows the latest generation chemistry undergoing continuous discharge at 100C and 200C while being compared to the baseline chemistry shown in Figure 1. The green line shows the original chemistry delivering the 60% capacity above 2.7V. The current generation chemistry delivers just 12% more capacity at the 100C rate. The capacity is delivered at half of the original cell impedance resulting in a higher average voltage. This is clearly illustrated by the dashed line which shows the performance of the cell at 200C being comparable to the original 100C discharge. All testing was performed at 30°C.

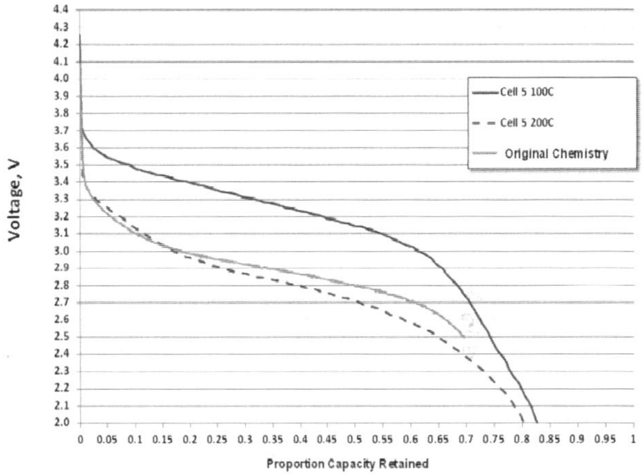

Figure 3. Original and Current Generation High Power Chemistry at 100C and 200C Discharge Rates

Operating above room temperature can greatly improve battery performance. As referenced in the previous papers, the thin prismatic cells can dissipate heat over fifteen times faster than a thick/wound cell of similar capacity. The ability to move heat quickly reduces the peak core temperature that a cell will reach during operation and greatly reduces the time at elevated temperatures. This allows operation at higher starting temperatures without creating a safety risk or sacrificing battery life.

Figure 4 shows the pulse performance at two different temperatures. A generic, 0.5 second, pulse is used to avoid overlap with controlled information. The blue line, 25°C, was intended to be a 2000Amp discharge but only achieved 1850Amps because of cycler limitations. The green line is the same cell operating at 60°C. The higher operating voltage for the 60°C test allowed the cycler to achieve the full 2000Amps. The difference in current and voltage results in the 60°C test delivering ~28% more power. Correcting for the difference in current shows that the difference in temperature has resulted in a 50% reduction in impedance. It is noted that this is still not EaglePicher's highest rate technology. The highest rate cells are shown in Figure 5. This testing is also conducted at a favorable 60°C.

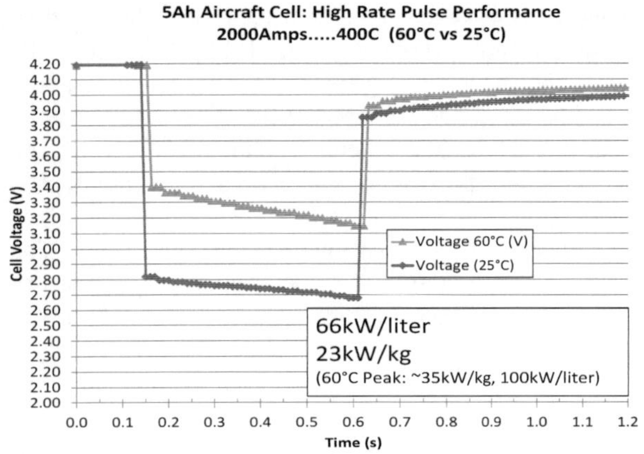

Figure 4. Original High Power Chemistry at 25°C and 60°C

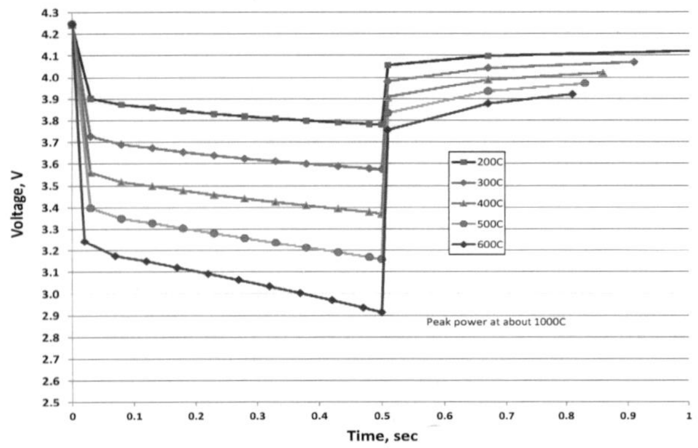

Figure 5. Current High Power Chemistry at 60°C and rates from 200C to 600C

This test was carried out in a small cell to avoid the high currents that would be associated with a large cell. However, this level of performance scales to 35kW/kg, 102kW/l in the same 5Ah cell tested in Figure 4. The idealized use of the capability is shown in Figures 6, Figure 7 and Figure 8. Figure 6 shows an example where a full size cell delivers 60% of its capacity in 20 seconds (i.e. 100C discharge rate). There is then a 15 second pause and the full cell capacity is returned in 100 seconds (i.e. 20C recharge rate). The cycle is repeated 150 times in fifteen hours with minimal change in the end of discharge voltage.

A 60C recharge rate was used in the next test. This data is shown in Figure 7. The cell started at 3.9V and the depth of discharge was limited to 40% to provide margin for polarization. The cell successfully ran the profile but the rising voltage cutoff and increased time in taper clearly shows that the cell was accumulating capacity. This was tracked down to differences in reporting accuracy between high discharge loads and lower charge loads. Over 70,000 rapid cycles were achieved in other tests. The ability to accept high charge rates without plating lithium required dramatic changes to anode material, electrolyte and separator. This capability was originally developed to accept high charge rates at the very low temperatures needed to support various space and aircraft applications.

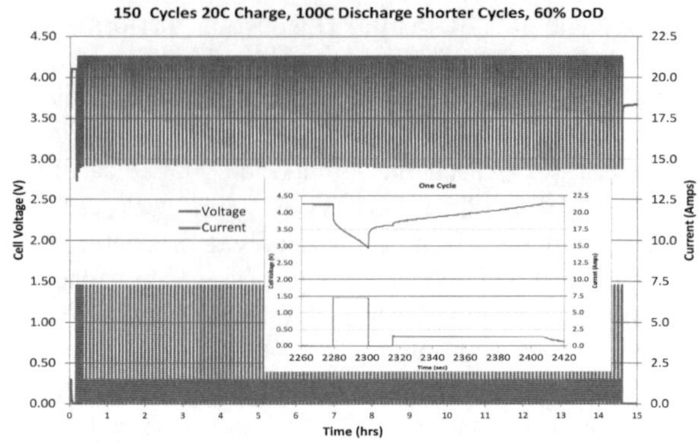

Figure 6. Example of a Mission with Long, 100C Discharges and Rapid Recharge

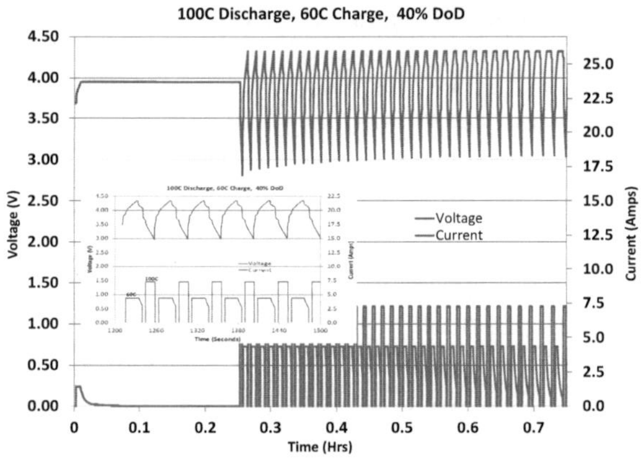

Figure 7. Example of a Mission with Long, 100C Discharges and Very Rapid Recharge

Figure 7 culminated in the creation of a hypothetical mission profile. The total magazine depth is about 60 seconds, 50 seconds of which is used in the profile. The results of this testing are shown in Figure 8 and Figure 9. A "full" sized cell was tested in this example. The battery is discharged for five seconds. After the first two discharges it is assumed that the system generator (GenSet) is operational. The discharge load to the battery is then commensurately reduced. The battery is recharged at a 38C rate for the 2.5 seconds between the pulses. The ability to fully accept the 38C recharging increases magazine depth by over 25%. The basic profile is shown in Figure 8. The energy balance for this profile allows for a total of ten pulses before a longer recharge time is needed to replenish the magazine. The allowed recharge time is ninety seconds and the battery is able to fully recover the capacity depleted within the ninety seconds. The battery would be capable of a limited number of additional full duration discharge pulses at any time during the recharge. Figure 9 shows the results for the ten discharge pulse regime repeated ten times for a total of one hundred discharges in twenty six minutes.

The combination of the high discharge capability, high charge capability and optimized thermal design results in a much smaller battery than would be otherwise needed. For example, a battery needed for a full size anti-drone system could be significantly smaller than a 6T battery size.

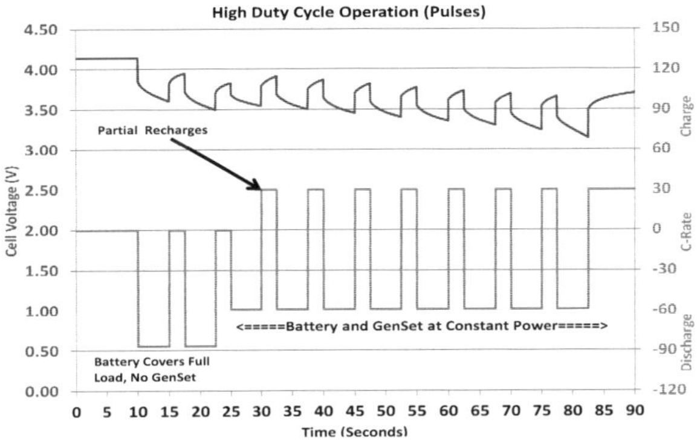

Figure 8. Operational Example (OE) with 5 Second Discharges and Continuous High Rate Recharge

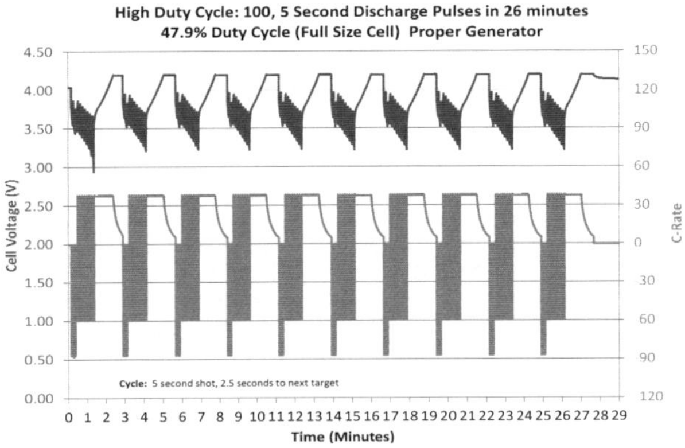

Figure 9. Rapid Repeat of the (OE) 10 Times to Demonstrate Rapid Thermal Dissipation

Aircraft Systems

The Directed Energy system originated from the need for aircraft systems to meet dead cold soak, high power requirements for tasks such as Auxiliary Power Unit (APU) start. The improvement in low temperature capability over the past several years is shown in Figure 10.

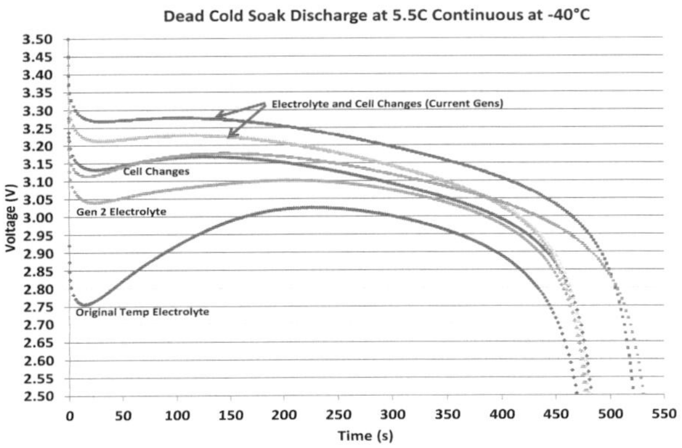

Figure 10. Current Generation Performance at -40°C

Aircraft systems often have both steady state and pulse requirements. A hybrid system can be preferred if pulse requirements drive the battery design. EaglePicher delivered a 270V, 200^{+}kW system to Northrop Grumman as part of the AirForce HESM program. An example of the basic system architecture is shown in Figure 11. Using the load profile provided for the HESM program, the HESM was able reduce voltage spikes on the aircraft bus by over 97%. The system is also, perhaps most importantly, a net thermal reduction.

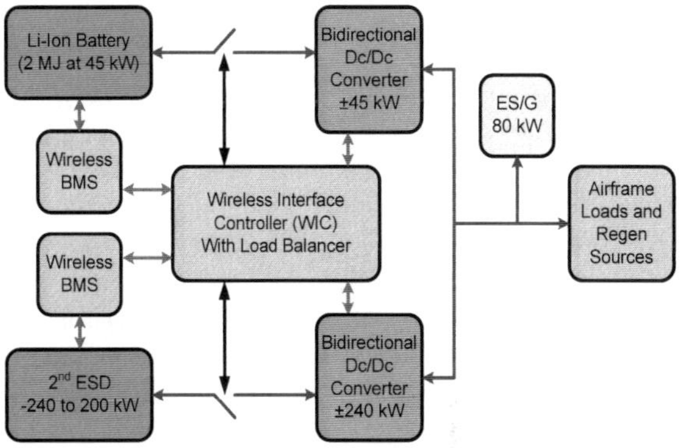

Figure 11. Design Option for the HESM System

Conclusion

High power and low temperature Li-ion chemistry, cell design, and battery design has matured greatly in the past several years. Pulse discharge power levels exceeding 100kW/l and 35kW/kg have been demonstrated, exceeding many capacitors. Charge capability still lags but has improved to the level of being able to support charge rates well in excess of 30C at room temperature resulting in demonstrated recharge times of less than 90 seconds in mission sized cells.

Acknowledgements

EaglePicher would like to acknowledge Wright Patterson Air Force Base for the use of the HESM data (USAF Release Approval 88ABW-2016-2908); NAVAIR, Patuxent River, for their original sponsoring of the high power program; General Atomics for their support and approval to discuss the system delivered to them in the presentation; the efforts of the entire Research and Development team whose hard work made this paper possible.

Development of Lithium Sulfur Cells Towards Commercialization

Simon C. Jones, Ratnakumar V. Bugga, John-Paul Jones, Frederick C. Krause and Jasmina Pasalic
Jet Propulsion Laboratory, California Institute of Technology
4800 Oak Grove Drive, Pasadena, CA 91109, USA
John-Paul.Jones@jpl.nasa.gov

Mary A. Hendrickson and Edward J. Plichta
US Army RDECOM CERDEC CP&I, Aberdeen Proving Ground, MD 21005, USA

David A. Ainsworth and Guillaume De Forton
OXIS Energy, E1 Culham Science Centre,
Abingdon, Oxfordshire, OX14 3DB, UK.

Abstract: *Electrochemical cells based on lithium/sulfur (Li/S) technology offer improved energy metrics compared to Li-ion; however much fundamental research in this area is performed using small developmental cells with limited relevance to commercial designs (for example, featuring very low active material loadings). We report the design of electrodes that cycle well at commercially-relevant material loadings, in particular when accompanied by modifications to the cell separator, and also the performance of pouch format commercial cells under a range of discharge conditions.*

Keywords: Lithium; sulfur; metal sulfide; blocking layer; specific energy; electrode; separator; pouch cell.

Introduction

Lithium sulfur (Li/S) batteries promise significant gains in energy density (3-5x) due to their high capacity cathode based on elemental sulfur and high capacity anode of lithium metal. Great strides have been made in the basic understanding of these cells by the research community on issues such as the polysulfide shuttle and how best to protect or cycle a lithium metal anode. Despite the incredible activity in academic environments, there have been few commercial cells tested in the literature, and even fewer that can deliver significant gains over commercial lithium-ion cells.

Our research has focused on making progress in cell technologies which could readily become commercialized. In that endeavor, we have developed high loading cathodes for Li/S cells by reducing the amount of carbon in the cathode to 15% and supplementing it with either TiS_2 or MoS_2.[1] Cathodes containing these disulfides can be coated with loadings greater than 10 mg/cm^2 and perform well in full cells, generally giving ~100 cycles at ~800 mAh/g initially based on S (Figure 1):

Additional performance improvements were observed through modification of separators with the intent of forming a blocking layer to constrain the soluble polysulfide species generated on discharge to the cathode portion of the cell.[2] Commercially-available alumina-coated separators showed some small improvement in cycle life and efficiency compared to baseline polyolefin separators; however, the largest improvements came from custom-made AlF_3-coated separators (Figure 2). Our current working hypothesis concerning these coated separators is that the ceramic materials interact chemically with the dissolved polysulfides and slow their progress through the electrolyte.

Furthermore, we have tested 19.5 Ah commercial lithium-sulfur (Li/S) pouch cells from OXIS Energy and report the testing of those cells here (Figure 3). The cells were subjected to a range of tests including cycle life, temperature characterization, impedance (both DC and AC), discharge and charge rate, and self-discharge as a function of depth of discharge (DOD). As-received, the cells delivered ~300 Wh/kg of specific energy when cycled at 20 °C and *C*/5, and retained over 11 Ah up to 100 cycles. Variable-temperature studies indicated that more than 60% of the 20 °C capacity was delivered down to -10 °C, although this was considerably reduced at -20 °C. Exposure of the cells to temperatures as low as -20 °C did not significantly affect the capacity retention of the cells cycling at 20 °C after variable-temperature testing.

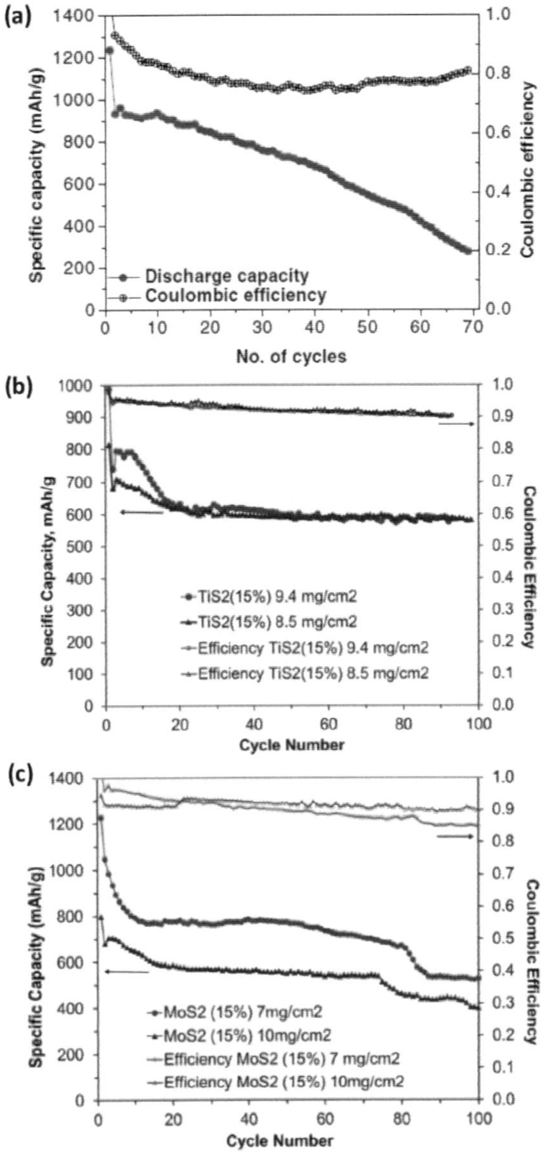

Figure 1. Cycling performance of a) conventional S cathode (S:C:PVDF 55:40:5, 6.2 mg/cm^2); b) S blended with TiS_2 and c) S blended with MoS_2 (S:MS_2:C:PVDF 65:15:15:5). Adapted and reproduced from Ref. 1.

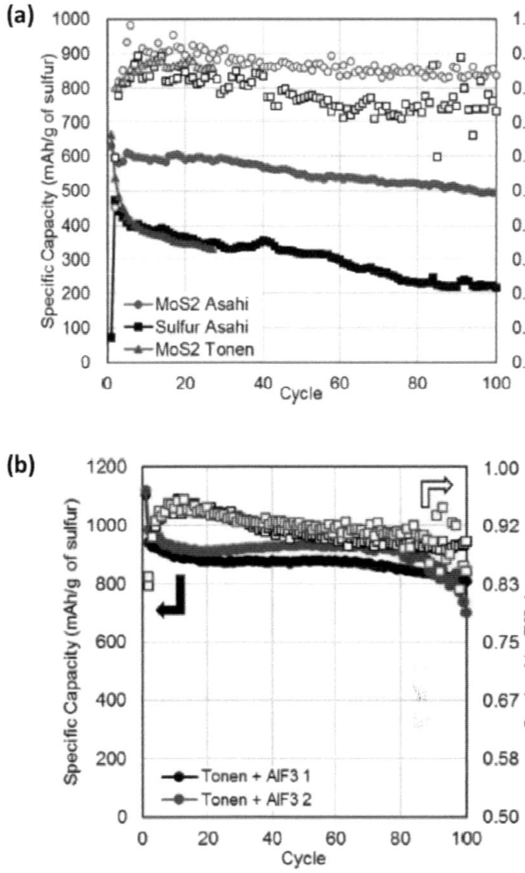

Figure 2. Cycling performance of a) Li/S pouch cells with Asahi Al_2O_3-coated separator and S (black squares) and S/MoS_2 cathodes (blue circles) compared to S/MoS_2 cathodes with uncoated Tonen polyolefin separator and b) Li/S coin cells with AlF_3-coated Tonen polyolefin separator (two duplicate cells shown). Adapted and reproduced from Ref. 2.

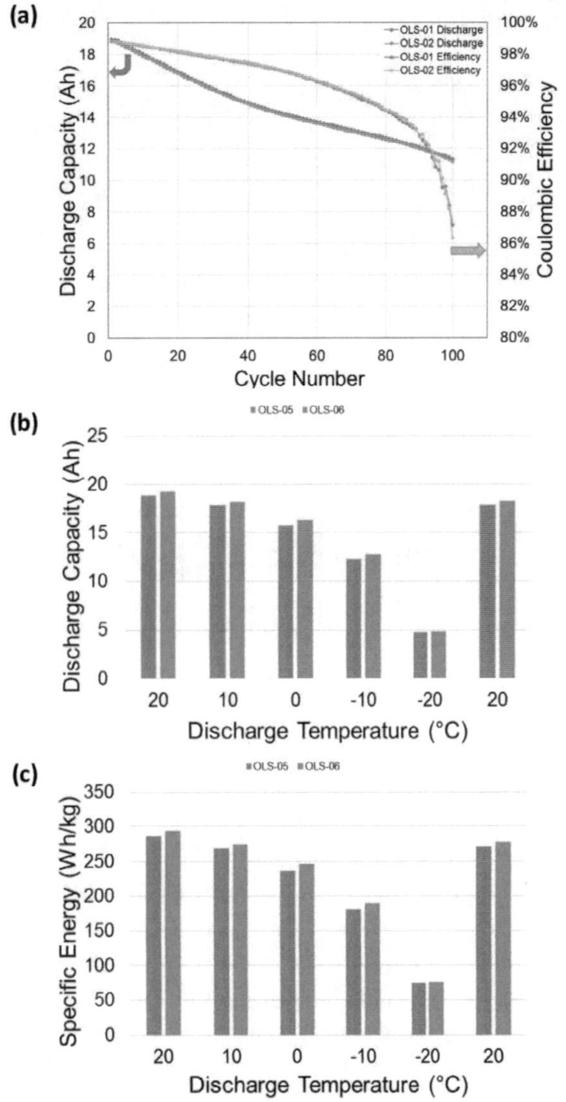

Figure 3. (a) Capacity retention and coulombic efficiency for OXIS pouch cells over 100 cycles at *C*/5 charge/discharge rates at 20 °C. (b) Delivered capacity and (c) specific energy from OXIS pouch cells at *C*/5 discharge rate at various temperatures. After each discharge, the cells were equilibrated at 20 °C and charged at *C*/5 rate at this temperature before the next discharge. The second set of 20 °C data correspond to observed performance after the indicated discharges down to -20 °C.

Acknowledgements

This research was carried out at the Jet Propulsion Laboratory (JPL), California Institute of Technology under a contract with the National Aeronautics and Space Administration (NASA). The authors acknowledge the funding support of NASA's Game Changing Development (GCD) Program, under the Space Technologies Missions Directorate (STMD).

References

1. Bugga, R. V.; Jones, S. C.; Pasalic, J.; Seu, C. S.; Jones, J.-P.; Torres, L. *J. Electrochem. Soc.* **2017**, *164* (2), A265.
2. Bugga, R.; Jones, J.-P.; Jones, S. C.; Krause, F. C.; Pasalic, J.; Ganapathi, D. S.; Hendrickson, M.; Plichta, E. J. *J. Electrochem. Soc.* **2018**, *165* (1), A6021.

The Hybrid Tiger: A Long Endurance Solar/Fuel Cell/Soaring Unmanned Aerial Vehicle

Richard O. Stroman[1], Daniel J. Edwards[2], Phillip Jenkins[3], Sam Carter[2], Daniel Newton[2], Matthew Kelly[2], Stearns Heinzen[2], Trent Young[2], Vladimir Dobrokhodov[6], Jack Langelaan[5], John Bird[5], P. Alex Reinecke[4]

[1]Chemistry Div., [2]Tactical Electronic Warfare Div., [3]Electronics Science and Tech. Div., [4]Marine Meteorology Div.
US Naval Research Laboratory, Washington, DC, USA, 20375
[5]Pennsylvania State University, Dept. of Aerospace Engineering, University Park, PA, USA, 16802
[6]Naval Postgraduate School, Dept. of Mechanical and Aerospace Engineering, Monterey, CA, USA, 93943

Abstract: The Hybrid Tiger is an Unmanned Air Vehicle currently in development at the US Naval Research Laboratory; it is designed to demonstrate long endurance (>2 d) and long range (>1000 nmi) in a relatively small (7.3 m wingspan, 25 kg GTOW) and tactically-relevant vehicle. The anticipated range and endurance are feasible due to a unique hybrid power train that incorporates a high specific energy (~1200 Wh/kg) PEM fuel cell system, high efficiency (+23%) solar arrays, and advanced autonomous soaring algorithms. Energy management is implemented onboard to coordinate the operation of each power subsystem and optimize the aircraft trajectory.

Keywords: solar, hydrogen, fuel cell, soaring, aircraft, unmanned, endurance, UAV, path planning

Introduction

The Hybrid Tiger is a Group 2 Unmanned Air Vehicle (UAV) currently in development at the US Naval Research Laboratory (NRL). The Hybrid Tiger is designed to demonstrate long endurance (>2 d) and long range (>1000 nmi) in a relatively small (7.3 m wingspan, 25 kg GTOW) and tactically-relevant vehicle. The anticipated range and endurance are feasible due to a unique hybrid power train that incorporates a high specific energy (~1200 Wh/kg) proton exchange membrane fuel cell (PEMFC) system, high efficiency (+23%) thin-film GaAs solar arrays, and advanced autonomous soaring algorithms. Energy management is implemented onboard to coordinate the operation of each power subsystem and optimize the aircraft trajectory. The Hybrid Tiger is a heavily modified version of the Ion Tiger UAV developed at NRL in 2009 to demonstrate fuel cell powered flight [1-4]. Ion Tiger is shown in Fig. 1 and Hybrid Tiger is shown in Fig. 2.

Aircraft which achieve long endurance by harvesting energy from the environment are not a new idea; Solar Impulse 2 [5], Zephyr [6], and Atlantik Solar [7] are prominent examples. Solar Impulse 2 and Zephyr are designed to fly at altitudes above 3,000 m where winds are consistent and few clouds obscure the sun. The Hybrid Tiger, in contrast, is a smaller and more robust vehicle which can fly at lower altitudes and endure a wider range of weather conditions. The increased mass of robust structures make storing sufficient solar energy to fly through the night infeasible, so the Hybrid Tiger cannot fly indefinitely like a pure solar electric aircraft. However, the Hybrid Tiger's hybrid electric propulsion system can exploit any available sunlight *and* operate in cloudy conditions by relying on the stored Hydrogen and PEMFC to supplement solar power, albeit at the cost of reduced range and endurance. Furthermore, by flying in the convective boundary layer of the atmosphere (below 3,000 m), the Hybrid Tiger can harvest energy from the atmosphere by exploiting thermals and other rising air.

Figure 1. The Ion Tiger UAV, predecessor of Hybrid Tiger.

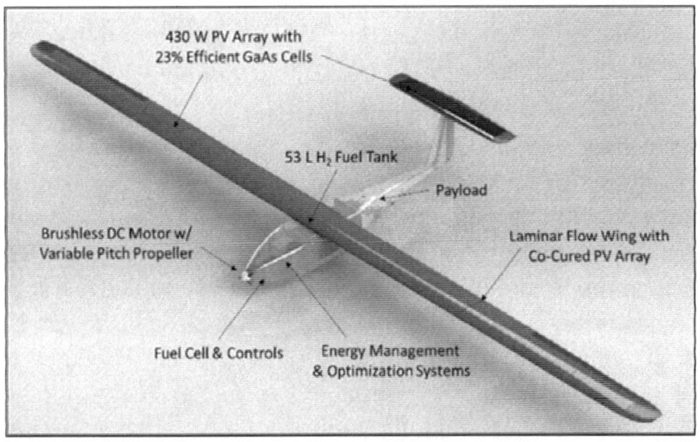

Figure 2. CAD model illustrating key energy-related elements of the Hybrid Tiger design.

Fuel Cell System: The PEMFC system has a traditional stack topology with a liquid cooling loop and produces up to 625 W at an efficiency of >40% (LHV of H_2). [4, 8] The 53 L hydrogen fuel tank stores 1221 g H_2 at 5,000 psia and 25°C.

The fuel tank is a Type-III aluminum lined, composite overwrapped pressure vessel which weighs <8 kg empty. A single stage pressure regulator reduces the H_2 pressure to 15 psig for consumption by the PEMFC system. The overall specific energy of the PEMFC and fuel tank is ~1200 Wh/kg, which is more than five times greater than Li-Ion batteries (~200 Wh/kg).

Solar Arrays: The Hybrid Tiger carries five thin-film GaAs solar arrays (four on the wing and one on the tail) and each has its own maximum power point tracker (MPPT). The array was divided this way to accommodate manufacturing variations between sub-arrays and differences in solar irradiation as the aircraft changes orientation with respect to the sun during maneuvers.

The solar arrays are co-molded with the wing and tail composite skins during vehicle fabrication to produce an integrated structure with a smooth surface. Total solar array system weight is 1.0 kg, approximately 5% of the vehicle gross take-off weight (GTOW).

Autonomous-Soaring: Algorithms that identify and exploit rising air to gain altitude are being employed to harvest energy from the atmosphere. Onboard algorithms use existing autopilot sensors to measure vertical wind motion, identify thermal updraft structures, and guide the aircraft into position to gain free altitude with the motor off [9].

Prior experimentation with auto-soaring techniques demonstrated +5 hours of endurance during the daytime with a sailplane [10] or offsetting over 50% of average propulsion energy over a multi-hour flight [11]. Soaring behaviors are integrated with the power management system to best leverage the energy capture opportunity balanced with the mission constraints.

Long Distance Path Planning: An algorithm that solves the task of energy (fuel) optimal trajectory planning between any two points in 4D space (3D position and time). The approach utilizes a prior given weather forecast of 3D wind and solar irradiance to produce the optimal path and the commanded airspeed along the path. The resulting trajectory serves as a reference of the achievable optimal performance of the vehicle along the route.

Drivetrain Efficiency: While the PEMFC system stores energy efficiently and the solar arrays and auto-soaring algorithms gather energy, another important contributor to the performance of Hybrid Tiger is the efficiency of its drivetrain. A variable pitch propeller (VPP) coupled to a six-phase brushless DC motor ensures that electric power is converted to thrust at maximum efficiency over a wide range of airspeeds and throttle settings. A full authority digital engine controller (FADEC) uses predetermined maps to look up the optimal VPP and motor configuration for the current flight conditions and throttle setting.

Airframe: The Hybrid Tiger is a high-wing monoplane with a large lift/drag ratio of ~21:1 designed to fly efficiently at 15 m/s. A spread-tow carbon fiber and foam sandwich composite skin construction enables robust and lightweight structures. The airframe is <30% of total takeoff mass, despite being designed for +6G ultimate loads. The wing and tail planforms are designed for high active solar area fractions, and the high-wing and T-tail reduce the likelihood of shading during maneuvers. Aerodynamics of the wing are highly tailored for low propulsion power required at a cruise speed reasonable to handle moderate environmental winds. The fuselage is direct from Ion Tiger [1-4] and the majority of available internal volume is dedicated to hydrogen storage.

Hybrid System Integration & Strategy

A major design constraint on long endurance (>12 h) pure solar electric aircraft is storing sufficient energy to fly through the night and having excess solar energy capture to recharge quickly during the daytime. The efficiency limits of practical photovoltaic technology and the specific energy limits of Li-ion batteries are major design drivers for such vehicles. The need to deploy large areas of solar array and lift large battery mass generally leads to designs with structures that are large and fragile.

The Hybrid Tiger, in contrast, does not attempt to store solar energy. Any energy gathered by the solar arrays offsets power production by the fuel cell to reduce the rate of fuel consumption. In some circumstances (clear skies, mid-day, and low latitude) there may be surplus solar power, in which case the Hybrid Tiger flies faster toward a range goal or climbs to store the energy in an “altitude battery”. The combination of reduced fuel consumption during daylight hours and high specific energy storage by the PEMFC system to continue flying at night enables this robust, long range and endurance vehicle.

Custom power management and distribution (PMAD) electronics integrate power from the solar arrays and fuel cell, and supply power to hotel loads and the propulsion system. A small 32 Wh Li-ion battery pack supplies power for the avionics in the event of an emergency, such that the aircraft can maintain control during descent and landing. A passive, voltage-staging approach is used to ensure all of the available solar power is absorbed before consuming finite hydrogen fuel resources via the PEMFC; the MPPTs provide power at 45 V, which is higher than the 31-45 V range of the fuel cell, which is higher than the 23-29 V range of the battery.

Energy-Optimal Path Planning

Flying within the convective boundary layer of the atmosphere creates several types of inhomogeneity in the energy environment. For example:

- Clouds cause the distribution of solar energy to vary both spatially and temporally, in addition to the diurnal cycle.
- Wind direction and magnitude vary both spatially and temporally. Winds are significant because they can

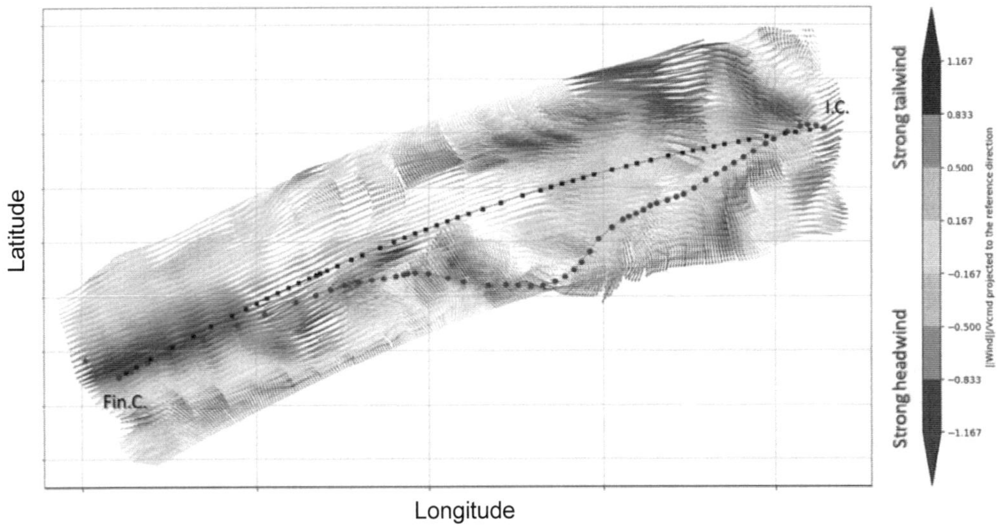

Figure 3. Example comparing great circle (blue dots) and energy optimal (red dots) routes through a wind field where favorable winds are red and unfavorable winds are blue. The optimal route also considers solar irradiance.

increase or decrease energy consumption, depending on the relative wind direction and vehicle trajectory.

- Rising (or sinking) air intensity varies spatially and temporally. Convective updrafts (i.e. thermals) form, drift, and dissipate as they interact with wind and the conditions which create them change.

The inhomogeneity of the energy environment presents an opportunity from a path planning perspective. Given a non-uniform distribution of energy sinks and sources, it is unlikely that the energy-optimal route for an energy harvesting vehicle will be the geographically shortest route. Simulations carried out at NRL and by partners at the Naval Postgraduate School (NPS) have indicated that significant energy savings can be realized by planning vehicle trajectories with energy in mind. The energy optimization problem has been cast as fuel consumption minimization over a flight between two fixed locations, but other formulations are possible as well. For example, the fight time could be minimized while respecting a constraint on the amount of fuel consumed so that sufficient fuel remains to carry out a mission upon arrival. The path planning process is decomposed into a global path planning problem and a local path planning problem to leverage different sources of environmental data and attack the problem at different scales.

The global path planner (GPP) uses weather forecasts produced by the NRL COAMPS numerical weather simulation [12] which include wind (u,v,w) and solar irradiance as functions of time and geographic position, on a 9 km and 3 h grid, produced in 6 h intervals. The GPP uses a Hybrid Tiger model to estimate the energy balance along a proposed path between two locations, given the predicted environment. The optimization task is formulated as a two point boundary value problem with an analytically synthesized optimal control laws which minimize energy consumption along the route; the analytical form of the solution allows for computationally efficient onboard implementation of the algorithm. The result, returned as the C^1 continuous polynomial, is discretized by a series of global waypoints with metadata describing the anticipated vehicle state (time of arrival, fuel remaining, etc.) at each waypoint.

Figure 3 presents an example that illustrates the resulting optimal route (red dots, x_t h flight) in comparison with the route along the great circle (blue dots, $1.51x_t$ h flight) between the initial and final position of the aircraft. The wind along the routes unfolds as the UAV flies along the optimal route. The wind direction and magnitude are color coded with red representing tail wind and the blue representing the headwind. The result illustrates that the optimal route heavily leverages wind in the desired direction of flight.

The local path planner (LPP) uses local observations of wind and solar irradiance to exploit energy harvesting opportunities and reduce energy expenditure [13]. The LPP drives the minute-by-minute operation of the Hybrid Tiger in response to environmental features that have too small a spatial or temporal resolution be captured by the weather forecast. The ultimate goal of the LPP is to fly the Hybrid Tiger to the next global waypoint and arrive with the aircraft in the anticipated state or in a state that improves the global prediction of the GPP solution. This gives the LPP some leeway to operate the Hybrid Tiger outside of the global path in search of improved energy harvesting opportunities or reduced energy expenditure, so long as it arrives at the next global waypoint on time and with sufficient energy. For example, the LPP can stop forward progress to gain altitude via autonomous soaring, trading free energy for time along route.

Energy management software is implemented onboard on an Odroid XU4 board computer. Disparate software functions such as the GPP and LPP were wrapped into Robot

Operating System (ROS) nodes to facilitate parallel development and robust interactions through a publish/subscribe model.

Vehicle Energy Simulation

A detailed Hybrid Tiger simulation was developed for component sizing, performance estimation, and energy management strategy analysis. The simulation steps through a flight in 1 min increments, calculating the vehicle energy balance and state at each step. Fuel cell performance measurements are used to relate fuel cell electrical power production to fuel consumption rate, and detailed solar array models predict solar power production as a function of solar irradiance and array temperature. A vehicle drag model estimates propulsion power consumption as a function of vehicle weight, airspeed, altitude, load factor, etc. Energy management behaviors are captured by the simulation, such as climbing to store surplus solar energy. The simulation can assume user-defined environmental conditions such as wind field, temperature profile, and celestially determined solar irradiance, or use COAMPS weather forecast data to simulate in a realistic environment.

Simulation results include metrics such as the fraction of total energy supplied by the solar arrays, fuel cell average efficiency, and fuel remaining as a function of time. The relationship between diurnal variation in solar irradiance and the rate of fuel consumption is evident in the results. For example, along a route near 32°N with takeoff on the summer equinox, the fuel tank fill fraction curve is flat for 2-3 h in the middle of each day indicating the solar arrays produce sufficient power to satisfy all vehicle power consumption during those periods. In simulations at moderate latitudes, the solar arrays supply ~20% of the energy consumed in a flight.

Conclusions

The Hybrid Tiger UAV is projected to achieve long range and endurance through a combination of high specific energy storage, energy harvesting from the environment, energy management, and energy-aware path planning. Flight testing of the full hybrid power system is anticipated in 2018 followed by a maximum endurance flight in 2019.

Acknowledgements

The authors thank DoD Operational Energy Capabilities Investment Fund for supporting this work, the USMC Expeditionary Energy Office for supporting development of solar-soaring algorithms at NRL, and the NRL 6.2 Base Program system for supporting basic research programs in fuel cells, solar co-molding integration, and autonomous soaring algorithm development.

References

1. K. Swider-Lyons, R. Stroman, et al., *The Ion Tiger Fuel Cell Unmanned Air Vehicle*, Proc. of the 44th Power Sources Conf., p. 561-563, Las Vegas NV, 2010.
2. K. Swider-Lyons, R. Stroman, et al., *Hydrogen Fuel Cell Propulsion for Long Endurance Small UAVs*, AIAA Centennial of Naval Aviation Forum "100 Years of Achievement and Progress", Aviation Technology, Integration, and Operations (ATIO) Conf., (2011).
3. R. Stroman, M. Schuette, K. Swider-Lyons, J. Rodgers, and D. Edwards, *Liquid hydrogen fuel system design and demonstration in a small long endurance air vehicle*, Int. J. of Hydrogen Energy, 39, 11279-11290 (2014).
4. K. Swider-Lyons, R. Stroman, J. Rodgers, B. Gould, J. Mackrell, M. Schuette, and G. Page, *Hydrogen Fuel Cells for Small Unmanned Air Vehicles, ECS Transactions*, 64 (3) 963-972 (2014).
5. Solar Impulse 2 (www.solarimpulse.com)
6. Zephyr (www.airbus.com/defence/uav/zephyr.html)
7. P. Oettershagen, *Perpetual flight with a small solar-powered UAV: Flight results, performance analysis and model validation*, IEEE Aerospace Conf., Big Sky, MT, June 2016.
8. Protonex Technology Corp. (www.protonex.com)
9. D. Edwards, *Autonomous Locator of Thermals (ALOFT) Autonomous Soaring Algorithm*, Formal Report, US NRL, Washington, DC, Apr 2015.
10. D. Edwards, and L. Silverberg, *Autonomous Soaring: The Montague Cross-Country Challenge*, Journal of Aircraft, Vol. 47, No. 5 (2010), pp. 1763-1769.
11. D. Edwards, *Integrating Hydrogen Fuel Cell Propulsion and Autonomous Soaring Techniques*, 2018 AIAA Guidance, Navigation, and Control Conf., AIAA SciTech Forum, (AIAA 2018-185).
12. Coupled Ocean/Atmosphere Mesoscale Prediction System, www.nrlmry.navy.mil/coamps-web/web/home
13. J. J. Bird., and J. Langelaan. *Design Space Exploration for Hybrid Solar/Soaring Aircraft*, 17th AIAA Aviation Technology, Integration, and Operations Conf. 2017.

Flexible Hybrid Energy System for Pulsed Power Applications

Brian Hennings, Jonathan Reeh & Jibi Ninan Varughese
Lynntech Inc.
2501 Earl Rudder Fwy, College Station, TX, U.S.A, 77845
brian.hennings@lynntech.com / 1-979-764-2234

Abstract: *This paper presents a brief analysis of hybrid energy systems for pulse power applications. This is accomplished by analyzing two power profiles of different energy and power requirements. The authors have also included test data from on-going and recent SBIR projects to provide the reader with proof-of-concept. The test data is included to show the reader the possibility of scaling the system in terms of power and energy for certain combinations of energy-power technologies.*

Keywords: Lynntech; fuel cell; hybrid; power; energy; scalable; flexible; battery, supercapacitor; ultracapacitor; pulse power; DEW; directed energy weapon; SBIR.

Introduction

There are mature portable energy-power storage options available today: batteries, capacitors, heat engines, and fuel cells. Each of these technologies comes with a drawback that is resolved by another energy storage technology. A hybrid system aims to balance these competing energy and power factors.

For example, in general, batteries have high specific energy but low specific power while capacitors/supercapacitor are poor energy storage devices but much more capable of high power charge and discharge as shown in Figure 1. By combining these technologies it is possible to achieve the best of both and mitigate the weaknesses.

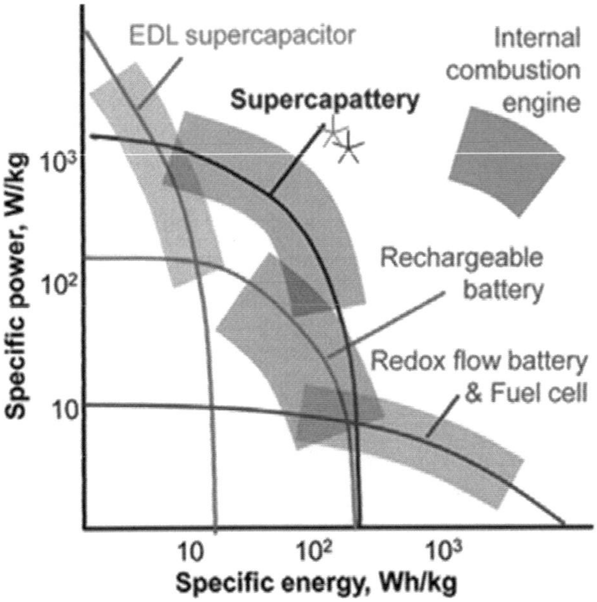

Figure 1: Ragone plot of different energy/power technologies [1].

Similarly, fuel cell systems have an advantage that energy stored as hydrogen can be optimized independent of the fuel cell itself which is the power producing component of a fuel cell system. A significant advantage of using fuel cell is that these systems operate quietly, at higher efficiencies and some can operate at temperatures much lower than seen in internal combustion engines making thermal management easier.

This paper aims to discuss the advantages of fuel cell-based hybrid power system currently under development for the Department of Defense and other hybrid systems that should be considered based on total energy, power, weight and volume requirements. A convenient way to compare such technologies is to compare specific power and specific energy. Specific power is the power provided by a system per unit weight. Specific energy is the energy delivered per unit weight. Using these metrics we shall consider the two pulse profiles shown in Figure 2 in this paper.

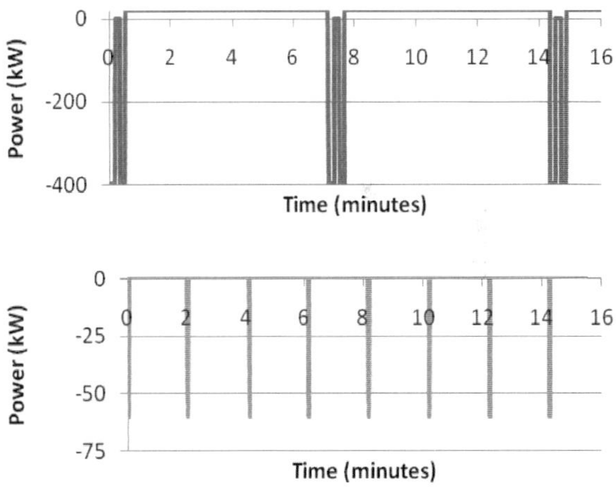

Figure 2: Representative pulse power profiles: Top to Bottom – Profile A & Profile B. Profile A consists of 40 total pulses (not shown), and profile B consists of 200 total pulses (not shown). Negative power represents discharge and positive power represents recharge. See following sections for profile details.

Non-Hybrid Systems

Consider Profile A: 400 kW of discharge power for 10 seconds 40 times from an energy system on an airborne application. This equates to 160 MJ or 44.4 kWh of energy.

A supercapacitor bank would need 35,000 Ioxus iRB1250K270CT supercapacitors to dissipate the energy required. The platform would have to haul approximately

10,000 kg into the air apart from balance of plant (BOP) required for thermal management and maintaining the health of the capacitors.

A battery pack made from Kokam SLPB4367114H6 would weigh 760 kg. This weight approximates the required thermal management components of the battery pack and other BOP.

For the same requirement, a Hamilton Sundstrand APS5000 APU will weigh ~560 kg including the weight of the aircraft fuel consumed in idle mode and during operation based on 18 hours of runtime.

Profile A Hybrid System

A hybrid fuel cell-battery power system will be one in which the battery acts as the power source capable of discharging the required 400 kW; the fuel cell sub-system provides energy to recharge the battery at a rate of ~4 minutes per power pulse from the battery.

Combining the same Kokam-based battery pack mentioned in the previous section with Lynntech's proprietary low temperature proton exchange membrane (LTPEM) fuel cell technology, the same system will weigh approximately 180 kg.

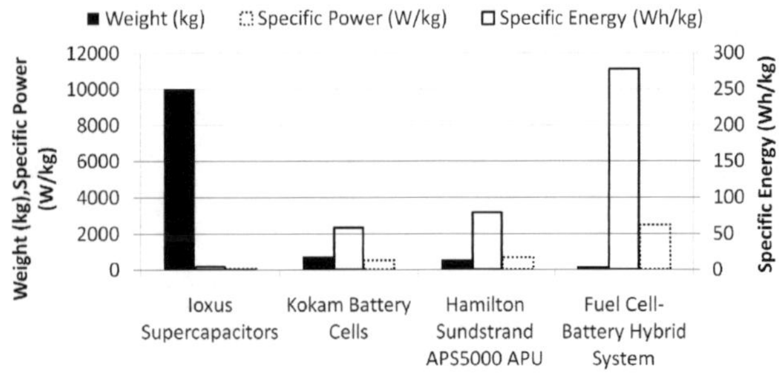

Figure 3: Comparison of hybrid and non-hybrid system for profile A

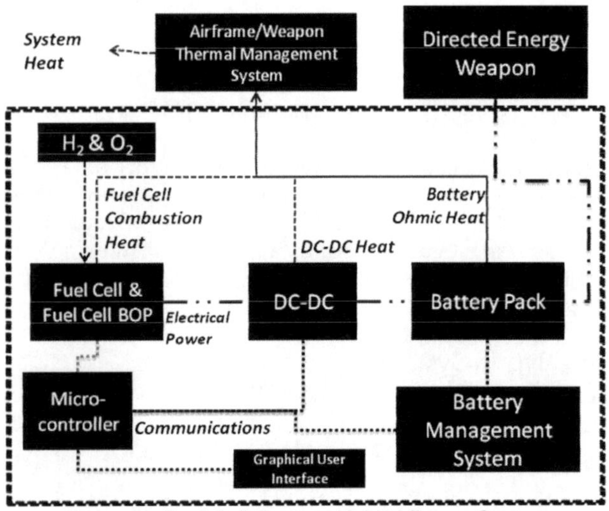

Figure 4: Fuel Cell-Battery Hybrid Power System

As shown in Figure 3 battery only option system will have a specific power of 526 W/kg and a specific energy of 58 Wh/kg. The LTPEM fuel cell, including fuel & oxidizer tanks, has a specific power of 250 W/kg. But the combination of the two technologies provides a specific power of 2500 W/kg and specific energy of 275 Wh/kg; this is more than three times the metrics of a non-hybrid system. Hence, by combining the right technologies significant gains can be made. The black star represents this system in Figure 1.

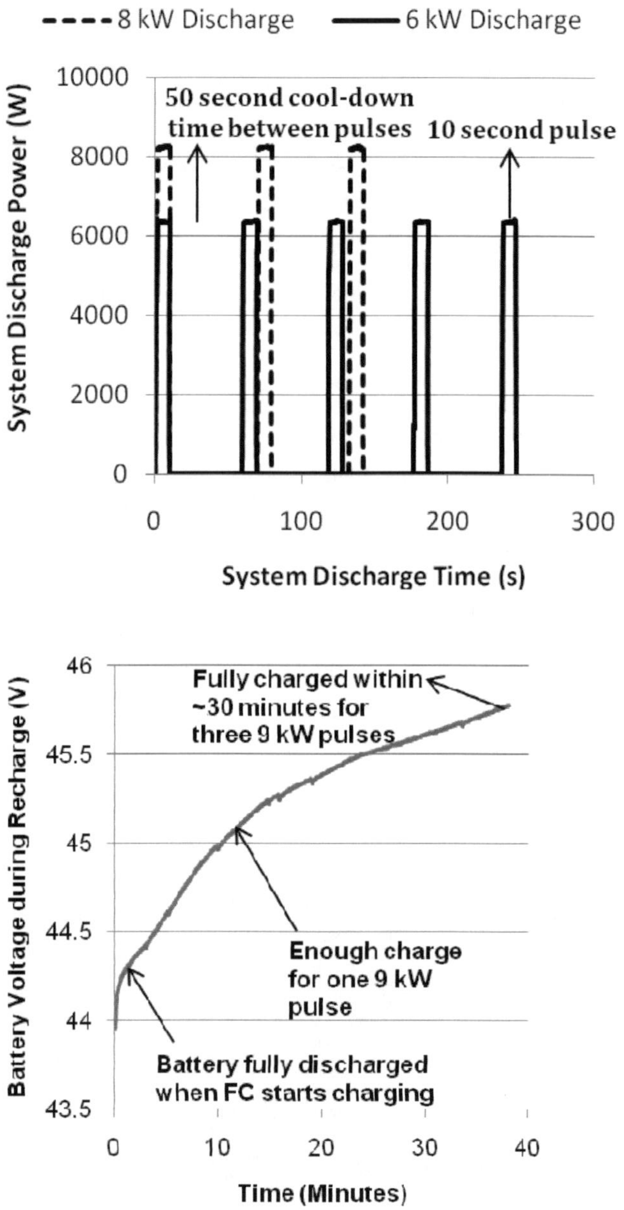

Figure 5: Phase I Proof-of-Concept: Top-Test data showing scalability and flexibility in terms of discharge. The discharge consisted of three 8 kW pulses followed by a recharge from the fuel cell and five 6 kW pulses. Bottom-Test data showing the battery being recharged by a low power fuel cell after the three 8 kW pulses

Lynntech integrated a Low Temperature Proton Exchange Membrane (LTPEM) with a battery pack at the end of an SBIR Phase I. The purpose of this system, shown in Figure 4, was to provide proof-of-concept and to prove scalability in terms of discharge power. This was successfully proven as shown by test data in Figure 5. The system was developed with an airborne Directed Energy Weapon (DEW) system as the target end user; however, owing to the nature of this system, it's flexible for integration with systems requiring different power requirements. As shown in Figure 5, Lynntech achieved a recharge rate of 10 minutes per pulse.

This project is currently in its Phase II stage where Lynntech aims to achieve a recharge time of 5 minutes per pulse. Lynntech has also scaled the system to discharge upto 100 kW from an NMC battery system. A ~5 kW LTPEM fuel cell has been fabricated and independently tested. As per current concept-of-operations (CONOPs), following the 100 kW discharge from the battery pack, the fuel cell will recharge it by stepping up the voltage through a Silicon Carbide (SiC) DC-DC converter. The SiC converter is based on an evaluation board; the board has been customized to step-up voltage from ~70-50 VDC to ~180-200 VDC. Even at these low voltages the converter is capable of 87%-90% efficiency.

The conclusion of the current Phase II will showcase charge-discharge cycles, the systems capability to be scalable in terms of discharge power and number of pulses and control & monitoring of this battery-fuel cell system.

The Phase III will be at full scale: two 400 kW discharges for 10 seconds with a 10 second off-period in between the pulses. The power discharges will be followed up by ~20 kW recharge from a high specific power fuel cell to recharge the battery in ~4 minutes per pulse. The projected system level mass is ~180 kg.

Profile B Hybrid System

Profile B represents a power system capable of a short discharge, providing mediocre total energy and low recharge power. Profile B is 200 pulses of 60 kW power discharges for 1.5 seconds followed by a two minute recharge between each pulse as shown in Figure 6.

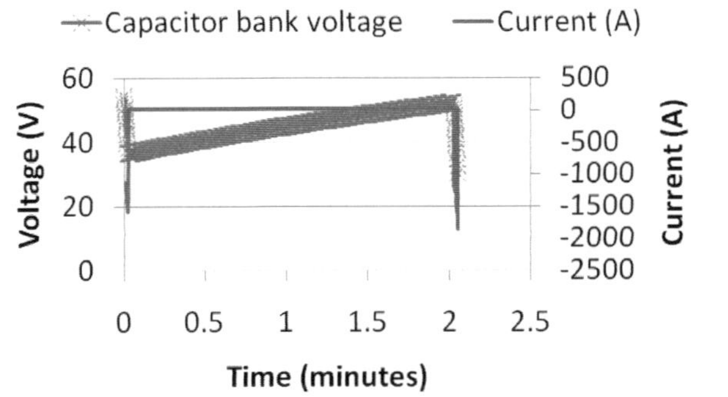

Figure 6: An Ioxus iRB1250K270CT Ultracapacitor-Fuel Cell Hybrid system's theoretical performance.

Figure 6 shows the performance of the fuel cell-supercapacitor hybrid system. The supercapacitor bank will consist of 40 Ioxus iRB1250K270CT supercapacitors in series and two of these serial banks in parallel. Since the pulse is just for 1.5 s and the rated pulse current discharge for the supercapacitor is 1300 A. A fuel cell capable of 750 W shall be capable of recharging the supercapacitor in two minutes. A boost converter or a buck-boost converter will be required between the supercapacitor and fuel cell. The supercapacitor bank will weigh less than 15 kg, the fuel cell including BOP, fuel and oxidizer tanks will weigh approximately 8 kg and the DC-DC converter will be approximately 0.5 kg. The specific power of such a system would be 2800 W/kg and specific energy would be 230 Wh/kg. The green star on Figure 1 represents system metrics to other technologies on the Ragone plot.

For perspective, let's compare a high energy battery system for this application. This application will require approximately 600 SAFT MP 176065 Integration high energy density cells which. Such a system will have a specific power of only 710 W/kg and specific energy of 60 Wh/kg; three times lower than the previous system.

Conclusion

Hybrid systems should be particularly considered if any one technology cannot meet energy and power requirements. As shown in this paper, a fuel cell-based hybrid system can provide tremendous advantages in terms of specific energy and specific power due to the engineer's capability to independently scale the energy and power source. Military or civilian applications that are severely constrained in weight should consider these hybrid options.

A test based proof-of-concept has been given to the reader to provide confidence in such systems and make them aware of developments in the hybrid power-energy arena.

Acknowledgements

Authors would like to acknowledge USAF contracts FA 9451-15-M0522 and FA9451-16-C-0528 for funding the SBIR Phase I & Phase II that helped the authors generate data for this paper.

Reference

1. George Z. Chen (2017) Supercapacitor and supercapattery as emerging electrochemical energy stores, International Materials Reviews, 62:4, 173-202, DOI: 10.1080/09506608.2016.1240914

BB-2590 Hybrid Electrical Energy Storage System

Stephen Cordova, Steven C. Arzberger and Weibing Xing
stephenc@adatech.com, stevena@adatech.com, weibingx@adatech.com
ADA Technologies, Inc.
11149 Bradford Rd.
Littleton, CO 80127
Phone: (303) 792-5615
Fax: (303) 792-5633

Abstract: *ADA Technologies, Inc. (ADA) demonstrated an unprecedented lithium ion (Li-ion)/supercapacitor Hybrid Electrical Energy Storage System (HEESS). It will afford significant pulse power (projected ~ 10 kW/kg) in a high-specific energy system (100 – 150 Wh/kg). A BB-2590 prototype was demonstrated, and a conformable wearable battery (CWB) is forthcoming. The HEESS is enabled via a constant-current regulator that isolates the battery from the supercapacitor to improve end-to-end efficiency from the battery to the load, while accounting for the relative diminutive rate capability of the high-energy Li-ion battery. The pulse power capability is provided by an ADA supercapacitor that possesses ~ 10x the energy (15 – 20 Wh/kg, at cell level) of commercial supercapacitor products. This leads to significantly improved duty cycle – duration, magnitude and pulse frequency.*

Keywords: Supercapacitor, ultracapacitor, hybrid, energy, Li-ion, battery, high energy, pulse power, BB-2590, conformal wearable battery, 6T

Introduction

A HEESS comprised of a supercapacitor to buffer/filter high rate pulse currents, and coupled to a high-energy battery, affords an efficient storage device that maximizes energy density and delivers pulse power characteristics (duty cycle, pulse amplitude, frequency, *etc.*). Such an HEESS would enable the combination of many disparate energy devices providing valuable mass and size savings.

In essence, supercapacitors serve as a compliment to a primary energy source (battery), which cannot repeatedly provide quick power bursts. Supercapacitors are capable of repetitive cycling (several hundreds of thousands of cycles) across a wide range of rate and temperature. This holds tremendous potential to extend the life of current systems and provide additional mass savings through the elimination of the heating/cooling architectures required by battery systems.

A hybrid device will permit high charge/discharge currents for acceptance via an isolated supercapacitor. Indeed this is important because a Li-ion battery can be compromised when rapidly charged at a high state-of-charge (SoC), which is known to lead to deteriorated performance and significant safety concerns.

ADA first demonstrated our HEESS technology in a benchtop demonstration based on the BB-2590 battery. We then transitioned the technology to a prototype BB-2590 HEESS. Hereafter we will incorporate our HEESS into a CWB to provide tactical advantages to the US soldier.

Identification & Significance of the Problem or Opportunity

Burden of Today's Soldier: Many electronic devices require high power, often pulse power, and high energy; a dichotomous pair that, until recently, required multiple energy storage devices. The high pulse power characteristics tend to compromise the life of high energy batteries. This necessitates inefficient oversizing of the battery and direct current-buss architecture. Alternatively, supercapacitors offer very high repetitive pulse power but historically suffer from very low energy density; this prohibits their sole use in many applications.

A BB-2590 (preferably conformable and wearable) hybrid energy storage architecture based on a supercapacitor, used to buffer/filter high rate pulse currents, and coupled to a high-energy battery is desirable. Such an energy storage device would provide power to the numerous mobile electronic devices carried by soldiers, thereby substantially reducing the soldier burden (**Figure 1**). This energy storage combination leads to a highly efficient storage device that maximizes energy density and offers pulse power characteristics (duty cycle). Thus, supercapacitors can serve as a complement to a battery energy source, which cannot repeatedly provide rapid power bursts. Supercapacitors are also capable of repetitive cycling (several hundreds of thousands of cycles) across a wide temperature range. This represents a tremendous potential to extend the life of current systems and reduce their mass. Substantial mass reductions are possible by the elimination of heating/cooling architectures. An ADA hybrid device further permits high charge currents for acceptance via an isolated supercapacitor, as opposed to a Li-ion battery. This is important because the performance safety of a Li-ion battery can be compromised when rapidly charged at a high SoC. A unique integration of the power system within the existing soldier load would further reduce the overall soldier burden. *A CWB-HEESS device that conformably couples the attributes of a Li-ion battery (high energy, low cost, etc.)*

with a supercapacitor (high power and specifically pulse power, long life, wide operational temperature range and safety -- especially during high charge currents), represents an unprecedented capability to provide US soldiers with unmatched safety and performance.

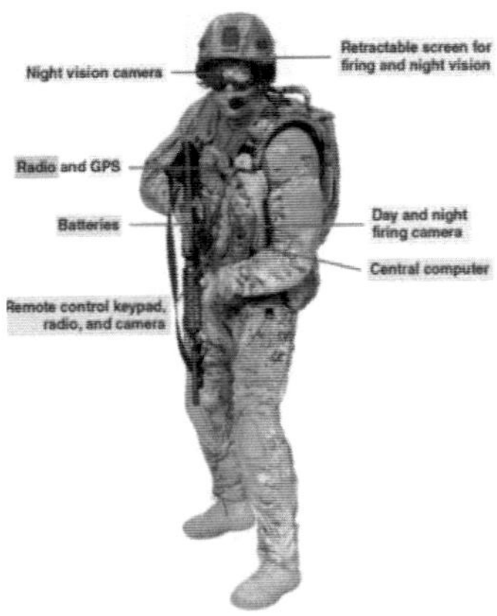

Figure 1. A modern soldier' electronic burden.

ADA HEESS Tech.

An ADA HEESS was conceptualized based on commercial high energy Li-ion battery cells, ADA high specific energy supercapacitor cells and a constant current regulator architecture. Analytical tools were used with empircal data inputs, leading to the predicted performance of a range of possible designs that represent an unprecedented combination of power (pulse power) and energy (*see* **Figure 2**). This results in the discreet isolation of each energy storage bank,[1] and the load. It also permits ADA HEESS performance tailorability charactercs, to address a range of applications. This is possible through design adjustments in the relative Li-ion/supercapacitor percentages to meet the specific pulse power requirement(s).

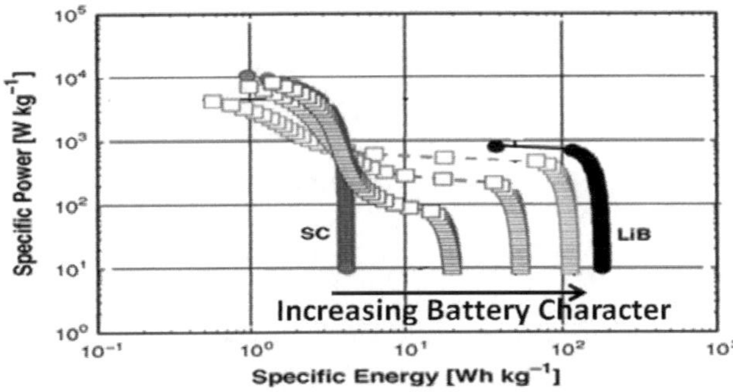

Figure 2. Ragone plot illustrating HEESS analytical model. Solid red profile depicts a supercapacitor (SC) and the solid black depicts a Li-ion battery (LiB).

ADA (and partners) defined three fundamental charge management policies: (1) a charge allocation from a power source to a set of EES banks,[2] (2) a charge replacement from EES banks to load devices[3] and (3) a charge migration between EES banks to improve the HEESS availability and responsiveness.[4] Optimal control policies based on convex optimization and heuristic search algorithms were derived.

We established effective logarithmic-time algorithms for HEESS fault detection and tolerance.[5] This led to the development of a state-of-health (SoH) joint charge management algorithm and HEESS models, leading to significant safety improvements.[6] This SoH model also provided meaningful extensions over prior SoH degradation models, which are limited to predictions for battery cycle life charge/discharge for arbitrary charge/discharge patterns. The models employ effective cycle decoupling techniques. SoH modeling provided a dynamic means to adjust charge allocation throughout life increasing the HEESS efficiency and safety characteristics.

The coupling of a high energy supercapacitor with a high energy Li-ion battery via a constant current regulator: (1) maximizes pulse power capability, (2) extends operational life, (3) maximizes operational temperature range and (4) maximizes safety characteristics. The device pulse power capability was enhanced with a higher energy supercapacitor. For example, ADA high specific energy supercapacitors that provide 10x the energy (15 – 20 Wh/kg, at cell level) of a commercial supercapacitor significantly improve the duty cycle—duration, magnitude and frequency of pulse characteristics. We can also tailor the energy storage banks and electronics architecture to a specific charge/discharge protocol to maximize capability.

ADA 20 F Supercapacitor

ADA developed and offers high energy supercapacitor electrodes and cells for large format applications. We demonstrated high specific energy (15 – 20 Wh/kg) supercapacitors with excellent rate and life cycle stability performance. Supercapacitor performance includes discharge capacity specific values of 88 – 92% at 1000 C rate and near complete capacity retention without fade for > 30,000 cycles.

ADA fabricated 20 F supercapacitor prototype cells (**Figure 3**) within a volume allotment for a commercial 10 F supercapacitor product. Our cells displayed more than double the capacitance, and more than triple the specific energy. We project an additional specific energy improvement of 2 – 4x will be achieved with cell material optimization and/or the selection of a high voltage electrolyte. This prototype development effort demonstrates the inherent potential of ADA supercapacitor technology.

Figure 3. An ADA 20 F supercapacitor prototype cell.

A rate evaluation of the ADA 20 F supercapacitor was performed in comparison to the 10 F commercial product (**Figure 4**). The ADA supercapacitor showed nearly double the capacitance at a lower mass than the commercial product. This led to a specific energy of 2 – 4x, which was rate dependent (as anticipated). The relatively high energy of the ADA supercapacitor was predicted to afford a substantial increase in pulse power capability.

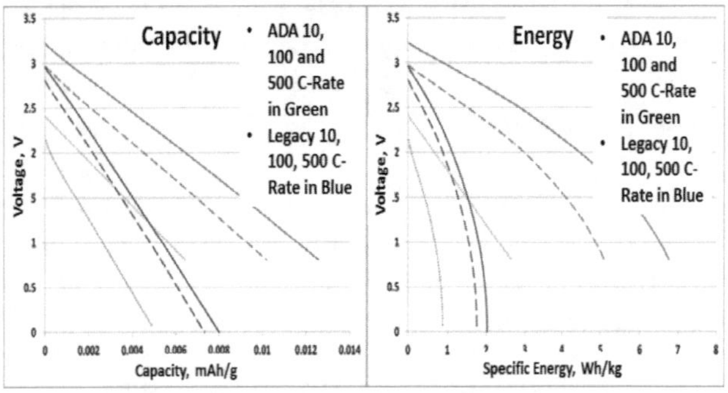

Figure 4. Rate comparison of the ADA 20 F supercapacitor (green) to commercial 10 F supercapacitor (blue); capacity (left) and specific energy (right) based data sets.

Design, Development and Demonstration of ADA High Energy Supercapacitors

ADA developed and optimized high energy supercapacitor electrodes and cells for large format applications. ADA demonstrated conformal nanoscale coatings on high surface area activated carbon (AC) powders and electrodes, which afford significantly improved supercapacitor behavior, when compared to pristine (*i.e.*, uncoated) materials.

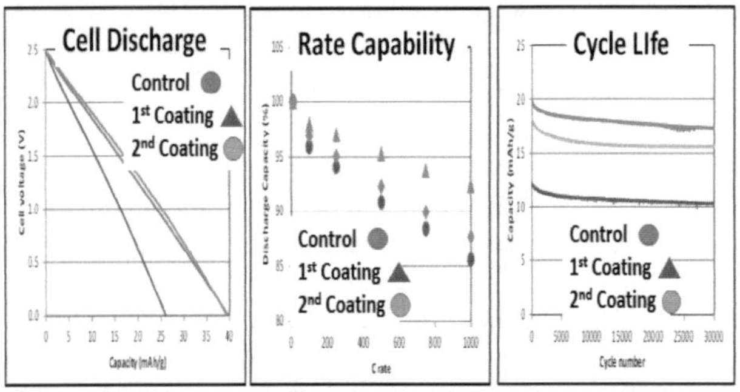

Figure 5. Summary of capacity (*left*), rate (*center*) and cycle life (*right*) data for electrodes fabricated from nano-coatings on high surface area AC powder.

Large Format Supercapacitors Based on BB-2590 Format

ADA designed and fabricated a large format, 280 mAh (325 F) supercapacitor cell (**Figure 6**, left). These cells were designed to fit efficiently within a BB-2590 enclosure. **Figure 6** (right) displays the cell discharge performance at various rates. This supercapacitor cell was observed to possess a specific energy of 11.5 Wh/kg at 10C rate, with little to no specific energy decrease with continuous rates up to 50C. Cell performance values were used to predict the performance of an ADA BB-2590 HEESS. The high capacitance and high power, including pulse and continuous, was predicted to yield significant HEESS pulse power. The design also included a large cell footprint with appreciable lead volume to efficiently dissipate joule heating generated from high currents.

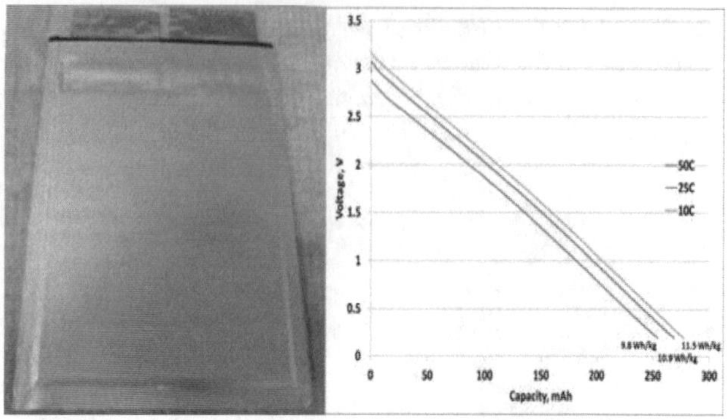

Figure 6. Supercapacitor (left) and discharge curves (right) for an ADA BB-2590 HEESS.

Demonstration of ADA BB-2590 HEESS

ADA developed an unprecedented performance BB-2590 HEESS. We paired custom, high-energy, large format Li-ion batteries and supercapacitors with a HEESS architecture to deliver a high energy (~ 160 Wh; comparable to the legacy ~ 200 Wh battery) pack with very high pulse power (> 100 Amps for up to 5 seconds; significant increase over 5 Amp limitation in legacy system). Our HEESS operates under the following principles (pictorially depicted in **Figure 7**, *left*):

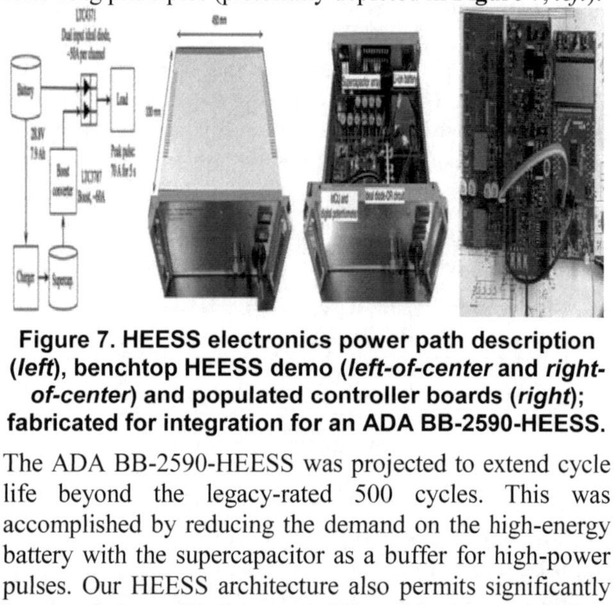

Figure 7. HEESS electronics power path description (*left*), benchtop HEESS demo (*left-of-center* and *right-of-center*) and populated controller boards (*right*); fabricated for integration for an ADA BB-2590-HEESS.

The ADA BB-2590-HEESS was projected to extend cycle life beyond the legacy-rated 500 cycles. This was accomplished by reducing the demand on the high-energy battery with the supercapacitor as a buffer for high-power pulses. Our HEESS architecture also permits significantly improved charge/discharge, enabling ubiquitous capability. We demonstrated all components in a benchtop setting, including the requisite electronics (**Figure 7,** center images) and energy storage devices (**Figure 6**).

Incorporation of HEESS Architecture into CWB

ADA (and partners) demonstrated the HEESS in a BB-2590 architecture. We also planned to extend this technology to deliver an enabling safe and high performance CWB-HEESS. The CWB-HEESS will incorporate three technologies to deliver an imperceptible, unprecedented power source to augment battlefield soldier' capabilities.

(1) CWB providing soldiers with ballistic-safe , ergonomic (comfort + maneuverability), power solution that reduces weight and the number of batteries for mission success.

(2) High-energy battery/supercapacitor banks manufactured using the ADA *Agile Manufacturing Environment*. Our supercapacitors currently incorporate ADA symmetric supercapacitors (~ 15 Wh/kg) with future systems to incorporate ADA asymmetric supercapacitors (~ 50 Wh/kg). The ADA *Agile Manufacturing Environment* affords custom (footprint/format, electrochemistry), energy storage offerings with high-throughput and agile, industrial automated equipment (IAE). ,

(3) HEESS to isolate energy storage banks, affording low continuous discharge + high pulse power.

We will advance legacy CWB products capabilities and extend cycle life while maximizing power delivery; this will be accomplished using custom high-energy storage banks.

Acknowledgements

The authors acknowledge the contributions and support of Dr. Ken K. Ho, Naval Facilities (NAVFAC; contract number N39430-14-C-1505) and Mr. David Chapman, Air Force Research Laboratories (AFRL; contract number FA9453-15-M-0493) in the development of the ADA high specific energy supercapacitor technology. We further acknowledge the contributions and support of Dr. Robert Mantz, Army Research Laboratories (ARL; contract number W911NF-15-P-0013) in the development of the ADA HEESS technology.

References

1. Siyu Yue, Di Zhu, Yanzhi Wang, Younghyun Kim, Naehyuck Chang and Massoud Pedram, "SIMES: A Simulator for Hybrid Electrical Energy Storage Systems," in Proceedings of IEEE/ACM International Symposium on Low Power Electronics and Design (ISLPED), pp. 33-38, 2013.
2. Q. Xie, Y. Wang, M. Pedram, Y. Kim, D. Shin, and N. Chang, “Charge replacement in hybrid electrical energy storage systems,” Proc. of Asia and South Pacific Design Automation Conference, Jan. 2012.
3. Y. Wang, X. Lin, Y. Kim, Q. Xie, M. Pedram, and N. Chang, “Sing-source, single-destination charge migration in hybrid electrical energy storage systems,” IEEE Trans. on VLSI Systems, vol. 22, no. 12, Dec. 2014, pp. 2752- 2765.
4. Y. Wang, X. Lin, M. Pedram, and N. Chang, “Online fault detection and fault tolerance in electrical energy storage systems,” Proc. of PES General Meeting, Jul. 2014, pp. 1-5.
5. Y. Wang, X. Lin, Q. Xie, N. Chang, and M. Pedram, “Minimizing state-of-health degradation in hybrid electrical energy storage systems with arbitrary source and load profiles,” Proc. of Design Automation & Test in Europe Conference & Exhibition, Mar. 2014, pp. 1-4.
6. Picture adapted from: D. Cericola, P.W. Ruch, R. Kötz, P. Novák, A. Wokau,n J. Power Sources, 195-9 (2010) 2731–2736, Simulation of a supercapacitor/Li-ion battery hybrid for pulsed applications.

Hybrid Energy Storage System for Tactical Microgrids

Frank W. Bohn, Joseph J. Vitale, Blane C. T. Wilson, David O. Teicher, Thomas F. Podlesak, Darren Z. Stephens, Michael L. Gonzalez, Stefan G. Siegfried, Bradley J. Stanley, Jaclyn A. Lynch

Communication, Electronics, Research and Development Engineering Center, US Army, Aberdeen Proving Ground, Maryland, USA, 21901

Abstract: *The US Army Communications, Electronics, Research and Development Engineering Center (CERDEC) Energy Informed Operations (EIO) Team has been investigating the use of energy storage systems on tactical microgrids in order to provide increased stability, reliability, efficiency, and resiliency. The team has integrated a battery storage device into the EIO Microgrid and demonstrated fuel savings and an increase in stability. Drawing on lessons learned from this battery storage integration, EIO has defined functionalities and capabilities necessary to fully realize an energy storage solution with customizable control for optimal use in any unique operation scenario. These functionalities and capabilities fed into requirements development for the Hybrid Resource Operational Energy Storage (HEROS). The HEROS system is a trailer mounted, hybrid battery and super-capacitor storage system with a capacity of 120kW 3 phase power at 208V. The HEROS system will be capable of responding to transients, shaving peak power, correcting power factor, and enabling operations such as silent watch. These capabilities will enable the HEROS system to drastically increase the stability, reliability, efficiency, and resiliency of the EIO Microgrid.*

Keywords: Energy Storage System; Supercapacitor; Battery; Microgrids; Tactical Microgrids; Power Quality; Controls; Power Management; Expeditionary; Generator; Efficiency; Microgrid Stability; Inverter; Mobility; Hybrid Power System; Hybrid Energy Storage System.

Background

The Energy Informed Operations (EIO) Microgrid was developed to increase the reliability, stability, and efficiency of the mobile Command Post (CP). The Army primarily uses spot generation where a single generator is placed at each set of loads based on peak-load and availability. Not only does this create a single point of failure, but the generators are frequently oversized and therefore run inefficiently and waste fuel. This suboptimal design is then repeated throughout the CP, lowering overall resilience. Along with increasing efficiency, reliability, and stability, the Army places great emphasis on enabling mobility. Putting a priority on mobility makes power solutions limited since complex infrastructures are not feasible.

In response to these issues, the EIO team developed the EIO Microgrid, an open source tactical microgrid capable of scaling from 60kW to 360kW. The microgrid includes a smart retrofit control kit for the diesel fueled 30kW and 60kW Tactical Quiet Generators (TQGs) that allows remote control through the EIO developed Intelligent Power Distribution (IPD) box. The EIO team developed a robust microgrid controller that monitors and controls all smart components on the microgrid. Each evolution of the EIO microgrid builds upon current functionality, eliminating points of failure and increasing sustainability in the field. These advances increase fuel savings and resiliency through optimized power generation and greater recovery algorithms that reduce the points of failures. The EIO Microgrid enables features such as load and source prioritization, load shedding, generator run-time optimization, prognostics and diagnostics, predictive algorithms, and a web-based application that increases situational awareness of the power associated with the command post.

Since the EIO Microgrid is small in scale with low inertia and since it must still comply with military frequency regulation, EIO choose to implement an isochronous/adaptive droop control strategy. In this strategy one generator acts as the isochronous, or grid-forming source and maintains the voltage and frequency of the microgrid at 208VAC and 60Hz, respectively. All other sources act as grid-following sources and are controlled though an adaptive droop algorithm that adjusts the frequency set point of each droop generator in order to control output power based on a predefined droop curve. This control strategy allows the frequency to remain at 60Hz and maintains power quality within the specifications outlined in MIL-STD-1332B [1].

One particular weakness of the grid identified through testing is the inability to maintain stability during large load changes. When large loads, such as environmental control units, turn on and off, they create a large transient response in the isochronous source and cause a frequency and voltage ripple. In response, the output of the droop sources fluctuate, further exacerbating the problem. Typically, the microgrid can stabilize, but on occasion, large transients have resulted in microgrid failure.

Introduction

One solution that EIO has implemented for this instability is the use of a battery storage system as the microgrid's isochronous source. EIO did this during an operational technology demonstration in 2016. The microgrid consisted of two 60kWand two 30 kW TQG's and the

Hybrid Energy System Rugged Energy Storage Containment Unit (HES-RESCU), a 60kW/106kWh inverter/battery system. The HES-RESCU was a ruggedized Tricon container that housed lead acid batteries, controls, and a prototype EPC Power inverter. The system was unable to be controlled by the microgrid controller and thus charged and discharged based on its internal control algorithm. The four generators were all placed in grid-following mode and were controlled though the microgrid controller. Even though the microgrid controller was not able to further optimize the HES-RESCU charge/discharge algorithm, the HES-RESCU still provided increased fuel savings and increased stability and resiliency, as the microgrid was able to handle a very large and frequent transient load. Although the HES-RESCU could be redesigned for mobile operations, the performance of a battery storage device integrated into the EIO microgrid led the EIO team to development requirements for a more ruggedized, intelligent, and mobile energy storage system that could seamlessly operate with the EIO Microgrid, reduce fuel consumption, and increase stability and resiliency.

Requirements

One of the three priorities of the Chief of Staff of the Army is to develop and enable the Future Fight and create an agile and adaptive Army [2]. From EIO's perspective, this is accomplished by further increasing the reliability, stability, adaptability, mobility, and ability of the EIO Microgrid components to be field ready. EIO's power and control expertise, matched with lessons learned from demonstrations allowed EIO to develop requirements for a hybrid energy storage system (HESS), some of which are summarized below:

1. Ability to operate in isochronous mode (while charging and discharging) and droop mode
2. Utilize both batteries and super-capacitors
3. Output power of 30kW with peak up to 60kW
4. Battery capacity exceeding 25kWh and super-capacitor capacity exceeding 2.5kWh
5. Configurable control architecture to allow the user to change the way the system responds in various scenarios

Hybrid Energy Storage – The batteries and super-capacitors both play an important role for a future HESS on the EIO Microgrid because of their different characteristics. The Army and Department of Defense have previously invested in battery based energy storage systems because of their high energy density. Battery energy storage systems allow for a large energy backup and can power loads for hours at a time. Research and development continues to increase energy density and manufacturability, and decrease costs of these battery systems.

Super-capacitors are about ten times more power dense than batteries. This can lead to a drastic weight reduction in scenarios where high power for short duration is needed. Super-capacitors also are capable of rapid charging and can charge at a higher rate than batteries. Super-capacitors also have a long cycle life, on the order of one-million cycles, compared to batteries which are on the order of one-thousand cycles. Most importantly, super-capacitors are well suited to respond to transients in power and improve the power quality of the microgrid overall [3].

By combining the capabilities of batteries and super-capacitors, EIO can increase the life of the system by utilizing the batteries for long duration charging and discharging and the super-capacitors for short-term transient response [3]. This combination also provides the possibility of eliminating transient power oscillations from the microgrid [4]. The use of a hybrid energy storage system will increase the efficiency, power quality, reliability and stability of the EIO Microgrid.

Test System – One of the most important requirements for the HESS is having a configurable control architecture to allow the system to serve as a robust test system. EIO will use the system to perform a wide variety of tests to determine the optimal controls and configuration that provide the greatest benefit to the microgrid. The depth of knowledge gained from this system will allow EIO to provide expertise and guidance to optimized future energy storage system acquisitions.

Use Cases

Integrating a HESS with the EIO Microgrid will increase the capability of the microgrid to respond to transients, allow for new capabilities, such as peak-shaving and silent operations, and ultimately increase the stability, reliability, and efficiency of the microgrid.

Transient Response – The tactical microgrid can have a number of large loads that cycle on and off very often. This quick load change causes a ripple in the frequency and voltage throughout the microgrid. This ripple can affect the performance of loads and can also adversely affect other sources on the microgrid. A HESS will be used to more effectively respond to these load changes, since it has a response quicker than a traditional diesel generator and will have minimal overshoot or undershoot. In order to effectively respond to these transients, the system will need to be the grid-forming source. As such, it will immediately respond to any change in load, while the grid-following generators on the microgrid will remain stable at the same output. The microgrid controller will then decide how to respond to the change in load. Depending on the current load, number and capacity of generators running, and state-of-charge of both the batteries and super-capacitors, the microgrid controller will transition the load to or from the hybrid energy storage system. Increasing the microgrid's capability to handle transient loads is important to maintain power quality and stability, however it becomes even more important as future systems are developed that have pulse power requirements.

Peak Shaving – A HESS will increase the efficiency of the microgrid through the use of peak-shaving techniques. This functionality can be utilized while the system is in either grid-forming or grid-following mode. With coordination from the microgrid controller, the HESS will be able to reduce the fuel consumed by the diesel generators by charging and discharging the batteries at optimal times. The microgrid controller will have the system charge in order to increase the generators' output to its peak efficiency point. On the other hand, if the generators are minimally loaded, the microgrid controller will have the HESS discharge and allow a generator to turn off. Charging and discharging the system at optimal times will greatly increase fuel efficiency of the microgrid.

Silent Operations – A HESS will allow the microgrid to operate in a silent operations mode. When a unit's mission requires silence, the microgrid can turn off all of the diesel generators and continue to maintain power to critical loads through the HESS. This capability helps keep the unit from being audibly detected by an adversary.

Power Factor Correction – A HESS will be able to provide power factor correction and further improve power quality of the microgrid. Many loads in a command post are inductive in nature and result in a non-unity power factor. The super-capacitors will effectively provide a filtering capability and move the power factor closer to unity. This will ultimately reduce the stress on the generators and increase fuel efficiency.

A hybrid energy storage system will enable a new suite of capabilities for the EIO microgrid that will ensure stability, decrease fuel usage, and increase mission effectiveness.

HEROS

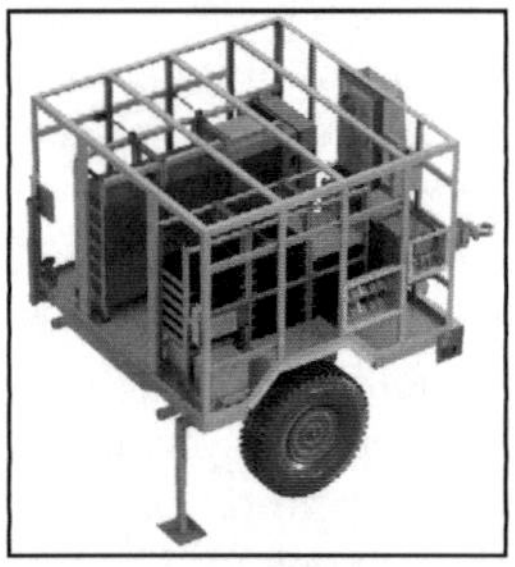

Figure 1. HEROS System Overview

The previously stated requirements and use cases were the basis for the development of the Hybrid Energy Resource Operational Storage (HEROS) system. The HEROS system is a HMMWV towable hybrid energy storage system comprised of both super-capacitor and battery storage.

The HEROS system operates at 208V 3-Phase AC. The system is capable of outputting up to 120kW, 60kW from the battery and 60kW from the super-capacitor. The storage capacity of the batteries is 29.3kWh and the capacity of the super-capacitor is 2.6kWh. This power is output through two bi-directional inverters to two sets of output ports. The HEROS system will be capable of operating in both grid-forming and grid-following mode and will be able to communicate with the EIO Microgrid controller in order to receive commands and send important system status updates.

Inverter – The HEROS system uses two bi-directional AC/DC inverters. Each inverter is capable of outputting 72kW at 208Vrms with a peak efficiency greater than 97 percent. Each inverter will connect to the battery modules and the super-capacitor modules independently and will connect on the output side to the same AC bus. The inverters are liquid cooled and operate between -20C to 40C, with derating between 40C and 60C. The inverters use a proprietary software to allow them to coordinate their outputs, but have an external CAN control interface to communicate with the rest of the HEROS system and the microgrid.

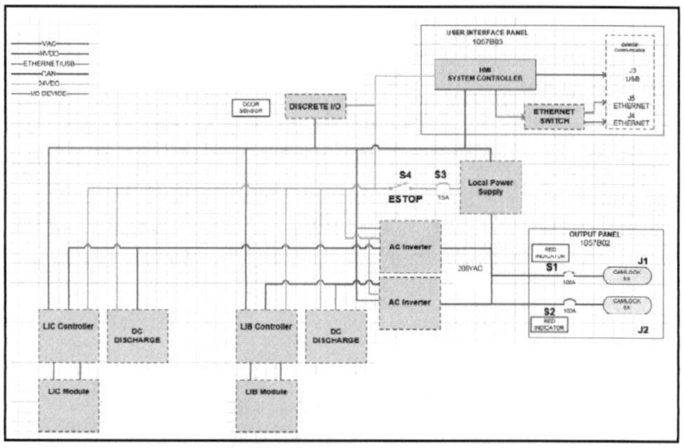

Figure 2. HEROS System Block Diagram

The inverters operate in three modes: grid forming, grid following, and generator emulation. Grid forming allows the inverters to be the stiff, isochronous voltage source. Grid following allows the inverters to receive real and reactive power commands from the microgrid controller. Generator emulation mode will put the inverter into droop control and will allow the droop setting to be changed. Setting the droop setpoint to 0 allows the inverter to emulate isochronous controls and allows the inverter to charge the batteries and super-capacitors while maintaining the microgrid voltage and frequency.

Modular Design – The batteries and super-capacitors in the HEROS systems are designed as modules to allow for easy access when replacing components. Each module is also complete with a sensor board allowing temperature sensing, available reserve charge gauging, communication connector sensing, cell sensing and balancing, and individual cell voltage monitoring. The system is comprised of a total of twenty super-capacitor modules and twenty battery modules, as well as a modular super-capacitor controller, a modular battery controller, and two modular DC discharge devices.

Super-Capacitor Modules – The lithium ion super-capacitors are built specifically for the HEROS system. Each module will be have an 8S4P configuration and will have a rated voltage of 24V and a total capacity of 41.6Ah. Together, the super-capacitor bank has a rated voltage of 480V and a total capacity of 2.6kWh.

Battery Modules – The battery modules consist of Lithium Iron Phosphate (LiFePO4) Energy Cells. Each module has a 6S20P configuration with a rated voltage of 19.8V and capacity of 74Ah. Together, the battery bank has a rated voltage of 396V and a total capacity of 29.3kWh.

Communications – The internal HEROS intra-device communication makes use of a high-speed Controller Area Network (CAN) bus. This CAN bus permits the exchange of control and diagnostic messages among the inverters, local power supply, battery and super-capacitor controllers, and the human-machine interface (HMI) system controller. Typical signaling messages provide for the charging and discharging of energy storage devices, regulation of inverter output, and status information.

Externally, HEROS exposes a SunSpec interface; an industry standard developed by the SunSpec Alliance solar and distributed energy resource trade group. SunSpec specifies the data models and communications protocols for the control and monitoring of compliant distributed energy systems. The models used by HEROS include 1 Common, 16 Simple IP Network, 103 Inverter (Three Phase), 802 Battery Base Model, and 804 Lithium-Ion String Model. These models are then mapped to Modbus registers exposed over an Ethernet TCP/IP connection [5].

Future Plans

Moving forward EIO plans to incorporate the HEROS system into the EIO Microgrid and understand the benefit it can provide. A test campaign has been devised to determine the optimal set points and parameters to operate in various operational scenarios and microgrid configurations. Microgrid controller development will continue in order to fully implement the functionalities and use cases of the HEROS system. Controller development will also include the development of a SunSpec to Tactical Microgrid Standard (TMS) adapter to permit interoperability with military microgrid systems. The TMS is being developed by the Tactical Microgrid Standards Consortium (TMSC) lead by the US Army Corps of Engineers' Engineering Research and Development Center (ERDC) Construction Engineering Research Laboratory (CERL) [6].

EIO intends to bring the HEROS system to field demonstrations and evaluations. The system brings new capabilities to the field that should be tested in various operational environments to validate expectations and assumptions. The HEROS system, being an inverter based source, would be ideal for microgrid demonstrations at both a traditional basecamp and in a mobile environment. At a basecamp level, it is important to show HEROS ability to improve microgrid power quality under operational conditions. In a mobile, ad-hoc environment, the HEROS capability can be fully exercised through adapting to load demand situations by leveraging both super capacitor and batteries. Demonstrations not only provide technical feedback on how to better integrate, tailor, and advance the technology, but also gives Soldiers the opportunity to experience technology solutions and inform research and development to enable a more effective, superior tactical product.

EIO will apply lessons learned from working with the HEROS system to future procurements of energy storage systems. An in-depth understanding of the important components and control parameters will be paramount for the development of future systems.

CERDEC is helping to enable the next generation of warfighters by providing high quality power, increased microgrid stability, and increased soldier effectiveness.

Acknowledgements

We would like to acknowledge UEC, as the developer of the HEROS system, for providing information and guidance. We would like to acknowledge Terrill Atwater for his help and expertise on batteries and super-capacitors. We would like to acknowledge Lawrence Valencourt from CECOM safety for providing guidance with the development of the HEROS system.

References

1. Department of Defense, MIL-STD-1332B, "Definitions of Tactical, Prime, Precise, and Utility Terminologies for Classification of the DOD Mobile Electric Power Engine Generator Set Family," 13 March 1973.
2. General Mark A. Milley, "39th Chief of Staff of the Army Initial Message to Army."
3. Huang Wei, Wang Xin, Guo Jianhua, Yang Jingyan, "Discussion on Application of Super capacitor Energy Storage System in Microgrid" Sustainable IEEE Power Generation and Std Supply Conference 2009.
4. Dehua Zheng, Dan Wei, Wei Zhang, Zhaojun Meng, "The Study of Supercapacitor' Transient Power Quality Improvement on Microgrid," IEEE PowerTech 2015 Eindhoven, Netherlands.
5. SunSpec Alliance, "SunSpec Technology Overview, v1.4, Document #12040," https://sunspec.org.
6. Department of Defense, MIL-STD-TMS, "Tactical Microgrid Standard," 23 March 2018, In Preparation, 2018.

Bidirectional Power Flow Control in Portable Hybrid Power Source for Pulsed Power Applications

Kyle G. Waterman, Joseph P. Tudino, Dr. Raymond B. Sepe

Electro Standards Laboratories
36 Western Industrial Drive
Cranston, RI 02921-3403

Contact Author Email: kwaterman@lab.electrostandards.com/1-401-943-1164

Abstract: *Investigation and development of portable hybrid systems have come into focus as peak power requirements of portable pulsed power applications have grown above capabilities of practical battery-only systems. A hybrid system has been developed that operates using an energy dense lithium ion battery and power dense lithium ion capacitor facilitated by power electronics and feedback controls. The utility of the existing hybrid system has been augmented through an improved algorithm and modified circuitry that support bidirectional power flow. This expands the capability of the system to act as both a source and portable energy harvesting device in the field. The hybrid system minimizes stress on the batteries by supplying or absorbing pulsed power required by the load resulting in greater power capability and extended lifetime.*

Keywords: hybrid; power; energy; portable; lithium ion; battery; capacitor; converter; bidirectional; feedback; controller; pulsed applications; sourcing; harvesting.

Introduction:

Problem

There is a general need for portable power sources that support pulsed power applications. Pulsed power applications are defined as those which exhibit a peak power pulse for a short duration followed by a low power draw over a longer duration. Typically, battery-only approaches are used to support these types of loads however, as peak power requirements increase, additional battery packs are required to satisfy the peak condition. This presents a logistics problem as costs rise, especially with single use primary type chemistries. Additionally, for applications utilizing portable power sources to operate equipment in the field, weight and volume burden may be exacerbated leading to decreased mobility and effectiveness. To address these concerns, hybrid power solutions have been developed that seek to improve system power density while maintaining sufficient levels of energy density.

Previous Work

Previous work conducted in battery hybridization yielded a system that integrated a lithium ion capacitor (LiC) and power electronics with a primary type lithium ion battery (LiB) [1]. The power electronics matched the LiC voltage to the battery voltage at the system bus level. A feedback controller was implemented that regulated the rate of energy out of the LiB in the presence of pulsed power loads maintaining the LiB within its regions of highly efficient operation. Doing so reduces battery stress and increases lifetime energy delivery. The LiC supplemented the additional power required during peak loads and was recharged by the LiB during times of low power draw. The power electronics circuitry and processor are implemented on the hybrid power management circuit board (HPMCB) shown in Figure 1 with the LiC mounted.

Figure 1: Hybrid Power Management Circuit Board with LiC Mounted

The system was shown to provide benefit with LiCFx/MnO2 primary chemistries by increasing power capability and therefore deliverable energy as well as reducing battery operating temperature. To build upon these previous successes and improve system utility, bidirectional power flow capability has been investigated and implemented in the hybrid system presented here.

Motivation

Bidirectional power flow is the ability to control the flow of energy into and out of each of the elements of the system, namely, the LiB, LiC, and device connected to the hybrid interface. Motivations for developing this functionality include integration of rechargeable battery chemistries in hybrid systems for pulsed power applications and also to influence the rechargeable battery design process. Currently, battery design consists of finding middle ground between satisfying power and energy requirements as they exhibit an inverse relationship. An increase in active material improves capacity but increases internal resistance and therefore reduces power capability. Decreasing active material reduces internal resistance improving power capability but sacrifices energy density. Designing batteries for hybridization allows for power requirements to be minimized allowing for energy optimization. Secondly, incorporating rechargeable cells into portable hybrid solutions implies cost reduction as both the energy dense LiB and the power dense LiC, are reusable. The integration of bidirectional power flow control also implies an added use case in the hybrid's ability to harvest energy. This capability proves useful especially in the case of mobile applications, as energy reserves may be replenished in the field. Specifically, the hybridization allows the system to harvest both constant and pulsed energy from incoming sources. Battery-only approaches to portable power are restricted to operate within the battery's capabilities as the battery is directly coupled to the external device. Multiple benefits in terms of utility may be realized through rechargeable batteries hybridized with a LiC.

Advanced Hybrid Algorithm

To facilitate bidirectional power flow between the load and the hybrid device, another layer of abstraction has been developed and is applied above the feedback controller. The algorithm termed the Advanced Hybrid Algorithm (AHA) is composed of several components that process system information and make decisions about hybrid operation. Figure 2 displays the flow and relationship between the components of the AHA where inputs are system measurements and outputs are converter control and hardware configuration signals. Several management system structures within the algorithm serve the purpose of monitoring the energy elements of the system through measurements to determine their state and other metrics such as health and stress. The management systems are composed of the energy management system (EMS), power management system (PMS), and hardware management system (HMS).

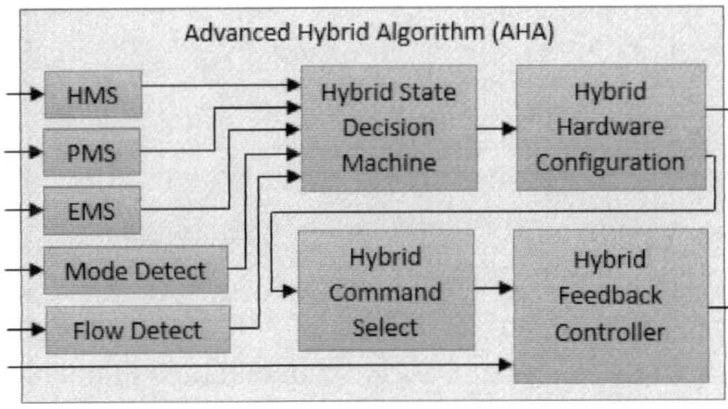

Figure 2: Advanced Hybrid Algorithm Flow

The EMS monitors the energy dense element of the system, typically the battery. The PMS monitors the power dense element of the system usually the super capacitor. The energy and power dense elements are not restricted to a battery and super capacitor, respectively. The device selection will be application dependent and may consist of any combination of energy or power devices such as two batteries of different chemistry types. The hybrid power management board power electronics circuitry design allows for this freedom in selection. Lastly, the HMS monitors the hardware to ensure conditions present in the electronics circuitry are within acceptable ranges. In addition to the management systems is the detection and decision machines. The detection components monitor conditions present at the hybrid interface to determine the appropriate mode of operation. The decision machine uses management system information and detection results to determine the appropriate hybrid state. The hybrid state defines how the hardware should be configured and how the feedback controller should operate. The resulting system is capable of determining whether the system should operate as a source or sink depending on conditions.

Test Setup, Procedures, and Results:

Test Setup

Initial testing was conducted to evaluate the performance of the algorithm under various modes of operation An Arbin cycler system was utilized for testing. The cycler performed as an external sink and source connected to the hybrid interface. Figure 3 shows an overview of the hybrid system and all of the major components of the HPMCB.

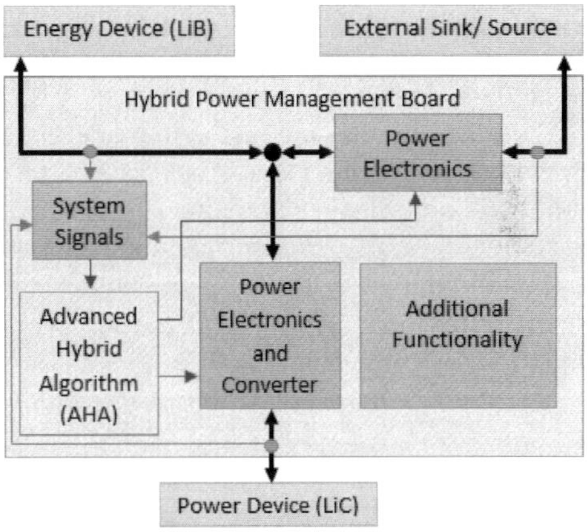

Figure 3: Hybrid System Overview

Commercially available LG18650MJ1 rechargeable LiB cells were used to create a 4 series 2 parallel (4S2P) battery pack. The cells feature some of the highest energy density in terms of commercial rechargeable chemistries. To evaluate the algorithm and demonstrate bidirectional power flow, the battery pack was connected to the input of the HPMCB through modified cabling that allowed for in line current measurements to be taken. The output of the hybrid power management board or hybrid interface was connected to the Arbin cycler. System measurements were captured using a DataQ data acquisition unit where battery current, hybrid current, battery voltage, hybrid voltage, and super capacitor voltage were recorded. The hybrid voltage and current are defined as those quantities measured at the output of the hybrid power management board. As a convention negative current represents charge leaving the LiB or LiC and entering the load and positive current represents charge entering LiB or LiC and leaving the load.

Hybrid Pulsed Discharge with the Load as a Sink

Pulsed discharge testing was conducted to verify the AHA's ability to operate the hybrid as a source. The pulsed discharge profile consisted of the Arbin sinking a 1 minute -2A pulse followed by a 6 minute -0.5A draw period. The test was designed to allow the hybrid to enter a discharge state that utilized both the LiC and the LiB to support the pulsed load demand. The controller was programmed to regulate the battery current to -1A such that the remaining power would be provided by the LiC. During the low power draw the hybrid enters a state in which the battery supports both the load and the recharge of the LiC in preparation of future peak pulses. The power management algorithm maintains the battery within its optimal discharging current range by utilizing the LiC to supply outgoing pulsed power. Figure 4 shows results from this testing. The behavior of the hybrid system during this test can be characterized by three distinct regions. In region 1, the load demands -2A, which is greater in magnitude than the LiB's -1A regulation point. The LiC provides the remaining -1A to the load. This is shown in that the LiB and LiC voltages both steadily decrease as they provide energy to the load. In region 2, the load demands -0.5A. Since the LiC is below its charge limit, and the load draw is lower than the LiB's regulation point, the LiB provides energy to both handle the load and recharge the LiC. This is shown in that the LiB voltage steadily decreases and the LiC voltage steadily increases. In region 3, the load is still demanding -0.5A, but the LiC has reached its charge limit, as shown by its voltage remaining constant. The LiC disconnects from the system, directly coupling the LiB to the load. The LiB provides -0.5A to the load. Note that the LiB current magnitude is always maintained within its commanded regulation point.

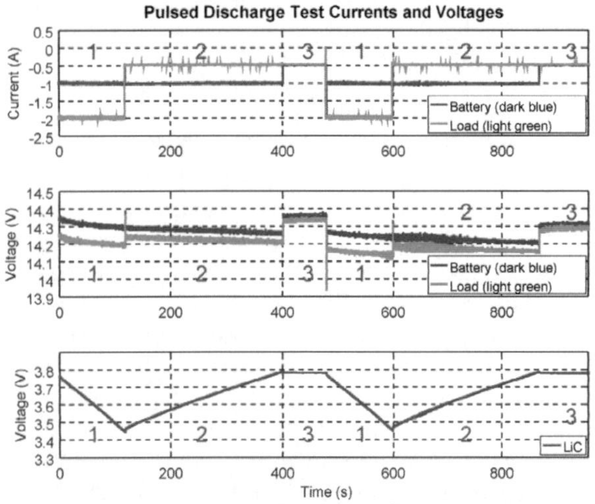

Figure 4: Pulsed Discharge Test Results

Hybrid Pulsed Charge with the Load as a Source

Pulsed charge testing utilizes the addition of bidirectional power flow capability. To demonstrate this mode of operation a pulsed charge test consisted of a 1 minute 2A pulse followed by a 6 minute 0.5A pull period. The test was designed to allow the hybrid to enter a charge state that utilized both the LiC and LiB to harvest the incoming peak pulse from the Arbin. The controller was programmed to regulate the battery current to 1A such that the remaining power would be absorbed by the super capacitor. During the low power pull portion, the hybrid enters a state in which the battery receives energy from both the external source and the LiC in order to drain the LiC in preparation of future incoming peak pulses. The power management algorithm maintains the battery within its optimal charging current range by utilizing the LiC to absorb incoming pulsed power. Figure 5 shows results from this testing. The behavior of the hybrid system during this test can be characterized by three distinct regions. In region 1, the load provides 2A, which is greater than the LiB's 1A regulation point. The LiC absorbs the remaining 1A from the load. This is shown in that the LiB and LiC voltages both steadily increase as they absorb energy from the load. In region 2, the load provides 0.5A. Since the LiC is above its discharge limit, and the current provided by the load is lower than the LiB's regulation point, the LiB absorbs energy from both the load and the LiC. This is shown in that the LiB voltage steadily increases and the LiC voltage steadily decreases. In region 3, the load is still providing 0.5A but the LiC has reached its discharge limit, as shown by its voltage remaining constant. The LiC disconnects from the system, directly coupling the LiB to the load. The LiB absorbs 0.5A from the load. Note that the LiB current is always maintained within its commanded regulation point.

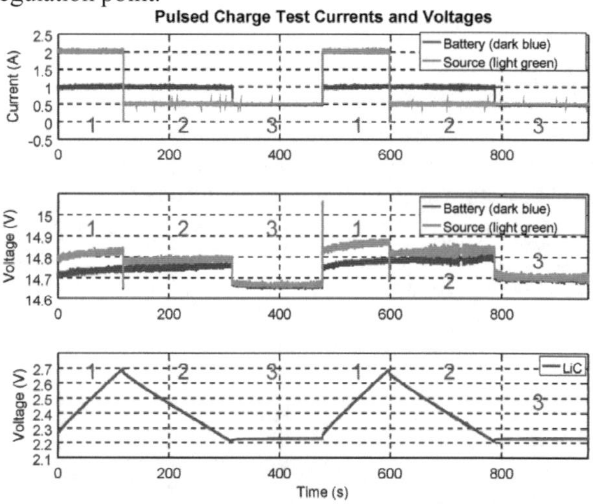

Figure 5: Pulsed Charge Test Results

Hybrid Bidirectional Mode with Sinking/Sourcing Load

To evaluate the AHA for continuous bidirectional operation, the pulsed discharge and pulsed charge test conditions were combined to create an alternating profile. The profile forces the algorithm to actively and correctly determine the appropriate operating state and configure the hardware properly. The discharge and charge conditions followed the same levels and time durations as described in the previous sections in the following order: low draw discharge, pulsed discharge, pulsed charge, low pull charge. This testing demonstrates the ability of the hybrid system to both source and harvest energy. The power management algorithm maintains the battery within its optimal charging and discharging current range creating an operating envelope by utilizing the LiC to absorb and source pulsed power from the load. Figure 6 shows results from this testing. The behavior of the hybrid system during this test can be characterized by four distinct regions. In region 1, the load demands -0.5A.

Like in the pulsed discharge test, the LiB provides its regulation point current of -1A which both supports the load and recharges the LiC. In region 2, the load demands -2A. Like in the pulsed discharge test, the LiB provides -1A and the capacitor makes up the remaining -1A to support the load. In region 3, the load provides 2A. Like in the pulsed charge test, the LiB absorbs 1A and the capacitor absorbs the remaining 1A. In region 4, the load provides 0.5A. Like in the pulsed charge test, the LiB absorbs 0.5A from the load and 0.5A from the discharging LiC. Note how during the test the LiB is always within its regulation point of 1A magnitude.

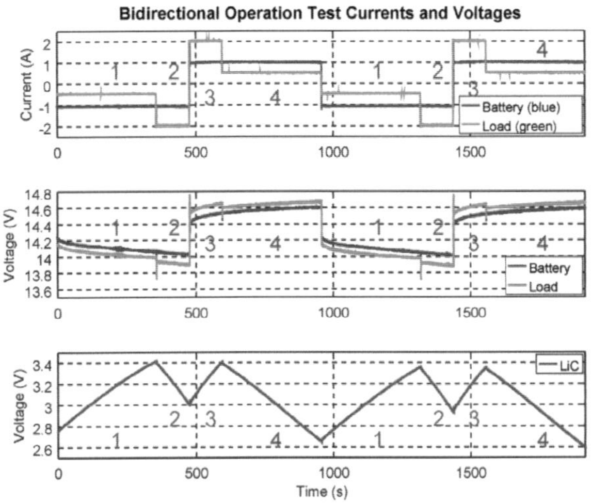

Figure 6: Bidirectional Operation Test Results

Hybrid Overloaded Discharge

An additional condition was tested to evaluate an operating state that allows for continued automated operation for unknown or unpredictable conditions at the hybrid interface. In this scenario a constant load greater than the battery operating point is continuously applied to the hybrid system. Given the conditions the LiC will eventually run out of charge to support the power requirements above the battery threshold. This forces the hybrid to periodically disconnect from the load and recharge the LiC internally before reconnecting to the load to continue operation. The mode eliminates need for user input and allows for tuning to minimize system downtime. Hybrid overloaded charge not shown here is the dual of this operating state. Figure 7 shows results from this testing. The behavior of the hybrid system during this test can be characterized by two distinct regions. In region 1, the load demands -2A, which is greater in magnitude than the LiB's -1A regulation point. Since the LiC is above its discharge limit, it provides the remaining -1A to the load. This is shown in that the both LiB and LiC voltages steadily decrease as they provide energy to the load. In region 2, the load still demands -2A, but the LiC has reached its discharge limit. Since the load is demanding a higher magnitude current than the LiB's regulation point, and the LiC can discharge no further, the hybrid system disconnects from the load. During this time, the LiB provides -1A to charge the LiC. This is shown by the LiB voltage decreasing as the LiC voltage is increasing. Once the LiC absorbs a significant amount of power for the application, the load is reconnected and the system provides power from the LiB and LiC to the load as in region 1. Note that during this test, the LiB current is always -1A.

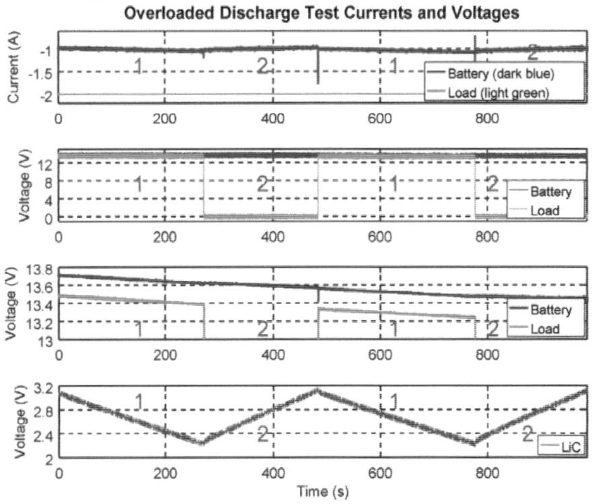

Figure 7: Overloaded Discharge Test Results

Conclusions and Implications

The AHA testing for bidirectional power flow capability successfully demonstrates the versatility of the portable hybrid power source solution presented. The hybrid device paired with the algorithm demonstrates the ability of the system to support both pulsed power discharge loads and pulsed power charge waveforms entering the system. The capability presents the potential for this hybrid device to act as a power source and as a portable energy harvesting device creating potential for use in a variety of pulsed power applications. Bidirectional support implies the hybrid's ability to operate with both primary and now secondary chemistries. In coordination with the work presented here, testing has begun to evaluate performance in rechargeable chemistries under battery only and hybrid conditions. Initial results have shown significant benefit in terms of energy delivered and recovered on a cycle by cycle basis. Results imply more efficient operation with hybridization of rechargeable chemistries and therefore significant improvement can be expected in terms of total energy delivered over cycle lifetime. Investigation and development continue towards full system level performance evaluation of rechargeable chemistry hybridization.

Acknowledgements

We would like to thank the Army for continued support in our portable hybrid power systems research.

References

Smith, P.H., Sepe, R. B., Waterman, K. G., Myron, J. L., "Development and analysis of a lithium carbon monofluoride battery- lithium ion capacitor hybrid system for high pulse-power applications ," *Journal of Power Sources*, vol. 327, pp. 495-506, Sept 2016.

5 V Phosphate Lithium-ion Cathode

Jan L. Allen, Samuel A. Delp, Jeff Wolfenstine and T. Richard Jow
Electrochemistry Branch, Sensor and Electron Devices Directorate
US Army Research Laboratory
Adelphi, Maryland, USA, 20783
jan.l.allen8.civ@mail.mil / 1-301-394-0291

Abstract: *With the rising need for higher energy batteries that are safe, 4.8 V $LiCoPO_4$ has emerged as a promising Li-ion cathode material which can deliver 800 Wh kg-1, almost 40% greater than commercialized $LiFePO_4$. Moreover, phosphate based cathodes may provide safety relative to high voltage oxides owing to the strong covalent P-O bond. However unmodified $LiCoPO_4$ has low intrinsic electronic conductivity and suffers a severe capacity fade upon multiple charge – discharge cycles owing to structure deterioration and electrolyte decomposition. Carbon coating has addressed the low electronic conductivity, partial cobalt substitution has been used to address both the capacity fade and the electrolyte decomposition. Additionally, new electrolyte formulations and additives have further increased the cycle life and discharge capacity. This paper will review our most recent efforts on LiCoPO4 electrode development and scale-up for improving the energy and abuse tolerance of Li-ion batteries. We will discuss synthesis, transport measurements, electronic structure and substitutional chemistry of $LiCoPO_4$ as well the initial scaled-up synthesis results.*

Keywords: Li-ion; cathode; 5 V; LiCoPO4; positive electrode

Introduction

The energy that can be stored in a battery is a product of its capacity and its voltage, thus $LiCoPO_4$ with a discharge voltage of about 4.8 V will provide about 40% improvement in energy stored relative to $LiFePO_4$ which has a similar capacity but a discharge voltage of only 3.5 V. $LiCoPO_4$ is compared to commercial Li-ion battery cathode materials in table 1 showing its potential as a high energy density Li-ion battery cathode. $LiFePO_4$ has been commercialized and its most noteworthy property is its abuse tolerance leading to high safety. However, its low discharge voltage considerably reduces the energy density. This provides strong motivation to work on the isostructural, higher voltage members of this family of compounds. $LiMnPO_4$ for example has a discharge voltage of 4.1 V [1]. $LiCoPO_4$ displays a voltage of 4.8V [2] and LiNiPO4 is a 5.1 V cathode [3]. The large enhancement in energy density of the higher voltage olivines provides strong motivation for effort to overcome the challenges to operating a $LiCoPO_4$ cathode at 5 V versus Li, a regime where electrolyte is unstable and the material itself can undergo loss of oxygen thus leading to capacity fade. The road to reaching this goal is long but we have come a long way towards addressing the challenges through substitutional chemistry of $LiCoPO_4$ to replace some of cobalt with Fe, Cr and Si which modifies the electronic structure to stabilize the charged state of the cathode material and reduces the reactivity with the electrolyte [4,5]. We have further explored novel electrolyte formulations which use either a new solvent or an additive which works at the surface of the electrode to stabilize the electrolyte [6]. At the lab scale we achieve greater 140 mAh g^{-1} capacity at an average discharge voltage of 4.8 V versus Li with stable cycling. The synthesis has been scaled to kilogram level and its performance has been tested in full cells versus a graphite anode [7]. Our work on understanding the electronic structural similarities and difference among the family of $LiMPO_4$ where M=Fe, Mn, Co and Ni has laid the groundwork for an approach to improvement of the properties of $LiCoPO_4$ [8]. In this work, the complete olivine series were synthesized and the valence band XPS spectra was recorded. These spectra were then compared to the computed spectra derived from the electronic structure calculated from density functional theory (DFT), thereby validating the model. Three main points were learned. First, the electronic conductivity arises from polarons. Electronic conductivity is achieved through hopping of a polaron which is a positive charge localized on the transition metal, a local M^{3+}, from site to site through the crystal. Second, the character at the valence band maximum, strongly affects the nature of the material upon delithiation (oxidation of the transition metal). Ideally, the Fe, Mn, Co or Ni undergoes an oxidation from formal divalency in $LiMPO_4$ to trivalency in MPO_4. Indeed, in the case of $LiFePO_4$, where the valence band maximum (VBM) shows a strong electronic contribution from the Fe d-orbitals a clear redox occurs on the transition metal. However, the valence band maximum shows an increasing oxygen 2p-orbital contribution as we move from Fe to Co to Mn to Ni. In the case of Ni, the overwhelming amount of oxygen 2p-orbital contribution precludes the formation of the localized state required to form a polaron charge carrier. The greater portion of oxygen like character at the VBM is more likely to lead to loss of oxygen during the charge rather than a redox reaction at the transition metal. This is the basis of the intrinsic instability of $CoPO_4$ and leads to its well known capacity fade [9-11]. Third, the mobility of the polaronic charge carrier was used to evaluate the differences in electronic conductivity. $LiFePO_4$ was found to be the most conductive, followed by $LiCoPO_4$ and $LiMnPO_4$. The poor polaronic conductivity of $LiMnPO_4$ can be explained by the fact that Mn^{3+} is a Jahn-Teller ion and in an octahedral coordination as is found in the $LiMnPO_4$ a distortion of the octahedron occurs which greatly reduces its polaronic mobility within the lattice since the distortion must hop from site to site.

Experimental

For small batches (10g) of all compositions, the starting components of appropriate stoichiometry, LiH_2PO_4, $FeC_2O_4.2H_2O$, Cr_2O_3, $Si(OCOCH_3)_4$ and 5 wt% acetylene black (based on final product mass) were high energy ball milled (Spex SamplePrep 8000 M Mixer/Mill) for 90 min. The milled powders were heated in a tube furnace at a rate of 10 °C per min. to 700 °C under N2, held at that temperature for 12 h and furnace cooled to room temperature. 1 kg / batch sample preparations were prepared based on the 10 g method.

For electrochemical testing, a PVDF-carbon–substituted $LiCoPO_4$ composite electrode was fabricated by a slurry coating method. Using N-methylpyrrolidone (NMP) as solvent, the slurry was coated onto an Al foil substrate after which the solvent was evaporated by heating. The electrodes were further dried under vacuum.

The electrolyte for both half and full cell data reported here was a 1.2 M $LiPF_6$ solution in a 3:7 (wt.%) mixture of ethylene carbonate (EC) and ethyl methyl carbonate (EMC) electrolyte with 2 wt% tris (trimethylsilyl) phosphite, a known high voltage stabilizing additive [6, 12–17]. Electrochemical testing was performed using a Maccor Series 4000 tester or VMP cycler.

Results and Discussion

The theoretical energy density of $LiCoPO_4$ is well known and the material has been under study for over 15 years by researchers trying to harness that potential but progress has been hindered by LCP's poor cycle life. The progression from $LiCoPO_4$ (LCP) to a Fe-substituted LCP (GEN 1 LCP through a Fe,Cr and Si substituted LCP (GEN 3 LCP) is shown in figure 1. Fe substitution dramatically stabilizes the cycling. Additional Cr and Si substitution of Fe-substituted $LiCoPO_4$ further stabilizes and increases the discharge capacity. Our strategy for stabilization was based on the viewpoint that substitution of LiCoPO4, even at a low level, can strongly change the electronic structure and stabilize the cycling and improve the electrochemical performance. The results are shown in figure 1 and a typical charge / discharge curve is shown in figure 2. In order to confirm the changes in electronic structure after substitution, we undertook synchrotron based spectroscopic measurements of GEN1 and GEN 3 substituted LCP [18]. The results of *ex situ* XAS through collaboration with ANL

Table 1. Characteristics of commercial Li-ion battery cathode materials relative to $LiCoPO_4$.

Material	Structure	V vs Li	mAh / g	Wh / kg
LiCoO2	layered	3.9	140	546
NCA	layered	3.8	200	760
NMC	layered	3.8	170	650
$LiMn_2O_4$	spinel	4.1	120	492
$LiFePO_4$	olivine	3.45	170	587
LiCoPO4	olivine	4.8	167	802

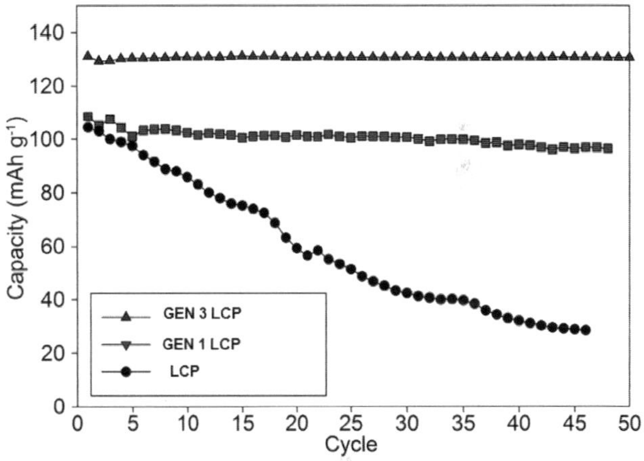

Figure 1. Comparison of capacity as a function of cycle for unsubstituted $LiCoPO_4$ (LCP) to Fe-substituted LCP (GEN1 LCP) and Fe,Cr and Si substituted LCP (GEN 3 LCP).

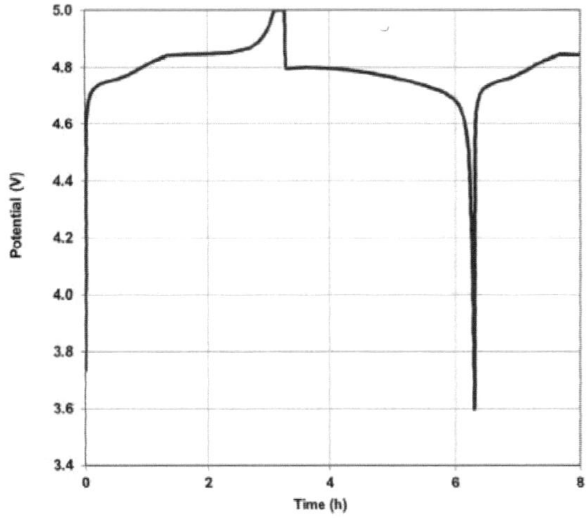

Figure 2. Typical charge/discharge curves of substituted (GEN3) LCP at C/3 rate.

and UI-Chicago led to the spectra shown in figure 3 ranging from pristine (P), Intermediate charge (I) through

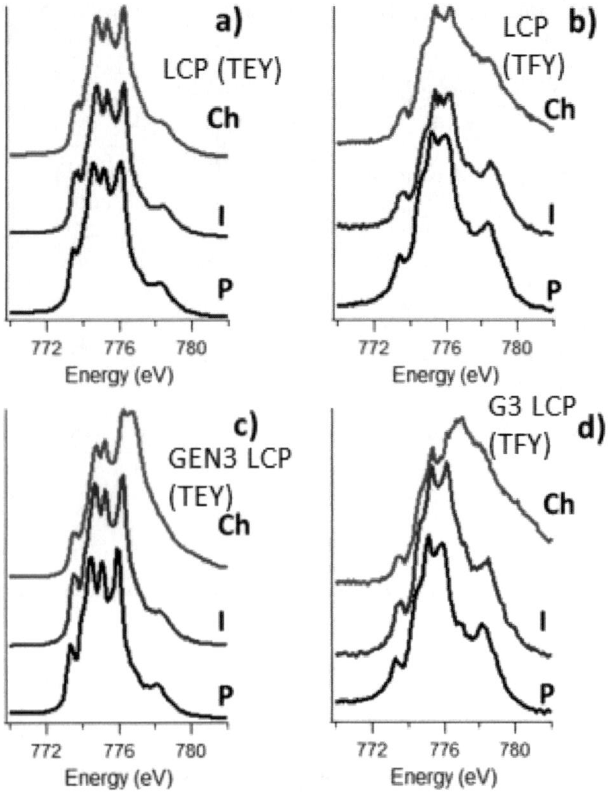

Figure 3. *Ex situ* XAS spectra collected during the first charge at the Co LIII edge for (a and b) LCP and (c and d) GEN 3 LCP electrodes. Spectra in panels a and c were collected in total electron yield mode (TEY), whereas spectra in panels b and d were collected in total fluorescence yield mode (TFY). Abbreviations: P, pristine; I, intermediate potential (4.79 or 4.87 V); C, fully charged (5.3 or 5.0 V). TEY is representative of the surface whereas TFY is representative of the bulk.

fully charged (Ch). First we consider the TEY spectra which are representative of the surface. In this case, we do not observe a big difference between the charged and pristine states and between the LCP and the GEN3 LCP. This indicates most likely that the surface is reduced by reaction with electrolyte upon charging in both cases. If we turn our attention to the TFY spectra we observe a much larger change in the pristine versus fully charged for both LCP and GEN3 LCP but the change is much more noticeable for GEN3 LCP confirming the changes in electronic structure of this material compared to unsubstituted LCP.

Finally, scale-up of the synthesis from grams to kilograms has been undertaken by Hydro-Québec. A pouch cell of GEN3-LCP full cell and its capacity as a function of cycle life is shown in Figure 4.

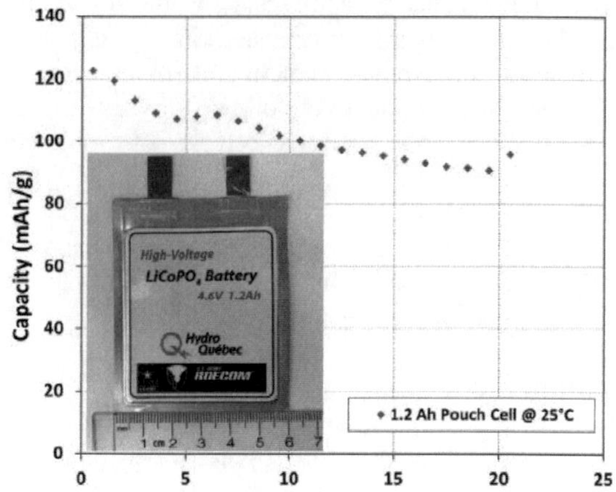

Figure 4. 1.2 Ah pouch type GEN3 LCP/Graphite full cell.

Conclusions

The substitution of cobalt by Fe, Cr and Si is a powerful method to improve the electrochemical performance of LCP. DFT suggests and *ex situ* spectroscopic measurements confirm changes in the electronic structure upon low substitution of Co. The electrochemical property is dramatically improved and in combination with new electrolyte formulations the promise of 5 V Li-ion chemistry can be envisioned. The synthesis is now scaled to kilogram levels and it is reasonable to believe that substituted LCP will be a promising next generation 5 V cathode material for high-energy lithium-ion batteries.

Acknowledgements

Ex situ XAS experiments were performed at Argonne National Laboratory through collaboration with J.W. Freeland (ANL) and were interpreted at University of Illinois-Chicago by J.G. Lapping and J. Cabana. DFT calculation were performed by M. Johannes (Naval Research Lab). Support was provided by the US Army ManTech and by Hydro-Québec for scale-up from grams to kilograms. DT Tran (ARL) provided characterization of GEN3 LCP.

References

1. Padhi, A.K., K.S. Nanjundaswamy, K.S., J.B. Goodenough, "Phospho-olivines as positive electrode materials for rechargeable lithium batteries," *J. Electrochem. Soc.*, vol. 144, pp. 1188-1194, 1997.
2. Amine, K., H. Yasuda, M. Yamachi, "Olivine $LiCoPO_4$ as 4.8 V electrode material for lithium batteries," *Electrochem. Solid State Lett.*, vol. 3, pp. 178-179, 2000.
3. Wolfenstine, J., J.L. Allen, "Ni^{3+}/Ni^{2+} redox potential in $LiNiPO_4$," *J. Power Sources*, vol. 142, pp. 389-390, 2005.

4. Allen, J.L., T.R. Jow, J. Wolfenstine, "Improved Cycle life of Fe-substituted $LiCoPO_4$," *J. Power Sources*, vol. 196, pp. 8656-8661, 2011.

5. Allen, Jan L., Joshua L. Allen, T. Thompson, S.A. Delp, J. Wolfenstine, T.R. Jow, "Cr and Si Substituted-$LiCo_{0.9}Fe_{0.1}PO_4$: Structure, full and half Li-ion cell performance," *J. Power Sources*, vol. 327, pp. 229-234, 2016.

6. Allen, Joshua L., Jan L. Allen, S.A. Delp, T.R. Jow, "Electrolyte additives for reducing the irreversible capacity loss, impedance and polarization of a doped $LiCoPO_4$ cathode," ECS Transactions, vol. 66, pp. 149-158 (2015).

7. Liu, D., W. Zhu, C. Kim, M. Cho, A. Guerfi, S.A. Delp, J.L. Allen, T.R. Jow, K. Zaghib, "High-energy lithium-ion battery using substituted $LiCoPO_4$: from coin type to 1 Ah cell," *J. Power Sources* vol. 388, pp. 52-56 (2018).

8. Johannes, M.D., K. Hoang, J.L. Allen, K. Gaskell, "Hole polaron formation and migration in olivine phosphate materials," Phys. Rev. B, vol. 85, pp. 115106-11512, 2012.

9. Bramnik, N.N., K.G.Bramnik, T. Buhrmester, C. Baehtz, H. Ehrenberg and H. Fuess, "Electrochemical and structural study of $LiCoPO_4$-based electrodes," *J. Solid State Electrochem.* vol.8, pp. 558-564, 2004.

10. Wolfenstine, J., U. Lee,B. Poese, J.L. Allen, "Effect of oxygen partial pressure on the discharge capacity of $LiCoPO_4$," *J. Power Sources*, vol. 144, pp. 226-230, 2005.

11. Bramnik, N.N., K. Nikolowski, D.M. Trots, H. Ehrenberg, "Thermal stability of $LiCoPO_4$ cathodes, *Electrochem. Solid-State Lett.,* vol. 11, pp. A89-A93, 2008.

12. Tranopolsky, V., "Electrolyte for Rechargeable Lithium Battery, and Rechargeable Lithium Battery Including Same," U.S. Patent 7,494,746 (2009).

13. Bhat, V.V., G. Cheng, S. Kaye, B. Li, R. Olugbile, J.-H. Yang, "Materials for Battery Electrolytes and Methods for Use," U.S. Patent 8,308,971 (2012).

14. Song, Y.-M. J.-G. Han, S. Park, K.T. Lee, N.-S. Choi, "A multifunctional phosphite-containing electrolyte for 5 V-class $LiNi_{0.5}Mn_{1.5}O_4$ cathodes with superior electrochemical performance," *J. Mater. Chem. A*, vol. 2, pp. 9506-9513 (2014).

15. Mai, S., M. Xu, X. Liao, J. Hu, H. Lin, L. Xing, Y. Liao, X. Li, W. Li, "Tris(trimethylsilyl)phosphite as electrolyte additive for high voltage layered lithium nickel cobalt manganese oxide cathode of lithium ion battery," *Electrochim. Acta*, vol. 147, p. 565-571 (2014).

16. Sinha, N.N., J.C. Burns, J.R. Dahn, "A high precision study of electrolyte additive combinations containing vinylene carbonate, ethylene sulfate, tris(trimethylsilyl) phosphate and tris(trimethylsilyl) phosphite in $Li[Ni_{1/3}Mn_{1/3}Co_{1/3}]O_2$/graphite pouch cells," *J. Electrochem. Soc.*, vol. 161, p. A1084-A1089 (2014).

17. Song, Y.M., C.K. Kim, K.E. Kim, S.Y. Hong, N.S. Choi, "Exploiting chemically and electrochemically reactive phosphite derivatives for high-voltage spinel $LiNi_{0.5}Mn_{1.5}O_4$ cathodes," *J. Power Sources*, vol. 302, pp. 22 (2016).

18. Lapping, J.G., S.A. Delp, Joshua L. Allen, Jan L. Allen, J.W. Freeland, M.D. Johannes, L. Hu, D.T. Tran, T.R. Jow, J. Cabana, "Changes in electronic structure upon Li deintercalation from $LiCoPO_4$ derivatives," *Chem. Mater.* Vol. 30, pp. 1898-1906 (2018).

Lithium-Oxygen Batteries using Phthalocyanine as Catalyst

Padmakar Kichambare[1], Stanley Rodrigues[2], and Lawrence Scanlon[2]
[1]UES Inc., 4401 Dayton-Xenia Road, Dayton, OH 45432.
[2]Air Force Research Laboratory, Aerospace Systems Directorate
Wright-Patterson Air Force Base, Ohio 45433-7252.

Abstract: *Hierarchically porous carbon (HPC) cathodes with tetra-butyl ammonium lithium phthalocyanine (TBA-LiPc) as soluble catalyst and lithium bis-(tri-fluoromethylsulfonyl) imide (LiTFSI salt) in tetra-ethylene glycol dimethyl ether (TEGDME) has been evaluated for application in lithium-oxygen batteries. Cyclic voltammetry (CV) on TBA-LiPc in oxygen saturated TEGDME electrolyte reveals the oxygen reduction reaction (ORR) activity at 2.27 and 2.72 V and oxygen evolution reaction (OER) activity at 3.17 and 3.96 V vs Li/Li$^+$. Under oxygen atmosphere at room temperature, a full cell exhibited first discharge and charge capacity of 14,226 and 14,142 mAh/g, respectively, (normalized to weight of carbon). These values relate to areal discharge and charge capacity of 3.92 and 3.90 mAh/cm^2, respectively. High discharge and charge capacity values suggest that TBA-LiPc is a promising catalyst for the ORR and OER in TEGDME.*

Keywords: hierarchically porous carbon; scanning electron microscopy; tetra-ethylene glycol dimethyl ether; tetra-butyl ammonium lithium phthalocyanine; lithium-oxygen battery

Introduction

Lithium-oxygen batteries have drawn significant interest due to their high energy density [1]. Although these cells operate on a simple chemical reaction between lithium ion and oxygen radical species, there are significant technical challenges that need to be overcome for successful development of these cells. Oxygen cathode structure, electrolyte decomposition, and significant overpotential on charging due to slow kinetics of dissociation of the reaction products are some of the challenges. Therefore, the cathode of the cell requires the use of efficient bifunctional catalysts that are active for both ORR and OER.

Various cathode catalysts, such as noble metals, metal oxides, carbon based nanomaterials, etc., have been investigated. Among the non-precious catalysts, phthalocyanine is attracting interest. Cobalt phthalocyanine has been used to lower the activation energy for O_2 reduction [2]. High discharge capacity was reported when dilithium phthalocyanine was employed as cathode catalyst [3]. Sun *et al* has employed a solution-phase bifunctional iron phthalocyanine (FePc) catalyst dissolved in TEGDME and dimethyl sulfoxide (DMSO) based electrolytes. This catalyst acts as a molecular shuttle of $(O_2)^-$ between the surface of carbon cathode and insulator Li_2O_2, product of discharge [4]. The reversible redox property of the central transition metal ion is generally considered as the source for catalysis.

In continuation of our work on lithium-oxygen cells [3,5], we report here the use of HPC as oxygen cathode with TBA-LiPc as soluble catalyst in TEGDME electrolyte. TEGDME was selected due to its low volatility, high boiling point, good oxygen solubility (4.43 mM/cm^3) and electrochemical stability over wide potential window.

Experimental Details

The synthesis of HPC was carried using zinc oxide nanoparticles as hard template [6]. This HPC powder was used to fabricate the oxygen cathode. LiTFSI (Sigma-Aldrich) was dried overnight under a vacuum at 120 °C. TBA-LiPc catalyst was synthesized and provided by Wright State University. The catalyst was vacuum dried at 110 °C before use. The electrolyte was prepared by mixing TEGDME (Sigma-Aldrich), LiTFSI and TBA-LiPc in a dry room. The concentration of LiTFSI and TBA-LiPc were controlled at 0.1M and 2 mM, respectively. A scanning electron microscope (SEM), (JEOL JSM-6060) was used to observe the morphologies of the specimens. The surface area of the specimen was determined by nitrogen adsorption / desorption measurements at 77 K (Micromeritics ASAP 2020). The porosity of cathode material was characterized by a gas pycnometer (Micromeritis, Accu Pyc II 1340). X-ray diffraction (XRD) of cathode specimens were obtained using Bruker D8 Discover diffractometer operated at 40 kV & 40 mA with CuKα over the 2θ range of 10 to 80° in the steps of 0.05. Galvanostatic charge-discharge measurements of the specimens were conducted using a computer controlled VersaSTAT 4 (Princeton Applied Research) electrochemical workstation. Cyclic voltammetry (CV) measurements were performed in a standard three-electrode cell configuration using electrolyte solution of TEGDME, LiTFSI and TBA-LiPc at 25 °C with a scan rate of 5 mVSec^{-1}. A graphite rod was used as working electrode for CV measurements. Li foil was used as the counter and reference electrode. CV measurements were first performed in argon saturated followed by oxygen saturated electrolyte.

To fabricate the oxygen cathode, HPC powder was mixed and dispersed in N-methyl-2-pyrrolidone (NMP) using sonication for 90 min. This process was carried to load cathode material in the open voids of nickel foam that is used as current collector. The mass of HPC present in the cathode was about 0.4 mg. Subsequently, specimen was dried overnight at 120 °C under vacuum. A cell with a 1.2 cm^2 active area was fabricated using a Swagelok type cell in a dry room. Nickel foam with HPC was used as working cathode, lithium metal as anode and a glass fiber (Whatman, GF-A) separator soaked with TBA-LiPc as soluble catalyst in LiTFSI-TEGDME electrolyte. The cells were discharged with constant current of 50, 100, 150 and 200 μA at 25 °C. After the discharge these cells were then charged with constant current of 25, 50, 75 and 100 μA at 25 °C. Electrochemical impedance spectroscopy (EIS) measurements were conducted before and after discharge. All electrochemical tests on these cells were carried under oxygen atmosphere.

Results and Discussion

The morphology of the working cathode examined under SEM reveals a porous architecture with interconnected pore channels. This favorable morphology facilitates oxygen transport, maximizes the availability for the catalytic sites, and diffusion of electrolyte in the cathode matrix. Nitrogen adsorption–desorption isotherm measurements were carried at 77 K. The Brunauer-Emmett-Teller (BET) surface area of HPC was found to be 1533 m^2/g with porosity of 47%. The pore size distribution indicates a wide variation of pore size from 2 nm to 137 nm. The remarkable nitrogen uptake above the relative pressure ratio of 0.40 was observed in BET isotherm and is due to condensation of nitrogen in HPC matrix. Such high porosity helps to improve cell capacity.

The electro-catalytic ability of TBA-LiPc in oxygen saturated TEGDME electrolyte was evaluated by CV. Figure 1 shows typical cyclic voltammogram for TBA-LiPc in oxygen saturated TEGDME electrolyte with well-defined OER peaks at 3.17 and 3.96 V (vs Li/Li^+) with total anodic current density of 0.015 and 0.024 mA/cm^2, respectively. In addition to the anodic peaks, broad and weak ORR peaks at around 2.27 and 2.72 V vs Li/Li^+ with total cathodic current density of 0.019 and 0.013 mA/cm^2, respectively, are found. It is clearly observed that anodic peaks are significantly stronger than the cathodic peaks.

There is asymmetry in the anodic and cathodic peaks locations and intensities. This asymmetry may be due to kinetic hindrance to the transport of O_2 and asymmetric activation energy for the involved reactions. The anodic peaks at 3.17 and 3.96 V are attributed to the subsequent oxidation of reduction products formed at 2.72 and 2.27 V during the cathodic scan.

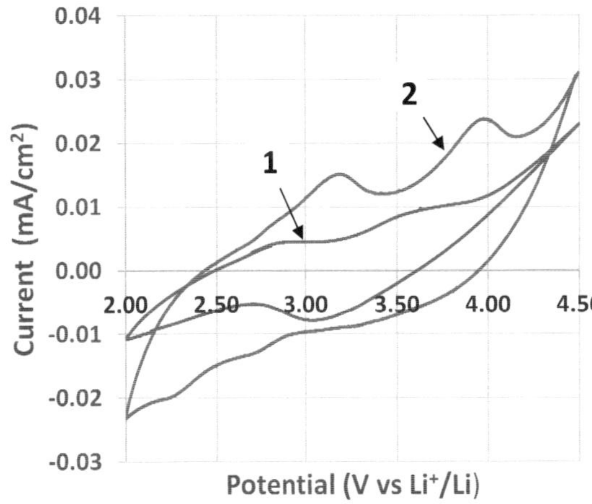

Figure 1. Cyclic voltammograms of TBA-LiPc in LiTFSI-TEGDME electrolyte saturated with (1) argon and (2) oxygen

This indicates that the oxygen reduction in the presence of TBA-LiPc is reversible. The site for oxygen interaction with TBA-LiPc is at the lithium ion which is located at the center of lithium-phthalocyanine anion [7]. The oxygen complex formed, prior to electrochemical reduction, is due to electrostatic interaction between oxygen and the lithium-ion resulting in an elongation of the oxygen-oxygen bond to a calculated value of 1.32 Å. In the model used for the theoretical calculations, it is shown that the TBA^+ cation is located above the anionic $LiPc-O_2$ complex providing stabilization for this complex. It is perhaps this type of complex that is involved in the reduction of oxygen to super-oxides and subsequent re-oxidation of super-oxides to oxygen. No significant anodic and cathodic peaks are observed in argon saturated TEGDME electrolyte solution. This clearly demonstrates the electro-catalytic activity of TBA-LiPc towards oxygen reduction and evolution in oxygen saturated TEGDME electrolyte.

Based on the high surface area with porous structure of HPC and electro-catalytic activity of TBA-LiPc towards oxygen reduction and evolution, cells with 1.2 cm^2 active area were fabricated. The electrochemical performance in oxygen atmosphere was evaluated. Figure 2 shows the discharge-charge profiles of the cells in the potential range 2 - 4 V. The cell was reversibly discharged and charged using current of 50 and 25 μA, respectively, at 25 °C. The charging process was carried till cell recovers it capacity during respective discharge run. The open circuit voltage (OCV) of cell was 3.24 V. Initial discharge and charge cell capacity was found to be 14,226 and 14,142 mAh/g, respectively. These values relate to areal discharge and charge capacity of 3.92 and 3.90 mAh/cm^2, respectively. Cell capacity for cathode decreased continuously with cycling and delivered capacity of 7933 mAh/g (2.19 mAh/cm^2) at the end of 3rd cycle.

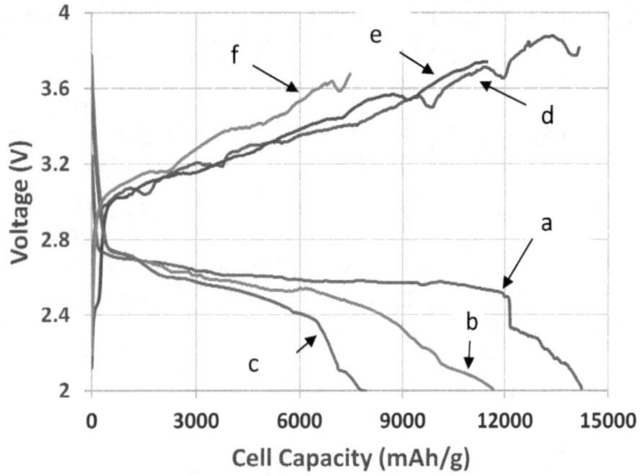

Figure 2. Discharge-charge profiles of cell at 25 °C (1st discharge and charge: a and d; 2nd discharge and charge: b and e; 3rd Discharge and Charge: c and f)

The high cell capacity is attributed to synergistic effect of high ORR and OER catalytic activity of TBA-LiPC and porous structure of HPC cathode. This cathode composition provides wide variation of pore size, easy diffusion of oxygen in the cathode matrix, increases the electrochemically available surface area and electrolyte transportation paths in the electrode resulting in high discharge capacity.

Cyclic stability was investigated with controlled depth of discharge at 2.6 V as shown in Fig. 3. The discharge and charge currents for the cell shown in Fig 3 were 50 and 25 μA, respectively, at 25 °C. The cell showed good cycle performance over 10 cycles with stable reversible capacities within discharge and charge voltage of 2.6 and 4 V, respectively. It also exhibited increase in overpotential during cycling.

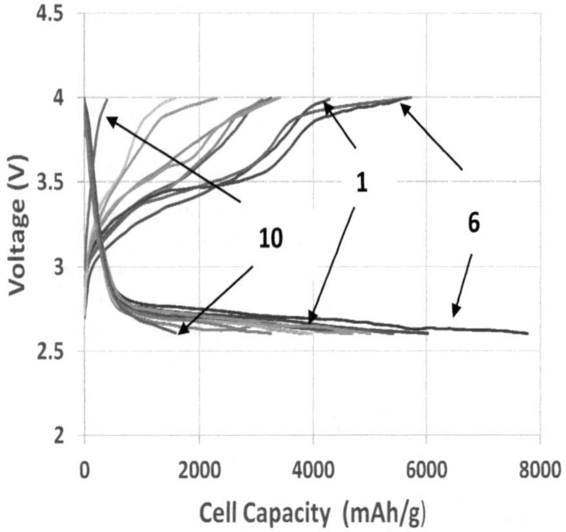

Figure 3. Discharge-charge profiles for 10 cycles under voltage limitation at 25 °C

Shown in Figure 4 are the discharge profiles at various rates using currents of 50, 100, 150 and 200 μA in oxygen atmosphere at 25 °C and with OCV's of 3.24, 3.38, 3.36 and 3.35 V, respectively. The difference in OCV is due to internal series resistances between various cell components and activation polarization of the cathode. At higher discharge currents of 100, 150 and 200 μA, the initial discharge capacity decreases to 8362.14 mAh/g (2.30 mAh/cm^2), 3072.62 mAh/g (0.85 mAh/cm^2), and 825.79 mAh/g (0.23 mAh/cm^2), respectively.

Typical Nyquist plots before and after first discharge at current of 50 μA are shown in Fig. 5. Plots before initial discharge exhibit charge-transfer resistance of 494 Ω (593 Ω/cm^2). There is a large increase in charge-transfer resistance to a value of 1179 Ω (1415 Ω/cm^2) after discharge.

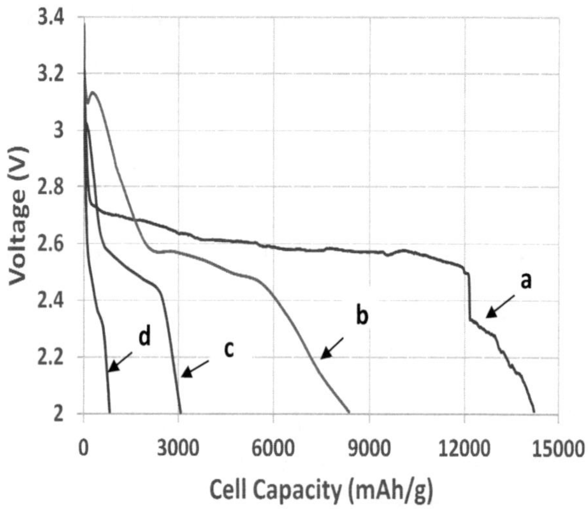

Figure 4. Discharge profiles of cell at discharge current of (a) 50 μA, (b) 100 μA, (c) 150 μA and (d) 200 μA

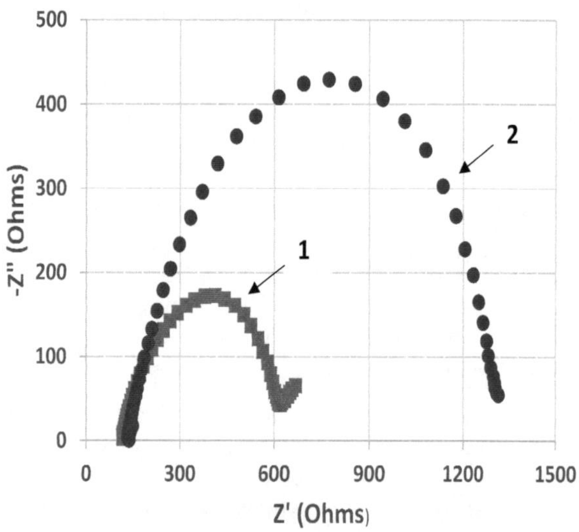

Figure 5. Nyquist plots of cell at 25 °C at the discharge current of 50 μA before (1) and after (2) discharge, respectively, in oxygen atmosphere

To confirm the reversible formation and decomposition of discharge products, XRD patterns were collected on the discharged cathodes. The XRD spectrum (Fig. 6) reveals the presence of Li_2O_2 and Li_2CO_3 crystalline phases indicating a two-electron reduction process during the discharge.

EIS results combined with CV measurements and discharge characteristics lead to the conclusion that the oxygen cathode with TBA-LiPc as soluble catalyst in TEGDME electrolyte has excellent catalytic activity towards ORR and OER with good cell capacity.

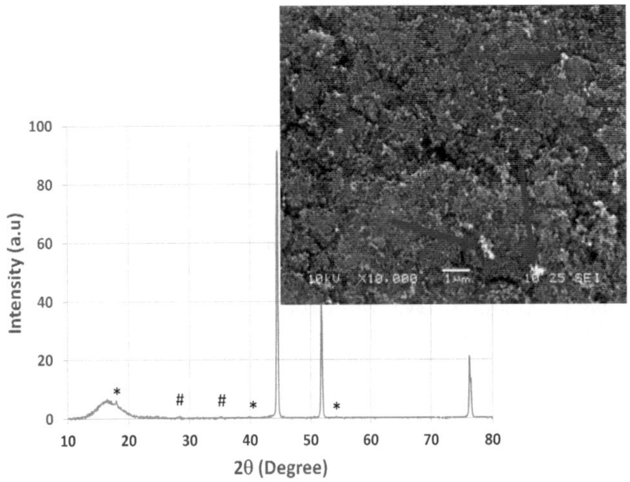

Figure 6. XRD pattern of discharged cathode when cell discharged to 2V at 50 µA. Li_2O_2 and Li_2CO_3 peaks are shown by * and #, respectively. Inset shows the SEM image of this cathode and discharge products are shown by arrows

The reactions that take place during ORR and OER are shown below.

$$\text{TBA-LiPc} + O_2 \rightleftarrows \text{TBA-LiPc}^{+\delta}\text{-} O_2^{-\delta}$$

$$\text{TBA-LiPc}^{+\delta} - O_2^{-\delta} + 2\,e^- \rightleftarrows \text{TBA-LiPc} + O_2^{2-}$$

Conclusion

In conclusion, this work demonstrates catalytic activity of TBA-LiPc for ORR and OER in a Li-O_2 cell. The cell exhibits high initial discharge and charge capacity of 14,226 mAh/g and 14,142 mAh/g, respectively. This work highlights the importance of novel catalyst as well as cathode architecture and opens up a promising approach to develop efficient rechargeable lithium-oxygen cells.

Acknowledgements

This research was supported by the Air Force Research Laboratory, Wright-Patterson Air Force Base, Ohio. We thank Professor William Feld, Department of Chemistry, Wright State University for generously providing TBA-LiPc.

References:

1. Abraham, K.M. and Z. Jiang, "A Polymer Electrolyte-Based Rechargeable Lithium/Oxygen Battery", *J. Electrochem. Soc.*, vol. 143, pp. 1-5, 1996.
2. Trahan, M.J., Q. Jia, S. Mukerjee, E.J. Plichta, M.A. Hendrickson, and K.M. Abraham, "Cobalt Phthalocyanine Catalyzed Lithium-Air Batteries", *J. Electrochem. Soc.,* vol. **160**, pp. A1577-A1586, 2013.
3. Selvaraj, C., N. Munichandraiah, and L.G. Scanlon, "Dilithium Phthalocyanine as a catalyst for Oxygen Reduction in Non-Aqueous Li-O_2 Cells", *J. Porphyrin Phthalocyanines.,* vol. **16**, pp. 255-259, 2012.
4. Sun, D., Y. Shen, W. Zhang, L. Yu, Z. Yi, W. Yin, D. Wang, Y. Huang, J. Wang, D. Wang, and J.B. Goodenough, "A solution-Phase Bifunctional Catalyst for Lithium-Oxygen Batteries", *J. Am. Chem. Soc.,* vol. **136**, pp. 8941-8946, 2014.
5. Kichambare, P. and S. Rodrigues, "Graphene Nanosheets Based Cathodes for Lithium-Oxygen Batteries", *C- J Carbon Research,* vol. **1**, pp. 27-42, 2015.
6. Strubel, P., Thieme, S., Biemelt, T., Helmer, A., Oschatz, M., Bruckner, J., Althues, H., and S. Kaskel, "ZnO Hard Templating for Synthesis of Hierarchical Porous Carbons with Tailored and High Performance in Lithium-Sulfur Battery", *Adv. Funct. Mater.,* vol. **25**, pp. 287-297, 2015.
7. Balbuena, P.B., Texas A&M University, College Station, USA, (Private Communication).

Rechargeable Zn–Air Batteries Enabled by Multifunctional Air Cathodes and Zn Sponge Anodes

Joseph F. Parker,[1] Jesse S. Ko,[2] Debra R. Rolison,[1] and Jeffrey W. Long[1]

[1]Surface Chemistry Branch – Code 6170
[2]NRL-NRC Postdoctoral Associate
U. S. Naval Research Laboratory
Washington, DC 20375, USA
Contact Author Email: jeffrey.long@nrl.navy.mil

Abstract: *Zinc–air batteries deliver high specific energy due to their use of lightweight positive electrodes that harvest molecular oxygen from the air, catalyze its reduction, and offer the additional benefits of low-cost, low-toxicity components. Yet, rechargeability of Zn–air cells has been historically limited by challenges at both the zinc anode and the air-breathing cathode, which must efficiently catalyze oxygen reduction (on discharge) and oxygen evolution (on recharge). While oxygen reduction is readily handled by manganese oxides, nanoscale nickel–iron oxides (nickel ferrites, NiFeOx) have emerged as promising electrocatalysts for oxygen evolution. We recently explored the electrocatalytic properties of a family of sol–gel-derived NiFeOx, where both the metal ratio and pore–solid architecture could be readily tuned, with corresponding impact on oxygen-evolution performance assessed by rotating-disk electrode measurements. Herein, we investigate performance trends for related materials, but as expressed in a more practical powder-composite electrode structure, interfaced with a specially designed three-electrode air-breathing cell that mimics conditions experienced in a Zn–air battery.*

Keywords: zinc–air battery; electrocatalyst; oxygen evolution; nickel–iron oxides

Introduction

Zinc–air batteries have the potential to overcome many of the disadvantages of leading market competitors, including those with safety concerns associated with toxic and flammable active materials, high costs, and moderate specific energy (<200 Wh kg^{-1}). Zinc–air provides high specific energy (up to 475 Wh kg^{-1}) while using safe, low-cost components, and aqueous electrolytes. Although commercially successful in single-use, primary mode, broader implementation is hindered by performance limitations at both the zinc anode and the air cathode. We recently introduced a 3D Zn "sponge" design that solves many long-standing issues with Zn anodes in alkaline electrolytes, including the propensity for dendrite formation on extensive recharging and passivation during discharge.[1,2,3,4]

With an effective Zn anode in place, we have turned our attention to solving lingering issues at the air-breathing cathode, which must serve multiple functions, namely oxygen reduction during discharge and oxygen evolution during recharge. Therefore, electrocatalysts must be identified that perform one or both reactions efficiently and durably. While manganese oxides are established oxygen-reduction catalysts, they may not be sufficiently stable and active to catalyze the reverse reaction. As an alternative, we have explored nanostructured nickel–iron oxides as prospective electrocatalysts, with promising results for the oxygen-evolution reaction, and even moderate activity for oxygen reduction. These materials are prepared by a flexible sol–gel chemistry route that can be adapted to produce oxides of tunable stoichiometry ($Ni_yFe_{1-y}Ox$, where $y = 0.1 - 0.9$), which are then expressed in different pore–solid architectures (xerogel, ambigel, and aerogel forms), yielding catalysts of varying specific surface area and pore size.

We recently reported on the electrocatalytic performance of a series of $Ni_yFe_{1-y}Ox$ nanomaterials as dispersed in inks at glassy carbon rotating-disk electrodes (RDE). Those measurements provided an initial assessment of activity as a function of stoichiometry, surface area, oxide crystallinity, and pore structure and found that an interplay between all four attributes affects performance.[5] Herein, we follow that initial investigation with a study on the activity of selected $Ni_yFe_{1-y}Ox$ materials, but now incorporated into more practical powder-composite electrode structures. We characterize these composite electrodes in our specially designed electroanalytical cell, where one face of the composite electrode is exposed to atmosphere and the other to an alkaline electrolyte containing reference and counter electrodes. With this cell configuration, we assess both oxygen-evolution and -reduction activity, and find trends that are similar to those previously reported for RDE experiments. The results of such measurements will be used to down-select the most promising electrocatalysts for incorporation into the air cathodes of next-generation rechargeable Zn–air batteries.

Experimental

Synthesis of $Ni_yFe_{1-y}Ox$ nanoarchitectures: Nickel–iron oxide powders were prepared using a previously established protocol.[5,6] Briefly, amorphous gels were prepared using an epoxide-initiated sol–gel method carried out with Ni:Fe stoichiometry set at 1:2 ($NiFe_2Ox$) and 2:1 (Ni_2FeOx) using nickel (II) chloride hexahydrate and iron (III) chloride hexahydrate as the respective Ni and Fe precursors. In order to yield $NiFe_2Ox$ ambigels, the wet gels were rinsed thoroughly with hexanes for 3 d before drying at 50 °C under flowing nitrogen. To process aerogels of $NiFe_2Ox$ and Ni_2FeOx, the wet gels were thoroughly rinsed with acetone for 6 d before supercritical drying with carbon dioxide. These three dried $Ni_yFe_{1-y}Ox$ nanoarchitectures were then heated for 2 h at 300 °C under flowing argon to crystallize into its respective inverse spinel/rock-salt crystalline phase.

Air-Breathing Electrode Assessment: Powder-composite electrode structures containing the $Ni_yFe_{1-y}Ox$ catalysts were prepared by ball-milling the oxide with XC-72 conductive carbon and PTFE polymer binder for 16 h using a roller mill. The ball-milled composite powder was then collected and evenly distributed between ½" nickel mesh and pressed to 1,750 psi for 1 min. The air cathodes were interfaced with an air-breathing electroanalytical cell[7] (Schematic 1) filled with 6 M KOH and equipped with independent reference and counter electrodes of zinc wire and platinum wire, respectively. To assess OER activity, chronoamperometric measurements were made by stepping the potential at (*i*) 25 mV intervals from 1.425 V to 2.000 V *vs.* Zn/Zn^{2+}. To evaluate the corresponding ORR activity, the potential was stepped down from 1.425 V to 1.300 V in 5 mV intervals and from 1.300 V to 1.000 V in 25 mV intervals.

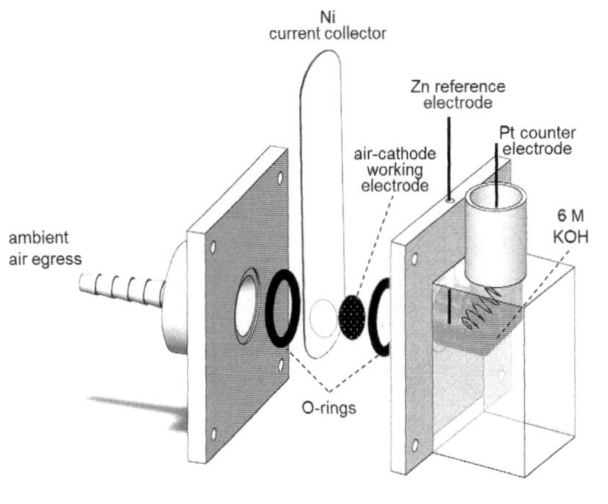

Schematic 1. Illustration of the three-electrode air-breathing electroanalytical cell.

Results and Discussion

On the basis of our prior RDE investigations of sol–gel-derived $Ni_yFe_{1-y}Ox$ powders as electrocatalysts for OER and ORR, we down-selected three representative samples for additional testing: $NiFe_2Ox$ aerogel, $NiFe_2Ox$ ambigel, and Ni_2FeOx aerogel. With these electrocatalysts, we prepared powder-composite electrode structures in which the active $Ni_yFe_{1-y}Ox$ powder was milled with polymer binder and conductive carbon, similar to preparing an air cathode for a practical Zn–air battery. The prototype air cathodes were interfaced with a three-electrode cell where one side sees atmosphere, and the other contacts a liquid electrolyte (6 M KOH). This cell design mimics the operating conditions of an air-breathing cell while allowing for measurement versus an independent reference electrode (Zn wire quasi-reference) and counter electrode.

With this experimental set-up, we first assessed the OER activity of the three $Ni_yFe_{1-y}Ox$-based electrodes. Steady-state currents were measured as the electrode was stepped positively in 25-mV intervals from 1.400 V to 2.000 V *vs.* Zn/Zn^{2+} (for fundamental interpretation, we also present these data in terms of overpotential, η). For this series, we varied either the pore–solid architecture (ambigel *vs.* aerogel) or the Ni:Fe ratio. With $NiFe_2Ox$ compositions, OER activity is primarily determined by the pore–solid architecture (Fig. 1); we find that the aerogel form exhibits greater OER activity due to its higher specific surface area (187 *vs.* 70 $m^2\ g^{-1}$).[5] The low density and friable nature of the aerogel, compared to the moderately densified ambigel, may also result in finer powders with the former, and ultimately more homogeneous distribution of the NiFeOx catalytic domains within the powder-composite structure.

The most active electrode contains Ni_2FeOx aerogel, with the onset of OER current by 1.6 V, whereas the other two electrocatalyst examples do not exhibit significant activity until ~1.8 V. For a given pore–solid architecture (aerogel), higher OER activity correlates with greater Ni content (2:1;

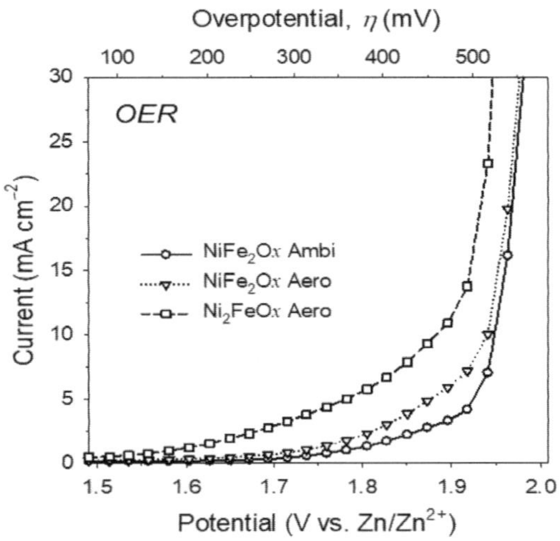

Figure 1. Current–potential response over the OER potential window (1.4–2.0 V *vs.* Zn/Zn^{2+}) in 6 M KOH under static air for $NiFe_2Ox$ ambigel and aerogel, and Ni_2FeOx aerogel.

Ni:Fe), as previously shown in our RDE characterization,[5] and in investigations of other related $Ni_yFe_{1-y}Ox$ materials.[8]

Following the initial assessment of OER activity of these $Ni_yFe_{1-y}Ox$-based cathodes, we then evaluated their ORR activity by stepping the potential in the reverse direction from 1.300 V to 1.000 V *vs.* Zn/Zn^{2+} in 25-mV intervals. With a fixed Ni:Fe stoichiometry ($NiFe_2Ox$), we find a similar response for ORR activity, where the expression of higher specific surface area and pore volume leads to greater electrocatalytic behavior. Moreover, with the aerogel nanoarchitecture, the magnitude of the current is higher across the potential range from 1.000 – 1.200 V, indicating that the increased Ni content also plays a role in reducing oxygen at the molecular level. Although the overpotentials for ORR at Ni_2FeOx are higher than typically observed for $MnOx$ electrocatalysts, this moderate ORR activity couples with high OER activity and stable operation. Thus, Ni_2FeOx may be desirable as a

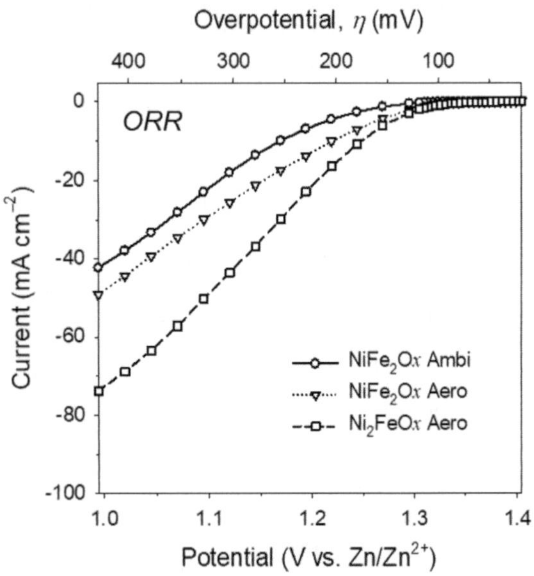

Figure 2. Current–potential response over the OER potential window (1.4–1.0 V *vs.* Zn/Zn^{2+}) in 6 M KOH under static air for $NiFe_2Ox$ ambigel and aerogel, and Ni_2FeOx aerogel.

bifunctional electrocatalyst for metal–air batteries.

The results of separate ORR and OER tests were also compared in order to assess charge/discharge voltage hysteresis, an important parameter that determines the round-trip energy efficiency of the ultimate Zn–air battery. We set a "figure-of-merit" for electrocatalyst activity at ± 10 mA cm^{-2}, with the difference in corresponding potential yielding the hysteresis value. The Ni_2FeOx aerogel air cathode expresses the lowest hysteresis at 631 mV, followed by $NiFe_2Ox$ aerogel (721 mV), and $NiFe_2Ox$ ambigel (773 mV). From such results we can identify promising electrocatalysts for further testing in prototype rechargeable Zn–air batteries.

Acknowledgements

The information, data, and work presented herein were funded by the U. S. Office of Naval Research.

References

1. Parker, J. F., Chervin, C. N., Nelson, E. S., Rolison, D. R., and Long, J. W., "Wiring Zinc in Three Dimensions Re-writes Battery Performance–Dendrite-Free Cycling." *Energy & Environmental Science*, vol. 7, pp. 1117–1124, 2014.
2. Parker, J. F., Nelson, E. S., Wattendorf, M. D., Chervin, C. N., Long, J. W., and Rolison, D. R., "Retaining the 3D Framework of Zinc Sponge Anodes upon Deep Discharge in Zn–Air Cells." *ACS Applied Materials & Interfaces*, vol. 6, pp. 19471–19476, 2014.
3. Parker, J. F., Pala, I. R., Chervin, C. N., Long, J. W., and Rolison, D. R., "Minimizing Shape Change at Zn Sponge Anodes in Rechargeable Ni–Zn cells: Impact of Electrolyte Formulation." *Journal of the Electrochemical Society*, vol. 163, pp. A351–A355, 2016.
4. Parker, J. F., Chervin, C. N., Pala, I. R., Machler, M., Burz, M. F., Long, J. W., and Rolison, D. R., "Rechargeable Nickel–3D Zinc Batteries: An Energy-Dense, Safer Alternative to Lithium-Ion." *Science*, vol. 356, pp. 415–418, 2017.
5. Ko, J. S., Chervin, C. N., Vila, M. N., DeSario, P. A., Parker, J. F., Long, J. W., and Rolison, D. R., "Electroanalytical Assessment of the Effect of Ni:Fe Stoichiometry and Architectural Expression on the Bifunctional Activity of Nanoscale $Ni_yFe_{1-y}Ox$." *Langmuir*, vol. 33, pp. 9390–9397, 2017.
6. Chervin, C. N., DeSario, P. A., Parker, J. F., Nelson, E. S., Miller, B. W., Rolison, D. R., and Long, J. W., "Aerogel Architectures Boost Oxygen-Evolution Performance of $NiFe_2Ox$ Spinels to Activities Commensurate with Nickel-Rich Oxides." *ChemElectroChem*, vol. 3, pp. 1369–1375, 2016.
7. Chervin, C. N., Parker, J. F., Nelson, E. S., Rolison, D. R., and Long, J. W., "CAD/CAM–designed 3D-Printed Electroanalytical Cell for the Evaluation of Nanostructured Gas-Diffusion Electrodes." *Nanotechnology*, vol. 27, pp. 174002, 2016.
8. Burke, M. S., Enman, L. J., Batchellor, A. S., Zou, S., and Boettcher, S. W., "Oxygen Evolution Reaction Electrocatalysts on Transition Metal Oxides and (Oxy)hydroxides: Activity Trends and Design Principles." *Chemistry. of Materials*, vol. 27, pp. 7549–7558, 2015.

Kinetics and Mechanisms of the Oxygen Electrode Reactions in Lithium-air Batteries

K. M. Abraham*, Amell Alsudairi, Sanjeev Mukerjee
Department of Chemistry, Northeastern University, Boston, MA 02115
*Telephone: 781-444-8453; E-mail: kmabraham@comcast.net

Edward J. Plichta and Mary A. Hendrickson
US Army RDECOM CERDEC C2D
Army Power Division, RDER-CCA Aberdeen Proving Grounds, MD 21005

Abstract: *When Li salts, LiX, are dissolved in organic solvents to prepare electrolytes, they form solvates of the formula, $Li^+(solvent)_nX^-$ which influence the kinetics of the O_2 reduction reactions and the stability of the intermediates formed in the discharge of Li-air batteries. In solvents with Guttmann Donor number (DN) of about 25 or more, the initial ORR reduction product O_2^- is stabilized as $Li^+(solvent)_{n-1}$-O_2^-, consistent with the HSAB theory. In solvents with DN less than about 20, the stable ORR reduction product is solid Li_2O_2. The solvent's Lewis basicity affects ORR catalysis also. Thus, an appropriate catalyst in the porous carbon cathode promotes ORR catalysis in low DN solvents while the same catalyst is less effective in high DN solvents. In the latter ORR reactions, the solvent promotes an outer Helmholtz plane charge transfer process even in the presence of the catalyst. Conversely, an inner Helmholtz plane reaction that promotes ORR catalysis takes place in electrolytes based on low DN solvents.*

Keywords: Li-air battery, non-aqueous electrolytes, dimethyl acetamide, dimethyl sulfoxide, Donor Number, HSAB concept

The non-aqueous Li-air battery composed of a Li metal anode and gaseous oxygen cathode, with a theoretical specific energy of 5200 Wh/kg, has been the subject of world-wide research and development in the last decade (1, 2). The four-electron O_2 reduction reaction (ORR) in non-aqueous electrolytes used in this battery proceeds through the intermediates LiO_2 and Li_2O_2 before converted to Li_2O. Our studies have revealed that the kinetics and mechanisms of the various chemical and electrochemical reactions in the overall reduction of O_2 to Li_2O are influenced by the electron donor-acceptor properties of the non-aqueous solvents used and the electron acceptor property of the solid catalyst employed in the porous carbon electrode in the Li-air battery (2-5).

When a Li salt is dissolved in a non–aqueous solvent to form an ion-conducting electrolyte, the Li^+ cation is complexed by the solvent to form solvates of the general formula $Li^+(solvent)_nX$, where n is usually 4. The solvation of Li^+ in turn modulates the Lewis acidity of Li^+ to make this normally hard Lewis acid to acquire increasing amounts of softness. Thus, Li^+ gains softer Lewis acid characteristics depending upon the basicity (DN) of the solvents with which it forms solvates. Electron donor solvents with High Guttmann Donor Number (DN) , i.e; DN >25, are strong Lewis bases which make Li^+ softer Lewis acids by solvation than Li^+ solvated by low DN solvents having DN <20. Two organic solvents with high DN are dimethyl sulfoxide (DMSO) (DN = 29.8) and dimethyl acetamide (DMAc) (DN=27). In the Li^+-conducting electrolytes formed in these solvents, Li^+ solvates behave as soft Lewis acids. The structural formula of the solvate formed in a $LIPF_6$ solution in DMAC is depicted in Scheme I where the solvate exists as a solvent-separated ion pair with the anion.

Interestingly, when the anion is triflate ($CF_3SO_3^-$) the solvate exists as a contact ion pair since both the solvent and the triflate anion bond with Li^+ (Scheme II).

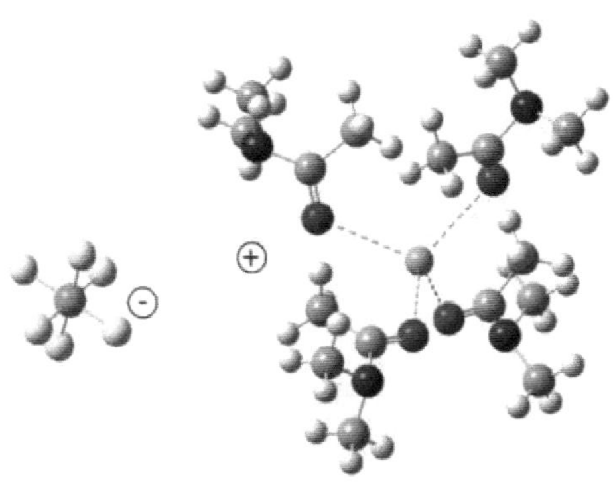

Scheme I: Molecular Structure of the solvent separated ion pair, $Li^+(DMAc)_4PF_6^-$ formed, in a solution of $LiPF_6$ in DMAc.

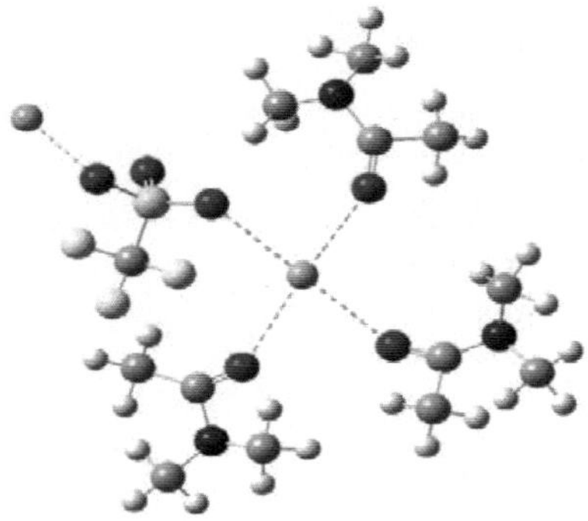

Scheme II: Molecular Structure of the contact ion pair, $Li^+CF_3SO_3^-(DMAc)_3$ in a solution of $LiCF_3SO_3$ in DMAc.

Two solvents with low DN useful in rechargeable Li batteries are dimethoxy ethane (DME) (DN=20) and tetraethyleneglycol dimethylether, (TEGDME (DN=16.5). In Li+-conducting electrolytes formed in these solvents, the Li^+ solvates behave as hard Lewis acids.

The oxygen reduction products O_2^-, O_2^{2-} and O_2^- are characterized by varying soft to hard Lewis base properties with O_2^- functioning as a soft Lewis base and O_2^{2-} and O^{2-} behaving as hard Lewis bases. Consequently, O_2 reduction reactions in non-aqueous solvents are governed by the Hard-Soft Acid-Base (HSAB) theory which state that hard Lewis acids want to combine with hard Lewis bases whereas soft Lewis acids want to combine with soft Lewis bases to form stable reaction products (2)

The overall conversion of O_2 to Li_2O in the electrochemical reduction of O_2 in a non-aqueous solvent proceeds through the intermediates LiO_2 and Li_2O_2 as shown in equations [1] – [4].

$$O_2 + Li^+(solvent)_n + e^- \longrightarrow Li^+(solvent)_n\text{--}O_2^- \quad [1]$$

$$2Li^+(solvent)_n\text{--}O_2^- \longrightarrow Li_2O_2(s) + O_2 + n\ solvent \quad [2]$$

$$Li^+(solvent)_n\text{--}O_2^- + e^- \longrightarrow Li_2O_2(s) + n\ solvent \quad [3]$$

$$Li_2O_2(s) + 2\ Li^+(solvent)_n + 2\ e^- \longrightarrow 2Li_2O(s) + nsolvent \quad [4]$$

Note that the reactions in equations [1]–[4] involve solvated Li^+ reactants. Similarly, the soluble initial one-electron O_2 reduction product superoxide, O_2^-, forms an ion-pair with solvated Li^+ whose life time, before decomposing according to reaction [2], depends on the electron donor property of the solvent as measured by its DN.

The four electron reduction of LiO_2 to Li_2O can be accomplished in potentiodynamic electrochemical reductions, such as cyclic voltammetry (CV) scans, in which the potential is swept to the region where the reaction in equation [4} occurs. On the other hand, solid Li_2O_2 is the final discharge product in Li-air cells because in these cells, the discharge under a continuous feed of O_2 gas takes place at a nearly constant potential so that the reaction mechanism is dominated by equations [1] and [2}. Because Li_2O_2 is insoluble in all of the solvents examined to date, it precipitates out in the pores of the carbon cathode. In low donor number solvents such as the aliphatic ethers DME and TEGDME (DN = 16.6 and 20) crystalline Li_2O_2 is formed even in a CV scan since the life time of $Li^+(solvent)_n\text{--}O_2^-$ is very low in these solvents and it decomposes quickly to Li_2O_2 as depicted in equation [2].

Our electrochemical data and NMR and Raman spectral results have revealed that soft Lewis acids such as the tetrabutyl ammonium (TBA) cation of TBA salts (e.g., $TBAPF_6$) or 1-ethyl-3-methylimidazolium imide (EMITFSI) cation of the room-temperature ionic liquid (RTIL) 1-ethyl-3-methylimidazolium bis(triflouromethanesulfonyl) imide (EMITFSI), stabilize the one-electron reduction product O_2^- in both high and low DN solvents (Scheme III) (2, 5). In these solutions further reduction of superoxide is very difficult which supports the validity of the HASAB concept.

We have found that ORR can be catalyzed by metal phthalocycanine such as cobalt and iron phthalocycanines (CoPC and FePC) appropriately dispersed in the porous carbon cathode (5, 7). The catalysis proceed via either a homogeneous (Outer Helmholtz Plane, OHP) or a heterogeneous (Inner Helmholtz Plane, IHP) reduction pathway depending on the Donor Number of the organic solvent and the d electron configuration of the metal phthalocyanine MPC catalyst. These are depicted in Figures 1 and 2. In these and later figures CoPC600 represents the active catalyst formed by heating the carbon-CoPC mixture at 600 °C (5, 7). In the case of CoPC, the Co(II) oxidation state with a $3d^7$ electronic configuration is the desired catalysts specie. When FePC is used, it is the Fe(I) oxidation state with the $3d^7$ electronic configuration that is desired for catalysis. A heterogeneous Inner Helmholtz Plane reaction catalyzed by the metal in the MPC is favored in the low DN solvent tetraethyleneglycoldimethyl ether, (TEGDME (DN=16.5) in which catalytic ORR is observed. In these Li-air cells, discharge occurs at a higher discharge voltage than in uncatalyzed cells (see figure 3) and the charge takes place at lower voltages (figure 4b).

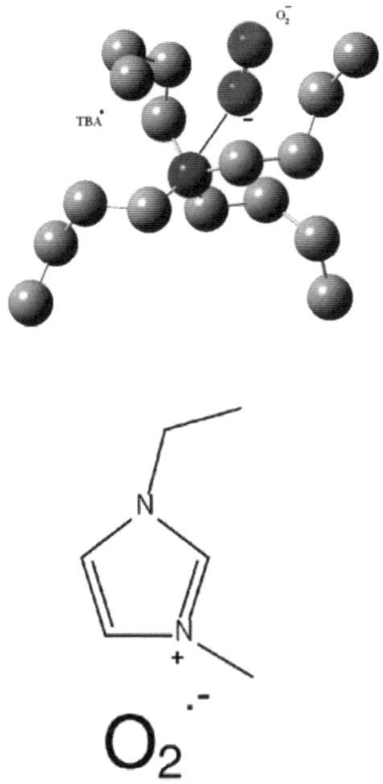

Scheme III: Stabilized superoxide (O_2^-) in TBA (upper in acetonitrile) and EMIImide (lower in EMITFSI) salt solutions

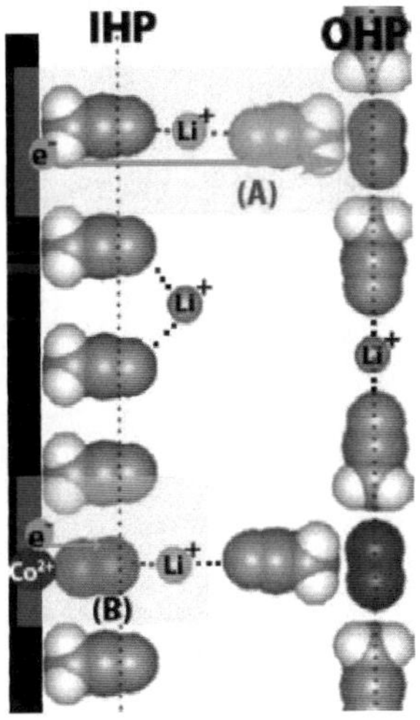

Figure 1: A schematic representation of the electrochemical double layer at the interface of a CoPC600 catalyzed carbon electrode in a Li^+-$(CH_3CN)_n$ electrolyte. Highlighted section A shows the outer Helmholtz plane one electron charge transfer as it occurs on an uncatalyzed surface. Highlighted section B shows inner Helmholtz plane charge transfer process facilitated by the presence of a catalyzed surface.

The higher discharge voltage of catalyzed cells is due to the catalyst lowering the charge transfer resistance of ORR, manifested as a lower iR drop in the cell discharge voltage. The catalyst doubled the cycle life of $Li-O_2$ battery cells cycled with the use of TEGDME-$LiSO_3CF_3$ electrolyte. These catalysts are less active in high DN solvent-based electrolytes such DMSO/$LiSO_3CF_3$ and DMAc/ $LiSO_3CF_3$ (5, 6).

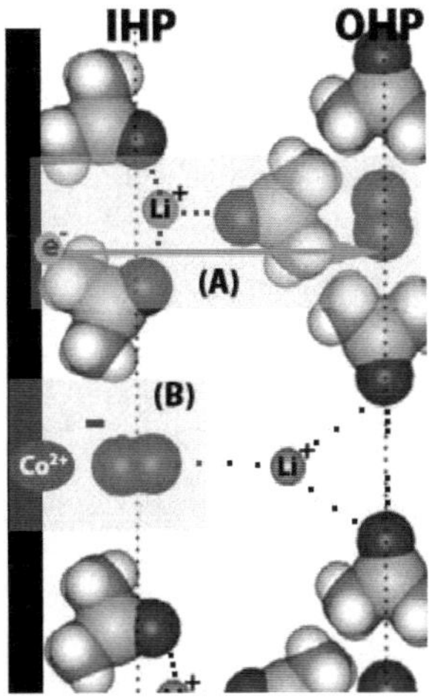

Figure 2: Electrochemical double layer at the interface of a CoPC600 catalyzed carbon electrode and a Li^+-DMSO or Li^+-DMAc electrolyte. Highlighted section (A) depicts outer sphere one-electron transfer. Highlighted section (B) shows the one-electron product superoxide chemisorbed to the Cobalt catalyst promoting further electrochemical reduction of O_2^-.

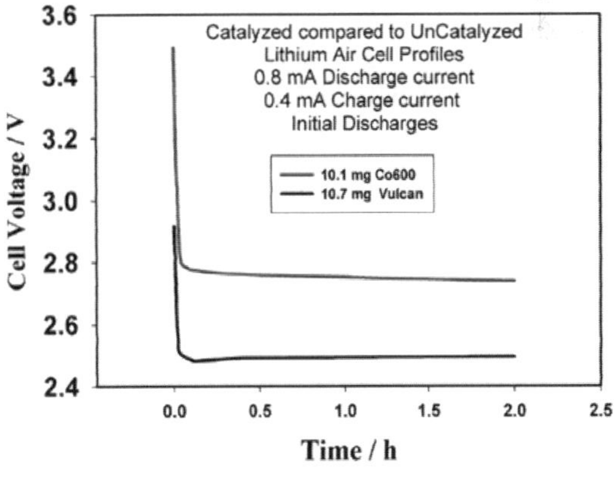

Figure 3: Discharge voltages of a Li-air cell with (upper) and without (lower) CoPC600 catalyst.

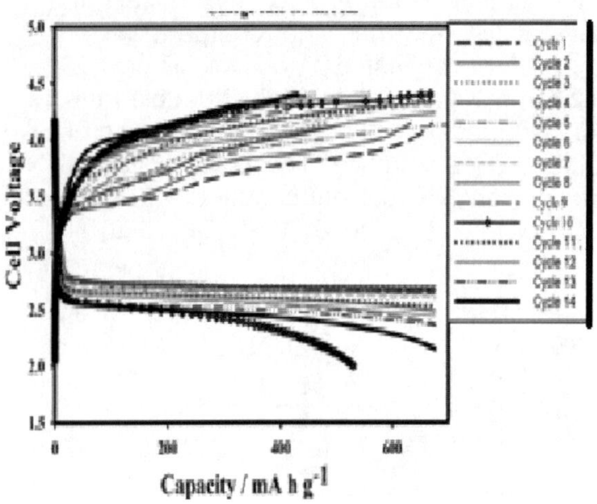

(a)

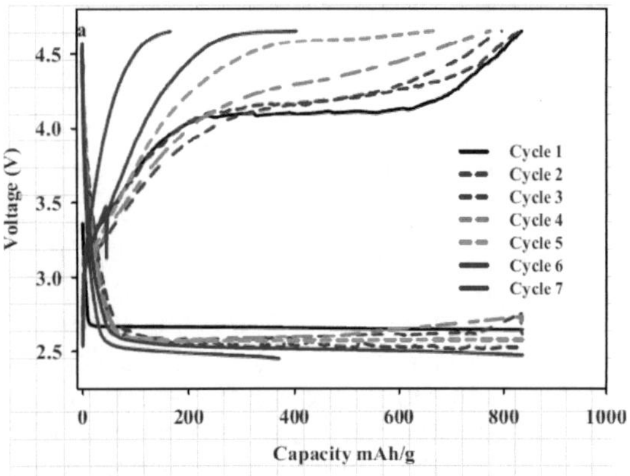

(b)

Figure 4: Li-air cell with (a) CoPC600 catalyzed Ketjenblack cathode and (**b**) uncatalyzed Ketjen black cathode with 1 M $LiPF_6$ in TEGDME electrolyte.

Acknowledgment: Financial support from the US Army CERDEC contract No: GTS-S-15-015 is gratefully acknowledged

References

1. Abraham, K. M.; Jiang, Z., Journal of the Electrochemical Society 1996, 143 (1), 1-5.
2. K.M. Abraham, J. Electrochemical Society, 2015, 162(2), A3021-A3031.
3. Laoire, C. O.; Mukerjee, S.; Abraham, K.; Plichta, E. J.; Hendrickson, M. A. *The Journal of Physical Chemistry C* **2009,** 113, (46), 20127-20134.
4. Laoire, C. O.; Mukerjee, S.; Abraham, K.; Plichta, E. J.; Hendrickson, M. A. *The Journal of Physical Chemistry C* **2010,** 114, (19), 9178-9186.
5. Trahan, M. J.; Gunasekara, I.; Mukerjee, S.; Plichta, E. J.; Hendrickson, M. A.; Abraham, K. M., Journal of The Electrochemical Society 2014, 161 (10), A1706-A1715.
6. C. J. Allen, J. Hwang, R. Kautz, S. Mukerjee, E. J. Plichta, M. A. Hendrickson and K. M. Abraham, The Journal of Physical Chemistry C, 2012, 116, 20755-20764.
7. Trahan, M. J.; Jia, Q.; Mukerjee, S.; Plichta, E. J.; Hendrickson, M. A.; Abraham, K. M., Journal of The Electrochemical Society 2013, 160 (9), A1577-A1586

Direct Recycling of Nickel Rich Scrap Cathodes

Steven Sloop[1], Michael Lerner[2], Wei Xu[2], James Trevey[3]
[1]OnTo Technology, LLC 63221 Service Road Suite F, Bend, OR USA, 97703 ssloop@onto-technology.com
[2] Oregon State University, Department of Chemistry,
153 Gilbert Hall, Corvallis, OR USA 97331, 541-737-6747, michael.lerner@oregonstate.edu
[3]Forge Nano, Inc., 1172 Century Drive Suite 240, Louisville, CO USA, 80027 jtrevey@forgenano.com

Abstract: *Nickel rich electrodes are of interest for use in next generation electric vehicle applications. With dilution of cobalt in these formulations, recycling for cobalt recovery may require fees. Direct recycling of the electrode particle does not have such constraints. Also, technical improvements in cathode manufacturing incorporate surface-treated electrode powders to improve cell performance. These systems can be adopted not only to improve 'first-life' cell performance, but also, when coupled with direct recycling technologies, facilitate the 'next-life' of low cost lithium-ion cathodes from scrap material. This paper demonstrates direct recycling of (bare) NMC 622 from used cells, and direct recycling of similar, surface treated material.*

Keywords: direct recycling; surface treated electrodes; design for recycle.

Lithium-ion batteries provide power to products ranging from electric vehicles (EVs) to energy storage systems (ESS) to smart phones. The growth of the industry is expected to reach \$98 billion worldwide by 2025. Challenges remain for these batteries in that the useful lifetime is limited by thermal reactivity of electrolytes,[1] and the consequent impedance rise in electrodes.[2] These attributes contribute to the relatively early battery end-of-life and costly disposal. An acceptable end of life liability is forecast to be 4% of the manufacturing coat of EV lithium-ion;[3] however, the lithium-ion battery disposal market is forecast to exceed \$14 billion globally by 2025, which is 14% of the industrial market.[4] This broadly highlights the current problem for the lithium-ion battery manufacturing and EV markets that there is no industrial scale, cost effective technology to recover materials at the end-of-life. However, the direct recycling technologies in combination with surface-treated electrode systems together have a unique potential to recover and return lithium-ion battery material to market in a cost effective manner.

Experimental: Lithium-ion batteries using NMC622 cathodes, and the baseline native cathode powders were obtained (2Ah, Pred Materials). To fade the cells, they were stored in a temperature controlled environmental oven held at 30°C and cycled at C/2 between 4.3-3.0 V until reaching 64% of original capacity. The capacity fade versus cycle number is shown in Figure 1 for NMC 622.

After reaching 80% of original capacity, the cells were discharged to 200mV to prepare for harvesting the electrodes. The batteries were opened the positive electrode was removed using methods taught elsewhere and summarized here;[5] the electrodes were placed into a blending-vessel with an aqueous basic (i.e. pH 10) wash-solution and delaminated from the current collector by activating the blender. The electrode materials were captured by filtration with an essentially quantitative yield. Other sample batteries were disintegrated in-whole to model other potential approaches in the recycling industry, such as shredding. The collected electrode particles are referred to as "harvested".

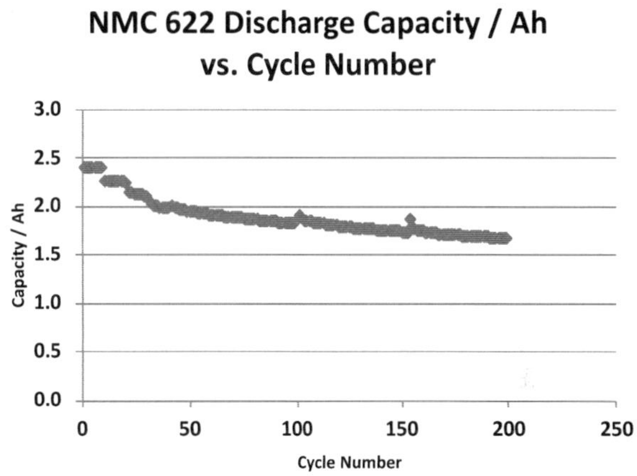

Figure 1. NMC-622 Source Cell Fade. The 2.5Ah cell was faded to 64% of original capacity by cycling at C/2 between 4.3-3.0V at 30°C.

The harvested material (i.e. 2 grams) was sealed in a pressure vessel (Parr, 100 mL) with a saturated, high lithium-ionic strength aqueous solution (with various corresponding anions). Gram quantities of liquid or solid oxidizing agents were added to the reaction vessel, and in another experiment oxygen gas was added to a pressure of 300psi. After hydrothermal treatment, the electrode material was removed from the vessel, rinsed and dried under vacuum at 120°C. The reaction solution was reused in subsequent trials. Initial harvest data were measured including capacity, XRD, and other structural characterizations. The cathodes were then heated under cover gases ranging from air, nitrogen, or oxygen. The heating temperatures were as high as 900°C using 5°C/ min ramp rates and dwell times ranging from 45 min to 8 hours with various cooling rates.

Structural Characterization for NMC622:

In addition to the previous experimental section for structural characterization, X-ray Photoelectron Spectroscopy (XPS) measurements were performed with a Physical Electrons Quantera Scanning ESCA Microprobe with a focused monochromatic Al Kα X-ray (1486.6 eV) source for excitation.

After heating, the samples were transferred to an atmosphere controlled drybox. Button size test cells were constructed using the cathode materials against lithium as described in the experimental section on recycling of NMC532.

Processing of Scrap, Native NMC622 Electrode Material: Surface treated and untreated electrode powders were obtained from Forge Nano and stored in a dry-box. Multi-gram samples were removed and exposed to air for several days and recycle-processed; the major difference was an abbreviated and much lower heat-treatment than employed on previous samples (including baseline, un-treated NMC622). Half cells were constructed and cycled to assess capacity and rate capability.

Results and Discussion:

Faded State: Nickel rich cathodes describe NMC formulations with greater than 50% nickel content, these include formulations such as NMC 622, NMC 811 and others.

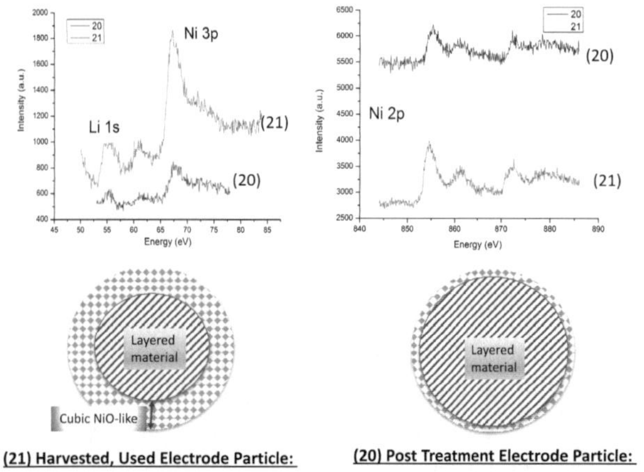

Figure 2. XPS and Particle Models. Cubic layers develop during cycling, and are reversed with the recycle treatment process.

The degraded NMC622 electrode material used in this study was harvested from the cell shown in Figure 1, in which the capacity was faded to 64% of the original state. The cut-off voltage of 4.3V is high enough to trigger electrolyte decomposition, and so the cell degradation may be slanted towards that factor over cathode decomposition. That said, the Figure 2 post mortem analyses of the harvested (untreated) cathode particles using XPS indicates a relatively high Ni^{2+} signal at 67eV for sample 21, the harvested material. That signal is due to a nickel 3p transition that occurs with population of those orbitals with a reduced (i.e. 2+) nickel.

Divalent nickel is an indicator of cubic nickel oxide that is a very poor lithium-ion conductor that inhibits the exchange current at the particle surface and contributes to capacity fade. The cubic material is likely within the first 100 nm of the surface of the electrode particle since the excitation X-ray in this XPS method only samples surface regions. This characterizes the state of the harvested, faded electrode particle as suffering from capacity fade due to non-conducting moieties forming in the surface region.

Reviving Harvested Particles: After treatment of the electrode material, the surface region of nickel is returned to an oxidized state. In Figure 2 the XPS signal for the treated sample (20) has a much lower intensity at 67eV. The use of oxidizing agents in the treatment must have oxidized nickel from Ni^{2+} to Ni^{3+}. The trivalent nickel indicates a layered metal oxide with a high conductivity for lithium-ions resulting in better exchange current density at the particle surface and therefore, higher capacity.

The half-cell specific capacity measurements of treated and untreated electrode materials supports the XPS measurement and model. Figure 3 shows that the capacity of harvested NMC622 without oxidizer in the treatment is very low (P1). The use of oxidizing agents improved the capacity of the product. Lithium chlorate (P2), hydrogen peroxide (P3 and P4) all improve the capacity of the used cathode material, even resulting in higher capacity than the baseline.

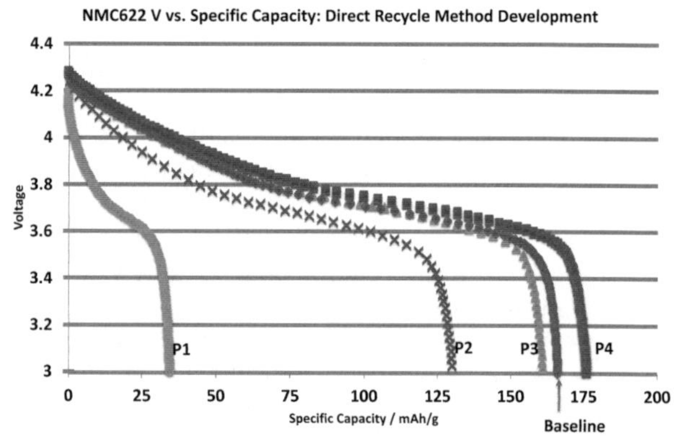

Figure 3. NMC-622 Specific Capacity after Treatments. The use of oxidizers improves the specific capacity of the degraded, harvested electrode material.

The improvement of capacity above the baseline material is plausible due to calendaring of the out-of-the-bottle material. That is, the baseline material has aged since original synthesis, and the treatment process has essentially reversed aging to a maximum extent, resetting the "born-on date" for the material.

The rate capability of the revived particles is shown in Figure 4. As a function of current density, the capacity of the revived material is slightly higher than the baseline, from the bottle, material. Processing of aged, baseline materials revives them, resulting in higher capacity on par with the harvested, recycled materials. The next section demonstrates that observation using surface-treated electrodes.

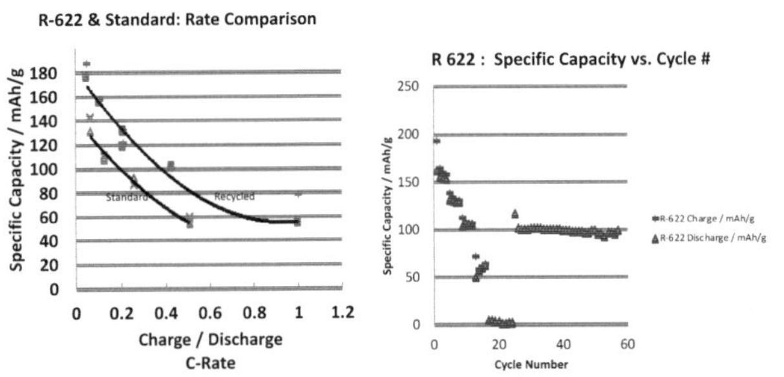

Figure 4. Rate Capability and Cycle Life. The left hand graph shows the recycled material has higher rate capability than the baseline, and the right hand figure shows good cycle life of the half-cell test for recycled NMC622.

Reviving Calendared Particles: Surface-treated NMC-622 powder became scrap after long term exposure to air. In Figure 5, the discharge graph, "ALD 622 after air exposure", shows low capacity. Simple hydrothermal processing followed by heating the material revived the capacity to 175mAh/g, which is (1) higher than the baseline, out-of-the-bottle, bare NMC 622 and (2) equal to the harvested, revived material in Figures 3 and 4. This provides evidence the recycle process reverses NMC ageing characteristics from air exposure and cell cycling.

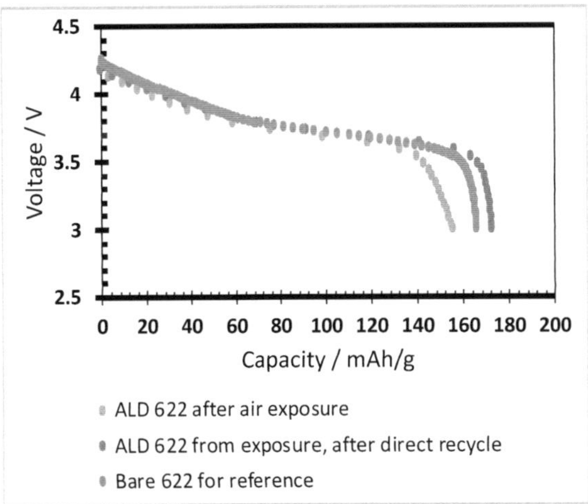

Figure 5. Direct Recycle of Surface Treated NMC. ALD-NMC622 had low capacity after air exposure. Hydrothermal/heat-dry treatment returned the specific capacity to ~175 mAh/g, which has higher capacity than uncoated, bare NMC 622.

The surface-treated NMCs were revived at lower temperature than the bare NMCs, which shows the surface-treated material is easier to recycle than the uncoated material. This result shows the potential for design for recycling using surface treated electrodes along with tdirect recycling as a strategy to reduce lifetime costs by planning for multiple lifetime uses of lithium-ion battery cathodes.

Conclusion:

Used NMC-622 harvested from 64% faded cells was directly revived using hydrothermal and heating processes. The resulting material had to equal performance to new NMC622 (without calendar time). The cost estimate for low temperature material production is less-than $10/kg.

The methodology was extended to surface coated NMC-622. The originally manufactured cathode material had low capacity due to calendaring. The capacity was revived through similar processing, but at lower temperatures, which reduces the cost estimate further for direct recycling. An originally designed battery using surface-coated electrodes, followed with direct recycling at end-of-life has the potential to enable low cost, multiple lifetime, lithium-ion cathodes.

Acknowledgements

The authors acknowledge the support and funding for this research effort from the Defense Logistics Agency through contract DLA SP4701-15-C-0097.

References

1. S.E. Sloop; J. K. Pugh; S. Wang; J. B. Kerr, K. Kinoshita *Electrochemical ans Soid-State Letters,* **4** (4) A42-A44 (2001)
2. X. Zhang, P. Ross Jr., R. Kostecki, F. Kong, S. Sloop, J. B. Kerr, K. Striebel, E. Cairns and F. McLarnon "Diagnostic Characterization of High-Power Lithium-Ion Batteries for Use in Hybrid Electric Vehicles" *Journal of the Electrochemical Society (*2001), 148, A463.
3. (i.e. 4% of manufacturing cost) T. Mackintosh, "Lithium Ion Battery Recycling Challenges" Battery Show, Novi MI (September 18, 2014)
4. Orian Research Consultants, www.orianresearch.com, (2018)
5. Sloop, S. E. US Patent #9,825,341 B2 Recycling Positive-Electrode Material of a Lithium-ion Battery (2017); Sloop, S. E.; Allen, M. US Patent #9,484,606 B1 Recycling and Reconditioning of Battery Electrode Materials (2016); Sloop, S. E. US Patent #9,287,552 B2 Reintroduction of lithium into recycled battery materials (2016); Sloop, S. E. US Patent #8,846,225 B2 Reintroduction of lithium into recycled battery materials (2014); Sloop, S. E. US Patent # 8,497,030 B2 Recycling of Battery Electrode Materials (2013)

Evaluation and Characterization of COTS Li-ion Cells for Military Applications

Svetlana Trebukhova, Chad Deroy, Frank Puglia, Rob Gitzendanner

EaglePicher Technologies -Yardney Technology Center
2000 South County Trail
East Greenwich, RI 02818
rob.gitzendanner@eaglepicher.com / 1-401-471-6580

Abstract: *The energy and power capabilities of Commercial off-the-shelf (COTS) Lithium-ion cells continue to increase as applications such as electric vehicles and power tools continue to push the envelope on performance requirements. Some high quality COTS cells are meeting the demands of several military applications, including Directed Energy Weapons and aircraft. The tradeoff between COTS and custom developed cells is often driven by more than just costs; with safety and scalability becoming important design factors. To fully evaluate and characterize the performance thresholds of COTS cells, they must be tested to profiles beyond the recommended limits of their manufacturers. Exceeding these barriers will provide better insight into the true capabilities and limitations of the cells – design engineers need to know where the cliffs are to better optimize system-level performance. This paper will review some of the "out of bounds" performance testing of COTS cells and provide insight on the optimization strategies used to evaluate the trade differentials between available COTS cells and custom designs for new applications.*

Keywords: Lithium-ion; Commercial off the Shelf; 18650; 26650; Directed Energy Weapons; Aircraft; Energy Storage Systems.

Introduction

Commercially available Lithium-ion cells have continued to improve in quality, reliability, and performance, meeting many of the requirements for military and aerospace applications. The advantage of using Commercial off-the-shelf (COTS) cells in a military battery application include lower cost, design flexibility/interchangeability, good power and energy density, and cell availability. High volume production, high levels of automation, and strong commercial pressure keeps cell costs low, typically \$1-\$0.20/Wh. By packaging small units of standard sizes, design engineers have more flexibility in arrangements of cells and modules and distribution of the power sources throughout their system. Some level of interchangeability is also achieved if the design application can utilize cells from multiple vendors. As material and production enhancements have allowed manufacturers to achieve higher capacities in the same form-factor, commercial energy densities are exceeding 250Wh/kg. The first commercial cells, available from Sony in the 18650 standard size were only a little over 1Ah capacity; today's leading cells exceed 3.5Ah in the same packaging [1].

However, there are disadvantages to relying on a foreign-source supply chain; especially one that is primarily aimed at a consumer electronics market. While packaging form factors have not changed significantly (though recently new sizes are being adopted, especially driven by Tesla's utilization of a '21700' size cell[2]), the materials within the cells, and the manufacturing procedures and operations used to assemble them do change regularly; often without any notification to the customers or even changes to the designated part number. For a Qualified military or aerospace program, these changes may present a problem for design heritage, manufacturing traceability, or baseline control. Additionally, there are almost no commercial vendors of COTS cells in North America, there are some exceptions, though typically a majority of the cells are produced overseas (Tesla currently utilizes all of the production from the Gigafactory in Nevada internally). Reliance on COTS cells requires acceptance of Asian sources of supply, with any of the political/economic issues that may bring during wartime.

For these reasons, a broad characterization of COTS cells, from multiple vendors, is advantageous to provide a clear understanding of performance capabilities and limitations, more than can be gleaned from a product data sheet, and to identify opportunities for alternative cells, should a single source of supply become compromised. The performance of different cells and vendors needs to be compared to provide data for optimized cell selection for any given application based on specific driving performance factors, be those high rates, low temperature operation, or longer life. EaglePicher Technologies produces several custom cells of different sizes and chemistries, but also recognizes the potential advantages of utilizing COTS cells for some applications. Therefore, we have begun a program to fully characterize Lithium-ion COTS cells from multiple vendors, in a standard set of test profiles and conditions, to better identify optimal cells for each mission, and provide data and confidence in the performance of those cells relative to the mission needs. The characterization test plans include a combination of power and energy performance, at different rates and different temperatures, evaluation of life cycling and stand characteristics, and always include a cell dissection, or Destructive Physical Analysis (DPA), to understand the mechanical construction of the cells, electrode tabbing, weld quality, and electrode and separator sizing and overlap. Through these tests we are building a library of information that can be shared with our customers to provide a better level of confidence in the cell selection and battery design process, and offer directly comparative information if the cell design, or manufacturer, has to be changed.

Vendor Selection

To ensure reliability of supply, minimize design variations, and provide performance stability, cells for evaluation were only selected from larger, reputable vendors with a strong history of providing high quality cells with little Lot to Lot variation and little volatility. Efforts were focused on Korean and Japanese vendors, such as Samsung and LG, though cells from Chinese manufacturers, such as A123, are being evaluated as well. These vendors deliver through numerous, reputable and well regarded distributors both domestically and overseas. Vendors usually produce cells at multiple factories, across different countries, so, where possible, we made an effort to identify manufacturing locations for batches of cells obtained, and are comparing cells from different factories as well as different date codes or Lots. The designed intent of the COTS evaluation program allows the addition of new cells, and cell vendors, at any time to continue to expand the library of performance data and stay current with available product offerings.

Test Profiles

Test profiles, or test plans, were developed with four main focuses – Power, Energy, Life and Safety. As the current focus at EaglePicher is on high power systems for Directed Energy Weapons (DEW) and aircraft applications, the current efforts have predominantly tested power cells. For each test, the rated capacity (C) is taken from the vendor data sheets. Each vendor applies different capacity deratings to their cells, however, maintaining consistency in design and discussions required accepting the vendor ratings as our test baseline to minimize confusion about performance and testing. Min and Max voltage limits are tailored to each cell based on the recommendations of the vendor. Typical test profiles start with a basic Cell Acceptance Test (CAT), which is repeated throughout the test life of the cell to track capacity degradation and impedance changes.

A typical Power profile test will include:

- Unless otherwise specified, charging at C/5 rate with a taper to C/50
- Different constant current discharge rates from C/5 to 30C (or higher if the subject cell can support the load).
- Pulse discharges for 5 seconds and 2 seconds, at rates from 1C to 50C and possibly up to 100C or greater (again, depending on the cell's performance)
- Charge and discharge (both continuous and pulse) performed at different temperatures from -20°C to +60°C
- DC Impedance tests by applying a high rate pulse over a constant current discharge as a function of State of Charge (SOC)
- Open circuit voltage (OCV) stand tests from 72 hours up to several weeks to gauge self-discharge characteristics.

Another key test is the variable temperature life cycling, during which the cells are 100% charged 1C and discharged 2C for rapid cycling; with 5 cycles at 25°C, 10 cycles at -5°C and 40 cycles at 60°C. This thermal profile is repeated as the cells continue cycling. This test acts as an accelerated life test as the high temperature exposure degrades the cells, and the impact can be clearly seen on the low temperature performance.

All tests are run using standard MACCOR cell test equipment. For some of the low temperature tests, especially high power testing, the cells are shielded from direct airflow and partially insulated to better simulate in-battery performance.

Data and Results

Typical CAT data for 18650 and 26650 cells are shown in Figure 1 and Figure 2 respectively. Both cell types are identified as power cells and rated at approximately 2.4Ah by their manufactures. The 26650 cells are typically Lithium Iron Phosphate (LFP) cathode cells; and these cells, as can be seen in the figures, do not perform as well at low temperatures.

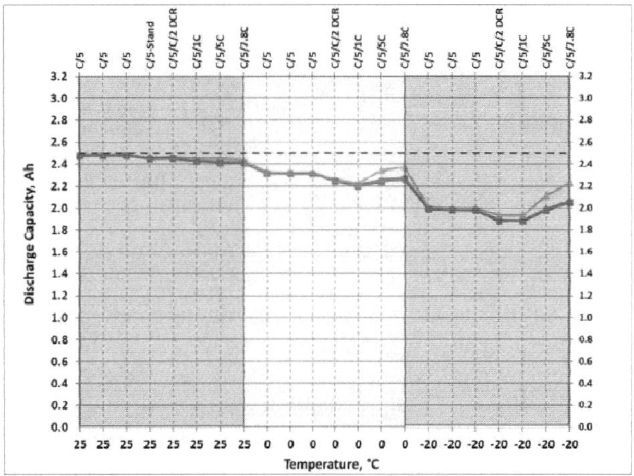

Figure 1. CAT testing of sample 18650 Power Cells

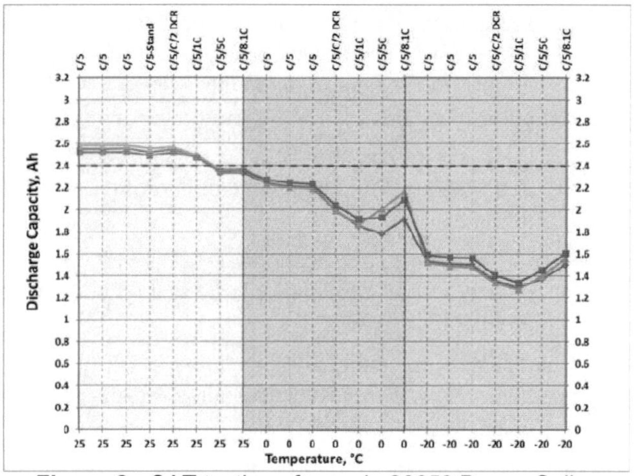

Figure 2. CAT testing of sample 26650 Power Cells

The continuous discharge rate capability of cells is characterized by comparing the capacity delivered as a percentage of the capacity at 1C. This provides a normalized comparison between cells of different sizes and capacities. The rate capability of a cell is often a function of not just the cell chemistry, but also the mechanical design with size, and number, of electrode tabs and weld designs having a significant effect on the ability of the cell to deliver high currents. Figure 3 shows the rate capability of select cells, note that only some cells support discharge rates above 5C or 10C.

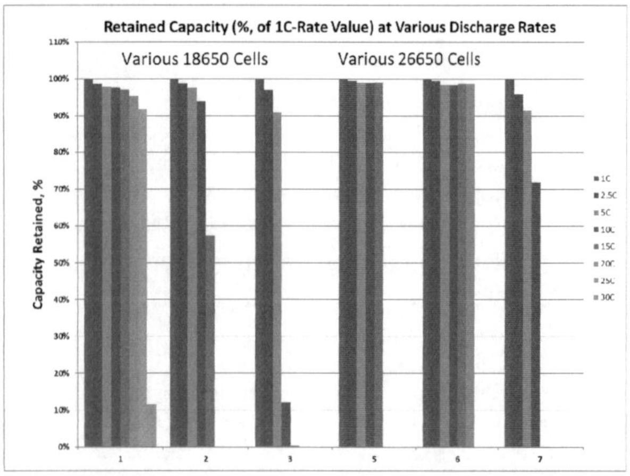

Figure 3. Continuous rate discharge results for select cells at 25°C

Pulse discharges are characterized by the minimum voltage during the pulse. C-rates are standard, per the vendor ratings, so this provides a clear indication of a cell's ability to support the high rate pulse. All pulses are limited to a minimum voltage of 1.8V to prevent cell reversal and minimize impact to the cell performance for subsequent tests. Figure 4 shows the pulse capability of a number of cells. Some COTS cells are able to easily support high pulse rates, up to 30C, which is useful for Directed Energy Weapons, aircraft or other high pulse power applications.

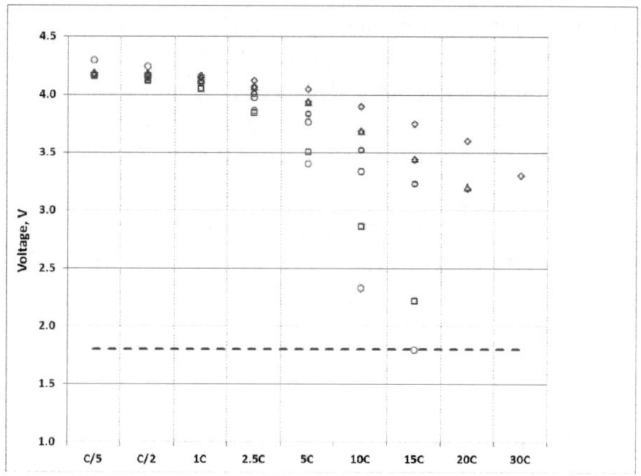

Figure 4. End of Pulse Discharge voltage for select cells at 30°C

The DC resistance of the cells is measured as a function of State of Charge, with data taken at in 10% SOC steps, and at different temperatures. This provides insight into the rate capability of the cells, but also provides valuable information for modeling the cells in a battery application. Understanding the internal impedance allows for modeling heat generation, which is used in designing the thermal management systems for the battery. Comparative data is typically examined at 50% SOC, Figure 5, as this is the flattest part of the resistance vs. SOC curve.

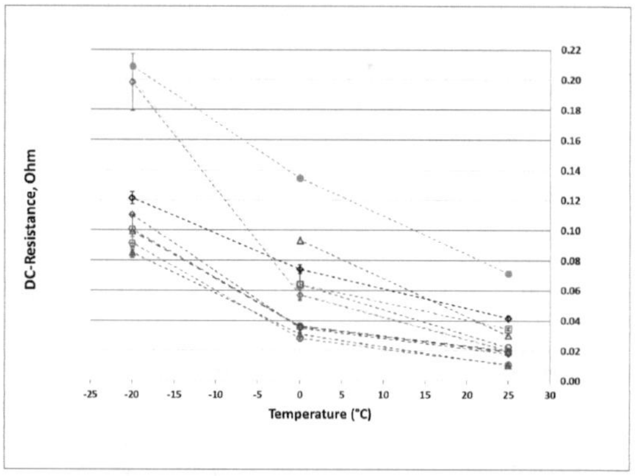

Figure 5. DC Resistance of select cells at 50% SOC over a range of temperatures from -20°C to +25°C.

The self-discharge rate of a cell can often show manufacturing defects, or other issues with cells. The OCV of all cells are measured upon receipt and outliers, cells that have discharged during storage and transport, are flagged for DPA and other testing. During testing, self-discharge rates are measured with cells in the fully charged state, 100% SOC. After charge and taper, the cells are allowed to stand open circuit for a minimum of 72 hours. The first two hours of data are typically ignored to allow the cells to equilibrate after charge, so the voltage loss is measured between hours 2 and 72, Figure 6. Notable outliers in self-discharge performance can be attributed to quality of construction and cleanliness, or material selection – typically ultra-thin separators providing a poorer electrical isolation.

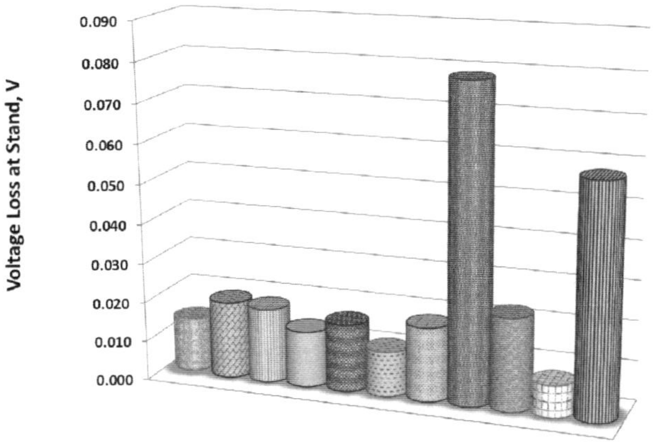

Figure 6. Voltage Drop, self-discharge rate, of various cells tested at 25□C.

As described, the variable temperature life cycle testing can be used as an accelerated life test, and provides good insight into the long-term performance of the cells. Many real-world applications, especially military, operate over broad ranges of temperatures and are exposed to different temperatures over the course of a single mission. Consider the thermal environment of an application, which may be quite cool, or ambient temperature, at the beginning of a mission, but quickly heat up as engines operate or other systems turn on. This type of thermal change has a noticeable impact on the performance of the cells and battery. These impacts are often most readily observed at very low temperatures. Depending on the chemistry or design of the cell, the increase in cell impedance, caused by operation or exposure to high temperatures, may actually improve low temperature operation initially as the cell experiences increased self-heating. The Coulombic Efficiency trend (Amphours Out divided by Amphours In) can be a good indicator of the life of the cell as the charge capacity is lost to decomposition and other parasitic reactions. Figure 7 shows the variable temperature cycles of one cell, clearly demonstrating the accelerated performance degradation of this test profile as significant capacity is lost after only 300 cycles, note the rate of capacity loss at -5□C is higher than at +60□C.

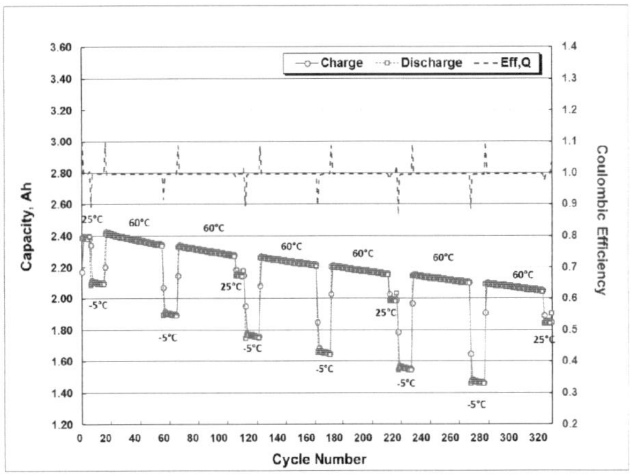

Figure 7. Variable temperature life cycle testing.

Conclusions

The evaluation and characterization of Lithium-ion COTS cells is an ongoing activity to provide a reasonably comprehensive database of available cell types and designs. By performing standard tests, and pushing the test conditions beyond the recommendations in vendor data sheets, EaglePicher is establishing a true vision of cell characteristics and performance capabilities (and limitations) to allow for optimized selection for various applications. The advantages and disadvantages of COTS solutions can easily be compared with custom designs and specifically formulated cells to provide a useful trade study. This enables a true evaluation of customer needs and power and energy solutions to provide mission-enabling systems.

Acknowledgements

The authors would like to thank their coworkers at EaglePicher, including those at the Lithiumstart facility, for help in selecting, procuring, and collecting data sheets and information on the cells. All this work is funded by EaglePicher as an IRAD effort.

References

1 Reddy, Thomas B., and David Linden. *Linden's Handbook of Batteries.* McGraw-Hill, 2011

2 Weintraub, Seth (July 28, 2016). "Tesla Gigafactory tour roundup and tidbits: 'This is the coolest factory in the world'". *Electrek.* Retrieved 2018-04-20.

Advances in Electrochemistry Development at Saft

Joong Sun Park, Carine L. Margez, Xilin Chen, Kostyantyn Kylyvnyk, Thomas A. Greszler*
Saft America, Space and Defense Division,
107 Beaver Court, Cockeysville, MD 21030
* Thomas.Greszler@saftamerica.com, +1-410-568-2590

Abstract: *SAFT has successfully applied Li-ion electrochemistry to defense, space, and commercial applications which require very high power and safety. By optimizing both the electrochemical and electro-mechanical cell designs, Saft has developed a range of Li-ion products that can deliver power pulses of 50 kW/kg or more for Joint Strike Fighter or racing car applications, or >250 Wh/kg for applications requiring high energy content. This paper summarizes advanced Li-ion electrochemistry research and development efforts underway at Saft. In particular, high power Lithium titanium oxide (LTO) based chemistry was successfully developed for 12V Start-Stop. The cells offer superior low temperature cranking performance and can meet the power needs of directed energy laser weapons. Improved energy and cycling stability without compromising safety is achieved via 4V olivine-class Lithium manganese iron phosphate (LMFP) cathode materials. Furthermore, extremely safe cell chemistries, such as water-in-salt aqueous batteries and all solid-state batteries, are in development.*

Keywords: High Power; High Safety; LTO; LMFP; Water-in-Salt; Solid-State Battery; Saft

Introduction

Saft has been manufacturing Li-ion batteries for 30 years and is a worldwide provider of high-quality, safe Li-ion systems for demanding applications in commercial, defense and space markets. Our products evolve to match the requirements of the market with a focus on high performance over a wide temperature range, long life, high quality and reliability, and rugged systems that can operate in uncontrolled and abusive environments. Saft continues to improve current Li-ion batteries and develop next-generation energy storage devices. Here, we highlight the results and status of Saft's research and development efforts on high power LTO chemistry, safe Li-ion based on LMFP cathode and beyond Li-ion batteries.

High Power LTO Chemistry

Saft has investigated the use of LTO as a replacement for traditional graphite as the negative electrode material in Li-ion batteries since 2012. LTO has the benefit of enabling symmetric fast charge/discharge plus extremely long cycle life [1-3]. Its ability to deliver high power makes the LTO chemistry attractive for numerous military and space applications such as (but not limited to) directed energy laser weapons and low earth orbit satellites that require extremely high power within a short period of time and aggressive cycling (continuous charge/discharge with a fast charge rate). Despite these benefits, LTO has historically suffered from high impedance growth and gassing at elevated temperatures [4, 5].

Saft developed a high power LTO-based chemistry as part of a US Advanced Battery Consortium / US Department of Energy (USABC/DOE) funded program for 12V Start-Stop applications. The main objectives of the program were to pass cold crank testing at -30°C and achieve 15 years of cell life at 45°C. Significant efforts were dedicated to a) optimizing the electrode composition and structure along with selecting an electrolyte that passes cold crank, while simultaneously b) reducing gassing during high temperature operation. Prototype cells have been produced, in a pouch format, with nominal voltage and capacity of 2.5V and 1.5Ah, respectively. At 25°C, these pouch cells have ~60Wh/kg specific energy and 10kW/kg specific pulse power (1s, 100% SOC).

Figure 1 summarizes the cold crank performance improvements over the course of the program, where final Lithium manganese oxide (LMO)/LTO chemistries pass cold crank (three 4.5s pulses: 0.5s 6kW pulse followed by a 4s 4kW pulse at the 12V module level). Results are shown for 1.5Ah cells at ~40% SOC. We found that 70% of the impedance came from the LTO electrodes during pulse; therefore optimization of the LTO electrode resulted in significant improvements in low temperature performance. To the best of our knowledge, this is the first successful demonstration of LMO/LTO based chemistry that passes cold crank performance testing, as outlined by USABC, at relatively low SOC.

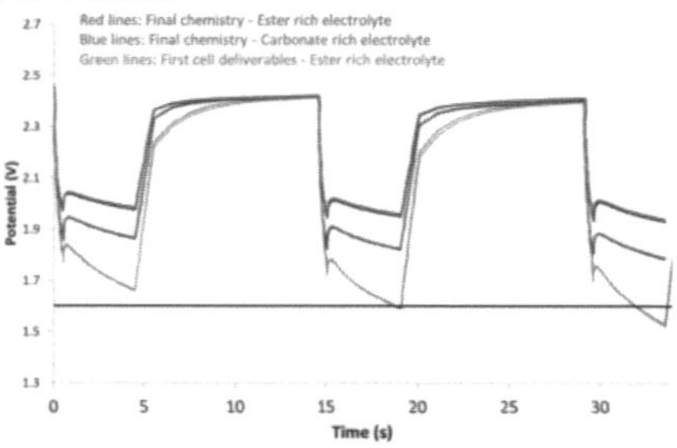

Figure 1. Cold-crank performance comparisons between first cell deliverables (green) and final prototypes (red: ester-rich electrolyte, blue: carbonate-rich electrolyte) after removing scaled 360Wh corresponding to ~40% SOC; target voltage/cell (black line) is 1.6V (5S1P configuration)

Challenges associated with LTO chemistry use include high temperature cell swelling (caused by gassing) and impedance growth. The gas generation rate of an LMO/LTO cell is largely dependent on the intrinsic physical properties of its electrolyte solvent. Solvents with low boiling points (such as nitriles and esters) typically generate more gas. As a result of selective electrolyte design, we developed a final cell chemistry with ester-rich electrolyte and a three-fold reduction in gas generation compared to the first cell deliverables, and a carbonate-rich electrolyte with ten-fold reductions, as shown in Fig. 2.

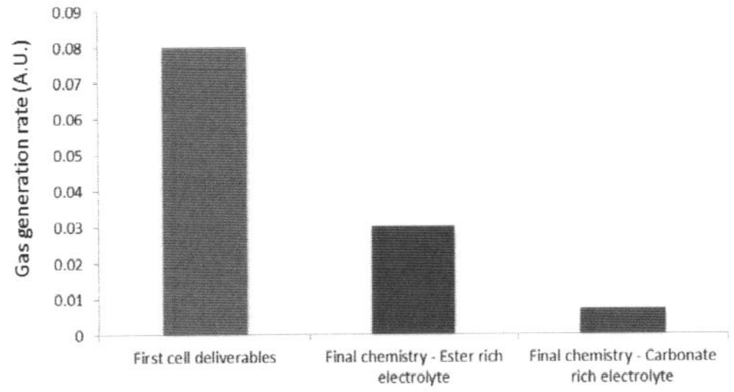

Figure 2. Gas generation rate comparisons measured at 60°C, 100% SOC between cells with baseline (green) and final selected chemistry with two electrolytes (red and blue)

Long-term cycling results for the first LMO/LTO cell deliverables are illustrated in Fig. 3. USABC micro-cycling at 45°C consists of a 1-minute discharge (59s at 1.3C rate and 1s at 6.5C) followed by a 1-minute 2.2C charge with taper to the target voltage. The cells had no capacity loss and only 20% impedance growth after 180,000 cycles (~8 months). Results for the final/improved cell chemistry are likely to exhibit even lower impedance growth because impedance growth and gas generation rates at high temperature are positively correlated (cycling results still ongoing).

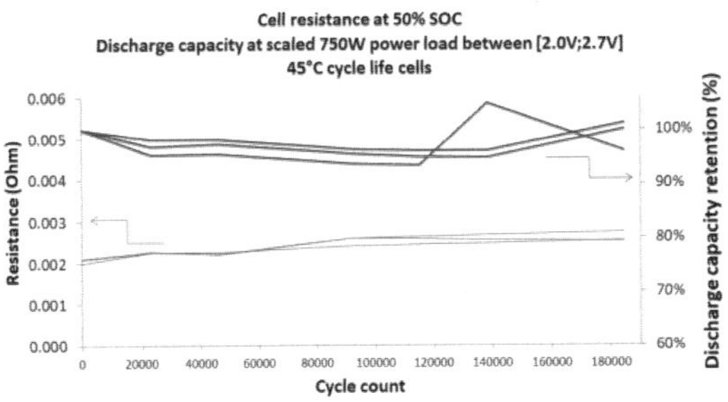

Figure 3. Discharge capacity and impedance growth during USABC micro-cycling procedure at 45°C for over 8 months

As a final deliverable to USABC, A4 size pouch cells (nominal capacity: 46Ah) were manufactured and assembled into a prototype module as shown in Fig. 4. Each prototype module includes a battery monitoring system that transmits voltage, temperature, and cell balancing data. Electrochemical characterizations, including cold-crank performance, verify successful scale-up of 1.5Ah small pouch cells to 46Ah large pouch cells.

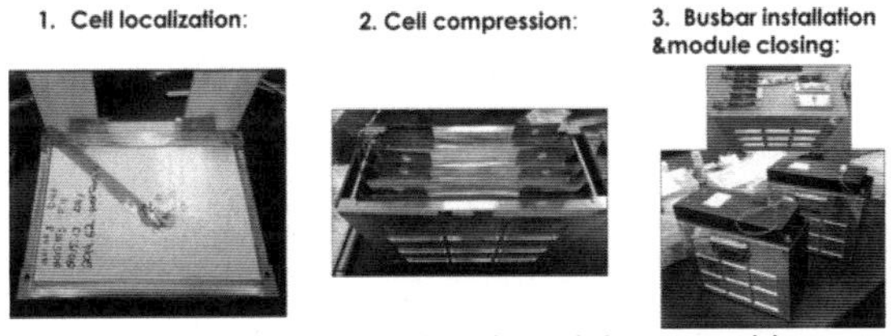

Figure 4. A4 size 46Ah cell and module assembly process

The high power and fast charging capabilities of the LTO electrode chemistry could be an attractive battery solution for directed energy weapon systems. Accordingly, the same LTO electrode was coupled with Lithium nickel manganese cobalt oxide (NMC) cathode material and evaluated. NMC/LTO cells were tested using two different procedures, current ramping and constant current, as depicted in Fig. 5. The current ramping profile is: both charge and discharge pulses spike to 250A and ramp to 0A over 3 seconds with a 20-second rest between each pulse. Pulses are 7% depth of discharge (DOD) with an average rate of 83C. For the constant current procedure, discharges are 150A for 10 seconds and charges are 50A for 30 seconds with no rests between pulses. Pulses are 28% DOD, with 100C and 33.3C rates, respectively.

Preliminary results, shown in Fig. 5, plot the voltage responses for both test profiles. For the current ramping pulse procedure, delivery of 8kW/kg was available during 3 seconds of peak power over 600W pulse (~150C) at 25°C. Cells experienced negligible capacity fading (<1%) or impedance growth (<3%) after 10,000 cycles. The cells subjected to the constant current pulse procedure, which used DOD ranges four times higher than that for the current ramping pulse test, experienced 14% capacity fading and 22% impedance growth after 5,000 cycles. The cell temperatures remained below 30°C for both pulse tests, which is 10°C -15°C lower than temperatures recorded for Saft VL5U cells that have graphite-based anode.

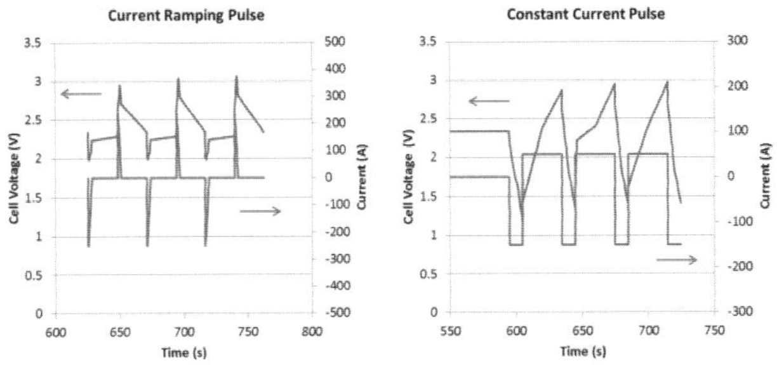

Figure 5. Current profiles over time and corresponding voltage response during (L) current ramping and (R) constant current procedures for directed energy weapon application

Enhanced Safety with Mn-Phosphate

Lithium manganese iron phosphate (LMFP) offers the safety of Lithium iron phosphate (LFP) and the energy density of NMC because of its olivine crystal structure and high operational potential, around 4V [6]. This chemistry can deliver more than 20% increased energy compared to Saft's current Super Phosphate™ technology. Drawbacks to commercializing the LMFP technology are i) poor ionic/electronic conductivity, and ii) poor cycle life, due in part to distortion of the Jahn-Teller active Mn^{3+} ion and transition metal dissolution. Saft has improved this electrochemistry–especially its rate capability, cycle life and manufacturing/process quality–by optimizing the electrode formulation and choosing the most suitable anode materials. Cells with different formats (i.e., cylindrical, hard case prismatic, and pouch) were assembled and evaluated for different applications.

Evaluation of 32Ah LMFP cells in abuse conditions did not lead to thermal runaway during nail penetration (Figure 6) or 1C overcharge, confirming the intrinsic stability of the LMFP materials compared to layered oxides. Also, a 3.3Ah LMFP/graphite pouch cell shows excellent capacity retention (>80% after ~1400 cycles), as depicted in Fig. 7.

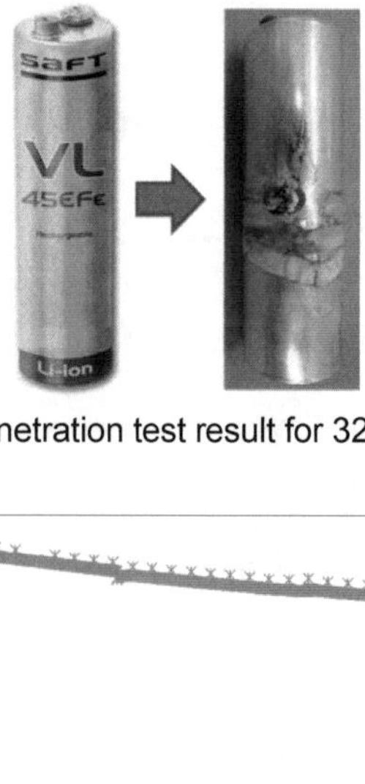

Figure 6. Nail penetration test result for 32Ah cylindrical cell

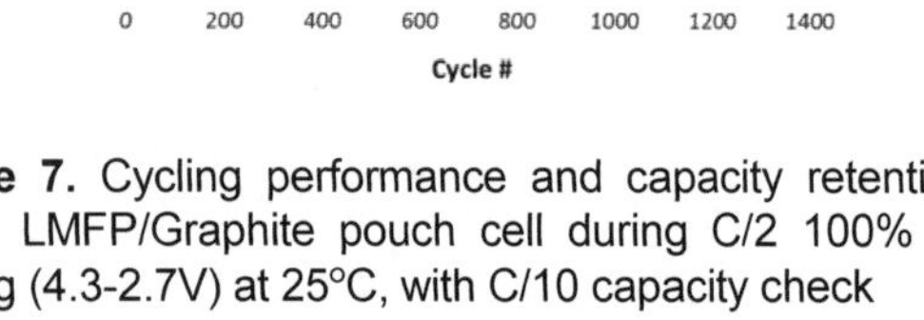

Figure 7. Cycling performance and capacity retention of 3.3Ah LMFP/Graphite pouch cell during C/2 100% DOD cycling (4.3-2.7V) at 25°C, with C/10 capacity check

To better understand the capacity fading mechanism for LMFP/graphite cells, Saft performed differential capacity and voltage analyses. The data showed a slight shift of LiC_6 to LiC_{12} transition peak and Mn redox capacity in the differential voltage (dV/dQ) of an aged cell, which corresponds to ~3% of total capacity.

Further analysis through differential-voltage signature showed that active lithium loss during cycling is the main cause of capacity fading, which is described well in an earlier report [7]. The result is further supported by half-cell capacities from harvested electrodes. There was only 1%-2% capacity loss in aged cathodes and anodes. In addition, we observed an increased amount of Mn in aged graphite anodes. These changes in solid electrolyte interface (SEI) might be due to the presence of Mn, which could be consuming the active lithium during cycling (as reported in other Mn-containing cathode materials [8]). Further cycling performance improvements are expected as Saft works with suppliers to improve the stability of Mn and optimizes the electrolyte additives.

High Energy Aqueous Li-ion Batteries

"Water-in-salt" electrolyte utilizes non-flammable water as an electrolyte. Non-flammable water is achieved by dissolving lithium bis(trifluoromethane sulfonyl)imide (LiTFSI), at extremely high concentrations (molarity > 20M), in water. This leads to an anion-containing Li^+ solvation sheath, forming a dense interphase on the anode surface mainly arising from anion reduction. This highly concentrated water-in-salt electrolyte, with its substantially reduced electrochemical activity, provides an expanded electrochemical stability window of ~3.0V [8]. LMFP with various negative electrodes is currently being investigated as a part of a DOE Advanced Research Project Agency-Energy (ARPA-E) program that seeks to develop an intrinsically safe aqueous system.

All Solid-State Battery

Replacement of flammable liquid electrolyte with solid-state electrolyte could revolutionize energy storage system safety and energy density, and could lead to bipolar module designs. A breakthrough in the ionic conductivity of solid-state electrolytes based on polymer, ceramic, or hybrids could enable the use of metallic lithium, which could increase energy density up to 500Wh/kg and 1000Wh/L. We envision incremental advances from the current lithium-ion cell architecture to all solid-state batteries with lithium metal [10].

Saft is actively investigating and determining the best strategy and schedule for implementing this technology. We have identified the most promising technologies currently available, notably from start-ups and our partners in joint development and strategic investments. We expect to build the first prototype based on all-solid-state batteries in 2018.

Conclusions

Saft has developed an advanced LTO-based electrochemistry for high power applications. Performance tests confirmed that LTO chemistry is an ideal solution for applications requiring high power, long cycle life, and 0V storage. Advances in LMFP technology via optimizations in electrode formulation and architecture, choice of electrolyte and additives allow significant enhancements in cycle life and power capabilities with excellent safety. Next-generation battery chemistries that use highly concentrated (>20M) aqueous electrolytes and solid-state electrolytes are under development–potentially enabling batteries with even higher energy capabilities and unprecedented safety.

Acknowledgements

Support for this work from the USABC program and the U.S. Department of Energy, Office of Energy Efficiency and Renewable Energy, is gratefully acknowledged.

The authors also acknowledge the support from DOE ARPA-E (DEAR0000389).

References

1. Colbow, K. M., Dahn, J. R., and Haering, R. R., "Structure and Electrochemistry of the Spinel Oxides LiTi2O4 and Li4/3Ti5/3O4," *J. Power Sources*, vol. 26, pp. 397–402, 1989.
2. Ferg, E., Gummow, R. J., Kock, A. de, and Thackeray, M. M., "Spinel Anodes for Lithium-Ion Batteries," *J. Electrochem. Soc.* vol. 141(11), pp. L147, 1994.
3. Amine, K., Belharouak, I., Chen, Z., Tran, T., Yumoto, H., Ota, N., Myung, S. T., and Sun, Y. K., "Nanostructured Anode Material for High-Power Battery System in Electric Vehicles," *Adv. Mater.*, vol. 22 (28), pp. 3052–3057, 2010.
4. Chen, Y., Greszler, T., and Deveney, B., "Lithium Titanite Oxide as Negative Electrode in Li-Ion Cells," US 2015/0333371 A1 2015.
5. Han, C., He, Y-B., Liu, M., Li, B., Yang, Q., Wong, C-P., and Kang, F., "A review of gassing behavior in Li4Ti5O12-based lithium ion batteries," *J. Mater. Chem. A*, vol. 5, pp. 6368-6381, 2017.
6. Martha, S.K., Grinblat, J., Haik, O., Zinigrad, E., Drezen, T., Miners, J.H., Exnar, I., Kay, A., Markovsky, B., and Aurbach, D., "LiMn0.8Fe0.2PO4: An Advanced Cathode Material for Rechargeable Lithium Batteries," *Angew. Chem. Int. Ed.*, vol. 48, pp. 8559-8563, 2009.
7. Keil, P., Schuster, S. F., Wilhelm, J¨., Travi, J., Hauser, A., Karl., R. C., and Jossen, A., "Calendar Aging of Lithium-Ion Batteries I. Impact of the Graphite Anode on Capacity Fade," *J. Electrochem. Soc.* vol. 163(9), pp. A1872-A1880, 1994.
8. Gilbert, J. A, Shkrob. I. A, and Abraham, D. P., "Transition Metal Dissolution, Ion Migration, Electrocatalytic Reduction and Capacity Loss in Lithium-Ion Full Cells," *J. Electrochem. Soc.* vol. 164(2), pp. A389-A399, 2017.
9. Suo, L., Borodin, O., Gao, T. Oliguin, M., Ho, J., Fan, X., Luo, C., Wang, C., and Xu, K., ""Water-in-salt" electrolyte enables high-voltage aqueous lithium-ion chemistries," *Science,* vol. 350, pp. 938-943, 2015.
10. Janek, J. and Zeier, W. G., "A solid future for battery development," *Nat. Energy*, vol. 1, pp 1-4, 2016.

SAFT's Pouch Product and Capability

Carine Margez, Jian Dong, Serena Peterson, Saori Tokuoka, Thomas A. Greszler*,
Saft America, Space and Defense Division,
107 Beaver Court, Cockeysville, MD 21030
*Thomas.Greszler@saftamerica.com

Abstract:

Saft has developed Li-ion technology for space, defense and commercial applications, offering high energy cells and high power cells based on customers' requirements. While a number of our standard products are in cylindrical format, Saft has also successfully integrated pouch cells into our product line. Over the past five years our pouch proficiencies have expanded in terms of custom size factor availability and performance. Saft can design, build, and deliver Li-ion pouch cells for a broad range of high power to high energy applications. The high power cells are used for Formula 1 car racing applications and are being considered for laser weapons applications, while the high energy cells are suitable for the Navy, E-type racing(i.e., fully electric cars)and more applications. In parallel, novel Li-ion chemistries have been developed to improve cell safety. For example, lithium titanium oxide (LTO) and lithium manganese iron phosphate (LMFP) have been extensively investigated in pouch cell format and tested under abuse conditions. Extremely safe cell chemistries, such as all solid-state batteries in pouch cell format, are under development. Saft's vision is to provide electrochemical solutions and custom-made pouch cell manufacturing capabilities to meet our customers' needs.

Keywords: Pouch Cell; High Power; High Energy; Safety, Saft

Introduction

Saft has been manufacturing Li-ion batteries for 30 years and is a world leader in providing Li-ion systems for demanding applications in commercial, defense and space markets. Our products have evolved to match the requirements of the market, focusing on high performance over a wide temperature range, long life, high quality and reliability, and rugged systems that can operate in uncontrolled and abusive environments. Saft continues to improve current Li-ion batteries and develop next-generation energy storage devices. Here we highlight Saft's developments in pouch cell design and manufacturing for both high power and high energy applications. Saft works with customers for low- and high-volume needs.

Diverse Form Factor Capability

Pouch cells weigh less and offer more flexibility in cell size and shape than cylindrical cells. Saft has been developing pouch cell designs for the last few years with the first prototype cell in 2012 and commercial cell in 2014. We have experience manufacturing pouch cells ranging from 2Ah all the way to 50Ah and in sizes from 13cm ×8cm to 21cm × 28cm. Cell length, width and thickness can be tailored to each customer's request and designed to best fit the application. In addition, the chemistry (active materials and electrolyte) and power/energy can be tailored to meet most needs. Figure 1 shows the range of power and energy cells available.

Type	Specific Energy	Specific Power
High Energy	250 Wh/kg	2 kW/kg
Power	120 Wh/kg	6 kW/kg
Very High Power	80 Wh/kg	20 kW/kg
Ultra High Power	52 Wh/kg	40 kW/kg

Figure 1: Range of power/energy available from Saft cells.

High Power and High Temperature Pouch Cell

High power pouch cells are one of Saft's specialty products. These "power blocks" are optimized to power hybrid vehicles, directed-energy weapons, and specialty race cars. Saft continues to lead in high power cell applications through research & development and advanced manufacturing.

Our high temperature pouch cells can operate at 100°C and at extremely high rates (200C). Table 1 presents the specific energy and power performance capabilities of Saft's high power cells in cylindrical and pouch cell formats. Both cell formats have extremely high power-to-energy (P/E) ratios, over 500. Figure 2 shows capacity retention for Saft pouch cells discharged at different C-rates at room temperature (25°C). Figure 3 compares cell performance for several rate capabilities at three temperatures. The cell can discharge at a 50C rate and retain more than 85% capacity at 25°C. The cell capacity retention after 50C rate discharge increases to 91% at 45°C and to 96% at 60°C.

	Performance of Saft Cell	
	Saft 3.5Ah cylindrical cell	Saft 2Ah pouch cell
Wh/Kg	78	100
W/Kg	46,260	50,250

Table 1: Specific energy and power of high power cylindrical and pouch cells.

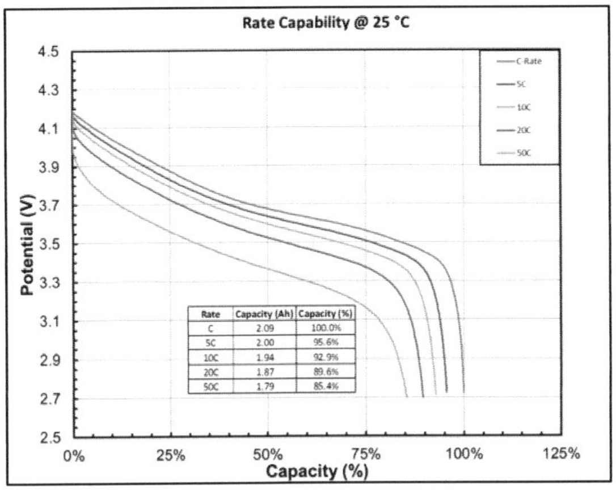

Figure 2: Rate capability of Saft pouch cell at room temperature, and cell size is roughly 100cm x 100cm x 2 mm.

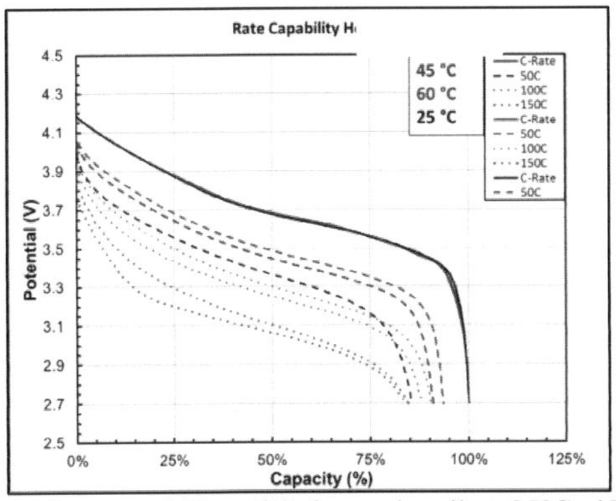

Figure 3: Rate capability of Saft pouch cell at 25°C, 45°C and 60°C. Cell size is roughly 100cm × 100cm × 2 mm.

In addition, Saft has been investigating LTO chemistry in a pouch format. Performance features such as high power, improved safety and fast charging capability are achievable with LTO chemistry leading to an attractive battery solution for directed energy weapon systems [1-3]. In parallel the pouch cell design improves packaging efficiency and reduces weight. LTO electrode was coupled with Nickel Manganese Cobalt (NMC) cathode material and the cells were tested using two different procedures, current ramping and constant current, as depicted in Figure 4. For the current ramping procedure, both charge and discharge pulses spike to 250A and ramp to 0A over 3 seconds, with 20 seconds of rest between each pulse. Pulses are 7% depth of discharge (DOD) with an average rate of 83C. For the constant current procedure, discharges are 150A for 10 seconds and charges are 50A for 30 seconds with no rest between pulses. Pulses are 28% DOD, 100C and 33.3C, respectively.

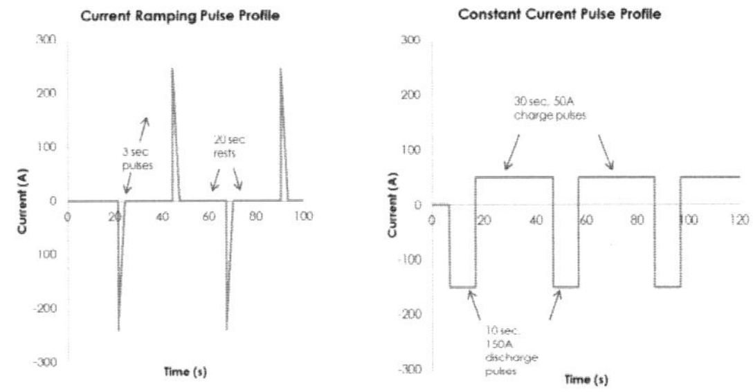

Figure 4: Current profiles over time during testing for direct energy weapons applications.

Preliminary results show that the current ramping test causes negligible capacity fading (<1%) and impedance growth (<3%) after 10,000 cycles. Constant current pulse testing, which utilizes four times higher DOD ranges, result in 14% capacity fading and 22% impedance growth after 5,000 cycles. The cell temperature stays below 30°C for both pulsing tests, which is 10°C-15°C lower than the results for Saft's VL5U cells (based on graphite anode).

High Energy Pouch Cell

Saft has developed very high energy pouch cells with excellent cycling performance. This work optimizes cell design in terms of electrode porosity, separator selection, and positive material screening. Compared to Panasonic's 3.4Ah 18650 Saft's pouch shows higher volumetric energy and significantly better cycling at 45°C, as shown in Figure 6.

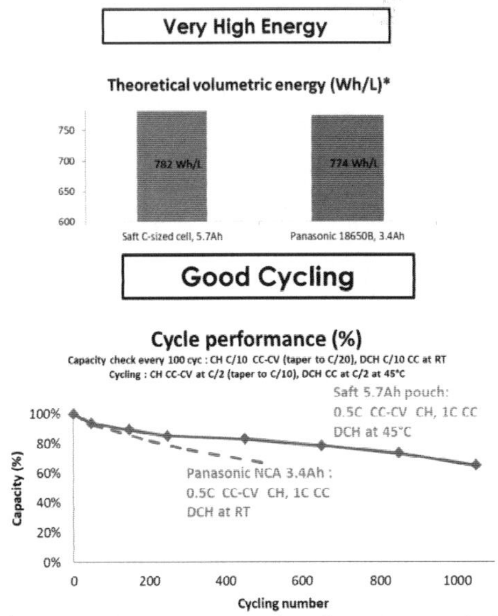

Figure 6: Saft's high energy pouch cell vs. Panasonic 18650B. The volumetric energy comparison excludes mechanical parts.

Furthermore Saft's high energy cells show high rate capability at room temperature, as depicted in Figure 7, with 68% capacity retention at a 2C rate. On top of having good charge / discharge performance the high energy pouch cells developed by Saft experience lower temperature increases during high rate discharges compared to an 18650 cell. This is possible because of the higher heat dissipation surface in the pouch cell format (Figure 8) [4].

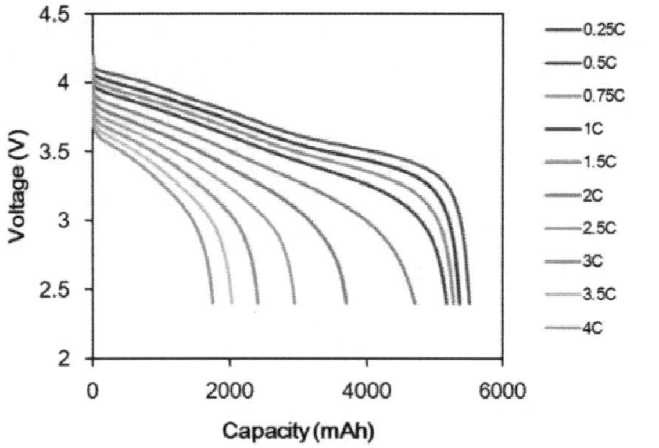

Figure 7: Rate capability testing at 25°C of Saft's high energy pouch cell.

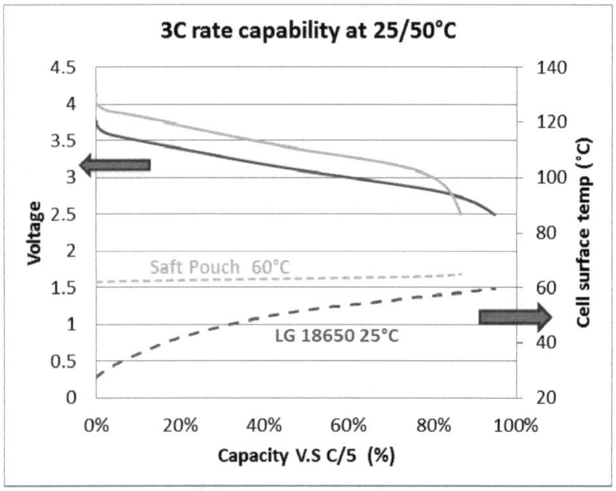

Figure 8: Temperature increase during rate capability testing.

Within the high energy market Saft developed a 4.9Ah (240Ah/kg) prototype high energy-high power pouch cell and compared the cell's performance to Sony's VTC6 18650 (240Ah/kg) commercially available cells. Based on hybrid pulse-power capability (HPPC) testing results, Saft's newly developed high energy-high power pouch cells deliver better power density at 25°C and 60°C compared to Sony's VTC6 18650 cell, as shown in Figure 9. HPPC consists of 10C discharge pulses for 10s at different states of charge (SOCs).

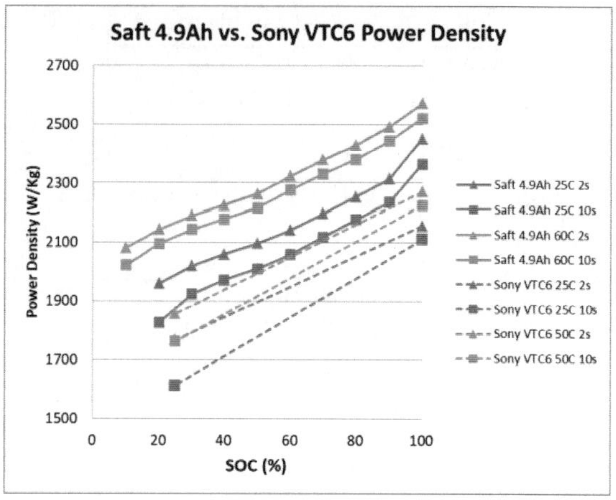

Figure 9: HPPC testing at 25°C (blue lines) and 60°C (pink lines) comparing Saft's 4.9Ah pouch cell (continuous lines) and Sony's 3Ah VTC6 18650 cell (dotted lines).

Compared to Samsung's 30Q 3Ah 18650 (240Ah/kg) cell, Saft's 4.9Ah cell shows better performance during electric race cycling tests. The Saft pouch does not heat up significantly (max. temp. 45°C vs. 67°C for the 30Q 18650 pouch) and shows much less impedance. See Figure 10.

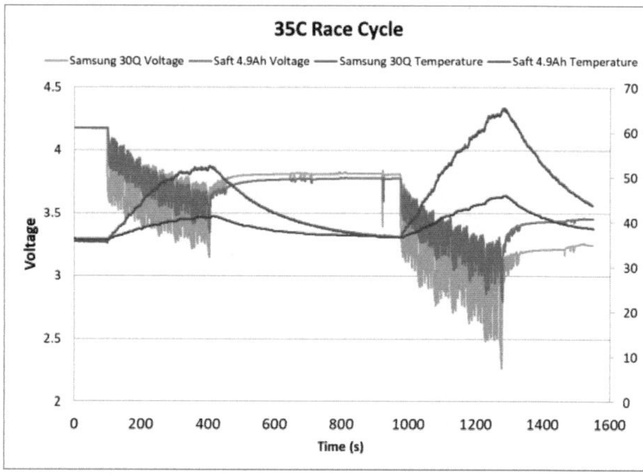

Figure 10: Results of Race Cycle testing that compare Saft's 4.9Ah (22-2) prototype pouch cell voltage and temperature performance to Sony's 3Ah 30Q pouch.

Pouch Cell Safety

Saft has also developed a high power Lithium Manganese Oxide (LMO)/LTO cell within the US Advanced Battery Consortium / US Department of Energy (USABC/DOE) funded 12V start-stop program. The chemistry was selected for its power capability and safety features. Saft built and tested 46Ah pouch cells using the LMO/LTO electrochemistry. These prototype cells showed extremely promising cold crank performance, passing three pulses at -30°C. One cell underwent nail penetration abuse testing. Some venting occurred from the nail penetration test, however no fire or disassembly took place, as shown in Figure 11.

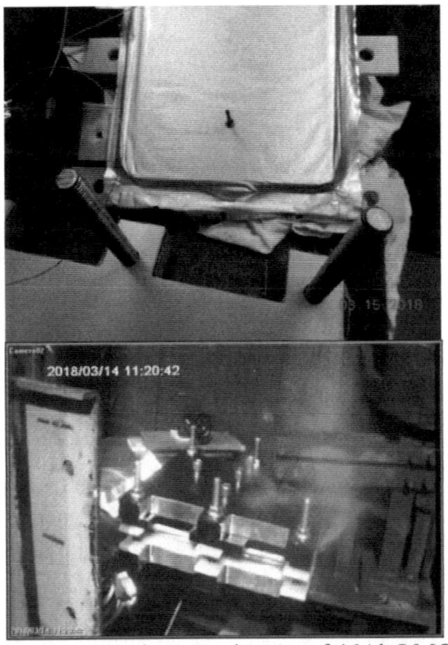

Figure 11: Nail penetration test pictures of 46Ah LMO/LTO cell. Cell was charged to 2.7V @ 46A tapered to 2.3A and placed into Nail Penetration fixture.

The LTO pouch cell design is very safe and is ideal for applications that require fast charging, low weight, better packaging efficiency and safety. In order to offer safer pouch cells to the high energy and high power markets, Saft is also developing LMFP chemistry in pouch cell format. LMFP offers the same safety as Lithium Iron Phosphate (LFP) and the energy density of NMC because of its olivine crystal structure and high operating voltage, around 4V [5]. This chemistry can deliver more than 20% higher energy compared to Saft's current Super Lithium Iron Phosphate (SLFP) technology. Previous overcharge and nail penetration tests with hard case prismatic and cylindrical cell format cells did not show thermal runaway. Abuse testing is planned for the pouch cell configuration.

Solid-State Batteries for Ultra High Energy

"All solid-state" batteries could revolutionize energy storage systems in terms of safety, energy density, and bipolar design. Saft is actively investigating and determining how and when to implement the technology. We have identified the most promising technology and are partnering, through joint development and strategic investments, to develop prototypes for performance and safety testing. We expect to have a prototype cell based on all solid-state batteries in 2018. Saft's knowledge in pouch cell manufacturing and our full-service cell / battery production facilities are assets that lower startup costs and risks associated with solid-state battery prototyping and evaluation of solid-state technology scale up prospects.

Conclusions

Saft has been developing lithium ion pouch cells since early 2012. Pouch cell manufacturing capability offers a range of different form size factors, tailored to meet each customers' program-specific needs. Saft's pouch cells are competitive in the high power markets, with graphite chemistry delivering 200C rates at 100°C and LTO delivering 83C at room temperature. Within the high energy domain, Saft's pouch cells offer better cycling capability than Panasonic's 18650 with better heat dissipation. Beyond Lithium-ion batteries, Saft is investigating all solid-state cell technology. Given the extent of Saft's knowledge in processing pouch cells and our capability to transform concepts into prototypes, and then test performance and safety in house, we are a cost-effective source for evaluating solid-state technology efficacy and product scale up manufacturability.

References

1. Colbow, K. M., Dahn, J. R., and Haering, R. R., "Structure and Electrochemistry of the Spinel Oxides LiTi2O4 and Li4/3Ti5/3O4," *J. Power Sources*, vol. 26, pp. 397–402, 1989.
2. Ferg, E., Gummow, R. J., Kock, A. de, and Thackeray, M. M., "Spinel Anodes for Lithium-Ion Batteries," *J. Electrochem. Soc.* vol. 141(11), pp. L147, 1994.
3. Amine, K., Belharouak, I., Chen, Z., Tran, T., Yumoto, H., Ota, N., Myung, S. T., and Sun, Y. K., "Nanostructured Anode Material for High-Power Battery System in Electric Vehicles," *Adv. Mater.*, vol. 22 (28), pp. 3052–3057, 2010.
4. Kim Yeow, Ho Teng, Marina Thelliez, Eugene Tan, "3D Thermal Analysis of Li-ion Battery Cells with various Geometries and Cooling Conditions using abaqus", AVL Powertrain Engineering
5. Martha, S.K., Grinblat, J., Haik, O., Zinigrad, E., Drezen, T., Miners, J.H., Exnar, I., Kay, A., Markovsky, B., and Aurbach, D., "LiMn0.8Fe0.2PO4: An Advanced Cathode Material for Rechargeable Lithium Batteries," *Angew. Chem. Int. Ed.*, vol. 48, pp. 8559-8563, 2009.

High Performance Safe Li-Ion Battery Systems

Ryo Tamaki, Hiroshi Nakahara
EnerSys
12744 San Fernando Rd, Sylmar, California, USA, 91342
ryo.tamaki@enersys.com / 1-818-833-2028

Abstract: *EnerSys is proposing a novel lithium-ion cell design to mitigate the safety risk and increase energy density, while maintaining the minimum power density and wide operating temperature capability. In conventional lithium ion cells, one main type of active material for the cathode and anode is used to address often competing requirements such as power & energy density, safety, life and operating temperature range. Often trades are to meet the most important requirements first, while compromising on the other requirements.*

Keywords: multi-functional electrodes, high performance, safety, high power, high energy, energy cache, self-power pumping

Introduction

Instead of relying on a singular active material approach, EnerSys is proposing a multi-functional electrode design. In this design, we employ several active materials with different functionalities, i.e. different power and different energy capabilities. The approach is analogous to a flow of data in a computer, in which a computer is generally equipped with cache on the CPU, memory, and the hard drive. The fastest data exchange is done through cache. Intermediate data exchange through memory and slow and long term storage is taken care by hard drive. Similar to this data exchange, in our multi -functional electrode lithium-ion design, short term energy exchange is done through a High Power Material **A**, intermediate one by Energy Material **B** and the long term storage by High Energy Material **C** (**Figure 1**).

Use of multifunctional components itself is not new. For example, hybrid energy storage comprising of a super capacitor and a lithium ion battery is being used to provide a solution to meet both power and energy demand. However, these systems are made of multiple separate devices and require custom battery management systems to control flow and direction of energies and also power conversion to match the voltage ranges, resulting in increased complication, lower reliability and higher cost. Lately internal hybridization of capacitor materials and battery materials has also gained some attentions to achieve the same goal but with limited materials choices[1, 2, 3].

Our concept is less complex. We utilize multiple active materials in a single electrode and let them exchange energy electrochemically without implementing additional battery management electronics. Our design is also more flexible than the known hybrid electrode approaches; allowing us to combine multiple function components in a single electrode. The new electrode design will enable a smooth flow of energy among the different layers of active materials, through an electrochemical control of impedances and material capacities. At the battery or system power distribution level, the cell appears as a single storage device.

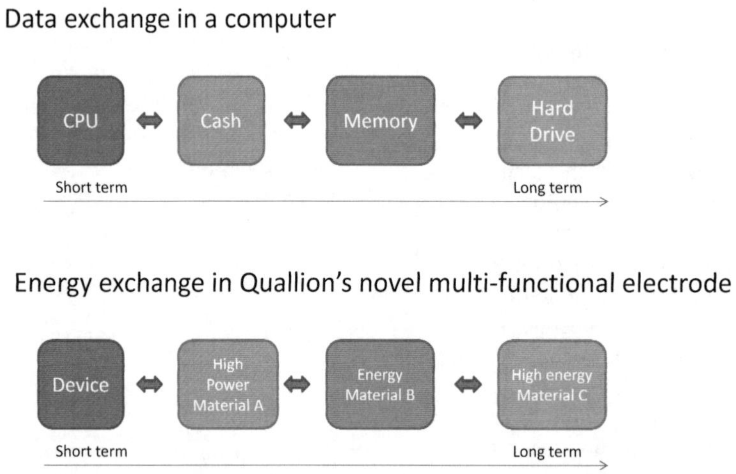

Figure 1. Comparison of EnerSys novel multi-functional electrode concept and data exchange in a computer.

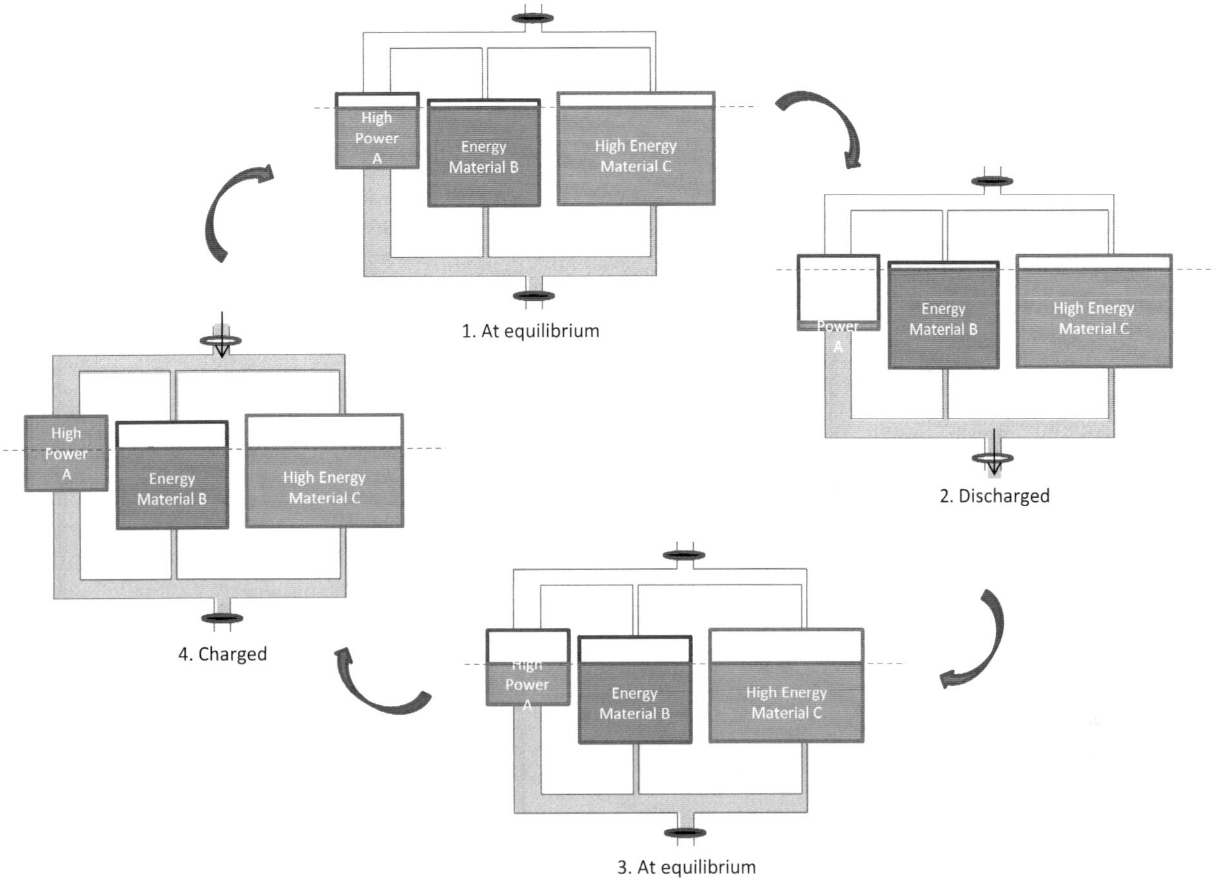

Figure 2. Description of EnerSys novel multi-functional electrode concept.

The concept can be described as in **Figure 2**. At rest (**Figure 2-1**), the energy levels of all the components are at the same level since they are connected in parallel within the electrode. When thee cell is discharged, the energy is drained from the highest power component, in this case from High Power Material A (**Figure 2-2**). Then when the cell is put at rest, the energy levels equilibrate again, energy flowing from Energy Material B/C to High Power Material A within the electrode design(**Figure 2-3**), essentially self-charging High Power Material A. In addition, when the cell is first charged from a low state of charge, High Power Material A initially absorbs the in rush energy (**Figure 2-4**). We achieve control of this energy flow through the interface of the ionic and electronic impedance of the active components and by careful selection of materials with proper voltage potential levels, and call the self-controlled flow of energy "self-power pumping".

Figure 3 describes a current flow in multi-active components electrode [3]. The positive current in y-axis indicates discharge current. The cell goes through 1 second discharge and 9 second rest, total of 4 pulses in the graph. The solid line corresponds to current flow from a high power component, the dotted line is for high energy component, and another dotted line for the total load current. During discharge, most of the load current is provided by the high power component, which gradually fades with a drain of the energy. Instead the high power component gradually increases its contribution.

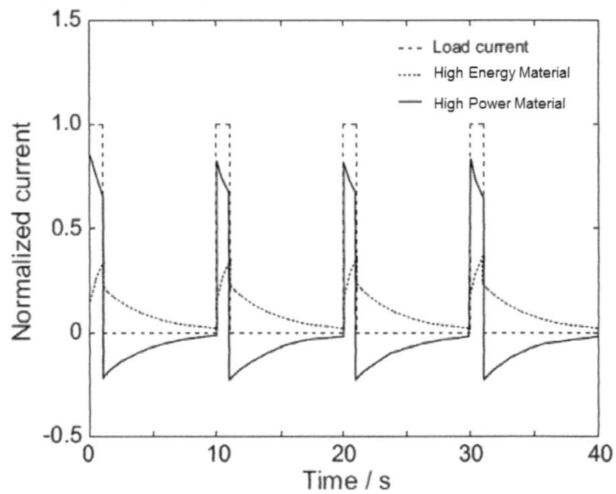

Figure 3. Energy flow in multi-functional electrode[3].

During rest, the energy flows from the high energy component to the high power component, as described in **Figure 2**, charging the high power component. Before the subsequent pulse discharge, the high power component is sufficiently charged to provide the high power performance.

Figure 4 shows our test result for the high power performance cell made with multi-functional electrode. Black line is a discharge curve for a conventional electrode during pulse discharge. The voltage immediately dropped below 2.1V due to a high internal resistance. Multi-functional electrode was prepared by adding a high power subcomponent to the electrode. The material is rechargeable material with low impedance. The cell with the multi-functional electrode (red line) experienced much less voltage drop during pulse discharge because the power was provided from the higher power component in the electrode. During rest, the high power component was regenerated by the high energy component for the next discharge event.

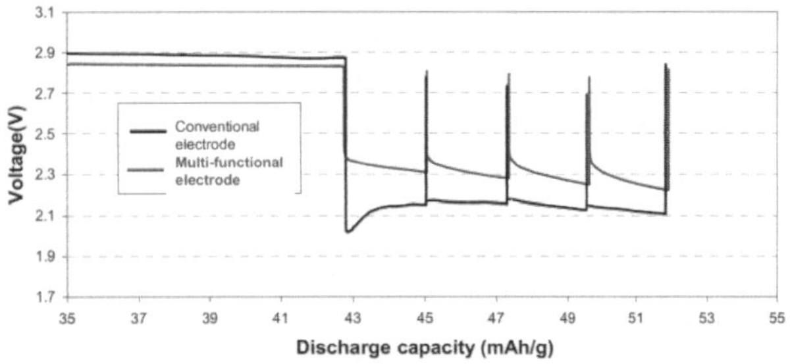

Figure 4. Example of enhanced power capability of multi-functional electrode (voltage changes during pulse discharge)

The above examples explain how the multi-functional electrodes could contribute to improvement in power performance. The multi-functional electrode can be design in a way so that the voltage drop would be suppressed. **Figure 5** shows an example of that concept. In this case, a standard electrode on a copper foil suffered a significant voltage drop during 3C discharge (red line). With implementation of multi-functional design, then the voltage drop was suppressed significantly (purple line) because of reduced internal resistance. The design could be applied even to a higher resistance current collector such as titanium foil. The multi-functional design on a titanium foil was able to provide the same level of performance as the copper foil based multi-functional electrode (black line).

The suppression of the voltage drop equates to the increase in the capacity in the same testing condition. While the standard electrode cell achieved only 7.7Ah at 3C rate discharge, the one with the multi-functional electrode design was able to increase the capacity of 12.3Ah, 60% increase from the original.

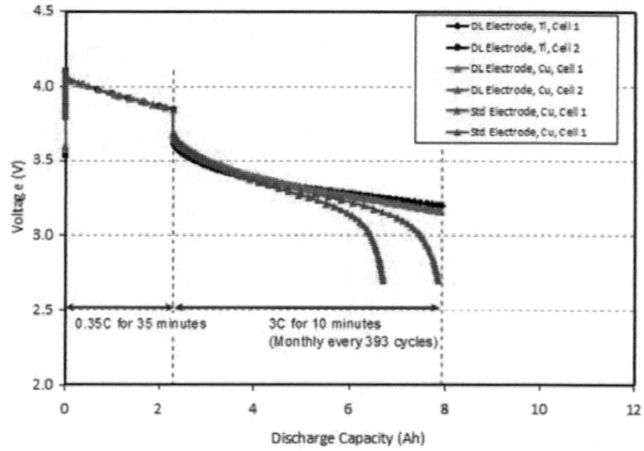

Figure 5. Reduction in voltage drop with multi-functional design.

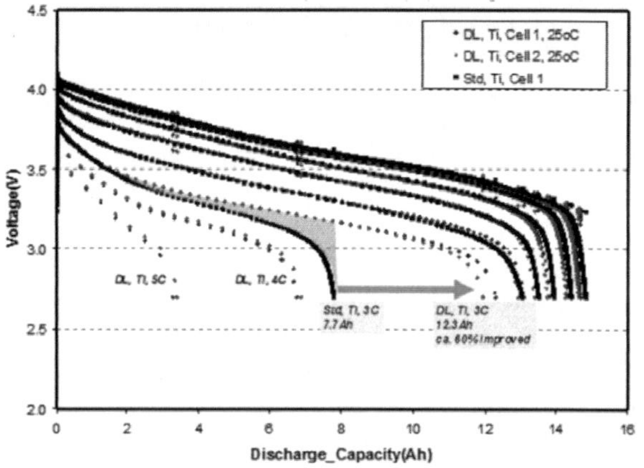

Figure 6. Increase in the capacity with multi-functional electrode design at 3C rate.

Another benefit of the multi-functional electrode design is the extension in the cycle life performance. Being able to absorb a rush of current, the multi-functional electrode homogenizes distribution of current through the entire electrode surface, minimizing local concentration of energy and the subsequent over-potential, which is normally the cause of decay of the materials in cells. With this effect, a cell with the multi-functional electrode design is able to achieve longer cycle life compared to cells with just high energy components. **Figure 7** demonstrates one example from a literature[1].

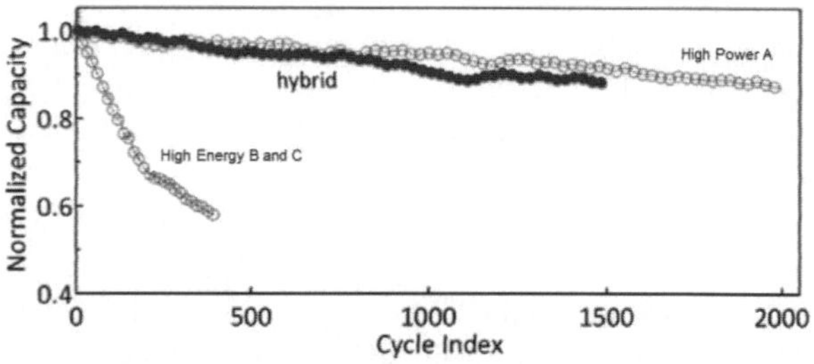

Figure 7. Cycle life improvement by the multi-functional electrode design[1].

The multi-functional electrode design is expected to improve the safety aspect of the cells, too. The design would minimize excessive heat generation during high rate charge and discharge by suppression of localized current and overall reduction in the internal resistance. The over potential reduction could also contribute in suppression of lithium dendrite formation under high current or low temperature charge conditions.

References

1. Vlad, A., Singh, N., Rolland, J. Melinte, S., Ajayan, P. M., "Hybrid supercapacitor-battery materials for fast electrochemical charge storage," *Scientific Reports*, vol. 4, no. 4315, pp. 1-7, 2014.
2. Cericola, D., Novák, P., Wokaun, A., Kötz, R., "Hybridization of electrochemical capacitors and rechargeable batteries: An experimental analysis of the different possible approaches utilizing activated carbon, $Li_4Ti_5O_{12}$ and $LiMn_2O_4$" *J. Power Sources*, Vol. 2011, pp. 10305-10313, 2011.
3. Cericola, D., Kötz, R"Hybridization of rechargeable batteries and electrochemical capacitors: Principles and limites" *Electrochimica Acta*, Vol. 72, pp. 1-17, 2012.

High Tech Cell Manufacturing of American Made Cells for Military Applications

Kevin Hykin, Felix Nunez, Chris Silkowski, Michael Wixom

Navitas Systems
4880 Venture Drive, Ann Arbor, MI 48108
FNunez@navitassys.com

Abstract: *American Manufacture Cells for military application is important for National Security and Military Readiness. The need of a consistent, American made supply of cells for military applications is critical for national security and to insure the readiness of our military and the support of their state of the are weapon systems. Navitas in partnership with Lockheed Martin has setup a Flexible pouch cell manufacturing line with the capability for cell sizes in the range of 20 mm to 200 mm and various shapes to maximize volume use. This new line is capable of 1+ Million Cells per year and is modular to increase the output if needed. This line is ideal for government programs, due to its flexibility. This cell line was setup to support military applications and to support qualified systems, to eliminate the need to qualify a different cell every time a commercial cell goes out of service. The cells produce on this line will support Portable Power communications systems, Unmanned Systems, and other where maximizing energy density is important.*

All-Solid-State Battery-Ultracapacitor Hybrid Devices Based on Nanostructured Materials

Elena Bekyarova,[1] Mikhail E Itkis,[1] Sergey Kalinin,[1] Jiaqi Dai,[2] Liangbing Hu,[2] Meng Li,[3] Chao Hu,[3] Mohan Sanghadasa[4]

[1] Carbon Solutions Inc., 1200 Columbia Ave., Riverside, CA 92507
[2] Department of Materials Science and Engineering, University of Maryland College Park, College Park, MD 20742
[3] Department of Mechanical Engineering, Iowa State University, Ames, IA 50011
[4] US Army Aviation & Missile Research, Development, and Engineering Center, Redstone Arsenal, AL 35898
bekyarova@carbonsolution.com / 1-951-682-5620

Abstract: *This work presents the design of a solid-state hybrid energy storage device that combines the advantages of a supercapacitor and a lithium-ion battery. The hybrid device is comprised of nano-materials: the capacitor-like electrode consists of a graphene - carbon nanotube composite and the battery-like cathode is comprised of a nano-$LiFePO_4$ (LFP) mixed with nanocarbon. The gel electrolyte utilizes a polymer membrane impregnated with organic electrolyte or ionic liquids. The electrochemical performance of hybrid devices fabricated with different gel electrolytes is presented and discussed. Compared with conventional supercapacitors and lithium-ion batteries, the hybrid devices exhibit high energy density exceeding 100 Wh/kg combined with high power density of >1 kW/kg. The devices retain their capacity after 1,000 cycles. The successful integration of electrical double-layer and electrochemical storage mechanisms affords devices with energy beyond the current state-of-art supercapacitors, while maintaining high power density, as well as cycling, chemical and thermal stability.*

Keywords: high power density; high energy density; battery-ultracapacitor hybrid device; gel electrolyte.

Introduction

Bridging the performance gap between batteries and supercapacitors has gain significant interest in recent years due to the growing number of advanced dynamic applications that require devices operating at different time scales. Traditional solutions make use of a combination of supercapacitors and batteries to satisfy the complex power-energy requirements, especially for applications with a high peak power demand. Achieving both high power and high energy in a single device is a very challenging task. A technology that combines the high energy density attributes of batteries and the rapid charge/discharge operation of ultracapacitors would solve a number of outstanding problems and opens new opportunities.

We discuss a battery-supercapacitor hybrid device which provides simultaneously high energy and power densities and operates safely within a light weight package. The battery-supercapacitor hybrid device is a unique energy storage system that bridges the performance gap between batteries (high energy density) and supercapacitors (high power density), providing an all-in-one solution. The device is comprised of a nano-carbon anode, a high-rate cathode and a gel electrolyte as illustrated in Figure 1.

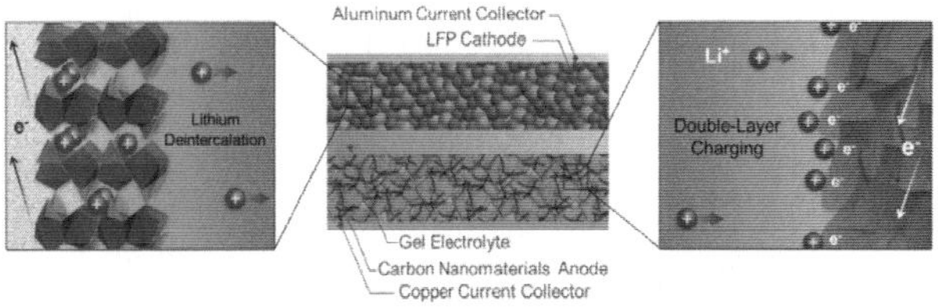

Figure 1. Schematic illustration of the hybrid cell components - $LiFePO_4$ (LFP) cathode, carbon nano-composite anode and ionic liquid-based gel electrolyte. Reproduced from Ref. 2 with permission from the Royal Society of Chemistry.

Results and Discussion

As a proof-of-concept, $LiFePO_4$ (LFP) was selected as the cathode for hybrid cells. The anode contains a composite of carbon nanotubes and graphene; it has been shown that proper engineering of the hybrid carbon nano-structures synergistically enhances the specific capacitance of symmetric supercapacitor devices [1]. The gel electrolyte was prepared by impregnation of a poly(vinylidene fluoride-co-hexafluoropropylene) [PVdF-HFP] membrane with electrolyte. Compared with conventional liquid electrolytes, gel polymer electrolytes have the advantages of comparable ionic conductivity at ambient temperature, good mechanical strength, stable electrochemical performances, and no liquid electrolyte leakage risks.

Electrochemical performance of ultra-light hybrid cell with gel organic electrolyte: In this study we designed a hybrid energy storage device consisting of $LiFePO_4$ (LFP) nanoparticles on an aluminum (Al) leaf current collector for the cathode and a free-standing reduced graphene oxide/carbon nanotube (RGO/CNT) nanocarbon membrane for the anode [2]. The ultrathin Al leaf with 1 μm thickness was used to reduce the mass of inactive materials. The PVdF-HFP membrane was impregnated with an organic electrolyte - 1M lithium hexafluorophosphate ($LiPF_6$) in ethylene carbonate (EC)/diethyl carbonate (DEC).

The electrochemical performance of a representative hybrid cell is shown in Figure 2a. The charge and discharge curves of the hybrid cell were recorded at 1C rate. The calculated energy density was about 180 Wh/kg, and the power density was about 218 W/kg, normalized to the total weight of the electrodes and current collectors. The hybrid cell exhibited an outstanding performance over 100 cycles with over 97% capacity retention (Figure 2b).

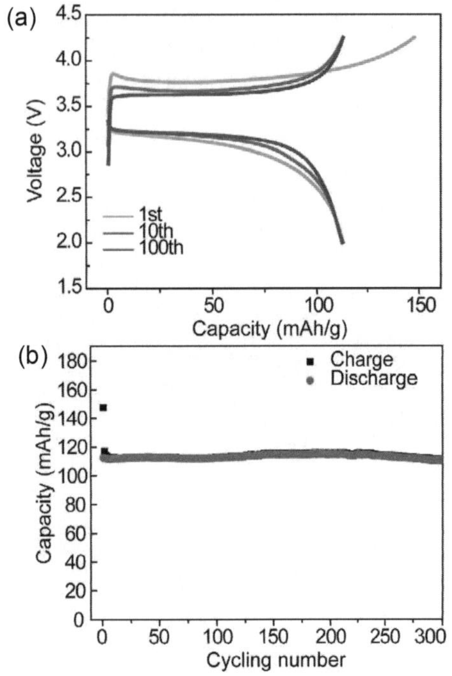

Figure 2. Electrochemical performance of the hybrid cell at 1C rate. (a) Voltage profile and (b) Cycling performance shows the stability and high capacity of the hybrid device. Reproduced from Ref. 2 with permission from the Royal Society of Chemistry.

The light-weight hybrid device exhibits a high energy density (180 Wh/kg) and a high power density (218 W/kg), outperforming conventional batteries and supercapacitors for future energy storage systems.

Electrochemical performance of hybrid cell with commercial standard current collectors and gel organic electrolyte: Prototype coin cells were prepared with the same anode and cathode materials as those used for the ultra-lightweight cells, however the electrodes were deposited on standard copper and aluminum current collectors. The cells were packed in a standard case LIR2025. The PVdF-HFP membrane was impregnated with 1M $LiPF_6$ in EC/DMC (DMC - dimethyl carbonate).

Charge-discharge curves for a representative battery-supercapacitor hybrid coin cell are shown in Figure 3a. The hybrid devices packed in a standard coin cell case have an energy density of about 250 Wh/kg at a current rate of 0.25 A/g (equivalent to ~ 4C). The cell shows stable cycling performance over 1,000 cycles with no obvious change of capacity as illustrated in Figure 3b. At current rate of 0.5 A/g the cells have energy density of ~ 200 Wh/kg and power density of 1,500 W/kg.

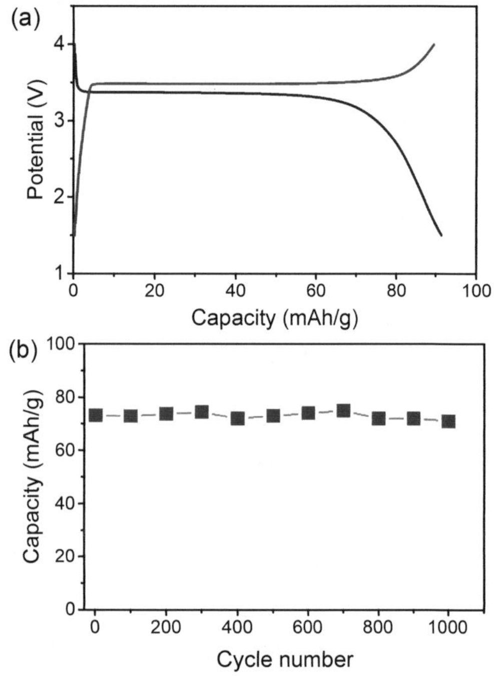

Figure 3. Electrochemical performance of the hybrid cell at 0.25 A/g. (a) Charge-discharge curves of a representative hybrid cell with gel organic electrolyte. (b) Cycling performance at room temperature.

Hybrid cells with gel ionic liquid electrolyte: Three different ionic liquids were used for the preparation of a gel electrolyte for battery-supercapacitor hybrid devices:

- diethylmethyl (2-methoxyethyl) ammonium bis(trifluoro-methylsulfonyl)imide: DEME– TFSI;
- 1-ethyl-3-methylimidazolium bis(trifluoromethyl-sulfonyl) imide: EMIM-TFSI;
- 1-ethyl-3-methylimidazolium bis(fluoromethyl-sulfonyl) imide: EMIM-FSI.

The structures of the ions comprising the ionic liquids are shown in Figure 4 and their main physicochemical characteristics are summarized in Table 1.

The main advantages of DEME-TFSI are the wide electrochemical window (ECW = 5.4 V) and low melting point (-91 °C), which make this ionic liquid attractive candidate for low temperature applications. The advantages of EMIM-TFSI and EMIM-FSI are the higher ionic conductivity and lower viscosity.

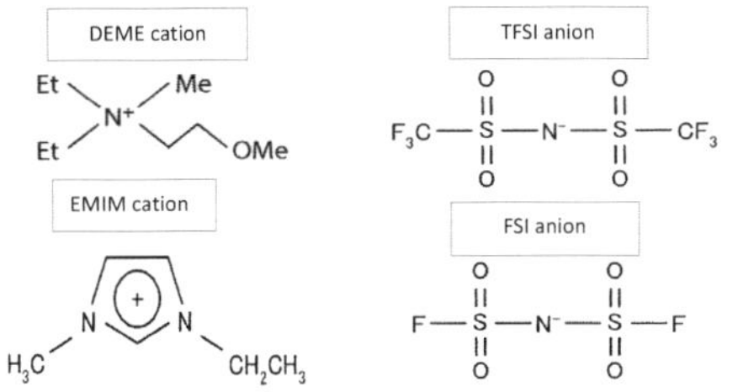

Figure 4. Structural formulas of the cations and anion of the ionic liquids used for gel electrolyte preparation.

Table 1. **Physicochemical properties of the ionic liquids.**

[Cation]$^+$ [Anion]$^-$	[EMIM] [TFSI]	[DEME] [TFSI]	[EMIM] [FSI]
Molecular Weight	391.31	426.4	291.3
Viscosity (mPa.s)	35.55	94	24.5
Melting Point (°C)	-17	-91	-13
Conductivity (S/cm @RT)	1.03x10^{-2}	4x10^{-3}	1.54x10^{-2}
ECW (V)	4.47	5.4	4.29

Cell configuration: To test the performance of hybrid cells assembled with ionic liquids, the device components were packed in a standard case LIR2025 and Li-TFSI was used to prepare 1M solution in the ionic liquids.

Electrochemical performance of hybrid cell with ionic liquid gel electrolyte: Two cells with each type of ionic liquid were utilized in these tests. The performance of the cells was compared based on the galvanostatic charge-discharge at a current rate of C/10. The test results of the hybrid coin cells fabricated with different ionic liquids are presented in Table 2. High energy densities in the range of 260 Wh/kg were observed for the hybrid cells built with all three ionic liquids.

Table 2. **Energy density of hybrid cells assembled with ionic liquid-based gel electrolyte.**

Ionic Liquid	**Energy Density at C/10 (Wh/kg)**
DEME-TFSI	264 ± 2
EMIM-FSI	274 ± 2
EMIM-TFSI	270 ± 20

Figure 5 shows the capacitance (blue) and Coulombic efficiency (red) of a hybrid cell fabricated with the ionic liquid DEME-TFSI for 500 charge-discharge cycles at a current rate of 0.25 A/g. The hybrid cells prepared with DEME-TFSI show significant performance stability; the Coulombic efficiency of the hybrid cell remained close to 100% after 1,000 cycles, while the energy density decreases by < 10%.

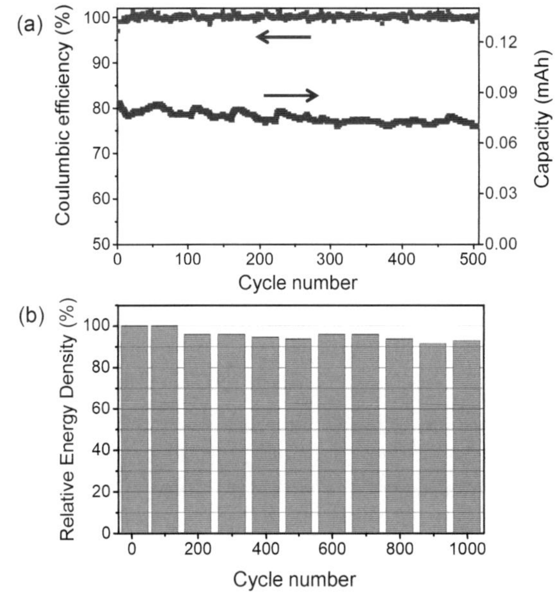

Figure 5. (a) Coulombic efficiency (red symbols) and specific capacitance (blue) of the hybrid cell prepared with DEME-TFSI as a function of cycle numbers at 0.25 A/g. (b) Relative energy density of the hybrid cells as a function of cycle number at 0.25 A/g.

Conclusion

We have demonstrated a battery-supercapacitor hybrid device, which exhibits high energy density of > 200 Wh/kg (the energy is equivalent to lithium-ion batteries) and a high power density of > 1.5 kW/kg (outperforming lithium-ion batteries). By appropriate selection of the gel (or solid state) electrolyte the devices can operate safely in a wide temperature range from sub-zero to +65 °C.

Acknowledgements

This work was supported by the US Army Small Business Innovation Research (SBIR) program under contract W31P4Q-15-C-0005.

References

1. Jha, N., P. Ramesh, E. Bekyarova, M.E. Itkis, and R.C. Haddon, "High Energy Density Supercapacitor Based on a Hybrid Carbon Nanotube–Reduced Graphite Oxide Architecture", *Adv. Energy Mater.*, vol. 2, pp. 438-444, 2012.
2. Dai, J., K. Fu, P. Ramesh, A. Gong, P. Glenn, R. Kornfeld, H. Zhu, M. Sanghadasa, E. Bekyarova, and L Hu, "High Power, High Energy Density Solid State Hybrid Energy Storage Device", *J. Mater. Chem. A*, vol. 5, pp. 15266-15272, 2017.

DISTRIBUTION A. Approved for public release: Distribution unlimited. UNCLASSIFIED

Hierarchical Power Management of Unmanned Aerial Vehicles

Luis Herrera[1], Charles Skipper[2], Michael Rottmayer[3], and Bang-Hung Tsao[2]

[1]Department of Electrical Engineering
Rochester Institute of Technology
Rochester, NY, USA

[3]Air Force Research Labs
Aerospace Systems Directorate
WPAFB, OH, USA

[2]University of Dayton Research Institute
Dayton, OH USA

Contact Author Email: lcheee@rit.edu

Abstract: *The development of Unmanned Aerial Vehicles (UAV) has increased significantly over the past decades. Hybrid electric UAVs typically incorporate engine and energy storage to increase efficiency, endurance, and flexibility. However, intelligent control techniques are needed to achieve these goals. In this paper, a hierarchical power management for series hybrid UAV is proposed. At the lowest/inner level, power electronics integrate multiple energy sources into a common dc bus while at the highest/outer level a model predictive controller manages the energy sources (battery and engine). Results illustrate how fuel consumption is different for different charging strategies while at the same time enhancing the capabilities of the UAV.*

Keywords: Unmanned Aerial Vehicles; power electronics; Model Predictive Control.

Introduction

Unmanned Aerial Vehicles (UAV) are becoming increasingly popular in a wide range of applications from agriculture to military. Typical energy sources for large UAV include gas engines and fuel cells. However, incorporation of other energy sources such as solar or battery (e.g. Lithium Ion cells), can increase the flexibility and endurance of these aircraft.

There have been several techniques proposed in recent years to manage UAVs with two or more different types of energy sources. For example in [1], a rule based approach prioritizing the state of charge of the energy storage was developed to coordinate a vehicle with solar, fuel cell, and batteries. In [2-3], fuzzy logic strategies are investigated to coordinate power between solar and energy storage. The solar system provided power to the propeller (dc motor) when sufficient power was available while the energy storage served as back up. In [4-5], a strategy was proposed to maximize the fuel cell's power in a hybrid fuel cell/battery UAV at a single time instant. However, the previous strategies focus on a fixed time without consideration for future load profile based on a specific mission. Towards this end, [6] proposed a Dynamic Programming (DP) approach for minimizing a cost function (e.g. fuel consumption) over an entire load profile. However, the load/mission data was assumed to be known a priori, which does not account for unforeseen scenarios (e.g. wind conditions).

In this paper, a hierarchical control strategy is proposed to consider the fast and slow electrical transients of a hybrid source UAV composed of a combustion engine and an energy storage. A master/slave controller is designed to regulate a common dc bus voltage and input current of one of the sources (hence its output power). A Model Predictive Controller (MPC) is then designed for the online and optimal power management to increase endurance and minimize fuel consumption.

This paper is structured as follows. First, the platform and high level diagram of the hybrid UAV is presented, detailing the electrical connection of the sources. Next, the inner level controllers are designed to regulate the common bus voltage and input current. A MPC is then formulated for optimal power management. The proposed MPC is a Quadratic Programming (QP) problem and details on its online implementation are presented. A case study is then shown for a specific load/mission profile and a conclusion and future work are presented.

Hybrid UAV Platform

A general overview of the series Hybrid UAV considered is shown in Fig. 1. As can be seen, the fuel/engine is coupled to the electrical network through a generator. The battery is then connected to a dc bus through power electronics in order to provide power to the main load. It is important to note that only the motor/propeller generates thrust taking power from either the engine and/or the battery.

One of the challenges of this type of UAV is the power management in order to maximize endurance. In this study it will be assumed that the generator/engine has limits on its minimum and maximum power output. Hence, the energy storage will have to provide more power when needed by the mission requirements.

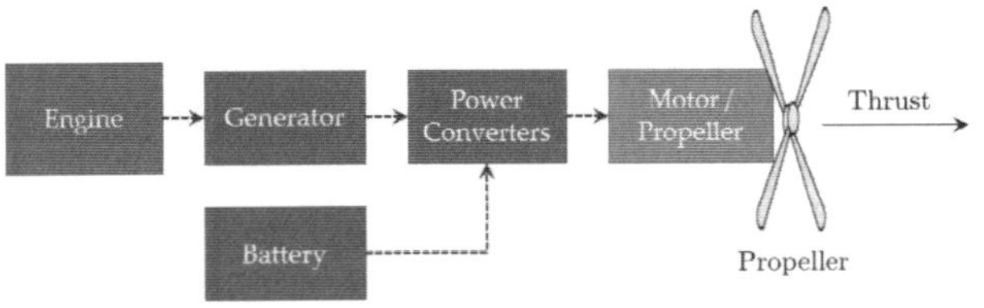

Figure 1. Series hybrid UAV architecture.

The electrical network and proposed higher level control strategy is shown in Fig. 2. Both energy sources are interfaced to a common dc electrical bus through power electronics converters. This brings the capability to decide and control the electrical power each source is providing to the load. The motor/propeller is a Permanent Magnet Synchronous Motor (PMSM) control through a DC/AC converter. It will be assumed that the inner-level control of the dc/dc converter of each source operates at a very high time steps (e.g. ns - µs)

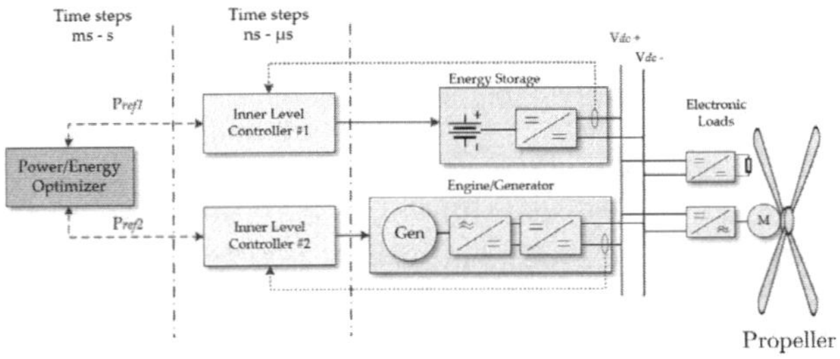

Figure 2. Hierarchical control architecture.

Inner Level Controller Design

The two sources (generator and battery) are interconnected to the dc bus through a power electronics converter. Depending on the input dc voltage of each source, a buck (step-down) or boost (step-up) converter will be used. The nominal output voltage of each converter is 50 V. A more detailed diagram of the power network with buck converters is shown in Fig. 3.

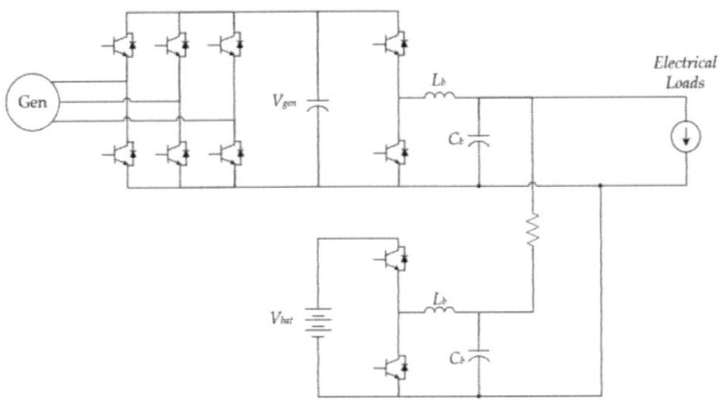

Figure 3. Electrical network for inner level controller design.

The buck converter inductance and capacitance are L_b = 200 µH and C_b = 50 µF. The input voltage of the battery and generator are 74 V. The switching frequency of the converters is F_{SW} = 100 kHz. One of the advantages of buck converters is that they have a linear state space representation as opposed to boost. In this paper, we consider a Master/Slave approach, where one of the sources regulates the dc bus voltage to nominal while the other controls its power/current output.

Current Controller Design

When a source is operating in current controlled mode, its output power can be regulated tightly. This implies the other source will make up the difference power needed to supply the load. The dynamic equations for a buck converter are as follows:

$$\begin{pmatrix} \dot{x}_1 \\ \dot{x}_2 \end{pmatrix} = \begin{pmatrix} 0 & \frac{-1}{L} \\ \frac{1}{C} & \frac{-1}{RC} \end{pmatrix} \begin{pmatrix} x_1 \\ x_2 \end{pmatrix} + \begin{pmatrix} \frac{1}{L} & 0 \\ 0 & \frac{-1}{C} \end{pmatrix} \begin{pmatrix} u \\ i_{\text{load}} \end{pmatrix} \tag{1}$$

where $u = dV$ with d as the duty cycle and V as the input voltage to the converter, x_1 is the inductor current and x_2 is the output capacitor voltage. In order to eliminate any error between a reference value for the current and its actual value, we introduce the following state (integrator):

$$\dot{e_I} = I_{\text{ref}} - x_1 \tag{2}$$

which increases the total order of the system as follows:

$$\begin{pmatrix} \dot{x}_1 \\ \dot{x}_2 \\ \dot{e_I} \end{pmatrix} = \begin{pmatrix} 0 & \frac{-1}{L} & 0 \\ \frac{1}{C} & -\frac{1}{RC} & 0 \\ -1 & 0 & 0 \end{pmatrix} \begin{pmatrix} x_1 \\ x_2 \\ e_I \end{pmatrix} + \begin{pmatrix} \frac{1}{L} \\ 0 \\ 0 \end{pmatrix} u + \begin{pmatrix} 0 \\ -\frac{1}{C} \\ 0 \end{pmatrix} i_{\text{load}} + \begin{pmatrix} 0 \\ 0 \\ 1 \end{pmatrix} I_{\text{ref}} \tag{3}$$

Assuming a change of coordinates from the operating condition, the system can be re-written simply as: $\dot{x} = Ax + Bu + Dh$ where $h = i_{load}$. Therefore, we can consider using state feedback such as $u = Kx$ where K is a 1x3 matrix of gains. To optimize the feedback gains we use an infinite horizon Linear Quadratic Regulator (LQR) such as:

$$J = \int_0^\infty x^T Q x + u^T H u \, dt \tag{4}$$

The optimal feedback matrix can then be computed by solving the following algebraic Riccati equation:

$$A^T S + SA - (SB)H^{-1}(B^T S) + Q = 0$$

and $K = -R^{-1}(B^T S)$.

Voltage Controller Design

For the source operating in voltage controlled mode (master), a similar approach is conducted in order to optimize the gains. Beginning with the open loop system in (1), the integral of the error state with respect to a voltage reference (e.g. 50 V) is added as follows:

$$\dot{e_V} = V_{\text{ref}} - x_2 \tag{5}$$

Expanding the open loop system to include this term as in (3), we can utilize a similar LQR in order to optimize the feedback gains for the output voltage control.

Parallel Operation

The parallel operation of the two converters in Master (voltage control) / Slave (current control) approach is presented in Fig. 4. In this example, the generator is used to

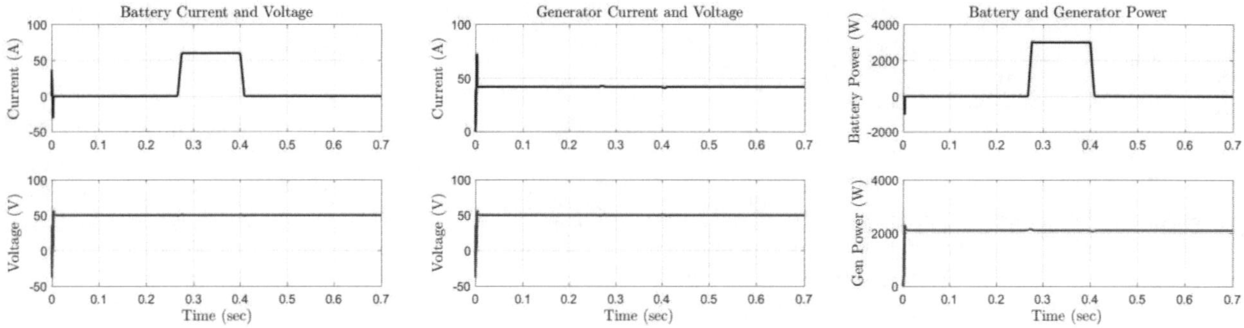

Figure 4. Example of Master/Slave control for voltage regulation and power management. The battery (left) controls its output current, the generator (middle) regulates the output voltage to 50 V, and the output powers are shown in the right.

control the output voltage while the battery controls its output power. This configuration is not required and a case where the battery regulates the output voltage instead can also be considered. In Fig. 4, right subfigure, it can be seen how the battery provides a pulse power of 3 kW, while the generator provides steady output power at 2 kW.

Higher Level Power Management

Since the thrust is generated electrically through a propeller (motor), the power is split between both the high energy source (engine + generator) and the high power source (battery). In this section, the main goal is to develop a high level power/energy management strategy to:

- Minimize fuel consumption
- Maintain State of Charge (SoC) levels of the battery within a desired margin
- Maintain power levels of generator and battery within limits
- Keep within limits the rise and fall rate of the generator power

Higher Level Dynamics

It is first important to define the dynamics at a higher level/slower time scales. In particular, the State of Charge (SOC) of the battery can be modeled as:

$$SoC(k+1) = SoC(k) - \kappa T_s P_{\text{bat}}(k) \tag{6}$$

where $\kappa = 1/E_{tot}$, E_{tot} is the total energy of the battery, and T_s is the sampling time of the higher level controller. Consider then a discrete state space system of the form [7]:

$$\begin{pmatrix} SoC(k+1) \\ P_{\text{gen}}(k) \end{pmatrix} = \begin{pmatrix} 1 & \kappa T_s \\ 0 & 1 \end{pmatrix} \begin{pmatrix} SoC(k) \\ P_{\text{gen}}(k-1) \end{pmatrix} + \begin{pmatrix} \kappa T_s \\ 1 \end{pmatrix} \Delta P_{\text{gen}}(k) + \begin{pmatrix} -\kappa T_s \\ 0 \end{pmatrix} P_{\text{load}}(k) \tag{7}$$

$$P_{\text{bat}}(k) = \begin{pmatrix} 0 & -1 \end{pmatrix} \begin{pmatrix} SoC(k) \\ P_{\text{gen}}(k-1) \end{pmatrix} - \Delta P_{\text{gen}}(k) + P_{\text{load}}(k) \tag{8}$$

where:

$$P_{\text{gen}}(k) + P_{\text{bat}}(k) = P_{\text{load}}(k),$$
$$\Delta P_{\text{gen}}(k) \triangleq P_{\text{gen}}(k) - P_{\text{gen}}(k-1)$$

To simplify the notation, equations (7) and (8) are placed in the following form:

$$\begin{aligned} x(k+1) &= Ax(k) + B_1 u(k) + B_2 w(k) \\ y(k) &= Cx(k) + D_1 u(k) + D_2 w(k) \end{aligned} \tag{9}$$

where $x(k) = [SoC(k), P_{gen}(k\text{-}1)]^T$, $u(k) = \Delta P_{gen}(k)$, $w(k) = P_{load}(k)$, and $y(k) = P_{bat}(k)$.

MPC Problem Formulation

The main idea behind MPC is to solve an optimization problem online at every time step and apply only the first input. This optimization problem considers a horizon (N) into the future where the load power can be either known (Prescient MPC/ PMPC) or kept constant (Frozen Time MPC/FMPC). The MPC is formulated as follows:

$$\begin{aligned} &\min_u \sum_{i=1}^{N} (x_i - x_{\text{ref}})^T Q (x_i - x_{\text{ref}}) + \sum_{j=0}^{N-1} u_j^T R u_j \\ &\text{s.t.} \\ &x_{j+1} = Ax_j + B_1 u_j + B_2 w_j \\ &y_j = Cx_j + D_1 u_j + D_2 w_j \quad j = 0, \ldots, N-1 \\ &A^x x \le b^x \quad x = (x_1, \ldots, x_N)^T \\ &A^u u \le b^u \quad u = (u_0, \ldots, u_{N-1})^T \\ &A^y y \le b^y \quad w = (y_0, \ldots, y_{N-1})^T \end{aligned} \tag{10}$$

where the cost function penalizes deviations of the states from a desired reference $x_{ref} = (SoC^* \, P_{gen}{}^*)^T$, and the input or rate of change of the generator power. The inequality constraints are linear in order to bound the SoC between 0.2 and 0.8, limit the generator power from 1.5 kW to 5 kW, limit the rate of change of the generator output power, and limit the charge and discharge rate of the battery power, typically 10 C and 20 C respectively. The MPC in (10) can be simplified further into the form:

$$\begin{aligned} &\min_u u^T H u + F^T u \\ &\text{s.t.} \\ &A_{\text{ineq}} u \le b_{\text{ineq}} \end{aligned} \tag{11}$$

which is a typical QP problem, without linear equality constraints. This type of optimization problems are convex and nowadays there are several packages available to solve the problem for real time and embedded implementations. This MPC has been successfully implemented in an Opal RT [8] system using the Qpkwik algorithm from Matlab.

The battery cells are ThunderPower, with nominal ratings of 3.7 V and 3.4 Ah [9]. Different configurations were used with 20 cells in series (74 V total) and multiple strings in parallel. The engine used is a 3W-56I B2 HFE FI.

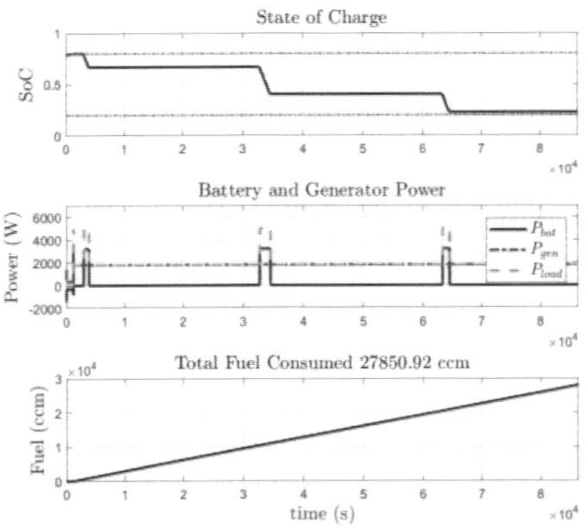

Figure 5. Case study with 24 battery strings in parallel and discharge only.

Case Study

Using the parameters for the battery and engine described in the previous section, different case studies were conducted in order to test the higher level controller under different battery configurations (e.g. number of strings in parallel) and different MPC gains.

We first consider a case with 24 strings in parallel were the total battery energy is sufficient to supply peak power during an entire load profile (~6.5 hours) without re-charging. The results for this case are shown in Fig. 5.

Next, a different configuration with only 12 strings in parallel is used with PMPC to charge/discharge the battery appropriately. This configuration significantly reduces weight and similar engine fuel consumptions can be seen, as shown in Fig. 6.

Moreover, only the electrical power extracted from the engine was used in the calculation of the fuel consumption. Therefore, the extra drag caused by the increased weight in the first scenario is not taken into account and could increase the fuel consumed in Fig. 5.

Conclusion and Future Work

In this paper a hierarchical control strategy to UAV power management was developed. At the lower/inner level, a Master/Slave approach to power sharing was developed where one source will control the dc bus voltage and the other will control its output current/power. LQR techniques were utilized in order to tune the controller gains. At the higher/outer level, a MPC approach was proposed in order to manage the charging and discharging of the battery. Future work will consider the actual implementation and testing of these controllers in a hardware testbed.

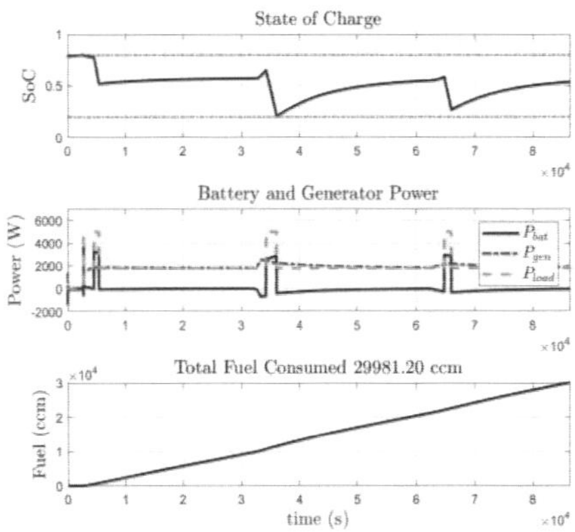

Figure 6. Case study with 12 battery strings in parallel and charging/discharging.

Acknowledgments

Luis Herrera would like to thank the support of the Air Force Summer Faculty Fellowship Program (SFFP) 2017.

References

1. B. Lee et al., "Active power management system for an unmanned aerial vehicle powered by solar cells, a fuel cell, and batteries," *IEEE Trans. on Aerospace and Electronic Systems*, vol. 50, no. 4, pp. 3167-3177, October 2014.
2. J. Shiau, Y. Wei, and M. Lee, "Fuzzy controller for a voltage-regulated solar-powered mppt system for hybrid power system applications", *Energies*, vol. 8, no. 5, 2015.
3. L. Karunarathne, J. T. Economou and K. Knowles, "Model based power and energy management system for PEM fuel cell/ Li-Ion battery driven propulsion system," *5th IET Int. Conf. on Power Electronics, Machines and Drives (PEMD 2010)*, 2010.
4. E. Bataller-Planes et al., "Power Balance of a Hybrid Power Source in a Power Plant for a Small Propulsion Aircraft," *IEEE Trans. on Power Electronics*, vol. 24, no. 12, pp. 2856-2866, Dec. 2009.
5. A. Savvaris, Y. Xie, K. Malandrakis, M. Lopez and A. Tsourdos, "Development of a fuel cell hybrid-powered unmanned aerial vehicle," *2016 24th Mediterranean Conf. on Control and Automation*, Athens, 2016,
6. E. Bongermino et al., "Model and energy management system for a parallel hybrid electric unmanned aerial vehicle," *2017 IEEE 26th Int. Symp. on Ind. Electronics (ISIE)*, 2017.
7. S. D. Cairano, D. Bernardini, A. Bemporad and I. V. Kolmanovsky, "Stochastic MPC With Learning for Driver-Predictive Vehicle Control and its Application to HEV Energy Management," *IEEE Trans. on Control Systems Tech.*, vol. 22, no. 3, pp. 1018-1031, May 2014.
8. Opal RT: https://www.opal-rt.com/
9. Thunderpower: http://www.thunderpowerrc.com/

Testing Spark Ignition Engines Converted to Operate on JP-8

Michael Seibert, Terry DuBois, Richard Scenna, Tony Thampan
US Army Communications, Electronics, Research, Development and Engineering Center (CERDEC)
Aberdeen Proving Ground, MD 21005

Abstract: *Testing was performed on commercially available 1 kW spark ignition generators that were modified to operate on JP-8 and other heavy fuels. This approach is motivated by the US Military mandate that only one fuel, JP-8, be taken to the battlefield, and the increased electrical demands at the squad and platoon level. Small units require a portable power source that can meet their energy demands, particularly battery charging. While diesel engines can operate on JP-8, their weight limits their mobility at the platoon level. Spark ignition engines have better power density at the 1 kW level, but must be modified to burn logistically available fuel.*

Multiple approaches have been pursued to enable these engines to operate on JP-8. In the present study, the longer term effects of three approaches are examined and compared to an unmodified spark ignition generator operating on gasoline. These approaches include A) chemically altering the fuel as it flows to the engine to create a higher octane mixture, B) modifying the carburetor and using ether starter fluid to preheat the cylinder, and C) electrically heating the cylinder while modifying the fuel system for direct injection. The different generators were characterized by oil sampling at 15 hour intervals. Oil testing included flash point, viscosity, wear elements, and additives. Oil quality and emissions vary with load. Different approaches to conversion perform better at different loads.

It was determined that multiple start-stop cycles with no load resulted in fuel dilution of the lubricating oil in several of the modified engines. Response varied with some of the modified engines maintaining low fuel dilution similar to the gasoline fueled engine while others indicated 15-20% fuel in the oil. During 100+ hours of operation at full load, the modified JP-8 burning generators showed 3-5% fuel dilution in the oil while the unmodified gasoline generator was less than 1%.

These experiments illustrated the challenges in developing portable, reliable JP-8 burning power sources. While further research and development is needed in each approach, it was shown that converted spark ignition engines are a promising path to portable logistic power. Oil analysis was shown to identify future research and development efforts to improve this technology

Keywords: SI engines; oil analysis; JP-8; portable power

Introduction

Increased technology capabilities of the modern soldier require increased power consumption on the battlefield. Logistic considerations require that the military transports only one fuel to the battlefield, JP-8[1]. JP-8, a kerosene, burns well in compression ignition engines, but like diesel, fairs poorly in spark ignition engines. The smallest diesel engine generators currently fielded by the Army is the 2 kW Military Tactical Generator (MTG) which weighs 120 lbs. However a smaller power solution that is compatible with JP-8 is desired. Commercial 1 kW spark ignition engines can provide sufficient power for a platoon at reasonable size and weight, but are unable to burn JP-8 directly. Rather than reduce the diesel engine's weight, recent R&D efforts have sought to modify SI engines to directly use JP-8. These approaches include A) chemically altering the fuel as it flows to the engine to create a higher octane mixture, B) modifying the carburetor and using ether starter fluid to preheat the cylinder, and C) electrically heating the cylinder while modifying the fuel system for direct injection. The present work examined these prototypes to assess the different conversion methods. Characterization was achieved primarily through analysis of the engine oil and emissions and compared to an unmodified engine. Similar approach have been used in predictive maintenance in fleet vehicles [2].

Analysis of the engine oil can be used to determine if engine modifications will degrade engine reliability and predict upcoming failures [3-5]. As oil lubricates the moving components within an engine, any wear particles generated will collect within the oil. The rate generated and metallurgical composition can be used to assess the health of an engine. In addition, measurement of additives and oil properties can also indicate if the oil is being depleted quicker than normal or if the oil properties are being altered such that it would lose its lubricity.

As the metallurgy of the engine is varied, the specific combination and levels can indicate regions of enhanced wear and potential sources of failure [6]. Aluminum particles indicate wear occurring on the piston skirts, but can also be derived from aluminum engine blocks, bearing, and heat exchangers. A common source of chromium is piston rings, which are in contact with the position and cylinder wall. Iron is commonly found throughout the engine (cylinder liner, camshaft lobes, crankshaft journal bearings and oil pumps. Iron is often cited to estimate wear of an engine [3,5,7]. Copper is found primarily bushings (cam shaft, piston wrist) and bearings (cranks shaft journal bearings, connecting rod). Lead is used as a surface coating within bearings. Tin is commonly found in journal bearings (crank shaft and camshaft), but also used within connecting rods. A bearing failure would be indicated by an increase of copper, lead, and iron over the base reading. Actual levels and metals will vary with engine metallurgical composition.

Analysis of the oil properties such as viscosity and flash point can give an indication if oil has been contaminated through fuel dilutions or particle buildup. Fuel dilution occurs by leaking injector seals, fuel pumps, idling, and unburnt fuel bypassing piston rings. Fuel dilution reduces oil viscosity and lubricity; decreasing the effectiveness of the oil. Oil replacement should be considered after 2.5-5% [8-9]. Another contaminate is soot, formed through combustion products. Literature indicated up to 3% volume is acceptable [9]. Water contamination is unlikely because the 1 kW generators are air cooled.

Experimental Set-up and Procedure

The generators were operated according to manufacturer instructions at each load level for one oil change interval (300 hours for the unmodified gasoline engine and Generator B, 100 hours for Generators A and C). Each day of operation, the generators ran until the fuel tanks were empty, 4-6 hours depending on the generator and the load. Oil samples were taken at approximately 15 hour intervals. 6 ml of oil was removed and replaced with fresh oil. Additional oil was added to the generator if necessary. Oil samples were taken at the beginning of the day when the engine block and oil plug did not present a burn hazard. The flashpoint test was done immediately, while the rest of the oil was labeled and stored for future testing.

Tests included: flashpoint to measure oil dilution, kinematic viscosity, atomic emissions spectroscopy measuring elemental content, and a Spectro Scientific Fluid Scan measuring TAN, TBN and water, soot, glycol, oxidation, nitration, and sulfation. Gaseous emissions were measured in a separate test.

Results and Discussion

Initial tests examined the fuel dilution in the oil in the worst case scenario, repeated starting and stopping. The generators were operated at idle for 8-10 minutes, and turned off. An oil sample was taken and flashpoint was measured. The generator was allowed to cool to ambient before the test was repeated. In all cases, the repeated starting and stopping caused fuel dilution in the oil as shown in Figure 1. At low cylinder temperatures, fuel that does not burn completely condenses on cylinder walls and passes the piston into the oil. Figure 1 shows that the gasoline engine experienced the least amount of fuel dilution because gasoline is more volatile, and evaporates more quickly than JP-8. Generator A had the lowest fuel dilution of the JP-8 generators because it partly reforms the fuel. The gaseous component is easily spark ignited which burns the remaining JP-8 droplets. Generator B uses thermal management to prepare the JP-8 for combustion, first using ether-based starter fluid, then controlling air flow through the housing. The short duration tests did not allow the cylinder to reach its steady operating temperature. This prevents fuel from fully evaporating, causing it to condense on the walls and enter the lubricant. In these short operations, Generator B had substantially more fuel dilution than the other units tested. The fuel dilution was visible when taking samples as the amount of oil in the sump continued to increase. Generators A and C are not as dependent on a heated cylinder for good combustion, thus fuel dilution was not as great.

At full load (Figure 2), the largest difference is between the gasoline and JP-8 fueled generators. Of the JP-8 fueled generators, Generator B has the lowest oil dilution. This is likely due to the thermal management door maintaining the engine temperature. Unlike the short duration runs, the loaded operation gives the generator time to reach steady state conditions.

Low power (100 W) operation shows changes in fuel dilution (Figure 3). Generator C experiences higher dilution while the dilution is reduced for Generators A and B. The unmodified gasoline engine dilution remained near 1%. The reduced dilution in Generator B is consistent with the increase in viscosity discussed below.

In general, operating at higher loads increased the oil viscosity over time due to the higher temperature promoting oxidation in the oil. Conversely, operating at lower loads reduced viscosity over time due to unburned fuel contaminating the lubricant. This viscosity behavior was observed in the unmodified gasoline generator and Generators A and C, as shown in Figures 4 and 5. However, the oil viscosity measurements differ in Generator B. As shown in Figures 4 and 5, viscosity increased rapidly over time at both high and low load. At both high and low load, the viscosity reached near 120 cSt before 100 hours. It then continued to increase, reaching above 160 cSt near 150 h. Beyond 150 h, the viscosity did not continue to increase. This generator has thermal control which maintains similar temperature under the range of loads. Similar temperature regardless of power output leads to similar oil conditions.

In Figures 7-9, wear metals illustrate additional differences between engine modification approaches. Of the three engines with the most hours, each showed a different metal with highest concentration, including chromium, molybdenum, and iron. Generator A showed the highest concentration of wear metals, particularly chromium. It is possible that this comes from the hydrogen gas created by the reforming process. Generators A and C showed similar levels of molybdenum, though this appears to have been in the fresh oil.

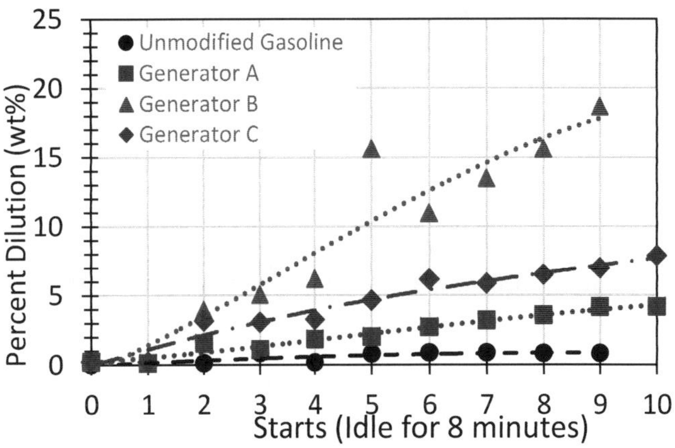

Figure 1: Dilution of oil with fuel over repeated start stop cycles

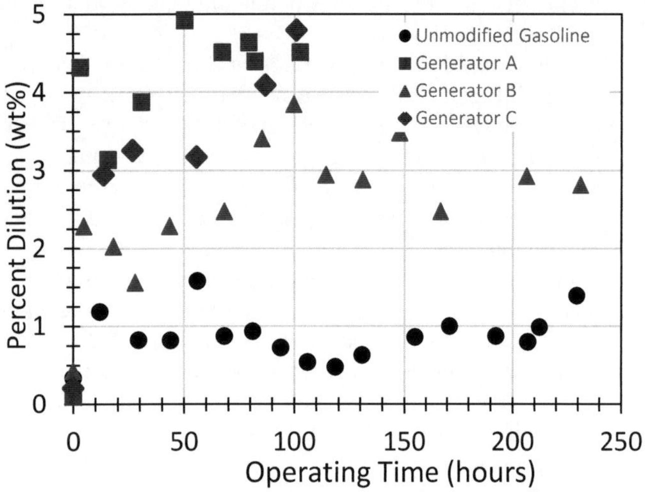

Figure 2: Dilution of oil with fuel at full load

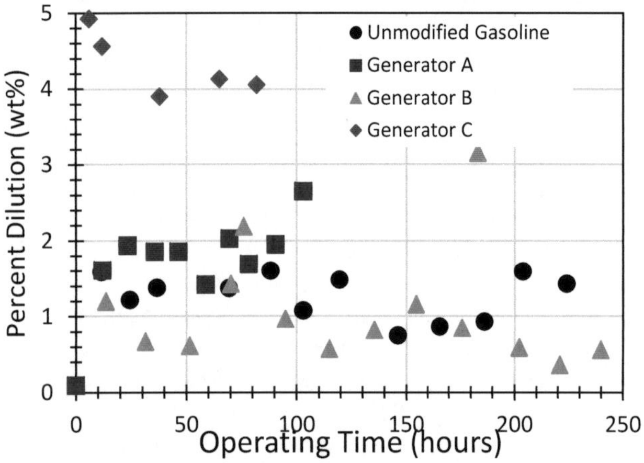

Figure 3: Dilution of oil with fuel at partial load.

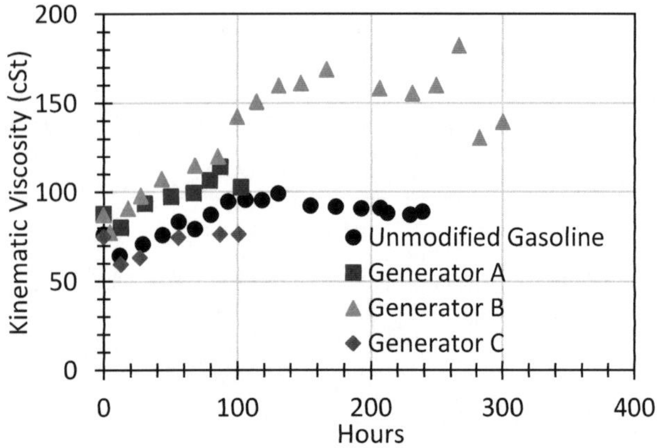

Figure 4: Oil viscosity of generators operated at full load

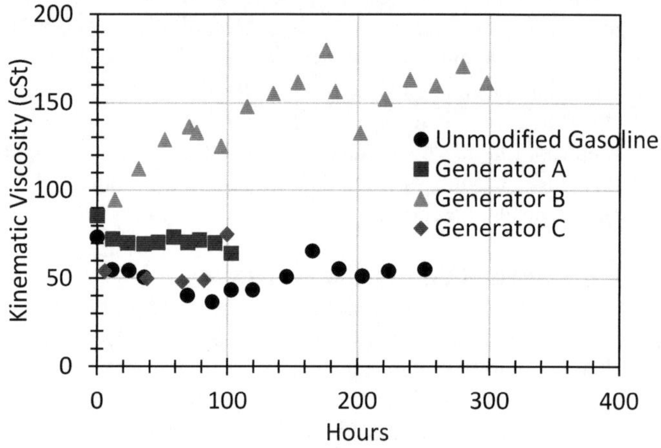

Figure 5: Oil viscosity of generators operated at low (100 W) load

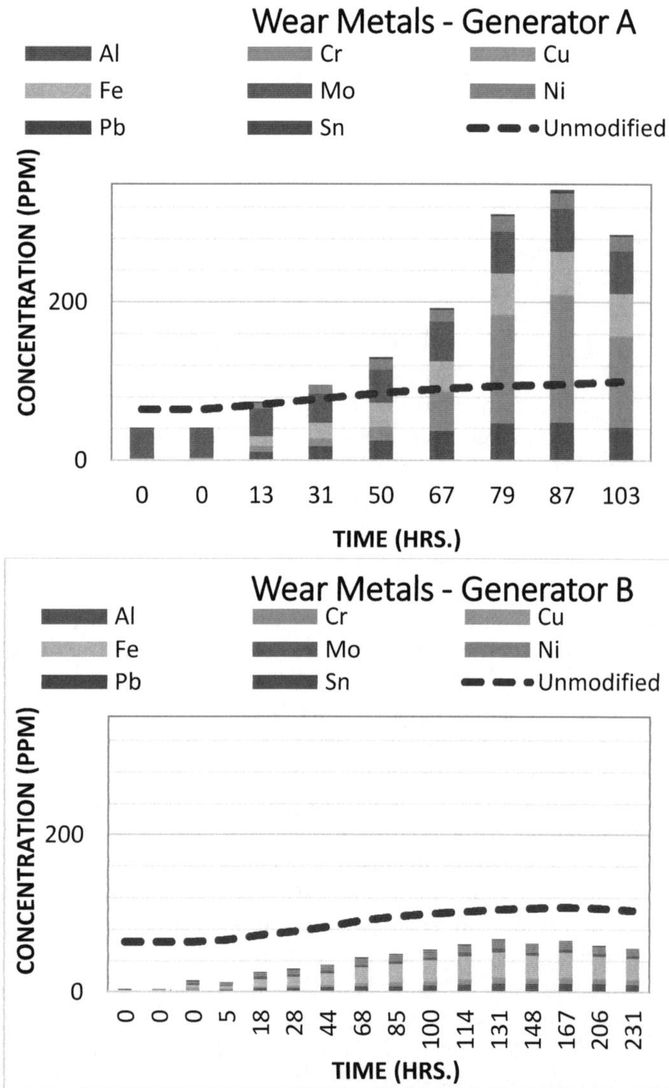

Figures 7-8: Wear metals at high load for Generators A and B

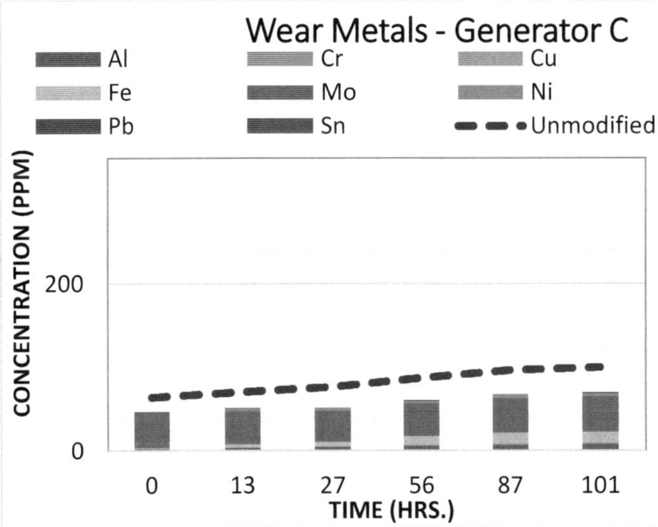

Figure 9: Wear metal at high load for Generator C

Summary

Three methods of modifying spark ignition engines to operate on JP-8 were analyzed using oil analysis and emissions measurements. Oil analysis showed cases of contamination with fuel, changes in viscosity, and the growth of wear metals.

Fuel dilution at idle conditions highlighted the challenge of completely burning the heavier JP-8 in an engine designed for gasoline. For example, relying on thermal management (Generator B) requires some warm up time to be fully effective, as shown by fuel dilution in the runs with startup, 8 min of idle, and shut down. When run for 4-6 hours at a time, Generator B showed the lowest fuel dilution of the modified generators.

The high temperature operation gave Generator B high viscosity and oil oxidation which are related, as the oxidation creates larger molecules, increasing viscosity. It is not clear if there is any relationship between the increased viscosity and the periodic losses of oil.

Generator C had lowest wear metals when considering molybdenum already present in the fresh oil. Chromium and iron in Generator A could be caused by hydrogen produced in the reformer. While it improves combustion, hydrogen is known to degrade steel.

Further investigation should evaluate the long term performance of these modified engines since these tests only included 2-3 oil change cycles. Extended operation may show issues unique to each approach. As part of the longer term study, the appropriate oil change and maintenance intervals should be re-evaluated. For example, Generator B's increased oxidation and viscosity indicate a shorter interval could be necessary. Further investigation should also identify the cause of Generator B's periodic oil losses. The chromium and iron wear should be monitored in Generator A, as well as the reliability of the fuel reformer which is critical to its operation. Generator C currently has the fewest hours of the three modified generators. Fuel dilution is a concern, but it has performed well on emissions and other oil qualitative measurements.

These results are preliminary in that all three modified generators are at different stages of development, and only one of each was tested. However, the tests do give insight into the merits of each approach and the potential of using spark ignition engines running on JP-8 as a portable power source.

References

1. Department of Defense, "DOD Directive 4140.3 'Single Fuel on the Battlefield Initiative.'" www.dtic.mil, 1988
2. California Integrated Waste Management Board, "Evaluation of High Efficiency Oil Filters in the State Fleet", Publication #IWMB-2008-020
3. Michael Holloway, "The Oil Analysis Handbook: A Comprehensive Guide to Using and Understanding Oil Analysis'"
4. Yuegang Zhao, "Oil Analysis Handbook for Predictive Equipment Maintenance" Spectro Scientific, 2014
5. Roger F. Haycock, Arthur J. Caines, John E. Hillier, "Automotive Lubricants Reference Book", 2004, page 159
6. Noria Corporation, "The Lowdown on Oil Breakdown", http://www.machinerylubrication.com/Read/475/oil-breakdown, Accessed 12/7/2017
7. Steffen Bots, "Establishing Elemental Limit Values for Motor Oils", Machinery Lubrication Magazine", www.machinerylubrication.com/, Accessed 12/7/2017
8. Techenomic International, "Test Explanations", http://www.techenomics.net/oil-fluid-analysis/test-explanations, Accessed 12/7/2017
9. Petroleum Technologies, "Petroleum Technologies" http://www.oil-lab.com/downloads/Petroleum_Technologies.pdf, Accessed 12/7/2017

Oil Analysis for Prognostic Diagnostics Applications

Richard Scenna, Terry Dubois, Michael Seibert
US Army Research, Development and Engineering Command, CERDEC, CPI

Abstract: *In order to assess the long-term effects of the Army's recent developmental efforts of microgrids and JP8 compatible spark ignition engines, engine oil analysis can be used.. A generator operating in a microgrid configuration could operate under variable load profiles, putting significant strain on one particular unit, while minimizing the load on others units. Another area of research has focused on modifying spark ignition engines to operate on JP8, which alters the combustion conditions, thus effecting engine wear. Engine oil analysis can be used to assess the current state of health of an engine within a generator[1]. As the engine is lubricated through oil, deviations from the unused oil can indicate potential problems and poor operating conditions.*

Keywords: Prognostic Diagnostic, Engine Oil, Oil Degradation, Microgrid, Modified Engine

Introduction

This paper discusses the mechanism of oil / engine failure. The Army's recent developmental efforts of microgrids and JP8 compatible spark ignition engines, may have induced unusual wear profiles within the engines. Engine oil analysis can be used to determine the effects of these modifications and predict potential failures without extensive engine testing. A generator operating within a microgrid configuration could operate under variable load profiles, which could induce unusual wear profiles in the engine. For example as the load peaks, a second generator is activated briefly, repeatedly turning on and off to help the first generator meet the load. This forces the second generator to continuously operate under cold start conditions. Alternatively one generator may inadvertently be favor of all the sets, putting significant strain on one particular unit, while minimizing the load on others unit.

Another area of research has focused on modifying spark ignition engines to operate on JP8, which the combustion conditions. The use of middle distillate fuels such as JP8 can have adverse effects due to the fuel properties. JP8 has significantly longer hydrocarbon changes and is considered more difficult to burn. JP8's higher sulfur concentrations may promote sulfation. Engine oil analysis can be used to assess the current state of health of an engine within a generator[1].

Engine oil analysis is a proven technology and has been in use for many years. As oil lubricates the moving components within an engine, any wear particles generated will collect within the oil. The rate and metallurgical composition of these particles can be used to assess the health of an engine. In addition, measurement of additives and oil properties can also indicate if the protective properties are being depleted at a faster rate than the unaltered engine or if the oil properties are being altered such that it would lose its lubricity.

Modern engine oils also contain additives which are used to minimize engine wear and prolong oil longevity. Corrosion inhibiters, anti-wear, detergents, and anti-oxidants are all common additives. It has been observed in the literature that the presence of wear metals rapidly increased after the additives were depleted [1]. Boron, zinc, and phosphorus are added to oil as anti-wear, anti-oxidant, and corrosion inhibitors. Sodium inhibits corrosion, but excessive levels can indicate a coolant leak. Calcium and Magnesium are both used as both detergents and dispersants of particulate matter. Calcium also maintains the reserve alkalinity. Barium acts as both a detergent as well as corrosion inhibiter. Sulfonates act as detergents, while thiophosphates act as anti-oxidants. Additive concentrations can fluctuate ±20% between samples so a long term trend must be observed [5]. Some of the oil additives are also common in engine metallurgy, meaning engine wear can increase concentrations within oil. Magnesium is a common engine component, but is added to oil as a detergent and dispersant.

Oil Degradation

Overtime the hydrocarbon structure of the oil degrades, reducing its lubricity, through oxidation, compressive heating, and thermal degradation. This is a direct change of the hydrocarbon structure of the oil, generally forming acidic compounds. Higher temperature fosters a more rapid decomposition. Additives, such as calcium, can mitigate these compounds. Petroleum technologies cited 75% as the limit for oxidation and nitration [5]. A general measure of the acidity and thus the degradation is ascertained by measuring the total acid base number of the oil.

The total base number (TBN) is a measure of how many mg of potassium hydroxide is required to neutralize the acidic components of the oil in a 1 gram sample (ASTMD974). TBN is used to assess the buildup of combustion products as they are primarily acidic. As combustion products tend to be acidic in nature, over time they will deplete the base nature of the oil. Unused Diesel oils typically have base numbers in the range of 8-12, but marine oils can have TBN as high as 80 [9]. The oil is considered for replacement when the base number drops below 6[9].

Oxidation is the chemical interaction of oil and oxygen, forming oxygenated compounds, particularly the carbonyl group. FTIR is a common method of detection, as the carbonyl group has a characteristic absorption at 1740cm-1 [2]. Oxidation occurs in three phases: initiation, propagation, and termination. In the initiation phase; temperature, pressure, or heat generate radicals. In the propagation phase, the radicals either react with the lubricant or react with oxygen to form peroxide radicals. In the termination phase, radicals will recombine to form a less reactive species. Anti-oxidants interrupt this process, reacting with the radicals to promote the termination phase. These products are typically acidic in nature (carboxylic acids), and can cause corrosion within the engine. The acid number of the oil also indicates oxidation of the fuel. Oxygenated products (hydroperoxides and carboxylic acids) can polymerize into larger molecules, increasing viscosity.

In thermal and compressive heating, the oil undergoes a rapid increase in temperature in the absence of oxygen. Thermal degradation occurs when oil interacts with hot surface temperature in excess of 200°C[2]. Compressive heating is the result of a rapid increase in temperature occurring from the adiabatic compression of entrained air bubbles. A pressure increase from 0 to 250 psig has been reported to increase temperature by as much as 400°C[2]. Under these conditions, the chemical structure of the oil will be altered. In extreme cases, these conditions will reduce the average length of the hydrocarbon chains, known as cracking, which decrease the oils viscosity. Gas chromatography can also be used to determine if cracking occurred. An observed shift toward lighter weight hydrocarbons indicates extreme thermal degradation.

Nitrogen oxides generated during combustion processes can interact with the oil, generating nitric acid. This is called nitration. This is more common under stoichiometric conditions (hotter), such as those that operate on natural gas. FTIR can also be used to detect nitrogenous molecules at (1600 to 1640 cm^{-1}) [2].

Sulfation is the interaction of oil and sulfur compounds. Sulfur containing additives, such as thiophosphates and sulfonates, become oxidized and interact with the fuel[10]. Another source is the combustion process, sulfur in the fuel oxidizes (SO_x) and interacts with the oil. These compounds are acidic in nature, which are corrosive to the engine components and can destroy other additives. Sulfation creates sludge and varnish and increases engine oil viscosity. Operating an engine on JP8 may cause increased sulfation issues, as JP8 has an allowed sulfur concentration of 3000pm, while conventional ultra-low sulfur diesel and gasoline have sulfur concentrations of 15ppm and 10pm, respectively. Heavier sulfur fuels require oils with higher TBN[11]. Testing is typically done through FTIR (1120 to 1180 cm^{-1}) [12] ASTM E2412 & ASTM D7415. Sulfur compounds can react with water to form H_2SO_4.

Hydrolysis is the chemical interaction of the water and oil. The water breaks down lubricating hydrocarbons, and reducing viscosity. This also leads to the formation of carboxylic acids. FTIR and acid test (ASTM D130) can be used to determine the presence of hydrolysis and water [13].

The electrical impedance of the oil will change as a result of the acids formed through nitration, sulfation and oxidation, water or other contamination, but cannot isolate a specific cause.

Wear Metals

Even under normal operation, the engine will generate predictable amounts of wear metals. Manufacturers set strict levels for acceptable wear metal concentrations, see Table 1-3. Under normal operation, these levels are consistent for a particular engine, but will vary between individual engines and oils. For detailed analysis it is best to observe the long term trend of an individual engine. However for diesel engines, copper and lead concentrations will be on the order of 30ppm, while tin, chrome and aluminum are typically detected at concentrations of 15 to 30ppm. Iron is typically detected at higher ranges of 60 to 80ppm. For spark ignition engines, wear metal concentrations are very similar except that copper has an allowed concentration of up to 120ppm. An increase beyond this amount would indicate the modification induced increased wear. As the metallurgy of the engine is unique, wear metals potentially can be used to indicate the components experiencing the increased wear.

Table 1. Normal wear metal profile.

Normal Operation	Cu	Fe	Cr	Al	Pb	Si
Oil Analysis Handbook[1]	50	80	25	30	50	25
machinerylubrication[7]	15	60	9	9	15	NA
Automotive Lubricants Reference Book[6]	25	70	10	20	40	20
Average	30.0	70.0	14.7	19.7	35.0	22.5

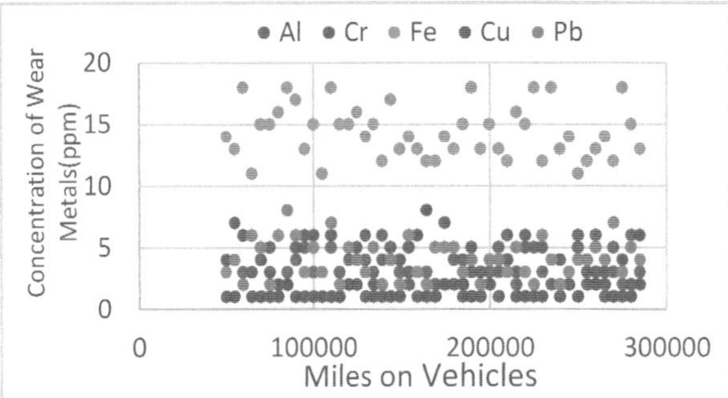

Figure 1. Wear metal analysis Ford 3.0L OHV[14]

When wear metals concentrations exceed the normal concentrations, within the recommended oil change interval, this indicates an issue has occurred. Manufactures and oil analysis groups have set limits on the allowed concentrations of wear particles for each engine configuration. This highlights the importance of establishing a base line for each engine. Tables 2 and 3 show the manufactures and test laboratories recommended limits for wear metals. More information was available on diesel engines, as these are common in fleet vehicles.

Table 2. Warning levels of wear metals for gasoline engines.

Warning Levels	Cu	Fe	Cr	Al	Pb	Si
Basics of Oil Analysis[5]	120	150	10	20	25	25
machinerylubrication[7]	60	180	60	55	30	30
Oil Analysis Handbook[1]	75	300	40	40	n/a	50
Average	85.0	210.0	36.7	38.3	27.5	35.0

Table 3. Warning levels for diesel engines

Warning Levels	Cu	Fe	Cr	Al	Pb	Si
Automotive Lubricants Reference Book[6]	50	100	20	25	50	25
http://www.machinery lubrication.com[2]	60	180	60	55	30	30
CT Analytical Services [3]	30	100	12	18	30	20
Chevron Lube Watch [3]	50	150	25	30	50	25
Herguth laboratories [3]	21	145	5	5	10	20
Chevron Diesel[3]	40	100	40	40	100	20
Cummins (ISX) [5]	25	150	15	15	35	15
Cummins (ISM)[5]	45	100	15	15	35	15
Caterpillar[5]	20	35	4	8	30	15
Caterpillar (3406E[5]	20	50	4	8	30	15
Caterpillar(C-12) [5]	100	75	8	8	30	15
Caterpillar(C-15)[5]	100	85	8	8	30	15
Detroit 60 Series[5]	25	85	4	10	35	15
Detroit 60 Series (new) [5]	40	150	10	15	35	20
Detroit 2 Cycle[5]	25	150	4	10	35	15
International[5]	45	100	4	12	35	15
Cummins 4BT & 6CT[5]	25	45	4	8	35	15
Mercedes Engines[5]	10	55	4	8	10	15
Volvo Engines[5]	40	100	10	25	35	20
Mack 300/350[5]	25	125	8	10	30	15
Average	39.8	104.0	13.2	16.7	35.5	18.0

A rapid increase in the presence of one or more wear metals indicates the emergence of a problem. As the metallurgy of the engine is varied, the specific combination and levels can indicate regions of enhanced wear and potential sources of failure [2]. Aluminum particles indicate wear occurring on the piston skirts, but can also be derived from aluminum engine blocks, bearing, and heat exchangers. A common source of chromium is piston rings, which are in contact with the piston and cylinder wall. Iron is commonly found throughout the engine (cylinder liner, camshaft lobes, crankshaft journal bearings, and oil pumps. Iron is often cited to estimate wear of an engine [1,6,7]. Copper is found primarily in bushings (cam shaft, piston wrist) and bearings (cranks shaft journal bearings, connecting rods). Lead is used as a surface coating within bearings. Tin is commonly found in journal bearings (crank shaft and camshaft), but also used within connecting rods. A bearing failure would be indicated by an increase of copper, lead, and iron over the base reading. Actual levels and metals will vary with engine metallurgical composition. Tables 4 and 5 show a sample base line and the corresponding increase in wear metals associated with each failure condition.

Table 4. Sample engine failures[8]

Mode	Cu	Pb	Sn	Fe	Na	Mg	Ca
Normal	15	20	5	48	10	500	2,000
Bearing Wear	68	71	15	10 8	10	500	2,000
Internal Coolant Leak	105	39	10	48	120	500	2,000
Leaching Oil Cooler Core	105	39	10	48	10	500	2,000
Oil Additive	200	20	48	10	10	1000	100

Table 5. Sample engine failures[8]

Mode	Fe	Al	Cr	Cu	Na	Si
Normal	35	8	3	15	12	15
Severe Dirt Entry	92	29	16	20	16	69
Internal Coolant Leak	38	9	4	124	243	101
Silicon Sealant	35	8	3	15	12	250
High Anti Foam	36	10	5	10	19	31
Piston Touching	105	134	5	10	19	31

Oil Contamination

Oil can also become contaminated with fuel, water, or combustion products (soot). The presence of these compounds can reduce the effectiveness of the oil. Fuel dilution occurs by leaking injector seals, fuel pumps, idling, and unburnt fuel bypassing piston rings. When fuel contaminates the oil, it reduces oil viscosity and lubricity; decreasing the oil protective capabilities. Oil replacement should be considered after 2.5-5% dilution [4-5]. Dilution is often detected by variation in flashpoint. Fuel dilution is often a sign of poor combustion conditions. Fuel dilution can lead to sulfation as sulfuric compounds in the fuel can react with the oil.

Water contamination is often the result of a coolant leak. This is less common. Water can lead to hydrolysis, which can result in a chemical change within the oil. Water itself can damage the engine through rusting. Contamination with water is limited to 0.3%, and primarily occurs through coolant contamination [5].

Carbonous deposits and soot are primarily formed through an incomplete combustion process can contaminate the oil. Soot contamination is more common in diesel engines. Literature indicated that up to 3% volume is acceptable [5].

Soot increases viscosity, and may have acidic properties. Detergents help keep the deposits in the suppression and suppress the formation of varnish and lacquers.

Possible Conditions

The following section discusses the potential conditions pertaining to the modified spark ignition engines and microgrids that could be observed using oil analysis.

Low temperature combustion resulting from altering the combustion conditions or improper load balancing (wetstacking) could present as fuel dilution. Fuel dilution will reduce the viscosity and reduce the flashpoint of the oil. Lower temperatures prevent proper sealing at piston rings and in extreme cases result in condensation of the fuel on the cylinder walls. This will be more pronounced under rapid starting and stopping as may occur in microgrids. Another sign of fuel dilution is an increase in volume of the oil reservoir. Fuel dilution of the oil can lead to sulfation. Sulfation will promote the formation of sludge and varnish, increasing the oil's viscosity. This may not be as pronounced on low sulfur JP8 (100ppm) but is expected to become more pronounced with high sulfur JP8 (3000pm).

Oxidization of the oil is possible especially in conditions where the generator is operating consistently at full load, in hot environments. It typically presents as increase in carbonyl acids, and an overall increase in viscosity due to polymerization. Nitration is less likely, as a low temperature conditions but can occur at full load.

Contamination of the oil may be prevalent depending on the conditions. Soot contamination may also form as both modified engine and wetstacking conditions can produce significant levels of hydrocarbons and soot. It is expected that this will occur under poor combustion conditions and low generator loading. Water related issues such as contamination or hydrolysis may impact larger generators in microgrids but are less relevant to the air cooled modified spark ignition engines

Wear metal analysis can be used to diagnose component failure, and be used to assess if a particular generator unit is overlay utilized in the microgrid. It is expected to see increase in iron over a shorter period of time, when compared to other generators in the grid.

Conclusion

Oil analysis provides a strong capability in predicating engine degradation and failure as a result of poor operating conditions. Oil properties can indicate a wide range of engine conditions ranging to oxidation, thermal degradation, nitration, sulfation, hydrolysis, and wear metals. In certain cases, using wear metal analysis the unique metallurgical composition of the engine will allow the determination of an upcoming failure. FTIR, gas chromatography, acidity, viscosity, and spectroscopy can provide a wide range of information on engine oil. For modified engines the most likely conditions stem from low temperature combustion. Increasing engine temperature may help alleviate this. Under microgrid configuration the issues result in rapid starting and stopping and improper load balancing.

To counter these issues the following should be considered: changing the oil change frequency, change to an oil that is more resistant to sulfur compounds, use oils high detergent concentrations to help mitigate contamination.

Acknowledgments

The authors acknowledge the support of the CERDEC CPI Power Division and E2S2.

Reference

[1] Michael Holloway, "The Oil Analysis Handbook: A Comprehensive Guide to Using and Understanding Oil Analysis"http://www.certifiedlabs.com/certified/vContent/4/documents/general/Oil_Analysis_Handbook.pdf

[2] Jim Fitch, Noria Corporation, Machinery Lubrication "The Lowdown on Oil Breakdown", 2015, http://www.machinerylubrication.com/Read/475/oil-breakdown

[3] California Integrated Waste Management Board, "Evaluation of High Efficiency Oil Filters in the State Fleet", Publication #IWMB-2008-020

[4] Techenomic International, "Test Explanations", http://www.techenomics.net/oil-fluid-analysis/test-explanations/

[5] Petroleum Technologies, "Petroleum Technologies" http://www.oillab.com/downloads/Petroleum_Technologies.pdf

[6] Roger F. Haycock, Arthur J. Caines, John E. Hillier, "Automotive Lubricants Reference Book", 2004, page 159

[7] Steffen Bots, "Establishing Elemental Limit Values for Motor Oils", Machinery Lubrication Magazine", www.machinerylubrication.com/

[8] John S. Evans, "Wear Limits Vs. Trends", Machinery Lubrication Magazine, www.machinerylubrication.com/

[9] Noria Corporation," What Oil Analysis Tests Tell Us", Machinery Lubrication Magazine, www.machinerylubrication.com/

[10] Anand Kumar Tripathi, Ravikrishnan Vinu "Characterization of Thermal Stability of Synthetic and Semi-Synthetic Engine Oils" Lubricants, 3, 54-79 2015

[11] Yuegang Zhao, "Oil Analysis Handbook for Predictive Equipment Maintenance" Spectro Scientific, 2014

[12]Analytical Testing Laboratory and Surveyors, http://www.labinspection.com/sulfation.html,

[13]Wes Cash, "Understanding Hydrolysis and Hydrolytic Stability", Noria Corporation, http://www.machinerylubrication.com/Read/29397/understanding-hydrolytic-stability, 2013

[14] David E. Newton, "Used Oil Analysis: How to decide what is normal" https://www.bobistheoilguy.com/used-oil-analysis-how-to-decide-what-is-normal/

Comparing Various Capacitor Types for High Power Applications

Kevin Chu, Yakira J. Howarth, Terrill B. Atwater
U.S. Army-RDECOM-CERDEC
Aberdeen Proving Ground, MD 21005

Abstract: *The increasing power and energy demands of Army equipment, from something as small as a radio to as large as a generator starter, have created a need for newer and better power solutions than what is currently provided by the traditional battery. The emergence of lithium-ion capacitors and the increasing development of supercapacitors – both of which are lighter, offer better cyclability, and have higher power densities than a battery – provide viable alternatives as power sources. Although supercapacitors are already being applied in systems such as power tools, electric vehicles, and elevators – as well as serving as an uninterrupted power supply in places like hospitals – and lithium-ion capacitors are being used in electric vehicles or as auxiliary power devices, neither supercapacitors nor lithium-ion capacitors are extensively used for military applications. While similar in many ways, supercapacitors and lithium-ion capacitors have a few key characteristic differences that cause them to behave in subtly yet vastly different ways. Data gathered from each technology will be used to examine these differences and to determine how best to optimize their respective strengths.*

Keywords
Supercapacitors, hybrid capacitors; lithium-ion capacitors; high rate electrochemical systems; asymmetric electrochemical capacitors

Introduction
With increasing advancements in technology as well as the Army's desire to increase mission time, Army equipment power and energy needs are rapidly outpacing the power and energy capabilities available from traditional power sources such as batteries. To satisfy these increasing power demands, the Army has begun to study systems that utilize alternative power sources, specifically supercapacitors and lithium-ion capacitors. On one hand, supercapacitors electrostatically store their charge on the surface of the electrode, while batteries store their charge in the bulk of the electrode[1]. Supercapacitors, usually composed of two electrodes made of the same material, have extremely high power density, capable of safely delivering over 5kW/kg[2,3,4]. Because supercapacitors lack high energy density, they need to be utilized in conjunction with another power source if the application is used for an extended period of time[5]. On the other hand, lithium-ion capacitors apply an asymmetric electrode system, meaning they will have two different types of electrodes. One electrode stores charge electrostatically – typically a graphite anode – while the other electrode stores its charge in a faradaic manner – usually using a lithium-doped activated carbon cathode[6,7]. Because this asymmetric electrode system uses a positive electrode that stores its charge in the bulk of the electrode itself, the energy of the system is up to ten times higher than that of a supercapacitor system[7]. Additionally, since rate capability – and therefore power density – of a lithium-ion capacitor is determined by the anode, the anode can be tailored to be more energy dense or more power dense depending on the application[3]. This paper will study two different lithium-ion capacitor cells – one more energy dense and the other more power dense – and compare them to a supercapacitor.

Experimental
Three different types of cells were tested for their performance at various rates and temperature ranges. One set of cells, Type A, were cylindrical supercapacitors, while the other two – Types B and C – were prismatic pouch lithium-ion capacitors. Type B was tailored to be more energy dense, while Type C was tailored to be more power dense. Type A cells had an average volume of 54cm^3 and an average weight of 60g. Type B cells had an average volume of 10cm^3 and an average weight of 20.8g. Type C cells had an average volume of 12 cm^3 and an average weight of 20.7g. All tests used an ARBIN MSTAT4 Battery Cycler System to cycle the cells and TPS Tenney TJR temperature chambers to evaluate performance at various temperatures. Before each series of tests, a baseline test of 20 cycles was conducted on each individual cell to establish its initial performance. For Type A cells, this consisted of charging and discharging the cells at a constant 1A rate between 0V and 2.7V, with a 5-minute rest period after each charge and discharge, for 20 cycles. For both Type B and C cells, the baseline test consisted of charging and discharging the cells at a constant 0.8A rate between 2.2V and 3.8V, also with a 5-minute rest period after each charge and discharge, for 20 cycles.

To assess performance at varying rates, three cells each of Type B and C were cycled, between their respective voltage ranges, at 1A for 20 cycles followed by 2A for 20 cycles. Type C cells were then tested at constant rates of 4A and 8A, with a baseline test run before and after the 8A test to see if the higher rate degraded their capacities. The Type B cells were tested at 3A due to their decreased performance at 2A. Neither type of cell was tested further because of the large decrease in capacity at 8A for Type C cells and the degradation at 3A for Type B cells. Three Type A cells were tested at 5A, 10A, and finally 20A since there was no significant decrease in performance at the higher rates. Then, to assess temperature performance, three fresh cells of each cell type were cycled at room temperature and then were slowly driven to more extreme temperatures. Each cell type was tested for 20 cycles, at 40°C, 10°C, 0°C, 50°C, -10°C, -5°C, and 55°C. Before and after the test at 55°C, the cells were also tested at 23°C to determine if the temperature tests had any impact on the cells.

Results

To easily compare the performance of all three cells at various rates and temperatures, not only to each other, but also to their respective baseline performances, graphs were made by plotting the discharge capacity of the cells in mAh/g. Specific discharge capacity was used as opposed to total discharge capacity to account for the differences in the weight of each type of cell. Using these graphs, specific discharge capacity and cell matching were analyzed. Additionally, any effects of the rate or temperature testing were also easily compared by ending each series of tests with a baseline test.

Figure 1 presents the specific discharge capacities of each cell type at various rates. Comparing the baseline discharge capacities, it can be seen that Type B cells had the highest specific discharge capacity, roughly 5 times higher than the specific discharge capacities of Type A and C cells. Although their specific discharge capacities were extremely similar to Type A cells, Type C cells possessed slightly higher specific discharge capacities.

Although possessing the lowest discharge capacities, Type A cells showed the least capacity loss when cycled at higher rates relative to baseline performance. When compared to the 1A baseline test, Type A cells retained an average capacity of 95.7% at 5A, 91.0% at 10A, and 82% at 20A.

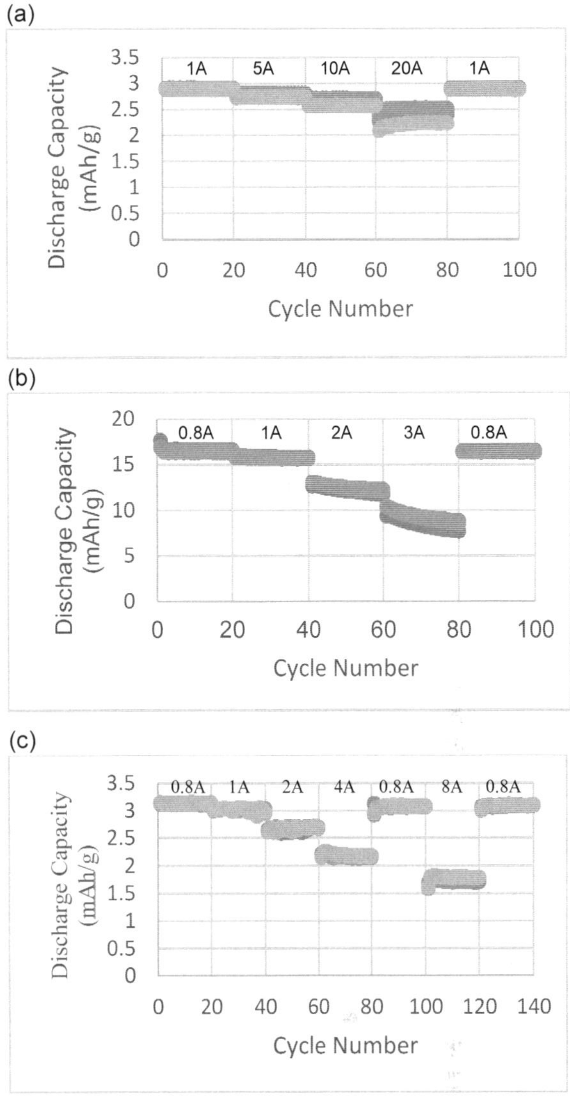

Figure 1: Specific discharge capacities for (a) Type A, (b) Type B, and (c) Type C cells at varying rates

Type B cells, while possessing the highest discharge capacities, also showed the highest decrease in performance at the higher rates. When compared to their 0.8A baseline test, they only retained an average capacity of 95.4% at 1A, dropping to 75.1% at 2A, and further dropping to 54.6% at 3A. Additionally, Type B cells showed a continual drop in capacity during their 20 cycles tested at 3A.

Lastly, Type C cells showed an average drop to 98.1% of baseline capacity at 1A, 87.1% at 2A, 71.4% at 4A, and 57.6% at 8A. Although all three cell types showed decreased performances as rates were increased, they performed at the same level as compared to the initial baseline capacities at the conclusion of the rate testing.

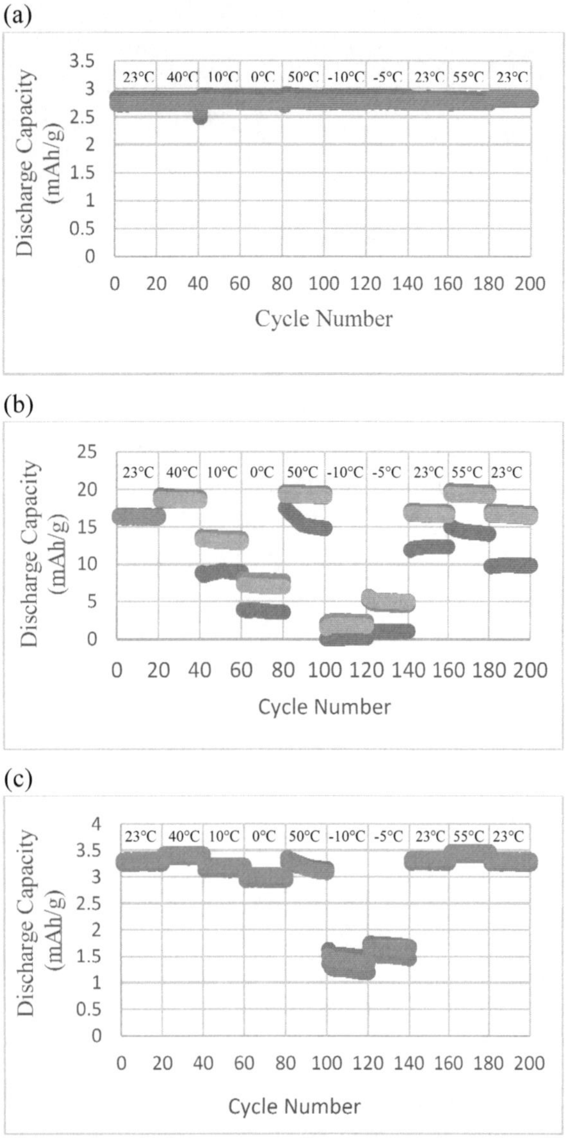

Figure 2: Specific discharge capacities for (a) Type A, (b) Type B, and (c) Type C cells at varying temperatures

Figure 2 presents the specific discharge capacities of the cell types at various temperatures when tested at their baseline rate. Comparing the baseline discharge capacities, it can be seen that Type B cells were the most affected by varying the temperature. Testing at temperatures above room temperature seemed to increase discharge capacity, with an average capacity increase of 14.4% at 40°C, 12.1% increase at 50°C, and 11.1% increase at 55°C. Additionally, it is interesting to note that a mismatched cell seemed to lose capacity as it was cycled at 50°C, while the other cells remained stable. However, testing at temperatures below room temperature had a negative impact on performance, with the cells only retaining an average capacity of 74.4% at 10°C, 40.3% at 0°C, 9.5% at -10°C, and 24.3% at -5°C. Additionally, testing the cells at -10°C caused one of the cells to become mismatched from the others.

Conversely, testing at varying temperatures seemed to have a negligible effect on the performances of Type A cells, with the capacities at all temperatures within 2% of their baseline performance.

Lastly, while not impacted as significantly as the performance of Type B cells, the performance of Type C cells was also impacted by testing at various temperatures. Similar to Type B cells, Type C cells saw a slight increase in capacity when tested at temperatures above room temperature, with a 3.5% increase at 40°C, negligible difference at 50°C, and a 5.6% increase at 55°C. Below room temperature, there was not a significant difference until the cells were tested below 0°C, with the cells retaining an average of 96.5% and 90.7% of baseline capacities at 10°C and 0°C, respectively. However, the performance decreased dramatically when tested below 0°C, with the cells only retaining 44% of baseline capacity at -10°C and recovering slightly at -5°C, retaining an average of 50.1% of baseline capacity.

It is important to note that with the exception of the one Type B cell that became mismatched while testing at 10°C, all the cells were able to achieve capacities that matched the initial baseline capacities when tested at baseline conditions at the end of the temperature tests.

Discussion

Two different prismatic lithium-ion capacitor cells were tested to compare their characteristics to those of cylindrical supercapacitor cells at higher rates as well as various temperatures. Unfortunately, due to availability, cells with the same configurations could not be tested. While both the lithium-ion capacitor cells had higher specific capacities than the supercapacitor, they both suffered, to varying extents, from being tested at higher rates as well as at low temperatures.

Type A cells were able to be cycled at rates as high as 20A while retaining most of their capacity, Type B cells were only able to be cycled at 3A while showing significant capacity loss, and Type C cells showed significant capacity loss at 8A. The same trend held when the cells were tested at various temperatures. The performance of Type A cells were marginally impacted by various temperatures, Type C cells showed poor performance at low temperatures, and Type B cells were barely able to be cycled at low temperatures. However, with the exception of one Type B cell, all cells were able to recover to their initial baseline capacity established at the beginning of the series of tests.

Furthermore, Type A and Type C cells showed good capacity matching throughout testing, only showing minimal drift at high rates for Type A and low temperatures for Types B and C

Conclusion

To solve the evolving power and energy demands of advancing equipment, the Army has started exploring supercapacitors and lithium-ion capacitors as potential solutions. These are viewed as solutions because, although they do not possess the energy density that batteries can provide, they can operate at wider temperatures and higher rates than batteries. Depending on the power and energy density demands of the system, the varying characteristics of each type of cell need to be considered.

Supercapacitors could be used if the system only needs a short, high rate burst of energy, or if the system allows them to be coupled with another power source that can provide a sustained output of energy. Additionally, if the system would be used at extreme cold or hot temperatures, the performance of Type A cells would not significantly affected. Type A cells would be well suited for generator or engine starting and lasers, where only a short, high power burst would be needed. Additionally, depending on where the generator or engine is deployed, they could be required to start in extremely low temperatures. Type B cells, possessing higher energy density but worse rate capabilities than the two counterpart cells tested, would be well suited for a system that demands high energy but only needs moderate rate capabilities – such as radios, where moderate energy is required while not in use but higher energy is required while in use. Type C cells do not seem to be preferable over the other two, as they do not possess the energy density of Type B cells or the rate capabilities of Type A cells. However, all the cells would need to be further tested according to the power profiles of various systems, as well as in the systems themselves, to confirm suitability.

Acknowledgements

The authors would like to thank our colleagues for having helpful discussions, editing this paper, helping with the various test set ups.

References

1. Sun, Fei et al. "A High Performance Lithium Ion Capacitor Achieved by the Integration of a Sn-C Anode and a Biomass-Derived Microporous Activated Carbon Cathode." *Scientific Reports* 7 (2017): 40990. *PMC.* Web. 17 Apr. 2018.
2. Du Pasquier, A. et al. "A comparative study of Li-ion battery, supercapacitor and nonaqueaous asymmetric hybrid devices for automotive applications," *Journal of Power Sources*, vol. 115.1, pp. 171-178, 2003
3. A. González, E. Goikolea, J.A. Barrena, R. Mysyk, "Review on supercapacitors: Technologies and materials," *Renewable and Sustainable Energy Reviews*, vol. 58, pp 1189-1206, 2016
4. Zhang, Y. et al. "Progress of electrochemical capacitor electrode materials: A review," *International Journal of Hydrogen Energy*, vol. 34.11, pp 4889-4899, 2009
5. Li, J. "Supercapacitors: Review of Materials and Fabrication Methods,"s *Journal off Energy and Engineering*, vol. 139, pp 72-79, 2013
6. Choi, H.S, Park, C.R, "Theoretical guidelines to designing high performance energy storage device based on hybridization of lithium-ion battery and supercapacitor", *Journal of Power Sources*, vol. 259, pp. 1-14, 2014
7. Cericola, D. and Kötz, R. "Hybridization of rechargeable batteries and electrochemical capacitors: Priciples and limits," *Electrochimica Acta*, vol. 72, pp. 1-17, 2012

Abuse Tolerant Electrolytes

Surya Moganty

CTO
NOHMs Technologies, Inc
Rochester, NY 14615

Abstract: *NOHMs Technologies is developing functional ionic liquid based hybrid electrolytes for high energy density, high voltage, and high power batteries for mobility and consumer applications. It is well established that the composition of electrolytes greatly affects cell performance from rate capability, lithium cycling efficiency, and capacity retention at various temperatures to tolerance against electrical, mechanical, and thermal abuses. Ionic liquids offer a host of attractive properties for electrolytes, including ultralow vapor pressure, high thermal stability, high ionic conductivity, and wide electrochemical stability. However, there are some physical property limitations that to-date has made them unattractive for lithium battery applications. High viscosity and the fraction of the ionic conductivity of the electrolyte arising from mobile lithium ions (i.e. the so-called lithium transference numbers) are typically low for these materials, which make cells assembled using ionic liquid electrolytes prone to large polarization during operation of the cell.*

These limitations can be easily overcome by blending functional ionic liquids with appropriate co-solvents. These hybrid electrolytes simultaneously overcome the poor thermal & electrochemical stability and safety problems that have plagued lithium battery electrolytes for years while still maintaining high conductivity. They provide a platform for engineering electrolytes with both chemical and interfacial tunability that beyond improving safety, expand the range of available battery form factors.

During the presentation, we will demonstrate how NOHMs' functional ionic liquid design impacts the SEI formation on the graphite anode, high temperature stability, and abuse tolerance of high nickel content cathode materials. We will discuss the following: 1) functional ionic liquid and co-solvent formulations to achieve an abuse tolerant electrolyte (nail pen and thermal ramp), 2) the relationship of capacity fade and operating temperature; and 3) how electrolyte formulations improve the abuse tolerance of large format pouch cells.

Below figure depicts the photographs of 5 Ah NMC532 cells underwent the nail penetration test at 100% SOC. Cells containing NOHMs electrolyte demonstrated excellent abuse tolerance compared to state of the art electrolytes.

High Energy/Power Density, Safe Lithium Battery with Nonflammable Electrolyte

Weibing Xing, Stephen Cordova and Steve C. Arzberger
weibingx@adatech.com, stevena@adatech.com, stephenc@adatech.com
ADA Technologies, Inc.
11149 Bradford Road, Littleton, CO 80127
Phone: (303) 792-5615 / Fax: (303) 792-5633

Abstract: *ADA Technologies (ADA) offers a high energy/power density, long cycle life, and safe lithium (Li) or lithium ion (Li-ion) battery, comprised from a room temperature ionic liquid (RTIL) based and/or fluorinated solvent based electrolyte and a nanoengineered, high voltage, high energy density cathode. ADA Li and/or Li-ion battery offers tremendous potential to meet the multifaceted performance requirements of advanced power sources with established advantages over state-of-the-art (SOA) Li or Li-ion batteries including unprecedented high energy density, high rate capability, wide temperature operation, long cycle life (at RT, and temperature extremes) and safety.*

Keywords: lithium battery; lithium-ion battery; nanoengineered cathode; high voltage high energy density cathode, nanoengineered lithium cobalt oxide; nonflammable room temperature ionic liquid based electrolyte; nonflammable fluorinated solvent based electrolyte.

Introduction

A high performance and safe Li battery with nonflammable electrolyte is highly desired for a range of US military and consumer applications. The ADA Li or Li-ion battery is comprised from a nonflammable, high performance, RTIL- and/or fluorinated solvent-based electrolyte and a nanoengineered, high voltage, high energy density cathode technology. The ADA Li or Li-ion battery offers tremendous potential to meet the multifaceted performance requirements for advanced power sources with established advantages over SOA Li or Li-ion batteries. This includes unprecedented energy density, high rate capability, wide temperature operation, long cycle life at RT and temperature extremes, and safety. Efforts are underway to transition this battery to meet a variety of advanced applications of interest to the US military and consumer markets.

The Need for High Performance and Safe Li or Li-ion Batteries

Advanced applications, such as, consumer electronics, defense, space, medical and electric drive vehicles, are becoming increasingly reliant on high energy density batteries, and particularly Li or Li-ion batteries. This is due to significant Li or Li-ion battery weight, density and storage capacity benefits. The mostly widely used Li or Li-ion batteries are activated via organic solvent-based electrolytes that are highly flammable. Unfortunately Li or Li-ion batteries with organic solvent-based electrolytes lack desired safety assurances; this represents a major impediment to large-format battery device implementation in safety critical systems. Under abuse conditions (e.g., internal short circuit, overcharge, overdischarge, and crush), Li or Li-ion batteries impose potential hazards associated with heat, fire, toxic material release and over-pressurization. These hazards represent substantial concerns for platforms populated by personnel, sensitive equipment and/or vital structures. Recent high-profile incidents involving energy dense batteries have increased public awareness resulting in intensified scrutiny for the processes used to develop, manufacture, certify and transport, and a renewed emphasis on quality, best practices and safety. Examples include Boeing 787 Dreamliner [1] and Samsung Galaxy Note 7 [2] battery fire incidents (**Figure 1**). These incidents underscore the fact that, despite a growing use of Li or Li-ion batteries in various applications, this battery class remains prone to complex failure modes, which can confound even the best fail-safe design practices. Therefore, there is a need to develop a high energy/power density Li or Li-ion battery based on a nonflammable, high performance electrolyte to mitigate/eliminate safety concerns associated with the flammable electrolytes in storage, transition and operation.

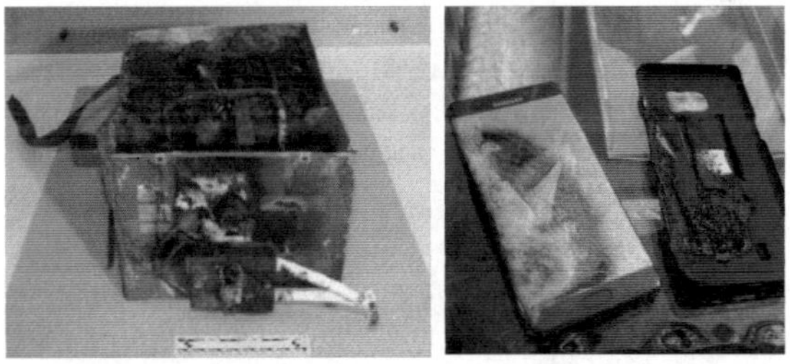

Figure 1. Boeing 787 Dreamliner (left) and Samsung Galaxy Note 7 (right) battery fire incidents.

ADA Nonflammable, High Performance, RTIL- and Fluorinated Solvent-Based Electrolytes

ADA employed various functional electrolyte components. This included conventional carbonate solvent based electrolyte (control), nonflammable RTIL-based electrolyte, and/or nonflammable fluorinated solvent-based electrolyte. **Table 1** summarizes a number of ADA electrolytes and flammability performance.

A combined Li salt approach was investigated. Li salts were selected to provide high ionic conductivity and enhanced extreme temperature performance. Conventional carbonate solvents were selected to provide passivation protection and high rate and wide temperature operation, with particular emphasis on extreme low temperatures (*e.g.*, -40°C). RTILs with low melting point (< RT) that were also known for nonflammability were selected to provide electrolyte nonflammable performance while being amenable to Li anode.

Table 1. ADA electrolytes and flammability test results

Electrolyte ID	Electrolyte Description	Flammability Test Result
Control	Li salt in carbonate solvents	Ignited with self-burning
RTIL-based	Li salt(s) in RTIL and carbonate solvents	Nonflammable
RTIL-based + additives	Li salt(s) in RTIL and carbonate solvents with additives	Nonflammable
Fluorinated solvent-based	Li salt(s) in fluorinated and carbonate solvents	Nonflammable

Fluorinated solvents represent attractive co-solvents in electrolyte formulations because they possess no flash point (nonflammable) and, offer high thermal stability and much lower viscosity than RTILs. These attributes are very helpful in achieving nonflammability while enabling high rate and operation at extreme temperatures. For this reason, a fluorinated solvent-based electrolyte was formulated and its electrochemical performance evaluated. A number of (carbonate and fluorinated carbonate based) additives were used to enhance cycle stability at elevated temperatures (*e.g.*, +75°C).

ADA Electrolyte Flammability Test

ADA conducted an electrolyte flammability evaluation. A lighter was used to ignite the electrolyte in a watch glass dish in open air. The control electrolyte (a conventional Li-ion battery electrolyte) was ignited and self-burning when the ignitor was moved away (**Figure 2**a). Each of the RTIL- and fluorinated solvent-based electrolytes did not ignite and, no combustion was observed (**Figure 2**b and 2c). We categorize the RTIL- and fluorinated solvent-based electrolytes as nonflammable electrolytes.

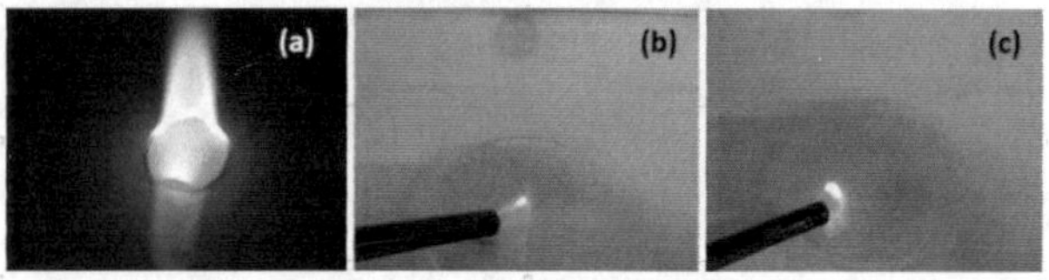

Figure 2. (a) Baseline, (b) RTIL-based and (c) fluorinated solvent-based electrolytes.

RTIL- and Fluorinated Solvent-Based Electrolytes: Capacity *vs.* Temperature Evaluation

In this study, coin cells were constructed using a Li metal anode and an ADA high voltage, high energy density cathode which is a nanoengineered, multifunctional material coated $LiCoO_2$ (denoted as HV-LCO). The nonflammable RTIL- and fluorinated solvent-based electrolytes were used in coin cells. **Figure 3** shows discharge voltage profiles of Li/HV-LCO cells as a function of temperature. An Espec environmental chamber (model BTZ-133) was used for temperature control. The cells were cycled between 3.0 – 4.6V (*vs.* Li/Li^+). At RT (23°C±0.5°C) and C/4 rate, the cells with the two types of nonflammable electrolytes delivered a high specific capacity ~ 205 mAh/g (based on the cathode active material weight). A cell level specific energy is estimated ~360 Wh/kg, ~50% increase over a Li/pristine LCO cell (~ 240 mAh/g), which can only be cycled at a lower voltage (3.0 – 4.2V) without rapid capacity fade.

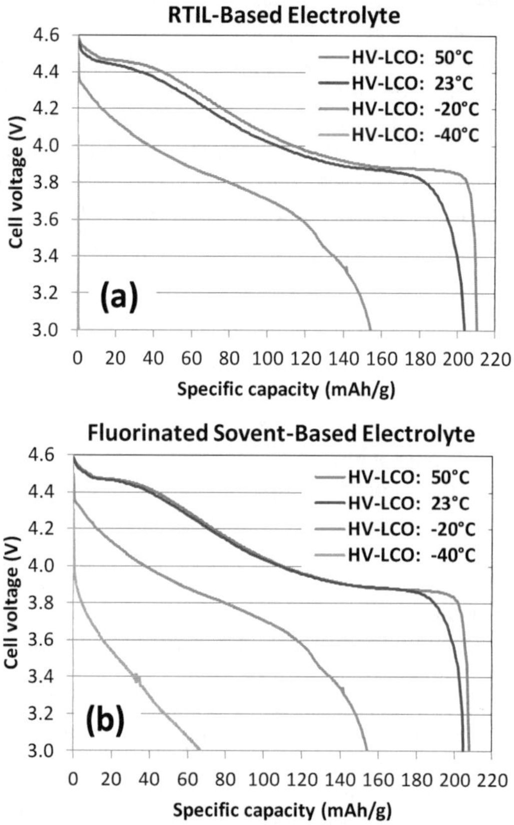

Figure 3. Discharge voltage profiles of Li/HV-LCO cells as a function of temperature: (a) RTIL- and (b) fluorinated solvent-based nonflammable electrolytes.

At 50°C and C/4 rate, the cells with the two nonflammable electrolytes delivered a slightly higher (1 – 3%) specific capacity, when compared to the data obtained at RT. Note the cells showed mostly overlapping discharge voltages between RT and 50°C; this indicates small direct current internal resistance (DCIR) afforded by the electrolytes.

After cooling to -20°C, the cells were cycled at C/10 rate. Each of the RTIL- and fluorinated solvent-based electrolyte cells delivered ~ 155 mAh/g specific capacity, ~ 75% of the capacity at RT. The cells showed noticeable lower discharge voltage profiles than at RT. The reduced capacity and lower voltages are attributed to increased electrolyte viscosity and reduced ionic conductivity at the low temperature. After further cooling to -40°C, the cells were cycled at C/20 rate. The RTIL-based electrolyte cell delivered a small specific capacity of 0.6 mAh/g. On the other hand, the fluorinated solvent-based electrolyte cell delivered a finite specific capacity (66.5 mAh/g), which was much higher than the RTIL-based electrolyte cell. The results will help guide our electrolyte design for extreme low temperatures.

RTIL-Based Electrolyte: Rate Capability Test

A rate capability evaluation (at RT) for Li/LCO cells with the RTIL-based electrolyte is shown in **Figure 4**. The cells were charged at C/4 rate and discharged at various C rates between 3.0 – 4.6V. The discharge capacities at each C rate are referenced to a low rate (0.25C rate). The RTIL-based electrolyte Li/LCO cells showed excellent rate capability with ~ 85% discharge capacity retention at 10C rate *vs*. C/4 rate.

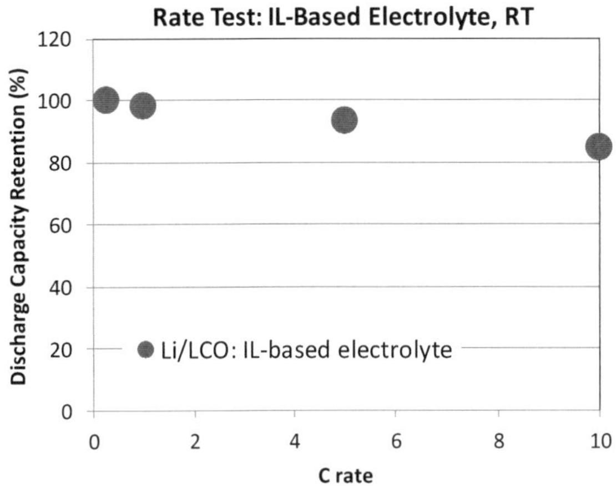

Figure 4. Rate capability test for Li/LCO cells using RTIL-based electrolyte.

RTIL-Based Electrolytes: High Voltage and High Temperature Cycle Life Tests

Figure 5a shows high voltage cycle life test for pristine-LCO and HV-LCO based Li cells using the RTIL-based electrolyte. The cells were cycled at 1C charge/2C discharge (1C/2C) rates, between 3.0 – 4.6V, at RT. The pristine LCO based cells experienced a rapid capacity fade upon the high voltage cycling, while the HV-LCO cells demonstrated excellent high voltage cycle life stability with > 92% capacity retention after 100 cycles. We attribute the excellent HV-LCO high voltage cycle performance to the nanoengineered, multifunctional material (e.g., a solid state electrolyte) coatings on LCO; such coatings effectively suppressed the degradation root causes, *i.e.*, the Co^{4+} dissolution and hexagonal to monoclinic phase transition [3].

We also carried out cycle life at an elevated temperature of 50°C. **Figure 5b** shows high voltage cycle life test data for pristine LCO and HV-LCO based Li cells using the RTIL-based electrolyte. The cells were cycled at 1C/2C rates, between 3.0 – 4.5V, at 50°C. The pristine LCO cells experienced a rapid capacity fade upon high voltage high temperature cycling, while the HV-LCO cells demonstrated excellent high voltage and high temperature cycle life stability with little capacity fade (98% capacity retention, *vs*. 28% of the pristine LCO) after 35 cycles. As in the case of stable high voltage RT cycle life performance demonstration, we attribute the excellent high voltage high temperature cycle stability to the nanoengineered, multifunctional material (e.g., a solid state electrolyte) coatings on LCO, which benefit stable high voltage cycle life at both RT and elevated temperatures.

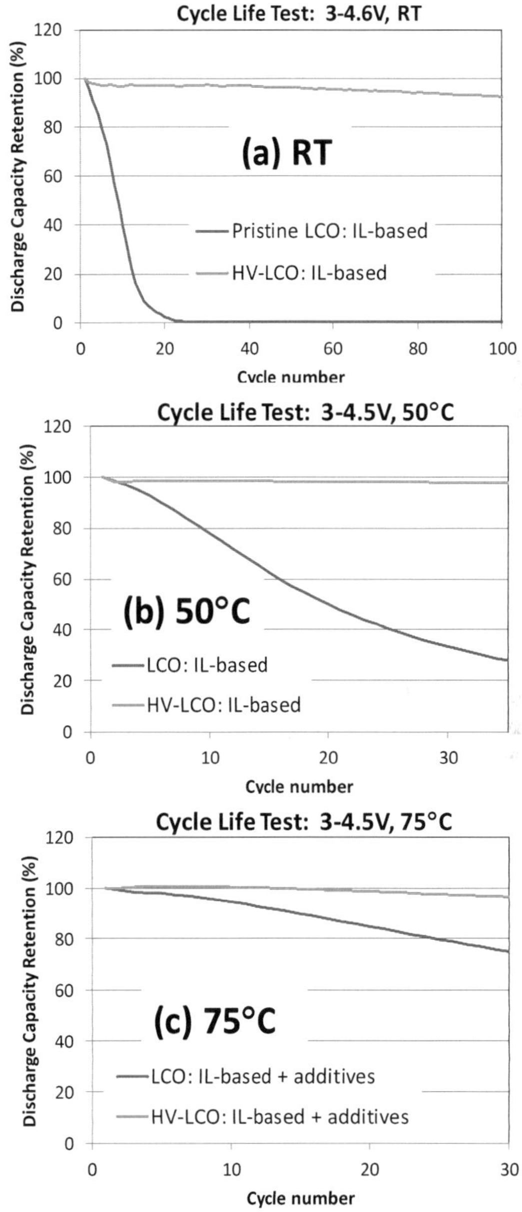

Figure 5. High voltage cycle life test for Li/LCO and Li/HV-LCO cells using RTIL-based electrolytes at (a) RT, (b) 50°C and (c) 75°C.

We further evaluated cycle life at an extreme high temperature of 75°C. **Figure 5c** shows high voltage cycle life test data for pristine LCO and HV-LCO based lithium cells, where carbonate and fluorinated carbonate additives were added to the RTIL-based electrolyte. The cells were cycled at 1C/2C rates, between 3.0 – 4.5V, at 75°C. It is interesting to note that the pristine LCO based Li cell showed a slower capacity fade rate at 75°C than at 50°C. We attribute this to the beneficial passivation protection afforded by the electrolyte additives. However, the pristine LCO based cell still experienced a much quicker capacity fade than the HV-LCO based cell; the latter exhibited an extraordinary high voltage high temperature cycle resiliency (97% capacity retention after 30 cycles, *vs*. 75% of the pristine LCO) even at the extreme high temperature of 75°C. We attribute the outstanding cycle stability at 75°C to the synergistic benefits of nanoengineered cathode and passivation protection from the electrolyte additives.

Our study highlights the importance of combining high performance, safe electrolyte with nanoengineered cathode to render the resultant lithium battery with unprecedented energy density (gained from the high voltage operation), high rate capability, safety (nonflammability) and robust cycle life over a wide temperature range particularly at the extreme high temperatures (*e.g.*, 75°C). We demonstrate here that our Li battery technology is ideally suited for many high energy density and safety demanding applications, such as, electric drive vehicles, consumer electronics, medical, space and military applications.

References

1. "FAA Grounds Boeing 787 Dreamliner for Battery Problems", Aviation International News, January 2013
2. https://www.scribd.com/document/368235555/Case-Study-Samsung-Galaxy-Note-7-Exploding-Batteries-PR-Response
3. Akira Yano, Masahiro Shikano, Atsushi Ueda, Hikari Sakaebe, and Zempachi Ogumi, J. Electrochem. Soc., 164, A6116 (2017).

Ultrathin Polymer Coatings to Improve Electrode Stability under Abusive Conditions

Rachel Carter[1,2], Jeffrey W. Long[1], Joseph F. Parker[1], Megan B. Sassin[1] and Corey T Love[1]
[1]Chemistry Division
U.S. Naval Research Laboratory
Washington, DC 20375 USA
corey.love@nrl.navy.mil

[2]NRL/NRC Post-doctoral Associate
U.S. Naval Research Laboratory
Washington, DC 20375 USA

Abstract: *The utility of an ultrathin polymer coating at battery negative electrodes was explored. Half-cell comparison of lithiation behavior in coated and uncoated graphite anodes suggest the polymer system provides advantages in electrolyte passivation and electrode stability, especially when tested at the extremities of conventional voltage operation (overcharge and overdischarge). The electrochemical stability and lithiating nature of the deposited polymer is thought to behave like a buffer to protect the graphite host substrate for enhanced performance. Further experiments are ongoing to better understand and exploit this behavior.*

Keywords: lithium-ion battery; battery safety, electrode coatings, overcharge, overdischarge, lithium dendrite

Introduction

Interfacial processes at the surfaces of charge-storing materials in Li-ion batteries have a great impact on such critical operational characteristics as rate capabilities, cycle and calendar life, and safety. Solid-electrolyte interphases (SEIs) that form spontaneously in situ serve to control surface reactivity in most Li-ion systems, yet can increase cell impedance and decrease performance. Recent advancements in deposition protocols for nanoscale coatings open new opportunities to pursue deliberately designed surface coatings at Li-on electrodes. Atomic-layer deposition has emerged as a popular tool to coat electrodes with nanoscale metal oxides (e.g., Al_2O_3) [1-3], but suffers from limitations related to the need for pre-deposition surface treatments and concerns regarding manufacturing scalability. Initiated chemical vapor deposition (iCVD) is a promising alternative route to generate coatings, in this case insulating polymers rather than metal oxides, with thickness control at the nanoscale, adaptability to non-line-of-sight deposition conditions, and compatibility with complex, porous substrates, while also being readily adaptable to large-scale manufacturing [4-8]. As a further benefit for electrochemical applications, the siloxane-based polymers most commonly generated by iCVD contain ether-like functionalities that support the solvation and transport of Li^+ salts, such that they can be readily transformed into Li-ion conductors. Exploiting these characteristics, iCVD-generated polymer coatings may be thought of as "artificial SEIs", thereby avoiding or minimizing the formation of spontaneously generated SEI layers present at the surfaces of active electrodes, such as graphite, in Li-based batteries. The incorporation of iCVD-polymer-modified graphite anodes into technologically relevant Li-ion battery systems pay provide the following performance advantages:

- enhanced tolerance to both overcharge and overdischarge excursions;
- greater electrode stability at elevated temperatures (e.g., for oxide-based cathodes);
- enhanced tolerance to H_2O impurities in the electrolyte;
- greater specific power compared to electrodes with spontaneously generated SEIs;
- suppression of Li dendrite formation at low temperatures and high charge rates.
- less oxygen loss on cathode during overcharge

In this work we demonstrate that nanoscale polymer coatings, deliberately applied to conventional Li-ion anodes using manufacture-friendly initiated chemical vapor deposition (iCVD) methods, yield substantial enhancements in lithiation performance, particularly in terms of cycling under abusive conditions.

Experimental Details

Commercial $LiCoO_2$ positive and graphite negative electrodes and lithium metal electrodes were used in this study. Graphite anodes were coated with poly-V3D3 using a commercial deposition chamber (GVD Corporation, Cambridge, MA). The monomer (1,3,5-trivinyl-1,3,5-trimethylcyclotrisiloxane: V3D3, >95%, Gelest) and the initiator (di-tert-butyl peroxide, TBPO 98%, Aldrich), were heated to 25°C and 50°C, respectively; lines from the source jars to the reaction chamber were held at 70°C to avoid vapor condensation. The flow of initiator was maintained at 2 sccm with a computer-controlled mass-flow controller. The V3D3 monomer was then introduced to the chamber using a manual regulator valve with the target chamber pressure set to 370 mTorr. Thermal excitation was achieved by resistively heating Nichrome wire at 35 V (~2 A). For the data presented herein, the deposition time was set at 40 min.

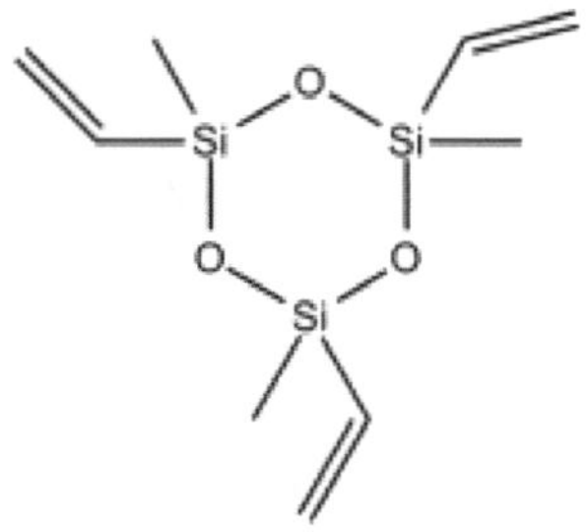

1,3,5-trivinyl-1,3,5-trimethyl-cyclotrisiloxane
"V3D3"

Electrochemical characterization was achieved using traditional potentiostat/galvanostat with impedance capability. Half cells of Li metal vs. graphite (coated and uncoated) were fabricated in coin cells (2320) with ultrahigh molecular weight polyethylene separators soaked in 1M $LiFP_6$ in EC/DEC (ethylene carbonate/diethyl carbonate) electrolyte. These cells were initially tested with cyclic voltammetry at 0.5mV/s. Cell impedance was also assessed before and after cycling with electrochemical impedance spectroscopy (EIS). Impedance data were collected over the frequency range, 1 MHz to 10 mHz, with a 10 mV AC amplitude. Overdischarge of the graphite electrode was assessed in this half-cell configuration by surpassing 3.0 V with linear sweep voltammetry (0.1mV/s). Finally, full cells with $LiCoO_2$ cathode and graphite anode were assembled to assess overcharge using linear sweep voltammetry was performed to 5.5 V at 0.1 mV s^{-1}.

Results

The lithiation of graphite with and without the poly(V3D3) coating was assessed using cyclic voltammetry at moderate scan rate (0.5 mV s^{-1}). First-cycle voltammograms are shown in Fig. 1, where multiple distinctions are noted. On the first negative sweep, current for the bare graphite increases sooner, at voltages (*vs.* Li) typical for the formation of an SEI layer at graphite (see Fig. 1, inset), while the onset of current at V3D3-graphite is shifted to lower voltage. At voltages <0.5 V, the increasing current is attributed to Li^+ intercalation, with the V3D3-graphite cell showing moderately higher current density. On the reverse scan, peaks for de-intercalation are observed in both cases, though the V3D3-graphite cell yields a larger and more well-defined peak. Four additional voltammetric cycles were collected, with the first three cycles for each cell show in Fig. 2 (the voltammetric signature was relatively constant after the third cycle).

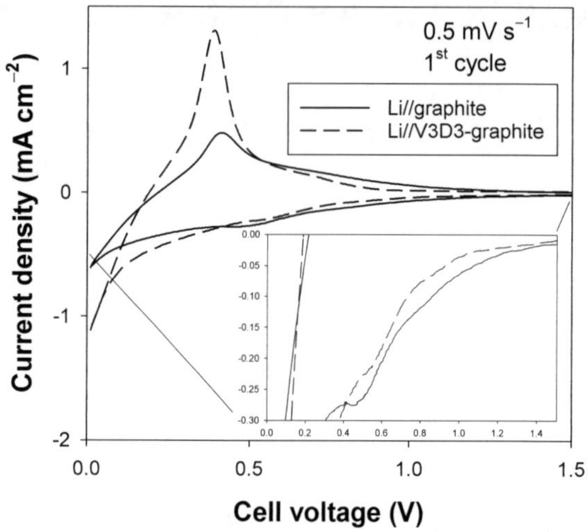

Figure 1. First-cycle voltammetry at 0.5 mV/s in lithium half cells, comparing uncoated and poly(V3D3)-coated graphite.

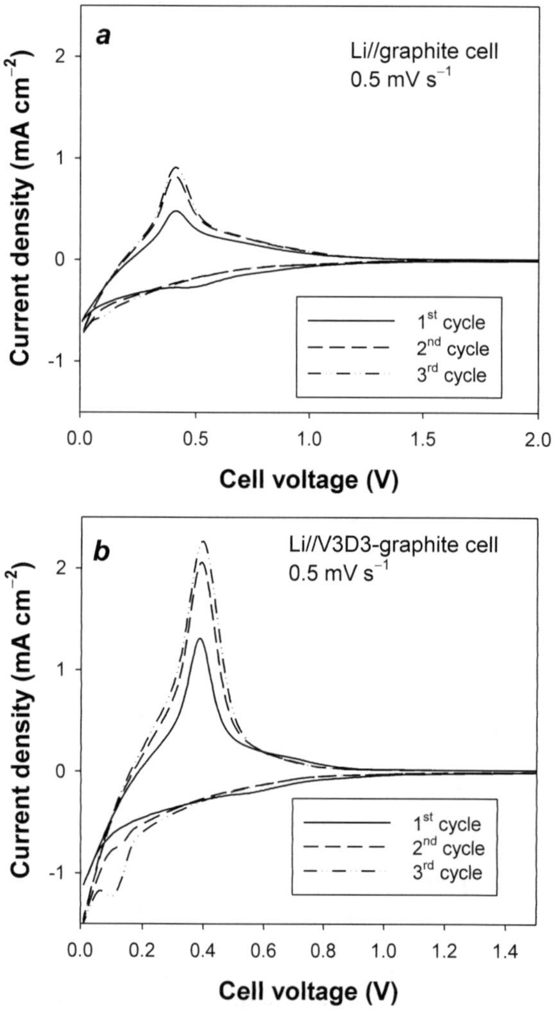

Figure 2. Cyclic voltammograms for the first three cycles in lithium half cells, comparing (*a*) uncoated graphite and (*b*) poly(V3D3)-coated graphite.

These initial cyclic voltammetry results confirm that the graphite electrode, beneath the nanoscale poly(V3D3) coating, readily undergoes reversible Li^+ intercalation, and does so with kinetics that are more favorable than for bare graphite electrodes. For further analysis of the interfacial characteristics of these graphite-based electrodes, we turned to electrochemical impedance spectroscopy (EIS). Impedance spectra were collected at open-circuit conditions (Fig. 3), first for uncycled cells of each type, and then for the same cells after they had been suggested to a five-cycle voltammetric "break-in" (see conditions noted above).

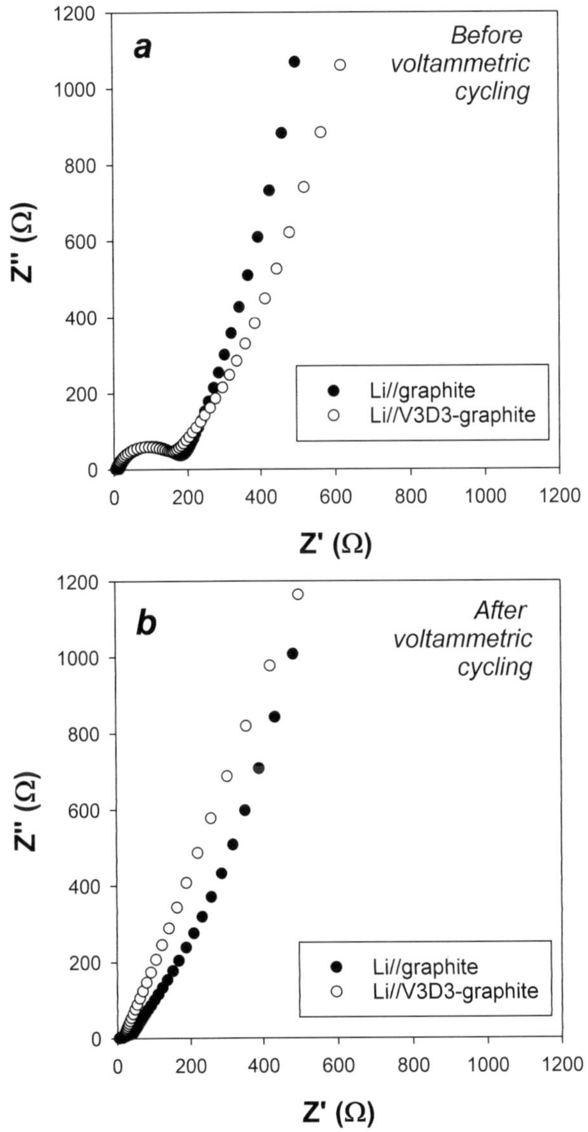

Figure 3. Electrochemical impedance spectra collected for uncoated graphite and poly(V3D3)-coated graphite, (a) in their initial uncycled state, and (b) after voltammetric cycling.

Cells with poly(V3D3)-coated graphite initially exhibit impedance higher than for cells with native graphite. The as-deposited poly(V3D3) coating does not contain lithium ions initially, and may require additional time or electrochemical driving force to achieve effective Li^+ distribution and transport through the polymer layer. After five electrochemical charge/discharge "break-in" cycles, the impedance of cells containing poly(V3D3)-graphite noticeably decrease, confirming the hypothesis noted above. Once the coatings lithiate they provide superior charge transfer to the native graphite alone. This distinction is likely due to resistances that arise from the SEI formed at bare graphite during initial cycling, whereas the poly(V3D3) coating may prevent the formation of the typical SEI under such conditions. The poly(V3D3) coating itself should ultimately serve as a more effective Li^+-transport layer [7,8] than the complex, heterogeneous SEI that is commonly generated at graphite surfaces.

In addition to mitigating SEI formation at graphite, iCVD-generated polymer coatings may also be effective for suppressing undesirable parasitic reactions that occur with either overdischarge or overcharge conditions in Li-ion batteries. Lithium half-cells were used for preliminary investigation of overdischarge protection properties. Cells were subjected to linear-sweep voltammetry tests, scanning from open-circuit to +3.55 V (Fig. 4). Oxidation of the copper current collector is the principle source of problems during overdischarge; such reactions are expected at ~3V vs. Li/Li^+. As the half-cell is swept through this voltage region, current density is higher for cells with bare graphite compared to the polymer-coated counterpart. Note that during the iCVD process, exposed copper surfaces on the electrode will also be coated with poly(V3D3). Passivation of exposed copper at the current collector results in the suppression of copper oxidation under these overdischarge conditions, as verified by lower current density in the voltage sweep.

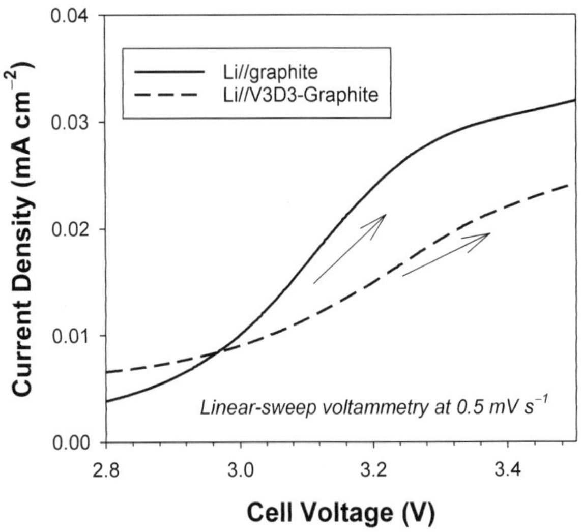

Figure 4. Linear-sweep voltammograms (0.1 mV s^{-1}) for half-cells with uncoated graphite and poly(V3D3)-coated graphite.

To simulate overcharge conditions, the bare and polymer-coated graphite electrodes were paired against $LiCoO_2$ electrodes in full cells. Following break-in cycling under galvanostatic conditions (five cycles at C/5 rate), these cells were subjected to linear-sweep voltammetry tests, with voltage excursions to an abusive 5.5 V value (Fig. 5). Both cells show the expected peaks for normal charging processes (Li^+-intercalation at the graphite and Li^+-de-insertion at $LiCoO_2$). Increased current density quantifies the activity of the electrodes in the cell. The 40-min coated electrodes show high activity just before 4.0 V indicating full capacity utilization of the $LiCoO_2$ electrode. But as the cell voltage passes ~4.7 V, current for the cell containing the poly(V3D3)-coated graphite is notably lower compared to the bare-graphite counterpart. Electrolyte decomposition reactions are expected in this voltage region, and the presence of the poly(V3D3) coating at the graphite anode appears to suppress such processes, which can lead to SEI breakdown, gassing, and electrode degradation.

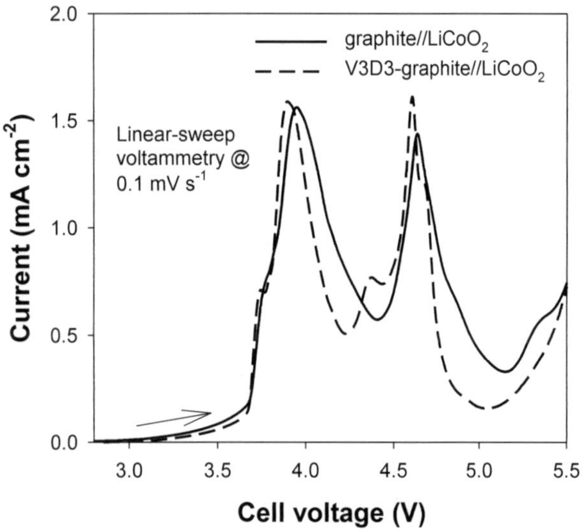

Figure 5. Linear-sweep voltammograms (0.1 mV s^{-1}) for full-cells with uncoated graphite and poly(V3D3)-coated graphite (and $LiCoO_2$ as the opposing electrode), scanned from 2.8 to 5.5 V.

Conclusions

The utility of an ultrathin polymer coating for battery negative electrodes was explored. The results suggest the polymer system may provide advantages to uncoated graphite, especially when cycled at the extremities of voltage operation or under overcharge and overdischarge. The *i*CVD polymer provides an alternative path for electrode coating compared to traditional atomic layer deposition (ALD) coating. The lithiating nature of the deposited polymer is thought to behave like an electrochemical buffer to allow sacrificial overlithiation during overcharge excursions to protect the graphite host substrate. Further experiments are ongoing to better understand and exploit this behavior.

Acknowledgements

The authors thank the U.S. Naval Research Laboratory for funding this work under the Institute for Nanoscience.

References

1. Jung, Y.S., A.S. Cavanagh, L.A. Riley, S-H Kang, A.C. Dillon, M.D. Groner, S.M. George and S-H Lee, "Ultrathin Direct Atomic Layer Deposition on Composite Electrodes for Highly Durable and Safe Li-Ion Batteries," *Advanced Materials*, vol. 2, pp. 2172–2176, 2010.
2. Jung, Y.S., A.S. Cavanagh, A.C. Dillon, M.D. Groner, S.M. George and S-H Lee, "Enhanced Stability of $LiCoO_2$ Cathodes in Lithium-Ion Batteries Using Surface Modification by Atomic Layer Deposition," *Journal of the Electrochemical Society*, vol. 152, iss. 1, pp. A75–A81, 2010.
3. Park, J.S., X. Meng, J.W. Elam, S. Hao, C. Wolverton, C. Kim and J. Cabana, "Ultrathin Lithium-Ion Conducting Coatings for Increased Interfacial Stability in High Voltage Lithium-Ion Batteries," *Chemistry of Materials*, vol. 26, iss. 10, pp. 3128–3134.
4. Murthy, S. K., Olsen, B. D., and Gleason, K. K., Langmuir, Vol. 18, pp. 6424–6428, 2002.
5. O'Shaughnessy, W. S., Gao, M., and Gleason, K. K., "Initiated Chemical Vapor Deposition of Trivinyl-trimethylcyclotrisiloxane for Biomaterial Coatings," Langmuir, Vol. 22, pp. 7021–7026, 2006.
6. Baxamusa, S. H. and Gleason, K. K., "Initiated Chemical Vapor Deposition of Polymer Films on Nonplanar Substrates," Thin Solid Films, Vol. 517, pp. 3536–3538, 2009.
7. Chen, N., Reeja-Jayan, B., Lau, J., Moni, P., Liu, A., Dunn, B., and Gleason, K. K.,"Nanoscale, Conformal Polysiloxane Thin Film Electrolytes for Three-Dimensional Battery Architectures," Materials Horizons, Vol. 2, pp. 309–314, 2015.
8. Reeja-Jayn, B., Chen, N., Lau, J., Kattirtzi, J. A., Moni, P., Liu, A., Miller, I. G., Kayser, R., Willard, A. P., Dunn, B., and Gleason, K. K., "A Group of Cyclic Siloxane and Silazane Polymer Films as Nanoscale Electrolytes for Microbattery Architectures," Macromolecules, Vol., 48, pp. 5222–5229, 2015.

Surface Chemistry Evolution in High-Power Lithium-ion Cathodes

Gordon H. Waller, Azzam N. Mansour, Christopher E. Hendricks, Jonathan K. Ko, Daphne A. Fuentevilla
Naval Surface Warfare Center, Carderock Division
9500 MacArthur Blvd, West Bethesda, MD 20817
gordon.waller@navy.mil / 1-301-227-1649

Abstract: High-energy cathode compounds $LiNi_{0.5}Co_{0.2}Mn_{0.3}O_2$ and $LiNi_{0.5}Mn_{1.5}O_4$ (NCM523 and LNMO) were cycled under various charge and discharge conditions to investigate the influence of high-rate operation on capacity degradation, impedance rise, and surface chemistry as analyzed by X-ray Photoelectron Spectroscopy (XPS). For the NCM523 cathodes it was found that high rates of charge were most detrimental to the electrodes, leading to a large decrease in coulombic efficiency with associated impedance rise and capacity fade. Meanwhile, the coulombic efficiency of LNMO was maximized with a slow charge and fast discharge while the impedance rise was lowest for the fast charge cells, presumably related to time spent in the potential region above the electrolyte stability window. XPS analysis was used to correlate the observed capacity, efficiency, and impedance changes to the cathode electrolyte interphase layer. For both electrodes materials, buildup of LiF was associated with increased impedance.

Keywords: Lithium-ion batteries; high-power; x-ray photoelectron spectroscopy

Introduction

Performance, safety, lifetime, and cost of lithium-ion batteries (LIB) are strongly influenced by the active materials used. As a result, cell chemistries are selected with the end goal in mind. For applications requiring superior power and safety, cells containing $LiFePO_4$ cathodes and graphite anodes with an organic liquid electrolyte are frequently used **[1]**. The major drawback of LIB cells designed for high-power is a relatively low energy density compared to high-energy cells, which conversely have poor rate capability.

While graphite anodes remain a constant in most commercial LIB, recent research has identified cathode materials which would potentially mitigate the tradeoff between power, energy, and safety. In particular, spinel structured $LiNi_{0.5}Mn_{1.5}O_4$ and layered nickel-rich compounds ($LiNi_xMn_yCo_zO_2$, $X \geq 0.5$) have reportedly high energy densities relative to $LiFePO_4$ while maintaining good power capability and thermal stability **[2] [3] [4] [5]**. While many published works have demonstrated that these compounds are capable of excellent high-power performance during discharge, particularly when nanostructured and carbon coated, very little work has been presented on the degradation mechanisms as a result of extended electrochemical cycling at high rates **[6] [7]**. In particular, over potentials produced when charging at high current densities can drive the upper cutoff voltage well above the ~4.5 V vs. Li/Li+ typically associated with electrolyte degradation **[8]**. Interestingly, even when cycled in identical electrolytes spinel and layered compounds have notably different responses to upper voltage cutoff. While the layered compound can be completely charged at low rates to a voltage less than 4.5 V vs. Li/Li^+ and cycling above this limit leads to rapid capacity loss, the spinel compound does not begin to accept charge until close to 4.7 V vs. Li/Li^+ and is comparatively less influenced by cycling above the potential for electrolyte oxidation.

This report will focus on analysis of the cathode-electrolyte interface, which is known to be a critical indicator of cell safety and lifetime, as a function of high-rate cycling and upper voltage cutoff. Capacity and electrochemical impedance measurements will be correlated with X-ray Photoelectron Spectroscopy (XPS) analysis used to analyze cathode surface chemistry. Results will be presented in the context of the cathode suitability for future development of high-power, high-energy, and safe LIBs.

Experimental

Electrodes were fabricated by tape-casting slurries containing 10 wt% PVDF binder, 10 wt% Timcal Super-P conductive carbon, and 80 wt% of active cathode material. Active materials were either $LiNi_{0.5}Mn_{1.5}O_4$ (LNMO, MTI) or $LiNi_{0.5}Co_{0.2}Mn_{0.3}O_2$ (NCM523, BASF). Powders were dissolved into N-Methyl-2-pyrrolidone and stirred for at least 3 hours at temperature of 70 °C until a homogenous slurry was formed which was spread onto sheets of aluminum foil using a doctor blade. Wet slurries were dried under vacuum over night at 150 °C and then cut into 15 mm diameter electrodes. Individual electrodes were then calendered under an applied load of 5 tons. Active material loading for each electrode was 5-6 mg/cm^2. Half-cells were assembled in an argon filled glovebox using a lithium metal counter electrode and glass fiber separators (Whatman GF/D) were soaked with 200 µL of electrolyte containing 1M $LiPF_6$ and a 3:7 blend of ethyl carbonate to ethyl methyl carbonate (BASF "A7" blend) in a 2032 coin cell. Coin cells were cycled on a potentiostat (Solartron 1480A Multistat) either in constant current - constant voltage (CC-CV) mode with currents normalized by the mass of the active cathode material and the nominal capacity (175 mAh/g for NCM523 and 100 mAh/g for LNMO) or by cyclic voltammetry (CV) at a scan rate of 100 µV/s. Following electrochemical cycling, cells were disassembled inside a glove box and rinsed with dimethyl carbonate (DMC) and then sealed inside an inert transfer vessel for analysis by x-ray photoelectron spectroscopy (XPS, PHI Versaprobe II).

Results

Cyclic voltammograms (Figure 1) collected for each electrode show that extraction of Li^+ from NCM523 (associated with the cell charging process) begins at approximately 3.6 V vs. Li/Li^+ with a peak current at 3.9 V vs. Li/Li^+. Lithium insertion (associated with the cell discharge process) is observed as a broad peak centered at 3.6 V vs. Li/Li^+. Continued electrode polarization of the NCM523 cathode above 4.7 V vs. Li/Li+ leads to the appearance of an irreversible oxidation peak in the CV plot, which is associated with deleterious side reactions not related to the charge storing capability of NCM523. Two closely spaced oxidation peaks are attributed to lithium extraction for LNMO, occurring at approximately 4.9 and 5.0 V vs. Li/Li^+, while lithium insertion occurs around 4.3 V vs. Li/Li^+. Meanwhile, no reversible redox activity is discernible for an electrode containing only conductive carbon and PVDF binder, and instead only an irreversible oxidation current is observed above 4.7 V vs. Li/Li+ and centered near 4.95 V vs. Li/Li^+. The oxidation current observed for the electrode containing only binder and conductive carbon is likely attributed to oxidation of the electrolyte, however no current is observed over the same potential region or a sheet of bare aluminum foil, which indicates that electrode components play an important role in the observation of irreversible side reactions.

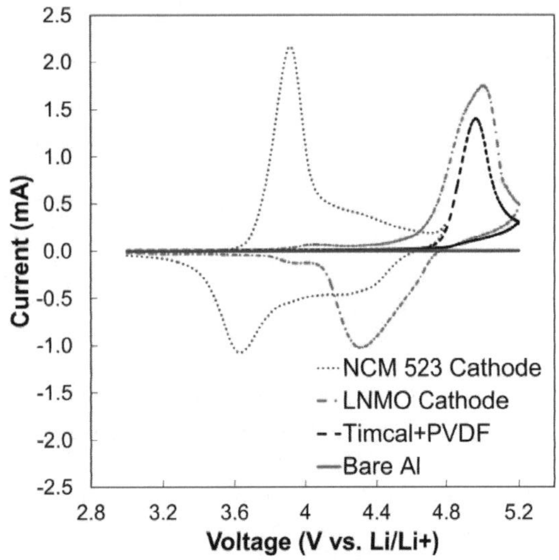

Figure 1. Cyclic Voltammograms (CV) comparing tape cast electrodes containing NCM523 cathode, LNMO cathode, an electrode containing binder and carbon only, and bare aluminum foil current collector.

Cycling of the NCM523 cathode to an upper voltage cutoff of 4.4V shows a strong dependence on rate for both the capacity retention and coulombic efficiency (Figure 2). When charged at a rate of 1C the coulombic efficiency is high (>99%), however as expected higher rates of discharge lead to less accessible capacity per cycle with less than 100 mAh/g accessible at a 5C discharge rate compared to ~140 mAh/g for the 1C discharge rate. Meanwhile, when comparing the capacity retention from the beginning C/10 cycles (formation) to the C/10 recovery cycles (after 200 cycles), <90% of the C/10 capacity was recovered for the electrodes with a 1C discharge regardless of charge rate compared to 96% capacity recovery for the 1C charge, 5C discharge electrode. Conversely, when charged at a rate of 5C a dramatic decrease in coulombic efficiency is observed leading to a rapid capacity fade from an initial 135 mAh/g to <60 mAh/g after 200 cycles. While all of the NCM523 electrodes recover most of their C/10 capacity, a notable difference is observed in the efficiency of these recovery cycles, with the 5C charge cells showing only <95% efficiency compared to >99% for the 1C charge, 5C discharge and ~97% for the 1C charge, 1C discharge cells. An identical trend is observed for impedance rise with the electrodes cycled at 1C charge and 5C discharge showing the smallest impedance after 200 cycles.

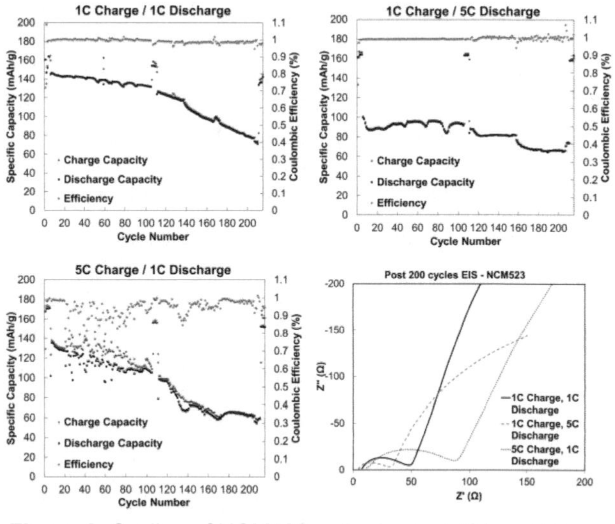

Figure 2. Cycling of NCM523 cathodes to 4.4V vs. Li/Li+ at charge/discharge rates of 1C/1C, 1C/5C, and 5C/1C. Impedance collected after 100 cycles was collected at 0% SOC.

LNMO electrodes cycled under identical rate conditions as NCM523 (relative to the specific capacity) are plotted in Figure 3. Like with the NCM523 electrode, charging at high rates leads to a large drop in coulombic efficiency, however in general the coulombic efficiency of LNMO is much lower than for NCM523. This is particularly noticeable during the formation cycles which were below 70% coulombic efficiency and indicated a large amount of electrolyte oxidation is occurring consistent with the CV plot in Figure 1. Also similar to NCM523, charging at a high rate leads to a further decrease in coulombic efficiency, however, regardless of the cycling conditions the capacity recovered after 200 cycles was comparable in all cases, and in fact slightly above the capacity observed during formation. The coulombic efficiency of the recovery cycles was also observed to improve relative to the formation cycles for electrodes charged at 1C with values near 95%, and slightly below this for the electrodes charged at 5C. An unexpected observation was that the impedance for the LNMO cathodes was found to be the smallest for the electrodes charged at 5C and highest for electrodes cycled at a low rate (1C charge and 1C discharge), which is opposite to the trend observed for NCM523 despite similarities in coulombic efficiency. This could indicate that while 5C charging leads to highly inefficient cycling, the side reactions occurring during charge are less detrimental to the conductivity of the electrode surface leading to lower impedance.

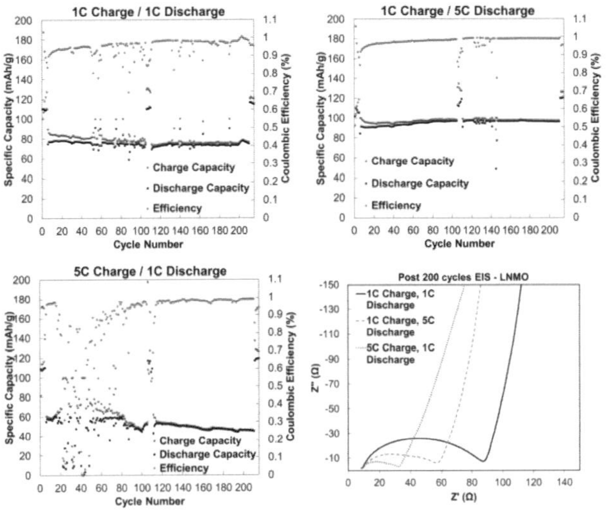

Figure 3. Cycling of LNMO cathodes to 4.8V vs. Li/Li+ at charge/discharge rates of 1C/1C, 1C/5C, and 5C/1C. Impedance collected after 100 cycles was collected at 0% SOC.

Following the cycling displayed in Figure 2 and Figure 3, cells were disassembled inside of an Ar filled glovebox, rinsed with DMC to remove electrolyte residue, and then sealed inside of an inert transfer vessel. This allowed the surface of the electrodes to be placed directly into the ultra-high vacuum conditions of the XPS chamber for analysis without exposure to ambient conditions. Summaries of the atomic percentages derived from survey scans of all elements observed in the cycled electrodes as compared to the uncycled electrodes are provided in Table 1 and Table 2.

For both electrodes initial oxygen content is expected to be associated with the transition-metal bonded oxygen in the cathode compounds as well as surface contaminants. Likewise, carbon content in the uncycled electrode is associated with the carbon black and PVDF binder inactive components. After cycling, the C1s and O1s content are found to experience the largest atomic % change out of all of the elements surveyed, while the transition metal content is generally seen to decrease. This is a strong indication of electrolyte breakdown leading to the formation of a surface film on the cathode active material, thereby decreasing their apparent concentration in the surface region of the electrodes.

General observations made from the changes in near-surface atomic concentrations are confirmed by reviewing the high-resolution multiplex scans collected for selected elements. As shown in Figure 4 for NCM523 and Figure 5 for LNMO, cycling conditions most associated with an increased impedance efficiency (5C charge / 1C discharge for NCM523 and 1C charge / 1C discharge for LNMO) lead to the greatest decrease in spectral features associated with the pristine electrode, namely the C1s, F1s, and O1s regions associated with carbon black, binder, and the transition metal oxide. Meanwhile, for an increase in LiF is observed directly correlating with increased impedance and capacity loss in both electrode material, however formed under different conditions.

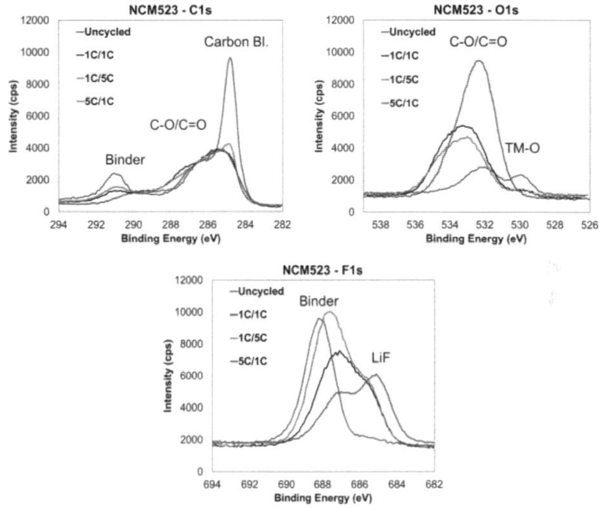

Figure 4. XPS analysis of C1s, O1s, and F1s regions of NCM523 cathodes cycled at various current densities.

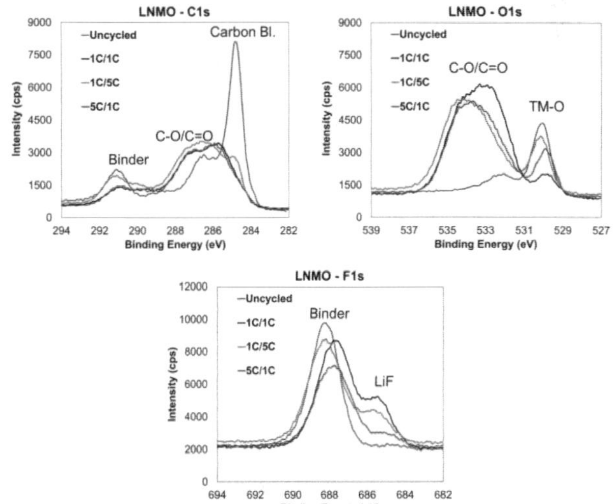

Figure 5. XPS analysis of C1s, O1s, and F1s regions of LNMO cathodes cycled at various current densities.

Table 1. Atomic percentages derived from XPS analysis of as-prepared and cycled NCM523 cathodes

Elemental Line	Uncycled	1C Ch / 1C Disch	1C Ch / 5C Disch	5C Ch / 1C Disch
C1s	65.5	44	47.4	37.8
O1s	8.7	21.7	25.4	31.6
F1s	18.9	21.3	15.1	14.9
Ni2p	3.4	2	2.6	1
Li1s	1.6	10.4	8.4	14.5
Mn2p	1.2	0.5	0.7	0.1
Co2p	0.7	0.2	0.3	0.1

Table 2. Atomic percentages derived from XPS analysis of as-prepared and cycled LNMO cathodes

Elemental Line	Uncycled	1C Ch / 1C Disch	1C Ch / 5C Disch	5C Ch / 1C Disch
C1s	62.8	39.9	48.6	46.7
O1s	10.4	29.5	25.6	28.7
F1s	20.1	23	19.8	16.8
Mn2p	3.3	1.8	2.4	2.6
Ni2p	3	0.9	2.1	2.2
Li1s	0.4	4.9	1.4	2.9

Conclusions

High energy cathode compounds $LiNi_{0.5}Mn_{1.5}O$ (LNMO) and $LiNi_{0.5}Co_{0.2}Mn_{0.3}O_2$ (NCM523) were cycled under high-power conditions for both charge and discharge. Regardless of the electrode choice, high rate charging (5C) was found to lead to a decrease in coulombic efficiency which correlated with an increased apparent formation of a cathode-electrolyte interphase layer. For NCM523, this increase interphase also correlated with decreased capacity retention and increased electrochemical impedance. Meanwhile, LNMO showed similar signatures of cathode-electrolyte interphase formation and impedance rise but this did not correlate with irreversible capacity loss, which implies that the native surface chemistry of LNMO, or perhaps the higher voltage of operation, can lead to a more stable and conductive interphase. Further research will focus on exploring the conditions in which the cathode-electrolyte interphase can be tailored for ideal performance.

Acknowledgements

The authors acknowledge financial support under the In-house Laboratory Independent Research (ILIR) program, managed by the NSWC Carderock Division Director of Research, Dr. Jack Price.

References

[1] E. Cairns and P. Albertus, "Batteries for Electric and Hybrid-Electric Vehicles," *Annual Review of Chemical and Biomolecular Engineering,* vol. 1, pp. 299-320, 2010.

[2] P. Rozier and J. Tarascon, "Review-Li-Rich Layered Oxide Cathodes for Next-Generation Li-Ion Batteries: Chances and Challenges," *Journal of the Electrochemical Society,* vol. 162, no. 14, pp. A2490-A2499, 2015.

[3] M. Noh and J. Cho, "Optimized Synthetic Conditions of LiNi0.5Co0.2Mn0.3O2 Cathode Materials for High Rate Lithium Batteries via Co-precipitation Method," *Journal of the Electrochemical Society,* vol. 160, no. 1, pp. A105-A111, 2013.

[4] J. Xiao, X. Chen, P. Sushko, M. Sushko, L. Kovarik, J. Feng, Z. Deng, J. Zheng, G. Graff, Z. Nie, D. Choi, J. Liu, J. Zhang and M. Whittingham, "High-Performance LiNi0.5Mn1.5O4 Spinel Controlled by Mn 3+ Concentration and Site Disorder," *Advanced Materials,* vol. 24, pp. 2109-2116, 2012.

[5] G. Q. Liu, L. Wen and Y. M. Liu, "Spinel LiNi0.5Mn1.5O4 and its derivates as cathodes for high-voltage Li-ion batteries," *Journal of Solid State Electrochemistry,* vol. 14, pp. 2191-2202, 2010.

[6] C. Yang, X. Zhang, M. Huang, J. Huang and Z. Fang, "Preparation and Rate Capability of Carbon Coated LiNi1/3Co1/3Mn1/3O2 as Cathode Material in Lithium Ion Batteries," *Applied Materials and Interfaces,* vol. 9, pp. 12408-12415, 2017.

[7] T. Yang, N. Zhang, Y. Lang and K. Sun, "Enhanced rate performance of carbon-coated LiNi0.5Mn1.5O4 cathode material for lithium ion batteries," *Electrochimica Acta,* vol. 56, pp. 4058-4064, 2011.

[8] J. Goodenough and Y. Kim, "Challenges for Rechargeable Li Batteries," *Chemistry of Materials,* vol. 22, pp. 587-603, 2010.

High-Nickel Cathode / Graphite Anode Cells for Diverse DoD Applications

Jane Rempel, Adrian Pullen, Daniel Kaplan, Brian Barnett, and Suresh Sriramulu
CAMX Power LLC
35 Hartwell Avenue; Lexington, MA 02421
e-mail: rempel.jane@camxpower.com, phone: (781)879-1238

Abstract: *CAMX Power has developed the CAM-7® cathode material platform that combines high specific energy with high rate capability. In this paper, we present data on the performance of CAM-7/graphite cells for DoD applications. We demonstrate CAM-7/graphite cells with high specific energy capable of superior performance, relative to COTS cells, at -40°C. We demonstrate life of the CAM-7/graphite cell chemistry in different form-factor cells including 18650 and soft pouch cells.*

Keywords: lithium ion, CAM-7; 18650 cells; pouch cells;

Introduction

Owing to its high energy content, Li-ion technology is attractive for many DoD applications including Rifleman Radios and Conformal Wearable Batteries. However, commercial off the shelf (COTS) cells frequently cannot meet all of the DoD specific operational requirements for energy and power capability across a broad range of operating conditions. The specific energy, energy density, and power capability of Li-ion cells are largely determined by the properties of the cathode active material used. Historically, lithium cobalt oxide (LCO) cathode paired with graphite anode has been the material of choice for high energy density cells. Continued questions around cobalt availability and cost volatility have forced displacement of LCO with lithium nickel cobalt aluminum oxide (NCA) and lithium nickel cobalt manganese oxide (NCM) platforms. However, even COTS cells containing NCA or NCM cannot meet all of the performance targets needed for DoD platforms. Higher nickel-content (hence higher energy) versions of NCA/NCM are in development now but suffer from poor cycle life. Furthermore, the rapid growth of electric drive vehicles (EDVs), which require large Li-ion batteries, is placing unprecedented strain on the supply of NCA and NCM materials. This trend is of particular concern to DoD, given that DoD batteries present a small fraction of the total global battery supply-chain and are not the focus of the major materials and battery producers.

We present an alternative high-nickel cathode material platform developed at CAMX Power, CAM-7, which is attractive for DoD Li-ion batteries not only because of its technical performance, but also because it can be produced in the US. CAM-7 is a dopant stabilized $LiNiO_2$-based cathode material that combines high capacity, high average discharge voltage, excellent rate capability, and long life. Discharge capacity for different CAM-7 compositions and their rate capability are shown in Table 1. CAM-7 can provide very high energy density when paired with graphite anode. The projected cell-level specific energy and energy density of CAM-7 compared to that of other commercial off-the-shelf cathode materials is shown in Figure 1.

Table 1. CAM-7 cathode materials platform combines high discharge capacity with high rate capability. Coin cell measurements with Li-metal anode, ~10mg/cm², 4.3-3.0V.

Cathode Material	Ni (mol %)	1st Cycle C/20 (mAh/g)		Discharge Rate Capability (mAh/g)		
		CHG	DCH	C/5	1C	5C
CAM-7.3	88	235	218	210	196	179
CAM-7.4	88	228	213	202	187	168
NCM-811	80	223	204	192	180	155
NCA	81	219	181	176	169	135
NCM-622	60	199	183	174	160	131

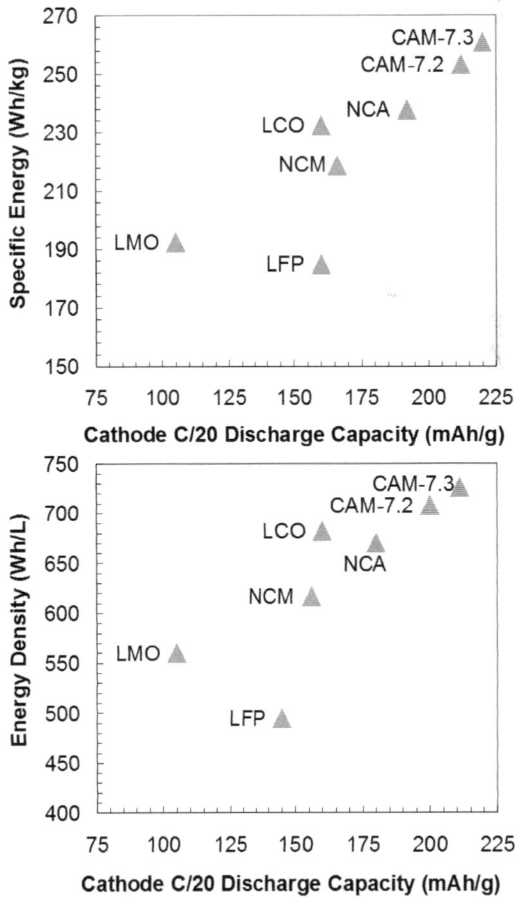

Figure 1. Comparison of the estimated cell-level specific energy (top) and energy density (bottom) of CAM-7 cathode materials with commercial off-the-shelf cathode materials in identically designed 18650 cells with graphite anode. LFP is $LiFePO_4$ and LMO is $LiMn_2O_4$.

Figure 2. Photograph of a 50 MT/y pilot plant for our CAM-7 cathode material located in Rowley outside of Boston MA.

CAM-7 Production

The synthesis of CAM-7 material has been scaled-up to pilot level. CAMX Power owns and operates a 50 MT/y pilot plant specifically designed for the production of CAM-7 cathode material (Figure 2). The plant can be easily upgraded to 300 MT/y with the addition of one piece of equipment. Following more than a decade of development, this material platform was recently licensed to both BASF and Johnson Matthey for scaled-up production primarily for the burgeoning EDV market. CAMX Power is continuing to develop advanced versions of this material targeting simultaneous achievement of higher capacity and longer life.

Cycle Life of CAM-7/Graphite Cells

CAM-7 is engineered to simultaneously offer high power capability as well as high energy and long life. Figure 3 shows representative cycle life data in two different cell formats – 18650 cells (plot on the bottom) and pouch cells (plot on the top) – at 45°C for full depth-of-discharge cycling (4.2V – 2.7V). Historically, it has not been possible to implement high-nickel cathode materials in laminate pouch cells because of unacceptable levels of swelling (gassing) when the cells were operated at high temperature. Recently, we have implemented CAM-7/graphite in pouch cells with excellent cycle life (as shown in Figure 3) and very low gassing.

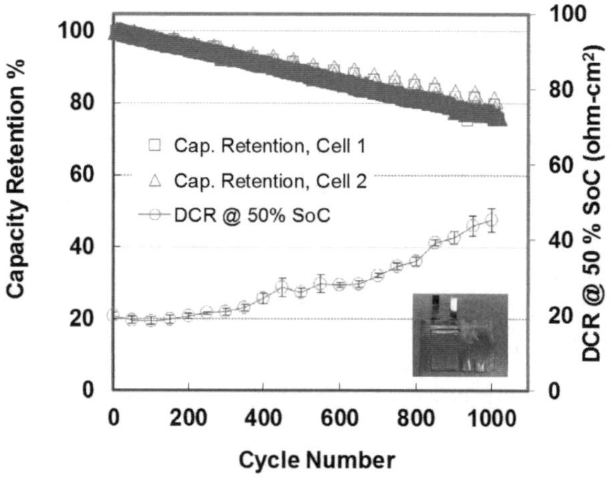

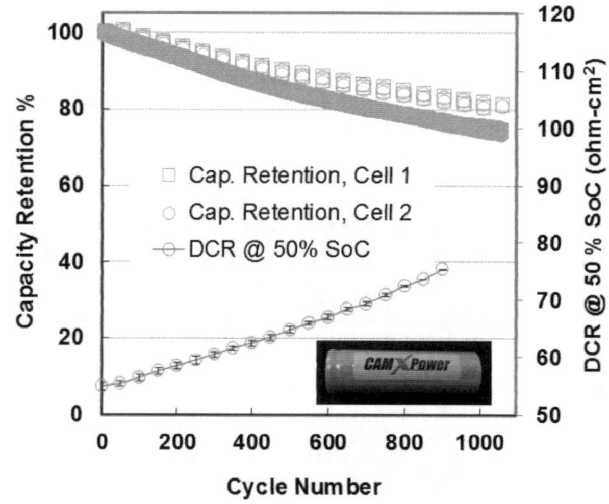

Figure 3. Demonstration of long life during cycle life testing at 45°C in pouch (top) and 18650 (bottom) cells containing CAM-7.3 high capacity cathode and graphite anode. 2.7-4.2V 1C-1C for pouch and 2.7-4.2V C/2-1C for 18650 cell cycling.

High-energy Cells with Excellent Low Temperature Performance

Specifically of interest to DoD is the development of high-specific energy cells that are capable of broad temperature range operation. As part of a program for U.S. Army, we developed a CAM-7/graphite cell chemistry and electrolyte combination capable of achieving high specific energy, long life, and excellent discharge performance even at -40°C. The discharge voltage curves for 18650 cells fabricated at CAMX Power are shown in Figure 4. The inset table in Figure 4 shows the measured specific energy and energy density both at the cell level and at the jelly roll level. These 18650 cells delivered 247Wh/kg (cell level) and 290Wh/kg (jelly roll level) at C/20 rate. Moreover, during continuous constant power discharge (1.15W, based on the Rifleman radio performance requirement), CAMX Power CAM-7/Graphite 18650 cells with high specific energy were able to deliver substantially more energy that commercial off the shelf (COTS) 2.9Ah 18650 cells (Figure 5). Note that further improvements in cell specific energy can be achieved for this cell chemistry by utilization of state-of-the-art 18650 cell hardware that is slightly lighter and bigger (~18mm vs. ~17.3mm inner diameter vs. CAMX cans) and contains more active material, while reducing the relative mass of inactive components. Moreover, by implementing more recent grades of CAM-7 cathode that have higher capacity than the material used in these 18650s, even higher energy densities can be obtained.

These CAM-7/graphite 18650 cells were also independently evaluated at the Army Research Laboratory (ARL), as part of a Phase II SBIR program, with the results summarized in an ARL report[i]. The rate capabilities of these cells at room temperature and at -20°C are shown in Figure 6. This ARL report concluded (for DoD use) *that these cells were ideal for applications where cycle life is imperative, even in extreme conditions.*

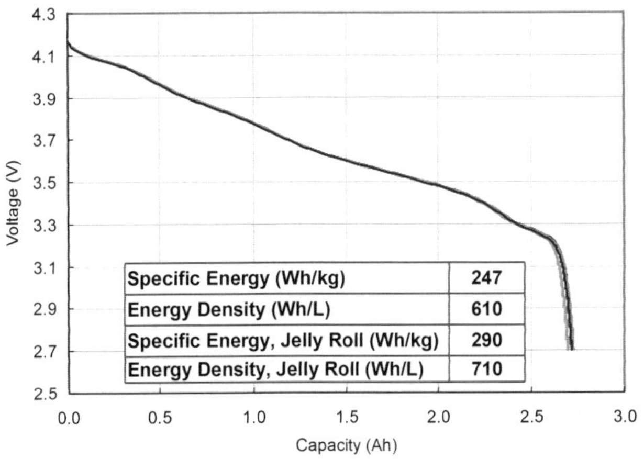

Figure 4. Discharge curves for CAM-7/graphite 18650 cells designed for very high specific energy. The cells were charged to 4.2 V and discharged to 2.7 V.

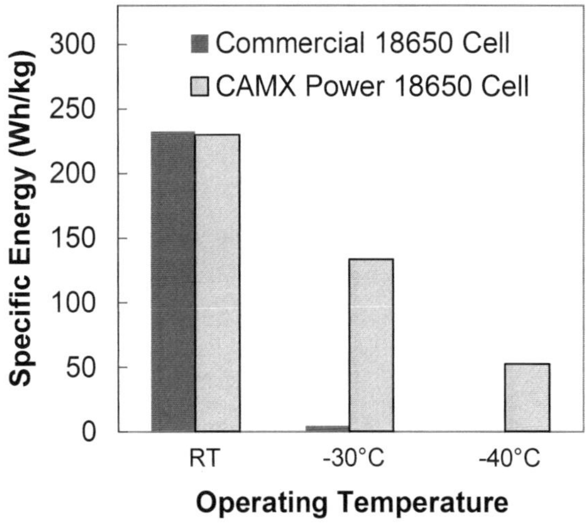

Figure 5. Comparison of delivered specific energy at different temperatures of COTS 2.9Ah 18650 cells with CAM-7/graphite high-energy 18650 cells. 4.2 V – 2.7 V discharge at 1.15W (power required for Rifleman radios).

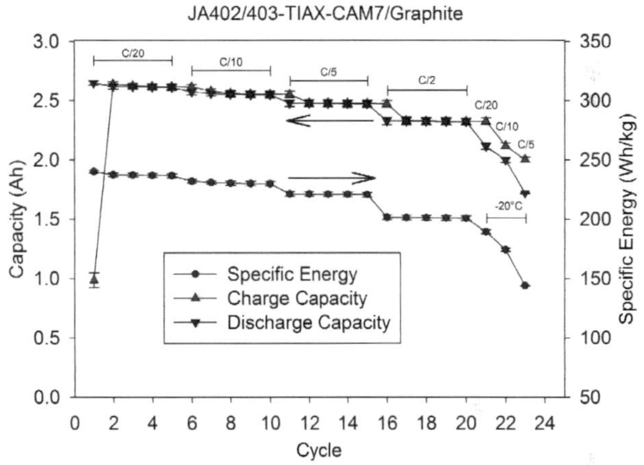

Figure 6. Measurements by ARL on CAM-7/graphite high-energy 18650 cells delivered to ARL as part of a Phase II SBIR project. Figure reproduced from ref. i. Room temperature (25°C, cycles 1–20) and low-temperature (–20°C, cycles 21–23) rate cycling of high energy 18650 cells.

CAM-7/Graphite Cells with Excellent Pulse Power Capability

Some applications, like hybrid (HEV) or plugin hybrid electric vehicle (PHEV) batteries require not only high specific energy, but also pulse power capability for acceleration or regenerative breaking that can be supported across a wide state-of-charge (SOC) range. Typically, lithium metal oxide cathode materials that suffer from high impedance at low states of charge can substantially reduce the operating SOC range and thus the 'available energy', requiring over-sizing the battery to meet power requirements. Because of its high rate capability, CAM-7 cathode material can support high rate pulse power discharge even at low SOCs.

We have implemented CAM-7 with a graphite anode in 18650 cells with low electrode loadings (~2mAh/cm²) that target PHEV operation. Using the hybrid pulse power characterization (HPPC) test developed by DOE, we measured the 1s and 10s discharge resistance during a constant current pulse for a batch of these 18650 cells. Data in Figure 7 show that these cells have low pulse resistance (DCR) suggesting high power capability over a wide range of state-of-charge, even down to 10%.

These cells also have excellent life, as demonstrated both during storage (Figure 8) and during cycling (Figure 9). Figure 8 shows that during storage at 4.1V at 45°C for a year, we observed only a minor decrease in capacity with little change in resistance measured at 50% SOC. Figure 9 shows that these cells maintain 80% of their capacity after 2000 cycles at room temperature across the full SOC range (2.7-4.2V).

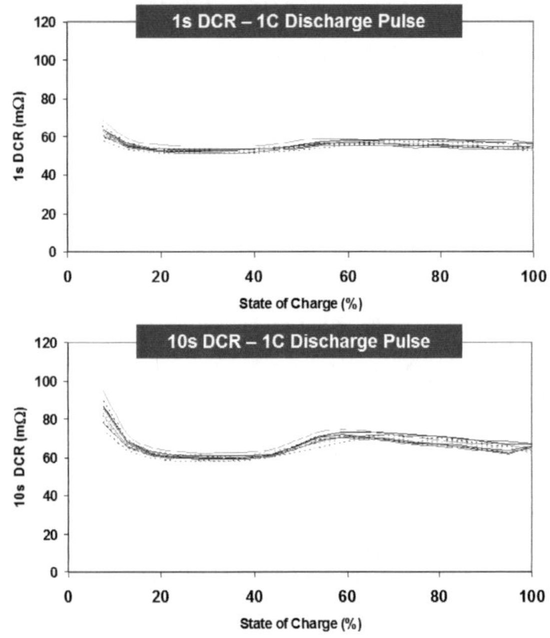

Figure 7. Discharge pulse power rate capability for a batch of CAM-7/Graphite 18650 cells designed for PHEV applications. Value for 1s (top) and 10s (bottom) direct current resistance shown as a function of SOC.

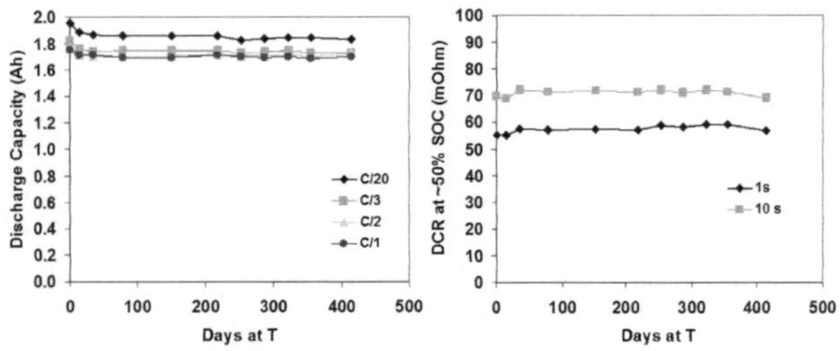

Figure 8. Capacity retention (left) and impedance rise (right) during storage of the CAM-7/ graphite 18650 cells at 4.1V at 45°C.

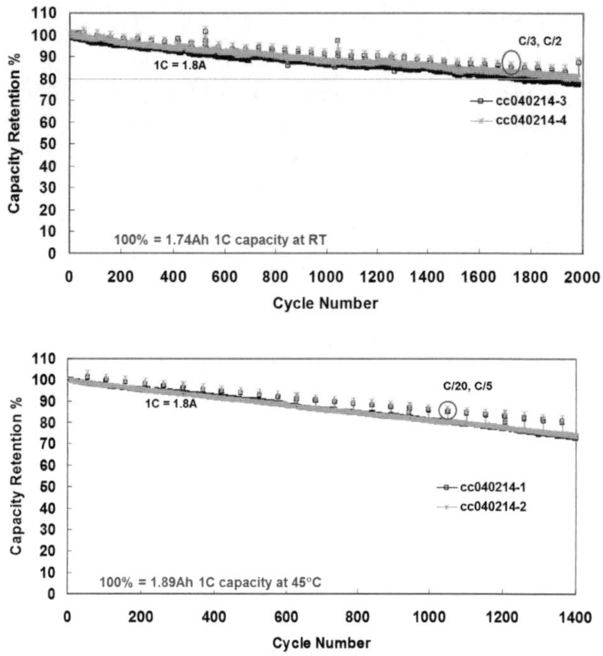

Figure 9. Cycle life of CAM-7/graphite 18650 cells designed for PHEV application. Cycling conditions: C/2 charge – 1C discharge 4.2 – 2.7V at room temperature (top) and at 45°C (bottom).

Summary

This paper demonstrates the versatility of the high energy and high power CAM-7 cathode material when implemented with graphite anode in cells designed for different end use scenarios. We show how long life can be achieved both in 18650 and in pouch cells during elevated temperature cycling. We show superior performance of this cell chemistry when combined with low-temperature-capable electrolytes for high specific energy delivery at -40°C. We also demonstrate excellent storage and cycle life for CAM-7/Graphite 18650 cells designed for applications that require pulse power capability over a wide range of SOC.

Acknowledgements

We gratefully acknowledge financial support for some of the work presented in this document from the U.S. Department of Energy under Contract No. DE-EE0006452 and U.S. Army under Contract No. W911QX-12-C-0001.

References

[i] Allen JL, Allen JL, Delp SA, Jow TR. (2014). Evaluation of TIAX High Energy CAM-7/Graphite Lithium-Ion Batteries at High & Low Temperatures, U.S. Army Research Laboratory.

High Energy Li-ion Cells with CAM-7® Cathode and Si-based Anodes

Jane Rempel, David Ofer, Adrian Pullen, Daniel Kaplan, Brian Barnett, and Suresh Sriramulu

CAMX Power LLC
35 Hartwell Avenue; Lexington, MA 02421
e-mail: rempel.jane@camxpower.com, phone: (781)879-1238

Abstract: *CAMX Power is developing Li-ion batteries that combine our proprietary high energy and high power CAM-7® cathode with Si-based anodes in different cell designs targeting applications that require high specific energy.*

Keywords: Li-ion, lithium ion, CAM-7; Si anode; 18650; pouch cells;

Introduction

Energy Storage is a critical component to meeting increasing electrical power demands of many DoD applications. Weight and volume constraints, along with requirements for long operational life, place stringent demands on the energy system of choice. Lithium-ion (Li-ion) battery technology is the current state-of-the-art rechargeable battery technology utilized in consumer electronics and electric drive vehicles due to its high gravimetric and volumetric energy density, good rate capability and long life. These attributes also make Li-ion technology increasingly favored for energy storage in DoD platforms. However, the highest specific energy Li-ion cells currently used for commercial portable power applications (approaching 270Wh/kg[i]) employ materials and cell designs that are not capable of providing specific rate, life, and temperature range needed to advance the capabilities of DoD systems. Implementation of next generation anode and cathode materials is needed to further increase gravimetric and volumetric energy of Li-ion cells while meeting rate and life targets.

CAMX Power developed a "stabilized" $LiNiO_2$-based cathode material, CAM-7, that combines the attributes needed for high energy cell designs: high capacity and high average discharge voltage with excellent high rate capability and long life. In a materials development effort spanning more than 15 years, CAMX Power resolved the challenges historically associated with high-nickel $LiNiO_2$ materials such as synthesis reproducibility, electrode slurry stability, high-temperature cycle life, and thermal stability. CAM-7 is now being commercialized for consumer applications worldwide by two global battery materials suppliers, BASF and Johnson Matthey, to whom we have licensed the technology for large scale production. In addition, CAMX Power operates a pilot plant located in Rowley, MA with a production capacity of 50 metric tons per year (expandable to 300 metric tons per year with the addition of one piece of equipment).

For increased specific energy cells, the high-capacity CAM-7 cathode needs to be combined with anodes based on Li alloying reactions to replace currently used low specific capacity graphitic anodes. While various metals and semiconductors can electrochemically alloy with Li, Si has been the focus of substantial research and development efforts because it offers the highest specific capacity among the alloys (approaching 3.6Ah/g Si) and due to its abundance and potential for low cost. As part of several Government and internally sponsored programs, CAMX Power has been working with a wide variety of Si-based anodes for Li-ion cells for over a decade by developing materials in-house, and by sourcing materials from multiple leading domestic and international silicon anode materials developers and implementing them in optimized electrode designs for high energy density. We have successfully developed high-performance Li-ion cells with Si-containing anodes paired with our CAM-7 cathode material.

High-Energy and High-Power Cell Design

Typical Li-ion cells containing a graphite anode designed to provide high specific energy normally cannot also support high rate continuous discharge. This constraint arises because such cells must use high-loading, thick electrodes to maximize cell specific energy and minimize the content of inactive components. Ionic transport limitations in such cells result in voltage polarization that also limits the discharge at high current. When high capacity and intrinsically high rate active materials are employed, high cell specific energy can be achieved with thinner electrodes that do not suffer from ionic transport rate limitations.

To demonstrate high specific energy combined with high rate continuous discharge capability, we combined CAM-7 with a high capacity silicon-carbon composite (sourced from a leading domestic supplier) anode, and a specially formulated electrolyte in custom-designed 48 x 30 x 5 mm pouch cells. The inset in Figure 1 shows a photograph of the pouch cell, which has a measured capacity of 1.1Ah at C/5 rate. The rate capability of this cell for continuous discharge at C/5, 1C, and 5C rate is shown Figure 1, demonstrating that this cell chemistry can deliver ~300Wh/kg at low rates, and ~270Wh/kg at 5C.

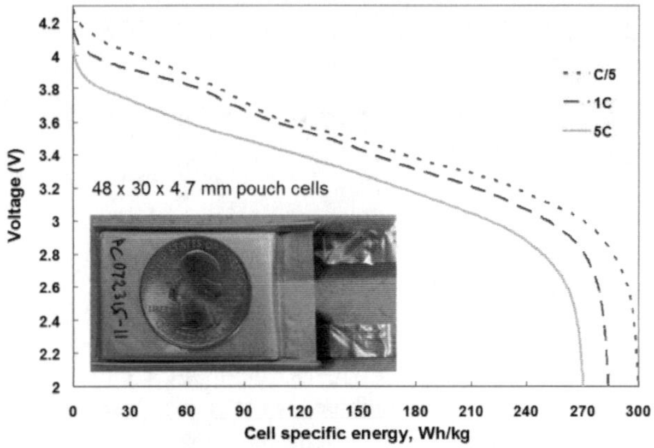

Figure 1. Discharge specific energy of the 1.1Ah CAM-7/Si pouch cell as a function of C-rate. The CAM-7/Si pouch cell delivers ~270Wh/kg at 5C rate.

CAM-7/Si 18650s for PHEV Applications

Applications such as plug-in hybrid electric vehicles (PHEV) require both high specific energy and high pulse power capability over a wide state-of-charge (SOC) range. CAM-7 cathode has low impedance over a broader SOC range than other competing cathode materials (e.g. NCA and NCM). By incorporating CAM-7 in cells and by blending small amounts of SiO with graphite anode, we were able to demonstrate 18650 cells with high specific energy and improved pulse power capability. Comparison of the delivered specific energy during continuous discharge at different C-rates is shown in Figure 2.

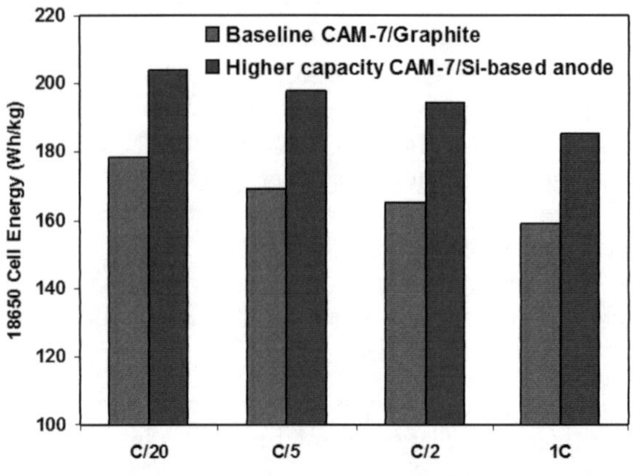

Figure 2. Comparison of specific energy between CAM-7/Graphite and CAM-7/Si-based anode 18650 cells during continuous discharge from 4.2V. Note that these cells use circa 2006 18650 cans that have slightly smaller diameter than state-of-the-art 18650 hardware.

DOE's hybrid pulse power characterization (HPPC) test is typically used to determine available energy for a particular pulse power target. Results for the HPPC test with a 5A 10s discharge and 3.6A 10s regen pulse are shown in Figure 3. The CAM-7/SiO-graphite blended anode cells can deliver ~180Wh/kg of available energy while providing 845W/kg pulse power at ~10% SOC. Note that further improvement in cell-specific energy can be achieved by implementing this cell chemistry and electrode design in more state-of-the-art 18650 hardware.

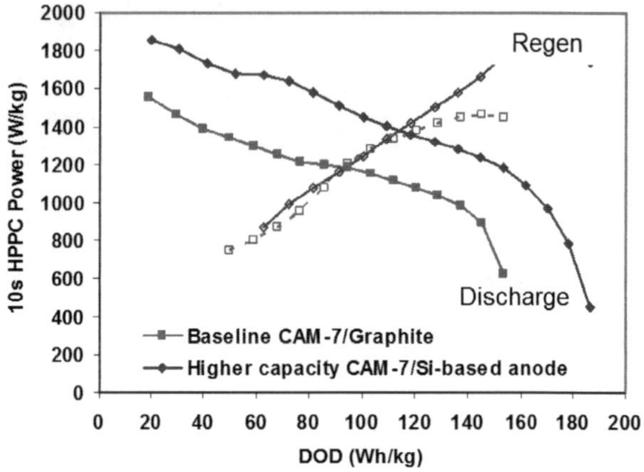

Figure 3. Comparison of rate capability during HPPC power delivery between the baseline CAM-7/Graphite and CAM-7/Si-based anode 18650 cells. HPPC power testing done using 5A 10s Discharge, 3.6A 10s Charge. V_{min} = 2.6V, V_{max} = 4.3V for HPPC power calculation. Si-based 18650 cells use lower resistance cell caps.

18650 cells with CAM-7 cathode and the blended SiO/graphite anode also have excellent cycle life. Capacity retention during room temperature cycling of these cells over a 90% SOC window (2.7V – 4.1V) is shown in Figure 4.

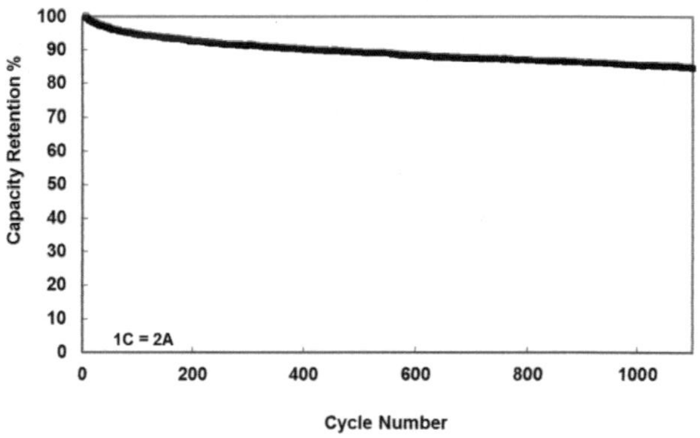

Figure 4. Cycle life of the CAM-7/Si-based anode in 18650 cells during 2.7-4.1V cycling at room temperature. C/2 charge and 1C discharge.

CAM-7/Si for 28V Navy Aircraft Applications

Implementation of CAM-7 with high SiO-content blended anodes can also be used to boost specific energy of Li-ion systems for use in aircraft applications that require high specific energy delivery during high current continuous discharge at room temperature and also during continuous discharge at low temperature. One down side of the high SiO-content anode electrodes is the low first cycle efficiency of the SiO. As a result, implementation of high content SiO/graphite blended anodes requires the use of pre-lithiation. In coin cell experiments, Figure 5, we demonstrated how anode pre-lithiation can be used to increase specific energy during continuous discharge operation between 4.04V and 2.86V (equivalent to 7-cell series for a 20-28.25V operation on a 28V aircraft DC bus). Moreover, higher discharge energy can be obtained by expanding the voltage range as shown in Figure 5. Impact of SiO content in the blended anode on the high current (4C) discharge rate capability and cycle life are shown in Figure 6.

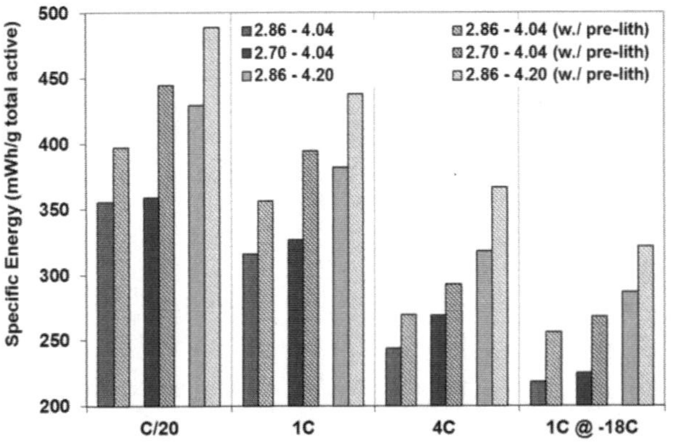

Figure 5. Impact of voltage ranges and pre-lithiation on the delivered specific energy as a function of rate at RT and -18°C for 45% SiO blended anode paired with a CAM-7 cathode. 4.04V corresponds to 28.25V for 7-series cells. Energy normalized by the total weight of the cathode and anode active materials. Cathode electrode formulated with 94:3:3 ratio of active:acetylene black:PVDF, ~3mAh/cm² loading, and nominal 1C = 200mAh/g. Anode matched based on 4.04V or 4.2V charge and pre-lithiated by 200mAh/g.

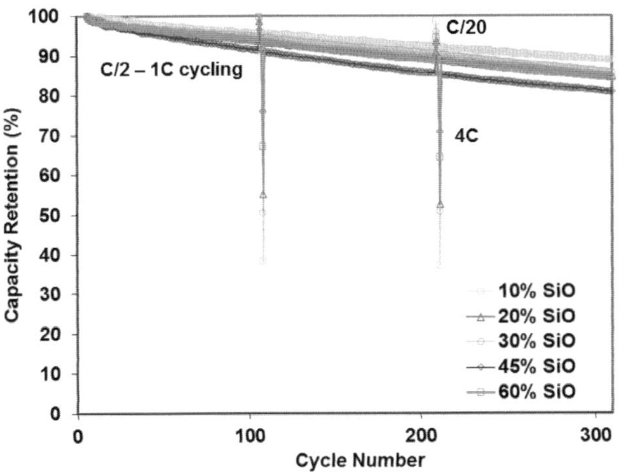

Figure 6. Impact of SiO content on 2.86-4.04V cycle life of pre-lithiated SiO/graphite blended anodes paired with a CAM-7 cathode. Cathode electrode formulated with 94:3:3 ratio of active:acetylene black:PVDF, active loading of ~3mAh/cm² and nominal 1C = 200mAh/g. Anode pre-lithiatiation based on SiO content.

To demonstrate life of the CAM-7/SiO high specific energy system, we implemented the chemistry in ~230mAh pouch cells. After initial formation and degassing, pouch cells were resealed and cycled at 45°C using 200mA charge and 400mA discharge between 2.86V and 4.04V. We observed >70% capacity retention after 1000 cycles at 45°C (Figure 7). Similar pouch cells were also stored at 45°C for almost two months. Capacity and rate capability retention after 4 weeks and 8 weeks of storage are shown in Figure 8.

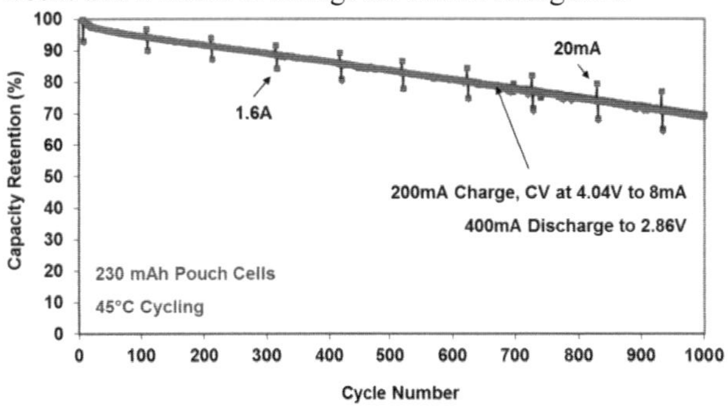

Figure 7. Elevated temperature cycle life of two ~230mAh pouch cells with CAM-7 and 60%SiO/graphite blended anode (no pre-lithiation). Pouch cells containing 3" x 3.5" electrodes with 1 double sided anode and 2 single sided cathodes. Cathode active loading of ~3mAh/cm². 1M $LiPF_6$ in EC:DMC:EMC 1:1:1 + 1%VC electrolyte.

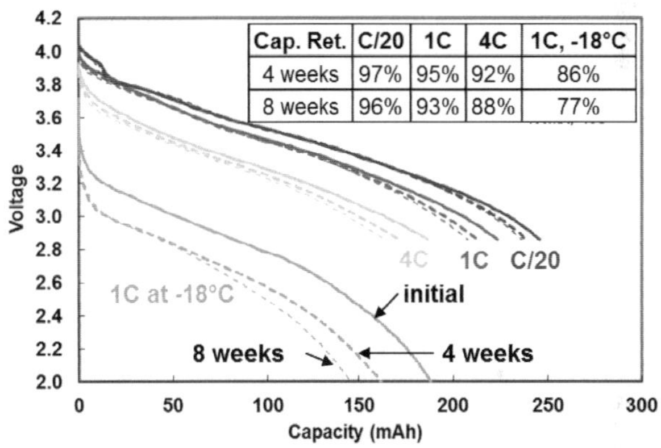

Figure 8. Elevated temperature storage at 4.04V of two ~230mAh pouch cells with CAM-7 and 60%SiO/graphite blended anode. Pouch cells containing 3" x 3.5" electrodes with 1 double sided anode and 2 single sided cathodes. Cathode active loading of ~3mAh/cm². 1M $LiPF_6$ in EC:DMC:EMC 1:1:1 + 1%VC electrolyte. 1C nominal of 400mA.

Cathode Pre-lithiation for High Energy Cells

In addition to implementing anode pre-lithiation for high specific energy cells that employ high SiO content anode electrodes, we have developed a novel proprietary method for introducing extra lithium into the cell by pre-lithiating the cathode electrode. As a proof of concept demonstration, we have prepared 200mAh pouch cells that incorporated 20%SiO/graphite blended anodes with CAM-7 cathodes with and without pre-lithiation. The resulting increase in specific energy due to pre-lithiation for this cell chemistry is shown in Figure 9. Moreover, we observed excellent capacity retention during full depth of discharge cycling (2.7-4.2V) at room temperature with >90% capacity retention after 200 cycles (Figure 10).

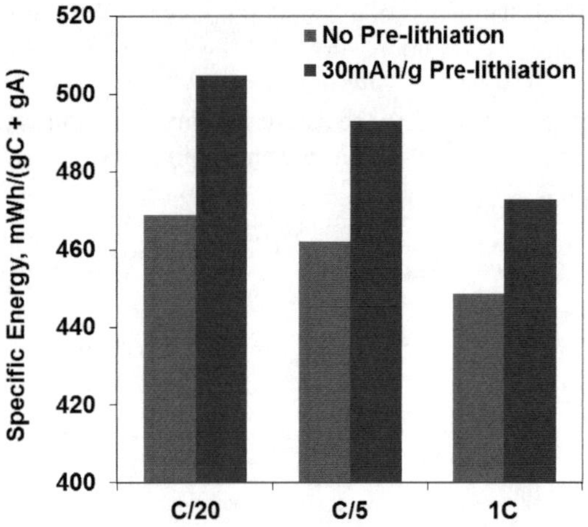

Figure 9. Comparison of active material only specific energy between two 200mAh pouch cells with and without 30mAh/g cathode pre-lithiation containing CAM-7 cathode and 20%SiO/graphite anode.

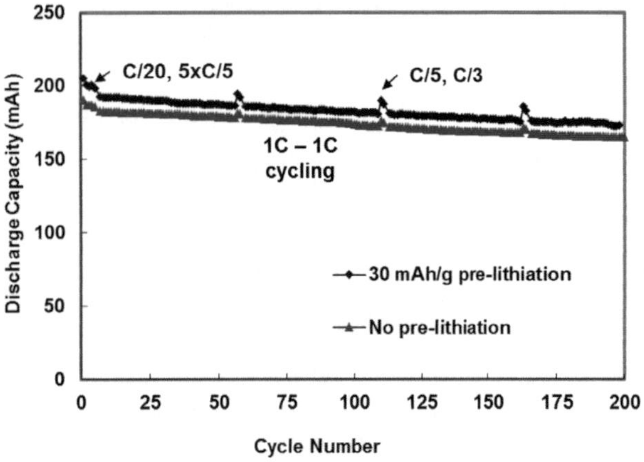

Figure 10. Room temperature cycle life of ~200mAh pouch cells with CAM-7 cathode and 20%SiO/Graphite blended anode with and without cathode pre-lithiation by 30mAh/g. Cathode electrodes with almost identical cathode active weight. 90% capacity retention after 200 cycles.

Conclusions

Combining CAM-7 cathodes with Si-based anodes enables development of very high specific energy cells for a range of applications that require high-specific energy, high pulse power or continuous discharge capability, and broad temperature range operation with long life. The examples shown in this paper highlight some of the applications:

- 18650 cells with high specific energy, long cycle life, and excellent pulse power capability, with measured available specific energy of >180Wh/kg while delivering >800W/kg pulse power at 10% SOC. This same chemistry implemented in a 15 Ah cell will deliver available energy >225Wh/kg while also providing >800W/kg at 10% SOC.
- Small pouch cells with specific energy of 300Wh/kg during continuous discharge at C/5 rate and 270Wh/kg at 5C.
- Long life, high specific energy cells incorporating SiO anode and pre-lithiation capable of high rate discharge at room temperature and delivering high specific energy at -18°C.
- High specific energy, long life cells incorporating high SiO anode and our proprietary cathode pre-lithiation technology.

Acknowledgements

We gratefully acknowledge financial support for some of the work presented in this document from the U.S. Department of Energy under Contracts No. DE-EE0006452 and DE-SC0017779 and the U.S. Navy under Contract No. N68335-16-C-0234.

References

---

[i] http://na.industrial.panasonic.com/products/batteries/rechargeable-batteries/lithium-ion/series/cylindrical-series/CS474

Higher Energy Density Li-Ion Battery Development

Christopher M. Lang and Peter D. Moran
Physical Sciences Inc.
20 New England Business Center
Andover, MA USA 01810-1077
lang@psicorp.com / 1-978-738-8125

Abstract: *Higher energy density batteries are required to power next generation technologies. New cell design techniques are required to minimize the mass fraction of inactive components and achieve improved energy density. This presentation will discuss Physical Sciences Inc.'s efforts to construct cells offering a 25% increase in cell energy density over the state of the art. This talk will focus on a low cost, rapid, high active (HA) coating technique that enables increased active material loadings and operating voltages. PSI will show this technology is scalable and applicable to the entire range of commercial active materials. Test results from multi-Ah pouch cells built for multiple applications will demonstrate the flexibility of the PSI technology. Finally, PSI will demonstrate that extended cycling to high voltages (4.4V) can be achieved with less than 10% fade over 1000 cycles.*

Keywords: Lithium ion; high energy; high voltage; energy density; cycle-life.

Introduction

"Electric vehicles ("EVs") represent a key pathway for reducing petroleum dependence, enhancing environmental stewardship and promoting transportation sustainability, while creating high quality jobs and economic growth."[1] However, in order for EVs to be commercially viable, higher energy density batteries are required to increase vehicle range, and lower cost batteries are needed to make the technology affordable. New approaches are required to reduce the inactive components in the battery and simplify cell production. Advances in these areas would increase the energy density and reduce the normalized ($/kWh) cost.

PSI has developed a rapid, low cost coating technique for active materials that enables increased active material loadings and operating voltages. Figure 1 illustrates the key advantages of this high active (HA) coating technology. The subsequent section briefly outlines the tests carried out by PSI to demonstrate that this technology is scalable and applicable to the entire range of commercial active materials. PSI's talk will provide more detail on the tests performed and the results achieved.

Results and Discussion

PSI has applied its HA coating to a large number of commercially available cathode materials. These materials include various grades of lithium iron phosphate, lithium cobalt oxide (LCO), lithium nickel cobalt aluminum oxide (NCA), and lithium nickel cobalt manganese oxide (NCM) cathode materials. For the NCM materials, PSI has demonstrated the HA coating can be applied to the entire range of metal ratios from 111 to 811. Electrochemical testing has demonstrated that the electrodes prepared with 98.5% HA material delivered equivalent performance to standard electrodes when normalizing for the active content. These electrodes are produced using 50% less solvent than traditional formulations and have increased density due to the reduction in the binder/conductor fractions. This directly impacts the electrode thickness resulting in >20% reduction which increases cell volumetric energy density.

PSI worked with a commercial cell manufacturer to construct 2.5+Ah lithium ion cells to demonstrate the scalability and performance of the HA technology. HA cells were built with a commercial anode and cathode electrodes both designed for operation at 4.2 and 4.4V. Extended cycling was carried out at a 1C charge/discharge rate and 100% depth of discharge (DOD). As shown in Figure 2, on cycling at 4.4V, the capacity retention at 1000 cycles is ~90%. 2200 cycles were achieved (with >86% retention) on cycling to 4.2V, demonstrating the robustness of the HA technology in the lithium ion environment.

Figure 1. PSI's HA technology increases performance while reducing cost.

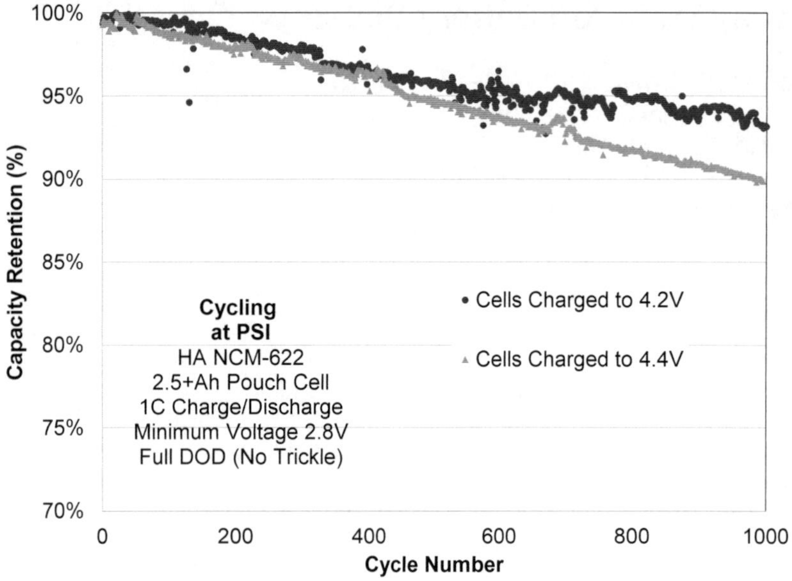

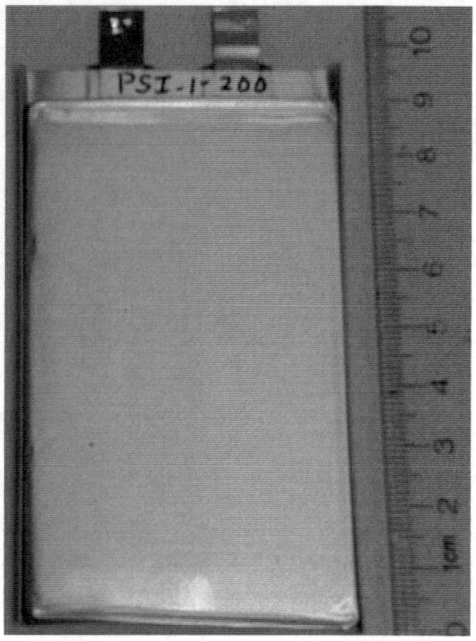

Figure 2. 2.5Ah HA cells show excellent capacity retention upon extended cycling to high voltages.

PSI designed larger high power HA cells for use in PSI's InstantEye® small unmanned aerial system. As shown in Figure 3, the HA cell on discharge at 5C delivers increased energy as compared to the baseline (the cell with the standard cathode). On controlled 1C discharge testing in the lab, the battery delivered 268Wh/kg. During dynamic simulated testing in the vehicle, the battery delivered 61.6Wh to the vehicle. (Note that this is actually lower than the value delivered from the battery due to the voltage drop over the vehicle connections.) This translates to an energy density of >244Wh/kg on 1 and 5C operation. This is a 47% increase over the theoretical energy (41.8Wh) delivered by the commercial battery currently in use. Both the cells and batteries passed all UN transportation tests. Successful operation demonstrates the HA coating can be used to design higher energy density batteries for dynamic load applications.

The conference talk will provide additional information on these tests and other tests carried out to demonstrate the advantages of the HA technology.

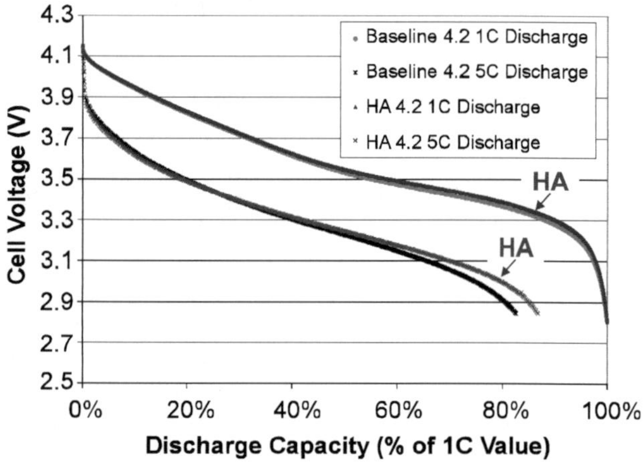

Figure 3. Performance of HA and traditional cells on discharge at 1 and 5C rates.

References

1. "One Million Electric Vehicles By 2015", DOE February 2011 Status Report.

Acknowledgments

This material is based upon work supported by the Department of Energy, Office of Science, Office of Electricity Delivery and Energy Reliability, under Award Number DE-SC0011877 and a Physical Sciences Inc. IRAD Contract.

Advanced Li-Ion Cell Development

Christopher M. Lang, Peter D. Moran, and Jake T. Herb
Physical Sciences Inc.
20 New England Business Center
Andover, MA USA 01810-1077
lang@psicorp.com / 1-978-738-8125

Abstract: *Higher energy density batteries are required to power next generation technologies. Lithium metal and silicon based anode systems offer the potential to improve cell energy density and performance. However, efficient utilization of these anodes has not been achieved to date due to first cycle limitations and lithium consumption. This presentation will discuss Physical Sciences Inc.'s (PSI) efforts to construct cells with lithium metal and silicon anodes. PSI will clearly illustrate the impact of each of these anodes on the realizable battery energy density. Test results from 50-2000+mAh pouch cells will highlight the scalability of PSI's cell designs.*

Keywords: Lithium ion; lithium metal; silicon; high energy; energy density.

Introduction

Higher energy density batteries are required to increase range and facilitate adoption of electric vehicles. Anode materials such as silicon or lithium metal offer the potential to reduce the mass of the electrodes, the final cell weight, and ultimately improve vehicle range. However, the increased voltage for delithiation and volume changes that occur during silicon cycling result in reduced cell energy density and cycle life. Lithium metal anodes offer the greatest potential operating voltage window and energy density. However, to date, efficient, safe and long term cycling of lithium metal cells as required for use in electric vehicles has not been demonstrated.

PSI has developed and scaled up cell designs with each of these anode material systems. This talk will provide an overview of these efforts, discuss the progress made to date, and outline the achievable energy densities.

Overview of Presentation: Silicon Anode Efforts

PSI has developed a patented composite silicon anode material that is formed by growing silicon whiskers on a commercially available carbon nanofiber (see Figure 1). PSI has demonstrated the scalability of its silicon composite anode material by successfully constructing and delivering to NASA twenty 30+Ah large format cells. These cells demonstrated the improved (>10%) energy density are realized by replacing the conventional graphite anode with silicon.[1] PSI has also successfully combined high voltage operation of commercial cathode materials with its existing silicon composite anode material to build and deliver Si-NCM 18650 cylindrical cells with a >20% increase in energy density.[2]

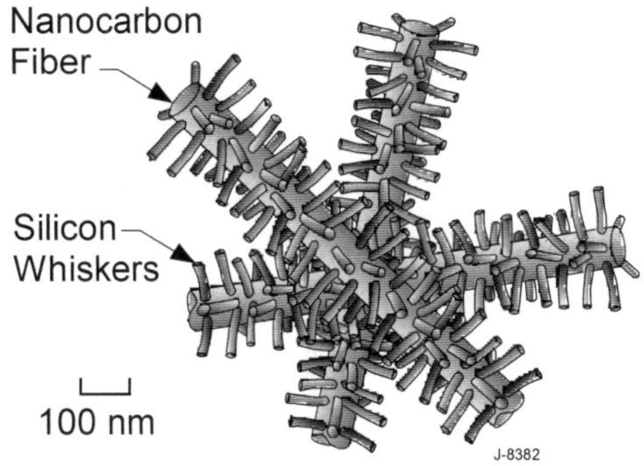

Figure 1. Schematic of PSI's silicon composite anode material.

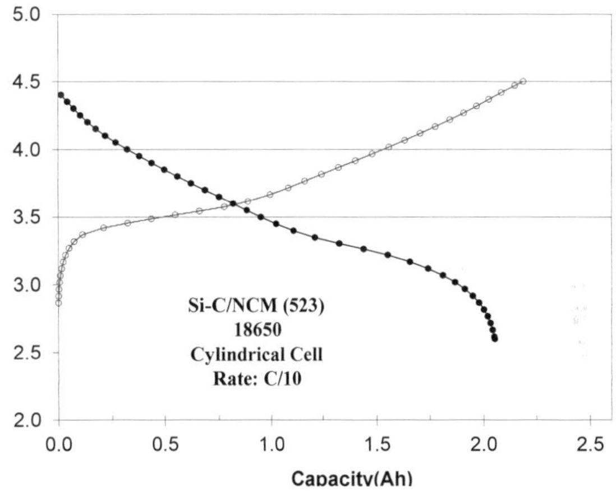

Figure 2. Energy densities of up to 178 and 173Wh/kg are achieved at the C/20 and C/10 cycling rates, respectively. This represents >20% improvement in the cell energy density as compared to the graphite control cells.

PSI has demonstrated that the cycle life performance of Si-NCM cells can be improved (30% improvement in the critical fade rate) using PSI's novel cathode electrode formulation techniques.[3] Specifically on testing at 40% depth of discharge (DOD) PSI has demonstrated:

- <2% fade in energy density over 50 cycles
- ~2.5% fade in energy density over 100 cycles
- <3% fade in energy density over 150 cycles
- <4% fade in energy density over 200 cycles

These results have been achieved at loadings that will support the construction of cells offering >265Wh/kg. The conference talk will provide additional information on these previous efforts and current efforts focused on developing high performance silicon based lithium ion cells.

Overview of Presentation: Lithium Metal Efforts

PSI has demonstrated a lithium metal cell architecture that can deliver >300Wh/kg at 1C rates in >2Ah prototype cells (see Figure 3). Further, PSI has demonstrated that this cell architecture supports charge rates up to 30C enabling system charge times of less than 10 minutes. Cells built using the PSI cell design approach have been demonstrated to utilize all the lithium ions available in the cathode material. In contrast, typical approaches result in inefficient lithium deposition that reduces the achievable energy density and cycling efficiency. PSI's design results in first cycle efficiencies equal to or greater than those achievable with graphite, silicon, or other advanced anode materials.

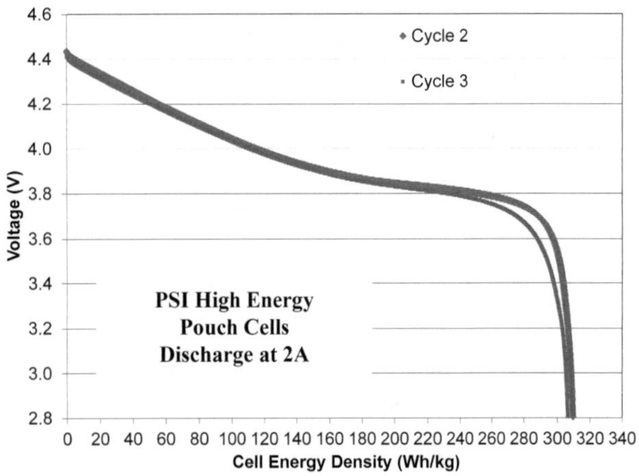

Figure 3. Demonstrated performance of prototype 2+Ah PSI lithium metal cell using HA $LiCoO_2$ cathode.

This portion of the conference talk will discuss these demonstration efforts and outline the achievable energy density with each candidate anode material.

Acknowledgments

This material is based upon work supported by NASA under contracts NNX09CD30P, NNX10CA51C, and NNX13CC41P and a Physical Sciences Inc. IRAD contract.

References

1. C.M. Lang, "Large Format Si-Whisker Cell Construction," Draft Final Report, NASA Phase III (NNC13CA10C), November 2013.
2. C.M. Lang, "Battery Construction with Silicon Whisker and Carbon Nanofiber Composite Anode," Final Report, NASA Phase III (NNC11QA96P), August 2013.
3. C.M. Lang and J.A. Vega, "Long Life, High Energy Cell Development," Final Report, NASA Phase I SBIR (NNX13CC41P), November 2013.

Development of High Energy and High Safety Lithium-ion Polymer Cells for Multifunctional Battery (MFB) Power Sources used in Battlefield Air Operations

Zhiqiang Xu* and Chul Chai
SKC Powertech, Inc.
Mt. Olive, NJ 07828
&
Thomas Howell, Michael Rottmayer, Lawrence Harrington and Stanley Rodrigues
U. S. Air Force, AFRL/AFMC, WPAFB, OH 45433

Abstract: *The objective of this project is to develop and demonstrate a high performance (greater than 200 Wh/kg), fail-safe, multifunctional battery (MFB) integrated into small arms protective insert (SAPI) hard body armor plate for improved weight reduction on the dismounted soldier.*
Through the efforts under the contracts, we have successfully developed high safety and high energy cells for the MFB. The cell developed in Phase I delivers 3.52Ah (13.07Wh) with an energy density of 236.8Wh/Kg; while the cell in Phase II has a larger dimension and delivers 5Ah (18.9Wh) with an improved energy density of 241.7Wh/Kg and enhanced low and high temperature performance. Both types of cells possess good electrical and temperature performance and excellent safety performance.The latest preliminary results demonstrated that cells with the same cathode but with graphite/silicon composite anode could reach an energy density as high as 270Wh/Kg (4.2V) even >320Wh/Kg(>4.2V).

Keywords: multifunctional battery (MFB); body armor; high safety; high energy

Introduction

High-energy density conformal (flexible and wearable) and rechargeable power sources have always been in demand by the U.S. military including theAirforce, battlefield, air operations,and Future Force Warrior (FFW) for use in communication systems. Despite the great performance offered by the current rechargeable Li-ion technologies (including SKCP's polymer Li-ion technology), the existing rechargeable batteries are heavier, bulkier, unsafe and have shorter runtime than what is required by US military during its training and combat missions.

The objective of this program is to develop a high performance (an energy density greater than 200 Wh/kg), fail-safe, multifunctional battery integrated into small arms protective insert (SAPI) hard body armor plate for improved weight reduction on the dismounted soldier. The battery shall adopt the existing charger which limits operating voltage of 4.2V/series. Therefore, the energy density of 200Wh/kg in battery level requires that cell energy be >240 Wh/kg, while possessing superb safety and temperature performance.

Due to the strict requirements, including charge voltage limit, high and low temperature performance, and particularly safety, it is clear that high capacity nickel contained materials, e.g. NCA, NCM, are not adoptable to this work. We have attempted to develop high-energy cells with dense LCO and/or its modified form with graphite or silicon composite graphite anode. The efforts in this work includecell development, electrical performance and safety assessment tests.

Experimental

$LiCoO_2$(LCO) or modified LCO materials were used as cathode material. Modified graphite or silicon-graphite composite served as anode material. Electrode manufacturing utilized slurry-coating technology with either polyvinylidene fluoride (PVDF) or Styrene Butadiene Rubber (SBR) as binder. The electrolytes contain LiPF6 in FEC/ EC/DEC/EMC/additives solution, gelled with SKCP process.[2]The separators used in these studies includedceramic coated polypropylene (PP),or PP/PE/PP,with a porosity ~ 40%. Cells were based on SKCP's pouch type design. The existing design employed a stacking process, in which electrodes were sandwiched in a Z-folded one-piece separator. Electrodes were vacuum-dried for at least 5 hours at 65°C-85°C prior to and after the assembly. While using activation machine, or inside a glove box, electrolyte was injected into the pouch to activate the cells. After allowing enough time to have electrodes and separator fully wetted, the cells were gelled at elevated temperatures, pre-charged, degassed, formed and aged. All cells were formed and tested on either Maccor 4000 or Arbin BT-2000.

For comparison purposes and also for pursuing higher energy density cell, >4.2V operating cells were also designed and made using the same fabrication, assembly and testing procedures.

Results and Discussion

Since C/Si composite anode materials are still under development, in this program we were focused on graphite

Approved for public release by US Air Force,
Review completed by Mr. James Mitchell (case # 88ABW-2018-1946)

based anodes. Although the cathode and anode active materials were fixed as $LiCoO_2$ and graphite respectively for this project, there are still many opportunities to increase the cell capacity by reducing the cell's weight and compressing the cell's thickness. These energy-limiting factors include:using thinner separator and current substrates;increasing active material loading;developing more suitable electrolyte with less irreversible capacity loss due to the formation of a SEI layer;finding more effective conducting additives for the electrodes;and searching for denser active materials.

Table 1. MFB Cell Basic Parameters and Performance Comparison

Cell format	765066 (Phase I)	965569 (Phase II)
Dimension (TxWxL, mm)	7.6x50x66	9.6x55x66
Weight(g)	56± 0.2	78.5± 0.2
Operation voltage (V)	4.2-2.5	4.2-2.5
Capacity(Ah) at C/4	3.57	5.06
Energy (Whr)	13.26	18.88
Gravimetric Energy Density(Wh/Kg)	236.8	241.7
Volumetric Energy Density(Wh/L)	528.7	518.2

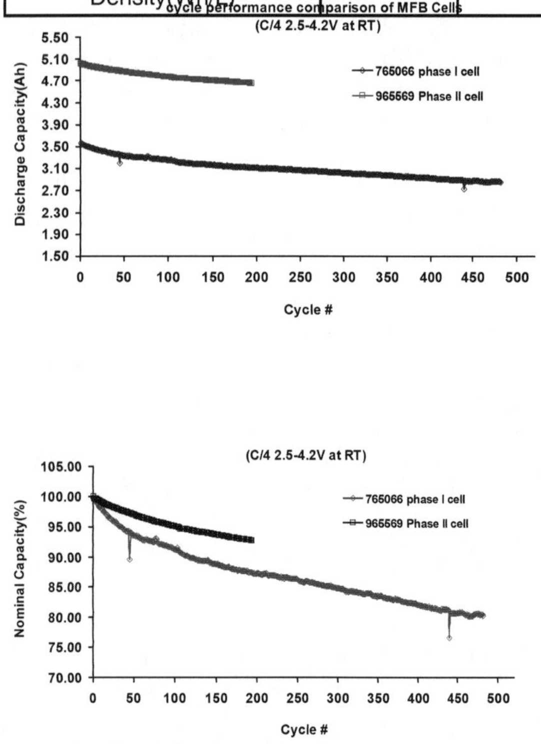

Figure 1. Cycle Performance Comparison (C/4 at RT) of the MFB Cells, top: Discharge vs. Cycle; bottom: Nominal Discharge Capacity vs. Cycle

Through extensive work on cell components, developments, and cell design optimization, we have developed two candidate cells for MFB applications as listed in **Table 1**. Both cells were designed for 4.2V operation.

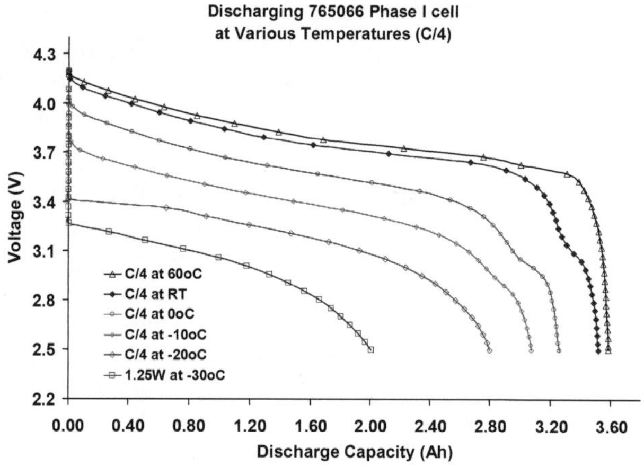

Figure 2. Temperature Performance of Phase I 765066 3.6Ah Cell.

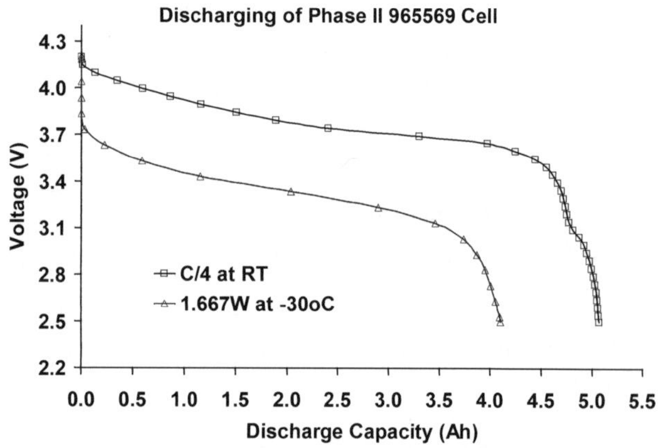

Figure 3. Temperature Performance of Phase II 965569 5Ah Cell

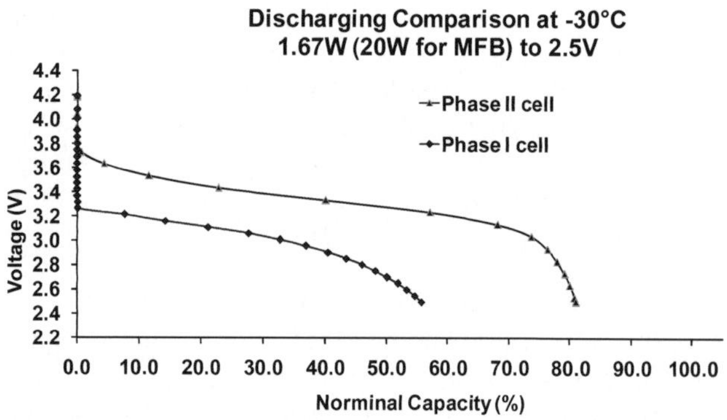

Figure 4. Comparison of Discharge Performance of MFB cells at -30°C

Approved for public release by US Air Force,
Review completed by Mr. James Mitchell (case # 88ABW-2018-1946)

Table 2. Safety Test Summary of 765066 Phase I cells

Test	Method	Results	Observation
Over-charge	5.04 V at 0.5 C	No Smoke, no fire, no explosion	Cell remained intact, Max temperature 24°C
Over-discharge	3.5Amp, -12V	No Smoke, no fire, no explosion	Cell swelled, voltage remained at -2 to -1V after a while, max. temperature reached 65°C
Shorting at 60°C and RT	~ 30 mΩ cable	No Smoke, no fire, no explosion. Sparking at 60°C	Cell swelled, front seal opened, and max. surface temperature reached 112°C for 60°C shorting and 92°C for RT shorting
150°C Oven	5°/min to 150°C and hold for 10 minutes	No Smoke, no fire, no explosion	Cell swelled, pouch seal opened at the front
130°C Oven	5°/min to 130°C and hold for 60 minutes	No Smoke, no fire, no explosion	Cell swelled, pouch seal opened at the front
Bar Crash	75 mm wide, 6 mm thick bar	No Smoke, no fire, no explosion	Cells were soft shorted. Temperature reached 46°C (Max) after 2 minutes and cooled down
Nail Penetration	3.5 mm diameter nail	No Smoke, no fire, no explosion	Cells remained intact. Temperature reached 110°C (Max) after 1 minute and cooled down
Altitude Simulation	0.114 atm (11.6 KPa), 6 hrs at RT	No Smoke, no fire, no explosion	Cells remained intact

At the end of Phase I of this project, SKCP has developed 765066 cells delivering 3.57Ah (0.25C) with an energy density of 236.8Wh/kg.Recent work under Phase II: we have designed 965569 format cells with higher capacity, 5.06Ah, and slightly improved energy density 241.7Wh/kg. Both cells were evaluated thoroughly in terms of the cycle life, and power capability at various temperatures. **Figure 1**to **4**showed that 5Ah Phase II cell has better cycle life and much improved low-temperature power capability compared with 3.6Ah Phase I cell, which match the requirements of this project.

At the same time, concentrated attention has been paid to safety performance through the entire program. Cell safety tests including shorting at RT and 60°C, over-heating to 130°C and 150°C, over-charge, over-discharge, bar crush and altitude simulation were conducted on both 3.6Ah (Phase I) and 5Ah (Phase II) cells.

Under above abuse test conditions, cells did not smoke/fire, which passed the safety test criteria in MIL-PRE-32052.**Table 2** summarizes the test results and observations on 765066 Phase I cells. Similar results and observations were obtained on Phase II cells with slightly higher peak temperatures.

Figure 5 and **6** showed the 3.6Ah 765066 cells after abuse tests

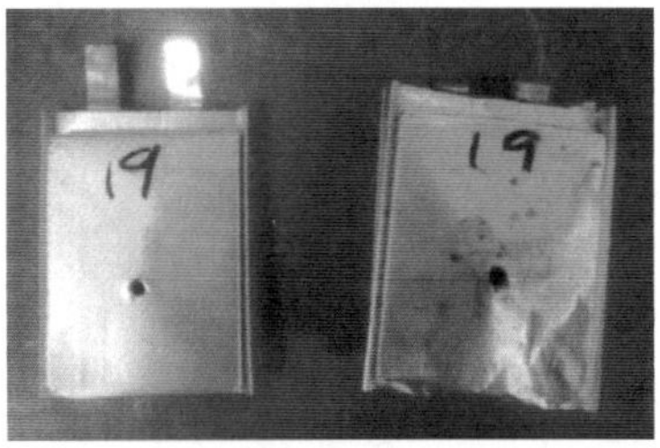

Figure 5. Nail penetration on single 765066 cell (left) and on Two (2) 765066 cells simultaneously (right)

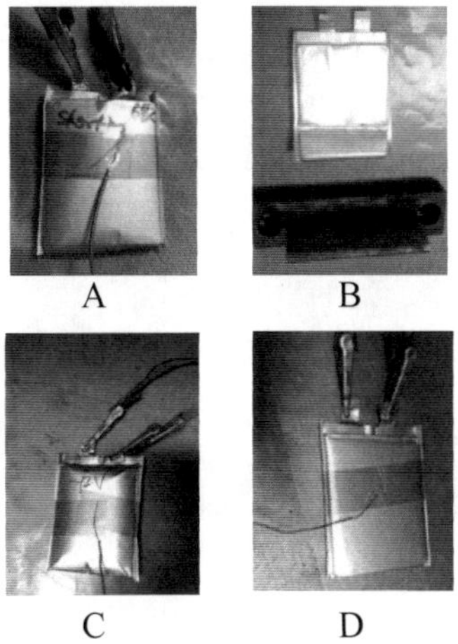

Figure 6. Safety Tests on 3.6Ah 765066 cell: External Shorting (A); Bar Crush (B); Reverse Over Discharge(C) and Over-Charge (D)

Approved for public release by US Air Force,
Review completed by Mr. James Mitchell (case # 88ABW-2018-1946)

To achieve high energy density, high voltage (>4.2V) operation is an effective strategy, especially true for$LiCoO_2$ based cells. Through our dedicated efforts including $LiCoO_2$ surface modification, and using high-voltage operation gel electrolyte et al., we have developed 285Wh/kg and 300Wh/kg large format cells as shown in **Table 3** and **Figure** 7and **8**. The 26Ah 120105130 cell, (153.5 grams)demonstrated excellent cycle life at low C-rate when being operated 2.5 to 4.45V (**Figure 9**).

Table 3. Basic Parameters of 120105130 Cellsat Various Charge Voltages.

Charge/ discharge Voltage (V)	Capacity (Ah) and Energy (Wh)	Energy Density (Wh/Kg)	Energy Density (Wh/L)
4.2 – 2.5	20.94(78.5)	221.76	479.2
4.3 – 2.5	22.89(86.68)	244.85	529.2
4.4 – 2.5	25.07(95.96)	271.07	585.8
4.45 – 2.5	26.23(101.1)	285.58	617.2
4.5 – 2.5	27.11(105.06)	296.78	641.4
4.5–2.5(0.1C)	27.13 (106.03)	299.53	647.3

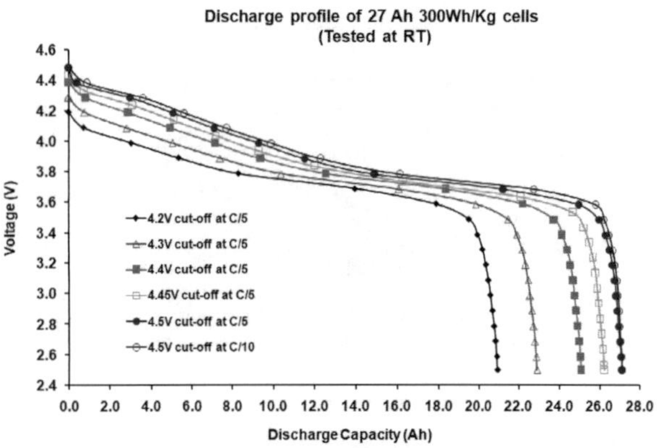

Figure 7. Discharge Profile of 120105130 Cells with Various Charging Voltages (C/4), Capacity View.

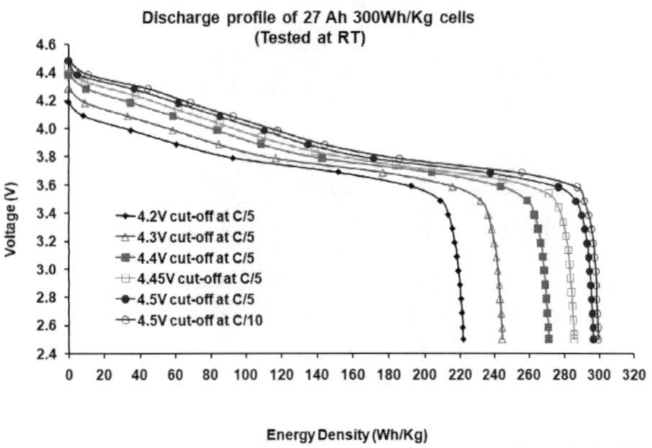

Figure 8. Discharge Profile of 120105130 Cells with Various Charging Voltages (C/4), Energy Density view.

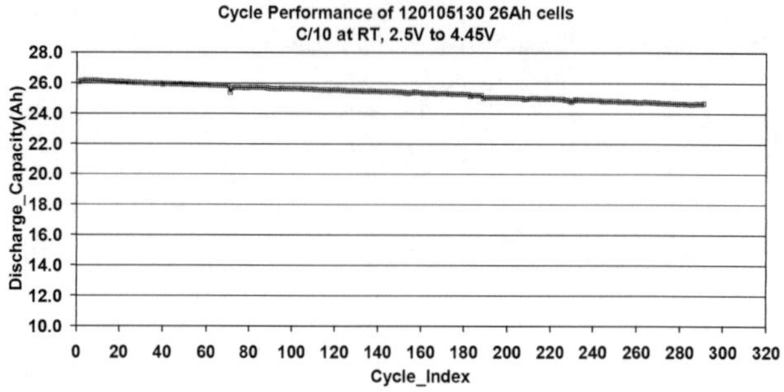

Figure 9. Cycle Performance (2.5 to 4.45V, C/4 RT) of the 120105130 High Energy Cell

Conclusions

Through intensive efforts on cell chemistries engineering optimizations, we have successfully developed two types of pouch cells formultifunctional batteries (MFB), i.e. 3.6Ah and 5Ah. Both have shown an energy density of ~ 240Wh/Kg at 4.2V operating charging volts. Those cells demonstrated enhanced over-charge, over-discharge, bar-crush, nail-penetration,and other safety and improved temperature performance.SKCP has also successfully developed 285Wh/kg higher energy cells technologies demonstrated by a larger format 26Ah 120105130 cells.
Current efforts in SKCP include developing 270Wh/kg high energy cells for MFB and other man-portable and rechargeable power sources, which means those high energy cells shall possess the same safety performance as the 965569 5Ah Phase II cell. Our concentrated efforts will also be spent to lift cell energy density to 300Wh/kg, even 320Wh/kg,by using high capacity anode, e.g. nano-sized silicon composite graphite anode, which is in progress in SKCP.

Acknowledgement

The authors gratefully acknowledge U.S. Air Force AFRL/AFMC for funding this work.

References

1. Zhiqiang Xu, Chi Kyun Park, Zhiwei Zhang, Chul Chai, *"Organic Lithium Salt Electrolytes Having Enhanced Safety for Rechargeable Batteries and Methods of Making the Same"*,US Patent 20060068295
2. "High Energy and High-Rate Rechargeable Lithium-Ion Battery",*SKC Powertech/USArmy Communications-Electronics CommandContract W15P7T-05-C-R009*
3. "The Development of Novel Electrolytes for Polymer Li-ion cells with wider operating temperature ranges", *SKC Powertech/US Army Communications-Electronics Command Contract W15P7T-06-D-A402*

Approved for public release by US Air Force,
Review completed by Mr. James Mitchell (case # 88ABW-2018-1946)

Novel Materials for High Voltage Thermal Batteries

[1]Joe Edington, [1]Zachary van Zandt, [1]Kenneth Haines, [1]Ivy Mills, and [2]Mohan Sanghadasa
[1]CFD Research Corporation, 701 McMillian Way NW, Suite D, Huntsville, AL 35806
[2]AMRDEC, US Army RDECOM, Redstone Arsenal, Huntsville, AL 35898
Contact Author Email: joe.edington@cfdrc.com

Abstract
The current state of the art thermal battery technologies will not be able to meet future requirements that call for higher power and capacity with a smaller footprint. The principal avenue for increasing the capacity of thermal batteries is to identify and develop new electrode materials that provide higher specific capacity and power performance. CFD Research Corporation has developed and demonstrated novel cathode and electrolyte materials that improve cell voltage and capacity over the current state-of-the-art sulfide-based cathode materials used in thermal batteries.

Cathode formulations have been optimized to produce >2.5 volts and c apacity exceeding 1000 am pere-seconds per gram of blended cathode while providing cell performance equivalent to or better than FeS_2 cathodes under constant current and pulse load profiles. Material performance at the battery level has been successfully demonstrated using 10-cell prototype thermal batteries.

Keywords: Thermal batteries; high capacity cathode; high voltage cathode

Introduction
Many thermal battery applications have strict size and weight constraints. With next-generation applications tending toward miniaturization, higher power needs, and longer ranges, advances in thermal battery technology are needed to support future applications. Game-changing improvements in thermal battery performance (operating life, energy density, etc.) can be achieved through technological advancements in thermal insulation, component manufacturing technology (thin film), and high voltage cell chemistries. CFD Research Corporation (CFDRC) has focused efforts on increasing thermal battery energy density by developing high voltage/high capacity cathodes and compatible electrolyte materials.

Cathode and electrolyte materials were developed that resulted in a h igher cell voltage and higher capacity. A baseline of 2.6 volts was obtained. Compared to the 1.85 volts of FeS_2, the height of the cell stacks in a battery can be reduced by 30%. The improved capacity gives the batteries a longer operating life, increasing the capabilities of thermal batteries for future applications.

Experimental
Individual cells were produced and tested across a temperature range of 400°C to 550°C. All testing and preparation was performed in a glovebox under an argon atmosphere with less than 0.5 ppm of water present. Lithium silicon (LiSi) was used as the anode material. Separator was prepared using magnesium oxide (MgO) powder as binder.

For single cell testing, cathode, anode and separator pellets were pressed into individual pellets 13 mm in diameter. The pellets were stacked between stainless-steel electrodes and placed in the heated platen apparatus shown in Figure 1. A BioLogic potentiostat with EC Labs software was used to control the applied current and record the voltage versus time.

Figure 1: Heated platen testing apparatus

Performance of Novel Cathode Material
The CFDRC cathode blend was tested and compared with FeS_2 to serve as a baseline. CFDRC's all-lithium electrolyte was used for all cells tested unless otherwise specified. The cathodes were discharged using constant current load profiles at 200 and 1000 mA/cm², a step profile, and a pulse load profile. The higher voltage of CFDRC is evident in every comparison.
Figure 2 shows the constant current performance of the cathodes. The capacity and voltage of CFDRC cathode cells

were higher than the FeS2 baseline under both 200 and 1000 mA/cm² loads. Table 1 shows the capacity of the CFDRC cathode at a cutoff voltage of 2 V. The capacity at 200 mA/cm² for the CFDRC cell exceeded the first plateau capacity of FeS_2 (840 amp-sec/gram) by 24%.

Table 1: Capacity of CFDRC cathode cells with a 2V cutoff

Current Density (mA/cm²)	Capacity (A s/g)
200	1039
1000	456

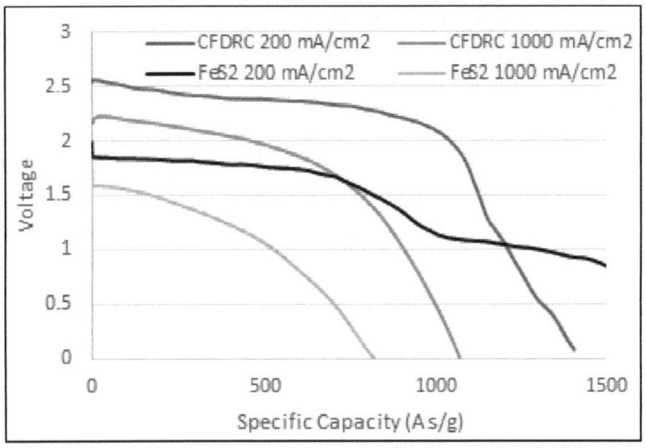

Figure 2: Constant current performance at 500°C

The CFDRC cathode cell performance was tested using a pulse load profile to measure pulse impedance under high current density pulses (Figure 3). Testing was performed using FeS_2 as a baseline for comparison (Figure 4). The pulse impedance was virtually identical for both the CFDRC cathode and FeS_2 tests. The equivalent cell impedance for the CFDRC cell translates to improved impedance at the battery level as the battery impedance is dependent upon the number of cells in the battery. At the battery level, an improvement in impedance of ~21% would be expected.

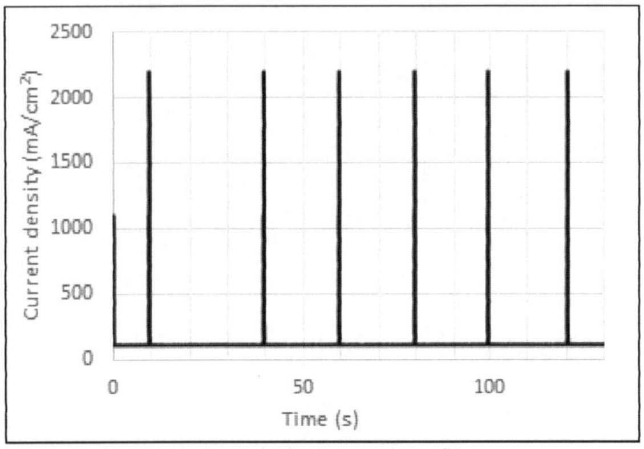

Figure 3: Pulse load profile

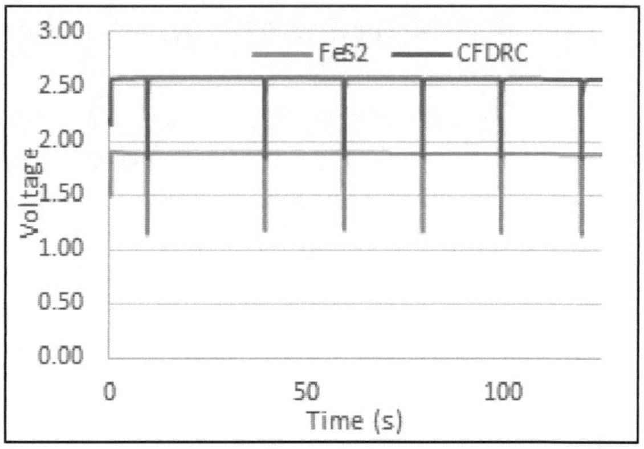

Figure 4: Pulse profile performance at 500°C

Figure 5 shows calculated pulse battery performance based on the pulse profile data above. The battery stack is designed to produce 142 volts under the pulse load. FeS_2 requires 76 cells while CFDRC cathode needs only 56 cells. The lower number of cells reduces the overall battery impedance and yields a smaller battery. The use of CFDRC cathode will reduce the length and volume by 20% and reduce the weight by 17% of the example battery shown in Table 2.

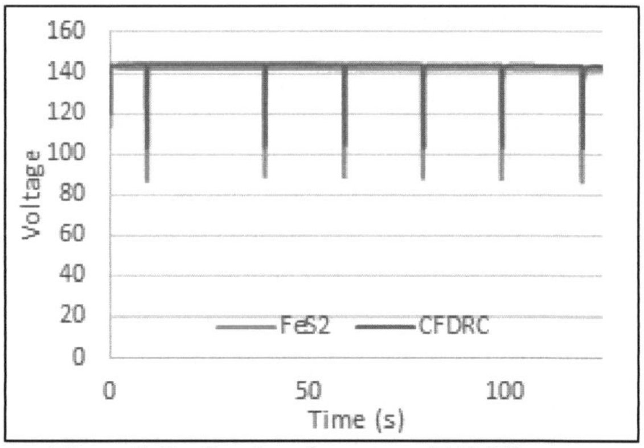

Figure 5: Predicted performance of 142 V battery.

Table 2: Dimensions of example battery

Material	Diameter (in)	Length (in)	Weight (lbs)
CFDRC	1.72	4.41	1.00
FeS_2	1.72	5.46	1.21

Performance of Electrolyte Materials

Along with the all-Li CFDRC electrolyte, a lower melting electrolyte was developed to extend operating life and improve rise times for batteries using high voltage cathode materials. Cooling tests were performed on the electrolytes by applying a constant load of 25 mA/cm² as the heated platens are cooled from an initial temperature of 550°C. Figure 6 shows the results of this test and gives an approximation of the minimum operation temperature for each electrolyte.

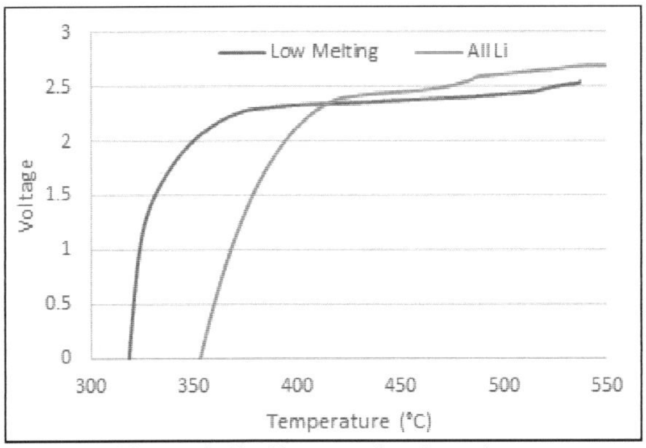

Figure 6: Cooling tests for electrolytes

The chemistry of the low melt salt would not be expected to perform as well under a heavy baseline load [2] due to lower lithium content. As a result, a profile with a baseline of 50 mA/cm^2 and pulses at 1000 mA/cm^2 was used to evaluate the electrolyte. The electrolyte was able to support 1000 mA/cm^2 pulses at temperatures down to 400°C, as shown in Figure 7 and Table 3.

Table 3: Pulse impedance for low melt salt cells at 400°C

Pulse	Impedance (Ohm)
1	0.400
2	0.469
3	0.721

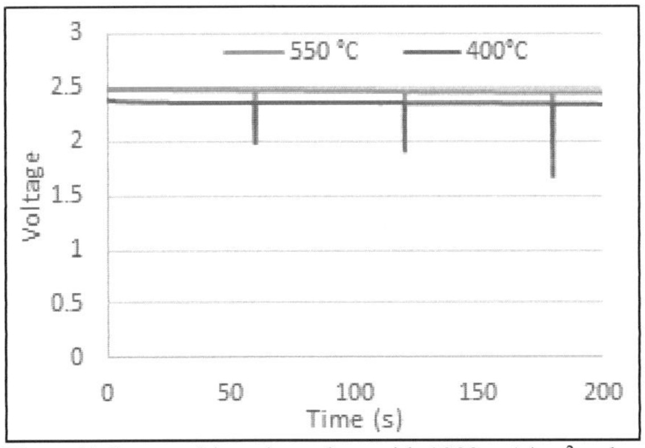

Figure 7: Low melting electrolyte with 1000 mA/cm^2 pulses

Prototype Battery Testing

Cell tests were performed using a step load profile that was selected for evaluating materials performance in the prototype batteries. The load profile was scaled to provide an equivalent current density for both the cell tests and prototype battery tests. The cell test performance (Figure 8) indicated that the CFDRC cell materials could easily support the prototype load profile. FeS_2 was tested as a baseline for comparison. P ulse impedance at 82 seconds and polarization under the high rate discharge step were comparable with FeS_2 but at a much higher voltage. The all-Li electrolyte was used for both the CFDRC cell and FeS_2 cell in these tests.

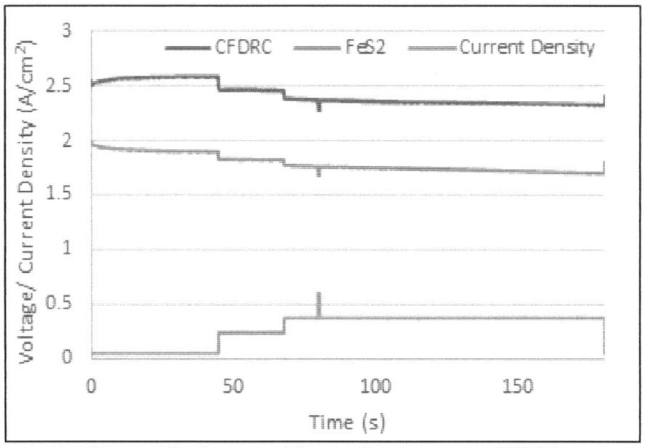

Figure 8: Step profile performance at 500°C

Battery materials were prepared and shipped to EaglePicher Technologies LLC to support prototype battery builds. All prototype batteries built with CFDRC materials contained a single stack of 10 cells. The batteries were 1.72" in diameter, and the cells had a 1.375" diameter with center hole ignition. Step and pulse load profiles were used with equivalent current densities as in the cell tests. The voltages of the battery
prototypes were comparable to a scaled version of the individual cell tests. Impedance and polarization of the batteries were satisfactory and similar to the individual cell tests.

The all-Li electrolyte was tested using the step profile (Figure 9). The test was allowed to run to zero volts (~600 seconds). The extended timeline showed that the battery remained stable throughout testing. No signs of shorting, off gassing or venting were observed during and after the operating life of the battery.

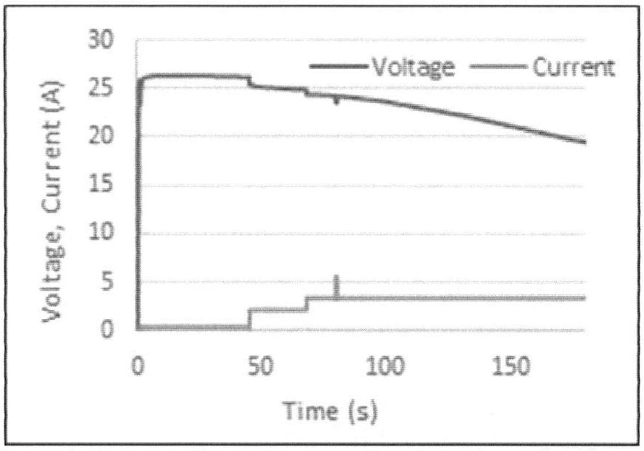

Figure 9: Step profile performance for all Li electrolyte battery prototype

Both the standard and low melting electrolytes were tested using the pulse profile shown above in Figure 3. The low melt electrolyte met the rise requirement of 0.65 seconds and provided excellent pulse impedance under heavy pulses for the 125 second operating life of the battery.

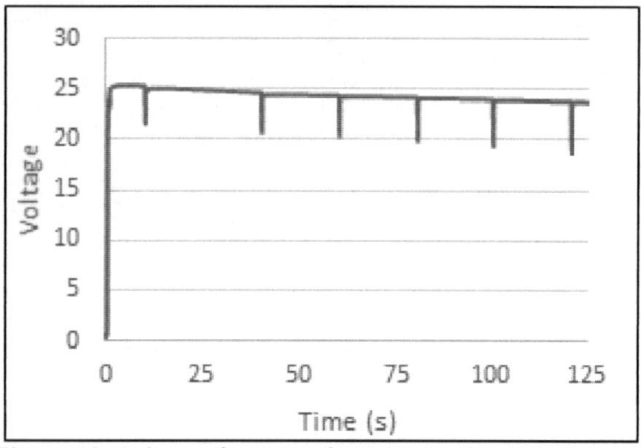

Figure 10: Pulse performance for prototype battery using low melt electrolyte

Figure 11 displays the first second of the pulse profile for prototype batteries using both the low melting electrolyte and higher melting temperature all-Li electrolyte. The lower melting temperature improved the rise time performance of the prototype battery and met the 0.65 second rise time requirement.

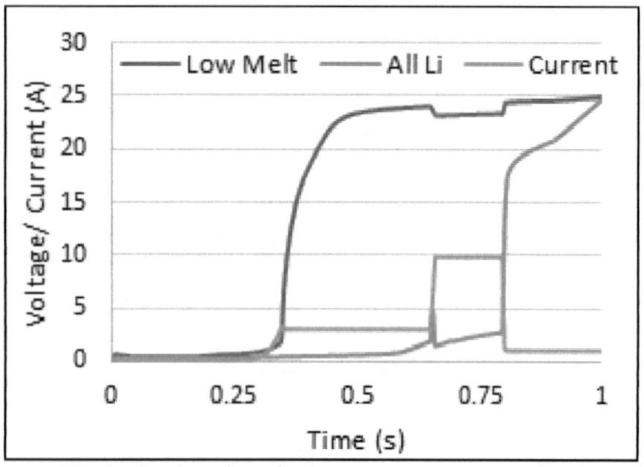

Figure 11: Activation time for battery prototypes under the pulse profile

Summary

The CFDRC cathode was developed and found to provide voltage and capacity advantages over FeS_2. The increased voltage and capacity yields a substantial increase in energy density. The low melting electrolyte was found to be useful in applications where a low operating temperature or a fast activation time is required. The standard electrolyte is suitable for batteries that require a high baseline current. Prototype batteries were built and showed stability and consistency to the individual cell tests.

Future Plans

Future development efforts will involve a manufacturability demonstration for the cathode and electrolyte powders as well as battery-level testing through temperature extremes and dynamic environments (vibration, shock, etc.)

Acknowledgments

This work was funded by the U.S. Army SBIR program (W31P4Q-16-C-0012).

DISTRIBUTION A. Approved for public release: Distribution unlimited. UNCLASSIFIED

References

[1] V. Klasons, C.M. Lamb, "Thermal Batteries" in *Handbook of Batteries,* 3rd ed, D. Linden, T.B Reddy, pp. 21.1-21.22, McGraw Hill, New York, NY, 2002

[2] R.A. Guidotti, F.W. Reinhardt, "Electrolyte Effects in Li(Si)/FeS_2 Thermal Batteries", Conference-950461-1, SAND94-1870

[3] M. Park, X. Zhang, M. Chung, G. Less, A.M. Sastry, "A Review of Conduction Phenomena in Li-ion Batteries", Power Sources (2010)

Full Scale Thermo Electric Model of Thermal Batteries

Ohad A. Shkury[1] and Ido Immer[2]

[1]Power Sources Department
Rafael LTD.
POB 2250, Haifa, Israel, 3102102
Contact information: ohadshk@rafael.co.il, +972-73-3350187

[2]Heat and Mass Transfer Department
Rafael LTD.
POB 2250, Haifa, Israel, 3102102

Abstract:

Molten salt thermal batteries are the traditional power sources for various military applications. The combination of wide operational temperature range, high power density, shelf life of more than 20 years and maintenance free storage are unsurpassed by any other battery technology.

In order to achieve optimized performance according to customer requirements a development of full thermoelectric model is required. Such a model would enable the designer to evaluate the effects of the different design parameters on the battery's performance. Moreover, the ability to propose and analyze several possible designs in a short time and at a minimum cost is of great benefit since it enables to evaluate strengths and weaknesses of the different solutions at early development stages.

In this paper, we present a 2D, axisymmetric thermal battery model validated by thermal and electrical measurements. The model is based on a multi physics system where electrical and thermal behaviors are interconnected to account for various reciprocal influences. Thermal and electrical properties of all critical battery materials were analyzed for their parameterization in the model. Optimization of the model was conducted using dedicated software in order to calibrate and adjust the various parameters. The resulted simulation enables prediction of the inner and outer battery temperatures, maximal and minimal voltage during operation, rise time and end of life within a small error margin.

Keywords: Finite Element Multi Physics Model; Thermal batteries; Heat transfer; Electric model

Introduction

Thermal battery modeling is a complex task which requires considering many physical phenomena such as: heat and mass transfer, electro chemical reactions, fluid flow, mechanical stresses etc. Coupling the various phenomena significantly increase model complexity and required computational power. As a result usually a few physical phenomena are taken into account depending on the required results. Previous work mainly focused on the performance sensitivity to various thermal properties, single cell multi physics models, electrolyte flow and electro chemistry reactions in LiSi/FeS_2 cells [1] [2] [3] [4] [5]. This work was focused on modeling and analysis of $FeS_2 - LiAl$ chemistry from the thermal and electrochemical perspective. Since the operation temperature window of LiCl-LiBr-LiF is smaller compared to LiCl-KCl the proper thermal balance of the first one is of higher importance in most of the currently developed models. Analysis of the influence of various parameters on the battery performance allowed excluding many phenomena which have minor influence on the studied battery performance. It was assumed, that in order to properly predict battery performance without undesired model complexity, the number of physical phenomena employed might be limited to heat transfer including the electrolyte phase transition and electrical behavior. Although many additional effects taking place during battery discharge such as electrochemical behavior, fluid flow, mechanical stresses etc are described in the literature [6], they were not implemented in the model in order to reduce the model's complexity.

The model development included several general steps. The first step included description of the phenomena with appropriate equations and boundary conditions. The material properties were obtained from the literature but the model results were not satisfactory. To improve prediction quality the actual material properties were measured using several techniques. All the obtained data was than implemented into a 2D axisymmetric model. Due to the materials properties variation and measurements errors additional calibration of the model was required. The model was validated by comparing its results to several new and existing batteries. A combination of finite elements solver and optimization software was used to fit the model for a case study battery measurement.

Methodology

Measurement of material properties. Initially, the different parameters were taken from the literature [8]. Thermal properties described in this paper were modeled as various polynomial expressions. In addition, measurements were conducted to compare the actual results to the proposed equations. It was found that the more appropriate approach is to replace the equations with actual measured data. Hence, the heat capacities and thermal conductivities were measured as a function of temperature for each material: Cathode (FeS_2), anode (LiAl), ceramic binder (MgO), electrolytes (LiCL-LiBr-LiF), insulations and heat pellets.

Heat capacity was measured using Differential Scanning Calorimeter (DSC) from room temperature (RT) to 500°C. Thermal conductivity was measured using Laser Flash technique in temperature range of $-50°C$ to $500°C$. Electrical resistivity was measured within temperature range of $400°C$ to $600°C$ in a single cell discharge system. Data for the rest of materials was taken from the literature, for example the thermal properties of stainless steel current collector [7].

Density dependence on the temperature was neglected except the step density variation of electrolyte phase transition from solid to molten state.

Model Geometry. To simplify the geometrical model from 3D to the 2D axi symmetric the "artifacts", such as the glass to metal seals, terminals and current collectors were neglected.

Figure 1 shows an example of a 2D model (a) with its corresponding mesh (b). Each domain was modeled with suitable thermal and electrical properties in accordance with the selected material. In general, to receive more accurate results the mesh should be as fine as possible. However, the smaller the mesh features are, the more time consuming is the model calculation. In order to reduce required computational power different battery components were meshed in accordance to their material, geometrical complexity and size. For example, due to their size and thermal properties of stainless steel separators between the cells were modeled as boundaries.

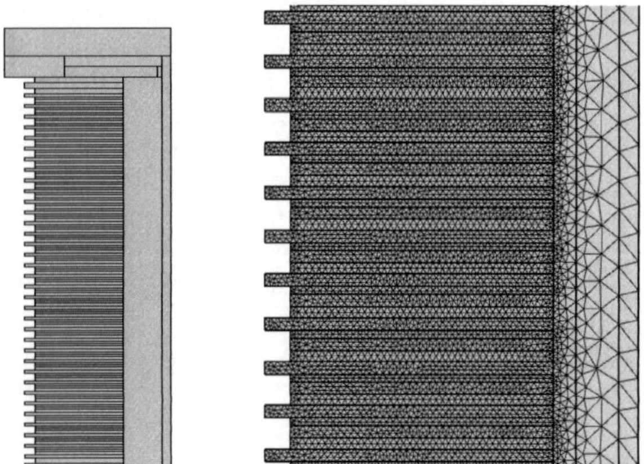

(a) (b)

Figure 1 – (1a) Geometrical 2D model of the battery. (1b) an example of the meshing method

Heat Transfer and phase transition. The thermal model is based on generic heat transfer equations such as Fourier Law (1), Newton's law of cooling (2) and phase transition (3)

$$(1)\ \rho C_p\left(\frac{\partial T}{\partial t}\right) - \nabla k \nabla T = Q$$

$$(2)\ \frac{dQ}{dT} = h \cdot A \cdot (T(t) - T_{env})$$

$$(3)\ \rho = \theta\rho_s + (1-\theta)\rho_l, k = \theta k_s + (1-\theta)k_l$$

Where ρ is the density$[\frac{kg}{m^3}]$, C_p is the specific heat capacity $[\frac{J}{kgK}]$, k is the thermal conductivity $[\frac{W}{mK}]$, Q- the volumetric heat power $[\frac{W}{m^3}]$, h is the thermal convection coefficient $[\frac{W}{m^2K}]$, A is the area $[m^2]$ and T is temperature $[K]$.

Both convective and radiative heat losses to the environment were assumed.

Electrochemical model. A simple model was proposed to describe dependency of open circuit voltage (OCV) and resistance on temperature and state of charge (SOC) with general formula shown below:

$$(4)\ V = V_{OCV}(T) - I \cdot R(T) - V(C)$$

While V_{OCV} is the OCV as function of the temperature, IR factor derived from the load current and the impedance as a function of temperature and V(C) is the SOC factor influencing the voltage.

To verify the model parameters a number of impedance measurements were conducted using single cell discharges at various temperatures, in a similar way described by Guidotti et.al [9]. Similar cells were also used in the case study battery for the thermal and electrical measurements. The OCV was taken from the impedance measurements, as a function of temperature as well. The experiment included discharge of case study batteries at different C rates to isolate the temperature and SOC role in the model.

Model calibration. A case study battery was chosen and several setups were built with thermocouples inside the batteries in order to compare, adjust and calibrate the model according to laboratory tested measurements. An example for such a setup is shown in Figure 2.

Figure 2 - One of the case study batteries built for inner temperature measurements

Results and discussion

Thermal model Calibration

Figure 3 shows average temperature inside the battery measured in experiment and prediction by the optimized model. It might be seen that the model and actual measurements are in good agreement.

The comparison between outer case temperatures at various points of interest is seen in Figure 4. The initial steep gradient of the measured temperature in the mid case and the bottom is in good agreement with the model. The maximum temperatures variation between the model and the actual performance doesn't exceed 5%. The model also gives a good prediction of the cooling rate, which confirms the assumption of heat loses to the surroundings by means of convection and radiation.

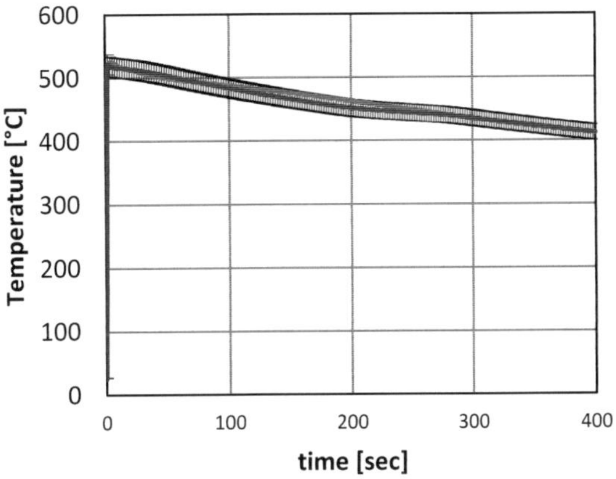

Figure 3 - Average temperature of the battery stack as measured experimentally (blue) and modeled (red). The error bars represent 3% error

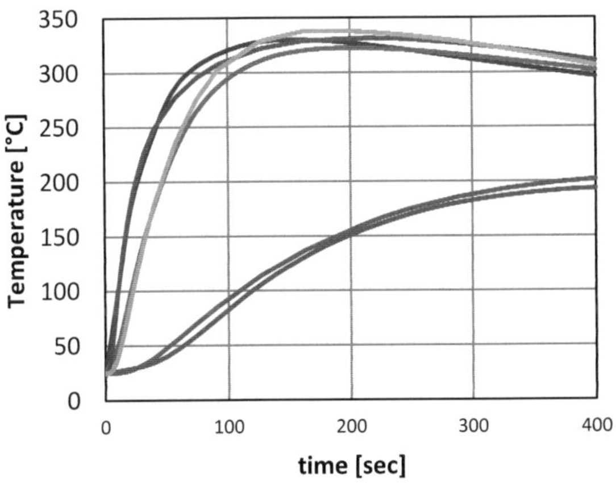

Figure 4 - Comparison of measured **outer temperature in three different sections of the battery: bottom, mid case and head (red, green and purple respectively) vs. modeled one (magenta, light green and blue). The maximal error margin is of 5%**

Electrical model calibration.

The model calibration was conducted using single cell discharges at various C rates and temperatures. The results of the impedance measurements were translated to conductivity.

The measurements of conductivity and OCV at various temperatures and SOC were used to calibrate the model described by expression 4. The dependency of conductivity on temperature was also compared to expression published by Guidotti et al [10] and was found to fit general behavior described in the paper.

As shown in Figure 5 there is a good agreement between the measured values and the model.

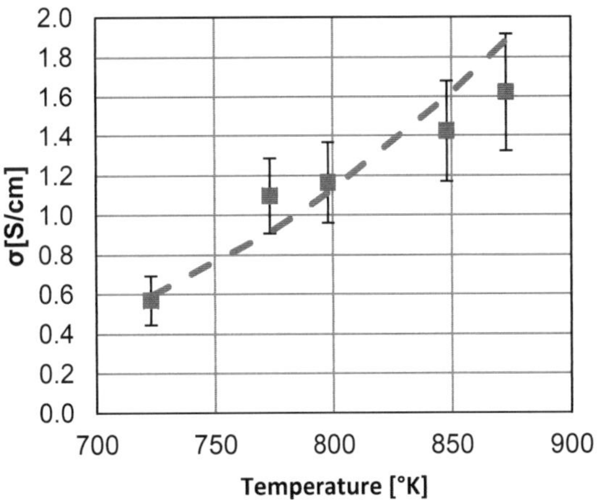

Figure 5 – Electrical conductance as function of temperature. The blue dashed line stands for the mathematical expression

An example of prototype battery discharge is shown at Figure 6. To compare results obtained from various C rate experiments the voltage was drawn as a function of the SOC. The figures revealed a strong correlation, regardless of temperature changes, as can be seen in Figure 7. It could be noted from Figure 7 that when measured at the SOC scale the coulomb efficiency of the 50C battery is better compared to the 15C battery. The difference is probably related to performance variations and to the battery's self discharge.

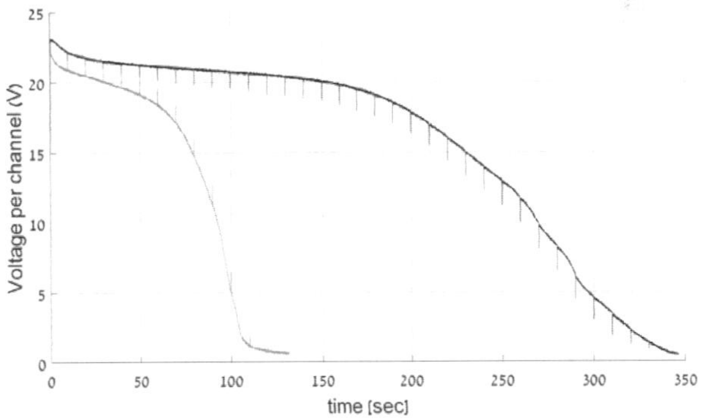

Figure 6 – Voltage as a function of time of the case study battery. Blue curve is 15C discharge rate and the light green curve is 50C discharge rate. The delta between the maximal voltages is of agreement to the IR factor

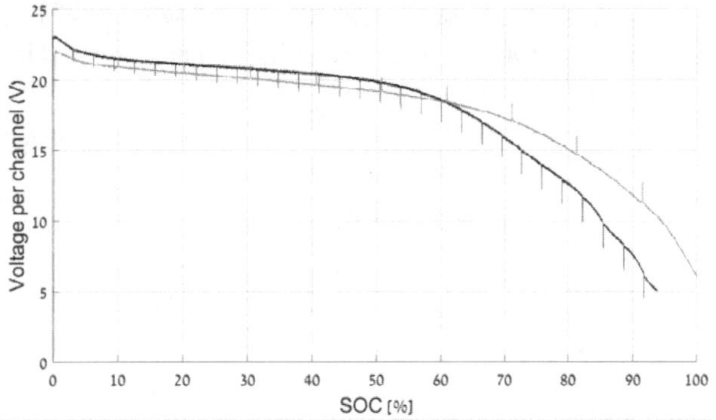

Figure 7 – Voltage as a function of State of charge. Blue curve is 15C and the green curve is 50C.

Model performance

To confirm the full thermal and electrical model a production battery with large experimental data available was simulated as can be seen in Figure 8. The electrical performance prediction is in good agreement with the actual experimental data. The voltage perturbations are related to the operational discharge profile so an averaged discharge profile employed for the simplicity of the model calculation.

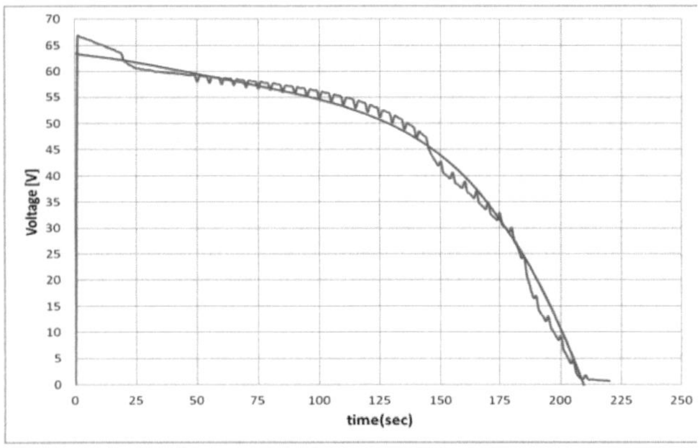

Figure 8 - Voltage of mass production battery (blue line) vs. simulated model (red line). The model neglected the pulses in the discharge profile.

Summary and Conclusions

A thermo-electric model was developed for thermal battery performance evaluation. The model accounts for thermal and electrical effects which were verified to have the most significant influence on battery performance. The 2D axisymmetric model permits calculation of battery inner and outer temperatures combined with electrical performance. Model validation was done by its implementation on existing and new products. Further model improvements will include 3D non symmetric features and addition of effects to improve prediction at various extreme conditions.

References

[1] E. S. Peikos, A. M. Grillet, N. D. Streeter and S. K. Showalter, "Assessing the Sesitivity of Thermal Battery Performance to Material Thermal Properties via Simulation," in *Power Sources Conference*, 2014.

[2] B. L. Tremback, S. R. Harris, E. S. Piekos and S. A. Roberts, "Uncertainty Quantification, Verification, and Validation of a Thermal Simulation Tool for Molten Salt Batteries," in *Power Sources Conference*, 2016.

[3] T. G. Voskuilen, J. C. Hewson, H. K. Moffat and S. A. Roberts, "Multi-Physics, Multi-Plateau Reaction Model for LiSi/FeS2 Batteries," in *Power Sources Conference*, 2016.

[4] S. A. Roberts, K. N. Long, J. R. Clausen, M. J. Martinez, E. S. Piekos and A. M. Grillet, "Towards a Coupled Multiphysics Model of Molten Salt Battery Mechanics," in *Power Sources Conference*, 2014.

[5] J. Hewson, H. Moffat and V. Brunini, "Model Parameterization for Electrochemical Predictions of LiSi/FeS2 Batteries," in *Power Sources Conference*, 2014.

[6] R. A. Guidotti and P. Masset, "Thermally activated ("thermal") battery technology," *Journal of Power Sources* , vol. 161, pp. 1443-1449, 2006.

[7] R. S. Graves, T. G. Kollie, D. L. McElroy and K. E. Glichrist, "The Thermal Conductivity of AISI 304L Stainless Steel," *International Journal of Thermophysics,* vol. 12, no. 2, pp. 409-415, 1991.

[8] N. Haimovich, D. R. Dekel and S. Brandon, "A Simulator for System-Level Analysis of Heat Transfer and Phase Change in Thermal Batteries," *Journal of the Electrochemical Society,* vol. 156, no. 6, pp. A442-A453, 2009.

[9] L. Redey, M. McParland and R. Guidotti, "Resistivity Measurments of Halide-salt/MgO Separators for Thermal Cells," in *International Power Sources Symposium*, 1990.

[10] P. Masset and R. A. Guidotti, "Thermal activated (thermal) battery technology Part II. Molten salt electrolytes," *Journal of Power Sources,* vol. 164, pp. 397-414, 2007.

Modeling of Pyrotechnic Combustion Behavior and Temperature Distribution for the Ignition Phase of Thermal Batteries

Tuğrul Koyuncu, Anıl Alkan, Kemal Sevim, Yener Yeşilırmak, Ender Ünsal and Ahmet Göçmez
TÜBİTAK SAGE
P.O. Box 16, Mamak/Ankara, Turkey, 06261
tugrul.koyuncu@tubitak.gov.tr

Abstract: *In this study, a two dimensional finite element model was generated using COMSOL Multiphysics to study and optimize the activation time of thermal batteries. Heat transfer and reaction kinetics are included and coupled in the model. The apparent activation energy, reaction model and Arrhenius constant for the combustion process were evaluated using differential thermal analysis experiments and several mathematical approaches like the Kissinger-Akahira-Sunose (KAS method and Málek's kinetic procedure [1]. Temperature dependent thermophysical properties of cell components were calculated by using optimization tool of COMSOL and experimental data. Thermal contact at the interfaces which plays an important role on heat transfer was also considered and included in the model. Spatial-temporal temperature profile, heat generation rate, reaction front movement, narrow reaction zone, ignition temperature, reactant conversion during the reaction and phase change distribution of electrolyte were obtained. Predicted results were compared with the experimental measurements to verify the accuracy of simulations. The model provided a reliable heat design tool for the activation phase of thermal batteries.*

Keywords: Thermal battery; activation; COMSOL Multiphysics; self-propagation.

Introduction

A proper heat generation mechanism and the management of heat distribution within a thermal battery has an importance to determine when the electrolyte is melted and maximum exposure temperatures are also of importance to ensure that cathode material is not degraded which causes undesired thermal runaway. The first case is related with the activation time of the thermal batteries. The activation time can be defined as the time between energy input to the igniter and the battery voltage reaching the minimum of the operation voltage while the battery discharged with the desired electrical load. Activation time is expected to be as small as possible especially when fast power discharge is required. It depends on how fast the heat pellets release sufficient amount of thermal energy for electrolyte melting and material properties (material type, thickness, theoretical density, etc.) of cell components. Thus, the amount of current that can be drawn from the battery within the activation time is restricted by the cross sectional area of molten regions of electrolyte pellets at different locations.

In this work, activation phase of the electrochemical system containing FeS_2/LiBr-LiCl-LiF(MgO)/LiSi electrochemical cell and Fe/$KClO_4$ heat pellet was studied and simulated. Time dependent temperature distributions, hence the ratio of molten electrolyte for all of the cells within the battery were evaluated using COMSOL Multiphysics software. Simulation results for temperature were compared with the experimental measurements and it is seen that the calculated data were consistent well with experimental values. It is concluded that the phase change of the electrolyte is the dominate factor for the activation time.

Model Description

In this study, a multiphysics modeling analysis based on self-propagating combustion waves and melting process of electrolyte have been established to predict the activation time of thermal batteries. The activation process of thermal batteries is divided into five steps: (1) activation of igniter; (2) heat pellet reaction; (3) heat transfer; (4) electrolyte melt; (5) electrochemical reaction. In our study we interested in steps (2), (3) and (4) which are the most rate determining and time consuming steps for activation.

Geometry

The geometrical structure of the model was created based on our experimental setup (Figure 4). A two dimensional and axisymmetric analysis was used to reduce the solution time due to cylindrical symmetry. Due to large temperature gradient across the heat pellets, smaller size mapped mesh was used for heat pellet to improve the model convergence (Figure 1). Remaining domains were mashed with more coarsely triangular mesh.

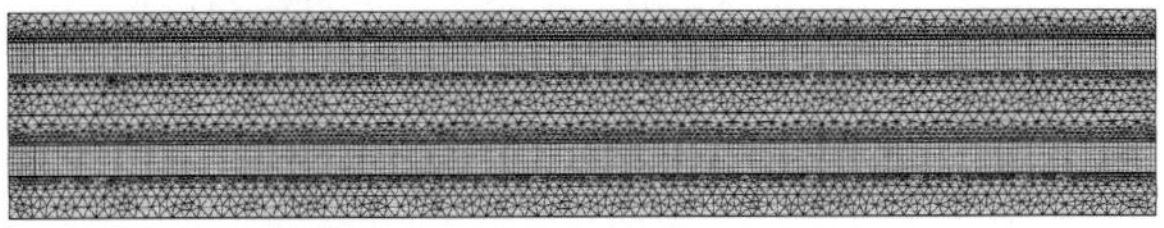

Figure 1. Mesh of the Geometry

Heat source (Q)

The pyrotechnic reaction of iron powder (Fe) and potassium perchlorate ($KClO_4$) are used as heat source in thermal batteries [2]

$$4Fe + KClO_4 \rightarrow 4FeO + KCl + Q \quad \text{(Eq. 1)}$$

The heat source term, Q, can be calculated from the mass density, reaction rate and the enthalpy of reaction:

$$Q = \rho \frac{d\alpha}{dt} \Delta H \qquad \text{(Eq. 2)}$$

where α is the conversion of the product. Enthalpy of reaction was obtained as -1242.6 J/g from calorimetry bomb experiments. Figure 2 illustrates the typical reaction characteristics of a self-propagating combustion wave in a pyrotechnic system.

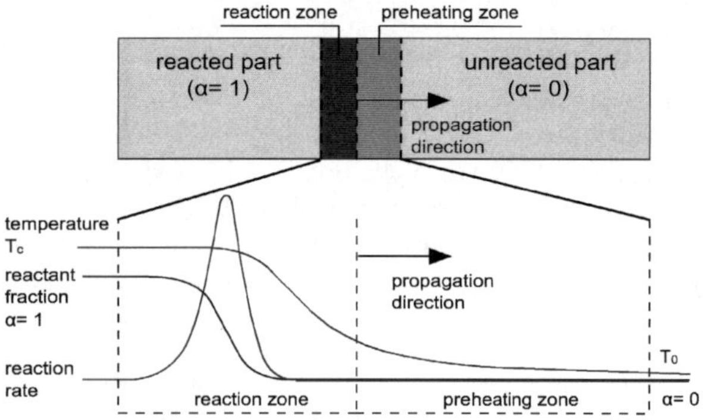

Figure 2. Combustion Wave Propagation

To obtain the best reaction model for $Fe/KClO_4$ binary mixture, kinetic studies were performed using Málek's kinetic procedure and it was concluded that Šesták Berggren reaction model gave the best fit with experimental data [1]. By assuming the Arrhenius chemical kinetics and Šesták Berggren reaction model, the reaction rate is given as

$$\frac{d\alpha}{dt} = \alpha^m (1-\alpha)^n A e^{-\frac{E_a}{RT}} \qquad \text{(Eq. 3)}$$

where m and n are Šesták Berggren parameters, E_a is the activation energy, R is the universal gas constant, and A is the pre-exponential factor. The reaction rate, enthalpy of reaction (calorific output), Šesták Berggren parameters and kinetic parameters (A and E_a) are affected by the mass ratio of mixture components in Eq 1. In our study we have used the mass ratio of 84/16 ($Fe/KClO_4$) where $KClO_4$ was the limiting reactant. All the kinetic data for this composition are listed in Table 1 [1].

Table 1. Kinetic Parameters Used in the Model

Parameter	Value
Šesták Berggren constant (m)	0.373
Šesták Berggren constant (n)	0.755
Activation energy (E_a)	217.0 kJ/mol
Arrhenius Constant (lnA)	29.16

Energy balance

For a multicomponent thermal battery system, a general differential equation of transient heat transfer has been formulated based on thermal energy balance

$$\frac{\partial(\rho C_p T)}{\partial t} = \frac{\partial}{\partial x}\left(k \frac{\partial T}{\partial x}\right) + Q \qquad \text{(Eq. 4)}$$

where t is the time, T is the temperature, ρ is the mass density, C_p is the specific heat, k is the thermal conductivity and Q is the exothermic heat of the pyrotechnic reaction (for heat pellet only). Also, thermal contact effects that are an important factor for the thermal conductivity of cell components were included in the model. The thermal contact resistance arises from the roughness of the surface and the gaps between the surfaces [3,4].

The temperature dependent thermophysical properties of thermal battery cell components were determined by using optimization tool of COMSOL and experimental data of inactive batteries. Figure 3 shows the good agreement of temperatures after optimization process. Goodness of the fit was found to be in the range of 0.987 – 0.999 using MATLAB's built in "corrcoef" script. All the thermophysical data for cell components used in the model was summarized in Table 2.

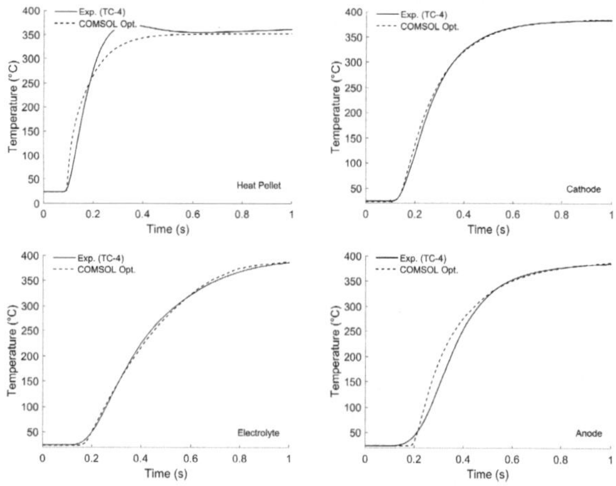

Figure 3. Comparison of Experimental and Theoretical Temperatures of Cell Components using Optimization

Mass Balance

Simple mass balance was used to model the conversion of reactants to products as the following equation

$$\frac{\partial c}{\partial t} = R_c = rV \qquad \text{(Eq. 5)}$$

$$-r = kC_A = k\alpha^m (1-\alpha)^n C_{A0} \qquad \text{(Eq. 6)}$$

Conversion expression can be expressed in terms of concentration and used in Eq. 6 by defining conversion as:

$$\alpha = 1 - \frac{C_A}{C_{A0}} \qquad \text{(Eq. 7)}$$

where C_{A0} is the initial reactant concentration. Since there is no mass transfer outside the heat pellet the boundaries were set to be insulation.

Experimental Setup

To determine unknown thermophysical properties, several inactive batteries that include only one cell component and stainless steel sheets were constructed and unknown data was obtained using optimization tool of COMSOL.

After optimization, 32-cell electrochemical system consisting of FeS_2 cathode, LiSi anode and LiCl-LiBr-LiF electrolyte with MgO binder was constructed and tested for the final verification of thermophysical data. For all of the batteries, Fe/$KClO_4$ heat pellet with the mass ratio of 84/16% was used as heat source. The resulting composite composite powders were then ground with a diameter of 50 mm. The densities of pellets are listed in Table 2. Pellets were stored in argon inert atmosphere until use. All the operations including the battery construction were performed in a dry room where dew point was below -45°C. The battery stack was surrounded by standard arrangement of thermal battery insulations and hermetically sealed container. The cells were activated by a standard 3.5A igniter in a temperature chamber at 24°C (to prevent forced convection effects) after conditioning of at least 3 hours for temperature stabilization. The battery was instrumented with internal and external K type thermocouples to provide a temperature waveform at selected locations as a function of time. Temperatures of the thermocouples were collected by a data acquisition system connected to a PC with DaqView software at a rate of 100 Hz. Details of the battery construction and instrumentation were given in Figure 4.

Table 2. Thermophysical Properties of Thermal Battery Cell Components

Material	ρ (g/cm3)	C_p (J/g.K)	k (W/m.K)
Anode (Li-Si)	1.083	$1.83x10^{-3}T+1.767$	$2.33x10^{-2}T-2.833$
Electrolyte (LiCl-LiBr-LiF + MgO)	2.414	0.85 (s) | 1.30 (l)	0.95
Latent Heat:	-	280 (J/g)	-
Cathode (FeS_2)	3.200	$4.28x10^{-4}T+1.331$	0.97
Heat Pellet (Fe/$KClO_4$)	3.380	1.01 (burned) | 0.43 (unburned)	20.39 (burned) | 9.32 (unburned)
Anode Protector (304 [solid, polished])	COMSOL Library	COMSOL Library	COMSOL Library

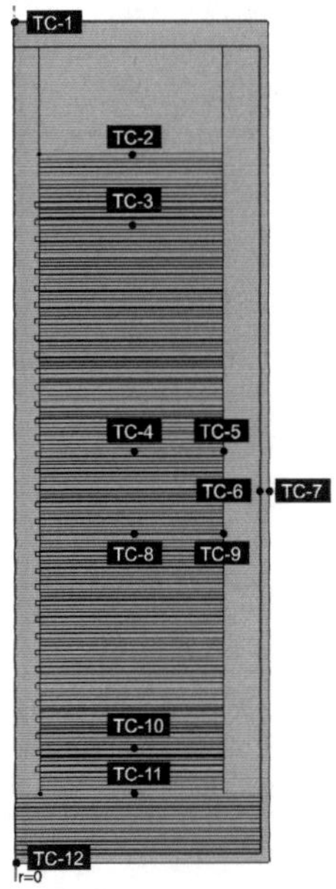

Figure 4. Battery Assembly and Location of Thermocouples

Results and Discussion

A heat design tool was developed to allow calculation of the activation time of thermal batteries. Heat generation rate of heat pellets, reactant conversion during combustion, speed of reaction front, spatial temperature distribution within the battery and the phase change profile of electrolyte pellets were calculated as a function of time during activation. The accuracy of the model was validated by comparing the predicted results with the experimental measurements. Figure 5 shows temperature simulation results match well with experimental data. Also the speed of burning front propagation was calculated as 11.5 cm/s in the experiments. This value was predicted as 10.97 cm/s by the model where the difference is smaller than 5%. Based on good fits between the experimentally measured values (temperature gradients at several locations and burning velocity) and model results, it is assumed that the unmeasured values (reaction rate, phase change profile, reactant conversion, etc.) were also calculated correctly.

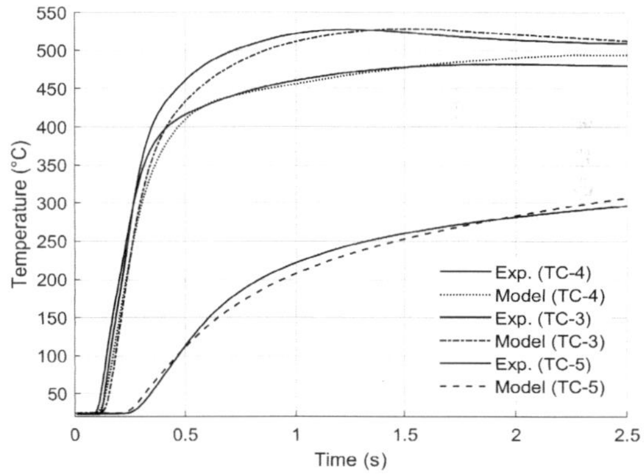

Figure 5. Temperature Comparison of Model Predictions and Experimental data for Full-Scale Thermal Battery

Within the activation time, the combustion reaction of heat pellets proceeds along radial direction while the released heat is transferred from it to the other cell components simultaneously. Once the temperature of electrolyte reached the phase change temperature, the electrolyte starts to melt and the voltage of the battery starts to increase. When the discharge voltage reaches the minimum cut-off voltage, the battery is assumed activated. This activation process is primarily influenced by material properties (thermophysical properties of cell components, melting point of electrolyte, calorific output of heat pellet, etc.) and the magnitude of electrical load applied. The higher the load, the more electrolyte need to be melted. Therefore, the dependency of the activation time on the electrical load is related to the amount of molten electrolyte that could be calculated by the model. After the model validation, the model calculations could be studied in detail to understand the physical phenomena during the activation phase. Figure 6 shows the local temperature profiles in the thru-plane direction for different time steps at $r=R_{pellet/2}$.

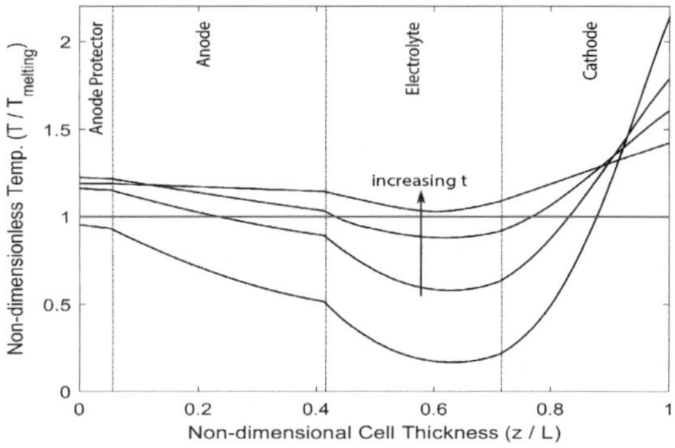

Figure 6. Thru-plane Temperature Profiles

According to the burning rate of the heat pellet, pyrotechnic combustion reaction was completed at 0.205 s but the electrolyte pellet is unlikely to reach molten point and thus thermal equilibrium at that time especially for $r=R_{pellet}$. As the time elapses, thermal diffusion occurs and thermal equilibrium is reached. This temperature change is followed by the phase change. Volume-averaged phase change distribution of the electrolyte pellet for several time values is presented in Figure 7. The percentage of molten electrolyte at any time could be calculated for any cell of the battery, thus it is possible to predict when the minimum voltage available that means activation time.

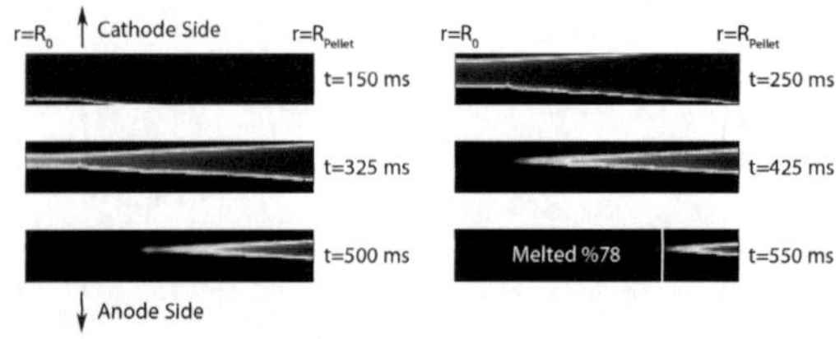

Figure 7. Volume-averaged Phase Change Distribution of Electrolyte Pellet at the Center Location of the Battery

The steps of activation in thermal batteries were discussed and summarized in model description chapter. Generation of ignition energy to ignite heat pellets are generally occurs within 20 milliseconds after the electric match subjected to external pulse in Step (1). So, the effect of Step (1) on the activation time had not been included in the model calculations. Also Step (5) was excluded from the calculations because it would depend on the electrical load to be applied and would occur after the activation phase completed. The effects of remaining steps (2, 3 and 4) have been studied in detail using the created model. According to the results, Step (2): combustion of heat pellets, Step (3): heat transfer and Step (4): phase changing times were calculated as 0.205, 0.240 and 0.494 ms respectively. Taking these results into account, we can conclude that Step (4) is the most rate-determining step for the activation process of thermal batteries. A schematical representation is given in Figure 8. The time delay between consecutive steps was calculated by the model.

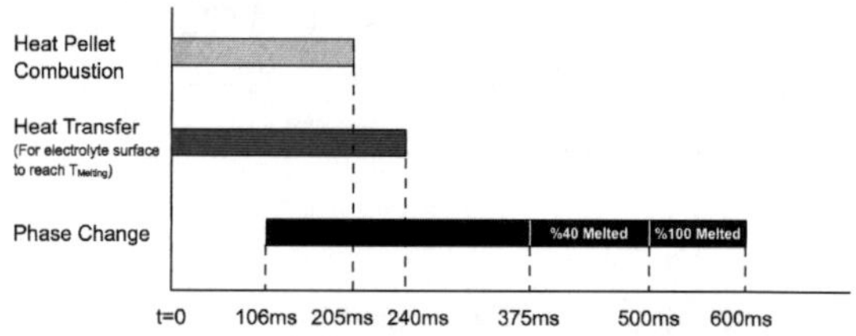

Figure 8. Duration of Activation Steps

Supplied thermal energy in thermal batteries should provide a temperature range between the melting point of the electrolyte and the thermal decomposition temperature of the cathode material. A sufficient supply of thermal energy can initiate electrolyte melting but an excessive amount may cause undesired thermal runaway. Time dependent temperature variations can be analyzed in detail at the component level using the model calculations.

Conclusion

Two-dimensional time-dependent computational model for the prediction of activation time in thermal batteries was developed with COMSOL Multiphysics. This model provides a design tool which was able not only to predict the effects of design variations on any of the activation steps and the total activation time but also to optimize the thermal management for a successful operation prior to prototyping. A prior prediction could increase the efficiency of the design and make cost down of production. When compared to experimental results, the agreement of local temperature evaluation profiles as a function of time and the combustion propagation speed were found to be quite favorable.

Acknowledgement

This work was supported and funded by TÜBİTAK SAGE that is a governmental institute under the Ministry of Science, Industry and Technology in Turkey.

References

1. Alkan, A. et al. "Determination of Kinetic Parameters for Fe/$KClO_4$ Pellets Used in Thermal Batteries," *Proceedings of the 48th Power Sources Conf.*, 2018.
2. Guidotti, R. A., "Development History of Fe/$KClO_4$ Heat Powders at Sandia and Related Aging Issues for Thermal Batteries," *Sandia Report*, SAND2001-2191.
3. Madhusudana, C.V., L.S. Fletcher, "Contact Heat Transfer," *AIAA Journal*, Vol. 24, Iss. 3, pp. 510-523.
4. Tovanovich, M.M., "Recent Developments in Thermal Contact, Gap and Joint Conductance Theo. and Exp.," *C.L. Tien et al, Eds., Heat Transfer-1986*, Vol. 1, Hemisphere, NY, 1986, pp. 35-45.

Experimental Characterization and Modeling of Thermal Battery Insulation Materials

Alexander Headley, Aron Robbins, Michael Hileman, Christine Roberts, Edward Piekos, Patrick Fleig, Ryan Solich, Adam Martinez
Diagnostic Science and Engineering Department
Sandia National Laboratories
Albuquerque, NM 87123
aheadle@sandia.gov / 1-505-844-5066

Abstract: *Thermal insulation is a key component for molten salt batteries. As electrolyte freeze-out is sometimes the limiting factor for battery life, accurate representation of the insulation thermal conductivity is essential to proper design. Though manufacturers report this for standard conditions, insulation is subjected to many extreme conditions in thermal batteries (compression, high temperatures, changing gaseous environments) that deviate the thermal conductivity from the nominal value. This work seeks to characterize the effect of various parameters experimentally and develop a model for the thermal conductivity of common thermal battery insulations to reduce the uncertainty in the larger battery model.*

Keywords: thermal battery; insulation; thermal conductivity

Introduction

Since thermal batteries are only active while the electrolyte is molten (>352 °C), they are insulated to maintain the necessary temperature. In long life batteries, properly applied insulation can provide battery lifetimes in excess of an hour [1]. However, in this application, the insulation is subjected to many conditions that significantly deviate from those tested for by the manufacturer. For example, the battery can is closed under a large stress (100-900 psi) and the stack is wrapped in fiberglass tape, compressing the insulation. Furthermore, although the free space in a battery is initially filled with dry air, residual water in the air slowly reacts away to form hydrogen. Since hydrogen is more conductive than nitrogen, the thermal resistance of the insulation degrades with aging.

Designing thermal batteries with a proper heat balance is necessary for proper operation and the safety of surrounding components. Batteries will undergo thermal runaway if their electrodes exceed threshold temperatures and will freeze before their mission is completed if insufficient insulation is included. Therefore, thermal models are important to understand design implications. The Thermally Activated Battery Simulator (TABS) model is a Sandia-developed multiphysics model for thermal battery operation in normal environments. This model includes electrochemical, mechanical, thermal, and electrolyte flow calculations and also predicts interactions between modules. Recent verification and validation efforts of this model have identified the uncertainty in the insulation thermal conductivity values as primary sources of model prediction uncertainty, especially when modelling the performance of long life batteries [2]. This is largely because the effects of compression, atmosphere, and temperature on the thermal conductivity of the insulation are not accounted for.

This paper summarizes the experimental and modeling efforts being performed to characterize three common thermal battery insulations, namely Fiberfrax T-30LR board, Fiberfrax 970-H wrap, and Min-K TE1400 board, for implementation in TABS. This includes a proposed thermal conductivity model framework, bulk thermal conductivity measurements with changing temperature and material strains, the calculation of anisotropic (axial and radial) thermal conductivities, X-ray CT scans, and pore size distribution measurements. Ultimately, this information will be used to improve the efficacy of the TABS model for thermally balancing battery designs.

Transient Plane Source Thermal Conductivity Measurements

Thermal conductivity data for all of the materials with respect to changes in temperature and compression level was collected using a Hot Disk AB TPS 2500s (Göteborg, Sweden) system. This device is based upon the transient plane source (TPS) technique. With this method, a spiral wound probe (typically nickel or molybdenum) that acts both as the heat source and temperature sensor is imbedded in the sample [3, 4]. Voltage is applied to the probe to generate heat in the center of the material while changes in the probe resistance are monitored to determine the temperature response of the probe, and consequently, thermal properties of the sample.

For these tests, the sensor was sandwiched between sheets of insulation. The samples and probe were held between plates with through holes for threaded guide rods. The compression of the materials was set by stacking gauge blocks of varying thicknesses between the plates as shown in Figure 1.

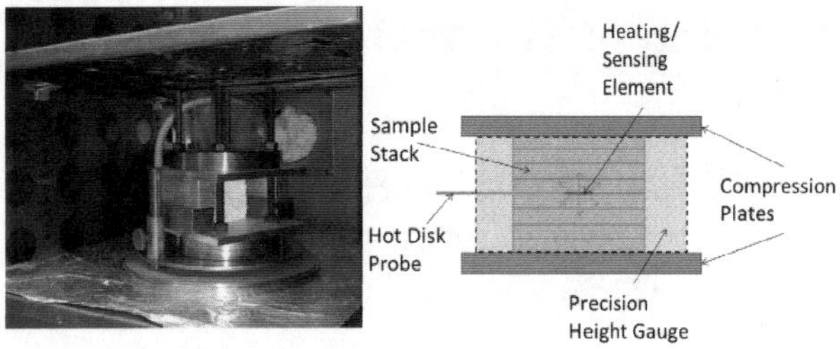

Figure 1: Test fixture and schematic

A load frame provided the necessary closing force to bring the plates to the gauge blocks, and care was taken to ensure that the plates were in full contact with the gauge blocks on all sides of the sample. The samples were tested at decreasing gap widths until 500 psi or more was required to close the plates to the final gap width in the case of the board materials (Min-K TE1400 and Fiberfrax T-30LR) or to the smallest gap that could be accommodated on the test setup (0.75in) in the case of Fiberfrax 970-H. Measurements were taken in sequence at 40°C, 100°C, 200°C, and 300°C. Data was taken in descending order as well at the same temperatures to check for any hysteresis that may have occurred due to water loss during the test. Four measurements were taken at each temperature.

Further experiments were conducted on the Min-K material to ascertain the effect of alternate gaseous environments. An additional chamber was designed to house the sensor and sample stack. The chamber was connected to a gas manifold with both a vacuum and gas port. Electrical connections were passed through the walls of the chamber with hermetic feedthroughs such that the purity of the gas in the chamber could be maintained. For these tests, measurements were taken both in a helium environment (ultra-high purity grade, 99.999% pure) and in partial vacuum (0.12 psia). Before each test, the stack gap was set in the same fashion as for the other tests.

Pore Size Distribution Measurements

Microporous insulations such as Min-K products are manufactured to have pore sizes on the order of the mean free path of air. This reduces the effectiveness of the gas phase conduction, thereby reducing the overall thermal conductivity of the insulation. To accurately model this effect, the pore size distribution of the material needs to be known to accurately capture the high Knudsen number regime effects. Furthermore, it is beneficial to know what percentage of the pores are in the high Knudsen number (pores less than ~70nm) and continuum regimes. Lastly, the effect of compression on the pore size distribution would need to be considered for a truly rigorous model.

To this end, BET (i.e. nitrogen sorption) measurements of Min-K samples were performed on a Micromeritics Tri-Star Plus instrument. The samples were prepared using the standard procedures outlined in the Micromeritics manuals. They were compressed to different thicknesses by holding them under pressures of 400 to 500 psi for varying lengths of time so that changes in pore sizes versus compression could be determined. Figure 2 shows the pore volume associated with each pore diameter up to 200nm measured by BET in Min-K samples compressed to different levels.

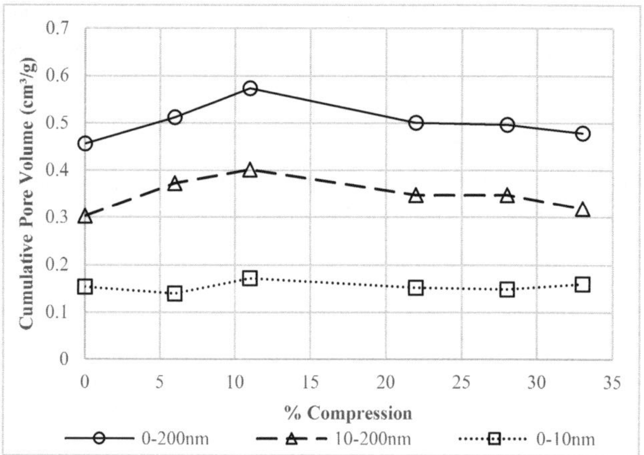

Figure 2: BET measured cumulative pore volume in various pore size ranges in pre-compressed Min-K TE1400

A few key points can be taken from this data. Firstly, pores less than 10nm in diameter are largely unaffected by compression up to 33%. Pores of this size contribute to heat transfer in the free-molecular Knudsen regime, and the contribution of these pores to the thermal conductivity of the material is unchanged by compression. From 10nm to 200nm, a peak in the cumulative pore volume occurs at ~11% compression. Pores of this size contribute to heat transfer in the "transitional" regime, and still significantly decrease conductivity. The peak in transitional pores at 11% for Min-K leads to a minimum thermal conductivity near this compression as will be seen in the following section.

Insulation Thermal Conductivity Model

The insulation conductivity model is based on published effective medium model for porous media [5]. For a two-phase medium, the effective thermal conductivity is calculated as:

$$\left(1-\varepsilon\right)\frac{k_s-k_e}{k_s+2k_m}+\varepsilon\frac{k_a-k_e}{k_a+2k_m}=0 \qquad (1)$$

where k_e, k_s, k_a, and k_m are the effective, solid phase, gaseous phase, and suspension medium thermal conductivities, respectively, and ε is the material porosity. The Series, Parallel, Maxwell-Eucken (ME) I and II, and EMT models, shown in Figure 3, can be represented explicitly by the proper selection of k_m (k_m=0, ∞, k_s, k_a, and k_e, respectively).

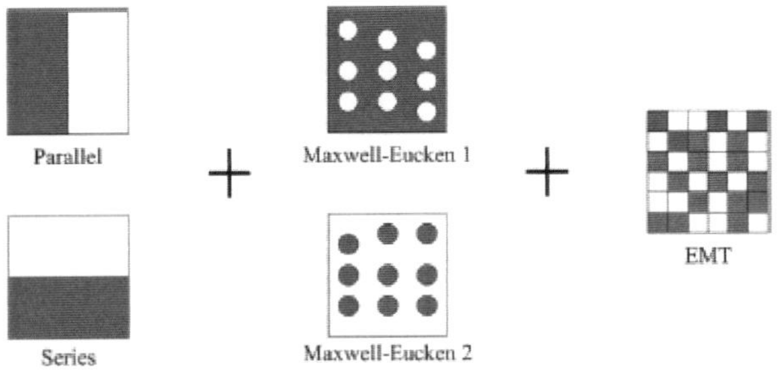

Figure 3: Fundamental effective medium material structures [5]. Heat transfer from bottom to top

The effect of compression is captured with changes to the porosity as:

$$\varepsilon = 1 - \frac{\rho_{bulk}}{\rho_{solid}} \frac{1}{(1-C)} \qquad (2)$$

where C is the compression ratio (i.e. sample strain). The effect of temperature is largely captured by the temperature dependence of the solid and gaseous phases. However, as k_m represents the thermal conductivity of the dispersing material, this parameter should not be constant with temperature. To this end, k_m was related to the solid and gas phase thermal conductivities through an additional material form factor as:

$$k_m(T) = \omega \cdot k_a(T) + (1-\omega) \cdot k_s(T) \qquad (3)$$

where ω is a constant material structure identifier. In this way, k_m can maintain a consistent material structure representation while also varying with changes in temperature.

Additional Considerations for Min-K

Min-K materials employ a nanostructure comprised of fumed silica particles. The features of the material structure are much smaller than the mean free path of most gases at standard temperature and pressure. This necessitates additional considerations to account for rarefaction effects on the gaseous thermal conductivity component.

The following equation proposed by Kaganer to estimate the gas thermal conductivity as a function of material pore diameter (i.e. Knudsen number) was used [6]:

$$k_{a,Kn} = \frac{k_{a,o}}{1 + 2\beta \dfrac{\lambda}{d_m}} \qquad (4)$$

where $k_{g,o}$ is the standard gas thermal conductivity, λ is the mean free path of the gas, and d_m is the pore diameter of the material and β is a function of the gas specific heat ratio and thermal accommodation coefficient [6]. The mean free path of the gas as a function of temperature and pressure can be estimated from kinetic theory as:

$$\lambda = \frac{RT}{\sqrt{2}\pi d_k^2 N_A P} \qquad (5)$$

where P and T are the environmental pressure and temperature, respectively, and d_k is the kinetic diameter of the gas molecules. This model has been shown to capture the effect of the Knudsen number on the thermal conductivity of air across a wide range of Knudsen numbers, and has also been used effectively to model conductivity through microporous materials [7].

For the material pore diameter, the BET measurement of the uncompressed material was referenced. Lastly, it was assumed that some fraction of the pores could be large enough so as not to be affected by Knudsen effects such that the final estimation of the gas thermal conductivity was:

$$k_{a,eff} = X_i \cdot k_{a,Kn} + (1 - X_i) k_{a,o} \qquad (6)$$

where X_i is the percentage of pores in the Knudsen conductivity regime.

Test and Modeling Results

The material form factor, ω, was tuned with the air data for each material. For Min-K, X_i was taken to be 0.97 (i.e. nearly all pores are in the free-molecular/transition Knudsen regimes). After tuning, the thermal conductivity model captures the main features of the data well, with the average difference between the model and data being 7% across all the cases. The modeled trend with changes in compression and temperature agrees with the trends seen in the experimental data for all the materials, though the model tends to overpredict the experimental results slightly, as can be seen in Figure 4.

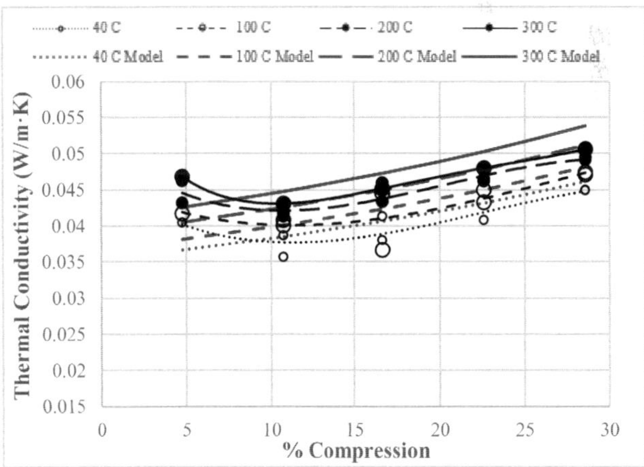

Figure 4: Experimental and modeled thermal conductivity of Min-K TE1400 in helium at varying compressions and temperatures

Figure 4 shows both the experimental and modeling results for Min-K in a helium environment. One shortcoming is that the model cannot predict the dip in thermal conductivity seen experimentally in air and helium environments with Min-K, likely caused by the peak in transitional Knudsen pore diameters in the material. A material compaction model and knowledge of the full pore size distribution in the material would be needed to model this effect. Further testing could enable such a modification; however, it is unrealistic to implement a thermal conductivity model into TABS that requires knowledge of the full pore size distribution.

Anisotropic Conductivity Estimates

If the specific heat of the sample is known, the axial thermal conductivity can be distinguished from the radial thermal conductivity with the results of TPS measurements [8]. The results of this calculation for the Min-K material are shown in Figure 5.

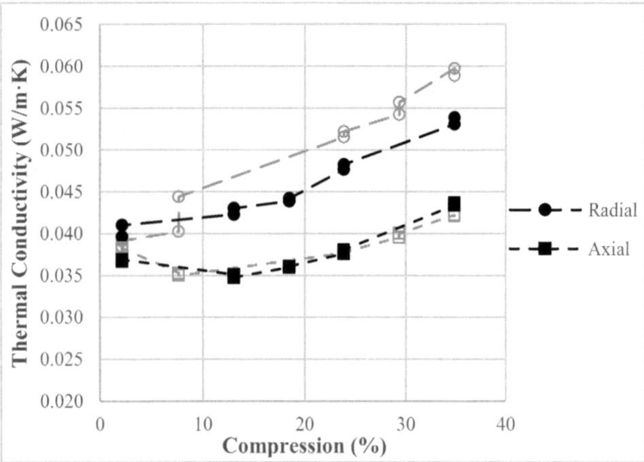

Figure 5: Axial and radial thermal conductivity calculations Min-K TE1400 at 200°C in air. Gray traces are from the first stack tested.

For all the materials tested, the radial thermal conductivity was higher than the axial thermal conductivity. This is in line with the CT scans of these materials, which show a preferential fiber alignment parallel to the material face (perpendicular to axial conduction), as shown in Figure 6.

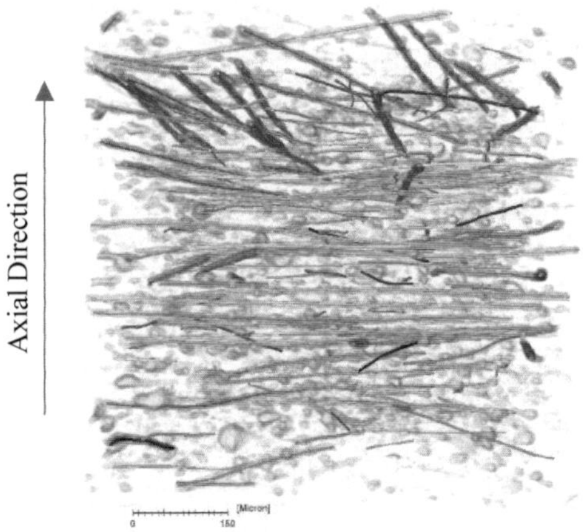

Figure 6: Analysis of fiber orientation from Min-K CT scan. Fibers are colored by their angle from the axial direction (darker is more in line with axial direction)

Conclusions

A number of efforts were applied to further the understanding of changes in insulation thermal conductivity with environmental conditions. To date, three materials have been characterized with respect to changes in temperature and compression. A model that captures these effects has been developed to improve insulation representations in TABS. Future work will include additional measurements in alternate environments and anisotropic modeling.

Acknowledgements

Sandia National Laboratories is a multimission laboratory managed and operated by National Technology & Engineering Solutions of Sandia, LLC, a wholly owned subsidiary of Honeywell International Inc., for the U.S. Department of Energy's National Nuclear Security Administration under contract DE-NA0003525. The views expressed in the article do not necessarily represent the views of the U.S. Department of Energy or the United States Government.

[1] R. A. Guidotti and P. Masset, "Thermally activated ("thermal") battery technology: Part I: An overview," *Journal of Power Sources,* vol. 161, no. 2, pp. 1443-1449, 2006/10/27/ 2006.

[2] S. A. Roberts, S. R. Harris, A. C. Hetzler, E. S. Piekos, B. B. Schroeder, and B. L. Trembacki, "Establishing the Credibility of the Thermally Activated Battery Simulator, Full-Battery Version 4: Verification, Validation and Uncertainty Quantification," Sandia National Laboratories, Albuquerque, NMSAND2017-3397, 2017, vol. SAND2017-3397.

[3] Y. Li *et al.*, "Improving the accuracy of the transient plane source method by correcting probe heat capacity and resistance influences," *Measurement Science and Technology,* vol. 25, no. 1, 2014.

[4] S. E. Gustafsson, "Transient plane source techniques for thermal conductivity and thermal diffusivity measurements of solid materials," *Review of Scientific Instruments,* vol. 62, no. 3, pp. 797-804, 1991.

[5] L. Gong, Y. Wang, X. Cheng, R. Zhang, and H. Zhang, "A novel effective medium theory for modelling the thermal conductivity of porous materials," *International Journal of Heat and Mass Transfer,* vol. 68, pp. 295-298, 2014.

[6] M. G. Kaganer, "Thermal insulation in cryogenic engineering," 1969.

[7] M. Andisheh-Tadbir, E. Kjeang, and M. Bahrami, "Thermal conductivity of microporous layers: Analytical modeling and experimental validation," *Journal of Power Sources,* vol. 296, pp. 344-351, 2015.

[8] M. Gustavsson and S. Gustafsson, "On the use of transient plane source sensors for studying materials with direction dependent properties," in *Thermal Conductivity 26: Thermal Expansion 14: Joint Conferences, August 6-8, 2001, Cambridge, Massachusetts, USA*, 2005, p. 367: DEStech Publications, Inc.

Soil-Science Mechanical/Capillary Pressure/Electrical Testing Methods applied to Molten-Salt Power-Source Separator Materials

Martin B. Nemer, Christine C. Roberts, Hans W. Papenguth, Patrick F. Fleig, Linda E. Johnson, Bernadette A. Hernandez-Sanchez, Alexander J. Headley
Sandia National Laboratories
Albuquerque, NM, USA, 87123
mbnemer@sandia.gov / 505-844-5754

Abstract: *Conventional Molten-salt-power-source designs often rely on non-cohesive-ceramic-granular materials (e.g. MgO powders) for the skeletal load-bearing portion of the separator pellet. The factors that quantitatively contribute to the ability of these materials to hold electrolyte under a mechanical load are not well understood. This lack of understanding can be rectified by applying soil mechanics to the problem. Applications of this theory include the development of new separator materials, understanding the behavior of separators in shock and vibration environments, and the development of alternative separator-pellet-processing methods.*

Keywords: thermal battery; molten-salt power source; separator; soil science; triaxial testing; uniaxial testing.

Introduction

Conventional molten-salt-power-source designs often rely on non-cohesive-ceramic granular materials (e.g. MgO powders) for the skeletal load-bearing portion of the separator pellet. The ceramic materials maintain electrical separation of the anode and cathode while allowing charge transfer via a (molten) liquid electrolyte that fills the pores between the skeletal grains. The factors that quantitatively contribute to the ability of the ceramic materials to hold electrolyte under a mechanical load are not well understood [1]. A scientific basis for separator behavior would enable searches for new materials, and would enable an understanding of current empirically obtained design limits.

Separator Axial-Deformation Tests: In 2016, axial-deformation testing was performed on 1.25" diameter salt/MgO separators over a range of salt/MgO mass ratios and at two axial loads of 8 psi and 14 psi. The separators were sandwiched between two thin mica sheets that were stapled in the corners (Figure 1). The sandwich was placed in between the two load-frame platens that were pre-heated to ≈ 500 °C. The mechanical load was fixed using a solid weight located at the top of the load frame ram. Axial displacement versus time was then measured via a Mitutoyo micrometer. The cold post-test radial displacement was measured through photography. Due to the presence of the mica sheets, flow of molten electrolyte was allowed radially but not axially.

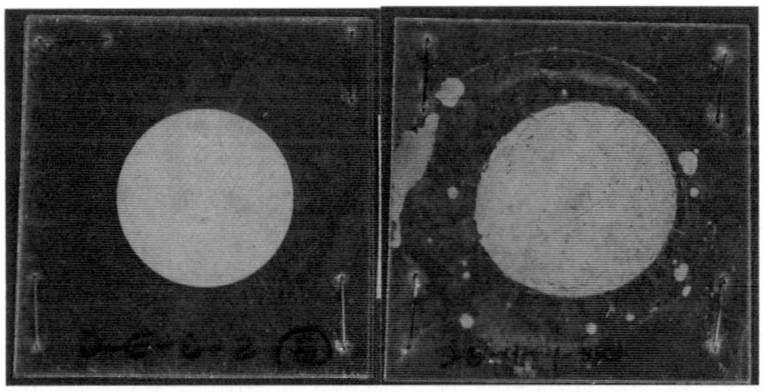

Figure 1. Cold separator pellets after deformation testing at an axial loading of 8 psi. The two pellets contained different amounts of initially air-filled porosity (24.4 %, 10.4 %, left-right respectively) and different liquid-filled void ratios after melting (e_l = 3.73, 4.64, left-right respectively). The scale of the two images is approximately equal.

The results of the separator deformation experiments are shown graphically in Figure 2 versus liquid-filled void ratio. Void ratio, *e*, is defined as the ratio of the void volume to the solid volume [2]. The liquid-filled void ratio e_l was calculated based on the initial salt/MgO mass ratio, and the decrease in density of the salt upon melting. According to Figure 2, above a liquid-filled void ratio of 3.73, the resulting deformation shows increasing axial deformation. As will be shown these observations can be explained through classical-soil-mechanics concepts of effective stress and dilation.

Effective Stress and Dilation Principles: To understand the observed axial-deformation-test results, consider a non-cohesive granular medium saturated or partially saturated with a wetting fluid as shown in Figure 3. Assume the mixture is subjected to an externally applied mean stress

$$p = \frac{1}{3}(\sigma_1 + \sigma_2 + \sigma_3), \quad (1)$$

and an externally applied shear (deviatoric) stress

$$q = \frac{1}{2}(\sigma_1 - \sigma_3), \quad (2)$$

where $\sigma_1 > \sigma_2 > \sigma_3$ are the principle externally applied stresses. In the case of a separator pellet, σ_1 scales with the axial load.

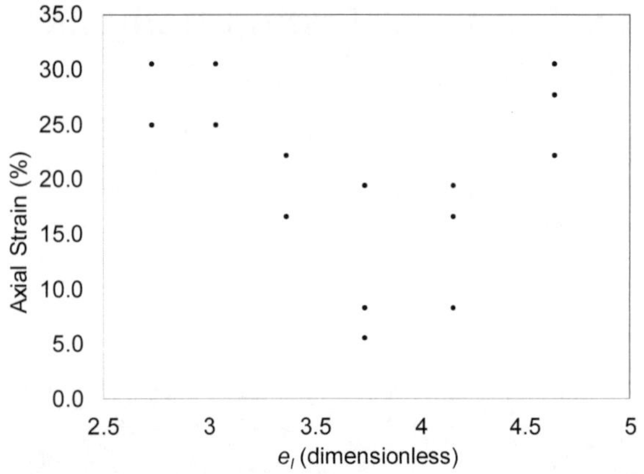

Figure 2. Separator deformation-test axial strain versus initial liquid-filled void ratio e_l. Note that in these samples air-filled porosity decreases with increased liquid-filled void ratio. All tests were performed at 8 psi of axial force.

Relative motion of the grain structure due to the applied stress is dominated by plastic rather than elastic deformations because of the large elastic modulus of the ceramic grains; i.e. significantly less work is required for the particles to slip past each other than for individual grains to deform. The resistance of the solid grains in the separator to shear motion is primarily controlled by inter-granular friction. This friction is affected by the mean stress p pressing the grains together and by the number/area of contacts between the grains.

Consider the effect of the mean stress. The larger the mean stress the greater the friction between the grains. However, in a saturated or partially saturated porous medium both the grain network and the fluid support the applied mean stress, because the fluid can support a pressure and requires time to drain due to the permeability of the medium. Only the solid grain network can statically support an applied shear stress, as a (Newtonian) fluid cannot withstand a shear stress without generating corresponding fluid motion.

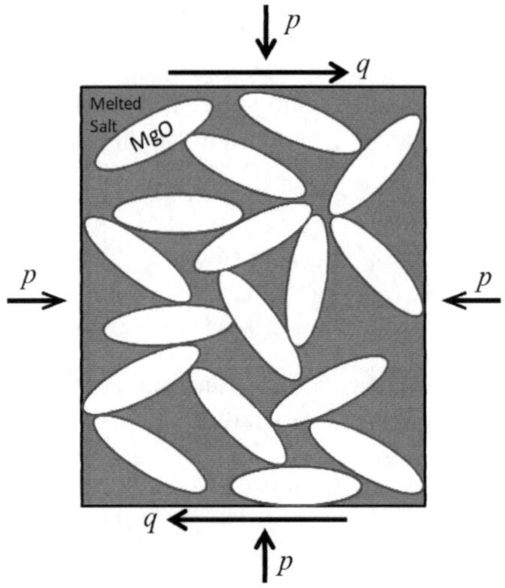

Figure 3. Schematic of a saturated granular medium under both a mean externally applied stress p and an externally applied shear stress q.

Thus when a mechanical load is rapidly applied to a saturated porous medium comprised of non-cohesive grains and a large fraction of fluid-filled porosity (e.g. a soil or a separator), the fluid pressure initially balances a significant portion of the externally applied mean pressure, reducing the friction between the solid grains. This effect is called the effective stress principle [3],

$$p = p' + p_{pore} \tag{3}$$

where p_{pore} is the fluid pressure in the pore space, and p' is the effective stress pressing the grains together. Hence if $p \approx p_{pore}$, and a shear stress also applied, the medium loses its cohesion and flows radially outward (e.g. Figure 1 right). The effective-stress phenomena is similarly used to explain landslides that occur after heavy rains [4].

Consider the effect of the number/area of contacts between the grains. This is affected by contraction and dilation of the medium as a whole. If the medium volumetrically contracts (e.g. by losing electrolyte to the anode and cathode under a mechanical load), the grains move closer together increasing interlocks that increase contact and thus friction to shear motion. The opposite effect occurs with dilation, where the grains move farther apart lessening the friction between them. It's well established that contractions and dilations cause large changes in the shear strength [5].

Interpretation of Separator Axial-Deformation Tests: Understanding gained from the soil-science literature clarifies why decreasing the air-filled pore space in a separator could cause deformation to increase. Less air-filled porosity provides less space for the increased volume of the salt upon melting. The separator must then either expel fluid or dilate. Because the fluid permeability of the separator is relatively low and fluid expansion upon melting is fast, dilation of the pellet occurs before the fluid can drain. Hence the separator expands (dilates) slightly, the grains move apart and the network is less able to support the shear stress compared to separators containing more air-filled porosity. The same argument can be made in the case of separators containing an increased salt/MgO mass ratio (i.e. liquid void ratio). Greater liquid-filled void space means that the particles are initially further apart, which equates to less inter-granular friction. Separators containing a higher salt/MgO mass ratio and less air-filled porosity will have more deformation than either effect alone, which corresponds to the case shown in Figure 1-Figure 2.

Soil-Science Testing Methods: With the success of applying soil mechanics to explaining separator-deformation-test results, a logical question is whether soil-mechanics-testing methods can be used to obtain additional information that would allow optimization of separator performance. Examples include diagnosing and understanding the bulk properties of separator/fluid combinations prior to building a battery or single-cell tests, comparing the mechanical and ionic permeability of different separator materials, comparing different salt/solid ratios, comparing different initial saturation levels, the ability to experimentally study shock and vibration, and modeling of existing batteries.

Traditional soil testing methods include tri-axial testing and uni-axial testing of saturated and partially saturated samples. In tri-axial testing a sample of material is first partially saturated and placed within a thin latex cylindrical membrane. The sample length should be at least twice the diameter to ensure that the stresses applied will be in the principle directions; i.e. that a shear plane does not develop normal to the cylinder axis. The sample plus membrane is placed in a tri-axial cell shown in Figure 4, which allows the sample to be subjected to an axisymmetric stress state

Figure 4. Image of an MgO sample loaded into the tri-axial apparatus. The sample diameter was 1.4".

with axial loading equal to σ_1, and the radial confining stress equal to $\sigma_2 = \sigma_3$. The pore pressure p_{pore} within the sample is independently controlled via a syringe pump, which can be used to simulate a separator that can allow fluid to flow axially (as in a battery), axially and radially, or not at all (similar to a deformation test); these configurations are called consolidated drained (CD) and consolidated undrained (CU) respectively in the soil-science literature [2]. The term consolidated here means that samples are initially subjected to a mean externally applied stress state $p = \sigma_3$, $q = 0$, where σ_3 is the confining stress that will be applied during the shear portion of the test. Fluid is allowed to drain from the sample during consolidation such that constant pore-pressure is maintained. Consolidation is performed to ensure that shearing (deviatoric) portion of the test ($q > 0$) begins with the sample in a state of mechanical equilibrium with the initial condition of $p = \sigma_3$, $q = 0$.

Uni-axial testing involves putting a sample into a rigid cylinder with porous axial end caps. This setup allows control over the axial load and in some systems the pore pressure, but no control over the radial confining stress. Instead, the boundary condition is no radial strain. Electrical conductivity and impedance spectroscopy can be accomplished with this cell by means of an electrically conductive non-aqueous fluid such as propylene carbonate plus LiBr; the confining cylinder (a.k.a confining ring) is made out of a non-conductive material for electrical measurements.

Triaxial Results

Tri-axial experiments were performed using apparatus obtained from Trautwein Soil Testing Equipment Co. Clearco 5cSt Silicone fluid was used as the permeant, and the same fluid was used to apply the confining stress. Silicone fluid was chosen because it strongly wets the MgO and is non-reactive. Samples were jacketed using a thin latex membrane. The MgO plus silicone oil were mixed together using a spatula and then gently molded into a cylinder using a Teflon mold and Teflon piston. The sample was assembled in layers, per ASTM guidelines on tri-axial testing of soils [6]. Alumina (Al_2O_3) porous frits were placed on the two axial ends of the sample.

Prior to testing, the sample was fully saturated (i.e. air was removed) by applying liquid backpressure to the pore space until the B-test value was nearly equal to one, per ASTM guidelines [6]. The idea is to increase the fluid pressure in order to force gas remaining in the pore space to dissolve into the permeant fluid; silicone oil can dissolve a significant volume of air as the pressure is increased [7].

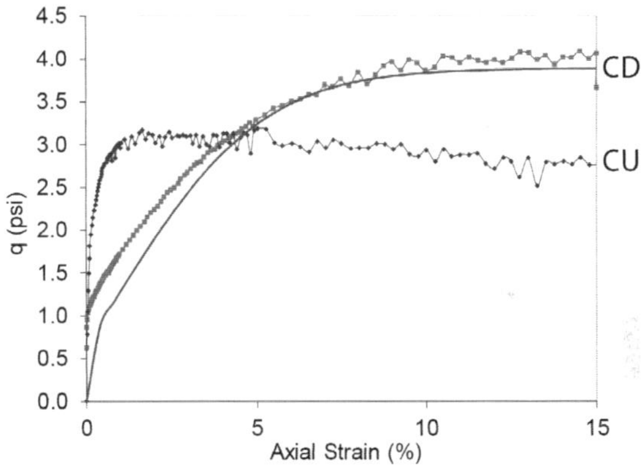

Figure 5. Tri-axial shear data on an MgO under constant-volume (CU; blue symbols) and constant pore-pressure (CD; red symbols) conditions, modeled using Cam-Clay (red solid line). The confining stress was 1.5 psi in both runs. Note that the CU experiment was run to 30% axial strain with the data past 15% not shown.

Figure 5 shows a typical tri-axial test of MgO under constant volume (CU) and constant pore pressure (CD) conditions, with a confining stress of 1.5 psi, which is close to the minimum confining stress that can be accurately measured with the equipment used. The blue symbols shows data for constant volume (CU) conditions, and the red symbols shows data for constant pore pressure (CD) conditions. The red solid curve (no symbols) is the result of an elastic-plastic simulation using the Cam-Clay yield surface [2] in ABAQUS. Ultimate failure is defined as the point where the slope of the curve goes to zero, i.e. increasing deformation can continue at a constant shear stress. The plot shows that the shear strength at failure is similar (3-4 psi) for the two samples, however the constant volume (CU) sample fails almost immediately in axial strain whereas the constant pore-pressure (CD) sample fails gradually and is not completely flat at 15% axial strain.

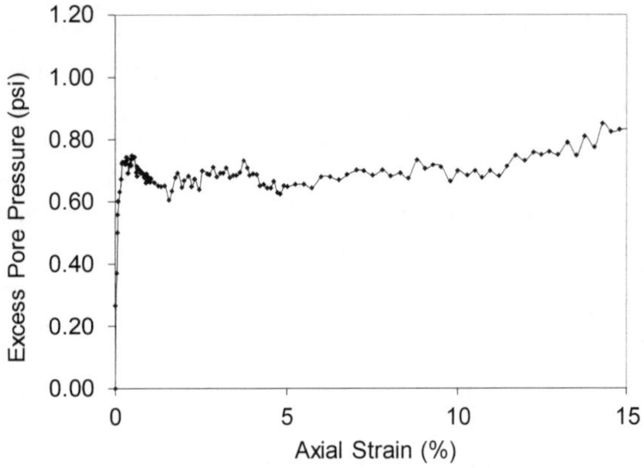

Figure 6. Pore pressure response of the CU sample.

The pore-pressure response of the CU samples is shown in Figure 6. The pore-pressure rises rapidly at small axial strain and then grows slightly with further strain. The magnitude of the pore pressure in Figure 6 is significant as with a confining stress of 1.5 psi, the pore-pressure has reduced the initial effective stress on the grains by more than half. Simultaneously, the shear stress continues to increase per the test configuration. Hence it's understandable that the material fails quickly.

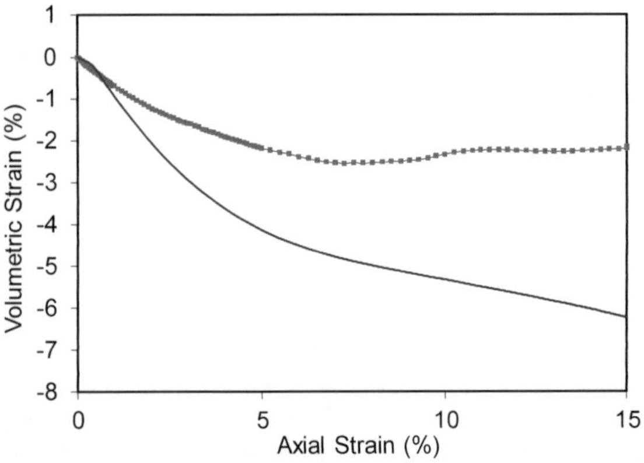

Figure 7. Volume response of the CD sample (red symbols), modeled using Cam-Clay (red solid line).

The volumetric drainage of the CD sample is shown in Figure 7, with symbols from the experimental data, and the solid line (no symbols) from the ABAQUS simulation. The sample contracts until 7-8% axial strain at which point it begins to dilate. This point corresponds to the beginning of failure for the CD sample as seen in Figure 5. While the sample is contracting it gains shear strength due to the increasing interlocking of grains. Once the sample can no longer contract, the friction between the grains stops significantly increasing while the externally applied shear stress continues to increase, which accounts for this point being the onset to failure. Future work will include improving the model, particularly with respect to volumetric contraction.

Conclusions

Herein we have demonstrated that classical soil-science concepts can explain observations on the mechanical behavior of thermal-battery separator pellets that rely on non-cohesive-ceramic-skeletal materials. We have also shown that triaxial testing, which is well established in the soil-science community, provides a more complete assessment of separator behavior compared to traditional deformation testing. This understanding is critical for understanding current design performance and will enable improvements in battery designs.

Acknowledgements

Sandia National Laboratories is a multimission laboratory managed and operated by National Technology & Engineering Solutions of Sandia, LLC, a wholly owned subsidiary of Honeywell International Inc., for the U.S. Department of Energy's National Nuclear Security Administration under contract DE-NA0003525. The views expressed in the article do not necessarily represent the views of the U.S. Department of Energy or the United States Government.

References

1. Guidotti, R.A. and F.W. Reinhardt, "Characterization of Electrolyte-Binder Mixes for Use in Thermal Batteries," Albuquerque, NM: Sandia National Laboratories, SAND90-2103, 1991.
2. Wood, D.M., "Soil Behavior and Critical State Soil Mechanics," Cambridge, U. K.: Cambridge University Press, 1990.
3. Terzaghi, K., "Theoretical Soil Mechanics," New York, New York: Wiley, 1943.
4. Holtz, R.D., W.D. Kovacs, and T.C. Sheahan, "An Introduction to Geotechnical Engineering," Second Edition, New Jersey: Pearson, 2011.
5. Jin, Y.-F., et al., "Estimation of Critical State-Related Formula in Advanced Consitutive Modeling of Granular Material," *Acta Geotechnica,* vol 12, pp. 1329-1351, 2017.
6. ASTM International, "Standard Test Method for Consolidated Undrained Triaxial Compression Test for Cohesive Soils," D4767-11, 2011.
7. Roberts, C.C., et al., "Physical Properties of Low-Molecular Weight Polydimethylsiloxane Fluids," Albuquerque, NM: Sandia National Laboratories, SAND2017-1242, 2017.

Advanced Electrolyte Solvents to Enable High Energy Lithium Ion Batteries

Tobias O. Johnson, Monica L. Usrey, Peng Du, Deborah J. Gilbert
Silatronix®, Inc.
3587 Anderson St, Suite 108, Madison WI 53704
tjohnson@silatronix.com / 1-608-661-1961

Abstract: *Silatronix® has developed new organosilicon (OS) solvent materials with molecular designs targeted for superior electrochemical characteristics. The inclusion of Si in the molecule has proved essential for improved thermal and electrochemical stability. Several OS solvent materials have demonstrated excellent performance in Lithium Ion Battery (LIB) systems. Silatronix® has now commercialized production of an advanced OS solvent "OS3®" that provides exceptional thermal, and high voltage electrochemical stability in current commercial LIB systems up to 4.5V; and fundamental oxidation stability up to 7V. OS3® is a strong coordinator of Li salts in electrolyte solution and prevents $LiPF_6$ salt decomposition and catalytic production of HF; which is critical to enablement of high energy LIB systems with long calendar life and excellent high temperature performance. Comprehensive LIB cell performance benefits have been observed with OS solvents; including excellent HT cycling stability, reduced impedance growth, improved calendar life rate capability, reduced gas generation, reduced pouch cell swelling, improved safety / abuse response, and improved low temperature rate capability.*

Keywords: electrolyte; Lithium Ion; solvent; organosilicon; OS; OS3®; LIB; high voltage; high temperature; thermal stability; oxidation; reduction; impedance; safety; solvation; $LiPF_6$; Lithium; SEI; solid electrolyte interphase; energy storage; DSC; ONR; NCA; Silicon; Si; SiO; NMC; graphite; gassing; LTO; NAVAIR; ONR; Office of Naval Research; Navy; DOD; battery; cell; molecule; electrochemical; electrochemistry; fluorine; anode; cathode; cycling; calendar; activation; energy

Introduction

Silatronix® has developed a series of new organosilicon materials over years of improvements to molecular design and targeted electrochemically functional characteristics. Design of unique organosilicon molecules includes selection of specific ion coordinating functional groups, degree of fluorination, and optimization of geometric structure to balance molecular polarity, ionic conductivity, and viscosity. The inclusion of Si in the molecule has proved to be essential for maintaining improved thermal and electrochemical stability. Geometric design of the molecule directly affects solvation sphere coordination in electrolyte solution, and activation energy for solvation/de-solvation and intercalation into electrode structures. Fortunately, several OS solvent materials have demonstrated excellent performance in Lithium Ion Battery (LIB) systems.

Currently Silatronix® has commercialized production of an advanced OS solvent "OS3®" that provides exceptional thermal, and high voltage electrochemical stability in LIB systems up to 4.5V in current commercially available electrode materials; and fundamental oxidation stability up to 7V in a platinum cell. OS3® also has low viscosity, good ionic conductivity, a high flash point >80°C, and low freezing point <-55°C. The most comprehensive performance benefits have been observed at <5% OS3® composition, which is fortunate for commercialization of OS3®, as this level fits comfortably within the additive market space of the LIB industry.

OS3® is a strong coordinator of Li salts in electrolyte solution and has proven to prevent both decomposition of $LiPF_6$ and catalytic production of HF in particular; which is critical to enablement of the high energy LIB systems with long calendar life and excellent high temperature performance. This mechanism protects many components in LIB cell systems and long-term impedance growth is systematically reduced. Additionally, DSC thermal response of charged cathode materials with OS electrolytes have shown reduced peak heating rate and delayed exotherm onset temperatures.

Several commercial cell development partners in the US, Asia, and Europe have observed practical improvements to comprehensive battery cell performance; including excellent HT cycling stability, reduced impedance growth, improved calendar life rate capability, reduced gas generation, reduced pouch cell swelling, improved safety / abuse response, and improved low temperature rate capability. Benefits have been observed in various cathode and anode systems including LCO, NMC, LFP, NCA, graphite, LTO, SiO, Si, and composites; among others. There is a specific synergy between Si anodes and OS3® for improved cycling stability, lower impedance, and protection of the Si anode structure.

Full format cell level testing and fundamental research of OS technology has been completed with ONR funding on several programs, including both shipboard and NAVAIR targeted applications. Currently active ONR development programs include optimization of a new high energy NCA based MH-60 battery. OS3® has demonstrated improved cycling stability, low temperature rate capability, and lower impedance during the first half of the work; with full MH-60 battery module demonstration for safety improvements yet to come. Fundamental research of the LTO anode system is also in process and has already shown improvements to high temperature cycling stability, reduced solvation activation energy, and reduced impedance growth with OS3®.

Results and Discussion

OS Molecular Design for Thermal and Electrochemical Stability

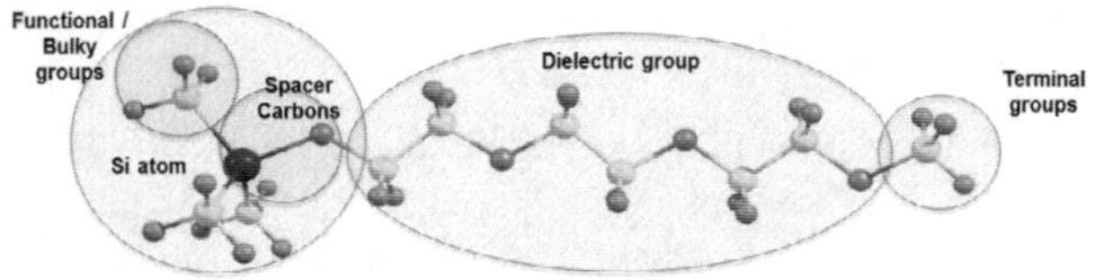

Figure 1. Organosilicon (OS) example molecular design

Organosilicon (OS) materials from Silatronix® feature intrinsic molecule design to target excellent thermal and electrochemical stability. These characteristics are well suited to state of the art Lithium Ion Battery (LIB) systems. To date, several OS solvent materials have demonstrated excellent performance in LIB cells. Silatronix® has commercialized their first product OS3® and is currently developing next generation cell designs with several cell manufacturing partners in the USA, Europe, and Asia. OS3® has demonstrated several fundamental improvements within LIB battery systems.

The fundamental OS3® mechanism stabilizes dissociated $LiPF_6$ salt within the electrolyte solution solvation structure, preventing $LiPF_6$ decomposition. OS3® also scavenges initial HF levels from the entire battery system and can reduce initial HF levels to <5ppm over time. Figure 2 shows HF levels in bulk electrolyte samples stored in NMR tubes at 100°C. Without OS3®, HF increased to >10,000 ppm after only 18 days. The control sample ruptured after 18 days due to excessive gas generation. HF is reduced to <5ppm for all OS3® containing electrolytes and samples remained intact for >1year. $LiPF_6$ salt is ubiquitous to most LIB systems, so OS3® can provide improvements to many chemistries.

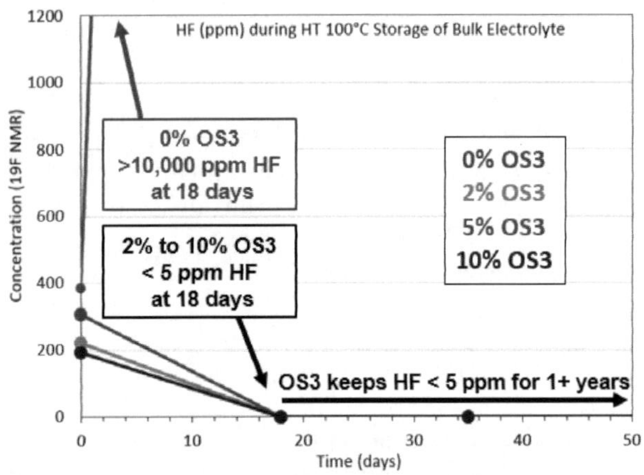

Figure 2. HF concentration in EC/DEC/$LiPF_6$/OS3® electrolytes during HT storage

The OS3® molecular structure includes nitrile functionality and fluorination. The full structure is balanced to provide excellent high voltage stability, reductive passivation, thermal stability, low reactivity, low viscosity, high conductivity, high flash point / boiling point, and low vapor pressure (Table 1).

Several variations within the same functional OS family are synthesized to target specific physical and electrochemical characteristics. Figure 3 shows fundamental oxidation stability (Pt) for several OS materials within the OS3® family.

Table 1. Physical Characteristics of OS3®

Dielectric	Flash	BP	FP	SG	Visc.
16.8	82°C	202°C	-57°C	0.93	2.0cP

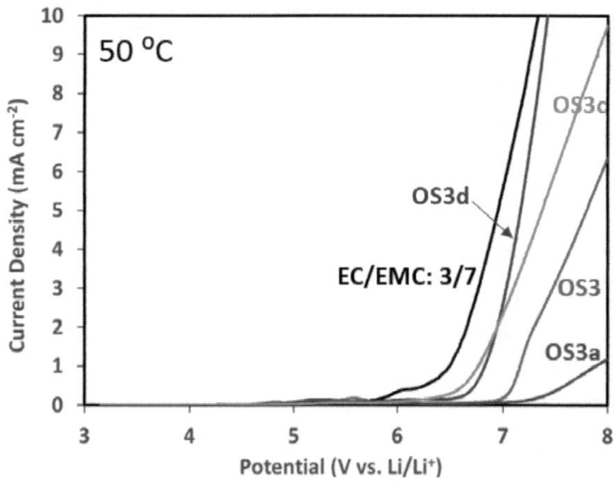

Figure 3. OS3® solvent family oxidative stability (Pt)

Table 2. Activation Energy with LTO anode

Electrolytes With 1M $LiPF_6$	E_{ct} Activation Energy (measured at -20°C to 20°C)
PC/EMC: 2/8v%	47.7 kJ/mol
+5% OS3®	45.0 kJ/mol

OS3® has strong solvation of Lithium salts in solution, and the activation energy for solvation of Li^+ into the anode is reduced when OS3® is added to a carbonate control electrolyte. The LTO anode system in particular shows a significant reduction in activation energy as shown Table 2.

OS3® does passivate reductively, but does not form an effective SEI on the anode. Thus, OS3® allows traditional film forming electrolyte components and additives to form an effective low impedance anode SEI. Furthermore, OS3® prevents continuous calendar life growth of SEI thickness, to maintain low cell impedance. Breakdown of $LiPF_6$ salt and carbonate co-solvents is prevented by OS3®, so decomposition products do not continuously deposit on the anode. This mechanism can provide fundamental thermal stability improvements to many LIB systems.

OS materials have also demonstrated the ability to reduce the thermal response of electrodes (DSC), with reduced peak heating rate and increased exotherm onset temperature, for improved safety and abuse tolerance in full format batteries. DSC testing of the high energy NMC622 cathode found much lower peak heating rates and increased onset temperature (Figure 4) with 20% OS3® solvent. Several cell development partners have reported improved safety test results with low concentrations of OS3®; in the 1% to 5% range.

Full format cell safety tests demonstrated improved nail penetration and ARC results with higher concentrations of OS solvents in the 4.2V NCA/graphite (nail), and 3.8V LFP/graphite system (ARC). ARC results in Figure 5 show reduced peak heating rate for OS electrolyte in LFP cylindrical cells. Current development seeks to continue validation of full format cell safety and abuse resistance at the module level in the NCA/graphite chemistry.

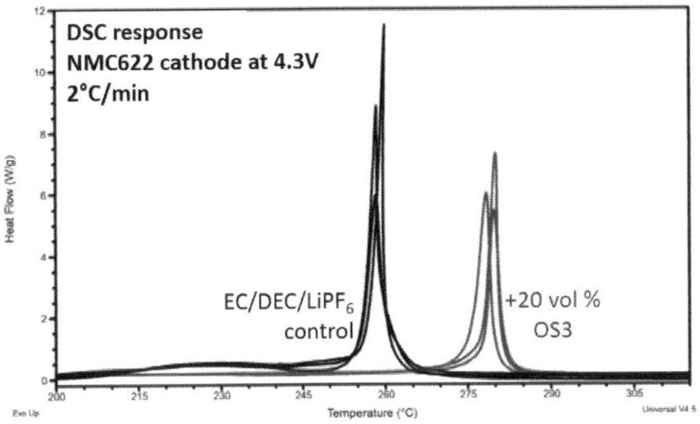

Figure 4. DSC response of OS materials with NMC cathode

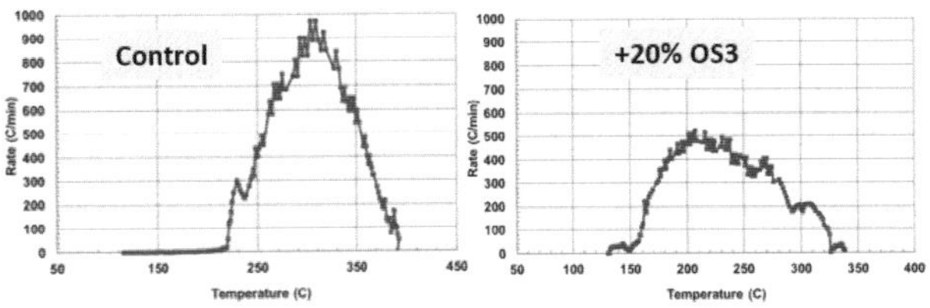

Figure 5. ARC heating rate for LFP/graphite cylindrical cells (Sandia National Lab testing for ONR contract)

Lithium Ion Battery (LIB) Cell Performance

OS solvents have demonstrated comprehensive performance improvements to several LIB cell systems. The most significant improvements have been found in high temperature and high voltage (>4.2V) applications with commercial LCO and high Nickel cathode materials. These systems are very attractive for portable and motive power applications that require high energy density. Observed full format cell benefits include HT cycling stability, reduced impedance growth, calendar life rate capability, reduced gas generation, improved safety / abuse response, and improved low temperature rate capability.

Recent testing has demonstrated an excellent balance of comprehensive cell performance at a low concentration of OS3®, in the 0.5% to 5.0% range. Individual system optimization is required in each case due to the wide variety of active materials, electrolyte formulation interaction, and other cell material interactions. Figure 6 shows the lowest initial impedance was found with 2% OS3® in the 4.30V NMC622/graphite system. After HT testing, impedance improvements with OS3® are often even larger. Figure 7 shows a major reduction in impedance growth with 2% and 1% OS3® after 300 cycles at HT in the 4.35V NMC622/graphite system.

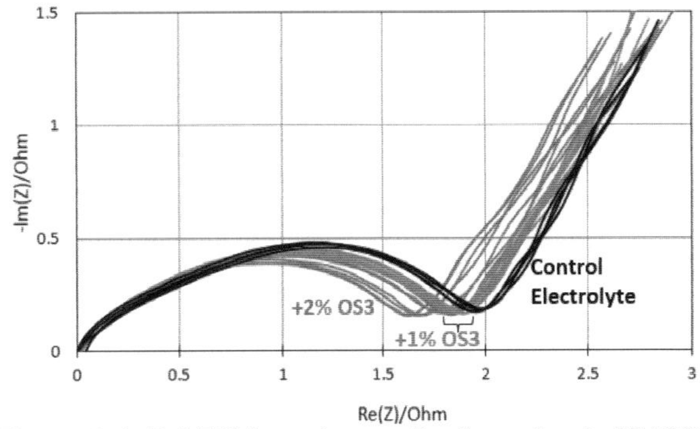

Figure 6. Initial EIS Impedance after formation in NMC622 /graphite (single layer pouch, 4.30V)

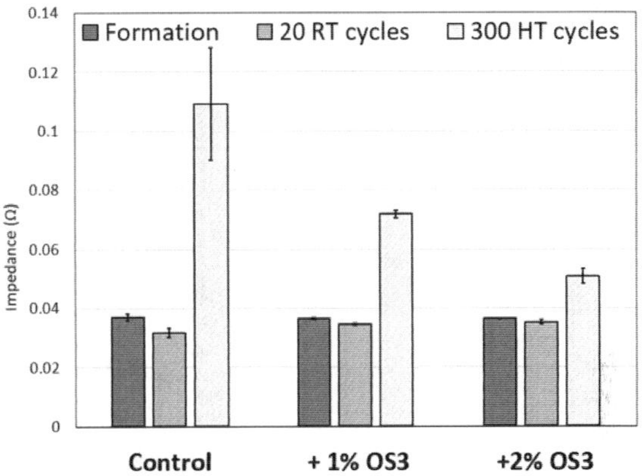

Figure 7. EIS Impedance after 300 cycles at 45°C NMC622/graphite (650mAh pouch cell, 4.35V)

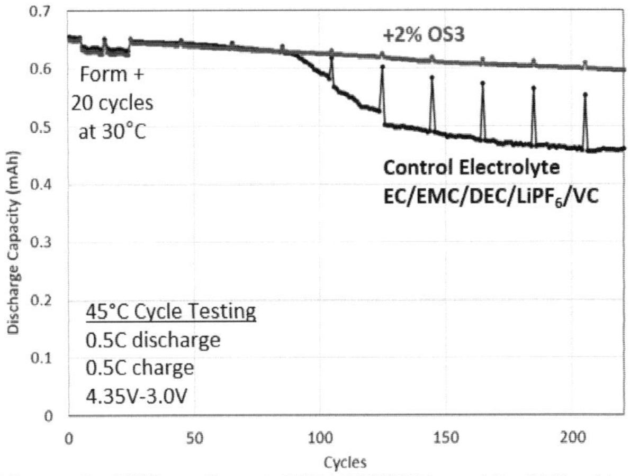

Figure 8. 45°C cycling, 4.35V NMC622/graphite 650mAh pouch cells

HT cycling stability is shown for the same 4.35V NMC622/graphite pouch system in Figure 8. OS3® enabled this high energy density, high nickel NMC622 cathode system to perform at high voltage and high temperature. Under very challenging conditions, the addition of only 2% OS3® to control electrolyte enabled excellent HT cycling stability, compared to rapid degradation of the control.

Significant commercial interest in OS3® is driven by reduced gassing, critical for high energy density pouch cells in consumer electronics and automotive applications. Reduced gassing has been observed in many LIB systems; including LCO/graphite, NMC/graphite, Si and LTO anode systems. Figure 9 shows significantly reduced pouch gassing after HT storage in the LCO / LTO system; as tested by Silatronix® within an ONR contract.

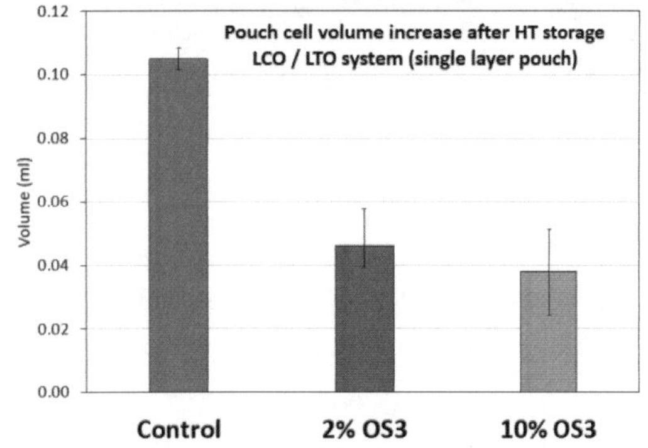

Figure 9. Pouch cell gassing after 70°C storage in LCO/LTO system (1 mo. at 2.8V, 100%SOC)

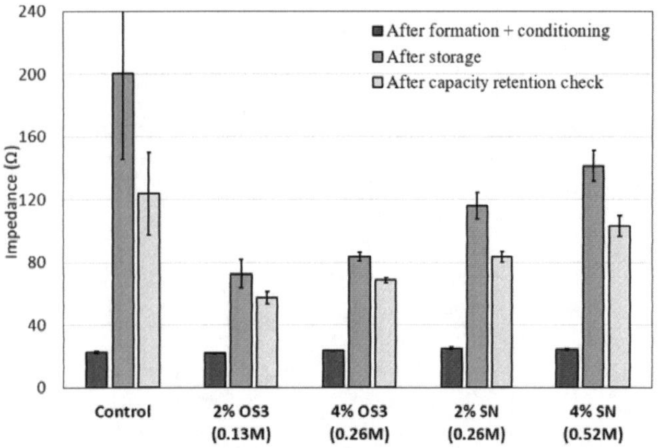

Figure 10. Cell impedance after 60°C Storage in LCO/graphite system (1 mo. at 4.40V, 100% SOC)

OS3® is often benchmarked for performance compared to traditional Nitrile additives due to their popularity in HV systems. Silatronix® has found that OS3® has the capability to demonstrate similar improvements to cycling stability and reduced gassing at HV, but with significantly reduced impedance compared to commercial nitrile additives like succinonitrile (SN) or adiponitrile (ADN). In the HV LCO/graphite system OS3® significantly lowered impedance after HT storage, compared to both SN and control variations (Figure 10).

Conclusions

Organosilicon (OS) solvents have demonstrated excellent performance in Lithium Ion Battery (LIB) systems. Silatronix® commercial product "OS3®" provides exceptional thermal stability, and high voltage electrochemical stability. OS3® is a strong coordinator of Li salts in electrolyte solution and prevents $LiPF_6$ salt decomposition and catalytic production of HF; which is critical to enablement of high energy LIB systems with long calendar life and excellent high temperature performance. Comprehensive LIB cell performance benefits have been observed with OS solvents; including excellent HT cycling stability, reduced impedance growth, improved calendar life rate capability, reduced gas generation, reduced pouch cell swelling, improved safety / abuse response, and improved low temperature rate capability.

Acknowledgements

The authors wish to thank the Office of Naval Research (ONR), and the Department of Energy (DOE) for funding development contracts to advance organosilicon technology. These include ONR contracts N00014-15-C-0031, N00014-16-C-2025, and N00014-17-C-2031; and DOE contract DE-EE0007232. Additional thanks to The University of Wisconsin – Madison, Argonne National Lab, Army Research Laboratory, Sandia National Lab, and NSWC Carderock for their collaboration.

References

1. Xu, K., Lam, Zhang, Jow, Curtis, "Solvation Sheath of Li+ in Nonaqueous Electrolytes and Its Implication of Graphite/Electrolyte Interface Chemistry", *The Journal of Physical Chemistry*, 111, pp 7411-7421, 2007.
2. Yamada, Y.; Iriyama, Abe, Ogumi, "Kinetics of Lithium Ion Transfer at the Interface between Graphite and Liquid Electrolytes: Effects of Solvent and Surface Film", *Langmuir*, *25* (21), pp 12766–12770, 2009.
3. Xu, K., Cresce, Lee, "Differentiating Contributions to "Ion Transfer" Barrier from Interphasial Resistance and Li+ Desolvation at Electrolyte/Graphite Interface", Langmuir, 26 (13), pp 11538–11543, 2010.

Analysis of the Aging Mechanisms in a Commercial $LiFePO_4$/Graphite 26650 Cylindrical Cell by FIB-SEM Tomography

Roberto Scipioni[a,b]***, Peter S. Jørgensen***[b]***, Daniel I. Stroe***[c]***, Reza Younesi***[d]***, Søren B. Simonsen***[b]***, Poul Norby***[b]***, Johan Hjelm***[b]***, and Søren H. Jensen***[b]

[a] Department of Material Science and Engineering, Northwestern University, 2220 Campus Drive, Evanston, IL 60208, USA
[b] DTU Energy, Department of Energy Conversion and Storage, Technical University of Denmark, Frederiksborgvej 399, 4000 Roskilde, Denmark
[c] Department of Energy Technology, Aalborg University, Fredrik Bajers Vej 5, 9100 Aalborg, Denmark
[d] Department of Chemistry, Ångström Laboratory, Uppsala University, SE-751 21 Uppsala, Sweden
roscip@northwestern.edu / 1-847-644-8359

Abstract: *This work focuses on the understanding of the aging mechanisms that occur in a commercial $LiFePO_4$/Graphite 26650 cylindrical cell upon cycling. Two cylindrical cells, labeled "Fresh" and "Aged", were cycled respectively 5 and 22000 times and subsequently disassembled in a glovebox to harvest the electrodes. The morphological and structural changes in the $LiFePO_4$ and Graphite samples were investigated by FIB/SEM tomography, XRD and XPS. The most significant aging mechanism observed was a 1μm thick CEI (cathode electrolyte interface) layer at the electrode/electrolyte interface of the aged $LiFePO_4$ electrode. Additionally, large agglomerates of decomposition products from the electrolyte were observed on the graphite surface.*

Keywords: Battery; Li-ion; Cathode Electrolyte Interface; Degradation Mechanisms; Focused Ion Beam; Scanning Electron Microscopy.

Introduction

Limited lifetime is still a challenge for several lithium ion battery (LIB) materials and the relation between degradation mechanisms and loss of performance is still not fully understood. Loss of lithium inventory (LLI), loss of active material (LAM), loading mismatching between electrodes and decrease of the active electrode surface area are among the most common degradation processes responsible for the performance loss of Li-ion batteries [1]. However, strong links between several of the observed degradation mechanisms and the operation of the battery are still not fully established. This paper presents a comparative study of a fresh and a cycling-aged commercial $LiFePO_4$/graphite 26650 cylindrical cell. The morphology changes in the electrodes due to cycling are characterized by Focused Ion Beam (FIB) – Scanning Electron Microscopy (SEM).

Experimental

Battery cycling: Two commercial $LiFePO_4$/Graphite 26650 cylindrical cells with a nominal capacity of 2.5Ah were tested and characterized. The first battery, labeled "fresh", was cycled 5 times between 0% and 100% state-of-charge at room temperature and constant C-rate of 0.1C (250mA). The second battery, labeled "aged", was cycled 22000 times between 25% and 75% SOC at room temperature and constant C-rate of 4 (10A) and showed a capacity loss equal to 22.5%.

Battery disassembly: The two cylindrical cells were discharged to 2.8V at 250mA and subsequently disassembled in an argon filled glovebox to harvest the positive and negative electrodes. Fig. 1 shows a schematic representation of the unrolled battery configuration. The batteries consist of a 1.5m $LiFePO_4$/carbonaceous additive (LFP/CB) positive electrode casted on both sides of an aluminum foil, a 1.5m graphite (Gr) negative electrode casted on both sides of a copper foil and 2 polymeric separators soaked with liquid electrolyte.

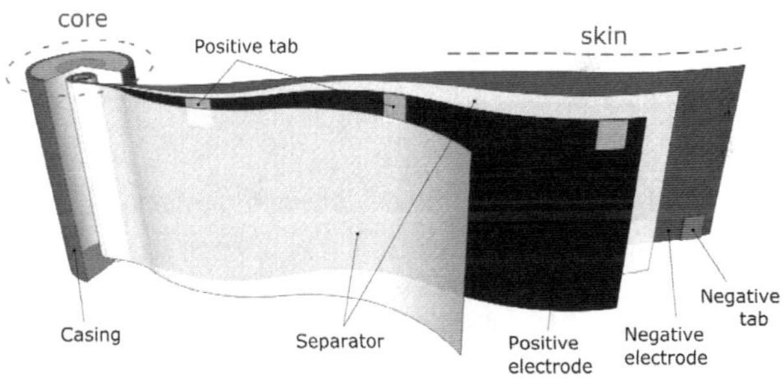

Figure 1. Schematic representation of the unrolled 26650 $LiFePO_4$/Graphite battery packaging design

Sample set preparation: The two electrode foils harvested from each cell were rinsed with diethyl carbonate and vacuum dried at 120°C for 2h to remove the liquid electrolyte. From the four electrode foils six couples of samples were cut. Two couples were cut from the fresh battery: one from the cathode foil (labeled LFP_F) and one from the anode foil (labeled Gr_F). The sample couples harvested from the aged cell were labeled with respect to their position in the foil: "_S" for the samples cut from the skin of the battery and "_C" for the ones cut from the core. Table 1 gives an overview of the couples of samples and the testing conditions for the examined cylindrical cells.

Each couple was prepared for microscopy analysis and x-ray photoelectron spectroscopy (XPS).

Table 1. Test conditions for the examined samples.

Battery	*Fresh*		*Aged*			
Cycle number	5		22000			
C-rate	0.1		4			
SOC range	0 – 100 %		25 – 75 %			
Comment	Before disassembling, fresh and aged cells were discharged to 2.8V at 250mA. Samples were cut from the washed and dried electrode rolls.					
Samples	*LFP_F*	*Gr_F*	*LFP_S*	*LFP_C*	*Gr_S*	*Gr_C*

FIB-SEM tomography: The six electrode samples were prepared for FIB-SEM analysis by vacuum infiltration with a silicon resin (Wacker Chemie) for 30 minutes to improve the phase contrast between CB particles and pores [2]. The samples were then infiltrated with epoxy resin to enable high-quality grinding and polishing of the sample. The FIB tomography and SEM imaging was carried out on a Zeiss 1540XB CrossBeam microscope, using a lateral E-T (Everhart-Thornley) detector. A Gallium FIB slicing probe of 2nA was used to mill the LFP electrodes. For the softer Gr electrodes, the current had to be reduced to 1nA to enable high-quality imaging. Table 2 shows the volume and voxel sizes of the six 3D datasets.

Image processing: Segmentation of the 3D FIB/SEM image data was performed with the program ImageJ (NIH). The Sauvola algorithm [3] was used to perform local thresholds of the data because of uneven illumination. The particle and void size distributions (PSD) in all the samples were analyzed based on the method introduced by Münch et al. [4]. Visualizations of the 3D reconstructions of the analyzed data were performed with the program Avizo (FEI).

Table 2. Volumes of the collected datasets.

Dataset	Volume (voxels) X x Y x Z	Voxel size (nm^3) X x Y x Z
LFP_F	80 x 850 x 400	27 x 15 x 15
LFP_S	81 x 870 x 450	32 x 15 x 15
LFP_C	185 x 800 x 360	14 x 15 x 15
Gr_F	328 x 750 x 150	14 x 49 x 49
Gr_S	197 x 489 x 164	15 x 59 x 59
Gr_C	381 x 920 x 130	23 x 59 x 59

X-ray photoelectron spectroscopy (XPS): The six samples were also prepared in the argon filled glove box. They were sealed under vacuum in a pouch bag and transferred into the analyzing chamber of the XPS instrument without any exposure to atmosphere using a special transfer cup. All the measurements were conducted at an in-house spectrometer (PHI 5500) using monochromatized Al Kα radiation. The XPS spectra were energy calibrated by setting the adventitious carbon peak to 285 eV.

Results

FIB-SEM: Figure 2 shows cross-sectional SEM images of the 6 electrode samples. The images were recorded with a lateral E-T detector and 1 kV acceleration voltage after FIB milling. As guidelines, on the top of Figure 2, five circles with the numbers 1,2 and 3a, 3b, and 4 are shown. The SEM images are vertically arranged such that (1) indicates an area in the SEM image showing a current collector, (2) indicates an area showing the anode, (3a) displays the region adjacent to the anode where the electrolyte filled separator sat before the battery was disassembled, (3b) show the same as 3a, but adjacent to the cathode, and (4) shows the cathode.

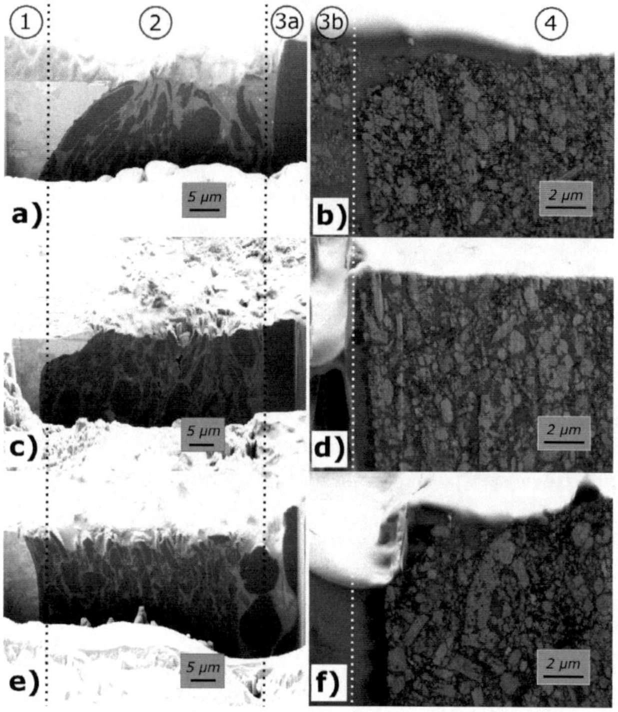

Figure 2. SEM images at 1 kV recorded with Lateral E – T detector of a) Gr_F, b) LFP_F, c) Gr_S, d) LFP_S, e) Gr_C, f) LFP_C.

All the individual SEM images are characterized by a bright region on top, which is the polished sample surface. On the front face three different phases could be distinguished in the LFP samples: light gray $LiFePO_4$ particles, dark gray pores (infiltrated with silicon resin) and black CB particles. A dark layer at the electrode/electrolyte interface of LFP_S and LFP_C is observed (Fig. 2d,f). It is assumed to be carbon and CEI layer formed by electrolyte decomposition products. This layer is thickest and most homogeneous in LFP_C. The remaining separator area in (3b) is filled with silicon resin (dark gray bulk) or epoxy resin (black bulk).

The Gr samples consist only of two phases: dark graphite particles and gray pores infiltrated with silicon resin. The darker regions on the right of the electrode areas are filled with epoxy resin, while the larger brighter areas with

Figure 3. 3D reconstructions of the segmented datasets: a) LFP_F, b) LFP_S, c) LFP_C

silicon resin. A porous structure of graphite grains characterizes all the electrode samples. However, Gr_S and Gr_C show smaller graphite particles than Gr_F, as confirmed below with PSD. Additionally, big black agglomerates are observed at the electrode/electrolyte interface of Gr_C (Fig. 2e).

3D reconstruction and structure analysis: The three-dimensional reconstructions of the segmented datasets for the 3 LFP electrodes are shown in Figure 3. The light gray particles represent LFP grains, black particles signify CB, and transparent blue show pores. For LFP_S and LFP_C a dark layer is observed at the electrode/electrolyte interface (Fig. 3b,c). The layer is approximately 0.5 μm and 1 μm thick for LFP_S and LFP_C respectively. The average sizes for particles, pores and agglomerates were retrieved from the reconstructions, and are presented in Table 3. Due to the high uncertainty on these values, no significant changes in particle size can be confirmed from this analysis.

Figure 4 shows the three-dimensional reconstructions of the segmented datasets for the 3 Gr electrodes. The orange region represents the copper current collector. In the electrode part two phases can be distinguished. Dark gray particles are graphite grains. Pores are represented as transparent blue. At the electrode/electrolyte interface of Gr_C (Fig. 4c) large agglomerates with a diameter between 5-10 μm in diameter are seen. The average sizes for particles, pores and agglomerates were retrieved from the reconstructions, and are presented in Table 3. The average Gr particle size is observed to be smaller in both the aged samples.

Table 3. Average particle diameters for the electrodes.

Phase	Average diameter [nm]		
	LFP_F	***LFP_S***	***LFP_C***
$LiFePO_4$	76	71	68
CB Additive	49	28	42
Pores	39	45	48
Agglomerates	-	141	169
	Gr_F	***Gr_S***	***Gr_C***
Graphite	1096	370	564
Pores	159	220	302
Agglomerates	-	-	875

XPS: Figure 5 shows F 1s and O 1s spectra for fresh, skin and core samples collected from both LFP and Gr electrodes. The fluorine signal is mainly generated by the PVdF binder and LiF formed by decomposition of the $LiPF_6$ salts (Figure 5a) [5]. The peak at 685 eV, attributed to LiF, has high intensity on all the graphite samples and on LFP_C. The O 1s spectra (Fig. 5b) contain at least two peaks, one at about 532 eV attributed to C=O bond in carbonates and carboxylates generated by decomposition of solvent, and another one at 534 eV attributed to C-O containing species [6]. In all the LFP sample is observed the presence of $-CO_3$ containing species on their surfaces, but a higher amount of C-O species (534 eV peak) is observed in the aged samples.

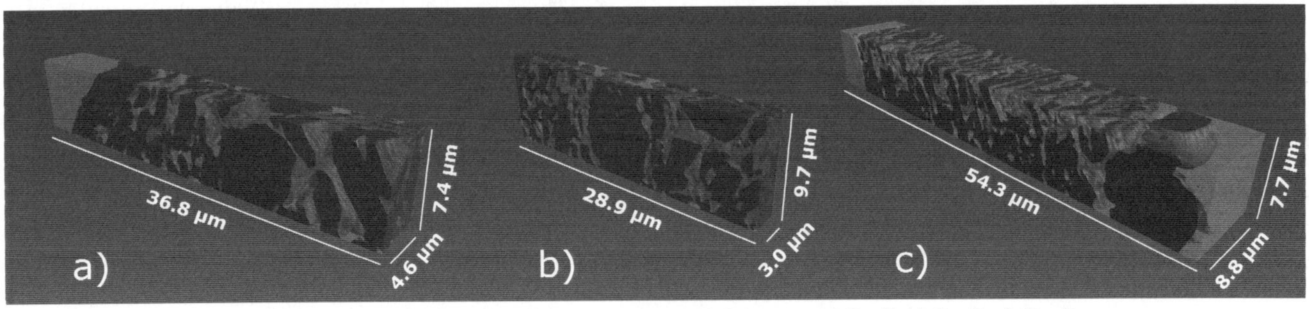

Figure 4. 3D reconstructions of the segmented datasets: a) Gr_F, b) Gr_S, c) Gr_C

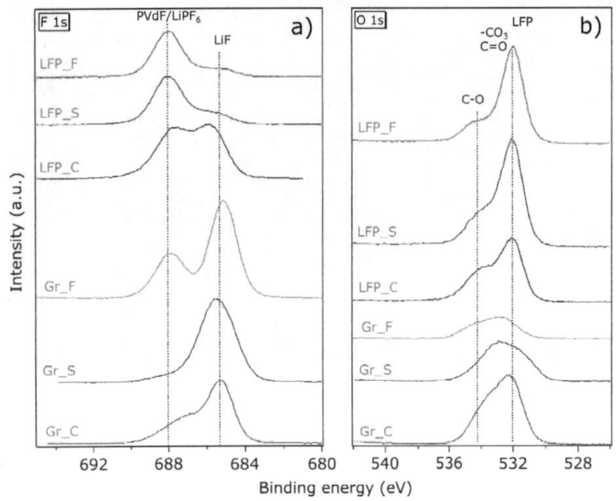

Figure 5. a) F1s and b) O1s spectra of fresh, skin center and core center samples.

Discussion

The most important degradation process seems to be the formation of a CEI layer at the electrode/electrolyte interface of the aged LFP cathode. The layer is possibly a mixture of CB and decomposition products from the electrolyte, i.e. Li-organic species, fluorophosphates and LiF [7] and could thus in part explain the loss of lithium inventory (LLI). This was confirmed by XPS results which showed a higher amount of LiF and alkoxides on the aged electrodes surface. The CEI layer is found to be thickest in the sample collected from the core of the cylindrical battery, which could be an effect of the accelerated degradation of the electrolyte caused by the higher temperature [8] developed in the core of the cylindrical cell [9]. Large agglomerates are also present at the electrode/electrolyte interface of the Gr_C electrode as revealed by FIB/SEM tomography. They are most likely a mixture of SEI layer (LiF and carbonates), as again confirmed by XPS analysis (Fig. 5). From the PSD analysis of the Gr electrodes is also seen that the graphite particles are significantly smaller in the aged battery. This could probably be an effect of cracking of the Gr particles with cycling [10].

Conclusions

In this work FIB-SEM tomography was used to study the electrode degradation mechanisms in a commercial 2.5 Ah $LiFePO_4$/Graphite 26650 cylindrical cell. The analysis showed that the average particle diameter in the Gr anode is significantly smaller in the aged battery than in the fresh one, whereas no significant change in cathode LFP particle size could be observed. The decrease in the anode particle size could be an effect of mechanical stress during lithiation/delithiation process. Furthermore, the cycling seems to produce a layer of what is believed to be electrolyte decomposition products at the LFP electrode/electrolyte interface. A decomposition layer is also produced at the electrode/electrolyte interface of the cycled anode. The layers at the anode and cathode electrode/electrolyte interfaces are composed of LiF and Li-organic species as shown by XPS analysis and are believed to be the main degradation mechanism causing loss of lithium inventory (LLI) in the cylindrical cell. The layers are observed to be thicker on the core of the cylindrical cell, suggesting that the higher temperature accelerates the electrolyte decomposition.

Acknowledgment

The authors gratefully acknowledge financial support from the Danish Strategic Research Council through the project "Advanced Lifetime Predictions of Battery Energy Storage" (contract no. 0603-00589B).

References

[1] E. Sarasketa-Zabala *et al.*, "Understanding lithium inventory loss and sudden performance fade in cylindrical cells during cycling with deep-discharge steps," *J. Phys. Chem. C*, vol. 119, pp. 896–906, 2015.

[2] M. Ender *et al.*, "Quantitative Characterization of LiFePO4 Cathodes Reconstructed by FIB/SEM Tomography," *J. Electrochem. Soc.*, vol. 159, no. 7, pp. A972–A980, 2012.

[3] J. Sauvola and M. Pietikäinen, "Adaptive document image binarization," *Pattern Recognit.*, vol. 33, no. 2, pp. 225–236, 2000.

[4] B. Münch and L. Holzer, "Contradicting geometrical concepts in pore size analysis attained with electron microscopy and mercury intrusion," *J. Am. Ceram. Soc.*, vol. 91, no. 12, pp. 4059–4067, 2008.

[5] R. Younesi *et al.*, "Analysis of the Interphase on Carbon Black Formed in High Voltage Batteries," *J. Electrochem. Soc.*, vol. 162, pp. A1289–A1296, 2015.

[6] R. Mogensen *et al.*, "Evolution of the solid electrolyte interphase on tin phosphide anodes in sodium ion batteries probed by hard x-ray photoelectron spectroscopy," *Electrochim. Acta*, vol. 245, pp. 696–704, 2017.

[7] M. Cuisinier *et al.*, "Evolution of the LiFePO4 positive electrode interface along cycling monitored by MAS NMR," *J. Power Sources*, vol. 224, pp. 50–58, 2013.

[8] M. H. Ryou *et al.*, "Effects of lithium salts on thermal stabilities of lithium alkyl carbonates in SEI layer," *Electrochim. Acta*, vol. 83, pp. 259–263, 2012.

[9] L. H. Saw *et al.*, "Electrochemical-thermal analysis of 18650 Lithium Iron Phosphate cell," *Energy Convers. Manag.*, vol. 75, pp. 162–174, 2013.

[10] D. Liu *et al.*, "On the stress characteristics of graphite anode in commercial pouch lithium-ion battery," *J. Power Sources*, vol. 232, pp. 29–33, 2013.

Reversibility of the Lithium Insertion Process in Li-ion Batteries Studied by Electrochemical Impedance Spectroscopy

Roberto Scipioni, Dawei Ren, Scott A. Barnett

Department of Material Science and Engineering, Northwestern University, 2220 Campus Drive, Evanston, IL 60208, USA
roscip@northwestern.edu / 1-847-644-8359

Abstract: *In this project we use electrochemical impedance spectroscopy (EIS) to study the reversibility of the lithium insertion process in Li-ion battery materials and describe how charge vs. discharge influences the insertion process at the electrode/electrolyte interface. A $LiFePO_4$ electrode is investigated in a three-electrode configuration, in order to distinguish the cathode impedance contribution from the lithium anode. Galvanostatic Intermittent Titration Technique (GITT) is then performed, in combination with EIS, to study diffusion of lithium ions inside the electrode. A study on $LiFePO_4$ (LFP) was performed to study how state-of-charge (SOC) affects the charge transfer resistance Rct at the electrolyte interface, and the Li solid-state diffusion DLi within the particles*

Keywords: Battery; Li-ion; Electrochemical Impedance Spectroscopy; Lithium diffusion.

Introduction

Electrochemical Impedance Spectroscopy (EIS) is a powerful diagnostic tool for the study of electrochemical reactions and the characterization of interfaces and porous electrodes in many energy devices [1]–[3]. It is widely used for the investigation of aging mechanisms [4], [5] and for the extraction of kinetic and transport properties in electrode materials, relevant for the development of accurate battery lifetime models.

In this work we study the reversibility of the lithium insertion process in $LiFePO_4$ (LFP), one of the most common cathodic material for Li-ion batteries [6], by impedance spectroscopy. An equivalent circuit model (ECM), previously developed for the impedance response of a porous $LiFePO_4$ cathode [7], is used to investigate how lithium diffusion and charge transfer resistance vary with the battery state-of-charge (SOC). This ECM includes a transmission line model (TLM), commonly used to investigate the impedance response of a porous electrode infiltrated by a liquid electrolyte [8], [9].

Experimental

Electrode preparation: An electrode slurry was prepared by mixing commercial $LiFePO_4$ (LFP) powder (from Johnson Matthey), Super P (from Timcal) and Styrene-Butadiene Rubber / Carboxymethylcellulose (SBR/CMC) as binder, with the ratio 80:10:10. The slurry was casted on an aluminum foil and, after drying, an electrode with a diameter of 16mm and thickness of 40μm was punched out.

Battery assembly and testing: the LFP electrode was tested in a 3-electrode setup, using lithium metal foil counter electrode, lithium metal as reference electrode and a glass fiber separator soaked with a standard 1M $LiPF_6$ in 1:1 EC/DMC electrolyte. The cell was cycled using a Biologic SP-200 with Pstat/Gstat boards at a constant current of 200μA, corresponding to a C-rate of 0.2, between 2.8-4.0 V.

Impedance spectroscopy: The EIS measurements in three-electrode configuration for the LFP electrode were obtained at room temperature in a frequency range from 100 kHz to 10 mHz (10 points per decade) at different SOC (state-of-charge) from 0% to 100% SOC in the voltage range 2.8–4.0 V. All spectra were measured at OCV after the cell had reached steady state defined by a change < 5 mV/h.

Equivalent circuit model (ECM): The EIS spectra obtained from the LFP electrode were modeled using the ECM shown in Fig. 1.

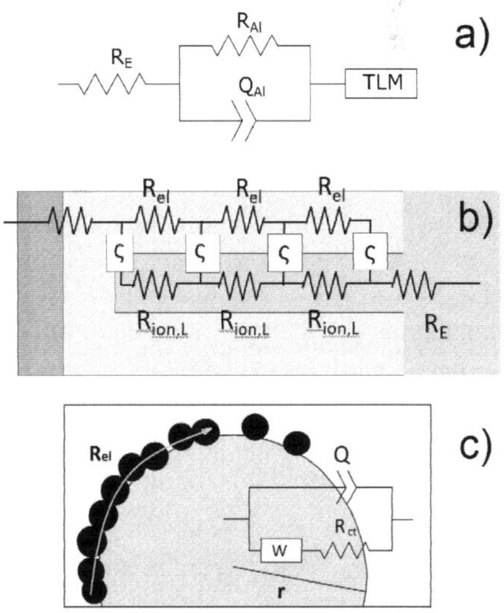

Figure 1. (a) Equivalent circuit used to model the impedance spectra, (b) Generalized Transmission Line model resembling the element TLM in (a), (c) Randles circuit used to model electrode/electrolyte interface with Li^+ diffusion (Warburg Finite Space element, W) within a particle with radius r.

The R_E-$R_{Al}Q_{Al}$ elements shown in Fig. 1a are used to model the high-frequency part of the impedance spectra, where R corresponds to a resistance and Q corresponds to a constant phase element. R_E represents the ionic resistance of the electrolyte, while the $R_{Al}Q_{Al}$ element denotes the aluminum/electrode interfacial polarization [10], [11]. The mid- and low-frequency part of the impedance spectra are modeled with a generalized TLM for a porous electrode [12], [13] (Fig. 1b). The model involves a cylindrical pore (with length L) filled with the electrolyte, and it is used to calculate the ionic resistance associate with lithium ions traveling in the pores $R_{ion,L}$, and the electron resistance through the electrode R_{el}. In this case R_{el} is associated with the Super P carbon network, as shown in Fig. 1c. The equivalent circuit element ς models the impedance of the electrode/electrolyte interface and the diffusion of lithium ions inside the LFP particles. It consists of a charge transfer resistance R_{ct} in parallel with a constant phase element Q modeling the apparent double layer capacitance of the insertion particles. R_{ct} is in series with a General Finite Space Warburg element $W_{GFS,1D}$ which models the impedance associated with lithium ion diffusion in the solid particles. More specifically $W_{GFS,1D}$ models a diffusion process along a one-dimensional diffusion path terminated by an impermeable boundary.

The impedance of the generalized TLM model is:

$$Z_{TLM} = \frac{R_{el}+R_{ion,L}}{R_{el}+R_{ion,L}}\left(L + \frac{2\lambda}{\sinh(L/\lambda)}\right) + +\lambda_{TLM}\frac{R_{el}^2+R_{ion,L}^2}{R_{el}+R_{ion,L}}\coth(L/\lambda_{TLM}) \quad [1]$$

With:

$$\lambda_{TLM} = \sqrt{\varsigma_{cat}/(R_{el}+R_{ion,L})} \quad [2]$$

As mentioned above the electrode/electrolyte interface (Fig. 1c) is modeled with the Randles circuit ς which includes the charge transfer resistance R_{ct}, a constant phase element (CPE) Q and the general finite space Warburg element $W_{GFS,1D}$. $W_{GFS,1D}$ has the impedance [5], [14], [15]:

$$Z_{WGFS,1D} = R_w\frac{\coth[(j\omega\tau_w)^{n_w}]}{(j\omega\tau_w)^{n_w}} \quad [3]$$

with the time constant:

$$\tau_w = \frac{r^2}{D} \quad [4]$$

R_w is polarization resistance, r is the particle radius, n_w is an exponent ($0<n_w<0.5$) reflecting the spread in the particle size distribution, and D is the diffusion coefficient of Lithium ion within $LiFePO_4$. The cylindrical pore length L (expressed in cm) is set equal to the electrode thickness.

Results

Battery cycling: The LFP/Li cell was initially tested at a constant C-rate of 0.2 between 2.8-4.0V for 2 cycles and showed a practical capacity of 150 mAh/g (Fig. 2a). The third cycle consisted of ten intermittent charge and discharge steps, followed by a relaxation period until reaching OCV (Fig. 2b).

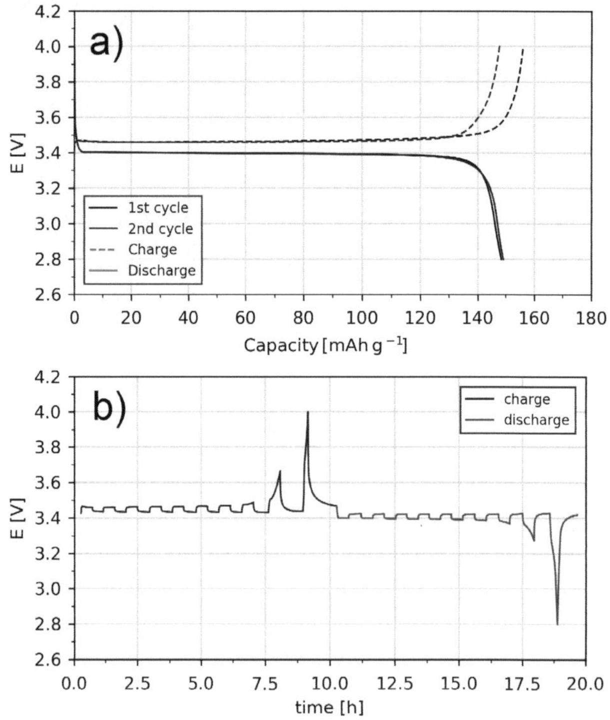

Figure 2. (a) Charge/discharge curves of the LFP/Li cell, (b) GITT charge/discharge steps of the LFP/Li cell.

Impedance spectroscopy: The normalized impedance spectra of the full cell, the LFP and Li metal electrodes are shown in Fig. 3a,b. The EIS spectra have been recorded at 0% SOC, after the first two cycles. The green line represents the impedance of the full cell, recorded in two-electrode setup, while the blue and red lines are the resolved spectra of cathode and anode, measured in three-electrode configuration. The impedance response of the LFP electrode (blue line) consists of a small semicircle in the high frequency range (above 1 kHz) and a low frequency branch characterized by a diffusive tail (with an angle of 45°). The EIS of Li metal (red line) is characterized by a large semicircle in the mid-frequency range (slightly above 100 Hz), relative to the solid electrolyte interface (SEI) layer resistance at the lithium surface [10]. Fig. 3c,d show instead the isolated LFP impedance spectrum (dots) with the modeling result (line) using the model presented in the experimental section.

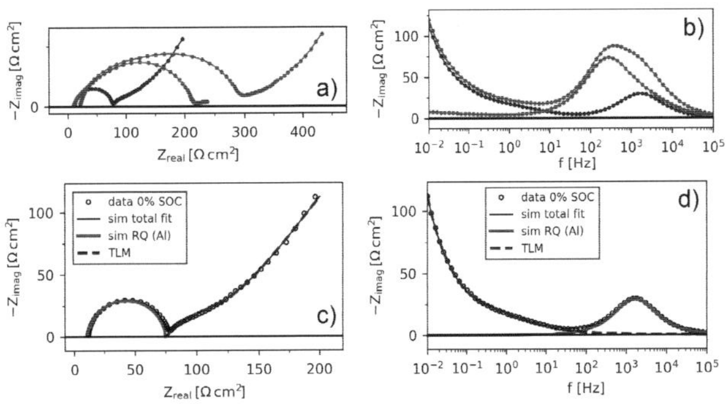

Figure 3. (a) Nyquist and (b) Bode plots of the LFP/Li cell, LFP cathode and Li anode at 0% SOC. (c) Nyquist and (d) Bode plots of the LFP cathode at 0% SOC, including fit using the equivalent circuit in Figure 1.

The high frequency side of the semicircle intersects with the x-axis at 10.9 Ωcm^2 (R_E). This value corresponds to the ionic resistance of the electrolyte between the cathode and the Li reference electrode. As mentioned in the experimental section, the high-frequency semicircle $R_{Al}Q_{Al}$ is assigned to the interface between the Aluminum current collector and the porous cathode [10], where R_{Al} corresponds to the contact resistance between current collector and the $LiFePO_4$ network, while Q_{Al} is the constant phase element which represents the double layer capacitance at this interface. The low-frequency part (TLM) of the Nyquist plot models the electrode/electrolyte interface and the resistances associated with the pore infiltrated with the electrolyte. Charge transfer resistance R_{ct} and Finite Space Warburg diffusion of Li^+ ions inside the LFP particle with radius r are calculated and reported in Table 1. Electron resistivity through the Carbon Black and the ion resistivity into the pore (with lenght L) filled with the electrolyte are also extracted (Table 1). The average LFP particle radius r used in the model is 200nm, as reported by the commercial supplier.

Table 1. Results from EIS fitting.

	R_E	$R_{Al}Q_{Al}$ element	Transmission Line Model			
			Randles element		Pore	Electrode
	R_E (Ωcm^2)	R_{Al} (Ωcm^2)	R_{ct} (Ωcm^2)	D (cm^2s^{-1})	$R_{ion,L}$ (Ωcm)	R_{el} (Ωcm)
LFP	10.9	64.0	10.3	$3.4 \cdot 10^{-11}$	1391	20

EIS at different SOC: Fig. 4 shows the normalized impedance spectra for the LFP electrode recorded at different SOCs in charging mode (Fig. 4a,b) and discharging mode (Fig. 4c,d). The high-frequency arc, related to the aluminum/electrode interfacial impedance is observed to not change with SOC, as also confirmed in literature [10]. The small arc at 10 Hz, modeled by the Randles circuit, represents the electrode/electrolyte interface. The size of the arc is subjected to a sudden drop as soon as the battery changes its SOC from 0% (Fig. 4a,b). When the process is reversed, the change is more gradual.

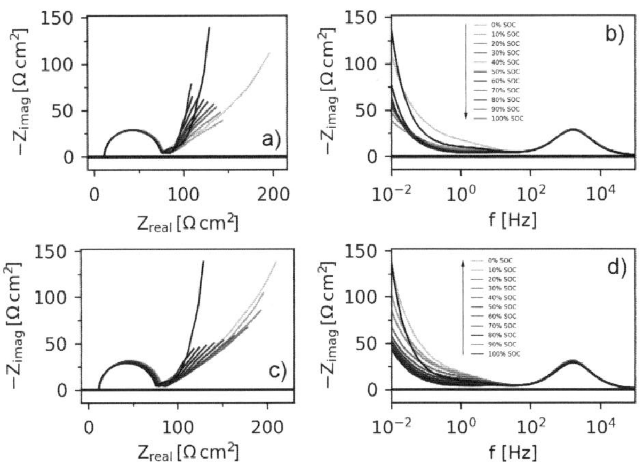

Figure 4. (a) Nyquist and (b) Bode plots of LFP cathode at different SOCs (Charging mode). (c) Nyquist and (d) Bode plots of LFP cathode at different SOCs (Discharging mode).

Figure 5 reports the R_{ct} and D_{Li} parameters extracted from the TLM after fitting of the EIS spectra at different SOC.

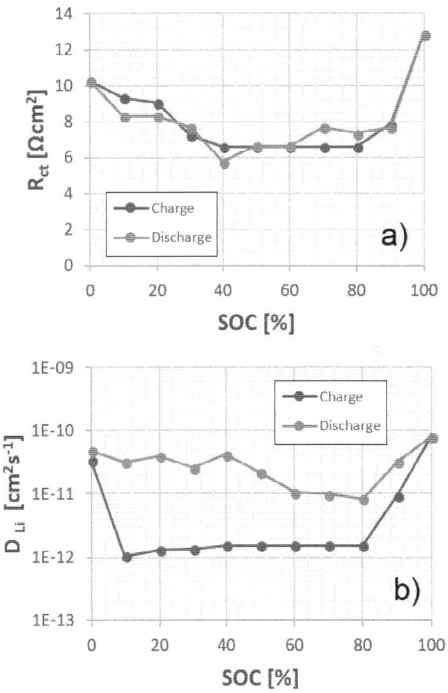

Figure 5. (a) Charge transfer resistance and (b) Lithium diffusion coefficient of LFP cathode at different SOCs.

Discussion

The impedance response of the LFP/Li cell (green line in Fig. 3a,b) consists of a large semicircle in the frequency range 10kHz – 10Hz and a diffusive tail with an angle of 45° at lower frequencies. The insertion of a lithium metal reference electrode permits to resolve the cathode impedance contribution from the anode one. It is observed that the LFP impedance spectra (blue line) is characterized by a high-frequency arc and a low-frequency diffusive tail.

The arc in the mid-frequency region represents the SEI layer on the lithium metal surface (red line), as reported in literature [10]. The EIS measurements of the LFP electrode at different SOCs show that the semicircle at 1 kHz does not change with SOC, confirming that it represents the aluminum/electrode interfacial polarization (Fig 4). A hysteresis is instead observed in the low-frequency branch, modeled by the Randles circuit. The small semicircle at 10 Hz is subjected to a sudden decrease in size when the LFP changes its SOC from 0%, and to a more gradual change when the process is reversed. This hysteresis, related to the sudden drop in the Li diffusivity when the lithium content in $Li_{1-x}FePO_4$ decreases [16], is not negligible: the D_{Li} is found to be an order of magnitude higher during the battery discharge (Fig. 5b). One hypothesis could be that the abundance of a Li-rich $Li_{1-x}FePO_4$ phase at the electrode/electrolyte interface during the discharge process could be characterized by a higher lithium diffusion coefficient than an electrode with a Li-poor phase at the electrode/electrolyte interface (during the charge process).

Conclusions

The reversibility of the lithium insertion process in $LiFePO_4$ is studied at different SOCs by electrochemical impedance spectroscopy. A LFP electrode is investigated in a three-electrode configuration, in order to distinguish the cathode impedance contribution from the lithium anode. The lithium diffusion coefficient D_{Li} in the $LiFePO_4$ cathode is found to be an order of magnitude higher during the lithiation process (or battery discharging). This hysteresis between the charging and discharging process is not fully understood yet, but it could be attributed to the abundance of a Li-rich or Li-poor phase at the electrode/electrolyte interface during the charge/discharge processes.

Acknowledgment

The authors gratefully acknowledge financial support from the Office of Naval Research (ONR) through the Research Grant # N00014-17-1-2688.

References

[1] S. H. Jensen, J. Hjelm, a Hagen, and M. Mogensen, "Electrochemical impedance spectroscopy as diagnostic tool," *Handb. Fuel Cells*, vol. 6, 2010.

[2] M. D. Levi and D. Aurbach, "Diffusion coefficients of lithium ions during intercalation into graphite derived from the simultaneous measurements and modeling of electrochemical impedance and potentiostatic intermittent titration characteristics of thin graphite electrodes," *J. Phys. Chem. B*, vol. 101, no. 23, pp. 4641–4647, 1997.

[3] J. Thevenin, "Passivating films on lithium electrodes. An approach by means of electrode impedance spectroscopy," *J. Power Sources*, vol. 14, no. 1–3, pp. 45–52, 1985.

[4] N. Mellgren, S. Brown, M. Vynnycky, and G. Lindbergh, "Impedance as a Tool for Investigating Aging in Lithium-Ion Porous Electrodes," *J. Electrochem. Soc.*, vol. 155, no. 4, p. A304, 2008.

[5] J. P. Meyers, M. Doyle, R. M. Darling, and J. Newman, "The Impedance Response of a Porous Electrode Composed of Intercalation Particles," *J. Electrochem. Soc.*, vol. 147, no. 8, p. 2930, 2000.

[6] A. K. Padhi, K. S. Nanjundaswamy, and J. B. Goodenough, "Phospho-olivines as Positive-Electrode Materials for Rechargeable Lithium Batteries," *J. Electrochem. Soc.*, vol. 144, no. 4, pp. 1188–1194, 1997.

[7] R. Scipioni, P. S. Jørgensen, C. Graves, J. Hjelm, and S. H. Jensen, "A Physically-Based Equivalent Circuit Model for the Impedance of a LiFePO $_4$ /Graphite 26650 Cylindrical Cell," *J. Electrochem. Soc.*, vol. 164, no. 9, pp. A2017–A2030, 2017.

[8] J. Illig, M. Ender, a. Weber, and E. Ivers-Tiffée, "Modeling graphite anodes with serial and transmission line models," *J. Power Sources*, vol. 282, pp. 335–347, 2015.

[9] N. Ogihara, S. Kawauchi, C. Okuda, Y. Itou, Y. Takeuchi, and Y. Ukyo, "Theoretical and Experimental Analysis of Porous Electrodes for Lithium-Ion Batteries by Electrochemical Impedance Spectroscopy Using a Symmetric Cell," *J. Electrochem. Soc.*, vol. 159, no. 7, pp. A1034–A1039, 2012.

[10] J. Illig, M. Ender, T. Chrobak, J. P. Schmidt, D. Klotz, and E. Ivers-Tiffee, "Separation of Charge Transfer and Contact Resistance in LiFePO4-Cathodes by Impedance Modeling," *J. Electrochem. Soc.*, vol. 159, no. 7, pp. A952–A960, 2012.

[11] M. Gaberscek, J. Moskon, B. Erjavec, R. Dominko, and J. Jamnik, "The Importance of Interphase Contacts in Li Ion Electrodes: The Meaning of the High-Frequency Impedance Arc," *Electrochem. Solid-State Lett.*, vol. 11, p. A170, 2008.

[12] G. Garcia-Belmonte, F. Fabregat-Santiago, J. Bisquert, M. Yamashita, E. C. Pereira, and S. Castro-Garcia, "Frequency dispersion in electrochromic devices and conducting polymer electrodes: A generalized transmission line approach," *Ionics (Kiel).*, vol. 5, pp. 44–51, 1999.

[13] R. D. Levie, "On porous electrodes," *Electrochim. Acta*, vol. 9, no. November 1963, p. 1231, 1964.

[14] F. Gao and Z. Tang, "Kinetic behavior of LiFePO4/C cathode material for lithium-ion batteries," *Electrochim. Acta*, vol. 53, no. 15, pp. 5071–5075, 2008.

[15] J. Song and M. Z. Bazant, "Effects of Nanoparticle Geometry and Size Distribution on Diffusion Impedance of Battery Electrodes," *J. Electrochem. Soc.*, vol. 160, no. 1, pp. A15–A24, 2013.

[16] A. V. Churikov, A. V. Ivanishchev, I. A. Ivanishcheva, V. O. Sycheva, N. R. Khasanova, and E. V. Antipov, "Determination of lithium diffusion coefficient in LiFePO4 electrode by galvanostatic and potentiostatic intermittent titration techniques," *Electrochim. Acta*, vol. 55, no. 8, pp. 2939–2950, 2010.

Unraveling Effects of Protective Coatings on $LiMn_2O_4$ Thin Film Cathodes for Lithium Ion Batteries

Xiankai Yu[1], Roberto Scipioni[1], Yao-bin Xu[2], Jingsong Wu[2], Scott A. Barnett[1*]
[1]Department of Materials Science and Engineering
Northwestern University
Evanston, IL 60208, USA
[2]NUANCE
Northwestern University
Evanston, IL 60208, USA
*E-mail: s-barnett@northwestern.edu / Phone: (847) 491-2447

Abstract: *The capacity fade of spinel $LiMn_2O_4$ (LMO) cathodes, which is primarily associated with Mn^{2+} dissolution into the liquid electrolyte, is a serious drawback of this otherwise promising lithium ion battery material. One of the main strategies that has been shown to help mitigate capacity fading is to apply a thin coating on LMO electrode. An all-thin-film geometry that is amenable to fundamental studies has been applied to explore LMO protective coating effects. It was found both thickness and crystallinity of coating layers notably affected LMO cathode performance. $La_{0.5}Sr_{0.5}CoO_3$ (LSCO), coating significantly improved LMO capacity retention with higher rate capability, indicating that the coating effectively prohibited Mn dissolution, especially at early cycling stage. With an annealed 2 nm thick LSCO coating, only 3% LMO capacity was lost over 300 cycles, while an uncoated LMO electrode suffered a 18% capacity loss. A larger amount of Mn^{2+} was observed by XPS at the coated versus the uncoated LMO surface, indicating that the LSCO layer prevented Mn^{2+} dissolution into the liquid electrolyte solution. ZnO coatings did not apparently improve capacity retention or high rate performance. It was presumed to be quickly dissolved and lose coating effects after certain cycles.*

Keywords: $LiMn_2O_4$; surface coating; manganese dissolution; thin films; lithium ion batteries.

Introduction

Although $LiMn_2O_4$ (LMO) lithium ion battery cathodes exhibit desirable characteristics including low cost, low toxicity, good structural and chemical stability, and fast charging rates[1,2], applications have been limited by severe capacity loss upon repeated electrochemical cycling, especially at elevated temperature[2]. The LMO capacity fading phenomenon has been attributed to several mechanisms including cooperative Jahn–Teller distortion at a deep state of discharge, electrochemical reactions with the liquid electrolyte, manganese dissolution into the liquid electrolyte, and etc. Although researchers have reported that it is the increased interfacial resistances rather than simple manganese dissolution that are responsible for the majority of cell capacity loss, manganese dissolution is considered to be a vital factor leading to the capacity fade since cell resistances are associated with manganese ion dissolution, migration and deposition (DMD) processes.[2,3] It's believed that dominant causes of manganese dissolution are Mn^{3+} disproportionation reaction due to attack of HF acid, irreversible loss of MnO to form more stable surface structures, and the existence of Mn^{2+} that is prone to be dissolved at certain truncated LMO surfaces.[3,4]

Although surface coating of LMO is a promising economical approach to improve capacity retention without sacrificing initial capacity[2,5], there is as yet little fundamental information on the mechanisms of how coatings inhibit Mn dissolution, migration and deposition processes. Here we report on the magnetron sputter deposition and characterization of LMO thin film samples that are ideal for studying surface effects, and the effect of coatings including $La_{0.5}Sr_{0.5}CoO_3$ (LSCO), ZnO and WO_3. LSCO is chosen in part because LSCO-coated LMO powder has been reported to promote electrode kinetics. In addition, perovskite LSCO has a high electrical conductivity that helps promote charge-exchange reactions. ZnO and WO_3 have been predicted to be promising LMO coating materials by DFT high-throughput computations.[6]

Experimental Section

Sample Preparation: Stoichiometric $LiMn_2O_4$, ZnO, and WO_3 targets (Kurt J. Lesker Company) and a fabricated LSCO target were used as the sputtering material. The substrates were sapphire with Au screen printed on the back, side, and part of the front surfaces, providing a back contact current collector. Before LMO deposition, the substrates were coated with 15 nm of Ti and 200 nm of Pt using DC sputtering. LMO films with nominal thicknesses of 100 nm or 25 nm were deposited using RF magnetron sputtering at room temperature. LMO films were annealed at 750 °C in air for 2 hours followed by LSCO, ZnO, or WO_3 deposition using the same sputter instrument. Some of coated LMO films were annealed at 450 °C in air for 2 hours to crystallize the coatings.

Sample Characterization: The surface morphology and roughness of all pristine and cycled thin films were observed by Atomic Force Microscopy (AFM, Bruker Dimension FastScan®). Grazing incidence X-ray diffraction was performed using ATX-G (Rigaku) with Cu Kα (λ = 1.5406 Å) radiation. Cross-sectional TEM samples of cycled thin films were prepared by a dual-beam focused ion beam (FIB, FEI Helios Nanolab 600). High resolution TEM (JEOL Co., JEM-2100F) observations were conducted at 200 kV with a field-emission gun electron source. X-ray photoelectron spectroscopy (XPS) measurements were performed on an ESCALAB 250Xi.

Electrochemical Measurement: The electrochemical tests on samples were performed using CR2025-type half coin cells with the lithium metal as the counter electrode. A mixture of 1 M $LiPF_6$ dissolved in ethylene carbonate (EC) and ethyl methyl carbonate (EMC) (v/v = 1:1) was used as the electrolyte. The cells were assembled in a glovebox filled with high-purity argon (O_2 <0.5 ppm). Galvanostatic cycling was done on an electrochemical testing system (Arbin Instrument) at a voltage range of 3.3 to 4.5 V with various current rates.

Results and Discussion

Figure 1 shows grazing incidence X-ray diffraction of a 100 nm LMO/200 nm Pt/15 nm Ti/c-Al_2O_3 film annealed at 750 °C in air. It can be seen that diffraction lines match with the lines from cubic spinel $LiMn_2O_4$ (space group Fd$\bar{3}$m, a = 8.248 Å, ICSD 99367) with a slight angle shift which is caused by Li deficiency in the LMO film. The lattice parameter calculated from LMO (111) peak at 18.74° is 8.195 Å.

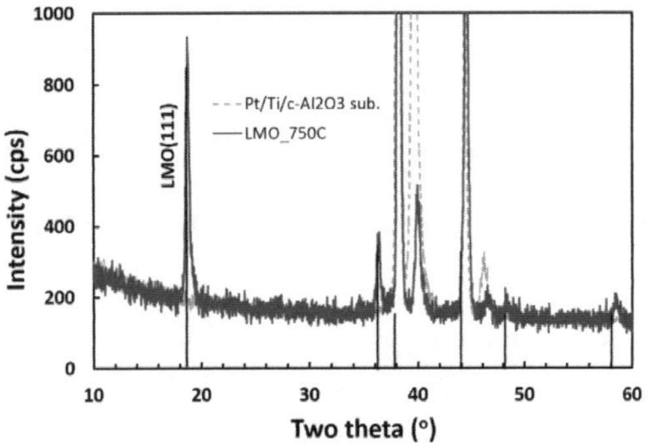

Figure 1. Grazing incidence X-ray diffraction pattern (red line) of a pristine 100 nm bare LMO film on Pt coated sapphire substrate annealed at 750 °C in air. Black reflection lines are from cubic spinel $LiMn_2O_4$ PDF.

Surface morphology of bare LMO film before and after 100 cycles between 3.5 – 4.3 V at 1C is shown in **Figure 2**a and b, exhibiting nano particles formed on large LMO grains during cycling. The interfacial structure of the cycled LMO film is depicted using TEM in **Figure 2**c. Smooth interface was achieved between LMO and Pt current collecting layer while LMO/electrolyte interface was much rougher with a RMS roughness of ~25 nm (**Figure 2**b). A dense CEI layer is formed at the LMO/electrolyte interface, marked by two red dash lines in **Figure 2**d. Manganese oxides were found within this thick dense CEI layer, verified by XPS measurements. It is discussed later in this section.

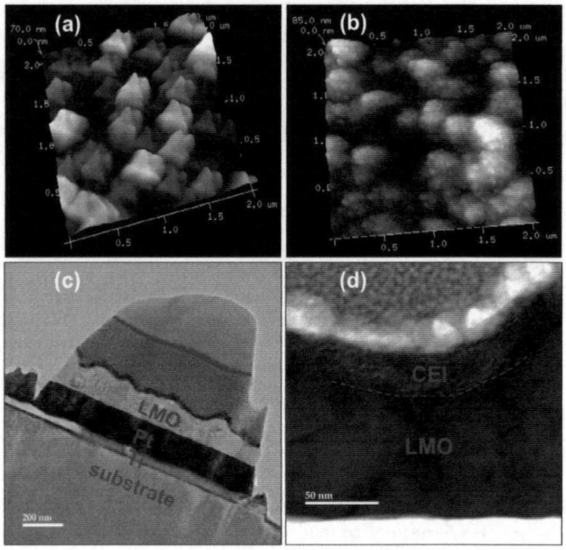

Figure 2. AFM images of a 100 nm bare LMO film (a) before and (b) after galvanostatic cycling over 100 times between 3.5 – 4.3 V at 1C. (c) and (d) are cross sectional TEM images of the cycled LMO film. A CEI layer is marked within red dash lines in (d).

Manganese dissolution of LMO cathode primarily occurs at deep states of charge/discharge or at relatively high/low electrode voltages. Thus, it is essential to decide proper cycling voltage window to clearly observe manganese dissolution effects. Capacity retention profiles of 100 nm bare LMO films cycled within various voltage windows are plotted in **Figure 3**a. It is apparent that discharging down to 2.5 V can severely damage LMO spinel structure resulting in large capacity loss. 3.5 – 4.3 V is commonly used voltage windows for LMO cathodes. As high as 98% capacity retention was achieved over 100 cycles at 4C. Herein, an extended voltage range of 3.3 – 4.5 V was applied to accelerate capacity fading while avoiding LMO structural damage (**Figure 3**a). It is widely recognized that LMO cathodes can also lose capacity when cycled at high C-rate due to constrained charge and Li^+ conductivities. **Figure 3**b demonstrates high rate test on a 25 nm bare LMO film at various current rates. A capacity of 116 mAh/g was obtained when first cycled at 1C. That capacity is smaller than theoretical spinel LMO capacity (148 mAh/g). It is due to measurement errors of LMO film thickness and area. Besides, a theoretical density of 4.28 g/cm^3 was used for calculations. It is remarkable that the LMO cathode reserved ~85% retention even at a current rate of 80C.

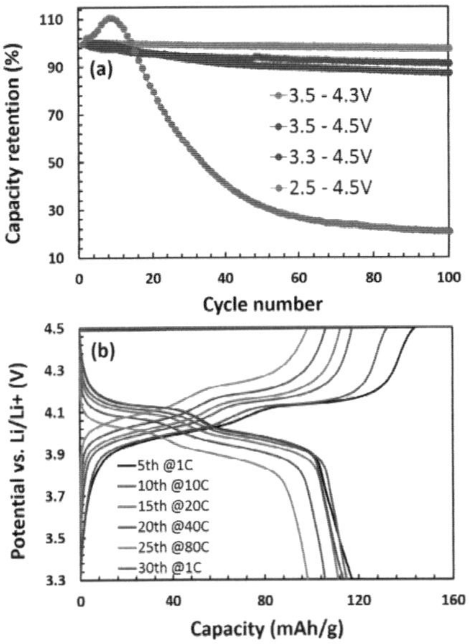

Figure 3. (a) Capacity retention of 100 nm bare LMO films cycled within various voltage ranges at a current rate of 4C. (b) 25 nm bare LMO film cycled between 3.3 – 4.5 V at various current rates.

Effects of LSCO and ZnO coatings were studied in terms of coating layer thickness and crystallinity. Discharge capacity retention of 25 nm thick LMO coated with LSCO or ZnO are shown in **Figure 4**a and b. All half cells were cycled between 3.3 – 4.5 V at 4C. It is clear that the 2 nm LSCO significantly improved LMO capacity retention, especially at the initial cycling stage where bare LMO suffered from drastic capacity fade. This may be a result of LSCO improving the electrode surface kinetics and/or reducing the Mn dissolution.

Figures 4d-f show capacity/potential curves of bare LMO and LSCO coated LMO films. By comparison, it can be seen that the LMO redox potential plateau became indistinct with LSCO coating, especially after annealing the coatings. It is possible that the LSCO promoted an LMO solid solution phase formation during LMO redox reactions.[7] **Figure 4**b shows that both unannealed and annealed ZnO of various thicknesses had little effect on LMO capacity fade. This is different than prior work on ZnO coatings on powder LMO cathodes, which were shown to improve capacity retention.[8] DFT high-throughput computations also indicate ZnO as a promising coating material.[6] One possible explanation is that the ZnO dissolved in the electrolyte after a number of cycles. This hence could illustrate the changing cycling voltage behaviors indicated by the potential profile in **Figure 4**c showing large polarization from the LMO redox potential plateau at initial stage and nearly symmetric redox potential plateau after 100 cycles (similar to bare LMO in **Figure 4**d).

In addition, Mn oxidation states and compositions of Mn ions at LMO surface were determined by deconvoluting the Mn2p XPS spectra shown in **Figure 5**. It was found much more Mn^{2+} existed at LSCO-coated LMO surface after cycling, indicating Mn^{2+} from Mn^{3+} disproportionation was prevented from dissolution into the liquid electrolyte.

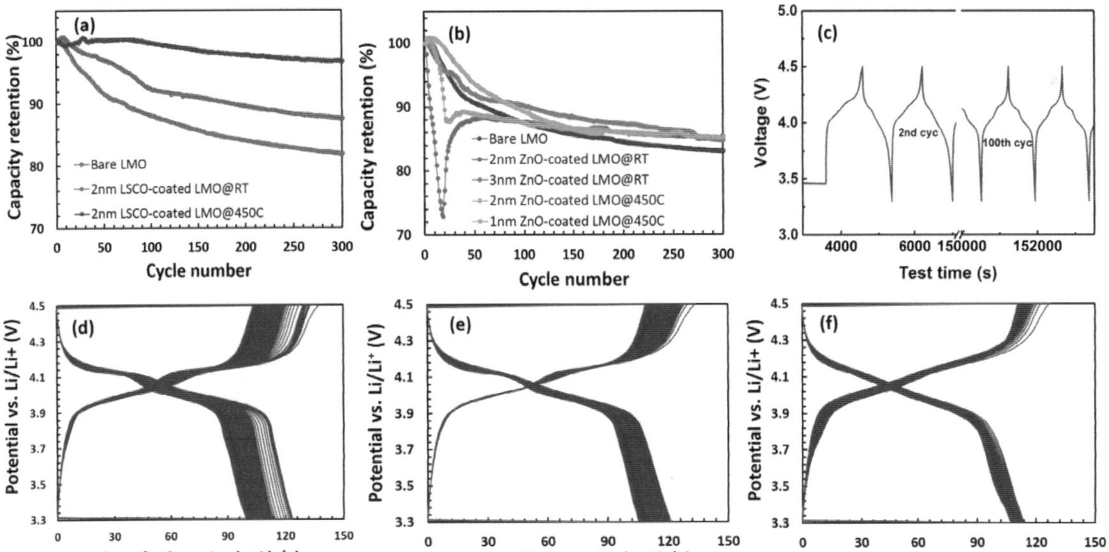

Figure 4. Discharge capacity retention of 25 nm LMO films with coating of (a) LSCO and (b) ZnO. All half cells were cycled between 3.3 – 4.5 V at a current rate of 4C. (c) shows two different shapes of the redox potential plateau during initial and later cycling of a 3 nm ZnO-coated LMO. (d) is charge/discharge curve from bare LMO while (e, f) are curves from coated LMO by 2 nm LSCO without and with annealing of the coating layer.

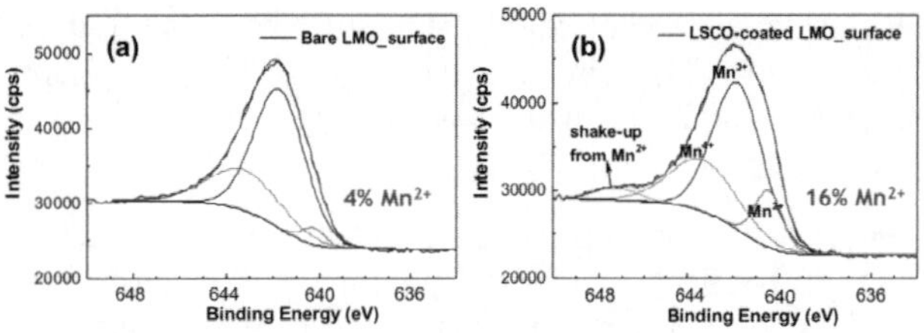

Figure 5. XPS spectra of $Mn2p_{3/2}$ from (a) cycled bare LMO and (b) cycled 2 nm LSCO-coated LMO. Data collected at LMO surface.

Conclusions

Thin-film LMO cathodes were studied to unravel the coating effects on mitigating LMO capacity loss. A 25 nm LMO/Pt/Ti/c-Al_2O_3 cathode demonstrated outstanding electrochemical performance. Capacity retention was 85% over 100 cycles even at 80C within an extended voltage window. Annealed LSCO coatings significantly improve LMO capacity retention, especially at early cycling stage. It was found manganese oxides existed within a dense and thick CEI layer formed on LMO surface, resulting in irreversible capacity loss. Deconvolution of Mn2p XPS spectra obtained near cycled LMO surface indicated that Mn^{2+} dissolution into the electrolyte was suppressed by the LSCO coating. ZnO didn't appear to enhance capacity retention. On the contrary, it tended to be quickly dissolved after certain cycles and then completely lost coating effects.

Acknowledgements

This work was supported as part of the Center for Electrochemical Energy Science, an Energy Frontier Research Center funded by the U.S. Department of Energy, Office of Science, Basic Energy Sciences. Research at the Advanced Photon was supported by DOE, Office of Science, BES. This work made use of the EPIC, Keck-II, and/or SPID facility(ies) of Northwestern University's NUANCE Center, which has received support from the Soft and Hybrid Nanotechnology Experimental (SHyNE) Resource (NSF ECCS-1542205); the MRSEC program (NSF DMR-1121262) at the Materials Research Center; the International Institute for Nanotechnology (IIN); the Keck Foundation; and the State of Illinois, through the IIN. This work also made use of Pulsed Laser Deposition Shared Facility at the Materials Research Center at Northwestern University supported by the National Science Foundation's MRSEC program (DMR-1121262).

References

1. Gummow, R. J., A. De Kock, and M. M. Thackeray, "Improved capacity retention in rechargeable 4 V lithium/lithium-manganese oxide (spinel) cells," *Solid State Ionics,* vol. 69, no. 1, pp. 59-67, 1994.
2. Lu, Jun, Chun Zhan, Tianpin Wu, Jianguo Wen, Yu Lei, A. Jeremy Kropf, Huiming Wu, "Effectively suppressing dissolution of manganese from spinel lithium manganate via a nanoscale surface-doping approach," *Nature communications,* vol. 5, pp. 5693, 2014.
3. Bhandari, Arihant, and Jishnu Bhattacharya, "Manganese Dissolution from Spinel Cathode: Few Unanswered Questions," *Journal of The Electrochemical Society*, vol. 164, no. 2, pp. A106-A127, 2017.
4. Lee, Yoon Koo, Jonghyun Park, and Wei Lu, "Electronic and Bonding Properties of $LiMn_2O_4$ Spinel with Different Surface Orientations and Doping Elements and Their Effects on Manganese Dissolution," *Journal of The Electrochemical Society,* vol. 163, no. 7, pp. A1359-A1368, 2016.
5. Jaber-Ansari, L.; Puntambekar, K.P.; Kim, S.; Aykol, M.; Luo, L.; Wu, J.; Myers, B.D.; Iddir, H.; Russell, J.T.; Saldana, S.J.; Kumar, R. "Suppressing Manganese Dissolution from Lithium Manganese Oxide Spinel Cathodes with Single-Layer Graphene," *Adv. Energy Mater.* vol. 5, pp. 1500646, 2015.
6. Aykol, Muratahan, Soo Kim, Vinay I. Hegde, David Snydacker, Zhi Lu, Shiqiang Hao, Scott Kirklin, Dane Morgan, and Christopher Wolverton, "High-throughput computational design of cathode coatings for Li-ion batteries," *Nature communications,* vol. 7, pp. 13779, 2016
7. Okubo, Masashi, Yoshifumi Mizuno, Hirotoshi Yamada, Jedeok Kim, Eiji Hosono, Haoshen Zhou, Tetsuichi Kudo, and Itaru Honma. "Fast Li-ion insertion into nanosized $LiMn_2O_4$ without domain boundaries," *Acs Nano,* vol. 4, no. 2, pp. 741-752, 2010.
8. Liu, Haowen, Cuixia Cheng, and Keli Zhang. "The effect of ZnO coating on $LiMn_2O_4$ cycle life in high temperature for lithium secondary batteries," *Materials chemistry and physics,* vol. 101, no. 2-3, pp. 276-279, 2007.

Lithium-Sulfur Battery with a Robust Sulfur Electrode and Mixed Conduction Membrane

Ahamed Irshad[a], Buddhinie S. Jayathilake[a], Rodrigo Elizalde-Segovia[a], Derek Moy[a], Edward. J. Plichta[b], Mary. A. Hendrickson[b] and S. R. Narayanan[a]
[a]Loker Hydrocarbon Research Institute, Department of Chemistry, University of Southern California, Los Angeles, California 90089, USA
[b]RDECOM CERDEC CP&I, Aberdeen Proving Ground, Maryland 21005, USA
srnaraya@usc.edu / 1- 213-740-5965

Abstract: *The development of robust cathode structure and prevent shuttling of the polysulfides are necessary for enhancing the cycle life and realizing the benefits of the lithium-sulfur battery. In the present study, we demonstrate a technique to prepare crack-free sulfur electrodes with different types of carbons. We also demonstrate that polysulfide shuttling can be avoided by using a nonporous mixed conduction membrane (MCM) made of lithium cobalt oxide (LCO). The MCM layer can be fabricated as thin as 20 microns when prepared from a sacrificial aluminum substrate. The MCM was found to be effective in suppressing the polysulfide shuttle and thus providing high capacity retention and extended cycle life.*

Keywords: Li-S battery; polysulfide shuttle effect; mixed conduction membrane; robust sulfur electrode; LCO

Introduction

Lithium-sulfur (Li–S) battery is an attractive technology for realizing high specific energy owing to the low cost and high theoretical capacity of sulfur (1675 mAh g^{-1}). However, the poor electronic conductivity of sulfur, large volume expansion, and high solubility of lithium polysulfides (PS) in the electrolyte lead to high polarization, rapid capacity fading, poor rate capability and low coloumbic efficiency.[1] The goal of our research is to develop a robust, high-capacity cathode structure and prevent the shuttling of the polysulfides to improve the electrical performance characteristics and cycle life of rechargeable Li-S batteries.

The insulating nature of the elemental sulfur requires that sulfur particles be embedded in an electrically conductive matrix of carbon to form an electrode. Consequently, the performance of the sulfur electrode is largely determined by the conductivity, porosity, pore diameter and surface area of the carbon matrix. When sulfur electrodes are made with different types of carbon such as acetylene black, carbon nanotubes, Ketjen black, the utilization of the active material increased with the surface area of the carbon. However, with high surface area carbon materials extensive cracks are formed in the electrode during the solvent evaporation step. This cracking eventually results in poor adhesion of the active material to the current collector, and non-uniform distribution of the electrolyte in the cathode. Thus, cracked electrodes resulted in electrode structures with variable and often poor performance. We found that the cracks in the electrode could be minimized by using the nanotubes of carbon, reducing the amount of solvent, and slowing the rate of solvent evaporation.

The suppression of the shuttling of polysulfides using a lithium cobalt oxide (LCO) based mixed conduction membrane (MCM) was reported in our previous studies.[1] The MCM is a non-porous membrane that restricts the soluble polysulfides to the positive electrode but allows fast lithium-ion conduction. To further improve the energy density and reduce the material cost, we developed a method to make a thinner membrane (~20 µm) using a thin foil of aluminium metal as the sacrificial substrate. The MCM was found to be effective in suppressing the polysulfide shuttle reactions and provide high capacity retention.

Experimental

Preparation of crack-free sulfur electrode: Sulfur (Aldrich, 99.5% purity), different types of carbon such as acetylene black (Alfa Aesar), carbon nanotube (Flotube 9000), ketjen black (Akzo Nobel EC 300J), N-methyl-2-pyrrolidone (NMP, Sigma-Aldrich) and polyvinylidene fluoride (PVDF) binder (MTI) were used as received. The cathode slurry consisted of sulfur (60 wt%), conductive carbon (30 wt%), and PVDF (10 wt%) in about 10 ml of NMP. The mixture was ball milled for 15 minute and coated onto an aluminum foil with a doctor blade. The cathode thickness was approximately 15 µm unless otherwise stated. The coated foil was heated at about 80 °C for 4 h to evaporate the solvent. Further evaporation at this temperature caused cracking of the electrode. Hence, blotting technique was used to remove traces of the solvent left in the coating. The blotting process was repeated several times to ensure the complete removal of the solvent. The electrode was then punched into 16 mm diameter disks and transferred to a glove box for overnight storage under Ar atmosphere. The sulfur loading in the cathode coating was approximately 2 mg/cm^2 for 15 µm thick electrodes.

Fabrication of mixed conduction membrane (MCM) layer. Lithiated cobalt oxide ($LiCoO_2$ from MTI) and PVDF were ball milled together in the proportion of 95% and 5% by weight, respectively, with NMP to form a slurry. The slurry was coated onto an aluminum foil substrate to a thickness of approximately 75 micrometers and dried at ~100 °C for 5 h in air. The coated substrate was then hot pressed at 180 °C at a pressure of 1.5 kg/cm^2 and again dried at 70 °C for 12 hours. The coated and pressed aluminum foil was punched into 16 mm diameter disks. Subsequently the aluminum foil substrate was peeled off to obtain a free-standing non-porous mixed conduction membrane layer. The peeling of the aluminum substrate caused mechanical damage to the film when the thickness was below 50 micrometers. In such cases, 1 M potassium hydroxide (KOH) solution was used to selectively etch out the aluminum substrate. The free-standing membrane so obtained was rinsed several times with distilled water, dried at 70 °C in an air oven and then transferred into the glove box where it was stored overnight under argon flow.

Coin cell fabrication. Coin cells of the 2032-type with aluminum clad cans (MTI) were assembled using lithium foil (MTI) as the anode, polypropylene separator (Celgard 2400) and the electrolyte consisting of 1 M lithium bis(trifluoromethanesulfonyl) imide (LiTFSI, Aldrich) dissolved in 1:1 (by volume) dioxolane/dimethyoxethane (Aldrich). Cells were made with and without MCM interlayer. For the cells with MCM, two different configurations were used. In one case a separator was placed between the sulfur electrode and MCM, whereas in the other type of cells, the sulfur cathode and the MCM layer were laid against each other in a "shorted" configuration. Each cell had an electrolyte volume of approximately 80 µL.

Results and Discussion

Cracking of Sulfur electrode. As described in the experimental section, we used different carbon materials such as acetylene black (AB), carbon nanotubes (CNT) and Ketjen black (KB) for the fabrication of the sulfur cathode. The use of solvents like NMP for preparing the slurry for coating leads to a step of evaporation of the solvent before cutting the electrodes and assembling the coin cell. As mentioned earlier, cracking of the electrode coating is a critical issue during the evaporation step. The cracking of coatings formed from slurries and pastes has been widely studied by Lee and Routh, 2004[2] and Kitsunezaki, 2011.[3] Some of the factors to consider for avoiding cracks on a film are; the homogeneity of the sample, the uniformity of the coating layer, the rate of drying or evaporation, the vapor pressure of the liquid, the equilibrium interactions at interfaces, the elasticity of the coating material, and the thickness of coated layer.

One of the common observations made on film cracking is that the space between the cracks increases in proportion to the thickness of the coating. Lee and Routh[2] introduced a hydrodynamic approach to explain the fractures on a drying film. This approach considers a film with its surface composed of several particles with fixed radius separated by the solvent. Between the particles, a meniscus is formed and it has a particular capillary pressure below the atmospheric. Consequently, the film is compressed by the atmosphere producing an exudation of the solvent. The sweating of the film is directly proportional to the magnitude of compression. The reduction of the solvent will decrease the capillary pressure between the particles. The fracturing process on the film starts at the regions of lower thickness. In our case, at the edges of the coating, the thicknesses are lower compared to the bulk or center of the coating. Thus, the particles are more compacted in the thinner layer and the evaporation of the liquid on this region will be faster compared to the bulk. The lack of solvent on the edges will lead to a flow of the solvent from the bulk to the edges creating a pressure gradient. Therefore, the cracks are produced by this applied force and the space between the cracks is determined by the distance travelled by the solvent.[3] While we agree with this general understanding of the cracking phenomenon, it is important to mention that besides the edges of the coating, any non-uniformity on the surface film will result in multiple flow gradients and therefore multiple cracking sites.

Blot-Evaporation process for crack-free electrode.
We seek to prepare a cathode free of cracks to guarantee good conductivity, mechanical stability and low variability of performance. Different thicknesses and evaporation rates were tested with NMP as the solvent. The formation of cracks in our experiments always occurred after complete evaporation of NMP. We observed that the formation of cracks starts at the edges (regions of lower thickness) and then propagated gradually to the bulk of the coating creating multiple fractures over the entire surface. Due to the difficulty of coating a perfect uniform surface and ensuring homogeneous evaporation of the solvent, we decided to introduce a blotting technique that will allow us to remove a significant fraction of the solvent and eliminating any flow or pressure gradient caused by the excess solvent. The absorption of the solvent by the external blotting medium eliminated the liquid in every region of the surface simultaneously. The blotting material should be inert and a possible compression of the coating is determined by the pressure applied to the absorbent film. We observed that the use of our blotting film on the wet surface of the electrodes does not damage the surface of the electrode. Consequently, we observed only signs of the solvent on the blotting film. By applying the blotting technique multiple times, we could obtain a relatively solvent-free electrode. As it is seen in Figure 1, regular air evaporation produces multiple large cracks in the film whereas the blotted sulfur electrodes (with CNT) are devoid of any macroscopic cracks on the surface.

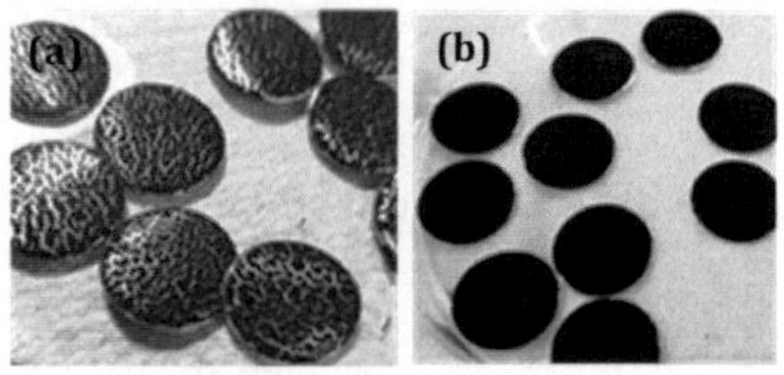

Figure 1. Sulfur electrodes based on 30 wt% CNT: (a) prepared by air evaporation and (b) by solvent removed by blotting.

We applied this blotting technique to all the carbon materials used in this work (KB, CNT and AB) and we found that cracking could be eliminated in all these cases.

Effect of carbon host on sulfur electrode performance. The surface area and pore size of the carbon can significantly affect the performance of the sulfur electrode. In general, higher surface area is desirable to achieve higher sulfur loading, utilization, and rate capability. While larger pores allow much higher sulfur loading, the areal contact between carbon and sulfur is reduced causing sulfur to be isolated from the surface of electrically conductive carbon, leading to lower utilization. Thus, a high performance sulfur electrode requires optimal surface area of carbon and also pore size distribution. The performance of the sulfur electrodes with different types of carbon materials such as AB, CNT and KB prepared by the same process are compared in Figure 2. In the very first discharge, the KB electrode gives the highest specific capacity close to 1000 mAh g^{-1} at C/50 discharge rate. On the other hand, AB based electrode shows extremely poor specific capacity of 170 mAh g^{-1} at the same rate. CNT based electrodes shows a moderate specific capacity of 630 mAh g^{-1}. These studies clearly indicate a strong dependence of the active material utilization on the properties of carbon host.

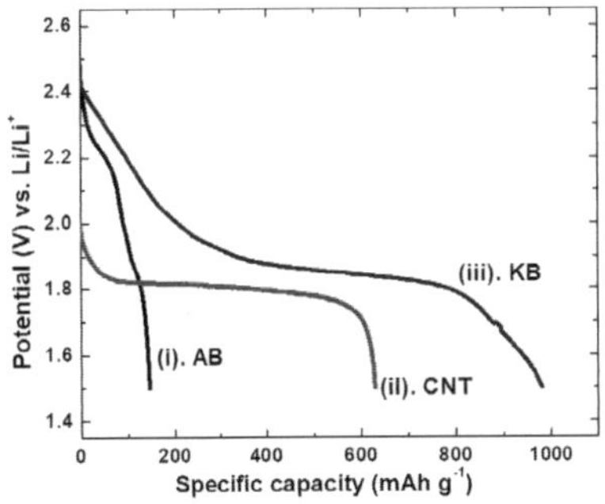

Figure. 2. Voltage-Capacity curves during the first discharge of lithium-sulfur coin cells with sulfur electrodes prepared from (i) acetylene black (AB), (ii). carbon nanotube(CNT) and (iii). ketjen black (KB). Discharge rate: C/50 and the thickness of the sulfur electrode: 50 μm

The high utilization of sulfur on the KB electrode is attributed to its high surface area of 800 m^2/g. The average pore size of KB is in the mesoporous range of 2-80 nm. The volume of pores is also high, close to 495 mL/100g. These properties make KB an ideal material to use as a sulfur host matrix. Acetylene black is a low surface area, of 50 to 60 m^2/g and an average pore size of 2.5 nm. These nano-pores are too small for sulfur to be incorporated into without thermal infusion. In the present study, AB and sulfur were mixed together with the solvent and binder by "wet" ball milling. Thus, such a mixing process is likely to result in a coating of sulfur on top of a network of AB particles without a significant quantity of sulfur was loaded into the nano-pores of the acetylene black (Fig. 3a). Similarly, the CNT used in this study, Flotube 9000, which has only a moderate surface area (200 m^2 g^{-1} with mostly mesopores of 11 nm in diameter. These are multi-walled nanotubes. Here again it is unlikely that a significant amount of sulfur was loaded into the nanotubes themselves. Instead, the sulfur was most likely deposited on the surface of the carbon nanotube network, similar to how the sulfur was deposited on the AB (Fig. 3a and b)

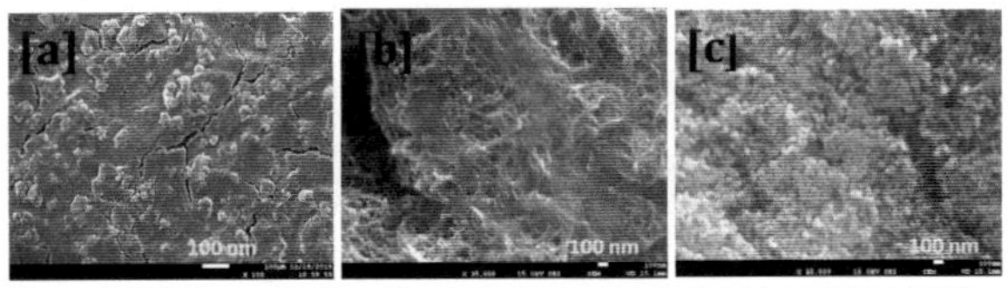

Figure. 3. SEM images for the sulfur electrodes prepared using (a). acetylene black, (b) carbon nanotube and (c) ketjen black

Suppression of polysulfide shuttle effect by the MCM layer: One of the major technical issues limiting the cycle life of the Li-S cell is the shuttling of the soluble polysulfides between the positive and negative electrodes. In recent studies we have shown that a novel type of lithium-ion conducting barrier layer can prevent the shuttling process[1]. Such a layer is called the mixed conduction membrane (MCM). The MCM has the following requirements: (1) a non-porous (2) lithium ion conductivity comparable to the liquid electrolyte, (3) electronic conductivity to support fast intercalation/de-intercalation of lithium ions, and (4) equilibrium potential for electrochemical lithium intercalation or insertion >2.7 V vs Li+/Li). A typical MCM material that meets these requirements would be a thin non-porous nanocomposite formed by combining lithiated cobalt oxide with a dense polymer binder such as polyvinylidene fluoride (PVDF). The MCM being non-porous does not allow the polysulfides to permeate. The electrochemical intercalation into the layered crystal structure of lithiated cobalt oxide allows for the rapid diffusion of lithium ions (Figure 4).

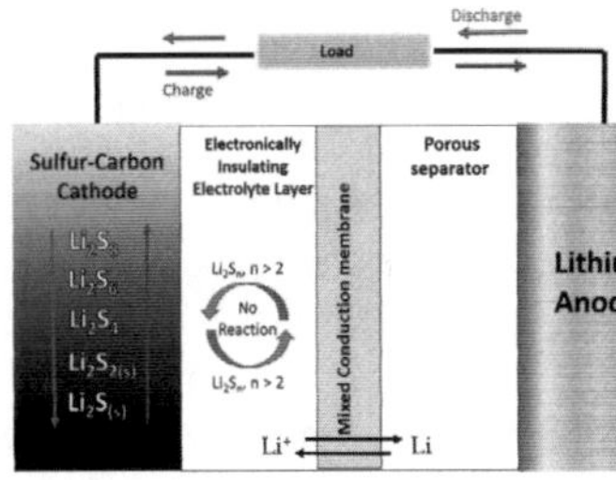

Figure 4. Schematic of a cell utilizing the mixed conduction membrane to encapsulate soluble polysulfides at the sulfur electrode without obstructing Li^+ movement

We have assembled Li-S coin cells with such an MCM barrier layer and studied them under galvanostatic charge/discharge cycling. In the case of cell without MCM barrier layer, initial discharge capacity of 1120 mAh g^{-1} was obtained at C/50 rate (Figure. 5a(i)). Such a high utilization of the active material was possible by using high surface area Ketjen black as the conductive host. However, the specific capacity of this cell decreased cycling to 1000 mAh g^{-1} by the third cycle (Figure. 5a(ii)). Thus, almost 120 mAh g^{-1} was lost just in three initial cycles, indicating a high degree of polysulfide shuttle and consequent active material loss from the cathode. In contrast, cells with MCM exhibited negligible capacity fade with cycling under similar conditions. As it is seen in Figure 5b curve (i), Li-S cell with membrane (ii) had slightly lower initial capacity close to 900 mAh g^{-1} at C/50 discharge rate. Although, slightly lower utilization value in the cells with membrane is unknown, such differences could be attributed to the unavoidable differences in the compression of the electrodes within the cells with and without MCM. Nonetheless, cell with MCM delivered almost same capacity as that of initial discharge capacity even in the third cycle (Figure. 5b(ii)). This result suggests that the MCM can be quite effective in preventing the capacity fade by by blocking of the polysulfide shuttle. This is further supported by the direct shuttle current measurement[4] for the cell with and without MCM. As it is seen from Figure. 5(c), the cells with MCM shows almost three times lower shuttle current at 90 % SoC compared to the cell without MCM. Long term cycling studies and rate capability tests on these cells are in progress.

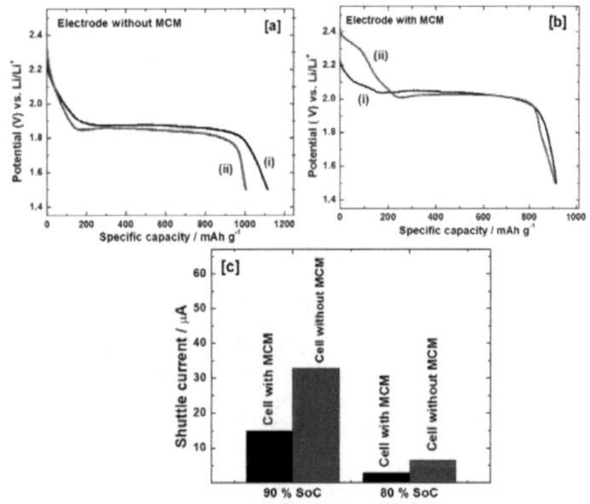

Figure. 5. Discharge curves at C/50 for the coin cells (a) without MCM and (b) with MCM. (i) is first cycle discharge curve and (ii) third cycle discharge curve. (c). Measurement of shuttle current at two different SoC for the cells with and without MCM

Electrochemical impedance measurement: Impedance measurements indicate that the high-frequency resistance of the cell with the MCM is comparable to that of the cell without the membrane (Figure 6). The high-frequency resistance at 10 kHz was 23 Ω for the cell with the MCM layer and 25 Ω for the cell without the membrane. Since these impedance values at high frequency are attributed to the ohmic resistance of the electrode, electrolyte and separator, we may conclude that the ion transport through MCM is not hindered relative to the cells without MCM. This conclusion is consistent with the behavior of lithiated cobalt oxide (the principal component in MCM) as a cathode offering high-rate capability in lithium ion cells.[1] In this regard, we note that other solid-state lithium-ion conductors that are not high-rate cathode materials can be expected to block the polysulfide shuttle but are likely to offer a higher resistance unless they can be made extremely thin. Thus, the MCM type barrier is unique in that it preserves the feature of high discharge rate capability of the lithium-sulfur cell while providing the benefit of blocking the polysulfide shuttle.

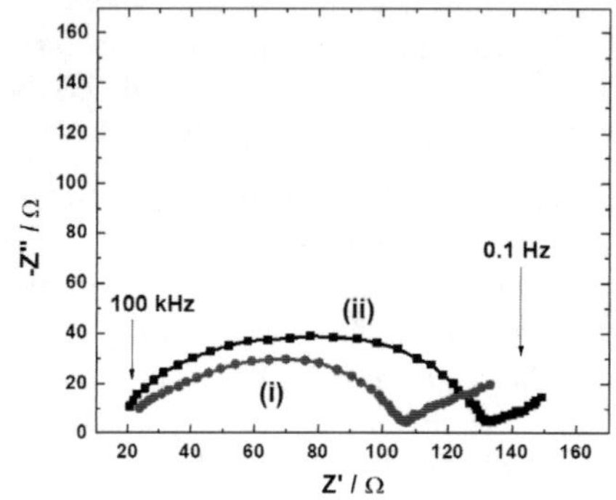

Figure. 6. Nyquist plots for the Li-S coin cells (i) with MCM and (ii) without MCM

Conclusions

We developed a simple blotting technique to minimize any flow and pressure gradient during the evaporation of solvent during the sulfur electrode coating process. This process ensured improved uniformity of evaporation and homogeneous surface without causing any visible cracks on the electrode surface. Using this blotting method, highly robust and reproducible sulfur electrodes could be made with different types of carbons such as acetylene black, carbon nanotube and Ketjen black. We observed that the sulfur utilization was improved with increase in the surface area of the carbon and highest specific capacity of 1120 mAh g^{-1} was obtained at C/50 rate for the electrodes made with Ketjen black. We also incorporated a lithium-cobalt oxide-based mixed conduction membrane into the Li-S cell that prevented polysulfide shuttle and gave high capacity retention during repeated cycling. We found that the in-house developed MCM offers a unique method to prevent the shuttling of the polysulfides without increasing the ionic resistance of the cell.

Acknowledgements

The authors acknowledge the financial support for this study from the U.S. Army RDECOM CERDEC CP&ID and the Loker Hydrocarbon Research Institute at USC.

References

1. Derek Moy and S. R. Narayanan. Mixed Conduction Membranes Suppress the Polysulfide Shuttle in Lithium-Sulfur Batteries. Journal of the Electrochemical Society 2017. 164, A560-566.

2. W. P. Lee, and A. F. Routh, Why Do Drying Films Crack, Langmuir, 2004, 20, 9885-9888.

3. S. Kitsunezaki, Crack growth in Drying Paste, Adv. Power. Technol, 2011, 22, 311-318.

4. Derek Moy, A. Manivannan, and S. R. Narayanan. Direct Measurement of Polysulfide Shuttle Current: A Window into Understanding the Performance of Lithium-Sulfur Cells. Journal of the Electrochemical Society 2015. 162, A1-A7.

Benefits and Limitations of E-Textile Power and Data Distribution Systems

Ethan Wise
Command, Power and Integration Directorate (CP&I)
U.S. Army Communications-Electronics Research, Development, and Engineering Center (CERDEC)
Aberdeen Proving Ground, MD, 21005

Abstract: *Power and data distribution systems are increasingly important for the modern Soldier given recent increases in power and data demands. An e-textile vest worn distribution system allows for easy connection to a single energy storage device and reduces the potential snag hazard. The vests tested, from two different vendors, include high power (up to 100 W) and USB 2.0 data interfaces on the same connector, which is not standard for USB devices. Therefore, it is important to validate the USB data interface under different power loads and characterize the performance of the high power connections. The CERDEC evaluation of both systems established that current systems represent potentially viable examples of integrated e-textile based power and data management systems. While there were issues with the implementation of USB data signals under load, allowing test mode functionality, and relatively high parasitic power consumption, the fundamental system and architecture show promise. The areas where the system performance fell short of the USB 2.0 performance specification are considered to be engineering issues that have the possibility of correction in future hardware and software revisions. These systems have the potential to provide a large burden relief to the Soldier, who has an increasing power and communications load with the fielding of Nett Warrior and other technologies still under development.*

Keywords: USB 2.0; e-textiles; power distribution; data distribution.

Background

Increasing Soldier lethality is a top priority for the Army, as stated by the Chief of Staff and Secretary of the Army in an October 2017 letter to the Army [1]. Specifically, Soldier lethality is one of six top priorities discussed in the letter, which also addresses upgrading the Army's network capability among several other priorities. When discussing Soldier lethality, the letter states, "[The Army] will field not only next generation individual and squad combat weapons, but also improved body armor, sensors, radios, and loadbearing exoskeletons." Almost all of these future capabilities and devices require some form of electrical power.

The Army is always looking to reduce the Soldier's physical load, reduce resupply, and facilitate better maneuverability. All of these factors combined with the increased focus on Soldier lethality have led to the increased importance of tactical, Soldier-worn power and data managers.

Power and data managers allow for a single energy storage device to be used to power all the dismounted Soldier's connected devices and simplify resupply by only requiring one replacement battery. Power and data managers also allow for power scavenging from various sources, e.g., solar panels or energy harvesters. By allowing for a larger central energy device and providing the capability to recharge, power and data managers support longer missions that can be completed with fewer batteries and less total weight.

Current power and data management solutions rely on external, cable-based technologies. E-textiles present a novel solution to the increased power and data demand on the dismounted Soldier. They allow for easy connection, distributed connecting points, reduced snag possibility, and possibly reduced weight.

However, e-textile managers provide high power (up to 100 W) and USB 2.0 data on the same connectors, which is not standard for USB devices [2]. The USB Implementers Forum (USB-IF) is the organization responsible for publishing the USB standards with which USB devices, hosts, cables, and hubs must be compliant. Along with the standards governing the data and electrical signals, the USB-IF provides a compliance test and certification procedure that commercial USB product vendors must undergo in order to ensure interoperability of their products. Thus, it is important to validate the USB data interface and interoperability under different power loads for any e-textile data and power managers.

Introduction

The U.S. Army Communications-Electronics Research, Development, and Engineering Center (CERDEC), Command, Power and Integration (CP&I) Directorate, Power Division, received e-textile vests from two vendors – referred to as Vendor A and Vendor B in this paper – for electrical testing. These vests represent two different implementations of an e-textile power and data manager.

Vendor A's e-textile vest was implemented using a traditional USB hub architecture, which discriminates between upstream devices and downstream devices. A downstream device cannot be plugged into an upstream port, and vice versa. This is the same architecture found in typical consumer USB hubs. Figure 1 shows an architectural diagram of a traditional USB hub.

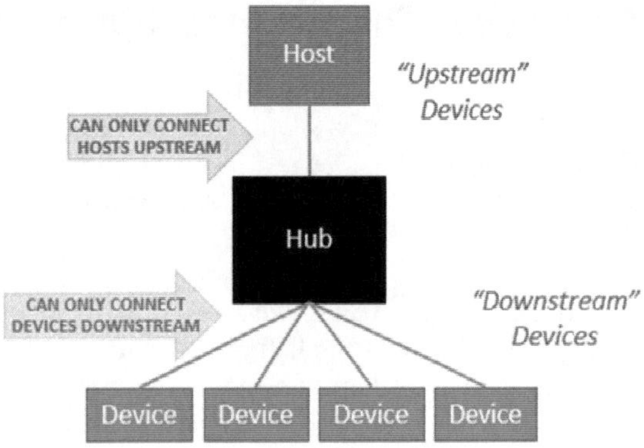

Figure 1. Notional diagram of a traditional USB hub's internal architecture (Vendor A).

Vendor B's e-textile vest implemented the technology using an embedded host architecture, which does not discriminate between upstream devices and downstream devices. All devices, downstream or upstream, can utilize any port on the vest. Figure 2 shows an architectural diagram of a USB embedded host.

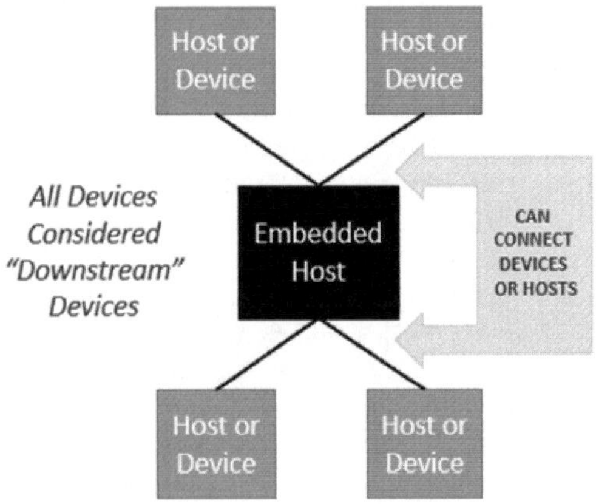

Figure 2. Notional diagram of USB embedded host's internal architecture (Vendor B).

Both the traditional hub and embedded host architectures have USB compliance tests, which determine whether or not the device, hub, or host conforms to the standards put forth by the USB-IF [3]. Vendor A's e-textile vest should comply with the USB host high-speed compliance tests, and Vendor B's vest should comply with the USB on-the-go (OTG) high-speed compliance tests.

Both vests were also tested to characterize their power usage and conditioning. Tests that were run include transient response to load, efficiency, and parasitic power consumption. The system weights were also compared, as reducing Soldier weight burden is a top priority for the Army. These results were then compared to the current baseline for dismounted Army power and data managers.

Results and Analysis

Using in-house USB certification testing equipment along with power characterization equipment, the Power Division tested both e-textile vest. The following sections discuss the results and their implications for the dismounted Warfighter.

System Weights: The weight of the system including the vest, excluding the vest, and the weight of the battery connector were compared. The data collected is provided in Table 1.

Table 1. Comparison of system weights.

System	System Weight With Vest	System Weight Without Vest	Connector Weight
Vendor B	5 lbs., 15.45 oz.	1 lb., 12.14 oz.	1.68 oz.
Vendor A	6 lbs., 10.58 oz.	2 lbs., 7.48 oz.	5.12 oz.
Baseline	NA	0 lbs., 6.90 oz.	NA

Vendor B's system weighed less in every category. A significant benefit of e-textiles is the potential for reduced weight by the removal of heavy cables, which allows for improved lethality, effectiveness, and stamina of the dismounted Soldier.

Efficiency: The overall efficiency is the amount of power lost from the input to the output of the system. This test is performed by applying a 14.8 V, 5 A supply at the input port and using a programmable DC load to step through increasing current values at the output port. The results, shown in Table 2, show that the vests have almost identical efficiencies. This is most likely due to the similar electrical architectures and the lack of any power (DC-DC or AC-DC) conversion. As e-textile design and manufacturing techniques improve, the efficiency will likely also improve. However, due to the parasitic power usage by the intelligence built into the system, it will likely not improve significantly over its current efficiency.

Table 2. Comparison of system efficiencies.

System	Efficiency
Vendor B	80%
Vendor A	79%
Baseline	91%

Efficiency is very important for dismounted Soldier technology as the Soldier only has access to a small amount of available energy. In many cases a dismounted Soldier will only have the energy he or she can carry. Any inefficiency in power usage is simply wasted and unusable to the Soldier. With better software and hardware engineering, the efficiencies of the e-textile vests could approach that of the baseline power and data manager.

Parasitic Power: This tests the amount of power consumed by the vest under no load, at 14.8 V input voltage. This is a very important metric because it determines the amount of power the vest will be consuming at all times (when an energy source is plugged in), regardless if the user is in fact using the vest or not. A high parasitic power consumption would deplete a Soldier's battery or other energy storage device much quicker than a lower parasitic power consumption. Table 3 shows the data collected on parasitic power usage.

Table 3. Comparison of system parasitic power usage.

System	Parasitic Power
Vendor B	1.41 W
Vendor A	2.01 W
Baseline	0.11 W

The Vendor A vest uses 0.60 W more than the Vendor B vest at idle. Due to the almost identical nature of the efficiencies of the vests, the e-textile cable assemblies and connectors of Vendor B must consume slightly less power under loading conditions when compared to the Vendor A vest. Both use more than ten times the current baseline manager. The parasitic power usage should be significantly decreased before fielding either vest.

Transient Response: This test measures the system's ability to handle a load switching on or off. A typical power system will experience a small dip in voltage in response to a load turning on. The goal of this test is to measure the magnitude and duration of that voltage drop to make sure it doesn't cause a power interruption for other connected devices. The load switching levels chosen for this test were 600 mA and 2700 mA. The results of this test are shown in Table 4.

Table 4. Comparison of system transient responses.

System	Transient Response
Vendor B	Negligible undershoot
Vendor A	1.6 V undershoot
Baseline	Negligible undershoot

Both the baseline and the Vendor B vest have a negligible undershoot when a load switches from 600 mA to 2700 mA. The Vendor A vest, however, has a 1.6 V undershoot, and takes 91 μs to recover. This could potentially impact peripherals connected to this vest if they are not properly internally protected.

USB Compliance Testing: The suite of tests for USB compliance depends on the type of USB device. Vendor A's vest was tested for all required USB hub certification tests [2], and Vendor B's vest was tested for all required USB on-the-go (OTG) tests [4]. All tests were run with at least two trials, one with no load attached, and one with a 35 W load attached to the vest.

Summary of Vendor A USB Test Results:

- The vest exhibited 15 total failures out of 47 total tests.
- Six of the failed tests are not required for certification or are considered for informational purposes only.
- Several of the failures only appeared under the loading condition.

Many of the failures could be due to a combination of the electrical characteristics of both the e-textiles and the connectors. Any stray capacitance/inductance or improper electrical separation of the power and data lines could impact the results of these tests. Overall, these failures are believed to be engineering issues that have the possibility of correction in future hardware and software revisions.

Summary of Vendor B USB Test Results:

- Not all tests were able to be performed; see paragraph below.
- Of the tests that could be performed,
  - Four resulted in failures.
  - Two of the failed tests are not required for certification or are considered for informational purposes only.

Any USB 2.0 compliant device must support test modes as defined in the USB 2.0 Specification [2]. In order to activate test modes necessary to complete USB 2.0 compliance testing, compliant embedded hosts must recognize a set of Vendor ID/Product ID (VIP/PID) pairs and enter their corresponding test modes. Vendor B's firmware did not support the VID/PID testing feature, and thus not all testing could be completed.

The other two known failures, while of concern, are believed to be engineering issues that could be corrected in future hardware or software revisions.

Conclusion

The evaluation of the two e-textile vests establishes that the system represents a potentially viable example of an integrated e-textile-based power and data manager with a USB host/hub capability. While there were some issues with the implementation, specifically with allowing test mode functionality and high parasitic power usage, the fundamental system and architecture show promise.

E-textile data and power managing hubs have the potential to provide a large burden relief to the Soldier, who has an increasing power and communications demand with the fielding of Nett Warrior and other new technologies under development.

Acknowledgements

The author would like to acknowledge the funding received from the Foreign Comparative Test (FCT) Office, as well as assistance from Dan Milliken, José Collazo, and Lauren Marzocca.

References

[1] M. A. Milley and R. D. McCarthy, *Modernization Priorities for the United States Army,* 2017.

[2] USB Implementers Forum, Inc., "Universal Serial Bus Specification, Revision 2.0," 27 April 2000. [Online]. Available: http://www.usb.org/developers/docs/usb20_docs. [Accessed April 2018].

[3] USB Implementers Forum, Inc., "USB-IF Compliance Program," [Online]. Available: http://www.usb.org/developers/compliance/. [Accessed April 2018].

[4] U. I. Forum, "On-The-Go and Embedded Host Supplement to the USB Revision 2.0 Specification," 27 July 2012. [Online]. Available: http://www.usb.org/developers/docs/usb20_docs. [Accessed April 2018].

Auto-Tuning for Tactical Microgrids: Model-Based Approach

Blane Wilson, Joseph Vitale, Frank Bohn, *Humberto Garcia, David Teicher, Jaclyn Lynch, Thomas Podlesak, Darren Stephens, Michael Gonzalez, Stefan Siegfried, Bradley Stanley
United States Army Communication - Electronics Research and Development Engineering Center, Aberdeen Proving Ground, MD
*Dynamic Cyber - Physical Systems Integration, Optimization & Resilient Controls Idaho National Laboratory, Idaho Falls, ID

Abstract: *Tactical microgrids have improved fuel efficiency for expeditionary operations in recent years; however, generator tuning remains a key challenge. Tuning requires specialized personnel who adjust generator control parameters to ensure that the microgrid can suitably respond to changing demand and maintain acceptable power quality. The current tuning process utilizes heuristic techniques, followed by trial and error, to achieve acceptable microgrid performance for a given topology.*

This process is not sustainable for the next generation of mobile command posts, which will leverage plug-and-play microgrids that draw power from a combination of generators manufactured by commercial and military vendors. To enable this capability, CERDEC - CP&I is developing a model-based system engineering (MBSE) methodology that uses model identification and control parameter optimization algorithms to give acceptable microgrid performance for any topology. These efforts will inform the development of an automated vendor-agnostic generator tuning solution for future power systems that can be operated by minimally-trained military personnel.

Keywords: Auto-Tuning; generator; microgrids; tactical microgrids; power quality; controls; power management; expeditionary

Background:

The United States Army primarily uses spot generation for power distribution within command posts. Spot generation is a distribution technique that uses a diesel generator to power a set of loads via a hierarchal system of feeder and distribution boxes. To meet peak demand for a given set of loads, soldiers select oversized generators that often operate below their optimal fuel efficiency. When supplying power to mission critical equipment, soldiers will often parallel generators to enable source redundancy; when one generator fails, the soldiers have another generator that can distribute power immediately [1]. This paralleling scheme is not only fuel inefficient, but also inflexible in that it requires both generators to be of the same make and model.
The Energy Informed Operations (EIO) program seeks to address these major issues through developing tactical microgrids that improve fuel efficiency and enable interoperability. These features will provide cost-savings with increased resilience and reliability for fielded power systems in the Army.

Introduction:

The EIO program focuses on tactical microgrids, with capacity ranging from 60kW to 360kW. The tactical microgrid is composed of 30kW and 60kW TQGs (Tactical Quiet Generators) which are connected via Intelligent Power Distribution (IPD) boxes that enable communication and control between the generators. In order to communicate with the IPDs, the TQG control kits were retrofitted with control kits that utilize an open communication protocol developed within the Tactical Microgrid Standard (TMS) [2]. To improve fuel savings, the EIO microgrid provides a supervisory control algorithm that minimizes the number of generators running, and allows running generators to operate at or near their peak efficiency. This algorithm manages the load balance across multiple generators and can also force the IPD to open a circuit breaker to shed a set of loads that may endanger its operation.

The supervisory control is implemented via a modified isochronous-droop control scheme, which emphasizes tight frequency regulation for loads in the field. The isochronous generator acts as a grid-forming source that maintains the nominal voltage and frequency on the grid, and is the first source to respond to a change in load. The supervisory control redistributes the change in load to the droop generators by adjusting their frequency setpoints. This can also be seen as translating the droop curve up or down, such that the desired output power corresponds to an engine speed that gives the nominal frequency.

The EIO microgrid has shown the ability to reduce fuel consumption at several test and demonstration events. One of the key challenges in preparing for each demonstration is tuning the TQGs to ensure that they can parallel and suitably respond to changing demand. The tuning process is a time and labor-intensive process that requires specialized personnel who use proprietary hardware and software provided by the manufacturers of the governor, automatic voltage regulator (AVR), and genset controller. The specialized personnel often resorts to heuristic techniques learned through experience, followed by trial and error, to tune the TQGs to operate acceptably in a microgrid (Acceptably is defined as meeting electrical performance metrics for Class 2C generator sets within MIL-STD-1332B [3]). This process is not sustainable for the next generation of mobile command posts, which will leverage plug-and-play microgrids that draw power from a combination of generators manufactured by commercial and military vendors.

To meet this need, the EIO program initiated the Auto-Tuning effort, which is divided into two thrusts. The first thrust is enabling centralized command of the control parameters for the different components of the TQG in order to automate the tuning process. This thrust will be done through a software tool that uses an open communications protocol that bypasses the proprietary software required to adjust the control parameters of the governor, AVR, and genset controller. The second thrust, the focus of this paper, is identifying models for the TQG components and determining their parameters, done through a close-study of the TQG components, literature review, and test series. These two thrusts will cumulate in a prototype, which runs an optimization algorithm that automatically adjusts a TQG's control parameters to give acceptable electrical performance in a microgrid.

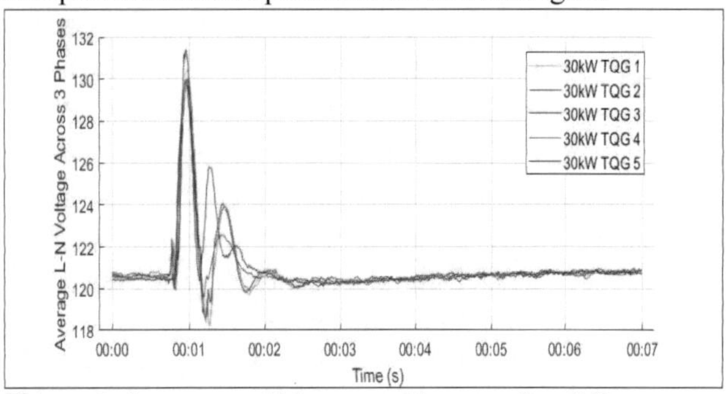

Figure 1: Same control kit swapped between five different generators

Preliminary Testing:

Two tests series were performed in order to demonstrate the instability of military microgrids and why Auto-Tuning is a necessity. The first test series featured five control kits, with the same control gains, swapped between five 30kW TQGs which each had the same model generator. The goal of this test was to determine if TQGs with the same control gains would have a similar response to a rated load step.

Figure 1 shows a segment of data from the first test series, where a rated load was applied to each TQG. TQG 2 and TQG 3 show notably different responses. Given the different responses for units that were built to the same specification and expected to perform similarly, there is a clear need for Auto-Tuning.

The second test series was developed to observe the instability within a microgrid with and without the supervisory control (see Figure 2). The results show a microgrid with two generators having large amounts of oscillation (see Figure 2 time mark 10:00-12:50). With a single generator, active power output is stable with little to no oscillations (see Figure 2 time mark 13:00-17:00). One cause of the large oscillations was the supervisory control adjusting the frequency setpoint too quickly. This was verified with communications data recorded during the testing.

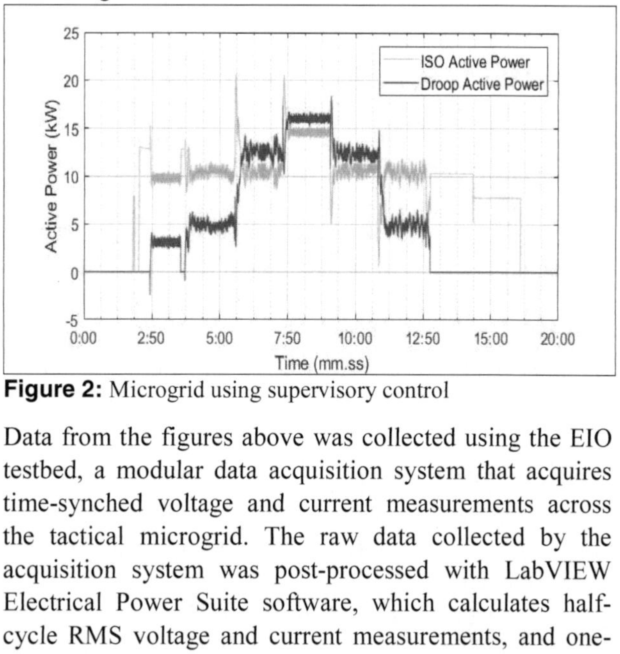

Figure 2: Microgrid using supervisory control

Data from the figures above was collected using the EIO testbed, a modular data acquisition system that acquires time-synched voltage and current measurements across the tactical microgrid. The raw data collected by the acquisition system was post-processed with LabVIEW Electrical Power Suite software, which calculates half-cycle RMS voltage and current measurements, and one-cycle power measurements. This software calculates the RMS and power data based on the IEC 61000-4-30:2008 Class A metrics for power quality measurement methods [4].

Generator Components:

The TQG consists of four main components, i) Engine Speed Governor (Woodward APECS 4500), ii) Excitation System with Automatic Voltage Regulator (McPherson EA08A AVR), iii) Synchronous Machine, iv) Woodward easYgen 2200 P2 genset controller, primarily used for paralleling generators. The components that control the voltage and frequency are the governor, AVR, and genset controller. Each component uses a PID controller, a common control scheme that uses a feedback mechanism. The governor has a PID loop for controlling the engine speed for frequency regulation while the AVR has a PID loop to control the excitation signal for voltage regulation. Lastly, the genset controller has PID loops for voltage and frequency, which act as a secondary control for the AVR and governor.

Model Selection and Implementation:

The methodology under development for Auto-Tuning is motivated by the need for model-based system engineering (MBSE). MBSE is becoming increasingly important for analyzing the performance of tactical microgrids, with variable loads being powered by diverse sources, including renewables and hybrid energy storage systems. To enable TQGs to more smoothly integrate with tactical microgrids, it is critical to develop models of its four main components that are verified and validated. These models allow the engineer to analyze the dynamic response of these generator sets, identify cascading effects under different operating conditions, and synthesize advanced monitoring approaches. The following sections briefly describe the models selected to characterize the main components of the TQG.

Engine Speed Governor:

The engine speed governor is responsible for maintaining the frequency of the output voltage of a generator set. In order to maintain the frequency, the governor regulates the fuel injected into the diesel engine, which converts the fuel's chemical energy into mechanical energy. The mechanical energy causes the rotor of the generator to rotate at a speed directly proportional to the frequency of the output voltage of the generator set. Three main components govern the dynamics of the engine-governor system; the governor, fuel control actuator, and diesel engine. While the dynamics of the governor can be adjusted, those of the actuator and the engine are both equipment specific. Different models of varying complexity were considered for modeling the main dynamics of the engine-governor system. The DEGOV Woodward Diesel governor model was selected, which specifies dynamics associated with the three main components [5]. The DEGOV model requires the values of ten parameters to be specified.

Excitation System:

The purpose of the excitation system is to provide the necessary field current to the rotor field winding of a synchronous machine, which creates the magnetic flux required to generate alternating current. The purpose of the AVR associated with the excitation system is to maintain constant voltage up to a certain level of load current, independent of generator speed and load. It is essential that the excitation system be modeled with sufficient detail, in order to accurately simulate and analyze the dynamic transient behavior of a generator's synchronous machine, when coupled with other energy sources and loads on a grid.

Ref. 6 presents a number of excitation system models suitable for use in system stability studies. These models are organized into three main types, i) Type DC, for direct current commutator rotation exciter, ii) Type AC, for alternator supplied rectifier excitation systems, iii) Type ST, for static excitation systems. A comprehensive literature review on these gensets suggested that the TQGs were constructed with excitation systems that are best modeled with Type AC models. In particular, these excitation systems use an ac alternator with either stationary or rotating rectifiers to produce the dc generator field requirements. Additional reviews revealed that these gensets have an ac rotating exciter with non-controlled rectifiers. According to Ref. 6, a non-controlled rectifier model requires the values of eight parameters.

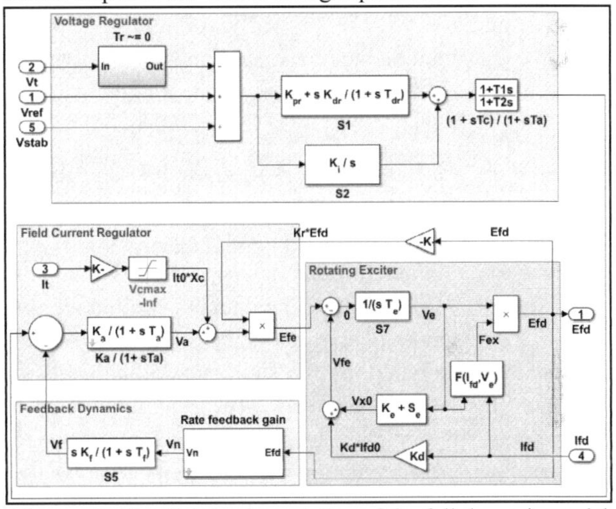

Figure 3: Simulink implementation of the full dynamic model for the AC3C excitation system and AVR.

The AC3C and AC5C models were considered to represent the TQG's excitation system. Ref. 6 indicated that AC5C was not only a simplified model for brushless generators but also suggested that it could be used to represent small excitation systems. However, an excitation system modeled using Type AC5C has the characteristic that the AVR's source is not affected by system disturbances. Such excitation systems typically use a permanent magnet generator or an external source that supplies power to the regulator. However, the TQG employs self-excitation, where the voltage regulator draws power from the TQG's voltage output terminals, and is affected by external transients. Only the AC3C model captured this characteristic, and was therefore selected for modeling and simulating the excitation system of the generator. The self-excitation behavior seen in the AC3C model is non-linear, represented by the multiplication block, shown in Figure 3. The AC3C model requires the values of twelve parameters to be specified.

Synchronous Machine:

The synchronous machine component of a genset, also referred to as the actual generator, converts the mechanical power output of its diesel engine into electrical power. The load supplied by the generator determines the voltage. The model selected to characterize the generator component of the TQG takes into account the dynamics of the stator, field, and damper windings, with its equivalent circuit represented in the rotor reference frame (qd frame), where the d-axis is the rotor direct axis and the q-axis is the quadrature axis. The synchronous machine dynamic model is based on the IEEE standard 1110-2002, with its electrical part represented by a sixth-order state-space model, where all rotor parameters and electrical quantities are viewed from the stator and identified by primed variables [7]. In order to utilize this model, the values of fourteen parameters need to be specified.

Future Work:

In total, there are forty-four parameters to be specified, i) ten from the DEGOV model, ii) eight from the non-controlled rectifier model, iii) twelve from the AC3C model and iv) fourteen from the synchronous machine model. The values of the parameters can either be estimated or experimentally determined. Experiments for determining parameters of the sub-components, such as the synchronous machine, are invasive [8]. Estimating the parameters, while quicker than experiments, may lead to less accuracy in simulating the performance of the generator set. In finding these parameters, the tradeoff between both approaches must be carefully considered. A test series is currently in progress to determine parameters for the governor and excitation system.

Conclusion:

Although the current generator tuning process is time-intensive, it remains the status-quo for commissioning sources for tactical microgrids. The status-quo for tuning is incompatible with the new operational paradigm for tactical power, which emphasizes mobility and plug-and-play capability. Addressing this problem requires developing a detailed model of the TQG components, which will enable automated calculation of the control parameters required to allow TQGs to perform acceptably in a microgrid. The MBSE methodology described in this paper can be applied to other generators and other sources. Applying this methodology on a large scale will build a comprehensive library of models, which can be used to quickly evaluate different microgrid topologies.

These models can be integrated into an Auto-Tuning prototype system, which will use an open communications standard (e.g. TMS), that supports mixed-source tactical microgrids. These features can prove the concept of plug-and-play, which is critical for ensuring interoperability for tactical microgrids that support The Warfighter.

References:

[1] "Mobile Electric Power Technologies for the Army of the Future: Engines, Power Source, and Electrical Aspects", Committee on Mobile Electric Power Plan Technologies, 1988.

[2] Department of Defense, MIL-STD. Tactical Microgrid Standard. 23 March 2018, In Preparation, 2018

[3] MIL-STD-1332B, Department of Defense, Definitions of Tactical, Prime, Precise, and Utility Terminology for Classification of the DoD Mobile Electric Power Engine Generator Set Family, 18 March 1973.

[4] International Electrotechnical Commission: 61000-4-30: Power Quality Measurement Methods, 2008

[5] IEEE PES-TR1, "IEEE Dynamic Models for Turbine-Governors in Power System Studies," IEEE Technical Report, 2014.

[6] IEEE Std. 421.5-2016, "IEEE Recommended Practice for Excitation Systems for Power System Stability Studies," 2016.

[7] IEEE Std. 1110-2002, "IEEE Guide for Synchronous Generator Modeling Practice and Applications in Power System Stability Analyses", 2002.

[8] IEEE Std 115-2009, "IEEE Guide for Test Procedures for Synchronous Machines. Part I: Acceptance and Performance Testing; Part II: Test Procedures and Parameter Determination for Dynamic Analysis," 2009.

Considerations of Generation and Energy Storage in an Emergency Microgrid

Pavan Penkey, Brian K. Johnson, and Herbert L. Hess
Department of Electrical and Computer Engineering
University of Idaho
Moscow, Idaho 83844-1023
hhess@uidaho.edu / 1-208-885-4341

Abstract: *This paper reports a feasibility study for forming a microgrid in the downtown area of a city in the Pacific Northwest. Improving the resilience of a microgrid to provide for high priority loads is the objective of the research. Generation is two hydroelectric units and a nearly equal amount of photovoltaics. The grid is defined and its elements identified. Models for each element in PowerWorld are presented. Simulations reveal that all critical loads cannot be served with available generation. The number of critical loads varies most with seasons and less with time of day. Battery storage is not really effective because cost allows too little to be proposed. Simulations show that steady state stability is readily achieved and maintained, including voltage and frequency stability.*

Keywords: microgrid; modeling of a microgrid; PowerWorld simulation of power system; battery storage

Introduction

A microgrid is a small-scale power grid that can isolate from the main grid and still be able to supply local loads using local distributed energy resources. The major components of a microgrid are electrical loads, generation resources, a microgrid controller, and an optional electrical energy storage system. Microgrids can be intentionally created, often in remote places, or they can be isolated and islanded during the prolonged grid outages. In either case, microgrids provide energy to loads within the microgrid footprint.[1] Likewise, tactical military installations may benefit greatly from such capacity. There is great resilience to be gained from establishing microgrids.

This paper describes a feasibility study for forming a microgrid in the downtown area of the city of Spokane, Washington, under emergency conditions created by loss of power transmission from the Bonneville Power Administration, as happened on November 17, 2015. The study's goal is to determine the level of improvement in resilience an established microgrid could provide for the known high-priority loads within the city's core. Electrically, this urban microgrid bears some similarities to a tactical military base. In the case at hand, two hydroelectric generators provide a total of 13 Megawatts without the energy storage of a dam. Rooftop solar generation adds a similar amount of generation capacity. Energy storage consists of vanadium flow batteries. Loads are typical high priority urban loads such as hospitals, police and jail, government offices, and a downtown business district.

The objective of this study is to improve the reliability of the microgrid once established, not to address the issues of establishing the microgrid under emergency conditions or its long term economics. From many years' public utility distribution and transmission data, a unified model of the downtown microgrid can be created. Using this model, steady state and transient studies may be performed. Voltage control, frequency stability, and power flow were important parts of this investigation. Voltage stability proves amenable to conventional means of reactive power control, such as tap changers and distributed capacitance. Renewable resources (hydro and solar) provide the sole sources of energy for this microgrid and its means of frequency control. Renewables' well-known seasonal or diurnal variations in availability encourage compensation from electrical energy storage. Conclusions of these studies provide understanding and insight into establishing, operating, and maintaining an urban microgrid.[2]

Understanding the distribution system

The project consisted of several tasks. First, to characterize the microgrid, it is necessary to identify energy resources and critical loads, obtain network data, and collect historical generation and load resource data. A microgrid is a controlled, coordinated unit within recognizable boundaries, not merely a piece of a distribution system with distributed energy resources (DER).[1] In the case at hand, the largest city between Minneapolis and Seattle along the northern tier of states plans to establish an urban microgrid downtown to serve critical loads during emergencies. Hydropower serves as the reason for inhabiting this location from the dawn of Native American cultures. Two hydroelectric turbines, operating nearly a century, sit along the continent's second largest urban waterfalls. Within the downtown core, planned photovoltaic arrays nearly match the energy capacity of the hydroelectric generators. Normally, hydroelectric generators on the Columbia River provide most of the city's power through a 500kV line. Loss of this line creates an incentive for an urban microgrid. A 115kV distribution loop and a set of substations, as illustrated in Figure 1, serves downtown electrical demand. Breakers B1, B7, B8, and B13 delineate an urban microgrid.[2]

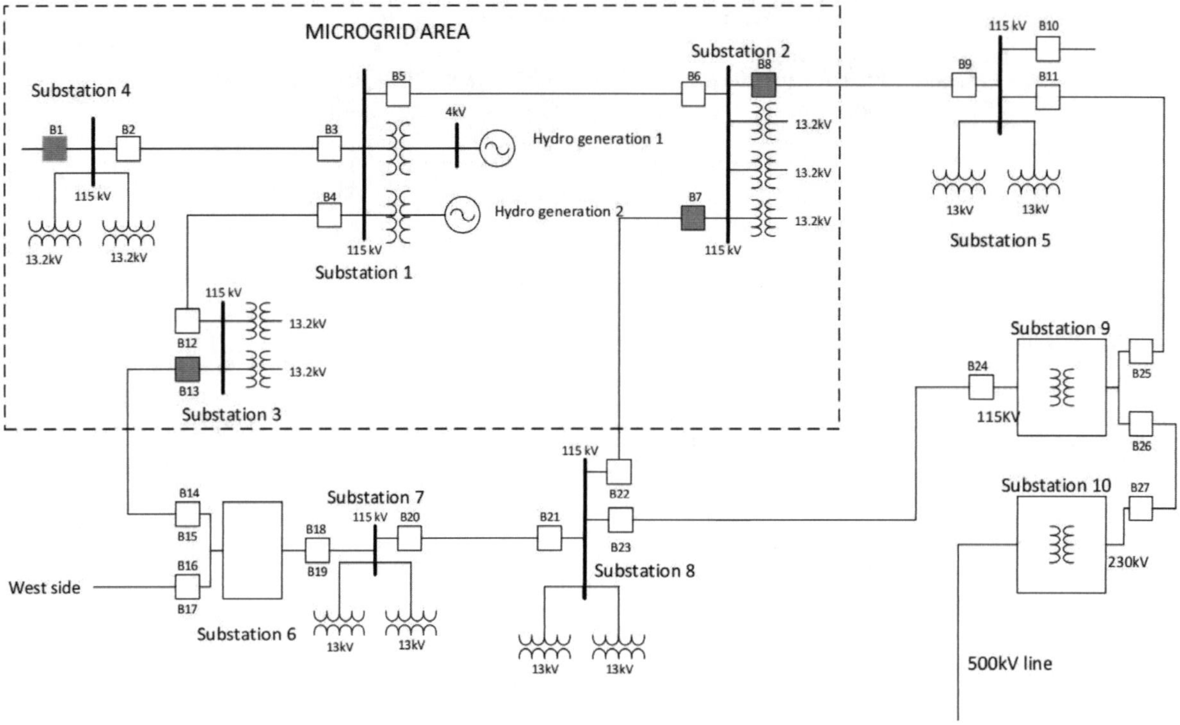

Figure 1. Downtown Electrical Distribution Loop.

Hydroelectric resources are "run of the river". There is no dam for water and hence, energy storage. Discharge rates are remarkably consistent since recordkeeping began in 1891. Flow is strongly seasonal. Flow in spring months of April, May, and June are more than ten times flow in August through October. Solar radiation is likewise strongly consistent. Insolation in May through September is nearly ten times insolation of November through February.[3] This presents an imperfect opportunity for balancing energy resources by season as shown in Figure 2.

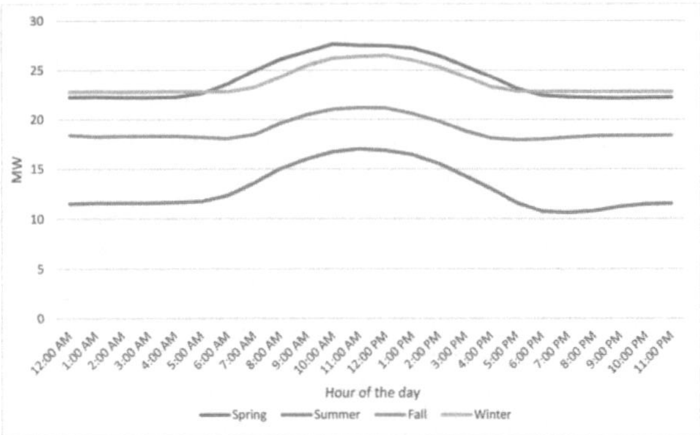

Figure 2. Combined Hydroelectric and Solar Energy Capacity by Season and Time of Day.

There are nine critical loads within the downtown microgrid area, such as hospitals, jails and police stations, government buildings at every level, emergency communications, etc. Metering data for each load dates back to when each was created. Three years' data accurately characterizes each load. Each load has its own switchgear that can be operated on site and remotely. All nine loads show similar seasonal and daily characteristics with strong summer and afternoon peaks. The public utility has installed vanadium flow batteries for energy storage in locations outside the downtown area, but they are considering such an installation just to the east of downtown. Cost currently limits such battery storage to about one or two megawatts of power and to one to two megawatt-hours of energy.[2]

Modeling the Microgrid

Second, a validated model of the microgrid is necessary. Appropriate models exist for each element of the microgrid but in different simulation packages. Generator and transmission line models are in PowerWorld as part of the larger Western Electricity Coordinating Council (WECC) transmission model.[4] Some of the distribution network is also modeled in PowerWorld, but most of it is modeled in SynerGEE.[5] Though a little tedious to convert, this SynerGEE section when converted to PowerWorld completed a unified PowerWorld model.[4,5]

Critical loads are mostly at the ends of distribution lines. Feeders that supply critical loads also have many non-critical loads as well.

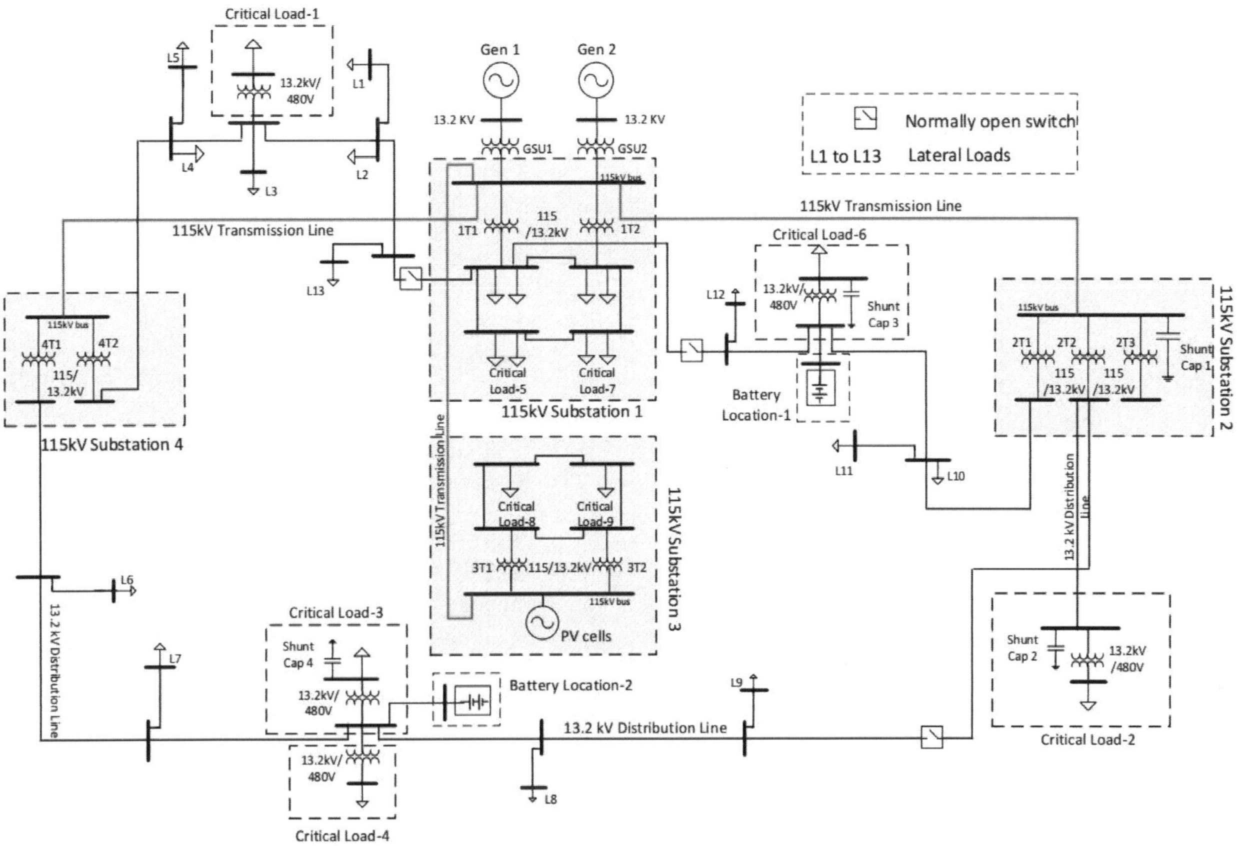

Figure 3. Final PowerWorld Model of Microgrid.

Some switchgear in appropriate places can isolate and serve critical loads, but additional switchgear is necessary to truly identify and serve critical loads alone. The model includes the influence of these non-critical, difficult to shed, loads.

Models for individual elements are of the standard variety. Lines are modeled as impedances with values known to the electric utility. One of the two generators has known models derived from testing during the most recent maintenance interval. These models include the machine itself, its exciter, and its governor and connections to the grid. The other generator's parameters are not known. A complete set of estimates were adapted from known parameters of other, similar generators within the public utility's territory. Frequency control is by droop methods. Transformers have standard models, including tap changers.[2] PowerWorld uses a CBEST model for batteries such as the Vanadium Flow Battery proposed for this microgrid.[2]

Constant power models are assigned in PowerWorld for all loads. Loads are priority designated by number from one (highest) to nine (lowest). Loads are aggregated as much as possible to simplify the analysis. More than one feeder supplies each critical load. Sometimes, a load may be recalculated if a feeder that supplies it goes out of service. A final PowerWorld model is shown in Figure 3.

PowerWorld Simulation

Third, PowerWorld simulation using the models as described proves the microgrid's steady state feasibility. Using historic profiles from the past three years, specifications for operation can be developed. It soon became obvious that not all critical loads could be supplied all the time. Loads must be scheduled for shedding or reclosing based on their own demand and on available generation. Generation that depends on river flow causes the most significant variation by season. Carefully considering season, time of day, and priority yields a set of expectations. There is a gap between available generation and critical load demand year round, but this gap is particularly greater in the summer. Battery storage could make up some of the shortfall, discharging during peak demand times during the day and recharging near sunrise and sunset. For two seasons, Figure 4 shows the use of generation, load shedding, and storage to meet demand.[2]

Steady state stability analysis performed within PowerWorld shows that appropriate load shedding and capacitor placement in coordination with available generation maintains system steady state stability. This is true in all four seasons. Only the loads that are shed are different in each case.

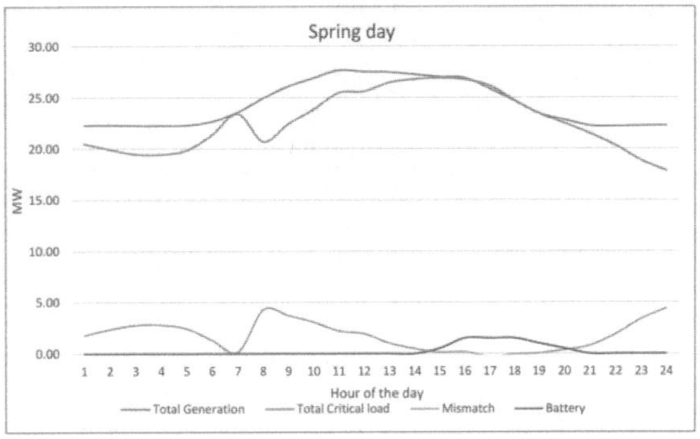

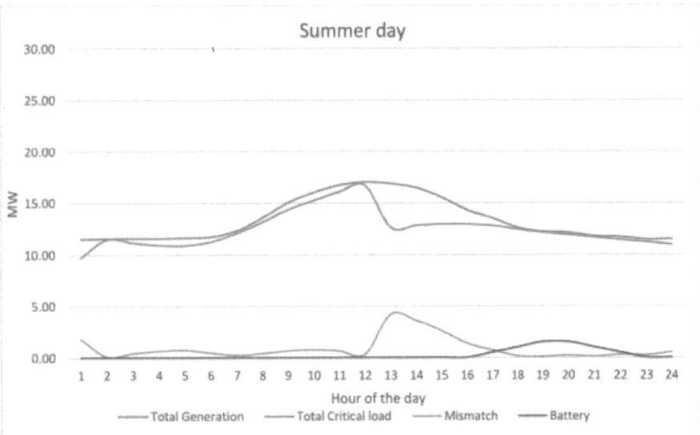

Figure 4. Total Load and Total Generation on a Spring or Summer Day Including Load Shedding.

Master control technology and its adaptation to microgrid control techniques were studied. Voltage magnitude and frequency are fundamental to master control of a microgrid.[2] Based on those results, voltage and frequency control schemes are developed for centralized and decentralized control of the microgrid. The results are in [2] and are the subject of a future paper.

Conclusions

This paper describes an investigation into establishing a microgrid in an urban downtown area. Appropriate boundaries are delineated and the distribution system within those limits and its contents are identified. Models for each element within the microgrid are created or adapted from existing models within the public utility's system. All models are restated in Powerworld. Simulation of the entire microgrid yields specifications for load shedding because generation does not always exceed total load demand. In fact, it rarely does. Seasonal variations and diurnal cycles affect both generation and load and therefore, which critical loads can be supplied. Because some non-critical loads cannot be easily separated from feeders that supply critical loads, more switchgear is needed to compartmentalize loads better. Some balance between hydroelectric and photovoltaic generation can be achieved, particularly in autumn and winter. Cost makes battery storage less than effective. This microgrid is expected to be stable in steady state and quite capable of supplying its critical loads to the degree that this investigation determined.

References

1. IEEE Standard for Interconnecting Distributed Resources with Electric Power Systems, IEEE Std 1547-2003, (Piscataway, New Jersey: IEEE Press, July 28 2003).
2. Penkey, P., "Critical Load Serving Capability by Microgrid Operation," Master of Science Thesis, University of Idaho, 2016.
3. National Renewable Energy Laboratory, 'Solar Energy and Capacity **Value,' [online] Available: http://www.nrel.gov/docs**/fy13osti/57582.pdf, accessed on: 06/21/2016.
4. PowerWorld, PowerWorld Simulator Overview, [Online]. Available: http://www.powerworld.com/products/simulator/overview, accessed on 05/09/2016.
5. SynerGEE Electric, Power distribution analysis and optimization - Synergi Electric, Available: https://www.dnvgl.com/services/power-distribution-analysis-and-optimization-synergi-electric-5005, accessed on 05/09/2016.

Acknowledgements

This research was funded by a technology development grant from Avista Corporation and its ratepayers, the University of Idaho Faculty of Excellence in Electric Power Endowment, and by alumni and faculty donations to the University of Idaho Department of Electrical Engineering. Students who worked on this project were Nathan Gaul, Matt Phillips, and Kennedy (Ned) Caisley.

Accelerated Aging of Li(Si)/CoS_2 Thermal Batteries

Daniel E. Wesolowski*, Margaret Sanchez, Ashley Allen, Chad Staiger, Nancy Missert, Andrea Ambrosini, Russell Jarek, Travis Anderson
Power Sources Technology Group
Sandia National Laboratories
Albuquerque, NM 87185-0614, USA
Contact author: dewesol@sandia.gov / 1-505-845-0614

Abstract:. *Accelerated aging of simulated thermal batteries using CoS_2 and FeS_2 cathodes was performed. Moisture and temperature were used as accelerating factors. A full suite of characterization was performed on the simulated thermal batteries, including evolved gas sampling, IR spectroscopy, thermal analysis (TGA/DSC) on active materials, calorific output on heat pellets, cell capacity and impedance, and microanalysis (SEM/EDS). The primary aging mechanism appears to be sulfur migration from the cathode leading to active material depletion at both electrodes. Cell capacity in both CoS_2 and FeS_2 cathode units was reduced by as much as 10% in dry samples, but no less than 15% and as much as 60% in moist samples. CoS_2 cathodes are susceptible to degradation without additional moisture over standard dry room conditions. Large amounts of hydrogen accumulated quickly in sealed batteries and di ssipated slowly. A reduction in calorific output with aging appears independent of moisture content for heat pellets. Microanalysis and s pectroscopy were used to define a probable reaction pathway for capacity fade through shelf-life aging. revealing that hydrogen sealed in thermal batteries may exacerbate cathode deterioration*

Keywords: molten salt, Arrhenius; lithium silicon; iron and cobalt disulfide; Fe/$KClO_4$; iron/potassium perchlorate.

Introduction

The Li(Si)/FeS_2 thermal battery system was developed in the early 1980's as a long operational life replacement for Ca/$CaCrO_4$ thermal batteries with lower intrinsic hazards [8]. The need for shelf stability is intrinsic to thermal batteries, so several accelerated aging studies were performed prior to the widespread use of this battery technology [1,2]. The studies identified the dominant aging mechanism as lithium oxidation from oxygen leaking through hermetic seals. Lithium oxidizes from water and oxygen trapped in the battery at time of production as well as leaking oxygen from air [2]. This early work focused on battery electrical performance, but a sampling of units was also examined before firing using analytical techniques.

Previous work [1] performed leak acceleration by leaving the battery open then flowing water and oxygen over it at elevated temperature to achieve a predetermined lithium oxidation content, based on measured activation energies of the lithium reaction. This acceleration technique presumes lithium oxidation is the predominant aging reaction. It was established previously that this reaction occurs [1], but the open configuration eliminates the possibility of observing other reactions that may occur from the interaction between constituents.

This earlier work did not use gas sampling as a methodology for examining the batteries before firing, and microanalysis was limited to surface analysis rather than polished cross-sections [3]. The present work revisits accelerated aging with a focus on analysis of the battery state before firing. This focus is due to the availability of field returns from batteries exceeding the anticipated 30-year lifetime. Accelerated aging is a way to refine analytical techniques to determine what we should expect to find in batteries that have experienced real-time aging.

The accelerating factors for this study were temperature and water vapor. Oxidation of lithium by molecular oxygen is considered the primary mechanism of thermal battery aging [1]. Water vapor also can leak into the battery, although given the slow rates of leakage molecular oxygen is assumed to be the predominant source of oxygen for lithium corrosion. Note that there is strong evidence that thermal batteries do not leak at the rates suggested by the helium bomb test [4]. These tests are go/no go tests for batteries because the leak rates are within the noise of the technique. Gas sampling of units after helium bomb has demonstrated that the observed leak rates could not have been present because the amount of residual helium in the sealed battery is not high enough to explain the leak rate. It must be assumed the observed leak rate is real at the time of product acceptance, but if longer lifetimes are required the leak test can be adjusted to become more sensitive. Examination of the reactions between only the sealed constituents is therefore of interest.

Temperatures for aging were selected based on practical criteria. 75°C is approximately the upper limit of use conditions for thermal batteries. 130°C is the temperature of previous accelerated aging studies [2]; it is based on the high temperature FeS_2 decomposition activation energy. 180°C was the upper practical limit for storage in available environmental chambers.

One year of detailed aging studies was undertaken with limited additional units pulled at two years. This means a 30x acceleration factor was desirable to mimic the lifetime of current field return units. Assuming a 40°C storage temperature, the activation energy required to get a 30x acceleration is 86 kJ/mol at 75°C, 32 kJ/mol at 130°C, and 24 kJ/mol at 180°C. These will be compared to possible aging reactions in the discussion section.

Experimental Procedures

Li(Si)/FeS_2 and CoS_2 thermal battery materials (anode, cathode, separator, heat pellet, and insulation) were hermetically sealed in stainless steel cans with known quantities of water and dry air. All materials were stored under argon after fabrication until simulated battery assembly. Battery cases were fabricated from two steel end plates and steel tubing cut to length; glass-to-metal seals were omitted to minimize leak paths. All steel was baked and vacuum dried. Fiberfrax (Unifrax, Latham NY) felt insulation was used to wrap the cells to provide a snug fit into the can. Fiberfrax board insulation was used for shims on the ends of the stack to provide some closing force on the assembly. Insulation material was dried as normal at high temperature. However, half of the material was then exposed to room temperature moist air by sealing the insulation in an enclosure such as a desiccator with a pan of water (H_2O for FeS_2 batteries). Batteries with this insulation were identified as "wet". In the CoS_2 cathode study, the pan of water was replaced with deuterium oxide (D_2O) so deliberately added water could be identified in mass spectroscopy from water residue from assembly.

The cell stack was comprised of a stainless steel collector, heat pellet, collector, cathode, separator, and anode repeated four times and capped with another collector. A 200 PSI closing force was supplied; shims were stainless steel or dried Fiberfrax board. Leak checking was performed to ensure the batteries had less than $5x10^{-9}$ sccs He leak rate.

The electrolyte for the FeS_2 batteries was standard KCl/LiCl eutectic, but a low melting electrolyte was selected for the CoS_2 cells. This brominated electrolyte may retain more moisture when dried and stored in normal dry room conditions than the KCl/LiCl eutectic.

All units were helium leak checked before and after aging. Units were gas sampled by puncturing the battery case in a sealed volume after aging. Units were then disassembled and visually inspected prior to additional testing. Single-cell testing was used to determine electrochemical capacity. Tests were performed at a constant 0.125 A/cm^2 discharge rate with periodic pulses to assess internal resistance. Analytical techniques applied to the internal materials include cross-section microanalysis (SEM/EDS) [3], Fourier transform infrared spectroscopy (FTIR), fast neutron activation analysis (FNAA) for oxygen content of the anode, bomb calorimetry for heat pellet output, spatially resolved X-ray diffraction (XRD), and thermal analysis (DSC, TGA).

Results

A general linear model was used to determine if statistically significant effects were observed as a result of time, temperature, or water vapor for each of the analytical techniques. This analysis was performed for FeS2 cathode units; CoS_2 cathode units were only compared qualitatively at this point. The model has the form:

$$\hat{y} = \beta_0 + \beta_1 T(°C) + \beta_2 t(days) + \beta_3(Wet?) + \epsilon$$

β terms are least-squared defined regression defined coefficents and ε is the residual. Although this simple linear model is useful for determining if there are statistically significant changes it is not a predictive model.

Application of this model shows that the following had no change during the study: Heat capacity (cathode and separator), electrolyte melting point, heat of fusion, N_2 and Ar content.

The thermal analysis results appear to be unchanged by the accelerating factors, likely demonstrating the electrolyte is dessicated by the lithium in the anode and the cathode does not create soluble decomposition products.

Temperature alone was a sufficient accelerant to cause changes in total pressure, heat pellet calorific output, H_2, and O_2 content. The primary changes associated with overall gas composition are a complete consumption of oxygen in the can in just three months at 75°C, a reduction in water vapor, and a dramatic increase in hydrogen concentration in the can. Heat pellet calorific output is reduced at high temperature (180°C), but was independent of water content. However, heat pellets in units with high water vapor content were difficult to ignite; only one of three "wet" units yielded any output. Ignition sensitivity was not systematically explored in this study, but will be a subject of future investigation.

Water was an effective accelerant for the following measurements: anode oxidation, electrochemical capacity, impedance, and peak voltage. Enhanced anode oxidation was the expected outcome based on conclusions of previous studies. Not drying the insulation effectively increased the extent of anode oxidation from 3.5wt% oxygen to about 10wt% as shown in Figure 1. Anode oxidation was independent of time in this work, meaning the reaction of the anode with water went to completion faster than the lowest time and temperature (3 months at 75°C). Searcy [4] measured oxidation rates and found the activation energy for the lithium reaction with water to be about 24 kJ/mol. This is like a 30x acceleration factor for 180°C. Anode oxidation occurred so quickly even at 75°C that it was not possible to determine its rate constant.

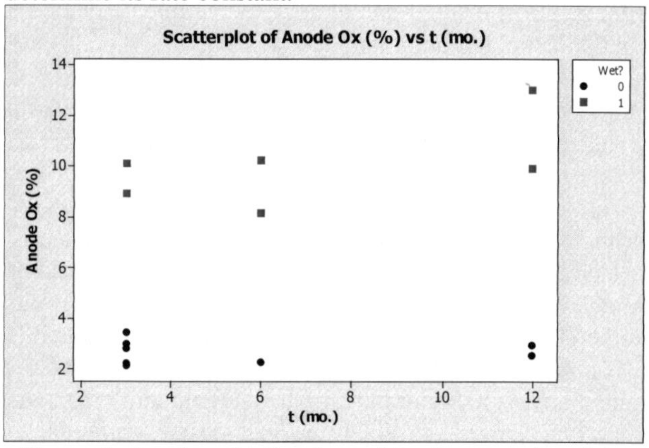

Figure 1. Anode oxidation for wet (red squares) and dry (black circles) sealed units

The capacity to 1.3V (approximately the voltage for complete conversion of all FeS_2 to FeS and $Li_{13}Si_4$ to Li_7Si_3) is shown in Figure 2.

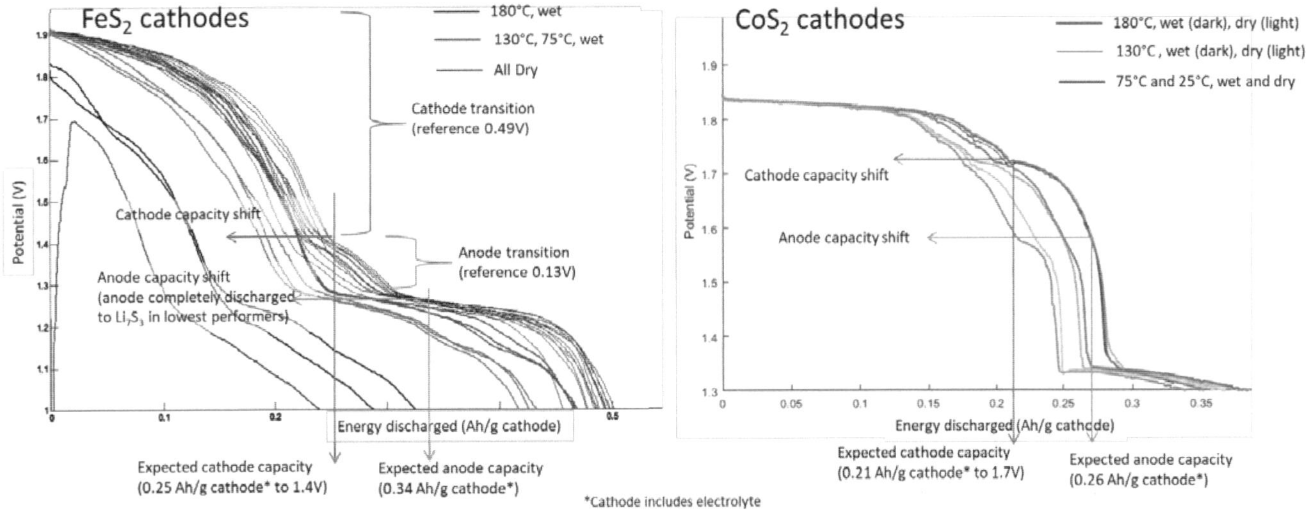

Figure 2. Single-cell discharge data (smoothed), 0.125 mA/cm^2.

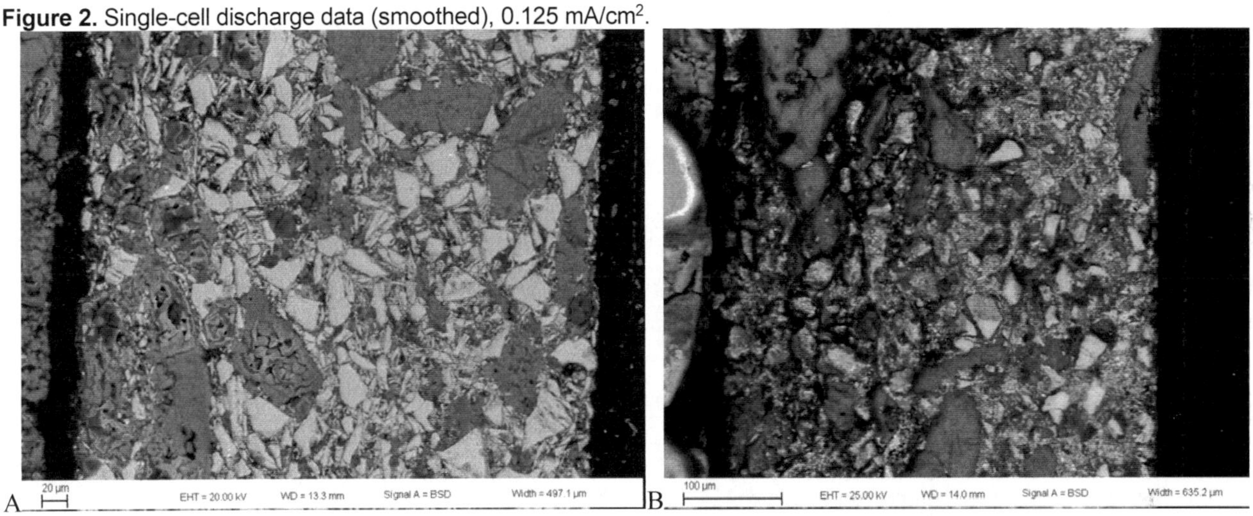

Figure 4. FeS2 Cathode after 6 months at 180°C. A) Dry B) Wet.

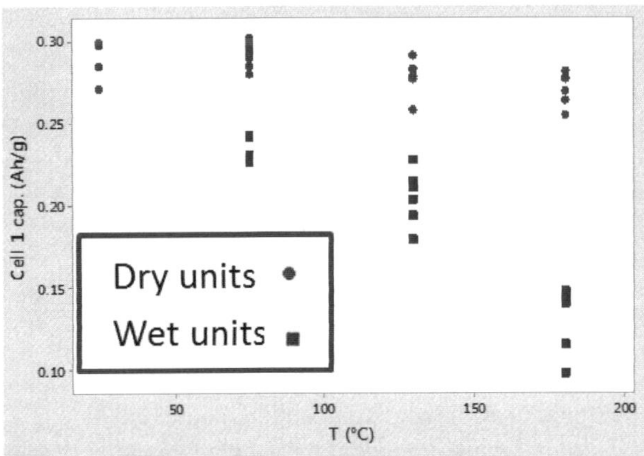

Figure 3. Capacity to 1.3V for single-cells

Electrochemical performance changes were not noted when temperature alone was used as an accelerant for FeS_2, but clear changes were observed for CoS_2. However, capacity, impedance, and peak voltage all changed when additional water was added to the sealed FeS_2 units (Figure 2). This degradation occurred despite a constant amount of anode oxidation (Figure 1), indicating the reaction was with the cathode. This is confirmed by examination of the cathode microstructure. The FeS_2 grains in 180°C wet samples are highly fractured and darker in color in backscattered electron mode (Figure 4), resembling discharged cathodes containing primarily FeS. CoS_2 grain morphology wasn't assessed.

Discussion

This study examines the behavior of the cathode when excessive water is trapped in the sealed volume. Lithium is oxidized by water to form hydrogen.

$2Li + H_2O = Li_2O + H_2$ $\Delta G°(100°C)$ -163 kJ/mol Li

The hydrogen content declines over time due to a secondary reaction; this could be absorption into the lithium silicon [5] or into the FeS_2 cathode [6]. However, the concentration of hydrogen stays high (up to 10%) for long periods of time. Elevated hydrogen content is a systematic observation in gas sampling of field return units, for instance.

Single-cell capacity loss measurements show a drop in cathode capacity as a function of temperature. The anode may also completely oxidize (showing a 0.13V drop in starting voltage), but this does not account for the remaining voltage change. Cathode decomposition could be the result of sulfate formation or SO_2 formation resulting in FeS. The sulfate reaction was suggested in the earlier, open-flow accelerated aging study [1]. However, both these reactions are limited by the oxygen in the battery, which drops to ppm levels due to gettering by lithium.

A more plausible reaction path is hydrogen enhanced FeS_2 decomposition:

$$FeS_2 + H_2(g) = FeS + H_2S(g)$$

$$\Delta G°(100°C)\ +27\ kJ/mol\ FeS_2\ [7]$$

This reaction consumes hydrogen but produces H_2S. Although this reaction is not thermodynamically favorable in a closed system, lithium readily getters H_2S.

$$2Li + H_2S(g) = Li_2S + H_2(g)$$

$$\Delta G°(100°C)\ -394\ kJ/mol\ Li_2S$$

This H_2S gettering by lithium produces an equilibrium pH_2S of 10^{-56} atm, thermodynamically making the FeS_2 decomposition reaction favorable even at room temperature. The activation energy for this decomposition is 88 kJ/mol, which results in approximately a 30x acceleration factor at 75°C and 25000x acceleration at 180°C.

Evidence for this reaction can be found in the microstructural analysis shown in Figure 5. EDS maps of the anode, separator and cathode show sulfur migration across the separator. No sulfur is present in the separator, indicating a low solubility of sulfur in the separator. The results are consistent with a gas phase mass transport of H_2S through a porous pressed powder compact separator.

Figure 5 also shows that a similar mechanism for sulfur transport is occurring in CoS_2 cells, but additional water is not required to drive this reaction. Maps in Figure 5 are from batteries made with dry room best practices.

A common concern with accelerated aging studies is that the acceleration effects are not applicable under normal circumstances. While this can't be discounted, sulfur migration was observed in the dry, 180°C, 12 month sample and extensively in CoS_2 units. Water accelerates the reaction, but occurs at pertinent battery water contents.

Conclusions

Lithium in thermal batteries getters water and oxygen to form lithium oxide and hydrogen. This is an important reaction and may limit battery lifetime if battery leak rates are sufficiently high. However, in well-sealed batteries hydrogen enhanced cathode decomposition may play an important role in determining the lifetime of the battery. Future studies will focus on determining the kinetic rate constants for these reactions.

Acknowledgements

Sandia is a multi-mission laboratory managed and operated by National Technology & Engineering Solutions of Sandia, LLC, a wholly owned subsidiary of Honeywell International, Inc., for the U.S. Department of Energy's National Nuclear Security Administration under contract DE-NA0003525.

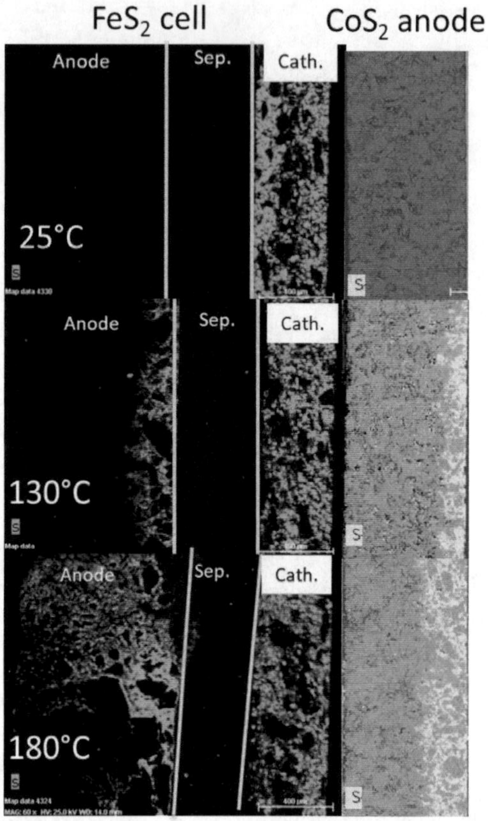

Figure 5. EDS Sulfur maps. FeS_2 maps are from wet cells, CoS_2 are from dry (anode only, overlaid on backscattered image). 25°C Control, 130C 6 months, 180°C 3 months.

References

1. J.Q. Searcy, J.R. Armijo. "Additional Experiments Relative to the Shelf-life of Li(Si)/FeS2 thermal batteries." Sandia Report SAND84-1510 (1984).
2. Searcy et al. "Lithium Oxide in the Li(Si)/FeS_2 Thermal Battery System." Sandia Report SAND81-1705 (1981).
3. Searcy, F.W. Reinhardt. "Reaction Rates of Atmospheric Gases with Lithium(Silicon) Alloy." Sandia Report SAND80-1363 (1980).
4. Beevers et al. "Hermeticity and Thermal Battery Lifetime." 45th Power Sources Conf. 34.5 (2014).
5. Searcy and Neiswander. "Aging Study of Li(Si)/FeS2 Thermally Activated Batteries." Sandia Report SAND80-0423 (1980).
6. Assink et al. "Hydrogen Sorption Studies of Materials Used in Li(Si)/FeS_2 Thermal Batteries." Sandia Report SAND87-3149 (1987).
7. Thomas et al. "Decomposition of Pyrite Under Coal Liquefaction Conditions: A Kinetic Study." Fuel, Vol. 61 761-764 (1982).
8. Guidotti and Masset. "Thermally activated ("thermal") battery technology Part I: An overview." Journal of Power Sources 161 (2006) 1443–1449

Advanced Nanostructuring and Enhanced Performance of Thermal Battery Cathode Materials

Lauren A. Morris[1*], Giuseppe L. Di Benedetto[1], David B. Swanson[2], Brian D. Wightman[2], Charles W. McMullan[1], and Richard Dratler[1]

[1] U.S. Army Armament Research, Development and Engineering Center, Picatinny Arsenal, NJ 07806.

[2] EnerSys Advanced Systems, Inc., 104 Rock Road, Horsham, PA 19044.

Contact author email and phone: Lauren.a.morris17.civ@mail.mil / 973.724.1946

Abstract: *For the U.S. Army, high-performance power sources are a critical technology for current and future gun-fired munitions and submunitions. Thermal batteries are the reserve power source of choice for many weapon systems due to their high power and power density, proven extreme shelf life, and capability to function across a wide range of operating environments. As development continues on future munitions, thermal batteries will need to supply a significantly higher level of power with longer run times while occupying less volume. The use of nanomaterials offers the potential to produce batteries with performance improvements, such as higher voltages at increased current densities. In this study, U.S. Army ARDEC and EnerSys Advanced Systems jointly investigated the optimization of nanostructured iron disulfide (FeS_2) for thermal battery manufacturing. Nanostructured FeS_2 was synthesized using a fully scalable method, and characterized utilizing SEM, EDS, XRD, ICP, BET, and other techniques. This study successfully used high energy milling to produce kilogram quantities of acceptable FeS_2 powder for cathode use in thermal batteries. The thermal properties and decomposition of the nanostructured FeS_2 powder was compared to that of the micron powder using TGA-DSC. Catholyte containing nanostructured FeS_2 was pressed into pellets, and characterized based on electrochemical performance as compared to the FeS_2 cathode pellets currently used in industry. Optimized single cell thermal battery techniques, discharge testing, and pulse load capability was used to compare cell performance between standard and nanostructured iron disulfides for better understanding of best-use applications for these materials.*

Keywords: nanomaterials; thermal battery; molten salt battery; cathode; nanoscale; iron disulfide; milling

Introduction

Thermal batteries are a mission critical defense technology required to power precision guided munitions, missiles, and other weapons systems in which it may be required that the power source remain dormant for several years, or even decades, prior to being activated for use. A thermal battery consists of a series of stacked cathode, separator, and anode pellets which become conductive when heated to their molten state by the activation of a pyrotechnic heat source. As weapons become more advanced the power requirements increase, creating a need for thermal batteries that can provide higher voltages and longer run times. Therefore, there is a strong need to manipulate materials to produce batteries with superior performance which can enable future weapons systems.

Recently, several research groups have reported on the use of nanoscale or nanostructured iron disulfide (n-FeS_2) as a replacement cathode material for conventional, micron-sized FeS_2 (μ-FeS_2) to improve performance of a thermal battery. Nanoscale FeS_2 has been synthesized by chemical hydrothermal synthesis [1, 2], and high energy ball milling [3]. Improved performance and material properties were reported including increased total power density, increased robustness of electrode pellets, and longer run times, attributed to the small particle size (< 100 nm) of the n-FeS_2 [4].

Our previous work has reported on the synthesis of nanoscale cathode materials (FeS_2, CoS_2, and NiS_2) by high energy ball milling [5, 6] and evaluating performance in single-cell thermal battery (SCTB) testing [5], wherein longer run times, higher capacities and higher voltages were demonstrated using n-FeS_2 in place of μ-FeS_2. Full sized thermal batteries were subsequently built with n-FeS_2, but, unfortunately, the performance increases demonstrated in SCTB testing were not realized in the full sized battery. It was hypothesized that changes in the thermal properties of the nanoscale cathode materials might require that the thermal balance of the battery be adjusted to compensate.

This work aims to scale up the previous high energy ball milling to increase batch sizes from 0.2 kg to 1 kg. Additionally, thermal analysis is performed on the μ-FeS_2 and n-FeS_2 and catholyte powders to fully characterize the effects of particle size on the thermal properties. SCTB testing is conducted at varying temperatures.

Experimental

Synthesis and Characterization

High energy ball milling was used to synthesize n-FeS_2 from commercially available micron sized powder. All powders (as received, and as synthesized) were stored in an inert argon environment with less than 10 ppm oxygen. Iron disulfide was milled in 1 kg batches down to nanoscale under argon in a horizontal attritor using yttria stabilized zirconia grinding media.

The synthesized nanoscale FeS_2 powder properties were characterized using a variety of techniques. Scanning Electron Microscopy (SEM) was performed using a Zeiss Supra V40 using in-lens and backscatter detectors at 15 kV. X-ray diffraction (XRD) was performed using a Rigaku Ultima with Cu-Kα source with MDI Jade software. Chemical analysis was performed using inductively coupled plasma optical emission spectroscopy (ICP-OES) and ASTM D1353 to determine Fe and S content by weight. The Barret-Emmet-Teller (B.E.T.) method for surface area analysis and particle size derivation was done using a Quantachrome Nova 4000e. Oxygen analysis was performed using a Horiba EMGA-620W oxygen/nitrogen analyzer. Particle size analysis was performed using a Horiba LA-950V2 to determine the d_{10}, d_{50}, and d_{90} on a volume basis. Complete thermal analysis was performed using a Netzsch STA 449F1 Jupiter: simultaneous thermogravimetric analysis and differential scanning calorimetry (TGA-DSC) was performed in a SiC furnace under Ar with a heating rate of 5 K/min; heat capacity (Cp) measurements were performed in a Pt furnace under Ar with a heating rate of 20 K/min using sapphire as a standard. Data analysis was performed using Proteus Analysis software and Cp was calculated using ASTM 1269.

Cathode Preparation and Single Cell Battery Testing

Catholyte powders were produced using micron and nanoscale FeS_2 as previously reported [5]. Under inert conditions FeS_2 was mixed with electrolyte powder and blended. After standard processing, grinding, sieving, and drying under vacuum the catholyte powder was pressed into pellets. Pressing of the cathode pellets was accomplished by hand in dry room conditions (< 3 % RH), all pellets used in this study were uniform in thickness, and free from defects.

A SCTB testing device clamps thermal battery pellets cathode-separator-andode between two thermostatically controlled metal platens at pressure, and allows voltage and current to flow between metal current collectors on each side of a cathode-separator-anode pellet stack. The cell is held at a constant temperature throughout testing.

Results and Discussion

Synthesis and Characterization

High energy ball milling to obtain n-FeS_2 was successful using a larger mill with 1 kg batch sizes. It was determined by XRD that all powders that were synthesized at this larger scale were phase pure pyrite (PDF reference: 01-071-1680) with peak broadening observed for milled n-FeS_2, an indication of particle size reduction (Figure 1). Electron microscopy confirmed particle size reduction and nanoscale features (Figure 2).

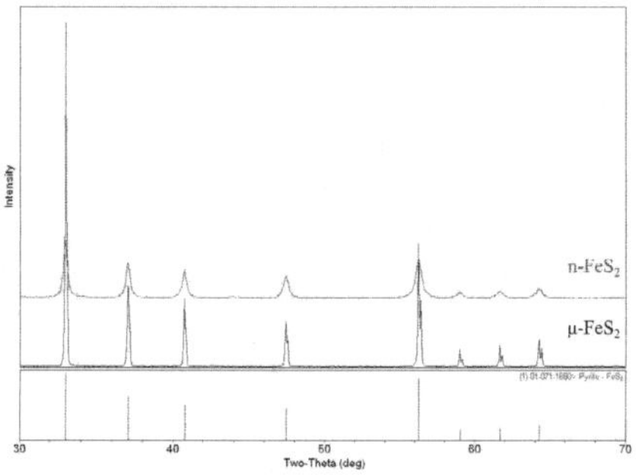

Figure 1: (a) XRD spectra of μ-FeS_2 and n-FeS_2 showing peaks corresponding to phase pure pyrite, FeS_2, in both samples and significant peak broadening in n-FeS_2.

a b c

Figure 2: In-lens SEM images of (a) μ-FeS_2 at 500 x, and n-FeS_2 synthesized by high energy ball milling at (b) 500 x and (c) 100 kx.

All lots passed ICP chemical analysis with empirical formulas within the acceptable limits ($FeS_{2.129}$ – $FeS_{1.882}$). Significant particle size reduction of the μ-FeS_2 was accomplished, resulting in a high surface area n-FeS_2 powder whose nominal particle diameter was calculated from BET to be 64.9 nm assuming uniform spherical particles.

The crystallite size of the μ-FeS_2 and n-FeS_2 were calculated from the XRD spectra using the Scherrer equation, and were > 500 nm and 48 nm respectively. Particle size analysis also confirmed particle size reduction. The chemical and physical properties of the μ-FeS_2 and n-FeS_2 are summarized in Table 1.

Table 1: Properties of micron and nanoscale FeS_2.

		μ-FeS_2	n-FeS_2
Empirical Formula		$FeS_{2.109}$	$FeS_{2.086}$
Specific Surface Area	(m^2/g)	0.491	19.665
BET Equivalent Diameter	(nm)	2600	64.9
Crystallite Size	(nm)	>500	48.2
Oxygen Content	(wt.%)	0.725	1.500
d_{10}	(μm)	11.97	0.348
d_{50}	(μm)	25.16	2.02
d_{90}	(μm)	43.38	18.378

The thermal stability of FeS_2 has been thoroughly investigated and it is widely understood that the overall mechanism is described by Equation 1 [7, 8], where pyrite undergoes an endothermic decomposition above 580 °C accompanied by mass loss due to evolved sulfur gas. Thermal batteries need to be heated to their molten state to be activated, but will undergo thermal runaway if they get too hot. Thermal stability of the μ-FeS_2 and milled n-FeS_2 powders was evaluated under inert atmospheres (see Figure 3a). The DSC data show both μ-FeS_2 and n-FeS_2 undergo thermal decomposition, although the process begins at much lower temperature (< 500 °C) in the n-FeS_2 powder, as is evident in the small endothermic peak that appears at prior to the onset of the main decomposition. The TGA data for n-FeS_2 looks similar to the data for μ-FeS_2, but the weight loss begins at much lower temperature in the n-FeS_2 as compared to the μ-FeS_2. The heat capacity was also calculated and is plotted in Figure 3b along with data from literature for pure pyrite [7].

$$(1-x)FeS_{2(s)} \overset{\Delta}{\rightarrow} Fe_{1-x}S_s(x=0-0.2) + \frac{1}{2}(1-2x)S_{2(g)} \quad \text{(Eq. 1)}$$

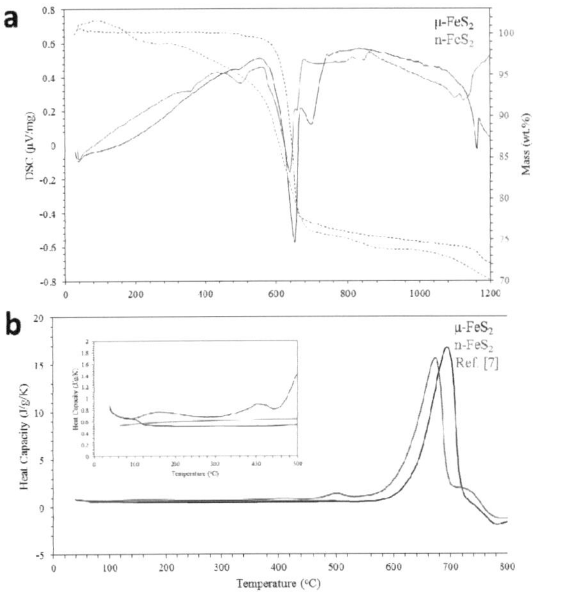

Figure 3: (a) DSC (solid) and TGA (dashed) of μ-FeS_2 and milled n-FeS_2 powders in argon and (b) heat capacity of μ-FeS_2 and n-FeS_2 plotted with data from literature [7] with inset showing zoomed in heat capacity data for T < 500 °C.

Cathode Preparation and Single Cell Battery Testing

The μ-FeS_2 and milled n-FeS_2 powders were mixed with electrolyte binder, heat treated, and ground into catholyte powders referred to as μ-catx and n-catx, respectively. Scanning electron microscopy in backscatter mode was used to image the catholyte powders (see Figure 4). The various elements in the catholyte powders are shown by different contrasts in the images in Figure 3; it is evident that the length scale of mixing is much smaller in the n-catx as compared to the μ-catx, showing shorter diffusion distances between constituents in the n-catx powders.

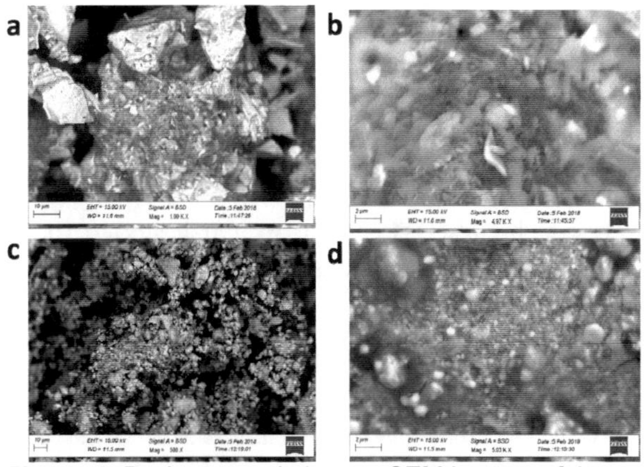

Figure 4: Backscattered electron SEM images of the μ-catx at (a) 1 kx and (b) 5 kx, and the n-catx at (c) 1 kx and (d) 5 kx.

Micron and nano cathode pellets were pressed from the μ-catx and n-catx powders shown in Figure 4. The pellet size and compaction force was maintained consistent with the commercial battery cathode. The separator and anode pellets that were used were standard to the commercial G3190B2 battery. Cathode, separator, and anode pellets were stacked into SCTBs (μ-SCTB and n-SCTB) and the performance of each was evaluated using the SCTB testing device.

The commercial G3190B2 battery is heated to its molten, conductive state using pyrotechnic heat pellets of varying energy output. Typically, it is operated with a current density of 50 mA/cm^2 which corresponds to a background load of 0.350 A in the SCTB test device. Due to the differences shown in thermal stability between the μ-FeS_2 and n-FeS_2 cathode powders, SCTB tests were conducted on μ-SCTB and n-SCTB at temperatures ranging from 425 to 625 °C to determine the effect of operating temperature under high loads. These experiments were performed with 0.350 A background load current with a 0.5 s, 7 A current pulse every 60 s. A cut off voltage of 1.4 V was used to determine end of life of the SCTBs, data acquisition was stopped when discharge voltages dropped below this threshold value.

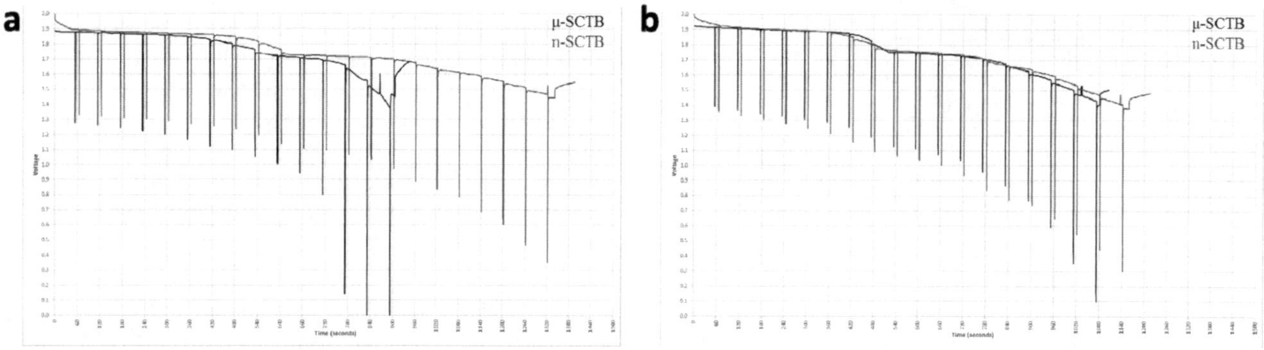

Figure 5: Single cell thermal battery discharge testing of μ-SCTB and n-SCTB with a 0.350 A background load current and 0.5 s, 7 A pulse every 60 s at platen temperatures of (a) 500 °C and (b) 550 °C

Figure 5a shows the discharge performance of the μ-SCTB and the n-SCTB with the platens heated to 500 °C and Figure 5b shows the performance at a slightly higher temperature of 550 °C. It was determined that the n-SCTB had a longer run time and higher voltage at both temperatures. The longest run time attained was 1080 s at 550 °C for the μ-SCTB and 1380 s at 500 °C for the n-SCTB. This data indicates that the n-SCTB has better performance when maintained at a 500 °C as compared with the μ-SCTB which performed better at 550 °C. The maximum cell voltages obtained in any test for μ-SCTB and n-SCTB were at the beginning of battery life and were approximately 1.9 and 2.0 V, respectively.

Conclusions

High surface area nanoscale FeS_2 with reduced particle size and acceptable chemical analysis was successfully synthesized in 1 kg batch sizes demonstrating a scalability of the high energy milling technique. Thermal analysis of the μ-FeS_2 and n-FeS_2 revealed that the thermal decomposition of the n-FeS_2 begins at lower temperature than in μ-FeS_2 powders. Micron and nano catholyte powders were synthesized and pressed into pellets for SCTB testing. SCTB testing under high pulsed current loads revealed that the n-SCTB showed higher maximum cell voltages and longer run times than the μ-SCTB at both 500 and 550 °C. The n-SCTB performed best at 500 °C while the μ-SCTB performed best at 550 °C. A 28% increase in run time, and 5% increase in maximum voltage was demonstrated using a nanostructured cathode and lower platen temperature.

Acknowledgements

This work is supported by the Power for Advanced Munitions effort on ARDEC's Fuze and Power Technologies for Munitions STO program, directly supporting the Army Modernization priority for Long Range Precision Fires (LRPF).

References

1. Guidotti, R. A., F. W. Reinhardt, J. Dai, and D. E. Reisner, "Preparation and Characterization of Synthetic Pyrite for Thermal-Battery Cathodes," *Proceedings of 40th Power Sources Conference*, p. 339, 2002.

2. Guidotti, R. A., P. J. Nigrey, F. W. Reinhardt, and J. G. Odinek, "Evaluation of Nanoparticulate Metal Disulfides in Thermal Batteries," *Proceedings of 40th Power Sources Conference*, p. 250, 2002.

3. Au, M., "Nanostructured Thermal Batteries with High Power Density," *Journal of Power Sources*, vol. 115, pp. 360-366, 2003.

4. Au, M., Y. Lei, and T. Yadav, "Thermal Batteries Made with Nanostructured Material," *NASA Tech Briefs*, vol. 23, no. 4, pp. 28-29, April 1999.

5. Di Benedetto, G. L., R. Carpenter, D. Swanson, and B. Wightman, "Enhanced Nanostructuring of Iron Disulfide for Thermal Battery Cathode Materials," *Proceedings of 46th Power Sources Conference*, pp. 469-472, 2014.

6. Carpenter, R., G.L. Di Benedetto, "Enhanced Nanostructuring Approach for Thermal Battery Cathode Materials," *Proceedings of 47th Power Sources Conference*, 2016.

7. Gronvold, F., E.F. Westrum, "Heat Capacities of iron disulfides Thermodynamics of marcasite from 5 to 700 K, pyrite from 300 to 780 K, and the transformation of marcasite to pyrite," J. Chem. Thermodynamics, vol.8, pp. 1039-1048, 1976.

8. Masset, P.J., R.A. Guidotti, "Thermal activated ("thermal") battery technology Part IIIa: FeS_2 cathode material," *Journal of Power Sources,* vol. 177, pp. 595-609, 2008.

Historical Production of Maglite S and the Development of a New Magnesium-Oxide Binder for Thermal Batteries

Hans W. Papenguth, Martin B. Nemer, Christine C. Roberts, Robert C. Moore, and Timothy J. Boyle
Sandia National Laboratories
Albuquerque, NM, USA 87123
hwpapen@sandia.gov / 1-505-844-3819

Abstract: *In the early 1980s, Sandia chose Maglite S MgO as the preferred binder in Li(Si)/FeS$_2$ thermal battery (TB) designs. Maglite S and later options such as Marinco OL MgO are no longer available, and the identification of alternatives has been the focus of many efforts. Over the past several years, Sandia has undertaken a large program to develop a new MgO for use in TBs. As an initial step, a historical study of MgOs was performed to better understand how Maglite S was manufactured, and to understand why substitutes for Maglite S have been so difficult to identify. This work has led to the determination of several physicochemical properties of Maglite S that allow it to function unusually well. Recent efforts at Sandia to create a new one-for-one substitute MgO material, including synthesis of the precursor material, are described.*

Keywords: MgO; magnesium oxide; separator; electrolyte binder; Maglite; Marinco; thermal battery

Introduction

Magnesium Oxide (MgO) has proven to be the material of choice for use as an electrolyte binder (EB) in pressed-powder separator pellets of modern TB designs. The general properties of MgO powder satisfy a myriad of requirements including reasonable shelf life before use; ability to fabricate high-quality, robust pellets; chemical compatibility with TB materials; and the absence of gas generation. At TB activation, the MgO binder must allow the separator pellet to release a predictable volume of E to the adjacent anode and cathode pellets, resist radial leakage, while maintaining a stiff structure to survive mechanical environments stresses. Moreover, the MgO binder must provide minimal resistance to ion transport between the anode and cathode. In the early 1980s, Sandia began using Maglite S no. 3331 MgO in Li(Si)/FeS$_2$ TB designs. Subsequent characterization work and searches for a substitute MgO [1] have consistently shown that Maglite S MgO enables superior TB performance, particularly under high load conditions. TB designs can be adjusted to accommodate suboptimal MgOs, but design or performance compromises must be made.

Over the past several years, Sandia has conducted a concerted effort to develop a replacement for Maglite S. While drawing on previous efforts at Sandia, the present effort is focused on developing a rigorous understanding of vintage MgO manufacturing methods, identifying why Maglite S performs so well, defining meaningful requirements for TB MgO, identifying materials available today made with relevant methods, and ultimately, developing synthesis techniques to produce a one-for-one substitute for Maglite S.

MgO Manufacturing Methods

A survey of MgO manufacturing methods was performed by compiling information from United States Geological Survey (USGS) Minerals Yearbooks from 1932-2008, patents from 1880-1980, and vintage trade journals. The evolution of companies and products listed in the USGS Yearbooks were used to guide reviews of patents. Insight was gained through interactions with current and former employees of companies that produce MgO. An extensive search was made of currently available MgOs from manufacturers and distributors in North America, Europe, Asia, and Australia. Physical properties were compiled for about 100 products (some recently discontinued), including product lines with tradenames MAGOX (Premier), MagChem (Martin Marietta Magnesia Specialties; MMMS), Maglite (Hallstar), Marinco and Elastomag (Rohm and Haas, Akrochem), Ossimag (Solvay), the RA series (Dead Sea Periclase, Scora), Baymag (Baymag), and Causmag (Causmag International).

MgO can be produced by calcining magnesite [$MgCO_3$] ore, which is economically practical in Australia and several Asian countries. In fact, the availability of low-cost MgO produced from ore had a negative impact on the economic viability of U.S. based MgO producers beginning in the 1980s. Other ores, such as brucite [$Mg(OH)_2$], can also be calcined to produce MgO, but those ore bodies are comparatively rare. More chemically pure MgO can be produced from a precursor made using a "one-step" precipitation process by reacting seawater or $MgCl_2$-rich brine with a base, typically lime [CaO] or dolime [($CaMgO_2$], produced from limestone [$CaCO_3$] and dolomite [$CaMg(CO_3)_2$], respectively. The brucite precipitate is recovered and calcined to MgO. Very chemically pure and morphologically unique MgO can be produced from a precursor made using a "two-step" process, in which brucite is dissolved with the aid of carbon dioxide to create a magnesium bicarbonate solution. The retrograde solubility (inverse with temperature) of carbonate phases is exploited as the solution is heated [2,3]. The magnesium carbonate (hydroxy) hydrate precipitate is recovered and calcined to MgO. The Pattinson process (BP 9,102; 1841) is a variant of the magnesium bicarbonate process, and uses dolomite as the source of magnesium. As demonstrated by the very limited discussion in a recent treatise on MgO [4], the two-step process is not currently of economic importance in the U.S.

About ten magnesium carbonate (hydroxy) hydrate phases have been identified in nature [5]. Compounds manufactured using the two-step process fall into two major categories (we will use mineral names for man-made compounds): neutral magnesium carbonate hydrates (NMCs) such as the trihydrate nesquehonite [$MgCO_3 \cdot 3H_2O$], and basic magnesium carbonate hydroxy hydrates (BMCs) such as hydromagnesite [$Mg_5(CO_3)_4(OH)_2 \cdot 4H_2O$]. In earlier patents and trade literature, BMCs were categorized using a wide range of stoichiometries, but in the absence of widespread availability of X-ray diffraction equipment, the values appear to have been based on inferences from thermogravimetric analyses. Through an examination of commercially available BMCs, we have concluded that differences in powder characteristics, such as bulk density, appear to be due to particle morphologies rather than phase differences.

Regardless of the MgO precursor, the temperature at which precursor is calcined affects the crystallinity and grain size of the resulting MgO. Maglite S would be categorized as light-burned or caustic-calcined material, which describes material processed at ~700-1000° C

Production of Maglite S MgO

Maglite S was originally manufactured in a plant located in South San Francisco CA, adjacent to San Francisco Bay (south of Point San Bruno Park). The South San Francisco plant began in 1927 as Marine Chemicals Co., changed names to Marine Magnesium Products Corp., was acquired as a division of Merck, later merged with Calgon Corp., and for its last several years was operated by a consortium of employees of Calgon and C.P. Hall Co., a distributor, as Marine Magnesium Co. Operations stopped in the early 1990s. Attempts to contact former employees of the plant were not successful. (Herein, we refer to the plant simply as "Marine" or "Merck.") In the early 1980s, Sandia acquired samples directly from Merck, but purchased material from distributors C.P. Hall Co. and Whittaker, Clark & Daniels, Inc. Products with the Maglite name are now distributed by the Hallstar Co. (which acquired C.P. Hall Co.).

A process flow diagram [3], shown in Figure 1, describes the operation of the Marine plant and the products produced. In the Maglite-S process-stream, brucite was precipitated from sea water and subsequently dissolved with the aid of carbon dioxide to create a magnesium bicarbonate solution. The bicarbonate solution was heated to precipitate a magnesium carbonate (hydroxy) hydrate suspension, which was subsequently recovered and calcined to MgO.

The MgO-CO_2-H_2O phase diagram shown in Figure 2 illustrates the thermodynamics of this process. Magnesite is thermodynamically favored over much of the phase diagram, but its formation is kinetically inhibited. Beginning with a magnesium bicarbonate solution in equilibrium with a sufficiently high partial pressure of CO_2 (e.g., 1 atm), as temperature is increased the metastability fields of the minerals lansfordite (NMC pentahydrate), nesquehonite (NMC trihydrate), and hydromagnesite (BMC) are encountered. To create light and extra-light BMCs, the metastability fields of the NMCs were quickly passed, avoiding their precipitation, to reach the metastability field where hydromagnesite would precipitate. This was accomplished by flash heating the magnesium bicarbonate solution using steam, which in the era when the Marine plant operated, was not cost prohibitive.

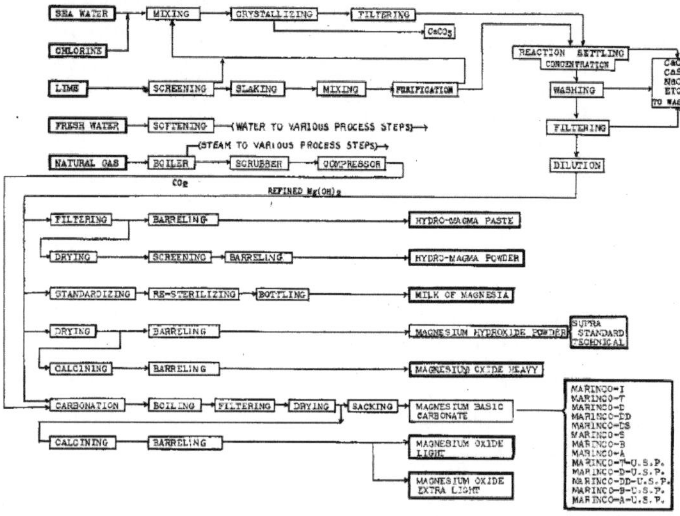

Figure 1. Marine Chemicals Co., plant flow diagram [3].

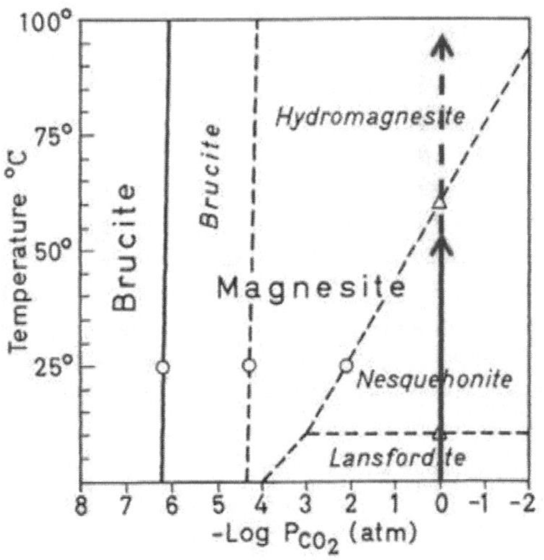

Figure 2. Tentative phase diagram of the system MgO-CO_2-H_2O [5].

After the Marine plant closed, the only remaining large-scale plant in the U.S. to produce MgO using a two-step process was Morton Salt Co. (Manistee, MI). Marinco OL MgO, identified as a candidate for use in TBs [1], had been produced using a two-step process at the Marine plant, but around the time that the plant closed, Morton, which was later acquired by Rohm & Haas Co., produced Marinco OL in Manistee until ~2004. The Morton plant is gone, as well as all other seawater plants in the U.S. (CA, DE, FL, MS, NJ, and TX). In fact, MMMS's plant in Manistee is the only remaining large-scale plant in the U.S. to produce MgO through a precipitation process.

Commercial uses

Commercial uses of MgO are remarkably diverse, including boiler-water and waste-water treatment, sugar processing, pulp whitening, animal-feed nutrient, soil conditioner, food additives, pharmaceuticals, cosmetics, refractories, insulation, rubber and plastic filler, paint pigment, abrasives, transformer-steel coating, CO_2 getter, cigarette filters, and smoke-stack gas scrubbing. Some of the early uses of brucite, BMC, and MgO were as health aids, canning additives, and food additives, such as anti-caking agents for table salt (BMC was replaced by calcium silicates in the 1940s). A key early enterprise of Marine was in supplying Morton Salt Co. (Manistee, MI) with BMC.

However, the greatest demand for magnesium carbonate (hydroxy) hydrate materials in the early 20th century was for manufacturing "85% Magnesia Insulation" to insulate pipes and boilers for the steam industry [6]. From ~1885 through ~1940, the insulation was manufactured by cold pressing a powder mix of 85:15 BMC:asbestos-fibers to create mechanically compacted shapes. Beginning in ~1935, the approach had evolved to casting a slurry of NMC (nesquehonite) and asbestos-fibers into shapes and then heating the casting for *in situ* conversion of NMC to BMC. This self-setting approach resulted in improved insulative properties, as well as a more durable product. During the era of cold-pressed 85% Magnesia Insulation, companies in the U.S. were at a peak in sophistication in producing light and extra-light BMCs. This included Ehret Magnesia Mfg. Co., Philip Carey Mfg. Co., Keasbey & Mattison Co. (PA); Johns-Manville Corp. (IL); and Plant Rubber & Asbestos Works/Parafinne Co. (CA). By ~1960 production of 85% Magnesia Insulation began to decline in the U.S., and ultimately was halted. As far as we could determine, Marine was not involved in the manufacture of 85% Magnesia insulation, but had extensive expertise in BMC production.

Excluding TBs, the only published use of Maglite S we have found is for a different Maglite product, Maglite S no. 3334 MgO. Several patents by authors associated with Calgon described the use of Maglite S no. 3334 as a coating for grain-oriented steel for transformers. It is plausible that no. 3331 was also marketed for that use.

Optimized MgO for TBs

The strikingly unusual characteristic of Maglite-S is its remarkably low "bulk density (loose)" of 5.5 pcf, listed on the Merck Product Data sheet. The uniqueness becomes apparent when compared to reported values for other contemporary commercial MgOs. Only Marinco OL and Ossimag MgO, which are also no longer available, have comparably low bulk densities. Bulk densities of other MgOs are typically greater by factors of 2-3 or more. A second unusual characteristic is the citric acid activity (CAA) value, which shows that the material is not as reactive as other relatively low-density MgOs. Gas adsorption (BET) surface area (SA) values of 30-35 m^2/g, which are not listed on the Data sheet but have been measured by Sandia, are low and consistent with the implication of CAA. In comparison, other caustic-calcined MgOs have SAs which may be 2-4 times greater.

Information in patents and trade journals shows that the key to creating extraordinarily low-density MgO powders is to begin with extremely low-density BMC powders [3] prior to calcination. MgO precursor phases have the unusual characteristic of retaining macroscopic morphologies as they transform to MgO [7]. The result is that relatively high density MgO powders result from calcining brucite, which has a blocky, tabular, pseudo-hexagonal habit. Relatively low density MgO powders result from calcining BMC, which can be manufactured as very thin plates. Extremely low density MgO powders occur with BMCs in which the very thin plates are manufactured with intersecting twinned plates or loose clusters, to create "propping" in the powder mass.

Figure 3. Micron-scale SEM image of Maglite S.

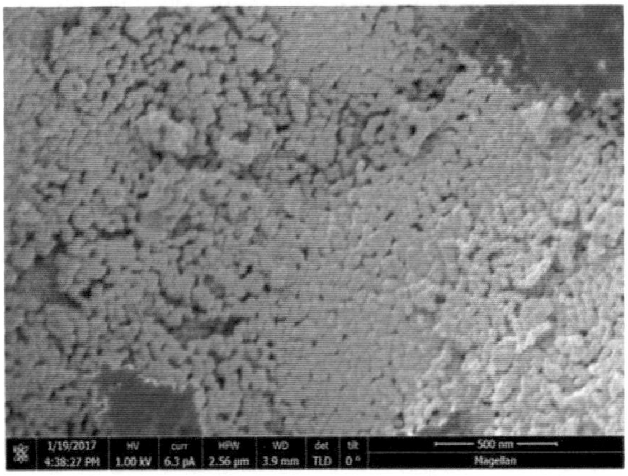

Figure 4. Nanometer-scale HR SEM image of Maglite S.

Micron-scale characterization of Maglite S using SEM shows that the powder is composed several types of grains. Most are plates (flakes) which have surface dimensions of 0.5-5 µm, with thicknesses of ~0.05-0.1 µm (Figure 3). Some larger plates are present. Many of the plates are twinned, such that they are joined at angles ("jacks"). Some of the grains are rosettes, consisting of many plates joined to form porous spheres with diameters of 5-10 µm.

Nanometer-scale characterization of Maglite S using high-resolution (HR) SEM shows that plates consist of blocky, nearly equant crystallites with smooth faces and edge dimensions of ~30-50 nm (Figure 4). The crystallites are linked such that plates consist of a single layer.

Since the outer dimensions of individual BMC grains are nearly retained during transformation from BMC to MgO, a great deal of porosity is created as water, hydroxyl, and carbonate groups are lost from BMC. Based on stoichiometry, theoretical porosity is as great as 73%. With HR SEM, porosity is evident between blocky, nearly equant MgO crystallites making up the former BMC grains.

The presence of micron-scale and nanometer-scale features creates two scales of porosity within Maglite S powder, resulting in high permeability and ionic conductivity for electrolyte in separator pellets. The porous nanostructure of Maglite S plates leads to through-particle transport. The thin, joined-plate microstructure of Maglite S leads to low packing fractions and minimal deformation at given stress levels and high retention of electrolyte. Electrolyte "binding" results exclusively from the morphological characteristics of the MgO powder [8,9].

MgO Synthesis at Sandia

We have completed batch hydrothermal BMC synthesis experiments using a laboratory steam generator, mimicking the two-step process, to explore the effects of magnesium concentrations, pCO_2, rates of heating, and process temperatures on BMC powder morphology (plate shape and size, twins, bulk density). The approach has been scaled-up to a small continuous-flow pilot-plant. We have produced BMC powders with micron-scale characteristics like Maglite S powder.

In parallel, we have pursued a precipitation approach using chemical reagents, based on methods described in the literature. The most successful approach has been through heating solutions of $MgCl_2$, $Mg(OH)_2$, and $NH_4(CO_3)_2$, which produces thin plates of BMC, although at the micron-scale, 3-dimensional features are not as prevalent as with hydrothermal synthesis. Scale-up has proven to be straightforward, but eliminating residual chloride, which affects calcination behavior, has been challenging.

Producing nanometer-scale features during calcining has proven to be equally challenging. For now, we are using a commercially available BMC to explore controls on achieving the relatively large crystallite size observed in Maglite S. To accomplish this, we are calcining toward the high end of the temperature range for caustic-calcined MgO under controlled humidity, and are exploring the use of dopants.

Conclusions

Maglite S was manufactured using a BMC precursor made by flash heating a magnesium bicarbonate solution, calcined under conditions creating relatively large crystallites. The superior performance of Maglite S no. 3331 MgO in TBs appears to be due to its unusually low bulk density and dual porosity. Chemical and hydrothermal synthesis of BMC, mimicking the two-step process, and calcining to create a similar MgO, has been successfully demonstrated at Sandia.

Acknowledgements

Sandia National Laboratories is a multimission laboratory managed and operated by National Technology and Engineering Solutions of Sandia LLC, a wholly owned subsidiary of Honeywell International Inc. for the U.S. Department of Energy's National Nuclear Security Administration under contract DE-NA0003525. The views expressed in the article do not necessarily represent the views of the U.S. Department of Energy or the United States Government.

References

1. Guidotti, R.A., and F.W. Reinhardt. "Characterization of MgO Powders for Use in Thermal Batteries." SAND90-2104. Albuquerque, NM, Sandia, 1996.
2. Doerner, H.A., W.F. Holbrook, and O.W. Fortner. "The Bicarbonate Process for the Production of Magnesium Oxide." Tech. Rept. 684, U.S. Dept. of the Interior, Bureau of Mines, 1946.
3. Chesny, H.H. "Magnesium Compounds from Ocean Water." Industrial and Engineering Chemistry, vol. 28, pp. 383-390, 1936.
4. Shand, M.A. *The Chemistry and Technology of Magnesia*. Hoboken, NJ, John Wiley & Sons, Inc., 2006.
5. Lippmann, F. "Sedimentary Carbonate Minerals." Berlin, Springer-Verlag, 1973.
6. Macan, W.A. "Defend Your Steam with '85% Magnesia' Pipe and Boiler Covering." Philadelphia, PA, The Magnesia Association of America, 1920.
7. Eubank, W.R. "Calcination Studies of Magnesium Oxides." J. Am. Cer. Soc., vol. 34, pp. 225-229, 1951.
8. Nemer, M.B., C.C. Roberts, H.W. Papenguth, P.F. Fleig, L.E. Johnson, B.A. Hernandez-Sanchez, and A.J. Headley. "Soil-Science Mechanical/Capillary Pressure/Electrical Testing Methods applied to Molten-Salt Power-Source Separator Materials." Proceedings 48th PSC, 2018.
9. Headley, A., M. Nemer, C. Roberts, and R. Solich. "Capillary Pressure Versus Saturation Characterization of Molten-Salt Power Source Separator Materials." Proceedings 48th PSC, 2018.

Development of Multivalent Chemistries for Thermal Batteries

Stewart A. M. Dickson[1], Richard K. B. Gover[2], John T. S. Irvine[1]

[1]University of St. Andrews, School of Chemistry, North Haugh, St Andrews, Fife, KY16 9ST, UK
[2]AWE Plc., Aldermaston, Reading, RG7 4PR, UK

Contact Author Email: samd2@st-andrews.ac.uk

Abstract: *In this work, prototype cells for magnesium and calcium thermal batteries have been developed by selecting eutectic electrolytes which do not contain lithium and melt at ~500 °C. The electrolytes were analysed by various techniques to determine their suitability. Cells using these electrolytes were constructed and investigated galvanostatically at temperatures of 500 °C for magnesium-containing cells and 525 °C for calcium-containing cells.*

Keywords: thermal battery; multivalent batteries; magnesium; calcium; molten salts.

Introduction

Thermal batteries are electrochemical devices used to convert chemical energy in to electrical energy. Their ability to remain usable decades after production makes them ideal for key defence applications. The success of lithium chemistry in existing thermal battery applications has led to further investigation of the chemical interactions occurring,[1] whilst also sparking renewed interest in novel cathode materials to improve performance.[2,3] Whilst lithium-based thermal batteries are considered the 'gold-standard' of the technology, they still have limitations. The lithium silicide alloy, $Li_{13}Si_4$, which is widely used as the anode material, is limited by its reduced specific capacity when compared to lithium metal (485 mA h g^{-1} *vs.* 3860 mA h g^{-1}), and by the possibility of thermal runaway at elevated temperatures.[4]

A multivalent thermal battery could provide a greater variety of alternative chemistries for new applications, especially in the mining and aerospace industries. To increase this temperature window and the capacity, it may be possible to use magnesium or calcium as the ion-carriers in thermal batteries. Both metals have been utilised as anode materials in thermal batteries previously. The Mg // V_2O_5 and Ca //$CaCrO_4$ systems, that are very well-known as predecessors to the lithium thermal battery, were also controlled by lithium chemistry. This is due to the molten lithium halide electrolyte, which has much faster diffusion coefficients than the multivalent ions.[5]

This work involves studying alternative molten salt systems which could be used as electrolytes in multivalent thermal batteries. Both magnesium and calcium systems have been analysed, as both metals are able to withstand temperatures >500 °C and, therefore, could be used as the anode material. Careful selection of a compatible electrolyte is also required to produce a functioning cell. The electrolyte mixtures were selected by studying phase diagrams of possible binary halide-salt systems, which contained the ion of interest, excluding lithium. The key considerations included identifying systems with low enough melting points to be usable with the FeS_2 cathode material and a large molar window for melting if the composition of the salt changes during discharge. Figure 1 displays the two eutectic phase diagrams of the selected mixtures.

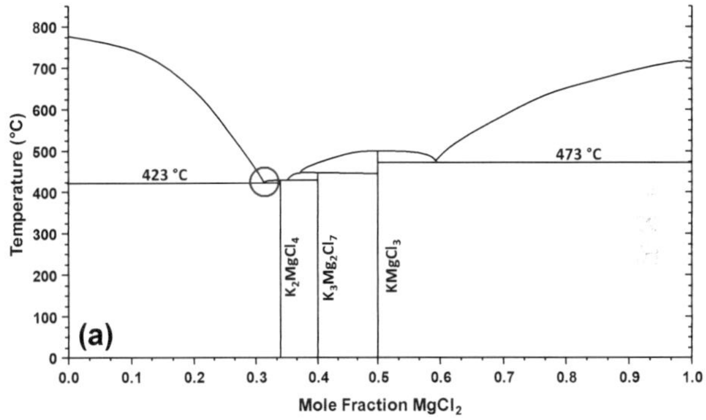

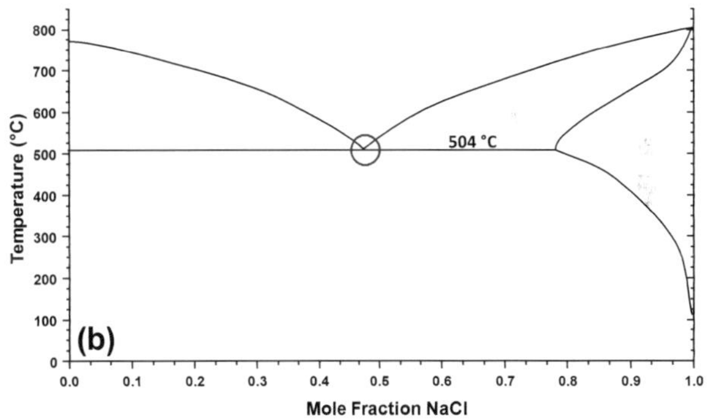

Figure 1. (a) The KCl-$MgCl_2$ phase diagram.[6] **(b)** The $CaCl_2$-NaCl phase diagram.[7] The eutectic points used in this study are circled.

The magnesium eutectic (Figure 1a) was a mixture of KCl and $MgCl_2$ with a eutectic point of 423 °C (69.2-30.7 mol%), whereas the calcium eutectic (Figure 1b) was a mixture of $CaCl_2$ and NaCl (52.1-47.9 mol%), which melts at 504 °C.

Experimental Procedure

Electrolyte Processing. The electrolytes were processed differently, due to solid solutions present in the magnesium eutectic phase diagram. Anhydrous KCl (Sigma-Aldrich, 99.9 %) and anhydrous $MgCl_2$ beads (Sigma-Aldrich,

99.99 %) were dried in a vacuum oven at 200 °C to remove hydrates, whilst preventing formation of oxides. The salts were weighed in an argon-filled glovebox to achieve the correct molar ratio, and then ball milled under argon for 2 h to afford the eutectic mixture.

For the $CaCl_2$-NaCl eutectic, the lack of solid solution formation allows for melt-quenching. Anhydrous NaCl (Alfa Aesar, 99.9 %) and anhydrous $CaCl_2$ (Alfa Aesar, 99 %) were dried at 200 °C overnight in a vacuum oven, then weighed. The mixture was then fused at 600 °C in a tube furnace under flowing argon overnight. The resultant melt was quenched by pouring on to a tantalum tray, with a stainless-steel block on top of the eutectic, to ensure even cooling. The melt was then transferred to an argon-filled glovebox and ball milled for 2 h under argon, to ensure a narrow particle size distribution

Powder X-ray Diffraction (PXRD). Powder X-ray diffraction was used to analyse the eutectics after processing, to ensure no formation of secondary phases. Patterns were collected with a PANalytical Empyrean diffractometer using Cu $K\alpha_1$ radiation (λ = 1.54068 Å), from 10 to 80° 2-theta. Samples were prepared in a glovebox using a zero-background silicon substrate. The holder was covered with Kapton film to protect samples from oxidation or water uptake during analysis, which gives a characteristic 'bump' at around 20° 2-theta.

Simultaneous Thermal Analysis (STA). The eutectics were analysed for their melting points and dryness by use of STA, which couples both thermal gravimetric analysis (TGA) with differential thermal analysis (DTA). The analysis was carried out using a NETSCH STA 449 Jupiter. The eutectic was added to an alumina crucible inside an argon filled glovebox. The samples were placed in to the STA and heated at 5 °C min^{-1} under an argon atmosphere (20 ml min^{-1}) from 50 to 600 °C.

Wetting Angle Measurements. Further analysis of the electrolytes was carried out on dense oxide binder pellets. The pellets of MgO, Al_2O_3, SiO_2 and ZrO_2 were pressed and sintered until dense. Small amounts of the eutectics were added and then the pellet placed in a bespoke tube furnace with quartz windows. The samples were heated under argon to the respective melting points and allowed to equilibrate, before photographs were taken to capture the wetting angle of the salt against the substrate. All contact angles were measured using ImageJ analysis software. Subsequently, cross-sectional analysis of the pellets was carried out using Scanning Electron Microscopy (SEM) with a JEOL 6900 FEG-SEM, to ensure adequate wetting of the salts on the dense substrate was achieved, rather than diffusion of the electrolyte in the pores.

Cell Preparation. Test cells were constructed inside an argon filled glovebox. The anodes used were either pure magnesium (Advent, 99.9 %) or calcium foils (Onyxmet, 99 %) cut to 13 mm discs. Prior to use, the foils were polished to remove any residual oxide layers, cleaned and dried. The separator was a mixture of magnesium or calcium eutectic and MgO (Hallstar) dried at 600 °C in a 55:45 wt.% ratio, pressed in to a 15 mm pellet. The cathode was raw FeS_2 powder (Sigma-Aldrich, -325mesh, 99.9 %), pressed in to a 13 mm pellet. Graphite foil was employed as a current collector for all electrodes. All components were stacked together in a ceramic cup and sealed inside a bespoke Swagelok® cell. During testing, magnesium-based cells were heated to 500 °C, whilst calcium-based cells were heated to 525 °C, allowed to stabilise at their open circuit voltage and then discharged galvanostatically using a MACCOR Model 5300 at a constant current of 15 mA cm^{-2}.

Results and Discussion

Figures 2 and 3 show the eutectic mixture PXRD patterns both before and after processing. All raw materials show no extra phases after drying. When processing, the KCl-$MgCl_2$ eutectic forms perovskite and Ruddlesden-Popper phases upon cooling, with formulae $KMgCl_3$ and K_2MgCl_4, which may be identified by the extra peaks present on the PXRD pattern (marked with •). For the ball milled mixture, these phases are absent, the only additional features are small amounts of peak broadening due to the comparatively decreased particle size and the loss of $MgCl_2$ peaks. This is likely due to formation of a glass-like mixture of both crystalline and amorphous phases.

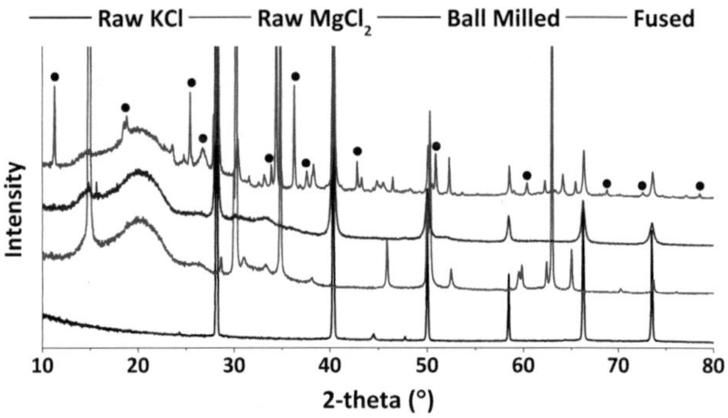

Figure 2. PXRD patterns of the raw and processed KCl-$MgCl_2$ eutectic.

For the $CaCl_2$-NaCl mixture, the opposite effect is seen. Both chlorides show clean PXRD patterns with no extra phases present. When melt quenched, the peaks are preserved, and the two salts co-exist with one another. However, upon ball milling at high speed, the formation of other phases was evident when studying the PXRD pattern in the 10° to 20° and 35° to 40° regions. Here, several peaks appear (marked with •) which do not match the raw materials. These phases could represent the perovskite and Ruddlesden-Popper phases seen in the previous eutectic mixture, as the chlorides usually favour these structures and peak positions in known phases are also similar, though this composition has never been previously reported.

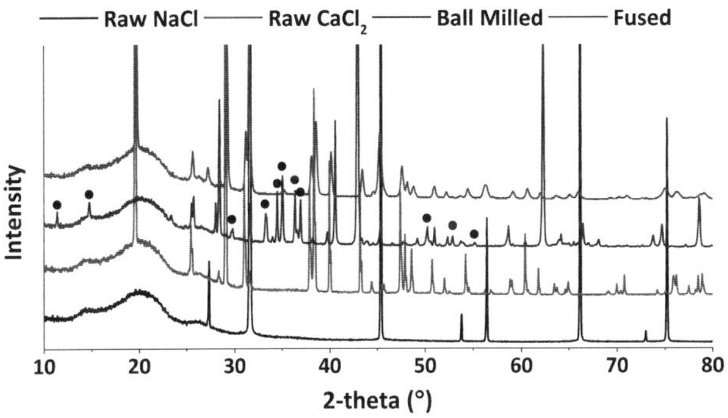

Figure 3. PXRD patterns of the raw and processed $CaCl_2$-NaCl eutectic.

The DTA traces in Figures 4 and 5 show comparable properties for both eutectics. The TGA displayed minimal mass losses from both eutectics, which identifies that both are free from bound water (though water is uptaken rapidly upon transferring to the instrument), nor do they undergo decomposition past the melting point and up to 600 °C. The DTA trace for the KCl-$MgCl_2$ eutectic in Figure 4 shows only one event which can be attributed to the melting point around 429 °C, slightly higher than is noted by the phase diagram because of the difficulty to achieve the exact molar percentages of reagents. For the $CaCl_2$-NaCl eutectic (Figure 5), the melting point is higher but as expected, 504 °C. The sharp peak given for both eutectics signifies a no interference from other phases or from other impurities.

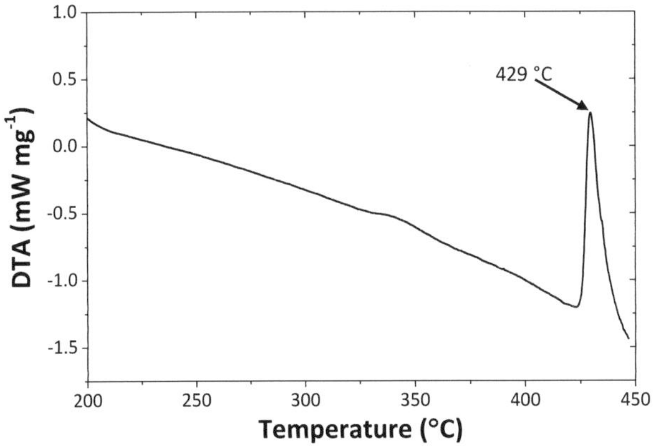

Figure 4. DTA analysis of the KCl-$MgCl_2$ eutectic.

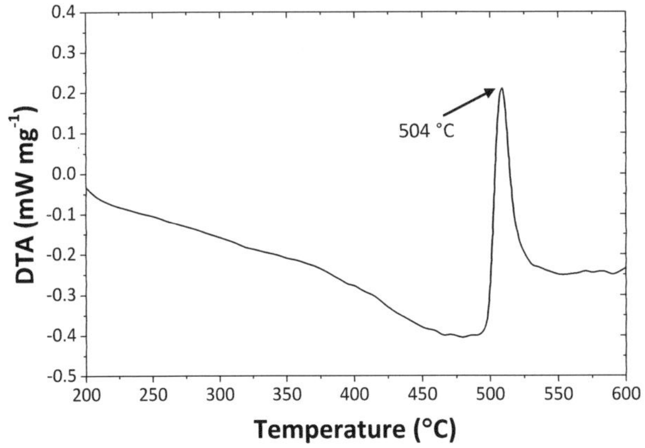

Figure 5. DTA analysis of the $CaCl_2$-NaCl eutectic.

Treatment of the eutectic with multiple melt/freeze cycles did not adversely affect the DTA curve for the calcium eutectic. However, for the magnesium eutectic, subsequent melting of the mixture gives two peaks, which can be attributed to the melting of the residual on-eutectic KCl-$MgCl_2$ along with the secondary phase K_2MgCl_4 which melts at around 435 °C.

Wetting of the eutectics on the dense oxide substrates identified differing properties for the two electrolytes. Using any of the oxide binders available for the $CaCl_2$-NaCl eutectic produced contact angles of near or exactly zero, meaning that full wetting of the substrate was achieved. This was confirmed by SEM micrographs of the pellets (Figure 6), which show the eutectic evenly and completely coating the dense pellets with a change of morphology occurring at the boundary between the melted eutectic and dense MgO. The contact angle of zero means that the affinity for the binder by the eutectic is infinite and as a result is unlikely to leach out of the separator pellet when melted during a discharge. This analysis was repeated for the other three oxides, the same result being achieved for all the binder candidates.

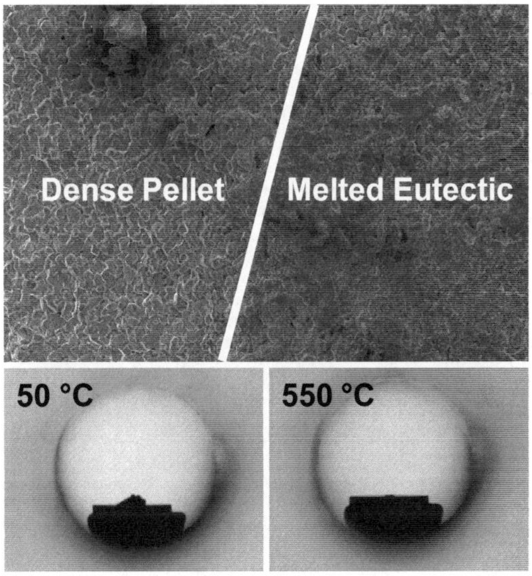

Figure 6. Contact angle measurement of the $CaCl_2$-NaCl eutectic on a dense MgO substrate and an SEM micrograph identifying two regions on the pellet surface.

The KCl-$MgCl_2$ salt exhibited contact angles of 20° to 40°. These are much smaller than the wetting angles for lithium-based salts on MgO, which have been reported to be 50° to 60° depending upon Li_2O content.[8]

The separator mixtures used in cell testing were prepared following the weight percentage of MgO estimated for that of the KCl-LiCl electrolyte. Equivalent volume and weight percentages are presented in Table 1. These values are higher than are considered optimal for lithium-based molten salt electrolytes, however they are greater than the 30 vol.% required for most electrolytes.[8] Further experiments to find optimal loadings are required.

Table 1. Calculated volume percentages of separator mixtures, compared to the KCl-LiCl separator.

Eutectic	wt.% MgO	vol.% MgO
KCl-LiCl	45	27.2
KCl-MgCl₂	45	32
CaCl₂-NaCl	45	33

Figure 7 shows the two galvanostatic discharge plots for the magnesium and calcium-based cells, respectively. For the magnesium cell (Figure 7a), the discharge shows a plateau around 1.4 V, with a capacity of approximately 150 mA h g^{-1}. The voltage achieved is expected as the potential of Mg is between 0.3 and 0.4 V lower than that of the LiSi alloy. The capacity equals 0.33 Mg, or 0.66 e^- transferred. Whilst both the potential and the capacity obtained is lower, the chemistry provides a good flat plateau. For the calcium cell (Figure 7b), two plateaux were achieved around 2.2 V and 1.8 V – higher than expected for the analogous lithium cells. This is unusual as the standard potential of calcium is lower than that of lithium, however other effects may be significant, *e.g.* in Ca // $CaCrO_4$ cells, the chemistry was found to be more complex. The cells reached capacities of 70 mA h g^{-1}, which corresponds to approximately 0.15 Ca, or 0.3 e^-.

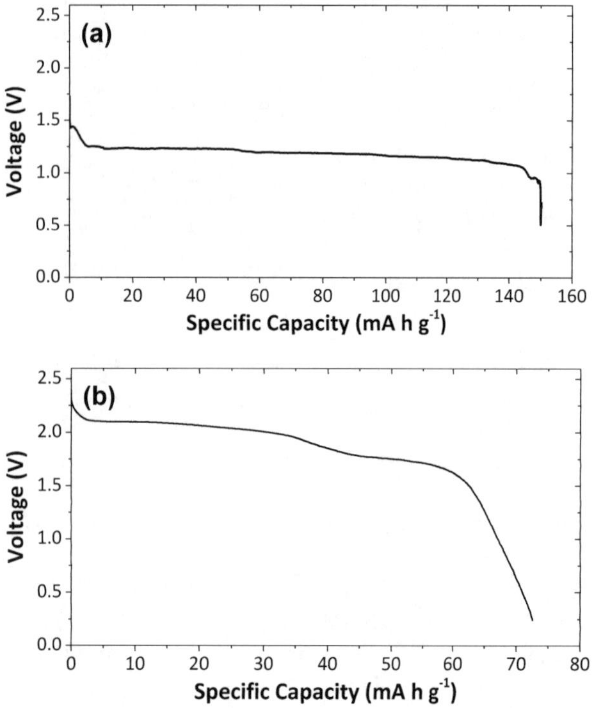

Figure 7. Galvanostatic discharge of the **(a)** Mg // KCl-$MgCl_2$ | MgO // FeS_2 and **(b)** Ca // $CaCl_2$-NaCl | MgO // FeS_2 cells, at constant current of 15 mA cm^{-2}.

Neither cell utilises the full capacity of the FeS_2 (~556 mA h g^{-1} in lithium thermal batteries), however as an initial concept, the cells show promise and were not yet modified with further additions to the electrodes. The limitations of the FeS_2 cathode material are due to its sensitivity to temperature where it begins to decompose around 550 °C. Therefore, the cells are limited by the test temperatures, and the performance of the cell and the electrolyte could be improved by increasing temperature further. By modifying these parameters, it may be possible to produce a cell which is suitable to certain applications in thermal battery technology.

Conclusions

Both the KCl-$MgCl_2$ and $CaCl_2$-NaCl salts presented in this work are potential candidates for multivalent thermal batteries. Their ideal wetting properties, on the selected oxide binders, and melting points mean that they have optimal behaviour for use as electrolytes. The first two multivalent cells constructed show promise, with capacities of at least one fifth the observed capacity of the FeS_2 cathode material. Expected voltage plateaux were achieved for magnesium-based cells, whilst plateaux for the calcium-based cells show opportunities to create for higher voltage thermal batteries. Further modifications to the prototype cells are required to determine whether their electrochemical behaviour can be controlled and improved, to make them more suitable for operation at higher currents. From this work it is also possible to broaden the scope of the cells to encompass cathode materials with higher voltage ranges, depending upon the redox stability of the electrolytes.

Acknowledgements

The authors would like to thank EPSRC and AWE plc. for contributing to and supporting this research.

References

1 J. L. Payne, J. D. Percival, K. Giagloglou, C. J. Crouch, G. M. Carins, R. I. Smith, R. Comrie, R. K. B. Gover and J. T. S. Irvine, *ChemElectroChem*, 2017, **4**, 1916–1923.

2 K. Giagloglou, J. L. Payne, C. Crouch, R. K. B. Gover, P. A. Connor and J. T. S. Irvine, *J. Electrochem. Soc.*, 2016, **163**, A3126–A3130.

3 C. Jin, L. Zhou, L. Fu, J. Zhu and D. Li, *Appl. Surf. Sci.*, 2017, **402**, 308–313.

4 H. Kim, G. Jeong, Y.-U. Kim, J.-H. Kim, C.-M. Park and H.-J. Sohn, *Chem. Soc. Rev.*, 2013, **42**, 9011–34.

5 P. J. Masset and R. A. Guidotti, *J. Power Sources*, 2007, **164**, 397–414.

6 K. Grjotheim, J. L. Holm and J. L. Roetnes, *Acta Chem. Scand.*, 1972, **26**, 3802.

7 E. M. Levin, C. R. Robbins and H. F. McMurdie, *Phase Diagrams for Ceramists*, 3rd edn., 1974.

8 P. Masset, *J. Power Sources*, 2006, **160**, 688–697.

Supporting Credibility of Single Cell Thermal Battery Modeling through V&V/UQ Activities

Benjamin B. Schroeder*, Eric Allcorn, John C. Hewson, Harry K. Moffat, Edward S. Piekos, Bradley L. Trembacki, Tyler G. Voskuilen, and Scott A. Roberts
Sandia National Laboratories, PO Box 5800, MS 0828, Albuquerque, NM, 87185-0828,
*Corresponding Author: bbschro@sandia.gov

Abstract: *When computational models are used for design, qualification, or product acceptance purposes, assessing and communicating the model's credibility to the end users is essential. Verification, validation, and uncertainty quantification (V&V/UQ) practices are used to monitor code reliability and pedigree, estimate uncertainties present in model predictions, and quantify the impact of model form errors through comparisons with experimental data. Previously, similar V&V/UQ practices have been used to establish the credibility of a thermal-only model of a molten salt battery. The current work now applies V&V/UQ practices including code verification, solution verification, uncertainty quantification, and model validation to a multi-physics model, consisting of thermal, electrochemical reactions, mechanical deformation, and fluid flow physics, of a single cell from a molten salt battery. Applying this process to establish model credibility can result in the identification of either modeling or experimental data gaps that need to be addressed.*

Following the identification of a gap in the model's electrochemical model parameterization and calibration, a mitigation plan was formulated. Through a new experimental campaign aligned with the modeling effort, single cell discharge data was gathered for a range of temperature and electrical load conditions, enabling calibration of thermodynamic and kinetic model parameters. Comparing the calibrated model with validation datasets allows the model's credibility story to be solidified, providing customers with a structured basis for understanding the model's utility.

Keywords: Thermal battery; molten salt electrolyte; single cell; calibration; validation; credibility

Introduction

A multi-physics modeling capability for thermally activated molten salt batteries has been developed over the last decade [1–3]. The current model variant includes capabilities to capture the coupling of thermal transport, electrochemical reactions, mechanical deformation, and fluid flow for single battery cells [4]. Motivating this capability development is the overarching goal of providing battery designers with a desktop tool that allows for exploration of battery design parameters and performance optimization; the Thermally Activated Battery Simulator (TABS) v5 is the graphical user interface version of this tool being distributed [5].

Previously, simulation predictions of engineering applications were presented as analysis results and it was acknowledged that significant modeling assumptions and simplifications were necessary when developing the simulations. The current paradigm of engineering simulations has begun to include both qualitative analysis of and quantification of the impact of such modeling simplifications and assumptions. To provide this type of information to the users of TABS, approaches and methods from the Verification, Validation, and Uncertainty Quantification (V&V/UQ) field were incorporated into the tool development process. A V&V/UQ study of a full battery setup of TABS v3, exercising only thermal physics, was previously completed [6]. Within that full battery study, prediction sensitivity and uncertainty caused by common geometric variabilities and uncertainty in material properties, as well as error caused by numerical discretization were quantified. Now, V&V/UQ processes are applied to a single cell model containing coupled multi-physics, such that the credibility of the product and resulting predictions can be provided to TABS users, enabling greater confidence in battery designs prior to physical builds.

Model Credibility

When establishing the credibility of the single cell modeling tool, elements of the Predictive Capability Maturity Model (PCMM) [7] process provide guidance as to what aspects of the simulation process should be addressed. The elements of PCMM are 1) ensure the code implementation of the math equations and numerical methods are tested (*code verification*), 2) establish the impact of simplifications used when describing the physical phenomena (*physics and material model fidelity*), 3) determine the impact of simplifications used when describing the physical system (*representation and geometric fidelity*), 4) evaluate the impact of numerical methods on the predictions of interest (*solution verification*), 5) consider the system's sensitivity to input uncertainty (*uncertainty quantification*), and 6) compare model predictions with experimental data to establish predictive capabilities (*validation*). Greater detail of how each element was applied to the TABS v4-v5 single cell model follow.

Code Verification: Regression tests were implemented to ensure that the impact of capability developments and refinements on prediction quantities of interest were understood when implemented. Version control was also used to transparently track code changes during development.

Physics and Material Model Fidelity: Impact of the fidelity of physics and material models included within simulations was studied and became an adjustable feature of the tool with documented impact on prediction quantities [4].

Representation and Geometric Fidelity: The single cell model uses a 2D axisymmetric representation. This simplification of a 3D object is perceived to be a good approximation due to the minimal expected axial variation and significant reduction in computational cost.

Solution Verification: Second order convergence of the spatial discretization (a 2nd order FEM scheme) was found for a user identified set of prediction quantities of interest. Relative error values due to the predictor-corrector tolerance used for the adaptive time-stepping scheme were also identified. Quantifying these numerical error sources allowed for informed default values to be set in the tool as well as guidance provided in the tool's documentation.

Uncertainty Quantification: Through a combination of expert elicitation and literature search, probabilistic uncertainties were derived for physical model parameters and material properties. Those uncertainties were then propagated through the single cell model using the stratified random sampling approach Latin Hypercube sampling, producing uncertainty estimates for single cell performance characteristics of interest. Sensitivity of the model responses to uncertain model inputs was characterized using global sensitivity measures, Sobol indices.

Validation: To test the predictive capability of the single cell model, single cell test data for a variety of load conditions was compared with corresponding model predictions. Multiple battery chemistries are supported by TABS, but the FeS_2/LiSi cathode/anode with LiCl−KCl electrolyte configuration is common and was used for current validation activities. Figure 1 shows how the model predictions using nominal parameter values compared with an experimental dataset at $500°C$, that included data under constant loads (2, 1, and 0.5 A/cm^2) as well as a pulsing load with a base load of 0.8 A/cm^2. For the constant load cases, significant under-prediction of the voltage, potentially attributed to incorrect parameterization of physics models resulting in loss mechanisms, is evident in all three cases and appears to be a function of load. The 0.2 A/cm^2 load case also indicates that the capacity of the experimental battery is significantly lower than predicted. Capacity loss could be

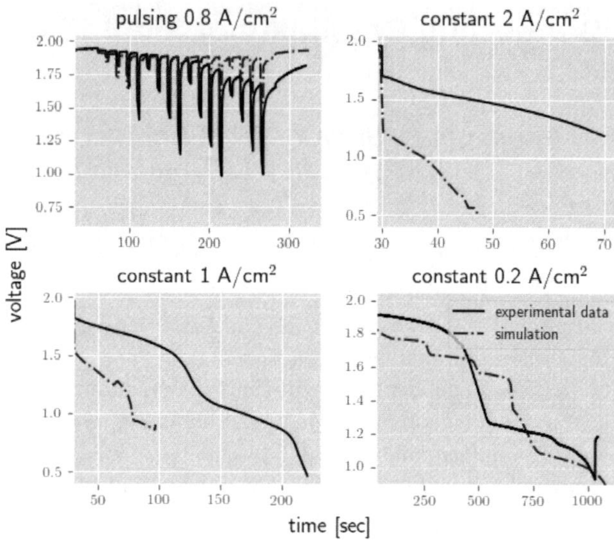

Figure 1. Validation comparisons of nominal simulation results with experimental data.

caused by unreacted FeS_2, which the model predicts to be completely consumed during the battery life.

Resulting from this V&V/UQ analysis was the identification of a gap in the model credibility. While five of the six aspects of model credibility considered were explored, analyzed, reported, and deemed to be acceptable for the customer, model validation illuminated a significant limitation with the tool's credibility. Parameter used for many of the important physics models within the single cell simulations, used values with limited physical derivation. To mitigate the gap in the tool's credibility, an experimental campaign was leveraged to provide a calibration basis for many of the model's important parameters. Once the model calibration has updated parameter values, the single cell model can be validated against additional datasets, solidifying its credibility.

Calibration

When approaching calibration of the multi-physics contained within the single cell framework, we took the approach of tackling the phenomena in the approximate order of impact on the prediction of interest, voltage traces. This approach was justified by the hierarchical relation among the physical phenomena, i.e., if the thermodynamics under-predict open circuit voltage, no reaction or diffusion process can force the voltage higher. Following that philosophy, thermodynamic open circuit predictions of the FeS_2/LiSi system are first considered, followed by reaction rates of the first cathode and anode plateaus. Simultaneous with the reaction rates, capacity loss mechanisms such as solid state diffusion rates must also be considered.

To calibrate the thermodynamic and kinetic mechanisms for the single cell chemistry of interest, a data gathering campaign in sync with those objectives was needed. This experimental campaign was designed to aid model calibration by holding open circuit for prolonged periods at the beginning of the cells' activation and testing cell performance over a range of temperatures to decouple reaction pre-exponential factors and activation energies. Single cells were loaded between hot platens, fixed at the temperature of interest; a programed current load profile was the applied with sheets of mica and then stainless steel collectors sandwiching the cell. 3 kilograms of compression was placed on the cells for testing. Replicates of each load and temperature condition were collected and pellet geometries were consistent across all experiments. The replicates were meant to enable characterization of unit to unit variability and measurement uncertainty.

The first model aspect investigated was the thermodynamic modeling of open circuit voltage (OCV). Thermodynamics using NASA 9 parameter and Shomate polynomials, previously described in [1], have been used to describe the FeS_2/LiSi single cell systems throughout the reaction process to equilibrium. When attempting to use the new datasets to observe OCV, issues arose due to physical phenomena not previously considered. Figure 2 shows voltage traces for three temperatures, where no load was applied until 30 seconds. The initial voltage spikes and

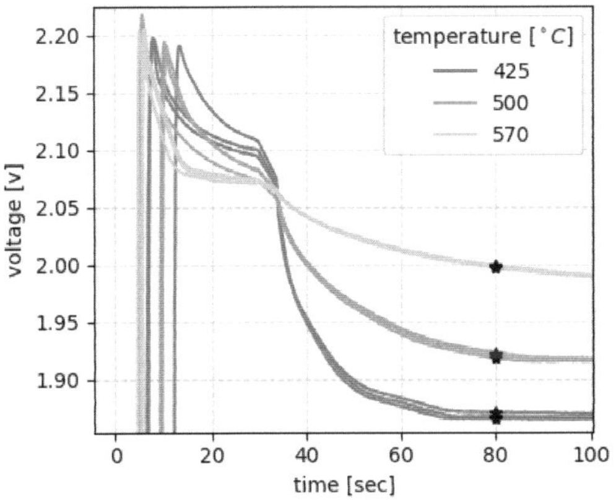

Figure 2. Experimental voltage data traces where the current was held at open circuit for 30 seconds, followed by a 50 mA/cm^2 load. Stars indicate where data for estimating the cell's initial OCV was extracted.

subsequent exponential behaviors are not fully understood and hypothesized to be a result of reactions with oxidized electrode materials that are not included within the current chemistry models. Lithiated cathodes have previously been found to reduce the initial voltage spiking behavior [8], but was not an aspect measured in the current campaign. Alternative reactions for the system involving oxidation products $FeSO_4$ and $Li_5Fe_2S_4$(s) [9] have been hypothesized, but have not been experimental found [8]. Then, once a low (50 mA/cm^2) load is applied, a new equilibrium voltage is not immediately reached, but transitioned to in a temperature dependent, exponential behavior. Due to the unaccounted for initial reactions, the system's initial OCV could not be extracted during the initial non-loaded period, but was instead extracted after an equilibrium voltage was approximately reached for the low loading condition (shown as stars in the figure).

To validate the thermodynamic model, OCV estimates from the new dataset (★) as well as other legacy datasets of lesser characterized derivation (□), are compared with the model over a range of applicable temperatures, as shown in Figure 3. The load associated with each data point

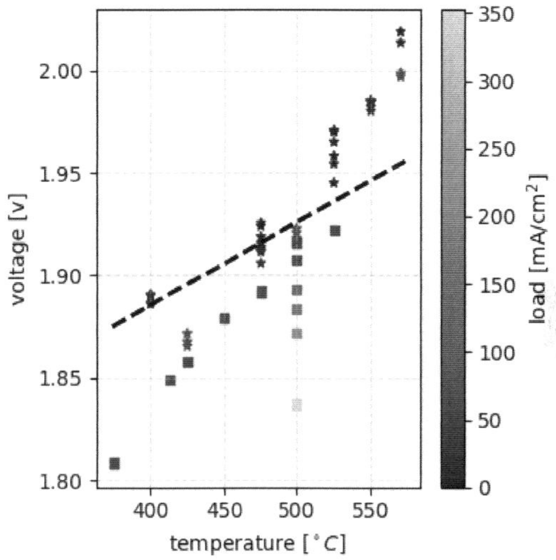

Figure 3. Comparison of experimental data used to approximate open circuit voltage with thermodynamic model (line) over a range of temperatures. Data with less known derivation shown as squares.

is shown as the color of the marker due to limitations in extracting OCV data previously mentioned. Comparing the available OCV data with the thermodynamic model shows that the data agrees well with the model between $450°C$ and $500°C$, but a significant discrepancy between the model and the data exists for temperature $550°C$ and above. Less concern was placed on the model's performance at temperatures $550°C$ and above, because it is believed that the cathode material starts to degrade in this temperature range, which the thermodynamic model does not capture.

To reduce the aforementioned problems with extracting OCV data, a final experimental dataset was designed to provide insight into the OCV trends of the single cells throughout the active lifetime. To accomplish this, 120 second periods without load and with 100 mA/cm^2 load are alternated, as shown in Figure 4. The initial spiking behavior followed by slow decay is still present, but now OCV values closely matching the thermodynamic model

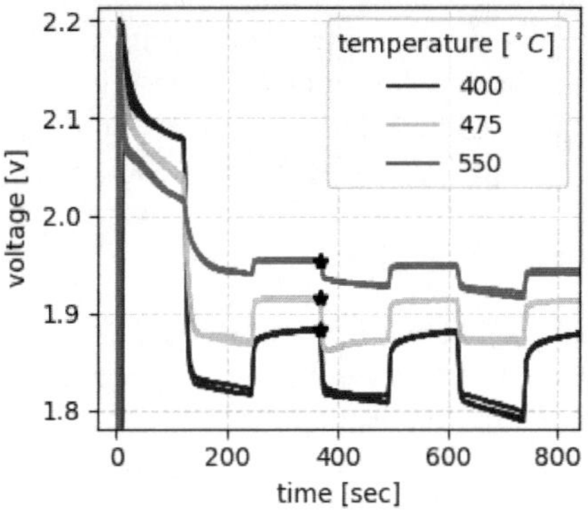

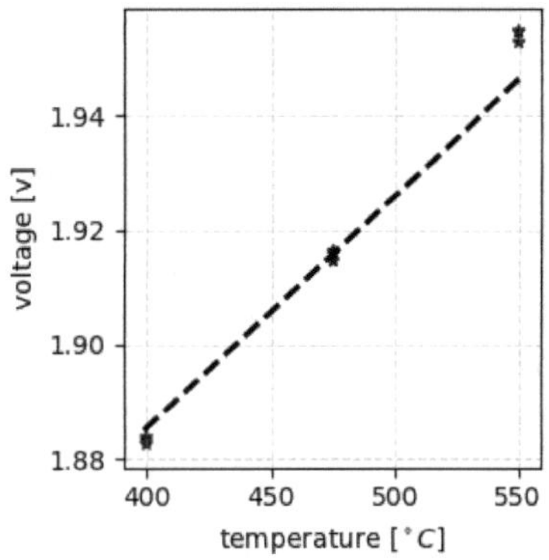

Figure 4. (Top) Experimental voltage traces over time with alternating open circuit and 100 mA/cm^2 every 120 seconds. (Bottom) Comparison of initial open circuit voltages (★) extracted from top plot with thermodynamic model over a range of temperatures.

are observed during the first two periods of open circuit after a load has been applied. This dataset shows close agreement with the thermodynamic model, with slight deviation at the higher temperature conditions that are known to possibly be beyond the physics described by the thermodynamic theory currently considered.

Summary

Credibility of the single cell thermal battery simulation tool TABS is being supported by V&V/UQ processes. Due to a gap in the model's predictive capabilities found during model validation, an experimental campaign was aligned with the calibration of thermodynamic and kinetic aspects of the single cell model. Following the validation of the thermodynamic model, kinetic reaction rates can now be calibrated to a subset of the datasets and the full single cell model can then be validated against the remaining datasets.

Acknowledgments

The authors gratefully acknowledge funding form the Joint Department of Defense/Department of Energy Munitions Technology Development Program. Sandia National Laboratories is a multi-mission laboratory managed and operated by National Technology and Engineering Solutions of Sandia, LLC., a wholly owned subsidiary of Honeywell International, Inc., for the U.S. Department of Energy's National Nuclear Security Administration under contract DE-NA0003525. The views expressed in this article do not necessarily represent the views of the U.S. Department of Energy or the United States Government. Unclassified Unlimited Release SAND2018-4408 C

References

1. Hewson, J., H. Moffat, C. Leuth, and D. Ingersoll. "Predicting Electrochemical Phenomena in Lithium Molten Salt Thermal Batteries." Proceedings of the 44th Power Sources Conference, 2010.

2. Hewson, J., H. Moffat, and V. Brunini. "Model Parameterization for Electrochemical Predictions of LiSi/FeS_2 Batteries." Proceedings of the 46th Power Sources Conference, 2014.

3. Voskuilen, T., J. Hewson, H. Moffat, and S. Roberts. "Multi-Physics, Multi-Plateau Reaction Model for LiSi/FeS_2 Batteries." Proceedings of the 47th Power Sources Conference, 2016.

4. Voskuilen, T., C. Jove-Colon, H. Moffat, B. Schroeder, B. Trembacki, and S. Roberts. "Multi-Physics Cost and Complexity Reduction Strategies for Modeling Thermally Activated Batteries." Proceedings of the 48th Power Sources Conference, 2018.

5. Roberts, S., C. Jove-Colon, H. Moffat, M. Neilsen, E. Piekos, B. Schroeder, B. Trembacki, and T. Voskuilen. "TABS : A Thermal Battery Desktop Design Tool." Proceedings of the 48th Power Sources Conference, 2018.

6. Trembacki, B., S. Harris, E. Piekos, and S. Roberts. "Uncertainty Quantification, Verification, and Validation of a Thermal Simulation Tool for Molten Salt Batteries." Proceedings of the 47th Power Sources Conference, 2016.

7. Oberkampf, W. L., M. Pilch, and T. G. Trucano. "Predictive Capability Maturity Model for Computational Modeling and Simulation." SAND2007-5948, Sandia National Laboratories, 2007.

8. Masset, P. and R. Guidotti. "Thermall activated (thermal) battery technology Part IIIa: FeS_2 cathode material." *J. of Power Sources*, vol. 177, pp. 596–609, 2008.

9. Aselage, T. and E. Hellstrom. "Multicomponent Phase Diagrams for Battery Applications II. Oxygen Impurities in the Li(Si)/FeS_2 Battery Cathode." *J. Electrochem. Soc.*, vol. 134, pp. 1932–1938, 1987.

Acoustic Monitoring of Thermal Batteries for Event Detection

Jennifer Dellinger, Chris Cassano, Travis Anderson, Summer Ferreira, Casey Keane, Armando Fresquez, Justin Serrano, Magdalana Heise, and Mara Schindelholz
Sandia National Laboratories
National Technology and Engineering Solutions of Sandia, LLC,
a wholly owned subsidiary of Honeywell International, Inc.
Albuquerque, New Mexico, USA, 87123
jdellin@sandia.gov / 1- (505) 845-1378

Abstract: *When off-normal performance of a thermal battery (TB) occurs, very little of the original hardware remains for post-mortem analysis to determine which portion of the train (igniter/primer/match, heat paper, heat pellet) failed to function as expected. Information on proper functioning of each portion of the thermal battery, along with the interaction of each section with the next, would aid in margin analysis, component aging assessment, and understanding of which component performed inadequately during a failure investigation. Although current and voltage outputs of the thermal batteries are monitored, little is known about the real-time behavior of the various processes, especially why some TBs hang fire, burn incompletely, or have reduced run times. Diagnostics to assess the individual events in thermal battery performance are being explored through acoustic and accelerometer sensor monitoring concurrent with electrochemical performance evaluations during battery firing. Initial studies were aimed at determining the feasibility of monitoring the acoustic emission of the disparate events from a thermal battery performance perspective, with subsequent signal processing data analysis and multivariate analysis. The kinetic energy of the firing pin was predicted from the acoustic data using partial least-squares (PLS) regression, a multivariate regression analysis technique, demonstrating the ability to use acoustic monitoring, not just for event detection, but also to distinguish details related to the performance margin.*

Keywords: thermal batteries; performance; percussion primer; acoustic emission; multivariate analysis.

Introduction

Thermal battery (TB) function is composed of a train (igniter/primer/match, heat paper (if present), heat pellet), with distinct events. These events include the electromechanical impact that initiates a percussion primer in a thermal battery and the percussion primer's creation of hot gases. For proper battery function, each section of the train must function within a given acceptable range. The characteristic times and frequency content of the acoustic and accelerometer signatures from these diverse events are likely to be widely different.

The shock response from thermal battery components is not typically studied with acoustics or accelerometers in a manner that lends itself to analysis of performance details, even though acoustic analysis of shock events (for the primer) and burning events (for the heat paper and heat pellets), is more common. The analysis of shock response on solids via accelerometers is commonly studied to protect buildings and other structures; one of the earliest analyses of shock damage by energetics is from the Gemini space program.[1, 2] These analyses focus on predicting damage response, not proper performance. In these analyses, rarely are the acoustic or accelerometer signals presented. Recent work predominately focuses on simulating the energetic events, not actually testing the energetics. Acoustic analysis of gunshots is very mature;[3] however, the focus is on determining the gun location via analysis of sound waves traveling through the air using geometrical acoustics, not as a diagnostic of a gun or primer firing. Although thermal battery acoustics may not be currently known, the acoustics monitoring of chemical reactions has been performed for decades and may inform this work.[4 5]

Distinct, transient events, such as a percussion primer firing, have distinctive acoustic emission (AE) signals. The characteristic signals of pulse-like noises, as opposed to continuous random noise, are characterized by a sharp rise, with a subsequent exponential decay.[6] The exponential decay has a ringing pattern due to resonance of the structure. The shock from the percussion primer creates a resonant decay response as the shock attenuates and reverberates along the battery and fixturing.

The characteristic signals in a thermal battery require the use of different sensors to optimally capture the relevant data. The accelerometer technique was employed to detect mechanical vibrations that fall approximately within the audible frequency range. A second method known as acoustic emissions testing (AET) was used to detect acoustic signatures containing ultrasonic frequencies that result from the rapid release of energy within a material.

This never-before attempted, non-parasitic diagnostic that is external to the component can evaluate proper subcomponent function within a thermal battery assembly. The aim of the research is to characterize these distinct events. This paper primarily focuses on the characterization of the percussion primer, with some work on the burning of a thermal battery.

Experimental

Neyer threshold tests[7] were performed on COTS percussion primers, with units preconditioned at 84°C and tested within 90 seconds of removal from the oven. A threshold test is used to determine the stimulus level at which it can be assumed that there is a 0.50 probability that any one of the units will fire. The Neyer method is a statistical approach that incorporates the go/no-go data into the analysis to determine the next stimulus level to be tested, thus providing a more efficient test than pre-determined stimulus levels. For these tests, the firing pin kinetic energy was varied and the resulting function, or lack thereof, was recorded. These tests were acoustically monitored with a S9215 sensor (Physical Acoustics/Mistras Group WD). Percussion primers (small pistol primer, Winchester Ammunition, Olin Corp.) were pressed into a plate similar to how they would be configured in a thermal battery. A schematic of the variable spring tester (VST) is given in Figure 1. The solenoid releases the firing pin and the two diodes are used to measure kinetic energy of the firing pin before it impacts the primer. The kinetic energy is tailored by adjusting the compression of the spring. The S9215 sensor is a wideband sensor with a flat frequency magnitude response of 50 kHz to 650 kHz and an operating temperature range of -200 to 540°C. A S9215 sensor was taped to the bottom of the variable spring force fixture with double sided Kapton adhesive film, the preamplifier gain was set at 40 dB, and a 1 kHz high pass filter was used to retain as much acoustic information as possible—even outside the frequency range of the sensor. To increase the resolution around the primer ignition, data was sampled at 10 Megasamples per second.

For the thermal battery tests, a thermal battery that has an ignition sequence that involves a primer simultaneously activating four center-activated heat pellets was chosen. The tester contains a percussion primer activation assembly that activated and monitored the battery via acoustics, accelerometer, output voltage, output current, and temperature. Fixturing to align the acoustic and accelerometer sensors were used for consistency, which is paramount because shock wave attenuation is highly dependent on distance of the sensor from the shock generated by the igniter/primer. The tests were acoustically monitored with a 7259B-10 sensor (Endevco). The 7259B-10 sensor has a ± 500g dynamic range and a flatband FRF from 1-30,000 Hz.

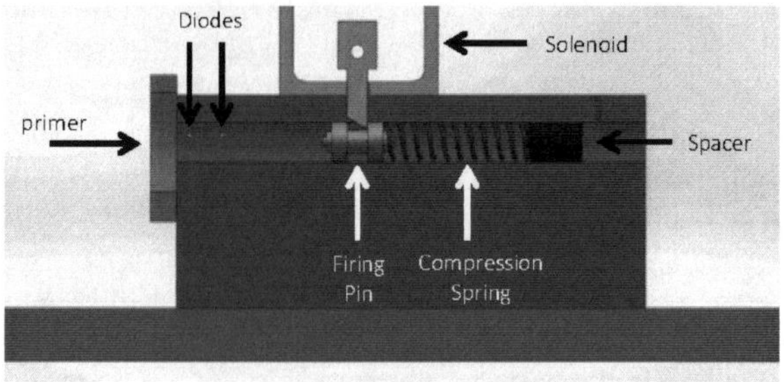

Figure 1. Schematic of the variable spring tester (VST) used for percussion primer testing with acoustic diagnostics.

Data Analysis

Because data was collected using a manual trigger, rather than a synchronized triggering signal, the signals collected were offset from each other by an arbitrary amount. This offset had no impact on the quality of the data, but made it significantly more difficult to process the large batches of test results in an efficient and uniform way. A modified version of the cross-correlation based on the wavelet transforms was developed to align the signals while accounting for the significant differences in primer function from that of the firing pin release (Figure 2). A method was developed to separate out the shock event from the subsequent resonant decay response by using a band pass filter and then enveloping the signal.

Multivariate analysis focused on answering questions, such as "was the impact force to the igniter and resulting impulse response as expected or close to the margin?" Partial least-squares (PLS) regression, a multivariate regression analysis technique, was used to predict the kinetic energy of the firing pin from the acoustic data.

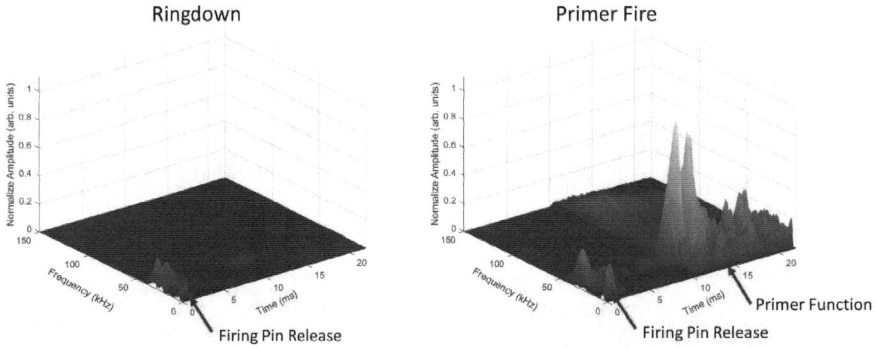

Figure 2. Continuous wavelet transforms of a ringdown and primer fire; data used to properly align signals.

Results and Discussion

Neyer threshold tests of COTS percussion primer tests had a 50% threshold of 79.3 mJ and a standard deviation of 20.9 mJ (Figure 3). The acoustic differences between pristine versus a previously functioned primer were demonstrated (Figure 4), along with acoustic differences created from diverse energies of the firing pin. The multivariate PLS model predicted the kinetic energy well from the acoustic data (Figure 5). This predictability is significant in that the ability to detect the proper kinetic energy of the firing pin to the percussion primer was demonstrated. In a failure investigation, the acoustic signature could be used, not just to verify that the primer functioned, but to determine the amount of margin. Of note, the acoustic emission signature is dominated by the primer function. Thus, the present analysis would elucidate primer margin, not firing pin kinetic energy.

Two other interesting observations were made: the first was from the residual analysis of the PLS model and the second was from observations of the acoustic signatures near threshold.

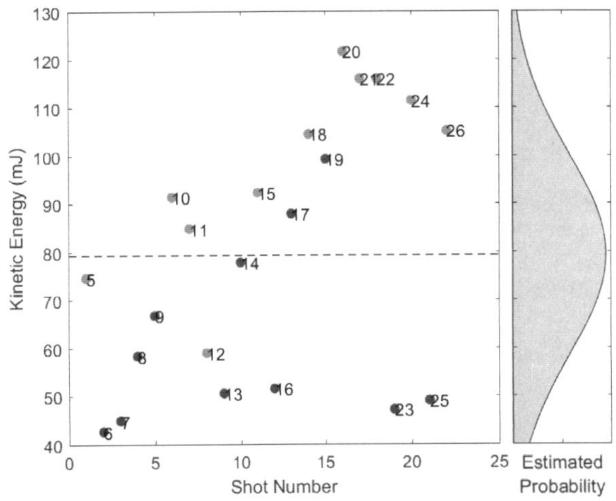

Figure 3. Go/no-go plot for COTS percussion primer testing, varied firing pin kinetic energy. Green data points functioned; red data points did not. Data points are labelled with the test number. Estimated probability to function is assumed to be normally distributed.

The data points with high residuals contain acoustic data features before the shock output that the other shots do not. The model will need to be improved to more accurately capture these data features. Interestingly, these features might be explained by a nuance of the tester, which is discussed below. The firing pin travels down a barrel, past the diodes used to measure kinetic energy, through the sample fixture, and then impacts the primer. Via separate experiments, it was determined that, due to a small amount of misalignment of the firing pin barrel and sample fixture, the kinetic energy that is actually delivered to the primer is slightly different than that measured by the diodes. It is theorized that the features in the acoustic data are the firing pin striking the lip of the fixture as it leaves the barrel.

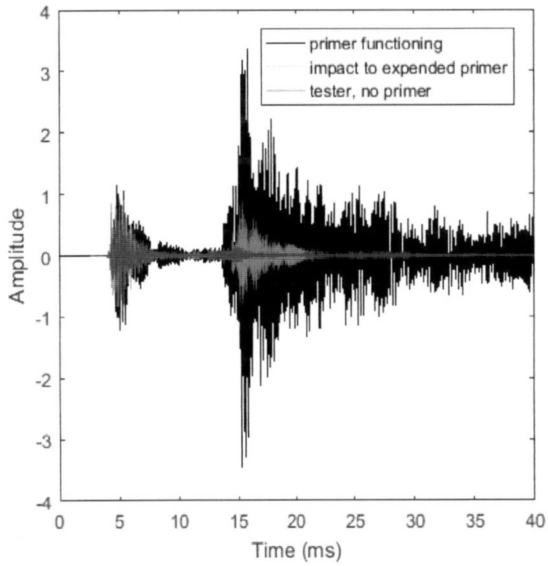

Figure 4. Clear difference in acoustic emission signature when a primer functions versus when an expended (inert) component is tested.

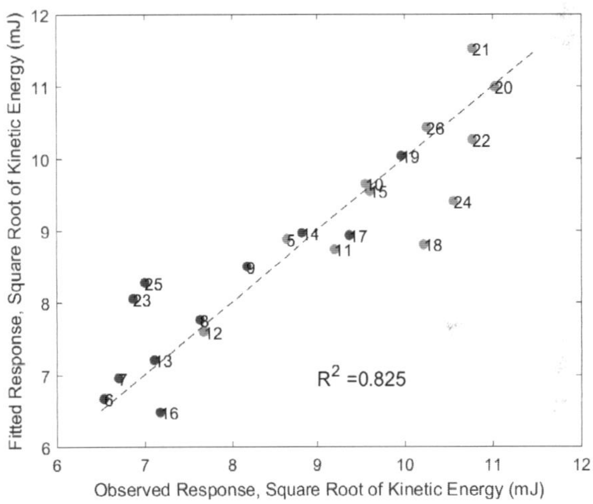

Figure 5. The observed square root of the kinetic energy of the firing pin versus that predicted with PLS. Green data points functioned, whereas red data points did not. Data points are labelled with the test number.

The acoustic signatures of a functioning primer from a high kinetic energy impact versus the signature of a non-functioning primer from a low kinetic energy impact are clearly different (Figure 6, A [high kinetic energy firing pin, functioning primer] and B [low kinetic energy firing pin, non-functioning primer]). Function near threshold yields a lower amplitude acoustic emission (Figure 6, C [firing pin kinetic energy near threshold, functioning primer]. The AE of one of the no-gos near threshold (Figure 6, D [mid-range kinetic energy firing pin, non-functioning primer with some function acoustic signature]) suggest that the primer might have initiated, but not to the full extent required to propagate.

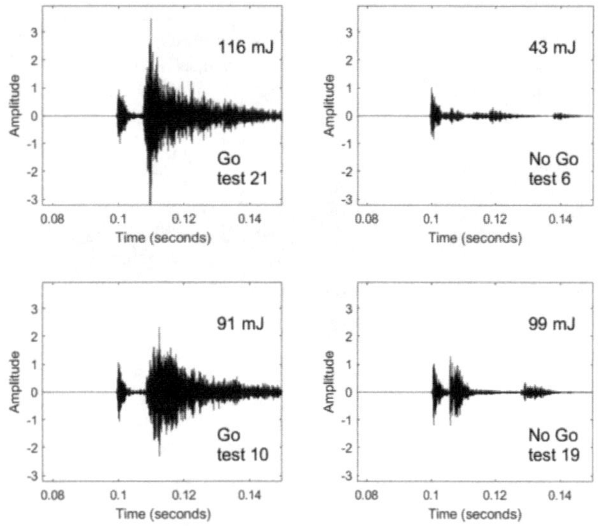

Figure 6. Acoustic emission signatures of functioning vs. non-functioning primers

Initial the thermal battery tests yielded accelerometer data with a clear signal for the primer function (Figure 7, top). After a delay of a little more than 0.1 seconds, the battery voltage began to rise. Signals at later times were detected (Figure 7, bottom); the specific events that these signals correspond to are not yet understood.

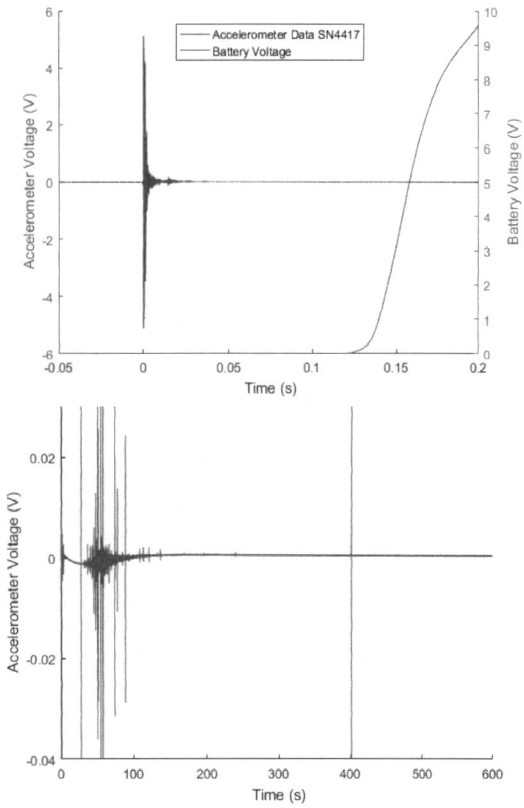

Figure 7. Acoustic emission signatures of a percussion primer activated thermal battery.

Summary/Conclusions

An initial demonstration in the development of a new diagnostic to assess the individual events in thermal battery performance has proved successful. Acoustic emissions signals were used to detect both expected and unexpected behaviors of percussion primers, in particular the misalignment of fixtures and what hints to be a primer that might have initiated but failed to propagate. Accelerometer evaluations at the thermal battery level to detect the burning of heat pellets are promising. Due to the noninvasive nature of the diagnostics, with continued tailoring of the acoustic and accelerometer sensors to the phenomenon of interest, this in-situ monitoring tool for multi-stage high energy reactions could be used for all thermal battery tests at the component and higher levels of assembly.

Acknowledgements

The views expressed in the article do not necessarily represent the views of the U.S. Department of Energy or the United States Government. Sandia National Laboratories is a multimission laboratory managed and operated by National Technology and Engineering Solutions of Sandia, LLC, a wholly owned subsidiary of Honeywell International, Inc., for the U.S. Department of Energy's National Nuclear Security Administration under contract DE-NA0003525.

References

1. J.A. Callahan, *Structural dynamics aspects of the Gemini program.* Journal of Spacecraft and Rockets, 1967. 4(1): p. 58-64.
2. V.S. Noonan and W.E. Noonan, *Structural Response to Impulsive Loading (Pyrotechnic Devices)*, in *Symposium on Shock, Vibration and Associated Environments*Office of the Director of Defense Research and Engineering.: New Orleans, Louisiana.
3. R.C. Maher. *Modeling and Signal Processing of Acoustic Gunshot Recordings.* in *2006 IEEE 12th Digital Signal Processing Workshop & 4th IEEE Signal Processing Education Workshop*. 2006.
4. D. Betteridge, M.T. Joslin, and T. Lilley, *Acoustic emissions from chemical reactions.* Analytical Chemistry, 1981. 53(7): p. 1064-1073.
5. R.M. Lec, P.A. Lewin, M. Musavi, S.W. Bang, S. Goel, S. Kwoun, and E. Radulescu. *Acoustic emission sensor for identification of chemical reactions*. in *Proceedings of the 1999 Joint Meeting of the European Frequency and Time Forum and the IEEE International Frequency Control Symposium (Cat. No.99CH36313)*. 1999.
6. K. Ono, *Acoustic Emission*, in *Springer Handbook of Acoustics*. 2014, Springer Publishing Company, Incorporated. p. 1209-1229.
7. B.T. Neyer, *A D-Optimality-Based Sensitivity Test.* Technometrics, 1994. 36(1): p. 61-70.

Thermal Battery Activation Using Heat Paper Fuses

Jeff Reinig, Benjamin Jantson
Advanced Thermal Batteries, Inc.
Westminster, MD 21158 USA
jeffre.reinig@atb-inc.com / 1-443-821-7829

Abstract: *Thermal batteries are primary reserve batteries that exhibit a long shelf life, high power density and excellent reliability. As a result, they are widely used in defense applications. The two common methods utilized to activate thermal batteries are igniter direct fire or heat paper fuse trains. This paper describes thermal battery activation by means of a heat paper fuse.*

Keywords: Thermal battery; fuse; heat paper; activation

Introduction

The use of heat paper to ignite thermal battery heat pellets is not a novel concept. Its origins can be traced all the way back to the earliest thermal battery designs (pre 1960's). Today, a heat paper fuse is used as either a flat fuse train configuration that is taped alongside the battery cell stack or a fuse roll configuration that is inserted down the center hole in the battery cell stack. Using both side fuse trains and center fuse roll can produce battery designs with very fast rise times. The fuse can be initiated by means of an igniter, electric match or a primer. The heat paper calorific output is variable and can be tailored to meet specific battery requirements. The use of heat paper fuses provides a level of flexibility in the battery design and improved reliability through redundancy.

Design Flexibility

Multiple Ignition Sources: Although the heat paper fuse itself is what ignites the battery's heat pellets, the heat paper itself requires an ignition source. The most common types of fuse ignition sources are igniters, electric matches and primers. Because the ignition source only ignites the heat paper fuse, the ignition source does not have to change from one battery design to the next. For example, in a battery that utilizes an igniter to activate heat pellets by directly firing down the center hole of the cell stack, the igniter's energetic output has to be taken into consideration for each battery design. For example, a very short, squat battery may not require the same energetic output as a very long, skinny battery.

Location/Placement of Ignition Source: Since the ignition source (igniter, match, primer) is only required to ignite the heat paper fuse, the ignition source can be placed anywhere in the battery assembly. For direct fire ignition methods, the initiator must be placed directly above the center hole in the cell stack. The ability to place the ignition source anywhere in the battery design provides an increased flexibility in the final battery design layout.

Ignition Source Orientation: Since the ignition source is not required to align with the center hole of the cell stack, the ignition source can be installed in any orientation that improves the design. For example, if the requirements for battery height are particularly challenging, the ignition source could be turned sideways effectively shortening the header assembly. The additional space achieved could be used to either shorten the battery or even potentially add cells increasing the battery's voltage within the same volume.

Location/Placement of Fuse: As stated in the introduction, the heat paper fuse can be placed either along the side of the cell stack or down the cell stack's center hole. For applications with aggressive rise time requirements, fuses can be placed in both locations to effectively increase the burn rate of the heat pellet. Improvements to rise time are possible because multiple heat paper fuses create multiple ignition sites as opposed to a single location. For example, when using an igniter for direct fire activation, the only ignition location is via the center hole of the battery cell stack. However, if you were to place multiple fuse strips alongside the cell stack as well as a fuse roll in the center hole, then the heat pellets would ignite from the sides and center locations causing the heat pellet to burn in its entirety more quickly. Activation times when using heat paper fuses can yield rise times as short as 50ms for small diameter batteries.

Increased Reliability

Redundant Ignition Sites: Similar to the use of a dual bridge wire igniter, the use of multiple heat paper fuses improves the overall battery operating reliability because it provides redundant initiation sites at the heat pellets.

Pellet Integrity: Unlike igniters, the heat paper fuse produces little to no brisance. Therefore, the potential to damage pellets during activation is nonexistent. Furthermore, since no damage to the pellets can occur, the failure mechanism associated with pellet debris (created during direct fire activation) is eliminated.

Conclusion

The use of a heat paper fuse to activate a thermal battery offers design flexibility in the type of ignition source as well as location and orientation. The rise time of the battery can be increased by utilizing multiple fuses at various locations within the battery design. Increased reliability is achieved through redundancy and damage to cells from the igniter's brisance is eliminated.

Thermal Battery Design Considerations for Hypersonic Vehicle Flight Temperature Environments

Benjamin Jantson, Jeff Reinig, Eric Scherzberg, James D. Briscoe
Advanced Thermal Batteries, Inc.
Westminster, MD 21158 USA
benjamin.jantson@atb-inc.com / 1-443-821-7899

Abstract: *Thermal batteries are rugged, highly reliable power sources that offer the highest power density of any available reserve battery technology. Conventional thermal batteries are designed to perform in defense applications that traditionally operate over a temperature range of -40°C to +70°C. However, more recently, thermal battery technologies are being used in hypersonic vehicles, where very high operating temperatures could prove problematic for the end user if the hypersonic environments are not properly conveyed to the thermal battery designer. This work describes the factors that must be considered when designing and testing a thermal battery to meet hypersonic vehicle temperature environments.*

Keywords: Thermal Battery; Hypersonic Vehicle; Thermal Management; Power Source

Introduction

The ability for hypersonic vehicles to travel at speeds greater than Mach 5 increases the vehicle's range and allows for the evasion of traditional defense systems. However, the advantage of hypersonic speed comes with a series of engineering challenges – one of which is dealing with the heat generated during flight. At hypersonic speeds, the heat generated from surface friction and air compression present a major design consideration for every element of the vehicle. One component impacted by the high heat experienced during flight is the thermal battery power source.

Thermal batteries are very rugged, highly reliable primary reserve power sources that offer the highest power density of any available (mature) reserve battery technology. The thermal battery is the power source of choice for defense applications that require high power, long shelf life and no storage maintenance. The battery design is capable of meeting these requirements because of its molten salt electrolyte. At room temperatures, the molten salt electrolyte is actually solid. In the solid state, the electrolyte has very high impedance and little if any ionic conduction will occur. It isn't until the battery is activated that the electrolyte becomes molten and the impedance drops significantly allowing for ionic conduction to take place.

Thermal Battery Activation: In order for the battery to provide power, the electrolyte must be driven from a solid state to a molten state. The traditional method to accomplish this is the ignition of heat pellets, which are positioned between each of the battery's cells. Upon ignition, either by means of a direct fire from an igniter or the flame front from a fuse strip, the burning heat pellets release heat into the surrounding cells resulting in the electrolyte melting.

Thermal Management: In order to deliver the power required by an application, the thermal battery design must have enough electrochemical capacity to meet the mission load. In addition, because the battery functions when the electrolyte is in the molten state, the battery must also remain "hot" long enough for the battery's capacity to be depleted. If the battery should prematurely cool, the electrolyte will begin to solidify and its impedance will increase until it is so great that no usable current flows forth from the battery. In the thermal battery community, the design process used to maintain the battery's core temperature is called *thermal management*.

Typical Thermal Battery Design Drivers

Capacity: The allowable voltage regulation, operating life and the load upon the battery will all be considered when determining the total capacity required.

Operating Temperature Extremes: The operating temperature extremes will have a direct impact on the thermal management of the battery design. The designer will consider the thermal mass of the cell stack, the thickness and type of axial and end insulation, as well as the necessary calorific output of the heat pellets. If the thermal management (or thermal balance as it is also sometimes referred to as) is less than adequate, the battery will suffer poor performance when functioning at one or the other temperature extreme. For example, if the core temperature of the battery is too low, the battery will perform poorly due to the electrolyte's high impedance. If however, the core temperature of the battery is too high, the battery will perform poorly due to high self-discharge or even cathode degradation (potentially leading to a thermal runaway event).

Electrochemistry: Probably the most important element of the design is the electrochemistry selected. There is no one anode/electrolyte/cathode combination that is perfectly suited for all thermal battery applications. Each application's performance requirements must be reviewed and the designer must select the combination of anode/electrolyte/cathode that provides the best battery performance to the stated requirements.

Mechanical Stress: The battery container and bracketry used to mount the battery in the next higher level assembly must be evaluated to ensure that the battery design will withstand the mechanical stresses imposed upon it during flight environments. The design is evaluated using the environments provided by the battery specification and the strength of the material used for the battery container.

Weight and Volume: The allowable weight and volume assigned to the battery in the next higher level assembly must permit for a design that meets all performance requirements and is producible.

Validating Testing: The final battery design is often qualified by subjecting the design to a series of environmental tests. The environmental testing is performed at both the high and low temperature extremes in order to validate the battery design across the required temperature spectrum.

Thermal Battery Design Considerations for the Extreme Temperature Related to Hypersonic Vehicle Flights

When engaging a thermal battery supplier to design and develop a power source solution for a hypersonic vehicle, critical system level requirements and expected engineering solutions associated with the extreme temperature must be shared and discussed with the battery designer. This will ensure that the final battery design will perform as expected during flight. The topics addressed in the following paragraphs may seem inconsequential at first, but each can have a negative impact on the battery's performance if not accounted for in the final battery design.

Note – Caution should be taken when using a thermal battery that was designed for another application in your hypersonic vehicle. Each battery design should be evaluated against your requirements to ensure that it will perform as expected during your specific flight scenario.

Operating Temperature Extreme - Preconditioning vs Ramp Rate: The first piece of information that should be conveyed to the battery designer is the anticipated operating temperature. More specifically, what should be conveyed is both the expected starting temperature (usually identified as precondition temperature) as well as any induced temperature that will be realized during the flight. The induced temperature environment is typically experienced as a temperature ramp up. In order to convey the true temperature environment that the battery will see, the precondition temperature should be conveyed along with a temperature profile that includes the temperature ramp as a "degree vs time" profile. The precondition temperature extremes will drive the battery thermal management design as will the temperature ramp up, but the latter may not have as big of an impact if the duration, magnitude or ramp rate is minimal. It should be stated that there are potential scenarios that exist for certain designs where the temperature extremes are so far apart that the thermal management of the battery becomes impossible. In this scenario, the designer and customer must work together to find the best possible solution available.

Heat Source & Heat Transfer: The second piece of information that should be conveyed to the battery designer is the source of the extreme heat. Is the source a thermal sink or a specific component (i.e. rocket motor) that the battery is located adjacent to. For example, a large thermal sink in the area of the battery will more than likely result in radiation heat transfer while attaching the battery to a component that is hot will result in conductive heat transfer. Heat transfer via conduction, convection, and/or radiation will impact the battery design differently and each type of heat transfer will be mitigated differently.

Temperature Effects on Chemistry: If the temperature extremes are significant, the designer may need to reevaluate the electrochemistry being used. For example, higher temperatures may lead to increased self-discharge which may result in the battery designer selecting a different electrolyte. If the temperature effects are great enough, the designer may switch to an anode that is more stable under high temperatures such as LAN. Similarly, a different cathode may be selected based upon its specific decomposition temperature. In the end, the designer will need to evaluate the proposed electrochemical design against the environments it will be subjected to in order to select the best possible solution that presents the least amount of performance impact possible.

Mechanical Stress: In the extreme temperature environment experienced in hypersonic vehicle flights, the temperature itself will become a stress upon the mechanical strength of the battery container and bracket. Therefore, any structural analysis performed on the battery mounting interface should take into account to what degree the extreme temperature affects the material strength properties.

Adding External Insulation: Often, at the system level, the decision is made to insulate the thermal battery, either to protect the system from additional heat generated by the battery or to protect the battery against heat produced by the system. In either case, prior to adopting this engineering solution, the system architect should discuss the approach with the battery designer. In certain circumstances, the addition of insulation material may cause the battery design to retain heat that is normally lost to the surrounding system. This retention of heat may result in poor performance or even thermal runaway. Often, those unfamiliar with the physics behind how the thermal batteries function believe, incorrectly, that the battery operates better when it is hotter. The fact is - thermal batteries function best when operated within the operating temperature range they were designed to work in.

Temperature Effects on Mass and Volume: Another common misconception is that the extreme heat from the hypersonic vehicle's flight environment could be used to thermally condition the thermal battery. The goal of using this available energy is to make the battery smaller and lighter since the battery would require thinner heat pellets. While in theory this is potentially possible, in reality it is not practical. The long conditioning period required to heat the core of the battery up to the proper operating temperature would be much longer than the hypersonic vehicle flight time. Furthermore, designing a battery to withstand the extreme heat would more than likely result in an increased mass and larger allowable volume. One potential solution could be a can in can battery design where the gap between the battery cans effectively thermally insulates the battery core from the outside case. The can in can design obviously adds both mass and weight when compared to the single battery can design. And of course, this solution would only be required in the extreme temperature case where the heat transferred was due to conduction or extreme radiation. Radiation alone ramped up over a certain time period may or may not have any significant impact to performance. In order to truly understand how the extreme temperature and how the heat is transferred to the battery have to be evaluated through thermal modeling and experimental testing.

Extreme Temperature Effects on Validation Testing: Even when the system operating temperature requirements are well defined, there may still be a problem validating the temperature effects on the battery design. This is because it may be difficult (if not impossible) to simulate the environment in a test lab. While it is possible to precondition a battery to a given temperature, it is often not possible to operate the battery while the temperature ramps up to the anticipated flight temperature. This reality often results in the battery performance being validated using a combination of thermal modeling and battery testing OR an over test condition where the battery is preconditioned to the starting temperature and then placed in a kiln set to the highest expected temperature. The latter is an extreme over test, but any battery that passes this extreme test would perform well in the real environment. However, a test failure in this scenario would not necessarily mean that the battery design would perform poorly in the real flight environment.

Conclusion

The predicted operating flight temperature environment in a hypersonic vehicle is unlike any traditional thermal battery operating temperature environment. Therefore, the vehicle system architect and the battery designer must work closely together to ensure that the designer understands the system and the architect understands the limitations of the battery design. While trades can be made to evaluate and select the best electrochemistry possible, there still may be certain performance requirements which are impossible to achieve. Identifying these issues early in the process will allow more time for the architect and designer to develop other solutions. When batteries designed for other applications are repurposed for use in a hypersonic vehicle, the architect must ensure that they understand the design limitations of the battery and that none of those limitations result in a poor performing battery. Furthermore, the cost and complexity of validating and testing this extreme temperature environment must be taken into consideration.

TABS: A Thermal Battery Desktop Design Tool

Scott A. Roberts[1*], Carlos F. Jove-Colon[1], Harry K. Moffat[1], Mitchell L. Neilsen[2], Edward S. Piekos[1], Benjamin B. Schroeder[1], Bradley L. Trembacki[1], and Tyler G. Voskuilen[1]

[1]Sandia National Laboratories, PO Box 5800, MS 0836, Albuquerque, NM, 87185-0836
[2]Kansas State University, 2184 Engineering Hall, 1701D Platt St., Manhattan, KS 66506
*Corresponding Author: sarober@sandia.gov, (505) 844-7957

Abstract: *The Thermally Activated Battery Simulator (TABS) is a computer modeling tool for assisting thermal battery designers in assessing design performance. This tool has been designed to run efficiently on a desktop computer and to present the user with an intuitive interface, allowing the designer to keep focused on the battery design, not the simulation details. The traditional TABS tool has been previously demonstrated to positively impact the battery design process at Sandia National Laboratories and has been integrated into regular workflows.*

In this paper, we demonstrate significant advancements to the capabilities and efficiencies of TABS. The traditional full-battery thermal model has been rebranded as TABS Full Battery (TABS-FB). Additionally, we have developed a second component to the modeling suite, dubbed TABS Single Cell (TABS-SC). This model focuses on a single thermal battery cell, providing the ability to predict the electrochemical performance (voltage and current) of the cell, with contributions from mechanical deformation, electrolyte flow, and thermal transport. A new materials database editor has also been developed that enables time-evolving properties for composite materials.

Keywords: Molten salt battery; modeling; simulation

The TABS Concept

The overarching goal of the TABS project is to create a computational tool to support thermal battery designers in creating and testing their designs virtually, reducing the number of design-build-test cycles required for qualification. Pursuing this goal, TABS is designed using the following principles:

1. Create a user interface intuitive to battery designers, not just for computational scientists,
2. Be computationally efficient, so many design iterations can be explored in a single work day on a standard computer,
3. Present the user with the most relevant quantities of interest, yet enable them to explore more deeply on their own, and
4. Have demonstrated credibility, such that the user knows when and how much to trust the solutions.

Two separate TABS modules are available in the current release (version 5.0, released May 2018). TABS-FB is a full battery thermal simulator (without electrochemistry or other physics), calculating the battery's internal temperature distribution from ignition to freeze-out. TABS-SC is a multiphysics simulator at a single-cell level, with the intent of predicting electrochemical performance by simulating heat generation and transport, mechanical deformation, two-phase porous electrolyte flow and species transport, electrical transport, and electrochemical reactions.

A typical TABS workflow is illustrated in Figure 1. The primary graphical user interface (GUI) is shown in the top-middle of Figure 1. Using this GUI, the user defines their battery design graphically and intuitively. After specifying the battery design dimensions, TABS automatically creates a discretized mesh using Cubit [1].

TABS contains a built-in, extensible database of thermophysical properties, shown via a series of snapshots in Figure 2. The database distributed with TABS is pre-populated with properties for many of the materials commonly used in thermal batteries. Through the editor window shown in Figure 2a, the user can add new materials or edit any of the properties of existing materials. Pressed-pellet materials common to the electrochemical cell are considered to be composite materials (editor shown in Figure 2b) comprised of solid, liquid (electrolyte), and gas phases, with each of these having its own distinct properties specified separately (Figure 2c). Additionally, the solid phase can be comprised of multiple materials (e.g. FeS_2, MgO, and Li_2O). This composite material behavior enables the properties to evolve over the course of the simulation (e.g. as electrolyte flows during startup, the cathode swells during discharge, etc.). In addition, the database contains the ability to store uncertainty values (for later use in uncertainty quantification studies) for each property and references for these values and uncertainties.

The mesh is combined with thermophysical properties for a physics simulation using Sierra/Aria [2]. For computational efficiency, the mesh and simulation are created assuming 2D axisymmetry common to most

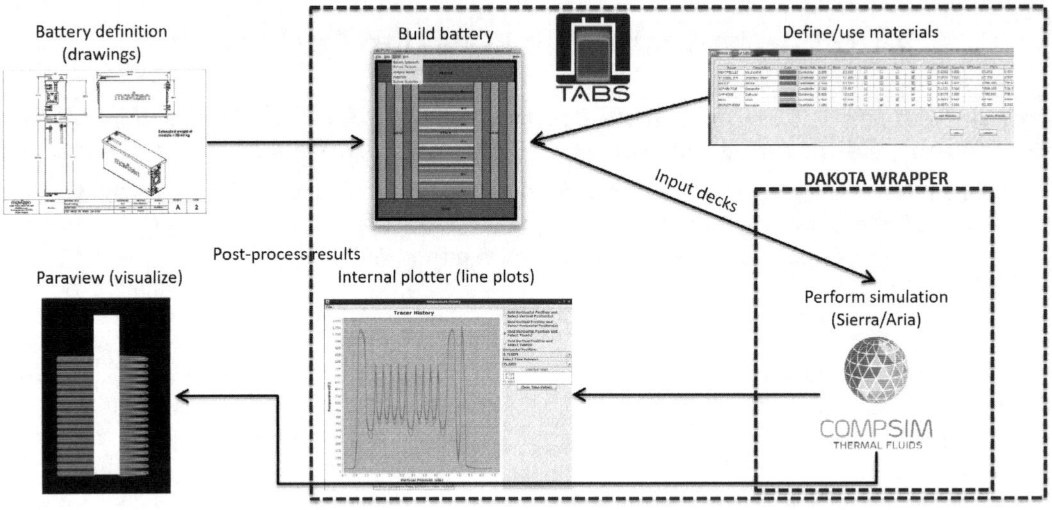

Figure 1. Overview of the TABS workflow showing steps to go from battery definition to solution

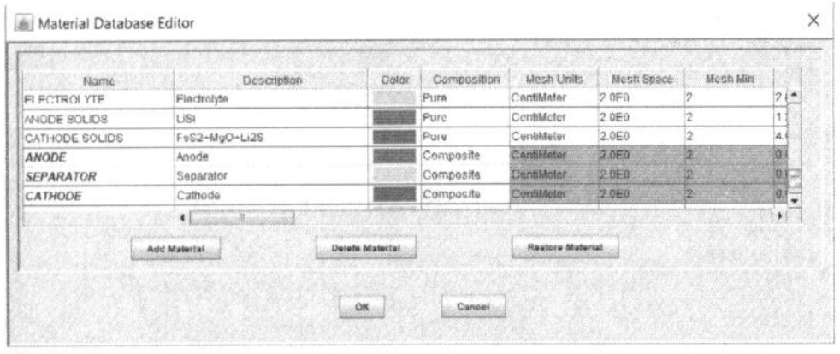

(a) Main database editor window

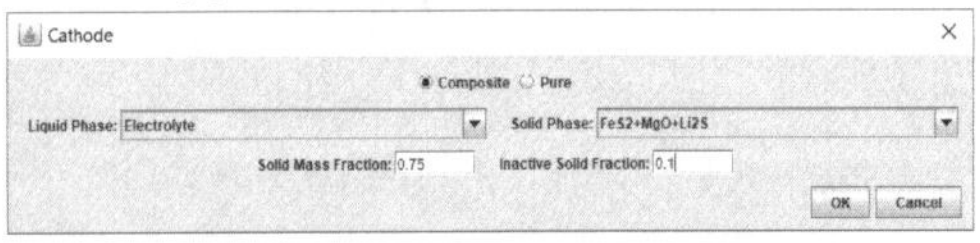

(b) Composite material editor

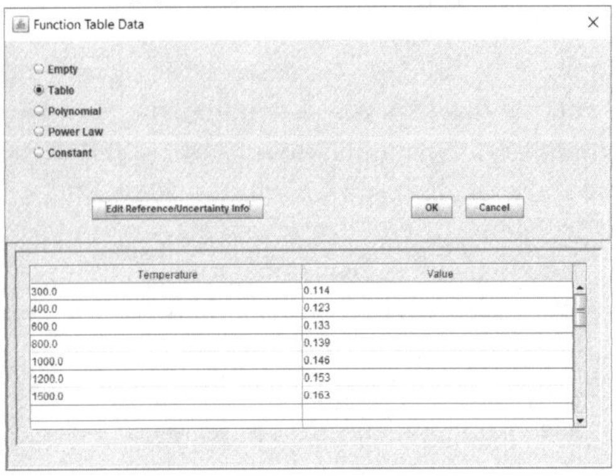

(c) Property entry editor

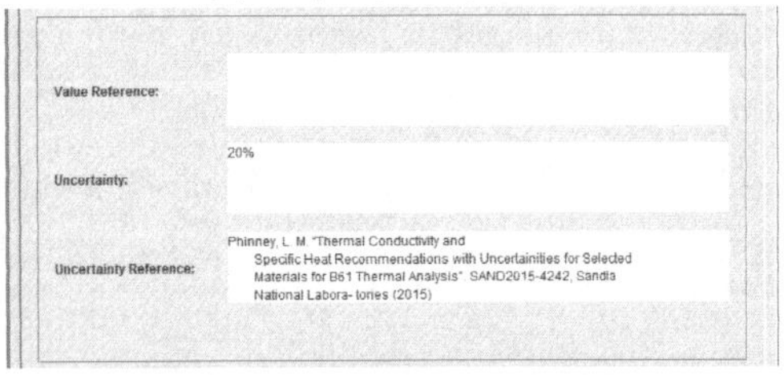

(d) Reference and uncertainty editor

Figure 2. Materials database editor

thermal batteries (which are typically right-circular cylinders). Depending on the resolution and physics chosen, simulations typically take less than one hour on a desktop workstation computer.

The fundamental output from a TABS simulation is a history of every fundamental physics quantity included in the simulation at every spatial point in the geometry for every time simulated. A number of convenient post-processing options are provided through the TABS GUI. First, global scalar quantities, such as battery rise and life times, are displayed directly in the TABS GUI window. Second, time-dependent scalar quantities, such as cell voltage and current, are saved as a comma-separated values (CSV) file viewable in spreadsheet editors. Additionally, TABS-FB contains a built-in plot generator, enabling spatial and temporal interrogation of the solution in the form of line plots. This plotting feature is currently under development for the next release of TABS-SC. Finally, Paraview [3] can be used for exploring the results in great detail, creating colored 2D images and movies.

TABS-FB: Full Battery Thermal Simulator

The original component to TABS is the TABS-FB full battery thermal simulator, whose main window is shown in Figure 3. The cell stack is designated as the combination of individual cells comprised of any number of materials, including heat pellets, collectors, cathodes, separators, and anodes. Identical cells may be repeated multiple times (note the "8x" in Figure 3) and combined with individually specified cells which are not identical. Radial insulation and wraps, axial insulation, header, footer, and can complete the battery definition. Center-hole fired or side-fired batteries can be specified.

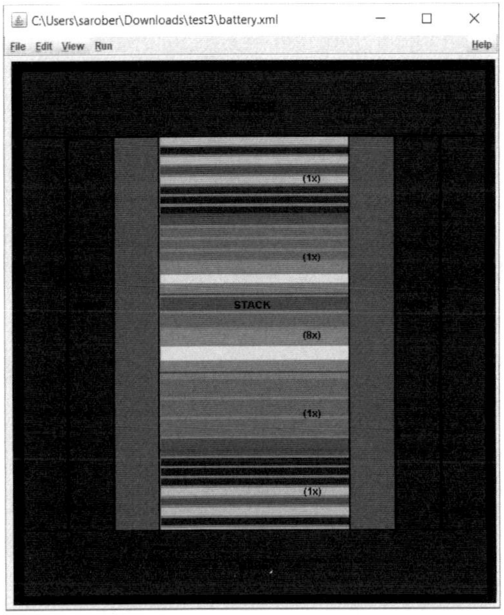

Figure 3. TABS-FB main window

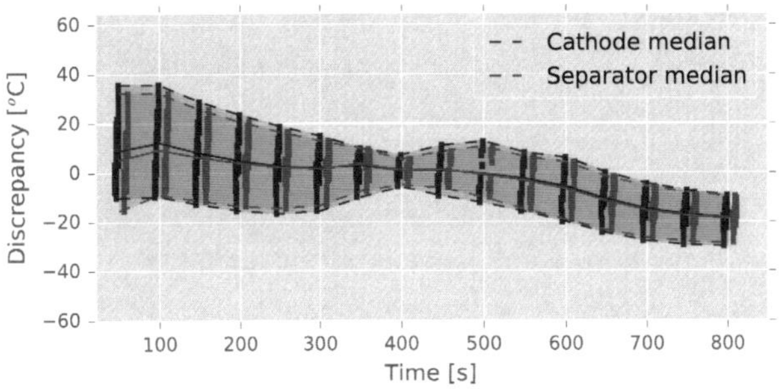

Figure 4. Example plot of TABS-FB experimental validation showing discrepancies between experimental data and nominal temperature for cathode and anode temperatures. The solid curves in the middle represent the median difference between experiment and simulation and the bands represent the range of values.

The TABS-FB physics model consists of heat generation and transport and has been previously described in detail [4]. For center-hole fired batteries, all heat pellets are simultaneously ignited at their centers. Side-fired batteries are initiated at the center of the heat pellet nearest the header, which then burns to ignite heat paper strips that burn axially and ignite the remaining heat pellets. Heat is lost through the can due to conduction, convection, and radiation.

The primary global scalar quantities of interest (QOIs) resulting from TABS-FB simulations are rise time, life time, and the maximum temperature in the cathode and anode. These QOIs are immediately available to the user through the TABS GUI without further post-processing. Additional temperature plots can also be easily created.

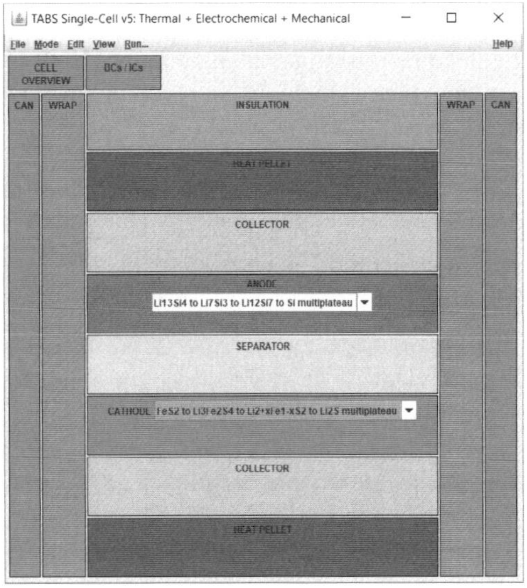

Figure 5. TABS-SC main window

TABS-FB has been subjected to a rigorous credibility assessment [4]. The underlying physics code has been verified using known solutions, and battery-specific problems have been subjected to solution verification, showing expected order-of-convergence with mesh resolution and time step size. These verification activities informed the default numerical parameters found in TABS-FB. Parameter uncertainties were quantified and propagated through the model. Resulting QOI uncertainties are relatively large due to highly uncertain values for insulation thermal conductivities, an area of active research [5]. Validation was performed against data from thermocouples embedded in a purpose-built model validation battery. The discrepancy between experiment and simulation (an example of which is shown in Figure 4) is always less than 50 °C, and typically much less (nominally 20 °C) during the majority of the battery's operational time.

TABS-SC: Single Cell Multiphysics Simulator

The newest component of TABS is the TABS-SC single cell multiphysics simulator, shown in Figure 5. The primary intent of this module is to predict the electrochemical performance of a battery cell. To do this, heat generation and transport, mechanical deformation, two-phase porous flow and species transport, electrical transport, and electrochemical reactions are modeled. Due to the complexity of these coupled physics, TABS-SC implements this capability only for single electrochemical cells. For the sake of computational efficiency, multiple levels of physics fidelities are offered in the form of simulation fidelity modes [6]. The electrochemical reactions are driven by specifying the cell load, either in the form of a current, voltage, or load resistance.

A large number of QOIs are available from TABS-SC in each of the physics areas simulated, both global and time-dependent scalars. Battery performance is primarily captured through the cell voltage and current, which are readily viewable in the output CSV file. Progress and spatial distribution of each electrochemical reaction, electrolyte distribution, and many other parameters are also available.

Credibility assessments of TABS-SC are ongoing. Code and solution verification show expected results and parametric uncertainties are quantified. Validation against experimental single-cell test data has also been completed, but agreement is currently poor, leading to ongoing research investments in improving the calibration of a number of electrochemical parameters [7]. More complete documentation of the TABS-SC physics model and credibility assessment is pending.

Obtaining and Using TABS

TABS is export controlled under EAR99 and is available to entities of the U.S. Government and their prime contractors from Sandia National Laboratories under a Government Use Notice. Concurrent licenses for Cubit [1] and Sierra/Aria [2] are also required.

TABS and its supporting codes are designed to be run natively under a Linux-based operating system, including MacOS. Windows computing environments can be supported via multiple non-native implementations, including virtual machines and the Windows Subsystem for Linux. TABS is capable of parallel processing, and the developers recommend running on a reasonably powerful multi-core desktop workstation for the best experience, although TABS-FB has been successfully run on laptop computers.

The Future of TABS

TABS continues to be actively developed. A minor version release (v5.1) is planned for the end of 2018, bringing additional post-processing capabilities to TABS-SC, improved electrochemical calibration, and an ability to use TABS-FB thermal profiles to define the temperature in TABS-SC. TABS v6.0 is slated for deployment in 2020 and will bring basic electrical simulation capabilities to the full battery scale. Future versions will improve the fidelity of full-battery electrochemistry and mechanics, including the ability to model battery performance in dynamic mechanical environments.

Acknowledgments

The authors gratefully acknowledge funding from the Department of Defense/Department of Energy Joint Munitions Technology Development Program (JMP). Sandia National Laboratories is a multi-mission laboratory managed and operated by National Technology and Engineering Solutions of Sandia, LLC., a wholly owned subsidiary of Honeywell International, Inc., for the U.S. Department of Energy's National Nuclear Security Administration under contract DE-NA0003525. The views expressed in this article do not necessarily represent the views of the U.S. Department of Energy or the United States Government. Unclassified Unlimited Release SAND2018-4243 C.

References

1. Blacker, T., S. J. Owen, M. L. Staten, R. W. Quadros, B. Hanks, B. Clark, T. Hensley, R. J. Meyers, C. Ernst, K. Merkley, R. Morris, C. McBride, C. Stimpson, M. Plooster, and S. Showman. "CUBIT Geometry and Mesh Generation Toolkit 15.3 User Documentation." Tech. Rep. SAND2017-6895 W, Sandia National Laboratories, Albuquerque, 2017.

2. SIERRA Thermal/Fluid Development Team. "SIERRA Multimechanics Module: Aria User Manual, Version 4.46." Tech. Rep. SAND2017-10427, Sandia National Laboratories, Albuquerque, 2017.

3. Ahrens, J., B. Geveci, and C. Law. "ParaView: An End-User Tool for Large Data Visualization." Tech. Rep. LA-UR-03-1560, Los Alamos National Laboratory, 2005.

4. Roberts, S. A., S. R. Harris, A. C. Hetzler, E. S. Piekos, B. B. Schroeder, and B. L. Trembacki. "Establishing the Credibility of the Thermally Activated Battery Simulator, Full-Battery Version 4: Verification, Validation, and Uncertainty Quantification." Tech. Rep. SAND2017-3397, Sandia National Laboratories, 2017.

5. Headley, A., M. Nemer, C. Roberts, and R. Solich. "Capillary Pressure Versus Saturation Characterization of Molten-Salt Power Source Separator Materials." Proceedings of the 48th Power Sources Conference, Denver, 2018.

6. Voskuilen, T., C. Jove-Colon, H. Moffat, B. Schroeder, B. Trembacki, and S. Roberts. "Multi-Physics Cost and Complexity Reduction Strategies for Modeling Thermally Activated Batteries." Proceedings of the 48th Power Sources Conference, Denver, 2018.

7. Schroeder, B., E. Allcorn, J. Hewson, H. Moffat, E. Piekos, B. Trembacki, T. Voskuilen, and S. Roberts. "Supporting Credibility of Single Cell Thermal Battery Modeling through V&V/UQ Activities." Proceedings of the 48th Power Sources Conference, Denver, 2018.

Multi-Physics Cost and Complexity Reduction Strategies for Modeling Thermally Activated Batteries

Tyler G. Voskuilen*, Carlos F. Jove-Colon, Harry K. Moffat, Benjamin B. Schroeder, Bradley L. Trembacki, and Scott A. Roberts

Sandia National Laboratories, PO Box 5800, MS 0828, Albuquerque, NM, 87185-0828

*Corresponding Author: tvoskui@sandia.gov, (505) 845-0390

Abstract: *Thermally activated LiSi/FeS_2 batteries undergo a series of coupled physical changes during activation, all of which can influence battery rise time and performance to some degree. These processes include burning of an energetic material, heat transfer, phase change, capillary-driven two-phase porous flow, ion transport, electrochemical reactions, electrical transport, and mechanical deformation.*

Several of these processes are strongly coupled and will have a significant effect on the simulation outcome, but others may have minimal impact or may be suitably represented by reduced-order models. Our prior investigations have focused on including as many of these processes as possible in order to improve the predictivity of the model, but this approach comes at a significant computational cost.

In this work, we first identify several quantities of interest (QOIs) that may be useful to model users and battery designers. We then define five categories of fidelity (simulation modes) that include different physical simplifications and assumptions, decoupling or removing physical processes from simulation. We compare the behavior of these modes in terms of computational cost, level of uncertainty, and effect on QOIs. Using this approach, we achieve an order-of-magnitude reduction in computational cost while preserving all the QOIs within an acceptable tolerance.

Keywords: thermal battery; primary lithium cell; molten salt electrolyte; iron disulfide; computational modeling

Introduction

Prior work on predictive modeling of thermal batteries has focused adding as many relevant physical phenomena to the model as possible in order to capture a variety of hypothesized effects [1–6]. These efforts have been successful in terms of producing a model capturing a rich set of physical processes, including heat transfer, electrochemical reactions, ion and species transport, porous flow, capillary effects, phase change, and mechanical deformation. However, the rich suite of models comes at a steep computational cost, even for a 2D axisymmetric domain.

In this work, we focus on assessing the effects of the different phenomena in the model and determining when and how the more costly portions of the model can be simplified without adversely affecting the solution outcome. Almost all model reductions will result in some change in the solution, so we will select several key quantities of interest (QOIs) to battery modelers and use those to evaluate the effect of different model reductions.

Methods

The model reduction approach used for this work is to start with the full-physics model and assess the relative computational costs and effects that the various model components have on predictivity. The top candidates for reduction are items identified as having high computational cost and low impact on predictivity. In this section, we briefly describe the full physics model and then outline the different reduced models we have developed. These reduced models are available in the Thermally Activated Battery Simulator (TABS) v5 [7].

Model: Many of the details of the current model have been described in our prior publications so we will describe these only at a high level [1–3, 8]. The key difference between the current model is the addition of mechanical deformation to the previously described model [1].

The model includes heat transfer, solid electrical conduction, species and ion transport in the molten electrolyte, electrochemical reactions, porous two-phase flow of electrolyte and trapped gasses, capillary wicking of liquid electrolyte, strain-dependent mechanical properties, and mechanical deformation. The model equations are applied to the single-cell 2D axisymmetric domain shown in Figure 1. The porous flow and electrochemical equations are evaluated in the anode, cathode, and separator, while deformation and heat transfer are evaluated over the entire domain.

Once the full-physics model was assembled, we used the results from the full analysis to direct the physics reduction. One thing in particular that drove the reductions was the fact that the full physics simulation spent a majority of its time resolving the first second

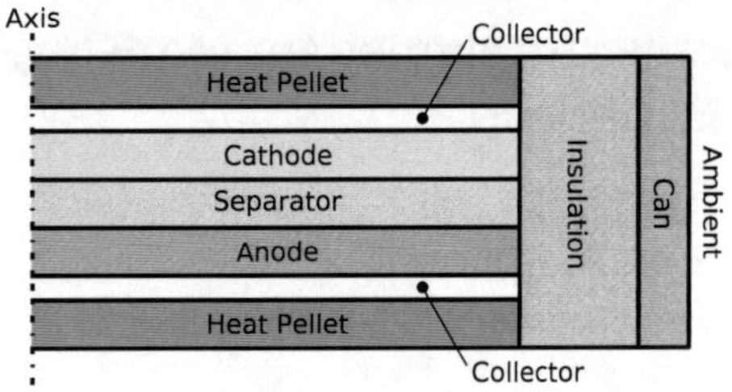

Figure 1. The 2D axisymmetric simulation domain for the multi-physics simulations (not to scale).

or two of the cell life. Many of the expensive phenomena were related to the cell transitioning from the as-manufactured configuration to the operational configuration. This included migration of the electrolyte out of the separator and deformation of the separator as the electrolyte melted. Once the battery was fully activated, these processes had minimal effect. As a result, the primary focus of the model reduction was on finding suitable approximations for the battery activation processes that did not involve a costly modeling step.

QOIs: To assess the proposed model reductions we have identified several key quantities of interest. These include rise time (time to reach a specified voltage), life time (time until voltage falls below a specified value), peak voltage, and peak temperature in the different battery components. The prior thermal model [2, 8] used temperature as a metric to indicate rise time and life time, so we can also compare the thermal model predictions with the full-physics predictions.

Model Reductions: We have broken the model into five levels of complexity, which we refer to as modes 1 to 5. The differences between these modes are described below. These modes are available in TABS for users to select from depending on their model fidelity requirements, available time, and computational resources.

Mode 1 is a 2D axisymmetric thermal model that includes the heat pellet burn as well as the latent heat of phase change of the electrolyte, but does not include electrochemistry, porous flow, or mechanical deformation.

Mode 2 is a one-dimensional model of the cell that includes Darcy flow and electrochemical reactions, but uses a prescribed temperature and neglects capillary effects and mechanical deformation. In this mode the temperature is specified by the user as a constant or time-varying function that is applied uniformly throughout the cell.

Mode 3 is a 2D axisymmetric reduced physics model. It includes heat transfer, electrochemical reactions, and porous flow, but neglects capillary forces and mechanical deformation. The user can specify an amount of separator strain that is applied by deforming the initial geometry and adjusting porosity and saturation initial conditions to preserve mass. Since this model does not resolve electrolyte migration during startup, the user can select from a number of options for how to change the saturations in the model from the as-manufactured state to the melted state.

The options for distributing the electrolyte are none (use the as-manufactured amounts in the anode, cathode, and separator), uniform (Eq. 2, preserve electrolyte mass and set equal saturation in the anode, cathode, and separator), or capillary equilibrium (preserve electrolyte mass and set the saturations in the anode, cathode, and separator to produce equal capillary pressure, Eq. 3 [9], by solving for saturations that minimize Eq. 4). The heights of the anode, cathode, and separator are defined as h_a, h_c, and h_s, respectively, and saturations (S_i) and porosities (ϕ_i) are indicated with the same subscript notation. The capillary pressure is noted as $p_{c,i}$ where i is the anode, cathode, or separator.

$$V_e = h_a \phi_a S_a + h_s \phi_s S_s + h_c \phi_c S_c \tag{1}$$

$$S_{eq} = \frac{V_e}{h_a \phi_a + h_s \phi_s + h_c \phi_c} \tag{2}$$

$$p_{c,i} = p_{ref,i} \left(S_i^{\left(\frac{-1}{1-\beta_i^{-1}} - 1\right)} \right)^{\frac{1}{\beta_i}} \tag{3}$$

$$E = |p_{c,a} - p_{c,s}| + |p_{c,c} - p_{c,s}| + |V_e - \sum \phi_i S_i h_i| \tag{4}$$

These options are valid to use in modes 1, 2, and 3, since none of those modes resolve the electrolyte migration during the melt phase.

Since mode 3 also neglects many of the transient processes during thermal battery activation, it makes sense to consider removing the heat pellet burn model as well and simply starting the cell at an elevated temperature. This option is referred to as "skip burn" and referred to as Mode 3 SB in the results.

Mode 4 is like mode 3, but adds in capillary forces for the liquid electrolyte. It does not include mechanical deformation, instead it allows the user to specify an amount of separator strain that is applied as an initial condition. Electrolyte migration during startup is

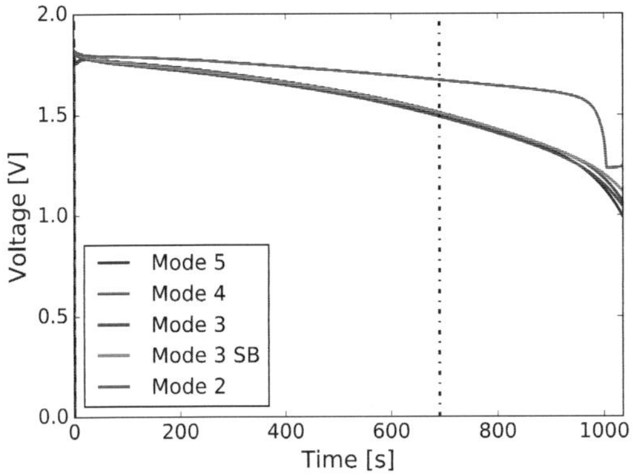

Figure 2. Predicted voltage vs. time for the different models, showing prediction of cell lifetime. The dashed line indicates when the full-physics model dropped below 1.5 volts.

captured by the model, so the electrolyte distribution approach is not relevant to mode 4.

Mode 5 is the full-physics model, and adds mechanical deformation to mode 4. Since separator strain is captured by the model along with electrolyte migration the user does not need to specify parameters for this.

Results

To assess the different model reductions, we compare the key quantities of interest for all the relevant models. The battery lifetime is defined by the time it takes for the cell to fall below a reference voltage. Comparing the cell voltage in Figure 2 for all the models that include electrochemistry (mode 1 is excluded here) it is apparent that the thermal model is key for predicting battery lifetime. Mode 2, which does not include a thermal model, has a considerably different lifetime prediction than the other modes, which are all quite consistent. The standard deviation in life time predictions is only 1.6 % of the mean.

Another important model prediction is the cell rise time. The rise time is not predicted for mode 2 and mode 3 SB, but they are shown for comparison in Figure 3. The rise times are also quite consistent, with a spread between the min and max rise time predictions of only 33 ms. It is also noteworthy that both mode 4 and 5 predict a small drop in voltage after startup while mode 3 does not. This voltage drop has also been observed experimentally. The spread in the predicted maximum voltage between simulation modes is also quite small, at around 20 mV.

The final set of scalar quantities are the mean temperatures in each component. These are compared in Figure 4. Mode 2 is shown for comparison here but since

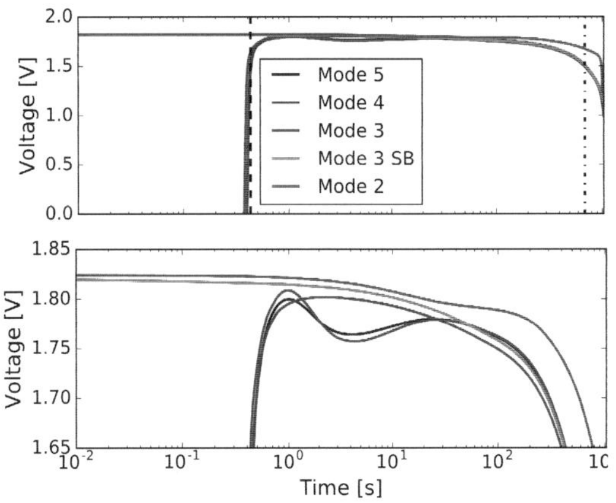

Figure 3. Comparison of voltage profiles vs. time (log scale) emphasizing the cell activation time. The dashed lines indicate when the full-physics model goes above 1.5 volts, then drops below 1.5 volts.

Table 1. Mode run times and speedup relative to mode 5

Mode	Run Time	Speedup
Mode 2	17 s	84.3
Mode 3 SB	235 s	6.1
Mode 3	815 s	1.76
Mode 4	1390 s	1.03
Mode 5	1433 s	-

it does not include a thermal solve the mean temperature is simply the prescribed condition. The temperature of the other modes are in good agreement however throughout the life of the battery. Even though mode 3 SB skips the cell startup, it does a reasonably good job of predicting the cell life time due to freeze-out. The spread in the max temperature on the cathode was 13 K and the spread between the min and max temperatures on the anode is 17 K.

The computational savings of the different modes varied as one might expect (Table 1). All timings shown were run for a full cell lifetime using 4 processors on a desktop computer. Mode 5 is used as a reference point for this comparison. Mode 4, which removed mechanical deformation, was 97 % of the run time of mode 5. Mode 3 including the heat pellet burn was 57 % of the run time of mode 5. Eliminating the burn front model from mode 3 decreased its time even further to 16 % of the mode 5 run time, a 6x speedup. Mode 2 was only 1 % of the mode 5 time, an 84x speedup although with a more significant loss of predictivity for a general battery configuration.

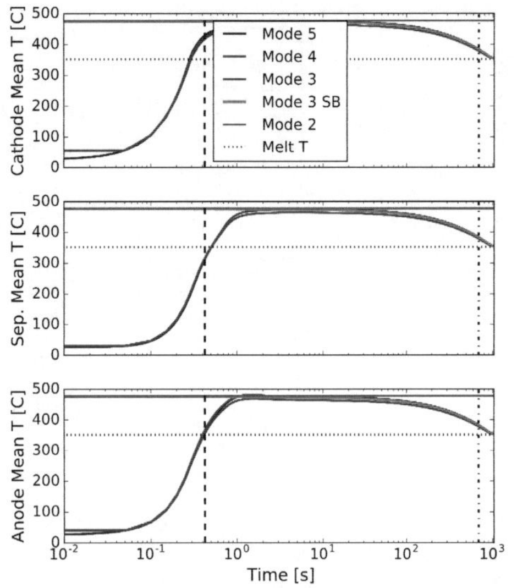

Figure 4. Comparison of mean temperature predictions per cell component with the different models. The vertical dashed lines indicate when the full-physics model goes above 1.5 volts, then drops below 1.5 volts.

Summary & Conclusions

The focus of our prior work was on adding as many of the potentially relevant physical processes to the TABS thermal battery model as was feasible. However, in order to make this a useful tool it also had to be able to run quickly. Therefore this work focused on using the results from the full-physics model to identify processes that were expensive to model and amenable to being replace with reduced order representations or modified initial conditions without significantly impacting key QOIs.

In this work we showed how five levels of model reduction compare in terms of computational cost and key quantities of interest; including battery rise time, life time, peak voltage, and peak temperature. The reduced physics model is between 6x and 84x faster than the full-physics model while preserving the QOIs to within 1 to 5 % of the predictions by the full-physics model.

Acknowledgments

The authors gratefully acknowledge funding from the Joint Department of Defense/Department of Energy Munitions Technology Development Program. Sandia National Laboratories is a multi-mission laboratory managed and operated by National Technology and Engineering Solutions of Sandia, LLC., a wholly owned subsidiary of Honeywell International, Inc., for the U.S. Department of Energy's National Nuclear Security Administration under contract DE-NA0003525. The views expressed in this article do not necessarily represent the views of the U.S. Department of Energy or the United States Government. Unclassified Unlimited Release SAND2018-4289 C

References

1. Voskuilen, T., J. Hewson, H. Moffat, and S. Roberts. "Multi-Physics, Multi-Plateua Reaction Model for LiSi/FeS_2 Batteries." Proceedings of the 47th Power Sources Conference, 2016.

2. Roberts, S. A., K. N. Long, J. S. Rath, L. A. Mondy, and A. M. Grillet. "Modeling Separator Deformation and Electrolyte Flow in Thermally-Activated Batteries." Proceedings of the 45th Power Sources Conference, 2012.

3. Roberts, S. A., K. N. Long, J. R. Clausen, M. R. Martinez, E. S. Piekos, and A. M. Grillet. "Towards a Coupled Multiphysics Model of Molten Salt Battery Mechanics." Proceedings of the 46th Power Sources Conference, 2014.

4. Hewson, J., H. Moffat, C. Leuth, and D. Ingersoll. "Predicting Electrochemical Phenomena in Lithium Molten Salt Thermal Batteries." Proceedings of the 44th Power Sources Conference, 2010.

5. Hewson, J., H. Moffat, C. Leuth, and D. Ingersoll. "Predicting Electrochemical Phenomena in Lithium Molten Salt Thermal Batteries." Proceedings of the 45th Power Sources Conference, 2012.

6. Hewson, J., H. Moffat, and V. Brunini. "Model Parameterization for Electrochemical Predictions of LiSi/FeS_2 Batteries." Proceedings of the 46th Power Sources Conference, 2014.

7. Roberts, S., C. Jove-Colon, H. Moffat, M. Neilsen, E. Piekos, B. Schroeder, B. Trembacki, and T. Voskuilen. "TABS : A Thermal Battery Desktop Design Tool." Proceedings of the 48th Power Sources Conference, 2018.

8. Piekos, E. S., A. M. Grillet, D. Ingersoll, N. D. Streeter, and D. R. Noble. "Modeling of thermal battery initiation using level sets." Proceedings of the 45th Power Sources Conference, 2012.

9. van Genuchten, M. T. "A closed-form equation for predicting the hydraulic conductivity of unsaturated soils." *Soil Science Society of America Journal*, vol. 44, pp. 892–898, 1980.

Advance Si Anode for High Energy Lithium Ion Cells

Pu Zhang, Michael Wixom

Navitas Systems
4880 Venture Drive, Ann Arbor, MI 48108
pzhang@navitassys.com

Abstract: *High Energy Dense lithium batteries are attractive power sources for military applications such as vehicle starting, Silent Watch, portable power units, Unmanned Systems, and other battlefield applications. Low cost and high performing Si anode material has been developed to enable high energy lithium cells at 300 Wh/kg and 600 Wh/L. High energy cathode, performance-enhanced electrolyte, and novel cell design are also developed to meet the high energy, low weight goals. All the electrodes are prepared using production processes and prototype, prismatic pouch cells are built in pilot scale and scale to production in Navitas cell manufacturing line. A cycle life of >300 has been demonstrated in the high energy cells. It will be applied for portable power Conformal Wearable Batteries (CWB), UAV battery packs.*

Effect of State of Charge and Depth of Discharge on the Cycle Life of LifePO4/Graphite Cell at Fast Charging for Electric Vehicle Application

Vallabha Rao Rikka[1], Abhijit Chatterjee[2], Raju Prakash[1], Raghavan Gopalan[1], Govindan Sundararajan[1]

[1]CAEM-International Advanced Research Centre for Powder Metallurgy & New Materials,
[2]Indian Institute of Technology (IITB)-Powai

Abstract: *Currently Lithium-ion batteries (LIBs) are the most promising energy storage devices for electric vehicle (EV) applications, which requires fast charging/discharging performance for convenient use in EVs. Among all lithium ion battery technologies, LiFePO4/Graphite cells are the most suitable ones for EV applications due to its high-power density, excellent structural stability and low premature aging for fast charge/discharge applications. Accelerated ageing studies at various temperatures, charge/discharge rates (C-rates), state of charge (SOC), depth of discharge (DOD) have been well established to determine the cycle life of LIB. Even though the effect of combination of SOC and DOD at a given C-rate plays a crucial role on the cycle life of LIB, which has not yet been investigated. Herein, we have studied for the first time that the cycle life of commercial LiFePO4/Graphite cells (3.2 V, 2.5 Ah) at various combination of SOC and DOD until the end-of-life (capacity retention of 80%). Tauguchi orthogonal test matrix was designed with different combination of SOC (80%-100%) and DOD (80%-100%) at a constant C-rate (4C). A tauguchi analysis of the data so generated will be presented and the relative impedance of SOC and DOD in determining the cycle life will be assessed.*

Conversion Mechanism of CuF_2 for Secondary Batteries

Kyler Carroll, Dee Strand, Bin Li
Wildcat Discovery Technologies
San Diego, CA, USA

Abstract: *The current generation of lithium-ion battery materials is quickly approaching its theoretical limit. Current commercial battery technology relies upon intercalation type layered oxides, such as NMC, which display a maximum achievable limit on capacity of only one lithium for every transition metal. As an example, NMC's theoretical capacity is 300mAh/g of cathode, however today's commercially available cells can only cycle around 0.6 to 0.7 lithium ions per transition metal, resulting in only 180-220 mAh/g of cathode. Therefore even if 100% lithium were utilized, todays commercial cathodes could only be improved by around 30-40%, clearly suggesting a new technology is needed if there is to be a stepwise change in battery technology.*

Metal fluoride (MF) conversion type materials are considered next generation cathodes, offering the potential for a threefold increase in energy density when compared to current technologies (Fig.1a). This potential is due their ability to cycle more than one lithium atom per transition metal. Copper fluoride, one of the most promising MFs, offers a tremendous potential for improvement in energy density due to its high capacity and reasonable operating potential (~3.5V), and these two properties taken together equate to an energy density on the order of 1800 Wh/kg or 7500 Wh/L (CuF2) – approximately three times that of today's commercialized NMC materials.

Wildcat Discovery Technologies has recently developed the first rechargeable CuF2 material with several patents granted. The rechargeable CuF2 demonstrated initial reversible capacity >240 mAh/g. To the best of our knowledge, CuF2 has not shown a reversible conversion reaction presumably due to the fact that the Cu nanoparticles after the lithiation are too large and the insulating LiF prevents electron migration to convert back to CuF2 (The reaction pathway for discharge is CuF2 + 2Li ? Cu + 2LiF). Our approach utilized high-throughput combinatorial research to improve the conductivity of CuF2 through surface coating. After evaluating hundreds of coatings, a two-step process creating a transition metal oxide coating allowed for 15 rechargeable cycles with greater than 80% retention (Fig.1b). To build on these results and improve cycling performance a better understanding of the local environment of the Cu and the metal oxide coating was needed. We utilized synchrotron X-ray absorption spectroscopy, at the Argonne National Laboratory, to provide a better understanding of the local atomic structure and phase progression of the metal oxide coated and uncoated CuF2. The results suggest that the metal oxide coating helps in the reversibility of the Cu to CuF2 conversion but is not electrochemically active (no coordination change or oxidation change). Additionally, we have utilized high resolution aberration corrected transition electron microscopy to visualize the distribution of Cu and LiF with that of the metal oxide coating. By utilizing both techniques we are able to improve our understanding of the metal oxide coating which will help guide the future direction of the conversion material.

Utilizing Custom and Commercial Li-Ion Cells for Space Applications

Blake Cardwell

Enersys
1751 S. Fordham St. Suite 100
Longmont, CO 80503

Abstract: *ABSL/Enersys is the world leader in Energy storage solutions for the Space marketplace. The extreme environments of space and the mission criticalities necessitate that the energy storage solutions utilized are robust and reliable. Battery cells destined for space must undergo extreme vibration, shock, temperatures, and radiation levels which often times are not considered as part of the product's design.*

ABSL/Enersys specializes in the design of cells tolerant to these conditions as well as the selection, screening and qualification of commercial technology to extend their operational envelopes to include the space environment. With over 1.6 Billion cell hours of operation in space without failure, ABSL/Enersys has a proven track record of excellence in this arena.

We will present the results of recently completed cell qualifications and the mission types for which each cell is of ideal use. We will also present the status of ongoing qualifications and plans for future qualifications. Additionally, we will discuss the qualification status and behavior of proprietary Li-Ion chemistry developed for the USG specifically for space missions.

Development of High Energy Li-ion Cell and Chemistry

Hyun Joo Bang, Xin Su, Anson Yang, Aadil Benmayza and Mario Destephen
Research and Development
EaglePicher Technologies, LLC
C&Porter Street, Joplin, MO 64801
Email: Hyun.Bang@eaglepicher.com / 1-471-623-8000

Abstract: *Demand for a high energy Li-ion battery is an increasing request for most applications due to limitation of energy density from conventional lithium ion chemistry. EaglePicher Technologies has developed high energy Li-ion chemistry delivering up to 300Wh/kg of energy density to provide a solution for a demand of high energy Li-ion battery under the awarded Title III Lithium Ion Battery Production for Military Applications (LIMA) Project by department of defense. EaglePicher research and development efforts have been focusing on development of high energy density lithium ion cells by incorporating new silicon anode and high specific cathode chemistries for automated production process.*

Keywords: Li-ion battery; high energy density; silicon carbon anode; high specific capacity cathode;

Introduction

In an effort to develop high energy Li-ion cell and chemistry, EaglePicher technologies (EPT) had developed Li-ion cell feasible for 300Wh/kg energy density through the Title III phase I project awarded by Department of Defense (DoD) in 2013. In 2014, encouraged by the demonstration of the high energy Li-ion cell performance from the Phase I, Title III Phase II project was awarded to EPT for establishing manufacturing capability for high energy Li-ion cell production. To support the Title III phase II, EaglePicher has also started a construction of a Li-Ion Center of Excellence (LiCoE) facility to produce various Li-ion cells. Technical efforts for high energy density lithium ion (Li-ion) cell production aim to establish high energy lithium ion cell production capability as well as the required cell chemistry including an incorporation of high specific cathode with reliable cell performance on a wide spectrum of applications [1]. The development efforts include cell designs and electrode chemistries which need to be suitable for a high rate automated production line.

Scope of project

The primary task of awarded Title III Lithium Ion Battery Production for Military Applications (LIMA) project is to establish manufacturing capability for producing Li-ion cells with the performance of more than 250Wh.kg^{-1} at 1C discharge rate. Major technical tasks are 1) identifying core cell and battery design to satisfy the needs, 2) establishing manufacturing facility and production line to produce the cored cells, 3) establishing material synthesis line for high specific capacity anode material, 4) establishing battery and electronics manufacturing capability to utilize cells for BAA applications. Two different sizes of cells are selected to conduct overall technical demands. Table 1 summarizes the detailed information for the selected two cells.

Table 1. Summary of cells under development range

Cells	Small Pouch cell	Medium pouch cell
Cell Model no.	SLC 201	SLC 203
Capacity nominal	1.85 Ah	10Ah
Specific Energy density	230 Wh/kg	300Wh/kg
Rate capability	1C-rate	2C-rate
Max Pulse rate	2C-rate	4C-rate
Shape	Prismatic	Prismatic
Operation temperature	-30°C to 50°C	-30°C to 50°C
Cell Dimension, W x H x T (mm)	50 x 57 x 70	115 x 101 x 70
Cell Packaging material	Polymer coated Al pouch	Polymer coated Al pouch
Target Applications	Portable power, UAV, etc.	Portable power, UAV, etc.

Cell and Chemistry development

Overall cell and chemistry development were directed to achieve the following technical goals which are 1) design flexibility for multi-size range of cell production, 2) cell design for production compatibility and flexibility for Z-folding stack design 3) flexibility to upgrade cell performance for high energy or high power cell, 4) compatibility to incorporate next generation chemistry (high specific capacity cathode material and high specific energy silicon anode material), 5) high conductive electrolyte with improved safety.

SLC 201 cell (small pouch cell) Development

Table 2 describes a specification of SLC 201 cell with detailed technical information. A picture of SLC-201 cell is shown in figure 1. SLC 201 is aim to provide high energy with medium power capability which can be operated in a wider temperature range of -30◦C to 50◦C as shown in table 2.

Table 2 Specification of SLC 201 cell

Model number	SLC 201
Nominal capacity	1.85Ah
Nominal specific energy	220Wh/kg
Nominal energy	6.8Wh
Cycle life	> 500 cycles
Size	50 x 57 x 70 mm
Weight	< 32g
Cell type	Prismatic
Cell packaging	Aluminum Pouch cell
Operation temperature	-30°C to 50°C
Max current/continuous	1.85A
Max current/Pulse	3.8A

Figure 1. Picture of SLC201 cell as assembled

Performance of SLC201 Cell

The performance of SLC 201 cell was evaluated to confirm that the developed SLC 201 cell meet all designed performance. One of target requirement for SL C201 cell is to meet the requirement for conformal wearable battery (CWB) for portable power application. Selected performance qualification results are shown in figure 2, 3 and 4.

Extreme low temperature test as shown in figure 2 is to determine cell discharge capability at extreme low temperature. The required performance is that the tested cell should deliver more than 51% (3.12Wh) of the discharge energy obtained at room temperature condition. The three tested SLC 201 cells delivered more than 4.5Wh discharge energy which exceeds the required energy of 3.12Wh by 44%.

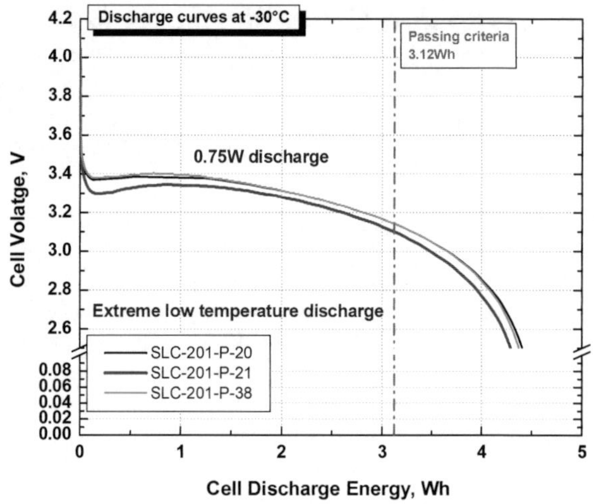

Figure 2. Extreme low temperature (-30◦C) discharge performance of SLC201 cells; three cells test results are shown, charge rate: C/3, discharge C-rate: C/2 in the voltage range of 2.5V-4.2V.

Extreme high temperature test results are shown in figure 3. A purpose of this test is to evaluate a stability of a cell stored and discharged at 55°C. Three tested SLC-201 cells delivered discharge energy from 6.35Wh to 6.63Wg which exceed the required energy of 5.42Wh by 17%~22.

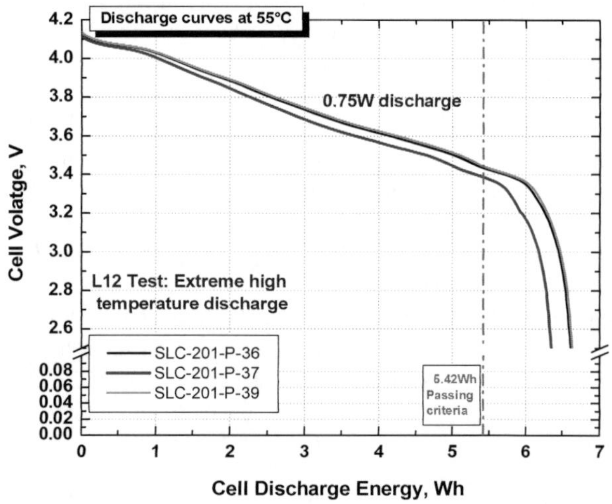

Figure 3. Extreme high temperature discharge performance of SLC201 cells I

Figure 4 shows the cycling performance of three SLC201 cells (SLC201-P-80, SLC201-P-82, and SLC201-P-83) cycled at 25°C. Initial discharge energy (or BOL energy) of three tested cells are approximately 6.9Wh as designed. Cycling test was carried out until discharge cell energy reached to 5.2Wh since the required cell minimum discharge energy for CWB application is above 5.2 for 224 cycles. As shown in figure 4, the tested three cells maintained discharge energy above 5.2 Wh for 600 cycles which exceeds the required cycling performance for CWB and also general Li-ion cell cycling retention requirement.

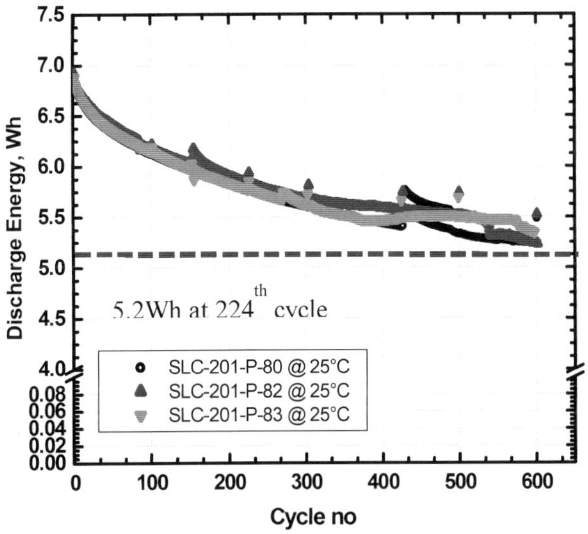

Figure 4 Cycling Performance of three SLC201 cell at room temperature; charge rate: C/3, discharge C-rate: C/2 in the voltage range of 2.5V-4.2V.

Another important qualification criterial is safety of the developed SLC201 cells. Safety qualification was carried out based on UN test protocol and the tests required by military standard such as nail penetration test. Table 3 summarized the safety test results of SLC201 cell.

Table 3. The results of Safety test for SLC201 cells

Inspection / Test	Test Item	Result
Altitude	UN T1 (L13)	PASS
Thermal shock	UN T2 (L14)	PASS
Vibration	UN T3(L15)	PASS
Mechanical shock	UN T4	PASS
Cell short circuit	UN T5 (L16)	PASS
Crush test	UN T6	PASS
Cell forced discharge	UN T8 (L17)	PASS
Cell nail penetration**	L18	All PASS
*L: tests required on Military specification **cells with 50%,100%, 110% state of charge (SOC)		

SLC203 cell development

Technical goal for SLC203 cell development is to achieve energy density more than 250Wh/kg at 1C discharge rate (10 ampere discharge) since SLC 203 cell and chemistry design is required to provide high energy density as well as high power capability for a wide spectrum of applications. Table 4 shows a preliminary specification of current SLC203 under development.

Table 4 Specification of SLC 203 Cell

Model number	SLC 203
Nominal capacity	10Ah
Max specific energy, C/10	300 Wh/kg
Specific Energy @ 1C-rate	250 Wh/kg
Target Cycle life	>100 cycles
Size	115 x 101 x 70 mm
Weight	~130g
Cell type	Prismatic
Cell packaging	Aluminum Pouch cell
Operation temperature	-30°C to 50°C
Max current/continuous	20A
Max current/Pulse	30A

Figure 5. Picture of SLC203 cell as assembled

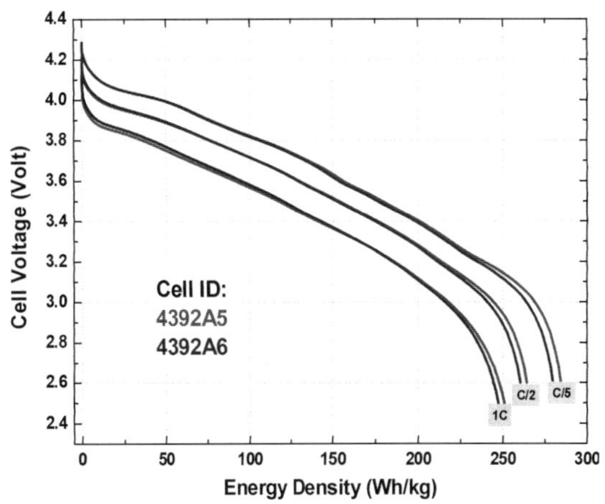

Figure 6 Discharge curves of SLC 203 cells tested at different C-rates to estimated cell energy; 1C current is 10A, the voltage range of 2.5V-4.2V

Figure 6 shows several discharge curves as a function of cell energy density tested at different C-rates to evaluate rate capability and overall energy density of SLC 203 cell. The test results of SLC203 were summarized in table 5.

Table 5 Summary of discharge energy density of SLC203 cell at different C-rate

C-rate, Discharge	Specific energy density	Average Voltage
C/hr	Wh/kg	Ave. V
C/5 rate	285	3.598
C/2 rate	261	3.513
1C rate	250	3.40

Production line establishment and validation

While validation of the cell design and chemistry is being carried out, the production line (equipment) installation and validation is also being conducted in parallel. The pictures in figure 7 are the installed production equipment for a production of SLC201 and SLC203 cell

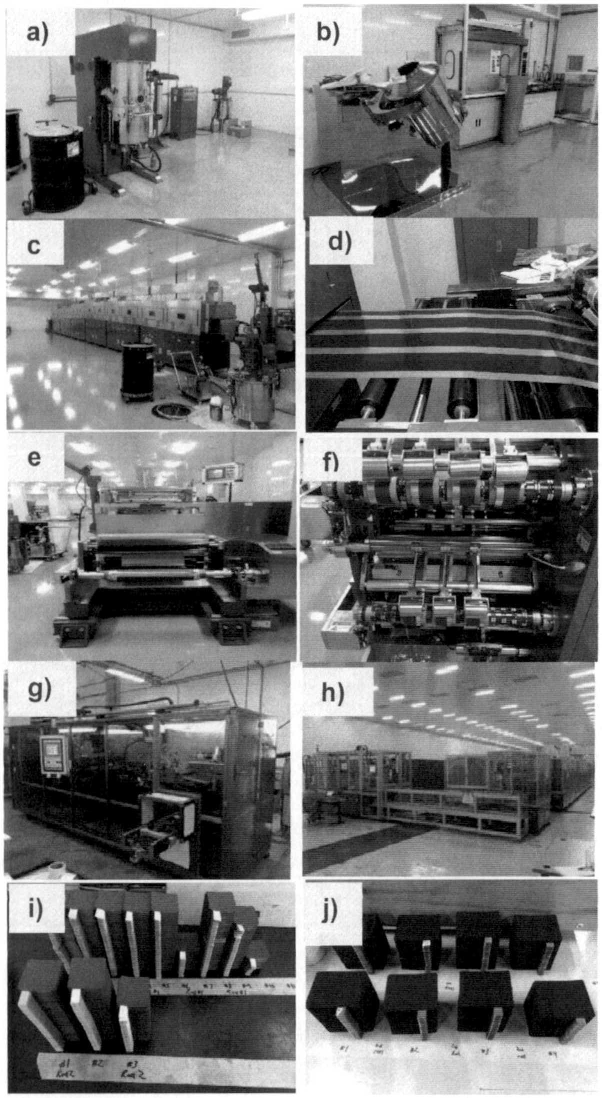

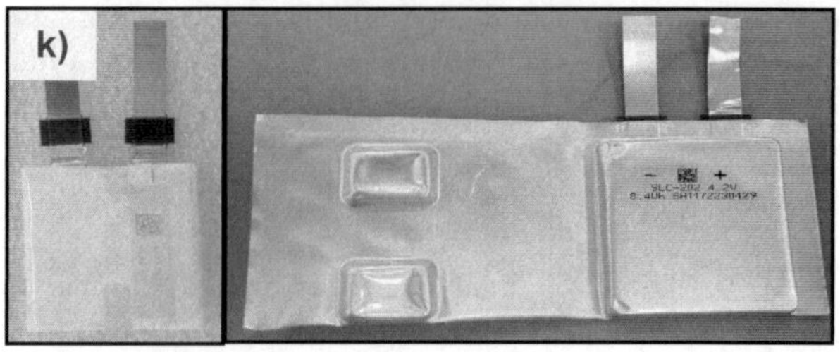

Figure 7. Installed production equipment for SLC cell production. a) slurry mixer, b) turbular powder mixer, c) electrode coater, d) lane pattern coated anode e) coater, f) electrode slitter, g) notching machine, h) automatic pouch cell assembly line, i) notched anode, j) notched cathode, k) assembled jelly roll and assembled pouch cell with gas pocket..

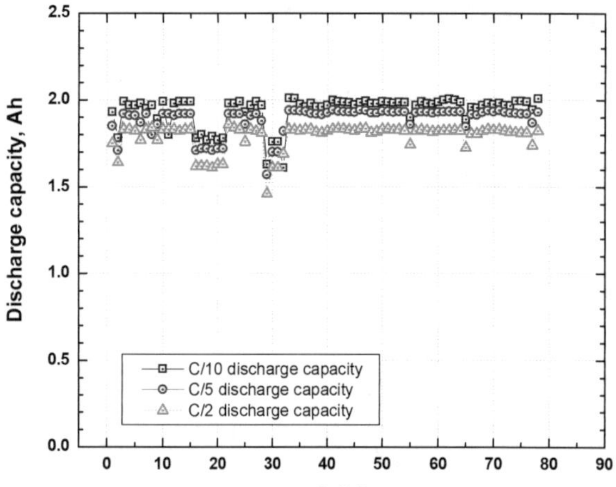

Figure 8. Validation of production cell performance, discharge capacity of the cells produced from manufacturing equipment in figure 7

Summary

EPT has been establishing next generation lithium ion cell production capability and also developed high energy density Li-ion cells. Currently two sizes of Li-ion cell are under development for high throughput production capability. The cells under development are demonstrating high energy and power capability as designed. Current technical effort is focusing on optimizing production equipment operation conditions and final cell design to produce the same performance through the production line.

Acknowledgement

"This material is released to the public domain in accordance with ITAR 22 CFR 120.11"

References

1. Bloom, I., S.A. Jones, V.S. Battaglia, G.L. Henriksen, J.P. Chrsitophersen, R.B. Wright, C.D. Ho, J.R.Belt, and C.G. Motloch, "Effect of cathode composition on capacity fade, impedance rise", *Journal Power Sources* vol. 124, pp. 538-550, 2003.

Novel High Sensitivity Cell Screening Technology for Reducing Formation Time and Improving Cell Sorting

Christopher H. McCoy[1], Thomas Kotwal[2], Suresh Sriramulu[1], and Brian Barnett[1]
[1]CAMX Power LLC
[2]TIAX LLC
35 Hartwell Avenue, Lexington MA 02421
mccoy.chris@camxpower.com

Abstract: *CAMX Power, with support from Defense Logistics Agency, has developed a new, ultra-high sensitivity cell screening technology that can substantially reduce the 7-28 day monitoring operation used in present Li-ion cell manufacturing practice with cost savings, safety and logistics benefits. In addition, the same technology can also be used to replace similar 14-day cell screening operations typically employed to screen cells immediately prior to battery pack assembly (in < 1 hour). The technology is based on a novel application and extension of a CAMX Power short detection technology that provides rapid, accurate, and sensitive detection of internal short circuits in Li-ion cells (and can also be employed to screen primary cells). CAMX Power is developing equipment that implements the hardware and the measurement algorithms for deployment in battery manufacturing as well as pre-pack assembly screening operations to achieve faster, more sensitive and higher sensitivity cell screening.*

Keywords: formation and aging; manufacturing cost; short detection; cell screening.

Introduction

Lithium-ion batteries are increasingly being deployed in DoD applications. However, despite the prevalence and high-volume production of Li-ion batteries in civilian applications (e.g., portable electronics and vehicles), manufacturing costs for Li-ion cells remain relatively high. A major portion of the non-material manufacturing cost of Li-ion batteries results from the long manufacturing cycle time and capital required for cell formation and aging following cell assembly, which is a gating factor in cell throughput for a cell manufacturing line. The formation process is an essential part of Li-ion cell production and ensures that cells operate with rated energy density, long shelf life and long operating life. The aging step is used to assess cell quality and to screen for internal short circuits that not only reduce cell performance, but in rare cases, can result in subsequent violent cell failure. A similar cell screening methodology is employed in the assembly of high reliability battery packs where quality control practices include 100% testing of incoming cells.

There is substantial variation in the duration and specifics of formation and aging processes used by different companies, and even (in our experience) between different plants within the same company. Discussions with industry experts and manufacturers suggest that depending on the chemistry, cell format, and the manufacturer, the formation and aging time is in the 7-28 day range, and is the major factor driving total cell manufacturing time. The process is rarely discussed in technical meetings, is not standardized, and does not appear to receive attention in university studies, all of which suggests an opportunity for improvements. Cost analysis carried out by CAMX Power in a multi-year project for the Department of Energy indicates that the formation/aging processes alone contribute up to 30 % of the total cost of non-material-based Li-ion cell manufacturing costs, which themselves amount to 30-40% of cell cost. Thus, the formation and aging process amounts to approximately 10% of Li-ion cell cost, constituting a significant portion of the cost burden to the DoD.

Most of the formation and aging time is associated with cell aging to check for any internal "soft" shorts that may be generated during electrochemical formation, and thus are not picked up by the Hi-Pot test which precedes electrolyte filling. In the aging process, cells are stored either at room temperature or at elevated temperature, and their open circuit voltage (OCV) is monitored to check for shorts. The longer the aging period, the greater the extent to which a cell will discharge through an internal short of given resistance, and thus the larger the cell's voltage decrease will be, and the better the chance of detecting the short. Cells with shorts, as indicated by OCV drop greater than a threshold magnitude, are rejected. The relative insensitivity of this method with respect to the required task of detecting internal shorts in early-stage development necessitates the extended diagnostic periods typically employed (e.g., 14-28 days). Larger, higher capacity cells require proportionally longer test periods to achieve a given level of detection sensitivity, thereby requiring either longer aging periods to be employed or lower standards of screening to be tolerated. Further, the small variations in cell voltage resulting from the effects of a minor internal short over time risk false-negative responses, permitting faulty cells to enter service and, in rare cases, fail in the field with catastrophic consequences. Thus, there is an opportunity to address key considerations in formation and aging protocols used for the manufacture of lithium-ion cells. These key considerations include the cost associated with manufacturing cycle time, which is driven primarily by the length of the aging period used to attempt to screen out cells with internal short circuits. Three main factors dictate the required time period: cell capacity, time required for internal shorts to develop to a level detectable by the monitoring means employed, and the detection sensitivity of the method used to monitor for internal shorts. Key considerations further include the fidelity and effectiveness of the currently practiced aging process in screening for the presence of internal shorts, specifically:

- False positives - cells that do not pass the aging protocol but do not actually contain internal shorts represent unnecessarily lost yield;
- False negatives - cells that pass the aging protocol but do actually contain internal shorts (i.e., below the detection limits for the aging protocol), represent risks including safety incidents and recall costs.

There are important limitations of screening for internal short circuits using cell voltage monitoring during an aging period. There is a minimum time period needed before an internal short can be definitively detected by monitoring decay in cell voltage (depending on factors including the short resistance and the cell chemistry and capacity). Because normal cells (free of internal shorts) naturally reside with a certain distribution in voltage after the aging period, it is necessary to set up pass-fail criteria that allow for this variation. Typically, cells that fall within a certain band of voltage at the conclusion of aging are graded "pass", while those residing at lower voltages are rejected. Thus, the monitoring technique is not quantitatively measuring the magnitude of the internal short, and a grey area of uncertainty is thus created in the outcome of the test.

Another situation where cell screening for internal short circuits is carried out involves pre-assembly quality checks on cells prior to incorporation into battery packs. This practice, currently limited to pack manufacturing operations where high reliability and safety requirements justify the cost and time expenditure associated with 100% screening of cells, could see far greater utilization if it could be rendered rapid, convenient, and less expensive. When pack assemblers screen cells prior to pack assembly, they utilize protocols similar to those employed in formation and aging quality control screening procedures, namely extended cell voltage monitoring to look for abnormal voltage decay over periods such as 14 days. Accordingly, a cell screening technology that can deliver even greater sensitivity in far less diagnostic time would render 100% cell screening in pack assembly economically viable for a much greater range of applications, enhancing battery pack reliability and safety as a result.

In work sponsored by the Defense Logistics Agency to reduce lithium-ion cell manufacturing costs, we have developed a rapid, ultra-high sensitivity cell screening technology that can identify and quantify internal short circuits in lithium-ion cells in a one-hour scan with more than an order of magnitude greater sensitivity than that achieved with typical 14-day cell voltage decay monitoring practices. This new cell screening technology utilizes a form of electrical monitoring that differs from simple cell terminal voltage tracking over extended time and delivers far greater resolution and sensitivity to the effects of internal shorts on cell electrical characteristics. We report test results and show examples of how our cell screening technology can be utilized to dramatically decrease the time required for formation and aging protocols in cell manufacturing and to render 100% pre-assembly cell screening for internal shorts in lithium-ion pack manufacture viable from both economic and process time perspectives.

Results and Discussion

We begin with test results for the common industry practice of long-term voltage monitoring to screen for internal shorts. Figure 1 shows test results for 2.6Ah 18650 cells held at rest for a period of 14 days with internal shorts over a range of resistance values electronically simulated. These "surrogate shorts" can take the form of either fixed resistance loads or time-variant resistance profiles created using electronic loads. Such techniques reproduce the equivalent circuit comprised by an internal short forming an electronically conductive path between the positive and negative electrodes of a cell of a given resistance. This method of electronic simulation of internal shorts provides high-fidelity replication of the presence of an internal short in a cell for all resistances of interest, with significant deviation from essentially identical replication of an internal short occurring only when internal short resistance approaches cell internal resistance (e.g., 0.05Ω for a typical 18650 cell, 0.001Ω for higher capacity, power-optimized cells). This is not a simulation scenario that is typically necessary or that we have every needed to employ.

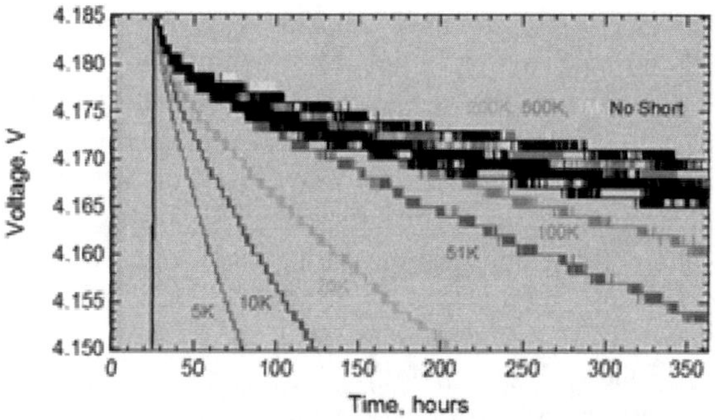

Figure 1. Example of cell screening results for common industry practice of long-term voltage monitoring. 2.6Ah 18650 cells were aged for 14 days after a formation-rate charge (C/20). Steps in the traces arise from the intrinsic resolution limit of the battery test equipment. Black traces show multiple cells with no simulated shorts, while other traces show cells with simulated shorts of the resistances indicated. Shorts from 5000 to 100,000 ohms were distinguishable from short-free cells over the 14-day monitoring period, while higher resistance shorts were not.

The data in Figure 1 show that the traditional 14-day voltage decay monitoring example used in the industry was able to distinguish resistances to 100,000Ω, while higher resistance shorts are not distinguishable from the normal cell-to-cell variability in voltage decay after charging. It should be noted that this test was conducted with commercially available cells that had already been formed (and screened by the manufacturer) prior to this test. This might, of course, tend to yield a *tighter* distribution in short-free cell voltage decay characteristics than might be expected in a population of newly formed cells (and thus higher sensitivity than might actually be achieved with newly formed cells). It is also important to recognize that by detecting internal shorts to the most sensitive levels possible during cell screening operations, cells can be eliminated from the supply chain that might otherwise see growth in severity of incipient internal shorts that ultimately can result in degradation in battery performance, battery failure, or in rare instances thermal runaway and catastrophic failure.

The CAMX Power Ultra-High Sensitivity Screening Technology

The CAMX Power technology for ultra-high sensitivity screening employs electrical diagnostics that are intrinsically much more sensitive to the presence of internal shorts in cells than long-term monitoring of cell voltage. Figure 2 shows test data demonstrating the contrast in sensitivity and diagnostic times achievable with our cell screening technology versus typical long-term voltage monitoring.

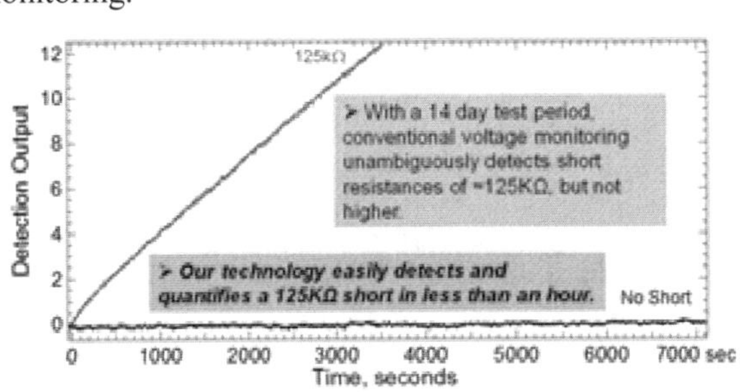

Figure 2. Test data showing response of our new technology for detection of internal shorts showing rapid detection of a 125,000 ohm short (about the limit of detection in the 14-day open circuit voltage monitoring used, for example, in lithium-ion cell manufacturing to screen for internal shorts). The 125,000 ohm internal short, simulated by application of a load resistance, is readily distinguished from the no-short condition in just a few hundred seconds of diagnostic scanning time.

We characterize the detection response obtained with our technology as a function of short resistance in a series of tests on commercially available 2.6Ah 18650 cells. Test results are shown in Figure 3. Short resistances from 32,000 to 1,000,000 ohms were simulated. In each case an unambiguous response, clearly distinguishable from the no-short condition, was obtained that further could be analyzed to provide a figure of merit that correlated quantitatively with the resistance of the short. Additional testing has shown that with detection times of a few hours, shorts as high in resistance as 8,000,000 ohms can be detected and quantified under appropriate test conditions. Not surprisingly, the ultra-high sensitivity of our diagnostic methodology requires that test conditions be regulated in certain respects to avoid factors that might cause measurement perturbation and/or drift. These factors include changing cell temperature and recent charge or discharge processes that create non-equilibrium cell conditions. While such factors do not prevent application of our methodology, well-equilibrated cells are a pre-requisite for maximum sensitivity, just as is the case for the common practice of simple cell terminal voltage monitoring to check for internal shorts.

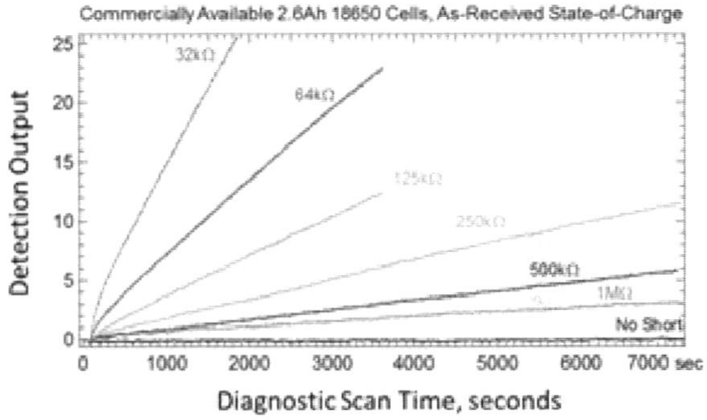

Figure 3. Detection response of the CAMX Power cell screening technology as a function of short resistances to 1 megohm (10^6 ohm) simulated using surrogate shorts as described.

We are developing prototype cell screening instrumentation to provide the high-sensitivity screening capability demonstrated by the data in Figure 2 and Figure 3. The ultimate equipment product being utilized for both lithium-ion cell manufacture and lithium-ion pack pre-assembly screening operations in which cells can be screened rapidly in a batch-wise continuous process. Some examples of cells screening tests and associated results are now presented.

Figure 4 shows test results in which we applied our rapid cell screening technology to evaluate cells from two different manufacturers for the presence of internal shorts. Both batches were commercially available cells with one batch (Manufacturer A) from a less-experienced manufacturer and the other batch (Manufacturer B) from a highly experienced manufacturer of 18650 cells. The contrast in test results was striking. The diagnostic output of our technology plotted in the figure comprises the basic raw data output of our detection algorithm. A value of -80, as seen for Manufacturer A for the worst cell, indicates a significant soft short. For the cells from Manufacturer A, five of six showed significant voltage loss (with complete self-discharge of cell F) in the 9 months following receipt, independently confirming our rapid screening results, obtained in just a few hours. In contrast, cells from

Manufacturer B were highly consistent in diagnostic score (between 0 and -0.08) and showed complete retention of voltage in the 12 months following receipt. These test results show how our rapid cell screening technology can accurately screen cells for quality and safety, detecting low-level soft shorts that were *not* identified at the factory. It can be understood that the soft shorts seen in the Manufacturer A cells in Figure 4 could result in decreased battery performance over time, and early battery failure in packs lacking cell balancing to correct for the self-discharge.

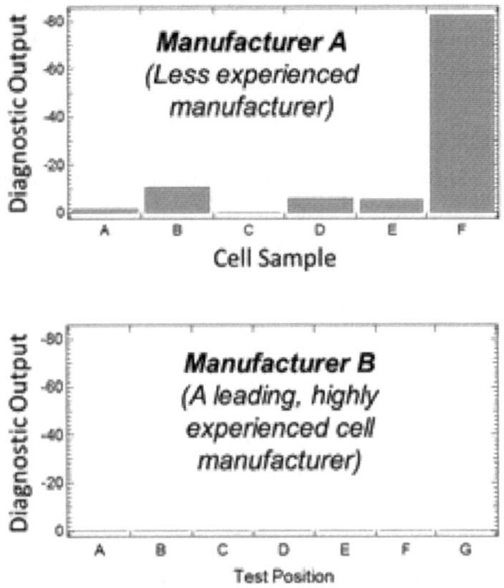

Figure 4. The cells from two manufacturers showed marked differences in rapid screening tests using our technology. Cells from manufacturer A vary considerably in diagnostic score and showed diagnostic output magnitudes indicating self-discharge (soft-shorting), while cells from manufacturer B were highly consistent in diagnostic score and yielded diagnostic outputs indicative of short-free status. Both results were entirely confirmed by independent long-term voltage monitoring of each batch of cells.

The rapid screening and quality/consistency assessment demonstrated by the data in Figure 4 illustrate how our technology can be employed to improve battery pack reliability and longevity by rejecting cells of reduced quality. We see further benefits in enabling 100% pre-assembly cell screening for battery pack manufacture in the ability to identify anomalous quality profiles in incoming batches of cells so that, as can be the case even for the most experience manufacturer, the negative consequences of transient quality control issues can be averted by identifying such issues *before* cells are sent into the field in finished batteries.

As we further develop our rapid, ultra-high sensitivity cell screening technology and the preferred protocols for its application, we continue to benchmark its performance against the typical industry practice of long-term voltage monitoring so that we have independent confirmation of our results. Examples of this work include:

- Application of our cell screening technology to check for materials contamination issues in different batches of cathode powder;
- Screening of 18650 cells produced on an in-house prototyping line;
- Evaluation of experimental cells, of a variety of form factors, for internal shorts in research and development programs.

The diagnostics provided in each of the aforementioned applications of our cell screening technology have been independently confirmed by follow-on long-term voltage monitoring, demonstrating that rapid and sensitive screening for internal shorts can be accomplished without extended monitoring for cell voltage decay.

In conclusion, we have developed technology for ultra-sensitive, rapid screening of lithium-ion cells for the presence of internal shorts that can detect even the most minor shorts, not detectable with present voltage drop methods, in diagnostic scan times of less than an hour. We have shown test results demonstrating these performance levels. We have shown how our screening technology can be used to assess cell quality and weed out short-containing cells in a manner that can make 100% pre-assembly screening of cells in battery pack manufacture viable by eliminating the throughput penalty of long-term voltage monitoring to screen cells for shorts.

Acknowledgements

The authors gratefully acknowledge the support of the Defense Logistics Agency under contract SP4701-17-C-0031.

Fast Charging Li-Ion Batteries

Shmuel De-Leon

Shmuel De-Leon Energy
shmuel@sdle.co.il
www.sdle.co.il

Abstract: *The demand to higher Li-Ion batteries energy and power density is high. But the energy and power density progress is in small steps of average 2-3% a year. Fast charging can close the gap until we will have batteries that standing the high requirements.*

Unfortunately the current Li-Ion technologies are not supporting fast charging because of safety and degradation concern. LTO can be charge fast and LFP can be charge in a moderate rate but the payment is a low energy density and high cost. New Li-Ion battery technologies should be developing for allowing fast charging.

We found that many players understood the importance of fast charging and start to develop new technologies that are covered by this market review.

Modeling the Thermodynamics and State of Health of High-Voltage Doped Li-Mn-Based Spinel

Terrill B. Atwater, Julianne S. Douglas, and Lauren M. Marzocca
U.S. Army Communications-Electronics Research, Development, and Engineering Center
Power Division – Command, Power, and Integration

Abstract: *CERDEC CP&I Power Division has demonstrated the beneficial impacts of incorporating chlorine (Cl) at the O-site and iron (Fe), cobalt (Co), and nickel (Ni) at the B-site of the lithium (Li)-manganese (Mn)-based AB_2O_4 spinel. This combination has resulted in extended cycle life with robust performance at potentials down to 2.25 V while retaining capacity with subsequent cycling in the 5.0 V to 3.5 V regime.*

By selectively controlling the stoichiometry of the Cl and the incorporation of Fe, Co, and/or Ni into the Li-Mn-based AB_2O_4 spinel, the thermodynamic characteristics of the spinel can be tailored. This tailored B- and O-doped spinel and the unique "fingerprint" of the material allow for precise and effective state of charge and state of health indication and calibration. An accurate model is needed for the differential capacity curve to aid in the development of a computer program for a future diagnostic/prognostic tool. Without a model, data is qualitative but not quantitative. The Gaussian curve has been used as the basis to model the peaks of the differential capacity curve. This data can then be used to predict cell state of charge and state of health.

This paper will present cell data demonstrating the utility and implementation of a precise and effective state of charge and state of health indicator. This is accomplished using the differential capacity curve for CERDEC-developed cathode material and the Gaussian curve model.

Keywords: state of health; safety; rechargeable; lithium-ion; battery

Introduction

A reliable diagnostic/prognostic indicator for electrochemical systems would allow for the prediction of cell failures, a function that would improve battery safety, efficiency, and quality assurance. The technique of differential capacity has proven to be a useful tool in the pursuit of this type of diagnostic/prognostic device. The plots resulting from the differential capacity technique provide a "fingerprint" of a battery system that can be tracked throughout its life, and changes in these plots give insight into the future behavior of the system.

Differential capacity tracks an electrochemical system's capacity increase on charge or decrease on discharge as a function of potential. Plotting differential capacity versus potential creates a snapshot "fingerprint" of the system that can be tracked throughout the system's life. These fingerprints show how characteristic features of the curve change and, unlike the traditional potential-versus-time curves, the differential capacity curve gives visual information regarding both the underlying thermodynamics and kinetics of the system.

Previous efforts by the authors have been presented at this conference[1-3]. These earlier efforts concentrated on the utility of the triple Gaussian curve superposition as a model for differential capacity data, and it was found that the technique is valid for a variety of electrochemistries. A three-curve Gaussian model was able to be transferred to different chemistries and cell types. Additionally, trends using two Gaussian curves to model differential capacity data during investigations using B- and O-doped spinel cathode material allowed for specifically formulated materials that exploited these trends. It is this data and analysis that will be presented here.

Background

Figure 1 gives a visual comparison between a standard potential-versus-time discharge plot and a differential capacity plot generated from the same test data. Monitoring the changes in a system's electrochemical properties through differential capacity can help predict capacity degradation and failure. This prognostic capability would be useful in preventing safety incidents while also ensuring that a cell or battery is removed from service only after being used to its fullest extent.

Through the Capability Needs Analysis (CNA) process, the U.S. Army derives a list of specific Warfighter requirements that are not currently being met. These requirements are known as CNA gaps. Two power- and energy-related CNA gaps state that "forces lack ability to accurately monitor and manage power demand and supply processes" and that "forces lack comprehensive, institutional awareness of the impact of energy use on operational effectiveness and need to consider efficient use of energy as a mission enabler."[4] The development of an effective battery diagnostic/prognostic device directly addresses both of these gaps.

Differential capacity was initially investigated as a quality assurance tool. Generating the differential capacity curves of two identical cells will yield nearly identical curves; therefore, the technique can be used to identify inconsistencies in a production environment. Analysis of this quality assurance data revealed the possibility for using differential capacity as a prognostic tool. Any changes made to the components of an electrochemical system (different electrodes, electrolyte, material ratios, etc.) as well as any changes in testing conditions (different rates, temperatures, abusive conditions, etc.) will cause changes in that system's fingerprint. This aspect of the differential capacity technique has inherent predictive capabilities that could be leveraged in a diagnostic/prognostic device.

Modeling: Previous work showed that using the Gaussian curve as the model basis for the differential capacity data provided useful computational information.[1-3] The general equation for the Gaussian function used to model the experimental data is given by Equation 1.

$$f(x) = ae^{-\frac{(x-b)^2}{2c^2}} + d. \quad (1)$$

For this particular application, *f(x)* equals the differential capacity at potential *x*. Coefficients *a*, *b*, and *c* are the curve-defining parameters, which were adjusted until the best fit was achieved, and *d* corresponds to the reaction equilibrium. Table 1 shows the relationship of each coefficient to its corresponding peak and details what physical values or processes dictate the coefficient values.

Table 1. Gaussian curve-defining coefficients.

Variables	Effect on Curve	Function of...
$f(x)$	Model	Differential capacity
a	Height	Theoretical capacity
b	Position	Theoretical potential (impedance, activation energy, polarization)
c	Width	Diffusion
d	Height Offset	Net-Zero Equilibrium
$\int f(x)$	Area	Theoretical capacity

For a spinel cathode, the two-curve Gaussian function model, as shown in Figure 2, captured the main features of the experimental data but allowed for significant error in certain areas, namely the flat portions of the curve at low and high potential and the area between the two peaks. To account for this, a third Gaussian curve was added to the model, as shown in Figure 3.[1-3]

Once the concept of using the change in the Gaussian function parameters to indicate state of health was established, the robustness and utility of the concept were evaluated. Electrochemical data was collected from 2.0 cm^2, 10 mAh spinel button cells constructed using internally developed B- and O-doped spinel cathode material.[7-11] Cells using this material were selected for this phase of the effort because the material characteristics are well-known and the cells are routinely taken to "failure" during evaluation.

During this verification effort, it became clear that a cathode material can be formulated to take advantage of the modeling capability and predictive nature of the Gaussian model fit to the differential capacity data.

Experimental

The behavior of the B- and O-doped spinel cathode material during charge and discharge exhibits distinct thermodynamic potential plateaus based on the ratio of Fe, Co, or Ni to Mn. These potential plateaus are resolvable and can be treated independently when modeled using a Gaussian function.

Manganese acetate, and either iron acetate, cobalt acetate, or nickel acetate were dissolved in distilled water in metal-based stoichiometric ratios. Ammonia hydroxide was added to the aqueous metal acetate solution to form a gel. The gel was dried and the residual was further heated until the material decomposed and self-ignited. The residual oxide was ground and calcined in air at 400 °C for two hours to form a manganese-based mixed metal oxide. The resultant manganese-based mixed metal oxide was then mixed with lithium perchlorate and lithium carbonate in stoichiometric ratios which determine the lithium and chlorine content of the final product. The mixture was ground in a high-energy mixer mill and then calcined in a furnace at 600 °C for four hours. This resulted in a chlorine O-site and Fe, Co, and/or Ni B-site Li-Mn-based AB_2O_4 spinel cathode material, which was coupled with lithium to yield the electrochemical cell used for the evaluation.

Performance experiments were designed to bring out cell characteristics and failure modes. The goal was to monitor changes in the differential capacity curve with each cycle of the test and to observe which characteristic feature(s) of the curve change as a result of performance degradation. Cells were charged and discharged between 5.0 V and 2.25 V at rates between 0.5 mA/cm^2 to 16 mA/cm^2. The differential capacity curves were tracked as the cell was cycled and the data was modeled using Gaussian function parameters.

Discussion

Figures 4 and 5 show the charge/discharge curves, and Figures 6 and 7 show the subsequent differential capacity curves for two variants of the B- and O-doped spinel cathode material. The formulas for the example spinel materials are $LiMn_{1.34}Fe_{0.08}Ni_{0.58}O_{4-d}Cl_d$ and $LiMn_{1.54}Fe_{0.12}Ni_{0.34}O_{4-d}Cl_d$, respectively. Figures 4 and 5 show three thermodynamic plateaus during charge and discharge. These plateaus are at approximately 4.5-5.0 V, 3.5-4.5 V, and 2.5-3.5 V. When the data is displayed as a differential capacity trace, it reveals that the 4.5-5.0 V thermodynamic region can also be divided further to allow for the resolution of two regions.

Comparing the data from the two formulations, the 3.5-4.5 V thermodynamic region is enhanced at the expense of the 4.5-5.0 V region, as the nickel content is reduced from a 0.58 to a 0.34 stoichiometry. This electrochemical behavior allows for the formulation of a cathode that has built-in calibration points. Additionally, using the Gaussian function as a model allows the user to infer the state of health of the system by interrogating any one of the thermodynamic regions.

Table 2. State of charge calculations for an electrochemical cell with a $LiMn_{1.34}Fe_{0.08}Ni_{0.58}O_{4-d}Cl_d$ cathode.

Cell Potential (V)	Capacity Remaining (mAh)	State of Charge (%)
5.0	205	100
4.7	170	82.9
4.4	**110**	**53.7**
3.5	99	48.3
2.25	0	0

Table 3. State of charge calculations for an electrochemical cell with a $LiMn_{1.54}Fe_{0.12}Ni_{0.34}O_{4-d}Cl_d$ cathode.

Cell Potential (V)	Capacity Remaining (mAh)	State of Charge (%)
5.0	210	100
4.7	184	87.6
4.4	**137**	**65.2**
3.5	89	42.4
2.25	0	0

Table 2 and 3 shows example state of charge calculations using the built-in calibration points for electrochemical cells with $LiMn_{1.34}Fe_{0.08}Ni_{0.58}O_{4-d}Cl_d$ and $LiMn_{1.54}Fe_{0.12}Ni_{0.34}O_{4-d}Cl_d$, respectively. Indexing lines to aid in the visualization of this property are included in Figures 4-7. The bold values in the tables represent the shift in the state of charge as a result of tailoring the cathode composition.

Coupling the state of charge information with information gained by generating a Gaussian model of the data and the known cycles of the system, a more comprehensive view of the state of health of the system can be achieved. This is accomplished by comparing the components of the model or any subset component with an established standard, based on theoretical capacity and/or initial forming cycle data. Shifts in model position and width, b and c in equation 1, will indicate an increase in impedance, which could manifest in reduced rate capabilities. Decreases in height and the integrated function when compared to the baseline will allow for quantification of the decrease in run time that can be expected.

Conclusion

This body of work shows that displaying an electrochemical cell's performance data as a differential capacity curve can enhance the predictive power of a state of charge/state of health monitor. By employing a Gaussian method of modeling, the ability to predict cell failure can be enhanced and, when coupled with tailored chemistry, state of charge and state of health accuracy can be improved.

Differential capacity curves can be accurately modeled using Gaussian curves. This type of model utilizes *a*, *b*, and *c* coefficients that relate directly back to the thermodynamics and kinetics of an electrochemical cell. Tracking these coefficients through the life of the cell allows the user to quantify and monitor changes. The ability to monitor and track changes is important if an in-use battery diagnostic/prognostic technique is to be implemented.

References

1. Marzocca, L.M. and Atwater, T.B., DTIC AD1018791, 2014.
2. Marzocca, L.M. and Atwater, T.B., *P. 46th Power Sources Conference*, 2014.
3. Atwater, T.B., Tavares, P.C., and Marzocca, L.M., *P. 44th Power Sources Conference*, 2010.
4. DiGiosaffatte, M. "Capability Needs Analysis." *Army Capabilities Integration Center.* http://www.arcic.army.mil/Articles/aid-Capability-Needs-Analysis.aspx.
5. Wright, R.B., et al. *P. 201st Meeting of the Electrochemical Society*, 2002.
6. Bloom, I., et al. *P. 204th Meeting of the Electrochemical Society*, 2003.
7. Ruth, A.L., Latorre, P.C., Wachsman, E.D., Atwater, T.B., ECS Trans. 2017 80(10): 125-133
8. Ruth, A.L., Latorre, P.C., Wachsman, E.D., Atwater, T.B., ECS Trans. 2017 80(10): 305-316
9. Atwater T.B., Latorre P.C., and Ruth A.L., DTIC AD1017821, 2016.
10. Ruth A.L., Atwater T.B., and Latorre P.C., DTIC AD1017827, 2016.
11. Latorre P.C., Ruth A.L., and Atwater T.B., DTIC AD1017833, 2016.

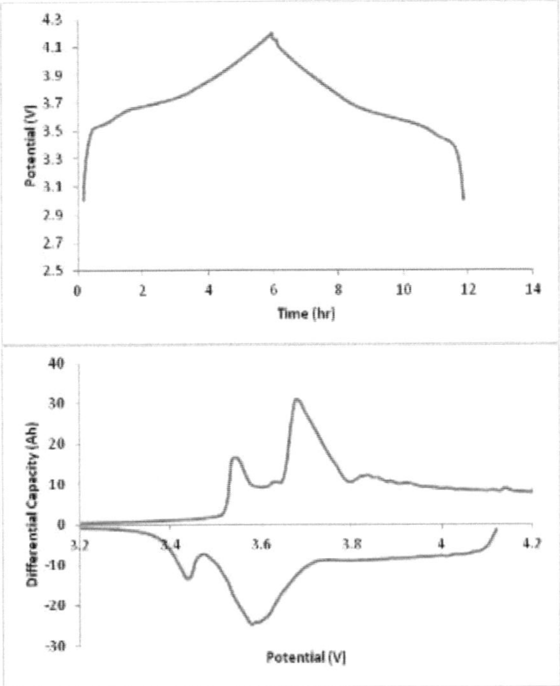

Figure 1. Standard potential vs. time discharge curve compared with corresponding differential capacity curve for a 2.4 Ah NMC 18650 cell.

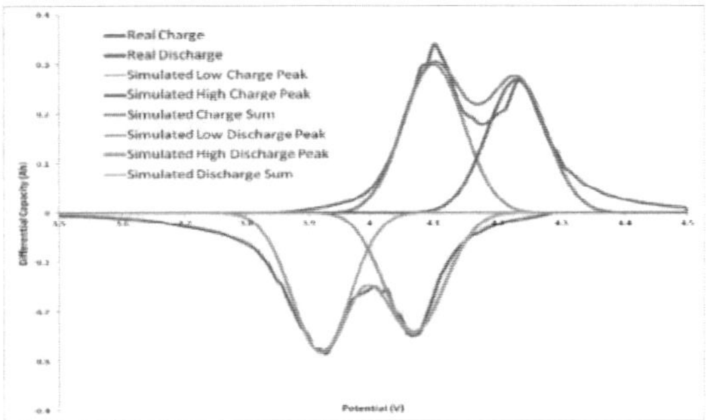

Figure 2. Differential capacity curve with its two-curve Gaussian model for a spinel button cell.

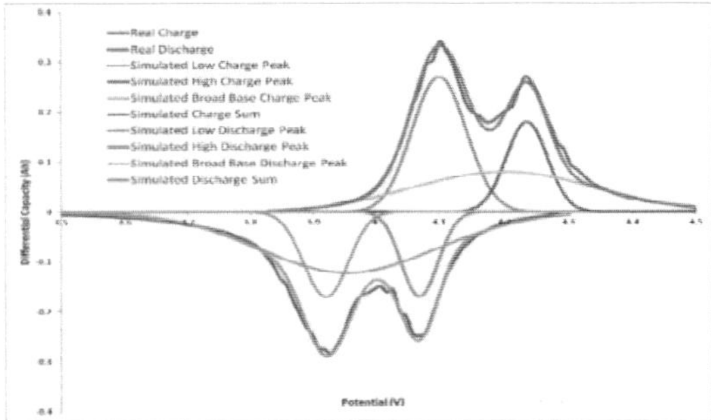

Figure 3. Differential capacity curve with its three-curve Gaussian model for a spinel button cell.

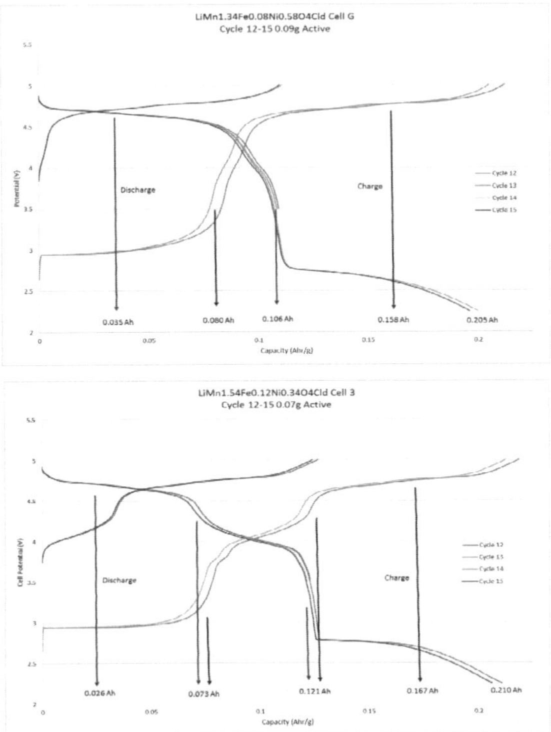

Figures 4 – 5. Electrochemical characteristics of Representative B- and O- doped spinel.

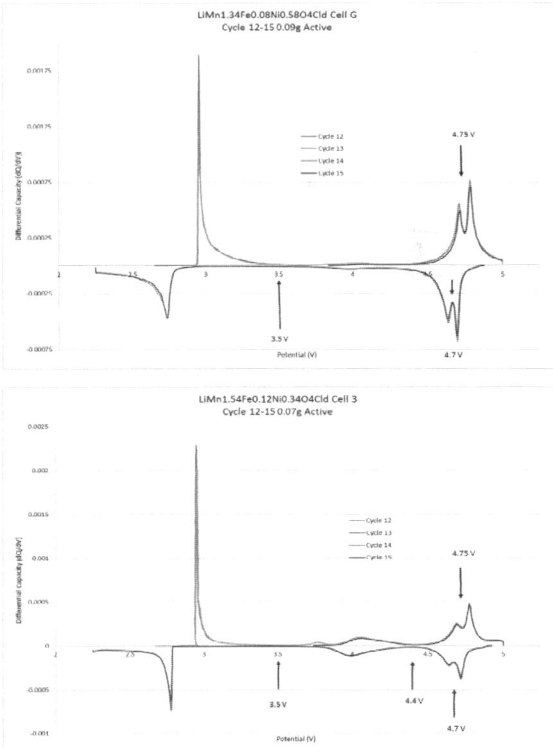

Figures 6 – 7. Differential capacity curve of representative B- and O- doped spinel.

Efficient On-line Control for Safe, Fast Charging of Li-ion Batteries

***Peter J. Weddle*[1]*, Tyrone Vincent*[2]*, Robert J. Kee*[1]**

[1]Department of Mechanical Engineering
Colorado School of Mines
Golden, CO 80401

[2]Department of Electrical Engineering
Colorado School of Mines
Golden, CO 80401

Contact Author Email: tvincent@mines.edu

Abstract: *Deposition of lithium metal at the anode/electrolyte interface can cause damage to separators, create internal short circuits, and decrease capacitance. It has been argued that during charging, deposition of lithium metal on the anode/electrolyte surface is favorable when the overpotential of the anode surface exceeds the open-circuit potential (OCP) of graphite vs. lithium metal. One method to mitigate lithium metal deposition, is to implement charging sequences that constrain the anode overpotential to this plating constraint. However, the anode overpotential and surface intercalation fraction cannot be directly measured on unmodified commercial batteries. In this paper, a method is developed to determine charging sequences that implicitly constrain the anode overpotential. The method can be divided into two main elements: accurate estimation of the anode overpotential and surface intercalation fraction at the separator, and the trajectory of the overpotential and surface intercalation fraction in response to a current perturbation.*

Keywords: Li-ion battery, State-space model, Model-predictive control, Lithium plating

Introduction

During charging lithium metal can be deposited on the anode/electrolyte interface. These deposits tend to create sharp, tree-like dendrites that can cause damage to separators, create internal short circuits, and decrease capacitance [1-4]. One mitigation technique to reduce propensity of lithium plating is to constrain the overpotential at the anode/electrolyte surface at the separator. As a first approximation, deposition of lithium metal on the anode/electrolyte surface is assumed to be favorable when the overpotential at the anode surface exceeds the open-circuit potential (OCP) of graphite vs. lithium metal [4]. Figure 1 illustrates the OCP of graphite vs. lithium metal as a function of intercalation fraction x.

In this paper, a method is developed to determine charging sequences that implicitly constrain the anode overpotential. The method can be divided into two main elements: accurate estimation of the anode overpotential and surface intercalation fraction at the separator, and the trajectory of the overpotential and surface intercalation fraction in response to a current perturbation. In this paper, physically-based battery models, implemented in Battery Design Studio (BDS), are used to estimate and predict the

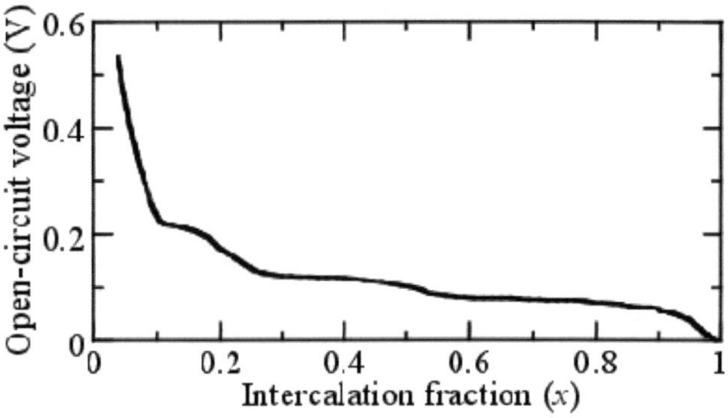

Figure 1. Open circuit potential of graphite vs. lithium metal as a function of intercalation fraction

trajectory of these immeasurable variables [5]. The responses of the anode overpotential and surface intercalation fraction are captured using system-identification techniques and incorporated into model-predictive control (MPC) algorithms.

Plating constraint

During charging, lithium ions in the electrolyte solution are assumed to plate on the surface (create dendrites) rather than intercalate into the bulk anode if the overpotential at the anode/electrolyte surface exceeds the OCP of graphite vs. lithium metal. Assuming that that the single charge-transfer reaction at the anode/electrolyte interface has equal symmetry factors, the overpotential can be expressed as

$$\eta = \frac{2RT}{F}\sin^{-1}\left(\frac{[\mathrm{LiC_6}]_{\mathrm{ed}}^{\mathrm{max}}}{F\sqrt{k[\mathrm{Li^+}]_{\mathrm{el}}}}\frac{i}{\sqrt{(1-x)x}}\right), \qquad (1)$$

where R is the universal gas constant, T is temperature, F is Faraday's constant, $[\mathrm{LiC_6}]_{\mathrm{ed}}^{\mathrm{max}}$ is the maximum concentration in the graphite, k is a reaction rate constant,
concentration in the graphite, k is a reaction rate constant,
$[\mathrm{Li^+}]_{\mathrm{el}}$ is the concentration of lithium ions in the electrolyte, and i is the exchange current density. Equation 1 indicates that the overpotential can be computed if the actuation and surface intercalation fraction are known. Figure 2 illustrates the *plating constraint* where the overpotential reaches the OCP of graphite. As illustrated the plating constraint depends on both the surface intercalation fraction and the current density demanded of the surface. Figure 3 illustrates the same concept as shown in Fig. 2 but as 3D surfaces. Illustrated in black is the OCP(x) of graphite and illustrated in color is the surface plot of Eq. 1. The

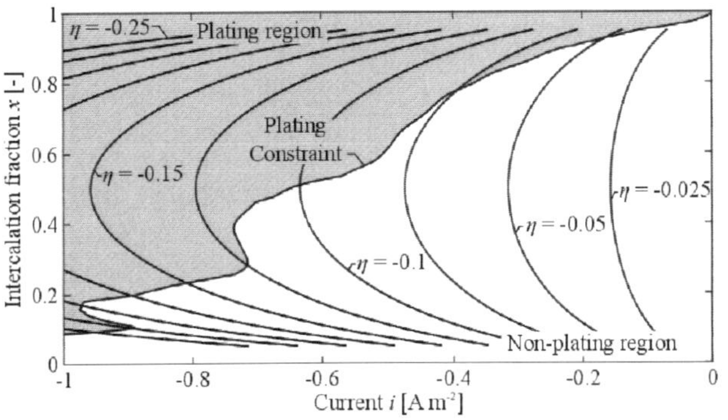

Figure 2. Contour plot of overpotential on the anode surface η with respect to surface intercalation fraction x and current density i. Overlaid is the line where the surface overpotential meets the open circuit potential. In this study, plating is assumed to occur when the anode overpotential at the separator exceeds the open circuit potential with respect to lithium metal.

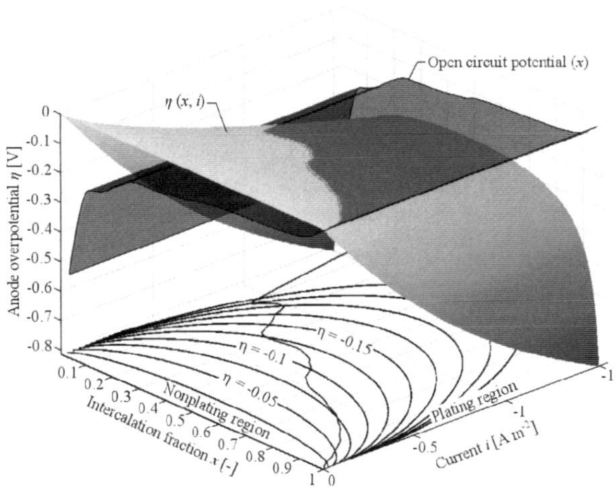

Figure 3. Surface plot of the anode overpotential η as a function of current density i and surface intercalation fraction x. Also illustrated is a surface plot of the open circuit potential of the anode with respect to lithium metal. The intersection of these surfaces is the plating constraint considered in this work.

intersection of these two plans is the plating limit. Projected on the x-i plane is the contour plot of overpotential and the plating constraint (equivalent to Fig. 2).

Estimating immeasurable variables

Since the anode surface intercalation fraction cannot be directly measured, it must be estimated from the available measurements (i.e. voltage, current, and temperature). The estimation technique presented here is based on a (known) relationship between open circuit voltage, surface concentration, and state of charge. That is, if there is no current, both the terminal voltage and surface concentration will reach equilibrium. These equilibria will each be function of the state of charge. The relationships between state-of-charge, steady-state voltage, and intercalation fraction can be estimated from either data or a model such that

$$v_{\text{oc}}(t) = f_v(s) \tag{2}$$

$$x_{\text{oc}}(t) = f_x(s) \tag{3}$$

where v_{oc} and x_{oc} are the terminal voltage and intercalation fraction at open circuit respectfully, and $f_v(s)$ and $f_x(s)$ are functions that relate the state of charge s to the terminal voltage and intercalation fraction respectfully.

A small signal, linear model is used to capture the deviation of x and v from their equilibra (x_{oc} and v_{oc}), due to the applied current. The voltage and surface concentration is then the sum of the open circuit value and a transient term i.e.

$$v(t) = v_{\text{oc}}(t) + y_v(t) \tag{4}$$

$$x(t) = x_{\text{oc}}(t) + y_x(t) \tag{5}$$

where $y_v(t)$ and $y_x(t)$ are the output of a dynamic system. The dynamic systems are represented as state-space models of the form

$$\begin{aligned} \dot{\zeta}(t) &= A\zeta(t) + Bu(t), \\ y(t) &= C\zeta(t), \end{aligned} \tag{6}$$

where $u(t)$ is the applied current and ξ determines the state. The parameters A, B, and C depend on the state of charge and temperature, and are identified by observing the system responses from psuedo-random binary current perturbations and are gain-scheduled between operating conditions [6].

Dynamic estimation of the surface intercalation fraction x can be achieved using the following steps

- Using measurements of the current and voltage, estimate $v_{oc}(t)$.
- Estimate the open circuit surface concentration as $x_{oc}(t) = f_x(f_v^{-1}(v_{oc}(t)))$.
- Using measurements of the current, and tentative future current, estimate $x(t)$.

Once the anode surface intercalation fraction is estimated, the controller will constrain the overpotential at that surface to respect the plating limit (see Eq. 1).

Model predictive control: Constrain plating

Battery charging can be considered as a problem of system control, where the system input is applied current. As the name suggests, Model Predictive Control operates by using a system model to predict the effect of possible system inputs, and optimization is used to select a specific input that satisfies necessary constraints while minimizing an objective function. The first part of this trajectory is applied to the system, and then the process is repeated after new measurements are obtained and the prediction updated. In this specific applications, the constraints will be linear constraints that keep the current/intercalation fraction within the nonplating region, and the objective function will be total charge delivered to the batter. Using the method described in the previous section, a prediction of

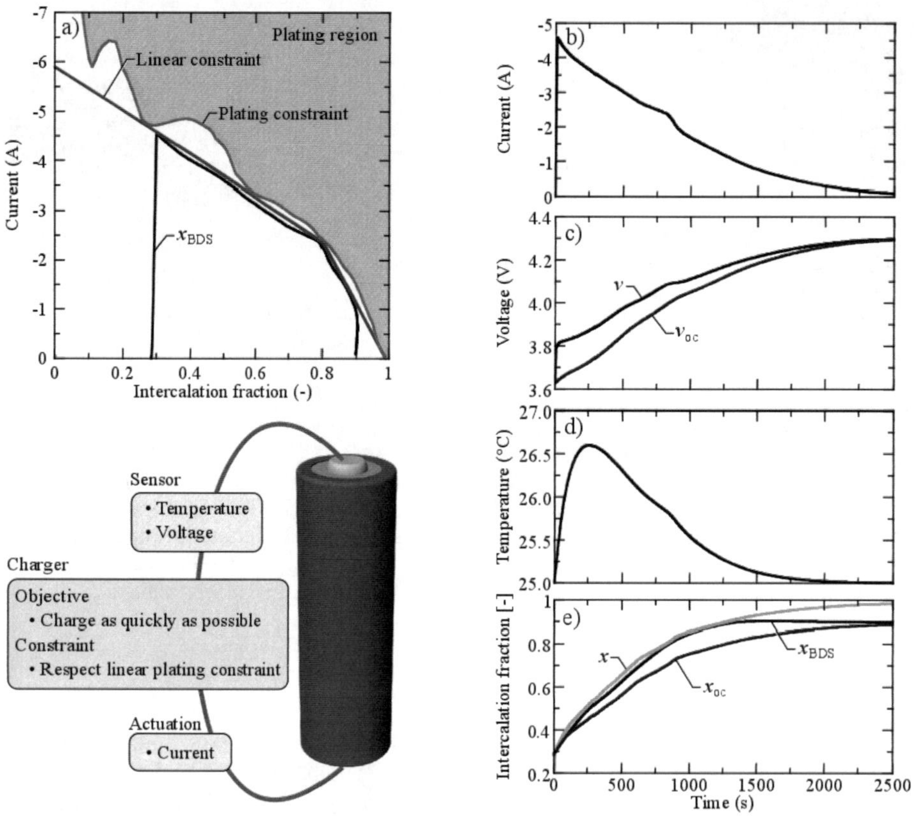

Figure 4. Results of MPC study that minimized charging time while respecting a linear plating constraint. Figure 4a illustrates the plating constraint with respect to the intercalation fraction on the anode surface at the separator (illustrated in blue). The plating constraint separates the plating region and nonplating region. To respect the plating constraint, a linear plating constraint is imposed in the MPC (illustrated in red). Illustrated in black is the model results from BDS. Figure 4b-e illustrate the control actuation, measured observed terminal voltage and temperature, and estimated intercalation fraction on the anode surface at the separator respectively with respect to time.

the anode surface intercalation fraction in response to future changes in current is available, and since the dynamic term $y_x(t)$ is the output of a linear system, this prediction is linear in the future current. Because of this, and because both the constraints and objective function are linear in current and intercalation fraction, the optimization problem to be solved is a linear program, which can be solved to a global minimum using efficient algorithms.

Several charging sequence examples are studied using the identified state-space models and subsequent MPC algorithms. Figure 4 illustrates the results of one of these charging sequence where the controller charges the battery as quickly as possible while respecting the imposed plating constraint. In this case study the plating constraint (illustrated in blue in Fig. 4a) is linearized to increase the speed of the controller (illustrated in red in Fig. 4a). Illustrated in black is the BDS results. It should be noted that the controller does not receive information on xBDS because this variable is immeasurable for real systems. From Fig. 4a, the controller is able to constrain the immeasurable intercalation fraction limit from measurable trajectories (i.e. C, v, T). Figure 4b illustrates the current demanded from the controller to charge the system while respecting the plating constraint. Figure 4c illustrates the terminal voltage v (measurable), and the predicted open-circuit voltage v_{oc}. Figure 4d illustrates the measured thermal response. Figure 4e illustrates the predicted intercalation fraction at the anode/electrolyte surface at the separator x, the predicted open-circuit intercalation fraction x_{oc}, and the actual intercalation fraction in the BDS model x_{BDS}. From these results it is evident that the controller is able to predict the immeasurable intercalation fraction and choose currents such that the plating constraint is respected.

Acknowledgements

This research was supported at CSM by the Office of Naval Research via grant N00014-16-1-2780.

References

1. Ahmed, S., I. Bloom, A.N. Jansen, T. Tanim, E.J. Dufek, A. Pesaran, A. Burnham, R.B. Carlson, F. Dias, K. Hardy, M. Keyser, C. Kreuzer, A. Markel, A. Meintz, C. Michelbacher, M. Mohanpurkar, P.A. Nelson, D.C. Robertson, D. Scoffield, M. Shirk, T. Stephens, R. Vijayagopal, and J. Zhang, "Enabling fast charging – A battery technology gap assessment," *J. Power Sources*, Vol. 367, pp. 250-262, 2017.

2. Love, C.T., O.A. Barurina, and K.E. Swider-Lyons, "Observation of lithium dendrites at ambient

temperature and below," *ECS Electrochem. Lett.*, Vol. 4, pp. A24-A27, 2015.

3. Hein, S., and A. Latz, "Influence of local lithium metal deposition in 3D microstructures on local and global behavior of Lithium-ion batteries," *Electrochim. Acta*, Vol. 201, pp. 354-365, 2016.

4. Legrand, N., B. Knosp, P. Desprez, F. Lapicque, and S. Raël, "Physical characterization of the charging process of a Li-ion battery and prediction of Li plating by electrochemical modeling," *J. Power Sources*, Vol. 245, pp. 208-216, 2014.

5. Battery Design Studio http://www.batdesign.com/batterydesign.html

6. Weddle, P.J., T. Vincent, and R.J. Kee, "Identifying and applying state-space models derived from high-fidelity physical models of Li-ion batteries," *ECS Meeting Abstracts*, 2017.

Two-Minute Charger Circuitry Design for Portable Phone

Brooks Prather, Keith Leitner, Robert Prew, and Herbert L. Hess
Department of Electrical and Computer Engineering
University of Idaho
Moscow, Idaho 83844-1023
hhess@uidaho.edu / 1-208-885-4341

Abstract: *Design of an electronic charging device that captures sufficient energy to charge a cell phone in less than two minutes. System architecture consists of a conventional rectifier facing 120V AC input to provide pulsed DC to a buck DC/DC converter serving as a regulated current source. Regulated current charges a bank of ultracapacitors to store captured energy. A conventional buck converter designed for interface from 6.5-27.0Volt input to 5.0 Volts USB cell phone battery charging unit transmits energy to the cell phone's USB input. Experimental results show ultracapacitor voltage performing as designed and cell phone charging as specified.*

Keywords: USB battery charger, ultracapacitor, cell phone charger

Introduction

Travelers often have little time between connecting flights in an airport. If their cell phone battery runs low on charge, this can be more than an inconvenience. Seatback USB charging ports have begun to appear on commercial aircraft, but anyone who has flown commercial knows that maintenance priorities lie elsewhere, not with small cell phone charger ports. The device described in this paper mitigates this problem.

These electronics use the fast charge capacity of the ultracapacitor to capture a designed amount of energy. The ultracapacitor then holds that energy until a cell phone is attached and the electronics can then move the energy into a cell phone battery at the phone battery's well-known and slower charging rate. The idea underlying this circuitry is to capture energy quickly when time is at a premium and energy is not. Then the circuitry moves that energy at a slower rate of use when energy is at a premium and time is not. In the example at hand, an airline passenger's cell phone has a low charge level, but the passenger has only a few minutes before boarding a flight. Such folks could really use a device that could capture enough energy to charge the phone. They would not mind if the device automatically and transparently dished out that energy in a controlled manner during the flight itself.

Putting enough energy into storage and moving energy from storage to the cell phone are two distinct operations for this power electronic converter. The concept is to acquire energy quickly, to capture enough to charge the cell phone in less than two minutes. This captured energy gets stored in an ultracapacitor bank that is large enough to hold it. The energy is then sent to the cell phone battery at a rate that it can safely accept. The system can both acquire energy and charge the cell phone battery at the same time, but charging the cell phone is by far the longer operation. To the user, charging may appear to take less than two minutes because moving energy from its ultracapacitor storage to the cell phone battery is automatic and transparent. In the following section of this paper, the system architecture of capturing, storing, and sending enough energy is presented.

System Architecture

A series of energy conversion and storage steps comprises the system architecture. The input is a standard commercial 120V AC, 60Hz, 20 Ampere supply. A diode rectifier converts this to a pulsating DC voltage. Due to the nature of the process at hand, this pulsating DC voltage needs not be filtered or regulated. A buck converter, or DC chopper, then converts the DC voltage into a direct current with a substantial ripple. Again, filtering of this current is not necessary, making the buck converter's inductor somewhat smaller than may be typical for similarly rated rectifiers. This direct current then flows into an ultracapacitor bank which stores the flow of charge. These ultracapacitors can tolerate a high current with substantial ripple, something that cell phone batteries cannot. In less than two minutes, the ultracapacitors store enough charge to recharge the phone's battery. When the ultracapacitors' voltage reaches a predetermined limit indicating enough stored charge, a sensor sends that information to a microcontroller which halts the flow of charge.[1,2]

The ultracapacitors then hold the charge until the cell phone is connected to the output portion of the system architecture. When the cell phone demands current on its USB charging port, a second buck converter begins sending current to the cell phone. Over the course of their designed operation, the ultracapacitors may have a wide range of voltage from discharged to down to 6.5 Volts to fully charged. The buck converter takes this variable voltage and converts it to a regulated 5.0VDC for the USB input port. Cell phones have an internal charging circuit to regulate flow of charge to their battery. This process of charging the phone's battery from the ultracapacitor bank through the second buck converter and the cell phone's charge regulator can take an hour or more, depending on the initial state of charge of the battery.

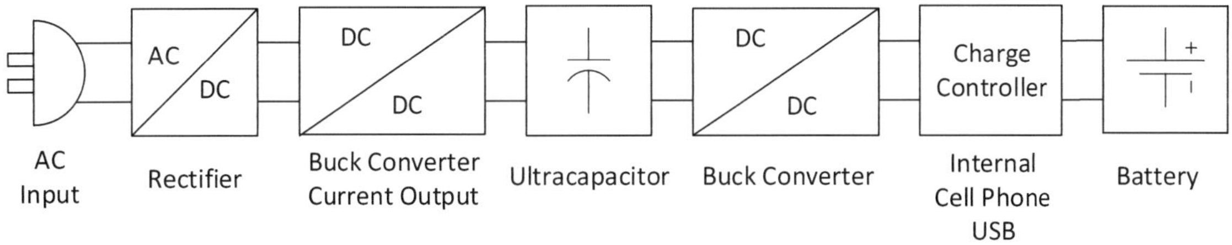

Figure 1. Two-Minute Charging System Architecture.

However, the output portion of the system architecture operates automatically and transparently from the user's perspective. Indeed, it may still take that hour or more to charge the phone's battery, but the user needs only connect the cell phone to the charging system's output to begin the output charging cycle. The charging system takes care of the rest automatically. [1,2] System architecture is illustrated in block diagram form in Figure 1. Each subsystem is explained in subsequent sections of this paper. A complete schematic appears in Figure 2.[2]

Subsystems: AC Input and Rectifier

This charging system captures its energy from commonly available electrical receptacles. Its input is 120V AC, 60 Hertz, 20 Amperes typical of a commercial electrical service in North America. The design is readily adaptable for universal input: 100V to 265V, 50/60 Hertz.

The rectifier is a commonly available four-diode bridge circuit. Diodes are rated for the expected input voltage and current range. Because the input power conditioning circuitry charges an ultracapacitor, the rectifier needs not filter the input voltage. This voltage can remain a pulsating DC voltage, reducing the current distortion at the input. Because the next subsystem is a buck DC/DC converter, there will be switching frequency noise in the system's input current.[3] Appropriate EMI filtering of the input must be provided.

Subsystems: Buck Converter

The next subsystem is a buck DC/DC converter. A buck converter provides a reduction in voltage and appropriate current control. In fact, this buck converter is designed to operate as a current source. A small resistor in series with the main current path serves as a simple sensor. The resulting voltage is fed through a resistor network into an A/D port on an Arduino microcontroller.[4] Within the Arduino, this indication of current level is compared to a reference in a hysteresis control algorithm. The Arduino sends a pulse width modulated signal to the buck converter's main switching transistor. This PWM signal is intended to keep the current level constant within a substantial but tolerable ripple. The result is a controlled current source, not a regulated voltage.[5] The ultracapacitors determine output voltage.

The two-minute standard to charge the ultracapacitors means that an average input current of 7.9 Amps would be sufficient. This is a low current in light of a typical 20 Amp electrical service. A current of 12 Amps provides as much current as practicable without tripping the breaker on an otherwise typically moderately loaded 20 Amp service. This will charge an ultracapacitor bank to 28 Volts DC in 79 seconds. Setting the hysteresis regulator for a ± 10 Amp tolerance yields an inductor value of 23.5µH. Five 4.7µH inductors with 12A current capacity fit within the device size specified. A gate driver of the ratings specified has a significant lead time, but is otherwise satisfactory. A housekeeping supply, Tamura SPM0507SJ [6], starts and maintains the Arduino. Other components are readily available commercially and are specified on the final schematic as shown in Figure 2.

Subsystems: Ultracapacitors

A bank of ultracapacitors stores the captured energy quickly. A typical cell phone battery has a capacity of 1420 mAmp-hours at a rated voltage of 3.7 Volts. There are more energy-hungry phones, some of whose batteries exceed 2000 mAmp-hours. Using the typical values for design, the phone battery has a capacity of 5.18 Watt-hours or 18.9 kiloJoules. Ultracapacitors typically have a voltage rating of about 2.7 Volts. A capacitance of about 50 Farads will store the desired 18.9 kJ. Considering reasonable losses exist in the system, 70 Farads of capacitance at 2.7 Volts stores 25.5 kJ. A bank of two series strings of ten 350F capacitors yields 70F.[7] Those numbers are consistent with the 7.9Amps average current.

When the ultracapacitors charge to the 27 Volt DC limit, a voltage sensor alerts the Arduino microcontroller. The Arduino commands the buck converter's main switching transistor to assume a blocking state. Energy capture then ceases.

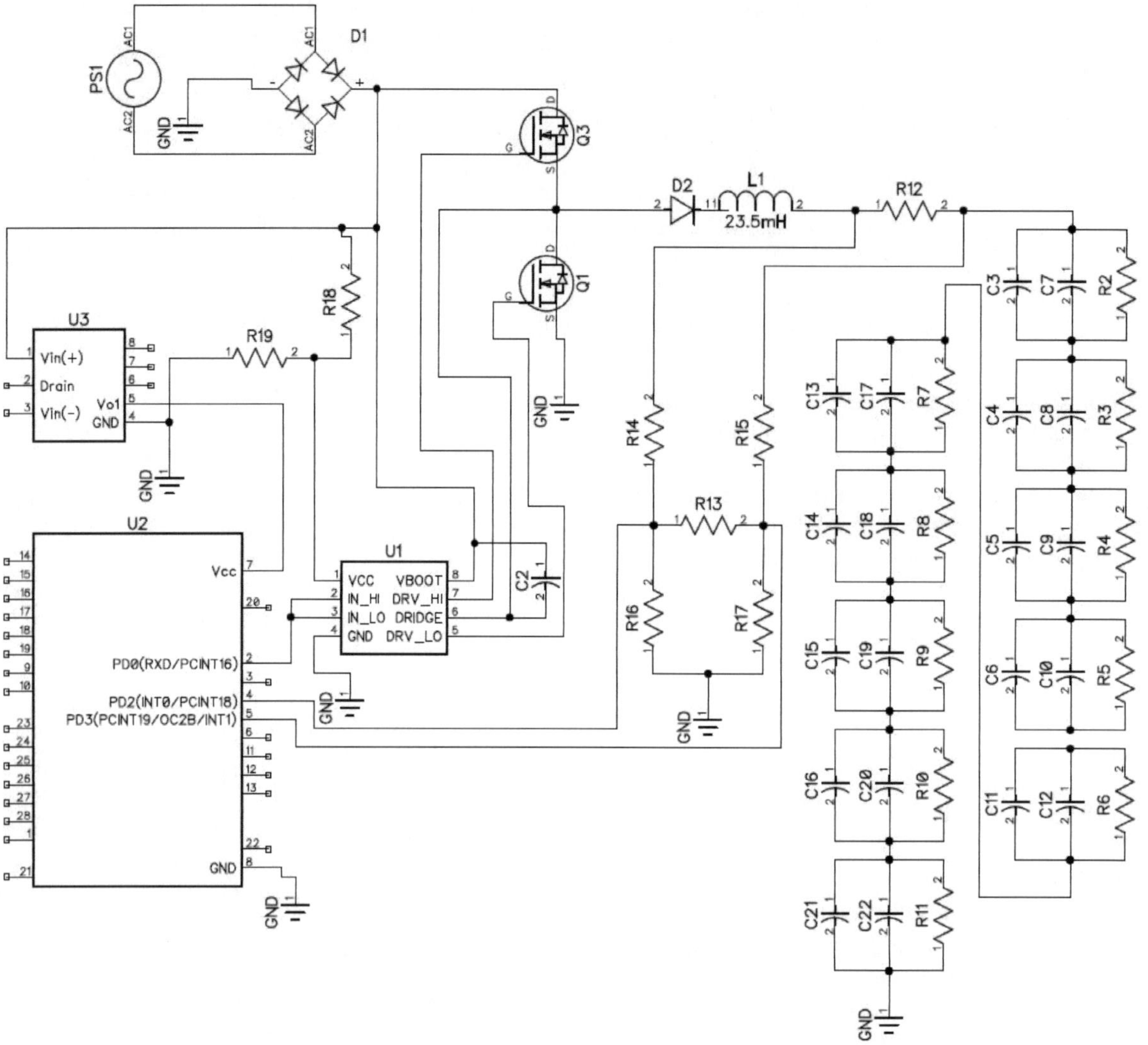

Figure 2. Complete Schematic Diagram.[2]

Subsystems: Charger Circuitry

A second buck DC/DC converter moves energy from the charged ultracapacitors to the cell phone charger. This is a pro forma task for a packaged buck converter. These are readily available from a host of suppliers. They cost about seven to ten dollars.[8] We chose several and all worked flawlessly with a charged ultracapacitor input.

A cost summary shows that the capacitors are the most expensive element. They retail for about $200 in lots of tenty. [7] The rest of the electronics retails for about $85.

Experimental Results

The power converter was tested under typical load conditions. The charging of the ultracapacitor bank is shown in Figure 3.[2] It shows a charge from 6.0 Volts to 20.0 Volts in 2.6 minutes. The cell phone was charged from the ultracapacitor bank. Its discharge curve is shown in Figure 4.[2] It shows a discharge of the ultracapacitors from a nominal 17 Volts to 6.5 Volts in 35 minutes.

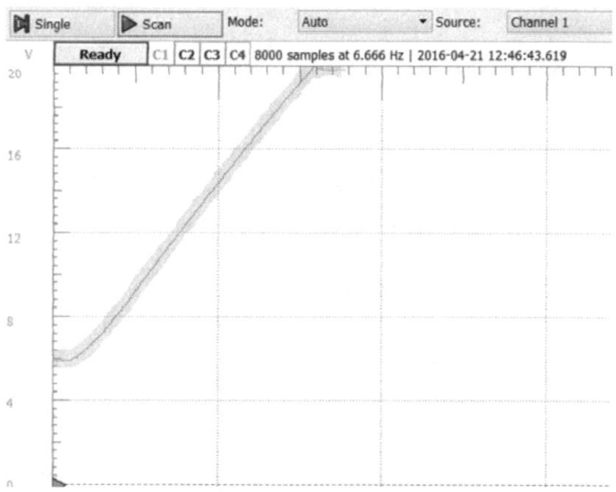

Figure 3. Experimental Results. Ultracapacitor Charging.[2]

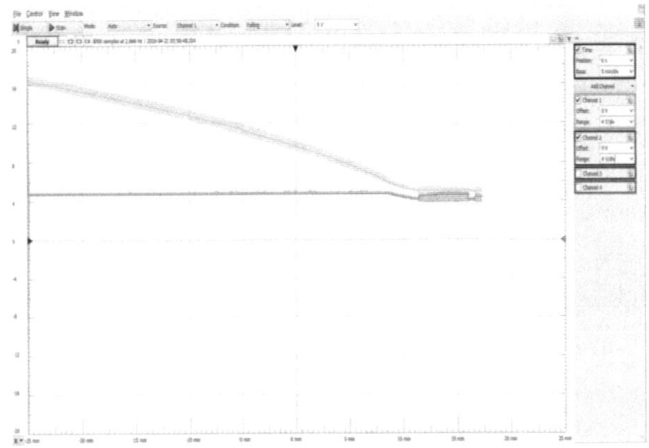

Figure 4. Experimental Results.
Ultracapacitor Discharging While Cell Phone Charges.

A photograph of the two-minute charger on the test bench is shown in Figure 5.[2] The ultracapacitor bank is on the right, the inductors are the black row of devices parallel to the ultracapacitors, the circuitry and electronics in the center,and the Arduino controller on the left. The ultracapacitors are exactly the size of a D-cell battery.

Figure 5.
Two-Minute Charger on the Test Bench.

Conclusions

Design of a two-minute charging device for cell phones was shown in this paper. It captures electrical energy in two minutes in an amount sufficient to charge a cell phone. Ultracapacitors store this captured energy. These ultracapacitors can handle the rapid charging even with substantial input current ripple. A buck DC/DC converter provides a controlled current source to regulate the charging process. From the ultracapacitors, ordinary USB chargers of several types showed that the cell phone's battery was charged automatically and transparently. An application for this device is an airline passenger whose cell phone is nearly discharged while his next flight is making boarding announcements.

Acknowledgements

This research was funded by the University of Idaho Faculty of Excellence in Electric Power Endowment and by alumni and faculty donations to the University of Idaho Department of Electrical Engineering. Thanks to Darion Marlin and Brian Patterson who worked on the finances and the construction, respectively.

References

1. Hess, H., F. Li, D. Marlin, B. Prather, and B. Patterson, "Airport Batttery Charger," http://mindworks.shoutwiki.com/wiki/Airport_Battery_Charger#Final_Report .
2. Hess, H., F. Li, K. Leitner, and R. Prew, "Battery Ultracharger," http://mindworks.shoutwiki.com/wiki/Battery_Ultracharger .
3. Hart, D., Power Electronics (New York: McGraw-Hill Education, 2010), chapter 6.
4. Arduino Uno, https://store.arduino.cc/usa/arduino-uno-rev3 , Accessed 20 April 2018.
5. Patel, R., "Power Conversion Design Guide," Austin, Texas: Texas Instruments, 2001.
6. Tamura Corporation, "SPM0507SJ Smart Phone, Tablet Housekeeping Supply," http://www.tamura-ss.co.jp/electronics/en/download/productssearch/serches_by_specifications_powermodule/spm0507sj/ , Accessed 20 April 2018.
7. Mouser Electronics, "Maxwell Technologies Ultracapacitor Series: 350F, 2.7V," https://www.mouser.com/search/refine.aspx?Ntk=P_MarCom&Ntt=101136366 , Accessed 20 April 2018.
8. Amazon.com, "HOMREE DC DC Converter Buck Module 12V/24V to 5V 3A USB Output Step Down Voltage Regulator Charge for Samsung Galaxy , iPad iPhone 4S 5 6/6 Plus etc (Standard USB)," https://www.amazon.com/HOMREE-Converter-Voltage-Regulator-Standard/dp/B01MEF293V , Accessed 20 April 2018.

Electrochemical & Thermal Analysis of the Thermal Battery

Jang Hyeon Cho, Byeong June Park, Ji Youn Kim, Sang-Hyeon Ha, Chae Nam Im
The 4th R&D Institute–4, Agency for Defense Development, Daejeon 305-600, Korea
jhcho4535@naver.com / 82-10-5050-4539

Abstract: *Both heat source exothermic reaction and discha rge resistance(joule heat) are the most detrimental failure ca uses of thermal batteries. To avoid thermal runaway and exp losion of the thermal battery, battery manufacturers rely hea vily on repetitive and empirical trial-error methods for the b attery component design. ADD has developed innovative sim ulation technology with the function of electrochemical & the rmal analysis for the high temperature thermal batteries. Thi s analysis technology is based on the commercial program ' COMSOL Multiphysics' that is efficient in the field of recipr ocal electrochemistry and heat transfer analysis, etc. This pa per provides electrochemical & thermal analysis results on t he thermal batteries with various heat source thickness. This analytical results would be useful for the design of electrodes , electrolytes, heat sources, insulator and the other compone nts. Additionally, this 'COMSOL' program analysis method could be applied to pure lithium typed thermal batteries, lithi um-ion batteries and packages.*

Keywords: thermal battery, electrochemical & thermal analysis, COMSOL, thermal design

Introduction

Thermal batteries for precision weapon system must be met stringent requirements such as high power, high energy density, long shelf-life and severe environmental conditions, etc.

These requirements of thermal batteries are mainly determined by the electrolyte(eutectic salts) which has excellent ionic conductivity at high temperatures(above 500 °C) but almost non-conductive at room temperature.

Once ignited, the temperature of a thermal battery rises above the electrolyte melting point owing to the internal heat source. As a result, the thermal battery exhibits high power density.

When the heat source is activated by the igniter, the internal temperature of a thermal battery is getting increased by the exothermic reaction of the heat source($Fe/KClO_4$). Here, $Fe/KClO_4$ is the main exothermic material and the most detrimental failure causes of thermal batteries.

As the ion conductivity of the electrolyte increases with rising temperature, the performance of the thermal battery is influenced by the temperature of various components inside the cell stack. Figure 1 shows the reaction concept of thermal battery(unit cell).

In general, the thermal battery is composed of anode(Li-Si alloy), electrolyte(LiCl-LiBr-LiF salt), cathode(FeS_2) and heat source.

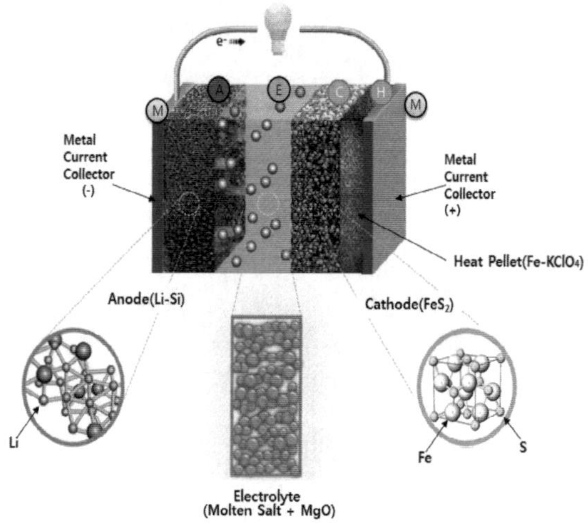

Figure 1. Concept of thermal battery(unit cell)

The electrolyte has the melting point of about 430°C. The decomposition temperature of the cathode FeS_2 varies depending on the condition such as particle size and shape, nevertheless is nearly about 550°C. For this reason, it is crucial to maintain the temperature of about 500~550°C for optimal performance of the thermal battery. Figure 2 shows the thermal runaway of thermal batteries.

Figure 2. Thermal runaway of thermal batteries

However, practically, all of unit cells in the thermal battery do not have the uniform temperature distribution due to shape, component arrangement and heat transfer effect. After all, it has different temperature distribution depending on where the unit cell is located and how the discharge time is elapsed. Therefore, the performance estimation obtained by unit cell testing at constant temperature conditions may differs from actual cell stacks.

Until now, the performance predictions of thermal battery has been performed mainly using SIMULINK and Lump Model. However, it seems that this model did not seem to have helped optimize the thermal battery design.

Therefore, in this study, the performance prediction of thermal batteries using 'COMSOL Multiphysics' is executed. 'COMSOL Mutiphysics'program has both an electrochemical model and a heat transfer analysis function.

Unit cell test

Prior to the performance prediction of a thermal battery, the unit cell discharge experiment was performed under various temperature conditions. The unit cell test equipment is shown in Figure 3.

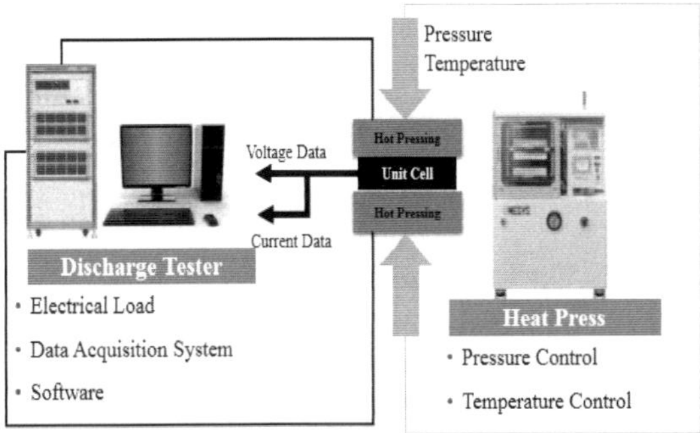

Figure 3. Unit Cell Discharge Test System

Thermal battery is composed of various components such as anode, cathode, electrolyte, heat source, insulator, igniter, case and so on. But, for unit cell testing, only cathode, anode and electrolyte are used. Table1 shows the physical properties of electrodes and electrolyte constituting the unit cell, all pellets were formed by cold pressing.

Table 1. Materials of unit cell

Material	Mass (g)	O.D (mm)	I.D (mm)	Thickness (mm)
Cathode (FeS_2)	1.81	44.67	8.32	0.38
Electrolyte (All-Li)	1.48	44.92	7.56	0.4
Anode (Li-Si alloy)	1.14	44.74	8.47	0.67

The experimental conditions are shown in Table 2.

Table 2. Unit cell discharge test cases(51 cases)

Test conditions			
Temperature(°C)	430°C ~ 590°C (10°C interval)		
Current(A) (Repetition profile)	7.6 A/2.4 s, 0 A/0.1 s	15.1A/2.4 s, 0A/0.1s	22.7A/2.4 s, 0A/0.1 s

When the temperature of the press is reached at setting point as shown in Figure 3, a unit cell was inserted between the upper plate and the lower plate, pressed to 250kg$_f$, and then was maintained for 2 minutes. Then, the stepwise discharge was performed according to the above Table 2.

The formula for calculating internal resistance of a unit cell is shown in Equation(1) published by Fujiwara et al., V_{ocv} is based on the voltage at 0.03 second after applying 0A and V_{ccv} is the voltage at 0.01 second after 0A discharge.

$$R_{tot} = \frac{V_{ocv}-V_{ccv}}{I_{ccv}} \quad \text{..... (1)}$$

The internal resistance is calculated using applied current values(I_{ccv}). The results of a unit cell discharge test(0.5A/cm^2, 1.0A/cm^2, 1.5A/cm^2) are shown in Figures 4, 5 and 6.

As the result of a unit cell discharge, it can be seen that the internal resistance of unit cell is very high when the temperature is less than 450℃. The reason is that viscosity of the electrolyte is too low and the conductivity is greatly lowered.

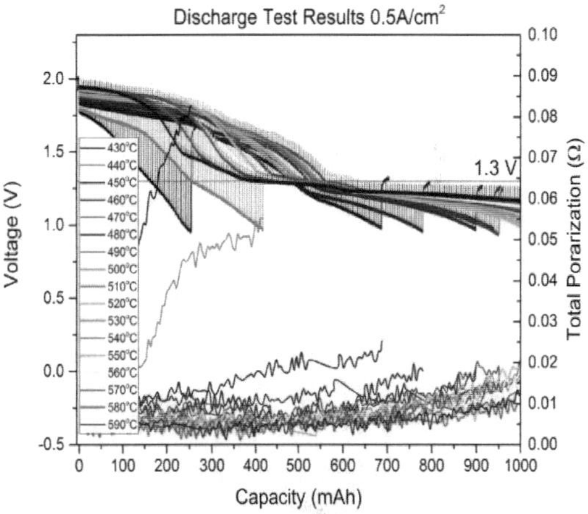

Figure 4. Unit cell discharge results (0.5A/cm^2)

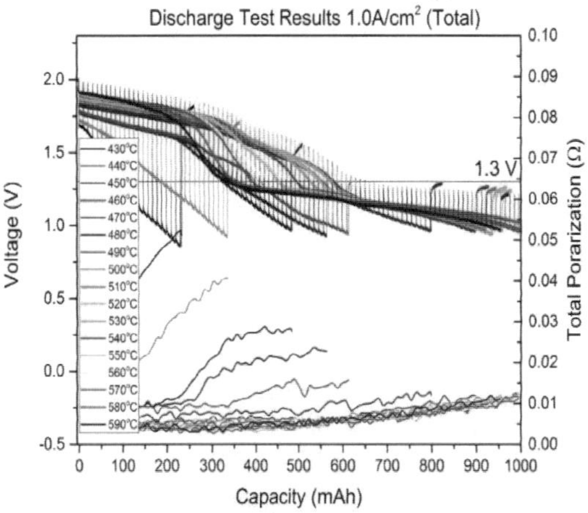

Figure 5. Unit cell discharge results (1.0A/cm^2)

Figure 7 shows the analysis results of the above discharge conditions(0.5A/cm^2, 1.0A/cm^2, 1.5A/cm^2).

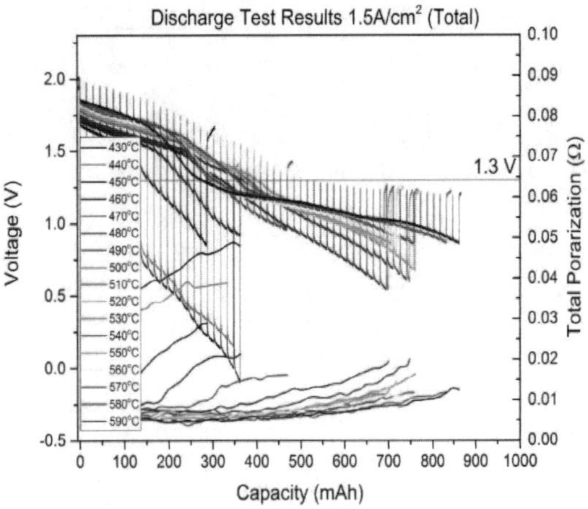

Figure 6. Unit cell discharge results (1.5A/cm^2)

Although there is a slight difference depending on the discharge rate, the optimal temperature range of a thermal battery is about 480~540°C.

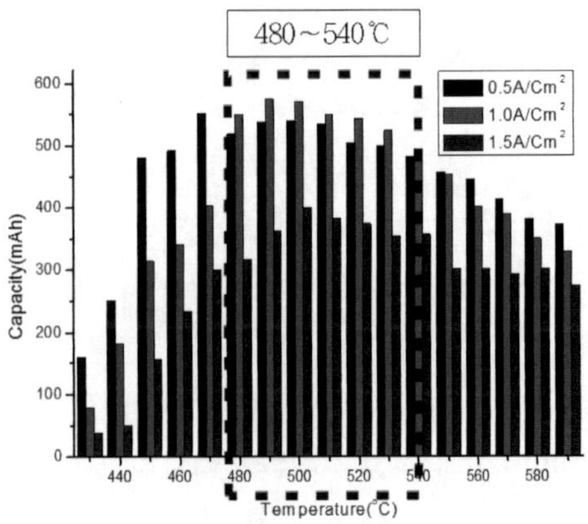

Figure 7. Unit cell discharge capacity results.

Thermal analysis of thermal battery

For optimal capacity of the thermal battery, the amount of the heat source must be carefully determined. If the amount of heat source in the thermal battery is too much, it may cause to overheat and rupture. On the other hand, if the amount of the heat source is too little, it is difficult to expect an optimum output because of low temperature.

In order to determine the amount of heat source for maintaining the optimal internal temperature of a thermal battery. The heat transfer & distribution inside the thermal battery was estimated using COMSOL program.

The component values and geometric shape for modeling is as Table 3 and Figure 8. The thickness of heat source are range from 0.8mm~1.5mm.

As shown in Figure 8, the temperature measurement points inside thermal battery are set at the middle of the cell stack(#4rdcell, red circle), cathode / electrolyte / anode / collector / heat source of #1stcell(dot line), insulator and cell case(red circle).

Table 3. Physical properties of a battery components.

Material	O.D (mm)	Density (g/cm^3)	Thickness (mm)
Cathode (FeS_2)	55.87	2.783	0.710
Electrolyte (All-Li)	56.24	2.240	0.430
Anode (Li-Si alloy)	56.08	1.060	1.000
Heat source ($Fe/KClO_4$)	56.17	3.300	0.8/0.9/1.0/1.2/1.5
Insulator (BF paper)		8.908	Ref. Figure 8
Case (SUS304)			Ref. Figure 8

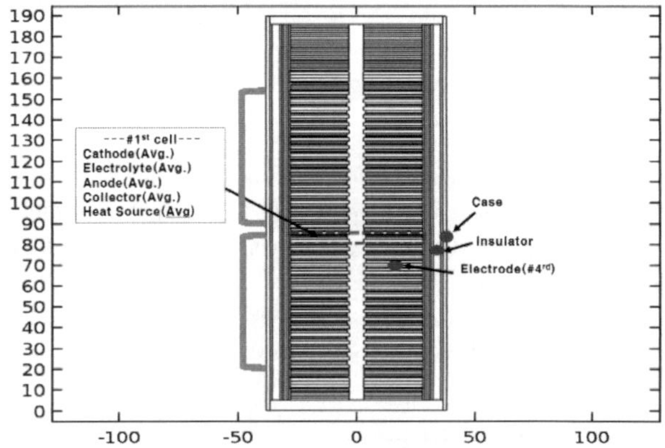

Figure 8. Temperature measurement point of thermal battery.

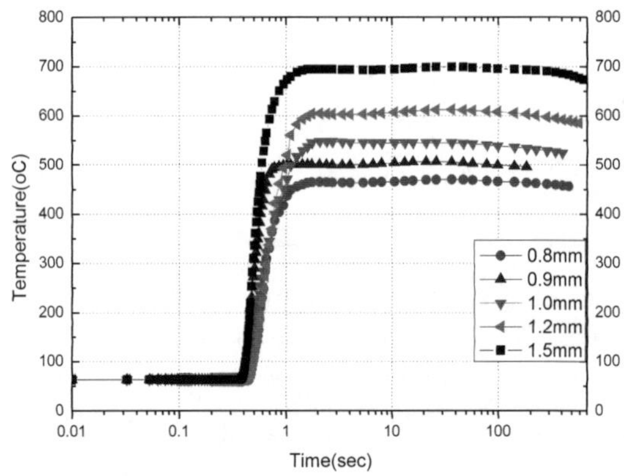

Figure 9. Temperature profiles of the #4th electrode of thermal battery(at 0.8~1.5mm heat source thickness)

Thermal analysis results

Through COMSOL program simulation, it was found that the temperature of electrode(#4rd) of a thermal battery differs according to the amount of heat source. As figure 7 shown, in the case 1.5mm thickness of heat source, the temperature of electrode rises up to 700°C. On the other hand, at 0.7mm, it was maintained at 460°C.

The optimal discharge performance was achieved when the thickness of heat source is 0.9~1.0mm. The rising time up to the temperature for optimal performance is about 1.0 sec. Figure 10 shows the average temperature of #1st cell vs. time. Here, #1st cell is located in the center of stack.

The highest average temperature of the heat source is 900°C (figure 10), but peak temperature reaches up to 1300°C at 0.2 second (figure 11).

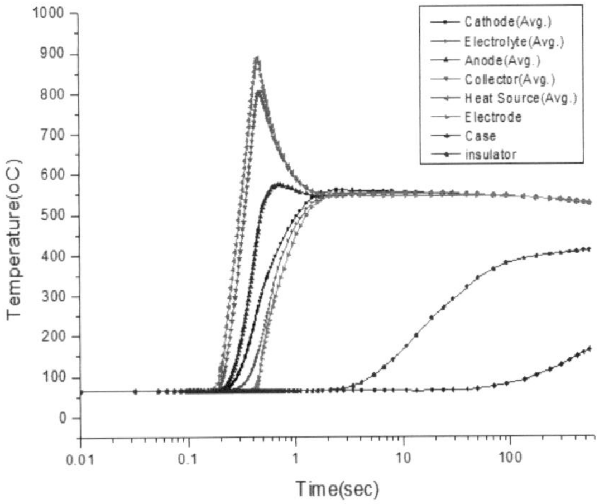

Figure 10. Temperature profiles of thermal battery components(at 1.0mm heat source thickness).

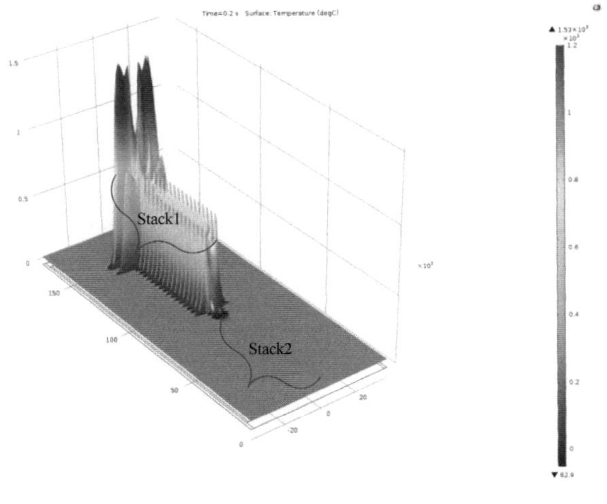

Figure 11. Temperature profiles of thermal battery components(0.2sec, at heat source 1.0mm, 45° view).

At the elapse of 10 seconds after the ignition, temperature profiles of thermal battery is as figure 12. The each side temperature of thermal battery reached above 800°C and that of central parts was up to about 600°C owing to the amount of dense heat source. The temperatures of stack1 and stack2 are maintained about 500~550°C.

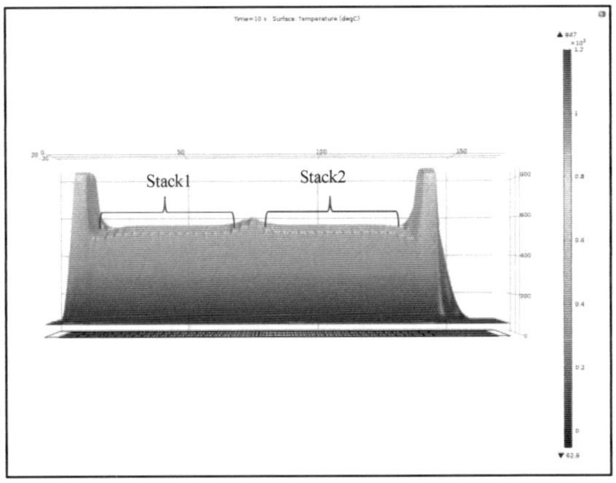

Figure 12. Temperature profiles of thermal battery components(10sec, at heat source 1.0mm, front view).

Acknowledgements

The authors wish to thank Sueng Soo Baek(ADD 4-4th Directorate) and electric power source team members of ADD. Also authors gratefully acknowledge funding from ADD defense S&T programs.

References

1. Seung Ho Kang, Ph.D Dissertation, 161, 1443 (2006).
2. H. W. Cheong, S. H. Kang, J. M. Kim, and S. B. Cho, Journal of Ceramic Processing Research, 13, 198 (2012).
3. Y. S. Choi, H. R. Yu, H. W. Cheong, S. B. Cho and Y. S. Lee, Appl. Chem. Eng. 25, 2, 161-166 (2014).
4. Freitas, C. S. Giancarlo, C. P. Fernando, and S. V. Ardson, Journal of Power Sources, 179.1, 424-429 (2008)
5. R. A. Guidotti, P. Masset, Journal of Power Sources, 183, 388-398 (2008)
6. H. J. Ji, Journal of the Korea Institute of Military Science and Technology, 11(1), 102-111 (2008)
7. S. Fujiwara, M. Inaba, and A. Tasaka, Journal of Power Sources, 196(8), 4012-4018 (2011)
8. A. G. Bergman, A. S. Arabadshan, Russ. J. Inorg. Chem. (English Trans.), 8(5), 369 (1963)
9. R. A. Guidotti, F. W. Reinhardt, Proceedings of the 33rd International Power Sources Conference, 369 (1988)
10. P. Masset, PhD Thesis, National Polytechnic Institute of Grenoble, Grenoble (2002)
11. J. R. Selman, D. K. DeNuccio, C. J. Sy, R. K. Steunenberg, Journal of Electrochemical Society, 124(8), 1160 (1977)
12. Y. S. Choi, H. R. Yu, H. W. Cheong, S. B. Cho and Y. S. Lee, Appl. Chem. Eng. 25, 1, 72-77 (2014).
13. S. Schoeffert, Journal of Power Sources, 142, 361-369 (2005)
14. S. Schoeffert, 40th Power Sources Conference, Cherry Hill-USA, June (2002).

Film Coating of Electrodes for High Power Density Thermal Batteries

Eric Allcorn, Ganesan Nagasubramanian, Bertha Montoya, Hannah Height, Chris A. Apblett, and Travis Anderson
Sandia National Laboratories
PO Box 5800, MS-0614, Albuquerque, NM 87185-0614
eallcor@sandia.gov

Abstract: *Molten salt thermal batteries are an integral piece of energy storage technology in modern munitions. The high conductivity of their molten salt electrolyte and high operating temperature enable extremely high discharge rates, providing a great deal of power over a short period of time. They are also capable of storing energy with little-to-no loss for several decades because the electrolyte salt is solid at room temperature, effectively halting any parasitic or self-discharge reactions during storage. Despite their widespread implementation, thermal batteries rely upon pellet-pressing for fabrication. This process is costly and time-consuming, while also restricting thermal batteries to a cylindrical form factor and requiring excessive electrode mass to produce mechanically robust pellets.*

We have developed a process to incorporate the FeS_2-based cathode and MgO-based separator materials of thermal batteries into slurries and coat into electrode films. This process can deliver higher throughput of thermal battery electrodes at a lower cost than pellet processing, and when employed with a foil-based anode, such as lithium-aluminum or lithium boron, can enable thermal batteries with smaller form factors and non-cylindrical geometries. The advantages of film processing have made this an attractive concept in the past. However, the high operating temperatures of thermal batteries and the high current density needed to meet power demands precludes the use of many film binders which either degrade at elevated temperatures or impede ion flow. Our process does not require the introduction of any foreign binder material into the electrode to produce high quality electrode films and thus has demonstrated the capability, in both single cells and batteries, to operate at high temperatures with less than 200 mV of polarization under a discharge current density of 2 A cm-^{2}. Figures 1 and 2 show, respectively, the high quality of electrode film produced as well as the effective discharge performance. This technology has the capability to lead to smaller, lower cost, and more geometrically diverse thermal batteries for a wide variety of applications.

Keywords: Thermal battery; molten salt electrolyte; high power; coated electrode

Introduction

Molten salt thermal batteries are primary reserve batteries that are desirable for munitions applications due to their high power density and extremely long shelf life. The most common chemistry for these batteries and the one reported on herein uses an FeS_2 cathode, a Li-Si alloy anode, an MgO separator, and a LiCl:KCl eutectic salt electrolyte.[1] These batteries are currently produced using a pellet-based fabrication approach in which individual cathode, separator, and anode pellets are pressed and assembled into stacks to form the battery. This pellet fabrication is time consuming and labor intensive, and restricts the form factor of batteries to near cylindrical shapes. In addition, to allow for ease of handling, these pellets must be fabricated with a significant excess of material, reducing the overall energy and power density of the batteries. Our goal with this work is to develop a film-based fabrication approach for thermal battery components, namely the cathode and separator, to enable more cost effective thermal battery production, more energy and power dense thermal batteries, and more geometrically flexible thermal battery form factors.

The advantages of film-based fabrication are well-known but their application to thermal batteries has been prevented thus far due in large part to the extreme operating environment of these battery systems. The batteries operate at temperatures in excess of 400°C and are hermetically sealed systems to enable long shelf life. This precludes the use of polymer binders commonly employed to produce electrode films in batteries, such as ambient temperature lithium-ion chemistries, due to thermal degradation and off-gassing of polymers at elevated temperatures. The selected binder system must also not impede the flow of current within the electrode films, as power density is a key metric for thermal batteries. Other concerns include chemical compatibility with active battery materials and electrochemical stability over the operational voltage window of the battery.

The approach targeted in this paper to meet all these needs is a LiCl salt binder system based on the electrolyte salt already present in the battery. This binder is thermally stable and non-gassing. In addition, upon battery activation the binder will melt to become a part of the electrolyte, thereby not impeding current flow and enabling the retention of high power density. Because it is already a constituent part of the thermal battery electrodes, LiCl is also proven compatible with the active materials within the cell and stable over the necessary voltage range. In this paper we detail the development and application of this LiCl binder to thermal battery cathodes and separators as well as the performance of the fabricated parts. Due to the need for organic solvents in processing and the strongly reducing nature of active anode materials, this binder system is not considered feasible for anode application.

LiCl Binder Development

The incorporation of LiCl as a binder into a thermal battery films is carried out by first solvating the LiCl in an organic solvent, mixing the active material powder into the solution mixture to form a slurry, coating the slurry to the thickness desired, and removing the solvent through a drying process to precipitate the LiCl out as the film binder. As the solvent is removed the LiCl will precipitate and bind the particles network into a coherent electrode film. A range of solvents were explored for the solvation of the LiCl binder as a numberof characteristics are required for effective application: appreciable solvation of LiCl, easily dried from coated film, and chemically compatible with active materials. The measured solubility of LiCl and reported boiling points for several different solvents are shown in Figure 1, where AN = acetonitrile, EC = ethylene carbonate, PC = propylene carbonate, GBL = γ-butyrolactone, NMF = n-methyl formamide, and DMSO = dimethyl sulfoxide. AN, EC, and GBL solvents can be seen from Figure 1a to have very low LiCl solubility, and showed in testing to yield loosely bound films that did not adhere to substrates. PC is shown in Figure 1b to have a very high boiling point of 242°C, making it unattractive from a drying standpoint. Meanwhile water, while offering moderate solvation of LiCl and a low boiling point, was proven chemically incompatible with both the FeS_2 cathode and MgO separator materials. NMF and DMSO offer the highest LiCl solvation among tested solvents as well as moderate boiling points of 182°C and 189°C, respectively. Functional cathodes were fabricated from both solvents. However, NMF proved chemically incompatible with the MgO separator material and yielded lower capacity cathodes, suggesting a degree of reactivity with the FeS_2 cathode, as well. As such, DMSO was selected as the solvent of choice for processing of the LiCl binder into thermal battery films.

The coating substrate is also an important consideration for LiCl thermal battery film development. The substrate will serve as the current collector for the deposited film so must be an electronically conductive material. In addition, it must be stable at thermal battery operating temperatures, electrochemically stable at electrode potentials, chemically stable to active materials, have good surface wetting and adhesion of coated films, and have a very small thickness. The materials identified for this application included 4 mil stainless steel foil, 3 mil Grafoil, and 5 mil carbon paper. While all of these materials were functional as coating substrates, the fully carbonized carbon paper (Spectracarb 2050A-0550) offered the strongest surface adhesion due to its porous structure that allowed for interpenetration of the electrode slurry. Without the incorporation of excessively high binder contents, the non-porous stainless steel and Grafoil both exhibited weak surface adhesion and frequent delamination of electrode films.

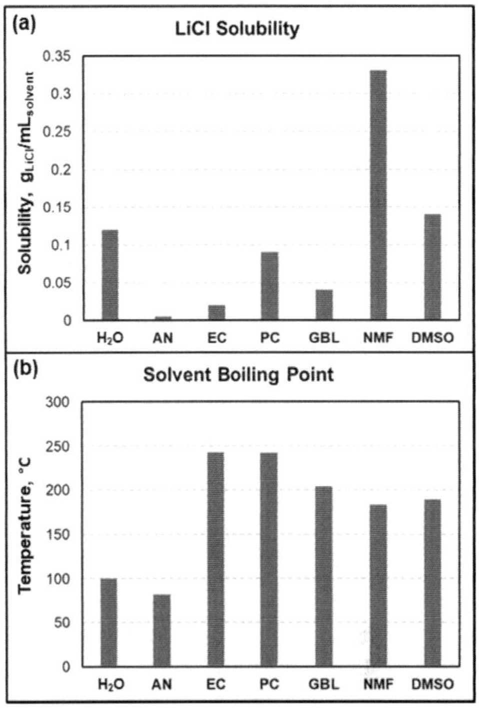

Figure 1. a) Measured solubility of LiCl salt in various organic solvents at STP. b) Reported boiling points for the same set of organic solvents.

Cathode Film Development

After the identification of an appropriate solvent and substrate for application of the LiCl binder into electrode films, fabrication of the FeS_2 cathode was investigated. Rheological characterization of cathode slurries was carried out to determine a slurry formulation that would work with the tape cast film deposition method chosen to fabricate these electrodes. Figure 2a shows the resulting curve of slurry viscosity as a function of solids content. A slurry formulation containing 25 vol.% solids was selected for its moderate viscosity of 200 cP, which is low enough to flow easily during the coating process with minimal flow after deposition.

The initial target in fabricating these cathode films was to maximize LiCl binder content to ensure a mechanically robust film. However, as Figure 2b shows, characterization of cathode impedance via an electrochemical pulse discharge method revealed a direct correlation between salt binder content – shown here in terms of the degree of solvent saturation prior to active powder addition – and electrode impedance. Lower impedance means a cell can deliver greater current at higher voltage so is a strong indicator of electrode performance. As such there were opposing drivers for the amount of binder to incorporate into the films. The adoption of the carbon paper substrate, shown in the inset of Figure 2c, enabled the reduction of binder content from 17 wt.% in early films, down to 4.9

wt.% with good film quality and adhesion. An example of one of our low-binder cathode films is shown in Figure 2c. The SEM inset shows a coherent and well-bound film microstructure while the larger photo shows the film can have electrodes punched from it with no cracking or delamination of the surrounding cathode. The cathode in this Figure was coated at a wet-film thickness of 10 mils and had a total dried thickness of 11 mils (including the 5 mil thick substrate).

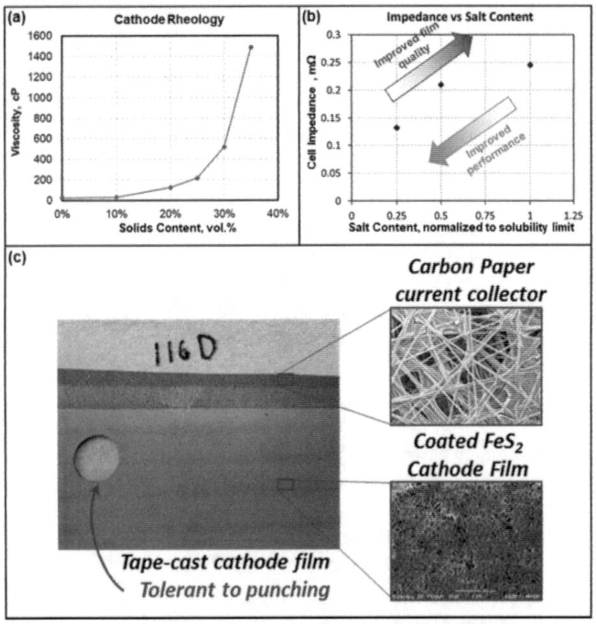

Figure 2. a) Measured rheology of DMSO cathode slurry. b) Competing trends of film adhesion and electrode impedance on salt binder content. c) Image of coated cathode film with inset SEM images of coating substrate and electrode surface.

After fabrication, we commenced with electrochemical testing of the cathode films in thermal battery single cells. These single cells are composed of a cathode, separator, and anode and allow for rapid assembly and testing of the discharge properties of the individual electrochemical components. Our coated film cathode is combined with a pellet separator and anode of, respectively, MgO and Li-Si to comprise a test cell. Baseline single cells of all pellet components were also fabricated and tested for comparison purposed. Electrochemical testing of these cells was conducted using a tester developed and built at Sandia National Laboratories for the high-temperature activation and discharge of thermal battery single cells under fixed temperature and pressure conditions in an inert environment. A standard discharge profile was selected for testing these single cells which involves heating them to 525°C and holding under open-circuit conditions for 10 to 30 seconds, followed by a low level discharge current of 50 mA/cm^2 with brief pulses at higher currents densities, up to a maximum value of 2 A cm^2.

Figure 3a shows the voltage curve of our film cathode subjected to this discharge profile, which is also included in the plot. A rapid rise in voltage is observed initially as the cell is activated by elevation above the eutectic salt melting point. This is followed by a voltage plateau at roughly 1.9 V, which corresponds to the initial discharge reaction of the FeS_2 cathode shown in equation 1

$$2FeS_2 + 3Li \rightarrow Li_3Fe_2S_4 \qquad (1)$$

As the high current pulses are applied, dips in the cell voltage are incurred due to polarization from impedance within the cell. The voltage change from these polarization dips are plotted in Figure 3b as a function of current density, yielding a linear trend with a slope that is proportional to the cell impedance. The polarization values for a similarly tested all-pellet single cell are also plotted here, showing that the film cathode has a lower impedance than the baseline pellet component under similar conditions. At the peak current density value of 2 A/cm^2 our film cathode has a polarization of ~180 mV, compared to ~300 mV for a pellet cathode. This confirms that our film cathode can deliver the high power densities necessary for thermal batteries and comparable to those from current pellet cathodes.

The capacity delivered from our film cathodes was also measured in single cell format and is shown in Figure 3c as a function of temperature. The upper plateau, associated with the reaction in equation 1, has a theoretical capacity of 335 mAh/g. Our film based cathode is significantly thinner and lighter than the pellet cathode but still delivers a capacity of >300 mAh/g, near theoretical, at temperatures below 500°C. When compared to similar measurements for pellet cathodes in Figure 3d, our film cathode shows no loss appreciable loss of delivered capacity. Both cathodes show a decrease in capacity at elevated temperatures due to FeS_2 decomposition. The lower voltage, secondary reaction plateau at roughly 1.5 V shows similar trends in these Figures as well.

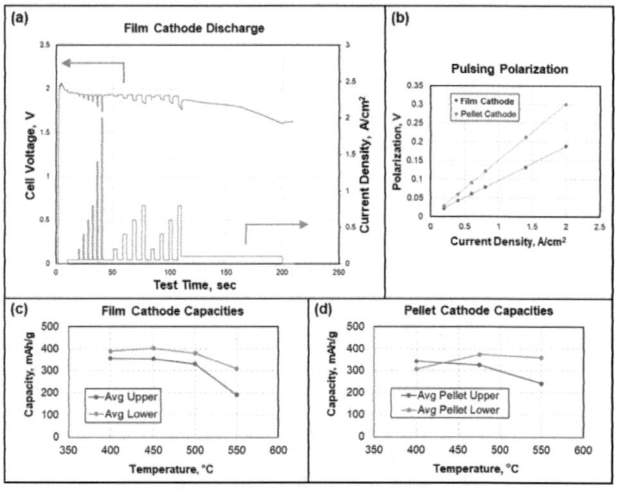

Figure 3. a) Discharge curve of a coated film cathode versus a Li-Si pellet anode at 525°C. b) Voltage polarization as a function of current density for film and pellet cathodes.

c) Specific capacity of film cathodes and (d) pellet cathodes as a function of operating temperature.

Separator Film Development

With the demonstration of functional cathode films using LiCl as a binder in organic DMSO solvent, the next effort was to extend this approach to the separator component of the thermal battery. Because the separator is located between the cathode and anode, a coated film separator would need to utilize either the cathode or anode as a coating substrate. The highly reducing anode materials are not compatible with organic solvents, including DMSO, so the cathode developed previously is utilized as the coating substrate for separator development. Thermal battery separators are composed of a high volume fraction of electrolyte salt as well as an MgO matrix that serves as both a physical separation between electrodes and as a porous framework to hold molten salt in place once a thermal battery is activated. To apply the separator film over the cathode undercoat both a tape cast and drop cast method were employed. The tape cast approach allows for fabrication of larger surface areas while the drop cast method enables a greater variety of sample control, which is very valuable during development. Both methods have yielded effective bi-layer films of cathodes and separators.

Figure 4a shows EDX mapping of the prepared bi-layer cathode and separator coated films. This confirms an intimate interface between the two layers with no cross-over of active material. Figure 4b shows an image of a tape-cast separator film over a cathode film substrate. Such a bi-layer film was assembled into single cells with a pellet anode and discharged under the standard discharge profile used previously. Figure 4c shows the discharge curve of the bi-layer film cathode and separator. There is an observed decrease in performance relative to the baseline in this case. The polarization at 2 A/cm^2 is higher at ~320 mV and the delivered capacity is lower at 151 mAh/g. However, the cell still supports a very high current density which further confirms the capability of the salt based binder to deliver coated thermal battery films with capability to support high power discharge. In addition, the separator component is still under ongoing development and we anticipate further improvement in both polarization and capacity.

Conclusions

Through DMSO solvent processing and tape cast deposition on a carbon paper substrate, we have fabricated thin, robust films of functional thermal battery cathodes and separators. The cathode has demonstrated improved electrochemical performance relative to a pellet baseline cathode and the separator has shown the capability to deliver high power with room for continued improvement. When paired with a novel anode material, such as a LiB foil anode, these film components could serve to realize a thermal battery with improved energy and power density.[2] This could also help to realize batteries of novel geometries not currently feasible using pellet-based thermal battery technology.

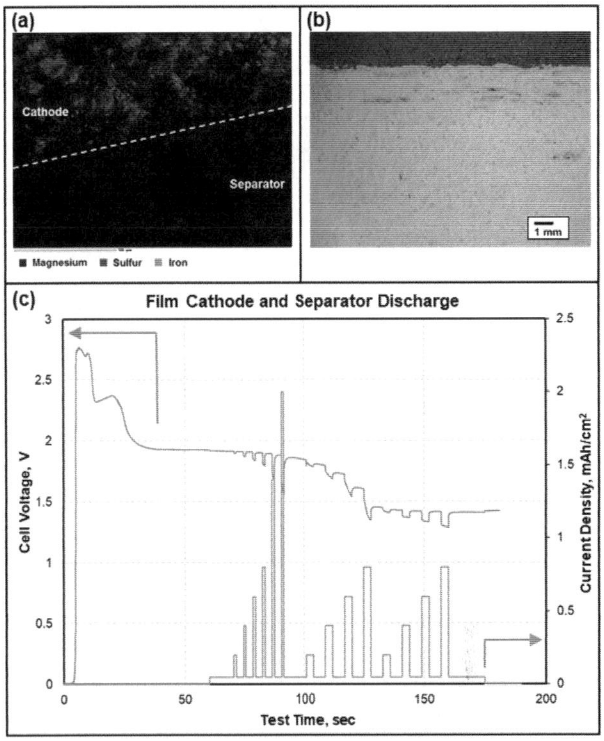

Figure 4. a) EDX mapping showing materials separation at the separator – cathode interface. b) Image of coated separator over a cathode film. c) Discharge curve of a coated film cathode and separator versus a Li-Si pellet anode at 525°C.

Acknowledgements

This project is graciously funded through the Joint Department of Defense / Department of Energy Munitions Program.

Sandia National Laboratories is a multimission laboratory managed and operated by National Technology and Engineering Solutions of Sandia LLC, a wholly owned subsidiary of Honeywell International Inc., for the U.S. Department of Energy's National Nuclear Security Administration under contract DE-NA0003525. The views expressed in this article do not necessarily represent the views of the U.S. Department of Energy or the United States Government. SAND2018-4783 C.

References

1. Guidotti, R. A. and P. Masset, "Thermally activated ("thermal") battery technology: Part I: An overview," *Journal of Power Sources*, Vol. 161, no. 2, pp. 1443-1449, October 2006.
2. Szwarc, R., R. B. Walton, S. Dallek and B. F. Larrick, "Dishcarge Characteristics of Lithium-Boron Alloy Anode in Molten Salt Thermal Cells," *Journal of the Electrochemical Society*, Vol. 129, no. 6, pp. 1168-1173, June 1982.

Improving Thermal Battery Performance through Model-Based Development and Improved Component Designs

Marc Kenton
Erigo Technologies LLC
POB 899, Enfield, NH 03748
marc.kenton@erigo.com

Dharmesh Bhakta
EaglePicher Technologies LLC
P.O. Box 47, Joplin, MO 64802

Abstract: *Even though thermal batteries are a relatively mature technology, continued improvements in performance are needed to support more challenging mission profiles. Erigo Technologies and EaglePicher are developing improvements in thermal battery capacity and power capabilities by a program that synergistically combines modeling and experiment to optimize battery designs.*

The modeling effort uses an advanced version of a physics-based computer code that has been continuously improved over the previous decade. The code is supported by an extensive property library that has been assembled using information from the literature, properties measured in the laboratory at EP, and that obtained by fitting predicted performance to a very wide range of EP cell data.

The experimental program consists of several efforts that directly support recent advances in the model's capabilities. One effort is directed toward obtaining a semi-mechanistic understanding of electrolyte transport between cell components during activation. This process can have a large impact on battery capacity as well as cell impedance. A second effort is aimed at achieving a more accurate representation of the thermal conductivity of an advanced insulation under actual operating conditions. These efforts are complemented by a separate program that is quantitatively characterizing the electrochemical properties of an advanced cathode additive developed by EP.

The current program will culminate in the construction, testing, and iterative improvement of batteries for a particularly demanding application. This will demonstrate the improved performance that can be achieved by leveraging advanced component technologies using a model-based development process.

Keywords: thermal batteries; electrochemical analysis; model-based design

Introduction

To meet ever more demanding applications, accurate, physics-based analytical models of thermal batteries are needed to shorten development cycles and optimize battery design. Thermal battery design and modeling are difficult because their performance depends on a number of complex phenomena. Moreover, the strong feedbacks between the phenomena, the high temperatures of operation, and the small size of thermal battery cells make it difficult to accurately study these processes in isolation.

A series of codes, developed at Erigo Technologies with funding from several SBIR programs, has long supported battery development at EaglePicher. The latest of these codes, named AllBatt, is currently being used as part of a development effort whose goal is to construct a very high performance thermal battery.

The battery development effort incorporates advances in component composition as well as recently developed, high performance insulation materials. The model-based development process being used on this program is considered particularly helpful when newly developed components are being employed, since relatively little direct experience with these is available to guide the design.

Description of the AllBatt Code

AllBatt is an improved version of several earlier battery modeling programs [Kenton et al, 2010]. The code consists of a 2-D or 3-D finite element thermal model coupled to a user-defined number of 1-D electrochemical models of individual battery cells. Considerable effort has been devoted to make this model easy to use by battery designers in an interactive, menu-driven manner.

The thermal model is relatively standard. The electrochemistry model is less conventional and consists of a species-based ion transport model coupled to a Butler-Volmer representation of electrochemical reactions and, where applicable, a solid-state diffusion model. The code tracks an arbitrary number of chemical species whose concentrations can change via an arbitrary number of user-input chemical reactions. The versatility of this framework is evidenced by the fact that the same code has been successfully used to simulate lithium-ion, lead-acid, thionyl chloride, and silver-zinc batteries, as well as several different thermal battery chemistries. The models are fully coupled so that electrochemical heating is fed back to the temperature calculations.

The specification of the electrical load applied to the battery stack is essentially arbitrary and can represent time-dependent voltage, current, power, resistance, or a combination of these. Individual sections of the stack can be operated in parallel by constraining the output voltages of sets of cells to be equal.

Development of AllBatt Material Property Library

Arguably the most challenging aspect of thermal battery modeling is assembling the physical properties library, and these have been determined from a variety of sources:

- The densities and thermal properties of the various solid species were obtained from the literature or in some cases using dedicated experiments conducted at EP for this purpose [e.g. Swift, 2011]. The molar volumes of the various ionic species were defined by fitting the species-based model to a wide assortment of NIST-published molten salt data.
- The diffusion coefficients and related parameters in the Stefan-Maxwell ion transport model have been estimated by fitting the predictions of the model to a wide assortment of published data on individual species mobility, molten salt mixture ionic conductivity, trace element diffusion, and self-diffusion. Aside from its generality, a strength of the species-based model is that it can account for the change in properties as the individual constituents of the electrolytes move within the cell.
- The open circuit potential of the various chemical reactions is generally based on the literature [e.g. Bernardi and Newman, 1987], but a few minor modifications were made to better fit the low-current single cell discharge data.

Among the more difficult parameters to estimate are those associated with the electrochemical reaction rate modeling, e.g. the exchange current density and symmetry coefficients for the various half-cell reactions. For thermal battery modeling, these are for the most part not available in the literature and were again estimated by fitting code predictions to a large set of single cell data taken at different temperatures, current profiles, and with variations in cell design. It was found to be very valuable to include in these tests cells containing either oversized anodes or cathodes: varying the relative amounts of active material in the anode and cathode makes it much easier to distinguish the contributions to overall cell impedance from the different reactions.

A special test series was conducted to estimate the open circuit potentials and reaction rate parameters needed to characterize a cathode additive developed by EaglePicher for which essentially no data was available in the literature. This additive reduces cell impedance for very demanding current profiles.

Empirical Modeling of Intra-cell Electrolyte Transport

Another key aspect of modeling the performance of thermal batteries is understanding the distribution of electrolytes in the cell following activation. Experience demonstrates that variations in the amount of electrolyte transferred from the separator to the anode and cathode can have a substantial impact on cell capacity and impedance.

A largely empirical approach has been taken to study this phenomenon. Single cell tests run at relatively low current densities (e.g. 100 mA/cm^2 or less) show clear inflection points when the cells transition from one half-reaction to another. Use of low current densities makes these transitions relatively obvious by suppressing the development of mixed potentials caused by multiple reactions occurring simultaneously in a component. The use of oversized anodes (or cathodes) is very useful in these studies since this again makes it relatively easy to maintain the cell on the first anode (or cathode) reaction plateau for most of the discharge.

In its current form, the AllBatt code requires that the user explicitly enter the fractions of the anode and cathode that are effectively wetted by electrolyte and can participate in chemical reactions. The volume of electrolyte that is transferred out of the separator (barring leakage to the periphery) can be calculated from these inputs and is assumed to reduce its thickness accordingly. Varying these two "wetting fraction" parameters until the computed cell voltage fits the data provides an indirect but valuable means for estimating the electrolyte inventories in the anode and cathode. Figures 1 and 2 demonstrate that the voltage behavior and inflection points of single cells can be quite accurately fit by the appropriate choice of wetting fraction. A set of over 60 such experiments was used to develop the reaction rate parameters for the property library and to study electrolyte migration phenomena. As described below, simulations of complete battery tests were performed to check the performance of the final model under realistic conditions.

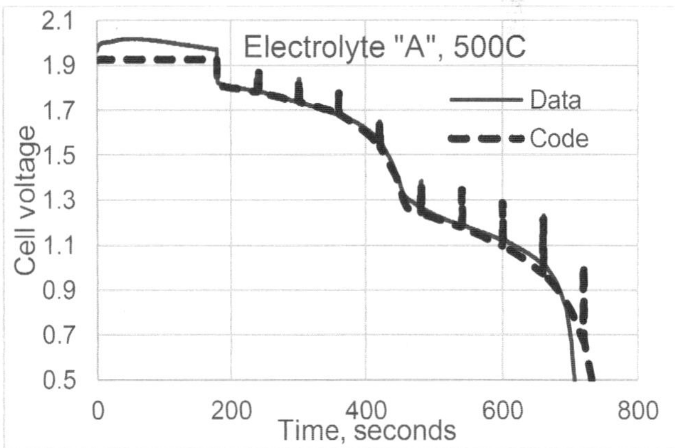

Figure 1: Code vs. data for single cell experiment with oversized anode. Nominal current density 500 mA/cm^2.

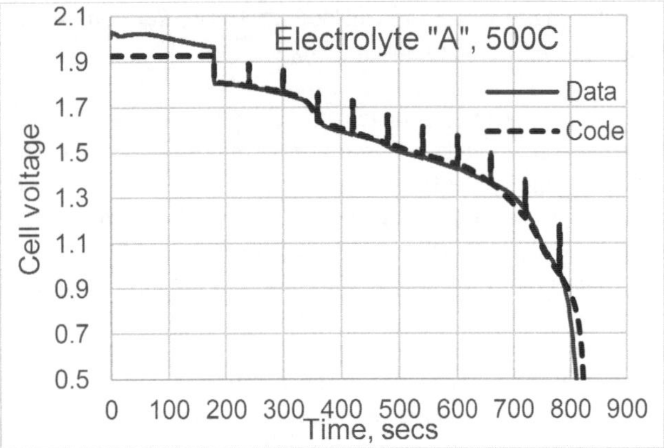

Figure 2: Code vs. data for single cell experiment with oversized cathode. Nominal current density 500 mA/cm².

Guidelines are needed to estimate the two wetting fractions so that accurate, a priori predictions of battery performance can be made for a new design. Such guidelines have been developed by analyzing the single cell data:

1) For a given electrolyte mixture and activation temperature, transport from the separator appears to be a reasonably consistent function of the total free volume available to receive electrolyte in the anode and the cathode and the initial EB volume in the separator. A possible explanation is that a high initial flow of EB from the separator, enabled by relatively high permeability in the anode and cathode, delays the formation of spanning clusters of binder particles that eventually support the cell against the imposed stack pressure to terminate the flow.
2) For cell designs in which the as-built cathode is already substantially filled with electrolyte, the wetting fraction needed to explain the detailed behavior of the early phase of the discharge (e.g. as shown in figure 1) is generally less than that corresponding to either the as-built inventory or the total exhibited cell capacity. This is attributed to the relatively high impedance the cathode presents to radial current flow: because of this impedance, the fraction of the cathode cross-section that undergoes chemical reactions is initially limited by the portion of the anode which is reacting, creating a strong correlation between the two wetting fractions (Figure 3).
3) At low current densities, lithium-silicon alloy anodes eventually exhibit a greater total capacity than is evident from the value of the wetting fraction needed to reproduce the timing of the transitions between reaction plateaus. This extra capacity is manifested by an unusually long period on the final reaction plateau:

$$Li_{12}Si_7 \rightarrow 12Li^+ + 7Si$$

There is also an inverse correlation of the impedance on the final plateau to the wetting fraction in the anode. Both behaviors are attributed to a hypothesized de-wetting phenomenon that causes electrolyte to migrate within the anode once silicon begins to be produced in the reaction shown above. This is believed to be qualitatively consistent with observations of catastrophic de-wetting in the middle of cell discharge when a wetting agent was added to anodes [Searcy et al, 1981]. This phenomenon, while not yet explicitly represented in the 1-D electrochemistry model, is typically unimportant in most demanding thermal battery applications.

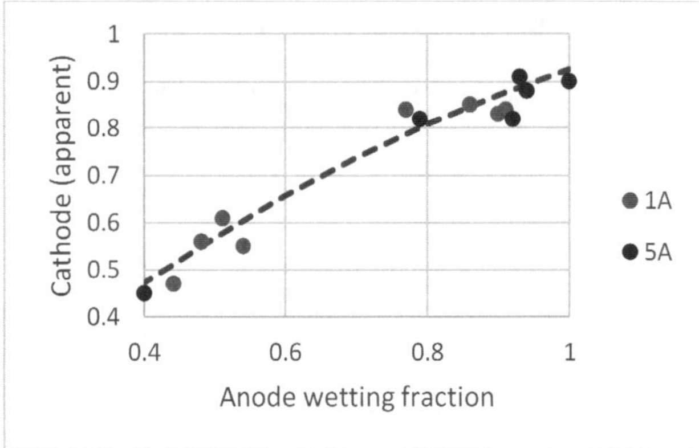

Figure 3: Correlation between apparent wetting fractions in anode and cathode caused by impedance effects.

A substantial variation in wetting fraction has been observed in our experiments, depending on electrolyte type, the activation temperature, and a few other parameters that are only partially understood. For design purposes, it appears that the wetting fractions can usually be estimated within about 10 percent using the guidelines outlined above. Variations in wetting fraction give rise to differences in cell capacity that can be erroneously attributed to unusually strong self-discharge reactions.

Testing on Complete Batteries

The true test of the code's predictive capabilities is, of course, modeling actual production batteries. This has been done using the property library described above with no modifications. At present, predictive calculations are performed using a range of wetting fraction values typical of those seen in the single cell tests, but a near-term goal is to estimate these explicitly using the electrolyte transport methodology. At that point, no adjustable parameters will in principal remain.

Figure 4 shows the prediction of the voltage behavior of an actual battery. This is a relatively difficult example since the electrical load is a specified power that yields a quite high current density. In such cases, errors in the predicted voltage have a positive feedback effect on the applied current, exaggerating the impact of errors on predicted battery lifetime. The excellent agreement between the code predictions and the data is encouraging.

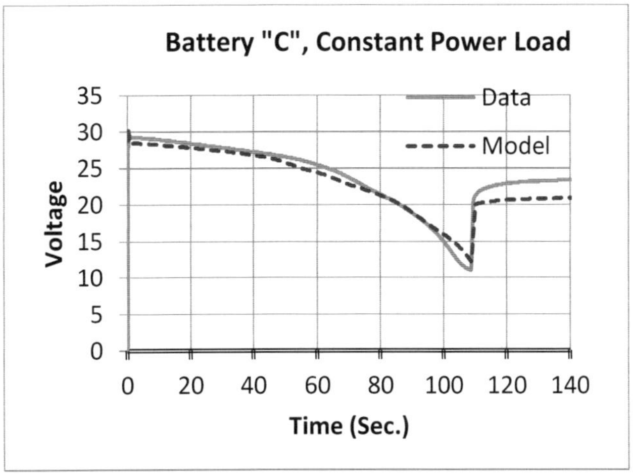

Figure 4: Comparison of model predictions to battery data with a specified-power boundary condition. Nominal current density varies from 600 to 1400 mA/cm^2. Wetting fractions entered manually.

Insulation Modeling

The AllBatt library contains a set of properties for commonly used insulation materials. These have proven accurate when simulating a highly instrumented thermal battery test [Ingersoll et al, 2008]. The lifetime of operational batteries operated at low current is usually limited by electrolyte freezing, and the timing can generally be predicted reasonably accurately if the compression of the insulation wrapper is accounted for.

We expect to investigate the use of recently developed, advanced insulation that may offer advantages for long life batteries with stringent constraints on battery size and weight. To this end, thermal properties measured in benchtop tests of these materials have been added to the property library, and the test program will include an effort to assess how accurately cell temperatures are predicted under actual operating conditions at relatively low electrical load. The use of a modest electrical load allows voltage to serve as a convenient surrogate for temperature. The measured external cannister temperature will also be compared to code predictions.

Model-based Optimization of Battery Design

A battery development process that leverages the capabilities of the analytical models is also being developed. The process leverages the detailed modeling capabilities of the AllBatt code, but a variety of lumped parameter and simplified 1-D models are also provided in the code to assist the designer. For example, a lumped parameter model is included that provides a fast, very accurate estimate for the post-burn cell average temperature to support design of the heat pellets. Another such model provides a rapid estimate for the stack temperature at end of life, given a proposed wrapper design.

We are commencing construction and testing of batteries for the target application that were designed using the draft model-based procedure. Refinements in the procedure will be developed as further experience is acquired.

Conclusion

A sophisticated, model-based capability has been developed to facilitate more efficient design of thermal batteries.

Acknowledgements

The authors acknowledge the valuable contributions of various colleagues who have contributed to the modeling efforts over the years. These include Mr. John Wilson (Erigo) and Dr. Joe Edington, Mr. Charley Lamb, and Mr. Eric Raub (EaglePicher).

References

1. Bernardi, Dawn, and J. Newman, 1987. Mathematical Modelling of Lithium(alloy), Iron Disulfide Cells, J. Electrochem. Soc., p1309-1318.

2. Ingersoll, D., J.T. Nakos, N.H. Clark, N. Streeter, and E. Listerud, 2008, "Highly Instrumented Thermal Battery for Thermal Model Validation," poster presented at the 43rd Power Sources Conference, Philadelphia, 7-10 July, 2008.

3. Kenton, Marc, J. Wilson, M. Miller, I. Yeaton, S. May, N. Elkouh, and D. Bhakta, 2010, A Comprehensive, Physics-Based Model for Thermal Batteries, Proc. 44th Power Sources Conference.

4. Searcy, J.Q., P.A. Neiswander, J.R. Armijo, and R.W. Bild, 1981, Lithium Oxide in the Li(Si)/FeS2 Thermal Battery System, SAND81-1705, Sandia National Laboratory.

5. Swift, G.A., 2011, Thermophysical Properties of Lithium Alloys for Thermal Batteries, Int. J. Thermophysics. 32, 2102-2111.

Ionic Conductivity and Thermal Stability of Lithium Salt / KF-HF Electrolytes for Molten Salt Batteries

Aliakbar Yazdani[1], Mohan Sanghadasa[2], Gerardine G. Botte[1]

[1]Department of Chemical and Biomolecular Engineering, Russ College of Engineering
Center for Electrochemical Engineering Research (CEER)
Ohio University
Athens, OH 45701

[2]Missile Research and Innovation Function
Weapons Development & Integration Directorate
Aviation and Missile Research, Development, and Engineering Center
U.S. Army RDECOM
Redstone Arsenal, AL 35898

Botte@ohio.edu / 1-740-593-9670

Abstract: *Commercial thermal batteries use an electrolyte that is a mixture of different lithium salts. To reduce the melting point and improve the performance of the electrolyte, these salts are mixed with eutectic point ratios. This research is focused on developing an electrolyte with a significantly lower melting point. To this end, three widely used lithium halides were mixed with potassium bifluoride (KF-HF) to prepare the electrolyte samples. The melting points and the ionic conductivity of the mixtures were tested at several composition ratios. These thermal and electrochemical data can be used to determine the correct ratio of each compound to maximize the battery performance.*

Keywords: Molten salt battery; Electrolyte; Ionic conductivity; Eutectic point; Thermal stability

Introduction

Molten salt batteries use an electrolyte that is solid at ambient temperatures. Because of the inactive electrolyte, these batteries can be stored with little to no power loss for long periods of time (>25 years). However, they could be activated within a fraction of a second to produce high power output ranging from watts to kilowatts. The design used to make the activation process possible is an internal pyrotechnic heat source. An exothermic reaction of the pyrotechnic material melts the electrolyte by significantly raising the temperature of internal components. Once the electrolyte is in liquid form, ions can pass through the electrolyte and the cell can deliver energy. [1]. The electrochemical and physical properties of the electrolyte such as the ionic conductivity and the melting point are the defining factors of the energy density and operational lifetime of the battery. Traditionally a eutectic mixture of different lithium salts is used as electrolyte [2].

The operating temperature of molten salt batteries is usually higher than 400 °C. These high operating temperatures require a complex thermal design of the battery casing [3]. An electrolyte with a lower melting point has several important advantages such as reduction in the activation time and a smaller amount of pyrotechnic material that is essential to activate the cell. The temperature drop is usually the limiting factor in operating lifetime of these energy storage devices [1]. The ability to operating at a lower temperature can increase the performance of these batteries by reducing the amount of heat loss while active.

Methodology

Materials

Based on the findings by Masset and Guidotti, three Lithium halide salts—LiF (ACROS Organics, purity 97%,), LiCl (ACROS Organics, purity ≥ 99%) and Li_2SO_4 (ACROS Organics, purity 99%)—were chosen as the initial candidates to be mixed with KF-HF (ACROS Organics, purity ≥ 99%)[2]. The mixture of these three lithium salts can be used as an electrolyte for thermal batteries, providing a reference point to which the new mixtures can be compared.

To remove any possible moisture from the materials, all the above chemicals were individually dried in an oven (Thermo Scientific Thermolyn Benchtop Muffle Furnaces, model# F47915) inside a glove box (under an argon atmosphere) before any mixing. Drying conditions for each material are presented in Table 1.

Table 1. Drying procedure (container, temperature and time) for each material

Material	Container	Temperature	Time
LiF, LiCl, Li_2SO_4	Alumina crucible	400 °C (673 K)	2 hours
KF-HF	Nickle crucible	150 °C (423 K)	2 hours

After the drying process, each material was cooled down and transferred to a closed plastic container. To eliminate any exposure to moisture or oxygen, none of the samples were removed from the glovebox at any point during the drying process, storage and mixing processes.

Infusion Process

The synthesis of an electrolyte with a combination of a Li-salt and KF-HF requires an infusion mixing process that involves the melting of KF-HF. The melting point of KF-HF is 238 °C[4]. The Li-salt/KF-HF mixture was infused at 250 °C for 2 hours and, after cooling down, was thoroughly pulverized to a very fine powder using mortar and pestle.

Lithium salt /KF-HF mixtures

Electrolyte samples were prepared from one Li-salt mixed with KF-HF using the infusion process described in the previous section. The choice of the Li-salt was dependent on its interaction with the KF-HF electrolyte and was optimized based on the melting point and ionic conductivity results from DSC and EIS measurements, respectively. The approach of this work to identify and consolidate the optimum Li-salt and electrolyte composition is shown in Figure 1. LiF, LiCl and Li_2SO_4 salts were systematically mixed with KF-HF. This flow chart (See Figure 1) illustrates the approach to experiment planning for this work.

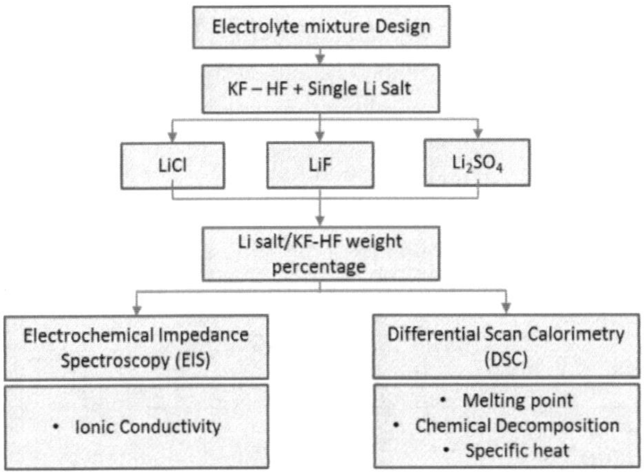

Figure 1. Experimental approach for the synthesis and evaluation of eutectic Li salt/KF – HF mixtures

Ionic conductivity measurement apparatus

The electrochemical impedance spectroscopy (EIS) test cell was designed based on a similar cell that has been widely used to measure the ionic conductivity of molten salts [5,6]. Detailed cell design was provided for similar fluoride mixtures in the literature [5]. A simplified version of it was built for the EIS tests.

For an accurate ionic conductivity measurement, electrolyte samples should have a significantly higher resistance in comparison to the cell resistance; this cell design can eliminate the error in measurement introduced by the resistance of the cell. A boron-silicate glass capillary tube (inner diameter 0.5 mm, length 6.0 cm), which is resistant to the corrosive nature of the electrolyte mixtures, was packed with the sample powder. A small rubber rod that could tightly fit inside the glass tube was used to pack the powder material. The lower electrode was used as a stand to stabilize the glass samples. The powdered sample was added to the tube and packed until the length of the sample inside the tube reach about 5.5 cm. Once the sample powder form melted down, the void spaces in the sample tube is eliminated since the air trapped in the void spaces can escape the sample tube. The upper electrode could freely move to keep the electrical contact despite the change in length of the electrolyte material inside the tube (see Figure 2). The length of the sample was measured after the experiment by a ruler, as the basis for resistivity calculations. Electrodes were made from Inconel. This nickel-based alloy could handle the temperature of the test while not reacting with the molten mixture. The tests should be run at temperatures above the melting point of the electrolyte. Figure 2 shows a schematic of the EIS test cell next to a picture of the cell inside the glovebox. The test apparatus was designed to fit inside the furnace in order to achieve different temperatures. The accurate temperature of the cell could be measured by a thermostat that was inserted into the furnace. Enough time was given between each step to ensure the temperature of the sample inside the sample tube was stabilized. The EIS test was conducted several times at each temperature to verify that the recorded values were stable, then the temperature of the furnace was increased by 5 to 10 °C and monitored by the digital thermostat. Once at least 10 minutes had passed, the EIS tests were initiated and the data were averaged to calculate the resistivity.

This EIS test can only measure the resistance of the electrolyte sample. The resistivity was calculated based on Pouillet's law, Equation (1). The conductivity of the mixtures was then achieved by dividing 1 by the resistivity.

$$R=(\rho . l)/A \quad (1)$$

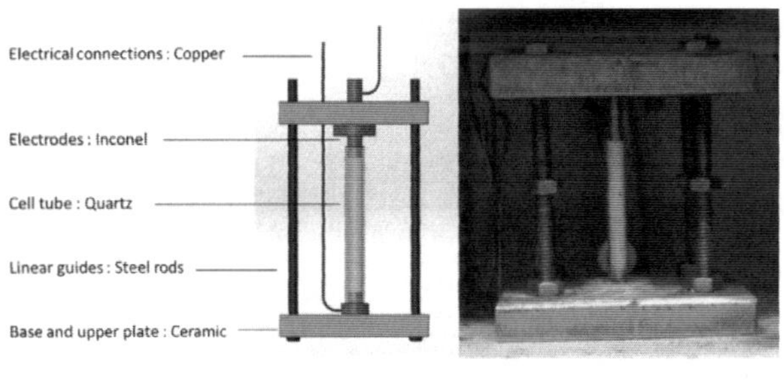

(a) (b)

Figure 2. (a) 3D model of the EIS fixture; (b) EIS test rig

A Gamry instrument was used to run the EIS test. Low resistance cables (procured from Gamry) connected the copper electrical contacts inside the glove-box to the Gamry instrument outside the glove-box. This setup made it possible to keep the processes of preparing the samples and testing them inside the glove-box while having the analytical tools operate outside. The EIS test conducted from 10^6 Hz to 1 Hz at 10mV AC voltage.

Thermal stability

From each batch of Li-salt/KF-HF mixtures, a small amount was reserved for thermal stability studies. Solid mixtures were pulverized to a very fine powder by mortar and pestle and well mixed to guarantee a homogenous distribution of materials in each sample. Differential scan calorimetry (DSC) was utilized to study the thermal stability of the tested materials. Hermetically sealed DSC pans (Perkin-Elmer Autosampler Sample Pans, Capacity: 50μL) were loaded with electrolyte samples inside the glove box to prevent any contact with air and moisture. DSC sample pans were weighed before and after the loading to record the exact sample size necessary to calculate the thermal capacity. Sample sizes were kept between 3 and 5 mg to prevent leakage and reactions with air because of thermal expansion at testing temperatures. DSC pans were hermetically sealed using a crimper press (PerkinElmer model# 139005 Universal Crimper) before removing them from the glovebox. All tests were conducted using PerkinElmer Pyris 1 DSC device. Samples were tested by scanning the temperature from room temperature (around 25 °C) to 400 °C at 10 °C/min scan rate. Heat flow vs temperature and derivative heat flow vs temperature diagrams were studied to determine the melting point, transition temperature and thermal decomposition of each electrolyte sample [7,8].

Results and Discussion

Ionic conductivity

LiF/KF-HF mixture with 40 wt.% LiF showed the highest ionic conductivity among different LiF mixtures with KF-HF. (see Table 2) Both LiCl and Li_2SO_4 mixtures with Kf-HF showed no benefit in terms of increase in ionic conductivity over pure KF-HF. Tables 3 and 4 showed the ionic conductivity of some of the LiCl/KF-HF and Li_2SO_4/KF-HF mixtures respectively.

Table 3. Ionic conductivity results for LiCl mixtures with KF-HF

LiCl wt. %	0	3	5	7
KF-HF wt. %	100	97	95	93
Ionic Conductivity (S/cm)	0.192 ±0.019	0.154 ±0.008	0.114 ±0.010	0.042 ±0.006

Table 4. Ionic conductivity results for Li_2SO_4 mixtures with KF-HF

Li_2SO_4 wt. %	0	3	5	7	10
KF-HF wt. %	100	97	95	93	90
Ionic Conductivity (S/cm)	0.192 ±0.019	0.137 ±0.010	0.081 ±0.002	0.075 ±0.003	0.030 ±0.004

Thermal stability

By increasing the weight percentage of LiF, decomposition temperature increased. Melting point results showed a eutectic point between 35 – 40 wt.% LiF (Table 5)

Increase in the weight percentage of LiCl increased the thermal decomposition temperature. The mixture has a eutectic point between 3 – 5 wt.% LiCl (Table 6)

Table 6. The melting point and thermal decomposition temperature of LiCl/KF-HF mixtures

LiCl wt. %	3	5	7	10	20	30
KF-HF wt. %	97	95	93	90	80	70
Melting Point °C	229.2 ±2.1	229.4 ±0.9	230.3 ±3.3	252.8 ±2.8	258.3 ±1.9	257.6 ±3.3
Decomposition Temperature °C	282.8 ±2.2	283.5	287.9 ±4.0	294.4	296.9	298.2 ±2.1

Table 2. Ionic conductivity results for LiF mixtures with KF-HF

LiF wt. %	0	5	10	15	20	25	30	35	40	50	60
KF-HF wt. %	100	95	90	85	80	75	70	65	60	50	40
Average Conductivity (S/cm)	0.192 ±0.019	0.121 ±0.008	0.165 ±0.010	0.221 ±0.025	0.174 ±0.011	0.197 ±0.024	0.240 ±0.009	0.220 ±0.030	0.260 ±0.031	0.084 ±0.008	0.040 ±0.004

Table 5. The melting point and thermal decomposition temperature of LiF/KF-HF mixture

LiF wt. %	0	10	15	20	25	30	35	40	50	60	70
KF-HF wt. %	100	90	85	80	75	60	65	60	50	40	30
Melting Point °C	238.5	232.2 ±4.0	230.6 ±3.0	228.1 ±1.8	229.2 ±1.1	229.4 ±2.5	228.4 ±2.8	228.9 ±3.7	231.3 ±3.8	234.1 ±3.8	235.7 ±5.2
Decomposition Temperature °C	276.7	279.2	285.8	291.3 ±5.6	296.4 ±1.9	295.4 ±7.5	295.1 ±2.0	294.3 ±3.5	300.9	303.6 ±4.7	307.9 ±6.2

Conclusions

The EIS test results prove that the conductivity of the electrolyte mixture can be increased significantly by an optimization of the salt/solvent mixture and that operating temperatures lower than 550 °C can be achieved. Further optimization is required to achieve similar conductivity compare to the standard electrolyte (1.56 S/cm) at 550 °C with the newly proposed mixtures but at much lower temperatures ~250-260 °C.

Acknowledgement

This work was partially funded by the Center for Electrochemical Processes and Technology (CEProTECH), a National Science Foundation Industry–University Cooperative Research Centers (IUCRC) program, award #IIP-1362075, U.S. Army AMRDEC Missile Science & Technology Program and Center for Electrochemical Engineering Research (CEER) at Ohio University.

References

[1] R.A. Guidotti, P. Masset, Thermally activated ("thermal") battery technology, J. Power Sources. 161 (2006) 1443–1449. doi:10.1016/j.jpowsour.2006.06.013.

[2] P. Masset, R.A. Guidotti, Thermal activated (thermal) battery technology, J. Power Sources. 164 (2007) 397–414. doi:10.1016/j.jpowsour.2006.10.080.

[3] P.B. Davis, C.S. Winchester, Limiting factors to advancing thermal battery technology for naval applications, NAVAL SURFACE WARFARE CENTER SILVER SPRING MD, 1991. http://www.dtic.mil/docs/citations/ADA247773 (accessed July 27, 2017).

[4] R.J. Ring, D. Royston, Australian Atomic Energy Commission, Research Establishment, A review of fluorine cells and fluorine production facilities, Australian Atomic Energy Commission, Research Establishment, Lucas Heights [N.S.W., 1973.

[5] E.W. Yim, M. Feinleib, Electrical Conductivity of Molten Fluorides I . Apparatus and Method, J. Electrochem. Soc. 104 (1957) 622–626. doi:10.1149/1.2428429.

[6] E.W. Yim, M. Feinleib, Electrical Condu Molten Fluorides II . Conductance of All Cryolites, and Cryolite -Base Melts, J. Soc. 104 (1957) 626–630. doi:10.1149/1

[7] G.H. Cady, Freezing Points and Vapor Pressures of the System Potassium Fluoride—Hydrogen Fluoride1, J. Am. Chem. Soc. 56 (1934) 1431–1434. doi:10.1021/ja01322a001.

[8] R.M. Bozorth, THE CRYSTAL STRUCTURE OF POTASSIUM HYDROGEN FLUORIDE, J. Am. Chem. Soc. 45 (1923) 2128–2132. doi:10.1021/ja01662a013.

Carbon Monofluoride Based High Voltage Thermal Battery Cathode

Brian Perdue, Chris Apblett, Linda Johnson, Eric Allcorn, Jonathan Leonard
Power Sources Technology Group, Sandia National Laboratories
P.O. Box 5800 MS 0613 Albuquerque, NM 87185
brperdu@sandia.gov / 1-505-845-8523

Abstract: *Current thermal batteries mainly utilize iron disulfide (FeS_2) as the cathode. Paired with a lithium/silicon anode, the voltage for these cells is only 1.94 V (slightly less in current systems) at 500 °C. Additionally, the FeS_2 systems suffer from low capacity, chemical instability over time and at temperature, have safety risks associated with thermal runaway. This translates into lower total run times, higher battery volumes, and increased aging risk.*

To overcome the deficiencies in these cathodes, we propose to develop a new thermal battery cathode based on lithium carbon monofluoride (Li-CF_x) chemistry that is safer, higher in capacity, and possesses higher voltage than the thermal battery cathodes used presently. Li-CF_x chemistries have been demonstrated previously with high capacity and high voltage in other, non-thermal battery architectures. By modifying the electrode processing of CF_x to make it compatible with thermal battery technology, we expect to develop a replacement for current thermal battery cathodes. The Li-CF_x thermal battery system should provide >2.7 V, 30% higher than existing chemistries (potentially higher if reaction mechanisms are different at thermal battery temperatures) and over 800 mAh/g (> 2x improvement from current chemistries). Results show that a CF_x thermal battery cathode can support a current load of 50 mA/cm^2, however cathode pelletization and cathode gas generation challenges remain.

Keywords: Molten Salt Batteries, Carbon Monofloride batteries

Introduction

Recent reports have warned of the inadequacy of the FeS_2 /LiSi electrochemical couple to provide continued support for the thermal battery systems. By utilizing an alternative cathode chemistry that has a proven record for lithium ambient battery systems, we can greatly increase the energy output of the current thermal battery technology with minimal changes to size, processing, and form factor.

CF_x must be synthesized by chemically reacting carbon and fluorine at elevated temperatures. This route offers a unique opportunity to control the cathode composition for different applications. Carbon monofluoride comprises a spectrum of compositions from below a 1:1 ratio of carbon to fluorine up to very high fluorine contents. While CF_x has been studied for use in Li-ion primary systems, performance of these materials at elevated temperature (up to 600°C), high rate (up to 3.5A/cm2), and in the presence of a highly corrosive molten salts has not been investigated.

The CF_x battery system is at present used in roughly 10% of all currently deployed power systems, including the widely utilized BA-5590 Department of Defense power system. Because the CF_x defluorination occurs at roughly 3.0V vs. Li at room temperature, the voltage per cell has the potential to increase from the present ~1.9V to ~3.2V per cell. CFx also has an energy density of ~800 mAh/g in Li primary systems, which compares favorably to 360 mAh/g (to first discharge plateau) for FeS_2. The net effect of this system is a substantial increase in overall energy output from our current thermal batteries.

The Li-CF_x system shows a moderate voltage between 2.7V and 3.2V depending on the discharge current at ambient temperatures as well as fluorination ratio. But the theoretical voltage of the lithium fluorine reaction should give close to 4.7 V open circuit voltage. To account for the depression in cell voltage, formation of a three membered ring (between carbon, lithium and fluorine) as an intermediate has been proposed. However, there is no information available on the mechanism of discharge reaction at high temperatures. If elevated temperature and the increased kinetics of the molten salt environment result in bypassing this intermediate compound, the cell voltage should be higher than 3.2 V.

While the CF_x system has traditionally been processed using either thin-film or slurry based cathodes, there is indication that this material would be amenable to processing in traditional pressed pellets formats (assuming similar binders and additives to current thermal batteries). Since the supporting structure is carbon, it may not require backing or substrate current collector material, making the battery more efficient. The low mechanical strength of the carbon fluoride together with the low mechanical strength of the binding LiCl/KCl electrolyte salt should provide the ability to press pellets of these materials and have them cohere.

This work aims to prove the feasibility of a CF_x cathode in a thermal battery. A few of the questions that will be addressed is the thermal stability of the CF_x, and the chemical stability of CF_x against a highly corrosive metal salt. We already possess the methods to evaluate electrochemical and thermal stability for FeS_2 by means of thermal battery single cell testing and thermogravimetic analysis, and we will apply these methods to the CF_x pellets to determine their durability and performance as a function of temperature and salt content. While potential side reactions and pitfalls do exist, the potential for a drop in replacement with almost two times the available gravimetric energy represents an excellent opportunity to advance the state of the art for these important power sources.

Experimental

Standard powder processing techniques were used for this work. The anode pellets used in this study were the standard

Li-Si alloy anode formulation with 44wt% Li in Si. These powders were dried, blended and pelletized on a variable tonnage hydraulic press with a pellet die to a diameter of 0.74 inches.

In this study three different molten salt eutectics were investigated. The first was the standard LiCl:KCl (ClLiK) prepared by mixing 44 wt% LiCl and 56 wt% KCl. The second electrolyte investigated in this study was the low melting LiCl:LiBr:KBr (low melt LM) prepared by mixing 12.05 wt% LiCl and 36.54 wt% LiBr and 51.41wt% KBr. The final eutectic investigated was LiF:NaF:KF or FLiNaK eutectic. prepared by mixing LiF/NaF/KF in a ratio 29.2 wt% LiF, 11.7 wt% NaF and 59.1 wt% KF.

Separator pellets consisted of a mixture of 65 wt% binder material and 35 wt% percent of the molten salt eutectic. Three different separator pellets were mixed and pelletized in this study. The first separator pellet was the standard separator pellet consisting of a MgO binder and the ClLiK eutectic. The final two separator pellets consisted of the FLiNaK eutectic and either Li_2O or Al_2O_3 binder material. All separator pellet mixes were then pelletized on a variable tonnage hydraulic press with a pellet die to a diameter of 0.75 inches.

Cathode pellet mixtures consisted of a of ratio of 75 wt% active material, 10 wt% binder material and 15 wt% eutectic. Similar to the separator pellets three cathode pellet formulations were generated. The first consisted of $CF_{0.96}$ as the active material mixed with the MgO binder and ClLiK eutectic in the proper ratios. The two cathode pellet mixture formulations consisted of CF1.01 active material FLiNaK eutectic and either Li_2O or Al_2O_3 binder material mixed in the proper ratios. All cathode pellet mixes were then pelletized on a variable tonnage hydraulic press with a pellet die to a diameter of 0.74 inches.

Once the anode separator and cathode pellets were pressed, they were assembled into thermal battery single cells and tested. This was accomplished by sandwiching an anode, separator, and cathode pellet stack between two stainless steel current collectors and mica sheets for structure. Once assembled, the single cell was tested in the thermal battery single cell tester by placing the cell between two heating elements equipped with temperature controllers and subjected to a compressive 9.6 kg load. Electrochemical measurements were collected with a Maccor battery tester.

Thermogravimetric analysis (TGA) was carried out using a TA Instruments Discovery TGA with Discovery MS quadrupole mass spectrometer attachment. Samples of ~1mg were loaded onto platinum pans and heated to 600 °C under flowing argon at a heating rate of 10 °C/min. Real time mass spectrometry data was captured for evolved gases during this heating step and the sample was subsequently cooled to room temperature at 50 °C/min.

Results and Discussion

In order to test the feasibility of the CF_x chemistry in a thermal battery environment, the cathode was first tested using the established material set currently used by the FeS_2 chemistry. This cell consisted of a LiSi composite anode, a separator containing an MgO binder with ClLiK eutectic electrolyte and a cathode containing $CF_{0.96}$ with MgO binder with ClLiK eutectic electrolyte. Empirical evidence from pressing cathode pellets shows very different behavior in the pelletization of CF_x containing and FeS_2 containing cathode pellet mixtures. Cathode pellet mixtures with FeS_2 behaves intuitively, with pellet density increasing with increased press tonnage, to the point at which maximum achievable density is obtained. In contrast, cathode pellet mixtures with CF_x has a much narrower functional range of press tonnage: increasing pressure does not result in more effective packing of material in the pellet due to flowing and breakage; too little pressure results in no formation of a pellet at all. Pellet density between the minimum (2 tons) and maximum (30 tonnage) tonnage was less than 10%. This is drastically different than the FeS_2 pellet mixtures. These challenges are exacerbated by the chemical nature of highly fluorinated CF_x which is mechanically similar to Teflon. Because of the lubricity of the $CF_{1.01}$ material, pelletization was difficult to achieve. The key challenge for this chemistry is that for it to be successful the pelletization of a lubricant must be achieved. For electrochemical testing a low level of fluorination was chosen $CF_x<1$ to decrease the lubricity of the active material and increase chances of pelletization. The consequence of this choice is that the voltage of these cells will not be as high as possible, however they would still demonstrate a substantial increase in voltage over the current FeS_2 chemistry. It is also worth noting that the ClLiK eutectic electrolyte is not the ideal electrolyte for CF_x as chlorine has the potential to cause parasitic side reactions. Cells with the were subjected to different current densities ranging from 0.05 mA/cm^2 to 25 mA/cm^2 at temperatures ranging from 375°C to 450 °C. Results are shown below in Figure 1

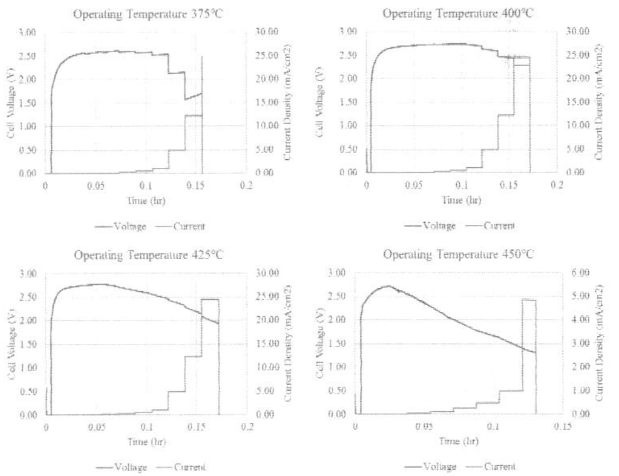

Figure 1: Current pulse testing of $CF_{0.96}$ single cell thermal batteries

The data in Figure 1, confirms that the CF_x chemistry is compatible in a molten salt thermal battery environment. When the temperature was increased to 475 °C a sharp spike to 2.7 V was observed followed by a sharp decline in voltage to 0.5 V. The cell was removed from the single cell tester and a black ring was observed around the current collector. The black ring is consistent with electrode material ejected out of the cell stack from gas generated from unwanted side reactions. This phenomenon is also consistent with the voltage profile observed. Gas generated from an unwanted side reaction broke the cathode pellet apart and ejected it away from the current collectors causing a loss in voltage.

When examining the data in Figure 1 the choice was made to perform further electrochemical testing at either 375 °C or 400 °C because these temperatures experienced the least voltage decay while executing the current pulses. Two experiments were conducted to determine if the CF_x formulation was able to support a 10-minute current draw. These tests consisted of a voltage equilibration step where no current was applied, a 10-minute current draw at 25 mA/cm^2 followed by a current pulse at 0.5 mA/cm^2 to extra capacity. In these tests the voltage equilibration time was longer for 375 °C than it was for 400 °C because 375 °C is very close to the eutectic melting temperature and needed more time for the electrolyte to effectively melt and wet the active material

These experiments demonstrated higher performance than anticipated. Typically, when a CF_x cathode is exposed to current densities above 0.05 mA/cm^2 over a volt of polarization is observed. The data in Figure 2 shows that we are orders of magnitude higher in current density and observe significantly less polarization confirming that increasing the operating temperature of CF_x increases its rate capability. For the final demonstration, a test was designed to simulate a discharge at relevant levels. Results for this demonstration can be found in Figure 2.

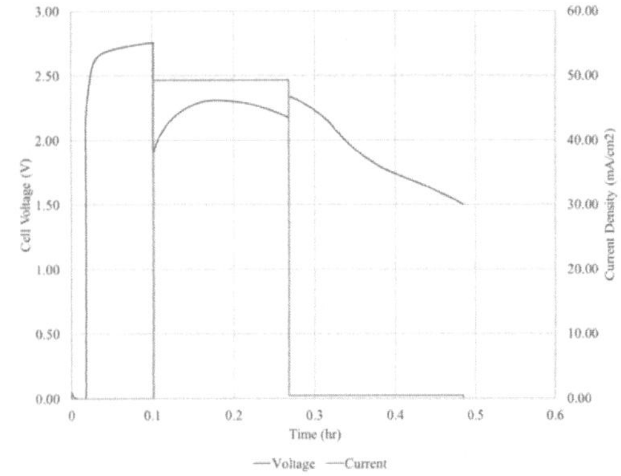

Figure 2: Discharge profile against CF_x MgO Binder LiCl:KCl Eutectic at 400 °C

The results in Figure 2 show that CF_x can support 50 mA/cm^2. It is worth noting that when the CF_x cell is supporting current it still exhibits a higher voltage than that of FeS_2. Additional testing also shows increased thermal stability (flat open circuit voltage) and voltage (cell voltage above 1.8 V) over current FeS_2 chemistry.

The electrochemical testing also allowed for insight on the role the fluorination level in CF_x plays in the observed voltage. When examining Figure 1,and 2, it its noted that a fluorination level of 0.96 results in a maximum observed voltage of 2.8V vs LiSi. When comparing the thermal battery voltage to the commonly achieved 3.4 V at room temperature a difference of 600 mV is observed. This is attributed to two major factors, the first is the lower fluorination ratio results in a lower voltage and the second is that thermal batteries reference a LiSi composite anode which is typically ~200 mV more positive than the Li potential. When switching to the 1.01 fluorination ratio and testing at 525 °C a voltage of approximately 3.2 V is observed before the pellet is broken apart by gas generation. The value of 3.2 V is consistent with the observed 3.4 V at room temperature when correcting for the 0.2 V shift between electrodes. This implies that increasing the fluorination ratio can raise the voltage. It is possible that a highly fluorinated cathode could poses a very high voltage (up to 4.5 V vs LiSi). This also suggests that at 525 °C we do not eliminate the proposed three membered ring an intermediate. Projecting a thermal battery build from this data assuming 3.2 V per cell and a pellet height of 0.019 inches, would reduce stack height by ~50% and would translate to a 28% reduction in full battery height.

When performing the original electrochemical performance evaluation, gas evolution was observed. This observation caused a change in focus, because a chemistry that generates gas in a hermetically sealed thermal battery will exclude its use. To do this TGA was performed on the available cathode powders. This was primarily done to to identify the gases generated by the side reactions. Two cathode pellet formulations were initially investigated, 75% wt $CF_{0.96}$ 15% wt ClLiK eutectic electrolyte and 10%wt MgO and a similar formulation with a LM eutectic electrolyte replacing the ClLiK eutectic electrolyte. TGA results of these two cathode powder formulations are shown in Figure 3.

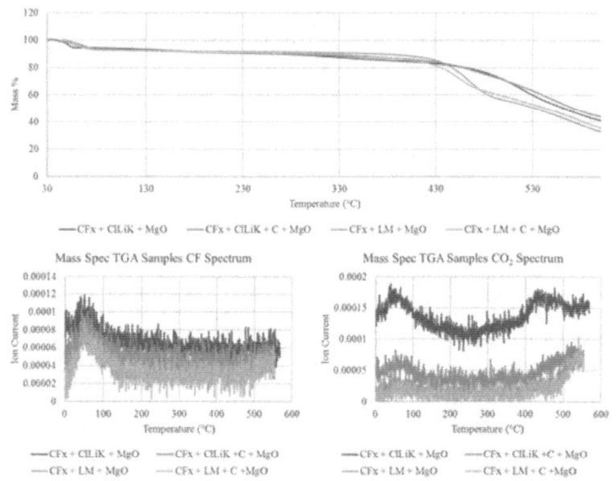

Figure 3: TGA analysis of initial cathode pellet formulations

Figure 3 shows that 5-10% of the total powder mass is converted to CF gas at around 80 °C and a large portion of the mass is converted to CO_2 at 475 °C. TGA is consistent with the observations made during the single cell thermal battery test leading to the ejection of electrode material observed. Based on these results, it was determined that the MgO binder in junction with Cl containing electrolytes are not stable with a CF_x cathode at elevated temperature.

Mixtures of CFx and potential binder systems were made and tested with TGA to measure their thermal stability and potential for gas generation. For these experiments $CF_{1.01}$ was used since increasing the fluorination level increases the overall stability of the compound. 50/50 wt% mixtures of

$CF_{1.01}$ and MgO, Li_2O, Al_2O_3, boron nitride (BN), boron carbide (BC) as well as LiF:KF were blended and analyzed. The results confirm that increasing the fluorination level in CF_x increases its thermal stability as it does not decompose at high temperatures. It is also worth mentioning that increasing the fluorination level will also increase its operational voltage. Despite these advantages $CF_{1.01}$ still off-gases harmful fluorene containing gasses. BN and BC are suitable binder candidates from a gas generation standpoint however their conductivity increases to unacceptable levels above 400 °C which eliminates them as candidates for potential binders. Moving forward the potential remaining two binder candidates are Li_2O, Al_2O_3.

Two final cathode pellet mixes were generated with the formulation 75 wt% $CF_{1.01}$ 15 wt% FLiNaK eutectic electrolyte and 10 wt% either Li_2O, Al_2O_3. These mixtures were tested and their results are shown in Figure 4.

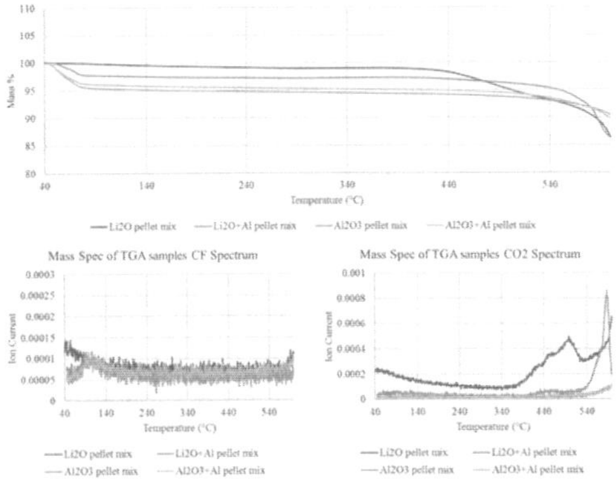

Figure 4: TGA of $CF_{1.01}$ Cathode Pellet Mixes

Li_2O when mixed with CF_x and a eutectic electrolyte will generate CO_2 at elevated temperatures thus eliminating it as a potential binder. Based on all the evidence collected from Based on the data collected from TGA, the recommended composition for a CF_x molten salt battery cathode is 75 wt% CF1.01 15 wt% FLiNaK eutectic electrolyte and 10 wt% Al_2O_3 for the cathode formulation in junction with a of 65 wt% Al_2O_3 and 35 wt% FLiNaK eutectic electrolyte separator pellet.

One of the major setbacks for this chemistry is that generates gas when heated. This setback could potentially exclude it from being used as a thermal battery material. When examining the TGA results it is apparent that generation of CO_2 is a major issue. When examining the inorganic literature, it is observed that $C + 2MgO \rightarrow CO_2 + 2Mg$. This usually happens at higher temperatures, however in a thermal battery pellet there are two very high surface area materials in contact which reduces the temperature at which this reaction can occur. This reaction is consistent with the observed results in Figure 3. The consequence of this is that MgO cannot be used as a separator material for CF_x. This also implies that a new binder must be found and optimized. This work only examined a small percentage of potential binder materials. Al_2O_3 is the current binder of choice as it eliminates CO_2 generation below 525 °C, however there is a large possibility that a better binder exists.

The other major setback for this chemistry is that it evolves F containing gas. This issue causes considerable safety concerns. The threshold limit value (TLV) for F_2 gas is $1.6 mg/m^3$. According to the TGA data 10% of the pellet mixture is converted to fluorene containing gas. That is to say the average pellet of mass 0.2 g will release 20 mg of F containing gas which is an order of magnitude above the TLV. This only gets worse considering that thermal batteries can contain many cells and if a battery ruptures there is potential for a large exposure. The TGA in Figures 3 and 4 suggest that baking the cathode pellet powder at 150 °C can remove the F containing gasses potentially eliminating the hazard for a battery, however the effects on performance after such a treatment is unknown.

Conclusion

This work demonstrates that the CF_x chemistry is a viable path forward to higher energy dense thermal batteries and represents the first potential advancement in thermal batteries in the last decade. The key results from this study show that CF_x was successfully mixed and pelletized with relevant ratios for drop in replacement for the FeS_2 chemistry. Electrochemical testing of CF_x shows that it can $50 mA/cm^2$. Further electrochemical testing of this system shows increased thermal stability and voltage over current FeS_2 chemistry. Projecting a thermal battery estimates a stack height reduction of 0.44" which is almost 50% and would translate to a 28% reduction in full battery height.

Despite these successes this chemistry suffers from a few key challenges. The first are the chemical incompatibilities that lead to gas generation. The CO_2 gas byproduct in junction with the fluorene gas by product can both disrupt cell continuity (loss of voltage or short) as well as create a rupture hazard in a full battery. These issues can be mitigated by baking the cathode pellet powder mixture to remove the fluorene gas hazard and switching the binder system to Al_2O_3 to minimize CO_2 production. The other key challenge is pelletizing a lubricant. As the fluorene content in CF_x rises it becomes more Teflon like which makes pelletization difficult. An in depth pelletization study of this issue would mitigate this problem.

Acknowledgement

This work was funded by the SNL exploratory express lab directed research and development program

Sandia National Laboratories is a multimission laboratory managed and operated by National Technology and Engineering Solutions of Sandia LLC, a wholly owned subsidiary of Honeywell International Inc. for the U.S. Department of Energy's National Nuclear Security Administration under contract DE-NA0003525.

Observations of Thermal Behavior in a Center-Fired Battery After a Missed Heat Pellet Ignition

Edward S. Piekos and Hans W. Papenguth
Sandia National Laboratories
P.O. Box 5800
Albuquerque, NM, USA 87185
espieko@sandia.gov / 505-845-7136

Abstract: *Center-fired thermal batteries, unlike their side-fired counterparts, lack a continuous path to sequentially ignite their pyrotechnic materials. The ignition process therefore depends on the flow of heated gases and particles down the center hole, which is sensitive to igniter properties as well as center hole geometry. Changes in these factors due to manufacturing variance, aging, or mechanical displacement raise the possibility of one or more heat pellets being missed by the initial ignition process. In this work, simulations are performed to examine the consequences of such an event. Its effect on the evolution of temperature at startup, as well as the timing of missed-pellet auto-ignition, are examined as a function of missed heat pellet position and number. Simulation results are also compared to measurements on a battery that displayed anomalous behavior and a good agreement is demonstrated.*

Keywords: thermal battery; simulation; center-fired; ignition; auto-ignition; auto-activation.

Introduction

Activation of a side-fired thermal battery typically follows a predictable process because the heat pellet ignition sequence is established by redundant heat paper strips that create a continuous fuse train. In contrast, a center-fired battery, when configured without heat paper in the center hole, has a less direct ignition process that depends on gas-phase and ballistic transport of energy down the center hole. The risk inherent to this arrangement is that one or more pellets will be missed by this energy flow and fail to ignite.

The flow of energy down the center hole is affected strongly by the hole geometry. Previous work [1], for example, has shown that this transport can be disrupted by stack misalignment. Even in a perfectly aligned battery, the hole is not typically cylindrical because different pellet types are often designed with differing center hole sizes. These features are intended to minimize damage due to the igniter while maximizing the probability of all heat pellets igniting.

This work explores the consequences of a missed heat pellet in terms of the subsequent temperature distribution, and therefore activation, of a thermal battery. The study was initiated in response to anomalous behavior observed in a constant-resistance test, the result of which is shown in Fig. 1. The anomalous battery showed a much-delayed rise time, as well as a lowered current. The rise time delay is consistent with a cold cell due to a missed heat pellet, which would prevent the entire battery from supporting a load because the cells are connected in series. In such a scenario, given sufficient heat from adjacent cells or auto-ignition of the missed heat pellet, the remaining separator eventually melts, allowing the battery to supply current.

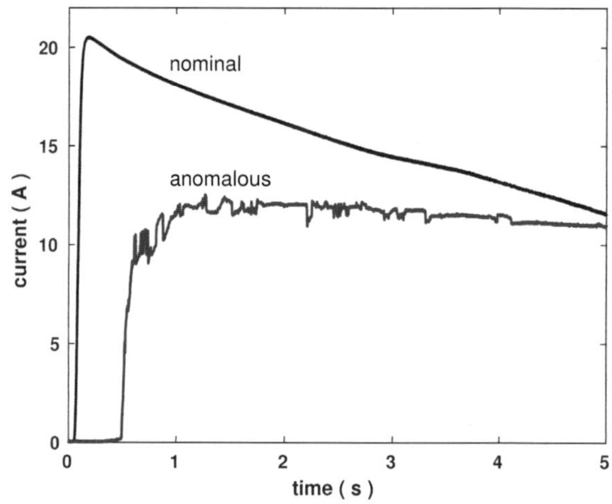

Figure 1. Measured current through a fixed resistance for nominal and anomalous batteries.

Methodology

The model was constructed using the Sandia Thermally Activated Battery Simulator, Full Battery (TABS-FB), version 5 [2]. Because TABS-FB allows only uniform outer and inner diameters among all pellets, the geometry was then manually modified in the Sandia Cubit [3] mesh generation toolkit to include the varying inner diameters of different pellet types to more accurately represent the center hole. The resulting geometry is shown in Fig. 2.

In the subject battery, the inner diameter of the collectors was intentionally made smaller to protect the adjacent heat pellets (red) and separator pellets (yellow) from damage by the igniter blast. The igniter (not shown) would be positioned at the top of the center hole in Fig. 2.

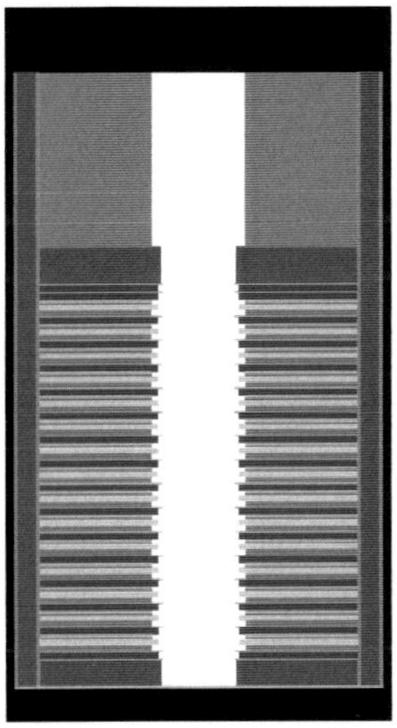

Figure 2. Battery geometry used in the simulations.

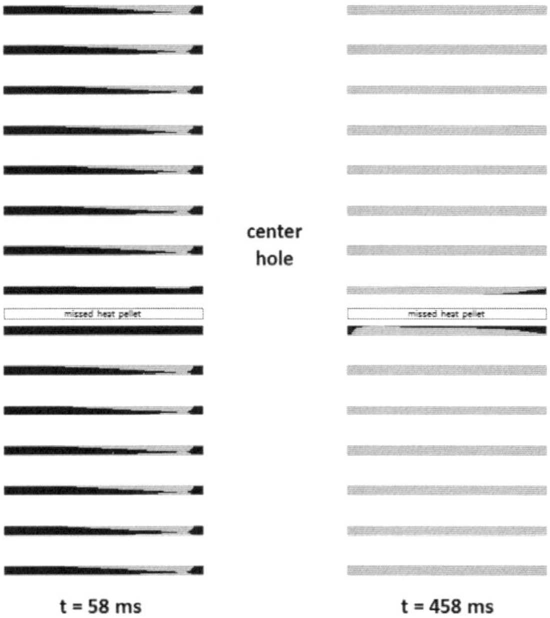

Figure 3. Separators at two different times from a simulation in which a heat pellet near the middle of the stack (outlined) does not ignite with the others at t=0. Frozen areas of the separator are shown in blue and melted areas are shown in orange.

The geometry shown in Fig. 2 was discretized with 376,969 quadrilateral elements. The simulation was performed with the Aria module [4] in the Sierra multiphysics simulation suite [5], solving the conservation of energy equation. Material properties were drawn from the TABS database. The heat pellet burn rate was set to 12.5 cm/s [6] but the results shown are relatively insensitive to this value. The separator consists of a mixture of LiCl-KCl eutectic electrolyte and magnesium oxide binder. An idealized electrolyte melting temperature of 352°C was used. All external boundaries were perfectly insulating, although at the short times considered here, the boundary conditions are expected to have little effect. The center hole was filled with air and initialized at 200°C to account for heat contributed by the igniter [7].

Because the simulations did not include electrochemistry, the voltage rise time could not be computed directly. As a surrogate, the rise time was defined as the the time at which all separators first provide a continuous path of molten electrolyte across their thickness. This is expected to be a reasonable approximation for when the battery would begin to provide a significant current through the constant resistive load applied in the test.

Results

Separators from a simulation in which a heat pellet near the middle of the stack fails to ignite are shown in Fig. 3. The left side of the figure shows the simulation at 58 ms, when the separators away from the missed heat pellet attain a melted path through their thickness. Because these separators are unaffected by the missed pellet, this would be the rise time of a normally functioning battery. This rise time agrees well with the approximately 55 ms measured for the nominal case shown in Fig. 1. The right side of Fig. 3 shows the separators at 458 ms, when the last separator (near the missed heat pellet) attains a melted path through its thickness. This value compares well with the anomalous rise time shown in Fig. 1 at approximately 492 ms.

The simulations of Fig. 3 assume a heat pellet auto-ignition temperature of 420°C. There is a wide range of reported values for this temperature [8, 9] so it has a large uncertainty. To examine its effect, Fig. 4 presents rise time and auto-ignition time as a function of auto-ignition temperature. Rise time is insensitive to auto-ignition temperature because the separator in the coldest cell is closer to a functioning heat pellet than the missed heat pellet is. Its electrolyte will therefore melt before auto-ignition occurs, even if the auto-ignition temperature is set as low as the separator melting temperature. Conversely, the auto-ignition time is very sensitive to auto-ignition temperature because more heat must diffuse through adjacent cells to reach a higher temperature, which is a relatively slow process.

To assess the sensitivity of these results to the position of the missed heat pellet, simulations were performed with each heat pellet in the stack missed in turn. The results, shown in Fig. 5, suggest that the rise time is insensitive to which heat pellet is missed, except for those very near the ends.

For the two closely spaced heat pellets at the top of the battery, missing one of them makes no difference because the missed pellet will almost immediately be ignited by its neighbor. In contrast, missing the bottom-most heat pellet

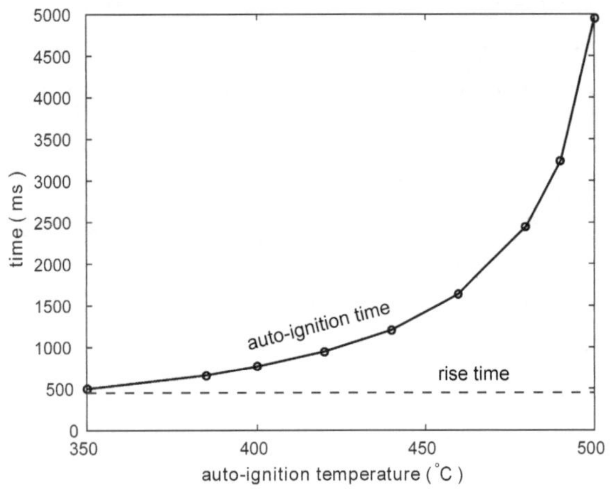

Figure 4. Auto-ignition time and rise time as a function of auto-ignition temperature.

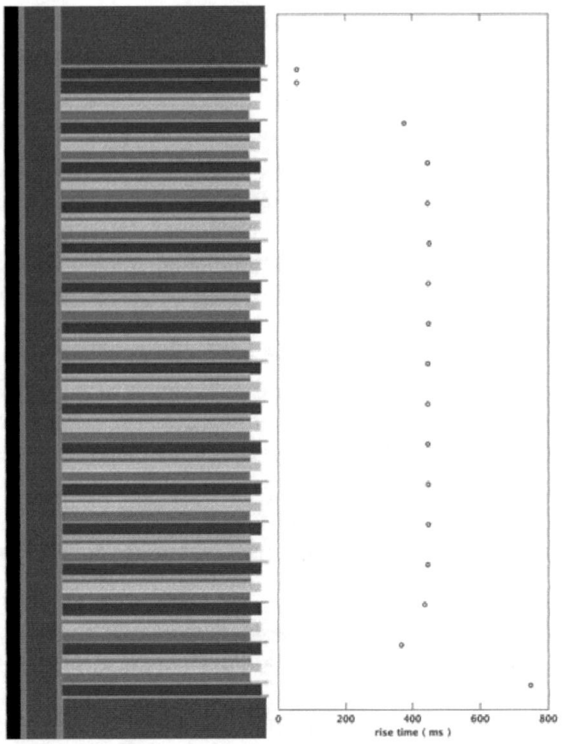

Figure 5. Rise time as a function of the vertical position of the missed heat pellet. The battery geometry is shown at left for reference with the heat pellets colored red.

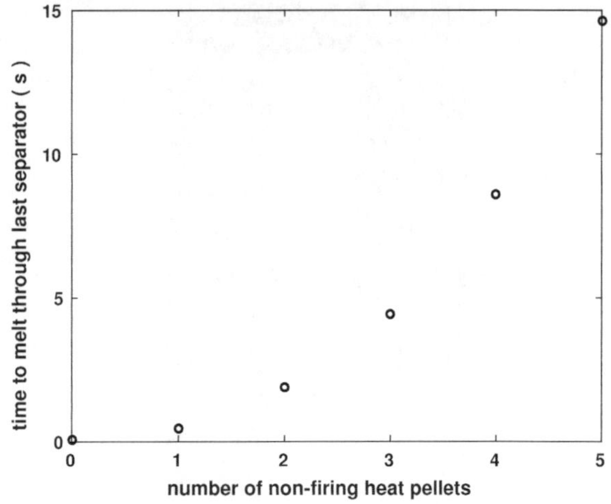

Figure 6. Rise time as a function of the number of missed heat pellets.

almost doubles the rise time because the separator above it then receives heat from only one side. Of the 17 heat pellets present in the subject battery, only one would therefore be expected to produce a rise time significantly worse than that observed in the anomalous case if it did not ignite at startup.

To determine the effect of multiple heat pellets being missed by the igniter, simulations were performed with an increasing number of adjacent missed pellets near the middle of the stack. Adjacent pellets were judged to be "worst case" because the separators between them would be furthest from a functioning heat source. The results of these calculations are shown in Fig. 6. The simulations predict a rise time of almost two seconds for a second missed heat pellet. Because the rise time in the anomalous battery is closer to half a second, it is unlikely that a second pellet was missed.

In addition to a late rise time, a missed heat pellet can induce excessive local temperatures when it finally burns. As shown in Fig. 7 for the nearest cathode, by the time the heat pellet auto-ignites, the battery has warmed far above a typical environmental temperature. In the studied case, in fact, the electrolyte has already melted. The heat input from the late-firing pellet therefore drives the surrounding materials to temperatures much higher than intended by the battery designer, which can induce melting or thermal decomposition and possibly lead to thermal runaway.

Conclusions

This work has shown that even a purely thermal simulation can provide significant insight into battery rise time behavior. In particular, simulations proved to be instrumental for determining the cause of an anomalous battery test. Within a simulation, a wide range of scenarios can be explored in a short time and at little cost. This investigation has shown that a problematic battery is very likely to support

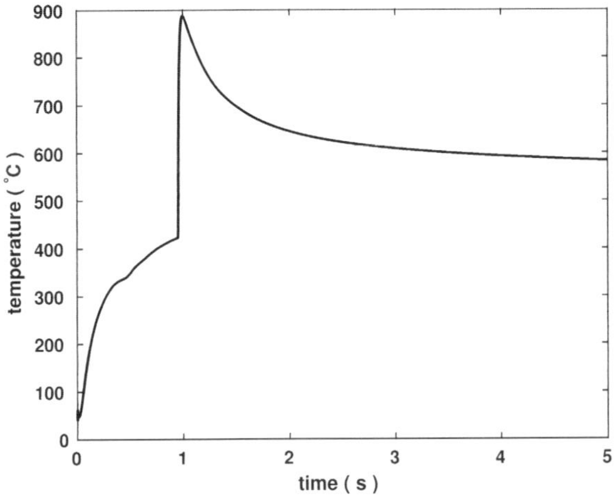

Figure 7. Temperature in a cathode near a missed heat pellet.

loads before the missed heat pellet auto-ignites, although performance is clearly suboptimal. Further, the position of the missed heat pellet has little effect on battery performance, unless it is at one of the ends. Finally, because the initially missed heat pellet burns in an already hot battery, it is likely to significantly overheat adjacent materials and could trigger a thermal runaway.

Acknowledgments

The authors gratefully acknowledge Tyler Voskuilen for implementing the temperature-dependent ignition mechanism in Aria and providing an example input deck.

Sandia National Laboratories is a multimission laboratory managed and operated by National Technology and Engineering Solutions of Sandia, LLC., a wholly owned subsidiary of Honeywell International, Inc., for the U.S. Department of Energy's National Nuclear Security Administration under contract DE-NA0003525.

This paper describes objective technical results and analysis. Any subjective views or opinions that might be expressed in the paper do not necessarily represent the views of the U.S. Department of Energy or the United States Government.

References

1. Edington, J. and J. Baumann. "Thermal Battery Igniter Activation Measurements and Flow Modeling." Proceedings of the 45th Power Sources Conference, Las Vegas, 2012.

2. Roberts, S., C. Jove-Colon, H. Moffat, M. Neilsen, E. Piekos, B. Schroeder, B. Trembacki, and T. Voskuilen. "TABS : A Thermal Battery Desktop Design Tool." Proceedings of the 48th Power Sources Conference, Denver, 2018.

3. Blacker, T., S. J. Owen, M. L. Staten, R. W. Quadros, B. Hanks, B. Clark, T. Hensley, R. J. Meyers, C. Ernst, K. Merkley, R. Morris, C. McBride, C. Stimpson, M. Plooster, and S. Showman. "CUBIT Geometry and Mesh Generation Toolkit 15.3 User Documentation." Tech. Rep. SAND2017-6895 W, Sandia National Laboratories, Albuquerque, 2017.

4. SIERRA Thermal/Fluid Development Team. "SIERRA Multimechanics Module: Aria User Manual, Version 4.46." Tech. Rep. SAND2017-10427, Sandia National Laboratories, Albuquerque, 2017.

5. Stewart, J. and H. Edwards. "A framework approach for developing parallel adaptive multiphysics applications." *Finite Elements in Analysis and Design*, vol. 40, no. 12, pp. 1599–1617, 2004.

6. Guidotti, R. A., J. Odinek, and F. W. Reinhardt. "Characterization of Fe/$KClO_4$ Heat Powders and Pellets." *Journal of Energetic Materials*, vol. 24, no. 4, pp. 271–305, 2006.

7. Evans, N. and N. Durand. "Heat Transfer Characteristics of Igniter Output Plumes." In *14th International Pyrotechnics Seminar*, pp. 173–184. Jersey, Channel Islands, UK, 1989.

8. Czajka, B., S. Styczyński, S. Tabat, D. Szal, and L. Wachowski. "Determination of Ignition Sensitivity of Selected Heat Powders." *Central European Journal of Energetic Materials*, vol. 8, no. 1, pp. 3–13, 2011.

9. Guidotti, R. A. "Development History of Fe/$KClO_4$ Heat Powders at Sandia and Related Aging Issues for Thermal Batteries." Tech. Rep. SAND2001-2191, Sandia National Laboratories, Albuquerque, 2001.

CAM-7®/LTO Lithium-Ion Technology for Structurally Integrated Vehicle Batteries

David Ofer, Mark Menard, Chris McCoy, Daniel Kaplan, Celine Yang, Brian Barnett, and Suresh Sriramulu
CAMX Power
35 Hartwell Avenue
Lexington, MA 02421

Abstract: *CAMX Power is developing Li-ion pouch cells and batteries based on our proprietary CAM-7® cathode material and commercially available lithium titanate (LTO) anode material. These cells provide high power, high charge rate capability, long life and outstanding, safety. Furthermore, they can offer broad configurational flexibility in military vehicle battery designs. The CAM-7®/LTO technology has excellent tolerance for cell voltage reversal and cell overcharge as well as having excellent elevated-temperature storage stability, making it well-suited for implementation in damage-tolerant, minimally managed, batteries that are structurally distributed and integrated in military vehicles.*

Keywords: pouch cell; lithium-ion; structural battery; CAM-7; lithium titanate.

Introduction

The energy storage capacities and resulting mission capabilities of current military vehicles can be substantially increased if unfilled spaces in a vehicle's structure that are not otherwise needed for personnel or equipment, such as those beneath external armor, are filled with batteries. However, implementation of such a distributed, structurally integrated battery on or beneath the surface of a military vehicle poses the unique challenges of essentially uncontrolled exposure to external environmental conditions and the high probability of incurring damage in battle or other operations.

Lithium-ion pouch cell technology employing our proprietary CAM-7® high capacity cathode material (licensed to BASF and Johnson Matthey) combined with lithium titanate (LTO) anode material offers unique advantages that we are exploiting to develop such a structurally integrated battery. Batteries at the uncooled surface of a vehicle must be particularly tolerant of high temperatures, which ordinarily will rapidly degrade conventional Li-ion cells, and therefore we are tailoring CAM-7®/LTO cell chemistry and design for enhanced elevated-temperature tolerance while relaxing high-rate performance capabilities.

With respect to damage tolerance, batteries distributed on the surface of a vehicle must incorporate redundancy and/or maintain function with some level of damage/disablement to individual cells. Furthermore, current-carrying elements and battery management elements can be more critically vulnerable than cells themselves, and therefore current collection should be as distributed as possible, current cutoff requirements should be minimized, and battery management should be minimized. When implemented in suitable cell designs, the CAM-7®/LTO chemistry is exceptionally tolerant of overcharge and overdischarge, making it well-suited for incorporation in structurally integrated batteries requiring minimal battery management and that can continue to function after absorbing significant battle damage.

CAM-7® is a high Ni content, $LiNiO_2$-class cathode material stabilized by innovative dopants to resolve the historical long-term stability concerns that have prevented exploitation of the high energy and power capability offered by this class of materials. CAM-7 has been developed by CAMX Power and its predecessor, TIAX, over 15+ years. CAM-7 is made by a readily scalable solid-state process, and its chemical composition, morphology, and synthesis procedures can be tuned to optimize it for specific applications and electrode processing conditions. In addition to the expected availability of CAM-7 from our licensees, we operate a 50 t/y pilot plant for producing CAM-7 in Rowley, Massachusetts.

$Li_4Ti_5O_{12}$ or LTO anode material has exceptional cycling stability. Nano-structured LTO is capable of very high rate performance as well, and can be lithiated (charged) very rapidly because at its high potential (~1.55 V vs. Li), passivating film (SEI) does not form on its surface, thus enhancing its rate capability. LTO's high potential further enables it to be charged at high rates without danger of Li metal plating. Because of its high potential, LTO can be coated onto Al foil current collectors rather than the oxidation-prone Cu foil used for conventional Li-ion anodes. Al current collector is essential for the resulting cells' tolerance of overdischarge and voltage reversal.

CAM-7®/LTO CELL ABUSE TOLERANCE

Damage tolerance in multi-cell batteries: Exceptionally robust cell technologies are required for structurally integrated multi-cell batteries to maintain functionality with some number of cells disabled while having minimal impact on the condition and life of remaining cells. To understand why this is the case, it is helpful to consider how cells in batteries can be configured in some collection of S-P and/or P-S cell connections, as illustrated for a 3x3 cell array in Figure 1, when discussing how the configuration of cell connections and the disablement of cells in a battery impacts the other cells and the overall battery performance.

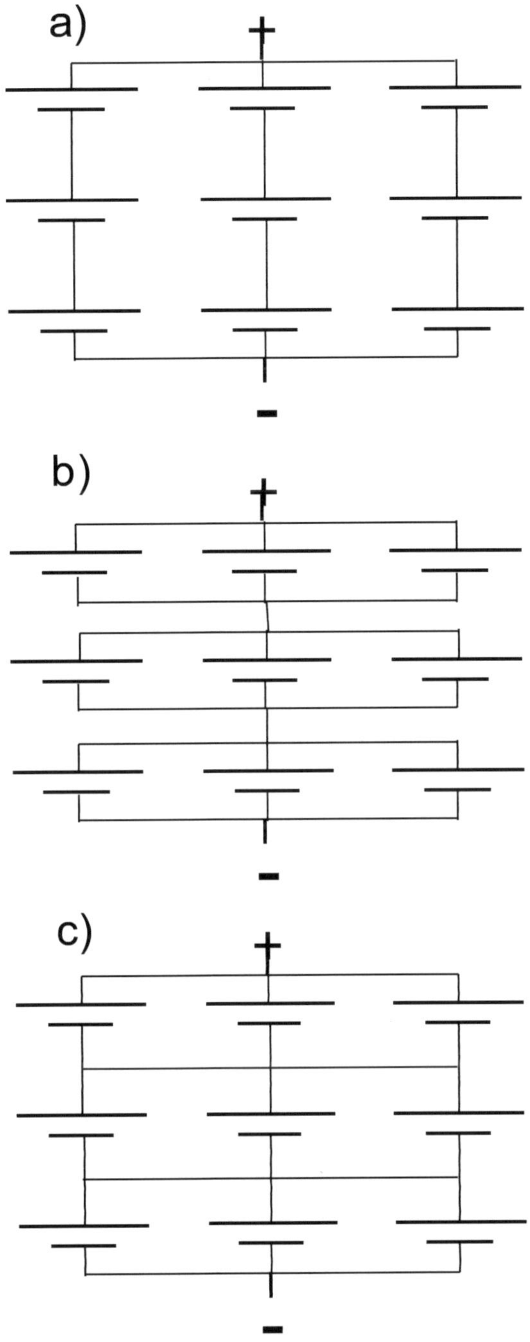

Figure 1. Cell connection configurations for a 3 series-cell, 3 parallel-cell battery. a) S-P configuration. b) P-S configuration. c) Matrix configuration.

In S-P configuration a:

- Few nodes carrying full battery current make for less critically vulnerable current distribution
- Cell failing open or disconnected takes out entire series string
- Hard shorted cell leads to series cell overcharge
- Soft shorted cell is vulnerable to reversal and causing milder overcharge of series cells

In P-S configuration b:

- More nodes carrying full battery current make for most vulnerable current distribution
- Cell failing open or disconnected subjects parallel cells to overcharge and overdischarge stress
- Hard shorted cell dissipates large fault currents, subjects parallel cells to reversal stress and series strings to overcharge stress
- Soft shorted cell and parallel cells are vulnerable to reversal and causing milder overcharge of series strings

In matrix configuration c:

- Least vulnerable current distribution
- Otherwise, cells in a matrix array are subject to same vulnerabilities as in P-S configuration b

Therefore, regardless of how its cells are topologically configured, for a multi-cell structural battery to maintain functionality even when damaged, it is desirable that its cells be tolerant of overcharge and of overdischarge and voltage reversal.

Cell reversal tolerance: The CAM-7®/LTO cell chemistry tolerates reversal to -3.5 V and by at least 5% of its capacity extremely well, as shown by the following data. Figure 2 shows cell voltage and individual electrode potentials for a CAM-7®/LTO pouch cell that underwent reversal by 5% of its capacity from an initial 0 V cell voltage.

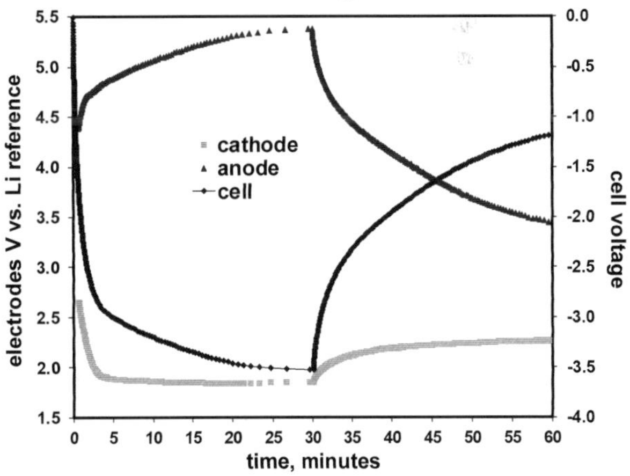

Figure 2. capacity/voltage characteristic and electrode potentials for a 130 mAh CAM-7/LTO pouch cell equipped with a Li metal reference electrode being reversed by 6.5 mAh capacity (5%) at 0.1C rate for 30 min. from 0V initial voltage, followed by 30 min. relaxation at open circuit.

The pouch cell shown in Figure 2 contained an electrolyte optimized for low-temperature performance rather than for abuse tolerance, but the cell nevertheless retained excellent power delivery capability at ambient and low temperatures, as shown by Figure 3. It is noteworthy that the cell appeared unaltered by the reversal, and that Figure 3 data were obtained with the cell free-standing and unconstrained, pointing to a lack of any significant gassing associated with cell reversal despite the extreme potential excursions made by the electrodes (Figure 2).

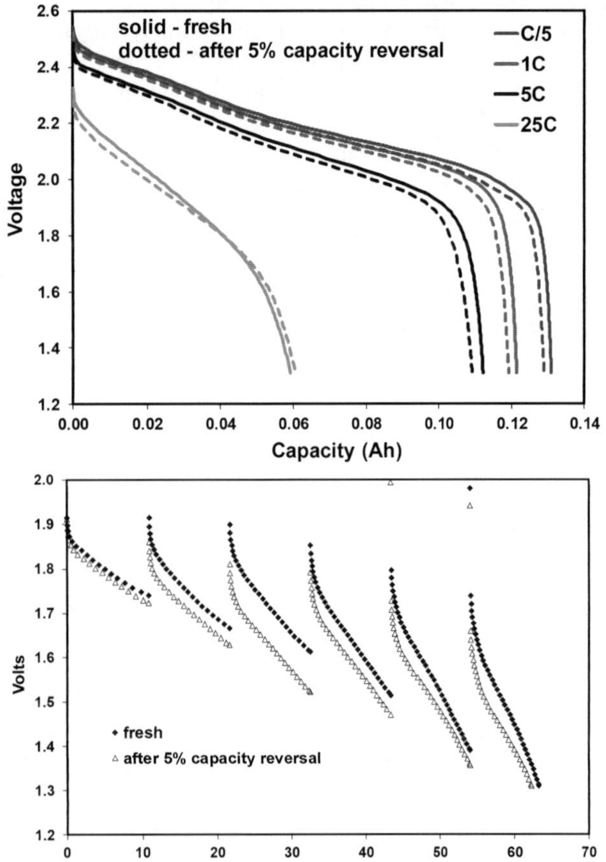

Figure 3. Top: Ambient-temperature constant current discharge characteristics of a 130 mAh CAM-7®/LTO pouch cell for discharge from 2.59V before and after being reversed by 5% of its ca[pacity. Bottom: Capacity delivered by the cell charged to 2.59V at RT and discharged at 10C for 30 sec. with 30 min. rest between pulses at -18 °C to 1.31V cutoff. All tests were run with the cell unconstrained (no clamps).

Cell overcharge tolerance: The CAM-7®/LTO cell chemistry tolerates overcharge to 3.5 V and up to 10% of its capacity extremely well, as shown by the following data. Figure 4 shows cell voltage and individual electrode potentials for a CAM-7®/LTO pouch cell that underwent overcharge by 10% of its capacity from an initial 2.59 V cell voltage. This cell too was filled with electrolyte optimized for low-temperature performance rather than for abuse tolerance, but the unconstrained cell still retained high power delivery capability after the overcharge, as shown by Figure 5.

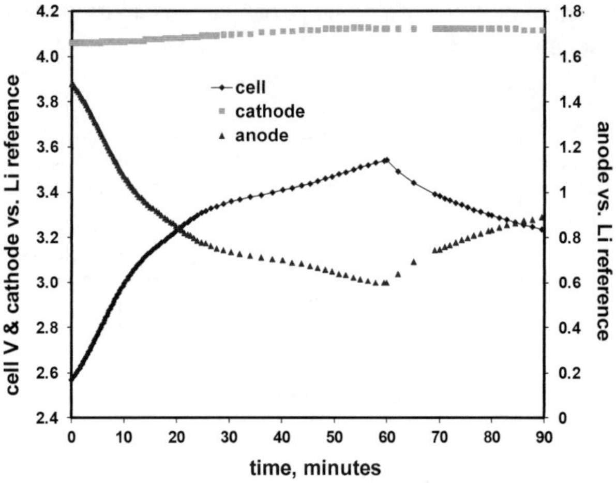

Figure 4. capacity/voltage characteristic and electrode potentials for a 130 mAh CAM-7/LTO pouch cell equipped with a Li metal reference electrode overcharged by 13 mAh capacity (10%) at 0.1C rate for 60 min. from 2.59V initial voltage, followed by 30 min. relaxation at open circuit.

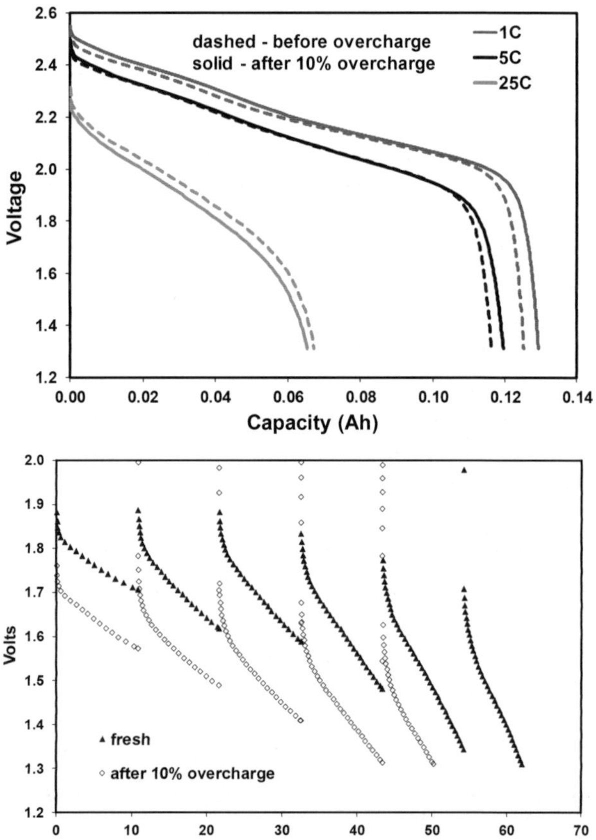

Figure 5. Top: Ambient-temperature constant current discharge characteristics of a 130 mAh CAM-7®/LTO pouch cell for discharge from 2.59V before and after being overcharged by 10%. Bottom: Capacity delivered by the cell charged to 2.59V at RT and discharged at 10C for 30 sec. with 30 min. rest between pulses at -18 °C to 1.31V cutoff.

The above overcharge tolerance shows that an 11-series-cell string of CAM-7®/LTO pouch cells interfacing directly with a 28.5 V vehicle bus voltage would be highly damage-tolerant in a structurally integrated vehicle battery architecture. Such an 11-series-cell string could function well with as many as 3 cells hard-shorted by battle damage, as shown by Table 1.

Table 1. Individual cell voltages of an 11-series-cell string charged to 28.5 V.

# of cells shorted	Remaining cells' charge V
0	2.591
1	2.850
2	3.167
3	3.563
4	4.071

With up to 3 cells shorted, voltages of remaining cells will not significantly exceed the 3.5 V value for which high tolerance is demonstrated in Figure 5 data. If individual cells in such a series string are soft-shorted, they can be subject to reversal stress in addition to the remaining cells being overcharged but, as shown in Figure 3 above, these cells would also tolerate reversal.

Elevated temperature tolerance: Batteries distributed on or just beneath the surface of a vehicle must be particularly tolerant of high temperatures, which ordinarily will rapidly degrade Li-ion cells. The CAM-7®/LTO cell chemistry and design can be tailored for enhanced elevated-temperature tolerance, particularly if high-rate performance capabilities are relaxed. This is illustrated by Figure 6, which shows the impacts of cell design (configuration) and electrolyte composition on performance retention of CAM-7®/LTO cells after lengthy high-temperature exposure.

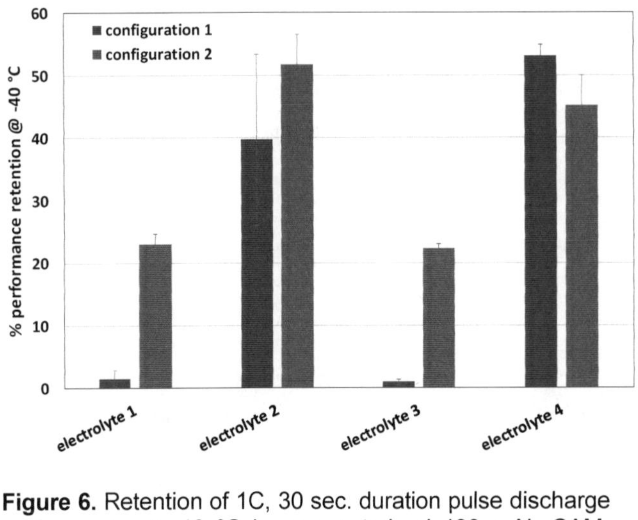

Figure 6. Retention of 1C, 30 sec. duration pulse discharge performance at -40 °C by unconstrained 130 mAh CAM-7®/LTO pouch cells after storage in charged state at 78 °C (172 °F) for 40 days.

POTENTIAL IMPLEMENTATIONS

Platform and design concept: Implementation of CAM-7®/LTO structurally integrated vehicle batteries could result in an order of magnitude increase in a vehicle's electrical energy storage capacity. For example, the estimated area behind the selected non-hinged armor pieces of an M1100 HMMWV shown in Figure 7 is up to ~7 m^2. At an estimated 2-3 cm thickness of space available beneath the armor, this area could provide over 140 liters of volume available for a battery. We estimate that filling this space with small, uniform CAM-7®/LTO pouch cell modules could provide 20+ kWh battery energy, as compared to the approximately 2 kWh expected for a CAM-7®/LTO 6T battery.

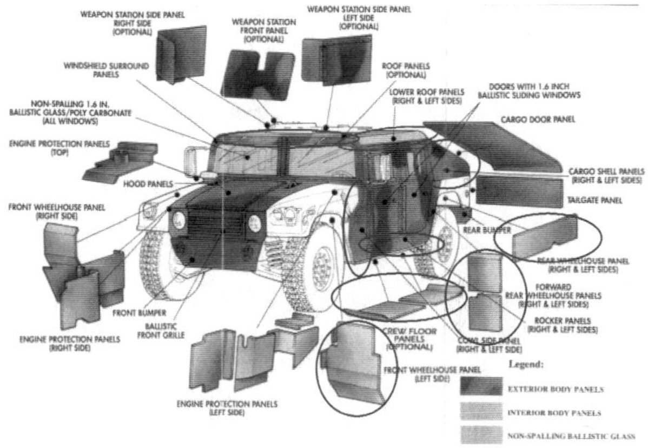

Figure 7. Selected non-hinged armor of an M1100 HMMWV that might accommodate a structural battery.

Conclusions

CAM-7®/LTO Lithium-ion cells can be the basis for a structurally integrated vehicle battery with high damage and environmental tolerance, and that would provide over an order of magnitude increase in energy storage relative to a 6T battery.

Acknowledgements: This material is based upon work supported by the U.S. Army under Contract No. W56HZV-16-C-0143 and by the Defense Logistics Agency under Contract No. HQ0147-15-C-8003.

Disclaimer: Any opinions, findings and conclusions or recommendations expressed in this material are those of the author(s) and do not necessarily reflect the views of any agency or branch of the United States Government.

CAM-7®/LTO Lithium-Ion Technology for Robust, High-Power Vehicle Batteries

David Ofer, Daniel Kaplan, Celine Yang, Sharon Dalton-Castor, Chris McCoy, Thomas Kotwal, Michael Rutberg, Brian Barnett, and Suresh Sriramulu
CAMX Power
35 Hartwell Avenue
Lexington, MA 02421

Abstract: *CAMX Power is developing Li-ion pouch cells and batteries based on our proprietary CAM-7® cathode material and commercially available lithium titanate (LTO) anode material to provide high power, high charge rate capability, long life, safety and configurational flexibility in military vehicle batteries. The CAM-7®/LTO technology can be discharged to 0 V and stored in that condition for extended periods with no loss in performance, making it ideally suited for batteries that can be logistically managed with little or no maintenance or environmental controls.*

Keywords: pouch cell; lithium-ion 6T; CAM-7; lithium titanate; LTO.

Introduction

Lithium-ion battery technology based on our proprietary high capacity CAM-7® cathode material (licensed to BASF and Johnson Matthey) combined with lithium titanate (LTO) anode implemented in pouch cells offers unique advantages for a variety of vehicular and energy storage applications. Among these advantages are the ability to be charged very rapidly and at very low temperatures (even at -50 °C), tolerance for extended periods of storage at 0 V, and very high stability, safety and long life. CAMX Power is developing CAM-7®/ LTO cells for military 6T vehicle batteries, start-stop vehicle batteries, and large-scale stationary storage batteries.

CAM-7® is a high Ni content, $LiNiO_2$-class cathode material stabilized by innovative dopants to resolve the historical long-term stability concerns that have prevented exploitation of the high energy and power capability offered by this class of materials. CAM-7 has been developed by CAMX Power and its predecessor, TIAX, over 15+ years. CAM-7 is made by a readily scalable solid-state process, and its chemical composition, morphology, and synthesis procedures can be tuned to optimize it for specific applications and electrode processing conditions. In addition to the expected availability of CAM-7 from our licensees, we operate a 50 t/y pilot plant for producing CAM-7 in Rowley, Massachusetts.

$Li_4Ti_5O_{12}$ or LTO anode material has exceptional cycling stability. Nano-structured LTO is capable of very high rate capability as well, and can be lithiated (charged) very rapidly because at its high potential (~1.55 V vs. Li), passivating film (SEI) does not form on its surface, thus enhancing its rate capability. LTO's high potential further enables it to be charged at high rates without danger of Li metal plating.

PROPERTIES OF CAM-7®/LTO CELLS

High Power: CAM-7® cathode, LTO anode cells can deliver exceptional rate capability for both charge and discharge. Figure 1 illustrates this high rate capability, showing constant power charge and discharge voltage characteristics for a small pouch cell made with low-loading electrodes to minimize electrolyte-based rate limitations and emphasize active materials characteristics. The cell was cycled between 2.59 V and 1.31 V, corresponding to the per-cell voltage range of an 11-series-cell 6T battery operated between 28.5 V and 14.4 V.

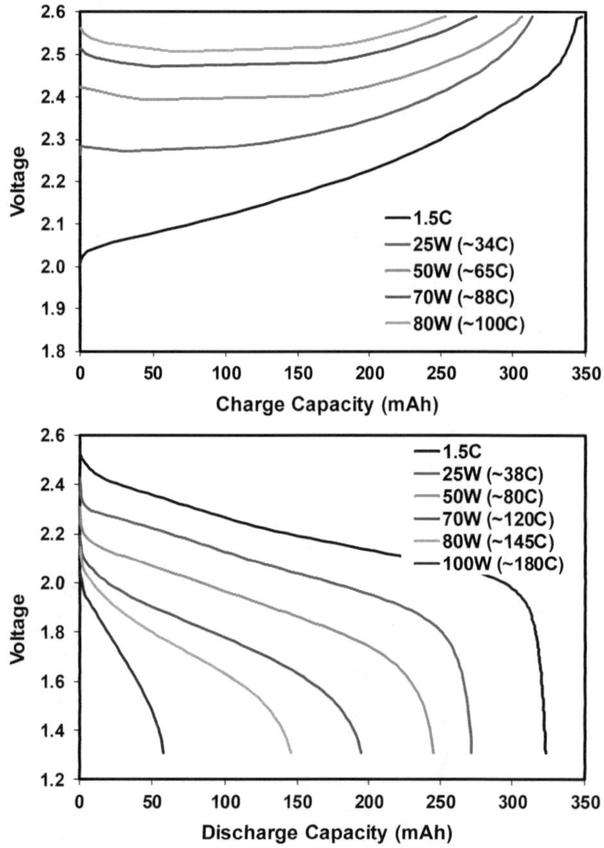

Figure 1. Continuous constant power charge (top) and discharge (bottom) characteristics of a 320 mAh, 0.5 mAh/cm² loading CAM-7®/LTO pouch cell at ambient temperature.

Extended temperature range performance and life: The CAM-7®/LTO cell chemistry can employ electrolyte formulations that are unsuitable for conventional Li-ion cell chemistries using low-potential anodes but can enable special benefits in CAM-7®/LTO cells, such as the outstanding low-temperature performance illustrated by Figure 2, which shows relatively high rate constant current charge and discharge performance of a pouch cell at -50 °C.

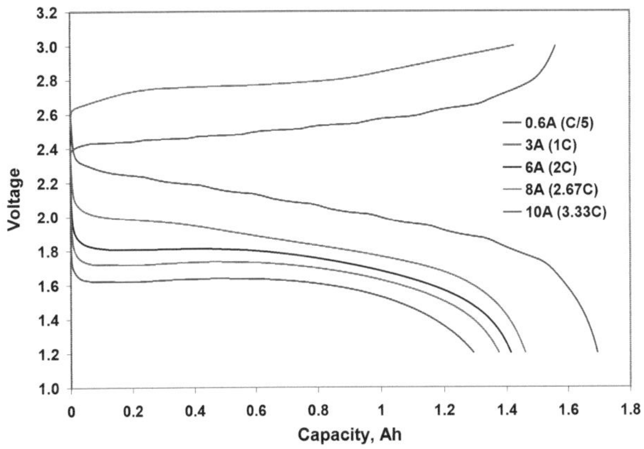

Figure 2. Continuous constant current charge and discharge characteristics of a 3 Ah, 1.7 mAh/cm^2 loading CAM-7/LTO pouch cell at -50 °C.

CAM-7®/LTO pouch cells filled with this same low-temperature-optimized electrolyte have excellent elevated-temperature stability. Figure 3 shows discharge capacity vs. cycle number for 10C/10C cycling of CAM-7®/LTO pouch cells at 45 °C between voltage limits for operation in a 6-series-cell start-stop vehicle battery, and a photograph of a cell after 1,000 full charge-discharge cycles showing that it did not gas or swell at all.

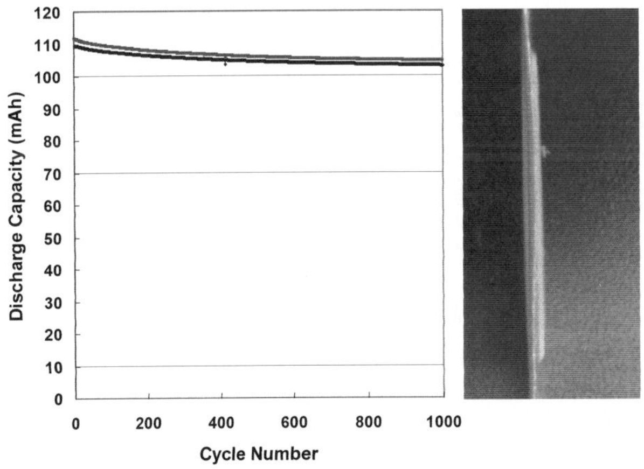

Figure 3. Left: Discharge capacity of 2 unconstrained 120 mAh CAM-7/LTO pouch cells cycled 1000 times between 2.43 V and 1.2 V at 10C/10C rate at 45 °C. Right: Side-on photograph of one cell after 45 °C cycling.

The Figure 3 data highlight this cell technology's rapid charge acceptance capability (10C charging) as well as its lack of elevated-temperature gassing. CAMX Power has found that despite the reputation of LTO-anode cells for gassing,[1] there is no gassing problem if adequately purified active materials and electrolyte are used in suitable cell designs.

CAM-7®/LTO cells have extremely long cycle life at ambient temperatures with excellent retention of low impedance and low-temperature performance, as shown in Figure 4.

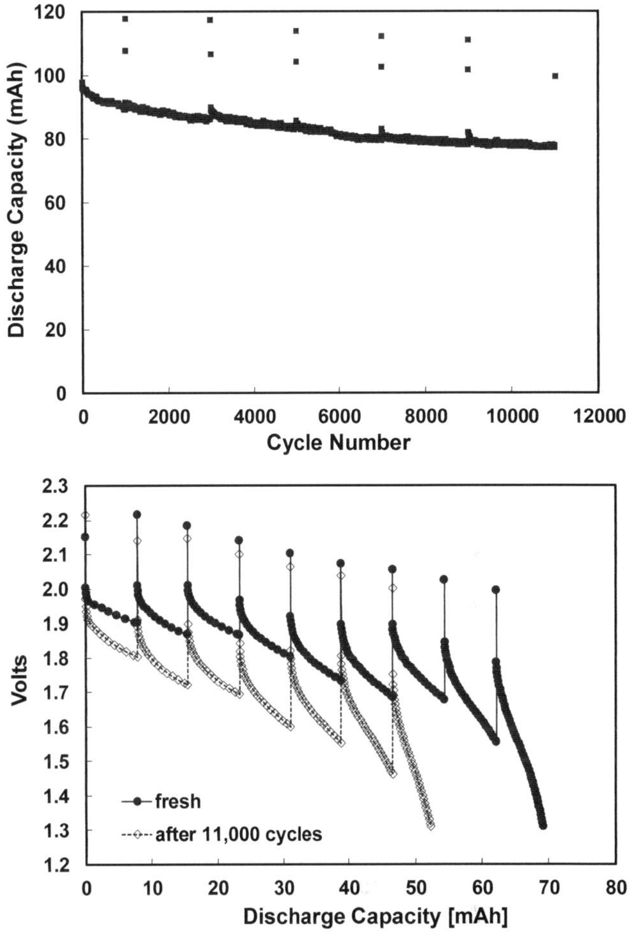

Figure 4. Top: Discharge capacity of an unconstrained 120 mAh CAM-7®/LTO pouch cell 10C/10C cycled between 2.59 V and 1.31 V at ambient temperature, with C/5 and 1C cycles at 2,000 cycle intervals. Bottom: Capacity and voltage for repeated 0.93A (~8C), 30 sec. pulsing of the cell to 1.31V cutoff with 30 min. rest between pulses at -18 °C.

The low-temperature pulse capability of the cell before and after 11,000 cycles, as shown in Figure 4, demonstrates its excellent retention of cold cranking performance at 0.93A current, which is scaled to correspond to the 600A requirement of the Li-ion 6T specification.[2] Note that cold cranking performance targets are especially difficult to achieve, and even slight increase in cell impedance can make it difficult to complete cold cranking pulses. Therefore, only slight change in the cold crank performance even after 1000 cycles at 45 °C is indicative of very low impedance increase by the cell

Safety: The safety of the CAM-7®/LTO pouch cell technology has been demonstrated in nail penetration tests. Figure 5 shows voltage and temperature results for nail penetration testing of a charged 2.7 Ah cell.

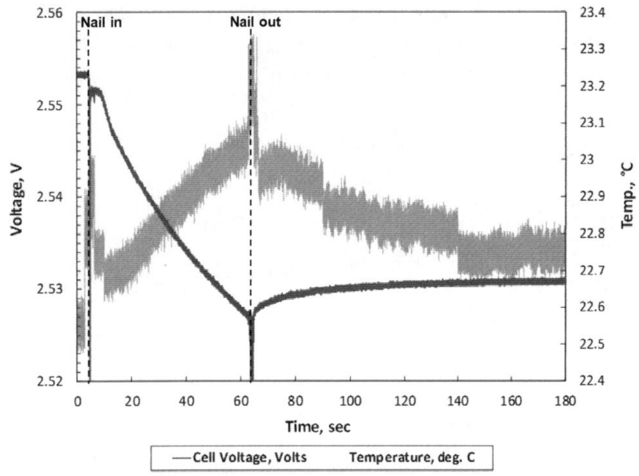

Figure 5. Voltage and surface temperature of a charged (2.65 V) 2.7 Ah CAM-7®/LTO pouch cell during penetration by a blunt 2 mm diameter nail at 1 cm/sec.

The Figure 5 data show that the short circuit induced by the nail penetration event has relatively high resistance and poses little or no safety threat. This abuse tolerance makes the technology very attractive for implementation in large military batteries.

0 V Stability: Unlike conventional Li-ion cells, CAM-7®/LTO cells can be discharged to 0 V and below (cell voltage reversal), which can enable batteries to be logistically managed in a completely de-energized condition in which they require no maintenance and present no electrical or thermal hazards. The long-term stability of CAM-7®/LTO pouch cells at 0 V is exceptional, as is demonstrated by the results in Figure 6, which show that the ambient-temperature performance of a cell was virtually unchanged by being fully cycled 1,000 times and stored for nearly 3 years in the 0V condition.

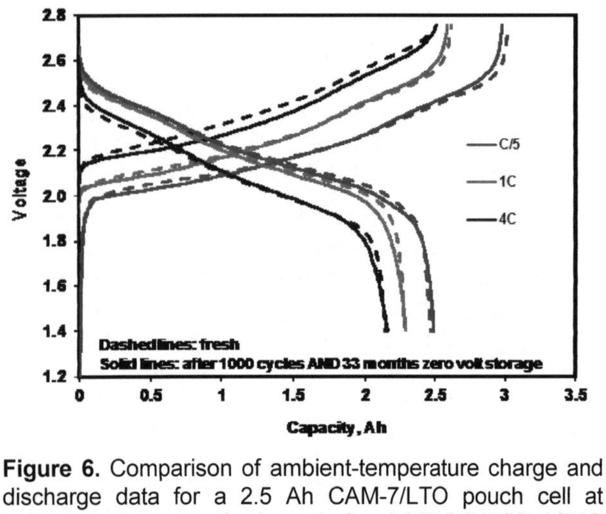

Figure 6. Comparison of ambient-temperature charge and discharge data for a 2.5 Ah CAM-7/LTO pouch cell at indicated rates when fresh, and after 1,000 full DOD 1C/1C charge-discharge cycles followed by 33 months' storage in 0 V condition at room temperature.

The thermal stability of CAM-7®/LTO cells is excellent when they are in the 0 V condition, as shown in Figure 7, suggesting that batteries employing them could be logistically managed with minimal environmental controls.

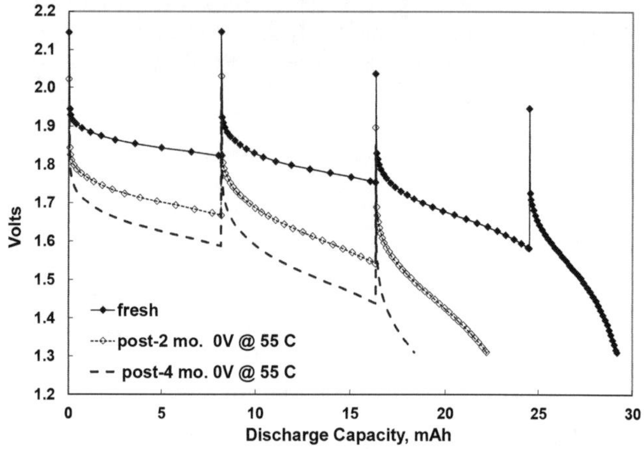

Figure 7. Repeated 0.93A, 30 sec. pulsing of an unfixtured low-loading 50 mAh CAM-7®/LTO pouch cell to 1.31V cutoff with 30 minutes rest between pulses at -18 °C, when the cell was fresh, after 2 months storage in 0 V condition at 55 °C, and after 4 months storage in 0V condition at 55 °C.

Figure 7 shows that even after extended exposure at 55 °C (131 °F), cells in the 0 V condition suffer relatively modest performance loss under the most demanding test conditions (low temperature and high rate approaching 20C). A battery's ability to tolerate discharge to 0V and storage at significantly elevated temperatures without damage to performance can greatly reduce the logistics burdens presented by Li-ion batteries because it eliminates needs for maintaining the batteries' charge status and controlling the environment in which they are stored, and also eliminates the safety concerns associated with storing and transporting large volumes of densely packed batteries.

6 Ah, 15 V CAM-7®/LTO MODULE

6T scaling: The majority of CAM-7®/LTO technology development efforts to date have been directed towards the 6T battery application. 6T military vehicle batteries currently employ lead-acid chemistry, but the need for longer run times and cycle life in Silent Watch missions is driving the development of Li-ion 6T batteries. However, there are safety concerns for Li-ion batteries, particularly with respect to transportation of military vehicles aboard Navy vessels. Therefore, although it has lower energy density than conventional graphite-anode cell chemistry, CAM-7®/LTO chemistry may prove to be more readily implemented in 6T batteries than conventional Li-ion chemistry, both because of the LTO-based cell chemistry's greater safety in the charged state, and because CAM-7®/LTO cells can be completely de-energized (discharged to 0 V) for logistical operations. Our CAM-7®/LTO cells have specific energy of about 90 Wh/kg, which is over twice that of currently employed lead-acid technology.

A 6-series-cell, 6 Ah module was made from CAM-7®/LTO pouch cells to test against scaled requirements for a Li-ion 6T battery per the Li-ion 6T specification, and was cycled between 15.55 V and 7.86 V, corresponding to the per-cell voltage of an 11-series-cell 6T. Figure 8 shows the opened module case prior to final assembly

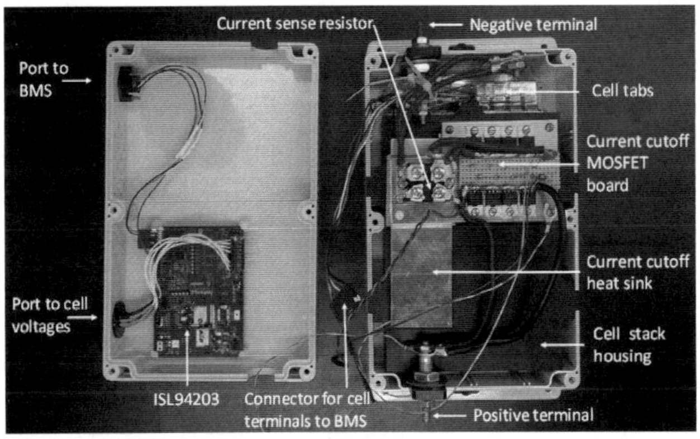

Figure 8. Photograph of 6-series-cell, 6 Ah module.

Figure 9 shows the module's charge and discharge characteristics at ambient temperature and demonstrates its excellent rate capability.

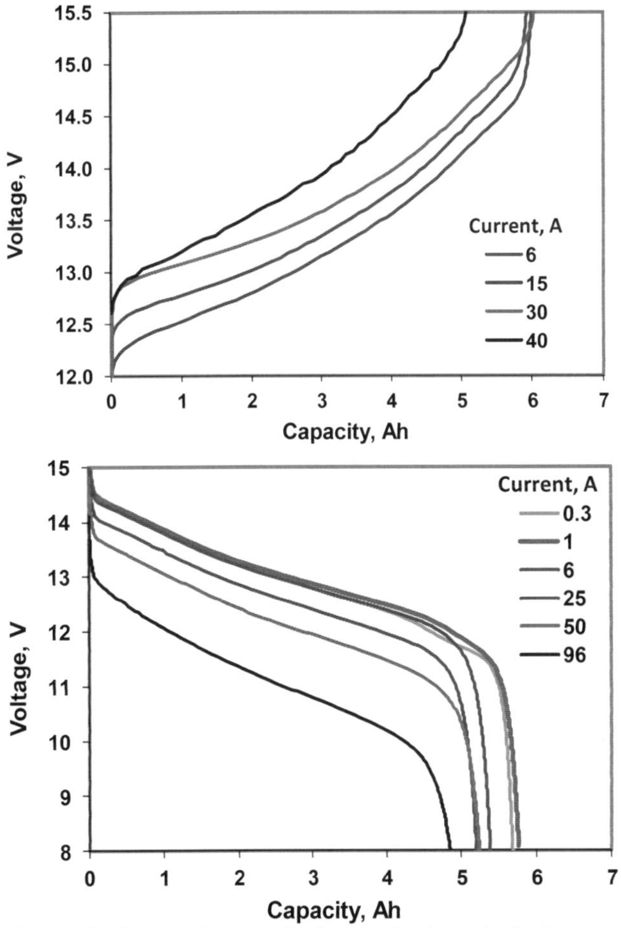

Figure 8. Constant current charge (top) and discharge (bottom) characteristics of 6-series-cell, 6 Ah module.

The module was also tested against the low-temperature pulse performance requirements of the Li-ion 6T specification, with the results shown in Figure 9. At -18 °C, the module delivered 600 A-scaled pulse discharge performance as required for Types 1 and 2 batteries by the Li-ion 6T specification, and delivered 1100 A-scaled pulse performance at -11 °C. At -40 °C, the module delivered 400 A-scaled pulse performance as the specification requires for Type 3 batteries.

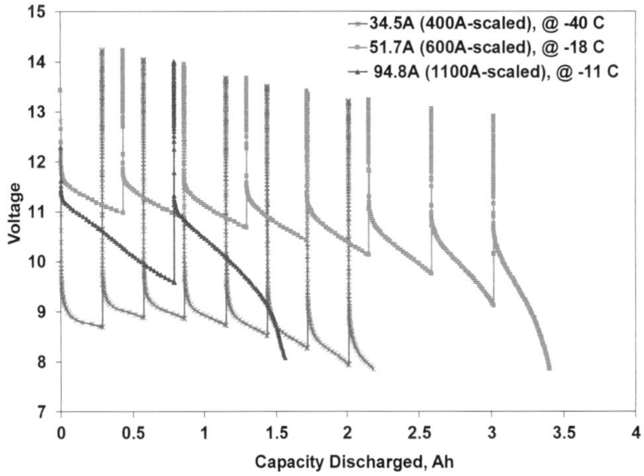

Figure 8. 600 A-scaled, 1100 A-scaled and 400 A-scaled 30 sec. pulse capacity delivered by 6 Ah module at -18 °C, -11 °C and -40 °C, respectively.

This module demonstrated that the CAM-7®/LTO technology is ready for demonstration and testing in full-scale prototype 6T batteries. A 6T battery having 62% of its volume occupied by 18.6 kg of cells based on the design used in the module would be expected to have 66 Ah capacity and 1600 Wh energy, and meet the Li-ion 6T specification's Type 1 and Type 2 battery requirements.

Conclusions

CAM-7®/LTO Lithium-Ion technology offers an excellent combination of high power, high energy density, long life and safety for many applications including 6T military vehicle batteries.

Acknowledgements: This material is based upon work supported by the U.S. Army under Contract No. W56HZV-11-C-0065, by the Navy under Contract No. N39430-14-C-1506, by the Defense Logistics Agency under Contract No. HQ0147-15-C-8003, and by the Department of Energy under Contract No. DE-FOA-0001227.

References

1. a) M. He, E. Castel, A. Laumann, G. Nuspl, P. Novak, E. J. Berg, *J. Electrochem. Soc.* **162**, A870 (2015). b) C. R. Fell, L. Sun, P. B. Hallac, B. Metz, B. Siska, *J. Electrochem. Soc.* **162**, A1916 (2015).
2. "Performance Specification: Battery, Rechargeable, Sealed, 6T Lithium-Ion", MIL-PRF-32565A.

Safe Lithium-ion 6T Development for Fighting Vehicles

John Perry, Kevin Andrew Paterson, Glyn Stanton, Simon Peter Marker
Denchi Power Ltd
Thurso Business Park, Thurso, Caithness, UK, KW14 7XW
john.perry@denchipower.com / (+44)1847808013

Abstract: Size Weight and Power (SWaP) are key concerns for military vehicle designers. Current vehicles use lead-acid for engine start and silent watch, therefore in order to achieve the silent watch mission time, many batteries must be included within a very constrained space. The increasing vehicle electrical load often means that the lead-acid solution is no longer viable or alternatively, a generator must be deployed. A novel design is proposed for a low weight, lithium-ion 6T battery, ensuring that maintainability, ruggedness and safety are enhanced, with the inclusion of status monitoring, multiple layers of electronic over watch and a ground up approach to cell choice and mechanical construction.

Keywords: lithium-ion; Li-ion; 6T; silent watch; military vehicle; engine start; fighting vehicle; longer mission time; operationally versatile; safe operation.

Introduction

The conflicting requirements of weight, safety, space constraints, mission capability and cost necessitated a holistic approach to the 6T design, removing any historical design bias as well as considering a solution which best fits the current operating environment. Consequently, the cells are chosen to ensure that the best energy density is achieved, that they are matched to mission requirements, achieve power requirements, cycle life and safety. Electronic design defines multiple layers of safety, each assuming the previous layer has failed together with communications to the vehicle, informing the crew of the status of the battery and the control of graceful degradation. Mechanical design considers the structural integrity of the battery, ensuring that the weight is minimized, fire propagation is limited and gasses are released in a controlled manner. The firmware design process must be well documented, rigorous and structured with module testing conducted at every opportunity. Encompassing this is a design philosophy which embraces virtual engineering, thermal simulation, circuit simulation and testing at all development levels.

Challenges with Current 6T Installations

Choosing Lithium-ion: Current 6T batteries in military vehicles utilize lead-acid chemistry. The battery bank provides power to start the diesel engine and during 'Silent Watch' to power a whole range of on-board systems such as communications, night sights, thermal imagers, jammers and laser range finders. The preferred solution is to accomplish this without the engine running or portable generators.

Lead acid batteries have a number of limitations that restrict the evolution of silent watch:

- They have a limited cycle life especially when cycled at 100% depth-of-discharge (DoD).
- When discharged at moderate to high loads, suffer from significantly reduced available capacity in an environment which is demanding ever higher current draw.
- Suffer from significantly reduced capacity when discharged at low temperatures.

Format: The challenge was therefore to design as close a drop-in replacement for the lead-acid 6T as possible which is more cost effective, makes integration easy by supporting a data rich interface and has been designed with safety as a priority. The battery had to support both engine start and silent watch, show significant improvements of performance at cold temperature, cycle life and achieve the reduced weight of 25kg. This weight saving was further enhanced by rating the output voltage at 25.9V, making it compatible with the voltage bus on most Military vehicles, allowing one Denchi 6T to be fitted in place of two lead-acid batteries, hence freeing up valuable space within the vehicle.

The principle driver to address the above is cell choice.

Cell Choice

Safety: The principle cell consideration is the safety and robustness of the cell packaging and therefore the 18650 format was chosen.

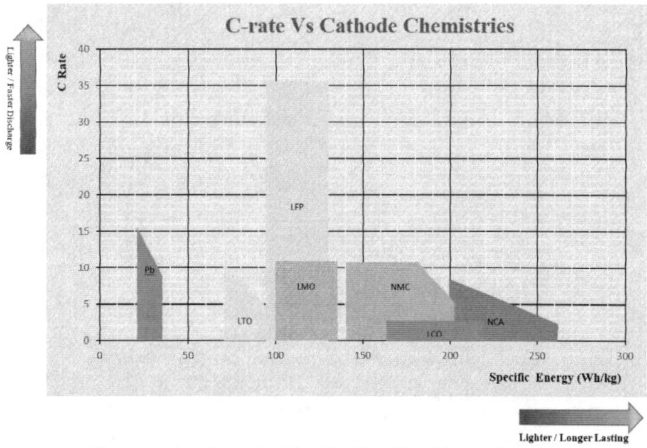

Figure 1. C-rate Vs Cathode Chemistries

This format will remain as the industry standard for a wide range of applications for many years giving the most straight forward upgrade path for improved performance and allowing mitigation of any future obsolescence issues. This size also allows a compartmentalization of the energy, reducing the probability of fire progression throughout the pack. The effects of an over temperature, an internal gas buildup, electrical or electronic protection within the cell, how the gas exits the cell were considered. The solutions to this are heavily dependent on the level of testing conducted by the supplier as well as their provenance, depth of knowledge and the availability of data.

Low Internal Series Resistance (ISR): For engine start, a cell was chosen with minimal series components and ISR, to keep the overall battery internal resistance low.

Small or Large Format: The choice of a large format cell minimizes connections, however it becomes difficult to limit the effect of an event to that cell and the size of that event is larger. With a pouch format, we can achieve a higher energy density and larger format size but the lack of robustness means that fire progression is quick and difficult to control. This can be mitigated by choosing a chemistry with a lower energy density however this impacts mission duration and capability.

Chemistry: Referring to figure 1 and the mission requirement, a lithium nickel manganese cobalt oxide (NMC) 18650 cell from an established quality supplier was chosen. This chemistry was considered to offer the optimum solution between, between power, energy, safety, cost, cycle-life and availability.

Electronic

Safety Architecture: The overall electronic safety architecture is shown in figure 2, where a multilevel, overlapping safety approach was used together with a modular and hence versatile solution, allowing application to non 6T formats.

The battery is split into 3 semi-autonomous modules. This allows safety to be further delegated with another level of redundancy. Multilevels of safety are employed extending from the module level through to controller. Refer to figure 2.

Within the module the first line of defense is the very fast acting analogue circuitry which acts on over/under voltage, over/under current as well as thermal input from the sensors.

There is also a redundant 2nd line which uses fast acting safety circuitry to blow a fuse if a fault with the primary circuit is detected. The next layer detects a longer, more sustained fault. This covers the lower energy fault condition which can damage the pack over a longer duration, also acting on a concerning thermal trend.

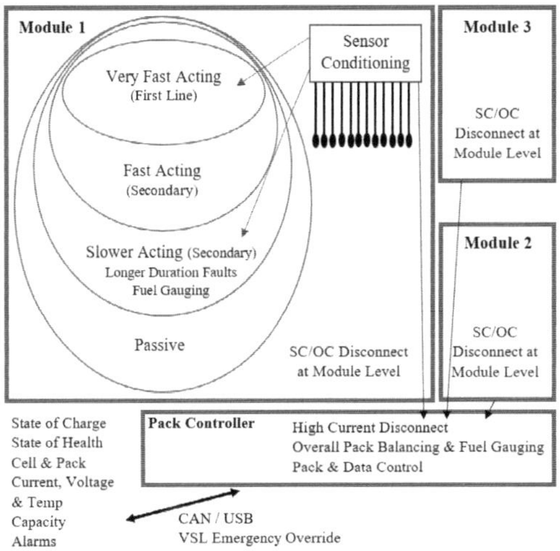

Figure 2. Overall Electronic Safety Architecture

The module is therefore able to autonomously disconnect short circuit and over current conditions. If all these levels fail there is a final module safety level with passive devices.

Monitoring: The use of sensors throughout the battery has allowed extensive real time monitoring and control, therefore with the multi-layer safety approach, a robust and detailed level of reporting battery status can be adopted. This allows the users within the military vehicle to manage available power in real time, matching this to the threat level at the time. This solution gives the vehicle enhanced silent watch capability giving a confidence from the reported battery status to start the engine, particularly in the situation where vehicle movement could draw fire. When the batteries are located in inaccessible areas within the vehicle, a detailed battery condition analysis or fault diagnoses can be conducted giving confidence in mission readiness and the ability to pinpoint any fault without having to extensively disassemble the vehicle. This was achieved through the use of detailed system analysis at the earliest stages of the design.

Charging control: There is a charger fitted to each module hence maintaining the autonomous nature of the module. This allows for easy integration without the need to add specialized lithium battery chargers and ensures that that charge rates are effectively controlled to maximize cycle life and safety. This also allows the battery to be incorporated into a wide range of vehicle platforms without affecting cycle life or safety since this adds another level of safety to the charging side of the circuit. Charge control is automatic, considering the pack temperature and the voltage on the bus before enabling. If there is an operational requirement to disable the charger, this can be enacted via a CAN message. In addition if the temperature of the pack is below 0°C, the charger will be disabled preventing the risk of lithium plating. The charge rate is also throttled at temperature extremes hence maximizing the cycle life of the cells.

Heating control: Heating is required to bring the battery mass up from –46°C and therefore, after consideration of multiple scenarios, the heating profile was determined in conjunction with the vehicle start procedure and charging requirements. This has resulted in fully automated heating control with manual override via CAN bus to allow the crew to control the current drawn during energy constrained scenarios.

Mechanical

Safety: In spite of all the electronic levels of protection, we also have to consider what would happen if a cell was to vent and possibly flame. Multiple packs will be located in a confined space where the crew cannot exit the vehicle without putting themselves under risk and therefore safety has to be paramount.

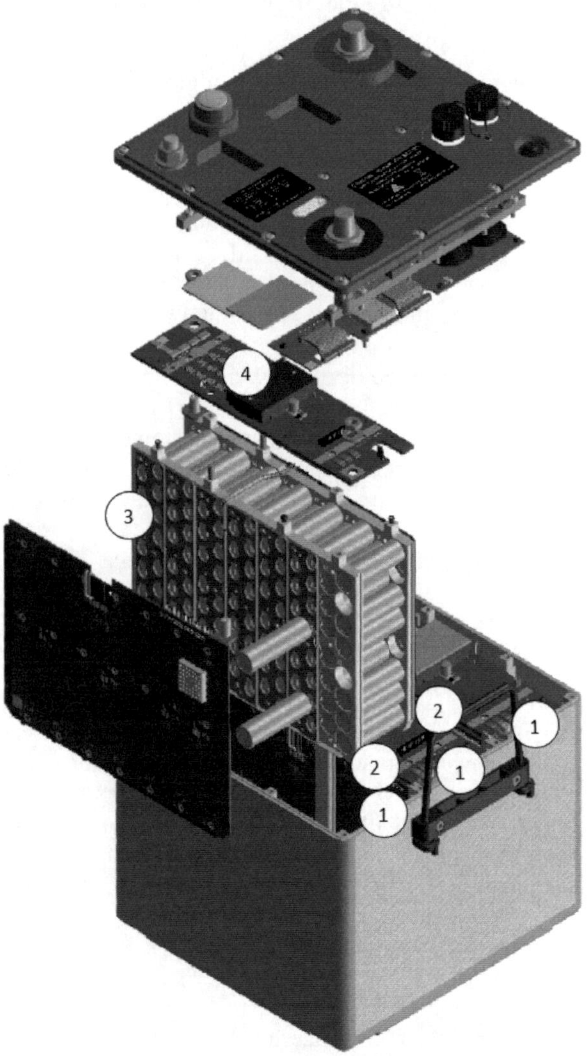

Figure 3. Exploded View of the Denchi 6T Battery

Referring to figure 3 the principle safety aspects of the design are:

1. High reliability due to separated modules. The failure of one module does not prevent the other modules from continuing to operate, if the battery is partially disabled.
2. Internal walls to prevent fire propagation between modules increasing safety.
3. Significant cell separation reduces the probability of cell to cell fire propagation. This was defined by the use of modelling and is confirmed by test.
4. Inbuilt charger in each module adding another level of safety and ability to address wider voltage range.

Robustness: An engineered aluminum outer case provides a robust mechanical solution for the battery enclosure that will protect the cell stacks and electronics within the demanding operating environment whilst still providing significant weight savings.

Thermal Management: The longevity of the pack depends principally on how stable the thermal profile can be maintained throughout the pack. This is achieved by extensive thermal modelling which defines the design of the heat sinking path, the mitigation of hotspots and the position of temperature monitoring. The array of thermistors tells the controller if there are any unexpected trends and the current thermal state of the pack.

Gas Management: If there is a gas release from one of the cells, the path to the vent must be considered to ensure that it is safely piped outside the pack and then the vehicle hence preventing any gas buildup which may lead to the possibility of ignition.

Firmware

Safety: The use of sensors throughout the battery has allowed extensive real time monitoring and control, therefore with the multi-layer safety approach, a robust and detailed level of reporting battery status has been adopted. This necessitates an initial decision as to which areas can be enacted by hardware or which are more over-watch and can be controlled by firmware.

Safe by Design: This is distilled into an overall architecture described with the aid of Unified Modelling Language (UML) [3]. Each firmware module interactions are defined and coding conducted to MISRA [2] standards. Test harnesses are then designed to test each module, exercising them to extreme scenario conditions and ensuring that each module is far more robust than testing in the target could accomplish. This ensures that where the batteries are located in inaccessible areas within the vehicle, a detailed battery condition analysis or fault diagnoses can be conducted giving confidence in mission readiness and the ability to pinpoint the fault without having to extensively disassemble the vehicle and that each module within the battery is as autonomous as possible.

The completed Product

Testing: Extensive environmental, performance (on various platforms), EMC, abuse and fire propagation testing has been conducted on the final product and will continue for most of the life of the product, especially cycle life testing.

Figure 4. Denchi Power Lithium-ion 6T battery

Validation of the early theoretical modelling, (based upon a combination of actual cell test data and early full battery modelling) confirms that the Denchi lithium-ion 6T will achieve the thermal performance targets. The predicted cycle life and reliability removes the need for costly re-supply via the logistics supply chain, significantly reducing through life costs.

Modular Design: The modular design has built-in redundancy, if one cell module goes down, the battery still works, albeit with reduced capacity. The modular approach also lends itself to applications in larger battery packs incorporating additional modules to additional modules to increase capacity or maximize the available power within an available space. See figure 5.

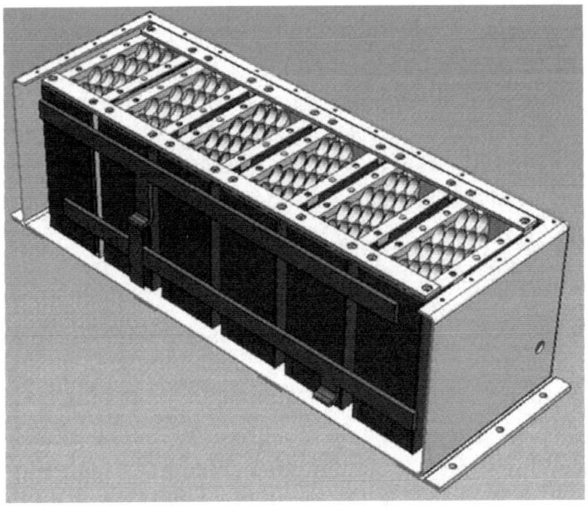

Figure 5. Scalable Modular Design

Operational Benefits of this Approach

- Multi-levels of safety within a mechanically robust enclosure.
- Selected cells optimize the highest achievable capacity, high rates of discharge, low temperature whilst maximizing cycle life.
- Significantly reduced weight and space within the vehicle.
- In-built charger allows retrofit to most existing vehicles.
- Current absorption during turret braking (up to 500A) is an available option.
- Battery Management System (BMS) provides real time data on battery performance, health status and built-in test facilities via CAN Bus.
- Operates with or without CAN Bus enabled.
- State of Charge/State of Health displays.
- Designed to MIL-STD-1275 [1] ensures compatibility with most vehicle power systems.
- In-built heater allows operation down to -46°C eliminating the need for an 'arctic kit'.
- A step change in performance against lead-acid.
- A major reduction in logistical burden.
- A much lower total cost of ownership.
- Modular design provides in-built redundancy.

The operational performance enables the Denchi lithium-ion 6T to undertake a main engine start even when the battery is close to empty, which could be life-saving when a quick getaway is essential. This has already been validated by customers in both Europe and the USA.

Acknowledgements

Thanks to Highland and Islands Enterprise and their support during this project. Thanks also to the wider Denchi team who have all contributed in some way to this project, small or large.

References

1. MIL-STD-1275E "Department of Defense Interface Standard Characteristics of 28 Volt DC Electrical Systems in Military Vehicles"
2. MISRA Compliance:2016 *"Achieving Compliance with MISRA Coding Guidelines"*, April 2016
3. Unified Modeling Language 2.5.1 *"A specification defining a graphical language for visualizing, specifying, constructing and documenting the artifacts of distributed object systems"* Dec 2017

Saft's Xcelion 6T® 28V Lithium Ion Battery for Military Vehicles

Scott Ferguson & Keith Hensley
Saft America, Inc.
Space and Defense Division
107 Beaver Ct.
Cockeysville, MD, 21234
scott.ferguson@saftbatteries.com / 1-410-568-2237

Abstract: *Saft has developed a competitively-priced lithium-ion replacement for the traditional lead-acid batteries for use in the next generation of military vehicles. Saft's 24 volt Xcelion 6T® delivers power at high rate that surpasses the delivered capacity of two lead-acid batteries. The battery design is tailored to support high rates, even at extreme cold temperatures, to support the mission needs for silent watch and starting for military vehicles. The product is now industrialized and commercially available for integration in the next generation of vehicles.*

Keywords: Lithium 6T; Lithium Iron Phosphate; between; your choice; of keywords. Including keywords is strongly encouraged because this section enhances the search functions of most electronic publications.

Introduction

As a design-compatible, drop-in alternative to traditional NATO 6T lead-acid batteries, the Xcelion 6T® provides increased energy density, measurable life cycle cost benefits and on-board diagnostics that monitor and manage output, performance and protections. The Xcelion 6T® weighs less than its lead-acid counterparts, delivers more power with greater reliability and requires no structural or interface design adaptation. The integral battery management system (BMS) is used for automated balancing and protection, offering CAN communication for advanced vehicles or operation as a standard battery for legacy vehicles. Advanced features of the BMS include real-time battery data monitoring with two-way communication between system and user, reserve protection to support starting at the end of a silent watch, and battle override to allow deep cycles and aggressive use beyond reserve levels.

The advanced Li-ion chemistry in the Xcelion 6T® not only provides more power, but reduces life-cycle cost and the total cost of ownership. The battery sustains significantly more deep-discharge cycles compared to legacy lead-acid, as much as 14 times more for shallow cycling and 25 times more for full depth of discharge. Longer battery life means fewer batteries to buy, replace, ship, store, and dispose and recycle and eliminates need for excess inventory. Reduced weight means one-person lifting and easier maintenance and replacement. Longer life and lighter weight reduces total spare inventory quantity and cost, shipping costs and other logistics burdens. The physical dimensions and connections of the Xcelion 6T® are identical to those of traditional NATO 6T batteries allowing for a direct drop in for today's applications.

Advantages Over Lead Acid

Batteries that incorporate lithium-ion (Li-ion) chemistries have demonstrated their ability to provide more power and to operate for significantly more deep discharge cycles. These advantages translate to a lower life-cycle cost compared to lead-acid batteries. The Xcelion 6T® is a Li-ion drop-in replacement for 28V systems that provides the power equivalent of two series lead-acid batteries. Physical dimensions and connections are identical to the standard NATO 6T lead batteries.

Lithium-ion batteries have a built-in battery management system (BMS) that communicates real-time diagnostic information about the battery's SOC to users. This provides the operator with confidence in knowing that after an extended silent watch sufficient power remains to start the engine. The battery system's Li-ion chemistry enhances the capabilities of today's military vehicles during silent watch operations and for supporting a multitude of power-hungry technologies vital to today's advanced vehicle operations and unit safety / survival.

The system provides power for SLI as well as devices critical to safety during silent watch missions. Li-ion technology safely powers electronics, communications, night sight and other silent watch devices while the vehicle is turned off. Additionally, the 24V, 60Ah design provides greater power density and energy efficiency with long-lasting performance that reduces logistical burdens to store, transport and distribute replacement batteries. It also features available CANBus communications that relay vital information, including SOC (%), battery and cell voltages, temperatures, and battery diagnostics.

One key advantage of the Xcelion 6T® is the ability to delivery capacity and energy at higher rates. Normally, a 120Ah battery label indicates that the battery could provide: 1A for 120 hours; 120A for 1 hour; or 20A for 6 hours – whatever combination of that gives 120Ah output. This is not the case with lead-acid batteries, normally rated at a 20 hour (C/20) discharge rate. Faster discharging reduces the available capacity of the lead-acid battery drastically. Peukert's law shows that the available capacity of a typical lead-acid battery against discharge time is stated for 20 hours at 100% capacity and that eh delivered capacity will diminish at higher than C/20 rates. In comparison, Saft's Xcelion 6T capacities vary only 4% of nameplate capacity at higher rate. Consistent capacity over various discharge rates results in a realized increase in energy density for lithium-ion batteries when compared to legacy lead-acid.

Figure 1 shows the energy delivered from a single 6T battery at various rates and temperatures. The lead acid battery delivers its capacity at 12V and the Xcelion 6T® delivers at 24V in a single 6T format package. The Xcelion 6T® delivers far more energy at these higher rates and is less sensitive to rate of discharge.

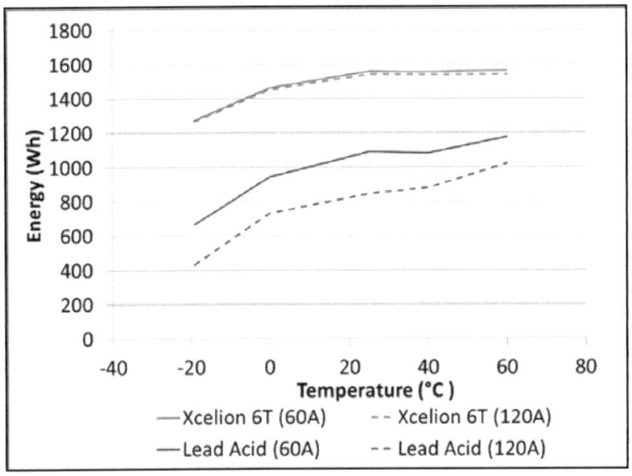

Figure 1: Delivered Energy of Xcelion 6T® vs. lead-acid

Saft's Xcelion 6T® is a 24V 6T lithium-ion equivalent that weighs 46lbs and provides 1.6 kWh of energy at C-rate discharge. Using the Xcelion 6T® rather than the lead-acid 6T option results in a 74% decrease in weight and a two-for-one replacement in volume per system (or 50% reduction.

The Xcelion 6T® delivers more capacity and Energy in comparison to the standard lead-acid AGM 6T battery. The available capacity of traditional lead-acid batteries is dramatically affected by faster charge and discharge rates and limited temperature ranges. By comparison, the increased usable energy density of Li-ion batteries provides consistent capability over various discharge rates and temperatures. Figure 2 shows the excellent rate capability of the Xcelion 6T® battery. Designed for high rate discharges, there is minimal effect on delivered capacity and energy when discharging at high rates. Even at a 240A discharge rate (4C) the Xcelion 6T® is able to deliver essentially all of its capacity. The low impedance of the battery also means less voltage drop under high loads, offering better stability for the 28V bus and a proven ability to dampen the effects of rapid load changes on the vehicle.

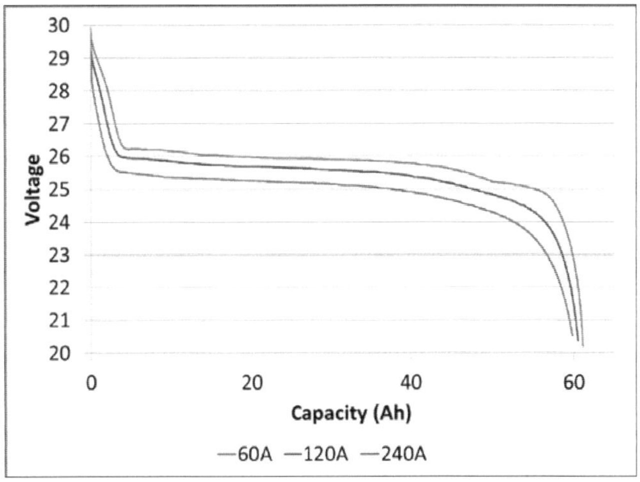

Figure 2: Rate Capability of Xcelion 6T® at Room Temperature

Additionally, use of the more the powerful Xcelion 6T® Li-ion batteries reduces the overall weight of the vehicles while amply meeting the power needs longer than the lifetime expectancy of the lead-acid units replaced. At 40kg per 12V battery, the lead-acid batteries create a high mass burden on the vehicle. The Xcelion 6T® battery is superior for delivery specific energy. Table I shows the specific energy of the Xcelion 6T® in comparison to its lead-acid counterpart. The table shows the energy delivered per unit mass at a 60A discharge rate.

Temperature (°C)	Lead Acid Energy (Wh/kg)	Xcelion 6T Energy (Wh/kg)
-19	17	61
0	24	71
25	27	75
40	27	75
60	29	76

Table I: Specific Energy of the Xcelion 6T® compared to lead-acid

The Xcelion 6T® can substantially reduce the mass burden of the batteries with each battery weighing less and the superior rate capability resulting in the need for fewer batteries to support normal vehicle loads. The weight savings allows for additional resources or capabilities to be outfitted on a vehicle.

Optimized for Power

In addition to energy density, it is also important to compare power density between the two electro-chemistries. The lead-acid 6T battery is required to provide 1,100 amps for 30 seconds at -18°C, and 400 amps for 30 seconds at -40°C. Saft's Xcelion 6T® can deliver this power capability without preheating. The Xcelion 6T®

includes Saft's proprietary Superphosphate® technology that offers excellent rate capability and power stability across state of charge.

Figure 3 shows the load response of the Xcelion 6T® across state of charge (SOC). An aged battery was tested under a 400A load for 30 seconds at each pulse. The battery was stabilized at 25°C between pulses. The data shows that the battery provides a reliable capability in delivering power for starting loads even at deep depths of discharge. This allows for the user to run a longer silent watch, discharging more energy from the battery, and still having enough power capability from the battery to start the engine. It has been demonstrated in real vehicle testing that a single battery at <10% SOC still provides the necessary power for an engine start.

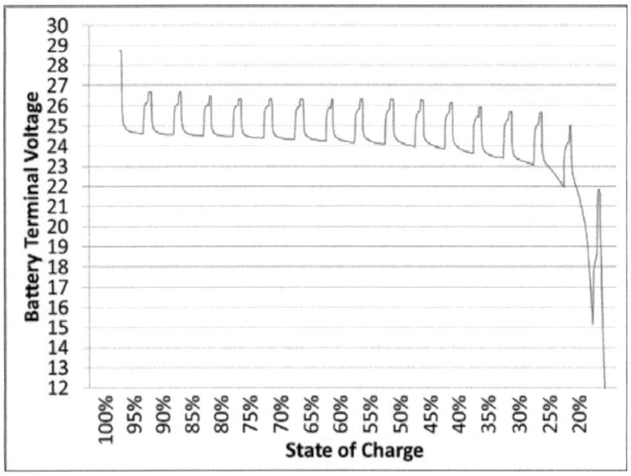

Figure 3: Pulse power capability of Xcelion 6T® across State of Charge

A key advantage of the Xcelion 6T® is the performance in arctic environments. The lead-acid 6T battery is required to provide 1,100 amps for 30 seconds at -18°C, and 400 amps for 30 seconds at -40°C. Other systems require preheating with a heating kit before starting below -40°C. The Xcelion 6T® can support a cold start at -40°C upon demand without any preheating. Additionally, the Xcelion 6T® automatically engages built-in heaters for optimum charging in extreme cold conditions.

Figure 4 shows the performance of the Xcelion 6T® battery under cold temperature cranking loads of 400A at -40°C. Without any preheating, the battery is capable of meeting minimum voltage requirements under load during the 30 second pulse. The voltage actually rises during the pulse due to self-heating of the cells from their internal resistance. The self-heating during cranking improves the performance further with subsequent pulse loads. The ability to provide this power capability at cold temperature on-demand allows for immediate availability without the delay of a preheating operation or the complication of running a secondary battery heater from an external power source to keep the batteries at 'start ready' temperatures.

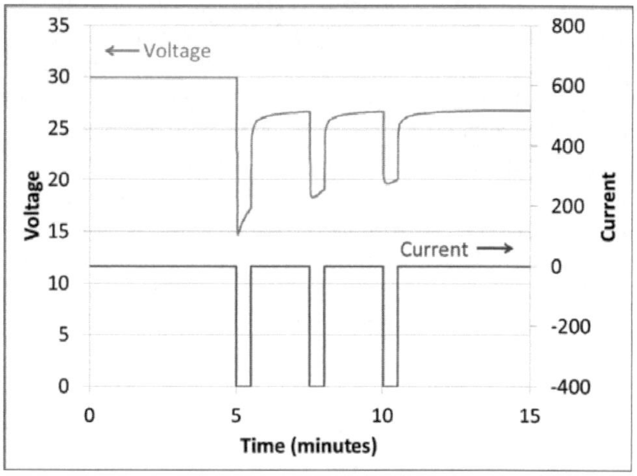

Figure 4: Xcelion 6T® performance under 400A/s30sec load at -40°C without preheating

The performance at -40° for supporting vehicle starting is superior to lead-acid battery performance. Figure 5 shows the comparison of loaded battery voltage for a single Xcelion 6T® battery compared to two (2) AGM lead-acid batteries in series. The single Xcelion 6T® battery is able to exceed the cold temperature capability of the baseline lead 6T batteries, at ¼ of the total battery weight and ½ the volume. The ability of a single battery to support cold temperature starting allows for fewer batteries to be installed in the vehicle.

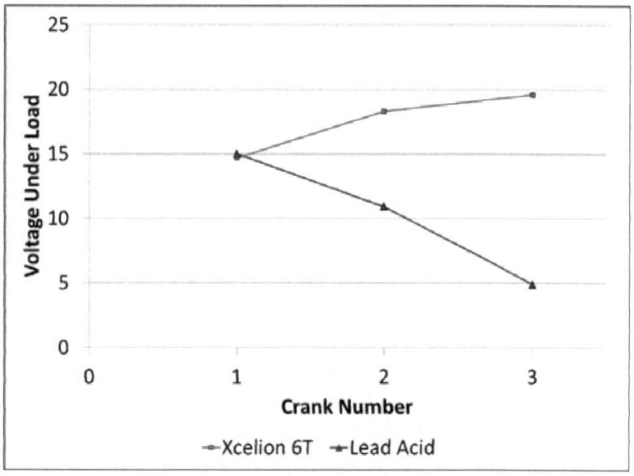

Figure 5: 400A/30sec pulse capability at -40°C

Designed for Long Life

The Superphosphate® cell chemistry used in the Xcelion 6T® battery has been optimized for life at high depth of discharge. Figure 6 shows the cycle life to 80% capacity loss for the Saft battery in comparison to lead acid and commercial 18650 lithium ion cells.

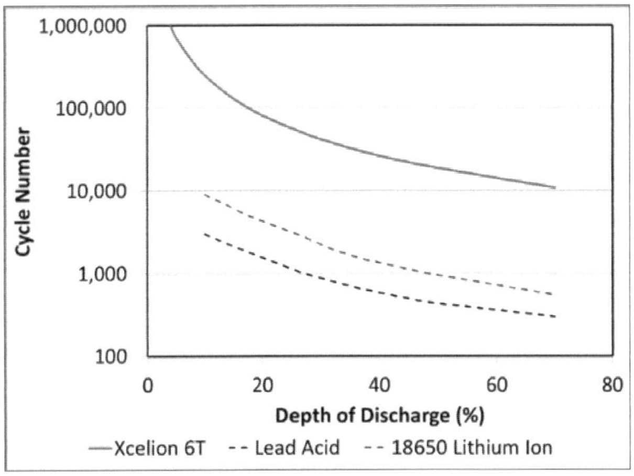

Figure 6: Cycle life comparison of battery technologies

The Saft Xcelion 6T® battery is able to support an order of magnitude more cycles than traditional batteries and is designed for the high depth of discharge demands required for effective silent watch.

In addition to cycle, life, the calendar life of the battery becomes important for long life batteries. Figure 7 shows the calendar life of the Xcelion 6T battery as a function of temperature.

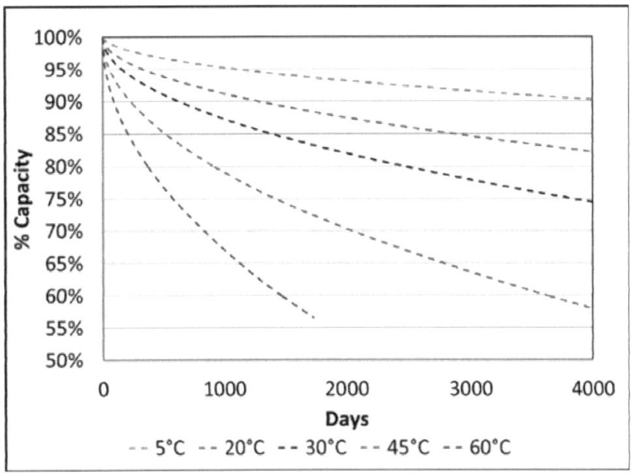

Figure 7: Calendar Life of Xcelion 6T®

The Xcelion 6T® is capable of many years of operation with little loss in capacity. Besides capacity loss as a function of calendar life, it is also important to understand impedance growth over the life of the battery. The impedance growth will affect the ability of the battery to support loads. Figure 8 shows the impedance growth of the Xcelion 6T® electrochemistry compared to normal 18650 lithium ion chemistry. The Superphosphate® chemistry used in the Xcelion 6T® batteries provides excellent impedance stability over the life of the battery. This means that it will still be able to support starting loads over the life of the vehicle. The ageing that occurs with typical batteries will mean that the loss in ability for the battery to support starting loads will likely be an end of life factor for that battery, even if it still has available capacity.

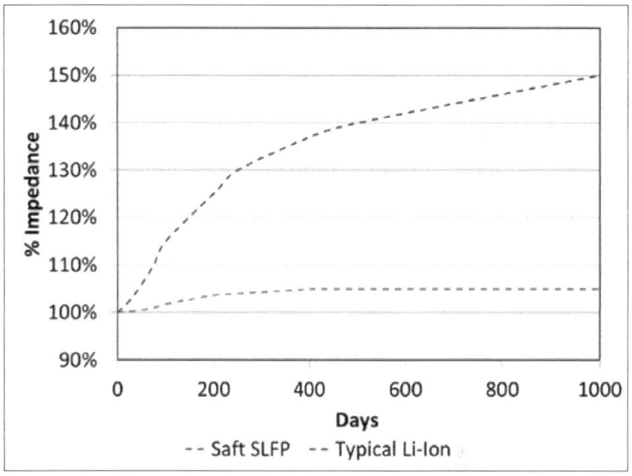

Figure 8: Impedance growth of Saft Superphosphate® in comparison to typical 18650 Li-Ion

The Xcelion 6T® battery offers its long life through excellent behavior for cycle life and impedance stability. The long cycle life and capacity retention means that it can still support silent watch missions even with years of battery use and the low impedance growth means that it will support vehicle starting with years of battery use and ageing.

CONCLUSIONS

The Xcelion 6T® is the result of several generations of battery design for military vehicles. The design has been industrialized with a substantial value engineering effort to reduce the overall cost. The resulting design is competitive with existing lead-acid battery pricing over the life of the vehicle. The cell design is tailored specifically for the application to guarantee performance for power, life, and overall performance. While the cells are customized for the application, they are produced in high volume by Saft. This allows for low cost cell manufacturing that is competitive with the commercial lithium ion market while also maintaining design control and guaranteed source of cells from the United States and Europe.

Acknowledgements

Saft would like to thank TARDEC for its continuing support and collaboration

Advanced Lead Acid – Designing to Stay Competitive

Michael D. Eskra, Rodney M. LaFollette, Richard T. Johnson
Eskra Technical Products, Saukville, WI 53080-1687
mikeeskra@aol.com / 1-262-707-5855

Abstract: *ETP under an Army Phase II SBIR has developed a bipolar lead acid wafer cell with significantly improved cycle life and specific energy. Typically well suited for high voltage applications, the design was directed towards the 6TAGM battery. Removing the lead grids and intercell connectors, the design increased the specific energy by a factor of two. The design lends itself well to higher power, higher voltage designs where further reductions in weight and increased capability naturally occur.*

The doubling of specific energy occurred with baseline active material utilization. Further benefits can be obtained as improvements in active materials are incorporated.

Keywords: Battery; Lead-Acid; Pseudobipolar; Titanium; SnO_2; Wafer Cell.

Introduction

High specific energy is a primary objective of designs of secondary batteries to be used in DOD applications. Lithium-ion (Li-ion) batteries are increasingly the choice for such applications due to their superior specific energy with respect to that of existing aqueous batteries. The disadvantages of Li-ion, such as cost and safety, have mandated reexamination of aqueous systems, particularly if increases in specific energy can be achieved.

Lead-acid batteries are still widely used, particularly when low cost and high power are needed, and the relatively low energy density is acceptable. Improvements in energy density of lead-acid batteries would greatly extend their market utility in many applications. Improved energy density can be achieved primarily through three approaches. The first is improvement in the utilization of the solid active materials (Pb and PbO_2). Utilization is typically limited to < 60%. This is caused by reduction in electrode porosity and electronic conductivity during discharge, caused by formation of (voluminous and resistive) $PbSO_4$ crystals. This can be mitigated in part through addition of conductive additives to the electrode masses, or through various means to retain high porosity. A second way to increase energy density is to decrease the mass of various components of the battery structure, such as electrode grids and connectors. Finally, energy density can be improved through more efficient battery geometries (rather than prismatic or spirally-wound cells having lead strap current collectors with welded intercell connections).

Under on-going sponsorship from the U.S. Army (Contract W56HZV-16-C-0059), Eskra Technical Products (ETP) is addressing the need for improved energy density lead-acid batteries. This is being done primarily through the second and third approaches mentioned; i.e. reduction in mass of battery components and improved construction. Improvements in active material have not been the focus of this program. ETP uses a "wafer cell" construction (Figure 1) that reduces the need for most of the supporting lead metal present in traditional lead-acid cells. This highly efficient design can potentially improve upon typical energy density by 100% or greater. The construction is similar to that of a true bipolar cell, except that both electrodes have their own supporting substrates. The individual cells, consisting of electrodes (active material supported on substrates), separator and electrolyte, are packaged in a polymer pouch, with open spaces on the back of both electrode current collectors as shown in Figure 1.

Individual cells are stacked next to one another, with external (metal) current collector discs placed in the open circular spaces on the backs of the electrodes. Current flows from one cell to its neighbor, by passing through the external current collector discs, improving on the inherent high power performance of lead-acid batteries by increasing the area of intercell connection and minimizing resistive losses by eliminating grids and providing multiple, high area/short path parallel current paths between adjacent cells. With this design there is significant savings in weight, due to reduction of the mass of intercell connections, with placement of current collector foils external to the outermost cell electrodes of each twelve volt block, connected via current collector discs through openings in the cell package on the outside of the electrodes. The twelve volt, six cell blocks are connected in parallel to copper straps leading directly to the base of the external terminals on top of the battery (Figures 2 and 3). This series-parallel arrangement of cells and blocks lowers the impedance of the battery radically.

An essential element of the design involves the substrates that support the active material in both electrodes. Lead metal can be used, although it has high specific weight (11.34 g/cm^3). Metals such as copper and titanium have lower specific weight, but are reactive in contact with the sulfuric acid electrolyte, and at the potentials encountered during battery operation. The material chosen for the substrates should be inert with respect to cell materials and environment. This is accomplished through application of various protective coatings to substrate materials. As long as the coatings completely cover the substrates, and are electrochemically stable, lighter weight materials (such as Ti foil) can be used to support the electrodes.

In this paper we present progress in efforts to build very high specific energy lead-acid batteries. The target application has been the 6TAGM battery. Titanium foil is one of the electrode substrates considered for both positive and negative electrodes. Various positive electrode coatings are used, with high conductivity and electrochemical stability being required coating attributes. The literature and our half-cell experiments show SnO_2 and other proprietary materials to be functional as applied to titanium, copper and other metallic substrates. Thin lead coating of substrates or carbon/graphite polymer composite layers are a favored coating for the negative electrode. Projected energy densities are presented to contrast the relative merits of different material choices. The wafer-cell cell and battery construction is used in these calculations.

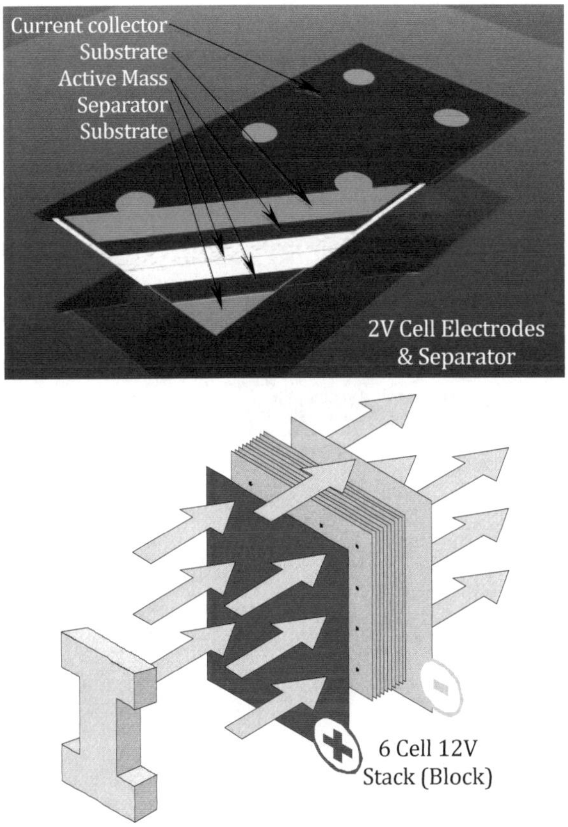

Figure 1. ETP Pseudobipolar "Wafer Cell"

ETP Battery Design

A battery of particular interest is the 6TAGM. A 12 V battery is constructed through parallel connection of multiple 12 V modules or blocks. Each 12 V block consists of six individual wafer cells, stacked adjacent to one another, and electrically connected in series. Figure 2 shows a 12 V battery schematically, consisting of five individual 12 V blocks/modules. Blocks are connected back-to-back, and are connected to battery posts as shown.

Figure 3 is a photograph of a high power, 450 volt Ni-MH battery, consisting of series-connected 48 volt blocks that contain multiple individual wafer cells. The construction is similar that that of the lead-acid battery described in this paper. Not shown are the current collecting straps that conduct current to the battery posts. This battery was built at Electro Energy, Inc., by one of the authors of this paper. It shows significant improvement in energy density (Wh/l) relative to commercial Ni-MH batteries, particularly in high voltage configurations. It was also capable of extremely high power output, > 1 MW.

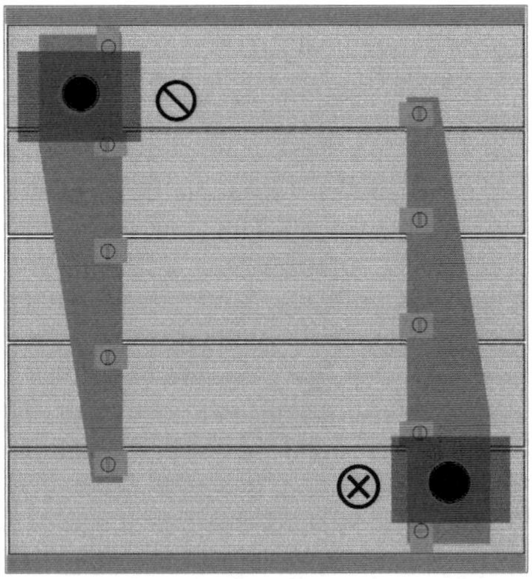

Figure 2. Wafer-Cell 6TAGM Construction Schematic, Top View of Block / Bus Configuration

Figure 3. Wafer-Cell NiMH Battery Construction

Design Calculations

ETP's wafer-cell construction is contrasted with that of traditional 6TAGM batteries through a series of design calculations. These calculations are for batteries such as depicted in Figure 2. Active material utilizations typical of automotive and commercial starting batteries are used. The baseline conditions for calculations are shown in Table 1.

Table 1. Construction Parameters (Data line 1, Table 2)

Parameter	Value
Capacity (Ah)	154
Voltage (V)	12
Positive Active Material Utilization, % Theor.	0.462
Negative Active Material Utilization, % Theor.	0.600
Acid Specific Mass (g/cm^3)	1.310
Separator Porosity (Compressed)	0.88
Acid Capacity/Solids Capacity	2.0
Temperature (Deg C)	25
Length, excluding handles (in)	10.000
Width (in)	10.512
Height (in) – excluding terminals	8.071
Packaging Thickness (in)	0.012
Number of Intercell Cu Connectors/Cell	4
Intercell Cu Connector Thickness (in)	0.004
Intercell Cu Connector Diameter (in)	0.92

Figure 4 shows results of calculations done to contrast the traditional 6TAGM design and the ETP wafer cell design. For the calculation, thin Ti foil (12 µm) was used as the positive electrode substrate, with a thin SnO_2 or equivalent coating (1.5 µm). For the negative, a 12 µm Cu foil was used, with an 85% graphite filled polyvinylidene fluoride (PVDF) coating (50 µm). The battery consisted of five, 12 volt modules, along with a metal housing, current collector straps, metal (steel) ribbed reinforcing plates at the ends of the battery, and a gas-inflated bladder to maintain pressure on the cells. As shown, the active material fraction is significantly higher in the ETP design. This is due to reduction in the weight of battery containment and conductive/connection components. This savings results in a 61% increase in specific energy (58 Wh/kg vs. 36 Wh/kg of the production 6TAGM).

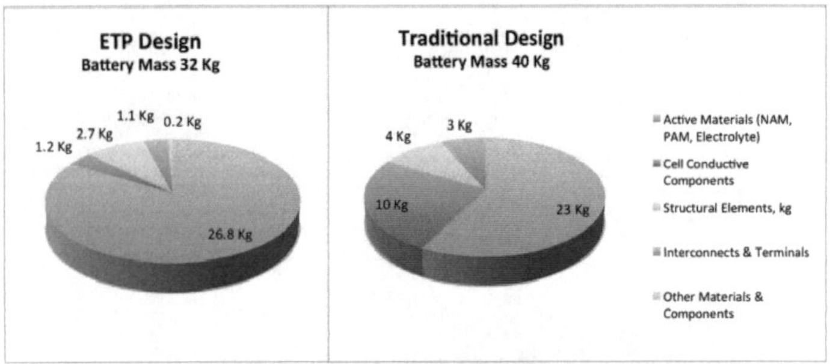

Figure 4. Mass Fractions of Battery Components for 6TAGM Lead-Acid Battery

Table 2 shows the effects of different supporting (non-active) materials, namely the material used in the housing (Titanium or Steel), and the electrode substrates. As shown, the use of thin titanium or copper for the electrodes improves specific energy by approximately 10-15% over 152 µm lead foil, which in turn offers a 40% increase over a conventional 6TAGM design. The housing material made a smaller difference. The designs use very conservative material utilization values typical of production 6TAGM batteries, and offer opportunities for ongoing, stepwise improvement in energy density, specific energy and specific power with further development of active material utilization strategies described in the literature.

Experimental

Full single pouch cells, such as shown in Figure 5 (electrode and substrate only) and Figure 6, were built to evaluate substrate performance. Cell construction initially used lead foil as the substrate for both electrodes for concept verification. Electrodes were prepared using standard pasting processes.

Table 2. Effects of Substrate Type, Block Count & Housing Material

12 Volt Blocks	Positive Substrate	Negative Substrate	Housing	Q Wh	Specific Energy Wh/kg	Energy Density Wh/l
5	12 µm Ti / 1.5 µm SnO_2	12 µm Cu/ 50 µm Graphite filled PVDF	Ti	1850	58.0	133
4	12 µm Ti / 1.5 µm SnO_2	12 µm Cu/ 50 µm Graphite filled PVDF	Steel	1830	55.8	132
5	152 µm Pb	152 µm Pb	Steel	1750	50.4	126
Present Production Lead-Acid 6TAGM:				1440	36	103

Figure 5. Single Full Scale 6TAGM Pouch Cell Electrode, Rear Current Collector Face with Round Intercell Connector Access Openings

As with the half cell tests, cells were held in compression (Figure 6) and evaluated using Arbin battery testers. After initial formation (C/20 to 2.55 V, 2.55 V for 36 hours), cells were subjected to repeated charge/ discharge cycles. Discharges were typically done at C/20 rate to 1.7 V, and charge was also done at C/20 rate, to 2.55 V, and then 2.55 V to C/30 cutoff current. After testing cells were disassembled and autopsied.

Figure 6. Full Scale 6TAGM Cells Under Test

Summary

A wafer cell construction of lead-acid batteries is proposed that will dramatically improve the specific energy over traditional designs. The pseudobipolar arrangement reduces the amount of support and conduction material (non-energy producing material) needed by 67%. The design approach to lead acid batteries greatly increases energy density and impressively eliminates the principle wearout modes of lead-acid – positive material cycling deterioration and in non-lead substrate implementations, does away with positive grid corrosion. Cycle life is multiplied by the high compression enabled by the design, and the design is ideal for high voltage batteries, which in contrast to conventional designs, result in elimination of interconnect and bus components, further reducing weight and freeing up additional volume for active materials. And experiments have shown the design capable of operating fully sealed, providing submodule and battery charge management capability via inexpensive pressure transducers.

The design is particularly suited to low and high voltage aircraft, heavy duty and tactical vehicles and other high vibration, high voltage and high power applications.

In contrast to other high performance batteries, this design approach is inherently safe, requiring minimal charge and discharge control subsystems and no supplemental containment in safety-critical applications.

Acknowledgements

The authors wish to thank the US Army for its support of this work, under SBIR Phase II Contract W56HZV-16-C-0059.

References

1. D.B. Edwards, C. Schmitz, Journal of Power Sources 85 _2000. 63–71
2. Kurisawaa, K. Fujitaa, M. Shiomib, S. Osumia, K. Matsuia, INTELEC 08, San Diego, CA, 14-18 September 2008, 147-152
3. Fujita, K, Kurisawa, US Patent 2010/0015517 A1, Jan (2010).

Li-Ion Conformal Wearable Battery

Rebecca Cragun, Caleb Buck, Shemaiah Khopang, Hyun Bang, Owen Crowther, and Mario Destephen

EaglePicher Technologies, LLC
1216 West C Street
Joplin, MO 64802, USA
Rebecca.Cragun@EaglePicher.com / 1-417-623-8000

Abstract: *This paper describes the continuing development of a Li-Ion conformal wearable battery by EaglePicher Technologies. It is designed to be robust, lightweight and flexible, with a nominal energy of over 154 Wh and a weight of less than 1.18 kg. The considerations in terms of balancing conformability, energy, and cell size will be discussed. The paper will also cover the battery management system, safety features and specific safety tests, and give examples of electrical battery performance.*

Keywords: Portable Power; Li-Ion Battery; Li-Ion Cell; Conformal Battery; Battery Management System; Safety; Overcharge; Nail Penetration; Pouch Cell.

Introduction

EaglePicher Technologies has been a leader in the development and production of cells and batteries for portable power applications. EaglePicher continues its development of next generation, lightweight, high energy density cells and batteries in both primary and secondary chemistries. In this regard, EaglePicher has continued the development of Li-Ion cell and battery technologies to decrease the wearable energy footprint of the Soldier. With higher energy density batteries, the Soldier will have increased energy availability to meet the rising energy demands of advanced gear. In addition to meeting the increasing energy demand, the batteries need to be flexible so the Soldier can locate them in convenient positions around other gear while maintaining comfort and load carriage distribution. The battery must also operate effectively and safely within the Soldier's temperature and other environmental operating conditions.

Li-Ion Conformal Wearable Batteries (CWB) deliver a lightweight energy solution in a conformal package leading to an improved energy density. This paper will give a brief description of advancements in Li-Ion cell and battery technology. It will describe some of the recent efforts involved in the analysis, design, and development of this battery. Trade-off considerations to show how conformability, cell size, electronics, and battery energy have to be balanced in order to achieve optimal performance based on the targeted goals will be discussed as well as improvements in the manufacturability of the cells. Results from safety and performance testing under various conditions are included.

Battery Description

The rechargeable conformal battery is a thin lightweight power source with a flexible form factor that is designed to match the contour of the Soldier's gear for improved mobility and agility. The case design and the layout of the battery are in Figure 1. As shown, the case has grooves that contribute to its flexibility as well as its manufacturability. The case design has a vent as well as a state-of-charge indicator. The main connector is on the lower right side while the charge pins are located on the back. The battery can be charged through either contact port. The battery provides a 14.4 V nominal voltage and delivers 154 Wh. Its operating temperature is from -20°C to 60°C. The battery delivers 10.5 Ah and operates in a voltage range from 10 to 17.2 V with a life expectancy of greater than 224 cycles. The battery assembly consists of Li-Ion pouch cells. A significant driver behind using pouch cells was the weight. Nominal weight for the battery is just below 1.18 kg and the energy density is 130 Wh/kg.

Figure 1: Case design and layout, showing grooves between cell compartments, vent, and state of charge indicator.

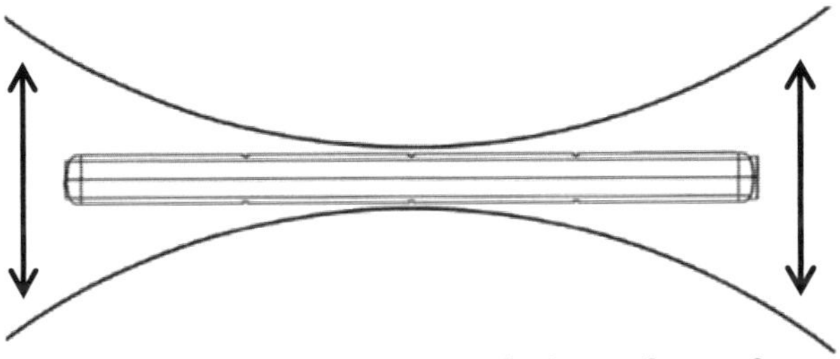

Figure 2: Required movement of edges of a conformal battery.

Conformability

Several challenges were overcome in enabling this design to fulfill the need of weight reduction while still supplying the required energy and power in a conformal package. The battery had to flex its edges a certain distance from its horizontal center axis repeatedly as shown in Figure 2 while still operating throughout the entire temperature range. To meet this challenge, multiple design factors were considered. The case material was selected based upon its flexibility, chemical compatibility, surface friction, durability, and strength characteristics. Many finite element analyses were performed on potential material and design combinations before one was selected.

Another challenge encountered during the development of the battery was the size and construction of the cells to use. Optimization of the cell size considered the energy requirements as well as the flexibility of the battery. If the selected cell filled a large portion of the interior volume of the case, the battery would not be as flexible as desired. If the cell size were small, the flexibility would be enhanced, but at the expense of decreased energy density. Once a balance between cell size and battery flexibility was determined, the final design underwent flexibility testing.

As shown in Figure 3, the battery was deflected 100+ times in both vertical directions, along both horizontal center axes. This test was performed at both room temperature and at -20°C. Noninvasive examination, electronics testing, and performance cycling was performed after the tests and confirmed that no damage was done to interior battery components.

Battery Management System

The conformal battery is a smart battery. Its Battery Management System (BMS) controls internal cell balancing, charge/discharge, and the state of charge indicator (SOCI) shown in Figure 4. The BMS is Smart Management Bus (SMBus) communications compliant and monitors temperature, current, and voltage fault conditions. To prevent cell damage during charge the BMS monitors virtual cell voltages and interrupts the charge when any virtual voltage exceeds a pre-set value.

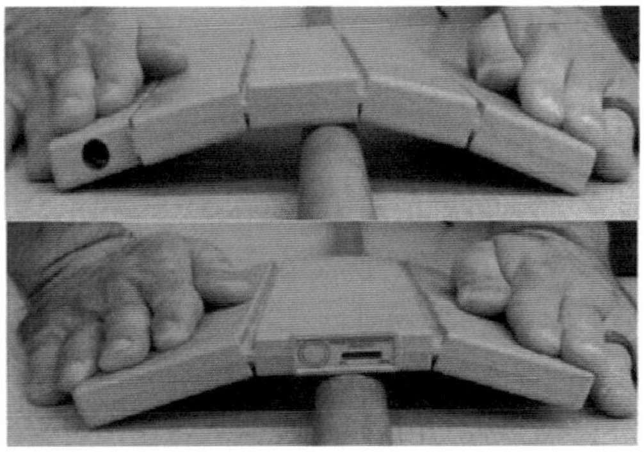

Figure 3: Battery subjected to conformability test of flexing the battery 100+ times in both vertical directions, along both horizontal center axes.

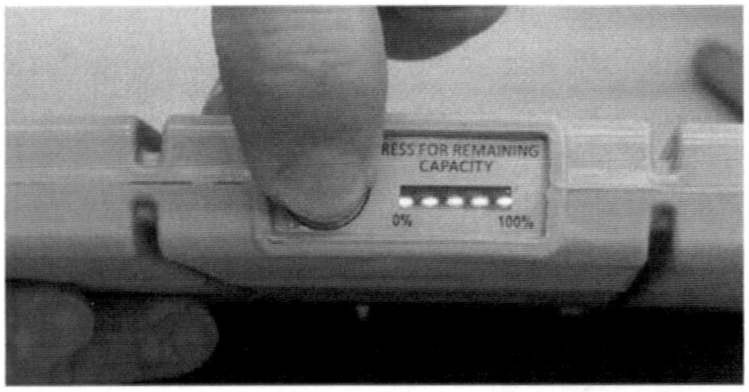

Figure 4: Temperature and rate compensated state-of-charge indicator with LED display.

In addition to the BMS protections, the battery contains other safety features, including both non-resettable and resettable thermal devices, current fuses, and a vent.

Safety Testing

As previously mentioned a pouch cell was used within the conformal battery. This was partly driven by the weight. In addition, the pouch approach provided enhanced safety. Fully charged cells were instrumented with thermocouples and subjected to the nail penetration test. As shown in Figure 5, the test was uneventful with the maximum temperature observed at about 94°C.

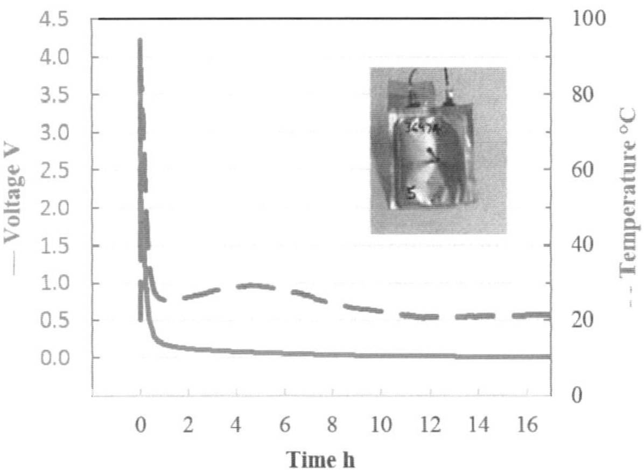

Figure 5: Image of pouch cell after nail penetration test and the temperature profile during testing.

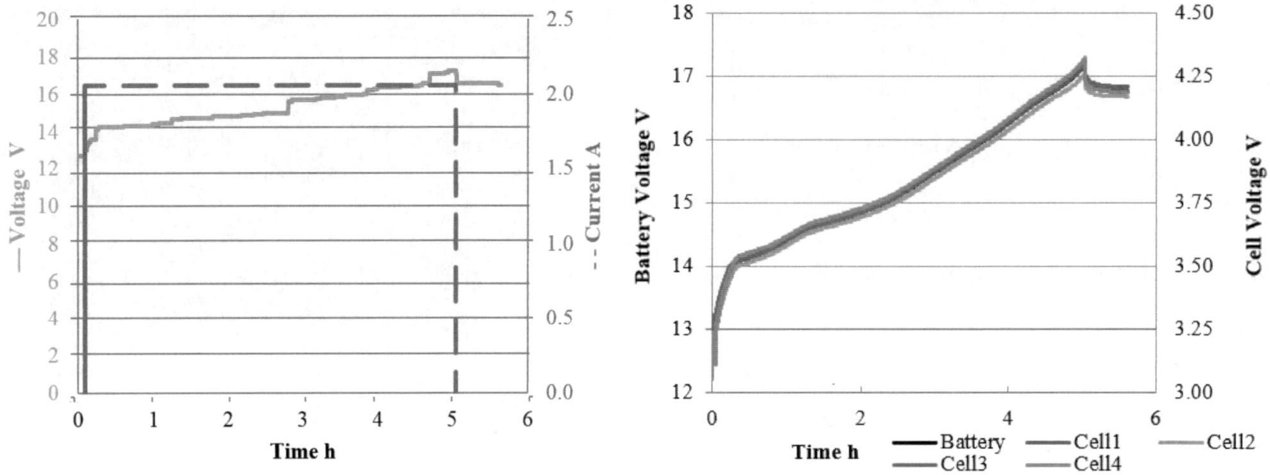

Figure 6: Overcharge test data.
Left – Battery voltage/current, Right – Measured cell voltages at battery voltage

Figure 6 shows battery test data recorded during an overcharge test. The battery was charged at a constant current of 2.1 A passed the recommended maximum voltage of 17.2 V until it reached 17.8 V. As shown in the figure, when the battery voltage reached 17.19 V the BMS stopped the charge. The maximum cell voltage reached was 4.3 V.

Discharge tests at the battery level shows that the battery will deliver over 154 Wh when discharged at a C/5 rate as shown in Figure 7. After charging at a 3.5 A (C/3) rate the battery was discharged at its maximum discharge rate of 5 A (C/2). The decrease in energy output was small with the battery delivering over 140 Wh.

The battery has also been subjected to cold temperature discharge testing. Figure 8 shows the discharge profile at -20°C after a cold soak of 4 hours at that temperature. At a rate of C/5 the battery delivers over 110 Wh.

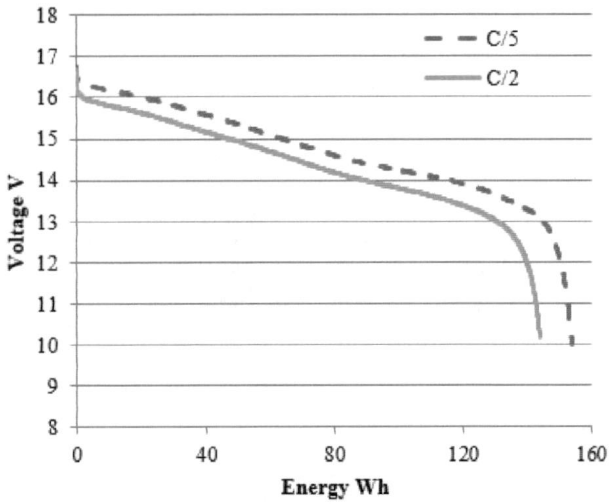

Figure 7: C/5 and C/2 discharge profiles during room temperature testing.

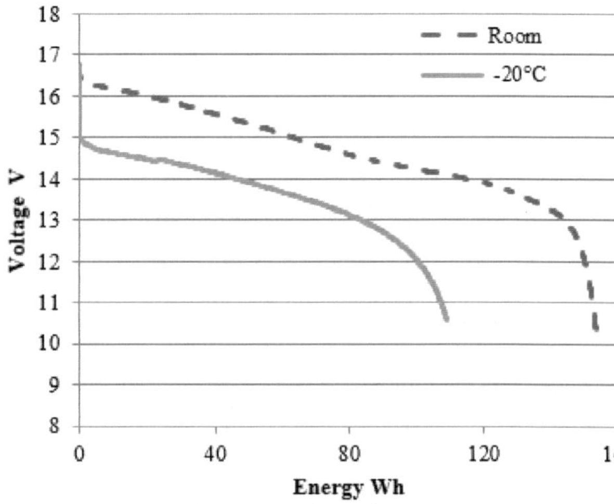

Figure 8: C/5 discharge profiles during room and -20°C testing.

Figure 9: EaglePicher SLC 200 series cells to power next generation of conformal batteries.

Figure 10: Li-Ion cell manufacturing equipment at EaglePicher.

Continued Development

EaglePicher Li-Ion cells are at the core of the conformal battery's performance. Development continues on the performance and manufacturing of these cells. EaglePicher with a Defense Production Act Title III program has expanded its facilities and created a production line to produce Li-Ion pouch cells as shown in Figure 9.

Having strong, reliable, domestic manufacturing in strategic areas is important to the United States. Not only does it encourage continued innovation, but it also provides a foundation to the country's economic future. The creation of this Li-Ion production line supports this foundation as a domestic source of quality, reliable Li-Ion pouch cells. Some of the production line equipment is shown in Figure 10.

SLC 200 series pouch cells, which are produced on this production line will power the next generation of conformal batteries. These pouch cells have an operating temperature range of -30°C to 60°C and an expected life of greater than 300 cycles. More information on available cell sizes and their capacity, weight, specific energy, and other performance data can be obtained through the EaglePicher website.

Conclusion

EaglePicher has developed a Li-Ion conformal battery that is flexible, weighs less than 1.18 kg, and will deliver over 154 Wh. It has a robust design with numerous tested safety features. With the creation of a new Li-Ion production line, EaglePicher continues to be a leader in the development and production of cells and batteries for next generation technologies.

Acknowledgement

Special thanks to CERDEC and to the Defense Production Act Title III program team for supporting the rechargeable conformal cell and battery development. This material is released to the public domain in accordance with ITAR 22 CFR 120.11.

High Power and High Rate Li/CF_x-MnO_2 Pouch Cell Hybrid Technology

Ernest Ndzebet, Mario Destephen, Dong Zhang, and David Darch

EaglePicher Technologies, LLC
1216 West "C" Street, Joplin, Missouri 64802
Phone: (417) 623-8000 Fax: (417) 680-7408

Contact Author: Ernest Ndzebet
Email: Ernest.Ndzebet@eaglepicher.com

Abstract: *EaglePicher Technologies has developed a Li/CF_x-MnO_2 pouch cell hybrid technology capable of delivering high energy at high discharge rates and very low temperatures. Performance of the hybrid pouch cells was validated at up to 2C continuous discharge rate in temperature range from -40°C and 60°C. These cells deliver a nominal specific energy of >400 Wh/Kg at room temperature which is >50% above current Li-ion cells. This technology offers a good opportunity for applications requiring a combination of high power and high energy such as Unmanned Aerial Vehicle (UAV). This paper will provide a general overview of recent progress on hybrid chemistry technology at EaglePicher Technologies, and discuss results from this pouch cell and battery work.*

Keywords: carbon fluoride; manganese dioxide; battery.

Introduction

Lithium/Carbon fluoride (Li/CF_x) is an attractive primary power source, because of its high specific energy, low self-discharge (less than 1% per year), excellent thermal stability, wide operating temperature range (-40 to 85°C), and improved abuse tolerance over other lithium systems. However, the obstacles that prevent a wider market penetration of Li/CF_x chemistry are its initial voltage delay at low temperature, thermal management issue at high discharge rates, and its material cost. Several approaches have been used to address these issues, including a partial substitution of CF_x by manganese dioxide to form hybrid cathode [1-2]. Using web-coating process similar to that in lithium-ion battery production, EPT has developed CF_x-MnO_2 hybrid cathode, which not only maintains all the favorable advantages of Li/CF_x but also provides the highest specific energy and excellent performance in wide temperature range as compared to other lithium primary chemistries.

This paper provides a general overview of recent developments on hybrid chemistry technology at EaglePicher Technologies, and discusses results from our work on pouch cells and batteries.

Experimental

The materials and cathode process were described previously [3-5]. Carbon fluoride (CF_x) and electrolytic manganese dioxide (MnO_2) used in this work were commercially-available materials. The hybrid cathodes were processed using EPT's advanced web coating equipment similar to that used in lithium-ion technology. The cathode composition and formulation were optimized to achieve high electrode density with enhanced rate capability.

Results and Discussion

EPT has developed a high-power and high-rate lithium primary cell technology that includes a web-coated CF_x/MnO_2 hybrid cathode and proprietary electrolyte formulations through extensive efforts over the last several years. The addition of MnO_2 in the cathode reduces the heat generation, eliminates voltage delay, and lowers the overall cathode material cost. The web coating process enables thinner cathodes with improved rate capability. The choice of carbon type used as conducting additive and its distribution within the cathode structure, as well as an optimized cathode porosity further enhance the cell rate capability. In order to extend the operating temperature of Li-CF_x/MnO_2 hybrid cell without sacrificing the rate capability, an electrolyte with low viscosity, low melting-point solvents and optimal lithium salt concentration was developed. This hybrid technology has been evaluated in both cylindrical and prismatic cells configurations. In this paper, we will discuss the performance of the hybrid Li/CF_x-MnO_2 pouch cell for high-rate applications in an extended temperature range.

High-Rate Hybrid Pouch Cell Development

Pouch cells with this hybrid chemistry were developed to maximize cell discharge rate capability, while maintaining the high energy density. The advantages for pouch cells include flexibility in size design, high specific energy, and inexpensive packaging material compared to hard case cells. The pouch cell format offers opportunities for better performance with reduced weight burden in portable power applications. The historic limitations for pouch cells include leakage and swelling due to gassing and CF_x electrode expansion during discharge. Among these limitations, the major challenge for hybrid pouch cells is cell swelling due to the well-known swelling behavior of the CF_x cathodes during discharge; the higher the amount of CF_x in the hybrid cathode, the higher the extent of swelling tends to be. The swelling will not only affect the battery integrity, but also will negatively impact the battery discharge performance in the pouch cell format. These limitations can be addressed through optimization of the electrolyte formulation, the choice of suitable CF_x materials, pouch material selection, and pouch sealing techniques. Figure 1 shows a drawing of the high-rate hybrid pouch cell (LCF-136) developed at EaglePicher.

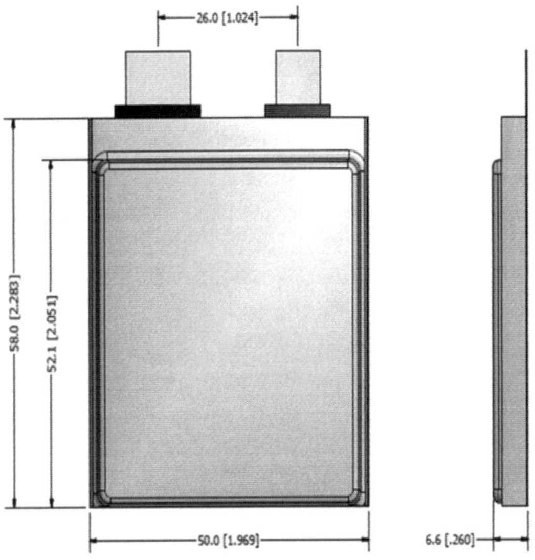

Figure 1. Li/CFx-MnO_2 Pouch Cell (dimension in mm)

The chemistry and design of the EaglePicher pouch cells were optimized by selecting the proper cathode active material, cathode composition, carbon conductive additives, and binder. Also, for the active materials, the ratio of the amount of MnO_2 to CF_x was optimized in terms of its effect on swelling, heat generation, and energy density requirement for the high-rate battery. The cathode loading was optimized according to the process capability, energy density, and power requirements for the battery. Cathode porosity was also optimized based on its effects on cathode swelling and energy density requirement for the battery.

Performance of the hybrid pouch cell was validated at up to a 2C rate for a wide range of temperatures. Figure 2 illustrates the performance of pouch cells at different temperatures. As can be seen, the pouch cells were able to deliver high efficiency from -40°C to 60°C.

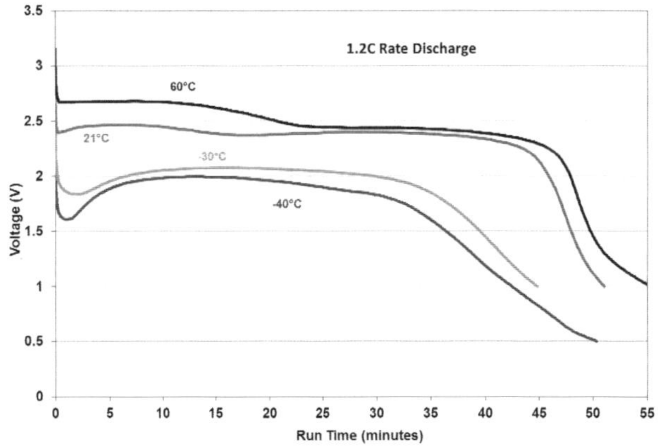

Figure 2. Discharge performance of pouch cells

Figure 3 shows the discharge curves of pouch cells on constant power discharge protocol at different temperatures. As can be seen, the cells exhibit a good start up power capability in the investigated temperature range. It has been demonstrated that batteries built with these cells achieved full power output at low temperature in short period of time, particularly when discharged at high rates due to cell self-heating nature.

The LCF-136 based Li/CF_x-MnO_2 pouch cells are suitable for applications requiring lightweight, maintenance free, high rate and long lasting power sources such as UAVs. Moreover, when stored at 20°C, they exhibit a low self-discharge of less than 0.7% per year. It is worth noting that the power capability of LCF-136 based batteries at -40°C has been demonstrated after 7 years of storage at 20°C.

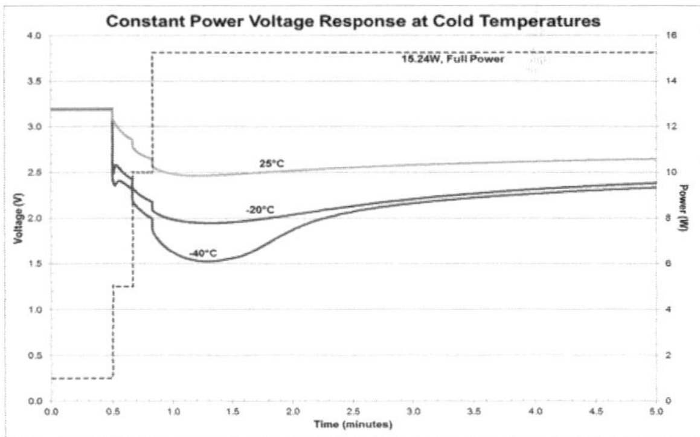

Figure 3. Performance of a LCF-136 pouch cell on constant power discharge protocol.

Figure 4 shows the performance of a single pouch cell (LCF-136) under a simulated UAV profile. The discharge profile includes a 1.5C discharge rate during take-off and a C/2 discharge rate during cruise discharge. It can be seen in the figure that the cell demonstrated the power capability required for this type of applications. Several battery packs have recently been developed for different applications including UAV (see Figure 5).

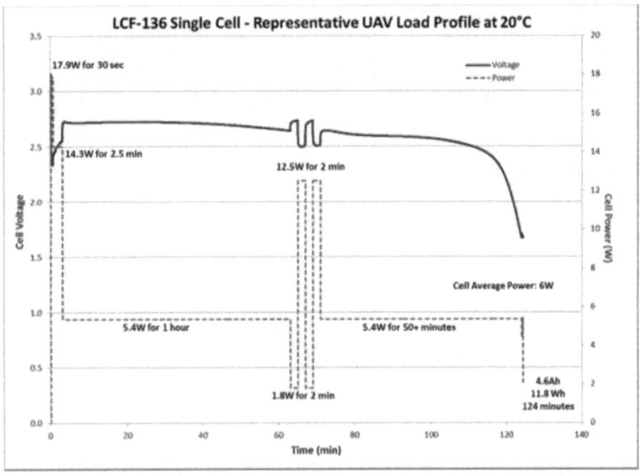

Figure 4. Performance of a LCF-136 pouch cell under a simulated UAV discharge profile

Figure 5. Example UAV packs with EaglePicher LCF-136 Li/CF_x-MnO_2 Cells (14, 24, and 56 cell packs)

In conclusion, EaglePicher has made great progress in developing a Li/CF_x-MnO_2 hybrid technology, which offers a combination of power and energy for military and space applications requiring high rate capability and long service life in an extended operating temperature from -40 to 60°C. The hybrid chemistry pouch cells provide an opportunity to develop lightweight, compact, and versatile batteries to address industry needs and requirements.

Acknowledgements

This material is released to the public domain in accordance with ITAR 22 CFR 120.11.

References

1. Marple, J. W., "Performance characteristics of Li/MnO_2-CFx hybrid cathode jellyroll cells" *Journal of Powers Sources*, vol. 19, pp.325-335, 1987.
2. Leger, V. Z., "Non aqueous cell having a MnO_2/polycarbon fluoride cathode," US patent 4327166, April 1982.
3. Zhang, D., E. Ndzebet, and M. Yang, "Advanced Battery Chemistry for Portable Power," *Proceeding of the 44th Power Sources Conference*, Las Vegas, Nevada, 14-17 June 2010.
4. Destephen, M., D. Zhang, H. Bang, J. Wang, U. Viswanathan, and E. Ndzebet, "Advanced Hybrid Battery Chemistry for Portable Power," *Proceeding of the 45th Power Sources Conference*, Las Vegas, Nevada, 11-14 June 2012.
5. Destephen, M., D. Zhang, H. Bang, and E. Ndzebet, "Advanced Li/CFx-MnO2 Hybrid Technology Development," *The 46th Power Sources Conference*, Orlando, Florida, June 9-12, 2014.
6. Read, J., D. Foster, J. Wolfenstine, and S. Zhang, "Microcalorimetry of Li/CFx Cells and Discharge Mechanism", *www.arl.army.mil/arlreports/2009/ARL-TR-5043.pdf*, 2009.

Primary Conformal Wearable Battery

David Darch and Mario Destephen

EaglePicher Technologies, LLC
1215 W. C Street
Joplin, Missouri, USA, 64802

Abstract: *This paper covers a description of the primary conformal wearable battery developed by EaglePicher Technologies. It is designed to be robust, lightweight and flexible, with a nominal energy of 250Wh when discharged at 20W continuous power. The weight of the battery is 0.94kg. The battery has been subjected to extensive safety and abuse testing and this will be discussed in details in this paper. The paper will also cover the battery management system, safety features, and examples of electrical battery performance.*

Keywords: Portable power; Li/CF_x-MnO_2 hybrid battery; Conformal Battery; Bullet penetration testing; Impact testing.

Introduction

There is an ongoing effort by the Army focused on enhancing the load carriage distribution for the Soldier with a reduced weight burden and increased comfort. In that regard, the Army is specifically interested in the development of a conformal battery system designed to slip in front and match the contour of a Soldier's SAPI body armor plate shown in Figure 6, providing the soldier with a lightweight power pack for the increasing energy/power demands in the electronic battlefields of the 21st century. EaglePicher Technologies, LLC (EPT) has designed and developed a primary version of the Conformal Wearable Battery (CWB) that will have a significantly reduced weight burden in a conformal package, as well as much higher energy density than that of a Li/MnO_2-based battery. This paper will give a brief description of the battery before describing results from safety and battery performance testing under various conditions, including impact testing and bullet penetration testing.

Battery Description

This primary CWB is a 24-cell 15V power pack based on a Li/CF_x-MnO_2 hybrid cell packaged in a flexible hermetic pouch. The pouch cell uses a CF_x-MnO_2 hybrid cathode, with paddle wound design in a flexible hermetic pouch. The conformal battery has dimensions of 19.5cm x 22.1 cm and is less than 2 cm thick. It weighs about 940 grams. The case design is shown in Figure 1 with a state-of-charge indicator (SOCI), a complete discharge device (CDD), and an electrical connector. As can be seen, there are grooves between the cell compartments. This is critical for achieving the right amount of conformability as required by the Army. While having these grooves is inconvenient from a cell size and cell layout and wiring perspective, it is necessary to give the battery the right amount of flexibility. A careful tradeoff study was conducted to establish the optimum balance between the conformability and the energy in the battery, driven by the allowable cell size. Once this had been determined, extensive flexibility testing with subsequent electric testing was performed. An example of this can be seen in Figure 2. In addition to strength and flexibility considerations, the surface friction of the case material must also be evaluated. The battery should not be difficult to insert and remove from its designated location next to the SAPI armor plates shown in Figure 6, thus the coefficient of friction of the outer case surface must be below a certain threshold. Another consideration in the case design is chemical compatibility. The battery case material has been exposed to electrolyte solvent, as well as kerosene. The chemical testing has shown no significant effect on the case.

The battery will deliver over 250 Wh at a nominal voltage of about 15V under a 20W continuous load. It has a discharge capacity of about 17.6 Ah above 9V. The energy density at this rate is about 266 Wh/kg. The maximum continuous power draw is about 75W or 5A. It will operate in a temperature range from -20°C to 60°C. This is further detailed later in the paper.

Figure 1. Case design and layout, showing grooves between cell compartments, connector, CDD location,and SOCI.

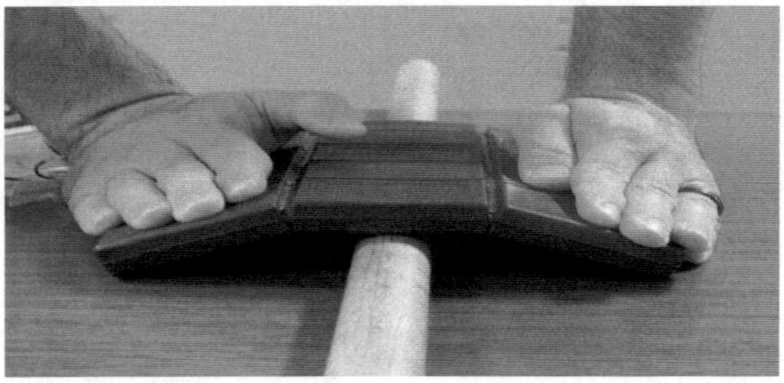

Figure 2. Battery flexibility testing along the short axis.

Battery SOCI and Protection System

EaglePicher Technologies has developed a battery protection and SOCI Printed Circuit Assembly (PCA) incorporating SBS/SMBus capability for the conformal battery pack. The PCA provides the following:

- Charge protection
- Over-current protection using fuses at both the cell and the battery level
- Temperature protection using multiple thermal fuses throughout the battery
- Complete Discharge Device (CDD)
- Temperature and Rate Compensated State-of-Charge Indicator (SOCI) with LED display. This can be seen in Figure 3. Testing of SOCI shows accuracy to within 10% of actual discharge data.
- Smart Battery Specification (SBS) 1.1 compliant communications interface (SMBus 1.1)

Figure 3: Temperature and Rate Compensated State-of-Charge Indicator (SOCI) with LED display.

Safety Evaluation

EaglePicher Technologies has conducted extensive safety and abuse testing of the primary CWB. Two of the more challenging tests that the Army requires the battery to pass are the bullet penetration and the impact tests.

Bullet Penetration Test

Three primary CWB batteries were exposed to the bullet penetration test as specified by the Army. These batteries were all at 100% SOC when subjected to the test and placed in front of a SAPI plate. Then each battery was shot three times using 7.62 mm ammunition. The last two were shot using 7.62 mm API tracer ammunition, one with the shots coming at an angle perpendicular to the battery surface, the other with the shots coming at a 45° angle to the surface. The back side of each of these two batteries can be seen in Figures 4 and 5, respectively. There were no sign of flames or fire in any of the three batteries. The maximum temperature observed in any of the batteries after the test was about 100°C.

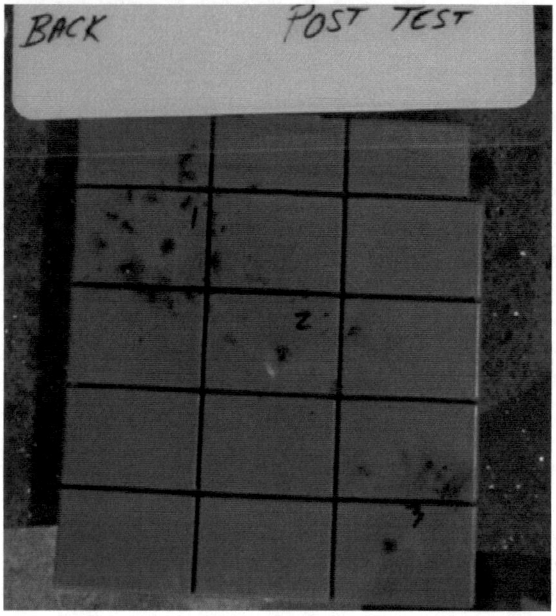

Figure 4. Backside of CWB battery after being shot three times with 7.62 mm API tracer ammunition at an angle perpendicular to the battery surface.

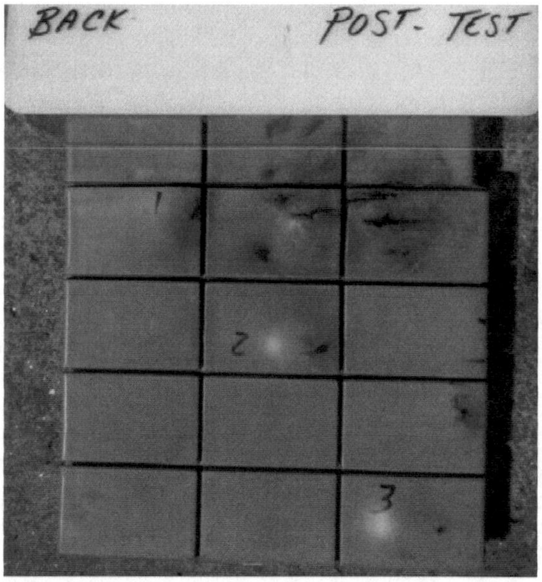

Figure 5. Backside of CWB battery after being shot three times with 7.62 mm API tracer ammunition at a 45° angle to the battery surface.

Each battery was still at 100% SOC after the test. This was observed by using both the SOCI and by measuring OCV through the connector. The battery has been designed to still be functional after being exposed to gunfire.

Impact Test

Several primary CWB batteries have been exposed to the impact test. This test involves dropping a 16lb bowling ball on to the surface of the CWB battery from 3 feet up. This is done three times for each battery. After the impact test the battery must remain functional. Figure 7 shows an image of a ball hitting a battery during a test. This particular battery was impacted five times. After impact testing the same battery was subjected to a 20 W constant power discharge. The voltage profile of this test can be seen in Figure 8. It delivers about 240Wh. The battery was instrumented with internal thermocouples, showing the temperature did not exceed 45°C.

Prior to exposing this battery to an impact test, this same battery was also exposed to conformability testing, mechanical shock, random vibration testing, and transit drop testing. The transit drop test had a 26-drop requirement. Throughout this testing the battery was subjected to several 1 minute 20W loads to evaluate if any damage had been done to the battery. This will need to be considered when looking at the discharge profile in Figure 8 and the output of 240Wh.

Battery Performance

The CWB have been tested at a variety of rates and various environmental conditions. One of the baseline tests that EPT performs is a 20W continuous power discharge at room temperature. Figure 9 (a, b) shows the outcome of two such tests. On Figure 9a is a continuous 20W discharge showing that the conformal battery will deliver 250Wh in room temperature conditions. The plot on the right (see Figure 9b) is the same test, except in this case the discharge was interrupted in order to perform other tests on the battery. The battery was discharged briefly at a 20W continuous load before it was exposed to 6 thermal cycles, similar to those specified for UN transportation testing. Subsequently it went through the UN sinusoidal vibration cycles 4 times in each axis. It was then discharged at 20W for another 3 hours. At this time the battery was subjected to a bend test of ninety deflection cycles, each cycle consisting of flexing the edges of the battery up and down a distance of 1in. from the centerline. This was then repeated along the other horizontal axes of the battery. After the bend test the battery was then fully discharged at 20W. It delivered 234Wh

Figure 10 (a, b) shows the discharge performance of the battery at 55°C (Fig. 10a) and -20°C (Fig. 10b). Prior to testing at 20 W constant power, these batteries were soaked for 4 hours either at 55 or -20°C. As can be seen, the battery discharged at 55°C delivered 260Wh and its skin temperature reached about 72°C (see Fig. 10a). Whereas the one discharge at -20°C delivered 194Wh and its skin temperature reached about 5°C (see Fig. 10b).

Figure 6. Slipping a conformal battery into the protective vest

Figure 7. Instrumented battery subjected to the impact test. Photo is taken with a high speed camera.The bowling ball is dropped on several locations from 36 inches above the battery.

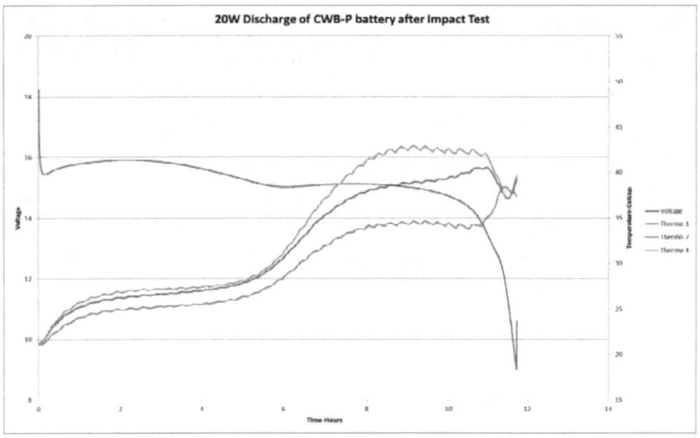

Figure 8. 20W continuous power discharge profile of battery after exposed to impact test.

Conclusion

EaglePicher has developed a primary conformal battery that is flexible, weighs less than 1.0kg, and will deliver 250Wh at room temperature. It will deliver over 190Wh at -20°C. It has a very robust design with numerous safety features that has been subjected to, and passed, bullet penetration and impact testing, in addition to numerous other safety tests.

Acknowledgement

Special thanks to CERDEC for supporting the primary conformal battery development. This material is released to the public domain in accordance with ITAR 22 CFR 120.11.

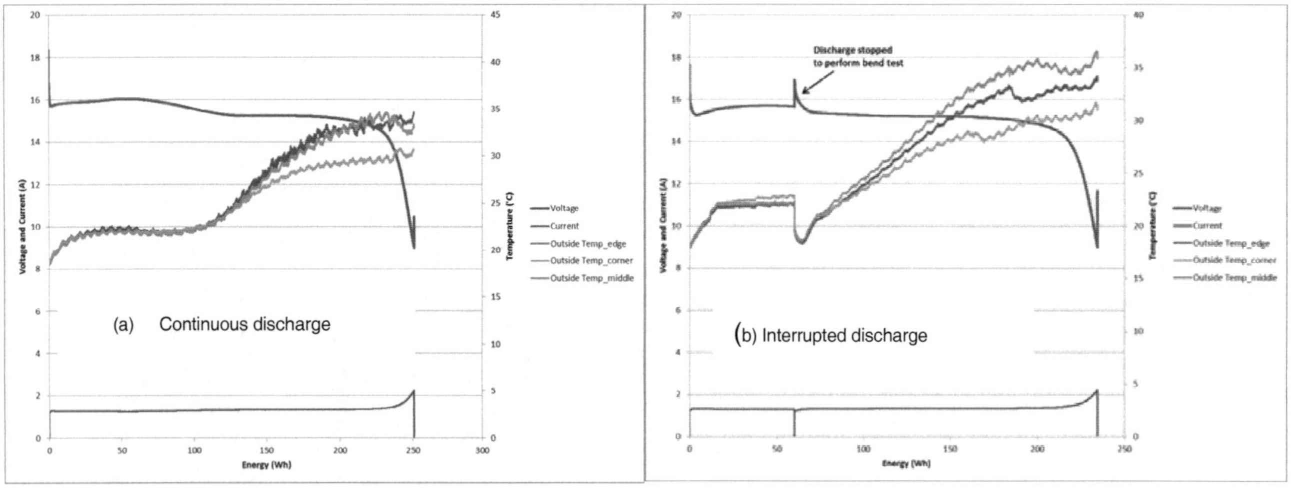

Figure 9(a, b). Discharge profile of CWB-P at 20W constant load in room temperature environment.

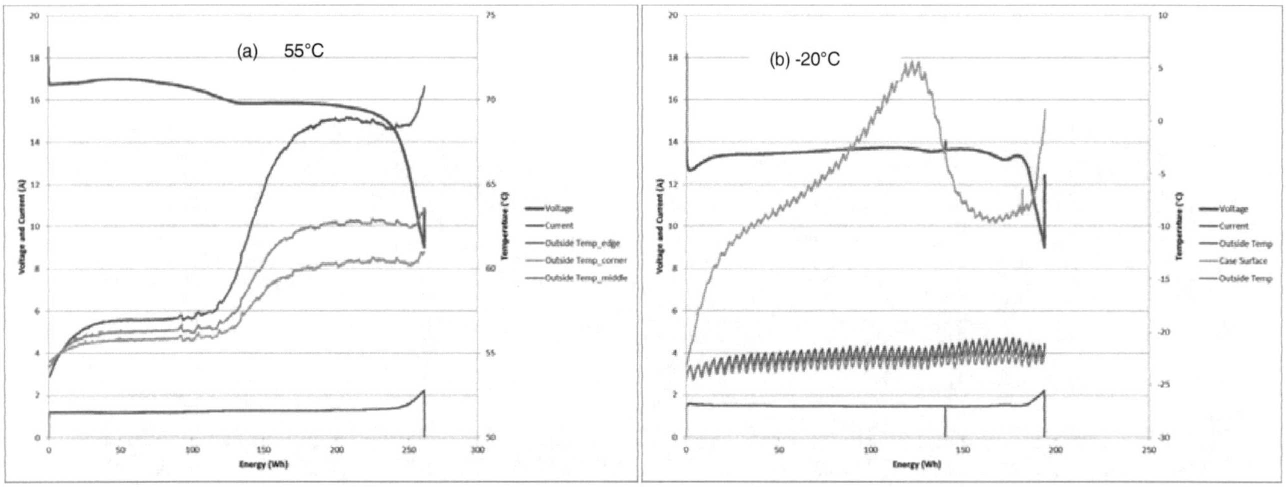

Figure 10(a,b). Discharge profile of CWB-P at 20W constant load at 55°C and -20°C.

NATO Standardization Efforts for Dismounted Soldier Power

Darren Jonathan Browning[1], Marc Gietter[2], Dan Milliken[2]

[1] Dstl, Platform Systems Division, Defence Science and Technology Laboratory, Salisbury, Wiltshire, UK, SP4 0JQ

[2] US Army CERDEC, Power Division, Command, Power and Integration Directorate, 6631 Cyber Street, Building 5100, Aberdeen Proving Ground, MD 21005-1852

Abstract: *NATO has an aim to enable greater interoperability between partner nations through standardization in all its various form. Specifically the NATO Land Capability Group on Dismounted Soldier Systems (LCGDSS) is tasked with implementing standardization and interoperability for the dismounted soldier. This is accomplished through the development of Standardization Agreements (STANAGS) and Standardization Recommendations (STANRECs) documents that when implemented will allow the sharing of power sources, data, and powered equipment between nations.*

The NATO Power Team of Experts (ToE) is a multinational group of subject matter experts (SMEs) that provide support to the NATO Land Capabilities Group on Dismounted Soldier Systems. Although the ToE works in the all areas of power generation, its current focus is developing those STANAGS and STANRECs related to the standardization and interoperability of the NATO dismounted soldier, both from a mechanical and electrical perspective. Current efforts include power and data standardization, multinational battery recharging, helmet, torso and weapon connectivity and soldier system architectures.

In particular this paper will describe work on a NATO standard power connector as defined in STANAG 4695 and the associated Allied Engineering Publication, AEP-95 and a proposal for a NATO standard battery charging interface as will be defined in STANREC 4819, along with some efforts planned for the future.

The Power Team of Experts is keen to socialize these standards and other efforts around the battery, connector and soldier system community to receive comments on their suitability and to drive wider adoption.

Keywords: standardization; interoperability; NATO; generic soldier architecture; STANAG 4695, STANREC 4819.

Introduction

Modern conflicts are generally undertaken by a coalition of forces consisting of elements from a number of partner nations. This trend is expected to increase in the future. In addition, dismounted soldiers are now carrying ever increasing amounts of electronic capabilities which must be seamlessly integrated within the soldier system, other platforms (vehicle, aviation) and with coalition partners. These trends lead to an increased importance for standardization (where mechanical and electrical characteristics are specifically defined) and interoperability (allowing different systems to interact). Without standardization, all solutions become single source which eliminates the ability for a "plug and play" capability. Interoperability is important to assure that the transfer of data between various systems/nations is seamless, as well as the sharing of energy resources. In reality there is no interoperability without some form of standardization

Within NATO, the Land Capability Group on Dismounted Soldier Systems (LCG DSS) is responsible for the standardization and interoperability of everything worn and utilized by the dismounted soldier, from weapons to clothing to actual tactics. This is accomplished by the creation and acceptance of Standardization Agreements (STANAGs) and Standardization Recommendations (STANRECs).

Due to the importance of energy to the success of the dismounted soldier's mission, LCG DSS established the Power Team of Experts (ToE). The ToE is a multinational group of subject matter experts (SMEs) tasked to author STANAGs and STANRECs, and provide technical support for all matters related to energy generation and distribution.

Power Interoperability Connectivity (NATO STANAG 4695)

NATO LCG DSS envisions that in coalition operations soldiers may find their batteries running low and will need to obtain energy from sources other than the system's native battery. These sources may include another nation's battery, some form of portable generator or even a mobile platform such as a vehicle. It assumes that the end item has the ability to use, or condition the energy provided in a safe manner.

To accomplish this will require a standardized connector and definition of expected power source parameters. Ideally coalition partners would standardize on a common set of soldier batteries. However, realistically this is seen as unlikely in the near to medium term. The enable the sharing of energy, the ToE authored STANAG 4695; "ELECTRICAL INTERFACE SPECIFICATIONS FOR DISMOUNTED SOLDIER SYSTEMS (DSS) LEVEL 2 POWER CONNECTOR INTEROPERABILITY"[1]. STANAGs tend to be overarching documents and much of the technical detail is provided in the associated Allied Engineering Publication (AEP) AEP 4695[2]. Both the STANAG and AEP has recently received sufficient votes from member nations and has been approved by the NAAG (NATO Army Armaments Group) for promulgation.

The adaptation of this STANAG requires that all power generation equipment designed in the future that might be available to the dismounted soldier have at least one output port that meets the requirements of the STANAG. However, it is expected that legacy equipment will remain for a considerable period of time.

Definition and implementation of a standard NATO soldier power connector means that if all partner nations need to carry a single cable that will allow them to connect their power source to the NATO power connector that this will enable interoperability without the need to carry adapters to every conceivable partner nation power source.

The NATO STANAG 4695 connector has been based around the US Nett Warrior power connector. It should however be noted that NATO does not specify a given manufacturer. The connector is already in use on a wide range of military power sources and equipment of a number of nations. This is one of the main reasons it was selected.

The key metrics for the connector are given below.

Table 1. Electrical characteristics of a STANAG 4695 compliant power source

	Level 2 Complaint Power Source
Voltage	8-32 V
Current	0-5 A
EMC	MIL-STD-461

Table 2. Pin assignments for a STANAG 4695 compliant connector

Contact location	Description	Terminal markings
1	V+ Battery Voltage	Batt +
2	V- Battery Voltage	Batt -
3	Charge +	Charge +
4	SMBus data	Data
5	SMBus clock	Clock
6	SMBus ID (10K Thermistor to Ground)	SB ID
7 (if present)	No connection or V+ Battery voltage	Blank/NC/Batt + (*2)

It should be noted that shielding to the connector casing is implied but not stated in this current version.

It should be noted that an edition 2 of this STANAG is now being written which includes some additional clarification and amendments. One change that is being made is that is being made is based on the concern that has been raised over having an optional centre pin (contact 7) since if the appropriate socket is not present on the receptacle then 2 connectors may not mate. Therefore in the second edition of AEP 4695 this centre connector has been removed. Since the document is being revised, industry and users are encouraged to contact their national representative if they believe changes need to be made to facilitate implementation. Copies of the document can be obtained from your national representative of by contacting one of the authors of this paper.

It is expected that in the first instance this STANAG will allow sharing of batteries but it is also intended to allow alternative power sources such as fuel cells and thermoelectric devices to be shared and ultimately energy harvesting devices such as solar panels and kinetic generators, although some form of power management will be needed to facilitate this.

Battery Charging Interoperability (NATO STANREC 4819)

For dismounted soldiers fighting side by side it was identified that there would be operational benefit in being able to charge one another's batteries. NATO War Gaming identified where soldiers from one nation on a joint exercise would end up at the forward operating base of another nation and be unable to recharge their equipment's batteries for the following day's mission.

Originally each new military battery was issued with its own dedicated charger that had the correct charging algorithm preprogrammed. This a proliferation of different, single application chargers which greatly complicates the logistics associated with charging batteries.

Recently such chargers have become more flexible by use of adapter trays. This allows one modular charger to be reconfigured for multiple different types of batteries by using different battery trays. This gives a nation flexibility in that it can buy battery chargers and then upgrade them to charge new batteries when required by buying new battery trays and reprogramming the charger. The charger knows which battery charge profile to use by recognizing the battery tray. This provides a nation some degree of charger standardization, but does little to implement charging interoperability between nations.

The implementation of STANAG 4695 allows for one nation to obtain energy/harvest from another energy source, but does not provide sufficient requirements to allow for interoperable battery charging. To enable this a charger must know and apply the correct charging profile for the battery.

STANREC 4819 addresses the need for interoperable charging by defining additional requirements for both military unique batteries and chargers based on commercial standards already established.

Different batteries have different charging requirements. This is because they use different chemistries or have different numbers of cells within them. For safety reasons and to maximize battery lifetimes they must be charged according to their required charging profile. The concept of interoperable charging is further complicated by the actual location of the charging contacts for a specific battery configuration. This makes interoperable charging very difficult.

However, industry has defined a smart battery charging specification which helps with this problem. The Smart Battery Charger Specification allows chargers to charge multiple different types of batteries by allowing battery-dependent charge profiles that are dictated by the smart batteries themselves. In effect the battery tells the charger how to charge it.

Therefore by using the industry standard SBC specification coupled to the STANAG 4695 connector both a standard connector and communication protocol is defined. This should allow one NATO partner nation to recharge their compliant batteries on another nation's compliant charger without any forward planning.

This concept has yet to be fully tested since the new smart level 2 and 3 chargers have only recently become available.

The NATO LCG DSS Power ToE would welcome comments from battery or battery charger manufacturers as to the viability of this approach and any additional information industry would wish to see in a future STANREC 4819.

Future Effort – Power and Data Connectivity

This connector defined in STANAG 4695 is for power and power related data i.e. SMBus only. There is also a desire for some systems to be able to pass power and tactical data at the same time using a single connector. This is especially important on a dismounted soldier system where requiring two separate connectors to pass power and data on a small device will add additional mass and bulk. NATO LCG DSS is therefore starting work on a combined power and data connector. This is considerably more difficult given the fact that a wide range of soldier systems are already in operation or development and the data requirements of peripherals can be different. The current debate is over whether USB or Ethernet should be selected as the data protocol. Any thoughts or solutions from industry or program managers would be very welcome and could be communicated to the authors of this paper in the first instance.

Future Work – Other Endeavors

NATO LCG DSS undertakes many other standardization activities and another one of these is the development of a NATO Generic Soldier Architecture (NGSA). This is following the ethos of the UK GSA but may make different design decisions to reach an acceptable compromise between partner nations. This work is relatively immature and will progress over the next couple of years.

Other efforts that are planned for the ToE include:

- Identification of potential connectors for use to connect helmet and weapon mounted systems
- Wireless (defined as the lack of cables) power and data transmission
- Including fuel cells into existing and future STANAGs and STANRECs

Conclusions

Future soldier systems are likely to be more integrated than they are today and if they are to remain flexible and upgradable an open architecture is required.

NATO LCG DSS is developing a range of STANAGS which will improve the interoperability of power sources and powered equipment between NATO nations. The first of these, STANAG 4695, defines a power and power related interface to allow batteries to be shared, either directly or via an adaptor.

The ToE welcomes and encourages academia and industry to participate in the development of the various documents.

Acknowledgements

The author would like to acknowledge all the hard working members of NATO LCG DSS

References

1. STANAG 4695 "Electrical Interface Specifications For Dismounted Soldier Systems (DSS) Type 2 Power Interoperability"
2. AEP 4695 "Electrical Connectivity Standards Between NATO Power Sources And Dismounted Soldier Systems (DSS) - Type 2 Connector To Worn/Carried NATO Power Sources"
3. Smart Battery Charger (SBC) Specification, Revision 1.1, December 11, 1998

AUTHOR INDEX